ANTITRUST
LAW
DEVELOPMENTS
(THIRD)

Volume II

Section of Antitrust Law
American Bar Association

This volume should be officially cited as:
"ABA Antitrust Section, Antitrust Law Developments (3d ed. 1992)."

Library of Congress Catalog Card Number: 92-71591
ISBN: 0-89707-638-9

Discounts are available for books ordered in bulk. Special consideration is given to state bars, CLE programs, and other bar-related organizations. Inquire at Publications Planning & Marketing, American Bar Association, 750 North Lake Shore Drive, Chicago, Illinois 60611.

97 96 95 94 93 5 4 3 2 1

CONTENTS

VOLUME I

Chapter I—Restraints of Trade

Page

A. Introduction 1
B. Elements of a Section 1 Violation 2
  1. Proof of a Contract, Combination or Conspiracy 2
    a. Distinguishing Unilateral from Concerted Action 2
      (1) Inferring Agreement Among Competitors 5
      (2) Inferring a Vertical Agreement 11
    b. A Special Case: Intraenterprise Conspiracy 17
  2. Proof That the Restraint Affects Interstate Commerce 22
  3. Proof That the Restraint of Trade Is Unreasonable 30
    a. The Per Se Rule 33
    b. The Rule of Reason 41
C. Horizontal Restraints of Trade 60
  1. Horizontal Arrangements Controlling or Affecting Price 62
    a. Direct Price-Fixing Arrangements 63
    b. Arrangements Indirectly Affecting Price 67
    c. Ancillary Price Restraints 74
    d. Joint Purchasing Agreements 74
  2. Horizontal Arrangements Among Competitors
     to Divide Markets or Allocate Customers 74
  3. Horizontal Arrangements Constituting
     Concerted Refusals to Deal 77
    a. Industry Self-Regulation 86
    b. Sports Leagues and Associations 90
    c. Health Care 91
    d. Noneconomic Boycotts 94
  4. Joint Ventures 95
  5. Other Horizontal Arrangements 95
    a. Conspiracies to Eliminate a Competitor
       by Unfair Business Conduct 95
    b. Covenants Not to Compete 98
D. Vertical Restraints of Trade 99
  1. Vertical Price Restrictions 100
    a. Consignment Arrangements 102
    b. Maximum Resale Price Fixing 103
    c. Dealer Terminations and Other Refusals to Deal 105
    d. Other Conduct 107
  2. Vertical Nonprice Restrictions 116
    a. Exclusive Distributorships 117
    b. Territorial and Customer Restrictions 119

c. Restrictions Imposed Under a Dual Distribution System 127
d. Location Clauses, Areas of Primary Responsibility,
    Profit Pass-Over Arrangements, and Related Restrictions 129
3. Tying Arrangements 131
    a. Elements of a Per Se Violation 136
        (1) Two Products 136
        (2) Proof of Conditioning 143
        (3) Sufficient Economic Power 148
        (4) Substantial Amount of Commerce in the Tied Product 157
        (5) Competitive Effect in the Market for the Tied Product 158
    b. Justifications and Defenses 160
    c. Rule of Reason 163
    d. Full Line Forcing 164
4. Reciprocal Dealing 166
5. Exclusive Dealing Arrangements 169
6. Vertical Refusals to Deal 179

Chapter II–Monopolization and Related Offenses

A. Introduction 195
B. "Monopolization" – Monopoly Power Plus an Element
    of Deliberateness 195
    1. Monopoly Power 196
        a. Definition of the Relevant Market 198
            (1) Relevant Product Market 199
            (2) Relevant Geographic Market 208
        b. Evidence of Monopoly Power 211
            (1) Market Share as an Indicator of Monopoly Power 212
            (2) Other Evidence of Monopoly Power 214
            (3) Regulation 218
    2. The "Deliberateness" Requirement – Intentional
        Anticompetitive Conduct 219
        a. Predatory Pricing 227
            (1) Price-Cost Analysis 227
            (2) Intent 234
            (3) Market Structure and Recoupment 236
        b. Price Squeezes 237
        c. Refusals to Deal 241
            (1) The Intent Test 242
            (2) The Essential Facilities Doctrine 246
        d. Leveraging 250
        e. New Product Introduction 253
        f. Abuse of Process 257

Page

C. Attempt to Monopolize 259
   1. Majority View on Proof of Dangerous
      Probability of Success 262
   2. Minority View on Proof of Dangerous
      Probability of Success 267
D. Monopoly by Combination and Conspiracy 270

Chapter III–Mergers and Acquisitions, Joint Ventures and Interlocking Directorates

A. Introduction 275
   1. Scope of Chapter 275
   2. Enforcement Mechanisms and Guidelines 277
B. Scope of Section 7 279
C. Market Definition 282
   1. Product Market Definition 282
      a. Judicial Approaches to Product Market Definition 282
         (1) Cross-Elasticity of Demand and Interchangeability of Use .. 282
         (2) Production Substitutability 287
         (3) Submarkets 288
         (4) Cluster Markets 289
      b. Department of Justice and FTC Approaches
         to Product Market Definition 290
      c. Competitive Effects of Imperfect Substitutes
         in the Same Product Market 293
   2. Geographic Market Definition 293
      a. Judicial Approaches to Geographic Market Definition 293
      b. Department of Justice and FTC Approaches
         to Geographic Market Definition 297
D. Horizontal Mergers 298
   1. Market Share and Concentration Measurement 299
   2. Assessment of Market Shares and Concentration 303
      a. Judicial Approaches 303
      b. Department of Justice and FTC Approaches 305
   3. Ease of Entry 307
   4. Other Qualitative Factors 311
   5. Failing Company and Related Defenses 313
      a. Failing Company 313
      b. Impaired Company 317
      c. Newspaper Preservation Act 318
   6. Efficiencies 319
E. Nonhorizontal Mergers 322
   1. Mergers Between Potential Competitors 322
      a. Elimination of Actual Potential Competition 324

    b. Elimination of Perceived Potential Competition 328
  2. Vertical Acquisitions 330
  3. Conglomerate Acquisitions 333
    a. Entrenchment 334
    b. Reciprocity 335
    c. Federal Agency Enforcement 337
F. Federal Agency Enforcement 337
  1. Premerger Notification 338
  2. Negotiated Settlements 344
  3. Preliminary Relief 351
    a. Actions by the Department of Justice 352
    b. Actions by the Federal Trade Commission 353
  4. Alternative Preliminary Relief 355
  5. Permanent Relief 358
G. Enforcement by Private Parties 361
  1. Standing 362
  2. Preliminary Relief 365
  3. Permanent Relief 370
    a. Injunctive Relief 370
    b. Damages 371
H. Enforcement by State Attorneys General 371
I. Joint Ventures 372
  1. Formation of a Joint Venture 372
    a. Integrative Efficiencies 372
    b. Creation of Market Power 376
  2. Analysis of Collateral Restraints 378
    a. General Principles 378
    b. Restraints on Price and Output 379
    c. Territorial and Customer Restraints 381
    d. Restraints on Access to the Joint Venture 384
    e. Department of Justice and FTC Approaches
       to Collateral Restraints 386
  3. Analysis of Particular Types of Joint Ventures 387
    a. Production Joint Ventures 387
    b. Joint Research Ventures 388
    c. Joint Buying and Selling Arrangements 389
J. Interlocking Directorates 392
  1. Interlocks Subject to Section 8 393
  2. Enforcement and Policy 398

Chapter IV—Robinson-Patman Act

A. Introduction 401
B. The Requirement of Commerce 402

C. Price Discrimination Prohibited by Section 2(a) 404
   1. The Requirement of Discrimination 405
   2. The Requirement of Sales to Two Purchasers 407
   3. The Requirement of Commodities 409
   4. The Requirement of Like Grade and Quality 410
   5. The Requirement of Competitive Injury 413
      a. Primary Line Injury 414
      b. Secondary Line Injury 415
D. Statutory Defenses to Section 2(a) Price Discrimination 417
   1. The Meeting Competition Defense 417
   2. The Cost Justification Defense 420
   3. The Changing Conditions Defense 426
E. Wholesaler Pricing and Functional Discounts 427
F. The Brokerage Provision 431
G. Allowances and Services Provisions 436
H. Buyer Liability 444
I. Exemptions 448
J. Injury to Plaintiffs Under Section 4 of the Clayton Act 449
K. Criminal Prohibitions 450

Chapter V—The Federal Trade Commission

A. Introduction 453
B. Jurisdictional Elements Under
   the Federal Trade Commission Act 454
   1. The "In or Affecting Commerce" Requirement 454
   2. The "Public Interest" Requirement 455
   3. Jurisdiction Over Nonprofit Organizations 455
C. Section 5 of the Federal Trade Commission Act
   as an Antitrust Law 457
   1. Practices That Violate the Sherman Act, the Clayton Act
      or the Robinson-Patman Act 457
   2. Practices That Do Not Violate the Sherman Act, the
      Clayton Act or the Robinson-Patman Act 457
      a. Earlier Decisions 458
      b. Later Decisions 460
D. Section 5 of the Federal Trade Commission Act as a
   Consumer Protection Law 464
   1. Deceptive Acts and Practices 464
      a. Scienter Not Required 464
      b. Actual Deception Not Required 464
      c. Failure to Have Substantiation
         for a Claim Is Deceptive 467
      d. Failure to Disclose Material Facts 468
      e. Determining Meaning of Representations 469

f. The Commission's 1983 Policy Statement
on Deception 471
g. Examples of Deceptive Practices 472
(1) Characteristics of Products 472
(2) Endorsements and Testimonials 474
(3) Pricing Claims 475
(4) Guarantees 475
(5) Origin of Products 476
(6) Business or Trade Status 477
(7) Business Torts — "Passing Off"
and False Disparagement 477
(8) Deceptive Business, Employment and
Sales Practices 478
(9) Special Problems of Television Advertising 480
2. Unfair Acts and Practices 482
a. General Standards 482
b. The Commission's 1980 Policy Statement 483
c. Examples of Unfair Practices 484
E. Commission Remedial Power 487
1. Cease and Desist Orders 488
a. Statutory Authority 488
b. Scope of Remedies Regarding Unlawful Conduct 488
c. Remedies Beyond Prohibitions of
Conduct Found to be Unlawful 490
(1) Restrictions on Business Practices 490
(2) Affirmative Disclosure 491
d. Limitations of Scope of Commission Orders 492
(1) First Amendment Concerns 492
(2) Reasonable Relation Standard 493
2. Trade Regulation Rules 495
3. Civil Penalties 495
a. Civil Penalty Proceedings Under Section 5(1) 495
b. Civil Penalty Proceedings Under Section 5(m) 497
4. Consumer Redress 498
5. Preliminary and Permanent Injunctions 501
a. Injunctions Against False Advertising
of Foods and Drugs 501
b. Injunctions Against Other Violations
of the Laws Administered by the Commission 502
F. FTC Enforcement Procedures 504
1. Precomplaint Investigation 504
2. Adjudicative Procedures 509
a. Separation of Functions Within the Commission 509
b. Adjudicative Discovery Procedures 510

    c. Intervention 512
    d. Evidence 513
    e. Privilege and Immunity 513
  3. Settlement Procedures 514
  4. Modification of Relief 515
  5. Protection of Confidential Information 516
  6. Judicial Review of Commission Actions 520
    a. Judicial Review of a Finding of Violation 520
    b. Review of the Remedial Provisions
       in a Final Cease and Desist Order 523
    c. Collateral and Interlocutory Proceedings
       in District Court 523

G. Rulemaking Proceedings 524
  1. Historical Exercise of Rulemaking Authority 524
  2. Magnuson-Moss Rulemaking 525
  3. Rulemaking Procedures 526
  4. Procedural Changes Resulting From the 1980 Amendments 527
  5. Judicial Review of Trade Regulation Rules 529

H. Other Commission Activities 530
  1. Advisory Opinions, Industry Guides and
     Statements of Policy 530
    a. Advisory Opinions 530
    b. Industry Guides 531
    c. Statements of Commission Enforcement Policy 531
  2. Competition and Consumer Advocacy 532
  3. Consumer Credit Enforcement 532
    a. Federal Trade Commission Act 532
    b. Truth-in-Lending Act 533
       (1) Overview 533
       (2) Federal Reserve Board Regulations 534
       (3) Fair Credit Billing Act 535
       (4) Consumer Leasing Act 535
    c. Fair Credit Reporting Act 535
    d. Equal Credit Opportunity Act 537
    e. Fair Debt Collection Practices Act 538
    f. Electronic Fund Transfer Act 539
    g. Holder in Due Course Rule 539
  4. Warranties 539
  5. Labeling Regulation 540
    a. Fair Packaging and Labeling Act 540
    b. Labeling of Wool, Textile, Fur, and
       Other Products 541
    c. Other Labeling Powers 541

I. Private Enforcement of FTC Law 542
J. State Analogues to FTC Act 543

Chapter VI–Department of Justice Administration and Enforcement

Page

A. Introduction 545
B. Relationship with FTC 547
C. Nonprosecutorial Activities 548
  1. Guidelines and Other Public Statements 548
  2. Business Review Letters 548
  3. Participation in Private Suits 551
  4. Participation in Other Forums 551
D. Investigations 552
  1. General Procedures 552
  2. The Decision to Proceed and Choice of Remedies 553
  3. Civil Investigations 556
    a. Civil Investigative Demands 556
    b. Merger Investigations 561
  4. Criminal Investigations 561
    a. Grand Jury Document Subpoenas 562
      (1) Legal Requirements 562
      (2) Modification 562
      (3) Motions to Quash 562
    b. Grand Jury Testimony 564
      (1) Role of Counsel 564
      (2) Abuse 566
    c. Decision on Indictment 568
E. Litigation 569
  1. Civil Litigation 569
  2. Civil Remedies 569
    a. In General 569
    b. Consent Decrees 569
      (1) Negotiations 570
      (2) Entry of Consent Judgments 572
      (3) Enforcement of Decrees 574
      (4) Interpretation, Modification, and Termination of Decrees ... 575
      (5) Intervention 578
  3. Damages Actions 579
  4. Criminal Actions 579
    a. Arraignment and Related Activities 579
      (1) Arrest Warrant or Summons 579
      (2) Arraignment 580
      (3) Pretrial Release 580
    b. Pleas and Plea Bargaining 580
    c. Pretrial Motions 583
    d. Discovery 586

Page

  e. Trial Considerations 591
   (1) Self Incrimination 591
   (2) Immunity 591
   (3) Statements of Coconspirators 593
   (4) Intent and Antitrust Compliance Programs 594
  f. Posttrial 595
   (1) Presentencing Reports 595
   (2) Sentencing 596
   (3) Posttrial Motions 598
   (4) Appeals 599
   (5) Factually Related Criminal and Civil Actions 600
   (6) Conflicts of Interest 600

Chapter VII–State Enforcement

A. Introduction 603
B. Enforcement of Federal Antitrust Laws by State Attorneys General ... 603
 1. Actions as a Private "Person" 603
  a. Treble Damage Suits 603
  b. Actions for Injunctive Relief 605
 2. Parens Patriae Actions 606
 3. Coordinated State Enforcement 608
  a. Coordinated Investigations and Litigation 609
  b. Amicus Briefs 613
  c. Legislative Positions 614
  d. NAAG Voluntary Pre-Merger Disclosure Compact 614
  e. Enforcement Guidelines 615
   (1) Vertical Restraints Guidelines 615
   (2) Merger Guidelines 617
  f. Cooperation Between Federal and State Authorities:
   The Executive Working Group for Antitrust 618
C. Federalism Issues Relating to State Antitrust Laws 619
 1. Scope of State Antitrust Laws 619
 2. Resolved Constitutional Challenges to State Antitrust Laws 621
  a. The Commerce Clause 621
  b. The Supremacy Clause 622
  c. The Equal Protection Clause 626
  d. The Due Process Clause 627
   (1) Statutory Vagueness 628
   (2) Extraterritorial Application 628
  e. The Double Jeopardy Clause 629
 3. Unresolved Constitutional Issues from Dual Antitrust
  Enforcement 629
  a. Double Recovery 629
  b. State Premerger Notification Statutes 632

Page

D. Differences Between State and Federal Antitrust Laws 633
   1. Substantive Antitrust Prohibitions 633
       a. Horizontal Restraints 634
       b. Vertical Restraints 634
       c. Attempts and Conspiracies to Monopolize, and
           Monopolization 635
       d. Price Discrimination 635
       e. Mergers and Acquisitions 636
   2. Exemptions and Defenses 637
       a. State Action 637
       b. Governmental Immunity 637
       c. *Noerr-Pennington* 638
       d. Primary Jurisdiction 638
       e. Labor 638
       f. Insurance 638
       g. Unclean Hands and In Pari Delicto 639
       h. Contribution 639
   3. Remedies 639
       a. Criminal 639
       b. Civil Penalties 640
       c. Damages 640
       d. Parens Patriae Actions 641
       e. Injunctions 641
       f. Forfeiture of Right to Do Business 641

Chapter VIII–Private Antitrust Suits

A. Introduction 643
B. Common Elements of Private Antitrust
    Suits Under Sections 4 and 16 643
    1. "Any Person" 643
        a. Actions by Private Persons 643
        b. Actions by Governments 645
    2. "Antitrust Laws" Defined 645
C. Standing Requirements of Section 4
    of the Clayton Act 646
    1. "Injured in His Business or Property" 647
        a. "Impact" or "Fact of Damage" 647
        b. "Business or Property" 647
    2. "By Reason Of" – Antitrust Injury 650
    3. Considerations of Remoteness 652
        a. The Pass-On/Indirect Purchaser Doctrine 653
        b. Other Cases Dealing with Remoteness Concerns 658
D. Standing Requirements of Section 16
    of the Clayton Act 663

E. Proof of Injury and Damages 665
   1. Proof of Injury 665
   2. Proof of Damages 667
      a. Burden of Proof 667
      b. Calculation of Damages 669
      c. Disaggregation 674
      d. Mitigation 675
F. Injunctive Relief 675
   1. In General 675
   2. Preliminary Injunctions 676
   3. Permanent Injunctions 679
   4. Divestiture 680
G. Defenses 680
   1. Statute of Limitations 680
      a. Uniform Statute of Limitations 680
      b. Tolling the Statute of Limitations 682
         (1) Government Actions 683
         (2) Fraudulent Concealment 688
         (3) Equitable Tolling 693
         (4) Class Action Tolling 695
   2. In Pari Delicto 697
   3. "Unclean Hands" 701
H. Practice and Procedure 702
   1. Summary Judgment 702
   2. Multidistrict Litigation 708
   3. Antitrust Class Actions 712
      a. Prerequisites to a Class Action 712
         (1) The Numerosity Requirement 713
         (2) The Requirement of Common Questions
           of Law or Fact 714
         (3) The Requirements for the Class Representatives 715
           (a) Typicality 715
           (b) Adequacy of Representation 717
      b. Additional Requirements to Maintain
        a Class Action 723
         (1) Rule 23(b)(1) Classes 723
         (2) Rule 23(b)(2) Classes 724
         (3) Rule 23(b)(3) Classes 724
           (a) Predominance 725
           (b) Superiority 729
      c. Procedure in Class Actions 733
         (1) Effect of Judgments in Class Actions 733
         (2) Procedure for Determining Class Certification 734
         (3) Notice and Costs 737
      d. Dismissal and Compromise 739

4. Selected Discovery Problems 745
   a. Relevant Time Period 745
   b. Scope of Relevant Market 747
      (1) Geographic Market 748
      (2) Product Market 750
   c. Discovery from Corporate Affiliates 752
   d. Discovery of Grand Jury Materials 754
      (1) Testimony 755
      (2) Documents 758
      (3) Proper Court 759
   e. Discovery of Debriefing Materials 760
   f. Attorney-Client Privilege 760
      (1) The Upjohn Test 760
      (2) The Crime/Fraud Exception 762
   g. Discovery Conditioned Upon Payment of Costs 766
   h. Sanctions for Failure to Make Discovery 767
   i. Fifth Amendment Problems 771
5. Complexity and the Right to Jury Trial 772
6. Bifurcation of Antitrust Trials 773
7. Use of Government Judgments and Decrees 775
   a. Collateral Estoppel 775
   b. Prima Facie Effect 777
I. Attorneys' Fees 780
   1. Successful Plaintiff 780
   2. Unsuccessful Plaintiff 787
J. Miscellaneous Topics 787
   1. Arbitrability of Antitrust Claims 787
   2. Rule 11 789
   3. Antitrust Violation as Defense to Contract Suit 791
   4. Effect of Death of a Party 793
   5. Contribution 793
   6. Tax Treatment of Treble Damages 794
      a. Plaintiff's Recovery 794
      b. Defendant's Payments 795

VOLUME II

Chapter IX–Antitrust Issues Involving Intellectual Property

A. Introduction 799
B. Patent-Antitrust Issues 799
   1. The Nature of Patents 799
   2. Developments in Patent-Antitrust Jurisprudence   800

3. Acquisition of Issued Patents as an Antitrust Violation 803
   a. Patents Obtained by Grant, Purchase or Assignment 803
   b. Patents Obtained by Grantbacks 804
4. Enforcement of Patents as an Antitrust Violation 806
   a. Patents Obtained by Fraud 806
      (1) The Requirement of Fraud: Inequitable
          Conduct Distinguished 808
   b. Enforcement of an Invalid Patent 811
5. Patent Misuse 813
   a. The Misuse Doctrine 813
   b. Patent Misuse and Contributory Infringement 816
   c. Nonuse and Refusal to License 818
6. Licensing Intellectual Property Rights as an
   Antitrust Violation 819
   a. Exclusivity 820
   b. Price and Quantity Limitations 821
   c. Royalties 823
      (1) Royalty Base 823
      (2) Different or Discriminatory Royalties 824
      (3) Preissuance and Postexpiration Royalties 825
      (4) Royalties Based Upon Use of an Article Purchased
          from the Patent Owner or His Licensee 826
      (5) Sharing and/or Fixing Royalties 827
   d. Territorial and Customer Restrictions 827
   e. Field of Use Restrictions 828
   f. Tying Arrangements 830
      (1) Introduction 830
      (2) Tie-ins as a Misuse 832
      (3) Tying as an Antitrust Violation 833
   g. Package Licensing of Patents and Copyrights 834
   h. Agreement Not to Contest Validity 835
7. Crosslicensing and Patent Pools 837
8. Concerted Boycott by Infringers or Licensees 839
9. Foreign Patent and Know-How Licensing 839
   a. Introduction 839
   b. Territorial Restrictions 841
      (1) Patents 841
      (2) Know-how or Trade Secrets 842
      (3) Trademarks and Copyrights 842
   c. Other Restrictions 843
C. Special Problems with Nonpatent Intellectual Property 844
  1. Copyrights 844
  2. Trademarks 847
  3. Trade Secret Licenses 849

Page

D. Procedural Aspects of the Antitrust–Intellectual Property
   Interface 851
   1. Jurisdiction 851
   2. Procedure 852
   3. Remedies 852
   4. Counterclaims 853
   5. Settlement of Infringement Actions and Interference
      Proceedings 854

Chapter X–Trade or Commerce with Foreign Nations

A. Introduction 855
B. Subject Matter Jurisdiction and Related Issues 855
   1. Sherman Act 855
      a. Jurisdiction 855
      b. Standing 858
      c. Comity Considerations 858
      d. Prudential and Other Considerations 863
   2. The Federal Trade Commission, Robinson-Patman
      and Clayton Acts 864
C. Venue, Personal Jurisdiction, and Service of Process 866
   1. Venue 866
   2. Personal Jurisdiction 871
   3. Service of Process 877
D. Discovery and the Conduct of Litigation in
   Foreign Commerce Cases 879
   1. Discovery Outside the United States 879
      a. Procedures Under U.S. Law for Obtaining Documents
         Located Abroad 879
      b. Foreign Laws Regulating Discovery Abroad 885
      c. The Effect of Foreign Laws and Comity
         Considerations on U.S. Discovery 886
E. Remedies and Relief 889
   1. Comity Considerations 890
   2. Reactions by Foreign Countries 892
   3. Arbitration 895
F. Application to Foreign Commerce of Certain
   Substantive Antitrust Rules 896
G. Relationship of U.S. International Trade
   Laws to Antitrust Laws 898
   1. Antidumping Act of 1916 898
   2. Use and Abuse of U.S. Trade Laws 898

Page

H. Exceptions and Defenses to Application of
Antitrust Laws in Foreign Commerce 899
   1. Sovereign Immunity 899
   2. Act of State 901
   3. Foreign Sovereign Compulsion 909
   4. Restraints Approved by the U.S. Executive Branch 911
   5. *Noerr-Pennington* Doctrine 912
   6. Statutory Exemptions Relating to Foreign Commerce 914
      a. Webb-Pomerene Act 914
      b. Certificates of Review 916
      c. National Defense 918
I. European Economic Community Antitrust Law 918
   1. Organization and Application 918
   2. General Goals 922
   3. Negative Clearance and Exemption 924
   4. Scope of Jurisdiction 927
   5. Trade Between Member States 928
   6. Article 85 (Restrictive Agreements) 930
      a. Horizontal Restrictions 932
      b. Vertical Restrictions 938
      c. Industrial Property: Patents, Know-how,
         Trademarks, and Copyrights 944
7. Article 86 (Abuse of Dominant Position) 949
8. Mergers and Acquisitions 957

Chapter XI–Exemptions and Regulated Markets

A. Introduction 963
B. Effect of Government Involvement 963
   1. Inducement or Approval by Federal Officials 963
   2. Restraints Imposed by State Action 965
      a. Basic Framework and Evolution of the
         State Action Doctrine 965
      b. The Clear Articulation Requirement 970
      c. The Active Supervision Requirement 973
      d. Limitations Upon the Availability of Immunity 976
      e. Restraints Imposed or Authorized by Political Subdivisions
         and Other Subordinate Government Entities 979
         (1) Clear Articulation 982
         (2) Active Supervision 985
      f. Local Government Liability for Treble Damages 987
   3. Solicitation of Government Action 989
      a. Basic Framework and Evolution of *Noerr* Immunity 989
         (1) *Noerr* 990
         (2) *Pennington* 991

Page

　　　　(3) California Motor Transport 992
　　　　(4) Allied Tube & Conduit 993
　　　　(5) Superior Court Trial Lawyers 996
　　　　(6) Omni Outdoor Advertising 996
　　b. Qualifications to *Noerr* Immunity 998
　　　　(1) Sham Exception 998
　　　　(2) Supplying False Information 1006
　　　　(3) Conspiracies with Public Officials 1008
　　　　(4) Commercial Exception 1009
　　　　(5) Tariff Filings 1011
　　c. Political Boycotts 1012
　　d. Evidentiary Issues 1014
　　e. Petitioning Foreign Governments 1015
C. Relationship Between Antitrust and Federal Regulation 1016
　1. Express Exemptions 1016
　2. Implied Exemptions 1018
　3. The Keogh Doctrine 1019
　4. Primary Jurisdiction 1021
D. Particular Industries and Markets 1024
　1. Agriculture 1024
　2. Communications 1028
　　a. Broadcasting 1029
　　　　(1) Licensing 1031
　　　　(2) Licensee Sales Practices 1032
　　　　(3) Ownership of Broadcast Licenses 1034
　　　　(4) Networks 1039
　　　　(5) Regulatory Efforts to Increase Broadcast Competition 1042
　　b. Common Carriers 1045
　　　　(1) Overview 1045
　　　　(2) Federal Regulation 1047
　　　　(3) State Regulation 1049
　　c. Cable Television 1050
　3. Energy 1055
　　a. Natural Gas 1055
　　　　(1) Regulatory History 1056
　　　　　(a) The Natural Gas Act 1056
　　　　　(b) The Natural Gas Policy Act of 1978:
　　　　　　　Competition at the Wellhead 1057
　　　　　(c) Open Access Transportation 1058
　　　　　(d) Bypass: A Consequence of Open Access 1060
　　　　(2) Litigation Under the Sherman Act 1062
　　　　(3) Mergers and Acquisitions 1066
　　b. Electric Power 1067
　　　　(1) Wheeling 1068
　　　　(2) Price Squeeze 1071
　　　　(3) Mergers and Acquisitions 1074

Page

    c. Oil Transportation 1079
    d. Nuclear Power 1080
    e. Competition and Federal Lands 1082
        (1) Antitrust Review Framework 1083
            (a) Federal Coal Leasing 1083
            (b) Outer Continental Shelf Oil and Gas Leasing 1085
            (c) Naval and National Petroleum Reserves 1086
        (2) The Statutory Standard 1087
4. Financial Institutions and Markets 1089
    a. Financial Institutions 1089
        (1) Joint Activities Under Sections 1 and 2
            of the Sherman Act 1090
        (2) Mergers and Acquisitions 1091
        (3) Tie-Ins 1097
        (4) Interlocking Directorates 1099
    b. The Securities Industry 1099
    c. Commodities Futures 1104
5. Government Contracts 1107
6. Insurance 1109
7. Organized Labor 1119
    a. The Statutory Exemption 1119
    b. The Nonstatutory Exemption 1121
8. Transportation 1126
    a. Motor Carriers 1126
    b. Rail Transportation 1131
        (1) National Rail Transportation Policy 1131
        (2) ICC Exemption Authority 1132
        (3) Regulation of Entry and Exit 1134
        (4) Regulation of Rates and Agreements 1135
        (5) Competitive Access and Related Isses 1140
        (6) Mergers and Acquisitions 1141
        (7) Section 10 of the Clayton Act 1145
    c. Air Transportation 1145
        (1) Regulatory History 1145
        (2) Civil Aeronautics Board and Department of
            Transportation Decisions in Merger,
            Acquisition and Control Cases 1147
        (3) Merger and Acquisition Decisions After January 1, 1989 ... 1149
        (4) Preemption 1152
        (5) Regulation of Unfair Competition 1153
    d. Ocean Shipping 1157
        (1) Regulation of Entry and Exit 1158
        (2) Regulation of Rates and Rebates 1159
        (3) Regulation of Agreements 1161

Page

Appendices 1167

A. Basic Antitrust and Trade Regulation Statutes 1167
   Sherman Act 1167
   Clayton Act 1169
   Robinson-Patman Act Section 3 1190
   Federal Trade Commission Act Section 5 1190
   Federal Trade Commission Act Section 13(b) 1195
   Federal Trade Commission Act Section 18 1195
   Federal Trade Commission Act Section 19 1202

B. 1984 U.S. Department of Justice Merger Guidelines 1205

C. Statement of Federal Trade Commission Concerning Horizontal
   Mergers 1229

D. 1987 Horizontal Merger Guidelines of the National Association
   of Attorneys General 1239

E. 1988 Antitrust Guidelines for International Operations 1255

F. 1992 Department of Justice and Federal Trade Commission
   Horizontal Merger Guidelines 1351

Table of Cases 1399

Index 1591

CHAPTER IX

ANTITRUST ISSUES INVOLVING INTELLECTUAL PROPERTY

A. Introduction

This chapter addresses the antitrust issues that arise from the acquisition, use, and enforcement of rights in intellectual property — i.e., patents, copyrights, trademarks, trade secrets, and other statutorily created rights.[1] This chapter is divided into three parts. Part B primarily discusses the antitrust issues related to patents, the subject of most of the decided cases. Part C discusses issues related to other types of intellectual property. Part D discusses various procedural issues that arise in patent-antitrust disputes.

B. Patent-Antitrust Issues

1. The Nature of Patents

Article I, section 8, clause 8 of the Constitution grants Congress the power to create a patent system. It provides:

> The Congress shall have Power . . . [t]o promote the Progress of Science and useful Arts, by securing for limited Times to Authors and Inventors the exclusive Right to their respective Writings and Discoveries.

A patent gives the inventor of any "new and useful process, machine, manufacture, or composition of matter," any "distinct and new variety of plant," or any "new, original, and ornamental design for an article of manufacture," or any patentable improvements to any of them, the right to exclude others from making, using, or selling the invention throughout the United States.[2] Patents have the attributes of

---

1. For example, Congress has created a right in creators of certain semiconductor "mask works" used in the fabrication of integrated circuits, to prohibit, for a limited time, the importation, reproduction, and distribution of such works. 17 U.S.C. §§ 901-944 (1988). The right of states to create intellectual property rights is qualified in that any state law scheme that is inconsistent with the federal patent system is preempted. Bonito Boats, Inc. v. Thunder Craft Boats, Inc., 489 U.S. 141 (1989). However, state law can, and does, create intellectual property rights not preempted by the patent law, such as trademarks and trade secrets.

2. 35 U.S.C. §§ 101, 154, 161, 171 (1988). The exclusive rights provided for in the patent laws are intended to offer an incentive for inventors to take risks in performing research and development. Kewanee Oil Co. v. Bicron Corp., 416 U.S. 470, 480-81, 484 (1974); Sears, Roebuck & Co. v. Stiffel Co., 376 U.S. 225, 229-30 (1964). The patent laws are also intended to encourage the disclosure of new ideas to the public which in turn may lead to the development of further

personal property.[3] The period of exclusivity of a United States patent is normally seventeen years from the date of issuance.[4]

Each patent contains one or more "claims." The claims are analogous to the "metes and bounds" of a deed. The claims alone define the scope of exclusivity granted to the patentee. The remainder of the disclosure in the patent, while required to comply with the statutory formalities for a patent, confers no exclusive rights.[5]

2. Developments in Patent-Antitrust Jurisprudence

Traditionally, patent-antitrust issues have been governed by the application of rules unique to patent cases. Even where the conduct addressed by patent law and antitrust law was similar or even identical, as in claims that a tie-in between a patented and an unpatented product constituted both an antitrust violation and a patent "misuse" causing the patentee to forfeit its right to enforce the patent, it was established law that the conduct could constitute patent misuse even if it did not violate the antitrust laws.[6] Recent court decisions and pronouncements of enforcement agencies, however, appear to indicate a greater willingness to test patent-antitrust issues by traditional antitrust principles. One court has stated, with regard to patent misuse:

> If misuse claims are not tested by conventional antitrust principles, by what principles should they be tested? Our law is not rich in alternative concepts of monopolistic abuse; and it is rather late in the day to try to develop one without in the process subjecting the rights of patentholders to debilitating uncertainty.[7]

Similar questions have been raised about the treatment of patents as

---

advances. Troxel Mfg. Co. v. Schwinn Bicycle Co., 465 F.2d 1253, 1258 (6th Cir. 1972), *later appeal*, 489 F.2d 968 (6th Cir. 1973), *cert. denied*, 416 U.S. 939 (1974). When the patent expires, the invention becomes freely available to the public without restriction. Brulotte v. Thys Co., 379 U.S. 29, 31 (1964); Special Equip. Co. v. Coe, 324 U.S. 370, 378 (1945). A patentee's remedies for infringment are specified in 35 U.S.C. § 271 (1988), and include rights against importers and exporters of goods covered by the patent. In addition, under Section 337 of the Tariff Act of 1930, as amended, 19 U.S.C. § 1337 (1988), a patentee may seek relief through the U.S. International Trade Commission against the importation of products that infringe a U.S. patent, subject to certain threshhold requirements relating to the existence of a domestic industry practicing the patent.

3. 35 U.S.C. § 261 (1988), first paragraph. The statutory provision was enacted to negate any inference that a patent was a "public trust" or "privilege." *See, e.g.*, Precision Instrument Mfg. Co. v. Automotive Maintenance Mach. Co., 324 U.S. 806, 816 (1945).

4. 35 U.S.C. § 154 (1988). Patents issued on applications filed after December 12, 1980 are subject to payment of maintenance fees four years, seven years, and twelve years after the patent issues. Failure to pay the maintenance fee will cause the patent's exclusivity to lapse. Under certain circumstances a patent's term may be extended if the patentee was also subject to review of his invention by the Food & Drug Administration. 35 U.S.C. § 155 *et seq.* (1988).

5. *See, e.g.*, 35 U.S.C. § 112 (1988).

6. *E.g.*, Zenith Radio Corp. v. Hazeltine Research, Inc., 395 U.S. 100, 140-41 (1969); Transparent-Wrap Mach. Corp. v. Stokes & Smith Co., 329 U.S. 637, 641 (1947), *on remand*, 161 F.2d 565 (2d Cir.), *cert. denied*, 331 U.S. 837 (1947); Morton Salt Co. v. G.S. Suppiger Co., 314 U.S. 488 (1942).

7. USM Corp. v. SPS Technologies, Inc., 694 F.2d 505, 512 (7th Cir. 1982), *cert. denied*, 462 U.S. 1107 (1983); *see also* Saturday Evening Post Co. v. Rumbleseat Press, Inc., 816 F.2d 1191, 1200 (7th Cir. 1987).

"monopolies." Historically courts have characterized a patent's power to exclude others from practicing the claimed invention as a "monopoly."[8] Thus, a number of cases have characterized the role of antitrust to be one of preventing the expansion or misuse of the "monopoly" granted a patentee.[9] This view of patents as monopolies was reflected in *Jefferson Parish Hospital District No. 2 v. Hyde*,[10] in which the Supreme Court stated, in dictum, that "if the Government has granted the seller [of a product] a patent or similar monopoly over a product, it is fair to presume that the inability to buy the product elsewhere gives the seller market power."[11] The Court added:

> Any effort to enlarge the scope of the patent monopoly by using the market power it confers to restrain competition in the market for a second product will undermine competition on the merits in that second market. Thus, the sale or lease of a patented item on condition that the buyer make all his purchases of a separate tied product from the patentee is unlawful.[12]

This view has been criticized. A concurring opinion in *Jefferson Parish*, joined by four Justices, termed the belief that a patent automatically confers market power a "common misconception," noting that "a patent holder has no market power in any relevant sense if there are close substitutes for the patented product."[13] The concurrence also questioned whether the presumption of market power was required by the Court's prior decisions.[14]

A number of lower court decisions have expressed views similar to the concurrence. In their view, whether a patent confers market power or monopoly power in the antitrust sense depends upon an assessment of the patent's exclusionary power in a relevant market.[15] Thus, while a patent grants its possessor the right to exclude others from practicing the claimed invention,[16] these courts tend to

---

8. *See, e.g.*, Zenith Radio Corp. v. Hazeltine Research, Inc., 395 U.S. 100, 135 (1969) (patentee possesses a "lawful monopoly"); Precision Instrument Mfg. Co. v. Automotive Maintenance Mach. Co., 324 U.S. 806, 816 (1945); Continental Paper Bag Co. v. Eastern Paper Bag Co., 210 U.S. 405 (1908); United States v. Aluminum Co. of Am., 148 F.2d 416, 430 (2d Cir. 1945) (patents are "lawful monopolies").

9. *See, e.g.*, Mercoid Corp. v. Mid-Continent Inv. Co., 320 U.S. 661 (1944); Mercoid Corp. v. Minneapolis-Honeywell Regulator Co., 320 U.S. 680 (1944); Brulotte v. Thys Co., 379 U.S. 29 (1964).

10. 466 U.S. 2 (1984).

11. *Id.* at 16 (citing United States v. Loew's Inc., 371 U.S. 38, 45-47 (1962)).

12. *Id.*

13. *Id.* at 37 n.7 (O'Connor, J., concurring) (quoting USM Corp. v. SPS Technologies, Inc., 694 F.2d 505, 511 (7th Cir. 1982), *cert. denied*, 462 U.S. 1107 (1983)).

14. *Id.* at 38.

15. Loctite Corp. v. Ultraseal, Ltd., 781 F.2d 861, 877 (Fed. Cir. 1985) ("the patent and antitrust laws are complementary"); American Hoist & Derrick Co. v. Sowa & Sons, 725 F.2d 1350, 1367 (Fed. Cir.) ("The patent system, which antedated the Sherman Act by a century, is not an 'exception' to the antitrust laws, and patent rights are not *legal monopolies* in the antitrust sense of that word.") (emphasis in original), *cert. denied*, 469 U.S. 821 (1984). Many courts continue to use the word "monopoly" as shorthand for the patent owner's power to exclude. *See, e.g.*, Dawson Chem. Co. v. Rohm & Haas Co., 448 U.S. 176, 180 (1980).

16. United States v. United Shoe Mach. Corp., 247 U.S. 32, 57 (1918); *see* United States v. Dubilier Condenser Corp., 289 U.S. 178, 186 (1933); Bement v. National Harrow Co., 186 U.S. 70, 91 (1902).

evaluate the existence of "market power" in the antitrust sense based on whether there are substitutes for the claimed invention,[17] the definition of the relevant market,[18] and an appraisal of the exclusionary power of the claimed invention in the relevant market.[19]

The Department of Justice's *Antitrust Enforcement Guidelines for International Operations* also express a view similar to the concurring opinion in *Jefferson Parish* on the effect of a patent on antitrust analysis.[20] The *International Guidelines* expressly reject the Department's earlier enforcement policy which proceeded on the assumption that intellectual property rights conflicted with the goals of the antitrust laws because intellectual property rights were thought to create "monopolies." The current position of the Department is stated in the *International Guidelines* as follows:

> Today, however, the Department recognizes that intellectual property – even a patent – does not necessarily confer a monopoly or market power in any relevant market. A patent, for example, is merely the right to exclude others from making, using, or reselling the product or process covered by the patent claims. The patented product or process remains subject to competition from products or processes outside the scope of the patent that are economic substitutes.[21]

The *International Guidelines* state further that for purposes of antitrust analysis, the Department regards patents and other intellectual property as essentially comparable

---

17. *See* Jefferson Parish Hosp. Dist. No. 2 v. Hyde, 466 U.S. 2, 37 n.7 (1984) (O'Connor, J., concurring) ("a patent holder has no market power in any relevant sense if there are close substitutes for the patented product") (quoting USM Corp. v. SPS Technologies, Inc., 694 F.2d 505, 511 (7th Cir. 1982), *cert. denied*, 462 U.S. 1107 (1983)); *cf.* Andewelt, *Antitrust Perspective on Intellectual Property Protection*, 30 PAT. TRADEMARK & COPYRIGHT J. (BNA) 319, 324 n.22 (July 25, 1985) (then Chief of Intellectual Property Section of the Antitrust Division stated that "patents seldom provide any significant power, much less actual market power"); Remarks of then Assistant Att'y Gen., J. Paul McGrath, Patent Licensing: A Fresh Look at Antitrust Principles in a Changing Economic Environment (before the International Conference on U.S. Patent Practice) (Apr. 5, 1984), *reprinted in* 4 TRADE REG. REP. (CCH) ¶ 13,130.

18. American Hoist & Derrick Co. v. Sowa & Sons, 725 F.2d 1350, 1367 (Fed. Cir.), *cert. denied*, 469 U.S. 821 (1984); SCM Corp. v. Xerox Corp., 645 F.2d 1195, 1207-08 (2d Cir. 1981), *cert. denied*, 455 U.S. 1016 (1982).

19. Walker Process Equip., Inc. v. Food Mach. & Chem. Corp., 382 U.S. 172, 177 (1965); *see* Brunswick Corp. v. Riegel Textile Corp., 752 F.2d 261 (7th Cir. 1984), *cert. denied*, 472 U.S. 1018 (1985); Consolidated Aluminum Corp. v. Foseco Int'l, Ltd., 716 F. Supp. 316 (N.D. Ill. 1989), *aff'd*, 910 F.2d 804 (Fed. Cir. 1990); Crucible, Inc. v. Stora Kopparbergs Bergslags AB, 701 F. Supp. 1157 (W.D. Pa. 1988); *cf.* Hennessy Indus. v. FMC Corp., 779 F.2d 402 (7th Cir. 1985) (rejecting attempted monopolization charge based on refusal to license where patentee and licensee accounted for less than 15% of industry sales); Handgards, Inc. v. Ethicon, Inc., 743 F.2d 1282, 1294 (9th Cir. 1984) (plaintiff proved " 'that the defendant patentee possessed or threatened to possess an ability to lessen competition in the relevant market' ") (quoting Handguards, Inc. v. Ethicon, Inc., 601 F.2d 986, 993 n.13 (9th Cir. 1979), *cert. denied*, 444 U.S. 1025 (1980)), *cert. denied*, 469 U.S. 1190 (1985); Papst Motoren GmbH v. Kanematsu-Goshu (U.S.A.) Inc., 629 F. Supp. 864, 871 (S.D.N.Y. 1986).

20. ANTITRUST DIV., U.S. DEP'T. OF JUSTICE, ANTITRUST ENFORCEMENT GUIDELINES FOR INTERNATIONAL OPERATIONS (1988) at § 3.6 [hereinafter INTERNATIONAL GUIDELINES]. The INTERNATIONAL GUIDELINES are *reprinted in* Appendix E to this treatise and 4 TRADE REG. REP. (CCH) ¶ 13,109.

21. *Id.*

to other forms of property created, transferred or used in the market.[22]

3. *Acquisition of Issued Patents as an Antitrust Violation*

a. PATENTS OBTAINED BY GRANT, PURCHASE OR ASSIGNMENT

A company does not violate the antitrust laws merely by acquiring patents based upon inventions made by its own employees.[23] Such procurement of patents does not normally violate the antitrust laws, even where the patents give their owner monopoly power in a relevant economic market.[24]

The assignment of a patent to another by the patentee is specifically authorized by the Patent Act.[25] Nonetheless, an assignment may violate the Sherman Act where the assignment constitutes unlawful monopolization or is part of an agreement by competitors to restrain trade. For example, in *United States v. Singer Manufacturing Co.*,[26] the Supreme Court found that the transfer of a patent in the context of a broader monopolistic scheme from a Swiss manufacturer to its American licensee to facilitate bringing infringement actions against Japanese competitors violated Section 1. Similarly, in *Kobe, Inc. v. Dempsey Pump Co.*,[27] the Tenth Circuit found that the acquisition, nonuse, and enforcement of "every important patent" in the field with a purpose to exclude competition together with other anticompetitive acts constituted a violation of Section 2 of the Sherman Act.

---

22. *Id.*; *see also* C. Rule, The Antitrust Implications of International Licensing: After the Nine No-Nos (Oct. 21, 1986), *reprinted in* 4 TRADE REG. REP. (CCH) ¶ 13,131; Andewelt, *Antitrust Perspective on Intellectual Property Protection*, 30 PAT. TRADEMARK & COPYRIGHT J. (BNA) 319 (July 25, 1985); Andewelt, *Analysis of Patent Pools under the Antitrust Laws*, 53 ANTITRUST L.J. 611 (1984); J. Paul McGrath, Patent Licensing: A Fresh Look at Antitrust Principles in a Changing Economic Environment (Apr. 5, 1984), *reprinted in* 4 TRADE REG. REP. (CCH) ¶ 13,130; Lipsky, *Current Antitrust Division Views on Patent Licensing Practices*, 50 ANTITRUST L.J. 515 (1981). In its VERTICAL RESTRAINTS GUIDELINES, the Department briefly discussed patent licensing but refrained from applying the GUIDELINES to it. DEPARTMENT OF JUSTICE, VERTICAL RESTRAINTS GUIDELINES at § 2.4 (1985), *reprinted in* 4 TRADE REG. REP. ¶ 13,105.

23. Automatic Radio Mfg. Co. v. Hazeltine Research, Inc., 339 U.S. 827, 834 (1950) ("mere accumulation of patents, no matter how many, is not in and of itself illegal"); *see* Cole v. Hughes Tool Co., 215 F.2d 924, 934 (10th Cir.), *cert. denied*, 348 U.S. 927 (1954).

24. SCM Corp. v. Xerox Corp., 645 F.2d 1195, 1206 (2d Cir. 1981) ("the procurement of a patent . . . will not violate § 2 even where it is likely that the patent monopoly will evolve into an economic monopoly"), *cert. denied*, 455 U.S. 1016 (1982); Cole v. Hughes Tool Co., 215 F.2d 924, 937 (10th Cir.), *cert. denied*, 348 U.S. 927 (1954); United States v. Aluminum Co. of Am., 148 F.2d 416 (2d Cir. 1945); Chisholm-Ryder Co. v. Mecca Bros., 1983-1 Trade Cas. (CCH) ¶ 65,406 (W.D.N.Y. 1982); United States v. E.I. du Pont de Nemours & Co., 118 F. Supp. 41, 214 (D. Del. 1953) (powers "granted under a valid patent are not powers on which plaintiff may rely to establish monopolization"), *aff'd*, 351 U.S. 377 (1956).

25. 35 U.S.C. § 261 (1988).

26. 374 U.S. 174 (1963).

27. 198 F.2d 416, 423-24 (10th Cir.), *cert. denied*, 344 U.S. 837 (1952). Prior to *Kobe* numerous cases dealt with patents in the context of broader monopolization schemes. *Singer*, 374 U.S. 174; United States v. United States Gypsum Co., 333 U.S. 364 (1948); Hartford-Empire Co. v. United States, 323 U.S. 386, *clarified*, 324 U.S. 570 (1945); United States v. Besser Mfg. Co., 96 F. Supp. 304 (E.D. Mich. 1951), *aff'd*, 343 U.S. 444 (1952); United States v. General Elec. Co., 82 F. Supp. 753, 816 (D.N.J. 1949); United States v. Vehicular Parking, Ltd., 54 F. Supp. 828, 839-40 (D. Del.), *modified*, 56 F. Supp. 297 (D. Del. 1944), *modified*, 61 F. Supp. 656 (D. Del. 1945); Stewart-Warner Corp. v. Staley, 42 F. Supp. 140, 146 (W.D. Pa. 1941).

Apart from such broader schemes to monopolize, the transfer of individual patents will raise antitrust concerns only infrequently. The transferability of a patent is often a necessary prerequisite to commercialization of the idea it embodies. In *SCM Corp. v. Xerox Corp.*,[28] the Second Circuit recognized that the role of investors in "both the inventive process and commercialization of inventions" is an important and procompetitive reality to be accommodated by the patent and antitrust laws.[29]

The acquisition of patent rights in connection with certain research and development joint ventures is covered by the National Cooperative Research Act.[30] If a venture qualifies under the Act, the conduct of the joint venture, including its acquisition of patent rights, is to be judged under the rule of reason.[31] Moreover, if the parties file the prescribed notice, treble damages will not be available in an action challenging the conduct of the venture.[32]

Patents and copyrights are "assets" for the purpose of Section 7 of the Clayton Act.[33] An exclusive license under a patent or a copyright is also an asset for that purpose.[34]

b. PATENTS OBTAINED BY GRANTBACKS

Patentees frequently seek to condition the grant of a license under their patents on the licensee's obligation to reassign to the patent holder any improvement patents secured by the licensee or on the licensee's obligation to license the patent holder under subsequently developed patents. Such a provision in a patent license is called a "grantback."

Grantbacks permit a patentee to license its technology without the risk that it will be foreclosed from the market by subsequent developments by its licensees.[35] The Supreme Court has found that grantbacks raise antitrust concerns primarily because of the possibility that they will discourage invention by the licensee.[36] In *Transparent-Wrap Machine Corp. v. Stokes & Smith Co.*,[37] the Supreme Court held that a rule of reason analysis should be used to test the grantback provision in an exclusive license agreement on a patented packaging machine. The grantback

---

28.   645 F.2d 1195 (2d Cir. 1981), *cert. denied*, 455 U.S. 1016 (1982).

29.   *Id.* at 1206 n.9.

30.   National Cooperative Research Act of 1984, 15 U.S.C. §§ 4301-4305 (1988); *see also* Statement of J. Paul McGrath, then Assistant Att'y Gen., Antitrust Division (1984), *reprinted in* 4 TRADE REG. REP. (CCH) ¶ 13,121 (explaining notification procedures).

31.   15 U.S.C. § 4302 (1988).

32.   *Id.*

33.   Crucible, Inc. v. Stora Kopparbergs Bergslags AB, 701 F. Supp. 1157, 1162-63 (W.D. Pa. 1988); SCM Corp. v. Xerox Corp., 463 F. Supp. 983 (D. Conn. 1978), *remanded on other grounds*, 599 F.2d 32 (2d Cir. 1979); *In re* Yarn Process Patent Validity & Antitrust Litig., 398 F. Supp. 31, 35 (S.D. Fla. 1974), *aff'd in part and rev'd in part*, 541 F.2d 1127 (5th Cir. 1976), *cert. denied*, 433 U.S. 910 (1977); Dole Valve Co. v. Perfection Bar Equip., Inc., 311 F. Supp. 459, 463 (N.D. Ill. 1970).

34.   *See* United States v. Lever Bros., 216 F. Supp. 887, 889 (S.D.N.Y. 1963); United States v. Columbia Pictures Corp., 189 F. Supp. 153, 181-82 (S.D.N.Y. 1960).

35.   Remarks of then Assistant Att'y Gen. B. Wilson Before the Fourth New England Antitrust Conference, Patent & Know-how License Agreements: Field of Use, Territorial, Price and Quantity Restrictions at 4 (Nov. 6, 1970); INTERNATIONAL GUIDELINES, *supra* note 20, at Case 11.

36.   *Hartford-Empire*, 323 U.S. at 400.

37.   329 U.S. 637 (1947).

provision required the licensee to assign to the licensor all patents for improvements applicable to the patented machine, leaving the licensee with only a nonexclusive, royalty-free license on the improvements. The Court recognized "the possibilities of abuse" and emphasized that it was holding only that grantbacks do not constitute per se violations.[38]

In *United States v. National Lead Co.*,[39] the Supreme Court approved a limited grantback provision in a decree against two defendants which together sold over 90% of titanium pigments in the United States. The decree required National Lead and du Pont to grant to any applicant a nonexclusive license under certain applicable patents at a "uniform, reasonable royalty," but permitted such licenses to "be conditioned upon the reciprocal grant of a license . . . at a reasonable royalty, under any and all patents covering titanium pigments . . . now issued or pending, or issued within five years from the date of this decree, if any, owned or controlled by such applicant."[40]

In applying a rule of reason analysis to grantback provision, the courts have identified a number of relevant factors: (1) whether the grantback is exclusive or nonexclusive; (2) if exclusive, whether the licensee retains the right to use the improvements; (3) whether the grantback precludes, permits or requires the licensor to grant sublicenses; (4) whether the grantback is limited to the scope of the licensed patents or covers inventions which would not infringe the licensed patent; (5) the duration of the grantback; (6) whether the grantback is royalty free; (7) the market power of the parties; (8) whether the parties are competitors; and (9) the effect of the grantback on the incentive for developmental research.[41]

Many cases hold that in the absence of anticompetitive intent or restrictive practices, the grantback of a nonexclusive license does not violate the antitrust laws or constitute misuse.[42] Exclusive grantbacks, standing alone, have also been

---

38. *Id.* at 646-48. On remand, the court of appeals found no illegality. 161 F.2d 565 (2d Cir.), *cert. denied*, 331 U.S. 837 (1947).

39. 332 U.S. 319, 335-36, 359-60 (1947).

40. *Id.* at 336.

41. *E.g.*, Santa Fe-Pomeroy, Inc. v. P & Z Co., 569 F.2d 1084, 1101 (9th Cir. 1978) ("the grantback was limited in time and subject matter . . . and therefore had no restrictive or 'chilling' effect on any improvements"); International Nickel Co. v. Ford Motor Co., 166 F. Supp. 551, 565-66 (S.D.N.Y. 1958); United States v. Associated Patents, Inc., 134 F. Supp. 74, 82 (E.D. Mich. 1955) (outside parties were foreclosed from obtaining improvement licenses, technological developments were discouraged), *aff'd mem. sub nom.* Mac Inv. Co. v. United States, 350 U.S. 960 (1956); United States v. E.I. du Pont de Nemours & Co., 118 F. Supp. 41, 224 (D. Del. 1953) (grantback agreements did not enhance du Pont's market power, scope of agreements was limited, no proof of refusal to license by du Pont), *aff'd*, 351 U.S. 377 (1956); United States v. Besser Mfg. Co., 96 F. Supp. 304, 310-11 (E.D. Mich. 1951) (purpose of unlawful agreements was "to make certain that these two giants of the industry didn't battle each other over patents any more"); United States v. General Electric Co., 82 F. Supp. 753, 815-16 (D.N.J. 1949) (GE acquired patents "to perpetuate a control over the incandescent electric lamp long after its basic patents expired"); United States v. National Lead Co., 63 F. Supp. 513, 524 (S.D.N.Y. 1945) (unlawful "agreements applied to patents not yet issued and to inventions not yet imagined"), *aff'd*, 332 U.S. 319 (1947).

42. Binks Mfg. Co. v. Ransburg Electro-Coating Corp., 281 F.2d 252, 259 (7th Cir. 1960), *cert. dismissed*, 366 U.S. 211 (1961); Barr Rubber Prods. Co. v. Sun Rubber Co., 277 F. Supp. 484, 506 (S.D.N.Y. 1967), *aff'd in part and rev'd in part*, 425 F.2d 1114 (2d Cir.), *cert. denied*, 400 U.S. 878 (1970); Well Surveys, Inc. v. McCullough Tool Co., 199 F. Supp. 374, 395 (N.D. Okla. 1961), *aff'd*, 343 F.2d 381 (10th Cir. 1965), *cert. denied*, 383 U.S. 933 (1966); International Nickel Co. v. Ford Motor Co., 166 F. Supp. 551, 565 (S.D.N.Y. 1958).

upheld.[43] Where license agreements combine grantbacks with other restrictions, both exclusive and nonexclusive grantbacks have been held to be illegal.[44]

The Department of Justice has consistently taken the position that a nonexclusive grantback of a license under subsequently developed technology is unlikely to raise antitrust concerns.[45] In 1970, the Department stated that it viewed as unlawful a provision in a patent license which required the licensee to assign to the patentee subsequently issued patents.[46] In 1981, the Department stated that where a patentee's exclusive grantback provision in licenses granted to all or most actual competitors of the patentee under which all technology in the field, whether or not an "improvement" on the licensed patent, was granted back to the patentee would be "clearly objectionable."[47]

More recent Department pronouncements tend to stress the procompetitive aspects of grantbacks.[48]

4. Enforcement of Patents as an Antitrust Violation

a. PATENTS OBTAINED BY FRAUD

The mere procurement of a patent from the Patent and Trademark Office (PTO) does not violate the antitrust laws.[49] However, the procurement of a patent through fraud on the PTO will render all of the claims of the patent unenforceable

---

43. Santa Fe-Pomeroy, Inc. v. P & Z Co., 569 F.2d 1084, 1101-02 (9th Cir. 1978) (many competitive alternatives and no evidence that the grantback had deterred improvements); Zajicek v. Koolvent Metal Awning Corp. of Am., 283 F.2d 127, 131-32 (9th Cir. 1960) (requirement that a licensee assign patents broader than those of licensor "substantially enhanced and extended" monopoly of the licensed patent), cert. denied, 365 U.S. 859 (1961); Swofford v. B & W, Inc., 251 F. Supp. 811, 820-21 (S.D. Tex. 1966), aff'd, 395 F.2d 362 (5th Cir.), cert. denied, 393 U.S. 935 (1968); Sperry Prods., Inc. v. Aluminum Co. of Am., 171 F. Supp. 901, 936-38 (N.D. Ohio 1959), aff'd in part and rev'd in part, 285 F.2d 911 (6th Cir. 1960), cert. denied, 368 U.S. 890 (1961). But see Duplan Corp. v. Deering Milliken, Inc., 444 F. Supp. 648, 700 (D.S.C. 1977), aff'd in part and rev'd in part, 594 F.2d 979 (4th Cir. 1979), cert. denied, 444 U.S. 1015 (1980).

44. United States v. Aluminum Co. of Am., 91 F. Supp. 333, 410 (S.D.N.Y. 1950); GE, 82 F. Supp. at 815-16 (nonexclusive grantbacks held illegal where court also found a broad scheme to monopolize an industry and to eliminate competition after basic patents expired); United States v. General Elec. Co., 80 F. Supp. 989, 1005-06 (S.D.N.Y. 1948) (grantbacks in conjunction with price-fixing agreements held to violate the antitrust laws).

45. Remarks of B. Wilson Before the Fourth New England Antitrust Conference, Patent and Know-how License Agreements: Field of Use, Territorial, Price and Quantity Restrictions at 4 (Nov. 6, 1970); see Rule, The Administration's Views: Antitrust Analysis after the Nine No-Nos., 55 ANTITRUST L.J. 365 (1986); Lipsky, Current Antitrust Division Views on Patent Licensing Practices, 50 ANTITRUST L.J. 515, 519-20 (1981). INTERNATIONAL GUIDELINES, supra note 20, at Case 11. See generally ABA Antitrust and International Trade and Practice Sections, Report on Draft Antitrust Guidelines for International Operations, 57 ANTITRUST L.J. 651, 676 (1988).

46. B. Wilson, supra note 35, at 4.

47. Lipsky, supra note 22, at 520.

48. C. Rule, supra note 22, at 12; INTERNATIONAL GUIDELINES, supra note 20, at Case 11.

49. FMC Corp. v. Manitowoc Co., 835 F.2d 1411, 1418 & n.16 (Fed. Cir. 1987); Brunswick Corp. v. Riegel Textile Corp., 752 F.2d 261, 265 (7th Cir. 1984), cert. denied, 472 U.S. 1018 (1985); see Oetiker v. Jurid Werke, GmbH, 556 F.2d 1 (D.C. Cir. 1977).

in an infringement action,[50] and may expose the patentee to liability for the defendant's attorneys fees under the Patent Act.[51] Such fraud may form the basis for a criminal prosecution under Sections 1 and 2 of the Sherman Act[52] and may also support an action for cancellation of the patent at the request of the United States.[53] Exploitation of a fraudulently procured patent may also constitute a violation of Section 5 of the FTC Act.[54] In addition, "inequitable conduct" less egregious than common law fraud may also render all of the claims of the patent unenforceable.

In *Walker Process Equipment, Inc. v. Food Machinery & Chemical Corp.*,[55] the Supreme Court ruled that the enforcement of a patent procured by fraud may form the basis for a cause of action under Section 2 of the Sherman Act exposing the patentee to a treble damage claim under Section 4 of the Clayton Act. In *Walker Process*, the defendant alleged that the patentee had procured the patent in suit by filing a false oath that failed to disclose to the PTO that a statutory bar to patentability existed.[56] The Supreme Court held that these allegations were sufficient to state a claim under Section 2 provided the remaining elements of a

---

50. Kingsdown Medical Consultants v. Hollister Inc., 863 F.2d 867, 877 (Fed. Cir. 1988) (en banc portion of decision), *cert. denied*, 490 U.S. 1067 (1989); J.P. Stevens & Co. v. Lex Tex Ltd., 747 F.2d 1553, 1560 (Fed. Cir. 1984) (Markey, Ch. J., five-member panel), *cert. denied*, 474 U.S. 822 (1985). This rule applies to inequitable conduct in reissuing patents. Hewlett-Packard Co. v. Bausch & Lomb, Inc., 882 F.2d 1556, 1563 (Fed. Cir. 1989), *cert. denied*, 493 U.S. 1076 (1990); *see* 35 U.S.C. § 288 (1988) ("Whenever, *without deceptive intention*, a claim of a patent is invalid, an action may be maintained for infringement of a claim of the patent which may be valid.") (emphasis added); Conceptual Eng'g Assocs. v. Aelectronic Bonding, Inc., 714 F. Supp. 1262 (D.R.I. 1989).

51. Fraud or inequitable conduct may form the basis for a finding that a patent case is "exceptional" justifying an award of attorneys' fees under 35 U.S.C. § 285 (1988). Kimberly-Clark Corp. v. Johnson & Johnson, 745 F.2d 1437, 1458 (Fed. Cir. 1984). "The trial standard of proving 'exceptional' is 'clear and convincing.'" Loctite Corp. v. Ultraseal Ltd., 781 F.2d 861, 878 n.12 (Fed. Cir. 1985).

52. *See* United States v. Union Camp Corp., 1969 Trade Cas. (CCH) ¶ 72,689 (E.D. Va. 1969) (consent decree) (indictment charged fraud on the courts in maintaining a patent infringement suit on a patent known to be invalid), *final judgment terminated*, 1990-1 Trade Cas. (CCH) ¶ 69,000 (E.D. Va. 1990); *see also* United States v. Markham, 537 F.2d 187 (5th Cir. 1976) (fraudulent statement and forged documents filed in an interference proceeding in the Patent Office to determine priority of invention), *cert. denied*, 429 U.S. 1041 (1977).

53. United States v. American Bell Tel. Co., 128 U.S. 315 (1888); United States v. Saf-T-Boom Corp., 164 U.S.P.Q. (BNA) 283 (E.D. Ark.), *aff'd per curiam*, 431 F.2d 737 (8th Cir. 1970).

54. 15 U.S.C. § 45 (1988); *see* Charles Pfizer & Co. v. FTC, 401 F.2d 574, 579 (6th Cir. 1968), *cert. denied*, 394 U.S. 920 (1969); American Cyanamid Co. v. FTC, 363 F.2d 757 (6th Cir. 1966), *on remand*, 72 F.T.C. 618 (1967), *later appeal sub nom.* Charles Pfizer & Co. v. FTC, 401 F.2d 574 (6th Cir. 1968), *cert. denied*, 394 U.S. 920 (1969).

55. 382 U.S. 172 (1965).

56. Under 35 U.S.C. § 102(a) (1988) an applicant is not entitled to a patent if his invention has been on sale for more than one year prior to the time the application for patent is made. At the time *Walker Process* was decided, the patent applicant was obligated to file an oath, prescribed by statute which, inter alia, required him to aver that no such "on sale" bar exists. *Id.* § 115. The allegation in *Walker Process* was that the patentee signed this oath with knowledge that an on sale bar existed.

monopolization claim were proven.[57]

In an attempted monopolization case under a *Walker Process* theory, the institution of the litigation by the patentee satisfies the specific intent element needed for attempted monopolization.[58] In addition, a plaintiff must prove: (1) that the patent was procured by fraud; (2) that the patent claims confer market power in a properly defined market;[59] (3) that the invention was not patentable;[60] and (4) that the party asserting the claim has antitrust standing and has suffered damages.[61] The allegations of fraud must comply with Rule 9(b) of the Federal Rules of Civil Procedure.[62]

(1) The Requirement of Fraud: Inequitable Conduct Distinguished

To establish the fraud element of a *Walker Process* claim, courts have required the proofs to adhere closely to the elements of common law fraud, i.e., a misrepresentation of a material fact, intentionally made to deceive, reasonably relied

---

57.   382 U.S. at 178. On the other hand, fraudulent procurement, standing alone, without assertion or enforcement, does not give rise to a treble damage claim. *See* Struthers Scientific & Int'l Corp. v. General Foods Corp., 334 F. Supp. 1329, 1332 (D. Del. 1971) (dictum); Oetiker v. Jurid Werke, GmbH, 671 F.2d 596 (D.C. Cir. 1982) (dictum).

58.   Brunswick Corp. v. Riegel Textile Corp., 752 F.2d 261, 265 (7th Cir. 1984), *cert. denied*, 472 U.S. 1018 (1985); *see also* Handgards, Inc. v. Ethicon, Inc., 601 F.2d 986, 993 (9th Cir. 1979), *cert. denied*, 444 U.S. 1025 (1980).

59.   *Walker Process*, 382 U.S. at 178; Technicon Instruments Corp. v. Alpkem Corp., 866 F.2d 417 (Fed. Cir. 1989); Hennessy Indus. v. FMC Corp., 779 F.2d 402 (7th Cir. 1985); *American Hoist*, 725 F.2d at 1366-67; *Brunswick*, 752 F.2d at 265; *see also* Handgards, Inc. v. Ethicon, Inc., 743 F.2d 1282 (9th Cir. 1984), *cert. denied*, 469 U.S. 1190 (1985); Crucible, Inc. v. Stora Kopparbergs Bergslags AB, 701 F. Supp. 1157 (W.D. Pa. 1988).

60.   *See Brunswick*, 752 F.2d at 265; E.I. du Pont de Nemours & Co. v. Berkley & Co., 620 F.2d 1247, 1274 (8th Cir. 1980); United States Movidyn Corp. v. Hercules, Inc., 388 F. Supp. 1146, 1155 (D. Minn. 1975); *see also* Norton v. Curtiss, 433 F.2d 779, 794 (C.C.P.A. 1970). In *Brunswick*, the Seventh Circuit reasoned that unless the patent was not patentable at all, whatever exclusionary power the patent possesses is not a concern of the antitrust laws. The requirement that the claimed invention not be patentable (as opposed to being procured as a result of dubious practices by the applicant for patent) is also manifested in the level of conduct need to prove "fraud."

61.   The party asserting the claim must have antitrust standing. Indium Corp. of Am. v. Semi-Alloys, Inc., 781 F.2d 879 (Fed. Cir. 1985) (no standing where plaintiff is not prepared to manufacture product covered by patent), *cert. denied*, 479 U.S. 820 (1986); Brunswick Corp. v. Riegel Textile Corp., 752 F.2d 261 (7th Cir. 1984), *cert. denied*, 472 U.S. 1018 (1985); Handgards, Inc. v. Ethicon, Inc., 743 F.2d 1282, 1295-97 (9th Cir. 1984) (standing found), *cert. denied*, 469 U.S. 1190 (1985); D.L. Auld Co. v. Park Electrochem. Corp., 1986-2 Trade Cas. (CCH) ¶ 67,309 (E.D.N.Y. 1986) (shareholder lacked standing). The requirement of damages is also an essential element. *See* Grip-Pak, Inc. v. Illinois Tool Works, Inc., 651 F. Supp. 1482 (N.D. Ill. 1986); Indium Corp. of Am. v. Semi-Alloys, Inc., 611 F. Supp. 379 (N.D.N.Y.), *aff'd*, 781 F.2d 879 (Fed. Cir. 1985), *cert. denied*, 479 U.S. 820 (1986); *cf.* Hu-Friedy Mfg. Co. v. Peerless Int'l, Inc., 1986-2 Trade Cas. (CCH) ¶ 67,197 (N.D. Ill. 1986) (ordinary requirements of § 2 case apply to claim attempted monopolization based on bad faith assertion of a trademark).

62.   A conclusory assertion that the patentee withheld material information "about pertinent prior art affecting patentability and validity of said Letters Patent and . . . knowingly and willfully present[ed] false and/or misleading arguments and materials . . . and in so doing perpetrated a fraud on [the PTO]" is insufficient. Papst Motoren GmbH v. Kanematsu-Goshu (U.S.A.) Inc., 629 F. Supp. 864, 871-72 (S.D.N.Y. 1986); *see* Erie Technological Prods. v. JFD Elec. Components Corp., 198 U.S.P.Q. (BNA) 179, 186 (E.D.N.Y. 1978).

upon by the party to whom the misrepresentation was made.[63] In one case, a district court described the element of fraud as follows:

> "knowing and willful fraud" as the term is used in *Walker*, can mean no less than clear, convincing proof of intentional fraud involving affirmative dishonesty, "a deliberately planned and carefully executed scheme to defraud . . . the Patent Office."[64]

Other cases likewise hold that specific intent to commit fraud, and not some lesser standard such as gross negligence, is necessary for a *Walker Process* claim to be made out.[65]

With regard to the materiality of the misstatement that forms the basis for the fraud, most courts have required "but for" materiality; that is, but for the misrepresentation the patent would not have issued.[66] Each of the elements of the fraud must be proven by clear and convincing evidence.[67]

Fraud sufficient to state a *Walker Process* claim must be distinguished from the

---

63. *See, e.g., Walker Process*, 382 U.S. at 177; Argus Chem. Corp. v. Fibre Glass-Evercoat Co., 812 F.2d 1381, 1383-86 (Fed. Cir. 1987); Korody-Colyer Corp. v. General Motors Corp., 828 F.2d 1572, 1577-78 (Fed. Cir. 1987); Kearny & Trecker Corp. v. Cincinnati Milacron, Inc., 562 F.2d 365 (6th Cir. 1977); Cataphote Corp. v. DeSoto Chem. Coatings, Inc., 450 F.2d 769, 770-71 (9th Cir. 1971), *cert. denied*, 408 U.S. 929 (1972); Jack Winter, Inc. v. Koratron Co., 375 F. Supp. 1, 67 (N.D. Cal. 1974).

64. *Cataphote Corp.*, 450 F.2d at 772 (quoting Hazel-Atlas Glass Co. v. Hartford-Empire Co., 322 U.S. 238, 245 (1944)).

65. In Argus Chemical Corp. v. Fibre Glass-Evercoat Co., 812 F.2d 1381 (Fed. Cir. 1987), the Federal Circuit, applying Ninth Circuit law, expressly refused to extend liability under the *Walker Process* doctrine to cases where the patent was held unenforceable for inequitable conduct less egregious than common law fraud. *Accord* American Hoist & Derrick Co. v. Sowa & Sons, 725 F.2d 1350, 1368 (Fed. Cir.), *cert. denied*, 469 U.S. 821 (1984); *see* Papst Motoren GmbH v. Kanematsu-Goshu (U.S.A.) Inc., 629 F. Supp. 864, 870 (S.D.N.Y. 1986) (*"Walker* and its progeny emphasize that to sustain [defendant's] antitrust counterclaim, 'deliberate fraud' is required: 'there must be allegations and proof of knowing, willful and intentional acts of misrepresentation to the Patent Office.' ") (quoting Erie Technological Prods. v. JFD Elec. Components Corp., 198 U.S.P.Q. (BNA) 179, 185 (E.D.N.Y. 1978)). *But cf.* Litton Indus. Prods. v. Solid State Sys., 755 F.2d 158, 166 & n.18 (Fed. Cir. 1985), where the court stated:
   > wholly inadvertent errors or honest mistakes, which are caused by neither fraudulent intent *nor by the patentee's gross negligence*, do not constitute the requisite level of intent. . . . This level of intent for *Walker Process* actions, where inequitable conduct . . . is used offensively for recovering damages, apparently corresponds to the level of intent required under Federal Circuit case law for asserting inequitable conduct defensively to render a patent unenforceable.

   (emphasis added) (citations omitted) (looking to Ninth Circuit law for guidance in interpreting Washington state law).

66. Litton Indus. Prods. v. Solid State Sys., 755 F.2d 158, 166 n.19 (Fed. Cir. 1985) ("the offensive use of such conduct before the PTO generally requires a higher level of materiality than that required for defensive purposes") (looking to Ninth Circuit law for guidance in interpreting Washington state law); Rohm & Haas Co. v. Dawson Chem. Co., 635 F. Supp. 1211, 1218 (S.D. Tex. 1986) ("The fraud must be material *in an antitrust sense* in that the alleged infringer/antitrust counterclaimant must show that but for the fraud no patent would have been issued to anyone.") (emphasis in original); *cf.* J.P. Stevens & Co. v. Lex Tex Ltd., 747 F.2d 1553, 1560 n.7 (Fed. Cir. 1984) ("Our discussion of the criteria for unenforceability does not encompass the test for a *Walker Process* type of claim.") (Markey, Ch. J., five-member panel), *cert. denied*, 474 U.S. 822 (1985).

67. Oetiker v. Jurid Werke, GmbH, 671 F.2d 596 (D.C. Cir. 1982); Handgards Inc. v. Ethicon, Inc., 601 F.2d 986, 996 (9th Cir. 1979), *cert. denied*, 444 U.S. 1025 (1980).

types of less egregious conduct that can render a patent unenforceable, often collectively termed "inequitable conduct." "The concept of inequitable conduct in patent procurement derives from the equitable doctrine of unclean hands: that a person who obtains a patent by intentionally misleading the PTO cannot enforce the patent."[68] The availability of this defense in a patent infringement or declaratory judgment action has been clear since at least as early as 1945, when the Supreme Court said, in *Precision Instrument Manufacturing Co. v. Automotive Maintenance Machine Co.,*[69] that patent applicants have "an uncompromising duty to report to [the PTO] all facts concerning possible fraud or inequitableness underlying the applications at issue."[70]

To make out an inequitable conduct defense, the accused infringer must show by "clear and convincing evidence"[71] a failure by the applicant[72] to disclose to the Patent Office material information known to him, or submission of false material information, with an intent to act inequitably.[73] Inequitable conduct as a defense can be made out by a showing of conduct less egregious than common law fraud.[74]

While inequitable conduct defenses and *Walker Process* counterclaims are frequently brought together, conduct sufficient to support an inequitable conduct defense, but not rising to the level of common law fraud, will not support a claim under Section 2.[75]

---

68.   Demaco Corp. v. F. Von Langsdorff Licensing Ltd., 851 F.2d 1387, 1394 (Fed. Cir.), *cert. denied*, 488 U.S. 956 (1988).

69.   324 U.S. 806 (1945) (failure to disclose to Patent Office the existence of perjury in an interference proceeding); *see* Hazel-Atlas Glass Co. v. Hartford-Empire Co., 322 U.S. 238, 240-51 (1944) (article used in support of a pending application was written by the applicant under a different name to deceive PTO); *see also* Kingsland v. Dorsey, 338 U.S. 318, 319 (1949) (concealment of participation of applicant's attorney in preparation of article used to support application); Shawkee Mfg. Co. v. Hartford-Empire Co., 322 U.S. 271, 273-74 (1944).

70.   324 U.S. at 818.

71.   SmithKline Diagnostics, Inc. v. Helena Labs., 859 F.2d 878, 891 (Fed. Cir. 1988); Specialty Composites v. Cabot Corp., 845 F.2d 981, 991 (Fed. Cir. 1988); FMC Corp. v. Manitowoc Co., 835 F.2d 1411, 1415 (Fed. Cir. 1987); *J.P. Stevens*, 747 F.2d at 1559.

72.   Knowledge of others having substantive involvement in the application is chargable to the applicant. 37 C.F.R. § 1.56(a) (1991); *Manitowoc*, 835 F.2d at 1415 n.8; *see* Kimberly-Clark Corp. v. Johnson & Johnson, 745 F.2d 1437, 1449-50 (Fed. Cir. 1984).

73.   *Manitowoc*, 835 F.2d at 1415; *see* Merck & Co. v. Danbury Pharmacal, Inc., 873 F.2d 1418, 1420 (Fed. Cir. 1989).

74.   Argus Chem. Corp. v. Fibre Glass-Evercoat Co., 759 F.2d 10, 12 n.3 (Fed. Cir.), *cert. denied.*, 474 U.S. 903 (1985) (*Argus I*). In *J.P. Stevens*, the Federal Circuit said:
        Conduct before the PTO that may render a patent unenforceable is broader than "common law fraud." It includes failure to disclose material information, or submission of false material information, with an intent to mislead. Because the "fraud" label can be confused with other forms of conduct, this opinion avoids that label and uses "inequitable conduct" as a more accurate description of the proscribed activity, it being understood that the term encompasses affirmative acts of commission, *e.g.*, submission of false information as well as omission, *e.g.*, failure to disclose material information.
        747 F.2d at 1559 (citation omitted).

75.   FMC Corp. v. Manitowoc Co., 835 F.2d 1411, 1417-18 (Fed Cir. 1987); Korody-Colyer Corp. v. General Motors Corp., 828 F.2d 1572, 1578 (Fed. Cir. 1987); Argus Chem. Corp. v. Fibreglass Evercoat Co., 812 F.2d 1381, 1384-85 (Fed. Cir. 1987); American Hoist & Derrick Co. v. Sowa & Sons, 725 F.2d 1350, 1368 (Fed. Cir.), *cert. denied*, 469 U.S. 821 (1984).

b. ENFORCEMENT OF AN INVALID PATENT

It is not a violation of the Sherman Act to bring a patent infringement suit, even if it is determined in the suit that the patent is invalid.[76] However, the commencement of litigation to enforce a patent known to be invalid may also give rise to antitrust liability, irrespective of whether the patent was obtained by fraud on the PTO.[77] In such a case, the specific intent required to support a Section 2 claim exists because the patentee instituted or maintained the litigation in bad faith — that is, with knowledge of the invalidity of the patent.[78] The other elements of the claim are the same as under the *Walker Process* theory.[79] Proof of the patentee's bad faith must be made by clear and convincing evidence.[80]

The close relation between a *Walker Process* Section 2 claim and one for bad faith enforcement of a patent is demonstrated by the leading case of *Handgards, Inc. v. Ethicon, Inc.*[81] In *Handgards*, the Ninth Circuit found that a violation of Section 2 occurred when a patentee instituted litigation with knowledge that its patent was

---

76. Atari Games Corp. v. Nintendo of Am., Inc., 897 F.2d 1572, 1576 (Fed. Cir. 1990) ("Congress has specifically granted patent owners the right to commence a civil suit in order to protect their inventions. 35 U.S.C. § 281."); Handgards, Inc. v. Ethicon, Inc., 601 F.2d 986, 993 (9th Cir. 1979) ("Patentees must be permitted to test the validity of their patents . . . ."), *cert. denied*, 444 U.S. 1025 (1980); *accord* Colortronic Reinhard & Co. v. Plastic Controls, Inc., 668 F.2d 1, 9 (1st Cir. 1981).

77. Handgards, Inc. v. Ethicon, Inc., 601 F.2d 986, 992-96 (9th Cir. 1979) (presumption of good faith in filing infringement action can be overcome by clear and convincing evidence to the contrary), *cert. denied*, 444 U.S. 1025 (1980); *see* Handgards, Inc. v. Ethicon, Inc., 743 F.2d 1282 (9th Cir. 1984), *cert. denied*, 469 U.S. 1190 (1985); Hart-Carter Co. v. J.P. Burroughs & Son, 605 F. Supp. 1327, 1347-48 (E.D. Mich. 1985); *cf.* Kearney & Trecker Corp. v. Cincinnati Milacron, Inc., 562 F.2d 365, 372 (6th Cir. 1977); Duplan Corp. v. Deering Milliken, Inc., 444 F. Supp. 648, 701 (D.S.C. 1977), *aff'd in part and rev'd in part*, 594 F.2d 979 (4th Cir. 1979), *cert. denied*, 444 U.S. 1015 (1980); Kellogg Co. v. National Biscuit Co., 71 F.2d 662 (2d Cir. 1934) (bad faith enforcement of trademark states a claim under § 2); *cf.* CVD, Inc. v. Raytheon Co., 769 F.2d 842 (1st Cir. 1985) (bad faith assertion of trade secret claims known to be invalid violated antitrust laws), *cert. denied*, 475 U.S. 1016 (1986); Boeing Co. v. Sierracin Corp., 108 Wash. 2d 38, 738 P.2d 665 (1987).

78. *Handgards*, 601 F.2d at 990; *accord* Tennant Co. v. Hako Minuteman, Inc., 651 F. Supp. 945 (N.D. Ill. 1986); *see also* Rohm & Hass Co. v. Dawson Chem. Co., 635 F. Supp. 1211, 1218 (S.D. Tex. 1986) ("[*Handgards*] held that the offense which is sanctioned by the antitrust laws is *not* the fraudulent procurement of a patent in circumstances that create monopoly power *but* the bringing of groundless suits of patent infringement.") (emphasis in original).

79. *See* Neumann v. Reinforced Earth Co., 786 F.2d 424, 427-30 (D.C. Cir.), *cert. denied*, 479 U.S. 851 (1986); Brunswick Corp. v. Riegel Textile Corp., 752 F.2d 261, 264-65 (7th Cir. 1984), *cert. denied*, 472 U.S. 1018 (1985).

80. In Argus Chem. Corp. v. Fibre Glass-Evercoat Co., 645 F. Supp. 15, 17 (C.D. Cal. 1986), *aff'd*, 812 F.2d 1381 (Fed. Cir. 1987), the district court stated the elements of a Section 2 attempt to monopolize claim under the *Handgards* theory:
    the defendant must prove (1) by clear and convincing evidence that the patent suit was pursued in bad faith; (2) that plaintiff had a specific intent to monopolize the relevant market; and (3) that a dangerous probability of success existed.
    Accord Loctite Corp. v. Ultraseal Ltd., 781 F.2d 861 (Fed. Cir. 1985) (bad faith in bringing infringement suit must be shown by clear and convincing evidence); Handgards, Inc. v. Ethicon, Inc., 743 F.2d 1282, 1294 (9th Cir. 1984), *cert. denied*, 469 U.S. 1190 (1985); Handgards, Inc. v. Ethicon, Inc., 601 F.2d 986, 996 (9th Cir. 1979), *cert. denied*, 444 U.S. 1025 (1980); Bendix Corp. v. Balax, Inc., 471 F.2d 149, 153 (7th Cir. 1972), *cert. denied*, 414 U.S. 819 (1973).

81. 601 F.2d 986 (9th Cir. 1979), *cert. denied*, 444 U.S. 1025 (1980).

invalid due to an "on sale" bar.[82] An "on sale" bar was the same basis that invalidity was alleged to invalidate the patent in *Walker Process*.[83] In *Walker Process*, the alleged antitrust violation occurred because the patentee sought to enforce a patent in court knowing it was procured by fraud before the PTO.[84] In a *Handgards*-type action, the defendant need not show that the patent was procured by fraud before the PTO. Rather, sufficient evidence of bad faith exists because the defendant learned sometime before suit was filed that the patent is not valid. In a similar vein, it has been held that institution of patent litigation against a defendant known by the patentee not to infringe may violate Section 2.[85]

Because the overt act in this type of case, filing a lawsuit, enjoys first amendment protection,[86] the *Noerr-Pennington* doctrine and first amendment principles will affect the burden of proof and the availability of a cause of action.[87] A few courts have discussed the applicability of the *Noerr-Pennington* doctrine to bad faith patent infringement actions.[88] Other courts, while not discussing *Noerr* specifically, have fashioned limitations on the cause of action consistent with *Noerr*'s precepts. For example, it has been held that a patentee is normally entitled to rely on the statutory presumption of validity in the Patent Law,[89] and hence proof of the patentee's bad faith must be made by clear and convincing evidence.[90] It has also been held that if the patent in suit is found valid, no antitrust counterclaim can be maintained.[91]

One court found that an infringement action commenced for the purpose of monopolizing a market, combined with other anticompetitive conduct, may violate Section 2 of the Sherman Act, even where there is a legitimate belief in validity and infringement. Thus in *Kobe, Inc. v. Dempsey Pump Co.*,[92] the Tenth Circuit found a plan of acquiring all present and future patents relevant to an entire industry, obtaining covenants not to compete from the sellers of the patents, threatening suits against all who dealt with infringers, and widely publicizing infringement suits was held to violate the Sherman Act. In such a case, however, the market the defendant sought to monopolize must be more than that which he may control by the exercise of his patent rights and the overt acts must be demonstrated independently, and must

---

82. *Id.* at 992. The patentees refusal to dismiss the litigation when invalidity became clear, together with certain discovery misconduct were also factors relied on by the court in finding a violation. *Id.*

83. *See supra* note 56.

84. *See supra* notes 55-57 and accompanying text.

85. United States v. Besser Mfg. Co., 96 F. Supp. 304, 312 (E.D. Mich. 1951), *aff'd*, 343 U.S. 444 (1952).

86. California Motor Transp. Co. v. Trucking Unlimited, 404 U.S. 508, 512 (1972).

87. See the discussion of the *Noerr-Pennington* doctrine in Subpart B.3 of Chapter XI of this treatise.

88. *See* Grip-Pak, Inc. v. Illinois Tool Works, Inc., 651 F. Supp. 1482 (N.D. Ill. 1986); Rohm & Hass Co. v. Dawson Chem. Co., 635 F. Supp. 1211 (S.D. Tex. 1986).

89. 35 U.S.C. § 282 (1988).

90. Handgards, Inc. v. Ethicon, Inc., 601 F.2d 986, 993, 996 (9th Cir. 1979), *cert. denied*, 444 U.S. 1025 (1980); *see* Handgards, Inc. v. Ethicon, Inc., 743 F.2d 1282, 1294 (9th Cir. 1984), *cert. denied*, 469 U.S. 1190 (1985); Bendix Corp. v. Balax, Inc., 471 F.2d 149, 153 (7th Cir. 1972), *cert. denied*, 414 U.S. 819 (1973); Tennant Co. v. Hako Minuteman, Inc., 651 F. Supp. 945 (N.D. Ill. 1986).

91. Darda, Inc. USA v. Majorette Toys (U.S.) Inc., 627 F. Supp. 1121 (S.D. Fla. 1986), *aff'd in part and rev'd in part on other grounds mem.*, 824 F.2d 976 (Fed. Cir. 1987).

92. 198 F.2d 416 (10th Cir.), *cert. denied*, 344 U.S. 837 (1952); *cf.* Kellogg Co. v. National Biscuit Co., 71 F.2d 662 (2d Cir. 1934) (involving trademarks).

consist of more than the filing of the infringement suit.[93]

At least one court has held that expenses of defending infringement actions are not recoverable as antitrust damages.[94] Other courts, however, have permitted the recovery of such expenses.[95]

5. *Patent Misuse*

a. THE MISUSE DOCTRINE

The term "patent misuse" is normally used to refer to conduct by the patentee that constitutes a defense to an action to enforce patent rights, either in an infringement action or in a contract action to collect royalties due under a patent license.[96] Throughout much of its existence, the doctrine of patent misuse has been applied to conduct by the patentee that also raises antitrust concerns. Historically, fixing the price of patented goods resold to the public[97] and tie-ins where the tying product was patented[98] were condemned by the Supreme Court as patent misuse when the conduct likewise was challengeable under the antitrust laws.[99] As the body of antitrust law developed, it continued to overlap the doctrine of misuse. As the Seventh Circuit observed in *USM Corp. v. SPS Technologies, Inc.*, "[s]ince the antitrust laws as currently interpreted reach every practice that could impair competition substantially, it is not easy to define a separate role for a [misuse] doctrine . . . ."[100]

The misuse doctrine grew out of the equitable doctrine of "unclean hands."[101] In *Morton Salt Co. v. G.S. Suppiger Co.*,[102] a patentee that tied the lease of his patented machines to the purchase of unpatented materials for use in the machines

---

93. *See* Handgards, Inc. v. Ethicon, Inc., 601 F.2d 986, 996 (9th Cir. 1979), *cert. denied*, 444 U.S. 1025 (1980).

94. Ansul Co. v. Uniroyal, Inc., 448 F.2d 872, 882-83 (2d Cir. 1971), *cert. denied*, 404 U.S. 1018 (1972).

95. Handgards, Inc. v. Ethicon, Inc., 743 F.2d 1281, 1297-98 (9th Cir. 1984), *cert. denied*, 469 U.S. 1190 (1985); Kearney & Trecker Corp. v. Cincinnati Milacron, Inc., 562 F.2d 365, 374 (6th Cir. 1977); Kearney & Trecker Corp. v. Giddings & Lewis, Inc., 452 F.2d 579, 597 (7th Cir. 1971), *cert. denied*, 405 U.S. 1066 (1972); American Infra-Red Radiant Co. v. Lambert Indus., 360 F.2d 977 (8th Cir.), *cert. denied*, 385 U.S. 920 (1966); Hart-Carter Co. v. J.P. Burroughs & Son, 605 F. Supp. 1327 (E.D. Mich. 1985).

96. Infringement Actions: Morton Salt Co. v. G.S. Suppiger Co., 314 U.S. 488, 492-94 (1942); B. B. Chem. Co. v. Ellis, 314 U.S. 495, 498 (1942).

   Actions to Collect Royalties: United States Gypsum Co. v. National Gypsum Co., 352 U.S. 457, 465 (1957); Park-In Theatres v. Paramount-Richards Theatres, 90 F. Supp. 730, 735 (D. Del.), *aff'd per curiam*, 185 F.2d 407 (3d Cir. 1950), *cert. denied*, 341 U.S. 950 (1951).

97. *See* Bauer & Cie v. O'Donnell, 229 U.S. 1 (1913).

98. Motion Picture Patents Co. v. Universal Film Mfg. Co., 243 U.S. 502 (1917).

99. *See* USM Corp. v. SPS Technologies Inc., 694 F.2d 505, 511 (7th Cir. 1982) (Posner, J.), *cert. denied*, 462 U.S. 1107 (1983). The influence of patent misuse law and the antitrust law of tie-ins was noted in the concurring opinion in *Jefferson Parish*. Jefferson Parish Hosp. Dist. No. 2 v. Hyde, 466 U.S.2, 37 n.7 (1984) (O'Connor, J., concurring).

100. *USM*, 694 F.2d at 511.

101. A recent discussion of the Federal Circuit suggests that an "unclean hands" defense exists separate and apart from established misuse authority. *See* Consolidated Aluminum Corp. v. Foseco Int'l, Ltd., 910 F.2d 804, 809-12 (Fed. Cir. 1990); *see also* Keystone Driller Co. v. General Excavator Co., 290 U.S. 240, 245-46 (1933).

102. 314 U.S. 488 (1942).

was found to have misused its patent. Invoking the equitable doctrine of unclean hands, the Supreme Court refused to enforce the patent against an infringer.[103]

The limits of the misuse doctrine have never been well defined. The doctrine has been applied to a variety of practices that also raise potential antitrust concern. For example, misuse has been found in certain cases where a patentee compelled a licensee of a patented process to purchase unpatented goods to use in the process,[104] compelled a licensee of one patent to take unwanted licenses under others,[105] or compelled the payment of royalties regardless of the licensee's use of the patent.[106]

Historically, patent misuse has also been applied to conduct that would not rise to the level of an antitrust violation.[107] Moreover, limitations on antitrust actions, such as standing and injury, have not been applied in misuse cases and the defense of misuse has been found to be available to one who is not directly affected by the patentee's conduct,[108] although it has usually been held that the misuse must relate to the patent in suit.[109]

---

103. *Id.* at 491. The *Morton Salt* Court viewed the patentee's conduct as an extension of the patentee's "monopoly." It stated: "a patent affords no immunity for a monopoly not within the grant, and the use of it to suppress competition in the sale of an unpatented article may deprive the patentee of the aid of a court of equity to restrain an alleged infringement." *Id.* (citations omitted); *see also* United States Gypsum Co. v. National Gypsum Co., 352 U.S. 457, 465 (1957).

104. B.B. Chem. Co. v. Ellis, 314 U.S. 495 (1942).

105. Hazeltine Research, Inc. v. Zenith Radio Corp., 388 F.2d 25 (7th Cir. 1967), *aff'd in part and rev'd in part*, 395 U.S. 100 (1969); American Securit Co. v. Shatterproof Glass Corp., 268 F.2d 769 (3d Cir.), *cert. denied*, 361 U.S. 902 (1959). *But cf.* Windsurfing Int'l, Inc. v. AMF, Inc., 782 F.2d 995 (Fed. Cir.) (not misuse to include in patent license an acknowledgment of the validity of the registered trademarks later found to be generic, or an agreement to avoid their use), *cert. denied*, 477 U.S. 905 (1986).

106. Zenith Radio Corp. v. Hazeltine Research, Inc., 395 U.S. 100, 133-40 (1969).

107. *Id.* at 140-41; Transparent-Wrap Mach. Corp. v. Stokes & Smith Co., 329 U.S. 637, 641, *on remand*, 161 F.2d 565 (2d Cir.), *cert. denied*, 331 U.S. 837 (1947); Morton Salt Co. v. G.S. Suppiger Co., 314 U.S. 488 (1942); Berlenbach v. Anderson & Thompson Ski Co., 329 F.2d 782, 784 (9th Cir.), *cert. denied*, 379 U.S. 830 (1964); Jack Winter, Inc. v. Koratron Co., 375 F. Supp. 1, 71 (N.D. Cal. 1974). *Compare* United States v. Studiengesellschaft Kohle, mbH, 670 F.2d 1122 (D.C. Cir. 1981) *with* Robintech, Inc. v. Chemidus Wavin, Ltd., 628 F.2d 142, 146-49 (D.C. Cir. 1980).

108. Morton Salt Co. v. G.S. Suppiger Co., 314 U.S. 488, 493-94 (1942); *see also* Ansul Co. v. Uniroyal, Inc., 448 F.2d 872, 880 (2d Cir. 1971) (holding patent unenforceable based upon territorial restraints and resale price fixing in marketing the patent product), *cert. denied*, 404 U.S. 1018 (1972); F. C. Russell Co. v. Consumers Insulation Co., 226 F.2d 373, 375-76 (3d Cir. 1955) (patent unenforceable based upon restrictions in distribution agreements); F. C. Russell Co. v. Comfort Equip. Corp., 194 F.2d 592, 596 (7th Cir. 1952) (patent unenforceable based upon restrictions in distribution agreements). The *F. C. Russell* cases were criticized in REPORT OF THE ATTORNEY GENERAL'S NATIONAL COMMITTEE TO STUDY THE ANTITRUST LAWS 251 (1955).

The defense apparently can be denied to a defendant who himself has acted inequitably and restrained trade. Touchett v. E Z Paintr Corp., 150 F. Supp. 384, 389 (E.D. Wis. 1957).

109. Morton Salt Co. v. G. S. Suppiger Co., 314 U.S. 488, 492-93 (1942); Kolene Corp. v. Motor City Metal Treating, Inc., 440 F.2d 77, 84 (6th Cir.) ("The misuse must be of the patent in suit.") (citations omitted), *cert. denied*, 404 U.S. 886 (1971); McCullough Tool Co. v. Well Surveys, Inc., 395 F.2d 230, 238-39 (10th Cir.), *cert. denied*, 393 U.S. 925 (1968); Republic Molding Corp. v. B. W. Photo Utils., 319 F.2d 347, 349 (9th Cir. 1963) ("misconduct in the abstract, unrelated to the claim to which is asserted as a defense, does not constitute unclean hands"); Binks Mfg. Co. v. Ransburg Electro-Coating Corp., 281 F.2d 252, 459 (7th Cir. 1960), *cert. dismissed*, 366 U.S. 211 (1961); Sperry Prods., Inc. v. Aluminum Co. of Am., 171 F. Supp. 901, 940 (N.D. Ohio 1959)

In 1988, Section 271(d) of the Patent Act was amended. It specifically declares that certain types of conduct shall not constitute "misuse or illegal extension of the patent right."[110] These include refusals to license a patent and certain acts relating to enforcement of a patent against contributing infringers.[111]

With regard to misuse claims based on tie-ins, Section 271(d)(5) provides that the:

license of any rights to [a] patent or . . . sale of a patented product on the [condition that the buyer take another] license to rights in another patent or purchase a separate product [shall not constitute misuse] unless, in view of the circumstances, the patent owner has market power in the relevant market for the patented product [which is the tying product.][112]

Thus, this statute places patented goods on a par with other tying products for misuse purposes.[113]

In the 1980s, two courts of appeals found that antitrust standards govern application of the patent misuse defense unless the Supreme Court's misuse decisions specifically condemn a practice. The Federal Circuit, applying Seventh Circuit law in *Windsurfing International, Inc. v. AMF, Inc.*,[114] found that a patent owner did not misuse his patent by inserting a provision in a license that required the licensee to acknowledge the validity of certain trademarks of the patent owner and to agree not to use them in any way. The court said:

To sustain a misuse defense involving a licensing arrangement not held to have been per se anticompetitive by the Supreme Court, a factual determination must reveal that the overall effect of the license tends to restrain competition unlawfully in an appropriately defined relevant market.[115]

In *USM Corp. v. SPS Technologies, Inc.*,[116] the Seventh Circuit held that, beyond "the conventional, rather stereotyped boundaries [of the patent-misuse doctrine]," misuse is tested by conventional antitrust principles, in particular the rule of reason. The court found no misuse because the party challenging the license failed to prove an "actual or probable anticompetitive effect in a relevant market," which would be

---

(misuse renders patents unenforceable), *aff'd in part and rev'd in part*, 285 F.2d 911 (6th Cir. 1960), *cert. denied*, 368 U.S. 890 (1961); Carter-Wallace, Inc. v. United States, 449 F.2d 1374, 1385-86 (Ct. Cl. 1971) (agreements relating to foreign patents do not render U.S. patents unenforceable).

110. 35 U.S.C. § 271(d) (1988) (as amended by Pub. L. No. 100-703, 102 Stat. 4676 (1988)).

111. *Id.* The misuse doctrine as it applies to contributing infringement actions is the subject of Section B.5.b of this chapter.

112. *Id.* § 271(d)(5).

113. The Supreme Court's decision in Jefferson Parish Hosp. Dist. No. 2 v. Hyde, 466 U.S. 2 (1984), generally requires a showing of market power in the tying product before a tie-in will be found to violate the Sherman Act. *See* Chapter I of this treatise. For a discussion of tie-ins involving patents, see Subsection B.6.f.(2) of this chapter.

114. 782 F.2d 995 (Fed. Cir.), *cert. denied*, 477 U.S. 905 (1986).

115. *Id.* at 1001 (footnote omitted). In Senza-Gel Corp. v. Seiffhart, 803 F.2d 661, 668 (Fed. Cir. 1986), the court emphasized that it was bound to adhere to existing Supreme Court guidance in the areas of patent misuse until otherwise directed by Congress or the Supreme Court.

116. 694 F.2d 505 (7th Cir. 1982) (Posner, J.), *cert. denied*, 462 U.S. 1107 (1983).

required under the rule of reason.[117]

Because the misuse doctrine is available as a defense to an action to collect royalties, anticompetitive conduct by the patentee can constitute a defense for a licensee in an action to collect royalties. In this respect the patent misuse defense differs from the rule in routine contract actions that antitrust violations by a seller do not support a defense to an action for payment of the purchased goods.[118]

Misuse renders a patent unenforceable, but the period of unenforceability ends if the patent owner can demonstrate "purge" of the misuse, i.e., that the misuse has been abandoned and the consequences of the misuse fully dissipated.[119] The courts divide on whether ceasing enforcement of an offending provision in a license or contract is sufficient to constitute abandonment of the offending agreement. Some find it sufficient.[120] In *Berlenbach v. Anderson & Thompson Ski Co.*,[121] the Ninth Circuit held that the patentee's failure to enforce an offending clause did not purge the misuse, because the clause remained in effect. Similarly, in *Ansul Co. v. Uniroyal, Inc.*,[122] the Second Circuit held that relaxation of price policing activities, without affirmative steps to convince distributors of their freedom to set prices, was held not to be a purge. A purge may effectively restore enforceability during the pendency of the infringement suit or after adjudication.[123]

b.   PATENT MISUSE AND CONTRIBUTORY INFRINGEMENT

To directly infringe a patent, it is necessary that a defendant make, use, or sell an article that meets each and every element of a claim of the patent in suit.[124]

---

117.   *Id.* at 511. *But see* Lasercomb Am., Inc. v. Reynolds, 911 F.2d 970 (4th Cir. 1990) (in recognizing the defense of copyright misuse, the court stated that such misuse need not rise to the level of a violation of the antitrust laws to constitute a defense to infringement).

118.   *See* Kelly v. Kosuga, 358 U.S. 516 (1959).

119.   Preformed Line Prods. Co. v. Fanner Mfg. Co., 328 F.2d 265, 278-79 (6th Cir.) (affirming findings that a patentee had abandoned misuse of patent and that the consequences had been dissipated by the date of the hearing on the purge question), *cert. denied*, 379 U.S. 846 (1964); White Cap Co. v. Owens-Illinois Glass Co., 203 F.2d 694, 698 (6th Cir.) (affirming a finding that misuse had been purged, where the objectionable clause in a contract was cancelled and a showing made that there were no adverse effects to be dissipated), *cert. denied*, 346 U.S. 876 (1953); Campbell v. Mueller, 159 F.2d 803, 807 (6th Cir. 1947) (no misuse where a minimum price clause included in a contract was never acted upon and had been cancelled upon renegotiation); Koratron Co. v. Lion Uniform, Inc., 409 F. Supp. 1019 (N.D. Cal. 1976); Printing Plate Supply Co. v. Crescent Engraving Co., 246 F. Supp. 654, 672-73 (W.D. Mich. 1965) (misuse purged by abandonment of offending practice where there had been no showing by defendant that there were effects to be dissipated); *see* United States Gypsum Co. v. National Gypsum Co., 352 U.S. 457, 465, 472-73 (1957); Morton Salt Co. v. G. S. Suppiger Co., 314 U.S. 488, 492-94 (1942); B. B. Chem. Co. v. Ellis, 314 U.S. 495, 498 (1942).

120.   Westinghouse Elec. Corp. v. Bulldog Elec. Prods. Co., 179 F.2d 139, 145 (4th Cir. 1950) (misuse purged by abandoning all efforts to enforce unlawful price control provisions); *cf.* Metals Disintegrating Co. v. Reynolds Metals Co., 228 F.2d 885, 889 (3d Cir. 1956) (no misuse where illegal provisions in a license agreement were not enforced).

121.   329 F.2d 782, 784-85 (9th Cir.), *cert. denied*, 379 U.S. 830 (1964).

122.   448 F.2d 872, 881-82 (2d Cir. 1971), *cert. denied*, 404 U.S. 1018 (1972).

123.   *E.g.*, Hensley Equip. Co. v. Esco Corp., 383 F.2d 252, 261 (5th Cir.), *modified per curiam* 386 F.2d 442 (5th Cir. 1967); Eastern Venetian Blind Co. v. Acme Steel Co., 188 F.2d 247, 253-54 (4th Cir.), *cert. denied*, 342 U.S. 824 (1951); *see* Printing Plate Supply Co. v. Crescent Engraving Co., 246 F. Supp. 654, 672-73 (W.D. Mich. 1965) (collecting earlier decisions).

124.   35 U.S.C. § 271(a) (1988).

Where a defendant sells an article that contains less than all of the elements of a claim, infringement liability may still exist under the doctrine of contributory infringement. The Patent Act provides:

> Whoever sells a component of a patented machine, manufacture, combination or composition, or a material or apparatus for use in practicing a patented process, constituting a material part of the invention, knowing the same to be especially made or especially adapted for use in an infringement of such patent, and not a staple article or commodity of commerce suitable for substantial noninfringing use, shall be liable as a contributory infringer.[125]

The fact that contributory infringement liability may permit a patentee to prevent defendants from selling unpatented components of patented inventions historically caused some courts to conclude that patent misuse could occur by "extension of the patent monopoly" to reach unpatented products.[126]

In the Patent Act, Congress specifically provided that certain conduct relating to the enforcement of a patent shall not constitute patent misuse. These include collecting royalties from acts that would constitute contributing infringment without a license and filing suit against contributing infringers[127] The legislative history of the statute makes it clear that in enacting this provision, Congress sought to overturn the result in prior cases where the assertion of a patent against a contributing infringer was found to constitute misuse.[128] The Supreme Court considered the effect of Section 271(d) on the misuse defense in *Dawson Chemical Co. v. Rohm & Haas Co.*[129] In *Dawson*, the Court concluded that the provisions of Section 271(d) confer upon a patentee "a limited power to exclude others from competition in nonstaple goods."[130] It further concluded that it was not patent misuse for the holder of a process patent to sue manufacturers and sellers of an unpatented chemical specially adapted for use in the process and having no other

---

125.   *Id.* § 271(c).
126.   *See, e.g.,* Mercoid Corp. v. Mid-Continent Inv. Co., 320 U.S. 661 (1944); Mercoid Corp. v. Minneapolis-Honeywell Regulator Co., 320 U.S. 680 (1944); Leitch Mfg. Co. v. Barber Co., 302 U.S. 458 (1939). In Carbice Corp. of America v. American Patents Development Corp., 283 U.S. 27, 34 (1931), the Supreme Court not only held that a contributory infringement action would not lie to preclude the sale of unpatented dry ice, but suggested that an attempt to do so would violate the Sherman Act. The earliest Supreme Court case on a similar point is Henry v. A. B. Dick Co., 224 U.S. 1, 25-36 (1912). There, the Court enjoined, as contributory infringement, the sale of unpatented ink for use in a patented mimeograph machine. Thereafter, in Motion Picture Patents Co. v. Universal Film Mfg. Co., 243 U.S. 502, 528 (1917), the Court overruled *A. B. Dick* and refused to enjoin, as contributory infringement, the sale of unpatented films for use with a patented motion picture projector. The Court relied in part on antitrust principles, including the enactment of the Clayton Act which had taken place in the five-year interim between the two cases. The development of the doctrine of contributory infringement is traced in Dawson Chemical Co. v. Rohm & Haas Co., 448 U.S. 176, 187-97 (1980). *See also* ABA ANTITRUST SECTION, ANTITRUST LAW DEVELOPMENTS (SECOND) at 507-08 (2d ed. 1984).
127.   35 U.S.C. § 271(d) (1988).
128.   Cases finding the assertion of a patent against contributing infringers to constitute a misuse include the Supreme Court's *Mercoid* cases, *supra* note 126. The legislative history of § 271(d) is discussed in *Dawson*, 448 U.S. at 202-12.
129.   448 U.S. 176 (1980).
130.   *Id.* at 201.

substantial use.[131] The patentee's refusal to grant licenses separately to those who wished to purchase the unpatented chemical from others and its insistence upon supplying all of the chemical for use in the process itself did not change the result.[132]

c. NONUSE AND REFUSAL TO LICENSE

Unlike many countries, the United States patent law contains no requirement that the patentee use or license his invention and creates no sanction for a patentee's nonuse or refusal to license his invention.[133] Rather, the essence of a patentee's right is the ability to exclude others from making, using, or selling the claimed invention.[134] Congress has specifically provided that it is not patent misuse for a patentee to refuse to use or license his invention.[135]

It has also long been held that a refusal to use or license a patent cannot form the basis for an antitrust claim.[136] In *Continental Paper Bag Co. v. Eastern Paper Bag Co.*,[137] the Supreme Court held that it was not unreasonable for a patent owner to use existing old machines rather than build new patented machines and that there was no requirement to license others to build the new ones:

> As to the suggestion that competitors were excluded from the use of the new patent, we answer that such exclusion may be said to have been of the very essence of the right conferred by the patent, as it is the privilege of any owner of property to use or not use it, without question of motive.[138]

---

131.   *Id.* at 186.

132.   *Id.*; *see also* Miller Insituform, Inc. v. Insituform of N. Am., Inc., 605 F. Supp. 1125, 1136 (M.D. Tenn. 1985) ("[A] tie-in usually would not exist when a patentee (or its licensee) conditions the right to use his patented process upon the vendee's purchase of nonpatented commodities that are necessary to the process, if such commodities have no effective, noninfringing use other than application in the patented process."), *aff'd*, 830 F.2d 606 (6th Cir. 1987), *cert. denied*, 484 U.S. 1064 (1988). On remand from *Dawson Chemical*, the district court found that § 271(d) also precluded a finding of an antitrust violation. Rohm & Haas Co. v. Dawson Chem. Co., 557 F. Supp. 739, 835-36 (S.D. Tex.), *rev'd on other grounds*, 722 F.2d 1556 (Fed. Cir. 1983), *cert. denied*, 469 U.S. 851 (1984).

133.   Most countries impose some obligation on a patentee to use his invention in the country or to license its use in the country. This is often referred to as a "working" requirement. In these countries, failure to "work" the patent within a specified number of years normally makes it available to others in some fashion, either through revocation of the patent, compulsory license, or some other relief. *See* Centrafarm B.V. v. Sterling Drug, Inc., 1974 EUR. COMM. CT. J. REP. 1147, [1974 Transfer Binder] COMMON MKT. REP. (CCH) ¶ 8246.

134.   35 U.S.C. § 154 (1988).

135.   *Id.* § 271(d)(4).

136.   Standard Oil Co. v. United States, 283 U.S. 163, 179 (1931); United States v. United Shoe Mach. Corp., 247 U.S. 32, 57-58 (1918); Extractol Process, Ltd. v. Hiram Walker & Sons, 153 F.2d 264, 268 (7th Cir. 1946).

137.   210 U.S. 405, 426-30 (1908). The *Continental Paper Bag* case was cited in Dawson Chemical Co. v. Rohm & Haas Co., 448 U.S. 176 (1980), where the Supreme Court noted that compulsory licensing is "a rarity in our patent system." *Id.* at 215 (footnotes omitted). *Dawson* refused to find a requirement that a patentee license suppliers of goods used to practice a patented process. *Id.* at 186.

138.   210 U.S. at 429 (citation omitted).

In *Hartford-Empire Co. v. United States*,[139] the Supreme Court set aside a decree provision that barred the defendant from applying for patents with an intent not to use the invention or to withhold it from others:

A patent owner is not in the position of a quasi-trustee for the public or under any obligation to see that the public acquires the free right to use the invention. He has no obligation either to use it or to grant its use to others. If he discloses the invention in his application so that it will come into the public domain at the end of the 17-year period of exclusive right he has fulfilled the only obligation imposed by the statute. This has been settled doctrine since at least 1896.[140]

Even where the patent owner has monopoly power in a relevant economic market, his refusal to license a patent to others will not provide the basis for holding he has violated Section 2 of the Sherman Act.[141] It has been held, however, that a patent owner may not agree with competitors not to use his patented invention.[142]

6. Licensing Intellectual Property Rights as an Antitrust Violation[143]

Patent license agreements can raise a number of antitrust issues. Such licenses are "contracts" within the scope of Section 1 of the Sherman Act. Moreover, licensing practices can give rise to monopolization allegations under Section 2 or constitute patent misuse and thereby a defense to an infringement action or action to collect royalties.[144]

Historically, the Department of Justice viewed certain patent licensing practices as illegal per se. The Department indicated that these practices, known colloquially as the "Nine No-Nos," would normally be challenged as per se violations of Section 1.[145] In recent years, the Department has been far more receptive to the

---

139.   323 U.S. 386, *clarified*, 324 U.S. 570 (1945).
140.   *Id.* at 432-33 (footnote omitted). More recent decisions reaffirming the patentee's right to refuse to license include United States v. Westinghouse Elec. Corp., 648 F.2d 642, 647 (9th Cir. 1981) (refusal to license does not violate the antitrust laws); Cataphote Corp. v. DeSoto Chem. Coatings, Inc., 450 F.2d 769, 774 (9th Cir. 1971) (calling this refusal to license an "untrammeled right" of the patentee), *cert. denied*, 408 U.S. 929 (1972); E.I. du Pont de Nemours & Co., 96 F.T.C. 705 (1980). *But cf.* Foster v. American Mach. & Foundry Co., 492 F.2d 1317, 1324 (2d Cir.) (nonuse considered relevant in denying injunction for infringement), *cert. denied*, 419 U.S. 833 (1974).
141.   SCM Corp. v. Xerox Corp., 645 F.2d 1195 (2d Cir. 1981), *cert. denied*, 455 U.S. 1016 (1982); Chisholm-Ryder Co. v. Mecca Bros., 1983-1 Trade Cas. (CCH) ¶ 65,406 (W.D.N.Y. 1982); GAF Corp. v. Eastman Kodak Co., 519 F. Supp. 1203, 1233 (S.D.N.Y. 1981).
142.   Blount Mfg. Co. v. Yale & Towne Mfg. Co., 166 F. 555, 560, 562 (C.C.D. Mass. 1909).
143.   For discussion of the Antitrust Division's views on patent licensing, see INTERNATIONAL GUIDELINES, *supra* note 20, at Case 11; C. Rule, The Antitrust Implications of International Licensing: After the Nine No-Nos (Oct. 21, 1986), *reprinted in* 4 TRADE REG. REP. (CCH) ¶ 13,131; Andewelt, *Antitrust Perspective on Intellectual Property Protection*, 30 PAT. TRADEMARK & COPYRIGHT J. (BNA) 319 (July 25, 1985).
144.   See Subpart B.5 of this chapter.
145.   *See, e.g.*, Remarks of B. Wilson Before the Fourth New England Antitrust Conference, Patent and Know-how License Agreements: Field of Use, Territorial, Price and Quantity Restrictions, (Nov. 6, 1970). The "Nine No-Nos" were:

    (i)   Tying the purchase of unpatented materials as a condition of the license;
    (ii)   requiring the licensee to assign back subsequent patents;
    (iii)   restricting the right of the purchaser of the product in the resale of the product;
    (iv)   restricting the licensee's ability to deal in products outside the scope of the

economic benefits that flow from patent licenses.[146]

In the absence of a naked restraint of trade, the Department of Justice views most patent license provisions under the rule of reason. In the *Vertical Restraints Guidelines*, the Department stated:

> [Restrictions in such licenses] often are essential to ensure that new technology realizes its maximum legitimate return and benefits consumers as quickly and efficiently as possible. Moreover, intellectual property licenses often involve the coordination of complementary, not competing, inputs. Thus, a rule of reason analysis is appropriate. Unless restrictions in intellectual property licenses involve naked restraints of trade unrelated to development of the intellectual property, or are used to coordinate a cartel among the owners of competing intellectual properties, or suppress the creation or development of competing intellectual properties, the restrictions should not be condemned.[147]

Likewise, the *International Guidelines* set out a four part rule of reason analysis of patent licensing transactions.[148]

a. EXCLUSIVITY

The Patent Act expressly provides that a patent is assignable: the patent owner may "grant and convey an exclusive right under his application for patent, or patents, to the whole or any specified part of the United States."[149] Although not expressly authorized in the statute, courts have long held that a patentee also may issue one or more patent licenses by agreeing to forbear from asserting his exclusive rights in an invention, typically in exchange for royalties.[150] Such licenses may be either exclusive or nonexclusive. A nonexclusive license is simply the patent owner's contractual waiver of his right to exclude the licensee from making, using, or selling the invention.[151] Such a license may arise from a course of conduct with no formal agreement.[152] In an exclusive license, the patent owner also agrees not to

---

<table>
<tr><td></td><td></td><td>patent;</td></tr>
<tr><td></td><td>(v)</td><td>a licensor's agreement not to grant further licenses;</td></tr>
<tr><td></td><td>(vi)</td><td>mandatory package licenses;</td></tr>
<tr><td></td><td>(vii)</td><td>royalty provisions not reasonably related to the licensee's sales;</td></tr>
<tr><td></td><td>(viii)</td><td>restrictions on a licensee's use of a product made by a patented process; and</td></tr>
<tr><td></td><td>(ix)</td><td>minimum resale price provisions for the licensed products.</td></tr>
</table>

146. *See* C. Rule, The Antitrust Implications of Patent Licensing: After the Nine No-Nos (Oct. 21, 1986), *reprinted in* 4 TRADE REG. REP. (CCH) ¶ 13,131.

147. VERTICAL RESTRAINTS GUIDELINES, *supra* note 22, at § 2.4.

148. INTERNATIONAL GUIDELINES, *supra* note 20, at § 3.62. *See generally* Subpart B.9 of this chapter.

149. 35 U.S.C. § 261 (1988).

150. Zenith Radio Corp. v. Hazeltine Research, Inc., 395 U.S. 100, 135-36 (1969); United States v. Studiengesellschaft Kohle, mbH, 670 F.2d 1122, 1127 (D.C. Cir. 1981).

151. *E.g.*, General Talking Pictures Corp. v. Western Elec. Co., 304 U.S. 175, 181 ("The Transformer Company . . . was a mere licensee under a nonexclusive license, amounting to no more than 'a mere waiver of the right to sue.' ") (quoting De Forest Radio Tel. Co. v. United States, 273 U.S. 236, 242 (1927)), *aff'd on reh'g*, 305 U.S. 124 (1938).

152. De Forest Radio Tel. Co. v. United States, 273 U.S. 236, 241 (1927) ("No formal granting of a license is necessary in order to give it effect."); Hunt v. Armour & Co., 185 F.2d 722, 729 (7th Cir. 1950); RCA v. Andrea, 90 F.2d 612, 615 (2d Cir. 1937) (license implied from patent owner's sale of a patented product, in the absence of express reservation of patent rights).

license others (and, not uncommonly, not to practice the patent himself).[153]   An exclusive license, as such, does not violate the antitrust laws or constitute misuse.[154]

b.   PRICE AND QUANTITY LIMITATIONS

In 1926, in *United States v. General Electric Co.,*[155] the Supreme Court held that General Electric did not violate the Sherman Act by granting a license to Westinghouse to make and sell patented lamps at prices established by General Electric. The Court stated the rationale for permitting the price restrictions as follows:

> Conveying less than title to the patent, or part of it, the patentee may grant a license to make, use and vend articles under the specifications of his patent for any royalty or upon any condition the performance of which is reasonably within the reward which the patentee by the grant of the patent is entitled to secure . . . . [M]ay [the patentee] limit the selling by limiting the method of sale and the price? We think he may do so, provided that the conditions of sale are normally and reasonably adapted to secure pecuniary reward for the patentee's monopoly.[156]

The Court thus held that it was reasonable for a patent owner who himself manufactures and sells the patented product to establish the price at which a licensee sells the product because that price "will necessarily affect" the price at which the patent owner can sell his own goods.[157]

The *General Electric* decision has been limited by subsequent decisions. In 1948, in *United States v. Line Material Co.,*[158] the Supreme Court held that where patents are crosslicensed, a provision in a sublicense establishing the sublicensee's price violated Section 1 of the Sherman Act. The Court distinguished *General Electric* but declined to overrule it.[159]   In 1965, in *United States v. Huck Manufacturing Co.,*[160] an equally divided Supreme Court again refused to overrule *General Electric*. In 1956, the Third Circuit in *Newburgh Moire Co. v. Superior Moire Co.*[161]

---

153.   Bement v. National Harrow Co., 186 U.S. 70, 94 (1902); *cf.* Sanofi, SA v. Med-Tech Veterinarian Prods., Inc., 222 U.S.P.Q. (BNA) 143 (D. Kan. 1983) (purchase of patented drug abroad does not create implied license to resell in U.S. in violation of third party's exclusive license).

154.   Virtue v. Creamery Package Mfg. Co., 227 U.S. 8, 36-37 (1913); SCM Corp. v. Xerox Corp., 463 F. Supp. 983 (D. Conn. 1978), *remanded*, 599 F.2d 32 (2d Cir.), *on remand*, 474 F. Supp. 589 (D. Conn. 1979), *aff'd*, 645 F.2d 1195 (2d Cir. 1981), *cert. denied*, 455 U.S. 1016 (1982); United States v. E.I. du Pont de Nemours & Co., 118 F. Supp. 41, 224 (D. Del. 1953), *aff'd*, 351 U.S. 377 (1956); *cf.* Smith Int'l, Inc. v. Kennametal, Inc., 621 F. Supp. 79, 89 (N.D. Ohio 1985).

155.   272 U.S. 476 (1926).

156.   *Id.* at 489-90.

157.   *Id.* at 490.

158.   333 U.S. 287, 293-97, 305-15 (1948).

159.   *Id.* at 299-304; *accord In re* Yarn Processing Patent Validity Litig., 541 F.2d 1127, 1135-36 (5th Cir. 1976) (price clauses in a license under crosslicensed patents held to be per se violations of the Sherman Act), *cert. denied*, 433 U.S. 910 (1977).

160.   382 U.S. 197 (1965).

161.   237 F.2d 283, 291-94 (3d Cir. 1956) (patentee had entered into price-fixing licenses with two of the five manufacturers in the industry); *see* Royal Indus. v. St. Regis Paper Co., 420 F.2d 449, 453-54 (9th Cir. 1969); Ansul Co. v. Uniroyal, Inc., 306 F. Supp. 541, 558-59 (S.D.N.Y. 1969), *aff'd in part and rev'd in part*, 448 F.2d 872 (2d Cir. 1971), *cert. denied*, 404 U.S. 1018 (1972); *see also* Tinnerman Prods., Inc. v. George K. Garrett Co., 185 F. Supp. 151, 157-59 (E.D. Pa. 1960), *aff'd*,

held that the grant of multiple licenses each containing price restrictions does not come within the *General Electric* doctrine, and without more violates Section 1 of the Sherman Act.

It is clear that *General Electric* does not permit the patent owner to fix the price of unpatented products of patented machines or processes.[162] Nor does *General Electric* permit a patent owner to establish the price on resale by expressly licensing "sale" of the patented product separately from manufacture and use. In *United States v. Univis Lens Co.*[163] and *Ethyl Gasoline Corp. v. United States*,[164] the Supreme Court declared unlawful practices whereby patent owners granted licenses to resell patented products and fixed the prices at which the products were to be resold. In *Ethyl*, the patent owner directly (or by one licensee) made and sold the patented product to another licensee for resale. In *Univis*, the patent owner sold the licensee an unpatented product useful only in making a patented product. In such situations, it is commonly said that the first sale of a product made under the teachings of a patent "exhausts" the patentee's exclusive rights, and restrictions on subsequent sales cannot be supported by reliance on the exclusive rights conferred in the patent statute.[165] A patent owner's ability to establish a licensee's prices for a patented article clearly does not include the right to do so in concert with other licensees or other patentees, and price restraints resulting from such combinations have been found per se violations of the Sherman Act.[166]

The Department of Justice has stated that it has sought a case in which to urge the overruling of *General Electric*.[167] However, it never found a price setting license that the licensor was prepared to defend in court.[168]

A few older decisions hold that a patent owner may limit the quantities produced

---

292 F.2d 137 (3d Cir.), *cert. denied*, 368 U.S. 833 (1961).

162. Cummer-Graham Co. v. Straight Side Basket Corp., 142 F.2d 646, 647 (5th Cir.), *cert. denied*, 323 U.S. 726 (1944); Barber-Colman Co. v. National Tool Co., 136 F.2d 339, 343-44 (6th Cir. 1943).

163. 316 U.S. 241, 243-45, 249-51 (1942).

164. 309 U.S. 436, 446-48, 452, 457 (1940).

165. *See, e.g., Univis Lens*, 316 U.S. at 249-51.

166. United States v. New Wrinkle, Inc., 342 U.S. 371, 378-80 (1952); United States v. United States Gypsum Co., 333 U.S. 364, 399-401 (1948); United States v. Masonite Corp., 316 U.S. 265, 276-80 (1942); Newburgh Moire Co. v. Superior Moire Co., 237 F.2d 283 (3d Cir. 1956); United States v. Vehicular Parking, Ltd. 54 F. Supp. 828, 837 (D. Del.), *modified*, 56 F. Supp. 297 (D. Del. 1944), *modified*, 61 F.Supp. 656 (D. Del. 1945).

167. *See* D. Turner, *Patents, Antitrust, and Innovations*, 28 U. PITT. L. REV. 151 (1966); *Conflicts between Patent and Antitrust Laws – A Panel*, 10 IDEA 33-35 (1966) (Remarks of D. Turner).

168. A former chief of the Intellectual Property Section of the Antitrust Division of the Department of Justice has stated:

> I and others in the Antitrust Division for many years sought an appropriate vehicle to overturn the 1926 *GE* case. I personally have found only three price-fixing clauses in patent licenses in thousands of licenses that I have read over the past ten years. Each time that such an agreement turned up, and we focused an investigation on it, the case was made moot – by abrogation of the agreements, by disclaimer of the patent, or the like. I have never yet found a patent lawyer who was willing to advise a client to litigate against us the legitimacy of a price-fixing clause in a license. I have given up any hope of ever finding a vehicle for overturning the *GE* case. If by some chance the Antitrust Division ever found such an agreement, I am sure it would try to seize the opportunity to bring such a case. But I doubt that this will ever happen.

Remarks of R. Stern, 377 PAT. TRADEMARK & COPYRIGHT J. (BNA) E-2 (May 4, 1978).

by a licensee.[169] A more recent decision suggests that quantity limitations in a patent license are not illegal per se.[170] Limitations on the quantity of unpatented products produced by a patented process have also been upheld.[171] However, in a case involving an alleged conspiracy among a patent owner and licensees, it was held that a provision causing royalties to increase as quantity increased violated the antitrust laws.[172]

c. ROYALTIES

A patent owner has the right to exploit his invention by requiring royalty payments,[173] and, in general, he may charge as high a royalty as he can obtain.[174]

(1) Royalty Base

A patent owner may base the formula for royalty payments on many different criteria. Royalties on patented articles manufactured by a licensee or on patented machines or processes used for manufacture are commonly based on utilization, either a fixed amount per unit on goods manufactured by the licensee under the patents or a fixed percentage of revenues received by the licensee for such goods. The criteria used to establish the royalty rate may raise antitrust or misuse issues where the royalty calculation is unrelated to the licensee's utilization of the patent and where that calculation is required by the patent owner. In *Zenith Radio Corp. v. Hazeltine Research, Inc.*, the Supreme Court held that "conditioning the grant of a patent license upon payment of royalties on products which do not use the teaching of the patent" was unlawful.[175] The Court stated that "patent misuse inheres in a patentee's insistence on a percentage-of-sales royalty, regardless of use, and his

---

169. United States v. Parker-Rust-Proof Co., 61 F. Supp. 805 (E.D. Mich. 1945); *see also* United States v. E.I. du Pont de Nemours & Co., 118 F. Supp. 41, 226 (D. Del. 1953), *aff'd*, 351 U.S. 377 (1956); Aspinwall Mfg. Co. v. Gill, 32 F. 697 (C.C.D.N.J. 1887)

170. Atari Games Corp. v. Nintendo of Am., Inc., 897 F.2d 1572, 1578 (Fed. Cir. 1990) (dicta).

171. Ethyl Corp. v. Hercules Powder Co., 232 F. Supp. 453, 460 (D. Del. 1963); Q-Tips, Inc. v. Johnson & Johnson, 109 F. Supp. 657 (D.N.J. 1951), *modified*, 207 F. 2d 509 (3d Cir. 1953), *cert. denied*, 347 U.S. 935 (1954).

172. United States v. General Elec. Co., 82 F. Supp. 753, 814 (D.N.J. 1949). *Contra* United States v. E.I. du Pont de Nemours & Co., 118 F. Supp. 41, 226 (D. Del. 1953), *aff'd*, 351 U.S. 377 (1956).

173. Hartford-Empire Co. v. United States, 323 U.S. 386, 413-16, *clarified*, 324 U.S. 570 (1945); Standard Oil Co. v. United States, 283 U.S. 163, 172, 179 (1931).

174. Brulotte v. Thys Co., 379 U.S. 29, 33 (1964); W.L. Gore & Assocs. v. Carlisle Corp., 529 F.2d 614, 623 (3d Cir. 1976); Warner-Jenkinson Co. v. Allied Chem. Corp., 477 F. Supp. 371, 397 (S.D.N.Y. 1979), *aff'd mem.*, 633 F.2d 208 (2d Cir. 1980). *But see* American Photocopy Equip. Co. v. Rovico, Inc., 359 F.2d 745 (7th Cir.) (issue of whether royalty was exorbitant remanded for trial), *on remand*, 257 F. Supp. 192, 201 (N.D. Ill. 1966) (royalty not exorbitant), *aff'd*, 384 F.2d 813 (7th Cir. 1967), *cert. denied*, 390 U.S. 945 (1968).

175. 395 U.S. 100, 135 (1969); *accord* United States v. United States Gypsum Co., 333 U.S. 364, 385-86, 397 (1948) (royalty provision which provided for percentage royalties based upon the sales of both patented and unpatented board held unlawful because purpose was to stabilize the price of patented board by eliminating the competition of unpatented board). *But cf.* Miller Insituform, Inc. v. Insituform of N. Am., Inc., 605 F. Supp. 1125, 1133-34 (M.D. Tenn. 1985) (upholding, without regard to reasonableness, royalty based on percentage of total contract price where contract was for patented process but also for preparatory and finishing work and nonpatented materials), *aff'd*, 830 F.2d 606 (6th Cir. 1987), *cert. denied*, 484 U.S. 1064 (1988).

rejection of licensee proposals to pay only for actual use."[176]

The Court in *Zenith*, however, was careful to note that royalties may be measured by sales of other than the patented products alone when the "convenience of the parties rather than patent power dictates the total sales royalty provision," and that no adverse inference is to be drawn from a total sales formula standing alone.[177] The Court thus clarified its earlier holding in *Automatic Radio Manufacturing Co. v. Hazeltine Research, Inc.*[178] in which it had upheld a royalty measured by total sales irrespective of whether any patents applied.[179]

(2) Different or Discriminatory Royalties

Generally, a patent owner is permitted to charge different licensees different royalties. Absent any anticompetitive purpose or effect, charging different royalty rates will not constitute misuse or an antitrust violation.[180] The Seventh Circuit has stated that "there is no antitrust prohibition against a patent owner's using price discrimination to maximize his income from the patent."[181]

Differential treatment of royalties in patent licenses does not implicate the Robinson-Patman Act where no commodities are sold with the license.[182] In evaluating whether the differing royalties are lawful, the Seventh Circuit requires only

---

176.　395 U.S. at 139.

177.　*Id.* at 138.

178.　339 U.S. 827, 834 (1950).

179.　*Id.* at 834. In Western Electric Co. v. Stewart-Warner Corp., 631 F.2d 333, 339 (4th Cir. 1980), *cert. denied*, 450 U.S. 971 (1981), the Fourth Circuit held that it was reasonable to base a royalty on the sale price of the finished products where substantially all the market value of the finished product was derived from the patented feature. *See also* Kearney & Trecker Corp. v. Giddings & Lewis, Inc., 306 F. Supp. 189, 200-01 (E.D. Wis. 1969), *rev'd on other grounds*, 452 F.2d 579 (7th Cir. 1971), *cert. denied*, 405 U.S. 1066 (1972).

180.　Standard Oil Co. v. United States, 283 U.S. 163, 179 (1931); USM Corp. v. SPS Technologies, Inc., 694 F.2d 505 (7th Cir. 1982) (Posner, J.), *cert. denied*, 462 U.S. 1107 (1983); La Salle St. Press, Inc. v. McCormick & Henderson, Inc., 445 F.2d 84, 95 (7th Cir. 1971); Honeywell, Inc. v. Sperry Rand Corp., 180 U.S.P.Q. (BNA) 673, 763 (D. Minn. 1973); Mobil Oil Corp. v. W.R. Grace & Co., 367 F. Supp. 207, 251 (D. Conn. 1973); Congoleum Indus. v. Armstrong Cork Co., 366 F. Supp. 220, 232 (E.D. Pa. 1973), *aff'd*, 510 F.2d 334 (3d Cir.), *cert. denied*, 421 U.S. 988 (1975); Bela Seating Co. v. Poloron Prods., Inc., 297 F. Supp. 489, 509 (N.D. Ill. 1968), *aff'd*, 438 F.2d 733, 738-39 (7th Cir.), *cert. denied*, 403 U.S. 922 (1971); Hanks v. Ross, 200 F. Supp. 605, 623 (D. Md. 1961); Pemco Prods., Inc. v. General Mills, Inc., 155 F. Supp. 433, 437 (N.D. Ohio 1957), *aff'd*, 261 F.2d 302 (6th Cir. 1958); Carter-Wallace, Inc. v. United States, 449 F.2d 1374, 1381-82 (Ct. Cl. 1971); *cf.* Akzo v. United States Int'l Trade Comm'n, 808 F.2d 1471, 1488-89 (Fed. Cir. 1986) (approving "value-in-use" pricing), *cert. denied*, 482 U.S. 909 (1987); Hennessy Indus. v. FMC Corp., 779 F.2d 402 (7th Cir. 1985). *But see* Allied Research Prods., Inc. v. Heatbath Corp., 300 F. Supp. 656, 657 (N.D. Ill. 1969) (patent owner's refusal to grant a license solely for personal rather than business reasons constituted unfair discrimination).

181.　USM Corp. v. SPS Technologies, Inc., 694 F.2d 505, 512 (7th Cir. 1982) (Posner, J.), *cert. denied*, 462 U.S. 1107 (1983); *see* Bela Seating Co. v. Poloron Prods., Inc., 438 F.2d 733, 738 (7th Cir.), *cert. denied*, 403 U.S. 922 (1971).

182.　La Salle St. Press, Inc. v. McCormick & Henderson, Inc., 293 F. Supp. 1004 (N.D. Ill. 1968), *modified*, 445 F.2d 84 (7th Cir. 1971); *see* Honeywell Inc. v. Sperry Rand Corp., 180 U.S.P.Q. (BNA) 673 (D. Minn. 1973).

that there exist a rational basis for the distinction between various licensees.[183] In order for a differential royalty licensing regime to violate Section 2, the challenger must show a demonstrable effect on competition.[184]

In the Shrimp Peelers cases,[185] several courts condemned a practice whereby a patentee with monopoly power in the market for shrimp cleaning machines licensed and leased his patented shrimp cleaning machines at different rates in different parts of the country. In a related proceeding, the FTC found that the discriminatory rates tended to insulate the patentee's own downstream shrimp cleaning business from competition from licensees and lessees of his machines, thereby violating Section 5 of the FTC Act.[186] To the extent the Shrimp Peelers cases have been read to suggest that differential royalty rates standing alone violate the antitrust laws, the decisions have been criticized.[187]

(3) Preissuance and Postexpiration Royalties

In *Brulotte v. Thys Co.*,[188] the Supreme Court found that patent misuse occurs when a patentee collects patent royalties beyond the expiration of the licensed patent.[189] The Court concluded that to collect such royalties was to "enlarge the monopoly of the patent" in a manner analogous to a patent tie-in. The Sixth, Seventh and Eleventh Circuit courts of appeal have held such patent licenses are unenforceable beyond the life of the patents.[190] The Sixth Circuit has held that it constitutes misuse to provide for postexpiration royalties whether or not such

---

183. Bela Seating Co. v. Poloron Prods., Inc., 438 F.2d 733 (7th Cir.), *cert. denied*, 403 U.S. 933 (1971); *see* La Salle St. Press Inc. v. McCormick & Henderson, Inc., 293 F. Supp. 1004 (N.D. Ill. 1968), *modified*, 445 F.2d 84 (7th Cir. 1971); Pemco Prods., Inc. v. General Mills, Inc., 155 F. Supp. 433 (N.D. Ohio 1957), *aff'd*, 261 F.2d 302 (6th Cir. 1958).

184. Honeywell, Inc. v. Sperry Rand Corp., 180 U.S.P.Q. (BNA) 673 (D. Minn. 1973); *see* National Foam Sys. v. Urquhart, 202 F.2d 659, 663-64 (3d Cir. 1953); Barber Asphalt Corp. v. La Fera Grecco Contracting Co., 116 F.2d 211, 214-16 (3d Cir. 1940). The vitality of these cases following Congress's amendment of 35 U.S.C. § 271(d) (1988) to limit the availability of the misuse defense in tie-in cases is unclear.

185. Peelers Co. v. Wendt, 260 F. Supp. 193 (W.D. Wash. 1966); Laitram Corp. v. King Crab, Inc., 244 F. Supp. 9 (D. Ala.), *modified*, 245 F. Supp. 1019 (D. Ala. 1965). *But cf.* Laitram Corp. v. Depoe Bay Fish Co., 549 F. Supp. 29 (D. Or. 1982) (rejecting argument that uniform royalty on unpeeled shrimp, where effect is unequal royalty on a peeled shrimp basis, is misuse).

186. Grand Caillou Packing Co., 65 F.T.C. 799 (1964), *aff'd in part and rev'd in part*, 366 F.2d 117 (5th Cir. 1966).

187. *See* Official Airline Guides, Inc. v. FTC, 630 F.2d 920 (2d Cir. 1980), *cert. denied*, 450 U.S. 917 (1981); Carter-Wallace, Inc. v. United States, 167 U.S.P.Q. (BNA) 667, 673 n.10 (Ct. Cl. 1970) (the Shrimp Peelers cases "stand the antimonopoly laws on their head"); *USM*, 694 F.2d at 513.

188. 379 U.S. 29 (1964).

189. *Id.* at 30-33. *See* Ar-Tik Sys. v. Dairy Queen, Inc., 302 F.2d 496, 510 (3d Cir. 1962); Shields-Jetco, Inc. v. Torti, 314 F. Supp. 1292 (D.R.I. 1970), *aff'd*, 436 F.2d 1061 (1st Cir. 1971).

190. Meehan v. PPG Indus., 802 F.2d 881 (7th Cir. 1986), *cert. denied*, 479 U.S. 1091 (1987); Boggild v. Kenner Prods., 776 F.2d 1315 (6th Cir. 1985), *cert. denied*, 477 U.S. 908 (1986); Pitney Bowes, Inc. v. Mestre, 701 F.2d 1365 (11th Cir.), *cert. denied*, 464 U.S. 893 (1983). *But cf.* Chromalloy Am. Corp. v. Fischmann, 716 F.2d 683 (9th Cir. 1983) ("hybrid" transfer of patent and of ongoing business unenforceable subsequent to repudiation of invalid patent, but compensation allowed for nonpatent assets such as know-how).

royalties were collected.[191] The Second Circuit has held, however, that a licensee may still collect royalties up to the expiration of the license, even if the *Brulotte* rule would invalidate the terminal portion of the license.[192]

With regard to preissuance royalties, some courts have held that such preissuance royalties for anticipated patents do not constitute misuse.[193] Where the license in question is a "hybrid" covering both trade secrets and anticipated patents, the collection of preissuance royalties has been upheld as not a misuse.[194]

(4) Royalties Based Upon Use of an Article Purchased from the Patent Owner or His Licensee

Generally the first authorized sale of a patented article by a patentee or his licensee exhausts the patentee's control over the article. Thereafter the patent owner may not ordinarily use the patent to control use or resale of the article sold.[195] A patent owner may, however, license use separately from manufacture and sale, and on that basis has been permitted to collect royalties for the use of a machine even though he has sold it.[196]

---

191.   Rocform Corp. v. Acitelli-Standard Concrete Wall, Inc., 367 F.2d 678 (6th Cir. 1966) (injunctive relief in an infringement action denied because license agreement provided for postexpiration royalties). Some courts have found misuse when royalties remained at a constant rate until the last of several licensed patents expired. *See id.*; Duplan Corp. v. Deering Milliken, Inc., 444 F. Supp. 648, 697-99 (D.S.C. 1977), *aff'd in part and rev'd in part*, 594 F.2d 979 (4th Cir. 1979), *cert. denied*, 444 U.S. 1015 (1980); *cf.* Clayton Mfg. Co. v. Cline, 427 F. Supp. 78 (C.D. Cal. 1976) (contract for royalties based on future sale of an entire line of products is not a per se violation of the Sherman Act). *But see* Hull v. Brunswick Corp., 704 F.2d 1195 (10th Cir. 1983); Cohn v. Compax Corp., 87 A.D.2d 364, 451 N.Y.S.2d 171 (2d Dep't 1982).

192.   Modrey v. American Gage & Mach. Co., 478 F.2d 470, 474-75 (2d Cir. 1973); *see* Veltman v. Norman Simon, Inc., 1977-1 Trade Cas. (CCH) ¶ 61,273 (S.D.N.Y. 1977).

193.   Painton & Co. v. Bourns, Inc., 442 F.2d 216, 223 (2d Cir. 1971); Congoleum Indus. v. Armstrong Cork Co., 366 F. Supp. 220, 234 (E.D. Pa. 1973), *aff'd*, 510 F.2d 334 (3d Cir.), *cert. denied*, 421 U.S. 988 (1975).

194.   Aronson v. Quick Point Pencil Co., 440 U.S. 257 (1979); *see* San Marino Elec. Corp. v. George J. Meyer Mfg. Co., 155 U.S.P.Q. (BNA) 617 (C.D. Cal. 1967), *aff'd*, 422 F.2d 1285 (9th Cir. 1970); *cf.* Reich v. Reed Tool Co., 582 S.W.2d 549 (Tex. Ct. App. 1979), *cert. denied*, 446 U.S. 946 (1980).

195.   Adams v. Burke, 84 U.S. (17 Wall.) 453, 457 (1873) ("when patented coffins] are once lawfully made and sold, there is no restriction on their use to be implied for the benefit of the patentee"); Bloomer v. McQuewan, 55 U.S. (14 How.) 539, 549 (1852) ("when the machine passes to the hands of the purchaser, it is no longer within the limits of the monopoly").

Wholly apart from the patent, a patentee may be able to place such "vertical restraints" on purchasers as the nonpatent antitrust laws permit. *See generally* Chapter I of this treatise.

196.   *In re* Yarn Processing Patent Validity Litig., 541 F.2d 1127 (5th Cir. 1976), *cert. denied*, 433 U.S. 910 (1977); Duplan Corp. v. Deering Milliken, Inc., 444 F. Supp. 648, 671-72 (D.S.C. 1977) (separately licensing the right to manufacture and sell and the right to use permissible, so long as there is no effect of fixing prices among competitors), *aff'd in part and rev'd in part*, 594 F.2d 979 (4th Cir. 1979), *cert. denied*, 444 U.S. 1015 (1980); Cold Metal Process Co. v. McLouth Steel Corp., 41 F. Supp. 487, 489-90 (E.D. Mich. 1931), *aff'd*, 170 F.2d 369 (6th Cir. 1948); *see also* General Talking Pictures Corp. v. Western Elec. Co., 304 U.S. 175 (notice of field of use restriction with purchase is enforceable), *aff'd on reh'g*, 305 U.S. 124 (1938). Extractol Process, Ltd. v. Hiram Walker & Sons, 153 F.2d 264, 267-68 (7th Cir. 1946); *cf.* Brulotte v. Thys Co., 379 U.S. 29, 33 (1964) (only that part of the license calling for royalties after all patents had expired was held unenforceable).

(5) Sharing and/or Fixing Royalties

In *Standard Oil Co. v. United States*,[197] the Supreme Court applied a rule of reason analysis to license agreements that required licensees to share sublicense royalties with the patent owners. However, in *In re Yarn Processing Patent Validity Litigation*,[198] the Fifth Circuit held that on the particular facts a royalty sharing arrangement involving royalties several times the magnitude of other costs constituted an unlawful price-fixing agreement. In *Congoleum Industries v. Armstrong Cork Co.*,[199] a district court held that a patent owner may agree with his licensee as to the royalty rate to be charged to sublicensees.

d.   TERRITORIAL AND CUSTOMER RESTRICTIONS

The Patent Act specifically provides that a patentee may grant exclusive licenses under his patent for use in the entire United States or "any specified part of the United States."[200]   In *Ethyl Gasoline Corp. v. United States*,[201] the Supreme Court held that a patentee may grant a license limiting the licensee's ability to "make, use, and sell" the patented invention to a particular territory within the United States, its territories and possessions.   In *Brownell v. Ketcham Wire & Manufacturing Co.*,[202] the Ninth Circuit held that a license to a United States licensee may prohibit exporting of the product. In addition, many courts have held that location clauses in licenses of patented processes are not per se unlawful.[203]

---

197.   283 U.S. 163, 170-71 (1931).
198.   541 F.2d 1127 (5th Cir. 1976), *cert. denied*, 433 U.S. 910 (1977).
199.   366 F. Supp. 220, 229 (E.D. Pa. 1973), *aff'd*, 510 F.2d 334 (3d Cir.), *cert. denied*, 421 U.S. 988 (1975); *see also* Hennessy Indus. v. FMC Corp., 779 F.2d 402 (7th Cir. 1985) (upholding agreement among patentee, its licensee, and its former licensee to deny license to industry leader unless that firm paid a disproportionately high royalty).
200.   35 U.S.C. § 261 (1988). For the definition of "United States" in the Patent Act, see *Id.* § 100(c).
201.   309 U.S. 436, 456 (1940) (a patentee "may grant licenses to make, use or vend, restricted in point of space or time . . . save only that . . . he may not enlarge his monopoly"); *see* Brownell v. Ketcham Wire & Mfg. Co., 211 F.2d 121, 128 (9th Cir. 1954) ("It is a fundamental rule of patent law that the owner of a patent may license another and prescribe territorial limitations."); *see* Bement v. National Harrow Co., 186 U.S. 70, 92-93 (1902); Miller Insituform, Inc. v. Insituform of N. Am., Inc., 605 F. Supp. 1125, 1130 (M.D. Tenn. 1985) ("as a matter of law, a patent licensor's use of geographic restrictions in a sublicensing scheme to divide territories into ones of primary or exclusive jurisdiction constitutes a lawful application of the rights derived from a patent grant"), *aff'd*, 830 F.2d 606 (6th Cir. 1987), *cert. denied*, 484 U.S. 1064 (1988); *cf.* Smith Int'l, Inc. v. Kennametal, Inc., 621 F. Supp. 79, 89-90 (N.D. Ohio 1985) (quoting *Brownell* with approval, but denying defense motion for summary judgment in case involving exclusive license, reciprocal exclusive distributorship, and requirements contract).
202.   211 F.2d 121, 129 (9th Cir. 1954) (holding that license prohibiting export of patented product does not violate the antitrust laws); *cf.* Atari Games Corp. v. Nintendo of Am., Inc., 897 F.2d 1572, 1578 (Fed. Cir. 1990) (restriction judged under rule of reason). The amendments to 35 U.S.C. § 271(f) (1988) tend to reinforce the correctness of this result. *But see* Extractol Process, Ltd. v. Hiram Walker & Sons, 153 F.2d 264, 267-68 (7th Cir. 1946) (suggesting that sale in the United States for use outside the United States is not infringement).
203.   United States v. Studiengesellschaft Kohle, mbH, 670 F.2d 1122 (D.C. Cir. 1981) (no per se violation of Sherman Act in limiting field of use of unpatented product made by patented process); Robintech, Inc. v. Chemidus Wavin, Ltd., 628 F.2d 142 (D.C. Cir. 1980); *see also In re* Amtorg Trading Corp., 75 F.2d 826 (C.C.P.A.) (a patented process used outside of the United States by a nonpatentee to make and export to the U.S. a nonpatented product is not an unfair method of competition), *cert. denied*, 296 U.S. 576 (1935).

Where territorial restraints involving patent licenses have been struck down, it has been because the license scheme has been found to be a pretext or sham in which the license is invoked to attempt to shield a naked market division scheme.[204] Likewise a territorial restraint imposed by a licensor in agreement with its licensees to insulate the licensees from competition has been found per se unlawful.[205] In characterizing the conduct, the origin of the restraint (i.e., with the patentee or its licensees) is central to an evaluation of its lawfulness.

A patentee may require a manufacturing licensee to sell only to prescribed customers,[206] to licensees under other patents,[207] or to licensees under different claims of the same patent.[208]

Some courts have held that it is patent misuse to require a licensee to refrain from dealing in competitive products.[209] At least one district court, however, has upheld a provision converting a license from exclusive to nonexclusive if the licensee handled competing products.[210]

The right of a patentee to impose territorial and/or customer restraints on his patentees is limited by the exhaustion doctrine.[211] Following the first authorized sale of a patented product, further restrictions on use and resale of a product implicate the law of vertical restraints addressed by the Supreme Court in *Continental T.V., Inc. v. GTE Sylvania Inc.*[212]

e.   FIELD OF USE RESTRICTIONS

Where a patent owner licenses the patent but restricts its use to a particular market or application, the limitation is sometimes termed a "field of use" restriction.

---

204.   *E.g.,* Timken Roller Bearing Co. v. United States, 341 U.S. 593, 598-99 (1951); United States v. Crown Zellerbach Corp., 141 F. Supp. 118, 126 (N.D. Ill. 1956); United States v. National Lead Co., 63 F. Supp. 513, 527 (S.D.N.Y. 1945), *aff'd*, 332 U.S. 319 (1947).

205.   *See, e.g.,* United States v. Sealy, Inc., 388 U.S. 350 (1967); International Wood Processors v. Power Dry, Inc., 792 F.2d 416 (4th Cir. 1986); Mannington Mills, Inc. v. Congoleum Indus., 610 F.2d 1059 (3d Cir. 1979); United States v. CIBA GEIGY Corp., 508 F. Supp 1118 (D.N.J. 1976), *final judgment*, 1980-81 Trade Cas. (CCH) ¶ 63,813 (D.N.J. 1981); *Crown Zellerbach*, 141 F. Supp. at 127-28.

206.   *In re* Yarn Processing Patent Validity Litig., 541 F.2d 1127, 1135 (5th Cir. 1976) (a license under product patents to make machinery and sell only to persons licensed by the patent owner to use the machinery does not violate the Sherman Act), *cert. denied*, 433 U.S. 910 (1977); Westinghouse Elec. & Mfg. Co. v. Cutting & Washington Radio Corp., 294 F. 671 (2d Cir. 1923).

207.   Deering, Milliken & Co. v. Temp-Resisto Corp., 160 F. Supp. 463, 478-82 (S.D.N.Y. 1958), *aff'd in part and rev'd in part*, 274 F.2d 626 (2d Cir. 1960). *But see* United States v. Univis Lens Co., 316 U.S. 241 (1942); Ethyl Gasoline Corp. v. United States, 309 U.S. 436 (1940).

208.   SCM Corp. v. RCA, 318 F. Supp. 433 (S.D.N.Y. 1970).

209.   Berlenbach v. Anderson & Thompson Ski Co., 329 F.2d 782 (9th Cir.), *cert. denied*, 379 U.S. 830 (1964); McCullough v. Kammerer Corp., 166 F.2d 759 (9th Cir.), *cert. denied*, 335 U.S. 813 (1948); National Lockwasher Co. v. George K. Garrett Co., 137 F.2d 255 (3d Cir. 1943); Krampe v. Ideal Indus., 347 F. Supp. 1384 (N.D. Ill. 1972).

210.   Naxon Telesign Corp. v. Bunker Ramo Corp., 517 F. Supp. 804 (N.D. Ill. 1981), *aff'd*, 686 F.2d 1258 (7th Cir. 1982).

211.   See Section B.6.b of this chapter.

212.   433 U.S. 36 (1977); *see* Munters Corp. v. Burgess Indus., 450 F. Supp. 1195, 1207-08 (S.D.N.Y. 1977). A former Department of Justice official stated that resale restrictions on patented goods "ought to be judged by the same standards as those that ought to be in use outside the patent field." Lipsky, *Current Antitrust Division Views on Patent Licensing Practices*, 50 ANTITRUST L.J. 515, 520 (1981).

In *General Talking Pictures Corp. v. Western Electric Co.*,[213] the owner of patents on amplifiers licensed its own subsidiary to make and sell equipment using the amplifiers for theaters, and separately licensed others to make and sell radio receivers using the amplifiers solely for use in private homes. The defendant, with actual notice of the limited license, purchased theater equipment from one of those licensed only to sell to the private home market. The Supreme Court upheld the field of use restriction and ruled that both the offending licensee and the purchaser were liable for infringement.[214]

Numerous cases have approved field of use restrictions in patent licenses. In *Benger Laboratories v. R.K. Laros Co.*,[215] for example, the Third Circuit approved two drug licenses.[216] Likewise, the Department of Justice has long recognized the procompetitive aspects of field of use licenses.[217]

In several older cases, courts have distinguished between field of use restrictions imposed upon a manufacturing licensee and those imposed upon a purchasing licensee, holding that a patent owner may not sell a patented product and limit the field of use of the purchaser.[218] To the extent that the distinction in these cases

213. 304 U.S. 175, *aff'd on reh'g*, 305 U.S. 124 (1938).

214. *Id.* at 181 ("Patent owners may grant licenses extending to all uses or limited to use in a defined field.") (citations omitted).

215. 209 F. Supp. 639 (E.D. Pa. 1962), *aff'd per curiam*, 317 F.2d 455 (3d Cir.), *cert. denied*, 375 U.S. 833 (1963).

216. *Accord* Automatic Radio Mfg. Co. v. Hazeltine Research, Inc., 176 F.2d 799, 802-03 (1st Cir. 1949), *aff'd*, 339 U.S. 827 (1950); Turner Glass Corp. v. Hartford Empire Co., 173 F.2d 49, 53 (7th Cir.) (restriction limiting licensee's use of patented machinery to make certain types of glassware upheld), *cert. denied*, 338 U.S. 830 (1949); Smith Int'l Inc. v. Kennametal, Inc., 621 F. Supp. 79 (N.D. Ohio 1985); United States v. CIBA GEIGY Corp., 508 F. Supp. 1118, 1149-51 (D.N.J. 1976), *final judgment*, 1980-81 Trade Cas. (CCH) ¶ 63,813 (D.N.J. 1981); Bela Seating Co. v. Poloron Prods., Inc., 297 F. Supp. 489, 503-04, 509-10 (N.D. Ill. 1968) (upholding requirement that chairs manufactured using the patent shall "be the same as or similar to the chairs currently manufactured by [the licensee]"), *aff'd*, 438 F.2d 733 (7th Cir.), *cert. denied*, 403 U.S. 922 (1971); Reliance Molded Plastics, Inc. v. Jiffy Prods., 215 F. Supp. 402, 405, 408-09 (D.N.J. 1963), *aff'd per curiam*, 337 F.2d 857 (3d Cir. 1964); *In re* Reclosable Plastic Bags, 192 U.S.P.Q. (BNA) 674, 679 (U.S. Int'l Trade Comm'n 1977).

217. *See, e.g.*, Remarks of B. Wilson Before the Fourth New England Antitrust Conference, Patent and Know-how License Agreements: Field of Use, Territorial, Price and Quantity Restrictions at 11 (Nov. 6, 1970): "[C]onsiderable justification can be made for a patentee reserving to himself a well-defined field of use and then offering to license others throughout the remaining fields of use without restrictions on his licensees. If the patentee could not thus protect himself, he might very well decide not to license at all."

218. Hensley Equip. Co. v. Esco Corp., 383 F.2d 252, 262-64 (5th Cir.) (license provision restricting use and sale of patented parts purchased from licensor constituted per se violation of the Sherman Act), *modified per curiam*, 386 F.2d 442 (5th Cir. 1967); Munters Corp. v. Burgess Indus., 450 F. Supp. 1195 (S.D.N.Y. 1977); United States v. CIBA GEIGY Corp., 508 F. Supp. 1118, 1126-47 (D.N.J. 1976) (supply agreement restricting purchasers of drug in bulk form from reselling in finished dosage form unless in combination approved by the seller violated the Sherman Act), *final judgment*, 1980-81 Trade Cas. (CCH) ¶ 63,813 (D.N.J. 1981); United States v. Glaxo Group, 302 F. Supp. 1, 4-11 (D.D.C. 1969) (agreement to supply patented drug in bulk form to a licensee-purchaser who agreed that it "will not, without first obtaining [the seller's] consent, resell or redeliver in bulk" violated the Sherman Act), *rev'd on other grounds*, 410 U.S. 52 (1973); Baldwin-Lima-Hamilton Corp. v. Tatnall Measuring Sys., 169 F. Supp. 1, 28-30 (E.D. Pa. 1958), *aff'd per curiam*, 268 F.2d 395 (3d Cir.), *cert. denied*, 361 U.S. 894 (1959). At least one court has declined to find misuse in this circumstance. Chemagro Corp. v. Universal Chem. Co., 244 F. Supp. 486, 489-90 (E.D. Tex. 1965) (sale of chemical restricted to reformulation for commercial market;

stemmed from a general judicial hostility against restraints on resale however, they may be affected by the 1977 decision of the Supreme Court in *Continental T.V., Inc. v. GTE Sylvania Inc.*[219] Prior to *Sylvania*, the Supreme Court in *United States v. Arnold, Schwinn & Co.*[220] had imposed a per se rule against many customer or territorial restrictions on the resale of a product, whether or not patented. The *Schwinn* decision was expressly overruled in *Sylvania*,[221] in which the Court held that nonprice vertical restrictions on resale are not per se violations of the Sherman Act but are to be judged under the rule of reason. Although *Sylvania* does not deal directly with the issue of resale restrictions in a patent license, the Court's rationale suggests that vertically imposed field of use restrictions in agreements for the sale of patented products will be tested by a rule of reason analysis.[222]

Two D.C. Circuit cases discuss restrictions on the field of use of unpatented products made by a patented process or machines. In *Robintech, Inc. v. Chemidus Wavin, Ltd.*,[223] it held that such restrictions constitute patent misuse. In *United States v. Studiengesellschaft Kohle, mbH*,[224] it held that such restrictions are to be tested by a rule of reason analysis.

f. TYING ARRANGEMENTS

(1) Introduction

As discussed in Chapter I of this treatise, a tying arrangement occurs when a seller offers a desirable item — the tying item — only on the condition that the purchaser also purchase another item, the tied item. To summarize the basic rule of law, a tying arrangement will be treated as per se unlawful under Section 1 of the Sherman Act and Section 3 of the Clayton Act, and thus prohibited without proof of an unreasonable anticompetitive effect, if it is established that (1) two separate products or services are involved; (2) there is a sale or agreement to sell one product or service "conditioned" on the purchase of another; (3) the seller has sufficient economic power in the market for the tying product to enable it to restrain trade in the market for the tied product; and (4) a not insubstantial amount of interstate commerce in the tied product is affected.[225] In the cases discussed in this section the "tying" item is in some way covered by a patent or copyright. That is, the tying

---

reformulation for home market prohibited). The *Chemagro* restriction was challenged by the Antitrust Division and abandoned in a consent decree. United States v. Farbenfabriken Bayer AG, 1969 Trade Cas. (CCH) ¶ 72,918 (D.D.C. 1969).

219.   433 U.S. 36 (1977).

220.   388 U.S. 365 (1967).

221.   433 U.S. 36, 58 (1977).

222.   *See* Munters Corp. v. Burgess Indus., 450 F. Supp. 1195, 1207-11 (S.D.N.Y. 1977).

223.   628 F.2d 142, 146-49 (D.C. Cir. 1980).

224.   670 F.2d 1122 (D.C. Cir. 1981). A former Department of Justice spokesman took a similar view in 1981. Lipsky, *Current Antitrust Division Views on Patent Licensing Practices*, 50 ANTITRUST L.J. 515, 523 (1981) ("[T]here is little point in worrying about the process/product distinction to the extent that control of the process necessarily confers control over the product or in circumstances in which no effective control over extra-patent items is threatened.").

225.   Northern Pac. Ry. v. United States, 356 U.S. 1, 6 (1958); Times-Picayune Publishing Co. v. United States, 345 U.S. 594, 608-09 (1953); *see* Jefferson Parish Hosp. Dist. No. 2 v. Hyde, 466 U.S. 2 (1984); Miller Insituform, Inc. v. Insituform of N. Am., Inc., 605 F. Supp. 1125, 1136 (M.D. Tenn. 1985), *aff'd*, 830 F.2d 606 (6th Cir. 1987), *cert. denied*, 484 U.S. 1064 (1988).

item is either a license under a patent owned by the licensor or a product made under a patent owned or licensed to the tying seller.

For many years courts have presumed that the seller has sufficient market power in the tying product where the tying item is patented or copyrighted.[226] Thus, in *IBM v. United States*,[227] the Supreme Court, in 1936, held that the lease of a patented tabulating machine on the condition the lessee also purchase paper cards for use in the machine violated Section 3 of the Clayton Act. Likewise, in 1947 in *International Salt Co. v. United States*,[228] a similar tying arrangement was held to violate Section 1 of the Sherman Act.

In recent years, the presumption that a patent or copyright confers sufficient market power in a tying case has been questioned by lower courts and by four Justices of the Supreme Court.[229] Proponents of this view argue that whether or not a patent truly confers any market power on its holder depends upon the availability of substitutes in the relevant market, and is not properly the subject of a blanket presumption.[230]

In 1988, Congress amended the Patent Act to provide that tying will not constitute patent misuse unless the patentee has market power in the tying items.[231] The amendment added Section 271(d)(5), which provides:

No patent owner otherwise entitled to relief for infringement or contributory infringement of a patent shall be denied relief or deemed guilty of misuse or illegal extension of the patent right by reason of his having done one or more of the following:

---

226. United States v. Loew's, Inc., 371 U.S. 38, 45 (1962) ("The requisite economic power is presumed when the tying product is patented or copyrighted.") (citations omitted); International Salt Co. v. United States, 332 U.S. 392, 395 (1947) (patented machine); Duplan Corp. v. Deering Milliken, Inc., 444 F. Supp. 648, 673 (D.S.C. 1977), *aff'd in part and rev'd in part*, 594 F.2d 979 (4th Cir. 1979), *cert. denied*, 444 U.S. 1015 (1980); *see also* Northern Pac. Ry. v. United States, 356 U.S. 1, 10 n.8, 18 (1958); Times-Picayune Publishing Co. v. United States, 345 U.S. 594, 608, 611-12 & n.30 (1953); Standard Oil Co. v. United States, 337 U.S. 293, 307 (1949).

227. 298 U.S. 131 (1936).

228. 332 U.S. 392 (1947).

229. *Jefferson Parish*, 466 U.S. at 37 n.7 (O'Connor, J., concurring) ("a patent holder has no market power in any relevant sense if there are close substitutes for the patented product"); *cf.* Data Gen. Corp. v. Digidyne Corp., 473 U.S. 908 (1985) (White, and Blackman, J.J., dissenting from denial of certiorari) ("this case raises several substantial questions of antitrust law and policy, including . . . what effect should be given to the existence of a copyright or other legal monopoly in determining market power"); A.I. Root Co. v. Computer/Dynamics, Inc., 806 F.2d 673, 676 (6th Cir. 1986) (holding that a copyright did not confer a presumption of market power for tie-in purposes; dismissing as "overbroad" the language in United States v. Loew's, Inc., 371 U.S. 38, 46 (1962) to the contrary).

Prior to the 1988 amendments, the Federal Circuit had declined to assume the existence of market power solely on the existence of a patent. *See, e.g.*, Windsurfing Int'l, Inc. v. AMF, Inc., 782 F.2d 995, 1001-02 (Fed. Cir. 1986) ("to sustain a misuse defense . . . a factual determination must reveal that the overall effect of the license tends to restrain competition unlawfully in an appropriately defined relevant market"), *cert. denied*, 407 U.S. 905 (1986); *cf.* Abbott Laboratories v. Brennan, 952 F.2d 1346 (Fed. Cir. 1991); USM Corp. v. SPS Technologies, Inc., 694 F.2d 505, 510-14 (7th Cir. 1982) (questioning per se treatment of patent misuse violations) (Posner, J.), *cert. denied*, 462 U.S. 107 (1983).

230. *See also* Lipsky, *Current Antitrust Division Views on Patent Licensing Practices*, 50 ANTITRUST L.J. 515, 518-19 (1981) ("while it is conceivable that patent tie-ins might be anticompetitive under peculiar conditions, a general rule prohibiting them is almost certainly counterproductive").

231. 35 U.S.C. § 271(d)(5) (1988) (as enacted by Pub. L. No. 100-703, 102 Stat. 4676 (1988)).

. . .

(5) conditioned the license of any rights to the patent or the sale of the patented product on the acquisition of a license to rights in another patent or purchase of a separate product, unless, in view of the circumstances, the patent owner has market power in the relevant market for the patent or patented product on which the license or sale is conditioned.[232]

Thus, to successfully assert the defense of patent misuse, a plaintiff must show that the patentee had market power in the tied item, in the same fashion that it must be shown in a nonpatent antitrust case.[233]

With regard to a tie-in as an antitrust violation, the situation appears to differ. In *Jefferson Parish Hospital District No. 2 v. Hyde*,[234] a majority of the Supreme Court reaffirmed, in dicta, that the presumption of market power will exist when the tying product is the subject of a patent.[235] Thus, an anomalous situation exists where a plaintiff must demonstrate market power to prevail in a misuse claim, but may rely on the existence of a patent to prevail in an antitrust claim.[236]

(2) Tie-ins as a Misuse

Section 271(d)(5) appears to reverse several Supreme Court decisions holding that the tying of an unpatented article to a patented article or patent license without more constitutes misuse.[237] Previously, misuse had been found where the lessor of a patented machine required the lessee to use only staple materials purchased from the patent owner with the machine,[238] where the patent tied unpatented materials for use in a patented process together with a license to use the patented process,[239] and where the patent owner sold an unpatented element of a patented combination, together with notice to customers that the purchase carried a license on the patented combination.[240] Section 271(d)(5) could be interpreted as

---

232.   *Id.*

233.   *See* 134 Cong. Rec. H10648 (daily ed. Oct. 20, 1988) (Statement of Rep. Kastenmeier) (expecting that with respect to market power, "the courts will be guided – though not bound – by the post and future decisions of the Supreme Court in the context of antitrust analysis of unlawful tie-ins").

234.   466 U.S. 2 (1984).

235.   *Id.* at 16.

236.   The Federal Circuit has recognized that patent misuse and antitrust violations based on the same conduct are not necessarily coextensive. *See* Senza-Gel Corp. v. Seiffhart, 803 F.2d 661, 665 n.5 (Fed. Cir. 1986) (observing that the test for determining whether two products exist is different under patent law than under antitrust law and stating that only Congress or the Supreme Court can make the two bodies of law consistent).

237.   Morton Salt Co. v. G. S. Suppiger Co., 314 U.S. 488, 490, 494 (1942); B. B. Chem. Co. v. Ellis, 314 U.S. 495 (1942).

238.   *E.g.*, Morton Salt Co. v. G. S. Suppiger Co., 314 U.S. 488, 491 (1942). *But see* Binks Mfg. Co. v. Ransburg Electro-Coating Corp., 281 F.2d 252, 259 (7th Cir. 1960) (no misuse where "the leasing arrangement is not imposed as a condition of licensing and licenses are available without equipment being leased from the defendant"), *cert. dismissed*, 366 U.S. 211 (1961).

239.   B. B. Chem. Co. v. Ellis, 314 U.S. 495, 496-97 (1942); *see also* Leitch Mfg. Co. v. Barber Co., 302 U.S. 458, 460-63 (1938).

240.   Mercoid Corp. v. Mid-Continent Inv. Co., 320 U.S. 661, 664-65 (1944); Mercoid Corp. v. Minneapolis-Honeywell Regulator Co., 320 U.S. 680, 682-84 (1944); B. B. Chem. Co. v. Ellis, 117 F.2d 829, 834-35 (1st Cir. 1941), *aff'd*, 314 U.S. 495 (1942); Philad Co. v. Lechler Labs., 107 F.2d 747 (2d Cir. 1939).

requiring a showing of market power in these situations as well.[241]

(3) Tying as an Antitrust Violation

Under the antitrust laws, it appears that the presence of a patent will meet the plaintiff's burden to establish market power in the tying market. The other elements of the offense must still be made out as if the tying product was not patented.[242]

A patent owner who sells any type of unpatented materials together with a license to practice a patent can avoid a claim of unlawful tying by offering a separate license under the patent using materials, parts or components supplied by others. In general, the terms of such separate license must be definite and as favorable as the terms of the license which the patent owner grants to his purchasers.[243] Moreover, in the misuse context several courts have found that misuse could be negated where the licensee never asked for a separate license and hence the patentee had no opportunity to offer one.[244] In such a circumstance, the availability of the licenses separated would negate the inference that the sale or license of one was conditional on the other.

Some courts have found that if the tied product is also covered by a patent, and thus both products are within the seller's control, the requisite restraint of trade in the tied product is missing.[245] In the *IBM* case, however, the Supreme Court

---

241. In Dawson Chemical Co. v. Rohm & Haas Co., 448 U.S. 176, 200-15 (1980), the Supreme Court read other parts of § 271(d) to effectuate Congress's intent even though the precise language of the statute did not cover the acts in question.

242. *See* Chapter I of this treatise.

243. *Compare* National Foam Sys. v. Urquhart, 202 F.2d 659, 662-64 (3d Cir. 1953); Dehydrators, Ltd. v. Petrolite Corp., 117 F.2d 183 (9th Cir.' 1941); Barber Asphalt Corp. v. La Fera Grecco Contracting Co., 116 F.2d 211, 214-16 (3d Cir. 1940); Ansul Co. v. Uniroyal, Inc., 306 F. Supp. 541, 563-64 (S.D.N.Y. 1969) (misuse where the offer to competitors to sell the unpatented material was unreasonable and discriminatory), *aff'd in part and rev'd in part*, 448 F.2d 872 (2d Cir. 1971), *cert. denied*, 404 U.S. 1018 (1972) *and* Urquhart v. United States, 109 F. Supp. 409, 411-12 (Ct. Cl. 1953) *with* United States Gypsum Co. v. National Gypsum Co., 387 F.2d 799, 802 (7th Cir. 1967) ("[t]here could be no misuse of the terms on which a license is available to those wishing to use [unpatented] tape manufactured by others are reasonably comparable to the terms for one who uses the patentee's tape"), *cert. denied*, 390 U.S. 988 (1968); Rohm & Haas Co. v. Owens-Corning Fiberglass Corp., 196 U.S.P.Q. (BNA) 726, 734, 742-43 (N.D. Ala. 1977); Watson Packer, Inc. v. Dresser Indus., 193 U.S.P.Q. (BNA) 552, 559-60 (N.D. Tex. 1977) *and* Congoleum Indus. v. Armstrong Cork Co., 366 F. Supp. 220, 236 (E.D. Pa. 1973), *aff'd*, 510 F.2d 334 (3d Cir.), *cert. denied*, 421 U.S. 988 (1975).

244. *See* Rex Chainbelt, Inc. v. Harco Prods., Inc., 512 F.2d 993, 1001 n.2 (9th Cir.) ("the fact that no one has yet asked for a direct license (and consequently no one was refused one) is evidence that there is no economic tying effect or misuse present; however, it is not conclusive of the point") (citations omitted), *cert. denied*, 423 U.S. 831 (1975); Federal Sign & Signal Corp. v. Bangor Punta Operations, Inc., 357 F. Supp. 1222, 1240 (S.D.N.Y. 1973); Ansul Co. v. Uniroyal, Inc., 306 F. Supp. 541, 562-63 (S.D.N.Y. 1969), *aff'd in part and rev'd in part*, 448 F.2d 872 (2d Cir. 1971), *cert. denied*, 404 U.S. 1018 (1972). *But see* B. B. Chem. Co. v. Ellis, 117 F.2d 829, 837-38 (1st Cir. 1941) (available license must not be on unreasonable and discriminatory terms), *aff'd*, 314 U.S. 495 (1942).

245. Federal Sign & Signal Corp. v. Bangor Punta Operations, Inc., 357 F. Supp. 1222, 1228 (S.D.N.Y. 1973) (no misuse where "plaintiff was proceeding in good faith to rely upon the validity of its Liston patent, which covers the VASCAR [tied] device" and had "never refused to grant any prospective purchaser a license under the [tying] patent"); United States v. Consolidated Car-Heating Co., 87 U.S.P.Q. (BNA) 20, 23-24 (S.D.N.Y. 1950) (no Sherman Act violation where a patent owner agreed to "loan" its licensee a patented electric furnace and required licensee to

suggested that a patent on the tied product, paper cards, would not have made any difference to IBM's liability for tying under Section 3 of the Clayton Act.[246]

g. PACKAGE LICENSING OF PATENTS AND COPYRIGHTS

Patent and copyright licenses frequently grant the licensee rights to practice under more than one of the licensor's patents or copyrights. Indeed, it is not unusual for a licensor to grant a license on all of its patents in a particular area of technology. In general, such package licenses are lawful and do not constitute misuse. For example, in *International Manufacturing Co. v. Landon, Inc.*,[247] the Ninth Circuit found no violation of the Sherman Act in package licensing where activities under one patent could not be carried out without infringing all patents in the group.[248]

When package licenses of intellectual property have been challenged, the concern has been that the licensor has leveraged his power over some patents to force the licensee to take less desirable licenses. In that regard, a line of Supreme Court decisions held that "block booking" of separately copyrighted films constituted a violation of Section 1 of the Sherman Act.[249]

In *Automatic Radio Manufacturing Co. v. Hazeltine Research, Inc.*,[250] the Supreme Court found no misuse where there was a single license for a number of patents and a fixed royalty based on a percentage of the licensee's sales that did not vary regardless of how many of the patents were used. Absent facts supporting a claim that the patent owner has refused to grant individual licenses, the Court refused to hold the licensing scheme constituted misuse.

Section 271(d)(5) of the Patent Act specifically applies to package licenses.[251]

---

purchase patented alloy for use in the furnace).

246.   IBM v. United States, 298 U.S. 131, 136-38 (1936); *see also* Baldwin-Lima-Hamilton Corp. v. Tatnall Measuring Sys., 169 F. Supp. 1, 31 (E.D. Pa. 1958) ("The monopoly which the patent law grants with respect to an article covered by one patent may not be utilized to aid the patentee to exploit another article even though it is covered by another patent."), *aff'd per curiam*, 268 F.2d 395 (3d Cir.), *cert. denied*, 361 U.S. 894 (1959); *cf.* Ethyl Gasoline Corp. v. United States, 309 U.S. 436, 458-59 (1940) ("The patent monopoly of one invention may no more be enlarged for the exploitation of a monopoly of another than for the exploitation of an unpatented article or for the exploitation or promotion of a business not embraced within the patent.") (citations omitted).

247.   336 F.2d 723 (9th Cir. 1964), *cert. denied*, 379 U.S. 988 (1965).

248.   *Id.* at 729-30; *see also* North Am. Philips Co. v. Stewart Eng'g Co., 319 F. Supp. 335, 350 (N.D. Cal. 1970); Binks Mfg. Co. v. Ransburg Electro-Coating Corp., 122 U.S.P.Q. (BNA) 74, 88 (S.D. Ind. 1959), *aff'd in part and rev'd in part*, 281 F.2d 252 (7th Cir. 1960), *cert. dismissed*, 366 U.S. 211 (1961).

249.   United States v. Loew's, Inc., 371 U.S. 38 (1962); United States v. Paramount Pictures, 334 U.S. 131, 156-59 (1948). In Broadcast Music, Inc. v. CBS, 441 U.S. 1, 24 (1979), the Supreme Court, without specifically addressing the package license question, held that agreements whereby holders of performance rights under numerous musical copyrights granted only "blanket" licenses covering multiple copyrights for a single royalty were not per se violations of § 1. The licenses were nonexclusive, i.e., the individual owners retained the right separately to grant individual licenses. On remand from *Broadcast Music*, the defendant prevailed. CBS v. American Soc'y of Composers, Authors & Publishers, 620 F.2d 930 (2d Cir. 1980), *cert. denied*, 450 U.S. 970 (1981); *see also* Buffalo Broadcasting Co. v. American Soc'y of Composers, Authors & Publishers, 744 F.2d 917 (2d Cir. 1984), *cert. denied*, 469 U.S. 1211 (1985).

250.   339 U.S. 827 (1950).

251.   35 U.S.C. § 271(d)(5) (1988) is applicable, inter alia, to cases where the patentee has "conditioned the license of any rights to the patent . . . on the acquisition of a license to rights in another patent."

Thus, when package licenses of patents are challenged as a misuse, the challenger must show that the licensor possesses market power in the market for "tying" patent.[252] The statute, by its terms, does not apply to copyrights, nor does it apply to actions under the Sherman Act.

Prior decisions provide mixed guidance regarding the question of evidence needed to establish coercion. Some courts found unlawful packaging where the licensor refused to license separately.[253] On the other hand, other courts have approved multiple licensing arrangements where the licensee failed to prove that he was refused the opportunity of taking licenses under less than all of the patents in the package.[254] Courts are divided on whether a simple requirement that a licensee pay the same royalty regardless of the number of patents licensed, without more, establishes the requisite coercion.[255] The patent owner is normally permitted to agree that a licensee will be given so-called "most favored nation" status, i.e., the benefit of more favorable terms granted in subsequent licenses.[256] An agreement by a patentee not to deal in other unpatented goods in competition with his licensee's goods was found unenforceable.[257]

h. AGREEMENT NOT TO CONTEST VALIDITY

A licensee is permitted to challenge the validity of the licensed patent.[258] While

---

252. *Id.*

253. Hazeltine Research, Inc. v. Zenith Radio Corp., 388 F.2d 25, 33-35 (7th Cir. 1967), *aff'd in part and rev'd in part*, 395 U.S. 100 (1969); American Securit Co. v. Shatterproof Glass Corp., 268 F.2d 769, 775-77 (3d Cir.), *cert. denied*, 361 U.S. 902 (1959); *see* Beckman Instruments, Inc. v. Technical Dev. Corp., 433 F.2d 55, 60 (7th Cir. 1970) (stating that if the plaintiff could prove coercion, it would have established misuse), *cert. denied*, 401 U.S. 976 (1971). *But see* United States v. Loew's, Inc., 371 U.S. 38, 55 (1962) (seller can try to sell a package and refuse to deal individually for a limited period while he exhausts possibility of a package sale).

254. Hensley Equip. Co. v. Esco Corp., 383 F.2d 252, 265 n.24 (5th Cir.), *modified per curiam*, 386 F.2d 442 (5th Cir. 1967); McCullough Tool Co. v. Well Surveys, Inc., 343 F.2d 381, 408-10 (10th Cir. 1965), *cert. denied*, 383 U.S. 933 (1966); Apex Elec. Mfg. Co. v. Altorfer Bros., 238 F.2d 867, 871-72 (7th Cir. 1956); Eversharp, Inc. v. Fisher Pen Co., 204 F. Supp. 649, 675 (N.D. Ill. 1961); Carter Prods., Inc. v. Colgate-Palmolive Co., 164 F. Supp. 503, 525-26 (D. Md. 1958), *aff'd*, 269 F.2d 299 (4th Cir. 1959).

255. Moraine Prods. v. ICI Am., Inc., 538 F.2d 134, 143-46 (7th Cir.) (such agreements not illegal per se but to be judged by rule of reason), *cert. denied*, 429 U.S. 941 (1976). For decisions applying a per se standard to a broad spectrum of anticompetitive conduct, see International Wood Processors v. Power Dry, Inc., 792 F.2d 416 (4th Cir. 1986); Mannington Mills, Inc. v. Congoleum Indus., 610 F.2d 1059, 1069-73 (3d Cir. 1979) (alleged conspiracy among patent owner and its foreign licensees to cancel foreign license of another licensee); United States v. Krasnov, 143 F. Supp. 184, 200-02 (E.D. Pa. 1956), *aff'd per curiam*, 355 U.S. 5 (1957); United States v. Besser Mfg. Co., 96 F. Supp. 304, 311 (E.D. Mich. 1951), *aff'd*, 343 U.S. 444 (1952). *But see* Miller Insituform, Inc. v. Insituform of N. Am., Inc., 605 F. Supp. 1125 (M.D. Tenn. 1985), *aff'd*, 830 F.2d 606 (6th Cir. 1987), *cert. denied*, 484 U.S. 1064 (1988).

256. General Tire & Rubber Co. v. Firestone Tire & Rubber Co., 349 F. Supp. 333, 344-45 (N.D. Ohio 1972); Technograph Printed Circuits, Ltd. v. Bendix Aviation Corp., 218 F. Supp. 1, 51 (D. Md. 1963), *aff'd per curiam*, 327 F.2d 497 (4th Cir.), *cert. denied*, 379 U.S. 826 (1964); *see also* United States v. United States Gypsum Co., 333 U.S. 364, 389 (1948).

257. McCullough v. Kammerer Corp., 166 F.2d 759 (9th Cir.), *cert. denied*, 335 U.S. 813 (1948).

258. Lear, Inc. v. Adkins, 395 U.S. 653, 671 (1969) (overruling with respect to licensee estoppel Automatic Radio Mfg. Co. v. Hazeltine Research, Inc., 339 U.S. 827, 836 (1950)). The Seventh Circuit has held that a copyright holder can estop a licensee by contract from contesting the validity of the licensed copyright, and that the *Loew's* decision did not apply to copyrights.

a license provision barring a licensee from contesting validity is unenforceable, courts have been reluctant to hold that such provisions violate the Sherman Act or constitute misuse.[259] The patent owner may not recover royalties that accrue while a licensee is challenging an invalid patent in court,[260] but where a licensee continues to practice the patent, a patent owner may exercise contractual termination rights for nonpayment of royalties.[261] Following a holding of invalidity, the licensee is not normally permitted to recover royalties paid prior to taking "an affirmative step that would prompt the early adjudication of the validity of the patent, such as filing an action contesting the patent's validity or notifying the licensor that the payments were being stopped because the patent was believed to be invalid."[262] Where a licensee can show that the patent owner fraudulently induced him to enter the license agreement, he can recover all royalties paid from the inception of the license.[263] Consent judgments entered in settlement of litigation that acknowledge validity and infringement have been given res judicata effect.[264] Although courts have disagreed on whether licensees under agreements entered in settlement of litigation may challenge validity and also retain the license, the Federal Circuit has held that termination of a license agreement is not always a precondition to suit.[265]

Saturday Evening Post Co. v. Rumbleseat Press, Inc., 816 F.2d 1191 (7th Cir. 1987) (Posner, J.).

259. Bendix Corp. v. Balax, Inc., 471 F.2d 149, 158 (7th Cir. 1972) (possible misuse because of post-expiration no contest agreement), *cert. denied*, 414 U.S. 819 (1973); Panther Pumps & Equip. Co. v. Hydrocraft, Inc., 468 F.2d 225, 232 (7th Cir. 1972), *cert. denied*, 411 U.S. 965 (1973); Congoleum Indus. v. Armstrong Cork Co., 366 F. Supp. 220, 233 (E.D. Pa. 1973), *aff'd*, 510 F.2d 334 (3d Cir.), *cert. denied*, 421 U.S. 988 (1975); *see also* Windsurfing Int'l, Inc. v. AMF, Inc., 782 F.2d 995 (Fed. Cir.) (agreement not to contest the validity of a trademark license found not a misuse), *cert. denied*, 477 U.S. 905 (1986).

260. Lear, Inc. v. Adkins, 395 U.S. 653, 673-74 (1969).

261. *See* Warner-Jenkinson Co. v. Allied Chem. Corp., 567 F.2d 184, 187-88 (2d Cir. 1977). *Contra* Lee v. Lee Custom Eng'g, Inc., 476 F. Supp. 361 (E.D. Wis. 1979). A court may require that post-challenge royalties be paid into an escrow account. *E.g.*, Precision Shooting Equip. Co. v. Allen, 646 F.2d 313 (7th Cir.), *cert. denied*, 454 U.S. 964 (1981).

262. Bristol Locknut Co. v. SPS Technologies, Inc., 677 F.2d 1277, 1283 (9th Cir. 1982) (footnotes and citations omitted); *see* Precision Shooting Equip. Co. v. Allen, 646 F.2d 313 (7th Cir.), *cert. denied*, 454 U.S. 964 (1981); Warner-Jenkinson Co. v. Allied Chem. Corp., 567 F.2d 184, 188 (2d Cir. 1977); Atlas Chem. Indus. v. Moraine Prods., 509 F.2d 1, 4-7 (6th Cir. 1974). *But cf.* Troxel Mfg. Co. v. Schwinn Bicycle Co., 465 F.2d 1253 (6th Cir. 1972) (absent fraud or misconduct, royalties may be recovered by a licensee who is not the party that established invalidity only from the time the patent is declared invalid), *later appeal*, 489 F.2d 968 (6th Cir. 1973), *cert. denied*, 416 U.S. 939 (1974).

263. *See* Nashua Corp. v. RCA Corp., 431 F.2d 220, 226 (1st Cir. 1970); SCM Corp. v. RCA, 318 F. Supp. 433, 470-72 (S.D.N.Y. 1970). *But see* Transitron Elec. Corp. v. Hughes Aircraft Co., 649 F.2d 871 (1st Cir. 1981) (fraud on patent office is insufficient, absent fraud in the inducement of the licensee).

264. Wallace Clark & Co. v. Acheson Indus., 532 F.2d 846, 849 (2d Cir.), *cert. denied*, 524 U.S. 976 (1976); Schlegel Mfg. Co. v. USM Corp., 525 F.2d 775 (6th Cir. 1975), *cert. denied*, 425 U.S. 912 (1976); USM Corp. v. Standard Pressed Steel Co., 453 F. Supp. 743, 747-48 (N.D. Ill. 1978), *aff'd in part and vacated in part*, 694 F.2d 505 (7th Cir. 1982), *cert. denied*, 462 U.S. 1107 (1983). *But see* Kaspar Wire Works, Inc. v. Leco Eng'g & Mach., Inc., 575 F.2d 530 (5th Cir. 1978) (consent judgment dismissing action by alleged infringer of action to declare patent invalid denied preclusive effect on question of validity).

265. C.R. Bard, Inc. v. Schwartz, 716 F.2d 874, 879-82 (Fed. Cir. 1983).

In *United States v. Glaxo Group,*[266] the Supreme Court held the United States may challenge the validity of a patent in a civil antitrust proceeding, where the patents are part and parcel of the alleged anticompetitive conduct.[267] The Court added, however, that it was not granting the government an "unlimited authority" to attack patents, nor was it investing the Attorney General with "a roving commission to question the validity of any patent lurking in the background of an antitrust case."[268]

7. Crosslicensing and Patent Pools[269]

When two or more owners of different patents agree to license one another or mutually select third parties under their respective patents, such an agreement may be termed a "patent pool," "crosslicense," or a "patent interchange." For analytical purposes under the antitrust laws, these terms are functionally identical. Patent interchanges are sometimes carried out by assigning the patents to a specially created entity.[270]

In *Standard Oil Co. v. United States,*[271] the Supreme Court held lawful a patent pool among competing oil companies. The agreements were accorded a rule of reason analysis and were considered reasonable because they were essential to permit each party to practice its own inventions. The patents were so-called "blocking patents" and one party could not practice under its patents without infringing the other parties' patents. Similarly, in *Carpet Seaming Tape Licensing Corp. v. Best Seam, Inc.,*[272] the Ninth Circuit noted that a "well recognized legitimate purpose for a pooling agreement is exchange of blocking patents."

Because they often involve horizontal agreements among competitors, the purpose of patent pools and crosslicenses is often important in a rule of reason analysis. Thus, in *Duplan Corp. v. Deering Milliken, Inc.,*[273] the Fourth Circuit held that

---

266. 410 U.S. 52 (1973).

267. *Id.* at 57-60; *see* United States v. United States Gypsum Co., 333 U.S. 364, 386-88 (1948); MacGregor v. Westinghouse Elec. & Mfg. Co., 329 U.S. 402 (1947); Sola Elec. Co. v. Jefferson Elec. Co., 317 U.S. 173 (1942); Baldwin-Lima-Hamilton Corp. v. Tatnall Measuring Sys., 169 F. Supp. 1, 27 (E.D. Pa. 1958), *aff'd per curiam*, 268 F.2d 395 (3d Cir.), *cert. denied*, 361 U.S. 849 (1959); *see also* United States v. Markham, 537 F.2d 187 (5th Cir. 1976) (criminal action brought by Antitrust Division for patent fraud), *cert. denied*, 429 U.S. 1041 (1977). Under the Lanham Act, 15 U.S.C. § 1064 (1988), the Federal Trade Commission is expressly empowered to institute proceedings to cancel trademarks that have become generic.

268. 410 U.S. at 59.

269. For a discussion of the Department of Justice's views of patent pools, see Andewelt, *Analysis of Patent Pools Under the Antitrust Laws*, 53 ANTITRUST L.J. 611 (1984).

270. *E.g.*, Baker-Cammack Hosiery Mills, Inc. v. Davis Co., 181 F.2d 550, 568 (4th Cir.), *cert. denied*, 340 U.S. 824 (1950); United States v. Vehicular Parking, Ltd., 54 F. Supp. 828 (D. Del.), *modified*, 56 F. Supp. 297 (D. Del. 1944), *modified*, 61 F. Supp. 656 (D. Del. 1945).

271. 283 U.S. 163, 170-77 (1931); *see* Apex Elec. Mfg. Co. v. Altorfer Bros., 238 F.2d 867, 873 (7th Cir. 1956).

272. 616 F.2d 1133, 1142 (9th Cir. 1980), *aff'd in part and rev'd in part*, 694 F.2d 570 (9th Cir. 1982), *cert. denied*, 464 U.S. 818 (1983); *see* International Mfg. Co. v. Landon, Inc., 336 U.S. 723, 729 (9th Cir. 1964) ("In a case involving blocking patents such an arrangement is the only reasonable method for making the invention available to the public.") (citations omitted), *cert. denied*, 379 U.S. 988 (1965); *see also* Cutter Labs. v. Lyophile-Cryochem Corp., 179 F.2d 80, 92-93 (9th Cir. 1949); International Nickel Co. v. Ford Motor Co., 166 F. Supp. 551, 565-66 (S.D.N.Y. 1958).

273. 540 F.2d 1215 (4th Cir. 1976).

settlement of patent litigation by crosslicensing agreement was lawful if entered into to resolve legitimate conflicting patent claims. On remand, however, the district court found that the settlement violated Section 2, because the parties had entered into the agreements to preserve their royalty structures and strengthen themselves against unlicensed outsiders.[274]

An important factor in determining the legality of a patent pool is whether the patents create monopoly power in an economic market. In *United States v. Krasnov*,[275] for example, companies that together had monopoly power formed a patent pool and agreed to refrain from licensing others without mutual consent, to allocate customers, to maintain prices established by the licensor, and to determine jointly the institution and maintenance of infringement suits. The district court held that this pool violated Sections 1 and 2 of the Sherman Act. In *United States v. National Lead Co.*,[276] the district court held that an agreement between the two largest companies in the titanium dioxide industry involving the exchange of nonexclusive licenses under all their patents, present and future, with the knowledge that such an arrangement would strengthen both parties to the exclusion of outsiders was held illegal.

A second important factor in determining legality is whether the pool is exclusive, i.e., whether the participants give up the right to license their own patents separately. In *Zenith Radio Corp. v. Hazeltine Research, Inc.*[277] the Supreme Court held that exclusive patent pools violate the Sherman Act even in the absence of monopoly power. *Zenith* involved a pool of Canadian patents formed to prevent the shipment of radio and television apparatus into Canada. "Once Zenith demonstrated that its exports from the United States had been restrained by pool activities, the treble-damage liability of the domestic company [Hazeltine] participating in the conspiracy was beyond question."[278]

Price-fixing clauses in crosslicenses have been held illegal, even though the patents covered complementary, noncompeting products or processes.[279] Likewise, agreements mutually to restrict such licenses to particular territories have been ruled

---

274. Duplan Corp. v. Deering Milliken, Inc., 444 F. Supp. 648 (D.S.C. 1977), *aff'd in part and rev'd in part*, 594 F.2d 979 (4th Cir. 1979), *cert. denied*, 444 U.S. 1015 (1980). In Carpet Seaming Tape Licensing Corp. v. Best Seam, Inc., 694 F.2d 570 (9th Cir. 1982), *cert. denied*, 464 U.S. 818 (1983), the Ninth Circuit held that the intent among pooling owners merely to enforce their patents was not sufficiently anticompetitive to support a claim of misuse.

275. 143 F. Supp. 184 (E.D. Pa. 1956), *aff'd per curiam*, 355 U.S. 5 (1957); *see* United States v. Besser Mfg. Co., 96 F. Supp. 304 (E.D. Mich. 1951), *aff'd*, 343 U.S. 444 (1952).

276. 63 F. Supp. 513, 531-32 (S.D.N.Y. 1945), *aff'd*, 332 U.S. 319 (1947); *see* United States v. Singer Mfg. Co., 374 U.S. 174 (1963); United States v. United States Gypsum Co., 333 U.S. 364 (1948); Hartford-Empire Co. v. United States, 323 U.S. 386, *clarified*, 324 U.S. 570 (1945).

277. 395 U.S. 100 (1969); *see* Honeywell, Inc. v. Sperry Rand Corp., 1974-1 Trade Cas. (CCH) ¶ 74,874 (D. Minn. 1973) (crosslicense found to be "de facto exclusive"); Mason City Tent & Awning Co. v. Clapper, 144 F. Supp. 754 (W.D. Mo. 1956). *But see* Kaiser Indus. v. Jones & Laughlin Steel Corp., 181 U.S.P.Q. (BNA) 193 (W.D. Pa. 1974) (where noninfringing processes could produce the same product as patented process, the industry was not dominated by the pooled patents and exclusive pooling agreement was lawful even if royalties charged were onerous), *rev'd on other grounds*, 515 F.2d 964 (3d Cir.), *cert. denied*, 423 U.S. 876 (1975).

278. 395 U.S. at 114 n.8.

279. United States v. Line Material Co., 333 U.S. 287, 305-15 (1948); *see* Subsection B.6.a.(2) of this chapter.

illegal.[280]

In *United States v. Automobile Manufacturers Association*,[281] the consent decree prohibited certain exchanges of technical information and royalty-free patent licenses among defendants. The government alleged a violation of the Sherman Act by reason of royalty-free crosslicensing of patents pertaining to emission control devices by the principal domestic automobile manufacturers, where the purpose of the crosslicense was to delay technical advancement.[282]

8. Concerted Boycott by Infringers or Licensees

The Third Circuit has distinguished between a mere "agreement to challenge the validity" of a patent, and the formation of a group for the purpose of " 'refusing to negotiate' " with the patent holder for licenses, holding the latter to be illegal.[283] In *Gould v. Control Laser Corp.*,[284] the district court held that competitors can agree to share the costs of litigating to have a patent declared invalid "even if the goal of the litigation is clearly anti-competitive." However, if the joint defense agreement goes further than sharing costs and restricts the rights of the parties to settle individually, antitrust liability could exist.[285]

9. Foreign Patent and Know-how Licensing

a. INTRODUCTION

The Department of Justice *Antitrust Enforcement Guidelines for International Operations*,[286] sets forth the Department's current enforcement policy with respect to international license agreements[287] and which includes three hypothetical examples demonstrating the application of this policy.[288] The *International*

---

280. United States v. Imperial Chem. Indus., 100 F. Supp. 504, 519-31 (S.D.N.Y. 1951); *see* United States v. Holophane Co., 119 F. Supp. 114, 117-19 (S.D. Ohio 1954), *aff'd per curiam*, 352 U.S. 903 (1956).

281. 307 F. Supp. 617 (C.D. Cal. 1969), *aff'd in part and appeal dismissed in part sub nom.* Grossman v. Automobile Mfrs. Ass'n, 397 U.S. 248 (1970).

282. A private action, based on the same theory, was dismissed for lack of a showing of an unreasonable restraint of trade. *In re* Multidistrict Vehicle Air Pollution, 367 F. Supp. 1298, 1303 (C.D. Cal.1973), *aff'd*, 538 F.2d 231 (9th Cir. 1976).

283. Jones Knitting Corp. v. Morgan, 361 F.2d 451, 459 (3d Cir. 1966) (quoting district court).

284. 462 F. Supp. 685, 693 (M.D. Fla. 1978), *aff'd in part and appeal dismissed in part*, 650 F.2d 617 (5th Cir. 1981).

285. *See* Lemelson v. Bendix Corp., 621 F. Supp. 1122 (D. Del. 1985); *Jones Knitting*, 361 F.2d at 459-60.

286. *Supra* note 20 (INTERNATIONAL GUIDELINES); *see also* C. Rule, The Antitrust Implications of International Licensing: After the Nine No-Nos (Oct. 21, 1986), *reprinted in* 4 TRADE REG. REP. (CCH) ¶ 13,131. *See generally* ABA ANTITRUST SECTION, MONOGRAPH No. 6, U.S. ANTITRUST LAW IN INTERNATIONAL PATENT AND KNOW-HOW LICENSING (1981).

287. INTERNATIONAL GUIDELINES, *supra* note 20, at § 3.6.

288. The three hypotheticals comprise Case 10, entitled "Vertical Restraints in a Patent License;" Case 11, entitled "Exclusive Patent Cross Licenses with Grantbacks;" and Case 12, entitled "Know-how Technology Transfer Agreement with Exclusive Territories."

Guidelines supersedes the Department's *Antitrust Guide for International Operations*.[289] The *International Guidelines* state that restrictions in intellectual property licensing arrangements hold significant procompetitive potential, and hence will be analyzed under a four-part rule of reason test.[290] Under that test the Department will examine (a) whether the license enhances or facilitates the exercise of market power; (b) whether there are spillover effects in other markets; (c) whether the license facilitates collusion; and (d) whether there are procompetitive efficiencies associated with the license.

Competitive restrictions in international license agreements are also affected by a number of statutes enacted in recent years which limit the scope or operation of the antitrust laws. These statutes include (1) the National Cooperative Research Act,[291] which accords rule of reason treatment for R&D joint ventures agreements properly notified to the Justice Department; (2) the Export Trading Company Act of 1982, under which recipients of export trade certificates from the Department of Commerce can obtain limited immunity under the antitrust laws for international licensing activities specified in the certificate;[292] (3) the Foreign Trade Antitrust Improvements Act,[293] which contains certain jurisdictional limitations on the application of the Sherman Act to nonimport foreign commerce; and (4) the Federal Arbitration Act[294] together with the Convention on the Recognition and Enforcement of Foreign Arbitral Awards,[295] which, as construed by *Mitsubishi Motors Corp. v. Soler Chrysler-Plymouth, Inc.*,[296] permit arbitration of antitrust aspects of international licensing disputes.

International patent and know-how license agreements may also be affected by antitrust statutes and regulations in other jurisdictions. The most comprehensive of these foreign regulatory systems is that implemented by the European Economic

---

289. ANTITRUST DIV., U.S. DEP'T OF JUSTICE (1977), *reprinted in* 4 TRADE REG. REP. (CCH) ¶ 13,110 (INTERNATIONAL GUIDE). The factual aspects of Cases I and F in the INTERNATIONAL GUIDE are similar to Cases 11 and 12, respectively, in the INTERNATIONAL GUIDELINES. Case 10 in the INTERNATIONAL GUIDELINES, which relates to competitive restrictions that extend beyond the scope of the licensed technology, has no analogue in the INTERNATIONAL GUIDE.

290. INTERNATIONAL GUIDELINES, *supra* note 20, at § 3.62. In prefatory language introducing this test, the Department states that it "will not challenge licensing arrangements that represent simply an effort by the creator of intellectual property to appropriate the full inherent value of that property" nor will it "require the owner of technology to create competition in its own technology." *Id.*

291. 15 U.S.C. §§ 4301-4305 (1988); *see* INTERNATIONAL GUIDELINES, *supra* note 20, at § 2.4.

292. 15 U.S.C. §§ 4001-4053 (1988); *see* INTERNATIONAL GUIDELINES, *supra* note 20, at § 2.6. Section V of Revised Guidelines issued under this Act by the Department of Commerce on January 11, 1985, 50 FED. REG. 1786, discusses technology licensing and includes a hypothetical international licensing situation.

293. 15 U.S.C. § 6a (1988). *See* INTERNATIONAL GUIDELINES *supra* note 20, at § 4.1 and Chapter X of this treatise; *see also* Eurim-Pharm GmbH v. Pfizer Inc., 593 F. Supp. 1102 (S.D.N.Y. 1984) (discussing this statute in connection with dismissal of claim involving in part an exclusive patent license).

294. 9 U.S.C. § 1 *et seq.* (1988).

295. 9 U.S.C. § 201 (1991 Supp.).

296. 473 U.S. 614 (1985).

Community under Article 85(3) of the Rome Treaty.[297]

In 1989, the Organization for Economic Cooperation and Development issued a report reviewing the competition policies relating to intellectual property licenses of a number of countries.[298] This organization, which only issues reports based upon the consensus of its member countries, recommended an approach to licensing competition policies that is quite similar to that set forth in the *International Guidelines*.

b. TERRITORIAL RESTRICTIONS

(1) Patents

A patentee is generally permitted to license the manufacture and sale of a product under its patents in one country but not another and also to provide by agreement that a foreign licensee will not infringe the licensor's U.S. patents. In *United States v. Westinghouse Electric Corp.*,[299] the Ninth Circuit approved reciprocal license agreements between Westinghouse and a Japanese electrical equipment manufacturer, Mitsubishi. Under the agreements, Westinghouse granted Mitsubishi an exclusive license for the manufacture of certain products in Japan under its patents and Mitsubishi granted Westinghouse nonexclusive licenses under Mitsubishi's patents and know-how to manufacture, use and sell certain products in all countries other than Japan. Concluding that "Westinghouse has done no more than to license some of its patents and refuse to license others,"[300] the Ninth Circuit affirmed the district court's dismissal of the government's case. In *Dunlop Co. v. Kelsey-Hayes Co.*,[301] the Sixth Circuit ruled that agreements between a licensor and its licensees in various foreign countries which forbade exportation of licensed products to the United States did not violate the antitrust laws. The court concluded that these were "merely territorial licenses granted by a patentee such as are permitted by 35 U.S.C. § 261."[302]

Territorial restraints in international licensing arrangements have been held unlawful when they have brought about a division of markets substantially beyond the scope and terms of the patents or involved pervasive schemes to restrain U.S. and

---

297. This regulatory system includes a group exemption regulation for patent license agreements, Commission Regulation (EEC) No. 2349/84, 17 O.J. EUR. COMM. (No. L 219) 15 (1984), *corrected*, 28 O.J. EUR. COMM. (No. L 1113) 34 (1985), *reprinted in* 2 COMMON MKT. REP. (CCH) ¶ 2747, and a group exemption regulation for know-how license agreements. O.J. EUR. COMM. (No.L 61/1) (1989), *reprinted in* 2 COMMON MKT. REP. (CCH) ¶ 2771. See Section I.6.C. of Chapter X of this treatise. These regulations in part implement several decisions of the European Court of Justice applying Article 85 to various licensing situations. *See e.g.,* Nungesser v. Comm'n, 1982 EUR. COMM. Ct. J. Rep. 2015, [1981-1983 Transfer Binder] COMMON MKT. REP. (CCH) ¶ 8805 ("Maize Seed" decision); Windsurfing Int'l, Inc. v. Commission, 1986 E. COMM. CT. J. REP. 611, [1985-1986 Transfer Binder] COMMON MKT. REP. (CCH) ¶ 14,271.

298. COMPETITION POLICY AND INTELLECTUAL PROPERTY RIGHTS (1989); *see* ABA Antitrust Section, *Antitrust* (Summer 1989).

299. 648 F.2d 642 (9th Cir. 1981).

300. *Id.* at 647.

301. 484 F.2d 407, 417-18 (6th Cir. 1973), *cert. denied*, 415 U.S. 917 (1974).

302. *Id.* at 417.

foreign commerce.[303]   Also, a patent pool among Canadian manufacturers that agreed not to license importers has been held to violate the U.S. antitrust laws.[304]

(2) Know-how or Trade Secrets

International know-how (trade secret) license agreements are discussed in the *International Guidelines*.[305]   The Department notes that "[b]ecause of the essentially similar roles that transfers of know-how and patent licensing play in the competitive process, the Department generally analyzes them in the same way."[306]

In the know-how licensing example of the *International Guidelines*, the Department stated that technology owners are free "to appropriate the full inherent value of [their] property," and are not required to create competition in that technology.[307] The Department analysis focuses on the application of a four-part rule of reason analysis to a restriction in the hypothetical know-how license which precludes sale of product in the United States utilizing technology *other than* the licensed technology.[308] It concludes, based on its rule of reason analysis, that enforcement action against the transaction would not be appropriate.

(3) Trademarks and Copyrights

Actions to bar the import of trademarked or copyrighted products are generally not found to conflict with the antitrust laws. While there have been substantial disputes as to the scope of exclusionary rights for imports of trademarked goods

---

303.   United States v. Singer Mfg. Co., 374 U.S. 174 (1963); United States v. Imperial Chem. Indus., 100 F. Supp. 504 (S.D.N.Y. 1951); United States v. Timken Roller Bearing Co., 83 F. Supp. 284 (N.D. Ohio 1949), *modified and aff'd*, 341 U.S. 593 (1951); United States v. General Elec. Co., 82 F. Supp. 753 (D.N.J. 1949); United States v. National Lead Co., 63 F. Supp. 513 (S.D.N.Y. 1945), *aff'd*, 332 U.S. 319 (1947). As discussed in Chapter X of this treatise, the Sherman Act no longer applies to restraints of export commerce which do not have a direct, substantial, and reasonably foreseeable effect on U.S. or export commerce. *See* Foreign Trade Antitrust Improvements Act, 15 U.S.C. § 6a (1988).

304.   *See* Zenith Radio Corp. v. Hazeltine Research, Inc., 401 U.S. 321, 326 (1971).

305.   *Supra* note 20.

306.   *Id.*, at Case 12; *accord* A. & E. Plastik Pak Co. v. Monsanto Co., 396 F.2d 710, 714-15 (9th Cir. 1968); ABA ANTITRUST SECTION, MONOGRAPH No. 6, *supra* note 286, at 35. The INTERNATIONAL GUIDE stated that "know-how licenses will in general be subject to antitrust standards which, if anything, are stricter than those applied to patent licenses." INTERNATIONAL GUIDE, *supra* note 289, at 34.

307.   INTERNATIONAL GUIDELINES, *supra* note 20, at § 3.63; *accord* A. & E. Plastik Pak Co. v. Monsanto Co., 396 F.2d 710, 714-15 (9th Cir. 1968) ("Thus, on its face, it does not appear to be an agreement between competitors not to compete, for absent the licensed know-how, A. & E. is in no position to compete.").
    The INTERNATIONAL GUIDE and earlier cases viewed know-how licenses as more suspect. INTERNATIONAL GUIDE, *supra* note 289, at 34; *cf.* Shin Nippon Koki Co. v. Irvin Indus., 1975-1 Trade Cas. (CCH) ¶ 60,347 (N.Y. Sup. Ct. 1975). *But cf.* United States v. E.I. du Pont de Nemours & Co., 118 F. Supp. 41, 218-22 (D. Del. 1953) (license since 1923 involving cellophane), *aff'd*, 351 U.S. 377 (1956); Foundry Servs. v. Beneflux Corp., 110 F. Supp. 857 (S.D.N.Y.) (license since 1934), *rev'd on other grounds*, 206 F.2d 214 (2d Cir. 1953). The INTERNATIONAL GUIDE obliged the defendant to show that "other, less anticompetitive actions would not achieve the same public benefits" with respect to the licensed technology. INTERNATIONAL GUIDE, *supra* note 289, at 30 n.56.

308.   INTERNATIONAL GUIDELINES, *supra* note 20, at Case 12.

under Section 526 of the Tariff Act of 1930,[309] it has become clear that the antitrust laws do not impede the exercise of rights under that section.[310] However, the use of trademarks as part of a broad scheme involving U.S. domestic or import commerce to limit output and raise prices is unlawful.[311] Some courts have held that bars to importation of copyrighted products did not raise antitrust concerns.[312]

c. OTHER RESTRICTIONS

The Foreign Trade Antitrust Improvements Act[313] exempts from the coverage of the antitrust laws those practices that do not have direct, substantial, and reasonably foreseeable effect on either domestic or import commerce or on the activities of a person exporting from the United States. Although the Act thus provides a jurisdictional test distinct from the comity-based approach of *Timberlane Lumber Co. v. Bank of America National Trust & Savings Association*[314] and *Mannington Mills, Inc. v. Congoleum Corp.*,[315] the legislative history of the Act leaves open the possibility that such comity-based tests could be used to decline jurisdiction where it would otherwise exist under the Act.[316]

Two of the hypotheticals in the *International Guidelines* involve nonterritorial restrictions. In Case 11 in the *International Guidelines*, the Department states that it would not challenge a patent crosslicense agreement involving exclusive grantbacks of rights under present and future patents between the second largest seller of a particular product in the United States and the largest seller of that product in Japan.[317] With respect to the exclusivity aspects of the license, the Department states that "[e]xclusive licensing provisions may also encourage licensees to maximize their promotion and utilization of the licensed technology without free-rider concerns and allow a patent owner to maximize the return on his investment in R&D efforts

---

309. 19 U.S.C. § 1526 (1988); *see* K-Mart Corp. v. Cartier, Inc., 486 U.S. 281 (1988).

310. *See, e.g.*, United States v. Eighty-Nine (89) Bottles of "Eau de Joy," 797 F.2d 767, 770 (9th Cir. 1986) ("Congress intended to make genuine goods excludable under Sec. 526 unless the American trademark owner consents to their importation."). In Coalition to Preserve The Integrity of Am. Trademarks v. United States, 790 F.2d 903, 916 (D.C. Cir. 1986), *aff'd in part and rev'd in part sub nom.* K-Mart Corp. v. Cartier, Inc., 486 U.S. 281 (1988), the Department of Justice and the Customs Service filed a joint amicus brief maintaining "that Section 526 raised no antitrust concerns." *See also* Osawa & Co. v. B&H Photo, 589 F. Supp. 1163, 1177-78 (S.D.N.Y. 1984).

311. Timken Roller Bearing Co. v. United States, 341 U.S. 593 (1951); *see* United States v. Topco Assocs., 405 U.S. 596 (1972).

312. *See* Hearst Corp. v. Stark, 639 F. Supp. 970, 981 (N.D. Cal. 1986); CBS v. Scorpio Music Distribs., 569 F. Supp. 47, 49-50 (E.D. Pa. 1983) (importer violated Copyright Act, 17 U.S.C. § 602 (1982)), *aff'd mem.*, 738 F.2d 424 (3d Cir. 1984).

313. 15 U.S.C. § 6(a) (1988); *see also* Subpart B.1 of Chapter X of this treatise.

314. 549 F.2d 597 (9th Cir. 1976). Applying *Timberlane*, the district court in United States v. Westinghouse Electric Corp., 471 F. Supp. 532, 542 (N.D. Cal. 1978), *aff'd in part and rev'd in part*, 648 F.2d 642 (9th Cir. 1981), rejected an effort by the Government to challenge the grant of exclusive rights by Westinghouse under its Japanese patents.

315. 595 F.2d 1287 (3d Cir. 1979) (requiring that a jurisdictional rule of reason test similar to that of *Timberlane* be applied in a case involving fraudulent procurement of foreign patents).

316. H.R. REP. No. 686, 97th Cong., 2d Sess. 13, *reprinted in* 1982 U.S. CODE CONG. & ADMIN. NEWS 2487, 2498 (Act "would have no effect on the courts' ability to employ notions of comity . . . or otherwise to take account of the 'international character of the transaction' ").

317. INTERNATIONAL GUIDELINES, *supra* note 20, at Case 11.

to acquire the patent."[318]

In Case 10 in the *International Guidelines*, the Department indicates that it would not challenge the grant by an automobile glass manufacturer of exclusive licenses to U.S. and British companies under its respective U.S. and EEC patents for the field of coated safety eyeglasses. Each of the licenses in the hypothetical includes provisions which forbid the licensee "from manufacturing and selling safety eyeglasses coated with any other material"[319] and which provide for the licensee "to pay royalties based on its total unit sales of safety eyeglasses, coated and uncoated."[320] In support of its determination not to take action against these provisions, the Department notes that a provision precluding the use of competing technologies "may be used to give [the licensee] a strong incentive to develop and aggressively market [the licensor's] technology"[321] and that a provision providing for royalties based on total sales "may save licensors the costs of determining how much its licensees' production utilizes the licensed technology."[322]

C. Special Problems with Nonpatent Intellectual Property

1. *Copyrights*

Copyrights are exclusively federal statutory grants[323] that provide exclusivity to an author's original expression of ideas.[324] Others may use the ideas expressed in a copyrighted work, but those who copy the original author's expression of those ideas may be liable as copyright infringers. If an identical work is independently created, there is no copyright infringement liability, in contrast to patent law where there may be infringement even if the infringement was unknowing.[325]

In spite of the differences between patents and copyrights, the Supreme Court has relied on its patent-antitrust decisions when resolving conflicts between the copyright

---

318. *Id.* In the INTERNATIONAL GUIDE, the Department had indicated that if the licensee were capable of competing in the United States, then the exclusive grantback "is likely to be per se illegal." INTERNATIONAL GUIDE, *supra* note 289, at 45. The Department also indicated that "[w]here the grantback obligation is narrowly defined, an exclusive grantback is in fact less likely to be anticompetitive." *Id.* at 44; *accord* United States v. National Lead Co., 332 U.S. 319 (1947); Duplan Corp. v. Deering Milliken, Inc., 444 F. Supp. 648 (D.S.C. 1977), *aff'd in part and rev'd in part*, 594 F.2d 979 (4th Cir. 1979), *cert. denied*, 444 U.S. 1015 (1980).

319. INTERNATIONAL GUIDELINES, *supra* note 20, at Case 10.

320. *Id.*

321. *Id.*

322. *Id.*

323. *See generally* 17 U.S.C. § 101 *et seq.* (1988). The 1976 revision of the Copyright Act specifically provides for federal preemption of all state laws directed to copyrightable subject matter. 17 U.S.C. § 301 (1988). Copyrights, as patents, are provided for in article 1, section 8, clause 8 of the Constitution.

324. 17 U.S.C. § 102(b) (1988) states: "In no case does copyright protection for an original work of authorship extend to any idea, procedure, process, system, method of operation, concept, principle, or discovery." *See* Mazer v. Stein, 347 U.S. 201, 217 (1954) ("protection is given only to the expression of the idea – not the idea itself").

325. Mazer v. Stein, 347 U.S. 201, 218 (1954) ("[A]bsent copying there can be no infringement of copyright."); *see* Kewanee Oil Co. v. Bicron Corp., 416 U.S. 470, 477-78 (1974). *Compare* 17 U.S.C. §§ 106-118, 501 (1988) *with* 35 U.S.C. § 271(a) (1988).

and antitrust laws. In *United States v. Paramount Pictures*,[326] for example, the Court held that producers and distributors of motion picture films engaged in an unlawful practice by requiring theatres to maintain minimum admission prices. The Court reasoned that "a copyright may no more be used than a patent to deter competition between rivals in the exploitation of their licenses."[327]

The doctrine of misuse is not as clear in copyright cases as in patent cases. Although the Supreme Court has made passing reference to the misuse of a copyright,[328] the Court has never squarely ruled that a copyright is not enforceable because it has been misused. In *Broadcast Music, Inc. v. CBS*,[329] the Court reversed a ruling of the Second Circuit that blanket copyright licenses were per se violations of the Sherman Act and constituted copyright misuse.[330] The Court remanded the case for an analysis under the rule of reason; the misuse question was not before it, nor was it mentioned by the Second Circuit on remand.[331]

Several circuits have acknowledged the existence of a doctrine of copyright misuse as a valid defense to copyright infringement. In *Lasercomb America, Inc. v. Reynolds*,[332] the Fourth Circuit reversed a damage award for copyright infringement on the ground that the plaintiff had engaged in copyright misuse by inserting a clause in its license prohibiting the licensee from developing competing software for ninety-nine years.[333] In expressly adopting a copyright misuse defense, the Fourth Circuit stated that copyright misuse need not rise to the level of an antitrust violation to constitute a defense.[334] It further held that the defense was available to one who was not a direct victim of the offending conduct.[335] Likewise, in *Tempo Music, Inc. v. Myers*,[336] the Fourth Circuit reversed a district court holding of infringement, ruling that the copyright owners had "unclean hands" for failing to notify licensees of beneficial provisions the owners were compelled to offer

---

326. 334 U.S. 131 (1948). *Paramount Pictures* was one of a series of cases before the Court in the 1940s dealing with arrangements between and among producers, distributors, and exhibitors of motion picture films. The exclusivity created by the copyrights on the films, while not always directly discussed in those cases, was always at least implicitly in issue because the copyrights prohibited anyone but the owners and their licensees from dealing in the copyrighted films. United States v. Griffith, 334 U.S. 100 (1948); Schine Chain Theatres v. United States, 334 U.S. 110 (1948); United States v. Crescent Amusement Co., 323 U.S. 173 (1944). See Section B.6.f of this chapter, for a discussion of the tying or "block booking" aspects of those cases; *see also* Broadcast Music, Inc. v. CBS, 441 U.S. 1 (1979).

327. 334 U.S. 131, 144 (1948). *See* Section B.6.b of this chapter. However, unlike the case in patent licenses, it has been held that a no-contest clause in a copyright license is enforceable unless it violates the Sherman Act. Saturday Evening Post Co. v. Rumbleseat Press, Inc., 816 F.2d 1191 (7th Cir. 1987) (distinguishing Lear, Inc. v. Adkins, 395 U.S. 653 (1969)); *see also* Straus & Straus v. American Publishers' Ass'n, 231 U.S. 222, 234 (1913). As with patents, it has also been held that the statutory grant is exhausted by the first authorized sale of a book or film that embodies the copyrighted work. Bobbs-Merrill Co. v. Straus, 210 U.S. 339, 350 (1908).

328. *See* Mazer v. Stein, 347 U.S. 201, 206, 218 (1954).

329. 441 U.S. 1 (1979).

330. CBS v. American Soc'y of Composers, Authors & Publishers, 562 F.2d 130, 141 n.29 (2d Cir. 1977), *rev'd and remanded sub nom.* Broadcast Music, Inc. v. CBS, 441 U.S. 1 (1979).

331. CBS v. American Soc'y of Composers, Authors & Publishers, 607 F.2d 543 (2d Cir. 1979).

332. 911 F.2d 970 (4th Cir. 1990).

333. *Id.* at 979.

334. *Id.* at 978.

335. *Id.* at 979.

336. 407 F.2d 503, 507 (4th Cir. 1969).

under a prior antitrust consent decree.

In *F.E.L. Publications Ltd. v. Catholic Bishop*,[337] the Seventh Circuit reversed a lower court ruling that a copyright holder had engaged in illegal licensing and tying arrangements and thus could not enforce a claim of infringement. Although the misuse defense was recognized by the circuit court, it held that "misuse" gives rise to a valid defense against infringement only after a "balancing of equities."[338] The Eighth Circuit, in *United Telephone Co. v. Johnson Publishing Co.*,[339] remarked that a claim of copyright misuse as an antitrust violation may be used as a defense to a charge of copyright infringement.

Many district courts have rejected the argument that a federal antitrust law violation provides the basis for an "unclean hands" defense to a copyright infringement suit.[340]

In a few cases a claim that a copyright owner's licensing scheme anticompetitively raised the prices for the copyrighted goods has been dismissed on the ground that the plaintiff failed to establish antitrust injury.[341] It also has been held that the institution of copyright litigation in good faith based on a valid copyright is immune

---

337.   1982-1 Trade Cas. (CCH) ¶ 64,632 (7th Cir.), *rev'g* 506 F. Supp. 1127, 1137 (N.D. Ill. 1981), *cert. denied*, 459 U.S. 859 (1982); *see also* Mitchell Bros. Film Group v. Cinema Adult Theater, 604 F.2d 852, 865 (5th Cir. 1979) ("In an appropriate case a misuse of the copyright statute that in some way subverts the purpose of the statute – the promotion of originality – might constitute a bar to judicial relief."), *cert. denied*, 445 U.S. 917 (1980).

338.   1982-1 Trade Cas. (CCH) ¶ 64,632, at 73,464 n.9.

339.   855 F.2d 604, 611 (8th Cir. 1988). In Bellsouth Advertising & Publishing Corp. v. Donnelley Information Publishing, 933 F.2d 952, 960-61 (11th Cir. 1991), the Eleventh Circuit suggested that it might apply the copyright misuse doctrine in an appropriate case. *See also* Eastern Publishing & Advertising, Inc. v. Chesapeake Publishing & Advertising, Inc., 831 F.2d 488, 493 (4th Cir. 1987), *vacated on other grounds*, 492 U.S. 913 (1989); Edward B. Marks Music Corp. v. Colorado Magnetics, Inc., 497 F.2d 285, 290-91 (10th Cir. 1974), *cert. denied*, 419 U.S. 1120 (1975); K-91, Inc. v. Gershwin Publishing Corp., 372 F.2d 1, 4 (9th Cir. 1967), *cert. denied*, 389 U.S. 1045 (1968).

340.   *E.g.*, Buck v. Cecere, 45 F. Supp. 441 (W.D.N.Y. 1942); Buck v. Newsreel, Inc., 25 F. Supp. 787, 789 (D. Mass. 1938); Vitagraph, Inc. v. Grobaski, 46 F.2d 813, 814 (W.D. Mich. 1931); M. Witmark & Sons v. Pastime Amusement Co., 298 F. 470, 480 (E.D.S.C.), *aff'd*, 2 F.2d 1020 (4th Cir. 1924); Harms v. Cohen, 279 F. 276, 280-81 (E.D. Pa. 1922). Those decisions predate Morton Salt Co. v. G.S. Suppiger Co., 314 U.S. 488, 493-94 (1942), where the Court refused to enforce a patent that had been misused. A number of district courts have ruled, in cases postdating the *Morton Salt* holding, that alleging an antitrust violation to defend a copyright infringement suit is "no defense." *See, e.g.*, Orth-O-Vision, Inc. v. Home Box Office, 474 F. Supp. 672, 686 (S.D.N.Y. 1979) ("As a general rule, it is no defense to a copyright infringement claim that the copyright owner is violating the antitrust laws."); Foreign Car Parts, Inc. v. Auto World, Inc., 366 F. Supp. 977, 979 (M.D. Pa. 1973) (doubtful that an antitrust violation creates a defense to an action for copyright infringement); Harms, Inc. v. Sansom House Enters., 162 F. Supp. 129, 135 (E.D. Pa. 1958), *aff'd sub nom.* Leo Feist, Inc. v. Lew Tender Tavern, Inc., 267 F.2d 494 (3d Cir. 1959). In certain of these cases, the decision may be based on the absence of any relationship between the patent and the violation in question. In *Morton Salt*, there was such a relationship between the patent and the violation. However, in United Artists Associated v. NWL Corp., 198 F. Supp. 953, 958 (S.D.N.Y. 1961), the court, after carefully reviewing the ruling in *Morton Salt* and noting the connection between the patent and the antitrust violation, still concluded that "it is a substantial question whether a like rule . . . is applicable to an action for infringement of *copyright*." (emphasis in original).

341.   Original Appalachian Artworks, Inc. v. Granada Elecs., Inc., 640 F. Supp. 928 (S.D.N.Y. 1986), *aff'd*, 816 F.2d 68 (2d Cir.), *cert. denied*, 487 U.S. 847 (1987); W. Goebel Porzellanfabrik v. Action Indus., 589 F. Supp. 763 (S.D.N.Y. 1984).

from antitrust scrutiny under the *Noerr-Pennington* doctrine.[342]

2. *Trademarks*

A trademark consists of "any word, name, symbol, or device or any combination thereof" used by a manufacturer or seller to distinguish his products from those of others.[343] Rights in a trademark are established by using the mark commercially on goods or with respect to services. In general, the first user of a mark is entitled to exclude others from using the same or a similar trademark where confusion of the purchasing public is likely.[344] A trademark differs significantly from a patent in that a trademark gives the owner no exclusive right to make, use or sell any good or service.[345]

The owner of a trademark may license others to use the mark, but as with patents and copyrights, certain ancillary restraints in the license agreement are subject to challenge under the antitrust laws. Thus, in *United States v. Sealy, Inc.,*[346] the Court struck down a territorial trademark licensing scheme on the ground that it was a horizontal agreement among competitors. The individual licensees jointly owned the licensor organization. Similarly, resale price maintenance cannot be justified on the ground that a product is trademarked.[347]

Although an early case held that a claim of trademark misuse is not a defense to trademark infringement actions,[348] a few courts recognize the defense.[349] Because of the significant differences between the exclusionary effects of patents and

---

342. Columbia Pictures Indus. v. Redd Horne, Inc., 749 F.2d 154, 161 (3d Cir. 1984); *see* Alberto-Culver Co. v. Andrea Dumon, Inc., 466 F.2d 705, 711 (7th Cir. 1972); Ansul Co. v. Uniroyal, Inc., 448 F.2d 872 (2d Cir. 1971), *cert. denied*, 404 U.S. 1018 (1972).

343. 15 U.S.C. § 1127 (1988). A trademark refers to a mark used in connection with goods. A mark used in connection with services is called a service mark. For convenience, the term "trademark" will be used to refer to both trademarks and service marks.

344. United Drug Co. v. Theodore Rectanus Co., 248 U.S. 90, 97-98 (1918); Hanover Star Milling Co. v. Metcalf, 240 U.S. 403, 412-15 (1916); Trade-Mark Cases, 100 U.S. 82, 92, 94 (1879). *See also* 15 U.S.C. § 1114 (1988).

345. Car-Freshner Corp. v. Auto Aid Mfg. Corp., 438 F. Supp. 82, 86 (N.D.N.Y. 1977); Seven-Up Co. v. No-Cal Corp., 183 U.S.P.Q. (BNA) 165, 166 (E.D.N.Y. 1974); Carl Zeiss Stiftung v. V.E.B. Carl Zeiss, Jena, 298 F. Supp. 1309, 1314 (S.D.N.Y. 1969), *modified on other grounds*, 433 F.2d 686 (2d Cir. 1970), *cert. denied*, 403 U.S. 905 (1971).

346. 388 U.S. 350, 356 (1967); *see also* United States v. Topco Assocs., 405 U.S. 596 (1972); Timken Roller Bearing Co. v. United States, 341 U.S. 593 (1951); Instructional Sys. Dev. Corp. v. Aetna Casualty & Sur. Co., 787 F.2d 1395 (10th Cir. 1986) (in reversing a grant of summary judgment for defendant, the court held that restrictions in a joint venture agreement beyond what was necessary to effectuate a trademark license (e.g., market division) could violate § 1 under the rule of reason), *modified on other grounds*, 817 F.2d 639 (10th Cir. 1987). A district court decision finding a probable violation of the *Sealy* consent decree and granting a preliminary injunction was reversed in Sealy Mattress Co. v. Sealy, Inc. 789 F.2d 582 (7th Cir. 1986).

347. United States v. Bausch & Lomb Optical Co., 321 U.S. 707, 721 (1944). Prior to the repeal, effective March 11, 1976, of the Miller-Tydings and McGuire Fair Trade Amendments to the Sherman Act, federal law permitted individual states, by statute, to exempt trademarked goods from the Sherman Act proscription against resale price maintenance. That subject is discussed in Chapter I of this treatise.

348. Folmer Graflex Corp. v. Graphic Photo Serv., 41 F. Supp. 319, 320 (D. Mass. 1941). The court did remark that such misuse may be a factor in determining equitable relief for the plaintiff.

349. Phi Delta Theta Fraternity v. J.A. Buchroeder & Co., 251 F. Supp. 968 (W.D. Mo. 1966); *see* Coca-Cola Co. v. Howard Johnson Co., 386 F. Supp. 330, 336 n.4 (N.D. Ga. 1974) (citing cases).

trademarks, the availability of the misuse defense is generally limited to situations where the trademark "itself has been the basic and fundamental vehicle required and used to accomplish the [antitrust] violation."[350] It has also been held that since trademarks, unlike patents, do not confer exclusionary power over products or services, excluding others from a trademark cannot support an attempt to monopolize claim.[351]

Section 33(b) of the Lanham Act provides that a mark that has become incontestable is conclusive evidence of the registrant's ownership, except when "the mark has been or is being used to violate the antitrust laws of the United States."[352] Some courts have suggested that Section 33(b) provides authority for finding trademark misuse.[353] These cases, however, have not discussed or recognized the difference between a possible defense to incontestability, which does not necessarily defeat the trademark owner's right to prevail, and a defense of misuse, which can defeat an infringement action.[354]

Several cases have discussed whether a trademark can be a separate product for the purpose of a tying analysis and the related question whether a trademark can be presumed to confer economic power. These tying cases express policy differences underlying the respective bodies of antitrust, trademark, and patent law. In *Siegel v. Chicken Delight, Inc.*,[355] the Ninth Circuit held that a franchisor may not license franchisees to use its trademark and business methods on condition that the franchisees purchase supplies and equipment from the franchisor. The trademark was held to constitute a distinct tying product and the presumption of economic power existing in patent cases was held by the court to apply equally to trademarks.[356] The court rejected the argument that the tying arrangements were justified by the franchisor's need to maintain quality control in connection with the

---

350.   Carl Zeiss Stiftung v. V.E.B. Carl Zeiss, Jena, 298 F. Supp. 1309, 1315 (S.D.N.Y. 1969), *modified on other grounds*, 433 F.2d 686 (2d Cir. 1970), *cert. denied*, 403 U.S. 905 (1971); *see also* G. Heileman Brewing Co. v. Anheuser-Busch Inc., 676 F. Supp. 1436, 1473 (E.D. Wis. 1987) (the test to be applied in determining whether a particular trademark use constitutes a § 2 violation is the same as in any other case where an unlawful monopoly, or attempt to monopolize, is alleged; § 2 is violated only when the trademark owner's "actions have led to or resulted in a dangerous probability that it will gain a monopoly over the relevant market"), *aff'd*, 873 F.2d 985 (7th Cir. 1989); Coca-Cola Co. v. Howard Johnson Co., 386 F. Supp. 330, 335-37 (N.D. Ga. 1974).

351.   Seven-Up Co. v. No-Cal Corp., 183 U.S.P.Q. (BNA) 165, 166 (E.D.N.Y. 1974); Alberto-Culver Co. v. Andrea Dumon, Inc., 295 F. Supp. 1155, 1158 (N.D. Ill. 1969), *aff'd in part and rev'd in part*, 466 F.2d 705 (7th Cir. 1972); *In re* Borden, Inc., 92 F.T.C. 669 (1978) (respondent not required to license ReaLemon trademark in spite of monopoly), *aff'd*, 674 F.2d 498 (6th Cir. 1982); *cf.* Original Appalachian Artworks, Inc. v. McCall Pattern Co., 649 F. Supp. 832 (N.D. Ga. 1986) (bad faith claim of sham trademark litigation cannot be made when prior trademark litigation was concluded successfully by trademark holder), *aff'd*, 825 F.2d 355 (11th Cir. 1987). *But see* Kellogg Co. v. National Biscuit Co., 71 F.2d 662, 665-66 (2d Cir. 1934).

352.   15 U.S.C. § 1115(b)(7) (1988).

353.   *See, e.g.*, G.D. Searle & Co. v. Institutional Drug Distribs., 151 F. Supp. 715, 720 (S.D. Cal. 1957); Carl Zeiss Stiftung v. V.E.B. Carl Zeiss, Jena, 289 F. Supp. 1309 (S.D.N.Y. 1969), *modified on other grounds*, 433 F.2d 686 (2nd Cir. 1970), *cert. denied*, 403 U.S. 905 (1971).

354.   *See* Coca-Cola Co. v. Howard Johnson Co., 386 F. Supp. 330, 335 (N.D. Ga. 1974).

355.   448 F.2d 43 (9th Cir. 1971), *cert. denied*, 405 U.S. 955 (1972).

356.   *Id.* at 47, 49-50.

use of its trademark.[357]

In *Krehl v. Baskin-Robbins Ice Cream Co.*,[358] the Ninth Circuit distinguished a "business format" franchise of the type in *Chicken Delight* from a "distribution type system," holding that the trademark in the latter was inseparable from the product. In *Redd v. Shell Oil Co.*,[359] the Tenth Circuit similarly refused to find the defendant's trademark to be separate from petroleum products sold under the mark, stating that "permissive trademark use did not . . . transform the mark into a separate product to be sold to plaintiff." In *Capital Temporaries, Inc. v. Olsten Corp.*,[360] the Second Circuit reached a similar result by refusing to presume the existence of economic power in a trademark (the tying product) necessary to a Sherman Act violation.[361]

In *Principe v. McDonald's Corp.*,[362] the Fourth Circuit held that the McDonald's franchise was not separable into tied and tying products, at least so far as the store location was alleged to be separable from the franchise. The court disagreed with the conclusion in *Chicken Delight* that the trademarks were the essence of a franchise. "Where the challenged aggregation is an essential ingredient of the franchised system's formula for success, there is but a single product and no tie-in exists as a matter of law."[363]

3. Trade Secret Licenses

State law, not federal law, protects trade secrets and know-how.[364] In *Kewanee*

---

357. *Id.* at 51; *accord* Northern v. McGraw-Edison Co., 542 F.2d 1336, 1345 (8th Cir. 1976), *cert. denied*, 429 U.S. 1097 (1977); Warriner Hermetics, Inc. v. Copeland Refrigeration Corp., 463 F.2d 1002, 1012-15 (5th Cir.), *cert. denied*, 409 U.S. 1086 (1972). *But see* Susser v. Carvel Corp., 332 F.2d 505, 519-20 (2d Cir. 1964) (the franchisor's trademark did not confer economic power and that tying arrangements were justified by the franchisor's need for quality control), *cert. dismissed*, 381 U.S. 125 (1965). The Lanham Act imposes an affirmative duty upon the trademark licensor to control the quality of goods and services. 15 U.S.C. §§ 1055, 1127 (1988).

358. 664 F.2d 1348, 1353 (9th Cir. 1982); *see also* Power Test Petroleum Distribs. v. Calcu Gas, Inc., 754 F.2d 91, 98 (2d Cir. 1985); Jack Walters & Sons Corp. v. Morton Bldg., Inc., 737 F.2d 698, 704 (7th Cir.), *cert. denied*, 469 U.S. 1018 (1984); Hamro v. Shell Oil Co., 674 F.2d 784, 788 (9th Cir. 1982) ("the nexus between the trademark and [gasoline] is sufficiently close to warrant treating them as one product"); Smith v. Mobil Oil Corp., 667 F. Supp. 1314 (W.D. Mo. 1987).

359. 524 F.2d 1054, 1057 (10th Cir. 1975), *cert. denied*, 425 U.S. 912 (1976). *But see* Bogosian v. Gulf Oil Corp., 561 F.2d 434 (3d Cir. 1977), *cert. denied*, 434 U.S. 1086 (1978).

360. 506 F.2d 658, 663 (2d Cir. 1974).

361. See Section B.6.f of this chapter.

362. 631 F.2d 303 (4th Cir. 1980), *cert. denied*, 451 U.S. 970 (1981).

363. *Id.* at 309. *But see* Roberts v. Elaine Powers Figure Salons, Inc., 708 F.2d 1476 (9th Cir. 1983) (franchise and bookkeeping service separate products).

364. The terms "trade secrets" and "know-how" are used interchangeably in this section. A trade secret can consist of any confidential information used by one firm in the conduct of business that gives that firm a competitive advantage over firms that do not have the information. Kewanee Oil Co. v. Bicron Corp., 416 U.S. 470, 474-75 (1974); Telex Corp. v. IBM, 510 F.2d 894, 928 (10th Cir.), *cert. dismissed*, 423 U.S. 802 (1975). The essence of trade secret protection stems from a motive to protect express or implied agreements to keep business information confidential. Unlike patents, trade secret law provides no rights against a person who independently develops or properly obtains the confidential information. Kewanee Oil Co. v. Bicron Corp., 416 U.S. 470, 490 (1974); Dr. Miles Medical Co. v. John D. Park & Sons, 220 U.S. 373, 400-02 (1911).

Oil Co. v. Bicron Corp.,[365] the Supreme Court held that trade secret protection is not preempted by federal patent law. Unlike patent license restrictions, however, restrictions in trade secret licenses cannot be justified on the ground that they serve the purposes of the patent statute or policy. In *CVD, Inc. v. Raytheon Co.*,[366] the First Circuit held that the bad faith assertion of trade secret claims, i.e., with the knowledge that no trade secrets exist, may violate both Sections 1 and 2 of the Sherman Act.[367]

Licenses to use trade secrets are lawful, as are restrictions that are reasonable and ancillary to such licenses. As the Ninth Circuit stated, "The critical question in an antitrust context is whether the restriction may fairly be said to be ancillary to a commercially supportable licensing arrangement, or whether the licensing scheme is a sham set up for the purpose of controlling competition while avoiding the consequences of the antitrust laws."[368] Field-of-use restrictions in a know-how license have been upheld.[369] Territorial restrictions in know-how licenses have been upheld where they were not an integral part of a general scheme to suppress competition.[370] In other cases, territorial restraints, when used as a part of a larger conspiracy to divide markets, have been held unlawful.[371] Trade secrets used to effectuate a package licensing scheme may raise antitrust concerns. Arrangements in which the licensing of trade secrets has been conditioned upon the licensing of patents and other trade secrets have been unlawful.[372] In *In re Data*

---

365.   416 U.S. 470, 491-92 (1974). In Aronson v. Quick Point Pencil Co., 440 U.S. 257, 265-66 (1979), the Supreme Court held that the patent laws do not preempt state enforcement of a contract for payment for know-how, even though the know-how was no longer secret at the time of suit. In Bonito Boats, Inc. v. Thunder Craft Boats, Inc., 489 U.S. 141, 157 (1989), the Supreme Court held that a state law (a Florida law that prohibited the use of a direct molding process to duplicate unpatented boat hulls) was preempted under the supremacy clause of the Constitution and thus reaffirmed the holdings in Sears, Roebuck & Co. v. Stiffel Co., 376 U.S. 225 (1964) and Compco Corp. v. Day-Brite Lighting, Inc., 376 U.S. 234 (1964).

366.   769 F.2d 842 (1st Cir. 1985) (upholding jury verdict for plaintiff), *cert. denied*, 475 U.S. 1016 (1986).

367.   *Id.* at 851 (plaintiff required to "prove, in addition to the other elements of an antitrust violation, by clear and convincing evidence, that the defendant asserted trade secrets with the knowledge that no trade secrets existed" where litigation "would have proved ruinous" to a new corporation and would have "effectively foreclosed competition," the court held that "the threat of unfounded trade secrets litigation in bad faith is sufficient to constitute a cause of action under the antitrust laws"). *But cf.* Boeing Co. v. Sierracin Corp., 108 Wash. 2d 38, 738 P.2d 665 (1987) (good faith, confidentiality clauses are lawful).

368.   A. & E. Plastik Pak Co. v. Monsanto Co., 396 F.2d 710, 715 (9th Cir. 1968); *see also* INTERNATIONAL GUIDELINES, *supra* note 20, at Cases 10, 11, 12 (enforcement policy of the Antitrust Division with respect to restrictions in know-how licenses between domestic companies and foreign companies).

369.   A. & E. Plastik Pak Co. v. Monsanto Co., 396 F.2d 710, 715 (9th Cir. 1968).

370.   Thoms v. Sutherland, 52 F.2d 592, 594-96 (3d Cir. 1931); Foundry Servs. v. Beneflux Corp., 110 F. Supp. 857, 860-62 (S.D.N.Y.), *rev'd on other grounds*, 206 F.2d 214 (2d Cir. 1953); *see also* United States v. E.I. du Pont de Nemours & Co., 118 F. Supp. 41, 219 (D. Del. 1953), *aff'd*, 351 U.S. 377 (1956); Shin Nippon Koki Co. v. Irvin Indus., 186 U.S.P.Q. (BNA) 296, 298 (N.Y. Sup. Ct. 1975).

371.   United States v. Imperial Chem. Indus., 100 F. Supp. 504, 519-31 (S.D.N.Y. 1951); United States v. Timken Roller Bearing Co., 83 F. Supp. 284, 315-16 (N.D. Ohio 1949), *modified and aff'd*, 341 U.S. 593 (1951) (the Supreme Court did not discuss the know-how issue).

372.   *See* Technograph Printed Circuits, Ltd. v. Bendix Aviation Corp., 218 F. Supp. 1, 50 (D. Md. 1963), *aff'd per curiam*, 327 F.2d 497 (4th Cir.), *cert. denied*, 379 U.S. 826 (1964).

General Corp. Antitrust Litigation,[373] a district court held that a trade secret does not necessarily convey the economic power required to establish unlawful tying.

D. Procedural Aspects of the Antitrust-Intellectual Property Interface

1. *Jurisdiction*

The United States Court of Appeals for the Federal Circuit has exclusive appellate jurisdiction over any complaint involving an antitrust claim and a claim arising under the patent laws.[374] In such a case, the court will apply the law of the originating circuit to the antitrust claim.[375] The First Circuit has held that where a nonfrivolous patent infringement counterclaim is filed in an antitrust action, exclusive jurisdiction rests in the Federal Circuit, notwithstanding the traditional rule that the plaintiff's complaint establishes the basis for district court jurisdiction.[376] Where the antitrust and patent claims are severed in the district court under Rule 42 of the Federal Rules of Civil Procedure, appellate jurisdiction over the antitrust claim normally will remain in the Federal Circuit.[377]

In *Christianson v. Colt Industries Operating Corp.*,[378] the Supreme Court ruled that 28 U.S.C. § 1295(a)(1) jurisdiction is evaluated by determining whether a claim arises under the patent law under 28 U.S.C. § 1338(a) in accordance with the well-pleaded complaint rule, which is based upon " 'from what necessarily appears in the plaintiff's statement of his own claim in the bill or declaration, unaided by anything alleged in anticipation or avoidance of defenses which it is thought that the defendant may interpose.' "[379] A suggestion that expired patents owned by Colt were invalid did not make the case as one "arising under" the patent law.[380] The case is interesting in that the Seventh Circuit insisted that the Federal Circuit had appellate jurisdiction and the Federal Circuit insisted that the Seventh Circuit had

---

373.   529 F. Supp. 801 (N.D. Cal. 1981), *aff'd in part and rev'd in part sub nom.* Digidyne Corp. v. Data Gen. Corp., 734 F.2d 1336 (9th Cir. 1984), *cert. denied*, 473 U.S. 908 (1985).

374.   28 U.S.C. § 1295(a) (1988); Atari, Inc. v. JS&A Group, 747 F.2d 1422 (Fed. Cir. 1984) (and cases cited therein); *see also* Handgards, Inc. v. Ethicon, Inc., 743 F.2d 1282, 1285-88 (9th Cir. 1984) (exploring but not resolving reach of this "perplexing statute"), *cert. denied*, 469 U.S. 1190 (1985).

375.   Argus Chem. Corp. v. Fibre Glass-Evercoat Co., 812 F.2d 1381 (Fed. Cir. 1987); Loctite Corp. v. Ultraseal Ltd., 781 F.2d 861, 875 (Fed. Cir. 1985); Bandag, Inc. v. Al Bolser's Tire Stores, 750 F.2d 903, 909 (Fed. Cir. 1984) ("mandate to unify intercircuit conflicts" limited to where exclusive subject matter jurisdiction); American Hoist & Derrick Co. v. Sowa & Sons, 725 F.2d 1350, 1366-67 (Fed. Cir.), *cert. denied*, 469 U.S. 821 (1984).

376.   Xeta, Inc. v. Atex, Inc., 825 F.2d 604 (1st Cir. 1987) (relying on *In re* Innotron Diagnostics, 800 F.2d 1077 (Fed. Cir. 1986) and Schwarzkopf Dev. Corp. v. Ti-Coating, Inc., 800 F.2d 240 (Fed. Cir. 1986)). The holding of the First Circuit here is consistent with the October 5, 1989 Order of the Federal Circuit in Aerojet-General Corp. v. Machine Tool Works, Oerlikon-Buehrle Ltd., No. 88-1351 that there was subject matter jurisdiction over a case where the plaintiff sued for trade secret violation and the defendant filed a patent infringement counterclaim.

377.   *See* Korody-Colyer Corp. v. General Motors Corp., 828 F.2d 1572 (Fed. Cir. 1987).

378.   486 U.S. 800 (1988).

379.   *Id.* at 809 (quoting Franchise Tax Bd. v. Construction Laborers Vacation Trust, 463 U.S. 1, 10 (1983) (quoting Taylor v. Anderson, 234 U.S. 74, 75-76 (1914))).

380.   486 U.S. at 806, 812-13.

jurisdiction. The Supreme Court agreed with the Federal Circuit.[381]

2. Procedure

When a suit involves both antitrust and patent claims, the case is frequently bifurcated for separate discovery or trial. A court is normally more willing to grant a motion for bifurcation if potentially dispositive issues are present. Antitrust issues are often postponed until patent rights are determined.[382] In some recent cases wherein a charge is made of inequitable conduct in the procurement of the patent, this matter is the first one tried.[383]

3. Remedies

In antitrust actions brought by the Attorney General of the United States alleging unlawful provisions in patent and copyright licenses, courts often have enjoined the defendant from further enforcement of the offending provisions or entering into similar agreements.[384] Compulsory licensing is an important additional remedy in such cases. In *United States v. Glaxo Group*,[385] the Supreme Court stated that "[m]andatory selling on specified terms and compulsory patent licensing at reasonable charges are recognized antitrust remedies." While noting that " '[t]he framing of decrees should take place in the District rather than Appellate Courts,'" the Court recognized " 'an obligation to intervene in this most significant phase of the case' when necessary to assure that the relief will be effective."[386]

A number of consent decrees call for royalty-free licensing.[387] A few courts have

---

381.   *Id.* at 818-19.

382.   *In re* Innotron Diagnostics, 800 F.2d 1077 (Fed. Cir. 1986).

383.   Gardco Mfg., Inc. v. Herst Lighting Co., 820 F.2d 1209 (Fed. Cir. 1987) (inequitable conduct hearing by court in advance of scheduled jury trial); Hemstreet v. Burroughs Corp., 666 F. Supp. 1096 (N.D. Ill. 1987) (summary judgment of unequitable conduct), *rev'd on other grounds in part and dimisssed in part mem.*, 861 F.2d 728 (Fed. Cir. 1988) (disputed factual issues).

384.   United States v. Glaxo Group, 410 U.S. 52, 64 (1973); United States v. United States Gypsum Co., 340 U.S. 76 (1950); United States v. Paramount Pictures, 334 U.S. 131 (1948); Hartford-Empire Co. v. United States, 323 U.S. 386, *clarified*, 324 U.S. 570 (1945); Ethyl Gasoline Corp. v. United States, 309 U.S. 436 (1940).

385.   410 U.S. 52, 64 (1973); *cf.* United States v. Imperial Chem. Indus., 105 F. Supp. 215 (S.D.N.Y. 1952) (du Pont and ICI ordered to grant reasonable royalty licenses with immunity under corresponding foreign patents). For a construction of the immunity provision, see United States v. Imperial Chem. Indus., 1956 Trade Cas. (CCH) ¶ 68,435 (S.D.N.Y. 1956). The Seventh Circuit has upheld a lower court's refusal to prohibit a defendant from further use of a trademark used to violate the antitrust laws. Switzer Bros. v. Locklin, 297 F.2d 39, 48 (7th Cir. 1961), *cert. denied*, 369 U.S. 851 (1962).

386.   410 U.S. at 64 (quoting International Salt Co. v. United States, 332 U.S. 392, 400-01 (1947) and United States v. United States Gypsum Co., 340 U.S. 76, 89 (1950)).

387.   United States v. General Motors, 1965 Trade Cas. (CCH) ¶ 71,624 (E.D. Mich. 1965) (royalty-free licenses on existing patents; reasonable royalties on patents obtained within five years); United States v. Pitney-Bowes, Inc., 1959 Trade Cas. (CCH) ¶ 69,235 (D. Conn. 1959); United States v. RCA, 1958 Trade Cas. (CCH) ¶ 69,164 (S.D.N.Y. 1958) (royalty-free licenses on existing patents, reasonable royalties on future patents); United States v. IBM, 1956 Trade Cas. (CCH) ¶ 68,245 (S.D.N.Y. 1956) (partly royalty free, partly at reasonable royalties, depending on product); United States v. Western Elec. Co., 1956 Trade Cas. (CCH) ¶ 68,246 (D.N.J. 1956) (partly royalty-free, partly at reasonable royalties, depending on identity of patentee); United States v. American Steel Foundries, 1955 Trade Cas. (CCH) ¶ 68,156 (N.D. Ohio 1955) (royalty-free licenses on existing

ordered royalty-free licensing or the dedication of existing patents to the public.[388] Other lower courts have chosen not to order royalty-free licensing or dedication.[389]

The Supreme Court has never ruled on whether dedication or compulsory royalty-free licensing is a proper remedy. In *Hartford-Empire Co. v. United States*,[390] the Court expressly declined to order dedication on the ground that "a patent is property, protected against appropriation both by individuals and by government." Later, however, in *United States v. National Lead Co.*,[391] the Court declared the issue concerning dedication and royalty-free licensing to be undecided.

Compulsory disclosure of know-how has also been ordered.[392] In doing so, however, courts have recognized the importance of secrecy to the property right.[393] When certain "joint research and development ventures" are reported in advance to the Antitrust Division and the FTC, plaintiffs challenging conduct (such as licensing) within the scope of such notification may recover only actual damages, plus costs (including reasonable attorneys' fees) and interest from the date of injury.[394]

4. Counterclaims

Antitrust counterclaims are frequently filed in response to patent infringement actions. An antitrust counterclaim may or may not be compulsory.[395] In *Xerox Corp. v. SCM Corp.*,[396] the Third Circuit held that a patent infringement action was not a compulsory counterclaim to a "massive antitrust suit" challenging "virtually every aspect of its business conduct." Antitrust counterclaims have been held to be compulsory where the complaint alleged copyright infringement and unfair trade

---

patents).

388. United States v. Greyhound Corp., 1957 Trade Cas. (CCH) ¶ 68,756, at 73,089 (N.D. Ill. 1957) (dedication of existing patents); United States v. General Elec. Co., 115 F. Supp. 835, 843-44 (D.N.J. 1953) (dedication of existing patents); United States v. American Can Co., 1950-51 Trade Cas. (CCH) ¶ 62,679, at 63,972-73 (N.D. Cal. 1950) (royalty-free license).

389. United States v. General Instrument Corp., 1953 Trade Cas. (CCH) ¶ 67,574 (D.N.J. 1953) (the government sought the dedication of defendants' patents; the court concluded that such drastic relief was unnecessary); United States v. Imperial Chem. Indus., 105 F. Supp. 215, 225 (S.D.N.Y. 1952) ("We hold that in the circumstances before us, compulsory royalty free licensing may not be decreed in the absence of legislative authority and the sanction of explicit interpretation of existing statutes by higher courts affirmatively permitting such action."); United States v. Vehicular Parking, Ltd., 61 F. Supp. 656, 657 (D. Del. 1945) ("I am unable to agree with the government's reading of *Hartford-Empire* . . . , that the court has *power* to mandate a royalty-free license where the patent has been used as an instrument in violation of the anti-trust laws.") (emphasis in original).

390. 323 U.S. 386, 415, *clarified*, 324 U.S. 570 (1945).

391. 332 U.S. 319, 338 (1947).

392. United States v. United Shoe Mach. Corp., 110 F. Supp. 295 (D. Mass. 1953), *aff'd per curiam*, 347 U.S. 521 (1954); United States v. General Elec. Co., 115 F. Supp. 835, 853-55 (D.N.J. 1953); United States v. Minnesota Mining & Mfg. Co., 1950-51 Trade Cas. (CCH) ¶ 62,724, at 64,115-16 (D. Mass. 1950); United States v. American Can Co., 1950-51 Trade Cas. (CCH) ¶ 62,679, at 63,974 (N.D. Cal. 1950).

393. United States v. National Lead Co., 332 U.S. 319, 357-58 (1947); Imperial Chem. Indus. v. National Distillers & Chem. Corp., 342 F.2d 737 (2d Cir. 1965); United States v. Imperial Chem. Indus., 254 F. Supp. 685 (S.D.N.Y. 1966).

394. National Cooperative Research Act of 1984, 15 U.S.C. §§ 4301-05 (1988); *see supra* note 30.

395. FED. R. CIV. P. 13(a).

396. 576 F.2d 1057, 1061 (3d Cir. 1978); *see also* Mercoid Corp. v. Mid-Continent Inv. Co., 320 U.S. 661, 670-71 (1944) (antitrust counterclaim not compulsory in patent infringement action).

practices, and the defendants claimed that plaintiff's suit was "one of a series of harassing maneuvers designed to interfere with defendants' proper exploitation of rights."[397] Under Federal Rules of Civil Procedure 42(b), infringement issues may be tried separately from antitrust counterclaims and misuse issues.[398]

5. Settlement of Infringement Actions and Interference Proceedings

In general, courts favor settlement of infringement and interference proceedings.[399] When these agreements involve horizontal competitors, they are carefully scrutinized for anticompetitive purpose or effect. In *United States v. Singer Manufacturing Co.*,[400] the Supreme Court found that the dominant purpose of a settlement was not to settle priority, but to exclude a mutual competitor of the parties.[401]

397. United Artists Corp. v. Masterpiece Prods., 221 F.2d 213, 216 (2d Cir. 1955); *see also* Koufakis v. Carvel, 425 F.2d 892, 898 (2d Cir. 1970).

398. *See* Helene Curtis Indus. v. Church & Dwight Co., 560 F.2d 1325, 1334-37 (7th Cir. 1977), *cert. denied*, 434 U.S. 1070 (1978); Components, Inc. v. Western Elec. Co., 318 F. Supp. 959, 965-68 (D. Me. 1970); Western Geophysical Co. of Am. v. Bolt Assocs., 50 F.R.D. 193 (D. Conn. 1970), *appeal dismissed*, 440 F.2d 765 (2d Cir. 1971); Henan Oil Tools, Inc. v. Engineering Enters., 262 F. Supp. 629 (S.D. Tex. 1966); Fischer & Porter Co. v. Sheffield Corp., 31 F.R.D. 534, 539-40 (D. Del. 1962); Zenith Radio Corp. v. Radio Corp. of Am., 106 F. Supp. 561, 576-77 (D. Del. 1952); Container Co. v. Carpenter Container Corp., 9 F.R.D. 89 (D. Del. 1949).

399. Standard Oil Co. v. United States, 283 U.S. 163, 171 (1931); Duplan Corp. v. Deering Milliken, Inc., 540 F.2d 1215, 1220 (4th Cir. 1976). *But cf.* Duplan Corp. v. Deering Milliken, Inc., 444 F. Supp. 648 (D.S.C. 1977), *aff'd in part and rev'd in part*, 594 F.2d 979 (4th Cir. 1979), *cert. denied*, 444 U.S. 1015 (1980).

400. 374 U.S. 174 (1963); *see* Hartford-Empire Co. v. United States, 323 U.S. 386, *clarified*, 324 U.S. 570 (1945) (interference settlement held unlawful as part of a scheme to monopolize). *But cf.* American Cyanamid Co. v. FTC, 363 F.2d 757 (6th Cir. 1966) (insufficient evidence of collusive settlement), *on remand*, 72 F.T.C. 618 (1967), *later appeal sub nom.* Charles Pfizer & Co. v. FTC, 401 F.2d 574 (6th Cir. 1968), *cert. denied*, 394 U.S. 920 (1969); Hutzler Bros. v. Sales Affiliates, Inc., 164 F.2d 260 (4th Cir. 1947).

401. *See also* Speed Shore Core Corp. v. Denda, 197 U.S.P.Q. (BNA) 526 (C.D. Cal. 1977) (scrutiny of settlement agreement by the district court a factor in determining the absence of impropriety), *aff'd*, 605 F.2d 469 (9th Cir. 1979).

CHAPTER X

TRADE OR COMMERCE WITH FOREIGN NATIONS

A. Introduction

Application of United States antitrust laws to international trade or commerce raises a variety of special issues. First, such application often raises fundamental questions concerning national jurisdiction to prescribe and enforce rules of law. Second, antitrust is but one of a number of national policies affecting international trade, and these other national policies, which are not always in harmony with each other, may at times be in tension with antitrust policies.[1] Third, the competition policies of other countries are not always in accord with U.S. antitrust policies. This chapter discusses many of these special issues.[2] In addition, the competition laws of certain other nations have increasing significance. Accordingly, Part I of this chapter provides a brief overview of the competition law of the European Economic Community.

B. Subject Matter Jurisdiction and Related Issues

1. Sherman Act

a. JURISDICTION

The Sherman Act applies to "every contract, combination . . . or conspiracy, in restraint of trade," and to every person who shall "monopolize, or attempt to monopolize, or combine or conspire . . . to monopolize" trade or commerce "among the several States, or with foreign nations." Congress refined this language by

---

1. Apart from the Sherman, Clayton, Robinson-Patman, and Federal Trade Commission acts, other competition or trade policy statutes applicable to foreign commerce include: the Omnibus Trade and Competitiveness Act of 1988, 19 U.S.C. §§ 2901-2906 (1988); the Export Trading Company Act of 1982, 15 U.S.C. §§ 4001-4021 (1988); the Webb-Pomerene Act, 15 U.S.C. §§ 61-66 (1988); the Wilson Tariff Act, 15 U.S.C. §§ 8-11 (1988); the Panama Canal Act, 15 U.S.C. § 31 (1988); § 801 of the Revenue Act, 15 U.S.C. §§ 71-77 (1988); § 337 of the Tariff Act, 19 U.S.C. § 1337 (1988); the "countervailing duties" law, 19 U.S.C. §§ 1671-1671f (1988); the "antidumping" provisions of the Trade Agreements Act, 19 U.S.C. §§ 1673-1677g (1988); § 301 of the Trade Act, 19 U.S.C. §§ 2411-2416 (1988); the antitrust provisions of the Shipping Act, 46 U.S.C. §§ 801-842 (1988); and the Merchant Marine Act of 1920, 46 U.S.C. § 885 (1988).

2. The Department of Justice's enforcement policies in cases involving international antitrust issues were articulated in its ANTITRUST ENFORCEMENT GUIDELINES FOR INTERNATIONAL OPERATIONS (1988), *reprinted in* Appendix E to this treatise and 4 TRADE REG. REP. (CCH) ¶ 13,109.10 [hereinafter INTERNATIONAL GUIDELINES].

enacting the Foreign Trade Antitrust Improvements Act of 1982 (FTAIA), which amended both the Sherman Act and Section 5 of the FTC Act.[3] The FTAIA limited the subject matter jurisdiction of those statutes over U.S. export commerce to conduct having a "direct, substantial, and reasonably foreseeable" effect on domestic U.S. commerce or U.S. import trade, or on the export commerce of a person engaged in such commerce in the United States.

Prior to that amendment, Sherman Act jurisdiction over foreign trade or commerce had been interpreted in various ways by a number of courts. The issue first came before the Supreme Court in *American Banana Co. v. United Fruit Co.*,[4] where the Sherman Act was construed to be inapplicable to conduct involving defendant's inducement of a military seizure of property outside the United States. In rejecting the claim Justice Holmes wrote:

> [T]he acts causing the damage were done, so far as appears, outside the jurisdiction of the United States . . . . It is surprising to hear it argued that they were governed by the act of Congress . . . . [T]he general and almost universal rule is that the character of an act as lawful or unlawful must be determined wholly by the law of the country where the act is done.[5]

This narrow interpretation of Sherman Act jurisdiction was limited in subsequent cases[6] and then largely rejected in 1945 in *United States v. Aluminum Co. of America.*[7] In *Alcoa*, the Second Circuit[8] held that the Sherman Act reached agreements entered into and consummated outside the United States by foreign companies "[i]f they were intended to affect [U.S.] imports and did affect them."[9] Judge Learned Hand wrote that "it is settled law — as [the defendant] itself agrees — that any state may impose liabilities, even upon persons not within its allegiance, for conduct outside its borders that has consequences within its borders which the state reprehends; and these liabilities other states will ordinarily recognize."[10]

Notwithstanding the Second Circuit's view of the "settled law," *Alcoa's* assertion of antitrust jurisdiction over wholly foreign conduct on the basis of the economic effects of that conduct within the United States proved controversial among foreign

---

3. Pub. L. No. 97-290, 96 Stat. 1246 (1982), *codified at* 15 U.S.C. § 6a (1988).
4. 213 U.S. 347 (1909).
5. *Id.* at 355-56.
6. *See, e.g.*, United States v. Sisal Sales Corp., 274 U.S. 268 (1927) (fact that control of production was aided by discriminatory legislation of foreign country did not prevent punishment of forbidden results of the conspiracy within the United States); Thomsen v. Cayser, 243 U.S. 66 (1917) (combination formed abroad was put into operation in the United States and affected U.S. foreign commerce); United States v. Pacific & Arctic Ry. & Navigation Co., 228 U.S. 87 (1913) (agreement between U.S. and Canadian firms to monopolize transportation routes partly in Canada); United States v. American Tobacco Co., 221 U.S. 106 (1911) (contracts dividing world markets executed in England by U.S. and British companies doing business in United States).
7. 148 F.2d 416 (2d Cir. 1945) (*Alcoa*).
8. The case was certified by the Supreme Court to the Second Circuit for want of a quorum of qualified Supreme Court justices. *Id.* at 421.
9. *Id.* at 444.
10. *Id.* at 443 (citations omitted).

governments.[11] It was nevertheless adopted by most U.S. courts.[12] Variations developed, however, as to the magnitude and type of domestic effect necessary for jurisdiction under U.S. antitrust laws.[13] The Department of Justice adopted the enforcement position that the Sherman Act applied only to transactions that had a "substantial and foreseeable effect on U.S. commerce."[14] Congress ultimately adopted this position in the FTAIA.

The FTAIA eliminated U.S. antitrust jurisdiction over conduct "involving trade or commerce (other than import trade or import commerce) with foreign nations unless (1) such conduct has a direct, substantial and reasonably foreseeable effect (A) on [domestic or import commerce], or (B) on export trade or export commerce . . . of a person engaged in such trade or commerce in the United States." Where jurisdiction is based only on subclause (B), the antitrust laws apply to that conduct "only for injury to export business in the United States."[15] The courts interpret this language literally, holding that conduct lacking the requisite domestic effect is exempt from United States antitrust laws even where the allegedly unlawful conduct takes place in the United States.[16]

Although the standard articulated by Judge Hand in *Alcoa* refers to "intended effects," the FTAIA employs the phrase "reasonably foreseeable." The legislative history also suggests that the standard adopted by Congress is "an objective

---

11.   *See* RESTATEMENT (THIRD) OF THE FOREIGN RELATIONS LAW OF THE UNITED STATES § 403 reporter's note 1 (1987); ABA ANTITRUST SECTION, REPORT OF THE SPECIAL COMMITTEE ON INTERNATIONAL ANTITRUST 208-11 (1991).

12.   *See, e.g.* Fleischmann Distilling Corp. v. Distillers Co., 395 F. Supp. 221, 226 (S.D.N.Y. 1975) ("direct and material adverse effect on interstate or foreign commerce"); Todhunter-Mitchell & Co. v. Anheuser-Busch, Inc., 383 F. Supp. 586, 587 (E.D. Pa. 1974) ("flow of commerce . . . was directly restrained"); Sabre Shipping Corp. v. American President Lines, 285 F. Supp. 949, 953 (S.D.N.Y. 1968) ("directly and materially affect . . . foreign commerce"), *cert. denied sub nom.* Japan Line v. Sabre Shipping Corp., 407 F.2d 173 (2d Cir.), *cert. denied,* 395 U.S. 922 (1969); United States v. Watchmakers of Switz. Information Center, Inc., 1963 Trade Cas. (CCH) ¶ 70,600, at 77,456 (S.D.N.Y. 1962) ("direct and substantial restraint on interstate and foreign commerce of the United States"), *order modified,* 1965 Trade Cas. (CCH) ¶ 71,352 (S.D.N.Y. 1965); United States v. General Electric Co., 82 F. Supp. 753, 891 (D.N.J. 1949) ("direct and substantial effect upon trade").

13.   *Compare* National Bank of Can. v. Interbank Card Ass'n, 666 F.2d 6 (2d Cir. 1981) (jurisdiction existed only where the effect upon U.S. commerce was foreseeable and appreciable) *with* Timberlane Lumber Co. v. Bank of Am. Nat'l Trust & Sav. Ass'n, 749 F.2d 1378 (9th Cir. 1984) (holding that magnitude of effect on U.S. commerce was separate factor to be considered apart from whether conduct had any effect on U.S. commerce), *cert. denied,* 472 U.S. 1032 (1985). In enacting the FTAIA, Congress adopted an approach that closely followed that of the Second Circuit in *National Bank of Canada.* Various tests of antitrust subject matter jurisdiction that developed among the circuits are described in Zenith Radio Corp. v. Matsushita Elec. Indus. Co., 494 F. Supp. 1161, 1177-89 (E.D. Pa. 1980).

14.   *See* ANTITRUST DIV., U.S. DEP'T OF JUSTICE, ANTITRUST GUIDE FOR INTERNATIONAL OPERATIONS (1977), *reprinted in* 4 TRADE REG. REP. (CCH) ¶ 13,110, at 20,645 [hereinafter INTERNATIONAL ANTITRUST GUIDE].

15.   15 U.S.C. § 6a(1) (1988).

16.   *See* McGlinchy v. Shell Chem. Co., 845 F.2d 802 (9th Cir. 1988) (antitrust claim dismissed for lack of subject matter jurisdiction where plaintiff failed to allege requisite "effect" under the FTAIA); McElderry v. Cathay Pac. Airways, 678 F. Supp. 1071, 1077 (S.D.N.Y. 1988) (antitrust claims dismissed for failure to meet requirements of the FTAIA and for reasons of comity); Eurim-Pharm GmbH v. Pfizer Inc., 593 F. Supp. 1102, 1106 (S.D.N.Y. 1984) (district court lacked jurisdiction when plaintiff failed to establish anticompetitive effect under the FTAIA).

one . . . [designed] to avoid — at least at the jurisdictional stage — inquiries into the actual, subjective motives of defendants."[17] The legislative history formulates the test, therefore, as "whether the effects [of the alleged unlawful conduct] would have been evident to a reasonable person making practical business judgments, [and] not whether actual knowledge or intent can be shown."[18]

b.   STANDING

In actions involving U.S. export trade, the FTAIA further limits recovery only to "injury to export business in the United States." Therefore, to have standing to sue under U.S. antitrust law a foreign company must demonstrate not only the requisite effect on United States export trade but also that it is within the class of injured United States exporters.[19]

Under Section 4 of the Clayton Act and cases interpreting its provisions, only persons or corporations injured while trading in U.S. foreign or domestic commerce have standing to bring claims for antitrust violations involving foreign commerce.[20] In *de Atucha v. Commodity Exchange, Inc.*,[21] the district court held that plaintiffs who traded *exclusively* on a foreign market did not have standing under U.S. antitrust law. However, foreign markets having even slight direct ties to U.S. commerce have been held not exclusively foreign. A person trading in such markets will have U.S. antitrust standing.[22]

c.   COMITY CONSIDERATIONS

Prior to the enactment of the FTAIA, some court decisions had modified the *Alcoa* effects test by requiring an analysis of international comity and other considerations.[23] A leading decision was *Timberlane Lumber Co. v. Bank of*

---

17.   H.R. REP. No. 686, 97th Cong., 2d Sess. 9 (1982), *reprinted in* 1982 U.S. CODE CONG. & ADMIN. NEWS 2487, 2491 [hereinafter HOUSE REPORT 686]; *Eurim-Pharm GmbH*, 593 F. Supp. at 1106 n.4; *McElderry*, 678 F. Supp. at 1077.

18.   HOUSE REPORT 686, *supra* note 17, at 9.

19.   The 'In' Porters, SA v. Hanes Printables, Inc., 663 F. Supp. 494, 500 (M.D.N.C. 1987) ("a foreign company can not demonstrate the domestic injury requirement by 'piggy-backing' onto the injury of a United States exporter").

20.   *See* Transnor (Bermuda) Ltd. v. BP N. Am. Petroleum, 738 F. Supp. 1472, 1476 (S.D.N.Y. 1990); de Atucha v. Commodity Exch., Inc., 608 F. Supp. 510, 517-18 (S.D.N.Y. 1985); *see also* Chapter VI of this treatise for a detailed discussion of the requirement of standing under Section 4 of the Clayton Act.

21.   608 F. Supp. 510, 518 (S.D.N.Y. 1985) ("Congress did not contemplate recovery under the antitrust laws by an individual who traded, and was injured entirely outside of United States commerce.").

22.   *See Transnor (Bermuda) Ltd.*, 738 F. Supp. at 1476. In *Transnor*, the location of the trading market was the relevant consideration; the location of the production, delivery, and contract points were considered much less relevant where the trading market itself was considered a U.S. market.

23.   "Comity" has been defined as "neither a matter of absolute obligation on the one hand, nor of mere courtesy and good will upon the other. But it is the recognition which one nation allows within its territory to the legislative, executive, or judicial acts of another nation, having due regard both to international duty and convenience, and to the rights of its own citizens or of other persons who are under the protection of its laws." Hilton v. Guyot, 159 U.S. 113, 163-64 (1895). Comity considerations that arise from general considerations involving international relations should therefore be distinguished from the narrower act of state doctrine (discussed in Subpart H.2 of this chapter).

America National Trust & Savings Association.[24] In that case the Ninth Circuit stated that the "effects test by itself is incomplete because it fails to consider other nations' interests" and because it fails to take into account the relationship between the actors involved and the United States.[25] The court therefore set forth three requirements for Sherman Act subject matter jurisdiction, explicitly including principles of international comity: first, "that there be *some* effect – actual or intended – on American foreign commerce before the federal courts may legitimately exercise subject matter jurisdiction"; second, that the restraint be "of such a type and magnitude so as to be cognizable as a violation of the Sherman Act"; and third, that "[a]s a matter of international comity and fairness, . . . extraterritorial jurisdiction of the United States [should] be asserted to cover [the restraint]."[26]

The factors to be weighed in making this third determination, according to *Timberlane*, include:

(1) the degree of conflict with foreign law or policy;

(2) the nationality or allegiance of the parties and the locations or principal places of business of corporations;

(3) the extent to which enforcement by either state can be expected to achieve compliance;

(4) the relative significance of effects on the United States as compared with those elsewhere;

(5) the extent to which there is explicit purpose to harm or affect American commerce;

(6) the foreseeability of such effect; and

(7) the relative importance to the violations charged of conduct within the United States as compared with conduct abroad.[27]

While some courts adopted the *Timberlane* approach,[28] others weigh *Timberlane*-type comity factors as a discretionary analysis in addition to, but distinct from, issues of subject matter jurisdiction.[29] In *Mannington Mills, Inc. v. Congoleum Corp.,*[30]

---

24. 549 F.2d 597 (9th Cir. 1976) (*Timberlane I*).

25. *Id.* at 611-12.

26. *Id.* at 613-15 (emphasis in original).

27. *Id.* at 614. On remand in *Timberlane*, the district court granted defendants' motion to dismiss for lack of subject matter jurisdiction, based on a modified version of the Ninth Circuit's comity analysis. 574 F. Supp. 1453, 1469-71 (N.D. Cal. 1983). The Ninth Circuit affirmed, but disapproved the district court's departure from the appellate court's first *Timberlane* opinion, stating that "[b]ecause this categorization does not sufficiently clarify the application of the seven factor analysis, we believe that district courts should continue to use the factors listed in *Timberlane I*." 749 F.2d 1378, 1383 n.3 (9th Cir. 1984), *cert. denied*, 472 U.S. 1032 (1985) (*Timberlane II*). Although Congress had enacted the FTAIA prior to the district court's opinion in *Timberlane II*, neither that court nor the Ninth Circuit discussed the effect, if any, of that statute or the continued applicability of the *Timberlane* analysis to cases governed by FTAIA.

28. *E.g.,* Montreal Trading Ltd. v. Amax, Inc., 661 F.2d 864 (10th Cir. 1981), *cert. denied*, 455 U.S. 1001 (1982); Dominicus Americana Bohio v. Gulf & Western Indus., 473 F. Supp. 680 (S.D.N.Y. 1979).

29. The distinction between conduct that does not confer subject matter jurisdiction under the Sherman Act and conduct that does not give rise to a cognizable claim is important because there are significant procedural differences between a dismissal for lack of subject matter jurisdiction and a dismissal for failure to state a claim. *See Timberlane I,* 549 F.2d at 601-02; *see also* Industrial Inv. Dev. Corp. v. Mitsui & Co., 671 F.2d 876, 884 n.7 (5th Cir. 1982) (defendants failed to show that *Timberlane* factors required summary judgment), *vacated on other grounds and*

the Third Circuit applied the *Alcoa* "intended effects" test, but ordered the district court on remand to engage in what it termed the *Timberlane* "balancing process" to determine "whether jurisdiction should be exercised."[31] In addition to the factors enumerated in *Timberlane*, the Third Circuit held that the jurisdictional analysis should consider any treaties governing the conduct at issue, the degree of harm to United States foreign policy that might result from asserting jurisdiction, the problems that might be created by any relief granted, and the availability of remedies abroad.[32] Similarly, the Seventh Circuit in *In re Uranium Antitrust Litigation*[33] ruled that subject matter jurisdiction should be determined under the *Alcoa* "intended effects" test, and, if that test is satisfied, a court "should consider additional factors to determine whether the exercise of that jurisdiction is appropriate," with the *Mannington Mills* factors providing an "adequate framework for such a determination."[34]

In *Industrial Investment Development Corp. v. Mitsui & Co.*,[35] however, the Fifth Circuit took issue with the suggestion by the Seventh Circuit in *In re Uranium Antitrust Litigation* that the decision whether to exercise jurisdiction is discretionary, holding that, as a matter of law (but *not* as an issue of subject matter jurisdiction), a court "should not apply the antitrust laws to foreign conduct or foreign actors if such application would violate principles of comity, conflicts of law, or international law."[36] Other courts had taken a variety of different approaches to jurisdiction prior to enactment of the FTAIA.[37]

---

remanded, 460 U.S. 1007, reaff'd, 704 F.2d 785 (5th Cir.), cert. denied, 464 U.S. 961 (1983); Zenith Radio Corp. v. Matsushita Elec. Indus. Co., 494 F. Supp. 1161, 1171-77 (E.D. Pa. 1980).

30. 595 F.2d 1287 (3d Cir. 1979).

31. *Id.* at 1294 (citations omitted); *cf. id.* at 1301-02 n.9 (Adams, J., concurring) (such discretionary abstention is narrowly limited).

32. *Id.* at 1297-98.

33. 617 F.2d 1248 (7th Cir. 1980).

34. *Id.* at 1255. The court affirmed a district court's exercise of jurisdiction over defaulting foreign defendants based on the complexity of the litigation, the seriousness of the antitrust charges, and, especially, the recalcitrance of the nonappearing parties. *See also* Pillar Corp. v. Enercon Indus. Corp., 694 F. Supp. 1353, 1361 (E.D. Wis. 1988) (denying defendant's motion to dismiss for lack of subject matter jurisdiction for failure to present evidence pertinent to the factors adopted in *In re Uranium Antitrust Litigation*).

35. 671 F.2d 876 (5th Cir. 1982), *vacated on other grounds and remanded*, 460 U.S. 1007, *reaff'd*, 704 F.2d 785 (5th Cir.), *cert. denied*, 464 U.S. 961 (1983).

36. *Id.* at 884.

37. The Second Circuit expressly rejected the *Timberlane* jurisdictional test in National Bank of Canada v. Interbank Card Association, 666 F.2d 6, 8-9 (2d Cir. 1981), finding that more than "some" effect upon U.S. commerce should be necessary to warrant jurisdiction under the U.S. antitrust laws. The court found that it did not have subject matter jurisdiction because the appellants had failed to demonstrate that the allegedly unlawful conduct could be foreseen as having any "appreciable" anticompetitive effect upon U.S. foreign or interstate commerce. While the Second Circuit had applied comity factors apart from its jurisdictional analysis in deciding whether to dismiss an antitrust action against a foreign corporation in Joseph Muller Corp. Zurich v. Societe Anonyme de Gerance et D'Armement, 451 F.2d 727 (2d Cir. 1971), *cert. denied*, 406 U.S. 906 (1972), it did not expressly sanction the comity factors set forth in *Timberlane* when it decided *National Bank of Canada*. *See also* Bulk Oil (ZUG) AG v. Sun Co., 583 F. Supp. 1134 (S.D.N.Y. 1983), *aff'd without pub. op.*, 742 F.2d 1431 (2d Cir.), *cert. denied*, 469 U.S. 835 (1984); Power East Ltd. v. Transamerica Delaval Inc., 558 F. Supp. 47 (S.D.N.Y.), *aff'd without pub. op.*, 742 F.2d 1439 (2d Cir. 1983).

In dictum, the D.C. Circuit in Laker Airways v. Sabena, Belgian World Airlines, 731 F.2d 909,

In enacting the FTAIA, Congress indicated neutrality on the role of comity. The *House Report* accompanying the legislation that became the FTAIA stated that "the bill is intended neither to prevent nor to encourage additional judicial recognition of the special international characteristics of transactions."[38] Citing *Timberlane*, the *Report* noted:

> If a court determines that the requirements for subject matter jurisdiction are met, this bill would have no effect on the courts' ability to employ notions of comity . . . or otherwise to take account of the international character of the transaction.[39]

Thus, the FTAIA may not prevent courts from employing notions of comity to decline jurisdiction even where the requirements of the FTAIA have been satisfied.[40] A recent Supreme Court decision casts some doubt upon the propriety of discretionary abstention from the exercise of U.S. antitrust jurisdiction, however.[41]

The *Restatement (Third) of the Foreign Relations Law of the United States*,[42] which

---

938 & nn.106-09 (D.C. Cir. 1984), indicated that facts relating to comity are appropriately considered both with respect to whether Congress intended to regulate the conduct in question and with respect to whether prescriptive jurisdiction exists. *Id.* at 948 & n.145. It held, however, that judicial interest balancing was inappropriate to resolve cases in which two nations properly have jurisdiction but their assertions of jurisdiction are contradictory and mutually inconsistent. *Id.* at 945-55.

38. HOUSE REPORT 686, *supra* note 17, at 13.

39. *Id.*

40. *See In re* Insurance Antitrust Litig., 938 F.2d 919 (9th Cir. 1991) (where the conduct meets the requirements of the FTAIA, comity will require abstention only in unusual cases; however since the FTAIA did not completely eliminate comity considerations, *Timberlane* analysis was applied to determine whether jurisdiction should be exercised); Transnor (Bermuda) Ltd. v. BP N. Am. Petroleum, 738 F. Supp. 1472, 1477-78 (S.D.N.Y. 1990) (defendant's motion for summary judgment failed when *Timberlane* analysis favored exercise of jurisdiction); McElderry v. Cathay Pac. Airways, 678 F. Supp. 1071, 1078-80 (S.D.N.Y. 1988) (jurisdiction declined on basis of international comity in spite of finding of sufficient anticompetitive effect on U.S. commerce).

41. In W.S. Kirkpatrick & Co. v. Environmental Tectonics Corp., 493 U.S. 400, 408-09 (1990), the Court rejected the proposition that the policies of "international comity, respect for the sovereignty of foreign nations on their own territory, and the avoidance of embarrassment to the Executive Branch in its conduct of foreign relations" should serve as a basis for interpreting the act of state doctrine to decline U.S. antitrust jurisdiction over anticompetitive conduct directed at the award of a contract by a foreign government. In so doing, the Court stated, "Courts in the United States have the power, and ordinarily the obligation, to decide cases and controversies properly presented to them." *Id.* at 409.

For a discussion of the *Kirkpatrick* decision and the act of state doctrine, see Subpart H.2 of this chapter.

42. The RESTATEMENT (THIRD) OF THE FOREIGN RELATIONS LAW OF THE UNITED STATES § 403 (1987) provides as follows:

Limitations on Jurisdiction to Prescribe

(1) Even when one of the bases for jurisdiction under § 402 is present, a state may not exercise jurisdiction to prescribe law with respect to a person or activity having connections with another state when the exercise of such jurisdiction is unreasonable.

(2) Whether exercise of jurisdiction over a person or activity is unreasonable is determined by evaluating all relevant factors, including, where appropriate:

(a) the link of the activity to the territory of the regulating state, *i.e.,* the extent to which the activity takes place within the territory, or has

followed the enactment of the FTAIA, would preclude "unreasonable" exercises of jurisdiction. Although the *Restatement* does not directly invoke "comity," the factors enumerated as relevant to an evaluation of unreasonableness are akin to those identified in *Timberlane*. A similar list of factors is considered by the Department of Justice in determining whether to assert jurisdiction in a case involving international commerce.[43]

In the *International Guidelines*, the Department of Justice has asserted the position that in suits to which the United States is a party, courts are precluded from ordering dismissal on the basis of comity because "[a] decision by the Department to prosecute an antitrust action amounts to a determination by the Executive Branch that the interests of the United States supersede the interests of any foreign sovereign and that the challenged conduct is more harmful to the United States than any injury to foreign relations that might result from the antitrust action."[44] In at

---

substantial, direct, and foreseeable effect upon or in the territory;

  (b) the connections, such as nationality, residence or economic activity, between the regulating state and the person principally responsible for the activity to be regulated, or between that state and those whom the regulation is designed to protect;

  (c) the character of the activity to be regulated, the importance of regulation to the regulating state, the extent to which other states regulate such activities, and the degree to which the desirability of such regulation is generally accepted;

  (d) the existence of justified expectations that might be protected or hurt by the regulation;

  (e) the importance of the regulation to the international political, legal, or economic system;

  (f) the extent to which the regulation is consistent with the traditions of the international system;

  (g) the extent to which another state may have an interest in regulating the activity; and

  (h) the likelihood of conflict with regulation by another state.

  (3) When it would not be unreasonable for each of two states to exercise jurisdiction over a person or activity, but the prescriptions by the two states are in conflict, each state has an obligation to evaluate its own as well as the other state's interest in exercising jurisdiction, in light of all the relevant factors, Subsection (2); a state should defer to the other state if that state's interest is clearly greater.

43.   The Department considers whether "significant interests of any foreign sovereign would be affected," and, more specifically:

  (1) the relative significance, to the violation alleged, of conduct within the United States as compared to conduct abroad;

  (2) the nationality of the persons involved in or affected by the conduct;

  (3) the presence or absence of a purpose to affect United Stated consumers or competitors;

  (4) the relative significance and forseeability of the effects of the conduct on the United States as compared to the effects abroad;

  (5) the existence of reasonable expectations that would be furthered or defeated by the action; and

  (6) the degree of conflict with foreign law or articulated foreign economic policies.

INTERNATIONAL GUIDELINES, *supra* note 2, at § 5 & n.170.

44.   INTERNATIONAL GUIDELINES, *supra* note 2, at § 5, at n.167; *cf.* Brief for the United States as Amicus Curiae Supporting Petitioners at 23-24, Matsushita Elec. Indus. Co. v. Zenith Radio Corp., 475 U.S. 574 (1986) (sovereign compulsion doctrine should not apply in suits brought by the

least one case, a district court has deferred to the State Department's consideration of a foreign government's objections,[45] and a number of other cases contain language that supports such deferrence.[46]

Even if a United States court has jurisdiction, a foreign court may also lawfully exercise jurisdiction.[47] A country may even exercise its jurisdiction when compliance with a court order may subject a person to liability in another country.[48] When a court exercises jurisdiction over a matter that is also pending in part before a foreign court, however, it may, in its discretion, stay its proceedings pending the outcome of the foreign litigation.[49]

d. PRUDENTIAL AND OTHER CONSIDERATIONS

The Department of Justice *International Guidelines*, while acknowledging that a U.S. court has jurisdiction under the FTAIA to reach conduct that has a direct, substantial, and reasonably foreseeable effect on export commerce, originally adopted an additional substantive and/or prudential limitation with respect to such cases. Under this limitation, "the Department is concerned only with adverse effects on competition that would harm U.S. consumers by reducing output or raising prices."[50] More recently, however, the Department has rescinded that policy.[51]

    United States); *In re* Grand Jury Proceedings the Bank of Nova Scotia, 740 F.2d 817, 832 n.23 (11th Cir. 1984) (act of state doctrine does not apply where executive branch announces that it does not oppose judicial inquiry), *cert. denied*, 469 U.S. 1106 (1985).

45. United States v. Baker Hughes Inc., 731 F. Supp. 3, 6 n.5 (D.D.C.) ("It is not the Court's role to second-guess the executive branch's judgment as to the proper role of comity concerns."), *aff'd*, 908 F.2d 981 (D.C. Cir. 1990).

46. In *Timberlane I*, for example, the Ninth Circuit specifically distinguished government cases, noting that in private suits "there is no opportunity for the executive branch to weigh the foreign relations impact, nor any statement implicit in the filing of the suit that that consideration has been outweighed." 549 F.2d at 613; *cf.* Laker Airways v. Sabena, Belgian World Airlines, 731 F.2d 909, 944 (D.C. Cir. 1984) (absence of executive branch's intervention or expression of affirmative United States interest does not bar or impede private plaintiff's antitrust suit against foreign corporation); United States v. Vetco Inc., 691 F.2d 1281, 1289 n.9 (9th Cir.) (enforcement of IRS summons) (quoting *Timberlane I*, 549 F.2d at 613), *cert. denied*, 454 U.S. 1098 (1981); Arthur Andersen & Co. v. Finesilver, 546 F.2d 338, 342 (10th Cir. 1976) (defendant cannot speak for United States in asserting international comity as a basis for its failure to comply with discovery order where such order could cause the defendant to violate foreign law), *cert denied*, 429 U.S. 1096 (1977).

47. *See* RESTATEMENT (THIRD) OF THE FOREIGN RELATIONS LAW OF THE UNITED STATES § 403 comments d-e (1987) (stating that one state's exercise of jurisdiction to prescribe is not conclusive that it is unreasonable for another state to exercise its own jurisdiction, but where the states' regulations conflict, each state is required to evaluate both its interests in exercising jurisdiction and those of the other state and to defer if the other state's interests are clearly greater); Laker Airways v. Pan Am. World Airways, 559 F. Supp. 1124 (D.D.C. 1983), *aff'd sub nom.* Laker Airways v. Sabena, Belgian World Airlines, 731 F.2d 909, 921-26 (D.C. Cir. 1984).

48. RESTATEMENT (THIRD) OF THE FOREIGN RELATIONS LAW OF THE UNITED STATES § 441 (1987).

49. *See* Mul-T-Lock Corp. v. Mul-T-Lock, Ltd., 1984-1 Trade Cas. (CCH) ¶ 65,855 (E.D.N.Y. 1984).

50. INTERNATIONAL GUIDELINES, *supra* note 2, § 4.1, at n.159.

51. Department of Justice Policy Regarding Anticompetitive Conduct That Restricts U.S. Exports, released April 3, 1992. The 1992 policy statement declares that the Department will, in appropriate cases, take enforcement action against conduct occurring overseas that restrains U.S. exports, whether or not U.S. consumers are harmed, if (1) "the conduct has a direct, substantial, and reasonably foreseeable effect" on exports, (2) the conduct involves activities that violate the antitrust laws, and (3) U.S. courts have personal jurisdiction. The statement notes that it will

The *International Guidelines* also provide a specific interpretation of the reach of the FTAIA with respect to export sales where the U.S. Government is the purchaser. The *Guidelines* take the position that Congress did not intend to place such conduct beyond the reach of the U.S. antitrust laws because "[t]o do so would have been to place the burden of anticompetitive pricing squarely on the shoulders of U.S. taxpayers."[52] This position is generally in accord with case law decided prior to enactment of the FTAIA,[53] although the *Guidelines* statement is more specific including all transactions where the U.S. Government bears "more than half the cost of the transaction."[54] The *Guidelines* do not specifically address, however, whether the "substantial" effects element of the FTAIA jurisdictional test must be independently satisfied.

2. The Federal Trade Commission, Robinson-Patman, and Clayton Acts

The Federal Trade Commission Act prohibits unfair methods of competition and unfair or deceptive acts or practices "in or affecting commerce."[55] Commerce is defined to include "commerce . . . with foreign nations."[56] However, in 1982 the Act was amended to prohibit only unfair methods of competition involving domestic commerce and import commerce, and other foreign commerce where the "methods of competition have a direct, substantial, and reasonably foreseeable effect" on U.S. domestic or import commerce, or on the export commerce of a person so engaged in the United States.[57]

In *Branch v. FTC*,[58] the Act was held to apply to false advertising overseas. The Seventh Circuit reasoned that although the Act did not protect overseas consumers from Branch's false statements, it did protect his U.S. competitors from the effects of his unfair practices.[59]

Section 1 of the Clayton Act defines "commerce" to include "commerce . . . with foreign nations."[60] Since Section 7 of the Act was amended in 1980 to apply to acquisitions or mergers between persons engaged "in commerce" or whose activities "affect commerce,"[61] many acquisitions and mergers involving foreign companies

---

continue its policy of considering international comity where another government's legitimate interests are affected. It also notes that if the conduct is unlawful under the importing country's antitrust laws, the Department "is prepared to work with that country if that country is better situated to remedy the conduct and is prepared to take action."

52.   INTERNATIONAL GUIDELINES, *supra* note 2, at § 4.1.
53.   *See* United States v. Concentrated Phosphate Export Ass'n, 393 U.S. 199, 208 (1968) (burden fell overwhelmingly on U.S. taxpayer; foreign elements "insignificant").
54.   INTERNATIONAL GUIDELINES, *supra* note 2, at § 4.1.
55.   15 U.S.C. § 45 (1988).
56.   *Id.* § 44.
57.   *Id.* § 45(a)(3).
58.   141 F.2d 31 (7th Cir. 1944); *see also* FTC v. Compagnie de Saint-Gobain-Pont-a-Mousson, 636 F.2d 1300, 1322 (D.C. Cir. 1980) (dictum) (FTC has jurisdiction under § 5 to investigate and regulate any activities of a foreign corporation that affect U.S. commerce).
59.   Foreshadowing the more recent repercussions abroad over the extension of U.S. jurisdiction to matters involving foreign commerce, the *Branch* court was careful to claim that its exercise of jurisdiction was "no invasion of the sovereignty of any other country or any attempt to act beyond the territorial jurisdiction of the United States." 141 F.2d at 35.
60.   15 U.S.C. § 12 (1988).
61.   *Id.* § 18. *See* Antitrust Procedural Improvements Act of 1980, Pub. L. No. 96-349, 94 Stat. 1154.

may now be covered by Section 7.[62]

Section 3 of the Clayton Act and Section 2(a) of the Robinson-Patman Act, on the other hand, reach only transactions in which the commodities or goods involved are sold "for use, consumption or resale in the United States."[63] In *In re Japanese Electronic Products Antitrust Litigation*,[64] the Third Circuit ruled that both sales that form the basis of a price discrimination claim under Section 2(a) must meet this test.[65] In *Paceco, Inc. v. Ishikawajima-Harima Heavy Industries Co.*,[66] the district court suggested that the "use" requirement could be satisfied where the goods that were the subject of the challenged discrimination were imported into the United States after sale and then "used" by being incorporated into a product sold in the United States. One district court has held that the "resale" requirement is met when the goods are sold in the United States and then resold domestically before being sold abroad, i.e., where two or more sales precede the export transaction.[67] Unlike Section 2(a), Robinson-Patman Act Sections 2(c), (d), (e), and (f) contain no requirement that the goods involved be used or resold in the United States. Thus, some courts have found that the export exemption of Section 2(a) is not applicable to Section 2(c). In *Baysoy v. Jessup Steel Co.*,[68] the district court specifically held that Section 2(c) applies to the sale of goods or commodities for export. Similarly, the district court in *Canadian Ingersoll-Rand Co. v. D. Loveman & Sons*[69] held that

---

62.   Even prior to its amendment, when Section 7 applied only to mergers involving corporations "engaged in commerce," the Clayton Act was applied both to acquisitions by U.S. companies of foreign companies with U.S. subsidiaries (*e.g.*, United States v. Jos. Schlitz Brewing Co., 253 F. Supp. 129 (N.D. Cal.), *aff'd*, 385 U.S. 37 (1966)), and to acquisitions by foreign companies of U.S. companies. *E.g.*, British Oxygen Co., 86 F.T.C. 1241 (1975), *set aside on other grounds and remanded sub nom.* BOC Int'l, Ltd. v. FTC, 557 F.2d 24 (2d Cir. 1977). For example, in a challenge of an acquisition of a Japanese corporation by an American corporation pursuant to a joint venture agreement, the FTC held that the Japanese corporation, which existed solely for the purpose of manufacturing motors for sale to its parent corporations (which were clearly engaged in U.S. commerce and which imported most of those motors into the United States for resale), was engaged "in commerce" under the Clayton Act. Brunswick Corp., 94 F.T.C. 1174, 1264-65 (1979), *aff'd as modified sub nom.* Yamaha Motor Co. v. FTC, 657 F.2d 971 (8th Cir. 1981), *cert. denied*, 456 U.S. 915 (1982).

63.   15 U.S.C. § 13(a) (1988); Shulton, Inc. v. Optel Corp., 1987-1 Trade Cas. (CCH) ¶ 67,436 (D.N.J. 1986); C.E.D. Mobilephone Communs. v. Harris Corp., 1985-1 Trade Cas. (CCH) ¶ 66,386 (S.D.N.Y. 1985).

64.   723 F.2d 238, 316-17 (3d Cir. 1983), *rev'd on other grounds sub nom.* Matsushita Elec. Indus. Co. v. Zenith Radio Corp., 475 U.S. 574 (1986).

65.   723 F.2d at 316-17; General Chems., Inc. v. Exxon Chem. Co., U.S.A., 625 F.2d 1231 (5th Cir. 1980); *see also* O. Hommel Co. v. Ferro Corp., 472 F. Supp. 793, 794-95 (W.D. Pa. 1979), *rev'd on other grounds*, 659 F.2d 340 (3d Cir. 1981), *cert. denied*, 455 U.S. 1017 (1982); Fimex Corp. v. Barmatic Prods. Co., 429 F. Supp. 978, 980 (E.D.N.Y.) (U.S. firm purchasing for export has no cause of action), *aff'd*, 573 F.2d 1289 (2d Cir. 1977).

66.   468 F. Supp. 256 (N.D. Cal. 1979). Although *Paceco* was brought under § 2(f), which prohibits a buyer from inducing unlawful price discrimination, the court read into this section the jurisdictional requirements contained in § 2(a). It did so to conform with the Supreme Court's ruling that buyer liability under § 2(f) is dependent on seller liability under § 2(a). Great Atl. & Pac. Tea Co. v. FTC, 440 U.S. 69 (1979).

67.   Raul Int'l Corp. v. Sealed Power Corp., 586 F. Supp. 349, 352-55 (D.N.J. 1984), *aff'd without published opinion*, 822 F.2d 54 (3d Cir. 1987).

68.   90 F. Supp. 303 (W.D. Pa. 1950). *But cf. Paceco*, 468 F. Supp. at 259-60 n.7 (§ 2(f) incorporates the jurisdictional requirements of § 2(a)).

69.   227 F. Supp. 829 (N.D. Ohio 1964).

there is no exemption under Section 2(c).

C. Venue, Personal Jurisdiction, and Service of Process

Whether a U.S. court may compel a foreign individual or corporation to appear before it and answer allegations of antitrust violations is a function of three distinct, but interrelated, concepts: personal jurisdiction, venue, and service of process. Generally, these concepts have the same meanings in the antitrust context as they do in other areas of the law. However, the antitrust laws contain several special venue provisions, which provide the starting point for analysis in this area. Courts have interpreted these provisions so expansively that in antitrust cases the issues of venue and personal jurisdiction in the Constitutional sense have become "virtually congruent."[70] Moreover, in the international context, in which the doctrine of forum non conveniens, rather than change of venue under 28 U.S.C. § 1404 would normally be applied, some courts have held that the special nature of antitrust laws makes that doctrine inapplicable to suits under those laws.[71]

1. Venue

The special antitrust venue provisions are contained in Sections 4 and 12 of the

---

70. Pacific Tobacco Corp. v. American Tobacco Co., 338 F. Supp. 842, 844 (D. Or. 1972); *accord* Cascade Steel Rolling Mills, Inc. v. C. Itoh & Co. (Am.), 499 F. Supp. 829, 835 (D. Or. 1980); *see* Square D Co. v. Niagara Frontier Tariff Bureau, 1984-1 Trade Cas. (CCH) ¶ 65,825, at 67,455 (D.D.C. 1984) (determination of personal jurisdiction also determinative of venue); Smokey's v. American Honda Motor Co., 453 F. Supp. 1265, 1267 (E.D. Okla. 1978) ("the jurisdictional issue hinges upon the determination regarding venue, to wit, if venue is proper so is in personam jurisdiction"); Humid-Aire Corp. v. J. Levitt, Inc., 1978-1 Trade Cas. (CCH) ¶ 61,846 (N.D. Ill. 1977) (three-part test for evaluating minimum contacts for purposes of jurisdiction analysis also determines whether venue is proper in a particular district); Industria Siciliana Asfalti, Bitumi SpA v. Exxon Research & Eng'g Co., 1977-1 Trade Cas. (CCH) ¶ 61,256, at 70,786 (S.D.N.Y. 1977); Zenith Radio Corp. v. Matsushita Elec. Indus. Co., 402 F. Supp. 262, 328 (E.D. Pa. 1975); Flank Oil Co. v. Continental Oil Co., 277 F. Supp. 357, 359 (D. Colo. 1967); *cf.* Dunham's, Inc. v. National Buying Syndicate, 614 F. Supp. 616, 624 (E.D. Mich. 1985) (concept of transacting business more lenient than minimum contacts standard).

   The general venue statute, 28 U.S.C. § 1391(c) (1988), provides that "for purposes of venue under this chapter, a defendant that is a corporation shall be deemed to reside in any judicial district in which it is subject to personal jurisdiction at the time the action is commenced."

71. Industrial Inv. Dev. Corp. v. Mitsui & Co., 671 F.2d 876 (5th Cir. 1982), *vacated on other grounds and remanded,* 460 U.S. 1007, *reaff'd,* 704 F.2d 785 (5th Cir.), *cert. denied,* 464 U.S. 961 (1983); Laker Airways v. Pan Am. World Airways, 568 F. Supp. 811 (D.D.C. 1983); El Cid, Ltd. v. New Jersey Zinc Co., 444 F. Supp. 845, 846 n.1 (S.D.N.Y. 1977) (motion denied "as frivolous since the plaintiff could not institute a Sherman Act or a comparable suit in Bolivia"); Ferguson v. Ford Motor Co., 77 F. Supp. 425, 430-31 (S.D.N.Y. 1948).

   The leading Supreme Court case addressing forum non conveniens in international litigation is Piper Aircraft Co. v. Reyno, 454 U.S. 235 (1981). In that case the Supreme Court ruled that the possibility that an alternative forum might apply law less favorable to the plaintiff "should ordinarily not be given conclusive or even substantial weight." *Id.* at 247. However, the Court also cautioned that "if the remedy provided by the alternative forum is so clearly inadequate or unsatisfactory that it is no remedy at all, the unfavorable change in the law [that would result from dismissal] may be given substantial weight," and it noted that "dismissal would not be appropriate where the alternative forum does not permit litigation of the subject matter of the dispute." *Id.* at 254 & n.22 (citation omitted).

Clayton Act.[72]   Section 4, which applies to individuals as well as corporations, authorizes private damage actions in any district "in which the defendant resides or is found or has an agent."[73]   Section 12 provides that a suit against a corporation "may be brought not only in the judicial district whereof it is an inhabitant, but also in any district wherein it may be found or transacts business."[74]   In cases involving foreign individuals or corporations, the critical terms of these provisions are (1) "found," (2) "agent," and (3) "transacts business."

In order to be "found" within a district, a corporation must be doing business in such a manner, and to such an extent, that actual presence is established.[75]   This has been held to require "proof of continuous local activities" in the district and consideration of whether or not the forum is "unfairly inconvenient."[76]

A corporation (or individual) has an "agent" in a district under Section 4 if an employee or other representative conducts business there on its behalf.[77]

The most expansive and, consequently, the most important basis for venue over corporations is provided by the "transacts business" language of Section 12.   The leading case applying this language to a foreign corporation is *United States v. Scophony Corp.*[78]   In *Scophony*, a British corporation asserted, and the district court agreed, that it did not transact business in the Southern District of New York within the meaning of Section 12 because its business was "manufacturing, selling and licensing of television apparatus," and, although a 50% owned U.S. subsidiary was engaged in this activity, Scophony was engaged only in protecting its interest as an investor.[79]   The Supreme Court reversed.   Referring to its landmark decision

---

72.   15 U.S.C. §§ 15, 22 (1988). The general federal venue statute, 28 U.S.C. § 1391(b)-(d) (1991 Supp.), which, inter alia, allows an alien to be sued in any judicial district, is discussed later in this subsection.

73.   15 U.S.C. § 15.

74.   *Id.* § 22.

75.   Eastman Kodak Co. v. Southern Photo Materials Co., 273 U.S. 359, 371 (1927). An individual defendant is "found" in a district, within the meaning of § 4, if he is physically present there when served with process. *See* Freeman v. Bee Mach. Co., 319 U.S. 448, 453-54 (1943).

76.   United States v. Watchmakers of Switz. Information Center, Inc., 133 F. Supp. 40, 43-46 (S.D.N.Y. 1955) (two Swiss corporations were "found" in the Southern District of New York, within the meaning of § 12, in view of the continuous activities in the district of their jointly owned subsidiary, which was found to have no independent business of its own and to have acted exclusively as the agent of its Swiss parents); *see also In re* Chicken Antitrust Litig., 407 F. Supp. 1285, 1299 (N.D. Ga. 1975) (out-of-state partnership was not "found" in the Northern District of Georgia within the meaning of § 4 because sporadic sales and purchases within the district did not constitute "continuous local activities").

77.   *See* Fooshee v. Interstate Vending Co., 234 F. Supp. 44 (D. Kan. 1964); Goldlawr, Inc. v. Shubert, 169 F. Supp. 677 (E.D. Pa. 1958), *aff'd*, 276 F.2d. 614 (3d Cir. 1960). In cases involving corporate defendants, the presence of an agent in the district is most often discussed as evidence that the corporation is "transacting business" there within the meaning of § 12, rather than as a separate basis for venue under § 4. *See, e.g.*, Sunrise Toyota, Ltd. v. Toyota Motor Co., 55 F.R.D. 519, 524 (S.D.N.Y. 1972).

       At one time, some courts employed the "agent" language of § 4 to conclude that a resident coconspirator was the "agent" of nonresident coconspirators for purposes of establishing venue. *See* Giusti v. Pyrotechnic Indus., 156 F.2d 351 (9th Cir.), *cert. denied*, 329 U.S. 787 (1946); Ross-Bart Post Theatre v. Eagle Lion Films, 140 F. Supp. 401 (E.D. Va. 1954). This line of reasoning has since been repudiated. Piedmont Label Co. v. Sun Garden Packing Co., 598 F.2d 491 (9th Cir. 1979) (citing cases).

78.   333 U.S. 795 (1948).

79.   United States v. Scophony Corp., 69 F. Supp. 666 (S.D.N.Y. 1946), *rev'd*, 333 U.S. 795 (1949).

applying the "transacts business" test to domestic corporations,[80] the Supreme Court observed that it had "sloughed off the highly technical distinctions" that had previously governed venue determinations and instead "substituted the practical and broader business conception of engaging in any substantial business operations. . . . The practical, everyday business or commercial concept of doing or carrying on business of any substantial character became the test of venue."[81] Thus the Court applied the "transact business" test to foreign as well as domestic corporations. The Court said that the determination of whether a corporation "transacts business" should not "be made for such an enterprise by atomizing it into minute parts or events, in disregard of the actual unity and continuity of the whole course of conduct."[82] In *Scophony*, the test was satisfied because a series of investment and licensing agreements "called for continuing exercise of supervision over and intervention in" the subsidiary's affairs,[83] and in fact individuals acting at least in part as Scophony's agents actively pursued its interests — beyond mere investment interests — in New York.

Determining whether a corporation "transacts business" is a "qualitative process" requiring an analysis of the contacts of the corporation in the district in which venue is sought to be laid.[84] Among the factors courts consider in making this determination are: (1) whether the activities of a defendant in the district are continuous and substantial;[85] (2) whether any contracts have been negotiated or consummated by the defendant in the district;[86] (3) whether the relationship between the defendant and a domestic subsidiary (or some related entity located in the district) is such that the related entity is merely carrying on the defendant's business in the district as its alter ego;[87] (4) whether the relationship between the

---

80. Eastman Kodak Co. v. Southern Photo Materials Co., 273 U.S. 359 (1927).

81. 333 U.S. at 807.

82. *Id.* at 817.

83. *Id.* at 814 (declining to decide whether Scophony could be "found" in New York by virtue of these agreements alone).

84. Buckeye Assocs. v. Fila Sports, Inc., 616 F. Supp. 1484 (D. Mass. 1985) (venue held to be improper under § 12 where Italian parent firm had no contacts with Massachusetts and subsidiary domestic firm did not have systematic, continuous or substantial contact with the state, although some of firm's products made their way into state); Chrysler Corp. v. General Motors Corp., 589 F. Supp. 1182, 1195-99 (D.D.C. 1984) (venue proper in Washington, D.C. even though government contact discounted); Lippa & Co. v. Lenox, Inc., 305 F. Supp. 175 (D. Vt. 1969). *See generally* Zenith Radio Corp. v. Matsushita Elec. Indus. Co., 402 F. Supp. 262, 317-28 (E.D. Pa. 1975).

85. United States v. Scophony Corp., 333 U.S. 795 (1948); Eastman Kodak Co. v. Southern Photo Materials Co., 273 U.S. 359 (1927); Black v. Acme Mkts., 564 F.2d 681 (5th Cir. 1977); Hunt v. Mobil Oil Corp., 410 F. Supp. 4, 8 (S.D.N.Y. 1975), *aff'd*, 550 F.2d 68 (2d Cir.), *cert. denied*, 434 U.S. 984 (1977).

86. *Hunt*, 410 F. Supp. at 8.

87. Codex Corp. v. Racal-Milgo, Inc., 1984-1 Trade Cas. (CCH) ¶ 65,853 (D. Mass. 1984); *Chrysler Corp.*, 589 F. Supp. at 1200-03; MCI Communs. Corp. v. AT&T, 1983-2 Trade Cas. (CCH) ¶ 65,652 (D.D.C. 1983); *see also* Dunham's, Inc. v. National Buying Syndicate, 614 F. Supp. 616, 625 (E.D. Mich. 1985) (venue proper where members of defendant buying syndicate are located in the district). *Compare* United States v. Scophony Corp., 333 U.S. 795 (1948); Tiger Trash v. Browning-Ferris Indus., 560 F.2d 818 (7th Cir. 1977), *cert. denied*, 434 U.S. 1034 (1978); Star Lines v. Puerto Rico Maritime Shipping Auth., 442 F. Supp. 1201 (S.D.N.Y. 1978); Zenith Radio Corp. v. Matsushita Elec. Indus. Co., 402 F. Supp. 262, 327-38 (E.D. Pa. 1975) *and* Fisher Baking Co. v. Continental Baking Corp., 238 F. Supp. 332 (D. Utah 1965) *with* Cannon Mfg. Co. v.

defendant and any seemingly unrelated company (an exclusive distributor, for example) is such that the company, in fact, is acting as the defendant's agent;[88] (5) the volume of sales the defendant is making, directly, in the district;[89] (6) whether the defendant carries on patent licensing activities in the district;[90] (7) whether the defendant has solicited business in the district,[91] maintains offices or employees in the district,[92] makes purchases in the district,[93] or advertises in the district,[94] and (8) whether its officers and executives have made business trips into the districts.[95] Courts will also evaluate the defendant's activities in the district as they relate to the specific allegations upon which the cause of action is based.[96]

In addition to the special antitrust venue provisions, the general federal venue statute[97] may provide a basis for venue in an antitrust action.[98] With respect to foreign defendants, whether individuals or corporations, the most pertinent provision of that statute is Section 1391(d), which provides that "an alien may be sued in any district."[99] In *Brunette Machine Works, Ltd. v. Kockum Industries*,[100] a patent infringement action, the Supreme Court observed that Section 1391(d) "is properly regarded, not as a venue restriction at all, but rather as a declaration of the long established rule that suits against aliens are wholly outside the operation of all the

---

Cudahy Packing Co., 267 U.S. 333 (1925); San Antonio Tel. Co. v. AT&T, 499 F.2d 349 (5th Cir. 1974); O.S.C. Corp. v. Toshiba Am., Inc., 491 F.2d 1064 (9th Cir. 1974); Sportmart, Inc. v. Frisch, 537 F. Supp. 1254 (N.D. Ill. 1982) *and* Williams v. Canon, Inc., 432 F. Supp. 376 (C.D. Cal. 1977).

88. Hoffman Motors Corp. v. Alfa Romeo, SpA, 244 F. Supp. 70 (S.D.N.Y. 1965). *Contra* Athlete's Foot of Delaware, Inc. v. Ralph Libonati Co., 445 F. Supp. 35 (D. Del. 1977).

89. Sunbury Wire Rope Mfg. v. U.S. Steel Corp., 129 F. Supp. 425 (E.D. Pa. 1955).

90. United States v. Scophony Corp., 333 U.S. 795 (1948).

91. School Dist. v. Kurtz Bros., 240 F. Supp. 361 (E.D. Pa. 1965); *cf.* AG Bliss Co. v. United Carr Fastener Co. of Can., 116 F. Supp. 291 (D. Mass. 1953) (foreign subsidiary of Massachusetts firm not doing business in Massachusetts where it has no place of business or employees in the state and does not solicit business there), *aff'd*, 213 F.2d 541 (1st Cir. 1954).

92. *Cf. AG Bliss Co.*, 116 F. Supp. at 294 (where Canadian corporation was subsidiary of Massachusetts corporation, the fact that it had Massachusetts residents as officers, among other factors, did not make it subject to service in Massachusetts).

93. McCrory Corp. v. Cloth World, Inc., 378 F. Supp. 322 (S.D.N.Y. 1974).

94. Runnels v. TMSI Contractors, Inc., 764 F.2d 417, 421 (5th Cir. 1985) (advertising in two Louisiana newspapers over a five year period constituted a contact); *cf.* San Antonio Tel. Co. v. AT&T, 499 F.2d 349, 351 n.5 (5th Cir. 1974) (national advertising that reaches a district is insufficient).

95. C.C.P. Corp. v. Wynn Oil Co., 354 F. Supp. 1275 (N.D. Ill. 1973).

96. Chrysler Corp. v. General Motors Corp., 589 F. Supp. 1182, 1203-06 (D.D.C. 1984) (Toyota had sufficient joint venture-related contacts with forum); *In re* Uranium Antitrust Litig., 1980-81 Trade Cas. (CCH) ¶ 63,678 (N.D. Ill. 1980) (alleged conspiratorial meetings took place in the district); *In re* Chicken Antitrust Litig., 407 F. Supp. 1285 (N.D. Ga. 1975). *But cf.* Sportmart, Inc. v. Frisch, 537 F. Supp. 1254, 1259 (N.D. Ill. 1982) ("The fact that Sportmart may have suffered injury here, without more, will not support the exercise of personal jurisdiction or create venue . . . .").

97. 28 U.S.C. § 1391 (1991 Supp.).

98. *Sportmart, Inc.*, 537 F. Supp. at 1257 (dictum); H & S Distribs. v. Cott Corp., 1980-2 Trade Cas. (CCH) ¶ 63,358 at 75,831 (D. Conn. 1980) (dictum); Ohio-Sealy Mattress Mfg. Co. v. Kaplan, 429 F. Supp. 139 (N.D. Ill. 1977); ABC Great States, Inc. v. Globe Ticket Co., 310 F. Supp. 739 (N.D. Ill. 1970); Edward J. Moriarty & Co. v. General Tire & Rubber Co., 289 F. Supp. 381 (D.C. Ohio 1967); Hoffman Motors Corp. v. Alfa Romeo, SpA, 244 F. Supp. 70 (S.D.N.Y. 1965).

99. 28 U.S.C. § 1391(d) (1991 Supp.).

100. 406 U.S. 706 (1973).

federal venue laws, general and special."[101]   Consistent with this rule, courts in antitrust cases have applied Section 1391(d) in rejecting claims of improper venue asserted by alien defendants, both individual[102] and corporate.[103]

The general venue statute, Section 1391(b), also permits venue in an antitrust suit to be laid in

(1) a judicial district where any defendant resides, if all defendants reside in the same State,
(2) a judicial district in which a substantial part of the events or omissions giving rise to the claim occurred, or a substantial part of property that is the subject of the action is situated, or (3) a judicial district in which any defendant may be found.[104]

Prior to the 1990 amendment, Section 1391(b) permitted venue to lie where "the claim arose."[105]   The previous language implied that there was only one district where the claim arose and thus encouraged litigation over which forum was proper in a multiforum transaction.   Under the amended clause, venue may be proper in

---

101.   *Id.* at 714. The constitutionality of § 1391(d) was challenged by the defendants but not decided by the district court in Zenith Radio Corp. v. Matsushita Elec. Indus. Co., 402 F. Supp. 262, 330 n.39 (E.D. Pa. 1975).

102.   *See* Scriptomatic, Inc. v. Agfa-Gevaert, Inc., 1973-1 Trade Cas. (CCH) ¶ 74,594 (S.D.N.Y. 1973); Edward J. Moriarty & Co. v. General Tire & Rubber Co., 289 F. Supp. 381 (S.D. Ohio 1967).

103.   Square D Co. v. Niagara Frontier Tariff Bureau, 1984-1 Trade Cas. (CCH) ¶ 65,825, at 67,454-55 (D.D.C. 1984) (venue in any district proper as to Canadian corporations); General Elec. Co. v. Bucyrus-Erie Co., 550 F. Supp. 1037 (S.D.N.Y. 1982); Centronics Data Computer Corp. v. Mannesmann, AG, 432 F. Supp. 659 (D.N.H. 1977); Hoffman Motors Corp. v. Alfa Romeo, SpA, 244 F. Supp. 70 (S.D.N.Y. 1965).
Of course, a conclusion that venue with respect to an alien defendant is properly laid under § 1391(d) does not necessarily mean that the defendant is amenable to suit. The jurisdictional question would still remain. *See* Chrysler Corp. v. Fedders Corp., 643 F.2d 1229, 1237-38 (6th Cir.), *cert. denied*, 454 U.S. 893 (1981); SCM v. Brothers Int'l Corp., 316 F. Supp. 1328, 1334 (S.D.N.Y. 1970) (in a patent infringement suit, a Japanese parent corporation, with respect to which venue was held to be properly laid under § 1391(d), was found amenable to suit in the forum district, not for that reason alone, but because it also had "sufficient contacts and activities in this jurisdiction to require [it] to defend an action commenced in this forum"); *see also* O.S.C. Corp. v. Toshiba Am., Inc., 491 F.2d 1064 (9th Cir. 1974) (after concluding that the defendant Japanese corporation was not transacting business in the district, the Ninth Circuit rejected the § 1391(d) argument, since the plaintiff had not shown that the alien corporation was amenable to suit in any U.S. district from a jurisdictional standpoint); Williams v. Canon, Inc., 432 F. Supp. 376 (C.D. Cal. 1977) (following *O.S.C.*). As discussed below, answering the jurisdictional question entails analysis of the alien defendant's contacts with the forum district and, perhaps, the United States as a whole – an analysis that does not significantly differ from that required by § 12 of the Clayton Act.

104.   28 U.S.C. § 1391(b) (1991 Supp.). Subsection 1391(a) of the statute applies only in cases in which jurisdiction is founded solely on diversity and thus is not applicable to federal antitrust claims since cases brought under the federal antitrust laws will always present a federal question.

105.   Under the pre-1990 statute, two tests existed for determining whether or not a claim "arose" in a particular district: (1) the "target area" test under which the claim arose in the district in which the target of the alleged violation suffered injury to its business, (*see, e.g.*, Centronics Data Computer Corp. v. Mannesmann, AG, 432 F. Supp. 659, 661 (D.N.H. 1977)), or (2) the "weight of the contact" test under which courts would look not only to the place in which the injury allegedly occurred, but also to other contacts between the defendants and the forum districts. *See, e.g.*, Caribe Trailer Sys. v. Puerto Rico Maritime Shipping Auth., 475 F. Supp. 711, 718-19 (D.D.C. 1979), *aff'd per curiam*, (D.C. Cir. 1980), *cert. denied*, 450 U.S. 914 (1981).

more than one district in a multiforum transaction.[106] Under Subsection (c), a corporate defendant may be sued in any district in which it is subject to personal jurisdiction at the time the action is commenced. If a corporation is amenable to jurisdiction in a state having several districts, venue is proper based on the districts with which the defendant has the most significant contacts.[107]

Finally, Section 1391(f) establishes special venue rules for civil action against foreign states.[108] Under these rules, venue in such actions may be laid in, among other places, any U.S. judicial district in which a substantial part of the events or omissions giving rise to the claim occurred, the district in which a substantial part of the property subject to the action is located, or in the District of Columbia.[109]

2. Personal Jurisdiction

No special rules of personal jurisdiction govern antitrust actions. Thus, in the antitrust field, as in other areas of law, *International Shoe Co. v. Washington*[110] provides the guiding principle: due process "requires only that in order to subject a defendant to a judgment *in personam*, if he be not present within the territory of the forum, he have certain minimum contacts with it such that the maintenance of the suit does not offend 'traditional notions of fair play and substantial justice'."[111]

---

106. *See* H.R. Rep. No. 734, 101st Cong., 2d Sess. (1990), *reprinted in* 1990 U.S. Code Cong. & Admin. News 6860, 6869.

107. 28 U.S.C. § 1391(c) (1988) provides that:

   For purposes of venue under this chapter, a defendant that is a corporation shall be deemed to reside in any judicial district in which it is subject to personal jurisdiction at the time the action is commenced. In a State which has more than one judicial district and in which a defendant that is a corporation is subject to personal jurisdiction at the time an action is commenced, such corporation shall be deemed to reside in any district in that State within which its contacts would be sufficient to subject it to personal jurisdiction if that district were a separate State, and, if there is no such district, the corporation shall be deemed to reside in the district within which it has the most significant contacts.

108. 28 U.S.C. § 1391(f) is a codification of part of the Foreign Sovereign Immunities Act of 1976, Pub. L. No. 94-583, 90 Stat. 2891.

109. *See, e.g.*, Kalamazoo Spice Extraction Co. v. Provisional Military Gov't of Socialist Ethiopia, 616 F. Supp. 660, 665 (W.D. Mich. 1985) (venue proper where accounts receivables totalling $2 million were located in the district and constituted a substantial portion of the assets of expropriated company which was subject matter of action); Schmidt v. Polish People's Republic, 579 F. Supp. 23, 28 (S.D.N.Y) (negotiation of original loan, negotiations after default, execution of agreement and payment of notes together make up a substantial part of events which give rise to claim to recover on defaulted notes, and all took place in the district), *aff'd*, 742 F.2d 67 (2d Cir. 1984).

110. 326 U.S. 310 (1945).

111. *Id.* at 316 (citations omitted). The *International Shoe* decision involved consideration of the adjudicatory power of state courts under the due process clause of the fourteenth amendment. Technically, in federal question cases, the due process clause of the fifth amendment controls. However, even in such cases courts frequently consult the Supreme Court's pronouncements on the jurisdiction of state courts for the "clearest guidance" on when the exercise of personal jurisdiction is permissible. *See, e.g.*, Max Daetwyler Corp. v. R. Meyer, 762 F.2d 290, 293 (3d Cir.), *cert. denied*, 474 U.S. 980 (1985); Buckeye Assocs. v. Fila Sports, Inc., 616 F. Supp. 1484, 1488 n.5 (D. Mass. 1985); Japan Gas Lighter Ass'n v. Ronson Corp., 257 F. Supp. 219, 232 (D.N.J. 1966). *But see* Dunham's, Inc. v. National Buying Syndicate, 614 F. Supp. 616, 619-23 (E.D. Mich. 1985) (in a federal antitrust action, personal jurisdiction is guided by standards of due process under the fifth amendment, rather than an *International Shoe* standard of minimum contacts with the forum; the proper inquiry is therefore whether service of process was adequate

In decisions subsequent to *International Shoe*, this principle evolved into a two-pronged test.[112] The first requirement is that there must be some "minimum contact" with the forum state (or district) resulting from an affirmative act of the defendant by which he "purposefully avails" himself of the privilege of conducting activities there and invokes the benefits and protections of the forum's laws.[113] The second requirement is that it be fair and reasonable to require the defendant to come into the forum state (or district) and defend the action.[114] A determination of whether the exercise of jurisdiction is reasonable will turn upon "the burden on

---

to give notice of the proceeding); *cf.* First Flight Co. v. National Carloading Corp., 209 F. Supp. 730, 736-37 (E.D. Tenn. 1962) (it is anomalous to limit federal court action by a constitutional provision applicable only to state action).

International Shoe considerations are applicable even for actions against foreign states. The Foreign Sovereign Immunities Act of 1976, 28 U.S.C. § 1330(b) (1988), states that personal jurisdiction is established whenever a court has subject matter jurisdiction and service of process has been made pursuant to the Act, but the courts have imposed a due process review. *E.g.*, Texas Trading & Milling Corp. v. Federal Republic of Nig., 647 F.2d 300 (2d Cir. 1981), *cert. denied*, 454 U.S. 1148 (1982); *Kalamazoo Spice*, 616 F. Supp. at 665; Transamerican S.S. Corp. v. Somali Democratic Republic, 590 F. Supp. 968, 976 (D.D.C. 1984), *aff'd in part and rev'd in part*, 767 F.2d 998 (D.C. Cir. 1985); *Schmidt*, 579 F. Supp. at 28; Ruiz v. Transportes Aeros Militares Ecuadorianos, 103 F.R.D. 458, 459 (D.D.C. 1984).

112.   *See* Product Promotions, Inc. v. Cousteau, 495 F.2d 483, 494 (5th Cir. 1974).

113.   *See* Burger King Corp. v. Rudzewicz, 471 U.S. 462, 474 (1985) ("the constitutional touchstone remains whether the defendant purposefully established 'minimum contacts' in the forum State"). In *Burger King*, the Supreme Court determined that personal jurisdiction in Florida over a Michigan franchise for breach of the franchise agreement was proper where defendant entered into a twenty-year relationship with wide-ranging contacts with Burger King's Miami headquarters and agreed that disputes would be governed by Florida law. These actions indicated a deliberate affiliation with the forum state and the reasonable foreseeability of possible litigation there. *See also* Chandler v. Barclays Bank PLC, 898 F.2d 1148 (6th Cir. 1990) (the issuance of a letter of credit naming a state resident as beneficiary is generally insufficient to confer jurisdiction). *Compare* FMC Corp. v. Varonos, 892 F.2d 1308 (7th Cir. 1990) (faxed transmissions into a forum, coupled with an attempt to avail oneself of that forum's benefits, provides sufficient basis for jurisdiction); Carter v. Trafalgar Tours Ltd., 704 F. Supp. 673 (W.D. Va. 1989) (sending travel brochures into forum sufficient to exercise jurisdiction) *and* World-Wide Volkswagen Corp. v. Woodson, 444 U.S. 286, 298 (1980) (dictum) (standard was not met) (the act of delivering one's products "into the stream of commerce with the expectation that they will be purchased by consumers in the forum state" subjects one to the assertions of jurisdiction by courts in that state) *with* Asahi Metal Ind. Co. v. Superior Court of Cal., 480 U.S. 102 (1987) (mere placement of goods into the "stream of commerce," with awareness that they would eventually reach the forum state is not, itself, sufficient to satisfy minimum contact requirement); Hanson v. Denckla, 357 U.S. 235 (1958) (the defendant trustee did not "purposefully avail itself of the privilege of conducting activities within the forum state" simply by sending checks to the settlor of the trust, who moved to the forum state after having established the trust in the defendant's home state) *and* Coblenz GMC/Freightliner v. General Motors Corp., 724 F. Supp. 1364, 1368-70 (M.D. Ala. 1989) (foreseeability of effect within a forum, absent intent, does not entitle the forum to exercise jurisdiction), *aff'd without pub. op.*, 932 F.2d 977 and 932 F.2d 978 (11th Cir. 1991).

114.   *See, e.g.,* Congoleum Corp. v. DLW Aktiengesellschaft, 729 F.2d 1240 (9th Cir. 1984) (would not comport with fair play and substantial justice to assert jurisdiction over a West German corporation in the distant forum of California on a claim that arises out of activities in Europe, where the corporation had no contact with California other than sales and sales promotion by independent nonexclusive sales representatives unrelated to the cause of action); Metrix Warehouse, Inc. v. Daimler-Benz Aktiengesellschaft, 1984-2 Trade Cas. (CCH) ¶ 66,129 (D. Md. 1984), *aff'd*, 828 F.2d 1033 (4th Cir. 1987), *cert. denied*, 486 U.S. 1017 (1988); *see also* McGee v. International Life Ins. Co., 355 U.S. 220 (1957).

the defendant, the interests of the forum state, and the plaintiff's interest in obtaining relief."[115]

The jurisdictional analysis required to evaluate due process is similar to the analysis required by the "transacting business" test for determining whether or not venue is proper under Section 12 of the Clayton Act. The factors that courts consider are virtually identical, including: (1) the continuity of the defendant's activities in the district;[116] (2) the volume of the defendant's business in the district;[117] (3) the relationship between the defendant's activities in the district and the nature of the case of action;[118] (4) activities in the district by a subsidiary controlled by the defendant;[119] (5) local telephone or other listings by defendant

---

115. *Asahi Metal*, 480 U.S. at 113.
116. Keeton v. Hustler Magazine, Inc., 465 U.S. 770 (1984) (out-of-state publisher's continuous and deliberate exploitation of the forum state market (i.e., regular monthly sales of thousands of magazines) was sufficient to support an assertion of jurisdiction in a libel action which arose out of the very activity being conducted in the forum state, regardless of plaintiff's limited contacts with the state); *see* Helicopteros Nacionales de Colombia, SA v. Hall, 466 U.S. 408 (1984) (in wrongful death action concerning helicopter crash in Peru, a contract negotiation session, helicopter purchases, and related training trips were insufficient contacts for the State of Texas to exercise *general* personal jurisdiction over Colombian corporation unrelated to forum contacts); Perkins v. Benguet Consol. Mining Co., 342 U.S. 437 (1952); International Shoe Co. v. Washington, 326 U.S. 310 (1945); Harran Transp. Co. v. National Trailways Bus Sys., 1985-2 Trade Cas. (CCH) ¶ 66,723 (D.D.C. 1985) ($37,800 in parts sales, four service calls, and sales of thirty-six buses not sufficient to meet more substantial contacts required for exercise of general jurisdiction); United States v. Imperial Chem. Indus., 100 F. Supp. 504 (S.D.N.Y. 1951); *In re* Shipowners Litig., 361 N.W.2d 112 (Minn. Ct. App. 1985) (personal jurisdiction lacking over state antitrust counterclaim against foreign counterdefendant where only contact with forum was a single meeting, instituted by counterclaimant to discuss possible settlement of contract dispute).
117. International Shoe Co. v. Washington, 326 U.S. 310 (1945).
118. *See* Perkins v. Benguet Consol. Mining Co., 342 U.S. 437 (1952); International Shoe Co. v. Washington, 326 U.S. 310 (1945); Pillar Corp. v. Enercon Indus. Corp., 1989-1 Trade Cas. (CCH) ¶ 68,597 (E.D. Wis. 1989) (federal district court could exercise personal jurisdiction over West German firm because firm's contacts with the forum, though minimal, gave rise to the cause of action). *Compare Burger King*, 471 U.S. at 472-73; *Keeton*, 465 U.S. 770; Calder v. Jones, 465 U.S. 783, 788-90 (1984) (personal jurisdiction was proper in California over Florida reporter and editor of *National Enquirer* where California was the deliberate focal point of the story and of the harm suffered by the plaintiff) *and* Widger Chem. Corp. v. Chemfil Corp., 601 F. Supp. 845 (E.D. Mich. 1985) *with Congoleum Corp.*, 729 F.2d 1240 (cause of action not related to defendant's activities in district); Mizlou Television Network v. NBC, 603 F. Supp. 677, 681-83 (D.D.C. 1984) (fact that party received legal advice regarding the transaction from attorney who operated from the district was not sufficient to confer personal jurisdiction) *and* McGlinchey v. Shell Chem. Co., 1985-2 Trade Cas. (CCH) ¶ 66,672 (N.D. Cal. 1984).
119. Call Carl, Inc. v. B.P. Oil Corp., 391 F. Supp. 367, 371 (D. Md. 1975), *aff'd in part and rev'd in part,* 554 F.2d 623 (4th Cir.), *cert. denied,* 434 U.S. 923 (1977); Kalamazoo Spice Extraction Co. v. Provisional Military Gov't of Socialist Ethiopia, 616 F. Supp. 660, 666 (W.D. Mich. 1985) (activities of expropriated company attributed to foreign state where state exercised direct control over operations by appointing majority of board of directors, requiring a government approved director to sign checks, and approving invoices); Dunlop Tire & Rubber Corp. v. PepsiCo, Inc., 591 F. Supp. 88 (N.D. Ill. 1984) (jurisdiction held to exist where foreign parent counterdefendant owned 100% of subsidiary counterdefendants, appointed common directors and holders of various high positions, and exercised control over capital expenditure and financial operations); United States v. Watchmakers of Switz. Information Center, Inc., 133 F. Supp. 40 (S.D.N.Y. 1955); United States v. Imperial Chem. Indus., 100 F. Supp. 504 (S.D.N.Y. 1951); *cf.* Behagen v. Amateur Basketball Ass'n, 744 F.2d 731 (10th Cir. 1984) (international association regulating amateur basketball maintained continuous and substantial activity in the forum state through the actions

in the district;[120] (6) the convenience of the forum chosen by plaintiff and the availability of other forums;[121] (7) the existence of directors' meetings, business correspondence, banking, stock transfers, payment of salaries, and purchasing of machinery in the district;[122] and (8) the attendance by the defendant at alleged conspiratorial meetings in the district.[123] If a defendant challenges jurisdiction but fails to comply with discovery orders, a court may sanction such noncompliance by finding jurisdiction to be established.[124]

Supreme Court decisions have expanded the exercise of personal jurisdiction by courts over nonresident individuals who purposefully direct activity toward the forum jurisdiction.[125] In *Keeton v. Hustler Magazine*[126] and *Calder v. Jones*,[127] the Court held that an individual who publishes an allegedly libelous article may become subject to the personal jurisdiction of a state in which the defamed individual

---

of its members), *cert. denied*, 471 U.S. 1010 (1985). *But cf.* Miller v. Honda Motor Co., 779 F.2d 769 (1st Cir. 1985) (no personal jurisdiction established over foreign parent in personal injury suit even though domestic subsidiary was wholly owned, sold the parent's products, and had two common board members with parent); Kramer Motors, Inc. v. British Leyland, Ltd., 628 F.2d 1175 (9th Cir. 1980) (no jurisdiction despite common directors between British parent and U.S. subsidiary where parent did not exercise day-to-day control), *cert. denied*, 449 U.S. 1062 (1981) (per curiam); Perfumer's Workshop, Ltd. v. Roure Bertrand du Pont, Inc., 1990-2 Trade Cas. (CCH) ¶ 69,102 (S.D.N.Y. 1990) (no personal jurisdiction over parent corporation of U.S. subsidiary where parent neither supplied product to, asserted control over, nor derived financial benefit from U.S. subsidiary); Savin Corp. v. Heritage Copy Prods., Inc., 661 F. Supp. 463 (M.D. Pa. 1987) (no personal jurisdiction over parent that was not alter ego of subsidiary); Camellia City Telecasters v. Tribune Broadcasting Co., 1984-2 Trade Cas. (CCH) ¶ 66,114, at 66,224-25 (D. Colo. 1984) (being part of national network of corporation insufficient to establish personal jurisdiction unless these facts justify piercing the corporate veil); Sportmart, Inc. v. Frisch, 537 F. Supp. 1254, 1258 (N.D. Ill. 1982) (jurisdiction denied where U.S. subsidiary was not "alter ego" of parent); Jamesbury Corp. v. Kitamura Valve Mfg. Co., 484 F. Supp. 533, 535 (S.D. Tex. 1980) (dictum) (unless subsidiary acts as an agent or parent lacks distinct legal existence, "mere transaction of business through a wholly owned subsidiary" is insufficient).

120. *See* Glick v. Empire Box Corp., 119 F. Supp. 224 (S.D.N.Y. 1954).

121. *See* Travelers Health Ass'n v. Virginia, 339 U.S. 643 (1950); Latimer v. S/A Industrias Reunidas F. Matarazzo, 175 F.2d 184 (2d Cir. 1949), *cert. denied*, 338 U.S. 867 (1949).

122. *See* Perkins v. Benguet Consol. Mining Co., 342 U.S. 437 (1952); Lanier v. American Bd. of Endodontics, 843 F.2d 901, 907 (6th Cir.), *cert. denied*, 488 U.S. 926 (1988). *But see* Helicopteros Nacionales de Colombia, SA v. Hall, 466 U.S. 408 (1984) (mere purchases, even if they included training sessions and were made at regular intervals, were not enough to warrant an assertion of general in personam jurisdiction; nor was it proper to consider the acceptance of checks drawn on a bank in the forum state in determining the existence of significant contacts, where the bank was unilaterally selected by another party or a third party).

123. *See* Ohio-Sealy Mattress Mfg. Co. v. Kaplan, 429 F. Supp. 139 (N.D. Ill. 1977); *cf.* McDonald v. St. Joseph's Hosp., 574 F. Supp. 123 (N.D. Ga. 1983) (allegedly defamatory statements made in telephone conversations with the forum state, which were not initiated by the nonresident defendant, not sufficient contact, even where conversations were basis of alleged conspiracy).

124. Insurance Corp. of Ireland, Ltd. v. Compagnie des Bauxites de Guinee, 456 U.S. 694 (1982). *See also* English v. 21st Phoenix Corp., 590 F.2d 723 (8th Cir.), *cert. denied*, 444 U.S. 832 (1979).

125. Burger King Corp. v. Rudzewicz, 471 U.S. 462 (1985); Keeton v. Hustler Magazine, Inc., 465 U.S. 770 (1984); Calder v. Jones, 465 U.S. 783 (1984); *see also* Karsten Manufacturing Corp. v. United States Golf Ass'n, 1990-1 Trade Cas. (CCH) ¶ 68,965 (D. Ariz. 1990) (foreseeability that activity might cause injury to the forum state is not sufficient to impose personal jurisdiction against one who did not purposefully direct its activities at the forum state).

126. 465 U.S. 770 (1984).

127. 465 U.S. 783 (1984).

lives,[128] does business, or otherwise may have suffered harm from the libelous act.[129] The import of these cases in antitrust actions involving foreign defendants is clear, particularly in the context of a Sherman Act violation: an agreement to restrain trade or an attempt to monopolize that is designed to affect the United States may give rise to personal jurisdiction by U.S. courts over the foreign conspirators or monopolist.

For example, in *Consolidated Gold Fields, PLC v. Anglo American Corp.*,[130] the purposeful activity doctrine was held to establish personal jurisdiction over a foreign defendant in the absence of general jurisdiction, where the defendant allegedly attempted to monopolize the international and U.S. gold market through a hostile tender offer that violated U.S. antitrust and securities laws. The district court held that "where [the defendant's] 'intentional and allegedly . . . [unlawful], actions were expressly aimed at' the United States . . . and the company knew and intended that its actions would have a direct impact on [the acquired entity] with whatever consequences that impact might have for competition in the United States, [the defendant] 'must reasonably anticipate being haled into court there to answer for' its actions."[131]

In antitrust cases, as in other cases involving federal questions, courts have generally held that the appropriate jurisdictional question is whether or not the nonresident defendant has had sufficient contacts with the district in which the court is sitting.[132] However, some courts have adopted a jurisdictional theory using an "aggregate contacts" or "national contacts" test to determine whether jurisdiction may be asserted over foreign defendants. This approach is grounded in the theory that if the defendant has sufficient cumulative contacts with the sovereign of which the court is an arm, the absence of contacts with the particular physical territory in which the court sits raises a question of venue rather than jurisdiction.[133] Because

---

128. *Calder*, 465 U.S. at 788.

129. *Keeton*, 465 U.S. at 777.

130. 698 F. Supp. 487 (S.D.N.Y. 1988), *aff'd in part and rev'd in part sub nom.* Consolidated Gold Fields, PLC v. Minorco, SA, 871 F.2d 252 (2d Cir.), *cert. dismissed*, 492 U.S. 939 (1989).

131. *Id.* at 496 (quoting *Calder*, 465 U.S. at 789, and World-Wide Volkswagen Corp. v. Woodson, 444 U.S. 286, 297 (1980)).

132. *See, e.g.*, Columbia Metal Culvert v. Kaiser Indus. Corp., 526 F.2d 724 (3d Cir. 1975); O.S.C. Corp. v. Toshiba Am., Inc., 491 F.2d 1064 (9th Cir. 1974); Leasco Data Processing Equip. Corp. v. Maxwell, 468 F.2d 1326 (2d Cir. 1972); Fraley v. Chesapeake & Ohio Ry., 397 F.2d 1 (3d Cir. 1968); Courtesy Chevrolet, Inc. v. Tennessee Walking Horse Breeders & Exhibitors' Ass'n of Am., 344 F.2d 860, 865 (9th Cir. 1965); Sportmart, Inc. v. Frisch, 537 F. Supp. 1254, 1260 (N.D. Ill. 1982); Superior Coal Co. v. Ruhrkohle, AG, 83 F.R.D. 414 (E.D. Pa. 1979); HumidAire Corp. v. J. Levitt, Inc., 1978-1 Trade Cas. (CCH) ¶ 61,846 (N.D. Ill. 1977). *See generally* Insurance Corp. of Ireland v. Compagnie des Bauxites de Guinee, 456 U.S. 694 (1982).

133. First Flight Co. v. National Carloading Corp., 209 F. Supp. 730, 738 (E.D. Tenn. 1962).
The Supreme Court has declined to rule on whether the aggregation of national contacts comports with the due process requirements of the fifth amendment. *See* Asahi Metal Ind. Co. v. Superior Court of Cal., 480 U.S. 102, 113 (1987) ("We have no occasion here to determine whether Congress could, consistent with the Due Process clause of the Fifth Amendment, authorize federal court personal jurisdiction over alien defendants based on the aggregate of national contacts, rather than on the contacts between the defendant and the state in which the federal court sits."). However, on an earlier occasion, the Court appeared to undermine the sovereignty approach to jurisdiction upon which the aggregate of contacts theory is premised. *See* Insurance Corp. of Ireland v. Campagnie des Bauxites de Guinee, 456 U.S. 694, 702 (1982) ("[T]he personal jurisdiction requirement recognizes and protects an individual liberty interest.

the Clayton Act authorizes worldwide service of process,[134] some courts have adopted the aggregate contacts theory in antitrust cases.[135] Other courts have rejected the aggregate contacts theory in the antitrust context,[136] and still others consider the aggregate of a defendant's national contacts in the context of a range of general principles of fair play and substantial justice.[137]

It represents a restriction on judicial power not as a matter of sovereignty, but as a matter of individual liberty."); *see also* Bamford v. Hobbs, 569 F. Supp. 160, 165 (S.D. Tex. 1983).

134. 15 U.S.C. § 22 (1988).

135. Go-Video, Inc. v. Akai Elec. Co., 885 F.2d 1406 (9th Cir. 1989); *In re* Plastic Bag Prod. Patent & Antitrust Litig., 1987-1 Trade Cas. (CCH) ¶ 67,561 (D. Mass. 1987); Newport Components, Inc. v. NEC Home Elecs. (U.S.A.), Inc., 671 F. Supp. 1525 (C.D. Cal. 1987); Amtrol, Inc. v. Vent-Rite Valve Corp., 646 F. Supp. 1168, 1172 (D. Mass. 1986) ("where a defendant is served pursuant to a congressional authorization of worldwide service of process, due process requires only that the defendant's aggregate contacts with the United States as a whole are such that 'maintenance of the suit does not offend traditional notions of fair play and substantial justice' ") (quoting International Shoe Co. v. Washington, 326 U.S. 310, 316 (1945)); Kalamazoo Spice Extraction Co. v. Provisional Military Gov't of Socialist Ethiopia, 616 F. Supp. 660, 665 (W.D. Mich. 1985) (application of national contacts standard to foreign state); Dunham's, Inc. v. National Buying Syndicate, 614 F. Supp. 616 (E.D. Mich. 1985); Paulson Inv. Co. v. Norbay Sec., Inc., 603 F. Supp. 615, 618 (D. Or. 1984); Transamerican S.S. Corp. v. Somali Democratic Republic, 590 F. Supp. 968, 976-77 n.5 (D.D.C. 1984) (same), *aff'd in part and rev'd in part,* 767 F.2d 998 (D.C. Cir. 1985); Ruiz v. Transportes Aereos Militares Ecuadorianos, 103 F.R.D. 458, 459-60 (D.D.C. 1984) (same); General Elec. Co. v. Bucyrus-Erie Co., 550 F. Supp. 1037 (S.D.N.Y. 1982); Scriptomatic, Inc. v. Agfa-Gevaert, Inc., 1973-1 Trade Cas. (CCH) ¶ 74,594 (S.D.N.Y. 1973) (contacts with forum district also shown); *cf. In re* Marc Rich & Co., 707 F.2d 663, 667 (2d Cir.) (personal jurisdiction for enforcement of grand jury subpoena should have been based on national contacts), *cert. denied,* 463 U.S. 1215 (1983); Texas Trading & Milling Corp. v. Federal Republic of Nig., 647 F.2d 300, 314 (2d Cir. 1981), *cert. denied,* 454 U.S. 1148 (1982).

136. Max Daetwyler Corp. v. R. Meyer, 762 F.2d 290, 294-95 (3d Cir.) (although "national contacts" theory might be constitutional, it is not authorized by statute), *cert. denied,* 474 U.S. 462 (1985); Neumann v. Vidal, 1982-2 Trade Cas. (CCH) ¶ 64,933, at 72,772 (D.D.C. 1981); Superior Coal Co. v. Ruhrkohle, AG, 83 F.R.D. 414, 419 (E.D. Pa. 1979) (holding that absent a federal statute or amendment of the Federal Rules of Civil Procedure evidencing a congressional intent to allow an aggregation of national contacts, courts are without authority to extend personal jurisdiction); *see also* Chrysler Corp. v. General Motors Corp., 589 F. Supp. 1182, 1202 n.11 (D.D.C. 1984).

137. Entek Corp. v. Southwest Pipe & Supply Co., 683 F. Supp. 1092 (E.D. Tex. 1988); Bamford v. Hobbs, 569 F. Supp. 160, 166 (S.D. Tex. 1983) (exercise of personal jurisdiction should not be decided solely on the basis of minimum contacts with the United States but on general principles of fair play and substantial justice, including the burden on a defendant of litigation in a distant forum, the character of defendant's business as national or regional, plaintiff's interest in obtaining convenient and effective relief, and the forum's effective resolution of controversies); *see also* Chrysler Corp. v. Fedders Corp., 643 F.2d 1229, 1238 (6th Cir.) (dictum) (stating that under certain circumstances it "may well be neither unfair nor unreasonable as a matter of due process to aggregate the nonforum contacts of an alien corporate defendant in order to establish personal jurisdiction"), *cert. denied,* 454 U.S. 893 (1981); Centronics Data Computer Corp. v. Mannesmann, AG, 432 F. Supp. 659, 664 (D.N.H. 1977) ("where an alien defendant is sued by an American plaintiff, and where there is no particular inconvenience due to the specific forum state, the fact that the defendant is an alien and that there is no other forum in which to litigate the claim should be taken into consideration for purposes of determining whether a finding of jurisdiction meets the requisite constitutional standards of fair play"); Edward J. Moriarity & Co. v. General Tire & Rubber Co., 289 F. Supp. 381 (S.D. Ohio 1967) (adopting aggregate contacts theory but holding that, in absence of federal statute providing for service upon an alien corporation, state long-arm statute will control, thereby requiring an analysis of contacts with the forum state).

3. Service of Process

A federal court's power to exercise authority over the parties is limited not only by Constitutional considerations, but also by the means granted by statute for securing the parties' attendance. In the case of a typical corporate defendant, Section 12 of the Clayton Act authorizes service of process "in the district of which it is an inhabitant, or wherever it may be found."[138] Thus, Section 12 authorizes extraterritorial service of process;[139] in *Hoffman Motors Corp. v. Alfa Romeo, SpA*, this authorization was held to permit service of process upon an alien corporation at its headquarters abroad.[140]

Under Rule 4 of the Federal Rules of Civil Procedure, extraterritorial service of process upon individuals (as well as corporations) is permitted when authorized by a statute or court rule of the state in which the district court sits.[141] Most states have so-called "long-arm" statutes that permit service abroad.[142]

Similarly, the specific means by which process may be served upon alien individuals or corporations abroad may be selected from among those provided by the laws of the state in which the district court is sitting.[143] Typically, such statutes permit service by registered mail addressed to an alien at his residence or principal place of

---

138. 15 U.S.C. § 22 (1988). There is authority suggesting that the authorization of service of process under § 12 is limited to cases where venue is established under that section or another venue statute. *See* Go-Video, Inc. v. Akai Elec. Co., 885 F.2d 1406 (9th Cir. 1989) (service of process may be effectuated under § 12 although venue is proper under 28 U.S.C. § 1391(d)); General Elec. Co. v. Bucyrus-Erie Co., 550 F. Supp. 1037, 1042 (S.D.N.Y. 1982); Scriptomatic, Inc. v. Agfa-Gevaert, Inc., 1973-1 Trade Cas. (CCH) ¶ 74,594, at 94,632 (S.D.N.Y. 1973); *cf.* Goldlawr, Inc. v. Heiman, 288 F.2d 579, 581 (2d Cir. 1961), *rev'd on other grounds*, 369 U.S. 463 (1963).

139. *See, e.g.*, Black v. Acme Mkts., 564 F.2d 681 (5th Cir. 1977); C.C.P. Corp. v. Wynn Oil Co., 354 F. Supp. 1275 (N.D. Ill. 1973); Luria Steel & Trading Corp. v. Ogden Corp., 327 F. Supp. 1345 (E.D. Pa. 1971); Goldlawr, Inc. v. Shubert, 169 F. Supp. 677 (E.D. Pa. 1958), *aff'd*, 276 F.2d 614 (3d Cir. 1960).

140. 244 F. Supp. 70, 79-80 (S.D.N.Y. 1965); *accord* Intermountain Ford Tractor Sales Co. v. Massey-Ferguson, Ltd., 210 F. Supp. 930, 939 (D. Utah 1962), *aff'd per curiam*, 325 F.2d 713 (10th Cir. 1963), *cert. denied*, 377 U.S. 931 (1964); *see also* Omni Capital Int'l v. Rudolf Wolff & Co., 484 U.S. 97 (1987) (in a case arising under the Commodity Exchange Act, the Court held that statutory limits on service of process in federal question cases must be observed, and that extraterritorial service of process is improper where not specifically authorized by statute).

141. FED. R. CIV. P. 4(e); *see, e.g.*, Meaamaile v. American Samoa, 550 F. Supp. 1227, 1231 (D. Haw. 1982) (complaint dismissed where no compliance with state's long-arm requirements).

142. *E.g.*, Uniform Interstate and International Procedure Act, § 1.03, 13 U.L.A. 355, 361-62 (1986) (adopted by six jurisdictions); *see* Engine Specialties, Inc. v. Bombardier Ltd., 454 F. 2d 527 (1st Cir. 1972); Fisons Ltd. v. United States, 458 F.2d 1241 (7th Cir.), *cert. denied*, 405 U.S. 1041 (1972); Meat Sys. Corp. v. Ben Langel-Mol, Inc., 410 F. Supp. 231 (S.D.N.Y. 1976).

143. *See* Black v. Acme Mkts., 564 F.2d 681, 685 (5th Cir. 1977); Chrysler Corp. v. General Motors Corp., 589 F. Supp. 1182, 1206 (D.D.C. 1984). However, the Convention on the Service Abroad of Judicial and Extrajudicial Documents in Civil or Commercial Matters, *done* Nov. 15, 1965, 20 U.S.T. 361, T.I.A.S. No. 6638, *reprinted in* 28 U.S.C.A. FED. R. CIV. P. 4, at 210 (1992), may limit the means of service available in certain countries. *See* Harris v. Browning-Ferris Indus., Chem. Servs., 100 F.R.D. 775, 777 (M.D. La. 1984) (service upon German corporation by direct mail pursuant to Louisiana long arm statute inadequate where Federal Republic of Germany had specifically objected to direct mail service pursuant to Hague Service Convention); Richardson v. Volkswagenwerk, AG, 552 F. Supp. 73, 78-79 (W.D. Mo. 1982); *cf.* Vorhees v. Fischer & Krecke, 697 F.2d 574 (4th Cir. 1983); Zisman v. Sieger, 106 F.R.D. 194, 199 (N.D. Ill. 1985) (service upon Japanese corporation by direct mail not contrary to Hague Service Convention as entered into by Japan).

business overseas or by personal service there.[144]   In addition, where service abroad is authorized by federal or state law, Rule 4(i) provides a number of possible alternative means of effecting it, including any means prescribed by the law of the foreign country in which service is to be made, letters rogatory, personal service, mail dispatched by the clerk of the court (signed receipt required), or as ordered by the court.[145]

While the Hague Service Convention provides for certain methods of service, the Supreme Court has held that state long-arm statutes were not superseded by the Convention, and that when state law does not define the applicable method of serving process as requiring the transmittal of documents abroad, the Convention does not apply.[146]

Finally, the activities of the subsidiary of a foreign parent in a district may support the conclusion that the parent is "found" in that district, within the meaning of Section 12, or that the subsidiary is acting as the parent's general agent, within the meaning of Rule 4(d)(3).[147]   If either conclusion is drawn, service of process upon the parent at the subsidiary's offices would be effective.   In other courts, the multinational character of corporate defendants has been considered as a factor

---

144.   *See, e.g., Hoffman Motors*, 244 F. Supp. at 78-80.

145.   *See id.* at 79-80; Sabre Farms v. Bergendahl, 103 F.R.D. 8 (D. Or. 1984) (service of process on individual by publication in two Australian cities per order of court; Rule 4(i)(1)(E)); *Harris*, 100 F.R.D. at 778 (provisions of Rule 4(i) intended to cover those instances where service in a foreign country is not prohibited by an international treaty). The Advisory Committee's Notes to the 1963 amendment of Rule 4(i) explain that "the authority for effecting foreign service must be found in a statute of the United States or a statute or rule of court of the state in which the district court is held."

    Service of process on foreign states is authorized in 28 U.S.C. § 1608(a) (1988), and may be made, among other ways, by having the court clerk mail a translated copy of a complaint, signed receipt required.

146.   Volkswagenwerk Aktiengesellschaft v. Schlunk, 486 U.S. 694 (1988); *cf.* SEC v. International Swiss Inv. Corp., 895 F.2d 1272, 1275 n.3 (9th Cir. 1990) (refusing to apply the Inter-American Convention on Letters Rogatory to a case that arose before its ratification, and declining to decide whether the subsequently ratified treaty superseded the Federal Rules of Civil Procedure with respect to foreign service of process).

147.   Volkswagenwerk Aktiengesellschaft v. Schlunk, 486 U.S. 694 (1988) (Hague Service Convention need not be used to serve process on a foreign corporation when service can be made on a U.S. subsidiary with a sufficiently close relationship to overseas parent); United States v. Scophony Corp., 333 U.S. 795 (1948); Lamb v. Volkswagenwerk Aktiengesellschaft, 104 F.R.D. 95, 97-101 (S.D. Fla. 1985) (control exercised by German parent corporation over wholly-owned American subsidiary sufficient basis for finding that parent transacted business in Florida or that subsidiary acted as parent's agent; objection of Federal Republic of Germany to direct mail service pursuant to Hague Service Convention inapplicable when service accomplished upon alter ego within United States); *Zisman*, 106 F.R.D. at 199-200 (service on local agent of foreign defendant; Hague Service Convention inapplicable when service accomplished within United States); Zenith Radio Corp. v. Matsushita Elec. Indus. Co., 402 F. Supp. 244 (E.D. Pa. 1975); *In re* Siemens & Halske AG, 155 F. Supp. 897 (S.D.N.Y. 1957); *In re* Grand Jury Subpoena Duces Tecum Addressed to Canadian Int'l Paper Co., 72 F. Supp. 1013 (S.D.N.Y. 1947). *But cf.* Southmark Corp. v. Life Investors, Inc., 851 F.2d 763, 773-74 (5th Cir. 1988) ("where wholly-owned subsidiary is operated as a distinct corporation, its contacts with the forum cannot be imputed to the parent"); FDIC v. British-American Corp., 726 F. Supp. 622, 629-30 (E.D.N.C. 1989) (presence of wholly-owned subsidiary does not definitively establish that the foreign parent corporation is under forum's jurisdiction); Williams v. Canon, Inc., 432 F. Supp. 376, 379-80 (C.D. Cal. 1977) (venue not established as to the parent merely by allegation that it participated in conspiracy with its subsidiaries).

relevant to the determination of the "convenience" prong of the *International Shoe* due process test.[148]

D. Discovery and the Conduct of Litigation in Foreign Commerce Cases

1. *Discovery Outside the United States*

American courts ordering discovery abroad or otherwise ordering or prohibiting conduct abroad affecting the conduct of litigation in the United States, often encounter conflicts with laws of foreign nations.[149] Extraterritorial application of U.S. discovery laws has given rise to considerable friction among nations.[150]

a. Procedures Under U.S. Law for Obtaining Documents Located Abroad

Rule 34 of the Federal Rules of Civil Procedure provides that when documents sought are in the "possession, custody, or control" of a party to the action, and the court has jurisdiction over the party, the location of the documents is not determina-

---

148. *See, e.g.*, Centronics Data Computer Corp. v. Mannesmann, AG, 432 F. Supp. 659, 664 (D.N.H. 1977) ("where an alien defendant is sued by an American plaintiff . . . and that there is no other forum in which to litigate the claim should be taken into consideration for purposes of determining whether a finding of jurisdiction meets the requisite constitutional standards of fair play").

149. A British court enjoined a British corporation from pursuing a U.S. antitrust action against two British defendants. British Airways Bd. v. Laker Airways (C.A. July 26, 1983), *reported in* 45 ANTITRUST & TRADE REG. REP. (BNA) 248 (Aug. 18, 1983). The decision was based in part on, and upheld, the English Protection of Trading Interests Act, which prohibited the British defendants from producing certain documents and information in the U.S. proceeding. *See* Protection of Trading Interests Act, *reprinted in* ANTITRUST & TRADE REG. Rep. (BNA) No. 959 (Apr. 10, 1980). The U.S. court responded to the British court's injunction by enjoining the other defendants "from taking any action in a foreign forum that would impair or interfere with the jurisdiction of this Court." Laker Airways v. Pan Am. World Airways, 559 F. Supp. 1124, 1139 (D.D.C. 1983), *aff'd sub nom.* Laker Airways v. Sabena, Belgian World Airlines, 731 F.2d 909, 921-26 (D.C. Cir. 1984) (stating that where two or more states have legitimate interests in a controversy, jurisdiction is not mutually exclusive; under principles of international law, territoriality and nationality often give rise to concurrent jurisdiction). The House of Lords discharged the British court's injunction on its appeal. British Airways Bd. v. Laker Airways Ltd., [1984] 3 W.L.R. 413, *reprinted in* 23 I.L.M. 727 (July 19, 1984). *But cf.* American Home Assurance Co. v. Insurance Corp. of Ireland, 603 F. Supp. 636, 642-43 (S.D.N.Y 1984) (enjoining litigants from pursuing simultaneous contests in foreign forum).

In another case involving an injunction by an English court against the prosecution of an antitrust claim in a U.S. court, the English Court of Appeals ruled that, although the complaint of an English person against an English subsidiary of an American company arising out of a contract in England had been properly enjoined, an amended complaint naming only the American parent should be allowed to proceed. Smith Kline & French Labs v. Bloch, The Times (C.A. Nov. 13, 1984).

150. RESTATEMENT (THIRD) OF THE FOREIGN RELATIONS LAW OF THE UNITED STATES § 442 reporter's note 1 (1987). Several countries have enacted legislation to restrict, or prohibit altogether, persons or corporations under their control from complying with foreign discovery orders. *See supra* note 11; *infra* note 178 and accompanying text.

tive of whether they must be produced.[151] The position of the United States is that persons who do business in the United States or otherwise bring themselves within the jurisdiction of United States courts are subject to the burdens as well as the benefits of United States law, including the laws on discovery.[152] However, the national interests of the State in which the documents are kept may affect a court's decision whether to exercise its power to order production or penalize nonproduction. Thus, before a court issues an order compelling discovery, it may

---

151. *See In re* Grand Jury Proceedings Bank of Nova Scotia, 740 F.2d 817, 828 n.17 (11th Cir. 1984) (law of situs of documents does not necessarily control in cases of conflict), *cert. denied*, 469 U.S. 1106 (1985); *In re* Marc Rich & Co., 707 F.2d 663, 667 (2d Cir.) *cert. denied*, 463 U.S. 1215 (1983); Cooper Indus. v. British Aerospace, Inc., 102 F.R.D. 918, 920 (S.D.N.Y. 1984); *In re* Uranium Antitrust Litig., 480 F. Supp. 1138, 1144 (N.D. Ill. 1979) (Marshall, J.); *In re* Grand Jury Subpoenas Duces Tecum Addressed to Canadian Int'l Paper Co., 72 F. Supp. 1013, 1029 (S.D.N.Y. 1947).

But note that § 442 of the RESTATEMENT (THIRD) OF THE FOREIGN RELATIONS LAW OF THE UNITED STATES (1987) would require discovery requests for documents or information located abroad to be issued by a court or agency authorized by statute or rule of court, not just a private party, and would impose a stricter relevancy test than is applicable to domestic discovery. The Attorney General and the Assistant Attorney General in charge of the Antitrust Division of the Justice Department are authorized by statute to issue civil investigative demands or subpoenas to persons outside the United States. Antitrust Civil Process Act, 15 U.S.C. § 1312(d)(2) (1988).

No general test of "possession, custody, or control" emerges from the case law. In foreign commerce cases, the most common dispute is whether a court may order a U.S. corporation to produce documents in the hands of a foreign affiliate. Courts have ordered production from controlled foreign subsidiaries of American corporations. *See, e.g., In re* Uranium Antitrust Litig., 480 F. Supp. 1138, 1144-45 (N.D. Ill. 1979) (ordering production from subsidiaries located in Australia, South Africa, Switzerland and Canada); *In re* Investigation of World Arrangements with Relation to the Prod., Transp., Ref. & Distrib. of Petroleum, 13 F.R.D. 280, 285 (D.D.C. 1952) (stating that parent corporations, having the power to control the directors of their subsidiaries, have the control necessary to secure documents). Where the U.S. corporation is a subsidiary of a foreign corporation, however, the courts have split on whether the American company controls the foreign parent for Rule 34 purposes. *Compare In re* Uranium Antitrust Litig., 480 F. Supp. 1138, 1145 (N.D. Ill. 1979) (stating that the test of control is less clear when an order is directed to a U.S. subsidiary of a foreign corporation, and rests finally on questions of fact) *with* United States v. Ciba Corp., 1972 Trade Cas. (CCH) ¶ 74,026, at 92,253-54 (D.N.J. 1971) (requiring corporation to make a good faith attempt to secure pertinent material in the hands of its foreign parent); *see also In re* Messerschmitt Bolkow Blohm GmbH, 757 F.2d 729, 733-334 (5th Cir. 1985) (no evidence that subsidiary was a sham or an alter ego or that it had custody or control of the documents), *cert. granted sub nom.* Messerschmitt Bolkow Blohm GmbH v. Walker, 475 U.S. 1118 (1986), *cert. granted and decision vacated*, 483 U.S. 1002 (1987); Laker Airways v. Pan Am. World Airways, 607 F. Supp. 324 (S.D.N.Y. 1985) (with respect to nonparties, documents regularly maintained in the United Kingdom could not be obtained by serving a U.S. branch office that had no connection with the matters in issue); Compagnie Française d'Assurance Pour le Commerce Exterieur v. Phillips Petroleum Corp., 105 F.R.D. 16, 33-35 (S.D.N.Y. 1984) (where agency of French government is a plaintiff and is affirmatively seeking the benefit of U.S. law, it is appropriate to require discovery of documents in the possession of other agencies of French government).

152. RESTATEMENT (THIRD) OF THE FOREIGN RELATIONS LAW OF THE UNITED STATES § 442 reporter's note 1 (1987); *see also* United States v. Germann, 370 F.2d 1019, 1023 (2d Cir. 1967) ("[A]nyone within the jurisdiction of the Court may be subpoenaed . . . . It makes no difference where he is resident or of what country he is a citizen."); *cf.* Commodity Futures Trading Comm'n v. Nahas, 738 F.2d 487, 493-95 (D.C. Cir. 1984) (in the absence of clear congressional direction to the contrary, statute authorizing court to enforce investigational subpoenas by the CFTC did not authorize enforcement of subpoena served on foreign citizen in foreign country in contravention of principles of international law).

evaluate the importance of the requested discovery, the degree of specificity of the request, the country of origin of the requested information, the availability of an alternative means of obtaining the requested information, and the extent to which important interests of the United States or a foreign country would be undermined by compliance or noncompliance.[153]

United States courts may also order production of documents in the possession of nonparties in the United States.[154] Moreover, Section 1783 of the Judicial Code authorizes service of subpoenas upon nonparties located abroad, if they are U.S. citizens or residents.[155]

In addition, courts may obtain documents located abroad by letters rogatory.[156] When documents are in the possession of a party, or a nonparty that can be served with a subpoena under Rule 45, a letter rogatory offers an additional method for obtaining the documents.[157] A letter rogatory is the only method available for obtaining documents from nonparties who cannot be served with subpoenas. Federal Rule 28(b) authorizes the District Court to issue a letter rogatory on the request of a party to the action. The letter may be transmitted directly to the foreign tribunal or it may be sent via the Department of State.[158]

---

153. Societe Nationale Industrielle Aerospatiale v. United States District Court, 482 U.S. 522, 546 (1987) (cautioning courts to exercise "special vigilance" to protect foreign litigants against undue burden and intrusiveness); *see also* RESTATEMENT (THIRD) OF THE FOREIGN RELATIONS LAW OF THE UNITED STATES § 442(1)(c) (1987); *cf.* United States v. First Nat'l City Bank, 396 F.2d 897, 901-03 (2d Cir. 1968) (affirming validity of subpoena requiring a New York bank to produce documents located at its branch in Frankfurt pursuant to the conclusion that the United States' interest in antitrust enforcement outweighed the German bank secrecy doctrine).

154. Discovery from nonparties is governed by Federal Rule of Civil Procedure 45, which sets out the rule for the issuance and service of a subpoena.

155. 28 U.S.C. § 1783(a) (1988) provides that:

A court of the United States may order the issuance of a subpoena requiring the appearance as a witness before it, or before a person or body designated by it, of a national or resident of the United States who is in a foreign country, or requiring the production of a specified document or other thing by him, if the court finds that particular testimony or the production of the document or other thing by him is necessary in the interest of justice, and, in other than a criminal action or proceeding, if the court finds, in addition, that it is not possible to obtain his testimony in admissible form without his personal appearance or to obtain the production of the document or other thing in any other manner.

156. A letter rogatory is:

the medium, in effect, whereby one country, speaking through one of its courts, requests another country, acting through its own courts and by methods of court procedure peculiar thereto and entirely within the latter's control, to assist the administration of justice in the former country; such request being made, and being usually granted, by reason of the comity existing between nations in ordinary peaceful times.

Tiedemann v. The Signe, 37 F. Supp. 819, 820 (E.D. La. 1941).

157. Thus, for example, where a party sought enforcement of a subpoena for bank records located in Canada and the parties differed on whether Canadian bank secrecy laws barred disclosure of the documents, the Second Circuit directed the party seeking the documents to proceed by letter rogatory in order to allow a Canadian court to decide the matter. Ings v. Ferguson, 282 F.2d 149 (2d Cir. 1960).

158. 28 U.S.C. § 1781 (1988). Department of State regulations governing letters rogatory and related matters are set forth in 22 C.F.R. § 92 (1991). With respect to countries that are signatories to the Hague Evidence Convention, letters of request are sent not to the foreign tribunal but to a Central Authority designated by each signatory. The Central Authority will transmit the request to the judicial authority competent to execute it. Hague Convention on the Taking of Evidence Abroad in Civil or Commercial Matters (Hague Evidence Convention), art. 2, *done* Mar. 18, 1970,

The Hague Convention on the Taking of Evidence Abroad in Civil or Commercial Matters (Hague Evidence Convention) expressly provides for the use of letters rogatory, which it terms "letters of request." Twenty-one countries, including the United States, are parties to the Convention.[159] Chapter 1 of the Convention sets out the procedures for issuing and executing letters of request.[160] Although the Convention provides procedures for obtaining evidence abroad, the current state of practice under the convention varies from country to country.[161]

The Convention's provisions for letters of request are somewhat tempered by several provisions that limit its usefulness in lending access to material for use in

---

23 U.S.T. 2555, T.I.A.S. No. 7444, *reprinted in* 28 U.S.C.A. § 1781 (1991 Supp.) *and in* MARTINDALE HUBBELL INTERNATIONAL LAW DIGESTS at IC-15 (1992) (entered into force for the United States Oct. 7, 1972).

159.   *Id.* The signatories are: Argentina, Barbados, Cyprus, Czechoslovakia, Denmark, Finland, France, Federal Republic of Germany, Israel, Italy, Luxembourg, Mexico, Monaco, Netherlands, Norway, Portugal, Singapore, Spain, Sweden, United Kingdom, and the United States. The Hague Evidence Convention is the latest in a series of multilateral treaties governing the collection of evidence abroad. The earlier two treaties, to which the United States is not a party, essentially codified existing international practice at the time. Because so few countries have acceded to the latest treaty, the earlier two are still important in international practice. They are: Convention Relating to Civil Procedure, *ratified* Apr. 24, 1909, 99 BRITISH AND FOREIGN STATE PAPERS 990 (1905); Hague Convention of 1954, 286 U.N.T.S. 266 (1958).

160.   The issuing country must indicate in the letter the nature of the action for which the evidence is sought, the parties to the action and whether any documents are sought. The country receiving the letter "shall apply the appropriate measures of compulsion in the instances and to the same extent as are provided by its internal law" for enforcing the letter. Hague Evidence Convention, *supra* note 158, art. 10.

161.   For example, because France views international judicial assistance as being rendered by courts for the benefit of other courts, it is preferable to send letters of request to the French Central Authority directly from the U.S. court, rather than from U.S. or local counsel. The Central Authority sends letters of request to the appropriate Ministère Publique, who directs the letter to the competent court. Upon authorization of the French judge, foreign counsel, their clients, and the U.S. judge may attend the execution proceedings and ask questions. French Civil Code [C. Pr. Civ.] art. 739. The parties or the Ministère Publique may appeal any adverse decision on execution to the Court of Appeals.

     In making requests of the United Kingdom, it is important to stress that the evidence is for use at trial. The English Central Authority forwards letters of request to a master of the Queens Bench Division of the High Court, who determines whether it is in accord with the Convention and the English Evidence (Proceedings in Other Jurisdictions) Act of 1975. The master, upon finding the request proper, will issue a summons to the witness to appear with the requested documents. Rules of the Supreme Court [R.S.C.] Order 70, § 2. The witness may in turn challenge the issuance of an order at the trial court level, then to the Court of Appeals and finally to the House of Lords. Judicial personnel only (as opposed to parties) of the requesting state may attend the execution of the letter of request. English courts have adopted a more liberal approach in dealing with requests for the taking of oral evidence than with requests for production of documents.

     The Federal Republic of Germany has designated eleven Central Authorities; the letter of request must be sent to the appropriate Authority. The issuing court should send the letter directly, because West German courts have criticized transmission from local counsel as contrary to Convention procedures. The Central Authority, which is always a Ministry of Justice, makes an initial review, and may request briefs and an informal hearing of the parties. The Ministry forwards approved requests to the local district court for execution. Members of the requesting court, including counsel, may be present for the execution, and may question and cross-examine the witnesses. Documentary evidence may not yet be obtained from Federal Republic of Germany under the Convention.

litigation in the United States. Most significant is Article 23 of the Convention, which permits a contracting state to declare that it will not execute letters of request that seek to obtain "pre-trial discovery of documents as known in Common Law countries."[162]   Of the twenty-one signatories, only Barbados, Cyprus, Czechoslovakia, Israel, and the United States have not issued such a declaration.[163] The tendency to make Article 23 declarations apparently arose from a widespread misunderstanding that American lawyers might seek, prior to the filing of a case, to determine whether evidence exists that could support the filing of an action.[164] Notwithstanding their Article 23 declarations, many contracting states will execute carefully drafted, specific document requests, particularly when the letter of request specifies that the requested documents are relevant to matters that will be in issue at trial. Indeed, after the civil law countries became aware that American discovery typically occurs only in a pending action, several of the largest nations clarified their Article 23 declarations, making it clear that they will execute requests for specific and identified documents.[165] In addition, Article 23 only applies to letters of request seeking documents. Thus, requests for deposition discovery by letters of request are not restricted by Article 23. Moreover, pretrial discovery of documents may be sought through consular or commissioner channels from voluntary witnesses where the compulsory power of the foreign state is not needed.[166]

The Hague Evidence Convention also provides that the person from whom the testimony or material is sought may refuse to give evidence insofar as he may claim a privilege under the law of the state sending the letter or the law of the state where

---

162.   Hague Evidence Convention, *supra* note 158, art. 23.

163.   *Id.*

164.   REPORT ON THE WORK OF THE SPECIAL COMMISSION ON THE OPERATION OF THE CONVENTION OF 18 MARCH 1970 ON THE TAKING OF EVIDENCE ABROAD IN CIVIL OR COMMERCIAL MATTERS, 17 I.L.M. 1425, 1428 (1978); REPORT OF THE UNITED STATES DELEGATION TO THE SPECIAL COMMISSION ON THE OPERATION OF THE CONVENTION OF 18 MARCH 1970 ON THE TAKING OF EVIDENCE ABROAD IN CIVIL OR COMMERCIAL MATTERS, 17 I.L.M. 1417, 1421 (1978).

165.   For example, the United Kingdom declaration under Article 23 states that:

In accordance with Article 23 Her Majesty's Government declare that the United Kingdom will not execute Letters of Request issued for the purpose of obtaining pretrial discovery of documents. Her Majesty's Government further declare that Her Majesty's Government understand "Letters of Request issued for the purpose of obtaining pre-trial discovery of documents" for the purposes of the foregoing Declaration as including any Letter of Request which requires a person:

a. to state what documents relevant to the proceedings to which the Letter of Request relates are, or have been, in his possession, custody or power; or

b. to produce any documents other than particular documents specified in the Letter of Request as being documents appearing to the requested court to be, or to be likely to be, in his possession, custody or powers.

Hague Evidence Convention, *supra* note 158, art. 23. Singapore, The Netherlands, Sweden, Finland, Norway and Denmark have made similar modifications to their Article 23 declarations. France has recently modified its declaration to state that it will honor document requests which are "enumerated limitively in the Letter of Request and have a direct and precise link with the object of the procedure." *Id.* at 18. The various countries' declarations are reprinted in MARTINDALE-HUBBELL INTERNATIONAL LAW DIGESTS, at IC-18-25 (1992). The Federal Republic of Germany and Italy have ratified the Convention while making broad reservations under Article 23, but the Federal Republic of Germany is currently considering regulations which would limit the scope of its Article 23 reservation.

166.   Hague Evidence Convention, *supra* note 158, art. 2.

execution is sought. In addition, a country may declare that it will respect privileges and duties existing under the laws of other countries.[167] Finally, Article 12 states that a nation may refuse to execute a letter if it "considers that its sovereignty or security may be prejudiced thereby."[168]

Some foreign courts have relied on the Hague Evidence Convention's limitations on letters of request to deny discovery requests from U.S. courts. For example, in *Rio Tinto Corp. v. Westinghouse Electric Corp.*,[169] the House of Lords cited the Convention in denying enforcement of a letter of request presented by Westinghouse Electric Corp. in the *Uranium Antitrust Litigation*. Canadian courts have also relied on the Hague Convention in refusing to enforce letters of request seeking evidence concerning an alleged uranium cartel.[170]

In *Societe Nationale Industrielle Aerospatiale v. United States District Court*,[171] the Supreme Court held, by a vote of five to four, that the Hague Evidence Convention does not displace the Federal Rules of Civil Procedure in matters of foreign discovery, but provides an alternative or supplementary means of obtaining information located abroad.[172] The decision directed the lower courts to engage in a detailed comity analysis in order to determine whether to order use of Convention procedures or to conduct discovery under the Federal Rules of Civil Procedure. Factors considered in the analysis include: (a) the competing interests of the governments involved (e.g., the U.S. interest in full discovery versus foreign principles of judicial sovereignty, and the interest of all signatories in maintaining a smoothly functioning international legal system); (b) the likelihood that Convention procedures would be effective; (c) the intrusiveness of the discovery requests (e.g., whether the requests seek trade secrets or matters affecting the national defense of a foreign sovereign); (d) the origin of the information being sought; (e) the costs of transporting the witnesses, documents, or other evidence to the United States; (f) the skill with which the requests are drafted (i.e., are they clear, specific, and limited to obtaining relevant information?); (g) the importance to the litigation of the documents or information sought; and (h) the availability of alternative means of securing the information.[173]

The Supreme Court stated that "[t]he exact line between reasonableness and unreasonableness in each case must be drawn by the trial court, based on its knowledge of the case and of the claims and interests of the parties and the

---

167.   *Id.* art. 11.

168.   *Id.* art. 12.

169.   [1978] 2 W.L.R. 81 (House of Lords 1977).

170.   Gulf Oil Corp. v. Gulf Can. Ltd., [1980] 2 S.C.R. 39, 1980-1 Trade Cas. (CCH) ¶ 63,285; *In re* Westinghouse Elec. Corp., 16 Ont. 2d 273 (Sup. Ct. 1977).

171.   482 U.S. 522 (1987).

172.   *Id.* at 538. Before *Aerospatiale*, decisions ranged from those holding that the Hague Evidence Convention was the preferred means of conducting foreign discovery (*see, e.g.,* Compagnie Francaise d'Assurance Pour le Commerce Exterieur v. Phillips Petroleum Co., 105 F.R.D. 16, 26-36 (S.D.N.Y. 1984); TH. Goldschmidt AG v. Smith, 676 S.W.2d 443 (Tex. Ct. App. 1984) (requiring litigants to pursue Hague Evidence Convention procedures as a matter of first resort)), to those that held that such discovery should ordinarily be conducted under the Federal Rules of Civil Procedure. *See, e.g., In re* Anschuetz & Co., GmbH, 754 F.2d 602 (5th Cir. 1985), *vacated*, Anschuetz & Co., GmbH v. Mississippi River Bridge Auth., 483 U.S. 1002 (1987).

173.   *Aerospatiale*, 482 U.S. at 555-56.

governments whose statutes and policies they invoke."[174] The Court emphasized the importance of careful supervision of discovery requests propounded to foreign litigants, cautioning courts to exercise "special vigilance to protect [them] from the danger that unnecessary, or unduly burdensome, discovery may place them in a disadvantageous position."[175]

Lower courts interpreting *Aerospatiale* have reached inconsistent conclusions in deciding which party has the burden of persuasion on whether to apply Hague Evidence Convention procedures or the Federal Rules.[176] Opinions also diverge as to whether foreign defendants objecting to U.S. court jurisdiction over them are subject to discovery under the Federal Rules on that issue.[177]

b. FOREIGN LAWS REGULATING DISCOVERY ABROAD

Efforts by U.S. litigants to obtain discovery abroad may conflict with the laws or interests of the country where the material sought is located. Several countries have enacted statutes that limit the extent to which a corporation or person subject to its jurisdiction may comply with requests for information abroad. In some instances, the legislative history of these laws makes it clear that the primary reason for passage was to block U.S. discovery requests.[178]

Among the countries that have passed "blocking statutes" are Australia, Canada, England, France and South Africa. In addition, Ontario and Quebec have passed their own statutes. The statutes vary greatly in scope and application. Some may be waived by government consent, while others may not. Some block discovery of material relating to certain industries; others apply to all commercial information. The Business Records Protection Act of Ontario[179] and the Business Concerns Record Act of Quebec,[180] appear to bar absolutely the removal of any documents from businesses in these two provinces in response to any judicial order. South Africa's Protection of Business Act prohibits compliance with any request for information arising from any act or business carried on in or outside South Africa,

---

174.   *Id.* at 546.

175.   *Id.*

176.   *Compare* Hudson v. Hermann Pfauter GmbH & Co., 117 F.R.D. 33, 38 (N.D.N.Y. 1987) (ruling that "the burden should be placed on the party opposing the use of Convention procedures to demonstrate that those procedures would frustrate" the interests of domestic litigants in pursuing evidence) *with* Sandsend Financial Consultants v. Wood, 743 S.W.2d 364, 366 (Tex. Ct. App. 1988) (holding that the Hague Evidence Convention "is a permissive supplement to the Texas Rules of Civil Procedure . . . [and] it is within the trial court's discretion to determine whether the Hague Convention procedures should be used as a first resort") *and* Scarminach v. Goldwell GmbH, 531 N.Y.S.2d 188 (N.Y. Sup. Ct. 1988) (holding that a German company had the burden of requiring the plaintiff to use the Convention instead of state discovery rules).

177.   *Compare* Jenco v. Martech Int'l, Inc., Civ. No. 86-4229 (E.D. La. May 20, 1988) (holding that evidence on the jurisdictional question regarding a Norwegian defendant should be taken under the Hague Convention) *with* Rich v. Kis Cal., Inc., 121 F.R.D. 254 (M.D.N.C. 1988) (allowing discovery to proceed under the Federal Rules against a French company objecting to jurisdiction).

178.   This is reflected most clearly in the legislative history of the United Kingdom's Protection of Trading Interests Act, 1980, ch. 22, *reprinted in* ANTITRUST & TRADE REG. REP. (BNA) No. 959, at F-1 (Apr. 10, 1980). *See* 404 PARL. DEB. H.L. (5th ser.) 554-60 (1980) (remarks of Lord Mackay); 972 PARL. DEB., H.C. (5th ser.) 1533-38, 1546 (1979) (remarks of John Nott).

179.   ONT. REV. STAT., ch. 54 (1980). *But see* Re Inter-City Truck Lines (Canada), 133 D.L.R.3d 134 (Ont. H. Ct. J. 1982) (Ontario attorney general did not object to removal of photostats).

180.   QUE. REV. STAT., ch. 278 (1964).

unless the Minister of Economic Affairs gives permission to comply.[181]   Statutes like the United Kingdom's Protection of Trading Interests Act,[182] Australia's Foreign Proceedings (Excess of Jurisdiction) Act,[183] and Canada's Foreign Extraterritorial Measures Act[184] permit removal unless a government official prohibits it. In addition, French law prohibits a French citizen, a resident of France, a French company, or a company with an establishment in France from providing documents or information of "an economic, commercial, industrial, financial or technical nature which might threaten France's sovereignty, security or basic economic interest."[185]

c.   THE EFFECT OF FOREIGN LAWS AND COMITY CONSIDERATIONS
     ON U.S. DISCOVERY

Under U.S. law, the effect of a foreign nondisclosure law, or of other foreign interests in conflict with discovery, is decided on a case-by-case basis. The starting point is *Societe Internationale Pour Participations Industrielles et Commerciales, SA v. Rogers.*[186]   In that case, Swiss bank secrecy laws had prevented the plaintiff from fully complying with the defendant's document request under Rule 34 of the Federal Rules of Civil Procedure. The plaintiff had sought a waiver of the Swiss law and had been partially successful; nonetheless, the plaintiff was unable to produce all the documents sought. As a result, the district court granted defendant's motion under Rule 37 to dismiss the action with prejudice.

The Supreme Court reversed, stressing that the plaintiff's inability to produce the documents was "fostered neither by its own conduct nor by circumstances within its control."[187]   Rule 37 should not be construed as authorizing dismissal, the court said, where "noncompliance . . . has been due to inability, and not to willfulness, bad faith, or any fault of petitioner."[188]   However, the Court stated that the plaintiff should not be allowed to benefit from nonproduction, and that on remand the district court possessed wide discretion, including the power to draw inferences adverse to plaintiff, to fashion an appropriate remedy.

In *Societe Internationale*, the Court drew a distinction between the power to order production in the face of a foreign nondisclosure law — which had been properly exercised — and the appropriate sanctions to apply for noncompliance. The Court found that the existence of the foreign law barring disclosure, and plaintiff's attempt

---

181.   Protection of Business Act No. 99 of 1978, § 1.
182.   Protection of Trading Interests Act of 1980, ch. 11, § 2, *reprinted in* ANTITRUST & TRADE REG. REP. (BNA) No. 959, at F-1 (Apr. 10, 1980).
183.   Foreign Proceedings (Excess of Jurisdiction) Act of 1984, No. 3, Austl. Acts (1984), *reprinted in* 23 I.L.M. 1038 (1984). The U.S. and several other governments have entered into antitrust cooperation agreements. *See* Subpart E.2 of this chapter.
184.   Foreign Extraterritorial Measures Act § 3, Can. Stat. 1984, ch. 49 (Dec. 21, 1984).
185.   Law concerning the Communication of Economic, Commercial, Industrial, Financial or Technical Documents or Information Law No. 80-538, 1980 Journal Officiel de la République Française [J.O.] 1799 (July 16, 1980). Other countries with nondisclosure laws include: Switzerland, STGB, CP, Cod. Pen. Art. 273 (disclosure of business or manufacturing secret prohibited except where all those with interest consent to waiver); and the Netherlands, Act of June 28, 1956, art. 39, S&G, 401, *as amended by* Act of July 16, 1958, S&G 413.
186.   357 U.S. 197 (1957).
187.   *Id.* at 211.
188.   *Id.* at 212 (footnote omitted).

to have it waived, "can hardly affect the fact of noncompliance and are relevant only to the path which the District Court might follow in dealing with petitioner's failure to comply."[189] This language led some courts to conclude that considerations of international comity are not relevant until the sanctions phase of the discovery proceeding.[190] That interpretation, however, does not appear to survive *Societe Nationale Industrielle Aerospatiale v. United States District Court*.[191]

Thus, in general, at some stage of the proceedings prior to ordering sanctions for noncompliance with the discovery order, most courts will consider a range of comity factors similar to those set forth in Section 437 of the *Restatement (Third) of the*

---

189. *Id.* at 208.

190. *See, e.g.,* Arthur Andersen & Co. v. Finesilver, 546 F.2d 338, 342 (10th Cir. 1976) (*Societe* "only indicates that the foreign law question goes to the imposition of a sanction for noncompliance with local law."), *cert. denied*, 429 U.S. 1096 (1977); Lasky v. Continental Prods. Corp., 569 F. Supp. 1227, 1228-29 (E.D. Pa. 1983) (stating in dictum that "while a court may have the power to order actions which are in violation of the laws of a foreign sovereign, the court must weigh considerations of international comity in determining . . . sanctions").

191. 482 U.S. 522, 545-46 (1987) (requiring courts to supervise discovery proceedings closely in accordance with the demands of comity). Although the Supreme Court did not articulate specific rules in *Aerospatiale* to guide this analysis, numerous courts, before and after *Aerospatiale*, had in fact engaged in a comity analysis in deciding whether to order production in the first instance. *See In re* Grand Jury Proceedings Bank of Nova Scotia, 740 F.2d 817, 826-29 (11th Cir. 1984) (in affirming contempt fine, court approved district court's balancing of factors in § 40 of the RESTATEMENT (SECOND) OF THE FOREIGN RELATIONS LAW OF THE UNITED STATES to determine whether subpoena enforcement was proper), *cert. denied*, 469 U.S. 1106 (1985); Minpeco, SA v. Conticommodity Servs., 116 F.R.D. 517, 522 (S.D.N.Y.) (comity analysis performed before deciding whether to order discovery barred by Swiss secrecy laws), *aff'd sub nom.* Korwek v. Hunt, 827 F.2d 874 (2d Cir. 1987); Garpeg Ltd. v. United States, 588 F. Supp. 1237 (S.D.N.Y. 1984) (refusing to quash IRS summons after balancing respective interests of each state); United States v. Chase Manhattan Bank, NA, 584 F. Supp. 1080, 1085-87 (S.D.N.Y. 1984) (enforcing IRS summons after examining RESTATEMENT (SECOND) § 40 factors); Garpeg, Ltd. v. United States, 583 F. Supp. 789 (S.D.N.Y. 1984) (same) (noting that factors other than those in § 40, suggested by the RESTATEMENT (REVISED), while relevant, have not yet been adopted by Second Circuit); Soletanche & Rodio, Inc. v. Brown & Lambrecht Earth Movers, Inc., 99 F.R.D. 269 (N.D. Ill. 1983) (declining to vacate order compelling answers to interrogatories, after balancing § 40 factors); *In re* Uranium Antitrust Litig., 480 F. Supp. 1138, 1148 (N.D. Ill. 1979) (issuance of production order held to be a "discretionary" act which, under *Société*, should be determined primarily by three factors: the importance of the U.S. statutes underlying plaintiff's claims; the importance of the information sought to the prosecution of such claims; and the degree of flexibility in the foreign nation's nondisclosure laws – all other considerations of comity deferred for sanctions hearing); *see also* Trade Dev. Bank v. Continental Ins. Co., 469 F.2d 35, 41-42 (2d Cir. 1972) (affirming decision not to order Swiss bank to seek customers' waivers of bank secrecy laws); United States v. First Nat'l City Bank, 396 F.2d 897, 904-05 (2d Cir. 1968) (potential civil liability in Germany for production of documents did not justify disobeying subpoena when German government did not oppose compliance); Application of Chase Manhattan Bank, 297 F.2d 611 (2d Cir. 1962); Ings v. Ferguson, 282 F.2d 149, 152-53 (2d Cir. 1960) (declining to call for production of bank records located in Canada when bank was merely a witness); Graco, Inc. v. Kremlin, Inc., 101 F.R.D. 503, 515 (N.D. Ill. 1984) (foreign state's flexibility should be considered at the sanctions stage); American Indus. Contracting, Inc. v. Johns-Manville Corp., 326 F. Supp. 879, 880 (W.D. Pa. 1971) (holding that notwithstanding Canadian blocking statute U.S. public policy demanded answers to interrogatories concerning Canadian subsidiaries of U.S. corporation when the subsidiaries sold their products in the United States).

Foreign Relations Law of the United States.[192]   When only the absence of permission by foreign authorities interferes with discovery, courts will often expect persons from whom discovery is sought to make a good faith effort to secure permission.[193]   When foreign secrecy laws require the consent by a subject of a

---

192.   RESTATEMENT (THIRD) OF THE FOREIGN RELATIONS LAW OF THE UNITED STATES § 437 (1987) would require a court to evaluate several factors before issuing an order compelling discovery, such as the importance of the information to the litigation, the degree of specificity of the request, the availability of alternative means of securing the information, and the interests of the countries involved. Where foreign law prohibits compliance with the discovery request, the party to whom the discovery is directed would be expected to make a good faith effort to secure permission for the discovery. When the party makes a good faith effort, the only sanction the RESTATEMENT would allow a court to consider for noncompliance is the entry of adverse fact findings.

See, e.g., United States v. Vetco Inc., 644 F.2d 1324, 1330 (9th Cir.) ("courts must balance competing interests in determining whether foreign illegality ought to preclude enforcement of an IRS summons") (summons enforced), cert. denied, 454 U.S. 1098 (1981); In re Westinghouse Elec. Corp. Uranium Contracts Litig., 563 F.2d 992, 997 (10th Cir. 1977) (contempt citation vacated); In re Grand Jury Proceedings, United States v. Field, 532 F.2d 404, 407 (5th Cir.), cert. denied, 429 U.S. 940 (1976); SEC v. Banca Della Svizzera Italiana, 92 F.R.D. 111 (S.D.N.Y. 1981) (discovery ordered). The case for sanctions is particularly strong where the nonproducing party has acted in bad faith, deliberately seeking a nondisclosure order or otherwise attempting to impede the discovery process. See General Atomic Co. v. Exxon Nuclear Co., 90 F.R.D. 290, 296 (S.D. Cal. 1981) (Infante, Mag.) (sanctions ordered where crucial documents were located only in Canada through the fault of defendant, to the prejudice of plaintiff); United Nuclear Corp. v. General Atomic Co., 96 N.M. 155, 629 P.2d 231 (1980), appeal dismissed, 451 U.S. 901 (1981); cf. In re Sealed Case, 825 F.2d 494 (D.C. Cir.) (reversing civil contempt order to grand jury witness where refusal to produce documents located in a foreign country would violate that country's laws), cert. denied, 484 U.S. 963 (1987); Sharon v. Time, Inc., 599 F. Supp. 538, 558-60 (S.D.N.Y. 1984) (plaintiff would not be precluded from testifying at trial about certain subjects in light of the extent and significance of the testimony given in discovery, the lesser importance of the testimony withheld, and the absence of prejudice to the defendant). But cf. In re Grand Jury Proceedings Bank of Nova Scotia, 740 F.2d 817, 828-29 (11th Cir. 1984) (comity factors considered, but court notes that it is not unfair for bank (which was not a target of the grand jury investigation) to have to choose between the conflicting commands of two sovereigns because it accepted that risk by electing to do business in numerous foreign host countries), cert. denied, 469 U.S. 1106 (1985); In re Marc Rich & Co., 736 F.2d 864 (2d Cir. 1984) (consideration of foreign secrecy law barred by prior agreement of parties; however, contemnor would still be permitted to show that it was physically impossible to comply with grand jury subpoena because Swiss government had seized documents); United States v. Chase Manhattan Bank, 590 F. Supp. 1160 (S.D.N.Y. 1984) (good faith and comity had been considered at enforcement stage and were not relevant to contempt sanctions); Garpeg, Ltd. v. United States, 588 F. Supp. 1240 (S.D.N.Y. 1984).

193.   See In re Grand Jury Proceedings, 691 F.2d 1384 (11th Cir. 1982) (contempt order affirmed where no good faith effort to comply), cert. denied, 462 U.S. 1119 (1983) ; United States v. First Nat'l Bank of Chicago, 699 F.2d 341 (7th Cir. 1983) (order enforcing IRS summons reversed, but trial court directed to consider order requiring good faith effort); Graco, Inc., 101 F.R.D. at 516 (ordering compliance with certain discovery requests and noting that potential sanctions may depend on whether party made reasonable attempt to secure permission); Soletanche, 99 F.R.D. at 271 (compulsion order required party to seek waiver); Compagnie Francaise d'Assurance Pour le Commerce Exterieur v. Phillips Petroleum Co., No. 81 Civ. 4463-CLB, slip op. at 13-14 (S.D.N.Y. Jan. 23, 1983), summarized in Compagnie Francaise d'Assurance Pour le Commerce Exterieur v. Phillips Petroleum Co., 105 F.R.D. 16, 23-24 (S.D.N.Y. 1984) (motion to compel held in abeyance while party directed to make good faith effort to obtain waivers); United States v. Standard Oil Co. (New Jersey), 23 F.R.D. 1 (S.D.N.Y. 1958) (defendants ordered to make good faith attempt to obtain information; failure will result in hearing to determine how to proceed); see also RESTATEMENT (THIRD) OF THE FOREIGN RELATIONS LAW OF THE UNITED STATES § 442(2)(a) (1987) (providing that if a foreign law blocks discovery, a court may require the

grand jury investigation before permitting a third party to respond to a subpoena, some courts have compelled the subject to give consent.[194]   In cases where the subject of an investigation has sought to prevent disclosure through litigation in a foreign jurisdiction, some courts have compelled the subject to terminate the foreign litigation.[195]

In one case the Federal Trade Commission found a compromise between U.S. and German interests; as an alternative to either quashing or enforcing a subpoena for German documents, the FTC allowed the documents to be transmitted to the German Foreign Office, ordering the parties to negotiate a depository arrangement permitting FTC complaint counsel to view but not take possession of the documents, so that the degree of confidentiality insisted upon by the German government could be maintained at least through most of the discovery period.[196]

E. Remedies and Relief

United States law provides courts in antitrust actions with broad powers to order affirmative relief in addition to damages.   The objective of injunctive antitrust remedies, as distinct from damages, is to terminate unlawful anticompetitive activity, prevent its revival, and destroy its effects by reestablishing competitive conditions insofar as they pertain to United States exports and imports.[197]   Courts tailor remedies to the facts of each case to minimize judicial supervision of the offenders' activities.   Applying U.S. remedies to conduct undertaken abroad, however, often reaches into the domain of foreign law and policy.   The resulting potential for conflict has spurred defensive reactions by some foreign countries[198] and gestures of comity by U.S. courts.

---

person to whom the order is directed to make a good faith effort to secure permission to make the information available).

194.   *In re* United States Grand Jury Proceedings, 767 F.2d 1131 (5th Cir. 1985); United States v. Davis, 767 F.2d 1025, 1033-36 (2d Cir. 1985); United States v. Ghidoni, 732 F.2d 814 (11th Cir.), *cert. denied,* 469 U.S. 932 (1984). *But cf.* Senate Select Comm. on Secret Military Assistance to Iran v. Secord, 664 F. Supp. 562, 564-66 (D.D.C. 1987) (witness need not order foreign banks to produce information); *In re* Grand Jury Investigation, John Doe, 599 F. Supp. 746 (S.D. Tex. 1984) (compelled waiver would acknowledge existence of and signatory authority over account and would violate fifth amendment), *aff'd,* 812 F.2d 1404 (5th Cir. 1987), *aff'd sub nom.* Doe v. United States, 487 U.S. 201 (1988); Garpeg, Ltd. v. United States, 583 F. Supp. 789, 799 (S.D.N.Y. 1984) (foreign corporation that was not a defendant or a target of an investigation would not be compelled to waive its rights under foreign bank secrecy law; bank would be compelled to respond to summons without benefit of waiver).

195.   *Davis,* 767 F.2d at 1036-39 (citing cases). *But see Garpeg,* 583 F. Supp. at 797-99 (injunction would not be issued where the issues in the two actions were not the same and the right of secrecy sought to be enforced in the foreign court was one arising under foreign law; bank would be compelled to respond to subpoena without being relieved of foreign suit by its customer).

196.   Volkswagen of Am., Inc., 103 F.T.C. 536 (1984).

197.   United States v. Imperial Chem. Indus., 100 F. Supp. 504 (S.D.N.Y. 1951), *supplemental opinion on remedies,* 105 F. Supp. 215, 238 (S.D.N.Y. 1952).

198.   *See, e.g.,* The United Kingdom's Protection of Trading Interest Act, 1980, Ch. 22, *reprinted in* ANTITRUST & TRADE REG. REP. (BNA) at F-1 (Apr. 10, 1980) (limiting recognition of foreign multiple damage judgments).

1. *Comity Considerations*

Comity most often manifests itself in refusals by U.S. courts to exercise jurisdiction over cases involving foreign interests.[199]   When courts exercise jurisdiction, however, they often consider foreign interests in determining the remedy that U.S. antitrust law requires.[200]   An antitrust remedy may reflect the foreign policy position of the United States government.[201]   In ordering relief, a U.S. court may also consider the difficulty of enforcing a U.S. antitrust decree abroad.   The effectiveness of United States judgments affecting foreign interests may very well depend on the recognition that foreign countries give them as a matter of comity.[202]   Variations in substantive and procedural rules from country to country may render U.S. judgments more difficult to enforce abroad and therefore less effective.[203]

Although U.S. antitrust courts tend to give deference to foreign laws and interests, they remain willing to order U.S. and foreign defendants headquartered abroad to take remedial action when necessary to redress U.S. antitrust violations.   Courts have ordered U.S. companies to divest themselves of stockholdings in foreign corporations,[204] to encourage their foreign subsidiaries to export to the United States,[205] to undertake reasonable efforts to sell abroad,[206] and to license foreign

---

199.   *See also* Section B.1.c of this chapter.

200.   It has been suggested that a state should limit its enforcement jurisdiction to measures that are reasonably related to the laws it is enforcing.   RESTATEMENT (THIRD) OF THE FOREIGN RELATIONS LAW OF THE UNITED STATES § 431 (1987).

201.   *See* United States v. Watchmakers of Switz. Information Center, Inc., 1963 Trade Cas. (CCH) ¶ 70,600 (S.D.N.Y. 1962), *order modified,* 1965 Trade Cas. (CCH) ¶ 71,352 (S.D.N.Y. 1965) (modifying decree at the request of the United States government).

202.   United States v. Imperial Chem. Indus., 100 F. Supp. 504 (S.D.N.Y. 1951), *supplemental opinion on remedies,* 105 F. Supp. 215, 229 (S.D.N.Y. 1952).

203.   *See* 56 ANTITRUST & TRADE REG. REP. (BNA) 232 (discussing 1989 OECD REPORT ON INTERNATIONAL MERGERS AND COMPETITION POLICY).

204.   United States v. National Lead Co., 332 U.S. 319, 363 (1947) (upholding decree requiring U.S. company to present a divestment plan because the foreign stock acquisitions had been part of territorial allocation agreements regarding the market for titanium products); *cf.* Pilkington Bros. PLC, 103 F.T.C. 707 (1984) (consent order under which British company agreed to sell certain interests in and forego certain control over float glass producers in Canada and Mexico, not to acquire any float glass producers in North America for ten years, and to keep detailed records regarding certain business dealings abroad).

205.   United States v. Everest & Jennings Int'l, 1979-1 Trade Cas. (CCH) ¶ 62,508, §§ VII-X (C.D. Cal. 1979) (consent decree requiring wheelchair manufacturer to take affirmative action to encourage its subsidiaries to export to the U.S. and to assist them in developing a distribution system in the United States).

206.   United States v. Diebold, Inc., 1977-2 Trade Cas. (CCH) ¶ 61,736, § VI (N.D. Ohio 1976) (consent decree requiring defendant to "promote in good faith" the firm's products in the United Kingdom and requiring a written explanation for every foreign sale refused); *see also* United States v. Norman M. Morris Corp., 1976-1 Trade Cas. ¶ 60,894, § VII(C) (S.D.N.Y. 1976) (obliging firm to notify distributors of their right to export), *decree terminated by consent,* 1983-1 Trade Cas. ¶ 65,442 (S.D.N.Y. 1981); United States v. R. Hoe & Co., 1955 Trade Cas. ¶ 68,215, § IX(A)-(B) (S.D.N.Y. 1955) (requiring the defendant to advertise the availability of its product abroad); United States v. United Engr. & Foundry Co., 1952-1953 Trade Cas. ¶ 67,368, § X (W.D. Pa. 1952) (same).

patents royalty-free.[207] United States courts have required foreign corporations to license U.S. patents,[208] and to refrain from enforcing foreign patents.[209] In addition, a U.S. court required a U.S. company and a British company to divest joint ownership of companies in third countries.[210]

The Supreme Court has affirmed the authority of U.S. courts to order affirmative relief abroad. In *United States v. Holophane Co.*,[211] a U.S. defendant was a party to an international producers cartel that had allocated among portions of the world market for prismatic glassware. The district court found that the allocation agreements violated Section 1 of the Sherman Act, and ordered the defendant to violate the unlawful agreements by using "reasonable efforts" to sell its products in countries from which the agreements had excluded it. An equally divided Supreme Court, realizing that compliance with the decree would subject the U.S. company to suits in foreign countries for violation of the agreement, nonetheless affirmed the judgment.[212]

Although U.S. courts may apply U.S. antitrust law to conduct in foreign countries, they have on numerous occasions shown deference to foreign interests, particularly when a foreign government expresses concern. For example, in *United States v. Watchmakers of Switzerland Information Center, Inc.*,[213] the district court modified its initial decree to accommodate concerns that the Swiss Government articulated as amicus curiae after the court had entered the decree.[214] Similarly, in *United States v. General Electric Co.*,[215] the district court permitted Canada to consult on the terms of the proposed consent decree, although it did not bend to all of Canada's concerns.

---

207. United States v. Inco, Ltd., 1978-1 Trade Cas. (CCH) ¶ 61,869, at 73,640 (E.D. Pa. 1978) (consent decree requiring U.S. and foreign battery manufacturers to license their patents without charge to anyone making a written request).

208. United States v. Imperial Chem. Indus., 100 F. Supp. 504 (S.D.N.Y. 1951), *supplemental opinion on remedies*, 105 F. Supp. 215, 227 (S.D.N.Y. 1952) (requiring British company to license its U.S. patents to redress antitrust violations arising from denial of licensing because of intervention and objection of United States company).

209. United States v. Inco, Ltd., 1978-1 Trade Cas. (CCH) ¶ 61,869 (E.D. Pa. 1978) (consent decree requiring defendants to license their patents and granting immunity to licensees of defendants' patent rights from suit under any other patent belonging to defendants); United States v. Imperial Chem. Indus., 100 F. Supp. 504 (S.D.N.Y. 1951), *supplemental opinion on remedies*, 105 F. Supp. 215, 228 (S.D.N.Y. 1952) (requiring British company to grant immunity under its British patents to licensees of its corresponding United States patents).

210. United States v. Imperial Chem. Indus., 100 F. Supp. 504 (S.D.N.Y. 1951), *supplemental opinion on remedies*, 105 F. Supp. 215, 237 (S.D.N.Y. 1952) (noting that "the harsh remedy of divestiture" was necessary not only to remove the means to restrain the market but also to eliminate the incentive not to compete).

211. 119 F. Supp. 114 (S.D. Ohio) (findings and conclusions), 1954 Trade Cas. (CCH) ¶ 67,679 (S.D. Ohio 1954) (judgment), *aff'd per curiam*, 352 U.S. 903 (1956).

212. 352 U.S. 903 (1956); *see also* United States v. National Lead Co., 332 U.S. 319, 335 (1947) (upholding a decree enjoining performance and renewal of anticompetitive agreements among U.S. companies, ordering compulsory licensing of patents, and requiring divestiture of stockholdings and other financial interests in foreign companies).

213. 1963 Trade Cas. (CCH) ¶ 70,600 (S.D.N.Y. 1962), *order modified*, 1965 Trade Cas. (CCH) ¶ 71,352 (S.D.N.Y. 1965).

214. 1965 Trade Cas. (CCH) ¶ 71,352, at 80,492-93.

215. 1962 Trade Cas. (CCH) ¶¶ 70,342, 70,428, 70,546 (S.D.N.Y. 1962) (enjoining home entertainment firms from undertaking activity restricting exports from the U.S. to Canada).

In addition, courts sometimes allow a defense of foreign government compulsion of the conduct at issue.[216] Moreover, U.S. courts typically omit from their remedial decrees conduct in a foreign country that is compelled by the laws of that country.[217]

2. Reactions by Foreign Countries

The willingness of U.S. courts to enforce antitrust laws extraterritorially has engendered concern on the part of foreign countries.[218] Many other countries do not place as high a priority on competition as does the United States. In addition, some foreign countries resent the use of U.S. antitrust laws against anticompetitive activities that the foreign governments themselves support. Moreover, many countries view the judicial function as an aspect of their own sovereignty, and they consider their sovereignty threatened when U.S. courts order acts to take place within their territory.

An early case, *United States v. Imperial Chemical Industries*,[219] illustrates the negative reaction of some foreign countries to perceived intrusion by U.S. courts. *Imperial Chemical* was an action brought by the Department of Justice against several international chemical companies for dividing world markets for chemicals and explosives. The court ruled in favor of the Department of Justice, and as part of the remedy for the antitrust violations enjoined a British company, Imperial Chemical Industries (ICI), from enforcing its English patents against licensees of its corresponding U.S. patents. ICI, however, had assigned its English patent rights to another British company. The assignee sued in an English court, which upheld the

---

216. Interamerican Ref. Corp. v. Texaco Maracaibo, Inc., 307 F. Supp. 1291 (D. Del. 1970); *see also In re* Japanese Elec. Prods. Antitrust Litig., 723 F.2d 238, 315 (3d Cir. 1983) (assuming, although the evidence was insufficient to establish compulsion, that "a government-mandated export cartel arrangement fixing minimum export prices would be outside the ambit of" the antitrust laws), *rev'd on other grounds sub nom.* Matsushita Elec. Indus. v. Zenith Radio Corp., 475 U.S. 574 (1986); Timberlane Lumber Co. v. Bank of America, 549 F.2d 597, 606 (9th Cir. 1976) (acknowledging the "often-recognized principle that corporate conduct which is compelled by a foreign sovereign is . . . protected from antitrust liability" but finding the defense not applicable to that case). *See generally* Subpart H.3 of this chapter.

The Antitrust Division may decline to prosecute certain activities if compelled by a foreign sovereign. *See infra* note 341.

217. *See, e.g.*, United States v. F.M.C. Corp., 1979-2 Trade Cas. (CCH) ¶ 62,901, § III (D. Mass. 1979) (decree not applicable to arrangements "required by the laws or regulations of the jurisdiction in which such conduct takes place"); United States v. United Fruit Co., 1978-1 Trade Cas. (CCH) ¶ 62,001, § VII (E.D. La. 1978) (the U.S. company subject to judgment would not be in contempt of judgment for undertaking activity required by the foreign country in which the activity takes place. Nor would failure to perform acts required by judgment constitute contempt if the foreign country forbids the activity); United States v. Watchmakers of Switz. Information Center, 1963 Trade Cas. (CCH) ¶ 70,600 (S.D.N.Y. 1962), *order modified*, 1965 Trade Cas. (CCH) ¶ 71,352, at 80,492 (noting that part of the basis for modifying the decree was the issuance of new Swiss regulations concerning export permits); *see also infra* note 341. The Oil Cartel courts went so far as to exempt from the decree acts done "pursuant to request or official pronouncement of policy" by the foreign government if the firm's failure to comply would subject it to loss of business in the foreign nation. *See, e.g.*, United States v. Standard Oil Co., 1969 Trade Cas. ¶ 72,742, § V(c)(2) (S.D.N.Y. 1968).

218. *See infra* notes 224-229 and accompanying text.

219. 100 F. Supp. 504 (S.D.N.Y. 1951), *supplemental opinion on remedies*, 105 F. Supp. 215 (S.D.N.Y. 1952).

contract rights of the assignee, in effect partially overturning the U.S. decree.[220]

Despite a trend toward incorporating foreign governments' concerns into U.S. antitrust decrees, some countries have passed blocking statutes limiting the extraterritorial application of U.S. antitrust judgments.[221] Generally, such foreign blocking statutes are motivated by the potential for the award of treble damages to private plaintiffs[222] resulting from conduct that occurred outside the United States, which conduct may even have been condoned or encouraged by a foreign government.[223] Blocking statutes limit discovery, the enforcement of U.S. judgments, or both. Among the countries that have acted to bar enforcement of U.S. judgments are the Philippines, the United Kingdom, Canada, Australia, and South Africa.[224] The Philippines' statute prohibits enforcement of foreign judgments for multiple damages without clearance from the Philippine President's representative.[225] In the United Kingdom, the Secretary of Trade may bar enforcement of foreign judgments for multiple damages, and British companies that have paid a "multiple damage" award may sue the successful plaintiff in an English court to recover the "excess" damages.[226] Canadian law permits its Attorney General to declare a foreign antitrust judgment nonrecognizable, or recognizable only up to a certain amount, and permitting Canadian citizens, residents and corporations to sue the successful plaintiff for the damages collected under the nonrecognizable portion of a judgment.[227] Australia's blocking statute allows the Australian Attorney General to declare a judgment rendered in a foreign antitrust

---

220. British Nylon Spinners Ltd. v. Imperial Chem. Indus., [1953] 1 Ch. 19 (C.A. 1952) (patents are "a species of property . . . which is English in character and is subject to the jurisdiction of the English courts; and . . . it is not competent for the courts of the United States, or of any other country, to interfere with those rights"), *made permanent*, [1954] 1 Ch. 37.

221. *See, e.g.*, Great Britain Protection of Trade Interest Act (1980) (barring enforcement of foreign multiple damage judgments); Foreign Proceedings (Excess of Jurisdiction) Act No. 3, Austrl. Acts (1984), *reprinted in* 23 I.L.M. 1038 (1984) (superseding Foreign Antitrust Judgments (Restriction of Enforcement) Act of 1979, No. 13, Austrl. Acts (1979)); Protection of Business Act No. 99 of 1978 [South Africa].

222. Section 4 of the Clayton Act, 15 U.S.C. § 15(a) (1988), provides that any person whose business or property is injured by reason of actions forbidden by the antitrust laws may recover treble damages.

223. *See, e.g.*, Amicus Curiae Memorandum of the Government of Australia, *In re* Uranium Antitrust Litig., 617 F.2d 1248 (7th Cir. 1980) (complaining that the treble-damage litigation will have "a very serious and detrimental effect on the [Australian] national interest").

224. *See* Section D.1.b of this chapter. Litigation against foreign uranium producers for participation in an alleged government-organized international uranium cartel was the major impetus for much of this legislation. Several governments stated in amicus briefs filed in a U.S. antitrust action stemming from the cartel's alleged activities that it was their policy that private uranium producers cooperate in those activities. *See, e.g.*, Brief for Amicus Curiae Government of Australia, at 3-4, *In re* Uranium Antitrust Litig., 617 F.2d 1248 (7th Cir. 1980); Brief for Amicus Curiae Government of Canada, at 3-4, *In re* Uranium Antitrust Litig., 473 F. Supp. 382 (N.D. Ill. 1979).

225. Presidential Decree No. 1718, § 1 (Aug. 21, 1980) (Phil.).

226. Protection of Trading Interests Act, §§ 5-6, 1980, ch. 11, *reprinted in* ANTITRUST & TRADE REG. REP. (BNA) No. 959, at F-1, 2 (Apr. 10, 1980).

227. Foreign Extraterritorial Measures Act, §§ 8-9, Stat. Canada 1984, ch. 49 (Dec. 21, 1984). A U.S. district court, in dictum, has indicated that U.S. courts should not normally interfere with such "clawback" recoveries. Laker Airways v. Pan Am World Airways, 559 F. Supp. 1124, 1136-37 (D.D.C. 1983), *aff'd sub nom.* Laker Airways v. Sabena, Belgium World Airlines, 731 F.2d 909 (D.C. Cir. 1984).

proceeding not recognizable in Australia,[228] and authorizes Australians to recover the full amount − not just the noncompensatory portion − of multiple damages imposed in foreign countries.[229]

In an effort to reconcile U.S. actions with the concerns of foreign countries, the United States, through the Justice Department and the Federal Trade Commission, has entered into bilateral antitrust cooperation agreements with some of its trading partners, notably Australia,[230] Canada,[231] and the Federal Republic of Germany.[232] The agreement with Australia requires the United States government to notify the Australian government when the Antitrust Division or the FTC "decides to undertake an antitrust investigation that may have implications for Australian laws, policies or national interests."[233] Conversely, the Australian government may notify the United States if Australia adopts "a policy that it considers may have antitrust implications for the United States."[234] Each government must respond to the other's communications with its own concerns,[235] while either may request consultations aiming to avoid potential conflicts between the countries' laws, policies, and national interests.[236] If the consultations do not prevent a conflict, each country may act to protect its own interests.[237] Each country agrees, however, to cooperate with the other's antitrust investigations and other actions that do not present a conflict. Discovery, the countries agree, never presents a conflict affecting a significant national interest. The agreement with Canada is similar to that with Australia, but does not require Canada to forbear in its use of discovery-blocking

---

228.   Foreign Proceedings (Excess of Jurisdiction) Act No. 3, Austrl. Acts (1984), *reprinted in* 23 I.L.M. 1038 (1984) (superseding the Antitrust Judgments (Restriction of Enforcement) Act of 1979, No. 13, Austrl. Acts (1979)).

229.   *Id.* at § 10.

    South Africa's Protection of Business Act provides that no foreign decree or judgment may be enforced at all in South Africa without the consent of the Minister of Economic Affairs. Protection of Business Act (No. 99) of 1978, § 1. Multiple and punitive damage awards are never enforceable in South Africa, and as in Britain and Canada, those who have paid damage awards imposed by foreign judgments may recover the noncompensatory portion. *Id.* § 1A to 1B.

230.   Agreement Between the Government of the United States of America and the Government of Australia Relating to Cooperation on Antitrust Matters, 4 TRADE REG. REP. (CCH) ¶ 13,502 (June 29, 1982) [hereinafter *Australian Agreement*].

231.   Memorandum of Understanding Between the Government of Canada and the Government of the United States of America as to Notification, Consultation and Cooperation with Respect to the Application of National Antitrust Laws (Mar. 9, 1984), *reprinted in* 4 TRADE REG. REP. (CCH) ¶ 13,503 [hereinafter *Canadian Agreement*]. Representations of the Canadian government under this agreement were the basis, in part, of a 1986 Justice Department decision to permit a merger of Canadian and U.S. tractor companies under the "failing firm" provisions of the 1984 MERGER GUIDELINES. ANTITRUST & TRADE REG. REP. (BNA) No. 1172 (June 26, 1986).

232.   Agreement Between the Government of the United States of America and the Government of the Federal Republic of Germany Relating to Mutual Cooperation Regarding Restrictive Business Practices, June 23, 1976, United States-Federal Republic of Germany, 27 U.S.T. 1956, T.I.A.S. No. 8291, *reprinted in* 4 TRADE REG. REP. (CCH) ¶ 13,501 [hereinafter *German Agreement*].

233.   *Australian Agreement, supra* note 230, art. 1, ¶ 2.

234.   *Id.* The *Agreement* permits Australia to request the U.S. to participate in private litigation relating to conduct of which Australia notified the U.S. In addition, Australia may request a written response to the request.

235.   *Australian Agreement, supra* note 230, art. 2, ¶¶ 1-2.

236.   *Id.* art. 1, ¶ 4.

237.   *Id.* art. 4, ¶ 2.

legislation.[238] The accord with the Federal Republic of Germany is less structured, providing for the exchange of any significant information coming to the attention of either party that may have a substantial effect on the other, for cooperation in discovery and for possible coordination of concurrent antitrust investigations.[239] The effectiveness of the agreement is tempered by the provision that either Germany or the United States may decline to comply with the agreement if it determines that compliance would be contrary to its law, public policy, or important national interests, or if it is unable or unwilling to comply with specific terms or conditions established by the other.[240]

On September 23, 1991, representatives of the United States and the Commission of the European Communities signed an antitrust cooperation agreement.[241] Although the agreement is similar to the agreements with individual countries, it appears to contemplate more intensive international enforcement cooperation. First, the U.S.-E.C. agreement expressly permits enforcement authorities of one party to notify and request enforcement action by the other where anticompetitive acts within the latter's territory affect the interests of the former.[242] Notification provisions have been broadened to include significant forms of competition authority intervention "in a regulatory or judicial proceeding that does not arise from . . . enforcement activities" where the interests of the other party may be affected.[243] Finally, the agreement provides a regular framework for continuing consultations between the parties, including "at least" biannual consultations, and a review of the operation of the entire agreement.[244]

These cooperation agreements may prove especially useful in light of the increasing aggressiveness of foreign countries in applying their own competition laws to international trade or commerce. Until recently, the most significant regime of antitrust laws affecting U.S. companies was U.S. law. Today enforcement agencies from other countries routinely investigate the conduct of foreign persons, including U.S. firms.[245] In particular, the U.S. antitrust authorities increasingly conduct investigations of international mergers simultaneously with foreign enforcement agencies.[246]

3. Arbitration

Although the lower courts had long held that rights under the antitrust laws are

---

238. *Canadian Agreement, supra* note 231.
239. *German Agreement, supra* note 232, art. 2.
240. *Id.* art. 3.
241. Agreement Between the Government of the United States of America and the Commission of the European Communities Regarding the Application of Their Competition Laws, *reprinted in* 61 ANTITRUST & TRADE REG. REP. 382 (BNA) (Sept. 26, 1991).
242. *Id.* art. V.
243. *Id.* art. II.5.
244. *Id.* art. III.2.
245. *See generally* ABA ANTITRUST SECTION, REPORT OF THE SPECIAL COMMITTEE ON INTERNATIONAL ANTITRUST (1991).
246. For example, antitrust authorities in the U.S. and Britain both investigated Minorco's attempted takeover of Consolidated Gold Fields. Consolidated Gold Fields, PLC v. Minorco, SA, 871 F.2d 252 (2d Cir.), *cert. dismissed*, 492 U.S. 939 (1989).

not arbitrable,[247] the Supreme Court in *Mitsubishi Motors Corp. v. Soler Chrysler-Plymouth, Inc.*[248] ruled that an agreement to resolve antitrust claims by arbitration is enforceable when that agreement arises from an international transaction.[249] The Court declared that

> [C]oncerns of international comity, respect for the capacities of foreign and transnational tribunals, and sensitivity to the need of the international commercial system for predictability in the resolution of disputes require that we enforce the parties' agreement, even assuming that a contrary result would be forthcoming in a domestic context.[250]

F. Application to Foreign Commerce of Certain Substantive Antitrust Rules

The substantive antitrust rules governing transactions in U.S. foreign commerce are generally identical to those applicable to domestic commerce. Thus, price fixing,[251] output restriction,[252] and market division[253] have generally been condemned per se, while vertical nonprice restraints,[254] joint ventures,[255] and mergers[256] have generally been examined under a rule of reason standard. There are, however, a variety of special issues that present themselves in foreign commerce settings.

First, as noted above, considerations of jurisdiction, comity, or prosecutorial discretion may limit the application of U.S. antitrust laws, even where blatant cartel activity is involved, if the activity is directed solely to overseas markets and has only incidental effects on U.S. commerce.[257]

---

247. *E.g.*, American Safety Equip. Corp. v. J.P. Maguire & Co., 391 F.2d 821 (2d Cir. 1968).

248. 473 U.S. 614 (1985).

249. *See* Subpart J.1 of Chapter VIII of this treatise regarding arbitration in private domestic antitrust suits.

250. 473 U.S. at 629. *Mitsubishi* was followed in High Strength Steel, Inc. v. Svenskt Stal Aktiebolag, 1985-2 Trade Cas. (CCH) ¶ 66,884 (N.D. Ill. 1985). *See also In re* Hops Antitrust Litig., 832 F.2d 470 (8th Cir. 1987).

251. *See, e.g.*, United States v. Timken Roller Bearing Co., 83 F. Supp. 284 (N.D. Ohio 1949), *modified and aff'd*, 341 U.S. 593 (1951); United States v. General Electric Co., 80 F. Supp. 989 (S.D.N.Y. 1948); *see also* Chapter I of this treatise.

252. *See, e.g.*, United States v. General Electric Co., 82 F. Supp. 753 (D.N.J. 1949); *see also* Chapter I of this treatise.

253. *See, e.g., Timken*, 83 F. Supp. at 284; United States v. National Lead Co., 63 F. Supp. 513 (S.D.N.Y. 1945), *aff'd*, 332 U.S. 319 (1947); United States v. Aluminum Co. of Am., 148 F.2d 416 (2d Cir. 1945); United States v. Holophane Co., 119 F. Supp. 114 (S.D. Ohio 1954), *aff'd per curiam*, 325 U.S. 903 (1956); *see also* Chapter I of this treatise.

254. *See, e.g.*, Continental T.V., Inc. v. GTE Sylvania Inc., 433 U.S. 36, 54-57 (1977); *see also* Chapter I of this treatise.

255. *See, e.g.*, Brunswick Corp., 94 F.T.C. 1174 (1979), *aff'd as modified sub nom.* Yamaha Motor Co. v. FTC, 657 F.2d 971 (8th Cir. 1981), *cert. denied*, 456 U.S. 915 (1982); *see also* Chapter III of this treatise.

256. United States v. General Dynamics Corp., 415 U.S. 486 (1973); *see also* Chapter III of this treatise.

257. *See* Part B of this chapter; Montreal Trading Ltd. v. AMAX, Inc., 661 F.2d 864 (10th Cir. 1981), *cert. denied*, 455 U.S. 1001 (1982); Alfred Bell & Co. v. Catalda Fine Arts, Inc., 74 F. Supp. 973 (S.D.N.Y. 1947), *interlocutory decree aff'd*, 86 F. Supp. 399 (S.D.N.Y. 1949), *modified*, 191 F.2d 99 (2d Cir. 1951). An anticompetitive agreement need not expressly include the United States to have exposure, if it is clear from the participants' actions that they intend to include the U.S. in

Second, in evaluating market power, it is sometimes necessary to take into account import quotas, currency fluctuations, or other constraints that effectively limit the competitive significance of a foreign firm's activities.[258]

Third, the implementing regulations under the Hart-Scott-Rodino Antitrust Improvements Act of 1976[259] exempt certain mergers that might otherwise be covered from the reporting requirements including:

(1) acquisitions by U.S. companies of certain foreign assets and of voting securities of foreign entities whose U.S. assets and sales do not meet minimum threshold requirements;[260]

(2) acquisitions by foreign companies:

    (a) of foreign assets,[261]

    (b) of voting securities of foreign companies not resulting in direct or indirect control over U.S. assets or corporations meeting minimum threshold requirements,[262]

    (c) when both parties to the acquisition are foreign and when their combined U.S. sales and combined U.S. assets are each less than $110 million;[263]

(3) acquisitions by foreign states, governments or agencies (other than corporations engaged in commerce);[264] and

(4) acquisitions by or from companies "controlled" by foreign governments of assets located in, or corporations organized under the laws of, that foreign state.[265]

Fourth, cases involving intellectual property are affected by the fact that the protection of intellectual property is governed by separate national regimes. Thus, "corresponding" or "parallel" patents — that is, patents in different countries covering the same invention — can be used in an international licensing arrangement to effect a territorial division of markets. The Department of Justice's 1977

---

their arrangement. *See* United States v. United States Alkali Export Ass'n, 86 F. Supp. 59 (S.D.N.Y. 1949); United States v. Timken Roller Bearing Co., 83 F. Supp. 284, 304-07 (N.D. Ohio 1949), *modified and aff'd*, 341 U.S. 593 (1951). The legislative history of the FTAIA noted that a U.S. export cartel may have a "spillover" effect that in time would have a direct, substantial and reasonable foreseeable effect on domestic commerce. HOUSE REPORT 686, *supra* note 17, at 13.

258.   *See* INTERNATIONAL GUIDELINES, *supra* note 2, at Case 2; *see also* Subpart C.2 of Chapter III of this treatise.

259.   *See* 15 U.S.C. § 18a (1988). *See* Subpart F.1 of Chapter III of this treatise for a description of the premerger notification requirements under the Hart-Scott-Rodino Act.

260.   16 C.F.R. § 802.50 (1991) exempts acquisitions of assets outside the United States to which no sales in or into the United States are attributable. It also exempts acquisition of assets to which sales in or into the United States are attributable unless, as a result of that acquisition (and any other acquisitions), the acquirer would hold assets of the acquired person to which sales of $25 million or more were attributable during the acquired person's most recent fiscal year.

261.   *Id.* § 802.51(a).

262.   *Id.* § 802.51(b), which establishes as thresholds obtaining control over an issuer holding U.S. assets with an aggregate book value of $15 million or more, or obtaining control over a U.S. issuer with annual net sales or total assets of $25 million or more.

263.   *Id.* § 802.51(d).

264.   *Id.* § 801.1(a)(2).

265.   *Id.* §§ 802.52. "Control" is defined at § 801.1(b). *Cf.* United States v. Tengelmann Warenhandelsgesellschaft, 1989-1 Trade Cas. (CCH) ¶ 68,623 (D.D.C. 1989) (consent decree, payment of $3 million for failing to comply with reporting and waiting period requirements).

International Antitrust Guide stated that an international territorial division created by selectively licensing patents in different countries would not itself be illegal under the antitrust laws.[266] In the 1988 *International Guidelines*, the Department has suggested that such arrangements initially be analyzed as an acquisition of technology, and that impact on other markets be addressed under its merger analysis standards. Finally, it suggested that even if there were threats to competition, it would then consider whether or not there were offsetting efficiencies.[267] The issues raised by international patent licensing and patent pools are more fully discussed in Chapter IX of this treatise.

G. Relationship of U.S. International Trade Laws to Antitrust Laws

1. Antidumping Act of 1916

The Revenue Act of 1916, more commonly known as the 1916 Antidumping Act,[268] creates a private cause of action for treble damages against importers and others who sell comparable articles in the United States at substantially less than their wholesale price or market value in their market of production (or other export market), where such pricing is "common" or "systematic," and is done with anticompetitive intent.[269]

In *In re Japanese Electronic Products Antitrust Litigation*,[270] the Third Circuit described the 1916 Act as the international analogue to the Robinson-Patman Act, prohibiting discriminatory pricing in international commerce. There have been few reported decisions under the 1916 Act.[271]

2. Use and Abuse of U.S. Trade Laws

A variety of trade laws, including those imposing customs duties to neutralize the effects of dumping[272] and subsidization[273] of imports, and imposing duties or quotas on imports that seriously injure a domestic industry[274] may be invoked by U.S. companies. Where a trade law claim is baseless or sham, and is used primarily to erect barriers to competition from foreign-origin products, such a claim could be the basis of antitrust liability under doctrines laid down in *California Motor Transport*

---

266. INTERNATIONAL ANTITRUST GUIDE, *supra* note 14, at Cases H-I. *See also* DEP'T OF COMMERCE, GUIDELINES FOR THE ISSUANCE OF EXPORT TRADE CERTIFICATES OF REVIEW (2d ed.), 50 FED. REG. 1786, 1798-99 (1985), *reprinted in* 4 TRADE REG. REP. (CCH) ¶ 13,300, at Part V.C.

267. INTERNATIONAL GUIDELINES, *supra* note 2, Case 11.

268. 15 U.S.C. §§ 71-74 (1988).

269. 15 U.S.C. § 72 (1988).

270. 723 F.2d 319, 324 (3d Cir. 1983).

271. *See* Western Concrete Structures Co. v. Mitsui & Co. (U.S.A.), 760 F.2d 1013 (9th Cir.), *cert. denied*, 474 U.S. 903 (1985); Isra Fruit Ltd. v. Agrexco Agricultural Export Co., 631 F. Supp. 984 (S.D.N.Y. 1986) (standing); Schwimmer v. Sony Corp., 471 F. Supp. 793 (E.D.N.Y. 1979), *aff'd*, 637 F.2d 41 (2d Cir. 1980) (standing); Outboard Marine Corp. v. Pezetel, 461 F. Supp. 384 (D. Del. 1978) (requirement of foreign sale); Bywater v. Matsushita Elec. Indus. Co., 1971 Trade Cas. (CCH) ¶ 73,759 (S.D.N.Y. 1971) (standing).

272. 19 U.S.C. §§ 1673 *et seq.* (1988).

273. 19 U.S.C. §§ 1671 *et seq.* (1988).

274. 19 U.S.C. §§ 2251 *et seq.* (1988).

and *Noerr-Pennington*.[275]

One court of appeals has also held that the sale of imported products at prices below a level that could give rise to liability under the antidumping law could be an antitrust violation. In *Western Concrete Structures Co. v. Mitsui & Co.*,[276] the Ninth Circuit held that a cause of action under Sections 1 and 2 of the Sherman Act was stated by a complaint alleging that a company in the post-tensioning concrete business had conspired with a supplier to import steel strand (used in the post-tensioning process) at a price below the lawfully established antidumping trigger price, thus allowing the defendant to underbid plaintiff and other competitors.

H. Exceptions and Defenses to Application of Antitrust Laws in Foreign Commerce

1. Sovereign Immunity

A foreign sovereign's immunity from suit in U.S. courts has long been recognized in the United States.[277] Until 1976, a question of sovereign immunity often would be addressed by both the executive and judicial branches of the government, with the views of the executive commonly being regarded as binding on the courts.[278]

In 1976, the Foreign Sovereign Immunities Act (FSIA) established that immunity does not extend to suits arising out of commercial activity in the United States by a

---

275. California Motor Transport Co. v. Trucking Unlimited, 404 U.S. 508 (1972); United Mine Workers v. Pennington, 381 U.S. 657 (1965); Eastern R.R. Presidents Conference v. Noerr Motor Freight, Inc., 365 U.S. 127 (1961). These cases and their subsequent history are discussed in detail in Chapter XI of this treatise. The *International Guidelines, supra* note 2, at § 7 and Case 18, set forth the Department of Justice's concerns; and at Case 17, the Department cautioned that the settlement of such an action may pose even greater peril. The then Acting Chairman of the Federal Trade Commission expressed a similar concern, stating that unjustified invocation of antidumping and similar laws could amount to nonprice predation reachable under the antitrust laws. Calvani, *Non-Price Predation: A New Antitrust Horizon*, 54 ANTITRUST L.J. 409 (1985). For a discussion of the issues raised by the interplay of competition and trade law, see *Task Force Report on the Interface Between International Trade Law and Policy and Competition Law and Policy*, 56 ANTITRUST L.J. 461 (1987).

276. 760 F.2d 1013 (9th Cir.), *cert. denied*, 474 U.S. 903 (1985).

277. Foreign sovereign immunity was first recognized in The Schooner Exchange v. M'Faddon, 11 U.S. (7 Cranch) 116 (1812) (Marshall, C.J.). *See also* L'Invincible, 14 U.S. (1 Wheat.) 238 (1816).

278. *See* Mexico v. Hoffman, 324 U.S. 30, 38 (1945); *Ex parte* Peru, 318 U.S. 578, 588-89 (1943); *cf.* United States v. Deutsches Kalisyndikat Gesellschaft, 31 F.2d 199 (S.D.N.Y. 1929) (defense of sovereign immunity rejected where there were private shareholders in a mining company controlled by the French government, French law permitted suits against the company in France, and the State Department had been silent). *But cf. In re* Grand Jury Investigation of the Shipping Indus., 186 F. Supp. 298 (D.D.C. 1960) (court reserved decision where State Department refused to recommend extension of sovereign immunity to shipping line nationalized by the Philippine government); *In re* Investigation of World Arrangements, 13 F.R.D. 280 (D.D.C. 1952) (sovereign immunity compelled quashing subpoena where oil company was found to be "indistinguishable" from the British government, which owned 35% of the capital investment, controlled one-half of the voting stock and had formed the company to assure an adequate supply of petroleum to the British fleet). *See generally* H.R. REP. NO. 1487, 94th Cong., 2d Sess. (1976), *reprinted in* 1976 U.S. CODE CONG. & ADMIN. NEWS 6604 (report to accompany bill that became Foreign Sovereign Immunities Act of 1976).

foreign sovereign.[279] The Act defines commercial activity as "either a regular course of commercial conduct or a particular commercial transaction or act," with character to be determined "by reference to the nature of the course of conduct or particular transaction or act, rather than by reference to its purpose."[280]

The determination of whether an activity is "commercial" is central to cases involving the FSIA. In *Texas Trading & Milling Corp. v. Federal Republic of Nigeria*,[281] the Second Circuit relied on the Act's legislative history, the case law in existence when it was passed, and international law in finding that commercial activity included a government purchase of cement on the open market, regardless

---

279.   Pub. L. No. 94-583, 90 Stat. 2891 (1976) (codified at 28 U.S.C. §§ 1 (note), 1330, 1332, 1391, 1441, 1602-11 (1988)); Ministry of Supply, Cairo v. Universe Tankships, Inc., 708 F.2d 80 (2d Cir. 1983); *see also* Alfred Dunhill of London, Inc. v. Republic of Cuba, 425 U.S. 682, 701-02 (1976) (White, J., plurality opinion) (noting U.S. policy is to decline to extend sovereign immunity to the "commercial dealings of foreign governments"); Barkanic v. CAAC, 822 F.2d 11, 13 (2d Cir.) ("a nexus is required between the commercial activity in the United States and the cause of action"), *cert. denied*, 484 U.S. 964 (1987); RESTATEMENT (THIRD) OF THE FOREIGN RELATIONS LAW OF THE UNITED STATES § 451 (1987) ("Under international law, a state or state instrumentality is immune from the jurisdiction of the courts of another state, except with respect to claims arising out of activities of the kind that may be carried on by private persons.").

   The FSIA also established that immunity does not extend to an act performed in the United States in connection with a commercial activity elsewhere, or to an act performed outside the United States in connection with a commercial activity elsewhere where "that act causes a direct effect in the United States." 28 U.S.C. § 1605(a)(2) (1988). *See* America West Airlines v. GPA Group, 877 F.2d 793, 798-99 (9th Cir. 1989); Rush-Presbyterian-St. Luke's Medical Center v. Hellenic Republic, 877 F.2d 574, 581 (7th Cir.), *cert. denied*, 110 S. Ct. 333 (1989); Gould, Inc. v. Pechiney Ugine Kuhlmann, 853 F.2d 445, 453 (6th Cir. 1988); Zedan v. Kingdom of Saudi Arabia, 849 F.2d 1511, 1515 (D.C. Cir. 1988); Zernicek v. Brown & Root, Inc., 826 F.2d 415, 417-18 (5th Cir. 1987), *cert. denied*, 484 U.S. 1043 (1988); Harris Corp. v. National Iranian Radio & Television, 691 F.2d 1344 (11th Cir. 1982); Texas Trading & Milling Corp. v. Federal Republic of Nig., 647 F.2d 300, 313 (2d Cir. 1981) ("The question is, was the effect sufficiently 'direct' and sufficiently 'in the United States' that Congress would have wanted an American court to hear the case?"), *cert. denied*, 454 U.S. 1148 (1982); Carey v. National Oil Corp., 592 F.2d 673, 676 (2d Cir. 1979) (per curiam) (dismissal of action against Libyan-government-owned oil company because the challenged conduct, consisting of alleged overcharges and breach of contract, concerned a contract between a foreign state (the oil company) and a Bahamian corporation, and because no "direct effect in the United States" had been shown, even though the Bahamian corporation was a subsidiary of a U.S. corporation; "direct effect" language "embodies the standard set out in *International Shoe*," and an indirect effect on a U.S. parent corporation did not meet this standard); Wyle v. Bank Melli, 577 F. Supp. 1148 (N.D. Cal. 1983) (demand on shipping company's American bank by Iranian guarantor bank for payment of letter of credit held to be an act causing a "direct effect" in the United States since assets would be removed from the United States, and an American bankruptcy estate would experience the loss). *Compare* Texas Trading & Milling v. Federal Republic of Nig., 647 F.2d 306, 308 (2d Cir. 1981), *cert. denied*, 454 U.S. 1148 (1982) *with* Verlinden BV v. Central Bank of Nig., 461 U.S. 480, 498 n.23 (1983) (overseas repudiation of letter of credit did not cause direct effect in United States).

   There is a split among the circuits as to whether the "direct effect" clause includes only effects that are "substantial and foreseeable." The Fifth, Sixth, Seventh, Ninth, and D.C. Circuits have all applied the "substantial and foreseeable" standard, while the Second Circuit has rejected it. *See* International Housing Ltd. v. Rafidain Bank Iraq, 893 F.2d 8, 11 n.2 (2d Cir. 1989) (citing cases).

280.   28 U.S.C. § 1603(d) (1988).

281.   647 F.2d 300, 308 (2d Cir. 1981), *cert. denied*, 454 U.S. 1148 (1982).

of the purpose to which the cement was put.[282]   In *Outboard Marine Corporation v. Pezetel*,[283] suit was brought against a Polish government trade organization engaged in the manufacture and sale of golf carts that were imported into the United States. The district court held that this activity was inherently "commercial."[284]

By contrast, in *International Association of Machinists and Aerospace Workers* (IAM) *v. Organization of Petroleum Exporting Countries* (OPEC),[285] the commercial activity exception was found inapplicable. Plaintiff argued that the defendants' price-fixing activities were commercial and thus susceptible to antitrust suits in U.S. courts. The district court disagreed, ruling that establishing terms and conditions for the removal of natural resources was a governmental prerogative entitled to sovereign immunity. Since OPEC was composed of a collection of countries "coming together to agree upon how they will carry on that activity," the district court found the cartel to be involved in noncommercial activities,[286] and the suit was accordingly dismissed. The Ninth Circuit affirmed, but did so on act of state grounds, expressly avoiding the issue of whether OPEC's activities were commercial.[287]

2. *Act of State*

"The act of state doctrine . . . merely requires that . . . the acts of foreign sovereigns taken within their own jurisdictions shall be deemed valid."[288]   Unlike sovereign immunity, which exempts the sovereign itself from suit by virtue of its status, the act of state doctrine does not exempt any party from the process of the courts. Rather, it establishes a presumption that the acts of a foreign government

---

282.   *Id.* at 310; *see also* Gibbons v. Udaras na Gaeltachta, 549 F. Supp. 1094, 1110-11 (S.D.N.Y. 1982) (promotional activities commercial).

283.   461 F. Supp. 384 (D. Del. 1978).

284.   *Id.* at 395-96. The court also held that the defendant, as a state agency, was not protected from treble-damage liability by 28 U.S.C. § 1606 (1988), which provides that "a foreign state except for an agency or instrumentality thereof shall not be liable for punitive damages." *Id.* at 394-95. *See also* Rush-Presbyterian-St. Luke's Medical Center v. Hellenic Republic, 877 F.2d 574, 581 (7th Cir.) (Greek government's execution of contract to reimburse physicians and organ bank for requested kidney transplants performed on Greek nationals in United States facilities was "commercial activity" under FSIA), *cert. denied*, 110 S. Ct. 333 (1989); Millen Indus. v. Coordination Council for N. Am. Affairs, 855 F.2d 879 (D.C. Cir. 1988) (remanded to determine whether defendant, an instrumentality of the Taiwanese government, was engaged in commercial activity under the FSIA or immune sovereign activity when soliciting U.S. citizens to establish commercial ventures in Taiwan); West v. Multibanco Comermex, SA, 807 F.2d 820 (9th Cir.) (Mexican bank's issuance of certificates of deposit held to be "commercial activity" despite Mexican government's institution of currency exchange controls), *cert. denied*, 482 U.S. 906 (1987); Practical Concepts, Inc. v. Republic of Bolivia, 811 F.2d 1543 (D.C. Cir. 1987) (consulting contract between U.S. firm and foreign government held to be "commercial activity"; commercial activity exception determined by "essential character" of activity in issue); Morgan Guaranty Trust Co. v. Republic of Palau, 702 F. Supp. 60 (S.D.N.Y. 1988) (loan by U.S. company to foreign government held to be "commercial activity"); American Bonded Warehouse Corp. v. Compagnie Nationale Air France, 653 F. Supp. 861 (N.D. Ill. 1987) (alleged scheme by defendant to eliminate competition in the freight forwarding industry held to involve "commercial activity").

285.   477 F. Supp. 553 (C.D. Cal. 1979), *aff'd on other grounds*, 649 F.2d 1354 (9th Cir. 1981), *cert. denied*, 454 U.S. 1163 (1982).

286.   *Id.* at 569.

287.   649 F.2d at 1358.

288.   W.S. Kirkpatrick & Co. v. Environmental Tectonics Corp., 493 U.S. 400, 409 (1990).

are valid.[289] Where plaintiff's theory turns on the invalidity of such acts, this rule of decision may permit a private or governmental party to avoid liability.

Whatever its original premises may have been,[290] the act of state doctrine is now seen primarily as an aspect of the separation of powers.[291] According to this view, a judicial declaration that an act of a foreign state is invalid, even for the limited purpose of adjudicating a dispute under U.S. law, may adversely affect the conduct of foreign relations[292] – a subject which the Constitution commits to the federal Executive Branch.[293] Thus, the act of state doctrine is concerned with the potential embarassment not of foreign states,[294] but of the United States government in its relations with foreign states.[295]

The precise scope of the act of state doctrine remained uncertain for many

---

289. In *Kirkpatrick*, the Court recognized "that the policies underlying the act of state doctrine should be considered in deciding whether, despite the doctrine's technical availability, it should nonetheless not be invoked . . . ." 493 U.S. at 409. Thus, the presumption of validity may be rebuttable or inapplicable. *See infra* notes 314-15 and accompanying text.

290. For other suggested rationales of the doctrine, and its history, see First Nat'l City Bank v. Banco Nacional de Cuba, 406 U.S. 759 (1972); Banco Nacional de Cuba v. Sabbatino, 376 U.S. 398 (1964); Oetjen v. Central Leathers Co., 246 U.S. 297 (1918); Ricaud v. American Metal Co., 246 U.S. 304 (1918); American Banana v. United Fruit Co. 213 U.S. 347 (1909); Underhill v. Hernandez, 168 U.S. 250 (1897).

291. Environmental Tectonics Corp. v. W.S. Kirkpatrick & Co., 847 F.2d 1052, 1058 (3d Cir. 1988) ("the core concern of modern act of state jurisprudence is preserving the separation of powers between the federal judiciary and the political branches of our government – especially the Executive Branch where primary responsibility for the conduct of foreign affairs is lodged"), *aff'd*, 493 U.S. 400 (1990); Industrial Inv. Dev. Corp. v. Mitsui & Co., 594 F.2d 48, 51 (5th Cir. 1979), *cert. denied*, 445 U.S. 903 (1980); *see* Banco Nacional de Cuba v. Sabbatino, 376 U.S. 398, 421, 423 (1964) ("We do not believe that the doctrine is compelled either by the inherent nature of sovereign authority, as some of the earlier decisions seem to imply, or by some principle of international law." Rather, the doctrine "arises out of the basic relationships between branches of government in a system of separation of powers.") (citations omitted); International Ass'n of Machinists & Aerospace Workers (IAM) v. Organization of Petroleum Exporting Countries (OPEC), 649 F.2d 1354, 1358-59 (9th Cir. 1981), *cert. denied*, 454 U.S. 1163 (1982); *see also* Associated Container Transp. (Austl.) Ltd. v. United States, 705 F.2d 53, 61 (2d Cir. 1983) ("In essence, courts have recognized that the conduct of foreign relations is within the province of the Executive Branch and have refused under certain circumstances to become embroiled in international political controversies."); Linseman v. World Hockey Ass'n, 439 F. Supp. 1315, 1324 (D. Conn. 1977); Occidental Petroleum v. Buttes Gas & Oil Co., 331 F. Supp. 92, 108-09 (C.D. Cal. 1971), *aff'd per curiam*, 461 F.2d 1261 (9th Cir.), *cert. denied*, 409 U.S. 950 (1972).

292. *Kirkpatrick*, 493 U.S. at 404.

293. *International Ass'n of Machinists*, 649 F.2d at 1358-59. The act of state doctrine is akin to the political question doctrine, which also may be occasionally implicated in antitrust suits involving foreign policy considerations. Unlike the act of state doctrine, however, the political question doctrine, if applicable, renders the entire dispute nonjusticiable. *See* Occidental, Inc. v. A Certain Cargo of Petroleum, 577 F.2d 1196, 1203 (5th Cir. 1978) (suit in conversion for crude oil extracted from disputed territory was nonjusticiable: "The ownership of lands disputed by foreign sovereigns is a political question of foreign relations, the resolution of which is committed to the Executive Branch by the Constitution."), *cert. denied*, 444 U.S. 928 (1979). *See generally* Goldwater v. Carter, 444 U.S. 996 (1979); Baker v. Carr, 369 U.S. 186 (1962).

294. *See Kirkpatrick*, 493 U.S. at 409.

295. *International Ass'n of Machinists*, 649 F.2d at 1358.

years.[296] Lower courts generally had engaged in a "case by case analysis of the extent to which the separation of powers concerns on which the doctrine is based were implicated."[297] Courts were more likely to apply the doctrine where a foreign state nationalized private property,[298] where the questioned government conduct was public rather than commercial in nature,[299] or where a judicial pronouncement might have potentially serious foreign policy ramifications,[300] such as where a court was asked to inquire into the validity of a foreign government's actions.[301]

In a 1990 decision, *W.S. Kirkpatrick, Inc. v. Environmental Tectonics*,[302] a unanimous Supreme Court clarified several aspects of the doctrine. The plaintiff alleged that a competitor had conspired, in violation of the Robinson-Patman, RICO, and New Jersey RICO Acts, to bribe Nigerian officials in order to obtain a

---

296.   The Supreme Court first addressed the act of state doctrine in an antitrust context in American Banana Co. v. United Fruit Co., 213 U.S. 347 (1909). In that case, plaintiff alleged that its competitor had induced the Costa Rican military to seize plaintiff's banana plantations. The Court held that the antitrust laws had no extraterritorial application. While this rendered unnecessary any consideration of the act of state doctrine, Justice Holmes nevertheless admonished that "a seizure by a state is not a thing that can be complained of elsewhere in the courts." *Id.* at 357-58. Persuading a foreign government to make such a seizure could not be illegal, according to Justice Holmes, because "it is a contradiction in terms to say that within its jurisdiction it is unlawful to persuade a sovereign power to bring about a result that it declares by its conduct to be desirable and proper." *Id.* at 358.

   The Supreme Court reversed the jurisdictional holding of *American Banana*, in Continental Ore Co. v. Union Carbide & Carbon Corp., 370 U.S. 690, 704 (1962). In *Kirkpatrick*, the Court described the act of state discussion in *America Banana* as dictum that did not survive United States v. Sisal Sales Corp., 274 U.S. 268 (1927). *See infra* notes 311-13 and accompanying text.

297.   Texas Trading & Milling Corp. v. Federal Republic of Nig., 647 F.2d 300, 316 n.38 (2d Cir. 1981), *cert. denied*, 454 U.S. 1148 (1982); *see* Republic of the Philippines v. Marcos, 862 F.2d 1355, 1361 (9th Cir.), *cert. denied*, 490 U.S. 1035 (1989); Allied Bank Int'l v. Banco Credito Agricola de Cartago, 757 F.2d 516, 521 (2d Cir.), *cert. dismissed*, 473 U.S. 934 (1985); Williams v. Curtiss-Wright Corp., 694 F.2d 300, 303-05 (3d Cir. 1982); Rasoulzadeh v. Associated Press, 574 F. Supp. 854 (S.D.N.Y. 1983), *aff'd without pub. op.*, 767 F.2d 908 (2d Cir. 1985); Sage Int'l, Ltd. v. Cadillac Gage Co., 534 F. Supp. 896 (E.D. Mich. 1981).

298.   *See* RESTATEMENT (THIRD) OF THE FOREIGN RELATIONS LAW OF THE UNITED STATES § 443 comment c (1987) (the doctrine "has been applied predominantly" to acts involving the taking of private property by foreign states); *cf.* Williams v. Curtiss-Wright Corp., 694 F.2d 300, 304 (3d Cir. 1982). *But see infra* note 324.

299.   *See infra* notes 326-29 and accompanying text.

300.   *See* International Ass'n of Machinists & Aerospace Workers (IAM) v. Organization of Petroleum Exporting Countries (OPEC), 649 F.2d 1354, 1360-61 (9th Cir. 1981) (noting that "the crucial element is the potential for interference with our foreign relations") (citation omitted), *cert. denied*, 454 U.S. 1163 (1982); Clayco Petroleum Corp. v. Occidental Petroleum Corp., 712 F.2d 404, 407-08 (9th Cir. 1983) (per curiam), *cert. denied*, 464 U.S. 1040 (1984); Hunt v. Mobil Oil Corp., 550 F.2d 68, 78 (2d Cir.), *cert. denied*, 434 U.S. 984 (1977); *cf.* Texas Trading & Milling Corp. v. Federal Republic of Nig., 647 F.2d 300, 316 n.38 (2d Cir. 1981) (act of state doctrine was not applied because defendants' challenged conduct did not threaten to embarrass the Executive Branch in its conduct of foreign relations), *cert. denied*, 454 U.S. 1148 (1982).

   In some cases, courts have declined to apply the act of state doctrine where the Executive Branch has stated that its application would not advance foreign policy interests. See discussion of the "Bernstein" exception, *infra* notes 330-33 and accompanying text.

301.   *See* Alfred Dunhill of London, Inc. v. Republic of Cuba, 425 U.S. 682, 697, 706 (1976) (plurality op.) (White, J.); Banco Nacional de Cuba v. Sabbatino, 376 U.S. 398, 428 (1964); *cf. Associated Container Transp. (Austl.) Ltd.*, 705 F.2d at 61 (doctrine not applicable where court not required to inquire into validity of foreign statutes).

302.   493 U.S. 400 (1990).

government construction contract.[303] The Court held that because the validity of
the contract award was not in issue and the act of state doctrine did not apply.[304]
The Court suggested that to place validity in issue a party must seek relief or invoke
a defense that "declare[s] invalid . . . the official act of a foreign sovereign."[305]

Kirkpatrick thus resolved a conflict among the circuits over whether the doctrine
bars judicial inquiry into the motivations of the relevant state actors,[306] or whether
the doctrine is limited to questions of validity of the foreign state's act.[307] Relying
upon the judicial duty to decide cases and controversies, the Court adopted the latter
view.

---

303.   Id. at 401-02.
304.   Id. at 405 ("Nothing in the present suit requires the Court to declare invalid, and thus ineffective
       as 'a rule of decision for the courts of this country,' . . . the offical act of a foreign sovereign.")
       (citations omitted).
305.   493 U.S. at 405.
306.   See Clayco Petroleum Corp. v. Occidental Petroleum Corp., 712 F.2d 404, 407-08 (9th Cir. 1983)
       (per curiam), cert. denied, 464 U.S. 1040 (1984); Hunt v. Mobil Oil Corp., 550 F.2d 68 (2d Cir.),
       cert. denied, 434 U.S. 984 (1977); Occidental Petroleum Corp. v. Buttes Gas & Oil Co., 331 F.
       Supp. 92, 110 (C.D. Cal. 1971), aff'd per curiam, 461 F.2d 1261 (9th Cir. 1972).
          In Hunt, for example, an independent oil producer alleged that the major oil companies, acting
       in concert, had manipulated their dealings with Libya so as to prompt the nationalization of
       plaintiff's Libyan oil interests. Plaintiff did not allege any wrongful conduct by the Libyan
       government. The Second Circuit nevertheless ruled that Libya's action was a necessary element
       in one of the antitrust counts, and Hunt's claim "was admittedly not viable unless the judicial
       branch examined the motivation of the Libyan action and that inevitably involves its
       validity" – which, under the act of state doctrine, a court should not do. 550 F.2d at 76-77. The
       court relied on a State Department analysis of the nationalization, in part to support its conclusion
       that the issues of motivation and validity were inextricably intertwined, and in part to show that
       the State Department had already decided those issues and thus a judicial inquiry "could only be
       fissiparous, hindering or embarrassing the conduct of foreign relations" – relations that the oil
       crises had moved to a delicate stage. Id. at 77-78.
          Similar concerns about judging the validity and motivation of acts of foreign governments led
       several other courts, often relying on Hunt, to invoke the doctrine. See O.N.E. Shipping Ltd. v.
       Flota Mercante Grancolombiana, SA, 830 F.2d 449, 452-53 (2d Cir. 1987) (antitrust claims arising
       from foreign cargo preference laws dismissed on basis of act of state doctrine), cert. denied, 488
       U.S. 923 (1988); International Ass'n of Machinists & Aerospace Workers (IAM) v. Organization
       of Petroleum Exporting Countries (OPEC), 649 F.2d 1354 (9th Cir. 1981), cert. denied, 454 U.S.
       1163 (1982); Occidental Petroleum Corp. v. Buttes Gas & Oil Co., 331 F. Supp. 92, 110 (C.D.
       Cal. 1971) (challenge of conduct "catalyzing" foreign sovereign's disruption of Mideast oil
       operations would require inquiry "into the authenticity and motivation of the acts of foreign
       sovereigns"), aff'd per curiam, 461 F.2d 1261 (9th Cir.), cert. denied, 409 U.S. 950 (1972); General
       Aircraft Corp. v. Air America, Inc., 482 F. Supp. 3, 6 (D.D.C. 1979) (following Occidental
       Petroleum); Van Bokkelen v. Grumman Aerospace Corp., 432 F. Supp. 329 (E.D.N.Y. 1977)
       (challenge to allegedly improper influencing of Brazil export license denial); see also RESTATEMENT
       (THIRD) OF THE FOREIGN RELATIONS LAW OF THE UNITED STATES § 443 & reporter's note 7
       (1987).
307.   See Associated Container Transp. (Austl.) Ltd. v. United States, 705 F.2d 53, 61 (2d Cir. 1983);
       Williams v. Curtiss-Wright Corp., 694 F.2d 300, 304 n.5 (3d Cir. 1982); Industrial Inv. Dev. Corp.
       v. Mitsui & Co., 594 F.2d 48, 54 (5th Cir. 1979), cert. denied, 445 U.S. 903 (1980); Sage Int'l Ltd.
       v. Cadillac Gage Co., 534 F. Supp. 896, 901-03, 909 (E.D. Mich. 1981); accord INTERNATIONAL
       GUIDELINES, supra note 2, at § 5 n.169. The Department of Justice has taken the position that the
       act of state doctrine should apply only in cases where the conduct "complained of is a public act
       of the foreign sovereign within its territorial jurisdiction on matters pertaining to its governmental
       sovereignty." Id. It should not be recognized as a defense "unless resolution of issues presented
       in the suit would call into question the validity of a specific foreign sovereign act." Id.

Act of state issues arise only when a court *must decide* – that is, when the outcome of the case turns upon – the effect of the official action by a foreign sovereign. . . .[308]

> The short of the matter is this: Courts in the United States have the power, and ordinarily the obligation, to decide cases and controversies properly presented to them. The act of state doctrine does not establish an exception for cases and controversies that may embarrass foreign governments, but merely requires that, in the process of deciding, the acts of foreign sovereigns taken within their own jurisdictions shall be deemed valid.[309]

The Court characterized as dictum[310] its previous discussion of the act of state doctrine in *American Banana Co. v. United Fruit Co.*,[311] and made clear that in any event, that dictum had not survived *United States v. Sisal Sales Corp.*[312] *Sisal* involved an alleged conspiracy that culminated in the enactment of discriminatory tax legislation in Mexico. The Supreme Court ruled that the antitrust laws apply notwithstanding the act of state doctrine where a conspiracy is formed in the United States, the conspirators took actions in the United States to further the conspiracy, and the restraint of trade results not from foreign sovereign acts alone, but from the "deliberate acts, here and elsewhere," of private parties.[313]

Further indicating a restricted view of the act of state doctrine, the Court in *Kirkpatrick* suggested that in cases where a judicial inquiry into the validity of the act of a foreign state would not compromise principles of comity, sovereignty, and the separation of powers that underlie the doctrine, a court may decline to invoke the doctrine.[314] While this ad hoc "balancing approach" may be deployed to operate "against application of the doctrine, for example, if the government that committed the 'challenged act of state' is no longer in existence," the Court emphasized that "it is something quite different to suggest that those underlying polices are a doctrine unto themselves, justifying expansion of the act of state doctrine . . . into new and uncharted fields."[315] In other words, courts have some discretion to contract, but none to expand, the scope of the doctrine.

Despite the Supreme Court's clarification of the doctrine in *Kirkpatrick*, various threshold questions remain uncertain. These include the definition of an "act of state." For example, in *Timberlane Lumber Co. v. Bank of America National Trust & Savings Association*,[316] defendants allegedly conspired to block plaintiff's efforts

---

308. *Id.* at 406 (emphasis in original); *see* Lamb v. Phillip Morris, Inc., 915 F.2d 1024, 1025, 1027 (6th Cir. 1990) (donations by U.S. firms to a charitable organization in exchange for tax deductions, the elimination of price controls on cigarettes, and a pledge not to raise excise taxes' because the adjudication "merely call[ed] into question the . . . parties' motivations and the resulting anticompetitive effects of the agreement"), *cert. denied*, 111 S. Ct. 961 (1991).

309. *Kirkpatrick*, 493 U.S. at 409.

310. *Id.* at 407-08.

311. 213 U.S. 347 (1909). *See supra* note 296.

312. 274 U.S. 268 (1927). The Court did not discuss the act of state doctrine by name, although its reasoning, appears to have been based on the doctrine.

313. *Id.* at 276; *see also* United Nuclear Corp. v. General Atomic Co., 96 N.M. 155, 629 P.2d 231, 258 (1980) (the mere fact that a foreign government played a role in an anticompetitive scheme is not dispositive; courts must examine "the nature of the role played by the foreign government"), *appeal dismissed*, 451 U.S. 901 (1981).

314. *Kirkpatrick*, 493 U.S. at 408-09.

315. *Id.* at 409.

316. 549 F.2d 597 (9th Cir. 1976).

to set up a plant in Honduras. The complaint alleged that defendants had instituted proceedings in Honduran courts solely to interfere with the operations of the plant. The district court dismissed the suit on the ground that the judicial decree that caused plaintiff's injury was an act of state. The Ninth Circuit reversed. Noting that the suit did not challenge any policy of the Honduran government, that a judicial determination of the legality of the offensive conduct would not threaten relations between Honduras and the United States, and that the judicial proceedings were not instituted by the sovereign, the court concluded that a foreign court judgment in a private civil suit was not an act of state.[317]

Similarly, in *Mannington Mills, Inc. v. Congoleum Corp.*,[318] the Third Circuit held that the act of state doctrine did not preclude judicial consideration of allegedly fraudulent methods used to obtain foreign patents. The court reasoned that the "ministerial" act of granting a patent was "not the kind of governmental action contemplated by the act of state doctrine."[319] Rather, the court observed that judicial abstention generally has been required only when the conduct being challenged is "a result of a considered policy determination by a government to give effect to its political and public interests — matters that would have a significant impact on American foreign relations."[320]

Other threshold questions include whether a determination as to the validity of an act of state is necessary to a decision,[321] whether the sovereign in question is one

---

317.   *Id.* at 608; *see* Dominicus Americana Bohio v. Gulf & Western, 473 F. Supp. 680 (S.D.N.Y. 1979).

318.   595 F.2d 1287 (3d Cir. 1979).

319.   *Id.* at 1294. In Williams v. Curtiss-Wright Corp., 694 F.2d 300 (3d Cir. 1982), the Third Circuit clarified that it did not create a "ministerial exception" in *Mannington Mills. Id.* at 303.

320.   595 F.2d at 1294 (citation omitted); *see also* Remington Rand Corp.-Delaware v. Business Sys., 830 F.2d 1260 (3d Cir. 1987) (act of state doctrine did not apply to foreign debtor's bankruptcy trustees, since they were not government officials); American Indus. Contracting, Inc. v. Johns-Manville Corp., 326 F. Supp. 879 (W.D. Pa. 1971) (statute of the Province of Quebec not covered by the doctrine because Quebec is not a nation-state). *Compare* Bernstein v. Van Heyghen Frères, SA, 163 F.2d 246 (2d Cir.) (*Bernstein I*) (L. Hand, J.) (subsequent war against, and destruction of, Nazi regime did not retroactively deprive pre-War actions by Nazi officials of act of state status), *cert. denied*, 332 U.S. 772 (1947) *with* Underhill v. Hernandez, 168 U.S. 250 (1897) (seizures by then-unrecognized revolutionary party, which by the time of suit had become the recognized government of Venezuela, accorded act of state status).

        Acts deemed to have been committed by foreign officials in their private capacity are not acts of state and thus receive no protection under the doctrine. *See, e.g.*, Republic of the Philippines v. Marcos, 806 F.2d 344, 358-59 (2d Cir. 1986) (*Marcos I*) (drawing distinction between "acts of Marcos as head of state, which may be protected from judicial scrutiny even if illegal under Philippine law, and his purely private acts," but noting the difficulty of distinguishing between the two); Jiminez v. Aristequieta, 311 F.2d 547, 557-58 (5th Cir. 1962) (former Venezuelan dictator, seeking to block extradition for embezzlement, could not invoke doctrine because his acts "were not acts of Venezuelan sovereignty." They were for "private benefit" only and "constituted common crimes committed by the Chief of State . . . . They are as far from being an act of state as rape . . . ."), *cert. denied*, 373 U.S. 914 (1963); United States v. Noriega, 746 F. Supp. 1506, 1521-22 (S.D. Fla. 1990) (former Panamanian dictator's participation in a conspiracy to import cocaine into the United States and protect money launderers was but "a series of private acts committed by the defendant for his own personal financial enrichment" and thus not immunized from prosecution by the act of state doctrine).

321.   *See supra* note 301 and cases discussed therein.

to whom the United States judiciary owes deference,[322] and whether the conduct has occurred within the foreign sovereign's jurisdiction.[323]

There are also several possible exceptions to the doctrine. Congress created one such exception with the Second Hickenlooper Amendment,[324] which reversed the Supreme Court's holding in *Banco Nacional de Cuba v. Sabbatino*[325] and required courts to determine the validity of expropriations under international law.

The precise status of other exceptions is less clear. In *Alfred Dunhill of London, Inc. v. Republic of Cuba*,[326] the Supreme Court, in a four-justice plurality opinion, stated that the act of state doctrine does not apply where the sovereign's action involves a commercial rather than a governmental function.[327] The Second Circuit and some other courts have adopted this commercial activity exception.[328] Other courts, however, have discounted the authority of the *Dunhill* plurality opinion.[329]

---

322. *See* Banco Nacional de Cuba v. Sabbatino, 376 U.S. 298, 408-412, 437-38 (1964) (rejecting the argument that the severance of diplomatic relations, imposition of an embargo, and freezing of assets manifested such hostility toward Cuba as to deprive that country of the privilege of suing in U.S. courts or raising the act of state doctrine as a defense: "This Court would hardly be competent to undertake assessments of varying degrees of unfriendliness . . . we are constrained to consider any relations, short of war, with a recognized sovereign power . . ." as sufficient.); Bernstein v. Van Heyghen Frères, SA, 163 F.2d 246, 249-51 (2d Cir.) (*Bernstein I*) (doctrine applied to pre-War acts of Nazi officials), *cert. denied*, 332 U.S. 772 (1947); *cf.* Republic of the Philippines v. Marcos, 862 F.2d 1355, 1360-61 (9th Cir.) (*Marcos II*) (deposed head of state cannot invoke the doctrine to immunize his past activities from inquiry in U.S. courts where the reigning sovereign authority is suing to reclaim assets allegedly misappropriated in violation of its municipal law), *cert. denied*, 490 U.S. 1035 (1989).

323. The act of state doctrine does not apply to extraterritorial assertions of jurisdiction. Thus, when a foreign state attempts to seize the property of its nationals located in the United States, "our courts will give effect to acts of state 'only if they are consistent with the policy and law of the United States.'" Republic of Iraq v. First Nat'l City Bank, 353 F.2d 47, 51 (2d Cir. 1965) (citation omitted) (Iraqi seizure of assets abroad), *aff'g* 241 F. Supp. 567, 574 (S.D.N.Y.), *cert. denied*, 392 U.S. 1027 (1966); *accord* Baudes v. Harlow & Jones, Inc., 852 F.2d 661, 666 (2d Cir. 1988) ("When another state attempts to seize property held here, our jurisdiction is paramount."); Tchacosh Co. Ltd. v. Rockwell Int'l Corp., 766 F.2d 1333, 1336 (9th Cir. 1985) ("Notions of territoriality run deep through the doctrine. . . . When property is located within United States territory . . . 'the policies mandating a hands-off attitude no longer apply with the same force.' ") (citation omitted); United Bank, Ltd. v. Cosmic Int'l, Inc., 542 F.2d 868 (2d Cir. 1976) (holding act of state doctrine inapplicable to Bangladesh's extraterritorial seizures); *see also* Banco Nacional de Cuba v. Sabbatino, 376 U.S. 398, 447 n.7 (1964) (White, J., dissenting) (collecting cases).

324. Foreign Assistance Act of 1961 (as amended § 62(e)(2), 22 U.S.C. § 2370(e)(2) (1988)).

325. 376 U.S. 398 (1964).

326. 425 U.S. 682, 695-706 (1976) (White, J., with Burger, C.J., Powell, J. & Rehnquist, J.).

327. The Foreign Sovereign Immunities Act contains a commercial activity exception. *See* Subpart H.1 of this chapter.

328. *See* Hunt v. Mobil Oil Corp., 550 F.2d 68, 73 (2d Cir.), *cert. denied*, 434 U.S. 984 (1977); *see also* Northrop Corp. v. McDonnell Douglas Corp., 705 F.2d 1030, 1048 n.25 (9th Cir.) ("purely commercial activity ordinarily does not require judicial forbearance"), *cert. denied*, 464 U.S. 849 (1983); Texas Trading & Milling Corp. v. Federal Republic of Nigeria, 647 F.2d 300, 316 n.38 (2d Cir. 1981) (declining to apply doctrine in part because government conduct was commercial), *cert. denied*, 454 U.S. 1148 (1989); Sage Int'l, Ltd. v. Cadillac Gage Co., 534 F. Supp. 896 (E.D. Mich. 1981).

329. *See* Van Bokkelen v. Grumman Aerospace Corp., 432 F. Supp. 329, 333 (E.D.N.Y. 1977); *cf.* International Ass'n of Machinists & Aerospace Workers (IAM) v. Organization of Petroleum Exporting Countries (OPEC), 649 F.2d 1354, 1360 (9th Cir. 1981) ("While purely commercial activity may not rise to the level of an act of state, certain seemingly commercial activity will trigger act of state considerations. . . . The 'touchstone' or 'crucial element' is the potential for

In *First National City Bank v. Banco Nacional de Cuba*,[330] a three-justice plurality adopted an exception that the Second Circuit had recognized in *Bernstein v. NV Nederlandsche-Amerikaansche Stoomvaart-Maatschappij*,[331] holding that courts need not invoke the doctrine where the Executive Branch has formally represented that its application "would not advance the interests of American foreign policy."[332]   Because the act of state doctrine did not apply to the facts of *Kirkpatrick*, the Court declined to address either the commercial activity or "Bernstein letter" exceptions.[333]

The burden of proof is on the party asserting the act of state doctrine.[334]   An act of state issue is a matter of federal law whether it arises in a federal or state court.[335]

The doctrine is not jurisdictional, but is a substantive rule of decision. Thus, as a matter of procedure, a motion to dismiss on act of state grounds lies under Rule 12(b)(6) of the Federal Rules of Civil Procedure, not under Rule 12(b)(1).[336]   The stage of the proceeding at which the doctrine is raised may affect its applicability. In *Associated Container Transport (Australia) Ltd. v. United States*,[337] the Second

---

interference with our foreign relations.") (citations omitted), *cert. denied*, 454 U.S. 1163 (1982).

330.   406 U.S. 759, 764-68 (1972) (Rehnquist, J., with Burger, C.J. & White, J.).

331.   210 F.2d 375 (2d Cir. 1954).

332.   *Id.* at 768; *see also* Banco Nacional de Cuba v. Sabbatino, 376 U.S. 398, 462 (1964) (White, J., dissenting); *cf.* Environmental Tectonics Corp. v. W.S. Kirkpatrick & Co., 847 F.2d 1052, 1061-62 (3d Cir. 1988) (State Department's views "entitled to substantial respect"), *aff'd on other grounds*, 493 U.S. 400 (1990). As with the commercial activity exception, courts have split on whether to adopt the "Bernstein letter" exception. *Compare* United Nuclear Corp. v. General Atomic Co., 96 N.M. 155, 629 P.2d 231 (1980), *appeal dismissed*, 451 U.S. 901 (1981) (state antitrust action) (Federal Executive's representations, while relevant, are not dispositive with respect to the applicabiity of the act of state doctrine) *and* Republic of the Philippines v. Marcos, 806 F.2d 344, 358 (2d Cir. 1986) (*Marcos I*) ("Whether to invoke the act of state doctrine is ultimately and always a judicial question.") (same) (citation omitted) *with* In re Grand Jury Proceedings the Bank of Nova Scotia, 740 F.2d 817, 832 n.23 (11th Cir. 1984) (act of state doctrine does not apply where the executive announces it has no objection to a judicial examination), *cert. denied*, 469 U.S. 1106 (1985).

The acquiescence or tacit consent of the State Department also may lessen a court's sensitivity to asserted foreign policy concerns. *See, e.g.*, Associated Container Transp. (Austl.) Ltd. v. United States, 705 F.2d 53, 55, 61 n.11 (2d Cir. 1983) ("State Department's failure to intervene makes us less wary of permitting the Justice Department" to proceed with its request for records of communications between defendants and the governments of Australia and New Zealand).

333.   *Kirkpatrick*, 493 U.S. at 404-05. Courts have also declined to apply the act of state doctrine to infamous conduct. *See, e.g.*, Liu v. Republic of China, 892 F.2d 1419, 1432-34 (9th Cir. 1989) (foreign intelligence officer who allegedly ordered assasination in the United States could not raise doctrine as a defense in a wrongful death action brought by widow), *cert. dismissed*, 111 S. Ct. 27 (1990); Letelier v. Republic of Chile, 488 F. Supp. 665, 671-74 (D.D.C. 1980) (assasination in Washington, D.C. allegedly ordered by foreign government); Filartiga v. Pena-Irala, 630 F.2d 876, 889-90 (2d Cir. 1980) (dictum) (torture committed by Paraguayan official not protected by the act of state doctrine, even though committed within the territory of a foreign state, because torture is a violation of universally recognized human rights).

334.   Alfred Dunhill of London, Inc. v. Republic of Cuba, 425 U.S. 682, 691 (1976); Linseman v. World Hockey Ass'n, 439 F. Supp. 1315, 1323 (D. Conn. 1977).

335.   Banco Nacional de Cuba v. Sabbatino, 376 U.S. 398, 425-27 (1964).

336.   Ricaud v. American Metal Co., 246 U.S. 304, 309 (1918); Lamb v. Phillip Morris, Inc., 915 F.2d 1024, 1026 n.3 (6th Cir. 1990), *cert. denied*, 111 S. Ct. 961 (1991); Timberlane Lumber Co. v. Bank of America Nat'l Trust & Savings Ass'n, 549 F.2d 597, 602 (9th Cir. 1976).

337.   705 F.2d 53 (2d Cir. 1983).

Circuit reversed the district court's decision to quash civil investigative demands of the Antitrust Division on *Noerr-Pennington*[338] and act of state grounds, holding that civil investigative demands could be enforced to compel production of communications to the Federal Maritime Commission and New Zealand and Australian Government agencies. The court emphasized that it was premature to foreclose inquiry, and specifically noted that its decision "in no way indicates that these doctrines may not properly be invoked at a later state of these proceedings should the Justice Department decide to bring formal charges."[339]

3. Foreign Sovereign Compulsion

Conduct by private parties in violation of the antitrust laws is not immunized from prosecution by encouragement or approval of a foreign sovereign.[340] However, courts generally will not impose antitrust liability if the offending conduct results from compulsion by a foreign government.[341] The defense of sovereign compulsion constitutes a judicial recognition that it would be unfair to assess liability against a private party compelled to act by the command of a foreign sovereign,[342] at least where a refusal to comply with the sovereign's command would result in the imposition of significant penalties or in the denial of significant benefits.[343]

---

338. *See* Subpart B.3 of Chapter XI of this treatise.

339. 705 F.2d at 62; *see* Cofinco, Inc. v. Angola Coffee Co., 1975-2 Trade Cas. (CCH) ¶ 60,456 (S.D.N.Y. 1975) (denying summary judgment motion because genuine issues of material fact existed concerning the act of state defense). *But see In re* Investigation of World Arrangements With Regard to Prod., Transp., Ref., and Distrib. of Petroleum, 13 F.R.D. 280 (D.D.C. 1952) (grand jury subpoena in Antitrust Division oil cartel investigation quashed).

340. Mannington Mills, Inc. v. Congoleum Corp., 595 F.2d 1287, 1293 (3d Cir. 1979); United States v. Watchmakers of Switz. Information Center, Inc., 1963 Trade Cas. (CCH) ¶ 70,600, at 77,456-57 (S.D.N.Y. 1962), *modified*, 1965 Trade Cas. (CCH) ¶ 71,352 (S.D.N.Y. 1965); *cf.* Continental Ore Co. v. Union Carbide & Carbon Corp., 370 U.S. 690, 704-07 (1962).

341. *See, e.g., Mannington Mills*, 595 F.2d at 1293; Timberlane Lumber Co. v. Bank of Am. Nat'l Trust & Sav. Ass'n, 549 F.2d 597, 606 (9th Cir. 1976); Interamerican Ref. Corp. v. Texaco Maracaibo, Inc., 307 F. Supp. 1291, 1296-98 (D. Del. 1970); United States v. Watchmakers of Switz. Information Center, Inc., 1963 Trade Cas. (CCH) ¶ 70,600, at 77,456 (S.D.N.Y. 1962), *modified*, 1965 Trade Cas. (CCH) ¶ 71,352 (S.D.N.Y. 1965); *see also* Letter from then Attorney Gen. W.F. Smith to Ambassador Y. Okawara of Japan (May 7, 1981) (compliance with Japanese automobile export limitations would not violate the U.S. antitrust laws), *reprinted in* 1981-1 Trade Cas. (CCH) ¶ 63,998.

The INTERNATIONAL GUIDELINES provide that the Antitrust Division will not prosecute when conduct has been compelled by a foreign government, if refusal to comply would have resulted in the imposition of penalties or the denial of substantial benefits. Foreign sovereign compulsion will not be recognized as a defense when the compelled conduct has occurred wholly or primarily in the United States. *Supra* note 2, at § 6.

342. Interamerican Ref. Corp. v. Texaco Maracaibo, Inc., 307 F. Supp. 1291, 1297-98 (D. Del. 1970); *see also* RESTATEMENT (THIRD) OF THE FOREIGN RELATIONS LAW OF THE UNITED STATES § 441 comment a (1987).

343. INTERNATIONAL GUIDELINES, *supra* note 2, at § 6. The Department has also stated that a foreign government's representation that such results would ensue would be sufficient to establish that the conduct has been "compelled." *Id.* However, the Department has taken the position that in cases where foreign governments coordinate voluntary price or export decisions of their country's exporters, the Department might prosecute these arrangements as unlawful export cartels. *Id.* Case 14. Nevertheless, the Department has conceded that such conspiracies would be prosecuted only if comity considerations allowed. *Id.*

The sovereign compulsion defense has generally been interpreted narrowly so as not to apply in situations involving conduct by a private party that was simply sanctioned or assisted by a foreign government, but not compelled. For example, in *United States v. Watchmakers of Switzerland Information Center*,[344] a number of Swiss watch manufacturers and sellers entered into private agreements in an attempt to protect the Swiss watch industry. One agreement, the Collective Convention, was devised in part to impede the growing watch industry in the United States. Although the companies were not compelled to enter into the Convention, the consortium was clearly sanctioned by the Swiss Government. One company involved in the formulation of the Convention was owned by a corporation in which the Swiss Government had a 37% interest. The government also adopted legislation to facilitate the implementation of the Collective Convention. The district court conceded that the agreements were approved by the government and were recognized in Switzerland as "facts of economic and industrial life."[345] However, absent a showing that the companies were forced to organize by the Swiss Government, the foreign sovereign compulsion defense was held inapplicable. Similar results have been reached in other cases.[346] In its *International Guidelines*, the Department of Justice has indicated, however, that even where a compulsion defense is unavailable, foreign government encouragement or permission may be taken into account in a comity analysis.[347]

The sovereign compulsion defense seems to have been employed successfully in only one reported case. In *Interamerican Refining Corp. v. Texaco Maracaibo, Inc.*,[348] the defendants were ordered by the Venezuelan Government not to sell oil to the plaintiff, and there was no evidence that the defendants had induced the Venezuelan Government to act. The district court stated:

> When a nation compels a trade practice, firms there have no choice but to obey. Acts of business become effectively acts of the sovereign. . . . Anti-competitive practices compelled by foreign nations are not restraints of commerce, as commerce is understood in the

---

344. 1963 Trade Cas. (CCH) ¶ 70,600 (S.D.N.Y. 1962), *modified*, 1965 Trade Cas. (CCH) ¶ 71,352 (S.D.N.Y. 1965).

345. 1963 Trade Cas. (CCH) ¶ 70,600, at 77,456.

346. In Continental Ore Co. v. Union Carbide & Carbon Corp., 370 U.S. 690 (1961), the Supreme Court held that a corporation was not immunized from antitrust liability by virtue of its position as an agent for the Canadian government. Although the alleged antitrust violation occurred while the corporation was acting as an agent, the Court found that the Canadian government had neither directed nor approved of the anticompetitive conduct and that it was not compelled by Canadian law. Absent compulsion, the corporation's actions were held susceptible to judicial scrutiny. *Id.* at 706-07.

    A number of cases arising out of the Uranium Antitrust litigation considered, but refused to apply, the sovereign compulsion defense in preliminary motions to dismiss. *In re* Uranium Antitrust Litig., 480 F. Supp. 1138 (N.D. Ill. 1979); United Nuclear Corp. v. General Atomic Co., 96 N.M. 155, 629 P.2d 231 (1980), *cert. dismissed*, 451 U.S. 901 (1981). Although the evidence showed extensive governmental involvement in the cartel, the courts were unable to find the requisite compulsion. This inquiry, however, was made more difficult by the refusal of the host governments of some of the defendants to permit them to participate fully in the discovery process. *See, e.g., In re Uranium Antitrust Litig.*, 480 F. Supp. at 1154; *United Nuclear Corp.*, 629 P.2d at 259-61.

347. INTERNATIONAL GUIDELINES, *supra* note 2, at § 6.

348. 307 F. Supp. 1291 (D. Del. 1970).

Sherman Act, because refusal to comply would put an end to commerce.[349]

The court granted summary judgment for the defendants, holding that compulsion by a foreign sovereign is a complete defense to an antitrust action. The case has been criticized, however, to the extent that it allows the compulsion defense with respect to conduct within U.S. territory.[350]

4. Restraints Approved by the U.S. Executive Branch

A defendant in an antitrust suit may seek to raise the defense that the challenged acts are requested or authorized by directives of an entity of the U.S. government. In contrast to the directives of foreign governments, domestic government directives immunize conduct only if they originate from statutory exemptions or from executive authority to permit activities otherwise violative of the antitrust laws.[351]

In *Consumers Union v. Rogers*,[352] the question of the extent of executive authority to immunize conduct was raised in an action charging violations of the Sherman Act in the steel import quota program, under which various foreign steel producers voluntarily limited sales. The State Department and the President actively participated in the negotiation of the voluntary steel import quotas. The Justice Department argued that the challenged restraints were valid, representing the lawful exercise of the President's constitutional powers, and thus could not violate the Sherman Act. By stipulation among the parties, the antitrust claim was dismissed. Nonetheless, the district court, ruling on motions for summary judgment, stated unequivocally that "[t]he President clearly has no authority to give binding assurances that a particular course of conduct, even if encouraged by its representatives, does not violate the Sherman Act or other related congressional enactments any more than he can grant immunity under such laws."[353] Acknowledging that the question was not directly before the court because of the stipulation, the court concluded that "very serious questions can and should be raised as to the legality of the arrangements" under the Sherman Act.[354]

On appeal, the holding of the district court concerning the President's authority to negotiate the agreements was upheld.[355] However, the D.C. Circuit repudiated the lower court's discussion of the antitrust issues and vacated that portion of the decision. Noting the "complex questions of fact and law" raised by the antitrust claim, the court determined that the potential antitrust ramifications from the

---

349. *Id.* at 1298.
350. The INTERNATIONAL GUIDELINES, without directly citing the case, state that the compulsion defense will not be recognized for conduct that has occurred "wholly or primarily in the United States." INTERNATIONAL GUIDELINES, *supra* note 2, at § 6; *see also* Sabre Shipping Corp. v. American President Lines, Ltd., 285 F. Supp. 949, 954 (S.D.N.Y. 1968) (even if sovereign compulsion were established, it "would not necessarily immunize [the defendants] from prosecution or civil responsibility for acts done in United States commerce"), *cert. denied sub nom.* Japan Line v. Sabre Shipping Corp., 407 F.2d 173 (2d Cir.), *cert. denied,* 395 U.S. 922 (1969).
351. *See, e.g.,* United States v. Socony-Vacuum Oil Co., 310 U.S. 150, 225-28 (1940).
352. 352 F. Supp. 1319 (D.D.C. 1973), *modified and aff'd sub nom.* Consumers Union v. Kissinger, 506 F.2d 136 (D.C. Cir. 1974), *cert. denied,* 421 U.S. 1004 (1975).
353. *Id.* at 1323.
354. *Id.* at 1324.
355. Consumers Union v. Kissinger, 506 F.2d 136 (D.C. Cir. 1974), *cert. denied,* 421 U.S. 1004 (1975).

agreement restricting imports were not ripe in view of plaintiff's decision to abandon that claim.[356]

The Justice Department has taken the position that U.S. government negotiators of import restraints by foreign governments should not incur antitrust liability for negotiating such restrictions.[357] However, the letter expressing this view did not address the potential liability of private participants in such negotiations.[358]

5. Noerr-Pennington Doctrine

A related question involves the extent to which the *Noerr-Pennington* doctrine[359] immunizes activities by private parties that are designed to influence a foreign government to engage in conduct in conflict with U.S. antitrust laws. The courts are in disagreement as to the applicability of this doctrine in the international context.[360]

In *Coastal States Marketing, Inc.* v. *Hunt*,[361] the Fifth Circuit found that the filing or joining in numerous foreign lawsuits was protected petitioning activity because at least one of the purposes of filing such suits was to establish ownership of the product involved.[362] The *Noerr-Pennington* doctrine protects the petitioning of foreign governments, the court reasoned, because the doctrine "reflects not only first amendment concerns but also a limitation on the scope of the Sherman Act."[363]

Other cases also have evidenced some willingness to employ the doctrine in an international context. In *United States* v. *AMAX, Inc.*,[364] the district court indicated the doctrine could be applied to an attempt by American corporations to influence the Canadian government. It chose not to do so, however, because the defendant's conduct, involving alleged private acts in the United States, was deemed beyond "the scope of the protection afforded by *Noerr-Pennington*."[365] In *Continental Ore v. Union Carbide & Carbon Corp.*,[366] the Ninth Circuit applied

---

356.   506 F.2d at 141. Prior to 1975, § 607 of the Trade Act of 1974, 19 U.S.C. § 2485 (1988), precluded state or federal antitrust liability arising from the voluntary limitation of steel exports to the United States at the request of the Secretary of State.

357.   *See* Letter from then Associate Att'y Gen. J. Shenefield to Senator C. Levin (Dec. 29, 1980), *reprinted in* [Current Comment 1969-1983 Transfer Binder] TRADE REG. REP. (CCH) ¶ 50,422.

358.   *But cf.* Letter from then Attorney Gen. W.F. Smith to Ambassador Y. Okawara of Japan (May 7, 1981) (foreign firms would not incur antitrust liability by complying with government directives), *reprinted in* 1981-1 Trade Cas. (CCH) ¶ 63,998.

           The Department has also stated that an agreement among domestic and foreign competitors to raise the price of products imported into the United States would constitute an antitrust violation even if the agreement was made to settle a dumping case. INTERNATIONAL GUIDELINES, *supra* note 2, at Case 17.

359.   United Mine Workers v. Pennington, 381 U.S. 657 (1965); Eastern R.R. Presidents Conference v. Noerr Motor Freight, Inc., 365 U.S. 127 (1961). For a more extensive discussion of this doctrine, see Subpart B.3 of Chapter XI of this treatise.

360.   *See, e.g.*, Associated Container Transp. (Austl.) Ltd. v. United States, 705 F.2d 53, 60 n.10 (2d Cir. 1983) (declining to resolve question but ruling that the doctrine should not block the discovery in issue).

361.   694 F.2d 1358 (5th Cir. 1983).

362.   *Id.* at 1372.

363.   *Id.* at 1364.

364.   1977-1 Trade Cas. (CCH) ¶ 61,467 (N.D. Ill. 1977).

365.   *Id.* at 71,799.

366.   289 F.2d 86 (9th Cir. 1961), *vacated and remanded*, 370 U.S. 690 (1962).

Noerr to find that efforts to influence a private corporation acting as an agent of the Canadian government were protected from the Sherman Act.[367] The Supreme Court reversed. It distinguished *Noerr*, but without mentioning the nationality of the government; instead, the Court pointed to the commercial nature of the activity being challenged.[368]

One case found the doctrine limited to the United States. The district court in *Occidental Petroleum Corp. v. Buttes Gas & Oil Co.*,[369] declined to apply the *Noerr-Pennington* doctrine to allegations that the defendant, through various activities designed to influence the foreign governments involved, had stimulated a border dispute in order to effect the displacement of plaintiff from an oil concession. The court ruled that the attempted persuasion of Middle Eastern states was "a far cry from the political process with which *Noerr* is concerned," and thus the "wholesale application" of the *Noerr-Pennington* doctrine appeared "inappropriate."[370] Another district court stated it is "questionable" whether the *Noerr-Pennington* doctrine protects attempts to influence foreign governments.[371] Yet another district court has expressed doubt about the applicability of *Noerr* directly, but declined on comity grounds to examine under the antitrust laws the petitioning of a foreign government.[372] A question has also arisen over the applicability of *Noerr* where the petitioning entity is itself owned by the foreign government.[373]

The Antitrust Division, noting the discrepancies in these decisions and the lack of a Supreme Court ruling on the issue,[374] has taken the position that it will not prosecute legitimate petitioning by foreign or U.S. firms in circumstances in which the United States protects such activities by its own citizens.[375] However, *Noerr* has been found not to apply to Department of Justice Civil Investigative Demands seeking discovery against foreign firms.[376]

---

367. *Id.* at 94.
368. *Continental Ore*, 370 U.S. at 707 ("Respondents were engaged in private commercial activity, no element of which involved seeking to procure the passage or enforcement of laws.").
369. 331 F. Supp. 92 (C.D. Cal. 1971), *aff'd per curiam*, 461 F.2d 1261 (9th Cir.), *cert. denied*, 409 U.S. 950 (1972).
370. *Id.* at 108.
371. Bulkferts, Inc. v. Salatin Inc., 1983-1 Trade Cas. (CCH) ¶ 65,272, at 69,605 (S.D.N.Y. 1983) (Carter, J., dictum) (disputed issues of fact prevented summary judgment); *see also* California Motor Transp. Co. v. Trucking Unlimited, 404 U.S. 508 (1972); Laker Airways v. Pan Am. World Airways, 604 F. Supp. 280, 287 n.20 (D.D.C. 1984); Dominicus Americana Bohio v. Gulf & W. Indus., 473 F. Supp. 680, 690 n.3 (S.D.N.Y. 1979) (Carter, J., dictum) (*Noerr*'s applicability to lobbying foreign governments is an "open question," but attempts to influence Dominican government were corrupt and coercive and thus would have fallen within the *Noerr* "sham" exception).
372. *Laker Airways*, 604 F. Supp. 280.
373. In dictum in an earlier decision in *Laker Airways*, the district court questioned whether an entity owned by a foreign government would have the same right to petition as would a private party, or whether the government's pecuniary interest might vitiate the arm's-length relationship normally assumed in petitioning. Laker Airways v. Pan Am. World Airways, 596 F. Supp. 202, 205 n.9 (D.D.C. 1984).
374. INTERNATIONAL GUIDELINES, *supra* note 2, at § 7.
375. *Id.*
376. *See* Australia/Eastern U.S.A. Shipping Conference v. United States, 537 F. Supp. 807, 812 (D.D.C. 1982) (enforcing CIDs because "[t]he Justice Department now explains that although the *Noerr-Pennington* doctrine is applied in foreign contexts in some cases for non-constitutional reasons . . . it is not applied across the board to all dealings with foreign governments"), *modifying*

6. *Statutory Exemptions Relating to Foreign Commerce*

This subpart discusses exemptions for export trading associations and export trading companies, as well as a national security exemption relating to preparedness, production, capacity and supply.[377]

a. WEBB-POMERENE ACT

The Webb-Pomerene Act[378] provides a limited exemption from the Sherman Act[379] for associations that are formed solely for the purpose of engaging in export trade, defined as "trade or commerce in goods, wares, or merchandise exported, or in the course of being exported" from the United States.[380] The statutory exemption, which was originally recommended by the Federal Trade Commission in order to permit U.S. companies to compete more effectively against foreign cartels,[381] is conditioned upon the export association's not being in restraint of trade within the United States, not restraining the export trade of any of its domestic competitors, and not acting so as to artificially or intentionally affect prices within the United States or substantially lessen competition therein.[382]

Few decisions have interpreted the Webb-Pomerene Act.[383] The decisions have

---

1982-1 Trade Cas. (CCH) ¶ 64,721, at 74,071 n.6 (D.D.C. 1981). *See generally* Associated Container Transp. (Austl.) Ltd. v. United States, 705 F.2d 53 (2d Cir. 1983) (enforcing CIDs because *Noerr-Pennington* was inapplicable at discovery stage of proceeding).

377. For a discussion of the protection that joint research ventures can receive under the National Cooperative Research Act of 1984, 15 U.S.C. §§ 4301-05 (1988), see Section I.3.b of Chapter III of this treatise.

378. 15 U.S.C. §§ 61-66 (1988).

379. Section 4 of the Act, 15 U.S.C. § 64 (1988), however, subjects such associations to scrutiny under § 5 of the FTC Act, 15 U.S.C. § 45 (1988).

380. 15 U.S.C. § 61 (1988). The product exported must be U.S.-produced and members must be U.S. citizens. Phosphate Export Ass'n, 42 F.T.C. 555 (1946). However, membership in an association by a U.S.-company owned or controlled by foreign interests would not, in and of itself, vitiate the exemption. International Raw Materials, Ltd. v. Stauffer Chem. Co., 716 F. Supp. 188 (E.D. Pa. 1989), *rev'd on other grounds*, 898 F.2d 946 (3d Cir. 1990); *see* FTC Advisory Opinion, 83 F.T.C. 1840 (1973).

381. FTC, REPORT ON COOPERATION IN AMERICAN EXPORT TRADE (1916). *See generally* FTC, WEBB-POMERENE ASSOCIATIONS: TEN YEARS LATER (Staff Analysis Nov. 1978); FTC, WEBB-POMERENE ASSOCIATIONS: A 50-YEAR REVIEW (Staff Report 1967).

382. 15 U.S.C. § 62 (1988). *But cf.* United States v. Minnesota Mining & Mfg. Co., 92 F. Supp. 947, 965 (D. Mass. 1950) ("Now it may very well be that every successful export company does inevitably affect adversely the foreign commerce of those not in the joint enterprise and does bring the members of the enterprise so closely together as to affect adversely the members' competition in domestic commerce. Thus every export company may be a restraint. But if there are only these inevitable consequences an export association is not an unlawful restraint.").

383. *See* United States v. Concentrated Phosphate Export Ass'n, 393 U.S. 199 (1968) (association cannot make A.I.D. sales); International Raw Materials, Ltd. v. Stauffer Chem. Co., 716 F. Supp. 188 (E.D. Pa. 1989) (association can consolidate members' goods, arranging joint shipment and distribution thereof for export), *reversed on other grounds*, 898 F.2d 946 (3d Cir. 1990), *on remand*, 767 F. Supp. 687 (E.D. Pa. 1991); United States v. Anthracite Export Ass'n, 1970 Trade Cas. (CCH) ¶ 73,348 (M.D. Pa. 1970); United States v. California Rice Exporters, Cr. 32879 (N.D. Cal. 1952); United States v. Minnesota Mining & Mfg. Co., 92 F. Supp. 947 (D. Mass. 1950); United States v. Electrical Apparatus Export Ass'n, 1946-47 Trade Cas. (CCH) ¶ 57,546 (S.D.N.Y. 1947); United States v. United States Alkali Export Ass'n, 58 F. Supp. 785 (S.D.N.Y. 1944), *aff'd*, 325 U.S. 196 (1945) (Justice Department as well as FTC can sue), *later proceeding*, 86 F. Supp. 59

generally involved joint conduct that did not qualify for the Webb-Pomerene exemption because it involved restraints on the export activity of other domestic firms or impermissible anticompetitive restraints within the United States. It has also been held that the act does not immunize cartel agreements entered into between a U.S. export association and foreign competitors.[384]

The most widely cited discussion of the Webb-Pomerene exemption is contained in *United States v. Minnesota Mining & Manufacturing Co.*[385] In that case, the district court found that the Webb-Pomerene Act did not grant Sherman Act immunity to an association that established and jointly operated manufacturing facilities abroad and thereafter restricted its exports in favor of making more profitable sales of product manufactured overseas.[386] However, it then went on to describe a wide variety of export practices that would be immunized by the Act, including: the creation of an export association by four-fifths of the firms in an industry; the use of an association as the exclusive foreign outlet of its members; the establishment of association export prices for its members' products; the allocation of export orders among association members; and the establishment of resale price and exclusive dealing restrictions on foreign distributors of the association's products. The district court found all of these to be normal features of any joint export enterprise essential to its stability and permissible under the Act, absent unfairness or oppressive character in a particular setting.[387]

More recently, in *International Raw Materials, Ltd. v. Stauffer Chemical Co.*,[388] the district court upheld an association's efforts to reduce distribution costs by consolidating goods and jointly negotiating for terminalling services. It held such activities were within the Webb-Pomerene Act's goals to promote economies of scale and that the Act's concerns about domestic trade restraints were aimed at protecting the interests of consumers, not domestic export service industries. In dismissing claims of horizontal price fixing and boycott brought by a terminal operator (who alleged he was made to change the association lower prices), the court further held that even if the association were found to be acting outside the scope of its exemption in other areas, that would not destroy the exemption for conduct in the

---

(S.D.N.Y. 1949) (associations cannot join overseas cartels nor can association attempt to control any terms or conditions of sale by members within U.S.); Phosphate Rock Export Ass'n, [1983-1987 Transfer Binder] TRADE REG. REP. (CCH) ¶ 22,059 (Aug. 1, 1983) (advisory opinion approving commodity barter arrangement); Carbon Black Export, Inc., 46 F.T.C. 1245 (1949) (office operations conducted jointly with domestic trade association not permitted); Pipe Fittings & Valve Export Ass'n, 45 F.T.C. 917 (1948); General Milk Co., 44 F.T.C. 1355 (1947) (agreements not allowed which precluded use of trademarks or labels within U.S.); Sulfur Export Corp., 43 F.T.C. 820 (1947) (nonmember exports cannot be deducted from association's export quota); Export Screw Ass'n, 43 F.T.C. 980 (1947); Phosphate Export Ass'n, 42 F.T.C. 555 (1946) (essential loading terminal use restricted to association members not covered); Florida Hard Rock Phosphate Export Ass'n, 42 F.T.C. 843 (1945) (domestic and export activities must be insulated from each other).

384. *See* United States v. United States Alkali Export Ass'n, 325 U.S. 196 (1945).

385. 92 F. Supp. 947 (D. Mass. 1950) (Wyzanski, J.).

386. While an association may not itself own overseas production, individual members may, provided they take care to keep those operations fully independent so as to avoid any artificial or intentional impact on domestic prices traceable to their foreign operations. *See* 92 F. Supp. at 962; FTC Advisory Opinion, *summarized at* 90 F.T.C. 1874-75 (Sept. 21, 1966).

387. 92 F. Supp. at 965.

388. 716 F. Supp. 188, 191-92 (E.D. Pa. 1989), *reversed on other grounds*, 898 F.2d 946 (3d Cir. 1990).

course of export trade.

In order to obtain the antitrust immunity provided by the Webb-Pomerene Act, associations must register with the Federal Trade Commission and file annual reports.[389] Association activities outside the scope of the immunity may be challenged at any time by the antitrust enforcement agencies or private parties.[390]

b. CERTIFICATES OF REVIEW

Title III of the Export Trading Company Act of 1982[391] creates a procedure by which any person engaged in export trade may request a Certificate of Review from the Secretary of Commerce that confers partial antitrust immunity.[392] Under Sections 303(a) and 303(b) of the Act, the Secretary must issue a Certificate of Review to any applicant that establishes that its export trade, export trade activities, and methods of operation will

(1) result in neither a substantial lessening of competition or restraint of trade within the United States nor a substantial restraint of the export trade of any competitor of the applicant,

(2) not unreasonably enhance, stabilize, or depress prices within the United States of the goods, wares, merchandise, or services of the class exported by the applicant,

(3) not constitute unfair methods of competition against competitors engaged in the export of goods, wares, merchandise, or services of the class exported by the applicant, and

(4) not include any act that may reasonably be expected to result in the sale for consumption or resale within the United States of the goods, wares, merchandise, or services exported by the applicant.[393]

To a large extent, standards for certification are a codification of the Webb-Pomerene exemption, discussed above.[394] However, unlike the Webb-Pomerene Act, a Certificate of Review can cover export of services, including the licensing of technology.[395] Export trade certification also affords some significant additional procedural safeguards and limitations of liability, discussed below. The Secretary of Commerce has issued Guidelines that "discuss the eligibility requirements, certification standards and analytical approach which the Departments of Commerce and Justice will utilize in determining whether to issue an export trade certificate of review."[396]

---

389. 15 U.S.C. § 65 (1988); 16 C.F.R. § 1.42 (1991). As of January 1992, twenty-one associations were registered with the FTC.

390. *See, e.g.*, United States v. United States Alkali Export Ass'n, 58 F. Supp. 785 (S.D.N.Y. 1944), *aff'd*, 325 U.S. 196 (1945).

391. 15 U.S.C. §§ 4001-4021 (1988).

392. Rules for applications for Certificates of Review are published at 50 FED. REG. 1804 (1985).

393. 15 U.S.C. § 4013(a) (1988).

394. *See* H.R. REP. NO. 637(I), 97th Cong., 2d Sess. 18-19 (1982), *reprinted in* 1982 U.S. CODE CONG. & ADMIN. NEWS 2431 at 2440-41; *see also* S. REP. NO. 27, 97th Cong., 1st. Sess. 10 (1981).

395. 15 U.S.C. §§ 4002(a)(2), (a)(3) (1988).

396. GUIDELINES FOR THE ISSUANCE OF EXPORT TRADE CERTIFICATES OF REVIEW (1985), *reprinted in* 4 TRADE REG. REP. (CCH) ¶ 13,300. These Guidelines contain several examples illustrating application of the certification standards to specific export trade conduct including the use of vertical and horizontal restraints and technology licensing agreements. To date, roughly 130 companies have been certified to export a number of products and services, including film (52

If the Certificate of Review is granted,[397] the holder is protected against criminal and treble damage liability under the antitrust laws for all conduct specified in the certificate that occurred while it was in effect.[398] Conduct outside the scope or in violation of the terms of the Certificate of Review remains subject to criminal sanctions as well as both private and government enforcement suits under the antitrust laws; and a certificate procured by fraud is void ab initio.[399]

Private parties injured by conduct engaged in under a Certificate of Review may seek "injunctive relief, actual [single] damages, the loss of interest on actual damages, and the cost of suit (including a reasonable attorney's fee) for the failure to comply with the standards" of Section 303(a).[400] However, there is a presumption that conduct specified in a Certificate of Review complies with those standards, and if a court finds that challenged conduct does so comply, it "shall award [the defendant] the cost of suit . . . (including a reasonable attorney's fee)."[401]

The Act provides that the Attorney General may also bring suit pursuant to Section 15 of the Clayton Act[402] "to enjoin conduct threatening clear and irreparable harm to the national interest."[403] The grant, denial, revocation, or modification or a Certificate of Review is subject to judicial review, based on and limited to the administrative record developed during the application process at the Commerce Department.[404]

FED. REG. 12,578 (Apr. 17, 1987)), machinery (54 FED. REG. 6312 (Feb. 9, 1989)), parts (53 FED. REG. 40,750 (Oct. 18, 1988)), chemicals (50 FED. REG. 4251 (Jan. 30, 1985)) and food products (50 FED. REG. 46807 (Nov. 13, 1985)), and to procure ocean shipping (51 FED. REG. 26,031 (July 18, 1986); 51 FED. REG. 20,873 (June 9, 1986)).

397. The Secretary of Commerce may not issue a Certificate until the Attorney General agrees that the eligibility standards are met. 15 U.S.C. § 4013(b) (1988). The Secretary must publish notice of the application and must act within 90 days of receiving the application. Expedited action is permitted where a special need for prompt disposition is indicated. *Id.* § 4013(c). The Secretary must state his reasons for denying an application, and an applicant may request reconsideration. *Id.* § 4013(d). All grants, denials, amendments, revocations, and modifications of Certificates of Review may be judicially reviewed. *Id.* § 4015. However, denial of any application, in whole or in part, is not admissible in evidence in any proceeding in support of any claim under the antitrust laws. *Id.* § 4016(b).

398. 15 U.S.C. § 4016(b) (1988). Antitrust laws are defined to include "any State antitrust or unfair competition law." *Id.* § 4002(a)(7).

399. *Id.* §§ 4017(a), 4013(f).

400. *Id.* § 4016(b). By allowing suits that allege unfair methods of competition, the act permits, for the first time, a private cause of action under a federal "unfairness" standard that may be similar to that of FTC Act § 5, 15 U.S.C. § 45 (1988). The FTC standard of unfairness is discussed in Chapter V of this treatise. The Commerce Department has stated that the Export Trading Company standard of unfairness is "narrower" than the FTC standard and any decisions expanding Section 5 of the FTC Act beyond the Sherman and Clayton Acts and applying to conduct only because of its affect on competitors, "while illustrative, have no precedential significance." GUIDELINES FOR THE ISSUANCE OF EXPORT TRADE CERTIFICATES OF REVIEW (1985), *reprinted in* 4 TRADE REG. REP. (CCH) ¶ 13,300, at 21,108.

401. 15 U.S.C. §§ 4016(b)(3)-(4) (1988).

402. *Id.* § 25.

403. *Id.* § 4016(b)(5).

404. *Id.* § 4015(a); *see* Horizons Int'l, Inc. v. Baldridge, 811 F.2d 154 (3d Cir. 1987). The Third Circuit in the *Horizons* case observed, however, that a challenge to a certificated export trading company's conduct is not limited to the administrative record or standards. *Id.* at 167.

c. NATIONAL DEFENSE

Section 708 of the Defense Production Act of 1950, as amended,[405] provides antitrust immunity for participation at the request of the President in national defense programs relating to preparedness, production, capacity, and supply. Since its enactment, the Act has on a number of occasions been used to grant antitrust immunity to joint action by American oil companies in their dealings with respect to foreign petroleum suppliers and tanker capacity, as well as for various national emergencies.[406] Acting in response to the 1973 oil embargo, Congress expanded the national defense exemption by providing immunity for voluntary agreements and plans of action for international allocation of petroleum products.[407] An elaborate system of record keeping is imposed on the participants in any allocation program and their agreements are subject to close monitoring by the antitrust enforcement agencies.[408]

I. European Economic Community Antitrust Law

1. Organization and Application

The European Communities (EC)[409] consist of three supranational institutions: the European Economic Community (EEC),[410] the European Coal and Steel Community (ECSC) and the European Atomic Energy Community (EURATOM). Since 1967 all three have been administered by a single Commission of the European Communities (Commission), with headquarters in Brussels.

The Commission is responsible for enforcement of Community antitrust policy through investigations and administrative proceedings designed to implement Articles 85 to 92 of the EEC Treaty and Council Regulation 4064/89 relating to the control of concentrations.[411] The Commission's action may lead to decisions involving fines and injunctions. It may begin investigations either on its own initiative or in response to formal or informal complaints brought by member states or private citizens. The Commission may impose fines if necessary information it has requested is not disclosed or if misleading information is submitted in connection with its investigations.[412] Upon issuing a decision of violation of Article 85 or 86 of the

---

405. 50 U.S.C. App. § 2158 (1988).
406. *See* U.S. DEP'T OF JUSTICE, REPORT OF THE TASK GROUP ON ANTITRUST IMMUNITIES 18 (1977).
407. 50 U.S.C. App. § 2158a (1988).
408. *Id.*
409. The twelve EC Member States are Belgium, Denmark, France, Germany, Greece, Ireland, Italy, Luxembourg, the Netherlands, Portugal, Spain, and the United Kingdom. The EC is sometimes called the "Common Market," a term less widely used than in the past.
410. The EEC was formed by the Treaty Establishing the European Economic Community, at Rome, Mar. 5, 1957, 298 U.N.T.S. 47 [hereinafter EEC Treaty].
411. Regulation 4064/89 on the Control of Concentrations between Undertakings, 33 O.J. EUR. COMM. (No. L 257) 1 (1990), 2 COMMON MKT. REP. (CCH) ¶ 2839 [hereinafter MERGER CONTROL REGULATION]. The scope and application of this regulation, relating to mergers, acquisition of control and concentrative joint ventures is discussed in Subpart I.8 of this chapter.
412. The Commission's enforcement action under Articles 85 and 86 is based upon Regulation 17, art. 15(1), 5 J.O. COMM. EUR. 204 (1962), 2 COMMON MKT. REP. (CCH) ¶ 2401 (amended 1962, 1963 and 1971); *see, e.g.*, Fabbrica Pisana and Fabbrica Lastre di Vetro Pietro Sciarra, 23 O.J. EUR. COMM. (No. L 75) 30 (1979), [1978-1981 Transfer Binder] COMMON MKT. REP. (CCH) ¶ 10,209.

EEC Treaty the Commission may, in cases of intentional or negligent violation, impose penalties of up to 1 million European Currency Units (ECU) or up to 10% of a group's previous year's sales, whichever is the larger.[413] The Commission may also issue cease-and-desist orders in respect of such violations and fine those who fail

---

The Commission's inspectors may appear without notice at the premises of a company that is the subject of an investigation. National Panasonic (UK) Ltd. v. Commission, Case 136/79, [1980] E.C.R. 2033, [1979-1981 Transfer Binder] COMMON MKT. REP. (CCH) ¶ 8682. The Commission is not under an obligation to obtain a search warrant before carrying out an investigation. There is no legal obligation to supply information or to submit to an investigation unless the Commission has taken a formal decision to that effect. The Commission may impose periodic penalty payments and fines on companies that refuse to comply with such a formal decision. The decision ordering an investigation must state clearly the object and the aim of the investigation. Further details as to the legal assessment of the alleged behavior or of the origin of the Commission's suspicion need not be described. If a company does not submit to an investigation the Commission must rely on the assistance of local authorities to enforce the decision. National authorities will act in accordance with local procedural rules. National judges or other local authorities called upon to enforce a Commission decision against a company have the power only to review whether the Commission decision is genuine and whether the measures proposed are arbitrary or disproportionate in relation to the aim to be achieved as stated in the decision. See Hoechst AG v. Commission, Joined Cases 46/87 and 227/88, [1989] E.C.R. 2859, [1991] 1 CEC (CCH) 280; see also Dow Benelux NV v. Commission, Case 85/87, [1989] E.C.R. 3137 and Dow Chemical Ibérica v. Commission, Joined Cases 97-99/87, [1989] E.C.R. 3165.

If a company subject to investigation claims that the information requested by the Commission is privileged, it must provide material sufficient to demonstrate that the information is entitled to protection. If the Commission is not satisfied with the evidence, it may, pursuant to Regulation 17, art. 15(1), 5 J.O. COMM. EUR. 204 (1962), 2 COMMON MKT. REP. (CCH) ¶ 2541 (amended 1962, 1963 and 1971), order production of the information and impose fines for noncompliance. Such an order may be appealed to the European Court of First Instance. See AM&S Europe v. Commission, Case 155/79, [1982] E.C.R. 1575, [1979-1981 Transfer Binder] COMMON MKT. REP. (CCH) ¶ 8757, at 9060-61.

In its THIRTEENTH REPORT ON COMPETITION POLICY 270-72 (1983), the Commission published the rules for investigation procedures. The Commission states that its inspectors are to inform the company of the scope and limits of their powers and of the company's right to consult its legal advisers, although such consultation may not unduly delay the investigation or impede its progress. The Commission also states that, subject to the obligation to respect the confidentiality of business secrets of other companies and of the need to preserve the confidential nature of its own documents, the Commission is to allow each company involved in an investigation to have access to the Commission's file in that case. Id. at 63-64. Similar procedural rules for the application of Articles 85 and 86 in the maritime and air transport sectors are contained in Regulation 4056/86, 29 O.J. EUR. COMM. (No. L 378) 4 (1986), 2 COMMON MKT. REP. (CCH) ¶¶ 2821-22c and in Regulation 3975/87, 30 O.J. EUR. COMM. (No. L 374) 1 (1987), 2 COMMON MKT. REP. (CCH) ¶ 2831. Similar rules also apply in connection with the EEC regulation on concentrations and its implementing regulation. MERGER CONTROL REGULATION, supra note 411, and Regulation 2367/90, 34 O.J. EUR. COMM. (No. L 219) 5 (1990), 2 COMMON MKT. REP. (CCH) ¶ 2840.

413.   Regulation 17, art. 15(2), 5 J.O. COMM. EUR. 204 (1962), 2 COMMON MKT. REP. (CCH) ¶ 2541 (amended 1962, 1963 and 1971). On December 30, 1991, U.S. $1.00 was equal to 1.34130 European Currency Unit (ECU). Heavy fines have been imposed in a number of cases. The heaviest so far imposed on a single company is that of 75 million ECU in Tetra Pak, Commission Press Release, IP (91) 715, (July 24, 1991) (fines for tying arrangements, discriminatory pricing and predatory pricing by a dominant company). Heavy fines have also been imposed for vertical restrictions leading to divisions between national markets, notably in the Pioneer case, where total fines of 3.2 million ECU were imposed on a Japanese electronics group and certain of its EEC distributors. Musique Diffusion Française SA v. Commission, Joined Cases 100-03/80, [1983] E.C.R. 1825, [1981-1983 Transfer Binder] COMMON MKT. REP. (CCH) ¶ 8880.

to comply up to 1,000 ECU per day.[414]   The Commission also has the power to issue interim orders.[415]   In addition to rendering decisions in individual cases, the Commission formulates regulations, issues policy notices and annual reports on competition policy setting forth its views on antitrust questions,[416] and issues press reports on both settled cases and formal decisions.

Private parties may seek enforcement of the EEC antitrust rules not only by registering complaints with the Commission but also by suing in national courts for damages or injunctions[417] and by raising EEC rules as a defense in national court proceedings. While private suits based on EEC rules have been infrequent, the right to bring such actions is generally recognized under national laws of the Member States.[418]

The European Court of First Instance, sitting in Luxembourg, hears challenges to Commission decisions (including the amount of any fines).[419] Requests for review of decisions of the Court of First Instance in respect of legal issues may be made to the European Court of Justice, which is the final interpreter of EEC and ECSC

---

414.   Regulation 17, art. 16(1), 5 J.O. COMM. EUR. 204 (1962), 2 COMMON MKT. REP. (CCH) ¶ 2551 (amended 1962, 1963 and 1971).

415.   See Peugeot-Ecosystem, Commission Press Release, IP (90) 233, (Mar. 27, 1990), aff'd sub nom. Automobiles Peugeot SA et Peugeot SA v. Commission, Case T-23/90R, [1990] E.C.R. II 195 and Automobiles Peugeot SA et Peugeot SA (Ct. First Instance 1991); BBI/Boosey & Hawkes, 30 O.J. EUR. COMM. (No. L 286) 36 (1987), [1985-1988 Transfer Binder] COMMON MKT. REP. (CCH) ¶ 10,920 (interim order to supply to assure that customer could go into same business as supplier); ECS/AKZO, 26 O.J. EUR. COMM. (No. L 252) 13 (1983), [1982-1985 Transfer Binder] COMMON MKT. REP. (CCH) ¶ 10,517 (interim order to supply on certain price terms to alleviate immediate effects of predatory pricing); Camera Care Ltd. v. Commission, Case 792/79R, [1980] E.C.R. 119, [1979-1981 Transfer Binder] COMMON MKT. REP. (CCH) ¶ 8645 (interim order indispensable to prevent a final Commission decision on the merits from becoming ineffectual); Ford of Europe Inc. v. Commission, Cases 228 and 229/82, [1984] E.C.R. 1129, [1983-1985 Transfer Binder] COMMON MKT. REP. (CCH) ¶ 14,025, at 14,411-12 (interim orders must be limited to measures necessary to prevent a final decision on the merits from becoming ineffectual and must come within the scope of relief that could be ordered in a final decision); see also FIFTH REPORT ON COMPETITION POLICY 60-61 (1975) (National Carbonizing Co.).

416.   In 1972 the Commission began publishing annual reports on Community antitrust enforcement, and this series constitutes an excellent research source. The series will hereinafter be referred to as FIRST REPORT, SECOND REPORT, etc. The year indicated for each Report indicates that to which it relates.

417.   Damages: An Bord Bainne v. Milk Mktg. Bd., [1984] 1 COMMON MKT. L. R. 519 (Q.B.), aff'd, [1984] 2 COMMON MKT. L. R. 584 (Eng. C.A.); Garden Cottage Foods Ltd. v. Milk Mktg. Bd. [1984] App. Cas. 130, [1983] 3 COMMON MKT. L.R. 43; BMW-Importe, BGH WuW 1643, GRUR 1980, 130.
        Injunctions: Cutsforth, Trading as for Amusement Only (Hull) v. Mansfield Inn Ltd., [1986] 1 W.L.R. 558, [1986] 1 COMMON MKT. L.R. 1 (Q.B.); NV Club and NV GB-Inno-BM v. NV Elsevier Sequoia, [1980] 3 COMMON MKT. L. R. 258 (Rechtbank van Koophandel, Brussels); FIFTEENTH REPORT ON COMPETITION POLICY 39-41 (1985).

418.   SIXTEEN REPORT 52-53 (1986).

419.   The Single European Act, which came into effect on July 1, 1987, provides in Article 168a for the institution of a Court of First Instance [hereinafter Tribunal] to hear antitrust cases and certain other cases previously heard by the Court of Justice. 30 O.J. EUR. COMM. (No. L 169) 1 (1987); see [1985-1988 Transfer Binder] COMMON MKT. REP. (CCH) ¶ 10,812. The Tribunal was first convened in September 1989.

Treaty provisions and regulations.[420]

Although both the EEC and ECSC treaties contain antitrust provisions, only the EEC Treaty's provisions (Articles 85 and 86) are of general applicability; the ECSC Treaty is limited to the coal and steel industries.[421] Article 85(1) of the EEC Treaty, which corresponds roughly to Section 1 of the Sherman Act, prohibits "agreements" and "concerted practices" that have as their object or effect the appreciable restriction of competition within the Community and that are subject to EEC jurisdiction because they may appreciably affect trade between Member States. Article 85(2) provides that any such prohibited agreement is void.[422] The Commission may issue exemptions from this prohibition, however, if it finds that the four conditions specified in Article 85(3) are satisfied. Article 86 is in some respects similar to Section 2 of the Sherman Act. It prohibits the abuse of a dominant position within the Community when such abuse may appreciably affect trade between Member States. Articles 85 and 86 are subject to a statute of limitations insofar as fines are concerned.[423] Council Regulation 4064/89 introduced a system for the control of mergers and acquisitions of a defined Community dimension.[424]

Most of the Member States have some form of antitrust rules.[425] EEC law, which is directly applicable in the Member States, prevails over conflicting national

---

420.   In antitrust matters, cases before the Community courts generally arise as challenges under Article 173 of the EEC Treaty to Commission decisions finding antitrust violations (which initially go to the Tribunal) or by referral of specific EEC law questions by national courts pursuant to Article 177 (which go to the Court of Justice). A private party may originate an action against the Commission in the Court of Justice under Article 175 when the Commission has failed to act within the time prescribed, e.g., with respect to that party's complaint to the Commission charging an antitrust violation by another person. See GEMA v. Commission, Case 125/78, [1979] E.C.R. 3173, [1978-1979 Transfer Binder] COMMON MKT. REP. (CCH) ¶ 8568, at 8259 (opinion of then Advocate General F. Capotorti, July 11, 1979). The cases other than appeals to the Court of Justice from the Tribunal are treated as original actions and can involve consideration of testimony and other new evidence. The right to review in the Tribunal includes review of Commission decisions rejecting complaints. See, e.g., British-American Tobacco Co. and R.J. Reynolds Indus. v. Commission, Joined Cases 142 and 156/84, [1987] E.C.R. 4487, [1987-1988 Transfer Binder] COMMON MKT. REP. (CCH) ¶ 14,405 (confirming Commission's rejection of complaints on Philip Morris shareholding in Rothmans); CICCE v. Commission, Case 298/83, [1985] E.C.R. 1105, [1983-1985 Transfer Binder] COMMON MKT. REP. (CCH) ¶ 14,157; Schmidt v. Commission, Case 210/81, [1983] E.C.R. 3045, [1983-1985 Transfer Binder] COMMON MKT. REP. (CCH) ¶ 14,009.

421.   The relevant ECSC Treaty provisions are Article 60 (price discrimination), Article 65 (restrictive practices) and Article 66 (concentrations). This chapter does not discuss ECSC cases, which are limited to a certain range of coal and steel products. The cases will sometimes be of interest, however, as an indication of the Commission's analysis of issues that arise under the EEC Treaty, in particular in regard to mergers and specialization and cooperation agreements.

422.   It is a question of national law whether the entire agreement or only the offending portion is void. Société de Vente de Ciments et Bétons de l'Est, S.A. v. Kerpen & Kerpen GmbH & Co. KG, Case 319/82, [1983] E.C.R. 4173, at 4184-4185, [1983-1985 Transfer Binder] COMMON MKT. REP. (CCH) ¶ 14,043.

423.   Regulation 2988/74, 17 O.J. EUR. COMM. (No. L 319) 1 (1974), 2 COMMON MKT. REP. (CCH) ¶ 2801; FOURTH REPORT 31-33 (1974).

424.   MERGER CONTROL REGULATION, supra note 411.

425.   Most of the Member States have adopted antitrust laws, the most active enforcement so far being in Germany, the United Kingdom and France. A summary of the legislative developments in the Member States in this field is published in the Commission's annual reports on competition policy. See supra note 416.

law. However, the application of national law is permitted so long as it does not prejudice the full and uniform application of EEC competition policy.[426] Thus, activity prohibited by EEC antitrust law is always illegal, but activity permitted by EEC law may be prohibited under national law in one or more Member States except where this would hamper the full and uniform application of Community policy. The latter situation might occur, for example, where the Commission has granted an exemption in regard to such activity.[427]

2. General Goals

Two principal goals underlie EEC antitrust policies. The first is the prevention of restrictive practices that interfere with the integration of the separate Member State economies into a unified common market.[428] Private agreements are not permitted to replace the regulatory barriers that existed in the past. Thus, restraints that hinder the free movement of goods or services between Member States are regularly condemned by the Commission and are usually the subject of substantial fines.[429] The Commission has frequently noted that price differences among the Member States that are not objectively justifiable may be indicative of restrictive practices and are undesirable in themselves.[430]

The second principal goal of EEC antitrust policy is the protection and promotion

---

426.   Wilhelm v. Bundeskartellamt, Case 14/68, [1969] E.C.R. 1, [1967-1970 Transfer Binder] COMMON MKT. REP. (CCH) ¶ 8056. In addition, national courts apply EEC antitrust rules in private actions and Member State officials are entitled to enforce the EEC rules based on Articles 85(1), 85(2) and 86. National antitrust authorities are precluded from applying EEC antitrust provisions where a proceeding involving the same parties and the same matter is pending before the Commission, but national courts are not. Belgische Radio en Télévisie v. SABAM, Case 127/73, [1974] E.C.R. 51, [1974 Transfer Binder] COMMON MKT. REP. (CCH) ¶ 8268. However, national courts may stay procedures or adopt provisional measures before applying Article 85(1) if an agreement has been notified to the Commission or if such notification is not required pursuant to Article 4(2) of Regulation 17 and the national court considers that the agreement meets the conditions to be granted an individual exemption under Article 85(3). Stergios Delimitis v. Henninger Bräu AG, Case 234/89 (Eur. Comm. Ct. J. 1991). The Commission has announced formal guidelines in regard to these matters. SIXTEENTH REPORT 42 (1986); FIFTEENTH REPORT 43 (1985).

427.   Procureur de la République and Others v. Bruno Giry and Guerlain SA, Joined Cases 253/78 and 1 to 3/79, [1980] E.C.R. 2357, [1979-1981 Transfer Binder] COMMON MKT. REP. (CCH) ¶ 8712. The Commission's determination that an agreement or practice falls outside the scope of Article 85(1) and thus does not need an exemption would not prevent the application of national law. SA Lancôme v. Etos, BV, Case 99/79, [1980] E.C.R. 2511, [1979-1981 Transfer Binder] COMMON MKT. REP. (CCH) ¶ 8714. The precise application of the rule of primacy of Community law in cases involving individual and block exemptions under Article 85(3) remains to be defined.

428.   See EIGHTEENTH REPORT 13 (1988); FIRST REPORT 13 (1971).

429.   See, e.g., Musique Diffusion Française SA v. Commission, Joined Cases 100-03/80, [1983] E.C.R. 1825, [1981-1983 Transfer Binder] COMMON MKT. REP. (CCH) ¶ 8880; Johnson & Johnson, 23 O.J. EUR. COMM. (No. L 377) 16 (1980), [1978-1981 Transfer Binder] COMMON MKT. REP. (CCH) ¶ 10,277.

430.   The Commission's block exemption regulation for certain selective distribution systems in the automobile industry provides in its Article 10 that the benefit of the block exemption may be withdrawn in a particular case where, inter alia, prices differ substantially as between Member States. 28 O.J. EUR. COMM. (No. L 15) 16 (1985), 2 COMMON MKT. REP. (CCH) ¶ 2751. The Commission's Notice on that regulation indicates that the Commission will not seek a withdrawal on the basis of such differences unless they exceed 12%. 28 O.J. EUR. COMM. (No. C 17) 4 (1985), [1982-1985 Transfer Binder] COMMON MKT. REP. (CCH) ¶ 10,655.

of "competition."[431]   The EEC conception of competition is not necessarily the same, however, as in U.S. antitrust law.   For example, the Commission has encouraged cooperation between small and medium-sized firms in order to help them to compete more effectively against larger units within and outside the Community.[432]   Also, the Commission has sometimes encouraged certain forms of cooperation among larger European firms, particularly in industries suffering from overcapacity, although such cooperation is subject to surveillance by the Commission to guard against market allocation or other restrictions of competition.[433]   Further, the Commission takes into account protection of consumers.[434]

Competition is further promoted through the protection of market structure.   The principal Community measure in this regard is the 1989 *Merger Control Regulation*, which is aimed at guaranteeing the maintenance of a market structure permitting "effective" competition.[435]

The two goals of market integration and preservation of competition are also pursued through implementation of the provisions of the EEC Treaty regarding State aids[436] and regarding undertakings that are entrusted with services of general economic interest or that are revenue-producing monopolies to which particular

---

431.   See FIRST REPORT 13 (1971).   The Commission often refers to ensuring "workable competition." *See, e.g.*, TWELFTH REPORT 1 (1982).

432.   *See* TWELFTH REPORT 35-37 (1982).   Measures taken by the Commission to promote cooperation between small and medium-sized firms include issuance of: (1) a Notice on Agreements of Minor Importance, 29 O.J. EUR. COMM. (No. C 231) 2 (1986), 2 COMMON MKT. REP. (CCH) ¶ 2700, expressing the Commission's view that certain agreements between small and medium-sized firms do not fall within Article 85; (2) a Notice Concerning Cooperation between Enterprises, 11 J.O. COMM EUR. (No. C 75) 3 (1968), 2 COMMON MKT. REP. (CCH) ¶ 2699, aimed primarily at facilitating cooperation among small and medium-sized firms; (3) a regulation providing for a block exemption from Article 85 applicable to certain categories of specialization agreements between small and medium-sized firms, 28 O.J. EUR. COMM. (No. L 53) 1 (1985), 2 COMMON MKT. REP. (CCH) ¶ 2743; and (4) individual decisions of negative clearance or exemption taking into account the size of the firms involved compared with that of competitors.   *See, e.g.*, Prym-Beka, 16 O.J. EUR. COMM. (No. L 296) 24 (1973), [1973-1975 Transfer Binder] COMMON MKT. REP. (CCH) ¶ 9609;   SAFCO, 15 J.O. COMM. EUR. (No. L 13) 44 (1971), [1970-1972 Transfer Binder] COMMON MKT. REP. (CCH) ¶ 9487. *See generally* FIFTEENTH REPORT 24 (1985); FOURTEENTH REPORT 33-34 (1984); ELEVENTH REPORT 33-35 (1981); SEVENTH REPORT 26-29 (1977).

433.   *See, e.g.*, Synthetic Fibres, 27 O.J. EUR. (No. L 207) 17 (1984), [1982-1985 Transfer Binder] COMM. COMMON MKT. REP. (CCH) ¶ 10,606.

434.   Thus, excessive pricing may be an abuse of a dominant position under Article 86, and in granting exemptions under Article 85(3) the Commission must take into account whether consumers will receive a fair share of the benefit resulting from the contemplated agreement. 85(3), 86.

435.   Regulation 4064/89, *supra* note 411, art. 2.

436.   Article 92(1).   State aids benefit activities or undertakings only in particular Member States and as such tend to affect investment decisions and to create artificial changes in the flow of goods or services between Member States. *See generally* ELEVENTH REPORT 111-15 (1981); FIRST REPORT 112-16 (1971).   The lists of objectives in paragraphs (2) and (3) of Article 92 concerning State aids are exhaustive. *See* Philip Morris v. Commission, Case 730/79, [1980] E.C.R. 2671, at 2690 [1979-1981 Transfer Binder] COMMON MKT. REP. (CCH) ¶ 8695.

State aids also interfere with the optimal allocation of resources and the effect of natural cost factors, thus normally distorting competition. *See* Philip Morris v. Commission, Case 730/79, [1980] E.C.R. 2671, at 2688 [1979-1981 Transfer Binder] COMMON MKT. REP. (CCH) ¶ 8695; Steinike & Weinlig v. Germany, Case 78/76, [1977] E.C.R. 595, at 612, [1977-1978 Transfer Binder] COMM. MKT. REP. (CCH) ¶ 8402. *See generally* ELEVENTH REPORT 111-15 (1981); FIRST REPORT 113 (1971).

tasks are assigned.[437] EEC policy in both these fields also recognizes certain other goals as legitimate, such as social, regional and industrial policy objectives.[438]

3. Negative Clearance and Exemption

The Commission has the power either to issue a "negative clearance" where it finds that there has been no violation of Articles 85(1) or 86 or to grant an "exemption" pursuant to Article 85(3) declaring Article 85(1) inapplicable. A negative clearance is a formal declaration by the Commission that, on the facts before it, there are no grounds to intervene under Article 85(1) (restrictive practices) or Article 86 (abuse of dominant position) with respect to a particular agreement or activity.[439] While a negative clearance is given only upon individual application, the Commission has issued several notices[440] stating that Article 85(1) is

---

437.   Article 90(2). Most of such undertakings enjoy special privileges, rights or a close relation with a Member State which can lead to distortions of competition and affect the unity of the market. *See generally* SIXTH REPORT 144-46 (1976); SECOND REPORT 111 (1972). *See also* Greek Ins. and Banks, 28 O.J. EUR. COMM. (No. L 152) 25 (1985) at 25.

The Commission has taken the view that in the case of "services of general economic interest" or "particular tasks," such interests or tasks must be consistent with and, in principle, expressly recognized in the EEC Treaty (e.g., in Articles 36 and 115), since Article 90(2) must be interpreted strictly. *See* Dutch Express Delivery Servs., Decision 90/16, 33 O.J. EUR. COMM. (No. L 10) 47 (1990), [1990] 1 CEC (CCH) 2038 (abuse of dominant position by Dutch Post Office by extending its monopoly over the basic postal service to the express deliveries market); SIXTH REPORT 143-46 (1976); *see also* TWELFTH REPORT 153 (1982). In practice, however, the range of such interests and tasks may be wide. The Court has held that in specific circumstances the activities of a public agency entrusted with a service of general economic interest may constitute an abuse of a dominant position under Article 86. Klaus Höfner and Fritz Elser v. Macrotron, GmbH, Case C-41/90, (Eur. Comm. Ct. J. 1991).

The Commission has been particularly active in regard to telecommunications. *See* Commission Directive No. 88/301, 31 O.J. EUR. COMM. (No. L 131) 73 (1988); the Commission's powers to issue this directive under Article 90(3) was in large part confirmed in France v. Commission, Case C-202/88, (Eur. Comm. Ct. J. 1991); Commission Directive 90/388, 33 O.J. EUR. COMM. (No. L 192) 10 (1990), Commission guidelines on the application of EEC competition rules in the telecommunications sector, 34 O.J. EUR. COMM. (No. C 233) 2 (1991).

438.   Examples include the improvement of the standard of living and the environment, the reduction of disparities between regions, economic stability, and technical innovation.

439.   Regulation 17, art. 2, 5 J.O. COMM. EUR. 204 (1962), 2 COMMON MKT. REP. (CCH) ¶ 2412 (amended 1962, 1963, and 1971). The Commission has announced that in appropriate cases it will be prepared to expedite proceedings involving either requests for negative clearances or exemptions by closing the proceedings upon issuance of a comfort or provisional letter to the effect that a negative clearance or exemption can in principle be granted. THIRTEENTH REPORT 61-62 (1983).

440.   Variously referred to as "notices," "communications," and "announcements," these policy statements are not binding on the Commission or the courts and may be modified at any time. Moreover, even though not formally revoked, notices may become outdated and therefore unreliable as guidance in light of the Commission's subsequent decisions or experience. Justified good faith reliance on a Commission notice may affect the imposition of a fine. *See* Miller Int'l Schallplatten GmbH v. Commission, Case 19/77, [1978] E.C.R. 131, [1977-1978 Transfer Binder] COMMON MKT. REP. (CCH) ¶ 8439 (opinion of then Advocate Gen. Warner); Coöperatieve Vereniging "Suiker Unie" UA v. Commission, Joined Cases 40-48, 50, 54-56, 111, 113 and 114/73, [1975] E.C.R. 1663, [1975 Transfer Binder] COMMON MKT. REP. (CCH) ¶ 8334. Since many of the notices are in particular designed to aid small and medium-sized enterprises, they sometimes apply only in instances of relatively small market shares. Attention must therefore be given to the relevant market in order to determine whether a notice's market share requirements are satisfied.

inapplicable to certain categories of agreements specified in such notices. These notices relate to agreements of minor importance,[441] agreements with commercial agents,[442] cooperation agreements[443] and subcontracting agreements,[444] among others.

The Commission may grant individual exemptions under Article 85(3) upon application by one or more of the parties to an agreement. In order to grant an exemption, the Commission must that all four conditions specified in Article 85(3) are satisfied.[445] These are: (1) an improvement in production or distribution or promotion of technical or economic progress, (2) an equitable sharing by consumers in the gains, (3) the indispensability of the restraints to the benefits sought, and (4) the absence of the elimination of competition with respect to a substantial part of the market.[446] Exemptions are valid only for the period specified in the exemption and are usually subject to specific conditions and surveillance by the Commission.

A negative clearance or an individual exemption can be granted only upon application to the Commission,[447] except in certain relatively limited categories of

---

For example, in Vaessen-Moris, 22 O.J. EUR. COMM. (No. L 19) 32 (1979), [1978-1981 Transfer Binder] COMMON MKT. REP. (CCH) ¶ 10,107, the Commission prohibited two clauses in a patent licensing agreement between two relatively small enterprises. The predecessor of the present Notice on Agreements of Minor Importance, 29 O.J. EUR. COMM. (No. C 231) 2 (1986), 2 COMMON MKT. REP. (CCH) ¶ 2700, was held inapplicable since the market share of one of the parties exceeded 5% in a market defined to include only sausage casings for Boulogne sausages, rather than for all sausages.

441. The Notice on Agreements of Minor Importance, 29 O.J. EUR. COMM. (No. C 231) 2 (1986), 2 COMMON MKT. REP. (CCH) ¶ 2700, expresses the Commission's view that Article 85(1) does not apply to agreements between firms engaged in the production or distribution of goods as to which both a 5% market share criterion and a 200 million ECU annual turnover criterion are met. *See infra* note 468.

442. The 1962 Announcement on Exclusive Agency Contracts, 5 J.O. COMM. EUR. 2921 (1962), 2 COMMON MKT. REP. (CCH) ¶ 2697, expresses the Commission's view that Article 85(1) does not apply to agreements, in particular exclusive agency agreements, made with bona fide commercial agents. The guideline is not an easy one to apply and subsequent case law seems to have limited the applicability of the notice. *See infra* note 522 and accompanying text. It is expected that a new notice will be issued.

443. The 1968 Notice on Agreements, Decisions and Concerted Practices Concerning Cooperation Between Enterprises, 11 J.O. COMM. EUR. (No. C 75) 3 (1968), 2 COMMON MKT. REP. (CCH) ¶ 2699, expresses the Commission's view that Article 85(1) does not apply to certain types of cooperation agreements. *See infra* note 480 and accompanying text.

444. The 1978 Notice on Subcontracting Agreements, 22 O.J. EUR. COMM. (No. C 1) 2 (1979), 2 COMMON MKT. REP. (CCH) ¶ 2701, expresses the Commission's view that Article 85(1) does not apply to certain subcontracting agreements.

445. The Court has found that the Commission's grant or refusal to grant an exemption cannot be overturned unless the applicant can show that the Commission has abused its discretion. *See, e.g.*, Verband der Sachversicherer v. Commission, Case 45/85, [1987] E.C.R. 405, [1987-1988 Transfer Binder] COMMON MKT. REP. (CCH) ¶ 14,413 (exemption refused for premium recommendation by German Association of Property Insurers).

446. EEC Treaty, art. 85(3), 2 COMMON MKT. REP. (CCH) ¶ 2051.

447. The process whereby copies of an agreement together with the prescribed Commission Form A/B, 28 O.J. EUR. COMM. (No. L 240) 1 (1985), 2 COMMON MKT. REP. (CCH) ¶ 2659, requesting a negative clearance or in the alternative an exemption are filed with the Commission is commonly referred to as "notification" of the agreement, although technically that term applies only to a request for an exemption.

agreements that are relieved from the notification requirement.[448] A proper notification immunizes the activity from fines imposed by the Commission between the date of notification and the Commission's decision, unless the Commission specifically shortens the immunity period by informing the parties that after a preliminary examination the application of Article 85(3) is not justified.[449]

Notification of an agreement gives it provisional validity as between the parties in certain limited cases.[450] Upon granting an exemption the Commission may give retroactive validity to an agreement to a date not earlier than that of notification.

The Commission has been authorized to issue "block" exemptions for certain categories of agreements.[451] When an agreement qualifies for such a block exemption, the agreement will have the benefit of an exemption without an individual Commission decision. Apart from the transportation sector[452] the Commission has issued eight regulations granting block exemptions that are currently

---

448. Regulation 17, art. 4(2), 5 J.O. COMM. EUR. 204 (1962), 2 COMMON MKT. REP. (CCH) ¶ 2431 (amended 1962, 1963 and 1971). Such agreements include those between parties of one Member State which do not relate to imports or exports between Member States, certain resale price maintenance agreements, and certain joint research and specialization agreements. This exception has been narrowly construed by the Commission. See Fonderies Roubaix v. Fonderies A. Roux, Case 63/75, [1976] E.C.R. 111, [1976 Transfer Binder] COMMON MKT. REP. (CCH) ¶ 8341; Brauerei A. Bilger Söhne GmbH v. Jehle, Case 43/69, [1970] E.C.R. 127, [1967-1970 Transfer Binder] COMMON MKT. REP. (CCH) ¶ 8076.

449. Regulation 17, art. 15(5)-(6), 5 J.O. COMM. EUR. 204 (1962), 2 COMMON MKT. REP. (CCH) ¶ 2541 (amended 1962, 1963 and 1971). See generally SA Cimenteries CBR v. Commission, Joined Cases 8-11/66, [1967] E.C.R. 75, [1967-1970 Transfer Binder] COMMON MKT. REP. (CCH) ¶ 8052; Vichy, Decision 91/153, 35 O.J. EUR. COMM. (No. L 75) 57 (1991), [1991] 1 CEC (CCH) 2062.

450. Special rules apply in respect of agreements existing prior to the time Regulation 17 came into force and in respect of agreements that became subject to Article 85 as a result of the accession of new Member States. See Regulation 17, art. 5, 6(2), 7, 9, 15(5)-(6) & 25, 5 J.O. COMM. EUR. 204 (1962), 2 COMMON MKT. REP. (CCH) ¶ 2442, 2451, 2462, 2482, 2542, 2633 (amended 1962, 1963 and 1971). With respect to such agreements that were notified to the Commission within the period specified by Regulation 17, Article 85(1) may not be invoked until such time as the Commission has indicated its view on the possibility of an exemption under Article 85(3). See SA Brasserie de Haecht v. Wilkin-Janssen, Case 48/72, [1973] E.C.R. 77, [1971-1973 Transfer Binder] COMMON MKT. REP. (CCH) ¶ 8170. Such agreements are thus referred to as "provisionally valid." The principal effect of this status is to prevent a challenge to the enforceability by one of the parties. The provisional validity of an agreement may be ended by a Commission decision informing the parties that after a preliminary examination the application of Article 85(3) is not justified. Provisional validity may also be ended by measures other than a decision, such as the closing of a Commission proceeding dealing with a notification. See SA Lancôme v. Etos BV, Case 99/79, [1980] E.C.R. 2511, [1979-1981 Transfer Binder] COMMON MKT. REP. (CCH) ¶ 8714.

451. Pursuant to its authority under Articles 85(3) and 87 of the EEC Treaty, the Council has enacted Regulation 19/65, 8 J.O. COMM. EUR. 533 (1965), 2 COMMON MKT. REP. (CCH) ¶ 2717, and Regulation 2821/71, 14 J.O. COMM. EUR. (No. L 285) 46 (1971) 2 COMMON MKT. REP. (CCH) ¶ 2741 (amended 1972), empowering the Commission by regulation to grant exemptions under Article 85(3) to certain categories of agreements (block exemptions). Pursuant to Regulation 19/65, the Commission may issue block exemptions applicable to categories of bilateral agreements: (1) for exclusive supply, exclusive purchase or for both, or (2) that include restrictions imposed with respect to the acquisition or use of industrial property rights. Under Regulation 2821/71, the Commission may issue block exemptions applicable to categories of agreements between undertakings that have as their object: (1) the application of standards or types, (2) research and development, or (3) specialization.

452. See infra note 493.

in effect: Regulations 1983/83 and 1984/83, which replaced Regulation 67/67, provide block exemptions for certain bilateral exclusive distribution agreements and exclusive purchasing agreements, respectively;[453] Regulation 417/85, a block exemption for certain specialization agreements among small and medium-sized firms;[454] Regulation 123/85, a block exemption for certain automobile distribution and servicing agreements;[455] Regulation 2349/84, a block exemption for certain patent licensing agreements;[456] Regulation 418/85, a block exemption for certain research and development agreements;[457] Regulation 556/89, a block exemption for certain know-how licenses;[458] and Regulation 4087/88, a block exemption for certain franchise agreements.[459]

4. Scope of Jurisdiction

From the early days of the Community, enforcement authorities and private parties have debated the extent of the Community's jurisdiction over acts that take place outside the Community and over companies that are not present within the Community. The EEC Treaty itself contains no indications other than the provisions of Articles 85 and 86, as interpreted by the Court, to the effect that to be subject to Article 85 agreements or concerted practices must have the object or effect of having an appreciable impact on competition within the EEC and must be capable of appreciably affecting trade between Member States and that to be subject to Article 86 the dominant position must be held within the EEC and the act challenged as abusive must be capable of appreciably affecting trade between Member States. Thus, the jurisdictional issue is primarily controlled by EEC case law, as it may be influenced by Community policy and any limitations of public international law.

The Commission has taken the position that Article 85 applies to acts or agreements that take place outside the EEC as long as there were the required effects within.[460] In *Wood Pulp*,[461] the Court held that agreements or concerted

---

453. 29 O.J. EUR. COMM. (No. L 173) 1 (1983), 2 COMMON MKT. REP. (CCH) ¶ 2730; 26 O.J. EUR. COMM. (No. L 173) 5 (1983), 2 COMMON MKT. REP. (CCH) ¶ 2733; *see infra* notes 505-06 and accompanying text.

454. 28 O.J. EUR. COMM. (No. L 53) 1 (1985), 2 COMMON MKT. REP. (CCH) ¶ 2743; *see infra* note 483 and accompanying text.

455. 28 O.J. EUR. COMM. (No. L 15) 16 (1985), 2 COMMON MKT. REP. (CCH) ¶ 2751; *see supra* note 430; *see also infra* note 514 and accompanying text.

456. 27 O.J. EUR. COMM. (No. L 219) 15 (1984), 2 COMMON MKT. REP. (CCH) ¶ 2747; *see infra* note 546.

457. 28 O.J. EUR. COMM. (No. L 53) 5 (1985), 2 COMMON MKT. REP. (CCH) ¶ 2753; *see infra* note 486 and accompanying text.

458. 32 O.J. EUR. COMM. (No. L 61) 1 (1989), 2 COMMON MKT. REP. (CCH) ¶ 2771; *see infra* note 556.

459. 31 O.J. EUR. COMM. (No. L 359) 46 (1988), 2 COMMON MKT. REP. (CCH) ¶ 2767; *see infra* note 516.

460. *E.g.*, Zinc Producer Group, 27 O.J. EUR. COMM. (No. L 220) 27 (1984), [1982-1984 Transfer Binder] COMMON MKT. REP. (CCH) ¶ 10,617 (firms outside Europe were not pursued because their participation did not have direct and substantial effects within the EEC); Franco-Japanese Ballbearings Agreement, 17 O.J. EUR. COMM. (No. L 343) 19 (1974), [1973-1975 Transfer Binder] COMMON MKT. REP. (CCH) ¶ 9697 (agreement between principal French and Japanese ballbearing producers restricting price competition); Dyestuffs, 12 J.O. COMM. EUR. (No. L 195) 11 (1969), [1965-1969 Transfer Binder] COMMON MKT. REP. (CCH) ¶ 9314 (concerted practices between companies located within and outside the Community affecting prices within the EEC),

practices among companies outside the Community, including those having no affiliates or agents within the Community, are within the jurisdiction of Article 85(1) when implemented within the Community.[462] Implementation takes place when non-EEC suppliers sell directly to EEC purchasers or act in concert with regard to EEC prices and sell at those prices. While the Court did not use the term "effects doctrine," its holding would in most cases produce substantially the same result.

Unlike the Sherman Act, Articles 85 and 86 have no "foreign commerce" clause. Thus, it is unclear under EEC antitrust law whether agreements concerned solely with exports into the EEC or from the EEC come within EEC jurisdiction. Apart from the question of jurisdiction discussed above, these issues relate essentially to the jurisdictional element of trade between Member States.

5. Trade Between Member States

Under Articles 85 and 86, in order for conduct to be a violation it must be capable of affecting trade between Member States. While the Court has followed different approaches in analyzing this requirement,[463] the requirement is now understood as a traditional jurisdictional requirement defining the sphere of application of Community rules.[464] The requirement is satisfied by the existence of an actual or potential effect, direct or indirect, on the flow or pattern of trade across borders

---

aff'd on other grounds sub nom. Imperial Chem. Indus. v. Commission, Case 48/69, [1972] E.C.R. 619, [1971-1973 Transfer Binder] COMMON MKT. REP. (CCH) ¶ 8161; SIXTH REPORT 31-33 (1976).

461.   Ahlström v. Commission (Wood Pulp), Joined Cases 89/85, 104, 114, 116, 117 and 125-129/85, [1988] E.C.R. 5193, [1987-1988 Transfer Binder] COMMON MKT. REP. (CCH) ¶ 14,491. The judgment dealt only with the jurisdictional issues raised in respect of the Commission's decision in *Wood Pulp.* 28 O.J. EUR. COMM. (No. L 85) 1 (1985), [1982-1985 Transfer Binder] COMMON MKT. REP. (CCH) ¶ 10,654 (restrictions found from concerted practices of non-EEC wood pulp producers in regard to sales into the Community). In previous judgments the Court had ruled upon jurisdiction in regard to defendants situated outside the Community but had not formulated a general rule. *See* Imperial Chem. Indus. v. Commission, Case 48/69, [1972] E.C.R. 619, [1971-1973 Transfer Binder] COMMON MKT. REP. (CCH) ¶ 8161, at 8031 ("by availing itself of its power of direction over its subsidiaries established in the common market [the parent] was able to apply its decision on that market"); Istituto Chemioterapico Italiano SpA and Commercial Solvents Corp. v. Commission, Joined Cases 6 and 7/73, [1974] E.C.R. 223, [1974 Transfer Binder] COMMON MKT. REP. (CCH) ¶ 8209 (foreign parent controlled an EEC affiliate); Béguelin Import Co. v. G.L. Import Export SA, Case 22/71, [1971] E.C.R. 949, [1971-1973 Transfer Binder] COMMON MKT. REP. (CCH) ¶ 8149 (dictum supporting the effects doctrine).

462.   *Wood Pulp,* [1988] E.C.R. 5193, [1987-1988 Transfer Binder] COMMON MKT. REP. (CCH) ¶ 14,491. The Advocate General had proposed that EEC jurisdiction would exist only when the effects were "substantial, direct and foreseeable." The Court gave some support to the proposition that the effects must be substantial and direct, but without so holding.

463.   *Compare* Völk v. Vervaecke, Case 5/69, [1969] E.C.R. 295, [1967-1970 Transfer Binder] COMMON MKT. REP. (CCH) ¶ 8074 *and* Hugin Kassaregister AB v. Commission, Case 22/78, [1979] E.C.R. 1869, [1978-1979 Transfer Binder] COMMON MKT. REP. (CCH) ¶ 8524 *with* Istituto Chemioterapico Italiano SpA *and* Commercial Solvents Corp. v. Commission, Joined Cases 6 and 7/73, [1974] E.C.R. 223, 252, [1974 Transfer Binder] COMMON MKT. REP. (CCH) ¶ 8209.

464.   Istituto Chemioterapico Italiano SpA and Commercial Solvents Corp. v. Commission, Joined Cases 6 and 7/73, [1974] E.C.R. 223, 252, [1974 Transfer Binder] COMMON MKT. REP. (CCH) ¶ 8209, at 8820.

within the EEC.[465] A potential effect on trade between Member States may be found, even though the conduct takes place in only one Member State,[466] when

---

465. Bureau Nat'l Interprofessionnel du Cognac v. Clair, Case 123/83, [1985] E.C.R. 391, [1983-1985 Transfer Binder] COMMON MKT. REP. (CCH) ¶ 14,160 (agreed minimum purchase price for intermediate material may affect trade between Member States in light of possible effect on flow of end product); Consten & Grundig v. Commission, Joined Cases 56 and 58/64, [1966] E.C.R. 299, [1961-1966 Transfer Binder] COMMON MKT. REP. (CCH) ¶ 8046 (agreement that constitutes a direct or indirect, actual or potential, threat to freedom of trade between the Member States within the jurisdiction of Article 85(1) even if such agreement encourages an increase in the volume of trade between Member States); *see also* Miller Int'l Schallplatten GmbH v. Commission, Case 19/77, [1978] E.C.R. 131, [1977-1978 Transfer Binder] COMMON MKT. REP. (CCH) ¶ 8439 (rejecting a "no-effect" argument based on limited export potential of German-language materials); Tepea BV v. Commission, Case 28/77, [1978] E.C.R. 1391, [1977-1978 Transfer Binder] COMMON MKT. REP. (CCH) ¶ 8467 (exclusive distribution right coupled with an exclusive trademark license enabled the parties to prevent parallel imports; the goods involved represented 15% of the relevant market in the Member State affected by the agreement); Vacuum Interrupters Ltd., 20 O.J. EUR. COMM. (No. L 48) 32 (1977), [1976-1978 Transfer Binder] COMMON MKT. REP. (CCH) ¶ 9926 (joint venture between competitors situated in one Member State affects trade between the Member States if each of the partners would otherwise have exported the products independently to other Member States); Reuter/BASF, 19 O.J. EUR. COMM. (No. L 254) 40 (1976), [1976-1978 Transfer Binder] COMMON MKT. REP. (CCH) ¶ 9862 (Commission disapproval of duration of noncompetition agreement in connection with sale of business).

466. *E.g.*, Belasco v. Commission, Case 246/86, [1989] E.C.R. 2117, [1990] 2 CEC (CCH) 912 (national price cartel can be effective only if the agreement provides for defensive measures against foreign manufacturers, thereby affecting importation from other Member States); Verband der Sachversicherer v. Commission, Case 45/85, [1987] E.C.R. 405, [1987-1988 Transfer Binder] COMMON MKT. REP. (CCH) ¶ 14,413 (German insurance industry practice can have the required effect on interstate trade either when there is an impact on the financial relationship between a German branch and its foreign head office elsewhere in the EEC or when the practice might affect insurers in other EEC countries which otherwise might be able to offer better rates through German branches); FEDETAB v. Commission, Joined Cases 209-15 and 218/78, [1980] E.C.R. 3125, [1979-1981 Transfer Binder] COMMON MKT. REP. (CCH) ¶ 8687 (agreement between members of a national trade association affects trade if it renders the sale of certain imported products more onerous than others); Vereniging van Cementhandelaren v. Commission, Case 8/72, [1972] E.C.R. 977, [1971-1973 Transfer Binder] COMMON MKT. REP. (CCH) ¶ 8179 (agreement covering all the territory of a Member State by itself prevents market penetration between Member States and therefore affects trade between the Member States); Brasserie de Haecht v. Wilkin (No. 1), Case 23/67, [1967] E.C.R. 407, [1967-1970 Transfer Binder] COMMON MKT. REP. (CCH) ¶ 8053 (agreements covering only one Member State may affect trade between Member States if combined with other agreements, such as a network); GERO-Fabriek, 20 O.J. EUR. COMM. (No. L 16) 8 (1977), [1976-1978 Transfer Binder] COMMON MKT. REP. (CCH) ¶ 9914 (system of fixed retail prices is likely to deflect trade flows between Member States from their natural channels). *But see* Groupement des Fabricants de Papiers Peints de Belgique v. Commission, Case 73/74, [1975] E.C.R. 1491, [1976 Transfer Binder] COMMON MKT. REP. (CCH) ¶ 8335 (Commission failed to meet its burden of proof); Kabelmetal-Luchaire, 18 O.J. EUR. COMM. (No. L 222) 34 (1975), [1973-1975 Transfer Binder] COMMON MKT. REP. (CCH) ¶ 9761 (restrictions on the resale of a product may not affect trade between Member States if the products are not suitable for marketing through intermediaries); Finnpap, 32 O.J. EUR. COMM. (No. C 45) 4 (1989) (restrictions on resale may not affect trade between Member States if reexportation is unlikely due to the bulky and fragile nature of the product).

Agreements covering the whole of the EEC between a company in the Community and one located outside it may also affect trade between Member States. *See* BBC Brown Boveri, Decision 88/541, 31 O.J. EUR. COMM. (No. L 301) 68 (1988), [1989] 1 CEC (CCH) 2234. Agreements may have an appreciable effect on trade between Member States even though the primary impact is outside the EEC. *See* Greenwich Film Production v. SACEM, Case 22/79, [1979] E.C.R. 3275, [1978-1979 Transfer Binder] COMMON MKT. REP. (CCH) ¶ 8567.

such conduct may deflect trade from the channels that it might otherwise follow.[467]

The Court requires that the actual or potential effect on Member State trade be "appreciable."[468] Restrictions on exports that impede the flow of products into the EEC or from the EEC can have an appreciable effect on trade between Member States. The Commission has held that export bans on duty-free products to EFTA countries may fall within Article 85(1) where transportation costs and the absence of customs duties permit the products to be re-imported into the EEC and thus potentially affect not only competition within the EEC but also trade between Member States.[469] The Court has indicated that an abusive act that limits exports to non-EEC areas may affect an EEC firm's industrial performance or existence and thus indirectly limit or preclude its potential shipments to other Member States, thereby bringing the abusive act under EEC jurisdiction. As a general matter, trade between Member States is clearly affected by a change in the competitive structure resulting from the elimination of a significant competitor.[470]

6. Article 85 (Restrictive Agreements)

Article 85[471] prohibits:

all agreements between undertakings, decisions by associations of undertakings and concerted practices which may affect trade between Member States and which have as their object or effect the prevention, restriction or distortion of competition within the common market, and in particular those which:

---

467. This effect will be found only where there exists, actually or potentially, a normal pattern of trade between Member States in the product in question. *See* Hugin Kassaregister AB v. Commission, Case 22/78, [1979] E.C.R. 1869, [1978-1979 Transfer Binder] COMMON MKT. REP. (CCH) ¶ 8524.

468. *E.g.*, Hasselblad (GB) Ltd. v. Commission, Case 86/82, [1984] E.C.R. 883, [1983-1985 Transfer Binder] COMMON MKT. REP. (CCH) ¶ 14,014; Société de Vente de Ciments et Bétons de l'Est, SA and Kerpen & Kerpen GmbH & Co. KG, Case 319/82, [1983] E.C.R. 4173, [1983-1985 Transfer Binder] COMMON MKT. REP. (CCH) ¶ 14,043; Völk v. Vervaecke, Case 5/69, [1969] E.C.R. 295, [1967-1970 Transfer Binder] COMMON MKT. REP. (CCH) ¶ 8074; Notice on Agreements of Minor Importance, 29 O.J. EUR. COMM. (No. C 231) 2 (1986), 2 COMMON MKT. REP. (CCH) ¶ 2700. In one case, a beer supply agreement that formed part of a network of agreements was held to have appreciable effects on competition as well as upon trade between Member States if it met two conditions: if there was significant entry barriers and the network of agreements significantly foreclosed third-party suppliers. The Court indicated, however, that if the reseller was free to purchase beer originating in other Member States and if as a practical matter there was a real possibility that it would be able to do so, then no appreciable potential effect on trade between Member States would be present. Stergios Delimitis v. Henninger Bräu AG, Case 234/89, (Eur. Comm. Ct. J. 1991).

469. *See* Junghans, 20 O.J. EUR. COMM. (No. L 30) 10 (1977), [1976-1978 Transfer Binder] COMMON MKT. REP. (CCH) ¶ 9912; *see also* De Laval-Stork, 20 O.J. EUR. COMM. (No. L 215) 11 (1977), [1976-1978 Transfer Binder] COMMON MKT. REP. (CCH) ¶ 9972; Kabelmetal-Luchaire, 18 O.J. EUR. COMM. (No. L 222) 34 (1975), [1973-1975 Transfer Binder] COMMON MKT. REP. (CCH) ¶ 9761; Dutch Engineers & Contractors Ass'n, 7 J.O. COMM. EUR 2761 (1964), [1965] COMMON MKT. L.R. 50.

470. Istituto Chemioterapico Italiano SpA and Commercial Solvents Corp. v. Commission, Joined Cases 6 and 7/73, [1974] E.C.R. 223, 252-53, [1974 Transfer Binder] COMMON MKT. REP. (CCH) ¶ 8209 (elimination of competitor as a result of an abuse of dominant position within EEC jurisdiction even when such competitor is mainly involved in exports to non-EEC countries, if the competitor would potentially have had significant exports to other Member States).

471. EEC Treaty, art. 85(1), 2 COMMON MKT. REP. (CCH) ¶ 2005.

(a) directly or indirectly fix purchase or selling prices or any other trading conditions;

(b) limit or control production, markets, technical development or investment;

(c) share markets or sources of supply;

(d) apply dissimilar conditions to equivalent transactions with other trading parties, thereby placing them at a competitive disadvantage;

(e) make the conclusion of contracts subject to acceptance by the other parties of supplementary obligations which, by their nature or according to commercial usage, have no connection with the subject of such contracts.

Like Section 1 of the Sherman Act, Article 85 does not apply to purely unilateral conduct; some "concerted" activity is required. The Court has ruled that a concerted practice can be found when the activity "consciously substitutes a practical cooperation for the risks of competition."[472] Thus, for example, the Court has held that indirect coordination of pricing through unduly early announcements of price increases can amount to a concerted practice.[473] However, both the Court and the Commission have rejected the intragroup or "bathtub" conspiracy doctrine in Article 85 cases, at least insofar as the agreements or practices relate to the "internal allocation of tasks" among members of a group under full common control.[474]

Moreover, Article 85 does not apply to agreements unless they can be expected to have an "appreciable" impact on competition within the EEC and as well satisfy the jurisdictional requirement of having an "appreciable" effect on trade between Member States.[475]

---

472. Imperial Chem. Indus. v. Commission, Case 48/69, [1972] E.C.R. 619, [1971-1973 Transfer Binder] COMMON MKT. REP. (CCH) ¶ 8161, at 8027; *see also* Züchner v. Bayerische Vereinsbank, Case 172/80, [1981] E.C.R. 2021, [1979-1981 Transfer Binder] COMMON MKT. REP. (CCH) ¶ 8706 (uniform debiting of a general service charge by all German banks on sums transferred by their customers to other Member States); Coöperatieve Vereniging "Suiker Unie" UA v. Commission, Joined Cases 40-48/73, 50, 54-56, 111, 113 and 114/73, [1975] E.C.R. 1663, [1975 Transfer Binder] COMMON MKT. REP. (CCH) ¶ 8334 (market-sharing agreement involving the Community's major sugar producers). In regard to application of Article 85(1) to "decisions by associations of undertakings," see, e.g., FEDETAB v. Commission, Joined Cases 209-15 and 218/78, [1980] E.C.R. 3125, [1979-1981 Transfer Binder] COMMON MKT. REP. (CCH) ¶ 8687; AROW/BNIC, 25 O.J. EUR. COMM. (No. L 397) 1 (1982), [1982-1985 Transfer Binder] COMMON MKT. REP. (CCH) ¶ 10,458 (Article 85(1) also applies to decisions by an association of associations of undertakings).

473. Imperial Chem. Indus. v. Commission, Case 48/69, [1972] E.C.R. 619, [1971-1973 Transfer Binder] COMMON MKT. REP. (CCH) ¶ 8161.

474. *See* Centrafarm BV v. Sterling Drug Inc., Case 15/74, [1974] E.C.R. 1147, [1974 Transfer Binder] COMMON MKT. REP. (CCH) ¶ 8246; Béguelin Import Co. v. G.L. Import Export SA, Case 22/71, [1971] E.C.R. 949, [1971-1973 Transfer Binder] COMMON MKT. REP. (CCH) ¶ 8149; Cekacan, Decision 90/535, 33 O.J. EUR. COMM. (No. L 299) 64 (1990), [1990] 2 CEC (CCH) 2,099 (agreements relating only to intragroup relations do not restrict competition); Christiani & Nielsen, 12 J.O. COMM. EUR. (No. L 165) 12 (1969), [1965-1969 Transfer Binder] COMMON MKT. REP. (CCH) ¶ 9308 (Article 85(1) does not govern relationships between a parent and a subsidiary which cannot take economic measures independently from the parent); FOURTH REPORT 34-36 (1974).

475. In regard to the criterion of appreciability, see *supra* note 468 and accompanying text. The Commission's Notice on Agreements of Minor Importance, 29 O.J. EUR. COMM. (No. C 231) 2 (1986), 2 COMMON MKT. REP. (CCH) ¶ 2700, states that Article 85(1) will not in principle apply when both the following requirements are met: (1) the products subject to the agreement (and identical products or products made by the parties which are considered by consumers to be similar on account of their properties, price or use) represent, in the area of the Community

a.   HORIZONTAL RESTRICTIONS

Article 85(1) has been enforced against "hard-core" horizontal restraints such as price fixing, market division, sales and production quotas, customer allocations and collective exclusive reciprocal dealing arrangements.[476]   The Commission has indicated that an exemption under Article 85(3) will rarely, if ever, be given to these restraints.[477]   In addition, agreements for exchange of confidential information between competitors, in particular that relating to prices and sales, have usually been found to violate Article 85(1) and ineligible for an exemption.[478]

---

affected by the agreement, not more than five percent of the total market for such products, and (2) the aggregate annual turnover of the enterprises participating in the agreement does not exceed 200 million ECU.   Article 85(1) remains inapplicable even if in the course of two consecutive financial years the above mentioned market share or turnover are exceeded by up to 10%.   The aggregate turnover to be taken into account under the Notice is the total turnover of the entire corporate group or groups to which the parties to the agreement belong, as defined in the Notice.

476.   *E.g.*, Stichting Sigarettenindustrie, Joined Cases 240-242, 261-62, 268 & 269/82, [1985] E.C.R. 3831, [1985-1986 Transfer Binder] COMMON MKT. REP. (CCH) ¶ 14,265 (market sharing and other practices); IAZ Int'l v. Commission, (ANSEAU-NAVEWA), Joined Cases 96-102, 104, 105, 108 and 110/82, [1983] E.C.R. 3369, [1983-1985 Transfer Binder] COMMON MKT. REP. (CCH) ¶ 14,023 (collective use of a seal of approval to impede parallel imports); VBBB v. Eldi Records BV, Case 106/79, [1980] E.C.R. 1137, [1979-1981 Transfer Binder] COMMON MKT. REP. (CCH) ¶ 8646 (collective resale price maintenance); Soda Ash-Solvay, ICI, Decision 91/297, 34 O.J. EUR. COMM. (No. L 152) 1 (1991), [1991] 2 CEC (CCH) 2003 (market sharing arrangement); LDPE/PVC, Decision 89/191, 31 O.J. EUR. COMM. (No. L 74) 2 (1989), [1989] 1 CEC (CCH) 2193 (price fixing in respect of petrochemical products); MELDOC, 29 O.J. EUR. COMM. (No. L 348) 50 (1986), [1985-1988 Transfer Binder] COMMON MKT. REP. (CCH) ¶ 10,853 (price fixing and market sharing in milk products); Roofing Felt, 29 O.J. EUR. COMM. (No. L 232) 15 (1986), [1985-1988 Transfer Binder] COMMON MKT. REP. (CCH) ¶ 10,805 (price fixing and market sharing involving insulation materials in construction industry); Polypropylene, 29 O.J. EUR. COMM. (No. L 230) 1 (1986), [1985-1988 Transfer Binder] COMMON MKT. REP. (CCH) ¶ 10,782 (price fixing and market sharing among fifteen petrochemical producers); Siemens/Fanuc, 28 O.J. EUR. COMM. (No. L 376) 29 (1985), [1985-1988 Transfer Binder] COMMON MKT. REP. (CCH) ¶ 10,765 (exclusive reciprocal dealing between a German and a Japanese producer of robotic tools); Aluminum, 28 O.J. Eur. Comm. (No. L 92) 1 (1985), [1982-1985 Transfer Binder] COMMON MKT. REP. (CCH) ¶ 10,658 (concerted channeling of Eastern European aluminum ingots onto the EEC market); AROW/BNIC, 25 O.J. EUR. COMM. (No. L 397) 1 (1982), [1982-1985 Transfer Binder] COMMON MKT. REP. (CCH) ¶ 10,458 (minimum prices); Zinc Producers, 25 O.J. EUR. COMM. (No. L 362) 40 (1982), [1982-1985 Transfer Binder] COMMON MKT. REP. (CCH) ¶ 10,447 (market-sharing and other practices); Italian Cast Glass, 23 O.J. EUR. COMM. (No. L 383) 19 (1980), [1978-1981 Transfer Binder] COMMON MKT. REP. (CCH) ¶ 10,285 (quotas); Industrieverband Solnhofener Natursteinplatten, 23 O.J. EUR. COMM. (No. L 318) 32 (1980), [1978-1981 Transfer Binder] COMMON MKT. REP. (CCH) ¶ 10,268 (export cartel); IMA Rules (Dutch Plywood Imports), 23 O.J. EUR. COMM. (No. L 318) 1 (1980), [1978-1981 Transfer Binder] COMMON MKT. REP. (CCH) ¶ 10,264 (market sharing); Pharmeceutische Handelsconventie, SNPE-LEL, 21 O.J. EUR. COMM. (No. L 191) 41 (1978), [1978-1981 Transfer Binder] COMMON MKT. REP. (CCH) ¶ 10,064 (limited market protection clause in cooperation agreement); White Lead, 21 O.J. EUR. COMM. (No. L 21) 16 (1978), [1978-1981 Transfer Binder] COMMON MKT. REP. (CCH) ¶ 10,111 (export quotas); EIGHTH REPORT 72-74 (1978) (market sharing and pricing).

477.   FIRST REPORT 24-39 (1971).

478.   The decided cases have so far related to oligopolistic markets and homogeneous products. *E.g.*, Fatty Acids, 30 O.J. EUR. COMM. (No. L 3) 17 (1987), [1985-1988 Transfer Binder] COMMON MKT. REP. (CCH) ¶ 10,841 (exchange of sales data allowing identification of participants permitted detailed knowledge of market shares); BP Kemi/DDSF, 22 O.J. EUR. COMM. (No. L 286) 32 (1979), [1978-1981 Transfer Binder] COMMON MKT. REP. (CCH) ¶ 10,165 (exchange of

Joint sales agencies that set common prices and other conditions of sale among competitors will generally be found to violate Article 85(1) and only rarely will be eligible for exemption.[479] Negative clearances have been granted, however, in regard to joint agencies limited to sales within one Member State and to exports outside the EEC when trade between Member States was not likely to be affected to an appreciable extent.[480] Joint purchasing agreements have been viewed more tolerantly than joint selling arrangements. They have been granted negative clearances or exemptions on several occasions.[481]

The Commission has shown a relatively permissive attitude toward less restrictive horizontal agreements. For example, the Commission has indicated that certain specified types of cooperation arrangements that promote efficiency and strengthen the participants — particularly when the participants are small and medium-sized

---

sales information introduced a system of coordination of market behavior on prices, customer allocation and market sharing); White Lead, 21 O.J. EUR. COMM. (No. L 21) 16 (1978), [1978-1981 Transfer Binder] COMMON MKT. REP. (CCH) ¶ 10,111 (cooperation agreement providing for the exchange of precise and up-to-date information on deliveries); Vegetable Parchment Producers, 20 O.J. EUR. COMM. (No. L 70) 54 (1977), [1976-1978 Transfer Binder] COMMON MKT. REP. (CCH) ¶ 10,016 (exchange of information on export quantities and sales prices relating to individual companies); COBELPA/VNP, 20 O.J. EUR. COMM. (No. L 242) 10 (1977), [1976-1978 Transfer Binder] COMMON MKT. REP. (CCH) ¶ 9980 (exchange of information on production, sales figures and prices between members of a trade association, coupled with an agreement to respect each member's distribution channels); SEVENTH REPORT 18-21 (1977).

479. *See, e.g.,* Ansac, Decision 91/301, 34 O.J. EUR. COMM (No. L 152) 54 (1991), [1991] 2 CEC (CCH) 2071 (exemption refused for export cartel of North American natural ash producers); Floral, 22 O.J. EUR. COMM. (No. L 39) 51 (1979), [1978-1981 Transfer Binder] COMMON MKT. REP. (CCH) ¶ 10,184 (fines imposed on three major French fertilizer manufacturers participating in joint sales agency); Central Stikstof Verkoopkantoor, 21 O.J. EUR. COMM. (No. L 242) 15 (1978), [1978-1981 Transfer Binder] COMMON MKT. REP. (CCH) ¶ 10,076 (prohibition order with respect to joint sales agency of two principal Dutch fertilizer producers); Nederlandse Cement-Handelmaatschappij NV, 15 J.O. COMM. EUR. (No. L 22) 16 (1972), [1970-1972 Transfer Binder] COMMON MKT. REP. (CCH) ¶ 9493 (exemption denied to a joint sales agency even when improvements in distribution resulted); SEVENTH REPORT 94-95 (1977) (Necomout); FIRST REPORT 31-35 (1971); *cf.* Kali und Salz AG v. Commission, Joined Cases 19 and 20/74, [1975] E.C.R. 499, [1975 Transfer Binder] COMMON MKT. REP. (CCH) ¶ 8284 (annulling, for failure to give sufficient reasons, Commission prohibition order and denial of exemption for sales coordination between the only two German potash producers).

480. *See, e.g.,* SEIFA, 12 J.O. COMM. EUR. (No. L 173) 8 (1969), [1965-1969 Transfer Binder] COMMON MKT. REP. (CCH) ¶ 9315; C.F.A., 11 J.O. COMM. EUR. (No. L 276) 29 (1968), [1965-1969 Transfer Binder] COMMON MKT. REP. (CCH) ¶ 9268. In addition, the Commission has granted a negative clearance to a joint sales agency composed of small French producers exporting to another Member State because the agency was necessary to permit those small producers to compete with larger competitors. SAFCO, 15 J.O. COMM. EUR. (No. L 13) 44 (1972), [1970-1972 Transfer Binder] COMMON MKT. REP. (CCH) ¶ 9487; *see also* 1968 Commission Notice on Agreements, Decisions, and Concerted Practices Concerning Cooperation Between Enterprises, 11 J.O. COMM. EUR. (No. C 75) 3 (1968), 2 COMMON MKT. REP. (CCH) ¶ 2699; *cf.* FIRST REPORT 32 (1971).

481. *See, e.g.,* National Sulphuric Acid Ass'n, Decision 89/408, 23 O.J. EUR. COMM. (No. L 260) 24 (1980), [1978-1981 Transfer Binder] COMMON MKT. REP. (CCH) ¶ 10,246, *exemption renewed,* 32 O.J. EUR. COMM. (No. L 190) 22 (1989), [1989] 2 CEC (CCH) 2006; Intergroup, 18 O.J. EUR. COMM. (No. L 212) 23 (1975), [1973-1975 Transfer Binder] COMMON MKT. REP. (CCH) ¶ 9759 (exemption). *See generally* FIRST REPORT 52-53 (1971).

firms — do not restrict competition.[482]   The Commission has issued a block
exemption covering certain types of specialization agreements between small and
medium-sized firms.[483]   This block exemption applies only to situations in which
the cooperating firms together have no more than 20% of the market and combined
annual sales of not more than 500 million ECU.   The Commission may grant
individual exemptions for specialization agreements that do not fall within the block
exemption when the four requirements of Article 85(3) are satisfied.[484]

Joint research and development agreements generally will be considered not to
violate Article 85(1) if they are between competitors that are relatively unimportant
in the market.   However, in other cases such activities will most likely be deemed to

---

482.   Notice on Agreements, Decisions, and Concerted Practices Concerning Cooperation Between
        Enterprises, 11 J.O. COMM. EUR. (No. C 75) 3 (1968), 2 COMMON MKT. REP. (CCH) ¶ 2699. The
        Notice expresses the Commission's view that Article 85(1) does not apply to certain types of
        cooperation agreements including certain joint research programs, joint use of production
        facilities, joint selling and after-sales and repair services for noncompeting enterprises, joint
        advertising, use of common quality standards and labeling, and cooperation in certain
        administrative and financial matters. This Notice is aimed primarily at facilitating cooperation
        among small and medium-sized firms. The views of the Commission set forth in the Notice are
        quite general and must be read together with subsequent individual decisions by the Commission.
        See, e.g., Beecham/Parke-Davis, 22 O.J. EUR. COMM. (No. L 70) 11 (1979), [1978-1981 Transfer
        Binder] COMMON MKT. REP. (CCH) ¶ 10,121 (joint research and development for the creation
        of pharmaceutical products); Henkel/Colgate, 15 J.O. COMM. EUR. (No. L 14) 14 (1972),
        [1970-1972 Transfer Binder] COMMON MKT. REP. (CCH) ¶ 9491 (establishment of a joint
        company for the coordination of research and development). In addition, the block exemption
        regulation on research and development agreements must be taken into account. 28 O.J. EUR.
        COMM. (No. L 53) 5 (1985), 2 COMMON MKT. REP. (CCH) ¶ 2753.

483.   Regulation 417/85, 28 O.J. EUR. COMM. (No. L 53) 1 (1985), 2 COMMON MKT. REP. (CCH)
        ¶ 2743. The block exemption applies to agreements in which firms mutually undertake (1) not to
        manufacture themselves or to have manufactured by others certain products and to leave to the
        other contracting parties the task of manufacturing such products or of having them manufactured,
        or (2) to manufacture or have manufactured certain products only jointly.

484.   FIRST REPORT 42-45 (1971). The Commission has issued a considerable number of individual
        decisions granting or renewing exemptions for specialization agreements which would not have
        been entitled to the benefit of the block exemption. E.g., ENI/Montedison, 30 O.J. EUR. COMM.
        (No. L 5) 13 (1987), [1985-1988 Transfer Binder] COMMON MKT. REP. (CCH) ¶ 10,860
        (specialization resulting from restructuring of Italian chemical industry in accordance with a
        government plan); Sopelem/Vickers, 21 O.J. EUR. COMM. (No. L 70) 47 (1978), [1976-1978
        Transfer Binder] COMMON MKT. REP. (CCH) ¶ 10,014 (specialization and reciprocal distribution
        with limited territorial protection); Bayer/Gist-Brocades, 19 O.J. EUR. COMM. (No. L 30) 13
        (1976), [1976-1978 Transfer Binder] COMMON MKT. REP. (CCH) ¶ 9814 (specialization
        arrangement combined with reciprocal long-term supply agreements); Rank/SOPELEM, 18 O.J.
        EUR. COMM. (No. L 29) 20 (1975), [1973-1975 Transfer Binder] COMMON MKT. REP. (CCH)
        ¶ 9707 (cooperation in research and development and production and exclusive distribution rights
        for the products developed in each party's territory); Prym-Beka, 16 O.J. EUR. COMM. (No. L
        296) 24 (1973), [1973-1975 Transfer Binder] COMMON MKT. REP. (CCH) ¶ 9609 (agreement to
        specialize where only one party continued to manufacture products); Lightweight Papers, 15 O.J.
        EUR. COMM. (No. L 182) 24 (1972), [1970-1972 Transfer Binder] COMMON MKT. REP. (CCH)
        ¶ 9523 (firms controlled 15%-50% of EEC production and even higher percentages of certain
        national markets); FN-CF, 14 (No. L 134) 6 (1971), [1970-1972 Transfer Binder] COMMON MKT.
        REP. (CCH) ¶ 9439 (reciprocal exclusive dealing permitted as an indispensable ancillary
        restriction); Jaz-Peter, 12 J.O. COMM. EUR. (No. L 195) 5 (1969), [1965-1969 Transfer Binder]
        COMMON MKT. REP. (CCH) ¶ 9317, exemption renewed, 20 O.J. EUR. COMM. (No. L 61) 17
        (1977), [1976-1978 Transfer Binder] COMMON MKT. REP. (CCH) ¶ 10,013 (market shares
        exceeded block exemption's limits).

result in a restriction of the parties' ability to compete by means of technical innovation and thus fall within the prohibition of Article 85(1), although they will be favorably considered for an exemption. An exemption is likely to be granted if individual research is not barred, if the results of the research are available without restriction to all participants and if the joint activity is confined to research and development without spillover effects leading to restraints in marketing or production.[485]

The Commission has issued a block exemption regulation[486] covering joint research and development, which permits agreement for joint exploitation of the results of prior research and development agreements. Joint exploitation, however, does not cover joint selling. In order to benefit from the block exemption the arrangements must conform to a number of conditions defined in the regulation. The only limitations in regard to the market position of the parties are that (1) when the parties are competitors at the time the agreement is entered into for products that may be improved or replaced by the results of the joint research and development, the exemption is available only if their combined production does not exceed 20% of the market and (2) the exemption will in any event continue to apply after five years only if the parties' combined production of the new product does not exceed 20% of the market.

Agreements concerning joint advertising have been permitted either by negative clearance or exemption.[487]   Agreements concerning the use of a common

---

485.   *See, e.g.*, KSB/Goulds/Lowara/ITT, Decision 91/38, 34 O.J. EUR. COMM. (No. L 19) 25 (1991), [1991] 1 CEC (CCH) 2009 (joint development and production of certain components of radial centrifugal pumps); Continental Zummi-Werke AG/Compagnie Générale des Etablissements Michelin, Decision 88/555, 31 O.J. EUR. COMM. (No. L 305) 33 (1988), [1989] 1 CEC (CCH) 2241 (joint development by two leading tire producers of a new run-flat tire wheel system); GEC-ANT-Telettra-SAT, 31 O.J. EUR. COMM. (No. C 180) 3 (1988), [1985-1988 Transfer Binder] COMMON MKT. REP. ¶ 11,005 (general program of cooperative R&D by four European telecommunications companies); Beecham/Parke Davis, 22 O.J. EUR. COMM. (No. L 70) 11 (1979), [1978-1981 Transfer Binder] COMMON MKT. REP. (CCH) ¶ 10,121 (payment of royalties on grant of licenses dropped at Commission request); Sopelem/Vickers, 21 O.J. EUR. COMM. (No. L 70) 47 (1978), [1976-1978 Transfer Binder] COMMON MKT. REP. (CCH) ¶ 10,014 (coordination of separate research and development, specialization in manufacturing activities, exclusive distribution rights for one of the parents and a sales joint venture in different areas of the EEC without limitation on passive sales exempted to allow competition with important competitors); Henkel/Colgate, 15 J.O. COMM. EUR. (No. L 14) 14 (1972), [1970-1972 Transfer Binder] COMMON MKT. REP. (CCH) ¶ 9491, *reexamined*, EIGHTH REPORT 77-78 (1978) (requirement of approval by joint venture partner for issuance of license to third parties opposed by Commission); SEVENTH REPORT 98 (1977) (EMI Electronics-Jungheinrich) (exclusive purchase obligation permitted in respect of products developed under joint development agreement); *see also* Notice on Agreements, Decisions and Concerted Practices Concerning Cooperation Between Enterprises, 11 J.O. COMM. EUR. (No. C 75) 3 (1968), 2 COMMON MKT. REP. (CCH) ¶ 2699. *But see* FIRST REPORT 45-49 (1971).
486.   Regulation 418/85, 28 O.J. EUR. COMM. (No. L 53) 5 (1985), 2 COMMON MKT. REP. (CCH) ¶ 2753.
487.   *See, e.g.*, Milchförderungsfonds, 28 O.J. EUR. COMM. (No. L 35) 35 (1985), [1982-1985 Transfer Binder] COMMON MKT. REP. (CCH) ¶ 10,649 (joint advertising of a general nature which is not brand oriented or based on the special features of the advertised product and not aimed at promoting a product on the basis of its national origin); A.S.B.L., 13 J.O. COMM. EUR. (No. L 153) 14 (1970), [1970-1972 Transfer Binder] COMMON MKT. REP. (CCH) ¶ 9380 (negative clearance); *see* Notice on Agreements, Decisions and Concerned Practices Concerning Cooperation Between Enterprises, 11 J.O. COMM. EUR. (No. C 75) 3 (1968), 2 COMMON MKT.

trademark have been exempted in certain cases when the users are not large and such cooperation has been judged necessary to permit them to compete against larger firms.[488] An agreement between a limited number of companies for use of a common application environment for software has been exempted because of its utility in creation of an open industry standard.[489] Also, a number of judgments, exemptions and negative clearances relating to agreements between banks,[490] traders on futures markets,[491] insurers,[492] and in the transportation sector[493]

Rep. (CCH) ¶ 2699. *But see* First Report 49-52 (1971).

488. *See, e.g.,* Transocean Marine Paint Ass'n, 10 J.O. Comm. Eur. (No. L 163) 10 (1967) [1965-1969 Transfer Binder] Common Mkt. Rep. (CCH) ¶ 9188 (exemption for joint advertising and common trademark when total market share approximately 5%), *renewed with conditions,* 17 O.J. Eur. Comm. (No. L 19) 18 (1974), [1973-1975 Transfer Binder] Common Mkt. Rep. (CCH) ¶ 9628, *rev'd in part,* Case 17/74, [1974] E.C.R. 1063, [1974 Transfer Binder] Common Mkt. Rep. (CCH) ¶ 8241, *revised,* 18 O.J. Eur. Comm. (No. L 286) 24 (1975), [1973-1975 Transfer Binder] Common Mkt. Rep. (CCH) ¶ 9783, *exemption renewed,* 23 O.J. Eur. Comm. (No. L 39) 73 (1979), [1978-1981 Transfer Binder] Common Mkt. Rep. (CCH) ¶ 10,186 (limited territorial protection of markets eliminated), *renewed,* Decision 88/635, 31 O.J. Eur. Comm. (No. L 351) 40 (1988), [1989] 1 CEC (CCH) 2003.

489. X/Open Group, 30 O.J. Eur. Comm. (No. L 35) 36 (1987), [1985-1988 Transfer Binder] Common Mkt. Rep. (CCH) ¶ 10,865.

490. Dutch Bankers' Ass'n, Decision 89/512, 32 O.J. Eur. Comm. (No. L 253) 1 (1989), [1989] 2 CEC (CCH) 2,033 (negative clearance for certain practices and an exemption in regard to simplified clearance procedures for checks denominated in guilders or foreign currencies); Irish Banks' Standing Committee, 29 O.J. Eur. Comm. (No. L 295) 28 (1986), [1985-1988 Transfer Binder] Common Mkt. Rep. (CCH) ¶ 10,829 (negative clearance); ABI, 29 O.J. Eur. Comm. (No. L 43) 51 (1986), [1985-1988 Transfer Binder] Common Mkt. Rep. (CCH) ¶ 10,846 (negative clearance in part and exemption in part for Italian banking agreements); Belgian Banking Ass'n, 30 O.J. Eur. Comm. (No. L 7) 27 (1987), [1985-1988 Transfer Binder] Common Mkt. Rep. (CCH) ¶ 10,847 (exemption).

491. Baltic Int'l Freight Futures Exch., 30 O.J. Eur. Comm. (No. L 222) 24 (1987), [1985-1988 Transfer Binder] Common Mkt. Rep. (CCH) ¶ 10,908; GAFTA Soya Bean Meal Futures Ass'n, 30 O.J. Eur. Comm. (No. L 19) 18 (1987), [1985-1988 Transfer Binder] Common Mkt. Rep. (CCH) ¶ 10,850; London Grain Futures Mkt., 29 O.J. Eur. Comm. (No. L 19) 22 (1986), [1985-1988 Transfer Binder] Common Mkt. Rep. (CCH) ¶ 10,850; London Potato Futures Ass'n, 29 O.J. Eur. Comm. (No. L 19) 26 (1986), [1985-1988 Transfer Binder] Common Mkt. Rep. (CCH) ¶ 10,850; London Meat Futures Exch., 29 O.J. Eur. Comm. (No. L 19) 30 (1986), [1985-1988 Transfer Binder] Common Mkt. Rep. (CCH) ¶ 10,850; Petroleum Exch. of London Ltd., 30 O.J. Eur. Comm. (No. L 3) 27 (1987), [1985-1988 Transfer Binder] Common Mkt. Rep. (CCH) ¶ 10,848 (all above decisions involving negative clearances).

492. Verband der Sachversicherer v. Commission, Case 45/85, [1987] E.C.R. 405, [1977-1988 Transfer Binder] Common Mkt. Rep. (CCH) ¶ 14,413 (nonbinding recommendation on the raising of premiums issued by a national insurers' association led to a uniform determination of rates and thereby restricted price competition); Concordato Incendio, Decision 90/25, 33 O.J. Eur. Comm. (No. L 15) 25 (1990), [1990] 1 CEC (CCH) 2053 (exemption in regard to recommendations to members of an association to use certain tariffs in setting rates and certain definitions and general terms and conditions); TEKO (German Machinery Breakdown Insurance), Decision 90/22, 33 O.J. Eur. Comm. (No. L 13) 34 (1990), [1990] 1 CEC (CCH) 2045 (exemption for cooperation needed in technical and limited reinsurance markets). A regulation enables the Commission to issue block exemptions for certain categories of agreements in the insurance sector. Regulation 1534/91, 34 O.J. Eur. Comm. (No. L 143) 1 (1991), 2 Common Mkt. Rep. (CCH) ¶ 2775. Under the regulation the Commission may issue block exemption regulations exempting certain categories of typical agreements or standardized terms of business frequently used by insurers as listed in its Article 1. The block exemption regulations issued under the regulation would provide for an opposition procedure for the rapid exemption of agreements not falling fully within the scope of the block exemption.

have established guidelines for permissible cooperation. A number of Commission exemptions relate to cooperation between competitors in times of crisis.[494] In some cases an exemption has not been required for the seller of a business to agree, for periods that have varied from two to five years, not to compete with the buyer when such a covenant is necessary to protect the value of know-how and goodwill included in the sale.[495]

The Commission generally considers cooperative joint ventures to be within the prohibition of Article 85(1) if they are between actual or potential competitors[496]

---

493. Regulation 3976/87 on the Granting of Block Exemptions for Certain Categories of Agreements in the Air Transport Sector, 30 O.J. EUR. COMM. (No. L 374) 9 (1987), 2 COMMON MKT. REP. (CCH) ¶ 2755, *amended by* Regulation 2344/90, 33 O.J. EUR. COMM. (No. L 217) 15 (1990), 2 COMMON MKT. REP. (CCH) ¶ 2755. The regulation enables the Commission to issue block exemption regulations applying Article 85(3) to certain categories of agreements relating to international air transport between Community airports. On the basis of Regulation 3976/87, the Commission adopted Regulation 2671/88 (31 O.J. EUR. COMM. (No. L 239) 9 (1988), 2 COMMON MKT. REP. (CCH) ¶ 2758) and Regulation 84/91 (34 O.J. EUR. COMM. (No. L 10) 14 (1991), 2 COMMON MKT. REP. (CCH) ¶ 2758), exempting from Article 85(1) agreements relating to joint planning and coordination of capacity sharing of revenue and consultation on tariffs and slot allocation at airports; Regulation 2672/88, 31 O.J. EUR. COMM. (No. L 239) 13 (1988), 2 COMMON MKT. REP. (CCH) ¶ 2761, and Regulation 83/91, 34 O.J. EUR. COMM. (No. L 10) 9 (1991), 2 COMMON MKT. REP. (CCH) ¶ 2761, exempting from Article 85(1) agreements relating to computer reservation systems for air transport services; Regulation 2673/88, 31 O.J. EUR. COMM. (No. L 239) 17 (1988) and Regulation 82/91 24, O.J. EUR. COMM. (No. L 10) 7 (1991), 2 COMMON MKT. REP. (CCH) ¶ 2764, exempting from Article 85(1) agreements relating to ground handling services.

494. Enichem/ICI, 31 O.J. EUR. COMM. (No. L 50) 18 (1988), [1985-1988 Transfer Binder] COMMON MKT. REP. (CCH) ¶ 10,962 (rationalization in polyvinylchloride market); BPCL/ICI, 27 O.J. EUR. COMM. (No. L 212) 1 (1984), [1982-1985 Transfer Binder] COMMON MKT. REP. (CCH) ¶ 10,611 (restructuring in the petrochemical industry); Synthetic Fibres, 27 O.J. EUR. COMM. (No. L 207) 17 (1984), [1982-1985 Transfer Binder] COMMON MKT. REP. (CCH) ¶ 10,606 (reduction of surplus capacity); International Energy Agency, 26 O.J. EUR. COMM. (No. L 376) 30 (1983), [1982-1985 Transfer Binder] COMMON MKT. REP. (CCH) ¶ 10,563 (cooperation among oil companies in a supply emergency); Shell/AKZO (Rovin), FOURTEENTH REPORT 72 (1984).

495. Remia BV, Case 42/84, [1985] E.C.R. 2545, [1985-1986 Transfer Binder] COMMON MKT. REP. (CCH) ¶ 14,217 (confirming in part Nutricia, 26 O.J. EUR. COMM. (No. L 376) 22 (1983), [1982-1985 Transfer Binder] COMMON MKT. REP. (CCH) ¶ 10,567); Reuter/BASF, 19 O.J. EUR. COMM. (No. L 254) 40 (1976), [1976-1978 Transfer Binder] COMMON MKT. REP. (CCH) ¶ 9862. The concept has been developed by the Commission in detail in its Notice on Ancillary Restrictions, 33 O.J. EUR. COMM. (No. C 203) 5 (1990), 2 COMMON MKT. REP. (CCH) ¶ 2841, issued in connection with the EEC MERGER CONTROL REGULATION. *See supra* note 411.

496. SIXTH REPORT 38-41 (1976); *e.g.*, Elopak/Metal Box-Odin, Decision 90/410, 33 O.J. EUR. COMM. (No. L 209) 15 (1990), [1990] 2 CEC (CCH) 2051 (dictum) (joint venture for the development, production and marketing of a carton-based container); United Int'l Pictures (UIP), Decision 89/467, 32 O.J. EUR. COMM. (No. L 226) 25 (1989), [1989] 2 CEC (CCH) 2019 (mainly distribution joint venture between major U.S. film producing companies); Iveco/Ford, 31 O.J. EUR. COMM. (No. L 230) 39 (1988), [1985-1988 Transfer Binder] COMMON MKT. REP. (CCH) ¶ 11,013 (joint production and sales of heavy vehicles); Olivetti-Canon, 31 O.J. EUR. COMM. (No. L 52) 51 (1988), [1985-1988 Transfer Binder] COMMON MKT. REP. (CCH) ¶ 10,961 (production joint venture in copying, facsimile machines, and laser printers exempted to achieve economies of scale, sharing of R&D and technology transfers); Mitchell Cotts/Sofiltra, 30 O.J. EUR. COMM. (No. L 41) 31 (1987), [1985-1988 Transfer Binder] COMMON MKT. REP. (CCH) ¶ 10,852 (exemption needed but ancillary restriction prohibiting joint venture from competing with parents found not to fall within Article 85); Optical Fibers, 29 O.J. EUR. COMM. (No. L 236) 30 (1986), [1985-1988 Transfer Binder] COMMON MKT. REP. (CCH) ¶ 10,813 (joint ventures involving

or if collaboration with respect to the joint venture is likely to affect competition between the parties in other areas.[497] However, the Commission regularly exempts joint ventures between competitors, sometimes subject to the condition that the parties drop certain distribution or licensing restraints that would not be acceptable in a simple bilateral contract.[498] In analyzing joint operations the Commission distinguishes between "concentrative" joint ventures, which are treated as mergers, and "cooperative" joint ventures, which are analyzed under Article 85(1) or Article 86 as potential horizontal restrictions.[499] The Court and the Commission consider minority share acquisitions in competitors to be violations of Article 85(1) where they allow the investor to exercise influence over the competitor or where they provide for commercial cooperation or create a structure likely to be used for such cooperation.[500]

b.   VERTICAL RESTRICTIONS

Postsale restraints generally are condemned in EEC antitrust law.[501] In light of

---

different parties in different countries exempted subject to certain conditions).

497.   See, e.g., WANO-Schwarzpulver, 21 O.J. EUR. COMM. (No. L 322) 26 (1978), [1978-1981 Transfer Binder] COMMON MKT. REP. (CCH) ¶ 10,089; GEC Weir (Sodium Circulators), 20 O.J. EUR. COMM. (No. L 327) 26 (1977), [1976-1978 Transfer Binder] COMMON MKT. REP. (CCH) ¶ 10,000; SEVENTH REPORT 117-19 (1977) (Imperial Chem. Indus. Ltd.-Montedison).

498.   See, e.g., United Int'l Pictures (UIP), Decision 89/467, 32 O.J. EUR. COMM. (No. L 226) 25 (1989), [1989] 2 CEC (CCH) 2019.

499.   It is often difficult to distinguish between a concentrative joint venture and a cooperative joint venture. Before adoption of the MERGER CONTROL REGULATION, supra note 411, the rule generally applied was that a concentrative joint venture (or partial merger) would be found only in exceptional cases where the parties to the joint operation, or at least one of them, completely and irreversibly abandoned business in the area covered by the joint venture and there is no weakening of competition in other areas where the parties remained independent of each other. See De Laval-Stork, 20 O.J. EUR. COMM. (No. L 215) 11 (1977), [1976-1978 Transfer Binder] COMMON MKT. REP. (CCH) ¶ 9972; SHV-Chevron, 18 O.J. EUR. COMM. (No. L 38) 14 (1975), [1973-1975 Transfer Binder] COMMON MKT. REP. (CCH) ¶ 9709; SIXTH REPORT 38-41, 89-92 (1976); FOURTH REPORT 67-69 (1974); cf. Himont, SEVENTEENTH REPORT 66 (1987), [1985-1988 Transfer Binder] COMMON MKT. REP. (CCH) ¶ 10,870 (not the subject of a formal decision); Amersham Buchler, 25 O.J. EUR. COMM. (No. L 314) 34 (1982), [1982-1985 Transfer Binder] COMMON MKT. REP. (CCH) ¶ 10,431.

        The Commission has formulated the distinction between concentrative and cooperative joint ventures in Article 3(2) of the regulation on concentrations. Under that formulation a cooperative joint venture is an operation that has as its object or effect the coordination of the competitive behavior of independent enterprises, while a partial merger involves a jointly-owned venture performing on a lasting basis all the functions of an autonomous economic entity that do not give rise to coordination of the competitive behavior of the parties amongst themselves or between them and the joint venture. This concept was developed by the Commission in its Notice Regarding Concentrative and Cooperative Operations, 33 O.J. EUR. COMM. (No. C 203) 10 (1990), 2 COMMON MKT. REP. (CCH) ¶ 2842; see infra note 597 and accompanying text.

500.   Philip Morris/Rembrandt/Rothmans (Commission decision not published, see FOURTEENTH REPORT 81-83 (1984)), aff'd sub nom. British-American Tobacco Co. and R.J. Reynolds Indus. v. Commission, Joined Cases 142 and 156/84, [1987] E.C.R. 4487, [1987-1988 Transfer Binder] COMMON MKT. REP. (CCH) ¶ 14,405.

501.   See, e.g., Bayo-n-ox, Decision 90/38, 33 O.J. EUR. COMM. (No. L 21) 71 (1990), [1990] 1 CEC (CCH) 2066 (prohibition to resell held contrary to Article 85(1) in the absence of evidence that German law prohibited customers from reselling the product), appeal dismissed, Bayer AG v. Commission, Case T-12/90, (Ct. First Instance 1991); SIXTH REPORT 129-133 (Beecham Pharma-Hoechst) (distribution agreement prohibiting resales in bulk form and requiring resale

the goal of market unification, territorial restraints receive careful scrutiny by the Commission. Article 85(1) prohibits virtually all territorial restrictions on sales across Member State boundaries,[502] including joint efforts of distributors and suppliers to discourage parallel trade.[503] Violations of this rule have been heavily fined.[504] The Commission has, however, recognized that certain territorial restraints are often justified, and has issued a regulation granting a block exemption for certain territorial restraints.[505] The exemption applies to exclusive distribution agreements where the supplier agrees to supply products for resale within all the EEC or within a defined part of it to only one distributor. With respect to sales within the EEC, the regulation allows a distributor to be prohibited from soliciting sales outside the contract territory and from maintaining supplies of goods outside the territory, but not from selling outside the territory. It also permits a distributor to be prevented from manufacturing or distributing competing products and to agree to purchase the products only from the supplier.[506] The exemption does not apply to agreements between competing manufacturers that do not exceed a minimum size threshold, or where the users of the goods have no alternative source of supply, or when the distributor and the supplier seek to prevent parallel imports.[507] The

only for human consumption and only in Germany). Article 85(1) may not, however, apply to a resale restriction in special situations such as a seed multiplication agreement or selective distribution. *See* SPRL Louis Eraw-Jacquery v. Société Coopérative la Hesbignonne, Case 27/87, [1988] E.C.R. 1919, [1989] 2 CEC (CCH) 637 (seed multiplication); *see infra* note 509 and accompanying text.

502.   *See, e.g.*, Sandoz, 30 O.J. EUR. COMM. (No. L 222) 28 (1987), [1985-1988 Transfer Binder] COMMON MKT. REP. (CCH) ¶ 10,907 (fines imposed when invoices in pharmaceutical trade bore words "export prohibited"), *aff'd sub nom.* Sandoz Prodotti Farmaceutici SpA v. Commission, Case 277/87, [1990] E.C.R. I 45; Tipp-Ex, 30 O.J. EUR. COMM. (No. L 222) 1 (1987), [1985-1988 Transfer Binder] COMMON MKT. REP. (CCH) ¶ 10,899 (distributor, also fined, was obliged not to sell to customers known to be intending to export), *aff'd sub nom.* Tipp-Ex GmbH & Co. KG v. Commission, Case 279/87, [1990] E.C.R. 261. This rule was from the beginning endorsed by the Court. Consten & Grundig v. Commission, Joined Cases 56 and 58/64, [1966] E.C.R. 299, [1961-1966 Transfer Binder] COMMON MKT. REP. (CCH) ¶ 8046.

503.   *E.g.*, Tepea BV v. Commission, Case 28/77, [1978] E.C.R. 1391, [1977-1978 Transfer Binder] COMMON MKT. REP. (CCH) ¶ 8467; Consten & Grundig v. Commission, Joined Cases 56 and 58/64, [1966] E.C.R. 299 [1961-1966 Transfer Binder] COMMON MKT. REP. (CCH) ¶ 8046. An agreement or concerted practice in violation of Article 85(1) can be found even when only one party to the agreement seeks to restrain parallel imports when that practice can be considered a part of the trading relationship. Hasselblad, 25 O.J. EUR. COMM. (No. L 161) 18 (1982), [1982-1985 Transfer Binder] COMMON MKT. REP. (CCH) ¶ 10,401, *aff'd sub nom.* Hasselblad (GB) Ltd. v. Commission, Case 86/82, [1984] E.C.R. 883, [1983-1985 Transfer Binder] COMMON MKT. REP. (CCH) ¶ 14,014.

504.   *See, e.g.*, SA Musiques Diffusion Française v. Commission, Joined Cases 100-03/80, [1983] E.C.R. 1825, [1981-1983 Transfer Binder] COMMON MKT. REP. (CCH) ¶ 8880 (total fines of 3.2 million ECU); Moët-Hennessy, 24 O.J. EUR. COMM. (No. L 94) 7 (1981), [1978-1981 Transfer Binder] COMMON MKT. REP. (CCH) ¶ 10,352 (fines of 1.1 million ECU).

505.   Regulation 1983/83, 26 O.J. EUR. COMM. (No. L 173) 1 (1983), 2 COMMON MKT. REP. (CCH) ¶ 2730. As of July 1, 1983, this regulation replaced Regulation 67/67 10 J.O. COMM. EUR. (No. 57) 849 (1967), 2 COMMON MKT. REP. (CCH) ¶ 2727. The Commission has also issued a Notice interpreting the new regulation. 27 O.J. EUR. COMM. (No. C 101) 2 (1984), [1982-1985 Transfer Binder] COMMON MKT. REP. (CCH) ¶ 10,548.

506.   Regulation 1983/83, arts. 1-2, 26 O.J. EUR. COMM. (No. L 173) 1-3 (1983) at 2-3, 2 COMMON MKT. REP. (CCH) ¶ 2730A, 2730B.

507.   *Id.* art. 3, 26 O.J. EUR. COMM. at 2-3, 2 COMMON MKT. REP. (CCH) ¶ 2730C.

Commission has also issued a number of individual exemptions for distributorships that do not qualify for a block exemption.[508]

EEC case law has developed the concept of "selective distribution" systems, in which a supplier limits the appointment of dealers to qualified resellers and requires those dealers to sell only to consumers or to other appointed dealers.[509] Selective distribution arrangements fall into three categories. First, a selective distribution system in which a supplier appoints its dealers solely on the basis of objective qualitative criteria in order to ensure that the distribution arrangements are appropriate to the nature of the product, such as criteria regarding the technical qualifications of the dealer's staff and the suitability of its premises, does not fall within Article 85(1) provided that the requirements are uniform and are applied without discrimination.[510] Second, a selective distribution system in which a supplier imposes additional criteria for the appointment of its dealers (such as the requirement that dealers accept certain promotional obligations or achieve certain sales levels) in general restricts competition in that it excludes dealers that meet the qualitative criteria but cannot or will not undertake additional obligations.[511] The

---

508. *See, e.g.*, Distillers, 28 O.J. EUR. COMM. (No. L 369) 19 (1985), [1985-1988 Transfer Binder] COMMON MKT. REP. (CCH) ¶ 10,750; Goodyear Italiana-Euram, 18 O.J. EUR. COMM. (No. L 38) 10 (1975), [1973-1975 Transfer Binder] COMMON MKT. REP. (CCH) ¶ 9708.

509. *See generally* NINTH REPORT 17-19 (1979); FIFTH REPORT 23-24 (1975).

510. *See, e.g.*, Binon & Cie SA v. Agence et Messageries de SA, Case 243/83, [1985] E.C.R. 2015, [1985-1986 Transfer Binder] COMMON MKT. REP. (CCH) ¶ 14,218 (selection criteria must not be based on the number of inhabitants in an area and must not discriminate in favor of supplier-owned outlets); AEG-Telefunken AG v. Commission, Case 107/82, [1983] E.C.R. 3151, [1983-1985 Transfer Binder] COMMON MKT. REP. (CCH) ¶ 14,018 (restrictive implementation of appropriate criteria will constitute a violation); Salonia v. Poidomani, Case 126/80, [1981] E.C.R. 1563, [1979-1981 Transfer Binder] COMMON MKT. REP. (CCH) ¶ 8758 (application to newspaper distribution); SA Lancôme v. Etos, BV, Case 99/79, [1980] E.C.R. 2511, [1979-1981 Transfer Binder] COMMON MKT. REP. (CCH) ¶ 8714 (permissible qualitative criteria must be established in light of the properties of the product); Villeroy & Boch, 28 O.J. EUR. COMM. (No. L 376) 15 (1985), [1985-1988 Transfer Binder] COMMON MKT. REP. (CCH) ¶ 10,758 (quality tableware); Ideal-Standard, 28 O.J. EUR. COMM. (No. L 20) 38 (1985), [1982-1985 Transfer Binder] COMMON MKT. REP. (CCH) ¶ 10,662 (sanitary equipment); IBM Personal Computer, 27 O.J. EUR. COMM. (No. L 118) 24 (1984), [1982-1985 Transfer Binder] COMMON MKT. REP. (CCH) ¶ 10,585; Kodak, 13 J.O. COMM. EUR. (No. L 147) 24 (1970), [1970-1972 Transfer Binder] COMMON MKT. REP. (CCH) ¶ 9378; TENTH REPORT 34-35; *cf.* AEG-Telefunken, 25 O.J. EUR. COMM. (No. L 117) 15 (1982), [1982-1985 Transfer Binder] COMMON MKT. REP. (CCH) ¶ 10,366 (fine imposed for discriminatory application of notified selective distribution system).

511. FIFTH REPORT 23 (1975). In Metro SB-Grossmärkte v. Commission, Case 26/76, [1977] E.C.R. 1875, [1977-1978 Transfer Binder] COMMON MKT. REP. (CCH) ¶ 8435, the Court considered in detail the application of Article 85(1) and 85(3) to a selective distribution system based on qualitative criteria with supplementary obligations that had been exempted by the Commission in SABA, 19 O.J. EUR. COMM. (No. L 28) 19 (1976), [1976-1978 Transfer Binder] COMMON MKT. REP. (CCH) ¶ 9802. Among the provisions that constituted restrictions of competition for which exemption was required were a prohibition on sales to nonapproved dealers with an accompanying request to keep detailed sales records to verify the identity of purchasers and a requirement that nonspecialist wholesalers open a special department suitable to the products. The Commission later granted a second exemption to a revised SABA distribution system. SABA, 26 O.J. EUR. COMM. (No. L 376) 41 (1983), [1982-1985 Transfer Binder] COMMON MKT. REP. (CCH) ¶ 10,568. When Metro, a wholesaler affected by the exemption, asked for review, the Court upheld the second SABA exemption. Metro SB-Grossmarket GmbH & Co. KG v. Commission, Case 75/84, [1986] E.C.R. 3021, [1985-1986 Transfer Binder] COMMON MKT. REP. (CCH) ¶ 14,326. *But see* Yves Saint-Laurent Parfums, 33 O.J. EUR. COMM. (No. C 320) 11 (1990) (selection criteria

Commission has stated that it is willing to consider the possibility of exemption under Article 85(3) in such cases.[512] Third, a selective distribution system in which a supplier imposes quantitative criteria so as to limit the number of appointed dealers. In regard to this category, exemptions have been granted only in exceptional cases.[513] Finally, the Commission has issued a special block exemption regulation governing selective distribution systems for automobiles which does allow limitation of the number of dealers.[514]

Franchise agreements are the subject of special treatment in light of their combination of distribution and industrial property features, to which the block exemption regulations concerning exclusive distribution and exclusive purchasing in principle will not apply.[515] The Commission has issued a block exemption regulation for distribution and service franchising agreements.[516]

In examining vertical arrangements of any kind, the Commission in particular will consider whether they relate directly or indirectly to territorial restrictions. Thus, it has condemned vertical pricing arrangements and differential warranty policies that tended to isolate national markets.[517]

---

including minimum annual turnover not caught by Article 85(1)).

512.   FIFTH REPORT 24 (1975); Junghans, 20 O.J. EUR. COMM. (No. L 30) 10 (1977), [1976-1978 Transfer Binder] COMMON MKT. REP. (CCH) ¶ 9912; SABA, 19 O.J. EUR. COMM. (No. L 28) 19 (1976), [1976-1978 Transfer Binder] COMMON MKT. REP. (CCH) ¶ 9802.

513.   FIFTH REPORT 23 (1975). Not since 1974 has the Commission issued an individual exemption for a selective distribution system based on quantitative criteria. Such exemptions were granted in Bayerische Motoren Werke AG, 18 O.J. EUR. COMM. (No. L 29) 1 (1974), [1973-1975 Transfer Binder] COMMON MKT. REP. (CCH) ¶ 9701; Omega, 13 J.O. COMM. EUR. (No. L 242) 22 (1970), [1970-1972 Transfer Binder] COMMON MKT. REP. (CCH) ¶ 9396.

514.   28 O.J. EUR. COMM. (No. L 15) 16 (1985), 2 COMMON MKT. REP. (CCH) ¶ 2751. The Commission has published a Notice interpreting the Regulation. 28 O.J. EUR. COMM. (No. C 17) 4 (1985), [1982-1985 Transfer Binder] COMMON MKT. REP. (CCH) ¶ 10,655. The Court interpreted the Regulation in VAG v. Magne, Case 10/86, [1986] E.C.R. 4071, [1985-1986 Transfer Binder] COMMON MKT. REP. (CCH) ¶ 14,390.

515.   Pronuptia, Case 161/84, [1986] E.C.R. 353, [1985-1986 Transfer Binder] COMMON MKT. REP. (CCH) ¶ 14,245. Individual exemptions in regard to franchising agreements have been granted in a number of cases. E.g., Moosehead/Whitbread, Decision 90/186, 33 O.J. EUR. COMM. (No. L 100) 32 (1990), [1990] 1 CEC (CCH) 2127; Charles Jourdan, Decision 89/94, 32 O.J. EUR. COMM. (No. L 35) 31 (1989), [1989] 1 CEC (CCH) 2003; ServiceMaster, Decision 88/604, 31 O.J. EUR. COMM. (No. L 332) 38 (1988), [1989] 1 CEC (CCH) 2287; Computerland, 30 O.J. EUR. COMM. (No. L 222) 12 (1987), [1985-1988 Transfer Binder] COMMON MKT. REP. (CCH) ¶ 10,906; Yves Rocher, 30 O.J. EUR. COMM. (No. L 8) 49 (1987), [1985-1988 Transfer Binder] COMMON MKT. REP. (CCH) ¶ 10,855; Pronuptia, 30 O.J. EUR. COMM. (No. L 12) 39 (1987), [1985-1988 Transfer Binder] COMMON MKT. REP. (CCH) ¶ 10,854.

516.   Regulation 4087/88, 31 O.J. EUR. COMM. (No. L 359) 46 (1988), 2 COMMON MKT. REP. (CCH) ¶ 2767. The regulation exempts clauses that give exclusive rights to operate a franchise in the territory, require the franchisee to operate only from the contract premises, require the franchisee to refrain from seeking customers outside the territory, and prohibit the franchisee from handling goods competing with the franchisor's products. The regulation does not allow control over resale prices.

517.   See, e.g., SA ETA Fabriques d'Ebauches, Case 31/85, [1985] E.C.R. 3933, [1985-1986 Transfer Binder] COMMON MKT. REP. (CCH) ¶ 14,276 (differential warranty treatment). But see Hasselblad (GB) Ltd. v. Commission, Case 86/82, [1984] E.C.R. 883, [1983-1985 Transfer Binder] COMMON MKT. REP. (CCH) ¶ 14,014 (additional distributor's guarantee not in violation when inapplicable to parallel imports); Distillers Co. v. Commission, Case 30/78, [1980] E.C.R. 2229, [1979-81 Transfer Binder] COMMON MKT. REP. (CCH) ¶ 8613 (pricing), aff'g 21 O.J. EUR. COMM. (No. L 50) 16 (1978), [1976-1978 Transfer Binder] COMMON MKT. REP. (CCH) ¶ 10,011; Zanussi, 21 O.J.

Although the Commission once stated that resale price maintenance is primarily a national problem because such arrangements in one country would only rarely affect trade between Member States,[518] it generally considers such arrangements to be violations of Article 85.[519] Moreover, even if an exemption were granted, resale price maintenance systems would be virtually impossible to enforce given the impossibility of excluding parallel imports and reexports of a firm's own products from other Member States. Although the Commission has not prohibited the use of suggested retail prices, it has indicated that it might find the use of such practice in combination with other activities, such as selective distribution, to be a violation of Article 85(1).[520]

In a number of proceedings the Commission has objected to agreements by which a user or reseller binds itself to obtain all or a substantial part of its requirements from a supplier. Exclusive purchasing contracts have been held to violate Article 85(1) when the supplier has a strong position in the relevant market, or when all suppliers that employ such contracts cumulatively account for a large percentage of supply and when the contract is for too long a term.[521] The Commission has

---

EUR. COMM. (No. L 322) 36 (1978), [1978-1981 Transfer Binder] COMMON MKT. REP. (CCH) ¶ 10,090 (differential warranty treatment); Pittsburgh Corning Europe, 15 J.O. EUR. COMM. (No. L 272) 35 (1972), [1970-1972 Transfer Binder] COMMON MKT. REP. (CCH) ¶ 9539 (pricing differential based on destination of goods); TENTH REPORT 82-83 (1980) (warranties); SEVENTH REPORT 24-26 (1977) (warranties). See also Ford Werke AG, 25 O. J. EUR. COMM. (No. L 256) 20 (1982), [1982-1985 Transfer Binder] COMMON MKT. REP. (CCH) ¶ 10,419 (interim order to prevent Ford from ceasing delivery of right-hand vehicles to its selective distribution system in Germany).

518. FIRST REPORT 62 (1971). A number of Member States have laws prohibiting or limiting resale price maintenance.

519. SIXTH REPORT 82-83 (1976). See, e.g., AEG-Telefunken, 25 O.J. EUR. COMM. (No. L 117) 15 (1982), [1982-1985 Transfer Binder] COMMON MKT. REP. (CCH) ¶ 10,366; Hennessy-Henkell, 23 O. J. EUR. COMM. (No. L 383) 11 (1980), [1978-1981 Transfer Binder] COMMON MKT. REP. (CCH) ¶ 10,283; GERO-Fabriek, 20 O.J. EUR. COMM. (No. L 16) 8 (1977), [1976-1978 Transfer Binder] COMMON MKT. REP. (CCH) ¶ 9914; Deutsche Philips GmbH, 16 O.J. EUR. COMM. (No. L 293) 40 (1973), [1973-1975 Transfer Binder] COMMON MKT. REP. (CCH) ¶ 9606; see also VBBB/VBVB (Dutch Language Books), 25 O.J. EUR. COMM. (No. L 54) 36 (1982), [1978-1981 Transfer Binder] COMMON MKT. REP. (CCH) ¶ 10,351.

520. Junghans, 20 O.J. EUR. COMM. (No. L 30) 10 (1977), [1976-1978 Transfer Binder] COMMON MKT. REP. (CCH) ¶ 9912.

521. See Schlegel/CPIO, 26 O.J. EUR. COMM. (No. L 351) 20 (1983), [1982-1985 Transfer Binder] COMMON MKT. REP. (CCH) ¶ 10,545 (five-year exclusive purchase agreement for intermediate material unduly foreclosed other suppliers of that material when purchaser held 12% of French market for end product); Dutch Cheese-Makers, 23 O.J. EUR. COMM. (No. L 51) 19 (1979), [1978-1981 Transfer Binder] COMMON MKT. REP. (CCH) ¶ 10,188 (obligation imposed on members of Dutch cheese makers' association to acquire all their rennet and coloring agent from the association found restrictive when it affected 90% of national consumption); EIGHTEENTH REPORT 67 (1988) (exclusive supply agreements between NutraSweet and the two major purchasers of its aspartame in the EEC amended to allow competitors to enter market); ELEVENTH REPORT 53-54 (1981) (soda ash suppliers obliged to reduce contract terms from five to two years and alter exclusivity to fixed tonnages); SEVENTH REPORT 104-05 (1977) (Billiton and Metal & Thermit Chemicals – EEC's largest producer and largest consumer of tin tetrachloride); see also BP Kemi-DDSF, 22 O.J. EUR. COMM. (No. L 286) 32 (1979), [1978-1981 Transfer Binder] COMMON MKT. REP. (CCH) ¶ 10,165 (six year exclusive purchase obligation contrary to Article 85(1) even if purchaser allowed to seek offers for annual requirements from third parties when supplier had right to supply upon meeting third party offers); Liebig, 21 O.J. EUR. COMM. (No. L 53) 20 (1978), [1976-1978 Transfer Binder] COMMON MKT. REP. (CCH) ¶ 10,017 (chain

issued a block exemption regulation covering agreements whereby a reseller contracts to purchase one type of good (or connected types) only from one supplier for a period of up to five years, provided that the supplier and reseller are not competing manufacturers meeting a minimum turnover threshold.[522]   Exclusive purchasing arrangements will normally constitute an abuse of a dominant position in violation of Article 86 if the supplier has a dominant position in the relevant market.[523]

Although tying arrangements are listed in Article 85(1) as one of the practices at which that provision is aimed, no decisions have applied this concept in a distribution agreement.   The Commission has, however, objected to a tying arrangement in a patent license agreement.[524]

Article 85 may apply to an agreement with a commercial agent, but in principle it will not apply when the commercial agent is small enough and dependent enough on the supplier to in effect be considered part of the supplier's marketing organization.[525]

The Commission has permitted restrictions imposed in subcontracting agreements, to the extent such restrictions are based on the contractor's patented or secret technology.[526]

---

retailers obliged to get from supplier all spice needs other than those bearing retailers' own brands).

522.   Regulation 1984/83, 26 O.J. Eur. Comm. (No. L 173) 5 (1983), 2 Common Mkt. Rep. (CCH) ¶ 2733. Special provisions of the regulation apply to beer supply and service station agreements. The Commission has issued a notice interpreting the regulation. 27 O.J. Eur. Comm. (No. C 101) 2 (1984), [1982-1985 Transfer Binder] Common Mkt. Rep. (CCH) ¶ 10,548.

523.   See infra note 574 and accompanying text.

524.   Vaessen-Moris, 22 O.J. Eur. Comm. (No. L 19) 32 (1979), [1978-1981 Transfer Binder] Common Mkt. Rep. (CCH) ¶ 10,107.

525.   See VZW Vereniging van Vlaamse Reisbureaus v. VZW Sociale Dienst, Case 311/85, [1987] E.C.R. 3801, [1987-1988 Transfer Binder] Common Mkt. Rep. (CCH) ¶ 14,499 (travel agent held to be an independent intermediary vis-à-vis a tour organizer when the agent worked with many tour organizers who in turn worked with many travel agents; the agent thus could not be considered an auxiliary organ integrated in the business group of any particular tour organizer); Coöperatieve Vereniging "Suiker Unie" UA v. Commission, Joined Cases 40-48, 50, 54-56, 111, 113, and 114/73, [1975] E.C.R. 1663, [1975 Transfer Binder] Common Mkt. Rep. (CCH) ¶ 8334; ARG/Rover/Unipart, 31 O.J. Eur. Comm. (No. L 45) 34 (1988), [1985-1988 Transfer Binder] Common Mkt. Rep. (CCH) ¶ 10,968 (distributor of automotive parts can be considered an agent for purposes of the rule even though buying and reselling); Pittsburgh Corning Europe, 15 J.O. Comm. Eur. (No. L 272) 35 (1972), [1970-1972 Transfer Binder] Common Mkt. Rep. (CCH) ¶ 9539 (Member State definition of commercial agent not binding). In 1962 the Commission issued a notice in regard to commercial agency agreements, 5 J.O. Comm. Eur. 2921 (1962), 2 Common Mkt. Rep. (CCH) ¶ 2697, but it is no longer up-to-date and is expected to be replaced. According to the notice, Article 85(1) does not apply to agreements with bona fide commercial agents, i.e., agents who do not assume any risk resulting from the transaction other than the usual del credere guarantee; when a nominal agent does assume such risks his function becomes akin to that of an independent trader and the application of Article 85(1) is not precluded.

526.   See 1978 Notice on Subcontracting Agreements, 22 O.J. Eur. Comm. (No. C 1) 2 (1979), 2 Common Mkt. Rep. (CCH) ¶ 2701. The Notice deals with the conditions under which a contractor may lawfully restrict the use by a subcontractor of particular technology or equipment provided by the contractor. In general, subject to the conditions set out in the Notice, in cases where a contractor supplies its distinctive equipment or its patented or secret technology to a subcontractor, the Notice permits, inter alia, a contractual requirement that the subcontractor will sell the products produced only to the contractor and that it will not reveal the contractor's secret technology or otherwise use it. The Notice would not, however, allow a requirement that the subcontractor sell only to the contractor in other circumstances or that the subcontractor must

c.　INDUSTRIAL PROPERTY:　PATENTS, KNOW-HOW,
　　TRADEMARKS, AND COPYRIGHTS

The Commission and the Court have given special and detailed attention to the application of the EEC Treaty to industrial property rights. The results often differ from those under U.S. law. The two principal issues have been: (1) the extent to which Article 30 of the EEC Treaty will prevent the enforcement of industrial property rights in certain situations and (2) the validity of restrictions in licensing agreements.

While the issue of the enforceability of the property right is not strictly a matter of antitrust law, the questions are closely related to the antitrust issues and in fact often arise in cases involving Article 85 or 86.[527] Article 30 provides in regard to Member State measures that "quantitative restrictions on imports and all measures having equivalent effect shall . . . be prohibited between Member States."[528] Although Article 36 permits such restrictions if they are "justified on the grounds of . . . the protection of industrial and commercial property [and are not] a disguised restriction on trade,"[529] the Court has severely limited the extent to which industrial property rights may be exercised to partition the Community. In 1991, the Tribunal defined in three related judgments, the limitation placed by EEC law on the scope of the exercise of law on a copyright granted under national law.[530] This limitation was based upon objectives of the Treaty, in particular the requirement of the establishment of a system of free competition as provided in Article 3(f) and embodied in Articles 85 and 86.

In regard to trademarks, on the basis of Article 30 the Court ruled in 1974 that a trademark holder could not use its rights under national law to block imports from another Member State if the products were put on the market in the other Member State by or with the consent of the trademark holder.[531] The same year the Court ruled that a common origin would prevent use of the trademark to block

---

　　　　not use in other fields know-how it develops while performing the subcontract.

527.　See, e.g., BBC v. Commission, Case T-70/89, (Ct. First Instance 1991) (limitations on the scope of a copyright granted under national law may derive from Article 86); Hoffmann-La Roche & Co. v. Centrafarm Vertriebsgesellschaft Pharmazeutischer Erzeugnisse GmbH, Case 102/77, [1978] E.C.R. 1139, [1977-1978 Transfer Binder] COMMON MKT. REP. (CCH) ¶ 8466 (an exercise of trademark rights that would not be permitted under Articles 30 and 36 may be contrary to Article 86). Similarly, because both Articles 85 and 30 of the Treaty are intended to prevent partitioning of markets, a practice involving industrial property rights which is inconsistent with Article 30 would, if engaged in pursuant to an agreement or concerted practice, normally also violate Article 85(1). See Advocaat Zwarte Kip, 17 O.J. EUR. COMM. (No. L 237) 12 (1974), [1973-1975 Transfer Binder] COMMON MKT. REP. (CCH) ¶ 9669.

528.　EEC Treaty, art. 30, 1 COMMON MKT. REP. (CCH) ¶ 322.

529.　EEC Treaty, art. 36, 1 COMMON MKT. REP. (CCH) ¶ 352.

530.　BBC v. Commission, Case T-70/89, (Ct. First Instance 1991) (television broadcasting organizations use of copyrights covering their weekly advance listings of forthcoming programs in Ireland and Northern Ireland to prevent independent publishers from reproducing all TV listings together in weekly guides); see also RTE v. Commission, Case T-69/89, (Ct. First Instance 1991) appeal filed; IIP v. Commission, Case T-76/89, (Ct. First Instance 1991) appeal filed.

531.　Centrafarm BV v. Winthrop BV, Case 16/74, [1974] E.C.R. 1183, [1974 Transfer Binder] COMMON MKT. REP. (CCH) ¶ 8247.

imports.[532]   However, in a 1990 judgment the Court overruled the second judgment based on common origin without expressly indicating what factors will control.[533] A trademark holder may in certain limited cases prevent such imports if the product has been repackaged and the trademark reaffixed.[534] A trademark holder also has the right to prevent a parallel importer from putting a different trademark on goods originally placed on the market in another Member State by or with the consent of the trademark holder.[535] The Court has also recognized the right of a trademark holder to block imports from another Member State if the trademark affixed is confusingly similar.[536] However, to prevent abuse of this right the Commission, acting under Article 85, has indicated that it will carefully examine agreements settling trademark disputes to ensure that there was a real risk of confusion between the marks and that the agreements are as nonrestrictive as possible.[537]

---

532.   Van Zuylen Frères v. Hag AG, Case 192/73, [1974] E.C.R. 731, [1974 Transfer Binder] COMMON MKT. REP. (CCH) ¶ 8230 (application of common origin doctrine despite circumstance of wartime confiscation).

533.   SA CNL-Sucal NV v. Hag GF AG, Case 10/89, (Eur. Comm. Ct. J. 1990). As a result of the second *Hag* judgment, it is no longer clear that consent is even the principal criterion in trademark enforcement cases involving blocking of imports of goods bearing identical parallel marks belonging to different owners, in view of the Court's emphasis on the essential function of the trademark as protecting the consumer from fraud and confusion. The judgment suggests that inability of the trademark owner seeking to block the imports to control the quality of the goods in question may be the primary condition permitting enforcement of the trademark. An entity holding a trademark in all the Member States may prevent imports from outside the Community, at least if it is not acting as a result of an agreement or concerted practice that has the object or effect of isolating or partitioning the Community. EMI Records Ltd. v. CBS Grammofon AS, Case 86/75, [1976] E.C.R. 871, [1976 Transfer Binder] COMMON MKT. REP. (CCH) ¶ 8351.

534.   Hoffmann-La Roche & Co. v. Centrafarm Vertriebsgesellschaft Pharmazeutischer Erzeugnisse GmbH, Case 102/77, [1978] E.C.R. 1139, [1977-1978 Transfer Binder] COMMON MKT. REP. (CCH) ¶ 8466; see also Pfizer, Inc. v. Eurim-Pharm GmbH, Case 1/81 [1981] E.C.R. 2913, [1979-1981 Transfer Binder] COMMON MKT. REP. (CCH) ¶ 8737 (trademark holder cannot prevent parallel import of product marketed by or with its consent in another Member State where the importer has repackaged the product in question by replacing the external package without affecting the internal packaging, has left visible the original trademark on the internal package, and has indicated on the external package the identity of the original manufacturer and the fact that it has repackaged the product).

535.   See Centrafarm BV v. American Home Prods. Corp., Case 3/78, [1978] E.C.R. 1823, [1977-1978 Transfer Binder] COMMON MKT. REP. (CCH) ¶ 8475 (trademark owner's right to prevent marketing of the product may constitute a disguised restriction on trade if it is established that the proprietor of the different marks has followed the practice of using such marks for the purpose of artificially partitioning markets).

536.   Terrapin (Overseas) Ltd. v. Terranova Industrie C.A. Kapferer & Co., Case 119/75, [1976] E.C.R. 1039, [1976 Transfer Binder] COMMON MKT. REP. (CCH) ¶ 8362.

537.   Syntex/Synthelabo, NINETEENTH REPORT 75 (1989); see, e.g., Sirdar-Phildar, 18 O.J. EUR. COMM. (No. L 125) 27 (1975), [1973-1975 Transfer Binder] COMMON MKT. REP. (CCH) ¶ 9741; Bayer/Tanabe, EIGHTH REPORT 94-96 (1978); Persil/Penneys, SEVENTH REPORT 108-111 (1977). The Commission has indicated that a defensive registration of a trademark by a company in a dominant position may violate Article 86 (Osram/Airam, ELEVENTH REPORT 66 (1981)), and has imposed a fine for a violation of Article 85 with respect to a no-challenge clause in a trademark delimitation agreement. See Toltecs/Dorcet, 25 O.J. EUR. COMM. (No. L 379) 19 (1982), [1982-1985 Transfer Binder] COMMON MKT. REP. (CCH) ¶ 10,459, aff'd sub nom. BAT Cigaretten-Fabriken GmbH, Case 35/83, [1985] E.C.R. 363, [1983-1985 Transfer Binder] COMMON MKT. REP. (CCH) ¶ 14,151.

With respect to patent rights, the Court has ruled that a patentee exhausts its rights in the EEC once the patented product has been marketed in the EEC by the patentee or by others with its consent.[538] On the other hand, the Court has indicated that a patentee may block imports into a Member State by a patent infringement action when those goods came from a Member State where no patent could be obtained because local law did not permit patenting, as long as the patentee did not make the product or authorize its manufacture in that state of origin.[539]

In the case of copyrights, the Court has ruled that a holder of sound reproduction rights granted under the laws of one Member State could not use them to prevent reimport and sale of sound recordings initially delivered by it to a distributor in another Member State.[540]

Article 85 has been applied in numerous cases to restrictive clauses in agreements concerning industrial property rights. An agreement that has a purpose or effect of isolating the Community or dividing it into exclusive marketing territories by license or transfer of industrial property rights is in principle prohibited under Article 85(1).[541] Thus, in the context of the assignment of trademark rights coupled with exclusive distribution rights, if an exclusive distributor receives an assignment of the local trademark and seeks to exercise those rights to prevent parallel imports, both the supplier and the distributor would be violating Article 85(1).[542]

---

538. Centrafarm BV v. Sterling Drug Inc., Case 15/74, [1974] E.C.R. 1147, [1974 Transfer Binder] COMMON MKT. REP. (CCH) ¶ 8246; *see also* Pharmon v. Hoechst, Case 19/84, [1985] E.C.R. 2281, [1985-1986 Transfer Binder] COMMON MKT. REP. (CCH) ¶ 14,206 (compulsory license does not constitute consent); Merck & Co. v. Stephar BV, Case 187/80, [1981] E.C.R. 2063, [1979-1981 Transfer Binder] COMMON MKT. REP. (CCH) ¶ 8707 (consent to marketing in Member State where law did not permit a patent for pharmaceuticals nevertheless constituted consent for purposes of rule).

539. Parke, Davis & Co. v. Probel, Case 24/67 [1968] E.C.R. 55, [1967-1970 Transfer Binder] COMMON MKT. REP. (CCH) ¶ 8054 (decided on the basis of Article 85); *see also* Merck & Co. v. Stephar BV, Case 187/80, [1981] E.C.R. 2063, [1979-1981 Transfer Binder] COMM. MKT. REP. (CCH) ¶ 8707 (decided on the basis of Articles 30 and 36); Centrafarm BV v. Sterling Drug Inc., Case 15/74, [1974] E.C.R. 1147, [1974 Transfer Binder] COMMON MKT. REP. (CCH) ¶ 8246 (also decided on the basis of Articles 30 and 36).

540. Deutsche Grammophon Gesellschaft GmbH v. Metro-SB-Grossmarket GmbH, Case 78/70, [1971] E.C.R. 487, [1971-1973 Transfer Binder] COMMON MKT. REP. (CCH) ¶ 8106; *see also* Musik-Bertrieb Membran GmbH v. GEMA, Joined Cases 55 and 57/80, [1981] E.C.R. 147, [1979-1981 Transfer Binder] COMMON MKT. REP. (CCH) ¶ 8670. In Polydor Ltd. v. Harlequin Record Shops, Case 270/80, [1982] E.C.R. 329, [1981-1983 Transfer Binder] COMMON MKT. REP. (CCH) ¶ 8806, the Court ruled that provisions similar to Articles 30-36 contained in the free trade treaty between the EEC and Portugal did not prohibit the owner of a copyright in a Member State from preventing parallel imports into the EEC of sound recordings which had been marketed in Portugal, at that time not a Member State, by a licensee.

541. *See, e.g.*, EMI Records Ltd. v. CBS Grammofon AS, Case 86/75, [1976] E.C.R. 871, [1976 Transfer Binder] COMMON MKT. REP. (CCH) ¶ 8351; Sirena Srl v. Eda GmbH, Case 40/70, [1971] E.C.R. 69, [1971-1973 Transfer Binder] COMMON MKT. REP. (CCH) ¶ 8101; Consten & Grundig v. Commission, Cases 56 and 58/64, [1966] E.C.R. 299, [1961-1966 Transfer Binder] COMMON MKT. REP. (CCH) ¶ 8046; Sirdar-Phildar, 18 O.J. EUR. COMM. (No. L 125) 27 (1975), [1973-1975 Transfer Binder] COMMON MKT. REP. (CCH) ¶ 9741; Advocaat Zwarte Kip, 17 O.J. EUR. COMM. (No. L 237) 12 (1974), [1973-1975 Transfer Binder] COMMON MKT. REP. (CCH) ¶ 9669.

542. *See, e.g.*, Tepea BV v. Commission, Case 28/77, [1978] E.C.R. 1391, [1977-1978 Transfer Binder] COMMON MKT. REP. (CCH) ¶ 8467; Consten & Grundig v. Commission, Cases 56 and 58/64, [1966] E.C.R. 299, [1961-1966 Transfer Binder] COMMON MKT. REP. (CCH) ¶ 8046. The Commission has, however, permitted restrictive trademark agreements in the form of exclusive

The Commission and the Court have also given detailed consideration to the application of Article 85(1) to licensing agreements. In a case that dealt only with plant protection rights but which had important implications for patent and other industrial property rights, a Commission decision applying Article 85(1) to an exclusivity clause[543] was overruled by the Court.[544] The Court held that a licensor's agreement not to compete with its licensee in the latter's exclusive territory and not to grant other licenses in that territory does not necessarily violate Article 85(1), in particular where such exclusivity is needed because a new product produced by means of a new technology is involved, provided there is no attempt to provide the licensee with absolute territorial protection. The Court referred to this type of exclusive license as an "open" one, contrasting it with a "closed" license which imposes limits on other licensees or parallel importers for the purpose of providing absolute territorial protection. The Court stated that the latter would violate Article 85(1) and would not be entitled to an exemption under Article 85(3).[545]

In individual cases and in its block exemption for certain patent licensing agreements,[546] the Commission has articulated in detail its position on various

---

trademark licenses when they qualified for an exemption under Article 85(3). Moosehead/Whitbread, Decision 90/186, 23 O.J. EUR. COMM. (No. L 100) 32 (1990), [1990] 1 CEC (CCH) 2127; Campari, 21 O.J. EUR. COMM. (No. L 70) 69 (1978), [1978-1981 Transfer Binder] COMMON MKT. REP. (CCH) ¶ 10,035.

543. Breeders' Rights-Maize Seed, 21 O.J. EUR. COMM. (No. L 286) 23 (1978), [1978-1981 Transfer Binder] COMMON MKT. REP. (CCH) ¶ 10,083.

544. Nungesser v. Commission, Case 258/78, [1982] E.C.R. 2015, [1981-1983 Transfer Binder] COMMON MKT. REP. (CCH) ¶ 8805. The Court has held with respect to the licensing of exclusive performance rights to a film that the exclusivity does not violate Article 85(1). SA Compagnie Générale pour la Diffusion de la Télévision Coditel v. SA Ciné Vog Films, Case 62/79, [1980] E.C.R. 881, [1979-1981 Transfer Binder] COMMON MKT. REP. (CCH) ¶ 8662.

545. The Court did not clearly delineate what restraints imposed on other licensees by the licensor or what acts by the licensee to exercise its rights would be deemed to give rise to a "closed" license. The approach taken by the Court in Télévision Coditel provides some support for the conclusion that acts by the licensee to protect its exclusivity which do not violate another provision of the EEC Treaty, such as Article 30, should not automatically convert an "open" to a "closed" license, thereby causing the exclusivity to violate Article 85(1) per se. The 1982 Télévision Coditel judgment involved performance rights to a film which come under Article 59 of the EEC Treaty, dealing with the freedom to provide services rather than with the free movement of goods under Article 30 which was involved in the Nungesser judgment. In a 1980 judgment involving the litigation relating to Coditel, the Court established that Article 59 does not prevent the assignee from exercising its rights to prohibit exhibition of the film in its territory, without its authorization, by means of a cable diffusion picked up and transmitted after a broadcast in another Member State by a third party with the consent of the original owner of the rights.

546. Regulation 2349/84; Block Exemption for Certain Patent Licensing Agreements, 27 O.J. EUR. COMM. (No. L 219) 15 (1984), as corrected, 28 O.J. EUR. COMM. (No. L 113) 34 (1985), 2 COMMON MKT. REP. (CCH) ¶ 2747; see FOURTEENTH REPORT 40-42 (1984). The regulation exempts patent licensing agreements under certain conditions when they contain the restrictions listed in its Articles 1-2. The exemption is not automatically available if the agreement contains any other restrictions, although it can become available through the "opposition" procedure if the agreement contains none of the restrictions listed in Article 3 of the regulation. The Commission in 1962 had expressed less restrictive views than are now contained in the block exemption. See Official Notice on Patent Licensing Agreements, 5 J.O. COMM. EUR. 2922 (1962), 2 COMMON MKT. REP. (CCH) ¶ 2698. Upon issuing the block exemption, the Commission withdrew the 1962 Notice. 27 O.J. EUR. COMM. (No. C 220) 14 (1984).

patent license restrictions.[547] The following restrictions have been considered permissible: exclusive territories for manufacture and sale in certain cases;[548] minimum royalty or quantity requirements;[549] prohibitions on sublicensing;[550] nonexclusive grantbacks;[551] and quality controls.[552] The Commission has disapproved the following restrictions: overly broad exclusive manufacturing and sales licenses; export bans; exclusive grantbacks; agreements not to contest the validity of the patent; and manufacture or sale restrictions extending beyond the life of the patent.[553] The Commission has also approved agreements not to divulge

---

547. While the Court has not yet expressly extended the prohibition on export bans to those ancillary to patent licensing, it has suggested that it agrees with the Commission's position that parallel licenses under the same basic patent to different licensees in different Member States, with the effect of partitioning EEC trade along national boundaries, may violate Article 85. Parke, Davis & Co. v. Probel, Case 24/67, [1968] E.C.R. 55, [1967-1970 Transfer Binder] COMMON MKT. REP. (CCH) ¶ 8054.

548. The Commission generally has been willing to grant exemptions for exclusive manufacturing licenses when competing products exist and when a reasonable showing is made that the licensee needs that exclusivity to encourage it to enter into production, but the Commission had been reluctant to recognize justifications for exclusive sales rights. See SEVENTH REPORT 105-07 (1977) (AGA Steel Radiators). The block exemption produced a substantial change by allowing each party to an agreement entitled to benefit from the block exemption to be protected from competition by the other throughout the duration of the agreement and in addition by allowing the licensee (1) full protection against competition from other licensees for up to five years from the time the product is first put on the market within the EEC, and (2) subsequent protection against other licensees' actively seeking to sell the product in the licensee's territory. Regulation 2349/84, supra note 546, art. 1(1).

549. See, e.g., Burroughs/Geha-Werke, 15 J.O. COMM. EUR. (No. L 13) 53 (1972), [1970-1972 Transfer Binder] COMMON MKT. REP. (CCH) ¶ 9486; Burroughs-Delplanque, 15 J.O. COMM. EUR. (No. L 13) 50 (1972), [1970-1972 Transfer Binder] COMMON MKT. REP. (CCH) ¶ 9485; Regulation 2349/84, supra note 546, art. 2(1)(2).

550. See, e.g., Davidson Rubber Co., 15 J.O. COMM. EUR. (No. L 143) 31 (1972), [1970-1972 Transfer Binder] COMMON MKT. REP. (CCH) ¶ 9512; Burroughs/Geha-Werke, 15 J.O. COMM. EUR. (No. L 13) 53 (1972), [1970-1972 Transfer Binder] COMMON MKT. REP. (CCH) ¶ 9486; Regulation 2349/84, supra note 546, art. 2(1)(5).

551. Davidson Rubber Co., 15 J.O. COMM. EUR. (No. 143) 31 (1972), [1970-1972 Transfer Binder] COMMON MKT. REP. (CCH) ¶ 9512; Regulation 2349/84, supra note 546, art. 2(1)(10).

552. See, e.g., Raymond-Nagoya, 15 J.O. COMM. EUR. (No. L 143) 39 (1972), [1970-1972 Transfer Binder] COMMON MKT. REP. (CCH) ¶ 9513; Burroughs/Geha-Werke, 15 J.O. COMM. EUR. (No. L 13) 53 (1972), [1970-1972 Transfer Binder] COMMON MKT. REP. (CCH) ¶ 9486; Regulation 2349/84, supra note 546, art. 2(1)(9). In addition to the restrictions mentioned above, the Regulation allows, inter alia: a requirement to use only the licensor's trademark; a requirement not to use the patent after termination of the license, certain field of use restrictions, a requirement not to divulge secret know-how and a requirement to use certain products or services in the exploitation of the patent.

553. AOIP/Beyrard, 19 O.J. EUR. COMM. (No. L 6) 8 (1976), [1976-1978 Transfer Binder] COMMON MKT. REP. (CCH) ¶ 9801 (finding no challenge clause, noncompetition clause, payment of royalties for nonuse, exclusivity and export ban to violate Article 85(1)). While most of the Commission's actions with respect to patent licensing have not led to formal decisions, the Commission has often indicated in its annual reports the types of clauses it opposes. See, e.g., TENTH REPORT 87-90 (1980) (Preflex/Lipski – royalties after expiration; Nodet Gougis/Lamazou – obligation to make licensor joint owner of improvement patent; Bramley/Gilbert – obligation of joint inventor to purchase requirements only from other joint inventor). The Commission also opposes inclusion of such clauses in agreements settling disputes over patent rights. See Zoller & Fröhlich/Télémécanique, NINTH REPORT 70-71 (1979); see also Regulation 2349/84, supra note 546, art. 3. The Commission has continued to decide or settle

know-how to third parties beyond the patent period[554] but has required that a licensee be allowed to use know-how after expiration of the license in return for a fee.[555]

The Commission has also issued a block exemption regulation for know-how licenses which is patterned closely upon the patent license block exemption regulation.[556] The know-how regulation will apply not only when that know-how alone is licensed but also when a combined patent and know-how license is granted and restrictions are imposed in regard to one or more Member States where no patents or patent applications exist. The rules provided in the know-how regulation are reflected in recent Commission decisions involving know-how licensing.[557]

7. *Article 86 (Abuse of Dominant Position)*

Article 86 prohibits "abuse" of "a dominant position" in a "substantial part" of the EEC.[558] No exemptions are possible. The Treaty lists several examples of abuse:

---

individual cases on the basis of the principles reflected in the Regulation. *See* Velcro/Aplix, 28 O.J. EUR. COMM. (No. L 233) 22 (1985), [1985-1988 Transfer Binder] COMMON MKT. REP. (CCH) ¶ 10,719 (violations found, inter alia, when licensee required to obtain equipment from a designated supplier and not to use equipment outside of territory); Windsurfing Int'l, 26 O.J. EUR. COMM. (No. L 229) 1 (1983), [1982-1985 Transfer Binder] COMMON MKT. REP. (CCH) ¶ 10,515, *aff'd sub nom.* Windsurfing Int'l Inc. v. Commission, Case 193/83, [1986] E.C.R. 611, [1985-1986 Transfer Binder] COMMON MKT. REP. (CCH) ¶ 14,271 (violations found when licensee required to use certain types of boards not covered by patents, component parts including the patented rigs not to be sold separately, royalties due on complete value of sailboard, notices of license to be affixed to the unpatented boards, licensees prevented from manufacturing in other parts of EEC where no patents existed, and no-contest clauses covering the patents and trademarks); FOURTEENTH REPORT 77 (1984) (UARCO – royalty cannot be exacted when all patents expired and all know-how in public domain); Knoll/Hille-Form, THIRTEENTH REPORT 91-92 (1983), (exclusivity and export restraints terminated).

554. Kabelmetal-Luchaire, 18 O.J. EUR. COMM. (No. L 222) 34 (1975), [1973-1975 Transfer Binder] COMMON MKT. REP. (CCH) ¶ 9761; Burroughs-Delplanque, 15 O.J. EUR. COMM. (No. L 13) 50 (1972), [1970-1972 Transfer Binder] COMMON MKT. REP. (CCH) ¶ 9485.

555. Cartoux/Terrapin, TENTH REPORT 90 (1980).

556. Regulation 556/89, Block Exemption for Certain Know-How Licensing Agreements, 32 O.J. EUR. COMM. (No. L 61) 1 (1989), 2 COMMON MKT. REP. (CCH) ¶ 2771; *see* EIGHTEENTH REPORT 43-44 (1988). The principal special features of the know-how regulation as compared with the provisions of the patent regulation are: (1) a time limit on the applicability of most of the block exemption provisions fixed at five or ten years from specified dates (art. 1(2)); (2) a limitation on the period of the licensor's use of the licensee's improvements if the licensee is prevented from using the know-how after the term of the agreement (art. 2(1)(4)); and (3) the licensee cannot be prevented from using the know-how after the term of the agreement where the know-how has meanwhile become publicly known, other than by the action of the licensee, or where it consists only of practical experience gained in working an expired patent previously licensed to the licensee (art. 3(1)).

557. Delta Chemie-DDD, Decision 88/563, 31 O.J. EUR. COMM. (No. L 309) 34 (1988), [1989] 1 CEC (CCH) 2254 (exclusive know-how license coupled with an initial exclusive distribution agreement); Rich Prod./Jus-rol, 31 O.J. EUR. COMM. (No. L 69) 21 (1988), [1985-1988 Transfer Binder] COMMON MKT. REP. (CCH) ¶ 10,956 (know-how license granting exclusive rights to manufacture the product in one Member State); Boussois/Interpane, 30 O.J. EUR. COMM. (No. L 50) 30 (1987), [1985-1988 Transfer Binder] COMMON MKT. REP. (CCH) ¶ 10,859 (know-how license granting exclusive rights to manufacture the product for five years).

558. EEC Treaty, art. 86, 2 COMMON MKT. REP. (CCH) ¶ 2101.

directly or indirectly imposing unfair purchase or selling prices or other unfair trading conditions;　limiting production, markets or technical development to the prejudice of consumers;　applying dissimilar conditions to equivalent transactions with other trading parties, thereby placing them at a competitive disadvantage;　and making the conclusion of contracts subject to acceptance by the other parties of supplementary obligations which, by their nature or according to commercial usage, have no connection with the subject of such contracts.

In applying Article 86 it is necessary to define the product and geographic markets in which a dominant position exists. In general the Court and the Commission have considered the relevant product market to include the market for the product in question and products readily substitutable for it.[559] Among the product markets accepted by the Court have been certain kinds of tires, specific vitamins, bananas, and certain metal containers and lids.[560] The relevant geographic market must be

---

559.　　The Court has in a number of cases laid down fairly standard criteria for the definition of the market. *See, e.g.*, Nederlandsche Banden-Indus., Michelin NV v. Commission, Case 322/81, [1983] E.C.R. 3461, [1983-1985 Transfer Binder] COMMON MKT. REP. (CCH) ¶ 14,031 ("the possibilities of competition must be judged in the context of the market comprising the totality of the products which, with respect to their characteristics, are particularly suitable for satisfying constant needs and are only to a limited extent interchangeable with other products. . . . The competitive conditions and the structure of supply and demand on the market must also be taken into consideration.").

　　　　An example of the Commission's application of the market definition criteria in connection with industrial equipment is found in Tetra Pak, 31 O.J. EUR. COMM. (No. L 272) 27 (1988), [1985-88 Transfer Binder] COMMON MKT. REP. (CCH) ¶ 11,015 (one market for the supply of machines incorporating technology for sterilizing cartons that can be used for filling under aspectic conditions with UHT-treated liquids, and a second market for the supply of cartons for such machines, both determined after examination of supply-side and demand-side substitutability, the latter taking into account the end-use of the liquids), *aff'd sub nom.* Tetra Pak Rausing v. Commission, Case T-51/89, [1990] E.C.R. II 309, [1990] 2 CEC (CCH) 409. A recent formulation by the Commission of a definition of the relevant product market is provided in Section 5 of the Form CO relating to the notification of a concentration:

　　　　A relevant product market comprises all those products and/or services which are regarded as interchangeable or substitutable by the consumer, by reason of the products' characteristics, their prices and their intended use. A relevant product market may in some cases be composed of a number of individual product groups. An individual product group is a product or small group of products which present largely identical physical or technical characteristics and are fully interchangeable. The difference between products within the group will be small and usually only a matter of brand and/or image. The product market will usually be the classification used by the undertaking in its marketing operations.

　　　　Regulation 2367/90, 34 O.J. EUR. COMM. (NO. L 219) 5 (1990), 2 COMMON MKT. REP. (CCH) ¶ 2840.

　　　　A further formulation for determining the relevant product market is stated in the Commission's Notice on Agreements of Minor Importance, 29 O.J. EUR. COMM. (No. C 231) 2 (1986), 2 COMMON MKT. REP. (CCH) ¶ 2700 (identical products or products which are considered by consumers to be similar on account of their properties, price or use; to this standard formulation the Notice adds that where the contract products are components which are incorporated into another product by the participating enterprises, reference should be made to the market for the latter product provided that the components represent a significant part of it; where the contract products are components which are sold to third parties, reference should be made to the market for the components).

560.　　*See* Nederlandsche Banden-Indus., Michelin NV v. Commission, Case 322/81, [1983] E.C.R. 3461, [1983-1985 Transfer Binder] COMMON MKT. REP. (CCH) ¶ 14,031 (new replacement tires for trucks, buses and similar vehicles); Hoffmann-La Roche & Co. AG v. Commission, Case 85/76,

at least a substantial part of the EEC, but this may be constituted by one of the smaller States (such as the Netherlands) or only a part of a larger Member State. The Court has accorded the Commission broad discretion in defining the geographic market.[561] A dominant position can exist with respect to either buyers or sellers in a particular market, and the behavior of a dominant buyer is also subject to the restrictions of Article 86.[562] A collective dominant position can exist with respect to two or more companies acting jointly.[563]

An enterprise is considered dominant if it is able to prevent effective competition or has the capacity to act, to an appreciable extent, independently of its competitors, suppliers and customers.[564]   A firm's market share is almost always the

---

[1979] E.C.R. 461, [1978-1979 Transfer Binder] COMMON MKT. REP. (CCH) ¶ 8527 (specific vitamins); United Brands Co. v. Commission, Case 27/76, [1978] E.C.R. 207, [1977-1978 Transfer Binder] COMMON MKT. REP. (CCH) ¶ 8429 (bananas found to be a relevant market by focusing on year-round substitutability for certain classes of end-users);   Europemballage Corp. and Continental Can Co. v. Commission, Case 6/72, [1973] E.C.R. 215, [1971-1973 Transfer Binder] COMMON MKT. REP. (CCH) ¶ 8171 (certain metal containers and lids).

In a number of cases the Court has recognized particularly narrow product markets. See, e.g., Hugin Kassaregister AB v. Commission, Case 22/78, [1979] E.C.R. 1869, [1978-1979 Transfer Binder] COMMON MKT. REP. (CCH) ¶ 8524 (market for spare parts for specific make of cash register);   General Motors Continental NV v. Commission, Case 26/75, [1975] E.C.R. 1367, [1975 Transfer Binder] COMMON MKT. REP. (CCH) ¶ 8320 (market for required safety certificates issued in respect of GM automobiles).

561.   See, e.g., Hoffmann-La Roche & Co. AG v. Commission, Case 85/76, [1979] E.C.R. 461, 1978-1979 Transfer Binder] COMMON MKT. REP. (CCH) ¶ 8527 (entire EEC);   United Brands Co. v. Commission, Case 27/76, [1978] E.C.R. 207, [1977-1978 Transfer Binder] COMMON MKT. REP. (CCH) ¶ 8429 (a six Member State area);   Coöperatieve Vereniging "Suiker Unie" UA v. Commission, Joined Cases 40-48, 50, 54-56, 111, 113, and 114/73, [1975] E.C.R. 1663, [1975 Transfer Binder] COMMON MKT. REP. (CCH) ¶ 8334 (Belgium-Luxembourg;   southwestern Germany);   ABG Oil Cos., 20 O.J. EUR. COMM. (No. L 117) 1 (1977), [1976-1978 Transfer Binder] COMMON MKT. REP. (CCH) ¶ 9944, rev'd on other grounds sub nom. BP v. Commission, Case 77/77, [1978] E.C.R. 1513, [1977-1978 Transfer Binder] COMMON MKT. REP. (CCH) ¶ 8465 (Netherlands). A recent and comprehensive Commission formulation is given in Article 9(7) of the MERGER CONTROL REGULATION:

The geographical reference market shall consist of the area in which the undertakings concerned are involved in the supply of products or services, in which the conditions of competition are sufficiently homogeneous and which can be distinguished from neighboring areas because, in particular, conditions of competition are appreciably different in those areas.   This assessment should take account in particular of the nature and characteristics of the products or services concerned, of the existence of entry barriers or of consumer preferences, of appreciable differences of the undertakings' market shares between neighboring areas or of substantial price differences.

Supra note 411; see also Section 5 of the Form CO relating to the notification of a concentration. Regulation 2367/90, 33 O.J. EUR. COMM. (No. L 219) 5 (1990), 2 COMM. MKT. REP. (CCH) ¶ 2840. Further, the Commission has held that the relevant geographic markets may be the areas within which members of a cartel have agreed that each will compete. Soda Ash-Solvay, ICI, Decision 91/297, 34 O.J. EUR. COMM. (No. L 152) 1 (1991), [1991] 2 CEC (CCH) 2003.

562.   See THIRD REPORT 60-61 (1973) (railway rolling stock).

563.   Italian Flat Glass, Decision 89/93, 32 O.J. EUR. COMM. (No. L 33) 44 (1989), [1989] 1 CEC (CCH) 2077 (horizontal restrictive practices and structural links between producers together holding 79% of one national market and 95% of another).

564.   See United Brands Co. v. Commission, Case 27/76, [1978] E.C.R. 207, [1977-1978 Transfer Binder] COMMON MKT. REP. (CCH) ¶ 8429;   see also Nederlandsche Baden-Indus., Michelin NV v. Commission, Case 322/81, [1983] ECR 3461, [1983-1985 Transfer Binder] COMMON MKT. REP. (CCH) ¶ 14,031 (dominance may be found when a company can behave to an appreciable extent

Commission's starting point for determining whether a firm has a dominant position. Dominance has been found when a company has a market share of from 40 to 45%, when its nearest competitors enjoy considerably smaller market shares, and when a number of other factors point toward dominance.[565]   Very large market shares in themselves may be taken as virtually conclusive evidence of a dominant position.[566] Other important factors have included technological superiority, a highly developed and specialized sales network and the absence of potential competition.[567]   A

---

independently of its competitors and customers); Europenballage Corp. and Continental Can Co. v. Commission, Case 6/72, [1973] E.C.R. 215, [1971-1973 Transfer Binder] COMMON MKT. REP. (CCH) ¶ 8171 (among factors considered were the company's technological position, its wide range of products that could not be duplicated by smaller competitors and its general financial strength).

In *United Brands*, the Court stated that in general a dominant position derives from a combination of factors which, when considered separately, are not necessarily determinative. The Court took into account the company's international economic strength as the largest and most vertically integrated producer and its control overall phases of production and marketing in a capital intensive industry. A decline in market share (from 45% to 41%) and a degree of nonprofitability did not prevent dominance. The Court noted that the company maintained its large market share despite the fact that its products were the most expensive. The Court also noted that the existence of a dominant position is perfectly compatible with fierce, albeit ultimately unsuccessful, competition. The mere possession of a copyright or trademark does not necessarily give a dominant position. Deutsche Grammophon Gesellschaft GmbH v. Metro-SB-Grossmarket GmbH, Case 78/70, [1971] E.C.R. 487, [1971-1973 Transfer Binder] COMMON MKT. REP. (CCH) ¶ 8106, at 7193 (copyright); Sirena Srl v. Eda GmbH, Case 40/70 [1971] E.C.R. 69, [1971-1973 Transfer Binder] COMMON MKT. REP. (CCH) ¶ 8101, at 7113 (trademark). *But cf.* RTE v. Commission, Case T-69/89, (Ct. First Instance 1991), *appeal filed*; BBC v. Commission, Case T-70/89 (Ct. First Instance 1991); ITP v. Commission, Case T-76/89 (Ct. First Instance 1991), *appeal filed* (broadcasting companies' exclusive rights under national copyright law to reproduce and market their program listings secured them a monopoly over the publication of their respective weekly listings and therefore were found to afford each company a dominant position on the market for its weekly listings and on the market for the magazine in which such listings are published).

565.   United Brands Co. v. Commission, Case 27/76, [1978] E.C.R. 207, [1977-1978 Transfer Binder] COMMON MKT. REP. (CCH) ¶ 8429. The Court noted that a trader can be in a dominant position in the market for a product only if it has succeeded in winning a large part of this market. *But cf.* Recital 15 of the regulation on concentrations. Merger Control Regulation, *supra* note 411, (market shares below 25% are an indication that effective competition will not be impeded); TENTH REPORT 103-04 (1980) (where the Commission states that a dominant position cannot be ruled out in respect of market shares between 20% and 40%).

566.   Hoffmann-La Roche & Co. v. Commission, Case 85/76, [1979] E.C.R. 461, [1978-1979 Transfer Binder] COMMON MKT. REP. (CCH) ¶ 8527. The Court in Hoffmann-La Roche seemed to consider that a rebuttable presumption of dominance operates when the market share is 60% or more. *But cf.* NINTH REPORT 28 (1979) (figure of 80% cited by Commission).

567.   *See* Hoffmann-La Roche & Co. v. Commission, Case 85/76, [1979] E.C.R. 461, [1978-1979 Transfer Binder] COMMON MKT. REP. (CCH) ¶ 8527. The Court rejected several indicia of dominance advanced by the Commission in this case, including retention of market share in the face of lively competition, production of a considerably larger range of products than competitors and holding a position as the world's largest manufacturer of the products. The Court did indicate, however, that the last two factors could be relevant to establishing dominance in an appropriate case. Among the relevant factors listed are: the number of other producers; the parties' manufacturing strength; the existence of upstream integration; the absence of competition from other Community producers; the exclusive or near-exclusive supply of all the major Community customers; the improbability of any new producer's entering the market; the protection afforded against non-Community producers by antidumping duties; the parties' role as price leader; the perception of the parties by other Community producers as the dominant

dominant position has also been found with respect to a producer's relationship with its normal customers during a severe shortage.[568]

The Commission has actively applied Article 86 to commercial practices of dominant companies and the Court has generally supported the Commission. It is not possible to discern any single standard by which an act of a dominant company might be judged to be a violation.[569] The Court has said that the concept of abuse

---

producers; and the reluctance of other producers to compete aggressively for the parties' traditional customers. Soda Ash-Solvay, ICI, Decision 91/297, 34 O.J. EUR. COMM. (No. L 152) 1 (1991), [1991] 2 CEC (CCH) 2003.

568.   ABG-Oil Cos., 20 O.J. EUR. COMM. (No. L 117) 1 (1977), [1976-1978 Transfer Binder] COMMON MKT. REP. (CCH) ¶ 9944, rev'd on other grounds sub nom. BP v. Commission, Case 77/77, [1978] E.C.R. 1513, [1977-1978 Transfer Binder] COMMON MKT. REP. (CCH) ¶ 8465.

569.   The category of possible abuses is not confined to the list of examples set forth in Article 86. The Commission has broadly stated that there is abuse of a dominant position when a dominant firm exploits its position to obtain advantages which would not have been possible had there been effective competition. FIRST REPORT 78-81 (1971); see also Hoffmann-La Roche & Co. v. Commission, Case 85/76, [1979] E.C.R. 461, [1978-1979 Transfer Binder] COMMON MKT. REP. (CCH) ¶ 8527, at 7553. The Court has held that a strengthening of a dominant position so as substantially to hamper competition may constitute an abuse. See ICI & Commercial Solvents Corp. v. Commission, Joined Cases 6 and 7/73, [1974] E.C.R. 223, [1974 Transfer Binder] COMMON MKT. REP. (CCH) ¶ 8209 (termination of supply to a competitor); Europemballage Corp. and Continental Can Co. v. Commission, Case 6/72, [1973] E.C.R. 215, [1971-1973 Transfer Binder] COMMON MKT. REP. (CCH) ¶ 8171 (acquisition of a potential competitor).

For a discussion of the application of Article 86 to mergers and acquisitions, see Subpart 1.8 of this chapter.

The Court has found that absent special circumstances the sole act of registering an industrial property right cannot in itself be considered abusive. AB Volvo v. Eric Veng (UK) Ltd., Case 238/87, [1988] E.C.R. 6211, [1987-1988 Transfer Binder] COMMON MKT. REP. (CCH) ¶ 14,498; Consorzio Italiano della Componentistica di Ricambio per Auto Veicoli (Consorzio) and Maxicar SpA v. Renault, Case 53/87, [1988] E.C.R. 6039, [1990] 1 CEC (CCH) 267. In specific circumstances, however, such registration may be abusive. In the Volvo and Renault cases, the Court went on to indicate that the exercise by a dominant company of exclusive rights resulting from the registration of an industrial property right can constitute an abuse if it involves arbitrary refusal to supply spare parts to independent repair shops, the fixing of prices for spare parts at an unfair level or a decision no longer to produce spare parts or a particular model when many vehicles of that model are still in circulation. In three related subsequent cases, upon review of a Commission decision, the Tribunal distinguished the automobile cases and held that the very refusal of a television station to furnish its weekly program listings to a third party for publication in a guide was an abusive exercise of the rights, in that the aim and effect of this refusal was to exclude any potential competition on the derivative market represented by the information on the weekly programs in order to continue to enjoy the monopoly held there by its own guide. RTE v. Commission, Case T-69/89, (Ct. First Instance 1991), appeal filed; BBC v. Commission, Case T-70/89, (Ct. First Instance 1991); ITP v. Commission, Case T-76/89, (Ct. First Instance 1991), appeal filed. In certain circumstances the Commission has found a trademark registration abusive. Osram/Airam, ELEVENTH REPORT 66 (1981) (registration of trademark by a dominant company when such trademark is used by a competitor in another country, thereby diminishing the competitor's ability to enter the market). The acquisition of an exclusive patent and technology license for the product in respect of which the acquiror holds a dominant position may constitute an abuse if it further hinders the degree of competition still existing on that market. Tetra Pak Rausing v. Commission, Case T-51/89, [1990] E.C.R. II 309, [1990] 2 CEC (CCH) 409. In Tetra Pak, the Court held that while the acquisition of the exclusive license by a dominant company did not in itself constitute an abuse, it could have such an effect depending on the circumstances. The fact that an exclusive license falls within the scope of a block exemption regulation does not preclude the application of Article 86, even when the benefit of the block exemption has not been withdrawn by the Commission.

is an objective one relating to behavior of a dominant undertaking that influences market structure and that a dominant position should not be maintained or improved by activity on the part of the dominant company which involves "methods different from those which condition normal competition."[570]   An act of a dominant company that would be a violation of Article 85(1) would often also violate Article 86.[571] An act by a dominant company that is likely to have the effect of protecting its market from imports from other Member States can be subject to attack under Article 86.[572]

Many findings of abuse of a dominant position involve refusals to continue dealing with a customer.[573] Under these cases, a dominant company may be held to have

---

570.   Hoffmann-La Roche & Co. v. Commission, Case 85/76, [1979] E.C.R. 461, [1978-1979 Transfer Binder] COMMON MKT. REP. (CCH) ¶ 8527, at 7553.

571.   See, e.g., Tetra Pak II, 35 O.J. EUR. COMM. (No. L 72) 1 (1992).

572.   See, e.g., British Leyland, 27 O.J. EUR. COMM. (No. L 207) 11 (1984), [1982-1985 Transfer Binder] COMMON MKT. REP. (CCH) ¶ 10,601, aff'd sub nom. British Leyland v. Commission, Case 226/84, [1986] E.C.R. 3263, [1985-1986 Transfer Binder] COMMON MKT. REP. (CCH) ¶ 14,336 (refusing to provide importers with type approval numbers); United Brands Co. v. Commission, Case 27/76, [1978] E.C.R. 207, [1977-1978 Transfer Binder] COMMON MKT. REP. (CCH) ¶ 8429 (limitations on parallel imports); General Motors Continental NV v. Commission, Case 26/75, [1975] E.C.R. 1367, [1975 Transfer Binder] COMMON MKT. REP. (CCH) ¶ 8320 (charging higher inspection fees on products arriving by parallel imports found by Commission to be an abuse but finding annulled by Court in light of particular circumstances); Hugin/Liptons, 21 O.J. EUR. COMM. (No. L 22) 23 (1978), [1976-1978 Transfer Binder] COMMON MKT. REP. (CCH) ¶ 10,007, rev'd on other grounds sub nom. Hugin Kassaregister AB v. Commission, Case 22/78, [1979] E.C.R. 1869, [1978-1979 Transfer Binder] COMMON MKT. REP. (CCH) ¶ 8524 (export bans). The EEC Treaty goal of creating a single common market has also led to the interpretation of Article 86 to prohibit discrimination by a dominant firm on the grounds of nationality. See GVL, 24 O.J. EUR. COMM. (No. L 370) 49 (1981), [1978-1981 Transfer Binder] COMMON MKT. REP. (CCH) ¶ 10,345, aff'd sub nom. Gessellschaft zur Verwertung von Leistungsschutzrechten (GVL) v. Commission, Case 7/82, [1983] E.C.R. 483, [1981-1983 Transfer Binder] COMMON MKT. REP. (CCH) ¶ 8910; GEMA, 14 J.O. COMM. EUR. (No. L 134) 15 (1971), [1970-1972 Transfer Binder] COMMON MKT. REP. (CCH) ¶ 9438; ELEVENTH REPORT 68-69 (1981).

573.   See SA Télémarketing v. Télédiffusion, Case 311/84, [1985] E.C.R. 3261, [1985-1986 Transfer Binder] COMMON MKT. REP. (CCH) ¶ 14,246 (following its ruling in Commercial Solvents, the Court held that a company holding a dominant position in one market may be found to commit an abuse if it reserves for itself or for a subsidiary an ancillary activity which might be carried out by another company on a neighboring but separate market when there is the possibility of eliminating all competition from that other company); United Brands Co. v. Commission, Case 27/76, [1978] E.C.R. 207, [1977-1978 Transfer Binder] COMMON MKT. REP. (CCH) ¶ 8429 (refusal to continue supply to a distributor that began handling a competing brand); ICI & Commercial Solvents Corp. v. Commission, Joined Cases 6 and 7/73, [1974] E.C.R. 223, [1974 Transfer Binder] COMMON MKT. REP. (CCH) ¶ 8209 (refusal to continue supply to a company competing downstream); Hugin/Liptons, 21 O.J. EUR. COMM. (No. L 22) 23 (1978), [1976-1978 Transfer Binder] COMMON MKT. REP. (CCH) ¶ 10,007, rev'd on other grounds sub nom. Hugin Kassaregister AB v. Commission, Case 22/78, [1979] E.C.R. 1869, [1978-1979 Transfer Binder] COMMON MKT. REP. (CCH) ¶ 8524 (refusal to continue supply to a company furnishing repair service in competition with the product manufacturer); cf. ABG-Oil Cos., 20 O.J. EUR. COMM. (No. L 117) 1 (1977), [1976-1978 Transfer Binder] COMMON MKT. REP. (CCH) ¶ 9944, rev'd sub nom. BP v. Commission, Case 77/77, [1978] E.C.R. 1513, [1977-1978 Transfer Binder] COMMON MKT. REP. (CCH) ¶ 8465 (refusal by a refiner to continue gasoline supplies during energy crisis); London European-SABENA, 31 O.J. EUR. COMM. (No. L 317) 47 (1988), (Decision 88/589) [1989] 1 CEC (CCH) 2278 (refusal to grant a competing airline access to a computer reservation system); British Sugar/Napier Brown, 31 O.J. EUR. COMM. (No. L 284) 41 (1988), [1985-1988 Transfer Binder] COMMON MKT. REP. (CCH) ¶ 11,015 (refusal to supply bulk sugar to a sugar merchant

an obligation to continue to deal with its regular customers when refusal to do so would threaten to result in a lessening of competition, for instance, by creating a significant change in market structure. There exist circumstances in which refusal by a dominant company to deal with or license a party with which it has not previously dealt will be found abusive.[574] Exclusive supply contracts regularly have been

---

in order to keep it out of the retail market); Boosey & Hawkes, 30 O.J. EUR. COMM. (No. L 286) 36 (1987), [1985-1988 Transfer Binder] COMMON MKT. REP. (CCH) ¶ 10,920 (interim order requiring supply to assure that customer could go into same business as supplier).

In *Télémarketing*, the company with monopoly television rights reserved telemarketing services to one of its affiliates. In *Commercial Solvents*, the Court upheld the Commission's finding of abuse of a dominant position by a manufacturer with a world monopoly of raw materials used in making a particular anti-tuberculosis drug. When the manufacturer decided to integrate forward and manufacture the drug itself, it sought to cut off its former customer and future competitor, one of the principal manufacturers of the drug in the EEC. In finding an abuse, the Court did not engage in a detailed analysis of the degree of anticompetitive effect on the market or of the impact on the terminated purchaser.

In *United Brands*, the Court again affirmed the Commission's finding of abuse of a dominant position based on an integrated banana producer's refusal to continue supplies to an independent distributor who had participated in advertising campaigns for competing bananas. The Court stated as a general principle that a firm in a dominant position for the purpose of marketing a product – which benefits from the reputation of a brand name known and valued by consumers – cannot stop supplying a long-standing customer who abides by regular commercial practice if the order placed by this customer is in no way out of the ordinary. The Court went on to find that a complete cut-off of supplies to the distributor was excessive in light of the behavior complained of and would have a chilling effect on a similar exercise of commercial independence (e.g., giving preference to a competitor's goods) by other small and medium-sized firms in their relations with the producer. The Court concluded that the producer's action was designed to have a serious effect on competition in the relevant market.

In *Hugin*, the Commission found that an integrated cash register manufacturer abused its dominant position in the market for its own spare parts by refusing to continue to supply such parts to an independent firm in the business of servicing, reconditioning, selling and renting cash registers of numerous makes. In the Commission's view, the manufacturer used its dominant position in the market for spare parts to eliminate a competitor in the maintenance, rental, repair and reconditioning of the manufacturer's own cash registers. The Court reversed the Commission's decision without ruling on the question of abuse on the ground that there was no effect on trade between Member States.

In *BP*, the Court accepted the principle put forward by the Commission that an integrated oil company could abuse its dominant position with respect to its own gasoline during the oil crisis in 1973-1974 when it terminated supplies to a large independent distributor while continuing to supply other customers. The Court disagreed with the Commission on the application of the principle to the facts, finding an objectively based and nondiscriminatory justification under the circumstances in a refusal to supply an occasional customer notwithstanding the continuation of supplies to traditional or regular purchasers.

In connection with a case settled in 1983 involving Polaroid's refusal to give price quotations to SSI Europe, the Commission stated that an objectively unjustifiable refusal to supply by a dominant company violates Article 86 and that a violation will also occur when the dominant company makes supply conditional on its having control of further processing or marketing. The case appeared to involve refusal to supply a company with which Polaroid had already dealt. THIRTEENTH REPORT 95 (1983).

574. Refusals to license under registered intellectual property rights raise special issues. The Court has held in regard to registered automotive body panels that the dominant owner of the right has no obligation to license third parties, even in return for a reasonable royalty. However, the Court added that refusal to sell these panels to a repairman would be abusive. AB Volvo v. Eric Veng (UK) Ltd., Case 238/87, [1988] E.C.R. 6211, [1987-1988 Transfer Binder] COMMON MKT. REP. (CCH) ¶ 14,498.

ruled violative of Article 86 when entered into by a dominant supplier.[575]

Violations of Article 86 often arise out of pricing arrangements. Thus, a dominant supplier's pricing mechanism designed to create an obstacle for other suppliers to obtain orders by the price or other terms they offer in any particular transaction will usually violate Article 86. Accordingly, "fidelity rebates,"[576] as well as rebates based on overall purchases of several lines of a dominant supplier's products,[577] will normally be prohibited. Also, excessive prices charged by a dominant company may violate Article 86,[578] although no such finding has so far been sustained by the Court. The Commission has also found predatory pricing violates Article 86.[579]

The Tribunal subsequently held that a refusal to license by a monopolist was abusive, when the applicant was prevented entry in a derivative market where the owner also held a monopoly position. BBC v. Commission, Case T-70/89, (Ct. First Instance 1991).

575. Hoffmann-La Roche & Co. v. Commission, Case 85/76, [1979] E.C.R. 461, [1978-1979 Transfer Binder] COMMON MKT. REP. (CCH) ¶ 8527; SIXTEENTH REPORT 76 (1986) (Istituto/IMC and Angus)(dominant supplier of aminobutanol agreed to terminate exclusive agreements and substitute contract for fixed amounts over a two-year period with automatic renewal for one year absent six months' notice); see NINETEENTH REPORT 62 (1989) (industrial gases); Hachette, EIGHTH REPORT 88-89 (1978).

576. See, e.g., Hoffmann-La Roche & Co. v. Commission, Case 85/76, [1979] E.C.R. 461, [1978-1979 Transfer Binder] COMMON MKT. REP. (CCH) ¶ 8527; Coöperatieve Vereniging "Suiker Unie" UA v. Commission, Joined Cases 40-48, 50, 54-56, 111, 113, and 114/73, [1975] E.C.R. 1663, [1975 Transfer Binder] COMMON MKT. REP. (CCH) ¶ 8334; Nederlandsche Banden-Indus., Michelin, 24 O.J. EUR. COMM. (No. L 353) 33 (1981), [1978-1981 Transfer Binder] COMMON MKT. REP. (CCH) ¶ 10,340, aff'd sub nom. Nederlandsche Banden-Indus., Michelin NV v. Commission, Case 322/81, [1983] E.C.R. 3461, [1983-1985 Transfer Binder] COMMON MKT. REP. (CCH) ¶ 14,031; Soda Ash-Solvay, Decision 91/299, 34 O.J. EUR. COMM. (No. L 152) 21 (1991), [1991] 2 CEC (CCH) 2029; Soda Ash-ICI, Decision 91/300, 34 O.J. EUR. COMM. (No. L 152) 40 (1991), [1991] 2 CEC (CCH) 2053, (exclusionary rebates tying customers to dominant suppliers); BPB Indus. (British gypsum), Decision 89/22, 32 O.J. EUR. COMM. (No. L 10) 50 (1989), [1989] 1 CEC (CCH) 2008 (loyalty rebates and priority in filling orders for exclusive purchasers). In addition to restricting the possibility for competition by other firms and the consequent consolidation of a dominant firm's position, a fidelity rebate may constitute a discriminatory abuse, within the example given in Article 86(c), insofar as two customers purchasing the same quantity of a product from a producer pay different net prices if one pays a higher price because he also purchases the product from another producer. See generally ELEVENTH REPORT 67-68 (1981); SEVENTH REPORT 21-23 (1977).

577. Hoffmann-La Roche & Co. v. Commission, Case 85/76, [1979] E.C.R. 461, [1978-1979 Transfer Binder] COMMON MKT. REP. (CCH) ¶ 8527.

578. United Brands Co. v. Commission, Case 27/76, [1978] E.C.R. 207, [1977-1978 Transfer Binder] COMMON MKT. REP. (CCH) ¶ 8429 ("unfair" prices are those with no reasonable relation to the "economic value" (based on cost) of the products supplied); see General Motors Continental NV v. Commission, Case 26/75, [1975] E.C.R. 1367, [1975 Transfer Binder] COMMON MKT. REP. (CCH) ¶ 8320 (a dominant supplier of a service may be abusing its position if the price is excessive in relation to the economic value of the service provided). The Court has indicated that abusively excessive prices under Article 86 exist when a dominant company imposes prices significantly higher than prices other companies charge in other Member States and that it is up to the dominant company to justify the difference on the basis of objective criteria. SACEM v. Lucazeau, Joined Cases 110, 241-242/88, [1989] E.C.R. 2811, [1990] 2 CEC (CCH) 856.

579. Akzo Chemie BV v. Commission, Case C-62/86, (Eur. Comm. Ct. J. 1991) (pricing of chemical product designed to foreclose competitor; predatory prices are presumed to exist, subject to proof to the contrary, when prices are below average variable costs; prices are also predatory when below average total costs when they are charged pursuant to a plan to eliminate a competitor). In a second decision involving Tetra Pak, the Commission found predatory pricing through sale

A dominant company is obliged under Article 86 not to sell on terms that are discriminatory and that may distort competition between competitors. Such a situation may arise when a dominant supplier is selling at different prices to distributors in different Member States and those distributors are actual or potential competitors with one another.[580]

A number of other practices have been found to constitute an abuse under Article 86,[581] including the imposition of overly restrictive and discriminatory provisions of membership in a national copyright organization,[582] the initiation of coercive patent infringement suits,[583] resale price maintenance,[584] discriminatory rates charged by a public authority in relaying telex and telephone messages,[585] restrictive provisions in industrial supply agreements,[586] and tying.[587]

8. *Mergers and Acquisitions*

EEC antitrust law in regard to mergers and acquisitions was until recently based on the concept of abuse of a dominant position under Article 86.[588] The law was

---

of aseptic products in Italy and the United Kingdom at a loss over a long period of time in order to eliminate competitors. Tetra Pak, Commission Press Release IP 715 (July 24, 1991).

580. United Brands Co. v. Commission, Case 27/76, [1978] E.C.R. 207, [1977-1978 Transfer Binder] COMMON MKT. REP. (CCH) ¶ 8429.

581. In its proceeding against IBM the Commission charged abuse of a dominant position by failing to supply other manufacturers early enough with interface information, by memory bundling, by software bundling and by refusing to supply certain software installation services to users of non-IBM central processing units (CPUs). These charges were settled by an undertaking by IBM to unbundle memory capacity from the sale of CPUs and to disclose certain information needed by other manufacturers. FOURTEENTH REPORT 77-79 (1984).

582. Belgische Radio en Tèlèvisie v. SABAM, Case 127/73, [1974] E.C.R. 51, [1974 Transfer Binder] COMMON MKT. REP. (CCH) ¶ 8269; GEMA, 14 J.O. COMM. EUR. (No. L 134) 15 (1971), [1970-1972 Transfer Binder] COMMON MKT. REP. (CCH) ¶ 9438; FOURTH REPORT 66-67 (1974); *cf.* GEMA Statutes, 25 O.J. EUR. COMM. (No. L 94) 12 (1982), [1978-1981 Transfer Binder] COMMON MKT. REP. (CCH) ¶ 10,357.

583. Commission Press Release in Zippers (1978), [1978-1981 Transfer Binder] COMMON MKT. REP. (CCH) ¶ 10,055. The Commission has also indicated that defensive registration of a trademark by a company in a dominant position could be deemed an abuse. Osram/Airam, ELEVENTH REPORT 66 (1981).

584. NV GB-INNO-BM v. Vereniging van de Kleinhandelaars in Tabak, Case 13/77, [1977] E.C.R. 2115, [1977-1978 Transfer Binder] COMMON MKT. REP. (CCH) ¶ 8442.

585. British Telecommuns., 25 O.J. EUR. COMM. (No. L 360) 36 (1982), [1982-1985 Transfer Binder] COMMON MKT. REP. (CCH) ¶ 10,443, *aff'd sub nom.* Italy v. Commission, Case 41/83, [1985] E.C.R. 873, [1983-1985 Transfer Binder] COMMON MKT. REP. (CCH) ¶ 14,168.

586. NINETEENTH REPORT 62 (1989) (industrial gases) (exclusivity, duration, storage equipment, prohibition on resale, right to meet competitors' offers, certain price indexation clauses and deposits for investment costs).

587. Tetra Pak, Commission Press Release IP 715 (July 24, 1991) (Tetra Pak obliged users of its packaging machines to use only its cartons and only original spare parts); Eurofix Bauco/Hilti, 31 O.J. EUR. COMM. (No. L. 65) 19 (1988), [1985-1988 Transfer Binder] COMMON MKT. REP. (CCH) ¶ 10,976 (dominant producer of nail guns and related equipment engaged in selective discriminatory pricing designed to damage competitors or alter market entry).

588. E.g., Continental Can Co., 15 J.O. COMM. EUR. (No. L 7) 25 (1972), [1970-1972 Transfer Binder] COMMON MKT. REP. (CCH) ¶ 9481, *rev'd on other grounds*, Europemballage Corp. and Continental Can Co. v. Commission, Case 6/72, [1973] E.C.R. 215, [1971-1973 Transfer Binder] COMMON MKT. REP. (CCH) ¶ 8171 (Commission and Court of Justice application of Article 86 to an acquisition).

changed by the adoption in 1989 of a Council regulation on concentration (*Merger Control Regulation*).[589] The present law can best be understood by first reviewing the background of the regulation.

In *Continental Can* the Court held that it was an abuse of a dominant position for an already dominant company to acquire a competitor if the freedom of choice of consumers was unduly limited as a result of the acquisition.[590] The Court later seemed to recognize that a dominant company may abuse its position through the acquisition of a minority shareholding in a competitor which enables it to control its competitor or at least to influence the competitor's commercial policy.[591] While the Commission since *Continental Can* has only infrequently applied Article 86 to a merger,[592] it has regularly reviewed mergers and acquisitions either on its own initiative or when brought to its attention by complainants.[593]

The Commission adopted the practice of applying Article 86 rather than Article 85 in large part because of the difficulties raised by the automatic nullity arising from Article 85(2) and the limitation on the periods of exemptions under Article 85(3). Also, Article 85(1) could not be applied other than to mergers and acquisitions arising out of an agreement or concerted practice.[594] However, Article 85(1) is now considered by the Court to apply to acquisitions of a minority equity interest in a competitor that provides the acquiror with the means to influence the commercial conduct of the other company which remains independent.[595]

Fully aware of the limited scope of its merger control power under Article 86, the Commission in 1973 proposed for adoption by the Council a regulation setting a new

---

589. MERGER CONTROL REGULATION, *supra* note 411.

590. Europemballage Corp. and Continental Can Co. v. Commission, Case 6/72, [1973] E.C.R. 215, [1971-1973 Transfer Binder] COMMON MKT. REP. (CCH) ¶ 8171 (abuse where a dominant enterprise strengthens its position by acquisition of a company capable of entering the same geographic market to the point that the only enterprises remaining in the market are dependent on the dominant enterprise).

591. British-American Tobacco Co. and R.J. Reynolds Indus. v. Commission, Joined Cases 142 and 156/84, [1987] E.C.R. 4487, [1987-1988 Transfer Binder] COMMON MKT. REP. (CCH) ¶ 14,405 (affirming Commission rejection of complaints against a minority share acquisition by Philip Morris in *Rothmans*). See the FOURTEENTH REPORT 81-83 (1984) for a description of the Commission decision.

592. A formal decision was reached in Tetra Pak, 31 O.J. EUR. COMM. (No. L 272) 27 (1988), [1985-1988 Transfer Binder] COMMON MKT. REP. (CCH) ¶ 11,015 (abuse of a dominant position through acquisition of a company holding technology rights needed by other companies for access to the market), *aff'd sub nom.* Tetra Pak Rausing v. Commission, Case T-51/89, [1990] E.C.R. II 309, [1990] 2 CEC (CCH) 409.

593. Commission activity in regard to merger review under Article 86 has been regularly reported in its annual REPORT ON COMPETITION POLICY.

594. These and others reasons why Article 85 could not apply to mergers and acquisitions were identified by the Commission in its MEMORANDUM ON THE PROBLEM OF CONCENTRATION IN THE COMMON MARKET, COMPETITION SERIES, STUDY NO. 3, (1966).

595. British-American Tobacco Co. and R. J. Reynolds Indus., Joined Cases 142 and 156/84, [1987] E.C.R. 4487, [1987-1988 Transfer Binder] COMMON MKT. REP. (CCH) ¶ 14,405. The Court stated that Article 85(1) may apply when one company acquires an equity interest in a competitor that serves as an instrument for influencing the commercial conduct of the companies in question, "in particular where, by the acquisition of a shareholding or through subsidiary clauses in the agreement, the investing company obtains legal or de facto control of the commercial conduct of the other company or where the agreement provides for commercial co-operation between the companies or creates a structure likely to be used for such co-operation." *Id.* at ¶ 38.

substantive standard and requiring prior notification. The *Merger Control Regulation* was adopted in 1989 and entered into force on September 21, 1990.[596]

The *Merger Control Regulation* declares as incompatible with EEC law any concentration with a Community dimension which creates or strengthens a dominant position as a result of which effective competition would be significantly impeded within the EEC or a substantial part of it. Notification of concentrations with a Community dimension is required within one week of the earliest of the conclusion of the merger agreement, the announcement of the public bid or the acquisition of a controlling interest. Absent derogation, the concentration cannot be carried out either prior to notification or for a period of three weeks following notification. Until revision in 1993, a Community dimension exists where aggregate worldwide turnover of the parties exceeds 5 billion ECU and at least two of the parties each has EEC turnover in excess of 250 million ECU, provided that no Community dimension exists when each of the parties has two-thirds of its turnover in one and the same Member State.

Under the *Merger Control Regulation*, an operation that can be classified as a "concentration" under EEC law will be subject to differing jurisdictional and substantive rules depending on the circumstances.[597] An operation is a

---

596.   MERGER CONTROL REGULATION, *supra* note 411.

    The implementing rules for the MERGER CONTROL REGULATION are set forth in Regulation 2367/90, 33 O.J. EUR. COMM. (No. L 219) 5 (1990), 2 COMMON MKT. REP. (CCH) ¶ 2840. The notification form, known as Form CO, has been published as an annex to the Commission's regulation. 33 O.J. EUR. COMM. (No. L 219) 11 (1990), 2 COMMON MKT. REP. (CCH) ¶ 2840. Commission Notices have been issued on (i) the distinction between concentrative joint ventures, which are subject to the new regulation, and cooperative joint ventures, still subject to Regulation No. 17 and Articles 85-86, 33 O.J. EUR. COMM. (No. C 203) 10 (1990), 2 COMMON MKT. REP. (CCH) ¶ 2842; and (ii) ancillary restrictions in connection with concentrations, 33 O.J. EUR. COMM. (No. C 203) 5 (1990), 2 COMMON MKT. REP. (CCH) ¶ 2841.

597.   Commission Notice regarding the concentration and co-operative operations under Council Regulation 4064/89, of 21 December 1989 on the control of concentrations between undertakings, 33 O.J. EUR. COMM. (No. C 203) 10 (1990), 2 COMMON MKT. REP. (CCH) ¶ 2842.

    The Commission's definition of control, the distinction between concentrative and cooperative joint ventures, as well as the substantive test of the regulation, are developed on a case-by-case basis. Decisions are published in the OFFICIAL JOURNAL only if they are adopted following a full inquiry of the compatibility of a transaction with the standards of the regulation. *E.g.*, Magneti Marelli/CEAc, Decision 91/403, 34 O.J. EUR. COMM. (No. L 222) 38 (1991), [1991] 2 CEC 2,146, (acquisition of control in a competitor leading to the creation of a dominant position in the French replacement market for starter batteries); Alcatel/Telettra, 34 O.J. EUR. COMM. (No. L 122) 48 (1991) (acquisition leading to very high combined market shares in Spanish transmissions market.) Unpublished decisions (i.e., those adopted following a first examination of the transaction, which must be issued within one month of the notification) are, however, made available to the public in a nonconfidential version and are summarized in a Commission press release. In addition, a notice of their adoption appears in the OFFICIAL JOURNAL. Unpublished decisions can be of considerable interest on difficult issues such as the distinction between cooperative and concentrative joint ventures. *See, e.g.*, Commission Press Release No. IP 42 (Jan. 23, 1992) (Ericsson/Kolbe); Commission Press Release No. 1079 (Dec. 3, 1991) (TNT/Canada Post et al.); Commission Press Release No. 1007 (Nov. 13, 1991) (UAP/Transatlantic/Sun Life); Commission Press Release No. 942 (Oct. 25, 1991) (Thomson/Pilkington); Commission Press Release No. IP 801 (Aug. 20, 1991) (Kelt/American Express); Commission Press Release No. IP 558 (June 6, 1991) (Sanofi/Sterling); Commission Press Release No. IP 127 (Feb. 14, 1991) (Baxter/Nestlé/Salvia-Werk); Commission Press Release No. IP 7 (Jan. 7, 1991) (Mitsubishi/ UCAR).

"concentration" within the meaning of the *Regulation* when:

> (a) two or more previously independent undertakings merge, or (b) one or more persons already controlling at least one undertaking, or one or more undertakings acquire, whether by purchase of securities or assets, by contract or by any other means, direct or indirect control of the whole or parts of one or more other undertakings.[598]

"Control" is defined as "the possibility of exercising decisive influence."[599] Decisive influence can be exercised jointly by different companies.

If it is a concentration by its nature, whatever its size, the Commission no longer has the authority to use the enforcement provisions of Regulation 17 to apply Article 85 or Article 86 to a concentration of any size or nature, or to any ancillary restrictions.[600] The Commission has exclusive jurisdiction to apply the rules of the Regulation to a concentration of a "Community dimension."[601] These concentrations are subject to prenotification to the Commission before implementation,[602] to the substantive standard of the *Regulation*,[603] and are not subject to the antitrust rules of Member States unless the Commission authorizes a Member State to act.[604] Concentrations that do not have a Community dimension are subject to application of the regulation by the Commission only when a Member State requests such application in its own territory.[605] Normally, such concentrations will be subject only to the antitrust rules of the Member States.

Under the *Merger Control Regulation*, Articles 85 and 86 are expected to play only a limited role with respect to mergers, acquisitions and joint ventures that qualify as concentrations. They will, however, continue to govern restrictions related to such operations that are not ancillary and those that affect third parties.[606] In addition, national courts may seek to apply Article 86 to concentrations under the *Continental Can* rule.[607] When, however, an operation is not a concentration within the meaning of the *Regulation*, the Commission can still act under Regulation 17 to enforce the substantive rules of Articles 85 and 86. For example, Articles 85 and 86 have been applied to a share acquisition which sufficient to give some significant influence but which falls short of giving "control" through giving decisive influence.[608] An agreement between competitors to acquire jointly another competitor for the purpose of sharing its assets among the acquirors could also be subject to Articles 85 and 86.[609]

---

598.   MERGER CONTROL REGULATION, *supra* note 411, art. 3(1).
599.   *Id.* art. 3(3).
600.   *Id.* art. 22(1).
601.   *Id.* art. 21(1).
602.   *Id.* art. 4(1).
603.   *Id.* art. 2(2).
604.   *Id.* arts. 9, 12(1).
605.   *Id.* arts. 22(3), 22(4).
606.   *Id.* art. 2(1) (MERGER CONTROL REGULATION only applicable to concentrations); *Id.* art. 3(1) (concentration defined).
607.   *See supra* note 590 and accompanying text.
608.   British-American Tobacco Co. and R.J. Reynolds Indus. v. Commission, Joined Cases 142 and 156/84, [1987] E.C.R. 4487, [1987-1988 Transfer Binder] COMMON MKT. REP. (CCH) ¶ 14,405. SEVENTEENTH REPORT 93-97 (1987).
609.   Such an operation does not fall within the definition of "concentration" under the REGULATION. *See supra* note 597.

For those "concentrations" that lack a "Community dimension," Regulation 17 does not apply and the Commission lacks effective enforcement powers.[610] Thus, enforcement of Articles 85 and 86 will be left to a large extent to Member State antitrust authorities. Moreover, private complainants may invoke Article 85 before a Member State's courts only after a finding by the Commission or by a national antitrust authority that Article 85 has been violated.[611]

---

610.   *See* MERGER CONTROL REGULATION, *supra* note 411, art. 22(2).

611.   *Compare* Ministère Public v. Asjes and Others, Joined Cases 209-213/84, [1986] E.C.R. 1425, [1985-1986 Transfer Binder] COMMON MKT. REP. (CCH) ¶ 14,287 (absent an implementing regulation such as Regulation 17, Article 85(1) has direct effect only with respect to agreements found in infringement by a Member State antitrust authority or the Commission, respectively, under Article 88 or 89) with Ahmed Saeed Flugreisen v. Zentrale, Case 66/86, [1989] E.C.R. 803, [1989] 2 CEC (CCH) 654 (permitting Member State enforcement of Article 86).

CHAPTER XI

EXEMPTIONS AND REGULATED MARKETS

A. Introduction

The antitrust laws are designed to promote competition. In areas of commerce where the government has adopted economic or social policies that conflict with free and open competition, accommodations must be made between the demands of the antitrust laws and the constraints of those other goals. In some instances Congress has resolved these conflicts by creating explicit statutory exemptions from the antitrust laws. In others, exemptions have been implied by the courts.

This chapter discusses the state action doctrine, under which the operation of a state regulatory scheme may preclude the imposition of antitrust liability; the *Noerr-Pennington* doctrine, which provides antitrust immunity for efforts to solicit government action that restricts competition; and antitrust exemptions that may result from federal regulation of an area of commerce. The chapter then discusses specific antitrust exemptions applicable to particular industries and the application of the antitrust laws and principles of competition in particular regulated markets.

B. Effect of Government Involvement

1. Inducement or Approval by Federal Officials

In *United States v. Socony-Vacuum Oil Co.*,[1] the Supreme Court rejected the argument that antitrust immunity was conferred by federal officials' knowledge of and acquiescence in the defendants' collaborative efforts to stabilize the price of refined petroleum products:

> The fact that Congress through utilization of the precise methods here employed could seek to reach the same objectives sought by respondents does not mean that respondents or any other group may do so without specific Congressional authority. . . . Though employees of the government may have known of those programs and winked at them or tacitly approved them, no immunity would have thereby been obtained. For Congress had specified the precise manner and method of securing immunity. None other would suffice. Otherwise national policy on such grave and important issues as this would be determined

---

1. 310 U.S. 150 (1940).

not by Congress nor by those to whom Congress had delegated authority but by virtual volunteers.[2]

Subsequent judicial decisions have reiterated the principle of *Socony* that federal officials have no independent authority to exempt conduct from the antitrust laws.[3] Such decisions are consistent with a separate line of cases that have established that federal officials acting beyond the scope of their actual authority ordinarily have no power to bind the government.[4]

Thus, as a general rule, it is no defense to an antitrust action that federal officials knew of, approved of, or induced the challenged conduct when such conduct was not undertaken pursuant to statutory authority.[5] Courts that have recognized immunity

---

2. *Id.* at 225-27.
3. In Otter Tail Power Co. v. United States, 410 U.S. 366 (1973), the Supreme Court rejected an electric utility's argument that federal officials had immunized its conduct by approving contractual restrictions that municipally-owned distribution companies claimed to violate the antitrust laws. The Court explained:

    The fact that some of the restrictive provisions were contained in a contract with the Bureau of Reclamation is not material to our problem for, as the Solicitor General says, "government contracting officers do not have the power to grant immunity from the Sherman Act." Such contracts stand on their own footing and are valid or not, depending on the statutory framework within which the federal agency operates.

    Id. at 378-79; *see also* California v. FPC, 369 U.S. 482, 487-89 (1962) (approval of acquisition by Federal Power Commission not bar to antitrust suit); United States v. RCA, 358 U.S. 334, 343-44, 351-52 (1959) (exchange of radio stations approved by Federal Communications Commission held subject to attack in antitrust proceedings); Eugene Dietzgen Co. v. FTC, 142 F.2d 321, 329 (7th Cir.) ("[P]etitioners cannot avoid liability for their actions because requested by some public official so to do. If such request could be shown it would have been of no more force than if spoken by a private citizen. Only Congress can lift the restrictions which find expression in the Sherman Act."), *cert. denied*, 323 U.S. 730 (1944); Consumers Union v. Rogers, 352 F. Supp. 1319, 1323 (D.D.C. 1973) (President lacks power to exempt conduct from antitrust laws unless Congress grants authority to do so), *vacated on this point for lack of actual controversy after stipulated dismissal of antitrust claim sub nom.* Consumers Union v. Kissinger, 506 F.2d 136 (D.C. Cir. 1974), *cert. denied*, 421 U.S. 1004 (1975); *cf.* Medical Ass'n v. Schweiker, 554 F. Supp. 955, 966 (M.D. Ala. 1983) ("private parties to the extent they are acting at the direction or with the consent of federal agencies also fall outside the pale of the [Sherman] act's prohibition"), *aff'd*, 714 F.2d 107 (11th Cir. 1983).
4. *See, e.g.*, Office of Personnel Mgmt. v. Richmond, 110 S. Ct. 2465, 2472 (1990) (federal government held not estopped from denying disability benefits to individual who relied upon misinformation provided by federal employee); Schweiker v. Hansen, 450 U.S. 785, 788 (1981) (per curiam) (estoppel not available to bind federal government for erroneous advice provided by Social Security Administration employee); Federal Crop Ins. Corp. v. Merrill, 332 U.S. 380, 385-86 (1947) (misinformation supplied by agent of federal government does not estop government from refusing payment of insurance benefits). Decisions dealing with the authority of federal employees have stopped short of saying there are no circumstances in which unauthorized acts of such employees could estop the government. *See Richmond*, 110 S. Ct. at 2472 (declining "to accept . . . an across-the-board no-estoppel rule").
5. *See, e.g.*, United States v. Socony-Vacuum Oil Co., 310 U.S. 150, 226 (1940) (approval by federal employees in absence of authority to provide immunity held to have no effect); *cf.* Hecht v. Pro-Football, Inc., 444 F.2d 931, 934-35 & n.6 (D.C. Cir. 1971) (citing, with approval, observation of dissent in Alabama Power Co. v. Alabama Elec. Coop., 394 F.2d 672, 685 (5th Cir. 1968) that "The cases do not support a proposition of general governmental [antitrust] immunity. If there is such a principle Congress has been proceeding for a long time under a misapprehension in providing for government officers, and those with whom they deal, exemptions which are specific in nature and varying in scope."), *cert. denied*, 404 U.S. 1047 (1972).

arising from the involvement of federal officials have done so on the ground that the government's employees had explicit or implicit authority to compel or approve conduct that otherwise might violate the antitrust laws.[6] In addition to challenges to the conduct of private actors, such disputes occasionally involve antitrust claims against federal agencies and their employees. Courts consistently have ruled that federal agencies and federal officials acting in their official capacity are immune from antitrust challenges.[7]

2. Restraints Imposed by State Action

Antitrust litigants sometimes allege that state or local government bodies have adopted policies that improperly limit competition. In such cases, firms or individual entrepreneurs typically argue that a public regulation or policy wrongly forecloses a commercial opportunity, unfairly discriminates among firms in determining access to markets, or otherwise unreasonably hinders the operation of the competitive process. Under the rubric of the "state action doctrine," the Supreme Court since the 1940s has permitted state governments and certain private economic actors to show that the operation of a state regulatory scheme precludes the imposition of antitrust liability. The state action doctrine also shields the decisions of political subdivisions (for example, cities and counties) to which the state has delegated authority to adopt competition-suppressing regulatory measures.

a. BASIC FRAMEWORK AND EVOLUTION OF THE STATE ACTION DOCTRINE

The foundation for state action jurisprudence is *Parker v. Brown*.[8] In *Parker*, the Supreme Court upheld, as an "act of government which the Sherman Act did not undertake to prohibit,"[9] a California program that regulated production and

---

6. *See, e.g.*, Alabama Power Co. v. Alabama Elec. Coop., 394 F.2d 672, 673, 676-77 (5th Cir.) (Congressional grant of authority to administrator of Rural Electrification Administration contemplated power to impose lending terms that formed the basis for plaintiff's antitrust claims; private party's conduct was immune because it resulted from "valid governmental action"), *cert. denied*, 393 U.S. 1000 (1968); Williams Elec. Co. v. Honeywell, Inc., 1991-1 Trade Cas. (CCH) ¶ 69,473, at 66,000-02 (N.D. Fla. 1991) (immunity recognized because provisions of Armed Services Procurement Act and Federal Acquisition Regulations gave Air Force purchasing official authority to direct contractors to engage in questioned conduct); Greensboro Lumber Co. v. Georgia Power Co., 643 F. Supp. 1345, 1364-66 (N.D. Ga. 1986) (electric utility's contracting practices immunized from antitrust challenge because Rural Electrification Administration required the contracts as condition for receiving federal loans; agency director's conduct was within discretion conferred by Congress), *aff'd*, 844 F.2d 1538, 1541 (11th Cir. 1988).

7. *See, e.g.*, Rex Sys. v. Holiday, 814 F.2d 994, 997 (4th Cir. 1987) (Department of the Navy and two Navy officials acting in their official capacities are not "persons" capable of being sued under the Sherman Act); Sea-Land Serv. v. Alaska R.R., 659 F.2d 243, 246-47 (D.C. Cir. 1981) (entity owned and operated by United States is immune from antitrust liability), *cert. denied*, 455 U.S. 919 (1982); *see also Williams Elec.*, 1991-1 Trade Cas. (CCH) ¶ 69,473, at 65,999 ("it appears well-settled that federal agencies and their officials acting in their official capacity are immune from federal antitrust liability").

8. 317 U.S. 341 (1943).

9. *Id.* at 352.

marketing of raisins by the state's growers.[10] The California legislature created the program by statute and delegated its implementation to an advisory commission on which the state director of agriculture participated ex-officio. The statute's declared purpose was to "'conserve the agricultural wealth of the State' and to 'prevent economic waste in the marketing of agricultural products.'"[11] The statute authorized programs to restrict competition among growers and to maintain prices in the distribution of agricultural commodities to packers. Marketing programs for individual products were administered by program committees consisting of producers, handlers, or packers. Although interested producers proposed and approved the marketing programs, the Court concluded that "it is the state, acting through the Commission, which adopts the program and which enforces it with penal sanctions, in the execution of a governmental policy."[12] Principles of federalism immunized such "state action" from antitrust attack. "In a dual system of government," the Court explained, "in which, under the Constitution, the states are sovereign, save only as Congress may constitutionally subtract from their authority, an unexpressed purpose to nullify a state's control over its officers and agents is not lightly to be attributed to Congress."[13] The Court found no such purpose in *Parker*.[14]

The *Parker* Court emphasized that competitive restraints qualify for antitrust immunity only to the extent that they constitute "state action or official action directed by a state."[15] The Court expressly noted that "a state does not give immunity to those who violate the Sherman Act by authorizing them to violate it, or by declaring that their action is lawful."[16] Thus, close analysis of the state's

---

10.   Courts traditionally have defined the state action doctrine in terms of immunity from Sherman Act scrutiny. In Cine 42nd Street Theater Corp. v. Nederlander Organization, 790 F.2d 1032, 1040 (2d Cir. 1986), the Second Circuit concluded that "the state action defense is [also] generally available to parties defending against a § 7 Clayton Act violation."

11.   317 U.S. at 346 (quoting § 3 of the California Agricultural Prorate Act).

12.   *Id.* at 352.

13.   *Id.* at 351; *see* City of Columbia v. Omni Outdoor Advertising, Inc., 111 S. Ct. 1344, 1349 (1991) (stating that *Parker* relied on "principles of federalism and state sovereignty" to hold that "the Sherman Act did not apply to anticompetitive restraints imposed by the States 'as an act of government.' 317 U.S. at 352"); Traweek v. City & County of San Francisco, 920 F.2d 589, 591 (9th Cir. 1990) (*Parker* "recognized that the free market principles espoused in the Sherman Antitrust Act end where countervailing principles of federalism and respect for state sovereignty begin").

14.   317 U.S. at 351 ("The Sherman Act makes no mention of the state as such, and gives no hint that it was intended to restrain state action or official action directed by a state."). *Parker* established that the Sherman Act did not bar the state from adopting a regulatory scheme that benefitted California raisin producers at the expense of consumers living in California and other states. In later cases, plaintiffs seeking legal grounds upon which to challenge such initiatives have remained free to argue that the conduct in question exceeds other limits upon the state's discretion to make economic policy. For example, certain forms of government intervention may be said to violate constitutional prohibitions upon measures that restrict free speech or unduly burden interstate commerce. *See, e.g.*, Preferred Communs. v. City of Los Angeles, 754 F.2d 1396, 1415 (9th Cir. 1985) (affirming, on state action grounds, dismissal of cable television firm's antitrust claims, but reinstating first amendment challenge to municipality's decision to award an exclusive cable television franchise), *aff'd*, 476 U.S. 488 (1986).

15.   317 U.S. at 351.

16.   *Id.* (citation omitted); *see Omni*, 111 S. Ct. at 1353 (*Parker* immunity "does not mean . . . that the States may exempt *private* action from the scope of the Sherman Act") (emphasis in original).

involvement in the restraint has been necessary to determine whether state action immunity serves to block the application of antitrust liability rules.[17]

In *Goldfarb v. Virginia State Bar*,[18] the Supreme Court held that adoption of minimum fee schedules by a county bar association and enforcement of the schedules through the prospect of disciplinary action by the State Bar constituted "essentially a private anticompetitive activity" which the *Parker* doctrine did not shield. Although the state supreme court had statutory authority to regulate the practice of law and the State Bar was an administrative agency of the court for purpose of enforcing rules and regulations adopted by the court, the Supreme Court found nothing in Virginia law or in the Virginia Supreme Court's rules that required minimum fee-setting. Rejecting an argument that adoption and enforcement of minimum fee schedules "complemented the objective" of ethical codes promulgated by the Virginia Supreme Court, the *Goldfarb* Court declared that in this context "[i]t is not enough that . . . anticompetitive conduct is 'prompted' by state action; rather, anticompetitive activities must be compelled by direction of the State acting as a sovereign."[19]

By contrast, in *Bates v. State Bar of Arizona*,[20] the Supreme Court held immune from antitrust attack a disciplinary rule restricting lawyer advertising because the regulation was both promulgated and enforced by the Arizona Supreme Court, which the state constitution authorized to regulate the practice of law.[21] The Court observed that the Arizona Supreme Court was "the real party in interest; it adopted the rules, and it is the ultimate trier of fact and law in the enforcement process."[22] The Arizona lawyer advertising rules "reflect[ed] a clear articulation of the State's policy with regard to professional behavior" and were "subject to pointed reexamination by the policy maker — the Arizona Supreme Court — in enforcement proceedings."[23]

---

17. *See* George R. Whitten, Jr., Inc. v. Paddock Pool Builders, 424 F.2d 25, 30 (1st Cir.) ("The [*Parker*] Court's emphasis on the extent of the state's involvement precludes the facile conclusion that action by any public official automatically confers exemption."), *cert. denied*, 404 U.S. 850 (1970). The state action doctrine's logic also has been invoked to curtail the ability of the Federal Trade Commission to use its consumer protection rulemaking authority to nullify state regulations. In California State Board of Optometry v. FTC, 910 F.2d 976 (D.C. Cir. 1990), the D.C. Circuit vacated a FTC rule that purported to create a defense to any state proceeding brought against an optometrist for violating certain state restrictions upon the practice of optometry. Relying upon *Parker* and later state action cases, the court stated that a federal agency "may not exercise authority over States as sovereigns unless that authority has been unambiguously granted to it." *Id.* at 982.

18. 421 U.S. 773, 792 (1975).

19. *Id.* at 791 (quoting respondent).

20. 433 U.S. 350 (1977).

21. A divided Court struck down the restrictions as a violation of the lawyers' first amendment right of free speech. *Compare id.* at 363-82 *with id.* at 386 (Burger, C.J., concurring and dissenting in part); *id.* at 389 (Powell, J., concurring and dissenting in part); *and id.* at 404 (Rehnquist, J., dissenting in part). The Court was unanimous, however, in finding antitrust immunity based on the *Parker* doctrine.

22. *Id.* at 361 (citation omitted).

23. *Id.* at 362; *see* Feldman v. Gardner, 661 F.2d 1295, 1306-08 (D.C. Cir. 1981) (*Bates* rule extended to Court of Appeals for District of Columbia, which, by act of Congress, has regulatory authority over admission of attorneys to bar of District of Columbia); Richardson v. Florida Bar, 1990-2 Trade Cas. (CCH) ¶ 69,111, at 64,110 (D.D.C. 1990) (in interpreting ethical rules governing practice of law, Supreme Court of Florida "acts for the sovereign and is therefore exempt from

The Supreme Court applied the logic of *Bates* in *Hoover v. Ronwin*.[24] Ronwin alleged that the Arizona Supreme Court Committee of Examinations and Admissions had violated the Sherman Act "by artificially reducing the number of competing attorneys."[25] Ronwin argued that although the Committee members were state officers, their actions were divorced from the Arizona Supreme Court's exercise of its sovereign powers and, therefore, were not immune from an antitrust action. The Supreme Court disagreed, holding that Ronwin's complaint had been properly dismissed for failure to state a claim upon which relief could be granted. Viewing the challenged Committee activities as functionally the activities of the Arizona Supreme Court, the Supreme Court said "this case turns on a narrow and specific issue: who denied Ronwin admission to the Arizona Bar? . . . [T]he incontrovertible fact [is] that under the law of Arizona *only* the State Supreme Court had authority to admit or deny admission to practice law . . . ."[26]

In *Cantor v. Detroit Edison Co.*,[27] a utility regulated by the Michigan Public Service Commission claimed immunity for its program of providing free light bulbs to electricity customers on the ground that the program was included in a tariff approved by the Commission. A majority of the Supreme Court denied immunity, finding that Commission approval of the program did not "implement any statewide policy relating to light bulbs,"[28] and that neither the Michigan legislature nor the Public Service Commission had actively considered the desirability of the free light bulb program.[29]

In *New Motor Vehicle Board v. Orrin W. Fox Co.*,[30] a statute that required state approval of the location of new automobile dealerships was challenged on the ground

---

antitrust liability for any anticompetitive rules and interpretations it may issue"); Foley v. Alabama State Bar, 481 F. Supp. 1308, 1311 (N.D. Ala. 1979) (disciplinary rules of Alabama State Bar "are in effect rules of the Supreme Court of Alabama" and are immune from antitrust challenge). In Princeton Community Phone Book, Inc. v. Bate, 582 F.2d 706 (3d Cir.), *cert. denied*, 439 U.S. 966 (1978), the court held that an ethics advisory panel's action was "not as clearly commanded as was the defendants' action in *Bates*." 582 F.2d at 719. Nonetheless, the court found that the close relationship between the advisory committee and the state's supreme court conferred immunity:

> The weaker the relationship between the state and the defendant, the more clearly the state must command the precise action taken by the defendant for the defendant to enjoy the state action exemption. Conversely, the closer the relationship between the state and the defendant, the less clearly the state need command the precise action for the defendant to enjoy the exemption.

Id.

24.   466 U.S. 558 (1984) (4-3 decision).
25.   *Id.* at 565. Ronwin argued that the Committee accomplished the artificial reduction by determining the number of new attorneys it wished to admit and by setting the passing score for the bar examination accordingly.
26.   *Id.* at 581 (emphasis in original).
27.   428 U.S. 579 (1976).
28.   *Id.* at 585.
29.   *Id.*; *accord* Winters v. Indiana & Mich. Elec. Co., 1979-2 Trade Cas. (CCH) ¶ 62,797 (N.D. Ind. 1979) (private power company's monopoly of electricity service gained by lease of facilities from city and approved by state commission held not exempt where no state body or policy required lease or resulting increase in power rates); Woolen v. Surtran Taxicabs, Inc., 461 F. Supp. 1025, 1031-33 (N.D. Tex. 1978) (city's award of exclusive franchise to provide taxi service to regional airport held not exempt; Texas Railroad Commission's grant of authority to municipality "did not require that Surtran carry on the permitted activities by means of an exclusive contract").
30.   439 U.S. 96 (1978).

that it gave effect to privately initiated restraints of trade. The statute required automobile manufacturers to advise existing franchisees of an intent to establish or relocate another dealership in the incumbent franchisees' market. If competing dealers protested, the statute provided for a hearing to determine the effect of the proposed intrabrand competition upon the existing franchisees and the public interest. The Court upheld the measure, finding it to be a "clearly articulated and affirmatively expressed" regulatory system designed to "displace unfettered business freedom in the matter of the establishment and relocation of automobile dealerships."[31]

In *California Retail Liquor Dealers Association v. Midcal Aluminum, Inc.,*[32] the Supreme Court held that there are "two standards for antitrust immunity" under the *Parker* doctrine: first, the challenged restraint must be " 'one clearly articulated and affirmatively expressed as state policy' " and, second, the policy must be "'actively supervised'" by the state itself.[33] *Midcal* involved a challenge to a California wholesale wine pricing system that functioned as a resale price maintenance program.[34] The Court held that, although the pricing system rested upon a clearly articulated state policy, the mechanism for overseeing its implementation was deficient:

> The State simply authorizes price setting and enforces the prices established by private parties. The State neither establishes prices nor reviews the reasonableness of the price schedules; nor does it regulate the terms of fair trade contracts. The State does not monitor market conditions or engage in any "pointed reexamination" of the program.[35]

---

31. *Id.* at 109. In Exxon Corp. v. Governor of Maryland, 437 U.S. 117 (1978), the Supreme Court considered a Maryland statute that barred producers or refiners of petroleum products from operating retail service stations within the state and required that certain price reductions provided by producers and refiners be granted uniformly to all stations they supply within the state. In holding that the Maryland statute was preempted by neither the Robinson-Patman Act nor the Sherman Act, the Court observed that "if an adverse effect on competition were, in and of itself, enough to render a state statute invalid, the States' power to engage in economic regulation would be effectively destroyed." *Id.* at 133.

32. 445 U.S. 97 (1980).

33. *Id.* at 105.

34. The California statute required wine producers and wholesalers to file fair trade contracts or price schedules with the state and provided for enforcement of the pricing system by fines and suspension or revocation of licenses. As such, the Court determined that the "legislative policy [was] forthrightly stated and clear in its purpose to permit resale price maintenance." *Id.*

35. *Id.* at 105-06 (citation omitted). The Court contrasted the California program with "the approach of those States that completely control the distribution of liquor within their boundaries," noting that "[s]uch comprehensive regulation would be immune from the Sherman Act . . . since the State would 'displace unfettered business freedom' with its own power." *Id.* at 106 n.9 (quoting New Motor Vehicle Bd. v. Orrin W. Fox Co., 439 U.S. 96, 109 (1978)) (other citations omitted); *see, e.g.,* Serlin Wine & Spirit Merchants, Inc. v. Healy, 512 F. Supp. 936, 939-43 (D. Conn.) (Connecticut's Liquor Control Act, even if constituting resale price maintenance, would be immune from Sherman Act), *aff'd sub nom.* Morgan v. Division of Liquor Control, 664 F.2d 353 (2d Cir. 1981); Hinshaw v. Beatrice Foods, Inc., 1980-81 Trade Cas. (CCH) ¶ 63,584 (D. Mont. 1980) (immunity established through comprehensive regulation of milk pricing under Montana Milk Price Control Act).

Thus, the Court held that the pricing system did not constitute active supervision.[36]

Midcal's two-pronged test has supplied the essential analytical framework within which subsequent decisions have determined the availability of immunity. Disputes concerning the application of the state action doctrine have focused upon satisfaction of the clear articulation and active supervision requirements, and the treatment of policies that emanate from public entities other than the state legislature.

b.   THE CLEAR ARTICULATION REQUIREMENT

The requirement that the challenged conduct must be undertaken "pursuant to a 'clearly articulated and affirmatively expressed state policy' to replace competition with regulation"[37] serves to ensure that the state has authorized regulatory departures from reliance upon market rivalry. For several years following *Midcal*, courts debated how extensively and specifically states must articulate a preference for competition-suppressing regulation. Some circuits concluded that a private entity claiming antitrust immunity must show that state law compelled the challenged anticompetitive conduct.[38] However, in *Southern Motor Carriers Rate Conference, Inc. v. United States*,[39] the Supreme Court examined the conduct of rate bureaus composed of common carriers in four Southeastern states. In each state the carriers were required to propose rates to a public regulatory commission for approval and were allowed, but not compelled, to agree on joint rate proposals before submitting the rates to the regulatory agency.[40] The Court held that *"Midcal's* two-pronged test [is] applicable to private parties' claims of state action immunity."[41] The Court said "a state policy that expressly *permits*, but does not compel, anticompetitive behavior may be 'clearly articulated' within the meaning of *Midcal.*"[42]

The rate bureau defendants in *Southern Motor Carriers* satisfied all elements of the *Midcal* test for state action. The government conceded the presence of active state supervision, as the state public service commissions actively oversaw the bureaus' collective ratemaking.[43] The rate bureaus established the existence of clearly

---

36.   In Fisher v. City of Berkeley, 475 U.S. 260 (1986), the Supreme Court considered an antitrust challenge to a municipal rent control scheme. The Court upheld the rent control program on the ground that the city had acted unilaterally to devise rent limits and to impose them upon landlords. *Id* at 266-67. Because the city had acted alone, there was no concerted action for Sherman Act § 1 purposes and no need to consider the availability of *Parker* immunity. The Court distinguished *Midcal* as an illustration of a non-unilateral, "hybrid" restraint through which the state enforced prices established by private parties without state oversight; *see also* Commuter Transp. Sys. v. Hillsborough County Aviation Auth., 801 F.2d 1286, 1291 (11th Cir. 1986) (no antitrust liability where defendant airport authority acted "unilaterally to achieve a legitimate public policy objective" and "not pursuant to any concerted action" with private parties).

37.   Hoover v. Ronwin, 466 U.S. 558, 569 (1984).

38.   *See, e.g.*, United States v. Southern Motor Carriers Rate Conference, Inc., 702 F.2d 532, 534 (5th Cir. 1983) (en banc), *rev'd*, 471 U.S. 48 (1985); United States v. Title Ins. Rating Bureau, 700 F.2d 1247, 1252 (9th Cir. 1983), *cert. denied*, 467 U.S. 1240 (1984); United States v. Texas State Bd. of Pub. Accountancy, 464 F. Supp. 400, 403-04 (W.D. Tex. 1978), *modified*, 592 F.2d 919 (5th Cir.), *cert. denied*, 444 U.S. 925 (1979).

39.   471 U.S. 48 (1985).

40.   *Id* at 51.

41.   *Id* at 61 (footnote omitted).

42.   *Id* (emphasis in original).

43.   *Id* at 62.

articulated, affirmatively expressed state policies to displace competition by showing that each state had enacted statutes that either explicitly permitted collective ratemaking by common carriers or indicated that intrastate rates were to be set by a regulatory agency, rather than by market forces.[44] Thus, *Southern Motor Carriers* established that state action immunity is available for public entities, public officials, and private parties whose conduct is authorized, but not compelled, by the state.[45]

Applications of the clear articulation test can require reviewing courts to make difficult judgments about whether state enactments display an intent to displace the

---

44.   *Id.*

45.   *See, e.g.,* Hancock Indus. v. Schaeffer, 811 F.2d 225, 233-34 (3d Cir. 1987) (county authorized to limit landfill dumping by clearly articulated state policy; county and county officials therefore held immune from antitrust liability); Woolen v. Surtran Taxicabs, Inc., 801 F.2d 159, 163-65 (5th Cir. 1986) (dismissing antitrust claims against private taxi operators who acted pursuant to directives of the cities of Dallas and Fort Worth and whose operations at Dallas/Fort Worth International Airport were actively supervised), *cert. denied,* 480 U.S. 931 (1987); Llewellyn v. Crothers, 765 F.2d 769, 771-73 (9th Cir. 1985) (fee-setting actions of Oregon Workers' Compensation Department and its private designate were immune from antitrust attack by chiropractors who objected to maximum fee schedule promulgated by the Department); Davis v. Southern Bell Tel. & Tel. Co., 755 F. Supp. 1532, 1538-40 (S.D. Fla. 1991) (state statute gave public service commission broad latitude to set terms for telephone service and contemplated commission's regulation of defendant's provision of inside wire maintenance service for residential customers); Metro Mobile CTS, Inc. v. New Vector Communs., 661 F. Supp. 1504, 1518 (D. Ariz. 1987) (state's constitution and statutes anticipated that state's corporation commission would have power to approve challenged tariffs of defendant), *aff'd on other grounds,* 892 F.2d 62 (9th Cir. 1989); Falk v. City of Chicago, 1986-1 Trade Cas. (CCH) ¶ 67,128 (N.D. Ill. 1986) (city and private bus company held immune from antitrust challenge to city's award of exclusive airport transportation contracts). *But cf. In re* Insurance Antitrust Litig., 938 F.2d 919, 931 (9th Cir. 1991) (defendants' agreements to refuse to reinsure were "neither a reasonable nor necessary consequence of the conduct regulated and approved by the state"); Medic Air Corp. v. Air Ambulance Auth., 843 F.2d 1187, 1189-90 (9th Cir. 1988) (immunity lacking where regulatory scheme neither gave private defendant an exclusive franchise nor showed intent to displace competition); Rosemont Cogeneration Joint Venture v. Northern States Power Co., 1991-1 Trade Cas. (CCH) ¶ 69,351, at 65,407 (D. Minn. 1991) (state action immunity rejected where defendant power company's conduct contradicted state policy favoring encouragement of cogeneration and small power production); Sweeney v. Athens Regional Medical Center, 709 F. Supp. 1563, 1576 (M.D. Ga. 1989) (rejecting immunity where statute did not authorize private anticompetitive conduct); Reynolds Metals Co. v. Commonwealth Gas Servs., 682 F. Supp. 291, 294 (E.D. Va. 1988) (rejecting state action defense to pipelines' refusal to wheel gas from independent producer over its lines to industrial user where there was no clearly articulated state policy countenancing such refusal); Wicker v. Union County Gen. Hosp., 673 F. Supp. 177, 185 (N.D. Miss. 1987) (rejecting immunity where statute expressed neutrality); Reazin v. Blue Cross & Blue Shield, 663 F. Supp. 1360, 1419 (D. Kan. 1987) (rejecting immunity for Blue Cross decision to terminate contracts with competing health care providers; state policy suggested no intent to displace competition), *aff'd in part and remanded in part,* 899 F.2d 951 (10th Cir.), *cert. denied,* 110 S. Ct. 3241 (1990); Jiricko v. Coffeyville Mem. Hosp. Medical Center, 628 F. Supp. 329, 332-33 (D. Kan. 1985) (state hospital's demotion of anesthesiology department head without hearing was not immune from antitrust attack at pleading stage where state statute concerning operation of state-owned hospitals did not expressly state that operation of hospital constituted public government function); New York Airlines v. Dukes County, 623 F. Supp. 1435, 1450-52 (D. Mass. 1985) (airport commission's refusal to permit airline to provide service not immune; statutes establishing commission evidenced no policy to displace competition and no indication that state was engaging in active supervision); Quinn v. Kent Gen. Hosp., 617 F. Supp. 1226, 1236 (D. Del. 1985) (hospital's refusal to grant physician full staff privileges not immunized by state peer review statute because no indication of state intent to displace competition in market for hospital facilities).

operation of market rivalry with regulation. In *Ticor Title Insurance Co. v. FTC*,[46] the Third Circuit reviewed an FTC order that barred title insurance companies from collectively using private rating bureaus to set rates charged by the insurers' attorney-agents for title search and examination services in six states. The FTC concluded that statutes in two states excluded amounts paid to attorneys from the definition of title insurance "fees" that insurers were to file with state regulators. The Third Circuit reversed, finding that the supreme court of each state would regard as reasonable, and would defer to, the view of state regulators who interpreted the statute as allowing regulation of attorney-agent's fees.[47]

The requisite state authority need not always antedate the challenged activity. For example, the Ninth Circuit has concluded that the state's authorizing legislation can shield conduct that occurred well before the measure was enacted.[48] However, immunity may be denied for past conduct when subsequent legislation cannot be said to have expressly provided authority that was implicit in earlier statutes or state policies.[49]

Private parties also may qualify for immunity by demonstrating reasonable reliance upon a state statute that the state's courts subsequently declare to be unconstitutional.[50]

---

46. 922 F.2d 1122 (3d Cir. 1991), *cert. granted*, 60 U.S.L.W. 3257 (U.S. Oct. 7, 1991) (No. 91-72).

47. 922 F.2d at 1132, 1134. *Ticor* is one of a number of decisions in which the antitrust court has looked to earlier state court decisions for guidance concerning the existence of the requisite state authorization for the challenged activity. *See* Town of Hallie v. City of Eau Claire, 471 U.S. 34, 44 n.8 (1985); Consolidated Television Cable Serv. v. City of Frankfort, 857 F.2d 354, 361 (6th Cir. 1988), *cert. denied*, 489 U.S. 1082 (1989); Campbell v. City of Chicago, 823 F.2d 1182, 1184-85 (7th Cir. 1987); Independent Taxicab Drivers' Employees v. Greater Houston Transp. Co., 760 F.2d 607, 611-12 (5th Cir.), *cert. denied*, 474 U.S. 903 (1985); Golden State Transit Corp. v. City of Los Angeles, 726 F. 2d 1430, 1433 (9th Cir. 1984), *cert. denied*, 471 U.S. 1003 (1985); Central Iowa Refuse Sys. v. Des Moines Metropolitan Solid Waste Agency, 715 F.2d 419, 421 n.5, 427 n.15 (8th Cir. 1983), *cert. denied*, 471 U.S. 1003 (1985); Pueblo Aircraft Serv. v. City of Pueblo, 679 F.2d 805, 810-11 (10th Cir. 1982), *cert. denied*, 459 U.S. 1126 (1983); Euster v. Eagle Downs Racing Ass'n, 677 F.2d 992 (3d Cir.), *cert. denied*, 459 U.S. 1022 (1982).

48. *See, e.g.*, California Aviation, Inc. v. City of Santa Monica, 806 F.2d 905, 909 n.5 (9th Cir. 1986) ("Statutes enacted after allegedly anticompetitive conduct [may] express pre-existing state policies to displace competition."); Mercy-Peninsula Ambulance, Inc. v. County of San Mateo, 791 F.2d 755, 757-58 (9th Cir. 1986) (giving effect to statutory intent to immunize conduct occurring before statute's enactment).

49. *Cf.* Tambone v. Memorial Hosp. for McHenry County, 635 F. Supp. 508, 513-14 (N.D. Ill. 1986) (subsequent enactment of supervisory mechanism for peer review system could not be said to endorse policies implicit in statutes in effect at time of challenged conduct), *aff'd*, 825 F.2d 1132 (7th Cir. 1987).

50. *See* Lease Lights, Inc. v. Public Serv. Co., 849 F.2d 1330 (10th Cir. 1988), *cert. denied*, 488 U.S. 1019 (1989):

> The constitutional invalidity of the attempted state regulation is not an appropriate basis for disregarding state action immunity. . . . Rather, there should be a defense for those reasonably relying on the appearance of legality when a state agency's exercise of power is unauthorized.

Id. at 1334 (citations omitted); *see also* Davis v. Southern Bell Tel. & Tel. Co., 755 F. Supp. 1532, 1542 (S.D. Fla. 1991) (interpreting *Lease Lights* to mean that immunity should be available whenever the defendant reasonably relies upon what ultimately proves to be an erroneous regulatory decision by the state entity).

c. The Active Supervision Requirement

Midcal's active supervision requirement is intended to ensure that state action immunity "will shelter only the particular anticompetitive acts of private parties that, in the judgment of the State, actually further state regulatory policies."[51] In *324 Liquor Corp. v. Duffy*,[52] the Supreme Court considered the implementation of a New York statute that promoted industry-wide resale price maintenance.[53] The statute required liquor retailers to sell liquor at a minimum of "price" plus a twelve percent markup and thereby forbade all price competition. "Price" was defined as the "posted" price established by liquor wholesalers in effect at the time of sale.[54] The Court held that state action did not immunize the liquor wholesalers.[55] A clearly articulated and affirmatively expressed state policy satisfied the *Midcal* test's first requirement, but there was no active state supervision of the prices set by the wholesalers.[56] The state simply authorized the actions of the wholesalers without either establishing the prices or reviewing their reasonableness, and thereby failed to satisfy *Midcal*'s second requirement.[57] Since the issuance of *Midcal* and *324 Liquor*, inquiries concerning state supervision require consideration of "whether private parties or public authorities made the operative decisions regarding the challenged anticompetitive conduct."[58]

In *Patrick v. Burget*,[59] a unanimous Supreme Court ruled that state action immunity did not apply to the conduct of Oregon physicians in participating on hospital peer review committees. In *Patrick*, a doctor alleged that a group of competing physicians had violated the Sherman Act by manipulating the peer review process to deny him privileges in the only hospital in Astoria, Oregon. The Ninth Circuit reversed a judgment against the defendants, ruling that their conduct was immune on state action grounds.[60] Among other points, the court of appeals concluded that the state actively supervised the operation of the peer review mechanism because a state agency had authority to review privilege termination decisions; peer review bodies were required to report all termination decisions to the state's medical examining board; and state courts ultimately exercised judicial review

---

51. Patrick v. Burget, 486 U.S. 94, 100-01 (1988).
52. 479 U.S. 335 (1987).
53. *Id.* at 341-43.
54. *Id.* at 339.
55. The Court also ruled that the twenty-first amendment did not protect the operation of the regulatory scheme from antitrust attack. *Id.* at 346-52.
56. *Id.* at 344-45; *see also* Kansas ex rel. Stephan v. Lamb, 1987-1 Trade Cas. (CCH) ¶ 67,521, at 60,191-92 (D. Kan. 1987) (applying *324 Liquor* to deny immunity to state minimum alcohol price law due to lack of active state supervision); *cf.* Miller v. Hedlund, 813 F.2d 1344, 1351-52 (9th Cir. 1986) (Oregon Liquor Control Commission and liquor wholesalers lacked immunity because state regulations concerning liquor prices did not provide adequate supervision), *cert. denied*, 484 U.S. 1061 (1988); Anheuser-Busch, Inc. v. Goodman, 745 F. Supp. 1048, 1052-54 (M.D. Pa. 1990) (no active supervision where state liquor control board lacked adequate control over implementation of price restraints).
57. 479 U.S. at 344-45. The Court noted, however, that a simple "minimum markup" statute might be entitled to immunity. *Id.* at 344 n.6. The Court also said a state's comprehensive regulation of liquor distribution within its boundaries would also be entitled to immunity. *Id.*
58. Municipal Utils. Bd. v. Alabama Power Co., 934 F.2d 1493, 1503 (11th Cir. 1991).
59. 486 U.S. 94 (1988).
60. Patrick v. Burget, 800 F.2d 1498 (9th Cir.), *rev'd*, 486 U.S. 94 (1988).

over termination matters.[61]

The Supreme Court found these safeguards inadequate. The Oregon peer review oversight process failed to provide the requisite active supervision because the state's role was limited essentially to regulating peer review procedures.   The Court observed that no state agency had "power to review private peer-review decisions and overturn a decision that fails to accord with state policy."[62]   To meet the active supervision test, state officials must "have and exercise power to review particular anticompetitive acts of private parties and disapprove those that fail to accord with state policy."[63]   The Court did not decide "whether judicial review of private conduct ever can constitute active supervision,"[64] but it concluded that the review available in Oregon's state courts failed to confer *Parker* immunity:

> [An Oregon] state court would not review the merits of a privilege termination decision to determine whether it accorded with state regulatory policy. Such constricted review does not convert the action of a private party in terminating a physician's privileges into the action of the State for purposes of the state action doctrine.[65]

At a minimum, *Patrick* indicated that extremely deferential forms of judicial review would not suffice to provide the requisite active supervision.[66]

Patrick's most specific and immediate impact has been to raise questions about the adequacy of many peer review mechanisms.[67]   More generally, *Patrick* has focused attention upon the level of state oversight that will satisfy the requirement that state instrumentalities in fact exercise their supervisory powers over private decisionmakers.   In *New England Motor Rate Bureau v. FTC*,[68] the First Circuit

---

61.   800 F.2d at 1506.
62.   486 U.S. at 102.
63.   *Id.* at 101.
64.   *Id.* at 104.
65.   *Id.* at 105.
66.   *Compare* Pinhas v. Summit Health, Ltd., 894 F.2d 1024, 1030 (9th Cir. 1989) (deferential state court review of peer review decisions insufficient to constitute active supervision), *aff'd on other grounds*, 111 S. Ct. 1842 (1991) *with* Bolt v. Halifax Hosp. Medical Center, 851 F.2d 1273, 1282-84 (11th Cir. 1988) (substantive state judicial review of private conduct satisfies active supervision requirement), *vacated en banc per curiam*, 874 F.2d 755 (11th Cir. 1989), *cert. denied*, 110 S. Ct. 1960 (1990) *and* Lender's Serv. v. Dayton Bar Ass'n, 758 F. Supp. 429, 438-39 (S.D. Ohio 1991) (extensive role of Ohio courts in reviewing disciplinary determinations concerning unauthorized practice of law, coupled with procedural safeguards provided to affected parties in initial administrative proceedings, deemed to constitute active supervision).
67.   *See, e.g.*, Miller v. Indiana Hosp., 930 F.2d 334, 337-39 (3d Cir. 1991) (administrative procedures for evaluating peer review process held insufficient to constitute active supervision); *Pinhas*, 894 F.2d at 1029-30 (no active supervision where state oversight body lacks authority to review privilege decisions; deferential state appellate review deemed inadequate supervision); Shahawy v. Harrison, 875 F.2d 1529, 1535 (11th Cir. 1989) (supervision of medical peer review process deemed inadequate despite existence of elaborate state monitoring mechanism; oversight of specific peer review decisions was delegated to state courts, which "merely review the board's decisions for procedural error and insufficient evidence"); Jiricko v. Coffeyville Mem. Hosp. Medical Center, 700 F. Supp. 1559, 1563 (D. Kan. 1988) (mere potential for judicial review does not constitute active state supervision of peer review process where state courts never had considered whether they could review merits of privilege termination decisions); Shah v. Memorial Hosp., 1988-2 Trade Cas. (CCH) ¶ 68,199, at 59,325-26 (W.D. Va. 1988) (no active supervision where judicial review limited to procedural fairness rather than merits of peer review process).
68.   908 F.2d 1064 (1st Cir. 1990).

examined the preparation and filing by private rate bureaus of collective tariffs for motor carriers in Massachusetts and other New England states. The FTC had concluded that state action immunity did not apply to these rate-setting activities in Massachusetts because the Massachusetts Department of Public Utilities (MDPU) had not sufficiently exercised its nominal power to conduct a substantive review of the merits of suggested rates. The FTC's decision emphasized that the MDPU never had disapproved a rate because of the suggested price, and never had obtained financial data to justify the suggested tariffs nor evaluated the relationship of the suggested tariffs to the carriers' costs. The FTC concluded that in practice, the MDPU reviewed collectively established tariffs only to ensure that they complied with technical filing requirements.

The First Circuit reversed the FTC's finding that the MDPU's oversight of the carriers' rate-setting activities was deficient. The court concluded that the Commission incorrectly had chosen to reassess policy decisions properly reserved for the state regulators:

> The FTC's position, at bottom, seems to be that the "active supervision" prong necessitates an inquiry by the FTC into whether a particular state's regulatory operation demonstrates satisfactory zeal and aggressiveness. The FTC would, in effect, try the state regulator. We think this goes too far. . . . It is not the province of the federal courts nor of federal regulatory agencies to sit in judgment upon the degree of *strictness* or *effectiveness* with which a state carries out its own statutes. It is sufficient that a meaningful scheme of regulation is in existence and that there are sufficient indications that active regulation under this scheme is taking place.[69]

In the First Circuit's view, the parties' stipulations established that the MDPU's failure to reject a rate indicated a determination that the rate had been found to meet the statutory "just and reasonable" criterion and that the MDPU would reject an unreasonable rate. *Patrick's* requirement that the state exercise its review power was satisfied because the state's oversight apparatus (1) was staffed, funded, and operational; (2) gave state overseers adequate power to monitor compliance with state regulatory policies; (3) was enforceable in the state's courts; and (4) showed a "basic level of activity" aimed at ensuring that private entities "carry out the state's policy and not simply their own policy."[70]

The Supreme Court has granted certiorari in *Ticor Title Insurance Co. v. FTC*,[71]

---

69. *Id.* at 1075-76 (emphasis in original); *see* Health Care Equalization Comm. v. Iowa Medical Soc'y, 851 F.2d 1020, 1027 (8th Cir. 1988) (active supervision of conduct of nonprofit health care service corporation satisfied by oversight process through which state's insurance commissioner reviews and approves all of the corporation's contracts and evaluates rates charged to subscribers); Lease Lights, Inc. v. Public Serv. Co., 849 F.2d 1330, 1334-35 (10th Cir. 1988) (active supervision of electric utility exists where state corporation commission sets guidelines for utility services and closely regulates rates), *cert. denied*, 488 U.S. 1019 (1989); Davis v. Southern Bell Tel. & Tel. Co., 755 F. Supp. 1532, 1540-41 (S.D. Fla. 1991) (active supervision requirement satisfied by existence and expansive use of procedures for state public service commission to oversee defendant telephone company's rates and service); Metro Mobile CTS, Inc. v. New Vector Communs., 661 F. Supp. 1504, 1519-20 (D. Ariz. 1987) (active supervision demonstrated by state corporation commission's close and continuing review of defendant's tariffs), *aff'd on other grounds*, 892 F.2d 62 (9th Cir. 1989).

70. 908 F.2d at 1071.

71. 922 F.2d 1122 (3d Cir. 1991), *cert. granted*, 60 U.S.L.W. 3257 (U.S. Oct. 7, 1991) (No. 91-72).

in which the Third Circuit reviewed a FTC ruling that the absence of effective state supervision denied state action immunity to the defendants. In *Ticor* the FTC found that public regulators in four states had failed to conduct any meaningful review of collectively established rates. State officials had allowed rates to go into effect without inquiring into insurer profitability, had not scrutinized insurer expenses, and had overlooked insurer failures to comply with requests for supporting data. In reversing the FTC's decision, the Third Circuit largely embraced the First Circuit's analytical approach in *New England Motor Rate Bureau*. The court said that the availability of immunity did not depend upon "the quality of state supervision,"[72] noting that the FTC's interpretation of the state action doctrine in effect required reviewing tribunals to try the state regulators.[73] The Third Circuit endorsed the *New England Motor Rate Bureau* criteria for evaluating the adequacy of state supervision and found that state insurance regulators had satisfied them. The court emphasized that the FTC could not use the active supervision requirement as a tool for repudiating disfavored policy judgments: "State action immunity is available not only when a state acts wisely; instead, the wisdom of a state's policy is immaterial."[74]

d. LIMITATIONS UPON THE AVAILABILITY OF IMMUNITY

In *Parker*, the Supreme Court intimated that the availability of state action immunity might depend upon the role the state plays in the market process and the manner in which private economic actors seek to elicit the state's intervention. At one point, the *Parker* Court observed that "we have no question of the state or its municipality becoming a participant in a private agreement or combination by others for restraint of trade."[75] In a separate passage, the Court observed that "[t]he state in adopting and enforcing the prorate program made no contract or agreement and entered into no conspiracy in restraint of trade or to establish monopoly but, as sovereign, imposed the restraint as an act of government which the Sherman Act did not undertake to prohibit."[76] Some lower courts interpreted these statements to create a "conspiracy exception" to state action immunity when public officials form

---

72.   922 F.2d at 1140.
73.   *Id.* at 1138.
74.   *Id.* at 1138-39; *see also* Hoover v. Ronwin, 466 U.S. 558, 574 (1984) ("The Court did not suggest in *Parker*, nor has it suggested since, that a state action is exempt from antitrust liability only if the sovereign acted wisely after full disclosure from its subordinate officers."); Fuchs v. Rural Elec. Convenience Coop., 858 F.2d 1210, 1214 (7th Cir. 1988) ("state action immunity is not dependent on the wisdom or extent of state regulation, only on whether the state is actually acting to displace free competition"), *cert. denied*, 490 U.S. 1020 (1989); Coastal Neuro-Psychiatric Assocs. v. Onslow Mem. Hosp., 795 F.2d 340, 342 (4th Cir. 1986) (publicly imposed restrictions upon competition "may or may not be a salutary result," but state action doctrine "restricts the power of federal courts to overturn that choice under the competitive principles embodied in the Sherman Act"); *cf.* Metro Mobile CTS, Inc. v. New Vector Communs., 661 F. Supp. 1504, 1520 (D. Ariz. 1987) (rejecting view that "the court should examine the substance" of state commission's regulation of rates), *aff'd on other grounds*, 892 F.2d 62 (9th Cir. 1989).
75.   317 U.S. at 351-52 (citation omitted).
76.   *Id.* at 352.

corrupt agreements with private parties.[77] In *City of Columbia v. Omni Outdoor Advertising, Inc.*,[78] the Supreme Court addressed the significance of these apparent qualifications to state action immunity. In *Omni*, a billboard company alleged that a rival billboard firm and the City of Columbia, South Carolina, had unlawfully conspired to hinder the plaintiff's ability to enter and compete in the local market for outdoor advertising. The plaintiff claimed that the defendant and various city officials collaborated to devise and enact a zoning ordinance to restrict the size, location, and spacing of billboards in Columbia. The ordinance impeded the plaintiff's efforts to construct new billboards and favored the defendant, which had a substantial inventory of existing structures. The plaintiff contended, and the Fourth Circuit agreed, that the existence of an anticompetitive conspiracy between the defendant and the city officials precluded the application of state action immunity.[79]

The Supreme Court reversed the Fourth Circuit and concluded that the defendant and the city were entitled to state action immunity for activities relating to the enactment of the challenged land use controls. After considering arguments that *Parker* withheld immunity for anticompetitive conspiracies between private actors and public officials, the Court ruled that "[t]here is no such conspiracy exception" to the state action doctrine.[80] The Court rejected as unadministrable a rule that would proscribe governmental actions that are "'not in the public interest'":[81]

> A conspiracy exception narrowed along such vague lines is . . . impractical. Few governmental actions are immune from the charge that they are "not in the public interest" or in some sense "corrupt." The California marketing scheme at issue in *Parker* itself, for example, can readily be viewed as the result of a "conspiracy" to put the "private" interest of the State's raisin growers above the "public" interest of the State's consumers. The fact is that virtually all regulation benefits some segments of the society and harms others; and that it is not universally considered contrary to the public good if the net economic loss to the losers exceeds the net economic gain to the winners.[82]

The Court feared that adopting a "public interest" standard would engage judges in "the sort of deconstruction of the governmental process and probing of the official

---

77.   *See, e.g.*, Westborough Mall, Inc. v. City of Cape Girardeau, 693 F.2d 733, 746 (8th Cir. 1982) (circumstantial evidence of illegal fraudulent acts deprived defendants of state action immunity), *cert. denied*, 461 U.S. 945 (1983); Fisichelli v. Town of Methuen, 653 F. Supp. 1494, 1499-1502 (D. Mass. 1987) (state action immunity lacking when public official conspired to prevent competition with his own pharmacy); *cf.* DiVerniero v. Murphy, 635 F. Supp. 1531, 1537 (D. Conn. 1986) ("To the extent that the municipal defendants may have conspired to inhibit lawful business activities by harassing legitimate vendors . . . they are subject to federal anti-trust laws. Nothing in the legislative grants of authority to the municipal defendants contemplates this kind of anti-competitive activity.").

78.   111 S. Ct. 1344 (1991).

79.   Omni Outdoor Advertising, Inc. v. City of Columbia, 891 F.2d 1127, 1133-34 (4th Cir. 1989), *rev'd*, 111 S. Ct. 1344 (1991).

80.   111 S. Ct. at 1351.

81.   *Id.* at 1352.

82.   *Id.*

'intent' that we have consistently sought to avoid."[83]

The Court also rejected, in dicta, the argument that state action immunity should be denied to governmental action procured by means of bribery or other unlawful behavior. The Court gave essentially two reasons for this position. First, the existence of unlawful, corrupt conduct does not establish that governmental action ultimately taken is not in the public interest.[84] Second, the Sherman Act was not designed to ensure that public officials abide by "principles of good government."[85] The Court stated that "Congress has passed other laws aimed at combatting corruption in state and local governments."[86] Thus, the Court disclaimed "any interpretation of the Sherman Act that would allow plaintiffs to look behind the actions of state sovereigns to base their claims on 'perceived conspiracies to restrain trade.'"[87]

Although it repudiated a "conspiracy exception" to the state action doctrine, the *Omni* Court suggested that immunity might not extend to public intervention when the state acts not as a regulator but instead behaves as a commercial entity. In restating the scope of *Parker*'s protection, the Court observed: "We reiterate that, with the possible market participant exception, *any* action that qualifies as state

---

83.   *Id.* (footnote omitted). In an earlier passage, the *Omni* Court observed that "*Parker* was not written in ignorance of the reality that determination of 'the public interest' in the manifold areas of government regulation entails not merely economic and mathematical analysis but value judgment, and it was not meant to shift that judgment from elected officials to judges and juries." *Id.*

84.   *Id.* at 1353. The Court explained:
        A mayor is guilty of accepting a bribe even if he would and should have taken, in the public interest, the same action for which the bribe was paid. . . . When, moreover, the regulatory body is not a single individual but a state legislature or city council, there is even less reason to believe that violation of the law (by bribing a minority of the decisionmakers) establishes that the regulation has no valid public purpose.
        Id.

85.   *Id*; *see* Buckley Constr., Inc. v. Shawnee Civic & Cultural Dev. Auth., 933 F.2d 853, 856 (10th Cir. 1991) ("Once a municipality establishes that it is entitled to state action immunity, the subjective motivation of the actors involved in the decisionmaking process should not come into play."); Traweek v. City & County of San Francisco, 920 F.2d 589, 592 (9th Cir. 1989) (allegedly malicious motivation does not deny immunity to acts by public officials when such acts otherwise are authorized by state statute); Consolidated Television Cable Serv. v. City of Frankfort, 857 F.2d 354, 362 (6th Cir. 1988) ("the sovereignty of state action must be respected without reference to the subjective motivations of persons implementing the state's policy"), *cert. denied*, 489 U.S. 1082 (1989); Hancock Indus. v. Schaeffer, 811 F.2d 225, 234 (3d Cir. 1987) ("subjective motivation of public decisionmakers is irrelevant to state antitrust immunity analysis"); *cf.* Sandcrest Outpatient Servs. v. Cumberland County Hosp. Sys., 853 F.2d 1139, 1146 (4th Cir. 1988) (in immunizing municipalities from damage suits, Local Government Antitrust Act "makes no provision for consideration of a defendant's motives.").

86.   111 S. Ct. at 1353.

87.   *Id.* (citation omitted); *see* Boone v. Redevelopment Agency, 841 F.2d 886, 890 (9th Cir.) (redevelopment agency with land use regulatory powers does not lose *Parker* immunity because it may have used its authority corruptly), *cert. denied*, 488 U.S. 965 (1988); Llewellyn v. Crothers, 765 F.2d 769, 774 (9th Cir. 1985) (directors of state agency with authority to set fee guidelines and maximum fee schedules do not lose *Parker* immunity if they act in bad faith); Northeast Jet Center, Ltd. v. Lehigh-Northampton Airport Auth., 767 F. Supp. 672, 680 (E.D. Pa. 1991) (allegation that municipal airport authority conspired with third parties to eliminate competition does not destroy state action immunity); Thillens, Inc. v. Fryzel, 712 F. Supp. 1319, 1327 (N.D. Ill. 1989) (*Parker* immunity applies even if legislature that passed statute controlling currency exchange had been corrupted).

action is 'ipso facto . . . exempt from the operation of the antitrust laws.' "[88] With little elaboration, the Court interpreted *Parker* to mean that "immunity does not necessarily obtain where the State acts not in a regulatory capacity but as a commercial participant in a given market."[89] The significance of the Court's brief mention of a possible "commercial participant" exception is uncertain.[90] The few previous cases that had considered this issue tended to reject distinctive treatment for "commercial" government intervention.[91]

e. RESTRAINTS IMPOSED OR AUTHORIZED BY POLITICAL SUBDIVISIONS AND OTHER SUBORDINATE GOVERNMENT ENTITIES

The predicate for state action immunity is a decision by the state to authorize the adoption of competition-suppressing policies. To apply this fundamental requirement, one must identify the instrumentalities whose decisions can be taken to provide the requisite authority to restrict competition. As indicated above, it is well-established that the state legislature and the state's highest court (when it performs legislative functions) have independent authority to permit departures from competition.

The status of decisions by state executive departments, agencies, or special authorities is less certain.[92] In *Southern Motor Carriers*,[93] the Supreme Court rejected the defendants' argument that a state public utility commission's approval of collective ratemaking constituted state authorization of departures from competition:

> The Public Service Commissions . . . permit collective ratemaking. Acting alone, however, these agencies could not immunize private anticompetitive conduct. . . . *Parker* immunity is available only when the challenged activity is undertaken pursuant to a clearly articulated policy of the State itself, such as a policy approved by a state legislature . . . or a State Supreme Court.[94]

The Court went on to find that the requisite authorization existed by virtue of a state

---

88. 111 S. Ct. at 1353 (citation omitted; emphasis in original).

89. *Id.* at 1351.

90. *Cf.* Paragould Cablevision, Inc. v. City of Paragould, 930 F.2d 1310, 1312-13 (8th Cir. 1991) (noting that *Omni*'s "market participant exception is merely a suggestion and is not a rule of law"), *cert. denied*, 112 S. Ct. 430 (1991).

91. *See* Limeco, Inc. v. Division of Lime of Miss. Dep't of Agric. & Commerce, 778 F.2d 1086, 1087 (5th Cir. 1985) (holding that there is no "commercial exception" to *Parker* doctrine; concluding that state-owned and -operated lime plants that sell limestone at actual cost are immune from antitrust challenge by private limestone supplier); *cf.* Wall v. City of Athens, 663 F. Supp. 747, 762 (M.D. Ga. 1987) (suggesting that Garcia v. San Antonio Metro Transit Auth., 469 U.S. 528 (1985), "effectively did away with the distinctions between 'governmental' and 'traditional' functions of a municipality as opposed to 'proprietary' or 'non-governmental' functions").

92. The analytical approach of Hoover v. Ronwin, 466 U.S. 558 (1984), suggests that decisions by the governor of a state will be deemed to be actions of the state. However, the *Hoover* Court did not address the question whether an executive official of a state "stands in the same position as the state legislature and [state] supreme court for the purposes of the state-action doctrine." 466 U.S. at 568 n.17.

93. Southern Motor Carriers Rate Conference, Inc. v. United States, 471 U.S. 48, 62-63 (1985) (citations omitted).

94. *Id.*

statute that permitted the state regulatory body to set just and reasonable rates. The implication of *Southern Motor Carriers* is that state public utility commissions, and perhaps other state agencies, require independent legislative authority to restrict competition.

Subsequent lower court decisions have reached varied results in considering whether state executive departments or agencies should be accorded a status similar to a state legislature or a state supreme court for state action purposes. A small number of decisions have concluded that state agencies are equivalent to the sovereign and require no additional authorization for their decisions to constitute state action. The most significant of these rulings is *Charley's Taxi Radio Dispatch Corp. v. SIDA of Hawaii, Inc.*,[95] in which the Ninth Circuit held that the decisions of the Hawaii Department of Transportation and its director were "entitled to *Parker* immunity for actions taken pursuant to their constitutional or statutory authority, regardless of whether these particular actions or their anticompetitive effects were contemplated by the legislature."[96] A number of contrary decisions have declined to equate certain state agencies and other public entities with the state, chiefly on the ground that the public instrumentality is not controlled by, or acts independently from, the state.[97]

---

95.   810 F.2d 869 (9th Cir. 1987).

96.   *Id.* at 876. An earlier Ninth Circuit decision, issued before *Southern Motor Carriers*, had reached essentially the same conclusion. *See* Deak-Perera Hawaii, Inc. v. Department of Transp., 745 F.2d 1281, 1282 (9th Cir. 1984), *cert. denied*, 470 U.S. 1053 (1985); *see also* Board of Governors of Univ. of N.C. v. Helpingstine, 714 F. Supp. 167, 176 (M.D.N.C. 1989) (treating state university as sovereign for state action purposes; noting that university was created in the North Carolina constitution to carry out "state purposes").

97.   *See, e.g.*, Washington State Elec. Contractors Ass'n v. Forrest, 930 F.2d 736, 737 (9th Cir.) (concluding that apprenticeship council that set and enforced minimum wage rates for apprenticeships is not a "state agency" because "[t]he council has both public and private members, and the private members have their own agenda which may or may not be responsive to state labor policy"), *cert. denied*, 112 S. Ct. 439 (1991); Benton, Benton & Benton v. Louisiana Pub. Facilities Auth., 897 F.2d 198, 203 (5th Cir. 1990) (special purpose public authority is a public corporation eligible for state action immunity, but the public authority is not the state itself), *cert. denied*, 111 S. Ct. 1619 (1991); Bolt v. Halifax Hosp. Medical Center, 891 F.2d 810, 824 (11th Cir.) (concluding that hospital district is not the state for *Parker* purposes; district had taxation authority, but neither the state's constitution nor its statutes provided for direct oversight of its conduct by the governor, legislature, or state supreme court), *cert. denied*, 110 S. Ct. 1960 (1990); Hass v. Oregon State Bar, 883 F.2d 1453, 1456 (9th Cir. 1989) (state bar was not the state, but instead was "merely an instrumentality of the state judiciary"), *cert. denied*, 110 S. Ct. 1812 (1990); FTC v. Monahan, 832 F.2d 688, 689 (1st Cir. 1987) (Massachusetts Board of Registration in Pharmacy deemed not to be the sovereign, but a "subordinate governmental unit"), *cert. denied*, 485 U.S. 987 (1988); Cine 42nd Street Theater Corp. v. Nederlander Org., 790 F.2d 1032, 1044 (2d Cir. 1986) (urban development corporation is not the state for *Parker* purposes; entity could not demonstrate that its actions were directed by the state because the entity's enabling legislation had provided it with substantial independence); Lender's Serv. v. Dayton Bar Ass'n, 758 F. Supp. 429, 437-38 (S.D. Ohio 1991) (because it enjoys discretion to decide whether to initiate complaints alleging unauthorized practice of law, state bar association committee deemed not to be the state); Anheuser-Busch, Inc. v. Goodman, 745 F. Supp. 1048, 1051 (M.D. Pa. 1990) (state liquor control board deemed to be "an agency, and not a legislature or sovereign body"); Midwest Constr. Co. v. Illinois Dep't of Labor, 684 F. Supp. 991, 994 (N.D. Ill. 1988) (Illinois Department of Labor and Capital Development Board deemed not to be the state because both enjoyed a "significant amount of independence in carrying out their governmental role"); Zapata Gulf Marine Corp. v. Puerto Rico Maritime Shipping Auth., 682 F. Supp. 1345,

The Supreme Court has made clear that political subdivisions such as counties, municipalities, and townships are not entitled to the same immunity from the antitrust laws as a state itself. In *City of Lafayette v. Louisiana Power & Light Co.*,[98] Justice Brennan, for a four-justice plurality, concluded that "[c]ities are not themselves sovereign."[99] *Lafayette* held that the *Parker* doctrine exempts only anticompetitive conduct engaged in as an act of government by the state as sovereign, or, by its subdivisions, pursuant to state policy to displace competition with regulation or monopoly public service.[100] The Court explained that a state's political subdivisions are entitled to immunity only when "the State authorized or directed a given municipality to act as it did."[101] The Court noted that "when the State itself has not directed or authorized an anticompetitive practice, the State's subdivisions in exercising their delegated power must obey the antitrust laws."[102]

The *Lafayette* plurality emphasized that, to provide immunity, the state policy must be one "clearly articulated and affirmatively expressed,"[103] but it stopped short of requiring "that a political subdivision necessarily must be able to point to a specific, detailed legislative authorization before it properly may assert a *Parker* defense to an antitrust suit."[104] The Court observed that "an adequate state mandate for anticompetitive activities of cities and other subordinate governmental units exists when it is found 'from the authority given a governmental entity to operate in a particular area, that the legislature contemplated the kind of action complained of.' "[105]

The Court further defined the exemption available to a state's political subdivisions in *Community Communications Co. v. City of Boulder*.[106] Although Colorado's home rule statute granted extensive powers to municipalities and may have authorized the City of Boulder to regulate cable television, the statute did not sufficiently articulate a state policy to confer immunity from the antitrust laws. The

---

1347-48 (E.D. La. 1988) (despite status as an agency of the Commonwealth of Puerto Rico, Puerto Rico Maritime Shipping Authority deemed not to be the state but only a subdivision); Massachusetts Bd. of Registration in Optometry, 110 F.T.C. 549, 612-13 (1988) (state board of registration of optometry deemed not to be the state; rejecting view that board's state-wide authority and rule-making powers for all state optometrists made it sovereign); *cf.* Fuchs v. Rural Elec. Convenience Coop., 858 F.2d 1210, 1217-18 (7th Cir. 1988) (unregulated, nonprofit rural electric cooperative deemed to be neither municipality nor state agency; some degree of state supervision deemed necessary to confer *Parker* immunity), *cert. denied*, 490 U.S. 1020 (1989).

98.   435 U.S. 389 (1978).
99.   *Id.* at 412.
100.   *Id.* at 413.
101.   *Id.* at 414.
102.   *Id.* at 416; *see also* Commuter Transp. Sys. v. Hillsborough County Aviation Auth., 801 F.2d 1286, 1291 (11th Cir. 1986) (to defeat *Parker* defense, plaintiff "must show a conspiracy not authorized by state law and thus beyond protection of state action immunity"); Central Telecommuns. v. City of Jefferson City, 589 F. Supp. 85, 88-89 (W.D. Mo. 1984) (where actions exceed grant of authority, no immunity exists).
103.   435 U.S. at 410.
104.   *Id.* at 415. *But cf.* Wall v. City of Athens, 663 F. Supp. 747, 763 (M.D. Ga. 1987) (state statute enacted to provide municipalities with immunity did not provide actual immunity since mere assertion that municipality's conduct is lawful does not make it so; immunity limited to actions "contemplated by the Georgia legislature").
105.   435 U.S. at 415 (quoting from opinion below, 532 F.2d 431, 434 (5th Cir. 1976)) (footnote omitted).
106.   455 U.S. 40 (1982).

Court characterized the statute as an expression of "mere *neutrality*" and held that when a state "allows its municipalities to do as they please [it] can hardly be said to have 'contemplated' the specific anticompetitive actions for which municipal liability is sought."[107]   The Court held that the general authority provided under Colorado's home rule statute did not immunize the City of Boulder from antitrust attack.

(1) Clear Articulation

Lafayette and *Boulder* demonstrated that counties, municipalities, and townships "are not entitled to all of the federalistic deference that the state would receive."[108] However, the two decisions created significant uncertainties about the application of the state action doctrine to these entities, and subsequent cases interpreting the exemption were inconsistent. Conflicting views were most apparent in judicial efforts to define how the state must delegate authority for political subdivisions to adopt competition-suppressing policies. Courts disagreed over whether the challenged activity need be compelled by state law[109] or merely be authorized.[110]

Cases also featured diverse standards concerning how specifically the state must authorize the challenged activity. Some courts required the state to indicate clearly that it contemplated the anticompetitive effects flowing from the subdivision's acts.[111]   Others immunized conduct whose anticompetitive impact was a "reasonable or foreseeable consequence of engaging in the authorized activity"[112]

---

107.   *Id.* at 55 (emphasis in original); *see also* Tri-State Executive Air, Inc. v. Tri-State Airport Auth., 1986-2 Trade Cas. (CCH) ¶ 67,257, at 61,327 (S.D. W. Va. 1985) (state's position was "mere neutrality"; government and airport authority's decision to reserve to the airport authority the exclusive right to sell aviation fuel was not antitrust-immune); *cf.* Central Iowa Refuse Sys. v. Des Moines Metro. Solid Waste Agency, 715 F.2d 419, 427 (8th Cir. 1983) ("although the state has left Iowa municipalities with a range of options . . . by no means has the state adopted an approach of indifference or 'mere neutrality' "), *cert. denied*, 471 U.S. 1003 (1985); Seay Bros. v. City of Albuquerque, 601 F. Supp. 1518, 1521-22 (D.N.M. 1985) (where intent could be inferred, authority was not "a neutral grant of power").

108.   Kurek v. Pleasure Driveway & Park Dist., 557 F.2d 580, 589 (7th Cir. 1977), *vacated*, 435 U.S. 992 (1978).

109.   *See, e.g.*, Ronwin v. State Bar of Ariz., 686 F.2d 692, 696 (9th Cir. 1981), *rev'd on other grounds sub nom.* Hoover v. Ronwin, 466 U.S. 558 (1984); *Kurek*, 557 F.2d at 590; Duke & Co. v. Foerster, 521 F.2d 1277, 1281 (3d Cir. 1975); Schiessle v. Stephens, 525 F. Supp. 763, 776 (N.D. Ill. 1982); United States v. Texas State Bd. of Pub. Accountancy, 464 F. Supp. 400, 402-03 (W.D. Tex. 1978), *modified*, 592 F.2d 919 (5th Cir.), *cert. denied*, 444 U.S. 925 (1979); *see also* Corey v. Look, 641 F.2d 32, 37 (1st Cir. 1981) (challenged activity must be "necessary to the successful operation of the legislative scheme that the state as sovereign has established").

110.   *See, e.g.*, Town of Hallie v. City of Eau Claire, 700 F.2d 376, 381 (7th Cir. 1983), *aff'd*, 471 U.S. 34 (1985); *Central Iowa Refuse Sys.*, 715 F.2d at 425-28; Community Builders v. City of Phoenix, 652 F.2d 823, 829-30 (9th Cir. 1981).

111.   *See, e.g.*, Westborough Mall, Inc. v. City of Cape Girardeau, 693 F.2d 733, 746 (8th Cir. 1982) (requiring state authorization for specific conduct in question), *cert. denied*, 461 U.S. 945 (1983); *Corey*, 641 F.2d at 37 (same); *Kurek*, 557 F.2d at 590 (same).

112.   *Hallie*, 700 F.2d at 381; *see also* Gold Cross Ambulance & Transfer v. City of Kansas City, 705 F.2d 1005, 1014 (8th Cir. 1983) (state policy deemed to authorize municipality to choose single provider of ambulance services); Century Fed., Inc. v. City of Palo Alto, 579 F. Supp. 1553, 1557-61 (N.D. Cal. 1984) (where state granted locality exclusive cable television franchising authority, specific reference to displacement of competition not necessary for immunity).

or granted exemptions if traditional municipal or governmental, as opposed to commercial, activities were involved.[113]

The Supreme Court resolved these conflicts in *Town of Hallie v. City of Eau Claire*.[114] In *Hallie*, the Court "fully considered . . . how clearly a state policy must be articulated for a municipality to be able to establish that its anticompetitive activity constitutes state action."[115] Unincorporated townships located next to the City of Eau Claire alleged that the city had violated the Sherman Act by using "its monopoly over sewage treatment to gain an unlawful monopoly over the provision of sewage collection and transportation services."[116] Although the city, which operated the only local sewage treatment facility, had refused to supply treatment services to the towns, it did supply those services to individual landowners who voted to have their properties annexed and to use the city's sewage collection and transportation services.

The Supreme Court examined the Wisconsin statutes that authorized cities to construct and operate sewage systems, to describe the districts to be served, and to refuse service to unincorporated areas. The Court unanimously rejected the plaintiff's contention that without express mention of anticompetitive conduct there was no evidence of a state policy to displace competition in the provision of sewage services. Instead, the challenged conduct was deemed "a foreseeable result of empowering the City to refuse to serve unannexed areas."[117] The Court said "it is clear that anticompetitive effects logically would result from this broad authority to regulate."[118] As one illustration of this approach, lower courts have applied

---

113. See City of Lafayette v. Louisiana Power & Light Co., 435 U.S. 389, 423-24 (1978) (Burger, C.J., concurring); see also *Hallie*, 700 F.2d at 384 (sewage and sanitation are traditional municipal activities); Pueblo Aircraft Serv. v. City of Pueblo, 679 F.2d 805, 810-11 (10th Cir. 1982), cert. denied, 459 U.S. 1126 (1983) (municipal airport deemed government function); Hybud Equip. Corp. v. City of Akron, 654 F.2d 1187, 1194 (6th Cir. 1981) (garbage collection and operation of incineration plants are traditional activities of local government), vacated mem., 455 U.S. 931 (1982), on remand, 1983-1 Trade Cas. (CCH) ¶ 65,356 (N.D. Ohio 1983), cert. denied, 471 U.S. 1004 (1985); Shrader v. Horton, 471 F. Supp. 1236, 1242 (W.D. Va. 1979) (water service deemed governmental undertaking), aff'd, 626 F.2d 1163 (4th Cir. 1980). But cf. Westborough Mall, 693 F.2d at 746 ("Even if zoning in general can be characterized as 'state action,'. . . a conspiracy to thwart normal zoning procedures . . . is not in furtherance of any clearly articulated state policy.") (citations omitted).

114. 471 U.S. 34 (1985).

115. *Id.* at 40.

116. *Id.* at 37.

117. *Id.* at 42.

118. *Id.* See Paragould Cablevision, Inc. v. City of Paragould, 930 F.2d 1310, 1313-14 (8th Cir.) (city's decision to enter cable television business in competition with existing private franchisee deemed "necessary and reasonable" consequence of state authorization for city to enter cable television business), cert. denied, 112 S. Ct. 430 (1991); Jacobs, Visconsi & Jacobs Co. v. City of Lawrence, 927 F.2d 1111, 1121 (10th Cir. 1991) (statutory power to zone and rezone has foreseeable anticompetitive effects); Hass v. Oregon State Bar, 883 F.2d 1453, 1457-59 (9th Cir. 1989) (legislation that authorized state bar to force attorneys to carry malpractice insurance and establish professional liability fund contemplated requirement that lawyers be compelled to pay money into liability fund), cert. denied, 110 S. Ct. 1812 (1990); Boone v. Redevelopment Agency, 841 F.2d 886 (9th Cir.) (state legislation that authorized city to control land use to prevent "blight" contemplated city's refusal to assist in financing plaintiff's proposed parking structure), cert. denied, 488 U.S. 965 (1988); Campbell v. City of Chicago, 823 F.2d 1182, 1184-85 (7th Cir. 1987) (conduct immunized as logical result of state authorization); Sterling Beef Co. v. City of Ft. Morgan, 810 F.2d 961, 963-65 (10th Cir. 1987) (city ordinance was a foreseeable result of state

Hallie's reasonable foreseeability standard to sustain grants of exclusive franchises when the state has authorized economic regulation without addressing the issue of exclusivity.[119]

In *City of Columbia v. Omni Outdoor Advertising, Inc.*,[120] the Supreme Court applied *Hallie*'s clear articulation standard in examining a dispute over municipal regulation of billboard advertising. *Omni* reiterated *Hallie*'s view that the clear articulation of state policy under which the municipality acts need not specifically authorize the suppression of competition. "We have rejected the contention," the Court stated, "that [the clear articulation] requirement can be met only if the delegating statute explicitly permits the displacement of competition. It is enough, we have held, if suppression of competition is the 'foreseeable result' of what the statute authorizes."[121] The Court added that the challenged zoning regulation "amply met" this requirement because "[t]he very purpose of zoning regulation is to displace unfettered business freedom in a manner that regularly has the effect of preventing normal acts of competition, particularly on the part of new entrants."[122]

Omni also considered whether a public body exceeds its delegated authority, and therefore forfeits state action immunity, whenever its regulatory conduct fails to adhere to all of the substantive and procedural requirements of the authorizing statute. The Court concluded that proof of such deficiencies did not necessarily negate immunity: "[I]n order to prevent *Parker* from undermining the very interests of federalism it is designed to protect, it is necessary to adopt a concept of authority broader than what is applied to determine the legality of the municipality's action

---

authorization and therefore warranted immunity); Coastal Neuro-Psychiatric Assocs. v. Onslow Memorial Hosp., 795 F.2d 340, 341-42 (4th Cir. 1986) (state statutes authorizing municipalities to build and operate hospitals contemplated anticompetitive effects); Auton v. Dade City, 783 F.2d 1009, 1011 (11th Cir. 1986) (legislation dealing with local water systems contemplated that municipalities would engage in anticompetitive conduct).

    For cases applying *Hallie* but declining to find an exemption, see Lancaster Community Hosp. v. Antelope Valley Hosp. Dist., 940 F.2d 397, 400-04 (9th Cir. 1991) (state's mandate to hospital district to provide hospital services did not authorize acts to exclude rival hospitals; state statutes showed intent to preserve competition among health care providers); Consolidated Gas Co. v. City Gas Co., 880 F.2d 297, 302 (11th Cir. 1989) (regulatory scheme deemed not to immunize horizontal division of territories by natural gas suppliers), *reinstated on reh'g*, 912 F.2d 1262 (11th Cir. 1990) (en banc; per curiam), *vacated as moot*, 111 S. Ct. 1300 (1991); Anheuser-Busch, Inc. v. Goodman, 745 F. Supp. 1048, 1051-52 (M.D. Pa. 1990) (state legislature's grant of authority to state liquor control board did not contemplate anticompetitive limits upon pricing of beer); Laidlaw Waste Sys. v. City of Ft. Smith, 742 F. Supp. 540, 542 (W.D. Ark. 1990) (although state legislature "intended to allow municipalities to authorize waste disposal monopolies, it did not intend to allow unfair competition by municipalities"); Wall v. City of Athens, 663 F. Supp. 747, 758 (M.D. Ga. 1987) (state statute enacted to provide municipalities with immunity did not provide actual immunity; "mere fact that [a municipal charter] has been adopted into Georgia Law does not mean that the state has considered every provision therein, and considers it to express state policy").

119.   *See, e.g.*, Monarch Entertainment Bureau v. New Jersey Highway Auth., 715 F. Supp. 1290, 1300 (D.N.J) (applying *Parker* to reject essential facilities claim), *aff'd mem.*, 893 F.2d 1331 (3d Cir. 1989); Hillman Flying Serv. v. City of Roanoke, 652 F. Supp. 1142, 1145-46 (W.D. Va. 1987) (statute allowing municipal regulation of local airport deemed to authorize choice of a single fixed base operator), *aff'd mem.*, 846 F.2d 71 (4th Cir. 1988).

120.   111 S. Ct. 1344 (1991).

121.   *Id.* at 1350 (citing *Hallie*, 471 U.S. at 41-42).

122.   *Id.* at 1350.

under state law."[123]   *Omni* suggests that eligibility for state action immunity requires the existence of authority to regulate — in *Omni*, zoning power over the installation of billboards — and does not depend upon the public body's fulfillment of all procedural and substantive commands of the authorizing statute.[124]

(2) Active Supervision

Lafayette, *Boulder*, and *Midcal* also raised the question of how actively a state must supervise a city's implementation of state policy. In *Midcal*, the Court had ruled that the state's oversight was inadequate where the state had "simply authorize[d] price setting and enforce[d] the prices established by private parties."[125]   The Court explained that "[t]he national policy in favor of competition cannot be thwarted by casting such a gauzy cloak of state involvement over what is essentially a private

---

123.   *Id.* Several lower court decisions have held that courts may not consider alleged bad faith motivation by public officials in determining whether the officials acted within their authority for purposes of state action immunity. *See, e.g.,* Traweek v. City and County of San Francisco, 920 F.2d 589, 592 (9th Cir. 1990) (judicial evaluation of "subjective motivation" inappropriate); Llewelyn v. Crothers, 765 F.2d 769, 774 (9th Cir. 1985) (*Parker* immunity "does not depend on the subjective motivations of the individual actors").

124.   Several lower court decisions preceding *Omni* had used similar rationales to reject arguments that immunity should be denied. *See, e.g.,* Boone v. Redevelopment Agency, 841 F.2d 886, 892 (9th Cir.) (public entities "do not forfeit their immunity merely because their execution of the powers granted to them . . . may have been imperfect in operation"), *cert. denied,* 488 U.S. 965 (1988); Kern-Tulare Water Dist. v. City of Bakersfield, 828 F.2d 514, 522 (9th Cir. 1987) ("Where ordinary errors or abuses in exercise of state law . . . serves to strip the city of state authorization, aggrieved parties should not forego customary state corrective processes."), *cert. denied,* 486 U.S. 1015 (1988); Interface Group v. Massachusetts Port Auth., 816 F.2d 9, 13-14 (1st Cir. 1987) (rejecting view that statute permitting port authority to make rules governing operation of airport authorized promulgation of "reasonable" rules only; expressing concern about analytical approach that "would force antitrust courts to review state administrative law disputes"); Falls Chase Special Taxing Dist. v. City of Tallahassee, 788 F.2d 711, 714 (11th Cir. 1986) (per curiam) (city's "slight departure" from authorizing statute's procedural requirements deemed insufficient to eliminate immunity); Scott v. City of Sioux City, 736 F.2d 1207, 1215-16 (8th Cir. 1984) ("The City's departure from state procedural requisites would have to be extreme to warrant the threat of antitrust liability. State authorization for antitrust purposes does not require administrative decisions that are free from ordinary errors."), *cert. denied,* 471 U.S. 1003 (1985); Davis v. Southern Bell Tel. & Tel. Co., 755 F. Supp. 1532, 1541 (S.D. Fla. 1991) (alleged deficiencies in otherwise comprehensive public service commission oversight of defendant held not to eliminate immunity; noting that "As a general rule, the federal courts do not probe for defects in the State's decision to authorize the anticompetitive conduct. . . . This applies to errors of law, fact, or judgment, errors of either substance or procedure.") (citations omitted); *cf.* Obendorf v. City & County of Denver, 900 F.2d 1434, 1437-39 (10th Cir. 1990) (rejecting plaintiff's claim that defendants' conduct was unauthorized because process of conceiving and implementing urban renewal plan was a "sham"); Preferred Communs. v. City of Los Angeles, 754 F.2d 1396, 1415 (9th Cir. 1985) (alleged violation of plaintiff cable television operator's first amendment rights did not deprive municipality of immunity against antitrust claims), *aff'd,* 476 U.S. 488 (1986). *But see* Kern-Tulare Water Dist. v. City of Bakersfield, 486 U.S. 1015, 1016 (1988) (White, J., dissenting from denial of certiorari to 828 F.2d 514 (9th Cir. 1987)) ("The Ninth Circuit's characterization of the alleged violation of state policy as an ordinary error or occasional abuse seems insufficient to insulate the municipality from liability for action that restrains competition."); Massachusetts Bd. of Registration in Optometry, 110 F.T.C. 549, 614 (1988) (respondent's conduct contradicted state command not to restrict advertising; state had not articulated policy "to displace competition by state regulation").

125.   California Retail Liquor Dealers Ass'n v. Midcal Aluminum, Inc., 445 U.S. 97, 105 (1980).

price-fixing arrangement."[126] Some later decisions distinguished *Midcal* and held that state supervision was superfluous when local governments created by state law carry out governmental functions pursuant to clearly articulated and affirmatively expressed state policy.[127] However, other courts required that the activities of governmental subdivisions meet the *Midcal* test of active state supervision.[128]

The Supreme Court's *Hallie* decision resolved the question as to the need for state supervision of local government activities. Holding that such supervision was unnecessary, the Court said that without it:

> The only real danger is that [the municipality] will seek to further purely parochial public interests at the expense of more overriding state goals. This danger is minimal, however, because of the requirement that the municipality act pursuant to a clearly articulated state policy. Once it is clear that the state authorization exists, there is no need to require the State to supervise actively the municipality's execution of what is a properly delegated function.[129]

Thus, the conduct of local government entities is immune even though the state does not supervise the exercise of authority it has delegated.[130] The *Hallie* Court suggested (but did not decide) that active supervision would be unnecessary for state agencies.[131] Several lower courts have concluded that *Hallie*'s logic dictates that the active supervision requirement does not apply to the actions of state agencies and departments.[132]

---

126. *Id.* at 106.
127. *See, e.g.*, First Am. Title Co. v. South Dakota Land Title Ass'n, 714 F.2d 1439, 1451 n.13 (8th Cir. 1983) (active state supervision not required for conduct by municipalities), *cert. denied*, 464 U.S. 1042 (1984); Gold Cross Ambulance and Transfer v. City of Kan. City, 705 F.2d 1005, 1014 (8th Cir. 1983) (same); Town of Hallie v. City of Eau Claire, 700 F.2d 376, 385 (7th Cir. 1983) (same), *aff'd*, 471 U.S. 34 (1985). In *Boulder*, Justice Rehnquist's dissent noted that "[i]t would seem rather odd to require municipal ordinances to be enforced by the State rather than by the city itself." Community Communs. Co. v. City of Boulder, 455 U.S. 40, 71 n.6 (1982).
128. *See, e.g.*, Corey v. Look, 641 F.2d 32, 37 (1st Cir. 1981) (no exception where provisions for state review lacking).
129. Town of Hallie v. City of Eau Claire, 471 U.S. 34, 47 (1985).
130. *Compare* Ambulance Serv. v. Nevada Ambulance Servs., 819 F.2d 910, 913 (9th Cir. 1987) (counties, hospitals, charitable corporation, and ambulance service immune from claims that grant of ambulance franchise by charitable corporation violated Sherman Act; charitable corporation, formed by county board of health, treated as instrument of municipality and, therefore, active state supervision not necessary) *with* Riverview Invs., Inc. v. Ottawa Community Improvement Corp., 899 F.2d 474, 479-82 (6th Cir.) (nonprofit corporation deemed to be private entity for *Hallie* purposes; private status found because city did not create corporation, establish its structure, control its activities, or appoint its board members), *cert. denied*, 111 S. Ct. 151 (1990).
131. *See Hallie*, 471 U.S. at 46 n.10 ("In cases in which the actor is a state agency, it is likely that active supervision would . . . not be required, although we do not here decide that issue.").
132. *See, e.g.*, Benton, Benton & Benton v. Louisiana Pub. Facilities Auth., 897 F.2d 198, 203-04 (conduct of special purpose public corporation need not be actively supervised by state for immunity to attach), *cert. denied*, 111 S. Ct. 1619 (1991); Hass v. Oregon State Bar, 883 F.2d 1453, 1460 (9th Cir. 1989) (state bar association deemed to be state agency and need not be supervised separately), *cert. denied*, 110 S. Ct. 1812 (1990); *Ambulance Serv.*, 819 F.2d at 913 (regional emergency medical services corporation created by the state for a county board of health deemed similar to a municipality; supervision not required); Interface Group v. Massachusetts Port Auth., 816 F.2d 9, 13 (state port authority treated as similar to municipality in Hallie; supervision not required) (1st Cir. 1987); Cine 42nd Street Theater Corp. v. Nederlander Org., 790 F.2d 1032,

f. LOCAL GOVERNMENT LIABILITY FOR TREBLE DAMAGES

Suits involving local governments are subject to distinctive limits upon remedies. The Local Government Antitrust Act of 1984[133] (LGAA) bars antitrust damage actions against local governments. Protection is afforded to any "city, county, parish, town, township, village, or any other general function governmental unit established by State law"[134] as well as to "a school district, sanitary district, or any other special function governmental unit established by State law in one or more States."[135] This legislation was enacted to stem the increase in litigation against local governments[136] that followed the decisions in *Lafayette* and *Boulder*.[137]

The LGAA precludes the recovery of damages from any local government official or employee "acting in an official capacity."[138] Private persons also enjoy immunity from damages under the Act in specified circumstances. No claim against a private party can be "based on any official action directed by a local government, or official or employee thereof acting in an official capacity."[139] The Act does not

---

1047 (2d Cir. 1986) (state statute immunized urban development corporation's alleged anticompetitive leasing of theaters; because corporation was political subdivision of state, active state supervision was not required); Humana of Ill., Inc. v. Board of Trustees of Southern Illinois Univ., 1986-1 Trade Cas. (CCH) ¶ 67,127, at 62,806-07 (C.D. Ill. 1986) (activities of state university not subject to active supervision requirement); Greensboro Lumber Co. v. Georgia Power Co., 643 F. Supp. 1345, 1383 (N.D. Ga. 1986) (electric authority consisting of numerous municipalities and one county was state agency for which active supervision was unnecessary), *aff'd*, 844 F.2d 1538 (1988). In some pre-*Hallie* decisions courts adopted similar reasoning. *See, e.g.*, Brazil v. Arkansas Bd. of Dental Examiners, 759 F.2d 674, 675 (8th Cir. 1985) (as state agency, board's conduct deemed immune from antitrust challenge without active supervision).

133. 15 U.S.C. §§ 34-36 (1988).

134. *Id.* § 34(1)(A).

135. *Id.* § 34(1)(B).

136. *See, e.g.*, Unity Ventures v. County of Lake, 1984-1 Trade Cas. (CCH) ¶ 65,883 (N.D. Ill. 1983) ($28.5 million judgment against two local governments and three local government officials individually under Civil Rights Act and Section 1 of Sherman Act), *judgment n.o.v. granted*, 631 F. Supp. 181 (N.D. Ill. 1986) (refusing to give retroactive effect to Local Government Antitrust Act, but granting judgment n.o.v. based on state action doctrine), *aff'd*, 841 F.2d 770 (7th Cir.), *cert. denied*, 488 U.S. 891 (1988). Before passage of the LGAA, some courts had recognized qualified immunity for local officials on the ground that their anticompetitive acts had never been clearly established as violating the antitrust laws. *See, e.g.*, Affiliated Capital Corp. v. City of Houston, 735 F.2d 1555, 1569-70 (5th Cir. 1984) (en banc) (reinstating jury verdict against private party defendant, but giving immunity to Houston's mayor), *cert. denied*, 474 U.S. 1053 (1986).

137. In Community Communications Co. v. City of Boulder, Justice Rehnquist noted that "[i]t will take a considerable feat of judicial gymnastics to conclude that municipalities are not subject to treble damages." 455 U.S. 40, 65 n.2 (1982) (Rehnquist, J., dissenting).

138. 15 U.S.C. § 35(a) (1988); *see, e.g.*, Thatcher Enters. v. Cache County Corp., 902 F.2d 1472, 1477-78 (10th Cir. 1990) (LGAA immunized public officials from damage liability when such officials acted in their public capacity); Fisichelli v. Town of Methuen, 653 F. Supp. 1494, 1502 (D. Mass. 1987) (Act barred damage awards against municipality and public officials acting in an official capacity; Act did not bar damage award against public officials acting in their private capacity); Montauk-Caribbean Airways, Inc. v. Hope, 1985-2 Trade Cas. (CCH) ¶ 66,660, at 63,104 (E.D.N.Y. 1985) (damage action barred), *aff'd on other grounds*, 784 F.2d 91 (2d Cir.), *cert. denied*, 479 U.S. 872 (1986).

139. 15 U.S.C. § 36(a) (1988). *Compare* Sandcrest Outpatient Servs. v. Cumberland County Hosp. Sys., 853 F.2d 1139, 1143-46 (4th Cir. 1988) (LGAA immunity held applicable to private hospital management company whose contract with county hospital's board of trustees permitted company to choose the hospital's suppliers, subject to review of individual decisions by the board of

affect injunction actions under Section 16 of the Clayton Act,[140] nor does it preclude the recovery of attorney's fees by plaintiffs who substantially prevail.[141]

The LGAA took effect on September 24, 1984, but it can be applied retroactively if "the defendant establishes and the court determines, in light of all the circumstances, including the stage of the litigation and the availability of alternative relief under the Clayton Act, that it would be inequitable not to apply [it] to a pending case."[142] Decisions that have applied the LGAA retroactively often have involved disputes in which pretrial discovery had not been completed, where equitable relief would adequately protect the plaintiff's interests, or where imposing a large damage award would significantly harm the municipality.[143] Decisions

---

trustees) *and Montauk-Caribbean Airways*, 784 F.2d at 94-95 (LGAA precludes damage suit against town board for refusal to allow air carrier to serve local airport year round; in enacting LGAA, Congress "intended that the phrase 'acting in an official capacity' be given broad meaning") *with* City Communs. v. City of Detroit, 660 F. Supp. 932, 936 (E.D. Mich. 1987) (LGAA immunity deemed inapplicable to private cable television firm that failed to establish that it had acted pursuant to official supervision).

140. *See* Wicker v. Union County Gen. Hosp., 673 F. Supp. 177, 186 (N.D. Miss. 1987) (Sherman Act claims against a county hospital were allowed to proceed, but only for equitable relief; Sherman Act claims for damages were barred by the Act); Montauk-Carribbean Airways, Inc. v. Hope, 1985-2 Trade Cas. (CCH) ¶ 66,660, at 63,104 (E.D.N.Y. 1985) (equitable claim against public officials could proceed), *aff'd on other grounds*, 784 F.2d 91 (2d Cir.), *cert. denied*, 479 U.S. 872 (1986).

141. *See* Lancaster Community Hosp. v. Antelope Valley Hosp. Dist., 940 F.2d 397, 404 n.14 (9th Cir. 1991).

142. 15 U.S.C. § 35(b) (1988).

143. *See* Opdyke Inv. Co. v. City of Detroit, 883 F.2d 1265, 1270-73 (6th Cir. 1989) (plaintiff failed to pursue its initial claim for injunctive relief when such a claim was available; imposition of multi-million dollar damage award would force the city to cut back on essential services); Woolen v. Surtran Taxicabs, Inc., 801 F.2d 159, 166-67 (5th Cir. 1986) (retroactive application appropriate where discovery was not completed, where injunctive relief remained available, and where treble damage recovery against the municipal defendants would be "totally at odds" with letter and spirit of Act), *cert. denied*, 480 U.S. 931 (1987); Kaplan v. Clear Lake City Water Auth., 794 F.2d 1059, 1062-63 (5th Cir. 1986) (retroactive application appropriate where discovery was not completed, where injunctive relief remained available, and where complaint was not amended to include antitrust claims until after passage of the Act); *Montauk-Caribbean Airways*, 784 F.2d at 95 (retroactive application granted to preclude damages; emphasizing "the desire of Congress to grant broad immunity from damages for noncriminal acts by local officials"); Pontarelli Limousine, Inc. v. City of Chicago, 623 F. Supp. 281 (N.D. Ill. 1985) (case had not progressed to such an advanced stage as to preclude application of the Act; not class had been certified, other parties were still liable for damages, and injunctive relief was still available); Driscoll v. City of New York, 650 F. Supp. 1522 (S.D.N.Y. 1987) (retroactive application appropriate because discovery was not completed and injunctive relief remained available); S. Kane & Son v. W.R. Grace & Co., 623 F. Supp. 162 (E.D. Pa. 1985) (retroactive application to city appropriate because little discovery had taken place and plaintiff could still obtain recovery from other defendants; claims against city employee not dismissed pending discovery into employee's involvement in the alleged conspiracy); Skepton v. County of Bucks, 613 F. Supp. 1013 (E.D. Pa. 1985) (retroactive application appropriate because pretrial discovery not completed); Miami Int'l Realty Co. v. Town of Mt. Crested Butte, 607 F. Supp. 448, 453-54 (D. Colo. 1985) (retroactivity appropriate for town officials acting under home rule authority where discovery was ongoing and broad injunctive relief was available; case was permitted to proceed against private parties); Jefferson Disposal Co. v. Parish of Jefferson, 603 F. Supp. 1125, 1129 (E.D. La. 1985) (where substantial discovery remained, refusal to grant immunity would have been inequitable in view of availability of injunctive relief); TCI Cablevision, Inc. v. City of Jefferson, 604 F. Supp. 845, 846 (W.D. Mo. 1984) (where plaintiff was pursuing alternative remedy and there had been no substantive

denying retroactive application have tended to emphasize the advanced stage of the proceedings (for example, the entry of a verdict) or the apparent absence of good faith on the part of the municipality or its officials.[144]

3. Solicitation of Government Action

Economic actors sometimes petition government entities to restrict the ability of their rivals to compete in the marketplace. When successful, these entreaties can have significant anticompetitive effects, particularly when firms persuade government authorities to exclude competitors from commercial opportunities. Even though such petitioning can pose serious competitive dangers, courts have conferred antitrust immunity upon a wide range of activities designed to induce government bodies to handicap competitors. Cases involving alleged misuse of the machinery of government implicate first amendment principles[145] and raise questions about whether Congress intended that antitrust regulate what might be characterized as the operation of the political process.

a. BASIC FRAMEWORK AND EVOLUTION OF NOERR IMMUNITY

Six Supreme Court cases from the post-World War II era have established the basic foundation for antitrust immunity for efforts to solicit government action that restricts competition. In essence, these cases distinguish government action from private conduct and immunize private efforts to elicit rivalry-suppressing government intervention.

---

development of the case before the Act's effective date, failure to apply Act retroactively would have been inequitable).

144. *See* Fisichelli v. Town of Methuen, 653 F. Supp. 1494, 1502-04 (D. Mass. 1987) (LGAA did not bar damage claim against town official sued in his individual capacity and alleged to have acted for his own personal financial gain); Unity Ventures v. County of Lakes, 631 F. Supp. 181, 187-88 (N.D. Ill. 1986) (refusing to give retroactive effect to LGAA where case had progressed to a jury verdict, but granting judgment n.o.v. on basis of state action defense), *aff'd*, 841 F.2d 770 (7th Cir.), *cert. denied*, 488 U.S. 891 (1988); Englert v. City of McKeesport, 637 F. Supp. 930 (W.D. Pa. 1986) (because case had begun before state's effective date and appeal already had been taken from earlier decision, retroactivity would have been inequitable); Huron Valley Hosp. v. City of Pontiac, 612 F. Supp. 654 (E.D. Mich. 1985) (retroactivity denied because defendants failed to meet burden of proving equities favoring preclusion of damages; suit had been filed in 1978, plaintiffs had not been dilatory in prosecuting, and injunctive relief would be inadequate), *aff'd in part and dismissed in part*, 792 F.2d 563 (6th Cir.), *cert. denied*, 479 U.S. 885 (1986).

145. The first amendment to the Constitution of the United States provides that "Congress shall make no law . . . abridging the freedom of speech, or of the press, or the right of the people peaceably to assemble, and to petition the Government for a redress of grievances." U.S. CONST. amend. I. In United Mine Workers v. Illinois State Bar Association, 389 U.S. 217 (1967), the Supreme Court observed:

We start with the premise that the rights to assemble peaceably and to petition for redress of grievances are among the most precious of the liberties safeguarded by the Bill of Rights. These rights . . . are intimately connected, both in origin and in purpose, with the other First Amendment rights of free speech and free press. "All these, though not identical, are inseparable."

Id. at 222 (citing Thomas v. Collins, 323 U.S. 516, 530 (1945)).

(1) Noerr

In *Eastern Railroad Presidents Conference v. Noerr Motor Freight, Inc.*,[146] the Court considered the application of the Sherman Act to a publicity and lobbying effort conducted by twenty-four railroads, an association of their presidents, and a public relations firm to obtain legislation to restrict competition from the trucking industry. The railroads carried out their campaign against the truckers through deceptive and unethical means,[147] and their sole aim in pursuing legislation was to destroy the competitive capability of the truckers.[148] Because "the railroads were making a genuine effort to influence legislation and law enforcement practices," the Court held that their conduct enjoyed absolute antitrust immunity.[149] The Court emphasized that there is an "essential dissimilarity" between agreements to petition for laws that would restrain trade and private agreements that directly restrain trade.[150]

The Court did not specify how much its refusal to impose liability for the railroads' lobbying efforts stemmed, respectively, from its assessment of the aims of the Sherman Act and its solicitude for first amendment petitioning rights. In one passage, the Court reasoned that to condemn the lobbying campaign "would impute to the Sherman Act a purpose to regulate, not business activity, but political activity, a purpose which would have no basis whatever in the legislative history of that Act."[151] At the same time, the Court stated that to hold otherwise would hinder the process by which constituents convey opinions to government officials and

---

146. 365 U.S. 127 (1961).

147. *Id.* at 145.

148. *Id.* at 129. Subsequent decisions have reiterated *Noerr*'s observation that the defendant's anticompetitive motive does not invalidate efforts to elicit government intervention that suppresses rivalry. In United Mine Workers v. Pennington, 381 U.S. 657, 670 (1965), the Court stated that "*Noerr* shields from the Sherman Act a concerted effort to influence public officials regardless of intent or purpose." *See also* City of Columbia v. Omni Outdoor Advertising, Inc., 111 S. Ct. 1344, 1354 (1991) ("That a private party's political motives are selfish is irrelevant . . . ."); *In re* Burlington Northern, Inc., 822 F.2d 518, 526 (5th Cir. 1987) (regardless of defendant's motives, filing of lawsuit was protected activity), *cert. denied*, 484 U.S. 1007 (1988); Razorback Ready Mix Concrete Co. v. Weaver, 761 F.2d 484, 487-88 (8th Cir. 1985) (petitioner's "invocation of adjudicative process to press legitimate claims is protected even though its purpose in doing so is to eliminate competition"; concluding that it is "immaterial" that petitioner's motives "may have been selfish or altruistic or mixed"); Greenwood Utils. Comm'n v. Mississippi Power Co., 751 F.2d 1484, 1499 (5th Cir. 1985) ("nor does the possibility that the companies had selfish or anticompetitive ends in mind when seeking to influence the government deprive them of *Noerr-Pennington* protection").

149. 365 U.S. at 144.

150. *Id.* at 136.

151. *Id.* at 137. The Court later observed:
> It is inevitable, whenever an attempt is made to influence legislation by a campaign of publicity, that an incidental effect of that campaign may be the infliction of some direct injury upon the interests of the party against whom the campaign is directed. And it seems equally inevitable that those conducting the campaign would be aware of, and possibly even pleased by, the prospect of such injury. To hold that the knowing infliction of such injury renders the campaign itself illegal would thus be tantamount to outlawing all such campaigns. . . . [T]his has not been done by anything in the Sherman Act.

> *Id.* at 143-44. *Cf.* City of Columbia v. Omni Outdoor Advertising, Inc., 111 S. Ct. 1344, 1354 (1991) ("the federal antitrust laws . . . do not regulate the conduct of private individuals in seeking anticompetitive action from the government").

"would raise important constitutional questions."[152] This ambiguity is significant, because conceptions about *Noerr*'s bases can affect judicial views about the appropriate reach of *Noerr* immunity.[153]

As it shielded genuine efforts to shape government policy, the Court cautioned that immunity would not extend to all activities seemingly designed to influence government behavior. The Court said "[t]here may be situations in which a publicity campaign, ostensibly directed toward influencing governmental action, is a mere sham to cover what is actually nothing more than an attempt to interfere directly with the business relationships of a competitor and the application of the Sherman Act would be justified."[154] As subsequent cases would demonstrate, the bounds of *Noerr* immunity would depend heavily upon how courts interpreted the decision's "sham" exception.

(2) Pennington

In *United Mine Workers v. Pennington*,[155] the Court held that *Noerr* applies to attempts to influence government administrative processes, as well as to legislative lobbying. In *Pennington*, large coal mine operators and the United Mine Workers Union collaborated to persuade the Secretary of Labor to establish higher minimum wages for workers supplying coal to the Tennessee Valley Authority and to induce the TVA to curtail certain spot market purchases.[156] The Court held this concerted activity to be exempt from the Sherman Act: "Joint efforts to influence public officials do not violate the antitrust laws even though intended to eliminate competition. Such conduct is not illegal, either standing alone or as part of a broader scheme itself violative of the Sherman Act."[157] The Court reached this conclusion even though there was considerable evidence that, in addition to seeking government intervention, the union and large coal operators had engaged in a

---

152. 365 U.S. at 137-38. The Court added that the "right of petition is one of the freedoms protected by the Bill of Rights, and we cannot, of course, lightly impute to Congress an intent to invade these freedoms." *Id.* at 138. Previously, in Continental Ore Co. v. Union Carbide & Carbon Corp., 370 U.S. 690, 707 (1962), the Court had stated that "imputing to the Sherman Act a purpose to regulate political activity . . . would have encountered serious constitutional barriers." *See also* Barton's Disposal Serv. v. Tiger Corp., 886 F.2d 1430, 1435-36 (5th Cir. 1989) ("The *Noerr-Pennington* doctrine recognizes that, under the First Amendment, business entities have the right to advocate policies to federal, state and local government bodies that may destroy competitors."); Zavaletta v. American Bar Ass'n, 721 F. Supp. 96, 98 (E.D. Va. 1989) (bar association "has a First Amendment right to communicate its views on law schools to governmental bodies and others"); County of Suffolk v. Long Island Lighting Co., 710 F. Supp. 1387, 1390 (E.D.N.Y. 1989) (rejecting antitrust liability and emphasizing *Noerr*'s protection of county's "exercise of its constitutional right" to oppose licensing of utility's nuclear power plant before the Nuclear Regulatory Commission), *aff'd in part and rev'd in part*, 907 F.2d 1295 (2d Cir. 1990).

153. This is true, for example, in determining the application of *Noerr* to petitioning before agencies of foreign governments or to petitioning behavior such as bribery that ordinarily lacks first amendment protection.

154. 365 U.S. at 144.

155. 381 U.S. 657 (1965).

156. *Id.* at 660-61.

157. *Id.* at 670; *see also id.* at 669 (observing that the "Sherman Act, it was held [in *Noerr*], was not intended to bar concerted action of this kind").

number of anticompetitive acts that did not involve petitioning activity.[158]

(3) California Motor Transport

In *California Motor Transport Co. v. Trucking Unlimited*,[159] the Court held that the *Noerr* exemption applies to attempts to influence judicial and other adjudicatory actions.[160] The *California Motor Transport* plaintiffs contended that the defendants, without regard to the merits of their claims, initiated court and administrative actions to defeat plaintiffs' applications to obtain and transfer motor operating rights.[161] Basing its analysis upon first amendment considerations, the Court stated:

> We conclude that it would be destructive of rights of association and of petition to hold that groups with common interests may not, without violating the antitrust laws, use the channels and procedures of state and federal agencies and courts to advocate their causes and points of view respecting resolution of their business and economic interest *vis-à-vis* their competitors.[162]

The Court, however, went on to find the conduct alleged, if proved, would fall outside *Noerr*'s protection. *Noerr* had noted that petitioning might incur Sherman Act liability if it was "a mere sham to cover what is actually nothing more than an attempt to interfere directly with the business relationships of a competitor."[163] The sham exception did not apply in *Noerr* because "the railroads were making a genuine effort to influence legislation and law enforcement practices."[164] In *California Motor Transport*, the Court said that "a pattern of baseless, repetitive claims . . . effectively barring respondents from access to the agencies and courts"

---

158. *Id.* at 660.
159. 404 U.S. 508 (1972).
160. Subsequent lower court decisions have extended *Noerr* immunity to petitioning designed to elicit intervention by police departments and other law enforcement bodies. *See, e.g.*, King v. Idaho Funeral Serv. Ass'n, 862 F.2d 744 (9th Cir. 1988) (*Noerr* immunizes trade association's efforts to alert state licensing agency that firm was retailing caskets illegally); Smith v. Combustion Eng'g, 856 F.2d 196 (6th Cir. 1988) (*Noerr* immunizes defendant's cooperation in police inquiry that led to plaintiff's guilty plea), *cert. denied*, 489 U.S. 1054 (1989); Ottensmeyer v. Chesapeake & Potomac Tel. Co., 756 F.2d 986 (4th Cir. 1985) (*Noerr* immunizes defendant's cooperation with police where such action yields anticompetitive result so long as actions were not taken purely for purpose of harassment); Forro Precision, Inc. v. IBM, 673 F.2d 1045 (9th Cir. 1982) (*Noerr* immunizes reports to police about alleged theft of trade secrets), *appeal after remand*, 745 F.2d 1283 (9th Cir. 1984), *cert. denied*, 471 U.S. 1130 (1985).
161. 404 U.S. at 509.
162. *Id.* at 510-11; *see also* Bill Johnson's Restaurants v. NLRB, 461 U.S. 731, 741 (1983) ("In [*California Motor Transport*] we recognized that the right of access to the courts is an aspect of the First Amendment right to petition the government for redress of grievances."); Monarch Entertainment Bureau v. New Jersey Highway Auth., 715 F. Supp. 1290, 1303 (D.N.J.) (observing that "*Noerr*'s first policy consideration" is "the government's need for access to information"), *aff'd mem.*, 893 F.2d 1331 (3d Cir. 1989).
163. 365 U.S. at 144.
164. *Id.*

would not qualify for immunity under the "umbrella of 'political expression.'"[165] The Court emphasized that conduct that would be immune if pursued before legislative bodies might be actionable if the setting in question was a forum for adjudication.[166] The Court also noted that the boundary between sham and legitimate conduct may be "a difficult line to discern and draw."[167]

(4) Allied Tube & Conduit

In *Allied Tube & Conduit Corp. v. Indian Head, Inc.*,[168] the Court considered the standard-setting activities of the National Fire Protection Association (NFPA), a private trade association that sets performance standards for electrical products, which standards are often incorporated into municipal fire codes. The *Allied* defendant, a producer of steel conduit, combined with independent sales agents and other manufacturers of steel conduit to recruit persons to join the NFPA, to attend the association's annual meetings, and to vote against proposals for the NFPA to approve polyvinyl chloride (PVC) electrical conduit in its model code.[169] After the defendant's campaign succeeded in defeating measures to include PVC conduit, a

---

165. 404 U.S. at 513; *see also* Otter Tail Power Co. v. United States, 410 U.S. 366, 380 (1973) (observing that, in *California Motor Transport*, the Court "held that the principle of *Noerr* may also apply to the use of administrative or judicial processes where the purpose to suppress competition is evidenced by repetitive lawsuits carrying the hallmark of insubstantial claims and thus is within the 'mere sham' exception").

166. The Court explained:
   There are many other forms of illegal and reprehensible practice which may corrupt the administrative or judicial processes and which may result in antitrust violations. Misrepresentations, condoned in the political arena, are not immunized when used in the adjudicatory process.
   404 U.S. at 513. The Court prefaced this observation with an enumeration of different types of conduct that, when performed in an adjudicatory setting, had been subject to condemnation:
   [U]nethical conduct in the setting of the adjudicatory process often results in sanctions. Perjury of witnesses is one example. Use of a patent obtained by fraud to exclude a competitor from the market may involve a violation of the antitrust laws, as we held in *Walker Process Equipment v. Food Machinery & Chemical Corp.*, 382 U.S. 172, 175-77. Conspiracy with a licensing authority to eliminate a competitor may also result in an antitrust transgression. *Continental Ore Co. v. Union Carbide & Carbon Corp.*, 370 U.S. 690, 707; *Harman v. Valley National Bank*, 339 F.2d 564 (CA9 1964). Similarly, bribery of a public purchasing agent may constitute a violation of § 2(c) of the Clayton Act, as amended by the Robinson-Patman Act. *Rangen, Inc. v. Sterling Nelson & Sons*, 351 F.2d 851 (CA9 1965).
   Id. at 512-13.

167. *Id.* at 513.

168. 486 U.S. 492 (1988).

169. Among other acts, the defendant recruited and purchased NFPA memberships for 230 individuals and arranged for them to attend the NFPA meeting in question. *Id.* at 496-97; *cf.* Schachar v. American Academy of Ophthalmology, 870 F.2d 397, 399-400 (7th Cir. 1989) (rejecting antitrust liability where professional association provided information but did not constrain others to adopt its views; stating that "an organization's towering reputation does not reduce its freedom to speak out. . . . If such statements should be false or misleading or incomplete or just plain mistaken, the remedy is not antitrust litigation but more speech – the marketplace of ideas."); Clamp-All Corp. v. Cast Iron Soil Pipe Inst., 851 F.2d 478, 488-89 (1st Cir. 1988) (declining to find antitrust liability for defendant's efforts to petition private standard-setting entity; plaintiff failed to prove that defendant's conduct constituted "a significant abuse of [the entity's] procedural standards or practices"), *cert. denied*, 488 U.S. 1007 (1989).

group of PVC conduit producers attacked the defendant's conduct under the Sherman Act. The Second Circuit rejected the defendant's defense of *Noerr* immunity,[170] and the Supreme Court affirmed.

The Court ruled that *Noerr*'s protection did not extend to the defendant's attempts to influence the NFPA's standard-setting activities:

> [A]t least where, as here, an economically interested party exercises decision-making authority in formulating a product standard for a private association that comprises market participants, that party enjoys no *Noerr* immunity from any antitrust liability flowing from the effect the standard has of its own force in the marketplace.[171]

The Court explained that the antitrust significance of efforts to suppress competition by influencing government bodies "depends . . . on the source, context, and nature of the anticompetitive restraint at issue."[172] The "source" element of the Court's test focused upon whether the trade restraint flowed from governmental or private action. The Court observed that private parties enjoy complete antitrust immunity when the anticompetitive restraints flow from government action.[173] The injury in *Allied* resulted from the plaintiff's exclusion from the trade association's model code and not from any government body's adoption of the code. The Court concluded that the "relevant context is thus the standard-setting process of a private association,"[174] an entity whose conduct ordinarily is subject to antitrust review.

---

170. Indian Head, Inc. v. Allied Tube & Conduit Corp., 817 F.2d 938 (2d Cir. 1987), *aff'd*, 486 U.S. 492 (1988).

171. 486 U.S. at 509-10.

172. *Id.* at 499.

173. *Id.* In Premier Electrical Construction Co. v. National Electrical Contractors Association, 814 F.2d 358 (7th Cir. 1987), the Seventh Circuit observed:

> [I]t is important to identify the source of the injury to competition. If the injury is caused by persuading the government, then the antitrust laws do not apply to the squelching (*Parker v. Brown*) or the persuasion (*Noerr-Pennington*). If the injury flows directly from the "petitioning" – if the injury occurs no matter how the government responds to the request for aid – then we have an antitrust case. When private parties help themselves to a reduction in competition, the antitrust laws apply.

Id. at 376; Midwest Constr. Co. v. Illinois Dep't of Labor, 684 F. Supp. 991 (N.D. Ill. 1988) (granting defendant's motion to dismiss where injury resulted from state agency's enforcement of in-state-labor preference law); Woolen v. Surtran Taxicabs, Inc., 615 F. Supp. 344, 354 (N.D. Tex. 1985) (conduct immune where "injuries were caused by the governmental action which the private defendants genuinely attempted to secure and succeeded in securing"), *aff'd per curiam*, 801 F.2d 159 (5th Cir. 1986), *cert. denied*, 480 U.S. 931 (1987); In re Airport Car Rental Antitrust Litig., 521 F. Supp. 568, 574 (N.D. Cal. 1981) (conduct immune where restriction on competition "flows, not from the joint action of defendants, but from the airport authorities' exercise of their statutory authority and duty to manage the facilities in their charge"), *aff'd*, 693 F.2d 84 (9th Cir. 1982), *cert. denied*, 462 U.S. 1133 (1983).

In Municipal Utilities Board v. Alabama Power Co., 934 F.2d 1493 (11th Cir. 1991), the Eleventh Circuit observed:

> This court has not recognized a ratification exception to the *Noerr-Pennington* doctrine. Moreover, such an exception would likely swallow the rule. It would permit the losers of legislative battles to claim that any coordination by their successful opponents amounted to a prior agreement which was then "ratified" by the legislature. If the *Noerr-Pennington* doctrine is to have any effect, plaintiffs cannot be allowed to use the mere existence of state legislation to bootstrap an antitrust claim against the supporters of that legislation.

Id. at 1505.

174. 486 U.S. at 499.

The Court also considered and rejected the defendants' argument that the NFPA should be treated as a "quasi-legislature" for purposes of *Noerr* analysis. Although it found that the challenged restriction resulted from "private action,"[175] the Court said that *Noerr* immunity nonetheless might be available if the trade association's refusal to endorse the use of the plaintiffs' conduit was "incidental to a valid effort to influence governmental action."[176] Even though the restriction stemmed from private action, *Noerr* immunity would apply if the nature of the conduct was chiefly political rather than commercial.[177]

Finally, *Allied* elaborated the dimensions of the sham exception. The Court stated that the sham exception is designed "to cover activity that was not genuinely intended to influence governmental action."[178] In doing so, the Court rejected the position taken in some lower court opinions that the sham exception applied to genuine attempts to influence government bodies when such efforts take the form of unethical petitioning.[179] The Court explained that "[s]uch a use of the word 'sham' distorts its meaning and bears little relation to the sham exception *Noerr* described to cover activity that was not genuinely intended to influence governmental action."[180]

---

175. *Id.* at 502.

176. *Id.*

177. The Court acknowledged problems that might arise in attempting to distinguish conduct that is primarily political from conduct that is primarily commercial:

>   It is admittedly difficult to draw the precise lines separating anticompetitive political activity that is immunized despite its commercial impact from anticompetitive commercial activity that is unprotected despite its political impact, and this is itself a case close to the line. For that reason we caution that our decision today depends on the context and nature of the activity.

>   *Id.* at 507-08 n.10. The Court noted that the activities in question in *Noerr* had taken place in the "open political arena, where partisanship is the hallmark of decisionmaking." *Id.* at 506. The Court contrasted this with private standard-setting that, from an antitrust perspective, had been "permitted at all . . . only on the understanding that it will be conducted in a nonpartisan manner offering procompetitive benefits." *Id.* at 506-07.

178. *Id.* at 508. Ten years earlier, in New Motor Vehicle Bd. v. Orrin W. Fox Co., 439 U.S. 96 (1978), the Court had held that a state regulatory scheme that permitted the delay of the establishment of new automobile dealerships whenever competing dealers protested did not improperly effectuate privately initiated restraints of trade. The Court observed that the automobile dealers' petitions to the state board opposing new car dealerships were protected unless such petitions were "sham protests" made for "the sole purpose of delaying the establishment of competing dealerships." 439 U.S. at 110.

179. *See, e.g.*, Sessions Tank Liners, Inc. v. Joor Mfg., 827 F.2d 458, 465 n.5 (9th Cir. 1987) (sham exception deemed applicable when "the defendant genuinely seeks to achieve his governmental result, but does so *through improper means*" [emphasis in original]), *vacated*, 487 U.S. 1213 (1988); *cf.* Central Telecommuns. v. TCI Cablevision, Inc., 800 F.2d 711, 722 (8th Cir. 1986) (upholding jury instruction stating that "The defendants are entitled . . . to use genuine efforts to influence public officials but if in fact defendant's lobbying activities included threats, intimidation, coercion or other unlawful acts, then you may find that such activities were not genuine efforts to influence public officials and you may consider those acts to have been unlawful conduct."), *cert. denied*, 480 U.S. 910 (1987).

180. 486 U.S. at 508 n.10.

(5) Superior Court Trial Lawyers

In *FTC v. Superior Court Trial Lawyers Association*,[181] the Court evaluated a refusal by a group of attorneys in the District of Columbia to accept assignments to represent indigent criminal defendants unless the city government increased the fees for such work. The Court ruled that per se condemnation was appropriate for the attorneys' boycott and rejected arguments that *Noerr* immunized the concerted refusal to deal. In particular, the Court emphasized that the boycott preceded government intervention:

> [I]n the *Noerr* case the alleged restraint of trade was the intended *consequence* of public action; in this case the boycott was the *means* by which respondents sought to obtain favorable legislation. The restraint of trade that was implemented while the boycott lasted would have had precisely the same anticompetitive consequences during that period even if no legislation had been enacted. In *Noerr*, the desired legislation would have created the restraint on the truckers' competition; in this case the emergency legislative response to the boycott put an end to the restraint.[182]

Thus, the source of the harm was the private boycott, not action by a government body.

In reaching this conclusion, the *Trial Lawyers* Court said *Noerr* does not shield all conduct that is genuinely intended to influence governmental action.[183] To do so would immunize price-fixing agreements aimed at government purchasing authorities, boycotts designed to induce government entities to pay higher prices to private suppliers, or boycotts justified as efforts to spur legislative action by dramatizing the plight of specific industries.[184] The Court also rejected the suggestion that the Court's first amendment jurisprudence protected the boycott as a lobbying effort designed to vindicate the sixth amendment rights of indigent criminal defendants.[185] Finally, the Court concluded that first amendment concerns raised by the boycott's "expressive component" did not foreclose application of a per se standard to condemn the collective refusal to deal.[186]

(6) Omni Outdoor Advertising

In *City of Columbia v. Omni Outdoor Advertising, Inc.*,[187] the Supreme Court considered immunity defenses based upon the state action[188] and *Noerr* doctrines. In *Omni*, a billboard firm alleged that a competitor and the City of Columbia, South Carolina conspired to restrict the plaintiff's ability to enter and compete in the market for outdoor advertising. Among other acts, the defendant and various

---

181. 493 U.S. 411 (1990).

182. *Id.* at 424-25 (emphasis in original).

183. *Id.*

184. *Id.*

185. *Id.* at 427.

186. The Court found that the expressive component of the boycott was "exaggerated," noting that all boycotts require communication among the boycott participants and therefore have some expressive features. *Id.* at 429-32.

187. 111 S. Ct. 1344 (1991).

188. *Omni*'s treatment of state action immunity issues is discussed at Section B.2.d and Subsection B.2.e(1) of this chapter.

municipal officials allegedly conspired to devise and enact a zoning ordinance that impeded the plaintiff's efforts to construct new billboards.[189] The plaintiff argued, and the Fourth Circuit agreed, that the defendants' conduct was not entitled to *Noerr* protection.[190]

In reversing the Fourth Circuit, the Supreme Court rejected two theories the plaintiff had advanced for withholding *Noerr* immunity. First, the Court concluded that the defendants' behavior did not fall within *Noerr*'s sham exception. The Court explained that the sham exception "encompasses situations in which persons use the governmental *process* — as opposed to the *outcome* of that process — as an anticompetitive weapon"[191] and reiterated *Allied*'s holding that sham conduct "involves a defendant whose activities are 'not genuinely aimed at procuring favorable government action'" at all.[192] The *Omni* defendant clearly had desired to exclude the plaintiff, but "it sought to do so not through the very process of lobbying, or of causing the city council to consider zoning measures, but rather through the ultimate *product* of that lobbying and consideration, viz., the zoning ordinances."[193] The sham exception applied only to "a context in which the conspirators' participation in the governmental process was itself claimed to be a 'sham,' employed as a means of imposing cost and delay."[194]

The *Omni* Court also refused to recognize an exception to *Noerr* immunity "when government officials conspire with a private party to employ government action as a means of stifling competition."[195] For the same reasons that it rejected a "conspiracy exception" to state action immunity,[196] the Court held that no such exception was available under *Noerr*:

> The same factors which . . . make it impracticable or beyond the purpose of the antitrust laws to identify and invalidate lawmaking that has been infected by selfishly motivated agreement with private interests likewise make it impracticable or beyond that scope to identify and invalidate lobbying that has produced selfishly motivated agreement with public officials.[197]

---

189. 111 S. Ct. at 1347-48.

190. Omni Outdoor Advertising, Inc. v. City of Columbia, 891 F.2d 1127 (4th Cir. 1989), *rev'd*, 111 S. Ct. 1344 (1991).

191. 111 S. Ct. at 1354 (emphasis in original).

192. *Id.* (quoting Allied Tube & Conduit Corp. v. Indian Head, Inc., 486 U.S. 492, 500 n.4 (1988)).

193. 111 S. Ct. at 1354 (emphasis in original).

194. *Id.* at 1355. The Court explained that to extend the sham exception "to a context in which the regulatory process is being invoked genuinely, and not in a 'sham' fashion, would produce precisely the conversion of antitrust law into regulation of the political process that we have sought to avoid." *Id.*

195. *Id.* Some lower court decisions previously had recognized a conspiracy exception to *Noerr*. See Affiliated Capital Corp. v. City of Houston, 735 F.2d 1555, 1566-68 (5th Cir. 1984) (en banc), *cert. denied*, 474 U.S. 1053 (1986); Duke & Co. v. Foerster, 521 F.2d 1277, 1282 (3d Cir. 1975).

196. *See* Section B.2.d of this chapter.

197. 111 S. Ct. at 1355. In dispensing with a conspiracy exception to *Parker* state action immunity, the Court observed:
   Since it is both inevitable and desirable that public officials often agree to do what one or another group of private citizens urges upon them, such an exception would virtually swallow up the *Parker* rule: All anticompetitive regulation would be vulnerable to a "conspiracy" charge.
   Id. at 1351.

The Court added that "'[i]t would be unlikely that any effort to influence a legislative action could succeed unless one or more members of the legislative body became . . . co-conspirators' in *some* sense with the private party urging such action."[198]

b. QUALIFICATIONS TO NOERR IMMUNITY

Courts have devoted substantial effort to defining the limits of *Noerr*'s protection. As a general matter, decisions have tended to confer immunity more expansively when the government body is performing legislative functions and less expansively when the government body is executing adjudicatory responsibilities.[199] Specific, recurring issues of interpretation are identified and treated below.

(1) Sham Exception

Decisions invoking the sham exception announced in *Noerr* and *California Motor Transport* to withhold immunity for petitioning activity ordinarily have concluded that the defendants' conduct was not designed to secure the benefits of government intervention, but rather to impose burdens upon rivals by forcing them to defend themselves or to incur substantial costs to gain access to the processes of government. A finding of sham conduct by itself ordinarily does not suffice to establish antitrust liability, as courts usually require the plaintiff to satisfy all elements of the asserted theory of antitrust liability.[200]

Courts have applied the sham exception in a variety of circumstances. As noted above, sham exception arguments have succeeded most frequently where the challenged conduct involves the alleged misuse of adjudicatory processes.[201] Sham

---

198.   *Id.* at 1355-56 (emphasis in original) (quoting Metro Cable Co. v. CATV of Rockford, Inc., 516 F.2d 220, 230 (7th Cir. 1975)).

199.   In California Motor Transport Co. v. Trucking Unlimited, 404 U.S. 508 (1972), the Court observed that misrepresentations "condoned in the political arena, are not immunized when used in the adjudicatory process." *Id.* at 513; *see* Clipper Exxpress v. Rocky Mountain Motor Tariff Bureau, 690 F.2d 1240, 1281 (9th Cir. 1982) (misrepresentations to adjudicatory bodies treated more severely because adjudicatory tribunals, unlike legislatures, depend more heavily on parties to verify the accuracy of information provided), *cert. denied*, 459 U.S. 1227 (1983).

200.   *See, e.g.*, Neumann v. Reinforced Earth Co., 786 F.2d 424 (D.C. Cir.) ("even if the litigation was a sham . . . [the plaintiff] must still prove the other elements of an illegal attempt to monopolize"), *cert. denied*, 479 U.S. 851 (1986); Consolidated Aluminum Corp. v. Foseco Int'l, Ltd., 716 F. Supp. 316 (N.D. Ill. 1989) (relevant market and dangerous probability of success must be established in claim based upon enforcement of patent known to be invalid), *aff'd*, 910 F.2d 804 (Fed. Cir. 1990); Conceptual Eng'g Assocs. v. Aelectronic Bonding, Inc., 714 F. Supp. 1262 (D.R.I. 1989) (same). *But see* Rickards v. Canine Eye Registration Found., 783 F.2d 1329, 1334 (9th Cir.) (despite finding of no anticompetitive effect and no per se offense, existence of sham lawsuit deemed to constitute Sherman Act § 1 offense because sham litigation "deserves all the chilling the law allows"), *cert. denied*, 479 U.S. 851 (1986).

201.   *See, e.g.*, Hufsmith v. Weaver, 817 F.2d 455 (8th Cir. 1987) (filing baseless state law claim for tortious interference with contractual relations); CVD, Inc. v. Raytheon Co., 769 F.2d 842, 851 (1st Cir. 1985) (despite awareness that it lacked a valid trade secret claim, defendant filed trade secret infringement suit to impede new entrant), *cert. denied*, 475 U.S. 1016 (1986); Handgards, Inc. v. Ethicon, Inc., 743 F.2d 1282, 1294 (9th Cir. 1984) (defendant filed suit "without probable cause and in complete disregard of the law in order to interfere with the business relationships of a competitor"), *cert. denied*, 469 U.S. 1190 (1985); Winterland Concessions Co. v. Trela, 735 F.2d 257, 263 (7th Cir. 1984) (strategically filing and withdrawing "John Doe" injunction actions);

behavior also has been found where the defendant filed baseless requests that a government body deny a rival's petition for regulatory approval,[202] commenced administrative proceedings to impede a rival's access to government processes,[203] or instituted administrative proceedings to inflict substantial costs of defense upon a rival.[204]

In these and other settings, courts have struggled to develop evaluative criteria for identifying conduct that falls outside *Noerr*'s protection. One criterion, suggested by the Supreme Court's language in *California Motor Transport*, is whether the challenged petitioning is "baseless." In *California Motor Transport*, the Supreme Court stated that "a pattern of baseless, repetitive claims may emerge which leads the factfinder to conclude that the administrative and judicial processes have been abused."[205] The Court also noted that the plaintiffs had alleged that their adversaries had "'instituted the proceedings and actions . . . with or without probable cause, and regardless of the merits of the cases.'"[206]

Some decisions have treated baselessness as a minimum (but not always sufficient) condition for invoking the sham exception.[207] However, other decisions have

---

Energy Conservation, Inc. v. Heliodyne, Inc., 698 F.2d 386, 389 (9th Cir. 1983) (defendant filed lawsuit to focus adverse media attention upon rival); Alexander v. National Farmers' Org., 687 F.2d 1173, 1200 (8th Cir. 1982) (mailing copies of complaint to rival's customers); *see also* Grip-Pak, Inc. v. Illinois Tool Works, Inc., 694 F.2d 466, 472 (7th Cir. 1982) (court's hypotheticals in which defendant used discovery to obtain rival's trade secrets; filed suit in order to compel rival to disclose potential liabilities and pay higher interest rates; initiated proceedings to impose disproportionate legal costs on rival to discourage entry), *cert. denied*, 461 U.S. 958 (1983).

202. *See, e.g.*, Litton Sys. v. AT&T, 700 F.2d 785, 811-12 (2d Cir. 1983) (despite having no realistic prospect for success, defendant sought regulatory agency's denial of permission for plaintiff to interconnect equipment with defendant's telephone network), *cert. denied*, 464 U.S. 1073 (1984); Clipper Exxpress v. Rocky Mountain Motor Tariff Bureau, 690 F.2d 1240, 1253-54 (9th Cir. 1982) (without regard to the merits of its actions, defendant consistently and automatically opposed rival's rate filings with administrative body), *cert. denied*, 459 U.S. 1227 (1983).

203. *See, e.g.*, Hospital Bldg. Co. v. Trustees of Rex Hosp., 691 F.2d 678 (4th Cir. 1982) (defendants participated in federal and state regulatory processes to prevent rivals from gaining access to government bodies), *cert. denied*, 464 U.S. 904 (1984); City of Kirkwood v. Union Elec. Co., 671 F.2d 1173, 1181 (8th Cir. 1982) (same), *cert. denied*, 459 U.S. 1170 (1983).

204. *See, e.g.*, Greenwood Utils. Comm'n v. Mississippi Power Co., 751 F.2d 1484, 1498 n.9 (5th Cir. 1985) (commencement of regulatory proceedings intended to impose burdens upon competitor rather than elicit favorable government action); MCI Communs. Corp. v. AT&T, 708 F.2d 1081, 1156 (7th Cir.) (forcing plaintiff to participate in proceedings before a multiplicity of forums in order to establish its rights), *cert. denied*, 464 U.S. 891 (1983); Landmarks Holding Corp. v. Bermant, 664 F.2d 891 (2d Cir. 1981) (defendant repeatedly commenced proceedings despite knowledge that it lacked standing).

205. California Motor Transport Co. v. Trucking Unlimited, 404 U.S. 508, 513 (1972).

206. *Id.* at 512.

207. *See, e.g.*, Opdyke Inv. Co. v. City of Detroit, 883 F.2d 1265, 1273 (6th Cir. 1989) (no sham where defendant initiated lawsuit "even if the suit proved to be without merit, absent a showing of clear abuse of process"); South Dakota v. Kansas City S. Indus., 880 F.2d 40, 51 (8th Cir. 1989) (sham exception applicable where defendant's resort to courts and agencies "'is so clearly baseless as to amount to an abuse of process'") (quoting Razorback Ready Mix Concrete Co. v. Weaver, 761 F.2d 484, 487 (8th Cir. 1985)), *cert. denied*, 493 U.S. 1023 (1990); Omni Resource Dev. Corp. v. Conoco, Inc., 739 F.2d 1412, 1414 (9th Cir. 1984) ("When the antitrust plaintiff challenges one suit and not a pattern, a finding of sham requires not only that the suit is baseless, but also that it has other characteristics of grave abuse, such as being coupled with actions or effects."); USS-Posco Indus. v. Contra Costa County Bldg. & Constr. Trades Council, 721 F. Supp. 239, 241 (N.D. Cal. 1989) (no sham where plaintiff failed to show that prior suit "'lacks a reasonable basis

suggested that, in some circumstances, a decision to prosecute a claim with some merit might be deemed sham conduct. In *Grip-Pak, Inc. v. Illinois Tool Works, Inc.*, the Seventh Circuit identified conditions in which a "baselessness" standard might be unduly restrictive:

> [T]he existence of a tort of abuse of process shows that it has long been thought that litigation could be used for improper purposes even when there is probable cause for the litigation; and if the improper purpose is to use litigation as a tool for suppressing competition in its antitrust sense, it becomes a matter of antitrust concern.[208]

Subsequent Seventh Circuit decisions have reiterated *Grip-Pak*'s view that lawsuits presenting colorable claims for relief nonetheless may constitute sham conduct if their chief aim is to encumber competitors, regardless of the outcome ultimately achieved in the litigation.[209]

The decisions are also divided on the question whether a single instance of baseless petitioning can support a finding of sham.[210]   In *Vendo Co. v. Lektro-Vend Corp.*,[211] a three-Justice plurality of the Supreme Court held that the Anti-Injunction Act, which generally bars federal courts from enjoining state courts, forbade the issuance of an injunction to halt a state court collection suit that was alleged to be sham action and a Sherman Act violation. Two concurring members of the Court believed that one baseless claim was insufficient to warrant an injunction but would have permitted an injunction if the plaintiff had proved a "pattern of baseless, repetitive claims."[212]   Four dissenters argued that a single baseless case could qualify for the sham exception.[213]

Some lower courts have interpreted *California Motor Transport* to preclude a finding of sham conduct on the basis of a single alleged instance of baseless petitioning.[214]   Other decisions have held that the filing of multiple lawsuits is not

---

in law and . . . was filed with an improper motive' "); Columbia Pictures Indus. v. Professional Real Estate Investors, Inc., 1990-1 Trade Cas. (CCH) ¶ 68,971, at 63,243 (C.D. Cal. 1990) (existence of probable cause precludes existence of sham), *aff'd*, 944 F.2d 1525 (9th Cir. 1991), *petition for cert. filed*, 60 U.S.L.W. 3482 (U.S. Dec. 23, 1991) (No. 91-1043); Spanish Int'l Communs. Corp. v. Leibowitz, 608 F. Supp. 178 (S.D. Fla.) (immunity protected attorney's representation of client before FCC where action before agency not baseless), *aff'd mem.*, 778 F.2d 791 (11th Cir. 1985); *cf.* Hydro-Tech Corp. v. Sundstrand Corp., 673 F.2d 1171, 1175-77 (10th Cir. 1982) (showing that lawsuit lacked probable cause, by itself, deemed insufficient to establish sham).

208.   694 F.2d 466, 471-72 (7th Cir. 1982), *cert. denied*, 461 U.S. 958 (1983).

209.   *See* Premier Elec. Constr. Co. v. National Elec. Contractors Ass'n, 814 F.2d 358, 372 (7th Cir. 1987); Winterland Concessions Co. v. Trela, 735 F.2d 257, 263 (7th Cir. 1984).

210.   In City of Cleveland v. Cleveland Electric Illuminating Co., 734 F.2d 1157, 1162-63 (6th Cir.), *cert. denied*, 469 U.S. 884 (1984), the Sixth Circuit observed that "[w]hether a single legal proceeding, even if found meritless, may be considered a basis of a 'sham' exception in light of California Motor Transport is not altogether clear."

211.   433 U.S. 623 (1977).

212.   *Id.* at 644 (Blackmun, J., concurring).

213.   *Id.* at 661-62 (Stevens, J., dissenting).

214.   *See* Hospital Bldg. Co. v. Trustees of Rex Hosp., 691 F.2d 678 (4th Cir. 1982), *cert. denied*, 464 U.S. 904 (1984); Loctite Corp. v. Fel-Pro, Inc., 1978-2 Trade Cas. (CCH) ¶ 62,204 (N.D. Ill. 1978); Mountain Grove Cemetery Ass'n v. Norwalk Vault Co., 428 F. Supp. 951 (D. Conn. 1977); Strategic Mktg. Servs. v. Cut & Curl, Inc., 1977-2 Trade Cas. (CCH) ¶ 61,788 (D. Conn. 1977); Central Bank v. Clayton Bank, 424 F. Supp. 163 (E.D. Mo. 1976), *aff'd mem.*, 553 F.2d 102 (8th

essential for invoking the sham exception and have found that a single lawsuit can suffice.[215] One subset of opinions has suggested that a single lawsuit might constitute sham conduct if the filing of the lawsuit was notably vexatious.[216] Some cases have indicated that threats of unfounded litigation and efforts to intimidate a rival's customers or suppliers with exaggerated reports of pending or contemplated lawsuits sometimes may be deemed sham conduct.[217]

Cir.), *cert. denied*, 433 U.S. 910 (1977); *cf.* Surgidev Corp. v. Eye Technology, Inc., 625 F. Supp. 800, 804 (D. Minn. 1986) ("it is extremely doubtful that the initiation of a single lawsuit can fit within the 'sham exception' "). A showing that the defendant engaged in a multiplicity of initiatives, by itself, does not ensure that its conduct will be found to be a sham. The court is likely to consider the quality, as well as the number, of litigation episodes. *Compare* Ad Visor, Inc. v. Pacific Tel. & Tel. Co., 640 F.2d 1107 (9th Cir. 1981) (64 claims that were neither baseless nor repetitive did not constitute sham) *with* Landmarks Holding Corp. v. Bermant, 664 F.2d 891 (2d Cir. 1981) (numerous baseless appeals and delay in their prosecution constitute sham).

215. *See, e.g.*, Village of Bolingbrook v. Citizens Utils. Co., 864 F.2d 481, 483 (7th Cir. 1988); Aydin Corp. v. Loral Corp., 718 F.2d 897, 903 (9th Cir. 1983); MCI Communs. Corp. v. AT&T, 708 F.2d 1081, 1093 (7th Cir.) ("multiple lawsuits are not a condition precedent to showing sham"), *cert. denied*, 464 U.S. 891 (1983); Energy Conservation, Inc. v. Heliodyne, Inc., 698 F.2d 386, 388-89 (9th Cir. 1983); Clipper Exxpress v. Rocky Mountain Motor Tariff Bureau, 690 F.2d 1240, 1255 (9th Cir. 1982) ("If the activity is not genuine petitioning activity, the antitrust laws are not suspended and continue to prohibit the violating activities . . . whether that activity consists of a single or multiple sham suits."), *cert. denied*, 459 U.S. 1227 (1983); Feminist Women's Health Center, Inc. v. Mohammad, 586 F.2d 530, 543 n.12 (5th Cir. 1978), *cert. denied*, 444 U.S. 924 (1979); Salomon SA v. Alpina Sports Corp., 737 F. Supp. 720, 725 (D.N.H. 1990); Brownlee v. Applied Biosystems, 1989-1 Trade Cas. (CCH) ¶ 68,425 (N.D. Cal. 1989); Collins & Aikman Corp. v. Stratton Indus., 728 F. Supp. 1570, 1580 (N.D. Ga. 1989); Grip-Pak, Inc. v. Illinois Tool Works, Inc., 651 F. Supp. 1482, 1498-99 (N.D. Ill. 1986) (plaintiff introduced sufficient evidence of bad faith in defendant's filing of single suit to avoid summary judgment); National Cash Register Corp. v. Arnett, 554 F. Supp. 1176 (D. Colo. 1983); Sage Int'l, Ltd. v. Cadillac Gage Co., 507 F. Supp. 939, 944-46 (E.D. Mich. 1981); Cyborg Sys. v. Management Science Am., Inc., 1978-1 Trade Cas. (CCH) ¶ 61,927 (N.D. Ill. 1978).

216. *See, e.g.*, Razorback Ready-Mix Concrete Co. v. Weaver, 761 F.2d 484, 487 (8th Cir. 1985) (because filing of single lawsuit did not involve serious misconduct, sham exception deemed inapplicable); Omni Resource Dev. Corp. v. Conoco, Inc., 739 F.2d 1412, 1414 (9th Cir. 1984) (single lawsuit deemed actionable only if suit is "baseless" and has "other characteristics of grave abuse"); Aircapital Cablevision, Inc. v. Starlink Communs. Group, 634 F. Supp. 316, 321 (D. Kan. 1986) (single lawsuit can be sham conduct "only if it involves a serious abuse, misuse, or corruption of the judicial process").

217. *See, e.g.*, CVD, Inc. v. Raytheon Co., 769 F.2d 842, 850-51 (1st Cir. 1985) (threat of unfounded litigation "is sufficient to constitute a cause of action under the antitrust laws, provided that the other essential elements of a violation are proven"), *cert. denied*, 475 U.S. 1016 (1986); Alexander v. National Farmers' Org., 687 F.2d 1173, 1200-03 (8th Cir. 1982) (*Noerr* immunity does not extend to threats to and harassment of customers regarding pending litigation). In Coastal States Marketing, Inc. v. Hunt, 694 F.2d 1358 (5th Cir. 1983), however, the Fifth Circuit observed:

> Given that petitioning immunity protects joint litigation, it would be absurd to hold that it does not protect those acts reasonably and normally attendant upon effective litigation. The litigator should not be protected only when he strikes without warning. If litigation is in good faith, a token of that sincerity is a warning that it will be commenced in a possible effort to compromise the dispute.

Id. at 1367; *cf.* Christianson v. Colt Indus. Operating Corp., 766 F. Supp. 670, 684 (C.D. Ill. 1991) (plaintiff raised question of material fact whether defendant's prelitigation threats "were limited to those reasonably and normally attendant upon effective litigation").

A second evaluative factor is the defendant's intent.[218] The Supreme Court has stated that the sham exception is designed "to cover activity that was not genuinely intended to influence governmental action."[219] The lower courts have used a variety of approaches to defining the requisite impermissible intent. In *Westmac, Inc. v. Smith*,[220] the Sixth Circuit embraced a comparatively narrow view of the conditions in which the defendant's intent will be deemed illegitimate.[221] The Sixth Circuit ruled that the "sham exception does not apply merely because a party files a suit with the principal purpose of harming his competitor."[222] The court framed the issue as whether the defendants (in filing a suit in state court) were "indifferent to obtaining a favorable judgment."[223] The court explained that "when a lawsuit raises a legal issue of genuine substance, it raises a rebuttable presumption that it is a serious attempt to obtain a judgment on the merits instead of a mere sham or harassment."[224] The Sixth Circuit affirmed summary judgment for the defendants, because the plaintiffs had failed to raise a triable issue with respect to this presumption.[225]

The Seventh Circuit has taken a more expansive view of the circumstances in which the defendant might be found to have acted with culpable intent. In *Premier Electrical Construction Co. v. National Electrical Contractors Association*,[226] the Seventh Circuit restated and refined the standard it first had articulated in *Grip-Pak, Inc. v. Illinois Tool Works, Inc.*:[227]

> We elaborated further in [*Grip-Pak*], holding that a suit brought only because of the costs litigation imposes on the other party also may fit the "sham" exception to the *Noerr-Pennington* doctrine. We explained: "Many claims not wholly groundless would

218. *See, e.g.*, Greenwood Utils. Comm'n v. Mississippi Power Co., 751 F.2d 1484, 1498 n.9 (5th Cir. 1985) ("determining whether the petitioning conduct was a sham often involves questions of motive or subjective intent").

219. Allied Tube & Conduit Corp. v. Indian Head, Inc., 486 U.S. 492, 508 (1988).

220. 797 F.2d 313 (6th Cir. 1986), *cert. denied*, 479 U.S. 1035 (1987).

221. Decisions that, like *Westmac*, have construed the sham exception narrowly also have tended to emphasize that plaintiffs who seek to invoke the sham exception should be held to higher standards of pleading. *See, e.g.*, Franchise Realty Interstate Corp. v. San Francisco Local Joint Exec. Bd., 542 F.2d 1076, 1082-83 (9th Cir. 1976) ("in any case, whether antitrust or something else, where a plaintiff seeks damages or injunctive relief, or both, for conduct which is prima facie protected by the First Amendment, the danger that the mere pendency of the action will chill the exercise of First Amendment rights requires more specific allegations than would otherwise be required"), *cert. denied*, 430 U.S. 940 (1977); Caplan v. American Baby, Inc., 582 F. Supp. 869, 870-71 (S.D.N.Y. 1984) (complaint alleging antitrust violations for conduct (such as filing a lawsuit) that enjoys prima facie first amendment protection "requires a greater degree of specificity . . . than would otherwise be the case" in order to avoid danger of chilling exercise of protected rights; plaintiff must make threshold showing of sham activity in order to go forward); City of Newark v. Delmarva Power & Light Co., 497 F. Supp. 323, 326 (D. Del. 1980) (antitrust plaintiff claiming sham behavior must "state the basis for this allegation in more than conclusory terms; his complaint must provide some basis for believing that what appears to be an exercise of the right to petition is in reality something else").

222. 797 F.2d at 317.

223. *Id.* at 318.

224. *Id.*

225. *Id.* at 319 n.9 ("It defies common sense to suggest defendants did not seek a favorable judgment.").

226. 814 F.2d 358 (7th Cir. 1987).

227. 694 F.2d 466 (7th Cir. 1982), *cert. denied*, 461 U.S. 958 (1983).

never be sued on for their own sake; the stakes, discounted by the probability of winning, would be too low to repay the investment in litigation." If the expected value of a judgment is $10,000 (say, a 10% chance of recovering $100,000), the case is not "groundless"; yet if it costs $30,000 to litigate, no rational plaintiff will do so unless he anticipates some other source of benefit. If the other benefit is the costs litigation will impose on a rival, allowing an elevation of the market price, it may be treated as a sham.[228]

By this test, a lawsuit could be deemed a sham unless a disinterested litigant would regard pursuit of the lawsuit as cost-justified.

A third formulation of the intent requirement is suggested in the Fifth Circuit's decision in *In re Burlington Northern, Inc.*[229] The Fifth Circuit held that litigation could be deemed a sham if it is "undertaken without a genuine desire for judicial relief as a significant motivating factor, or if there was no reasonable expectation of judicial relief, or if there was no reasonable basis for party standing."[230]

Burlington Northern also raised the question whether successful petitioning can be characterized as a sham. Although a number of decisions have concluded that

---

228. 814 F.2d at 372 (citation omitted); *cf.* City of Gainesville v. Florida Power & Light Co., 488 F. Supp. 1258, 1266 (S.D. Fla. 1980) (requisite impermissible motive consists of intent "to harm one's competitors not by the *result* of the litigation but by the simple fact of the *institution* of litigation") (emphasis in original).

229. 822 F.2d 518 (5th Cir. 1987), *cert. denied,* 484 U.S. 1007 (1988).

230. 822 F.2d at 533-34. *Burlington Northern* derived this standard in part from the Fifth Circuit's earlier decision in Coastal States Marketing, Inc. v. Hunt, 694 F.2d 1358, 1372 (5th Cir. 1983) (*Noerr* immunity exists for litigation "so long as a genuine desire for judicial relief is a significant motivating factor underlying the suit"). *See also* Original Appalachian Artworks, Inc. v. Granada Elecs., Inc., 816 F.2d 68, 74 (2d Cir.) (lawsuit not sham conduct "because there is no evidence that the suit was brought in bad faith, to harass, or in any way such that it would not be immune"), *cert. denied,* 484 U.S. 847 (1987); GTE Data Serv. v. Electronic Data Sys. Corp., 717 F. Supp. 1487, 1491 (M.D. Fla. 1989) (plaintiff adequately pled sham exception by alleging that defendant "in bad faith, knowing that the covenants were unenforceable, sued or threatened to sue its former employees to restrain competition"); Barq's v. Barq's Beverages, Inc., 677 F. Supp. 449, 453 (E.D. La. 1987) (*Noerr* immunity exists where "plaintiffs desire for judicial relief was a significant, motivating factor underlying the initiation of this lawsuit"); Disenos Artisticos Industriales, SA v. Work, 676 F. Supp. 1254, 1286 (E.D.N.Y. 1987) (lawsuit not sham conduct where not "brought in bad faith or without probable cause or to harass"); G. Heileman Brewing Co. v. Anheuser-Busch, Inc., 676 F. Supp. 1436, 1476 (E.D. Wis. 1987) ("the issue of intent that controls is whether the litigant wished to obtain its anticompetitive end through obtaining court-ordered relief or simply through the filing and maintenance of the lawsuit"), *aff'd,* 873 F.2d 985 (7th Cir. 1989); W.H. Brady Co. v. Lem Prods., 659 F. Supp. 1355, 1371-72 (N.D. Ill. 1987) (trademark action protected by *Noerr* when counterclaim plaintiff failed to show counterclaim defendant was not genuinely seeking relief); W. Goebel Porzellanfabrik v. Action Indus., 589 F. Supp. 763, 766-67 (S.D.N.Y. 1984) (antitrust immunity exists "[w]here holder of a valid copyright brings suit in good faith and based on reasonable grounds"); *cf.* United States v. Otter Tail Power Co., 360 F. Supp. 451, 451 (D. Minn. 1973) (sham existed where defendant's "repetitive use of litigation . . . was timed and designed principally to prevent the establishment of [competing] municipal electric systems and thereby to preserve defendant's monopoly"), *aff'd,* 417 U.S. 901 (1974). The *Burlington Northern* court also indicated that the act of defending a lawsuit can be treated as sham conduct. *See* 822 F.2d at 532-33 ("We perceive no reason to apply any different standard to defending lawsuits than to initiating them.").

successful litigation cannot be deemed a sham,[231] *Burlington Northern* held that litigation that ultimately succeeds can be treated as sham conduct.[232] This result appears to depend significantly upon the context in which the petitioning takes place. Courts have accorded less exculpatory weight to success when a defendant's procedural or substantive victory in a litigation forum may be an unreliable measure of the reasonableness of its claims.[233] Courts also have tended to discount the value of successful petitioning where the successful episode is offset by a large body

---

231.   *See, e.g.,* Eden Hannon & Co. v. Sumitomo Trust & Banking Co., 914 F.2d 556, 565 (4th Cir. 1990) (rejecting argument that a successful lawsuit can be a sham; stating that the defendant's "[i]ntent only becomes relevant once the invalidity of the legal claims is established"), *cert. denied,* 111 S. Ct. 1414 (1991); Columbia Pictures Indus. v. Redd Horne, Inc., 749 F.2d 154, 161 (3d Cir. 1984) (success on merits demonstrated validity of cause of action and precluded finding of bad faith); Pendleton Constr. Corp. v. Rockbridge County, 652 F. Supp. 312, 320 (W.D. Va. 1987) ("success belies any sham use of the governmental process"), *aff'd,* 837 F.2d 178 (4th Cir. 1988); WIXT Television, Inc. v. Meredith Corp., 506 F. Supp. 1003, 1032 (N.D.N.Y. 1980) ("by definition a successful claim cannot be a 'sham' "); *see also* Greenwood Utils. Comm'n v. Mississippi Power Co., 751 F.2d 1484, 1500 (5th Cir. 1985) ("in the absence of proof of a conspiracy with government officials, when a defendant succeeds in persuading the government to adopt his position, his petitioning conduct should not be considered sham activity"); *cf.* Allied Tube & Conduit Corp. v. Indian Head, Inc., 486 U.S. 492, 502 (1988) ("The effort to influence governmental action in this case certainly cannot be characterized as a sham given the actual adoption of the 1981 Code into a number of statutes and local ordinances."); Bill Johnson's Restaurants, Inc. v. NLRB, 461 U.S. 731, 747 (1983) (NLRB can enjoin only lawsuits that are brought with a retaliatory motive and lack a reasonable basis); Potters Medical Center v. City Hosp. Ass'n, 800 F.2d 568, 579 (6th Cir. 1986) ("relative success" of litigation "strongly suggests" no sham); Lender's Serv. v. Dayton Bar Ass'n, 758 F. Supp. 429, 440-41 (S.D. Ohio 1991) (defendants' success in prevailing before trial court and court of appeals is "further indication that defendants' suit was not baseless"); Baxter Travenol Labs. v. LeMay, 536 F. Supp. 247, 252 (S.D. Ohio 1982) (litigation success deemed "probably dispositive" of sham exception issue); Chest Hill Co. v. Guttman, 1981-2 Trade Cas. (CCH) ¶ 64,417, at 75,055 (S.D. Ohio 1981) (litigant's success on merits deemed "virtually conclusive" on sham exception issue).

232.   822 F.2d at 534; *see also* Video Int'l Prod., Inc. v. Warner-Amex Cable Communs., 858 F.2d 1075, 1083 (5th Cir. 1988) ("Although on its own . . . success might not be sufficient to prove that the petitioning activity is not a sham, . . . neither party seriously contends that [defendant] did not seek the end for which it petitioned."); Clipper Exxpress v. Rocky Mountain Motor Tariff Bureau, 690 F.2d 1240, 1254 (9th Cir. 1982) ("while success or failure . . . is not singularly determinative of a party's intent, this Circuit regards such success or failure as indicative of a party's intent"), *cert. denied,* 459 U.S. 1227 (1983); G. Heileman Brewing Co. v. Anheuser-Busch, Inc., 676 F. Supp. 1436, 1476-77 (E.D. Wis. 1987) (success creates strong but rebuttable inference that litigation is not a sham); Ross v. Bremer, 1982-2 Trade Cas. (CCH) ¶ 64,747 (W.D. Wash. 1982) (sham claim stated even though some of defendant's zoning cases were successful); Sunergy Communities Corp. v. Aristek Properties, Ltd., 535 F. Supp. 1327 (D. Colo. 1982) (success of action does not preclude finding that action was sham conduct).

233.   Success in satisfying a relatively lenient evidentiary or procedural standard may be deemed insufficient to preclude a finding of sham conduct. *See, e.g.,* Winterland Concessions Co. v. Trela, 735 F.2d 257, 263 & n.4 (7th Cir. 1984) (defendant's success in obtaining temporary restraining orders in ex parte proceedings deemed insufficient to preclude finding of sham conduct); Brownlee v. Applied Biosystems, 1989-1 Trade Cas. (CCH) ¶ 68,425 (N.D. Cal. 1989) (finding of sham not precluded by a court's refusal to dismiss a complaint in a prior suit); Shepherd Intelligence Sys. v. Defense Technologies, Inc., 702 F. Supp. 365 (D. Mass. 1988) (successful action for preliminary injunction could be deemed sham conduct owing to "rough justice" standard employed by state court).

of related failed claims.[234] Just as the fact of success is not always dispositive, a showing that the defendant's petitions have failed does not invariably produce a finding of sham behavior.[235] Finally, courts are likely to accord decisive weight to successful petitioning when the petitioning conduct is directed toward a legislative (rather than adjudicatory) body. Successful efforts to elicit legislative action typically preclude a finding of sham conduct.[236]

A third evaluative criterion is whether the petitioning in question serves to deny competitors access to government processes. In *California Motor Transport*, the Supreme Court described the defendants' repeated efforts to raise unmeritorious objections to the certification of competitors as "effectively barring . . . access" and eliminating "free and meaningful access" to state licensing authorities.[237] Some courts have interpreted these observations as limiting sham status to conduct that denies access to government bodies.[238] Most courts, however, have declined to

---

234. *See Burlington Northern*, 822 F.2d at 527-28. The litigation in *California Motor Transport* suggests that a nontrivial success rate in a large petitioning campaign may not invariably preclude a finding of sham conduct. In describing the boundaries of the sham exception in *California Motor Transport*, the Supreme Court emphasized that the defendant repeatedly had pressed claims "with or without probable cause." 404 U.S. at 515. The *California Motor Transport* defendants had initiated some forty proceedings to impede certification of the plaintiff's trucking operations. The trial court found that twenty-one of the forty proceedings "resulted in action favorable to the defendants." *See* Trucking Unlimited v. California Motor Transp. Co., 1967 Trade Cas. (CCH) ¶ 72,298, at 84,744 (N.D. Cal. 1967).

235. In CVD, Inc. v. Raytheon Co., 769 F.2d 842, 850 (1st Cir. 1985), *cert. denied*, 475 U.S. 1016 (1986), the First Circuit stated that "a patentee who has a good faith belief in the validity of a patent will not be exposed to antitrust damages even if the patent proves to be invalid, or the infringement action unsuccessful." *See also* First Am. Title Co. v. South Dakota Land Title Ass'n, 714 F.2d 1439, 1448 (8th Cir. 1983), *cert. denied*, 464 U.S. 1042 (1984); Alexander v. National Farmers' Org., 687 F.2d 1173, 1200 (8th Cir. 1982); Hydro-Tech Corp. v. Sundstrand Corp., 673 F.2d 1171, 1172-76 (10th Cir. 1982).

236. *See, e.g.,* Llewellyn v. Crothers, 765 F.2d 769, 775 (9th Cir. 1985) ("Since [petitioner's] lobbying efforts resulted in lawful action by the [legislature], we are presented with a required application of the *Noerr-Pennington* doctrine, and [petitioner's] conduct is immune from antitrust challenge."); Metro Cable Co. v. CATV of Rockford, Inc., 516 F.2d 220, 232 (7th Cir. 1975) (rejecting liability and emphasizing uncertainty about whether defendant's petitioning caused legislative outcome in question); Campbell v. City of Chicago, 639 F. Supp. 1501, 1509-10 (N.D. Ill. 1986) (sham exception rejected where defendant succeeded in persuading city council to enact favorable ordinance; sham not established by showing that city council rubber-stamped negotiated settlement between mayor and defendant), *aff'd*, 823 F.2d 1182 (7th Cir. 1987); First Nat'l Bank v. Marquette Nat'l Bank, 482 F. Supp. 514, 519 (D. Minn. 1979) (denying sham exception where defendant successfully petitioned legislative body), *aff'd*, 636 F.2d 195 (8th Cir. 1980), *cert. denied*, 450 U.S. 1042 (1981); *see also* Blank v. Kirwan, 39 Cal. 3d 311, 703 P.2d 58, 216 Cal. Rptr. 718 (1985) (in action under California's Cartwright Act, successful efforts of poker club to convince city council to restrict club licenses held immune; sham exception not applicable when lobbying efforts succeed).

237. 404 U.S. at 513, 515.

238. *See, e.g.,* Franchise Realty Interstate Corp. v. San Francisco Local Joint Exec. Bd., 542 F.2d 1076 (9th Cir. 1976) (dismissing complaint for failure to allege access barring), *cert. denied*, 430 U.S. 940 (1977); Racetrac Petroleum, Inc. v. Prince George's County, 601 F. Supp. 892, 910-11 (D. Md. 1985) (conspiracy between trade association and its members to oppose zoning application and special exception had neither purpose nor effect of barring access to government process; conduct deemed immune in absence of corruption of decisionmaking process by means of bribery or misrepresentation), *aff'd*, 786 F.2d 202 (4th Cir. 1986); Wilmorite v. Eagan Real Estate, Inc., 454 F. Supp. 1124, 1134-35 (N.D.N.Y. 1977) ("access-barring is the cornerstone to the sham

impose this requirement, chiefly on the ground that a complete denial of access is but one way in which vexatious petitioning can injure competition.[239]

A showing that petitioning has the effect of barring or restricting access does not mean that a sham characterization is appropriate. In *Omni*, the Supreme Court ruled that access-barring activities do not constitute a sham when they are conducted in the course of a genuine attempt to influence government action.[240] Proof that the defendant's lobbying for favorable government intervention precluded a government agency from considering the plaintiff's ideas did not establish a sham:

> Any lobbyist or applicant, in addition to getting himself heard, seeks by procedural and other means to get his opponent ignored. Policing the legitimate boundaries of such defensive strategies, when they are conducted in the context of a genuine attempt to influence governmental action, is not the role of the Sherman Act.[241]

Thus, *Noerr* immunity would appear to protect petitioning activity that genuinely seeks to elicit government intervention but also curbs a rival's access to public authorities.

(2) Supplying False Information

Noerr litigation sometimes involves claims that private parties have distorted government decisionmaking by providing public officials with false or misleading information. The *Noerr* Court held that a deceptive publicity campaign designed to persuade legislators and executive branch officials was immune from antitrust challenge.[242] *California Motor Transport* later observed that "[m]isrepresentations, condoned in the political arena, are not immunized when used in the adjudicatory process."[243] In *Allied*, the Court restated its rulings concerning the presentation

---

exception"), *aff'd mem.*, 578 F.2d 1372 (2d Cir.), *cert. denied*, 439 U.S. 983 (1978); Central Bank v. Clayton Bank, 424 F. Supp. 163 (E.D. Mo. 1976), *aff'd mem.*, 553 F.2d 102 (8th Cir.), *cert. denied*, 433 U.S. 910 (1977); *see also* Israel v. Baxter Labs., 466 F.2d 272 (D.C. Cir. 1972) (activities effectively precluding FDA consideration of plaintiff's application deemed sham conduct).

239. *See* Litton Sys. v. AT&T, 700 F.2d 785, 809 n.36 (2d Cir. 1983), *cert. denied*, 464 U.S. 1073 (1984); Clipper Exxpress v. Rocky Mountain Motor Tariff Bureau, 690 F.2d 1240, 1258-59 (9th Cir. 1982), *cert. denied*, 459 U.S. 1227 (1983); Ernest W. Hahn, Inc. v. Codding, 615 F.2d 830, 841 n.14 (9th Cir. 1980); Sage Int'l, Ltd. v. Cadillac Gage Co., 507 F. Supp. 939, 946-48 (E.D. Mich. 1981).

240. 111 S. Ct. at 1354-55.

241. *Id.* at 1355.

242. 365 U.S. at 140 ("Insofar as that [Sherman] Act sets up a code of ethics at all, it is a code that condemns trade restraints, not political activity, and . . . a publicity campaign to influence governmental activity falls clearly into the category of political activity.").

243. 404 U.S. at 513. In Walker Process Equipment, Inc. v. Food Machinery & Chemical Corp., 382 U.S. 172, 174 (1965), the Supreme Court held that the enforcement of a patent obtained through fraud on the Patent Office may violate § 2 of the Sherman Act. *Walker* contained no mention of the Court's earlier decisions in *Noerr* and *Pennington*, but it has provided a basis upon which some courts have concluded that providing spurious information to adjudicatory bodies can be actionable as monopolization or attempted monopolization. *See, e.g.*, Clipper Exxpress v. Rocky Mountain Motor Tariff Bureau, 690 F.2d 1240, 1261 (9th Cir. 1982) ("We hold that the fraudulent furnishing of false information to an agency in connection with an adjudicatory proceeding can be the basis for antitrust liability, if the requisite predatory intent is present and the other elements of an antitrust claim are proven."), *cert. denied*, 459 U.S. 1227 (1983); Woods Exploration & Prod. Co. v. Aluminum Co. of Am., 438 F.2d 1286, 1298 (5th Cir. 1971) (providing

of false or misleading statements to public officials and government bodies:

> A publicity campaign directed at the general public, seeking legislation or executive action, enjoys antitrust immunity even when the campaign employs unethical and deceptive methods. But in less political arenas, unethical and deceptive practices can constitute abuses of administrative or judicial processes that may result in antitrust violations.[244]

The *Allied* Court went on to observe that, in limited circumstances, misrepresentations in the legislative arena might not enjoy *Noerr* protection.[245]

Lower court decisions have emphasized the forum in which petitioning occurs in determining the antitrust significance of false or misleading speech. Misrepresentations designed to influence government bodies in performing what can be characterized as "legislative functions" tend to qualify for *Noerr* immunity.[246] By contrast, efforts to mislead officials performing adjudicatory functions or administrative duties in many instances have been denied *Noerr*'s protection[247] and

---

false information to state regulatory body performing adjudicatory tasks was "abuse of the administrative process" and did not warrant antitrust immunity), *cert. denied*, 404 U.S. 1047 (1972); Outboard Marine Corp. v. Pezetel, 474 F. Supp. 168, 179 (D. Del. 1979) (supplying false information with Treasury Department and Customs Service to induce government to impose duties and tariffs against foreign rivals).

244. 486 U.S. at 499-500; *cf. Omni*, 111 S. Ct. at 1356 (noting that in *Noerr*, "where the private party 'deliberately deceived the public and public officials' in its successful lobbying campaign, we said that 'deception, reprehensible as it is, can be of no consequence so far as the Sherman Act is concerned' ") (quoting *Noerr*, 365 U.S. at 145).

245. 486 U.S. at 504 (observing that "misrepresentations made under oath at a legislative committee hearing in the hopes of spurring legislative action" are not necessarily immune under *Noerr*).

246. *See, e.g.*, Boone v. Redevelopment Agency, 841 F.2d 886 (9th Cir.) (*Noerr* immunity applied to redevelopment agency's decision to cancel plans to build parking garage based upon false information provided by plaintiff's rivals; agency's action deemed "legislative" because city council reviewed its decisions), *cert. denied*, 488 U.S. 965 (1989); First Am. Title Co. v. South Dakota Land Title Ass'n, 714 F.2d 1439, 1447 (8th Cir. 1983) (antitrust plaintiff has "equal access to the legislature to lobby against the [proposed legislation] and to correct any 'misrepresentations' which may have been made"), *cert. denied*, 464 U.S. 1042 (1984); Mark Aero, Inc. v. TWA, 580 F.2d 288 (8th Cir. 1978) (rejecting claim that defendants provided false information to city officials); Metro Cable Co. v. CATV of Rockford, Inc., 516 F.2d 220, 228-29 (7th Cir. 1975) (misrepresentations immunized because they were made to city council, which "was a legislative body, acting as such, and the conduct challenged . . . thus occurred in a political setting"); Aurora Cable Communs. v. Jones Intercable, Inc., 720 F. Supp. 600, 602 (W.D. Mich. 1989) ("[M]isrepresentation in the political arena, as distinct from the judicial arena, is outside the scope of the Sherman Act.").

247. The Ninth Circuit's opinion in Clipper Exxpress v. Rocky Mountain Motor Tariff Bureau, 690 F.2d 1240, 1261 (9th Cir. 1982), *cert. denied*, 459 U.S. 1227 (1983), states the rationale for this view as follows:

> In the adjudicatory sphere, . . . information supplied by the parties is relied on as accurate for decision making and dispute resolving. The supplying of fraudulent information thus threatens the fair and impartial functioning of these agencies and does not deserve immunity from the antitrust laws.

See St. Joseph's Hosp. v. Hospital Corp. of Am., 795 F.2d 948, 955 (11th Cir. 1986) ("When a governmental agency such as [the State Health Planning Agency] is passing on specific certificate applications it is acting judicially. Misrepresentations under these circumstances do not enjoy *Noerr* immunity."); Israel v. Baxter Labs., 466 F.2d 272, 278 (D.C. Cir. 1972) (rejecting *Noerr* immunity for efforts to deceive the Food and Drug Administration into excluding plaintiff's drugs; stating that "No actions which impair the fair and impartial functioning of an administrative agency should be able to hide behind the cloak of an antitrust exemption."); Service Eng'g Co. v. Southwest Marine, Inc., 719 F. Supp. 1500, 1506 (N.D. Cal. 1989) (*Noerr* "privilege does not apply

may remain subject to antitrust scrutiny.[248]   Where *Noerr* immunity is denied, plaintiffs nonetheless may be required to show that the false information materially affected the government body's decisionmaking and caused the injury of which the plaintiff complains.[249]

(3) Conspiracies with Public Officials

Before *Omni*, some decisions had withheld *Noerr* immunity when private entities and public officials allegedly formed corrupt agreements to stifle competition.[250]

---

to the furnishing of false information to an agency or adjudicatory body – the First Amendment has not been interpreted to preclude liability for false statements"); Codex Corp. v. Racal-Milgo, Inc., 1984-1 Trade Cas. (CCH) ¶ 65,853, at 67,561 (D. Mass. 1984) (misrepresentation of facts to court and bad faith patent litigation could constitute sham conduct); TransKentucky Transp. R.R. v. Louisville & Nashville R.R., 581 F. Supp. 759, 770 (E.D. Ky. 1983) (refusing to dismiss claims of abuse of regulatory and judicial processes because "the commission of fraud and the knowing submission of false information do not enjoy immunity under the *Noerr* doctrine; plaintiffs need not allege "deprivation of access" in order to make out such claims).

248.   To the extent that *Noerr* immunity rests on the first amendment, such denial of *Noerr* protection appears to be in keeping with Supreme Court decisions denying first amendment value to deliverate misrepresentations of fact. *See* Hustler Magazine, Inc. v. Falwell, 485 U.S. 46, 52 (1988) ("False statements of fact are particularly valueless; they interfere with the truth-seeking function of the marketplace of ideas. . . . [The necessary] breathing space is provided by a constitutional rule that allows public figures to recover for libel or defamation only when they can prove *both* that the statement was false and that the statement was made with the requisite level of culpability.") (emphasis in original); McDonald v. Smith, 472 U.S. 479, 484 (1985) ("[P]etitions to the President that contain intentional and reckless falsehoods 'do not enjoy constitutional protection,' and may . . . be reached by the law of libel.") (quoting Garrison v. Louisiana, 379 U.S. 64, 75 (1964) (citation omitted)); Gertz v. Robert Welch, Inc., 418 U.S. 323, 340 (1974) ("there is no constitutional value in false statements of fact").

249.   *Compare* Interstate Properties v. Pyramid Co., 586 F. Supp. 1160, 1162-63 (S.D.N.Y. 1984) (misrepresentation to environmental agency that is not considered material to agency's decisionmaking and eventual conclusion deemed insufficient to constitute sham conduct) *and* Outboard Marine Corp. v. Pezetel, 474 F. Supp. 168, 178 (D. Del. 1979) ("[Plaintiff] faces substantial difficulties in proving the elements of the violation . . . that the material was indeed knowingly false, that the governmental agency relied exclusively or in large measure on false material in reaching its conclusion, and that antitrust injury actually flowed to [plaintiff] from the use of the data.") *with* Clipper Exxpress v. Rocky Mountain Motor Tariff Bureau, 690 F.2d 1240, 1261 (9th Cir. 1982) (even if false information did not mislead government agency, "the fraudulent furnishing of false information to an agency in connection with an adjudicatory proceeding can be the basis for antitrust liability"), *cert. denied*, 459 U.S. 1227 (1983).

250.   *See, e.g.,* Instructional Sys. Dev. Corp. v. Aetna Casualty & Sur. Co., 817 F.2d 639, 650 (10th Cir. 1987) ("bribery or misuse or corruption of governmental processes are outside the protection of the *Noerr-Pennington* doctrine"); Central Telecommuns. v. TCI Cablevision, Inc., 800 F.2d 711, 722 (8th Cir. 1986) (efforts to influence public officials not protected by *Noerr* when accompanied by "threats, intimidation, coercion or other unlawful acts"), *cert. denied*, 480 U.S. 910 (1987); Federal Prescription Serv. v. American Pharmaceutical Ass'n, 663 F.2d 253, 263, 265 (D.C. Cir. 1981) (observing "[t]hat a public official is persuaded by the entreaty of a lobbyist does not make him the lobbyist's co-conspirator," but stating that "[a]ttempts to influence governmental action through overtly corrupt conduct, such as bribes . . . are not normal and legitimate exercises of the right to petition, and activities of this sort have been held beyond the protection of *Noerr*"), *cert. denied*, 455 U.S. 928 (1982); Bieter Co. v. Blomquist, 1990-1 Trade Cas. (CCH) ¶ 69,083 (D. Minn. 1990) (bribery not entitled to *Noerr* immunity); Monarch Entertainment Bureau v. New Jersey Highway Auth., 715 F. Supp. 1290, 1303 (D.N.J.) (noting that "there are other possible exceptions to the [*Noerr*] doctrine such as the use of improper means, such as bribery"), *aff'd mem.*, 893 F.2d 1331 (3d Cir. 1989); *cf.* Oberndorf v. City & County of Denver, 900 F.2d 1434,

Judicial endorsement of what sometimes was labelled a "conspiracy exception" derived support from decisions such as *Allied*, in which the Supreme Court rejected the "absolutist position that the *Noerr* doctrine immunizes every concerted effort that is genuinely intended to influence governmental action."[251] In stating that the availability of *Noerr* immunity hinges upon "the source, context, and nature of the anticompetitive restraint,"[252] *Allied* indicated that the Court had "never suggested" that conduct such as bribery of public officials "merits protection."[253]

As discussed above,[254] *Omni* disavowed a conspiracy exception to *Noerr*.[255] In dicta, the *Omni* Court also suggested that *Noerr* immunity would extend to government intervention obtained by means of bribery or other illicit agreements between private actors and public officials.[256] *Omni* intimated that other regulatory mechanisms (such as anti-bribery statutes or conflict of interest prohibitions) are superior to the antitrust laws as tools for policing behavior in the political marketplace. *Omni* thus contradicts, without specifically addressing, the Court's earlier suggestion in *Allied* that bribery might not be entitled to *Noerr* protection.[257]

(4) Commercial Exception

Some courts have recognized a "commercial exception" to *Noerr* immunity where the government body acts in a purely commercial or proprietary capacity. Although it rejected a conspiracy exception to *Noerr* and state action immunity, *Omni*'s discussion of state action issues left open the possibility that *Parker v. Brown* immunity might be denied if the government acts "as a commercial participant in a

---

1440 (10th Cir. 1990) (pleading of conspiracy exception to *Noerr* deemed insufficient as plaintiffs submitted no "evidence indicating that any 'deal' was made, bribe taken"; noting that "bribery or misuse or corruption of governmental processes are outside the protection of the *Noerr-Pennington* doctrine; declining to address whether to adopt conspiracy exception); Sessions Tank Liners, Inc. v. Joor Mfg., 827 F.2d 458, 466 (9th Cir. 1987) (dictum) ("*Noerr-Pennington* does not extend to private parties who have entered into a 'conspiracy' with governmental actors"), *vacated on other grounds*, 487 U.S. 1213 (1988). *But see* Boone v. Redevelopment Agency, 841 F.2d 886, 897 (9th Cir.) ("*Noerr-Pennington* cannot be circumvented by merely alleging that a government official was involved in the alleged conspiracy."), *cert. denied*, 488 U.S. 965 (1989); Metro Cable Co. v. CATV of Rockford, Inc., 516 F.2d 220, 230 (7th Cir. 1975) (rejecting conspiracy exception to *Noerr* and noting that "[i]t would be unlikely that any effort to influence legislative action could succeed unless one or more members of the legislative body became such 'co-conspirators' ").

251. 486 U.S. at 503.
252. *Id.* at 499.
253. *Id.* at 504. The *Allied* Court also observed that dicta in *California Motor Transport*, 404 U.S. at 513, had stated that " 'bribery of a public purchasing agent' may violate the antitrust laws." 486 U.S. at 502 n.7.
254. *See* Section B.2.d of this chapter.
255. 111 S. Ct. at 1355; *see also* Municipal Utils. Bd. v. Alabama Power Co., 934 F.2d 1493, 1505 (11th Cir. 1991) ("[T]he Supreme Court has recently held that there is no 'public co-conspirator' exception to the *Noerr-Pennington* doctrine. *Omni, supra*. Accordingly, the Cities' claim under this theory is now foreclosed.").
256. 111 S. Ct. at 1353.
257. In *Allied* the Court said "one could imagine situations where the most effective means of influencing government officials is bribery, and we have never suggested that that kind of attempt to influence the government merits protection." 486 U.S. at 504; *California Motor Transport*, 404 U.S. at 513 (noting existence of "forms of illegal and reprehensible practice which may corrupt the administrative or judicial processes and which may result in antitrust violations").

given market."[258]   Because the Court used essentially the same reasoning in evaluating a proposed conspiracy exception under the *Noerr* and state action doctrines, one could infer that the *Omni* court might entertain a commercial participant exception to *Noerr* immunity.[259]

Lower courts decisions have taken divergent paths in considering a commercial exception to *Noerr*. The formative decision recognizing a commercial exception is *George R. Whitten, Jr., Inc. v. Paddock Pool Builders, Inc..*[260] In *Whitten*, the First Circuit addressed the defendant's efforts to persuade government purchasing agencies to specify its products for procurement under competitive bidding statutes. The court distinguished between activities designed to solicit change in procurement statutes (which would have received *Noerr* immunity) and efforts to influence the manner in which government purchasing officials exercised their discretion under existing statutes. Because the defendant engaged in the latter type of conduct, the court said it "should be subject to the same limitations as its dealings with private customers."[261]   Thus, the court concluded that "the immunity for efforts to influence public officials in the enforcement of laws does not extend to efforts to sell products to public officials acting under competitive bidding statutes."[262]

Other courts have rejected a commercial exception to *Noerr* immunity.[263]

---

258.   111 S. Ct. at 1351; *see also id.* at 1353 (mentioning "the possible market participant exception" to state action immunity).

259.   In *Allied*, the Court did not directly address the possibility of treating commercial activities differently. However, its "source, context, and nature" formula might be interpreted to withhold immunity when the government acts essentially as a commercial entrepreneur. 486 U.S. at 507.

260.   424 F.2d 25 (1st Cir.), *cert. denied*, 400 U.S. 850 (1970); *see* Federal Prescription Serv. v. American Pharmaceutical Ass'n, 663 F.2d 253, 263 (D.C. Cir. 1981), *cert. denied*, 455 U.S. 928 (1982); Israel v. Baxter Labs., 466 F.2d 272, 275-77 (D.C. Cir. 1972) (using *Whitten* framework to evaluate drug producers' efforts to persuade Food and Drug Administration to bar plaintiff's products from market); Hecht v. Pro-Football, Inc., 444 F.2d 931, 940-42 (D.C. Cir. 1971) (*Noerr* immunity inapplicable when petitioning deals with commercial activities of government that involve ministerial rather than policy-making functions), *cert. denied*, 404 U.S. 1047 (1972); Sacramento Coca-Cola Bottling Co. v. Chauffeurs, Teamsters & Helpers Local No. 150, 440 F.2d 1096, 1099 (9th Cir.) (approving commercial exception to *Noerr*), *cert. denied*, 404 U.S. 826 (1971); Hill Aircraft & Leasing Corp. v. Fulton County, 561 F. Supp. 667, 675-76 (N.D. Ga. 1982) (recognizing commercial exception to *Noerr*), *aff'd mem.*, 729 F.2d 1467 (11th Cir. 1984).

261.   424 F.2d at 33.

262.   *Id.; see also* United States v. North Dakota Hosp. Ass'n, 640 F. Supp. 1028, 1041-42 (D.N.D. 1986) (*Noerr* immunity unavailable when government acts as consumer); F. Buddie Contracting, Inc. v. Seawright, 595 F. Supp. 422, 439 (N.D. Ohio 1984) (withholding *Noerr* immunity for contractors who conspire with government purchasing officials to manipulate award of competitively bid contract); COMPACT v. Metropolitan Gov't, 594 F. Supp. 1567, 1572-73 (M.D. Tenn. 1984) (*Noerr* affords no "protection of *commercial* activity by businessmen when dealing with government in its *proprietary* capacity") (emphasis in original); City of Atlanta v. Ashland-Warren, Inc., 1982-1 Trade Cas. (CCH) ¶ 64,527 (N.D. Ga. 1981) (*Noerr* immunity held unavailable; city purchasing officials deemed to be performing commercial rather than policy-making functions). *But see* United States v. Johns Manville Corp., 259 F. Supp. 440, 453 (E.D. Pa. 1966) (immunity recognized for efforts to influence public officials to draft procurement specifications so narrowly that rivals are excluded).

263.   *See, e.g.*, Independent Taxicab Drivers' Employees v. Greater Houston Transp. Co., 760 F.2d 607, 612-13 (5th Cir.) (actions of taxicab company in obtaining exclusive control over airport's transportation service through contract with city upheld under *Noerr* despite "commercial" nature of firm's relationship with city), *cert. denied*, 474 U.S. 903 (1985); *In re* Airport Car Rental Antitrust Litig., 693 F.2d 84, 88 (9th Cir. 1982) ("There is no commercial exception to

Representative of this view is *Greenwood Utilities Commission v. Mississippi Power Co.*,[264] in which the Fifth Circuit evaluated an electric utility's efforts to contract with a federal agency to purchase all of the agency's output of electric power. Despite the defendant's anticompetitive aims in gaining exclusive access to the agency's generation capacity, the Court held that *Noerr* immunized the conduct. The Fifth Circuit found "no reason why the result should be different when the government's decision is embodied in a contract with a private entity rather than in a regulation or statute."[265] Administering a commercial exception to *Noerr* immunity would be "difficult, if not impossible . . . in a case . . . where the government engages in a policy decision and at the same time acts as a participant in the marketplace."[266]

(5) Tariff Filings

Noerr issues can arise when regulated firms submit tariffs to regulatory authorities. In such cases, regulated firms sometimes assert that *Noerr* immunizes the preparation and filing of tariffs with government regulators. One line of decisions has declined to recognize *Noerr* immunity. In *Litton Systems v. AT&T*,[267] an AT&T tariff compelled use of an AT&T interface device to connect non-AT&T telephone equipment into the Bell System network. AT&T had filed the challenged tariff with the Federal Communications Commission, which had not evaluated the propriety of the interconnection requirement. The Second Circuit concluded that *Noerr* was inapplicable:

> AT&T erroneously assumes that a mere *incident* of regulation – the tariff filing requirement – is tantamount to a request for governmental action akin to the conduct held protected in *Noerr* and *Pennington*. . . . The decision to impose and maintain the interface tariff was made in the AT&T boardroom not at the FCC. . . . The fact that the FCC might ultimately set aside a tariff filing does not transform AT&T's independent decisions as to how it will conduct its business into a "request" for governmental action or an "expression" of political opinion. Similarly, the FCC's failure to strike down a tariff at the time of its filing does not make the conduct lawful.[268]

Noerr-Pennington."), *cert. denied*, 462 U.S. 1133 (1983); United States Football League v. NFL, 634 F. Supp. 1155, 1179 (S.D.N.Y. 1986) (*Noerr* shields conduct "directed at government agencies acting in a proprietary capacity, even if such conduct may be characterized as anticompetitive"); Savage v. Waste Mgmt., Inc., 623 F. Supp. 1505, 1513 (D.S.C. 1985) (disposal firms' successful efforts to obtain exclusive contracts with county held immune, even if county's contractual relationship with private parties could be viewed as essentially commercial); Reaemco, Inc. v. Allegheny Airlines, 496 F. Supp. 546, 556 n.6 (S.D.N.Y. 1980) (efforts to prevent plaintiff from obtaining federal loans warranted *Noerr* immunity); BusTop Shelters, Inc. v. Convenience & Safety Corp., 521 F. Supp. 989 (S.D.N.Y. 1981) (*Noerr* immunity applied to deny claim of bus stop shelter franchisee who alleged injury as result of defendant's effort to apply pressure to government officials).

264. 751 F.2d 1484 (5th Cir. 1985).
265. *Id*. at 1505.
266. *Id*.
267. 700 F.2d 785 (2d Cir. 1983), *cert. denied*, 464 U.S. 1073 (1984).
268. *Id*. at 807-08 (emphasis in original); *see also* Jack Faucett Assocs. v. AT&T, 744 F.2d 118, 122-24 (D.C. Cir. 1984), *cert. denied*, 469 U.S. 1196 (1985); City of Kirkwood v. Union Elec. Co., 671 F.2d 1173, 1181 (8th Cir. 1982) (tariff filing "may not be used as pretext to achieve otherwise unlawful results"), *cert. denied*, 459 U.S. 1170 (1983); *In re* Wheat Rail Freight Rate Antitrust

Litton's approach is consistent with other authorities outside the tariff area that withhold *Noerr* immunity where collective action has substantial anticompetitive consequences and only incidentally involves governmental action.[269] Nonetheless, some decisions have identified circumstances in which *Noerr* immunity extends to tariff filings and related activities.[270]

c. POLITICAL BOYCOTTS

An important category of *Noerr* disputes has focused upon the circumstances in which immunity extends to concerted refusals to deal and other collective efforts using economic means to induce action by public officials. In *Noerr*, the Supreme Court emphasized that the railroads' lobbying efforts bore "very little if any resemblance to the combinations normally held violative of the Sherman Act."[271] Antitrust decisions dealing with collective activity usually focus upon "combinations ordinarily characterized by an express or implied agreement or understanding that the participants will jointly give up their trade freedom, or help one another to take away the trade freedom of others through the use of such devices as price-fixing agreements, boycotts, market-division agreements, and other similar arrangements."[272]

In *NAACP v. Claiborne Hardware Co.*,[273] the Court drew a distinction between collaborative arrangements undertaken to achieve noneconomic ends and boycotts to serve the economic interests of the participants. *Claiborne* involved a state tort law challenge to an agreement by black citizens to deny their patronage to white merchants in order to induce government officials and business leaders to meet a list of demands for equality and racial justice.[274] The Court ruled that the first

---

Litig., 579 F. Supp. 517, 537-38 (N.D. Ill. 1984) (ordinary tariff filing with ICC does not constitute request for government action and is not immune under *Noerr*), *aff'd*, 759 F.2d 1305 (7th Cir. 1985), *cert. denied*, 476 U.S. 1158 (1986).

269. In Continental Ore v. Union Carbide & Carbon Corp., 370 U.S. 690 (1962), the Canadian government appointed a wholly owned Canadian subsidiary of Union Carbide to be the exclusive purchasing agent for the government's Metals Controller. Continental Ore, a rival of Union Carbide, claimed that Union Carbide conspired with others to use its Canadian subsidiary and the purchasing authority delegated to that subsidiary to exclude Continental from selling in the market. The Supreme Court found that there was no evidence that the Canadian government approved the discriminatory purchasing of its agent. Moreover, the Court concluded that the conduct was "wholly dissimilar" to that in *Noerr* because the *Continental Ore* defendants "were engaged in private commercial activity, no element of which involved seeking to procure the passage or enforcement of laws." *Id.* at 707; *see also* F. Buddie Contracting, Inc. v. Seawright, 595 F. Supp. 422, 439 (N.D. Ohio 1984) (*Noerr* immunity inapplicable where award of competitive bid involved government body only incidentally).

270. *See, e.g.*, MCI Communs. Corp. v. AT&T, 708 F.2d 1081, 1155 (7th Cir.) (*Noerr* immunity applies to tariff filings unless the filing is "a pro forma publication perhaps required by law"), *cert. denied*, 464 U.S. 891 (1983); Clipper Exxpress v. Rocky Mountain Motor Tariff Bureau, 690 F.2d 1240, 1253-54 (9th Cir. 1982), *cert. denied*, 459 U.S. 1227 (1983); *cf.* United States v. Southern Motor Carriers Rate Conference, Inc., 672 F.2d 469, 477 (5th Cir. 1982) (*Noerr* immunity extends to rate filings and joint activities before public regulatory authorities, but not to prefiling collective efforts to devise proposed rates), *rev'd on other grounds*, 471 U.S. 48 (1985).

271. 365 U.S. at 136.

272. *Id.*

273. 458 U.S. 886 (1982).

274. The Mississippi Supreme Court previously had dismissed an antitrust cause of action. Thus, only the state tort claim was before the U.S. Supreme Court.

amendment shielded the boycott against the tort claim, even though the participants anticipated and intended that the boycott would impose economic harm upon the merchants:

> Unlike the railroads in [*Noerr*] . . . the purpose of petitioner's campaign was not to destroy legitimate competition. Petitioners sought to vindicate rights of equality and of freedom that lie at the heart of the Fourteenth Amendment itself. The right of the States to regulate economic activity could not justify a complete prohibition against a nonviolent, politically motivated boycott designed to force governmental and economic change and to effectuate rights guaranteed by the Constitution itself.[275]

The Court suggested that it might have reached a different result if the boycott's participants had been economic competitors.[276]

In *Allied*, the Court again explored the bounds of acceptable collective action to elicit adjustments in government agency behavior. The Court rejected the defendant's contention that *Noerr* shielded all collaborative efforts genuinely designed to shape government action:

> If all such conduct were immunized then, for example, competitors would be free to enter into horizontal price agreements as long as they wished to propose that price as an appropriate level for government ratemaking. . . . Horizontal conspiracies or boycotts designed to exact higher prices or other economic advantages from the government would be immunized on the ground that they are genuinely intended to influence the government to agree to the conspirators' terms. Firms could claim immunity for boycotts or horizontal output restrictions on the ground that they are intended to dramatize the plight of their industry and spur legislative action.[277]

The Court distinguished the *Allied* boycott participants from the *Claiborne* boycotters, who were "consumers who did not stand to profit financially from a lessening of competition in the boycotted market."[278]

The Court returned to the boycott issue in *Superior Court Trial Lawyers*, where it evaluated the defendants' concerted efforts to induce the District of Columbia to raise the hourly fees paid for representing indigent criminal defendants. The Court reiterated its observation in *Allied* that *Noerr* did not protect all concerted efforts to elicit government action; otherwise, the Court observed, *Noerr* could be invoked to immunize boycotts among rivals to obtain higher prices from government purchasers.[279] The Court also distinguished the trial lawyers from the *Claiborne* defendants:

> *Claiborne Hardware* is not applicable to a boycott conducted by business competitors who

---

275. 458 U.S. at 914; *see also* Missouri v. National Org. for Women, Inc., 620 F.2d 1301, 1315 (8th Cir.) (Sherman Act deemed inapplicable to use of boycott to influence legislation in noncompetitive political arena), *cert. denied*, 449 U.S. 842 (1980).
276. 458 U.S. at 915 (*Claiborne* boycott had neither been motivated by "parochial economic interests" nor "organized for economic ends").
277. 486 U.S. at 503 (citations omitted).
278. *Id.* at 508.
279. 493 U.S. at 427; *see also* Michigan State Medical Soc'y, 101 F.T.C. 191 (1983) (*Noerr* deemed inapplicable to coercive agreement by competing physicians not to participate in state Medicaid program unless reimbursement levels were increased).

"stand to profit financially from a lessening of competition in the boycotted market." No matter how altruistic the motives of respondents may have been, it is undisputed that their immediate objective was to increase the price that they would be paid for their services. Such an economic boycott is well within the category that was expressly distinguished in the *Claiborne Hardware* opinion itself.[280]

Finally, the Court concluded that the expressive content of the trial lawyers boycott was insufficient to preclude per se condemnation of the collective agreement to seek an increase in the lawyers' wages.[281]

d.   EVIDENTIARY ISSUES

Courts generally have held that the existence of a *Noerr* defense does not bar discovery of information relating to attempts to influence governmental action.[282] *Pennington* suggested that evidence of conduct immunized by *Noerr* may be admissible to establish the defendant's anticompetitive intent in engaging in other behavior that may be actionable under the antitrust statutes, provided that any prejudicial effect does not outweigh the probative value of the evidence.[283]   As interpreted by the Fifth Circuit in *Feminist Women's Health Center, Inc. v. Mohammad*,[284] *Pennington* establishes that the admissibility of evidence of protected activity "should be governed by a test that weighs the probativeness of and the plaintiff's need for the evidence against the danger that admission . . . will prejudice the defendant's first amendment rights."[285]

Courts generally have been wary of admitting such evidence, chiefly on the ground that the jury might impose liability on the basis of *Noerr*-immune conduct or that

---

280.   493 U.S. at 427 (citing *Allied*, 486 U.S. at 508).

281.   *Id.* at 429-32. The Court noted that "[a] rule that requires courts to apply the antitrust laws 'prudently and with sensitivity' whenever an economic boycott has an 'expressive component' would create a gaping hole in the fabric of [the antitrust] laws." *Id.* at 431-32.

282.   *See* Associated Container Transp. (Austl.), Ltd. v. United States, 705 F.2d 53, 58-60 (2d Cir. 1983) (discovery by Antitrust Division granted where civil investigative demand was claimed to be aimed at conduct protected by *Noerr*); North Carolina Elec. Membership Corp. v. Carolina Power & Light Co., 666 F.2d 50, 53 (4th Cir. 1981) (*Noerr* protection does not govern availability of discovery); Australia/Eastern U.S.A. Shipping Conf. v. United States, 537 F. Supp. 807 (D.D.C. 1982); *cf. In re* Burlington N., Inc., 822 F.2d 518, 533-34 (5th Cir. 1987) (attorney-client and work product privileges could be penetrated in discovery if legal advice had been given in the course of sham litigation unprotected by *Noerr*), *cert. denied*, 484 U.S. 1007 (1988).

283.   In *Pennington*, the Court stated:
    It would of course still be within the province of the trail judge to admit this evidence, if he deemed it probative and not unduly prejudicial, under the "established judicial rule of evidence that testimony of prior or subsequent transactions, which for some reason are barred from forming the basis for a suit, may nevertheless be introduced if it tends reasonably to show the purpose and character of the particular transactions under scrutiny."
    381 U.S. at 670 n.3 (citations omitted); *see also* United States Football League v. NFL, 842 F.2d 1335, 1373-75 (2d Cir. 1988).

284.   586 F.2d 530 (5th Cir. 1978), *cert. denied*, 444 U.S. 924 (1979).

285.   *Id.* at 543 n.7. The Fifth Circuit added that "[e]vidence of activity that is protected by the *Noerr* doctrine may be admitted to show the purpose and character of other activity." *Id.*; *see* MCI Commns. Corp. v. AT&T, 708 F.2d 1081, 1159-60 (7th Cir.), *cert. denied*, 464 U.S. 891 (1983); Coastal States Mktg., Inc. v. Hunt, 694 F.2d 1358, 1371 n.42 (5th Cir. 1983); Clipper Exxpress v. Rocky Mountain Motor Tariff Bureau, 690 F.2d 1240, 1263-64 (9th Cir. 1982), *cert. denied*, 459 U.S. 1227 (1983); United States v. AT&T, 524 F. Supp. 1336, 1354 n.7 (D.D.C. 1981).

broad admissibility of protected conduct will chill petitioning subject to first amendment protection.[286] Where the only probative evidence of a violation deals with activity protected by *Noerr*, courts usually will treat such evidence as inadmissible.[287] Cases admitting evidence of protected activity generally have involved evidence of antitrust violations other than *Noerr*-protected conduct.[288]

e. PETITIONING FOREIGN GOVERNMENTS

Requests for government intervention sometimes involve petitioning before instrumentalities of foreign governments. Antitrust disputes occasionally involve claims that abuses of foreign governmental processes facilitated the attainment of anticompetitive ends. The Supreme Court has not ruled whether *Noerr* immunity applies to petitioning of foreign government bodies, and lower court decisions have taken conflicting positions on this issue.[289] In its *Antitrust Enforcement Guidelines for International Operations*, the Department of Justice has stated that its policy "is

---

286. *See, e.g.*, Greenwood Utils. Comm'n v. Mississippi Power Co., 751 F.2d 1484, 1503 (5th Cir. 1985) (barring "[i]nferences of monopolistic conduct" from defendants' discussions with regulatory commission "because such conduct is protected by *Noerr-Pennington*"); Hospital Bldg. Co. v. Trustees of Rex Hosp., 691 F.2d 678, 688 (4th Cir. 1982) (rejecting jury instruction that withheld *Noerr* immunity for litigation "filed as part of an overall scheme to attempt to monopolize or exclude competition from the marketplace or otherwise violate the antitrust laws"), *cert. denied*, 464 U.S. 904 (1984); Feminist Women's Health Center, Inc. v. Mohammad, 586 F.2d 530, 543 n.7 (5th Cir. 1978) (first amendment interests deemed to outweigh plaintiff's need), *cert. denied*, 444 U.S. 924 (1979); United States Football League v. NFL, 634 F. Supp. 1155, 1181 (S.D.N.Y. 1986) ("evidence which by its very nature chills the exercise of First Amendment rights . . . is properly viewed as presumptively prejudicial"); United States v. AT&T, 524 F. Supp. 1336 (D.D.C. 1981) (evidence held not admissible). *But see* Lansdale v. Philadelphia Elec. Co., 692 F.2d 307 (3d Cir. 1982) (evidence held admissible for purpose of showing defendant's intent); *cf.* Cipollone v. Liggett Group, 668 F. Supp. 408, 411 (D.N.J. 1987) (in products liability case, presumption that evidence regarding protected activity would be prejudicial is "inappropriate" where petitioning was "ethically questionable").

287. *See, e.g.*, Bright v. Moss Ambulance Serv., 824 F.2d 819, 824 (10th Cir. 1987) (defendants' "enjoyment of the market share devolved from the protected activity cannot support allegations of market power"); Weit v. Continental Ill. Nat'l Bank & Trust Co., 641 F.2d 457, 467 (7th Cir. 1981) (denying admission of evidence concerning *Noerr*-protected activity where such evidence constituted the only direct evidence of alleged conspiracy), *cert. denied*, 455 U.S. 988 (1982).

288. *See, e.g.*, Alexander v. National Farmers' Org., 687 F.2d 1173, 1197-98 (8th Cir. 1982) (defendant engaged in anticompetitive conduct beyond protected activity); Webb v. Utah Tour Brokers Ass'n, 568 F.2d 670, 672 (10th Cir. 1977) (same); Household Goods Carriers' Bureau v. Terrell, 452 F.2d 152, 157-58 (5th Cir. 1971) (same). *But cf.* City of Cleveland v. Cleveland Elec. Illuminating Co., 734 F.2d 1157, 1164 (6th Cir.) (evidence of protected activity deemed inadmissible as being "cumulative" and "corroborative"), *cert. denied*, 469 U.S. 884 (1984).

289. *Compare* Coastal States Mktg., Inc. v. Hunt, 694 F.2d 1358, 1364, 1372 (5th Cir. 1983) (*Noerr* immunity deemed applicable to filing or joining in foreign lawsuits because *Noerr* doctrine "reflects not only first amendment concerns but also a limit on the scope of the Sherman Act") *and* United States v. AMAX, Inc., 1977-1 Trade Cas. (CCH) ¶ 61,467 (N.D. Ill. 1977) (*Noerr* immunity could be applied to attempts to influence Government of Canada) *with* Occidental Petroleum Corp. v. Buttes Gas & Oil Co., 331 F. Supp. 92, 107-08 (C.D. Cal. 1971) (declining to extend *Noerr* immunity to petitioning of foreign governments), *aff'd per curiam on other grounds*, 461 F.2d 1261 (9th Cir.), *cert. denied*, 409 U.S. 950 (1972) *and* Bulkferts, Inc. v. Salatin, Inc., 574 F. Supp. 6, 9 (S.D.N.Y. 1983) (same). *Cf.* Laker Airways v. Pan American World Airways, 604 F. Supp. 280, 287-94 & n. 20 (D.D.C. 1984) (holding that first amendment does not prevent enjoining a party from petitioning a foreign government, and citing with approval cases stating that *Noerr* does not apply to such petitioning, but declining to issue such an injunction on comity grounds).

not to prosecute the legitimate petitioning of foreign governments by foreign or U.S. firms in circumstances in which the United States protects such activities by its own citizens."[290]

C. Relationship Between Antitrust and Federal Regulation

The role of the antitrust laws in industries regulated under federal statutory schemes reflects the extent to which Congress intended to replace the antitrust regime with the regulatory regime. Where Congress has explicitly stated that the antitrust laws do not apply at all, or that they do not apply under the circumstances set forth in the regulatory statute, an express exemption is said to exist. There are also limited circumstances in which, despite the absence of an express statutory direction, exemption from the antitrust laws must be implied to preserve the integrity of a congressionally-mandated regulatory scheme. In still other circumstances, the possible application of the antitrust laws will be deferred under the doctrine of primary jurisdiction while the administrative agency with regulatory responsibility for the industry or area of commerce in question makes an initial determination of the dispute or an essential element thereof.

1. Express Exemptions

It is the exceptional instance in which a statute will contain a general exemption of an industry from the antitrust laws. In several industries, former statutory immunities disappeared with the advent of deregulation in those industries.[291] A general immunity conferred expressly by statute remains under a provision of the Shipping Act of 1984,[292] and the McCarran-Ferguson Act.[293]

Specific conduct may also be expressly exempted from the application of the antitrust laws under statutory schemes in which Congress has stated that agency approval confers antitrust immunity. For example, the Motor Carrier Act of 1980 and the Staggers Rail Act of 1980 both allow the Interstate Commerce Commission to approve industry rate bureaus that, in turn, are permitted to undertake certain joint rate-making and other limited activities with antitrust immunity.[294]

---

290. ANTITRUST DIV., U.S. DEP'T of JUSTICE, ANTITRUST ENFORCEMENT GUIDELINES FOR INTERNATIONAL OPERATIONS, at § 7 (1988), *reprinted in* Appendix E of this treatise and 4 TRADE REG. REP. (CCH) ¶ 13,109 (1988).

291. *See, e.g.*, Staggers Rail Act of 1980, Pub. L. No. 96-448, § 219, 94 Stat. 1926 (1980); Motor Carrier Act of 1980, Pub. L. No. 96-296, § 14, 94 Stat. 803, (1980); Airline Deregulation Act of 1978, Pub. L. No. 95-504, §§ 28, 30, 92 Stat. 1729, 1731 (1978).

292. 98 Stat. 72, 46 U.S.C. app. § 1706(a) (1988).

293. 59 Stat. 34, 15 U.S.C. §1012 (1988). The McCarran-Ferguson Act provides broad antitrust immunity for "the business of insurance" where regulated by state law, provided the conduct at issue does not constitute an agreement to or act of boycott, coercion or intimidation. *Id.* § 1013(b). See discussion at Subpart D.6 of this chapter.

294. Motor Carrier Act of 1980, Pub. L. No. 96-296, § 14, 94 Stat. 793, 803-08 (1980) (codified at 49 U.S.C. § 10706(b) (1988)); Staggers Rail Act of 1980, Pub. L. No. 96-448, § 219, 94 Stat. 1895, 1926-28 (1980) (codified at 49 U.S.C. § 10706(a) (1988)). The exempted activities are much more limited than under prior statutes. *See* Motor Carrier Act, 49 U.S.C. § 10706(b)(3)(D) (1988) (eliminating immunity for collective setting of single line rates and limiting immunity for collective setting of general rate increases or decreases); Staggers Rail Act, 49 U.S.C. §§ 10706(a)(3)(A)(i) and (ii) (1988) (eliminating single line rate immunity and limiting immunity for agreements on

The existence of express agency authority to confer antitrust immunity has not put an end to antitrust challenges in the industries for which such authority exists. Where conduct arguably within the scope of an agency's authority to immunize is challenged, courts are still required to determine whether the agency acted within its statutory authority in conferring immunity,[295] and whether the challenged activity fell within the immunity.[296]

Even where the responsible agency has not acted, whether because the matter has not been presented to the agency or because the agency has not made a decision, courts have sometimes found challenged conduct or transactions immune from antitrust prosecution. In these cases, the courts find that the agency's jurisdiction over the activity is "exclusive." Notwithstanding the absence of agency approval contemplated by the regulatory statute, these courts have deferred to the agency's experience with the effects of particular forms of anticompetitive practices in the industry, and to the need for uniformity in the treatment of issues of competition.[297] The Supreme Court has emphasized, however, that "exemptions from antitrust laws are strictly contrued . . . ."[298]

---

295. *See, e.g.,* FMC v. Seatrain Lines, 411 U.S. 726 (1973) (Commission's power to approve and thereby exempt intercarrier agreements did not extend to merger agreement); Coal Exporters Ass'n of U.S. v. United States, 745 F.2d 76 (D.C. Cir. 1984) (ICC improperly granted exemption for coal destined for export because of incorrect construction of "abuse of market power"), *cert. denied,* 471 U.S. 1072 (1985); Advanced Micro Devices v. CAB, 742 F.2d 1520 (D.C. Cir. 1984) (CAB grant of antitrust immunity to cargo rate agreement vacated for insufficiency of economic rationale); Arizona Pub. Serv. Co. v. United States, 742 F.2d 644 (D.C. Cir. 1984) (ICC finding of no market dominance and consequent lack of authority to scrutinize rates not the product of reasoned decision making); Brae Corp. v. United States, 740 F.2d 1023, 1054-55 (D.C. Cir. 1984) (ICC exceeded scope of Staggers Act exemption provision in adopting new car hire rules), *cert. denied,* 471 U.S. 1069 (1985).

296. *See, e.g.,* United States v. Bessemer & Lake Erie R.R. Co., 717 F.2d 593, 599-601 (D.C. Cir. 1983) (Interstate Commerce Act does not immunize illegal rate agreements which happen to coincide at points with legitimate actions of rate bureau); *cf.* Pinney Dock & Transp. Co. v. Penn Cent. Corp., 838 F.2d 1445, 1458-60 (6th Cir.) (court found Reed-Bullwinkle Act, 62 Stat. 472, 49 U.S.C. § 10706, and ICC policy immunized railroads' rate-making activities; court distinguished approach in *Bessemer*), *cert. denied,* 488 U.S. 880 (1988).

    Analysis of agency authority and regulatory scope is similarly employed in implied immunity cases, discussed in Subpart C.2 of this chapter.

297. *See* Pan Am. World Airways v. United States, 371 U.S. 296 (1963) (dismissing complaint in action contesting allocation of routes that predated Civil Aeronautics Board authority to approve routes that served the public interest); Far E. Conference v. United States, 342 U.S. 570 (1952) (dismissing complaint in action challenging rate agreement not filed with the Federal Maritime Commission).

298. FMC v. Seatrain Lines, 411 U.S. 726, 733 (1973) (citing United States v. McKesson & Robbins, Inc., 351 U.S. 305, 316 (1956)). Thus, for example, even though the *Pan American* and *Far East* cases found CAB and FMC jurisdiction to bar Justice Department efforts to obtain injunctions against the activities in question, the Supreme Court subsequently decided in Carnation Co. v. Pacific Westbound Conference, 383 U.S. 213 (1966), that the Federal Maritime Commission's "exclusive" jurisdiction over injunctive relief did not preclude a private treble damage action challenging an allegedly unfiled and unapproved rate agreement.

2. *Implied Exemptions*

A finding that an activity is exempt from the antitrust laws is not limited to matters in which agencies have express authority to approve and thereby immunize the activity. Where it appears to a court that a pervasive regulatory scheme would be disrupted by antitrust enforcement, the court may hold that the activity is impliedly immune.

Gordon v. New York Stock Exchange[299] illustrates this principle. In *Gordon*, plaintiffs challenged agreements by which New York Stock Exchange brokers fixed commission charges. Although these agreements were allowed under New York Stock Exchange rules, the Securities and Exchange Commission had statutory authority to alter the rules. The Supreme Court held that this authority to alter Exchange rules, supplemented by the SEC's actual review of commission charges, was sufficient to imply antitrust immunity for the commission-fixing agreements. The Court found that immunity was necessary to avoid the possibility of collision between the SEC's instructions to the Exchange and limits that might be imposed on the Exchange by an antitrust court.

In the implied repeal analysis, courts closely examine regulatory authority over the challenged activity to determine whether the statutory and regulatory framework is sufficiently comprehensive. The mere existence of complex regulation does not suffice to imply immunity.[300]

The courts have repeatedly relied on the Supreme Court's instruction that "[r]epeals of the antitrust laws by implication from a regulatory statute are strongly disfavored, and have only been found in cases of plain repugnancy between the antitrust and regulatory provisions."[301] The implication of repeal will be limited

---

299.   422 U.S. 659 (1975).

300.   *See, e.g.*, United States v. Rockford Memorial Corp., 898 F.2d 1278 (7th Cir. 1990) (hospitals not immune from antitrust merger restrictions), *cert. denied*, 111 S. Ct. 295 (1990); *In re* Wheat Rail Freight Rate Antitrust Litig., 759 F.2d 1305, 1313 (7th Cir. 1985) ("It was not true that rail carriers' activities were so pervasively regulated that the paradigm of competition had been foresworn by Congress for the rail industry." However, the court did find immunity under the *Keogh* doctrine.), *cert. denied*, 476 U.S. 1158 (1986); Southern Pac. Communs. Co. v. AT&T, 740 F.2d 980, 999-1000, (D.C. Cir. 1984) (no pervasive regulatory control over rates and interconnection decisions so as to conflict with antitrust laws), *cert. denied*, 470 U.S. 1005 (1985).

301.   United States v. Philadelphia Nat'l Bank, 374 U.S. 321, 350-51 (1963) (footnotes omitted); *see* Strobl v. New York Mercantile Exch., 768 F.2d 22, 27-29 (2d Cir.) (antitrust laws may not apply when they would prohibit an action the regulatory scheme might allow), *cert. denied*, 474 U.S. 1006 (1985); North Carolina v. P.I.A. Asheville, Inc., 740 F.2d 274 (1984) (antitrust immunity not implied in regulatory structure established by National Health Planning and Resources Department Act), *cert. denied*, 471 U.S. 1003 (1985); City of Kirkwood v. Union Elec. Co., 671 F.2d 1173, 1178 (8th Cir.) (no implied immunity because electric-utility regulatory scheme and antitrust laws not "plainly repugnant" to each other), *cert. denied*, 459 U.S. 1170 (1983); Phonetele, Inc. v. AT&T, 664 F.2d 716, 731-35 (9th Cir. 1981) (perceived repugnancy between antitrust laws and regulatory laws insufficient to establish finding of implied immunity; actual repugnancy must exist), *cert. denied*, 459 U.S. 1145 (1983); Marquis v. United States Sugar Corp., 652 F. Supp. 598 (S.D. Fla. 1987) (growers failed to show a "clear repugnancy" between antitrust laws and Department of Labor regulations); United States v. Braniff Airways, 453 F. Supp. 724 (W.D. Tex. 1978) (no implied immunity of agreement between airlines to eliminate competitor because there was not "plain repugnancy" between antitrust laws and Federal Aviation Act, which condemned cut-throat competition). *But see* Waldo v. North Am. Van Lines, 669 F. Supp. 722 (W.D. Pa. 1987) (exclusivity provisions in portions of trucking company's operating agreement with

to the activity challenged and will not extend to other conduct regulated by the same agency. As the Supreme Court emphasized in *Silver v. New York Stock Exchange*, "[r]epeal is to be regarded as implied only if necessary to make the [regulatory statute] work, and even then only to the minimum extent necessary. This is the guiding principle to reconciliation of the two statutory schemes."[302]

In *National Gerimedical Hospital & Gerontology Center v. Blue Cross*,[303] the Supreme Court applied this standard to refuse to exempt from antitrust scrutiny Blue Cross' exclusion of the plaintiff from an insurance plan, even though the decision was made in furtherance of a local health care planning scheme created in response to the National Health Planning and Resources Development Act.[304] Plaintiff had not sought approval of its plans to construct a hospital from the local advisory group created under the Act, and on this ground Blue Cross had rejected plaintiff's application to participate in the plan.[305] The Supreme Court denied Blue Cross immunity for its decision because, among other reasons, the local advisory group, although created and funded under federal law, was a private planning body, not a governmental agency charged with implementing a regulatory statute, and because no "clear repugnancy" between application of the antitrust laws to Blue Cross's decision and any provision of the Act or regulatory order was demonstrated.[306] The Court also expressly declined to create a "blanket exemption" for all conduct taken in response to the health planning process under the statute, finding this result consistent with its decisions in other industrial contexts.[307]

3. The Keogh Doctrine

In *Keogh v. Chicago & Northwestern Railway*[308] the Supreme Court held that a private shipper could not recover treble damages against railway companies that had set uniform rates duly filed with, and approved by, the Interstate Commerce Commission. The Court did not give the railway companies complete immunity from the antitrust laws — the Court expressly noted that Commission approval would not bar government antitrust proceedings[309] — but it held that a shipper could not recover antitrust damages from a carrier based on allegedly unreasonable rates. The Court rested its decision on four reasons, two of which demonstrate the Court's careful examination of the regulatory framework of the Interstate Commerce Act to

---

driver mandated by regulatory scheme of ICC, thereby providing antitrust immunity).

302. 373 U.S. 341, 357 (1963). Decisions applying these principles to various industries are discussed in Part D of this chapter.

303. 452 U.S. 378 (1981).

304. 42 U.S.C. §§ 300k-300n (1988).

305. 452 U.S. at 381.

306. *Id.* at 390-91.

307. *Id.* at 392 (citing Carnation Co. v. Pacific Westbound Conference, 383 U.S. 213 (1966) (maritime industry) and Otter Tail Power Co. v. United States, 410 U.S. 366, 373-74 (1973) (electric power industry)); *see also* City of Long Beach v. Standard Oil Co., 872 F.2d 1401, 1409 (9th Cir. 1989) (federal price control regulations do not supplant antitrust laws), *cert. denied*, 110 S. Ct. 1126 (1990). For a decision giving wide latitude to private regulatory bodies in amateur sports, see Behagen v. Amateur Basketball Ass'n, 884 F.2d 524 (10th Cir. 1989) (Amateur Sports Act directs monolithic control of amateur sports, therefore the actions of this association cannot be challenged on antitrust grounds), *cert. denied*, 110 S. Ct. 1947 (1990).

308. 260 U.S. 156 (1922).

309. *Id.* at 162.

support implied antitrust repeal.[310] First, the Court noted, the regulatory scheme allowed the recovery of damages for illegal rates in proceedings before the Commission. Although nothing in the statute explicitly precluded an antitrust remedy, the Court was persuaded that Congress could not have intended that there be an additional remedy for allegedly unreasonable rates. Second, the Court found that carrier rate regulation was primarily intended to prevent the charging of discriminatory rates. Uniform treatment of shippers could not be achieved if different measures of relief were available to different shippers in antitrust actions.

The vitality of the "filed rate" doctrine developed in *Keogh* was confirmed by the Supreme Court in *Square D Company v. Niagara Frontier Tariff Bureau*.[311] *Square D* involved a suit by shippers against the collective rate-making activities of an association of motor carriers. The Supreme Court first determined that the carriers' rates had been duly filed with the Interstate Commerce Commission and hence were lawful rates "in the same sense that the rates filed in *Keogh* were lawful."[312] The Court then turned to the question whether it should overrule *Keogh*. The Second Circuit had examined at some length the rationales set forth in *Keogh* and found most of them unpersuasive today, but nonetheless had applied *Keogh* to affirm dismissal of the shippers' treble damage claims.[313] The Supreme Court found persuasive Congress's failure to change the *Keogh* interpretation of the ICC statutory scheme when it had reexamined the same area of law only a few years earlier.[314] The Court reiterated, however, the limits of the "filed rate" doctrine, noting that *Keogh* does not create broad antitrust "immunity," but merely precludes treble damage recovery in an action by a private shipper arising from rates approved by the ICC.[315]

The filed rate doctrine is limited to allegations that rates filed and approved are unreasonable. The courts of appeal have declined to extend the doctrine to rates ultimately disproved,[316] to filed rates of which agency consideration was expressly postponed,[317] and to challenges to the mere adoption, as opposed to the reasonableness, of a filed rate.[318]

The courts of appeal are divided, however, on the applicability of the filed rate

---

310.   The Court's additional reasoning reflected its concern that a shipper's proof of damages would have to be premised on a hypothetical lower rate and further on speculation that the lower rate would have benefitted him.

311.   476 U.S. 409 (1986).

312.   *Id.* at 417.

313.   Square D Co. v. Niagara Frontier Tariff Bureau, 760 F.2d 1347 (2d Cir. 1985), *aff'd*, 476 U.S. 409 (1986).

314.   476 U.S. at 418-20.

315.   *Id.* at 422. The Supreme Court most recently confirmed the "filed rate doctrine" outside the antitrust context in Maislin Indus., U.S., Inc. v. Primary Steel, Inc., 110 S. Ct. 2759 (1990).

316.   City of Groton v. Connecticut Power & Light Co., 662 F.2d 921, 929 (2d Cir. 1981).

317.   Essential Communs. Sys. v. AT&T, 610 F.2d 1114, 1124 (3d Cir. 1979).

318.   Litton Sys. v. AT&T, 700 F.2d 785, 820-21 (2d Cir. 1983) (filed rate doctrine inapplicable when issue was not the reasonableness of interface tariff rate but whether the interface device requirement itself was reasonable), *cert. denied*, 464 U.S. 1073 (1984); *see also* Wileman Bros. & Elliott, Inc. v. Giannini, 909 F.2d 332, 337 (9th Cir. 1990) (failure of Secretary of Agriculture to disapprove standards implemented by private producers did not provide treble damages protection); City of Kirkwood v. Union Elec. Co., 671 F.2d 1173, 1179 (8th Cir. 1982) (allegations that interaction of filed rates created "price squeeze" not barred by filed rate doctrine), *cert. denied*, 459 U.S. 1170 (1983).

doctrine to actions brought by competitors rather than customers. Those declining to apply it to competitor lawsuits have held the view that the regulatory goal of achieving rate uniformity for customers is not undercut by affording the treble damage remedy in competitor suits.[319] The Sixth Circuit, however, extended the *Keogh* doctrine to a competitor lawsuit in *Pinney Dock & Transport Co. v. Penn Central Corp.*[320] Acknowledging that "the anti-discrimination arguments behind the *Keogh* doctrine lose their force" in lawsuits brought by competitors, the Sixth Circuit interpreted the Interstate Commerce Act as reflecting an assumption that the ICC takes competition policy into account in approving rates.[321] The court also noted that plaintiffs in the matter before it had the right to complain to the ICC about the challenged rates.[322] Analyzing plaintiffs' claims, the court held that those claims unrelated to the reasonableness of filed rates should be allowed to proceed, and that plaintiffs should be afforded opportunity to amend their complaint to clarify their allegations where the court could not determine whether *Keogh* applied.[323]

4. Primary Jurisdiction

Even when the antitrust laws are not entirely displaced by a regulatory scheme and a court declines to find that, expressly or impliedly, agency jurisdiction is exclusive, the court may defer consideration of antitrust issues until one or more regulatory agencies with "primary jurisdiction" has had an opportunity to consider a dispute. Deferring to the agency may avoid unnecessary or premature disturbance of a complex regulatory scheme by a court's application of the antitrust laws.[324] Deferral may also permit the agency to decide factual and legal issues within its particular expertise and aid the court in determining the application of the antitrust laws in the particular circumstances.[325] Courts asked to apply the primary jurisdiction doctrine will examine closely the nature of the relevant regulatory scheme to determine whether Congress "intend[ed] an administrative body to have the first word."[326]

"Primary jurisdiction" has been applied both to stay court antitrust proceedings until an agency has made an initial determination,[327] and to dismiss court

---

319. *See* City of Kirkwood v. Union Elec. Co, 671 F.2d 1173, 1179 (8th Cir. 1982), *cert. denied*, 459 U.S. 1170 (1983); City of Groton v. Connecticut Power & Light Co., 662 F.2d 921, 929 (2d Cir. 1981); Essential Communs. Sys. v. AT&T, 610 F.2d 1114, 1121 (3d Cir. 1979).

320. 838 F.2d 1445 (6th Cir.), *cert. denied*, 488 U.S. 880 (1988).

321. *Id.* at 1457.

322. *Id.*

323. *Id.* at 1457-58.

324. Mt. Hood Stages, Inc. v. Greyhound Corp., 616 F.2d 394, 399 (9th Cir.), *cert. denied*, 449 U.S. 831 (1980).

325. Ricci v. Chicago Mercantile Exch., 409 U.S. 289, 305-06 (1973); *Mt. Hood Stages*, 616 F.2d at 398-99.

326. United States v. General Dynamics Corp., 828 F.2d 1356, 1362 (9th Cir. 1987). *See generally* United States v. ABC, 1977-2 Trade Cas. (CCH) ¶ 61,580, at 72,371 (C.D. Cal. 1977); United States v. CBS, 1977-1 Trade Cas. (CCH) ¶ 61,327, at 71,139 (C.D. Cal. 1977); United States v. NBC, 1974-1 Trade Cas. (CCH) ¶ 74,885, at 95,992 (C.D. Cal. 1973).

327. *See, e.g.*, Segal v. AT&T, 606 F.2d 842 (9th Cir. 1979); Foremost Int'l Tours, Inc. v. Qantas Airways Ltd., 379 F. Supp. 88 (D. Haw. 1974), *aff'd*, 525 F.2d 281 (9th Cir. 1975), *cert. denied*, 429 U.S. 816 (1976).

proceedings without prejudice to recommencement after agency action.[328] Some courts have also applied the primary jurisdiction doctrine to stay or dismiss without prejudice an antitrust case pending consideration by state agencies.[329]

Some courts have tolled the four-year limitation period under equitable principles in order to prevent a party from being denied a chance to litigate its claim after an agency determination has been made.[330] More recently, however, courts have declined to do so.[331]

In *Ricci v. Chicago Mercantile Exchange*,[332] the Supreme Court set forth the circumstances under which a court should await initial agency review of an issue before deciding antitrust questions. Ricci claimed that the Chicago Mercantile Exchange had conspired with an Exchange member to prevent his trading on the Exchange. The action alleged a Section 1 restraint of trade and a violation of the Commodity Exchange Act. The Supreme Court held that the antitrust action should be stayed until the Commodity Exchange Commission had acted. It concluded that the antitrust court ultimately would have to determine whether any provisions of the Commodity Exchange Act were incompatible with antitrust enforcement, and that because "some facets" of the dispute were within the statutory jurisdiction of the Commodity Exchange Commission, the Commission's adjudication of the dispute

---

328. *See, e.g.*, Sea-Land Serv. v. Alaska R.R., 1980-2 Trade Cas. (CCH) ¶ 63,481, at 76,527 (D.D.C. 1980), *aff'd on other grounds*, 659 F.2d 243 (D.C. Cir. 1981), *cert. denied*, 455 U.S. 919 (1982); Luckenbach S.S. Co. v. United States, 179 F. Supp. 605 (D. Del. 1959) (dismissal on ground that courts must await ICC action before considering antitrust issues raised by filing of rate schedule), *aff'd in part and vacated in part per curiam*, 364 U.S. 280 (1960); *see also* City of Mishawaka v. American Elec. Power Corp., 616 F.2d 976 (7th Cir. 1980), *cert. denied*, 449 U.S. 1096 (1981); Meditech Int'l Co. v. Minigrip, Inc., 648 F. Supp. 1488 (N.D. Ill. 1986) (court stayed action but urged plaintiff to consider dismissal with unqualified leave to reinstate).

329. Industrial Communs. Sys. v. Pacific Tel. & Tel. Co., 505 F.2d 152 (9th Cir. 1974); United States v. Southern Motor Carriers Rate Conference, Inc., 439 F. Supp. 29 (N.D. Ga. 1977), *aff'd en banc on other grounds*, 702 F.2d 532 (5th Cir. 1983), *rev'd on other grounds*, 471 U.S. 48 (1985); Communications Brokers of Am. v. Chesapeake & Potomac Tel. Co., 370 F. Supp. 967 (W.D. Va. 1974). *But see* San Juan Racing Ass'n v. Asociacion de Jinetes de Puerto Rico, 590 F.2d 31 (1st Cir. 1979) (activities deemed not to be within primary jurisdiction of state racing administration); Litton Sys. v. Southwestern Bell Tel. Co., 539 F.2d 418 (5th Cir. 1976) (where state agencies merely acquiesce in activity, and no coherent state policy favoring it is indicated, doctrine of primary jurisdiction is inapplicable).

330. Mt. Hood Stages, Inc. v. Greyhound Corp., 616 F.2d 394, 399-400 (9th Cir. 1980) (even though plaintiff did not file suit until after the limitation period passed, court tolled the statute because it would have stayed or dismissed plaintiffs' antitrust claim pending an ICC determination; plaintiffs were not penalized for "proceeding in accordance with the integrated remedial scheme developed to accommodate the purpose of antitrust laws and the Interstate Commerce Act"), *cert. denied*, 449 U.S. 831 (1980). In Sea Land Service v. Alaska Railroad, 1980-2 Trade Cas. (CCH) ¶ 63,481 (D.D.C. 1980), the district court concluded dismissal was appropriate because plaintiffs suffered no past damages from the alleged antitrust violations and there was no imminent danger of the action being barred by the statute of limitations. *Id.* at 76,527.

331. Higgins v. New York Stock Exch., 942 F.2d 829 (2d Cir. 1991) (limitation period not tolled by proceeding brought before SEC by broker); Community Elec. Serv. v. National Elec. Contractors Ass'n, 869 F.2d 1235, 1241 (9th Cir. 1989) (limitation period not tolled because agency determination not a prerequisite to review in federal court), *cert. denied*, 493 U.S. 891 (1989); Brunswick Corp. v. Riegel Textile Corp., 752 F.2d 261 (7th Cir. 1984) (court did not toll the statute despite administrative proceeding, because alleged fraudulent procurement of patent not within the patent office primary jurisdiction), *cert. denied*, 472 U.S. 1018 (1985).

332. 409 U.S. 289 (1973).

"promise[d] to be of material aid [to the court] in resolving the immunity question."[333] Thus the Court established that deferral of an antitrust action pending administrative proceedings is proper when agency consideration of matters within the agency's jurisdiction will materially aid the court in resolving the antitrust issue.

Consistent with the *Ricci* standard, courts will not employ the doctrine of primary jurisdiction if the agency determination will not affect the status of the antitrust claim.[334] Thus, in *International Travel Arrangers, Inc. v. Western Airlines*,[335] the Eighth Circuit declined to apply the primary jurisdiction doctrine because a determination by the Civil Aeronautics Board (CAB) on unfair competition, an issue that fell within the CAB's regulatory authority, would not have clarified the antitrust questions presented.[336]

Courts also may refuse to defer to an agency if the questions involved are essentially legal and not factual, and thus are not peculiarly within the agency's special expertise.[337] If primarily legal questions are at issue, the courts have no need to "avail themselves of the aid implicit in the agency's superiority in gathering the relevant facts and in marshalling them into a meaningful pattern."[338] Some courts have also declined to defer to agency jurisdiction under the primary jurisdiction doctrine where the regulatory statute provides only partial or prospective regulation of the challenged conduct.[339]

---

333. *Id.* at 302. The Court noted that "[o]f course, the question of immunity, as such, will not be before the agency; but if Ricci's complaint is sustained, the immunity issue will dissolve, whereas if it is rejected and the conduct of the Exchange warranted by a valid membership rule, the court will be in a much better position to determine whether the antitrust action should go forward." *Id.* at 306.

334. *See* Telecom Plus v. Local No. 3, 719 F.2d 613, 615 (2d Cir. 1983) (deferral not appropriate where controlling issue in antitrust claim against union was wholly unrelated to the issue before the NLRB); International Travel Arrangers, Inc. v. Western Airlines, 623 F.2d 1255 (8th Cir.), *cert. denied*, 449 U.S. 1063 (1980); United States v. NBC, 1974 Trade Cas. (CCH) ¶ 74,885 (C.D. Cal. 1974) (nothing the FCC was empowered to adjudicate would resolve the issues before the court; FCC rules provided for future conduct and thus had no bearing on past antitrust violations); Marnell v. United Parcel Serv., 260 F. Supp. 391 (N.D. Cal. 1966) (an agency determination that rates and practices were just, reasonable and not unduly discriminatory would not be determinative or useful in determining the issue of monopoly presented in the case).

335. 623 F.2d 1255 (8th Cir.), *cert. denied*, 449 U.S. 1063 (1980).

336. *Id.* at 1259.

337. *See, e.g.*, Interstate Commerce Comm'n v. Big Sky Farmers & Ranchers Mktg. Coop., 451 F.2d 511, 515 (9th Cir. 1971); *see also* TransKentucky Transp. R.R. v. Louisville & Nashville R.R., 581 F. Supp. 759, 772 (E.D. Ky. 1983) (court refused to refer case to ICC under doctrine of primary jurisdiction where resolution of issues did not require special competence of agency).

338. *Ricci*, 409 U.S. at 305-06 (quoting Federal Maritime Bd. v. Isbrandtsen Co., 356 U.S. 481, 498 (1958)).

339. *See* City of Mishiwaka v. Indiana & Mich. Elec. Co., 560 F.2d 1314, 1324 (7th Cir. 1977) (award of antitrust damages for past conduct would not disrupt Federal Power Commission's authority to regulate future rates), *cert. denied*, 436 U.S. 922 (1978); Breen Air Freight, Ltd. v. Air Cargo, Inc., 470 F.2d 767, 774 (2d Cir. 1972) (affirming refusal to stay antitrust action pending administrative action by CAB when the issues were not technical in nature, there was no need to seek uniformity, and CAB could not award monetary damages sought by plaintiff), *cert. denied*, 411 U.S. 932 (1973); *see also* Long Lake Energy Corp. v. Niagara Mohawk Power Corp., 700 F. Supp. 186, 189 (S.D.N.Y. 1988) (primary jurisdiction not applicable where agencies lacked power to grant treble damages or broad injunction and legislative history of statute administered by agencies indicated that Congress did not intend that agency proceedings forestall antitrust actions);

D. Particular Industries and Markets

1. Agriculture

Congress has enacted a series of statutes granting agricultural producers the right to combine into associations and to engage in cooperative functions without violating the antitrust laws. Section 6 of the 1914 Clayton Act provides that:

> Nothing contained in the antitrust laws shall be construed to forbid the existence and operation of . . . agricultural, or horticultural organizations, instituted for the purposes of mutual help, and not having capital stock or conducted for profit, or to forbid or restrain individual members of such organizations from lawfully carrying out the legitimate objects thereof; nor shall such organizations, or the members thereof, be held or construed to be illegal combinations or conspiracies in restraint of trade, under the antitrust laws.[340]

In 1922, Congress expanded the cooperative exemption by passing the Capper-Volstead Act,[341] Section 1 of which provides that:

> Persons engaged in the production of agricultural products as farmers, planters, ranchmen, dairymen, nut or fruit growers may act together in associations, corporate or otherwise, with or without capital stock, in collectively processing, preparing for market, handling, and marketing in interstate and foreign commerce, such products of persons so engaged. Such associations may have marketing agencies in common; and such associations and their members may make the necessary contracts and agreements to effect such purposes

subject to specified limitations on the organizational structure of the cooperative. Section 2 of the Act, however, authorizes the Secretary of Agriculture to proceed against cooperative associations that have monopolized or restrained trade "to such an extent that the price of any agricultural product is unduly enhanced."[342]

The Cooperative Marketing Act of 1926 authorizes agricultural producers and associations to acquire and exchange "past, present and prospective" pricing,

---

Aloha Airlines v. Hawaiian Airlines, 349 F. Supp. 1064, 1068 (D. Haw. 1972) (declining to apply primary jurisdiction doctrine in case based on past conduct of airline when CAB had no power to award damages for past anticompetitive actions, but was limited to cease and desist orders against prospective conduct), aff'd, 489 F.2d 203 (9th Cir. 1973), cert. denied, 417 U.S. 913 (1974).

340.   15 U.S.C. § 17 (1988). The legislative histories of the Clayton Act § 6 and the Capper-Volstead Act (7 U.S.C. §§ 291-292 (1988)) are discussed in Maryland & Virginia Milk Producers Ass'n v. United States, 362 U.S. 458, 464-67 (1960) and Fairdale Farms v. Yankee Milk, Inc., 635 F.2d 1037, 1040-43 (2d Cir. 1980), cert. denied, 454 U.S. 818 (1981). See generally Tigner v. Texas, 310 U.S. 141 (1940), where the Court summarized the agricultural exemption legislation as follows:
>   [A]n impressive legislative movement bears witness to general acceptance of the view that the differences between agriculture and industry call for differentiation in the formulation of public policy. . . .
>   At the core of all these enactments lies a conception of price and production policy for agriculture very different from that which underlies the demands made upon industry and commerce by anti-trust laws.

Id. at 145-46 (footnote omitted).

341.   7 U.S.C. § 291 (1988). In 1934, fishermen were also granted the right to form cooperatives by the Fisherman's Collective Marketing Act, 15 U.S.C. §§ 521-522 (1988), which was patterned after the Capper-Volstead Act.

342.   7 U.S.C. § 292 (1988).

production, and marketing data.[343] Internal payments by cooperatives to their members are exempt from the Robinson-Patman Act.[344] The Agricultural Marketing Agreement Act of 1937 grants an exemption from the antitrust laws for marketing agreements between the Secretary of Agriculture and processors, producers, associations of producers, and others engaged in the handling of any agricultural commodity or product.[345] The Agricultural Fair Practices Act of 1967 makes it unlawful for "handlers" — defined to include both processors and producer associations — to coerce any producer in his decision whether to join a cooperative.[346]

In *United States v. Borden Co.*,[347] the Supreme Court upheld an indictment under Section 1 of the Sherman Act charging a dairy cooperative with having conspired with milk processors and distributors, a union, and local health officials to fix milk prices. The Court held that the Capper-Volstead Act, which exempts combinations of farmers from antitrust prosecution, did not authorize a cooperative to combine or conspire with persons outside the cooperative to fix prices or restrain trade.[348]

The Supreme Court addressed the Capper-Volstead exemption, as well as Section 6 of the Clayton Act, in *Maryland & Virginia Milk Producers Association v. United States*,[349] in which it concluded that a cooperative is not protected by the Capper-Volstead exemption when it monopolizes or attempts to monopolize by engaging in predatory or otherwise anticompetitive practices.[350] In such cases a cooperative is subject to the same antitrust liability as a private corporation.[351]

---

343. *Id.* § 455.

344. 15 U.S.C. § 13b (1988); 7 U.S.C. § 207(f) (1988).

345. 7 U.S.C. § 608(b) (1988); *see* United States v. Rock Royal Coop., 307 U.S. 533 (1939); *In re* Midwest Milk Monopolization Litig., 380 F. Supp. 880, 885 (W.D. Mo. 1974) (limiting exemption to marketing agreements and not marketing orders). *But see* Chiglades Farm v. Butz, 485 F.2d 1125 (5th Cir. 1973) (exemption also applies to marketing orders), *cert. denied*, 417 U.S. 968 (1974). *See generally* Berning v. Gooding, 820 F.2d 1550 (9th Cir. 1987) (administrative committee not liable under Clayton Act for its recommendations to Secretary of Agriculture pursuant to Agricultural Adjustment Act, 7 U.S.C. §§ 601-626 (1988)); United States v. Maryland & Va. Milk Producers Ass'n, 90 F. Supp. 681 (D.D.C. 1950), *rev'd on other grounds*, 193 F.2d 907 (D.C. Cir. 1951).

346. 7 U.S.C. §§ 2301-2306 (1988); *see* Michigan Canners & Freezers Ass'n v. Agricultural Mktg. & Bargaining Bd., 467 U.S. 461 (1984) (Agricultural Fair Practices Act preempts Michigan statute that accredited cooperative association as exclusive bargaining agent for all producers of a commodity); Newark Gardens, Inc. v. Michigan Potato Indus. Comm'n, 847 F.2d 1201 (6th Cir. 1988) (Agricultural Fair Practices Act does not preempt Michigan statute requiring payment of mandatory assessment to state commission for generic promotion of commodity).

347. 308 U.S. 188 (1939).

348. *Id.* at 204-05; *see* Tillamook Cheese and Dairy Ass'n v. Tillamook County Creamery Ass'n, 358 F.2d 115 (9th Cir. 1966); *cf.* Allen Bradley Co. v. Local 3, IBEW, 325 U.S. 797 (1945) (discussing parallel exemption for labor organization). In *Borden*, 308 U.S. at 203-04, the Supreme Court also rejected the contention that, under § 2 of the Capper-Volstead Act, 7 U.S.C. § 292 (1988), the Secretary of Agriculture has exclusive or primary jurisdiction over antitrust violations involving agricultural cooperatives, a position which was followed in Maryland & Va. Milk Producers Ass'n v. United States, 362 U.S. 458, 462-63 (1960). *See also* Sunkist Growers v. FTC, 464 F. Supp. 302 (C.D. Cal. 1979) (action to restrain FTC administrative proceedings dismissed).

349. 362 U.S. 458 (1960).

350. *Id.* at 465-67.

351. *Id.*

Following the lead of the Supreme Court, lower court decisions have found the Clayton Act Section 6 and Capper-Volstead exemptions inapplicable to charges of boycott,[352] predatory refusal to deal,[353] unfair rebates to favored customers,[354] discriminatory pricing,[355] coercion through picketing,[356] blacklisting,[357] coerced membership,[358] and acts of violence.[359] However, the Second Circuit reaffirmed that, absent predatory activity, Section 6 of the Clayton Act and the Capper-Volstead Act permit producers to seek, maintain and exercise monopoly power through the formation, growth, and combination of cooperatives.[360]

In three separate cases, the Supreme Court has sought to refine the *Borden* rule regarding concerted action with "outsiders." In *Sunkist Growers v. Winckler & Smith Citrus Products Co.*,[361] the Supreme Court granted Capper-Volstead immunity to conspiracy charges against three agricultural cooperatives which were legally separate

---

352. Boise Cascade Int'l, Inc. v. Northern Minn. Pulpwood Producers Ass'n, 294 F. Supp. 1015 (D. Minn. 1968).

353. North Tex. Producers Ass'n v. Metzger Dairies, 348 F.2d 189 (5th Cir. 1965), *cert. denied*, 382 U.S. 977 (1966); *see also* LaSalvia v. United Dairymen, 804 F.2d 1113 (9th Cir. 1986) (operators of independent dairy farm were proper parties to challenge dairy cooperative's allegedly anticompetitive behavior), *cert. denied*, 482 U.S. 928 (1987). *But cf.* Northwest Wholesale Stationers, Inc. v. Pacific Stationery & Printing Co., 472 U.S. 284 (1985) (purchasing cooperative's expulsion of member without notice or hearing did not mandate per se invalidation under § 1 of the Sherman Act as group boycott or concerted refusal to deal).

354. Bergjans Farm Dairy Co. v. Sanitary Milk Producers, 241 F. Supp. 476 (E.D. Mo. 1965), *aff'd*, 368 F.2d 679 (8th Cir. 1966).

355. Knuth v. Erie-Crawford Dairy Coop., 395 F.2d 420, 423-24 (3d Cir. 1968), *appeal after remand*, 463 F.2d 470 (3d Cir. 1972), *cert. denied*, 410 U.S. 913 (1973).

356. Otto Milk Co. v. United Dairy Farmers Coop., 388 F.2d 789 (3d Cir. 1967).

357. Bodker Dairy Co. v. Michigan Milk Producers Ass'n, Civil No. 23638 (E.D. Mich. 1963).

358. Gulf Coast Shrimpers and Oystermans Ass'n v. United States, 236 F.2d 658, 665 (5th Cir.), *cert. denied*, 352 U.S. 927 (1956).

359. Cincinnati Milk Sales Ass'n v. National Farmers' Org., 1967 Trade Cas. (CCH) ¶ 72,092 (S.D. Ohio 1967).

360. Fairdale Farms v. Yankee Milk, Inc., 715 F.2d 30 (2d Cir. 1983), *cert. denied*, 464 U.S. 1043 (1984); L. & L. Howell, Inc. v. Cincinnati Coop. Milk Sales Ass'n, 1983-2 Trade Cas. (CCH) ¶ 65,595 (6th Cir. 1983), *cert. denied*, 466 U.S. 904 (1984); Fairdale Farms v. Yankee Milk, Inc., 635 F.2d 1037, 1045 (2d Cir. 1980), *cert. denied*, 454 U.S. 818 (1981); GVF Cannery, Inc. v. California Tomato Growers Ass'n, 511 F. Supp. 711 (N.D. Cal. 1981) (no claim against cooperative under § 2 without pleading and proof of predatory acts); Kinnett Dairies v. Dairymen, Inc., 512 F. Supp. 608 (M.D. Ga. 1981) (judgment for defendant cooperative absent showing of predatory practices), *aff'd per curiam*, 715 F.2d 520 (11th Cir. 1983), *cert. denied*, 465 U.S. 1051 (1984); *see also* Marketing Assistance Plan, Inc. v. Associated Milk Producers, Inc., 338 F. Supp. 1019, 1023 (S.D. Tex. 1972) (plaintiff's allegations of predatory commercial activities could not be dismissed for failure to state a claim under antitrust laws); Cape Cod Food Prods. v. National Cranberry Ass'n, 119 F. Supp. 900, 907 (D. Mass 1954) (jury instructed that it "is not unlawful under the anti-trust acts for a Capper-Volstead cooperative . . . to try to acquire even 100 percent of the market if it does it exclusively through marketing agreements approved under the Capper-Volstead Act" (citation omitted)). *But see* Alexander v. National Farmers Org., 687 F.2d 1173, 1183 (8th Cir. 1982) ("Whether a co-op's given business practice is unlawful . . . is not merely a question of whether it is 'predatory' in a strict sense, *e.g.*, lacking a legitimate business justification."), *cert. denied*, 461 U.S. 937 (1983); United States v. Dairymen, Inc., 660 F.2d 192, 195 (6th Cir. 1981) ("An anticompetitive practice may have economic justification, but its use may be undertaken with unlawful intent and in the desire to achieve an unlawful goal. . . . However, the most important inquiry is whether these contracts were intended to stifle competition or were intended to meet legitimate business purposes.").

361. 370 U.S. 19 (1962).

entities but which had substantially the same members. The court reasoned that the three cooperatives were, in substance, a single economic unit and that the organizational distinctions between the groups were not of legal significance, because at any time the individual members and their cooperatives could have formed a single organization incapable of conspiring with itself.[362] Subsequently, upon a more complete record, the Court in *Case-Swayne Co. v. Sunkist Growers*,[363] held that the same "economic unit" was ineligible for exemption under the Capper-Volstead Act because 15% of its members were nonfarm corporations or partnerships rather than producers. Similarly, in its most recent consideration of the agricultural cooperative exemption, *National Broiler Marketing Association v. United States*,[364] the Supreme Court refused to grant the protection of the exemption to associations whose members could not all be classified as "farmers."

In actions concerning an alleged price-fixing conspiracy among California lettuce producers, the Federal Trade Commission and the Ninth Circuit have ruled that the activity of a cooperative that was formed and operated solely for the purpose of setting prices for its members' products was protected from attack under Section 1 of the Sherman Act.[365] The separate opinions rely heavily on an earlier Ninth Circuit case which held that associations of producers whose activities are confined to bargaining for prices are exempt from antitrust liability under Section 1 of the Sherman Act since setting a price for the sale of members' produce, without more, is "marketing" as that term is used in the Capper-Volstead Act.[366]

---

362. *See* Copperweld Corp. v. Independence Tube Corp., 467 U.S. 752, 773 (1984) (citing Sunkist Growers v. Winckler & Smith Citrus Prods. Co., 370 U.S. 19 (1962), in support of its holding that parent corporation is incapable of conspiring with its wholly owned subsidiary for purposes of Sherman Act § 1); Hudson's Bay Co. Fur Sales, Inc. v. American Legend Coop., 651 F. Supp. 819 (D.N.J. 1986) (cooperative association of mink ranchers incapable of conspiring with its subsidiary auction house under Sherman Act § 1).

363. 389 U.S. 384 (1967).

364. 436 U.S. 816 (1978). The Court ruled that in order for an association to enjoy the limited exemption of the Capper-Volstead Act, all of its members must be qualified as "farmers, planters, ranchmen, dairymen, nut or fruit growers." *Id.* at 823. Producers who own neither a breeder flock nor a hatchery and who maintain no grow-out facility do not qualify, and, therefore, the cooperative association of which they are members is not protected by the exemption. *Id.* at 827. *But see* Alexander v. National Farmers Org., 687 F.2d 1173, 1186-87 (8th Cir. 1982) (de minimis nonproducer membership of cooperative does not invalidate exemption when cooperative's activities were "conducted exclusively for true dairy farmers"), *cert. denied*, 461 U.S. 937 (1983).

365. *See* Northern Cal. Supermarkets v. Central Cal. Lettuce Producers Coop., 580 F.2d 369 (9th Cir. 1978), *cert. denied*, 439 U.S. 1090 (1979); Central Cal. Lettuce Producers Coop., 90 F.T.C. 18 (1977); *accord* Fairdale Farms v. Yankee Milk, Inc., 635 F.2d 1037, 1039-40 (2d Cir. 1980), *cert. denied*, 454 U.S. 878 (1981).

366. *See* Treasure Valley Potato Bargaining Ass'n v. Ore-Ida Foods, Inc., 497 F.2d 203 (9th Cir.), *cert. denied*, 419 U.S. 999 (1974); *see also* Holly Sugar Corp. v. Goshen County Coop. Beet Growers Ass'n, 725 F.2d 564 (10th Cir. 1984) (no antitrust violation stated where bargaining cooperative sought to take legal action to enforce marketing agreement with members); Washington Crab Ass'n, 66 F.T.C. 45, 105-14 (1964) (Capper-Volstead immunity applicable to cooperative which did not process, handle or sell members' products in competition with each other); *cf.* L. & L. Howell, Inc. v. Cincinnati Coop. Milk Sales Ass'n, 1983-2 Trade Cas. (CCH) ¶ 65,595 (6th Cir. 1983) (upholding joint proposing of handling fees to be paid), *cert. denied*, 466 U.S. 904 (1984).

2. *Communications*

Broadcast, common carrier, and other segments of the electronic telecommunications industry, and some aspects of the related equipment industry, are subject to regulation by the Federal Communications Commission (FCC) under the Communications Act of 1934 (the Communications Act), as amended.[367] The Act distinguishes broadcasters from common carriers and establishes a separate regulatory regime for each.[368] Intrastate common carrier communications are also subject to regulation by the states, except to the extent state regulation has been preempted by the FCC incident to its regulation of interstate and foreign communications.[369]

a. BROADCASTING

In *FCC v. Sanders Brothers Radio Station*, the Supreme Court observed that Congress intended "the field of broadcasting" to be an area of "free competition" and that the Communications Act "does not essay to regulate the business of the licensee."[370] Correspondingly, regulation of broadcasting under the Act has been, at times, confined to that necessary to allocate the limited broadcast spectrum.[371] Such regulations have focused, primarily through the licensing process, on conditions for entry and minimum standards for licensee performance designed, according to the statutory mandate, to serve the "public interest, convenience and necessity."[372] Conversely, the FCC's exercise of regulatory power over broadcast licensees has also been, at times, extensive and broadly defined. For example, in *Mt. Mansfield Television, Inc. v. FCC*, the Second Circuit observed:

> The Supreme Court has said that an important element in the Commission's consideration of the public interest is "the ability of the licensee to render the best practicable service to the community reached by his broadcasts." *Federal Communications Commission v. Sanders Brothers Radio Station*, 309 U.S. 470, 475, 60 S. Ct. 693, 697, 84 L. Ed. 869 (1940). The criterion of public interest is not limited to technological considerations but is the end to which the Commission's "comprehensive powers to promote and realize the

---

367. 47 U.S.C. §§ 151-757 (1988).
368. Title II of the Act applies to common carriers; Title III applies to radio transmission of energy, communications, or signals, whether for broadcasting, common carrier communications, or other purposes. *Compare* 47 U.S.C. §§ 201-224 (1988) (common carriers) *with id.* §§ 301-399B (radio).
369. *See* 47 U.S.C. §§ 152(b), 221(b) (1988); *see also* North Carolina Utils. Comm'n v. FCC, 537 F.2d 787, 793-94 (4th Cir.), *cert. denied*, 429 U.S. 1027 (1976).
370. 309 U.S. 470, 474-75 (1940).
371. The Supreme Court indicated that it might be willing to revisit the "scarcity of spectrum" rationale for broadcast regulation if the Congress or the FCC "signaled" that technological developments had advanced so far that some revision of the system of broadcast regulation may be required. FCC v. League of Women Voters, 468 U.S. 364, 376 n.11 (1984); *cf.* Syracuse Peace Council, 2 F.C.C. Rcd 5043 (1987), *recon. denied*, 3 F.C.C. Rcd 2035 (1988) (Fairness Doctrine found unconstitutional in part because "growth in both radio and television broadcasting . . . 'provide a reasonable assurance [of] sufficient diversity of opinion.' ").
372. 309 U.S. at 474-75; 47 U.S.C. § 309(a) (1988). Commercial advertising rates are not subject to Commission approval, although rates charged political candidates are reviewed by the Commission to determine whether the correct rate was charged. *See* 47 U.S.C. § 315(b) (1988).

vast potentialities of radio" should be directed. See National Broadcasting Co., Inc., *supra* 319 U.S. at 217, 63 S.Ct. at 1010.[373]

In recent years, however, the FCC has moved away from extensive regulation of broadcasters and broadcast services.[374]

Section 313(a) of the Communications Act[375] makes "all laws of the United States relating to unlawful restraints and monopolies and to combinations, contracts, or agreements in restraint of trade" applicable to interstate and foreign radio and television communications.[376] Section 313(a) also provides that if an FCC licensee is found guilty in a civil or criminal suit of violating the antitrust laws, the court may revoke its license.[377] Section 313(a) is the only provision of the Act under which a body other than the FCC may revoke an FCC license. Section 313(b) directs the FCC to refuse a license to any person whose license has been revoked by a court under this section.[378] The section does not prevent the Commission from granting a license transfer during the pendency of an antitrust suit but the new licensee may be joined as a party defendant in the antitrust suit.[379]

The FCC does not have the statutory power to grant antitrust immunity.[380] In *United States v. Radio Corp. of America (RCA)*, the Supreme Court held that in

---

373. 442 F.2d 470, 479 (2d Cir. 1971) (footnote omitted).
374. *See, e.g.*, Second Proposed Rulemaking, Network-Cable Cross-Ownership Rule, MM Dkt. no. 82-434, 57 FED. REG. 868 (1992); Further Notice of Proposed Rulemaking, amendment of part 26, subpart J, Section 76.501 of the Commission Rules Relative to Elimination of the Prohibition on Common Ownership of Cable Television Systems and National Television Networks, CT Dkt. No. 82-434 (Aug. 4, 1988); Tentative Decision and Request for Further Comments, 94 F.C.C.2d 1019 (1983) (proposed amendment of the financial interest and syndication rules); Deregulation of Radio, 84 F.C.C.2d 968 (1981), *aff'd in part and remanded in part sub nom.* Office of Communication of United Church of Christ v. FCC, 707 F.2d 1413 (D.C. Cir. 1983), *modified on remand*, 96 F.C.C.2d 930 (1984), *vacated and remanded*, 779 F.2d 702 (D.C. Cir. 1985), *modified on remand*, 104 F.C.C.2d 505 (1986); Revision of Programming and Commercialization Policies, Ascertainment Requirements, and Program Log Requirements for Commercial Television Stations, 98 F.C.C.2d 1076 (1984), *recon. denied*, 104 F.C.C.2d 357 (1986), *aff'd in part and remanded in part sub nom.* Action for Children's Television v. FCC, 821 F.2d 741 (D.C. Cir. 1987); Revision of Applications for Renewal of License of Commercial and Noncommercial AM, FM and Television Licensees, 87 F.C.C.2d 1127 (1981), *aff'd sub nom.* Black Citizens for a Fair Media v. FCC, 719 F.2d 407 (D.C. Cir. 1983), *cert. denied*, 467 U.S. 1255 (1984); Policy Regarding Character Qualifications in Broadcast Licensing, 102 F.C.C.2d 1179, 1200-03 (1986), *recon. denied*, 1 F.C.C. Rcd 421 (1986), *appeal dismissed sub nom.* National Ass'n for Better Broadcasting v. FCC, No. 86-1179 (D.C. Cir. June 11, 1987); Elimination of Unnecessary Broadcast Regulation, 50 FED. REG. 5,583 (1985) (During the course of these ongoing proceedings, the Commission has eliminated or modified what it has termed "regulatory 'underbrush' policies and rules [that] . . . are no longer warranted or required by the public interest."); Amendment of Section 73.3555 of the Commission's Rules Relating to Multiple Ownership of AM, FM and Television Broadcast Stations, 100 F.C.C.2d 74 (1985); Repeal of the "Regional Concentration of Control" Provisions of the Commission's Multiple Ownership Rules, 101 F.C.C.2d 402 (1984), *recon. denied*, 100 F.C.C.2d 1544 (1985); Amendment of Section 73.3555 of the Commission's Rules, the Broadcast Multiple Ownership Rules, First Report and Order, 4 F.C.C. Rcd 1723 (1989), Second Report and Order, 4 F.C.C. Rcd 1741 (1989).
375. 47 U.S.C. § 313(a) (1988).
376. *Id.* § 313(b). By statutory definition, radio includes television. *Id.* § 153(b).
377. *Id.* § 313(a).
378. *Id.* § 313(b).
379. A.H. Belo Corp., 43 F.C.C.2d 336, 338 (1973).
380. United States v. RCA, 358 U.S. 334, 346 (1959).

broadcasting, where "there [was] no pervasive regulatory scheme, and no rate structures to throw out of balance," there was no need to defer to the Commission's expertise.[381] Nevertheless, subsequent to *RCA*, courts have on occasion deferred to pending FCC action in cases involving antitrust claims.[382] The FCC, in turn, has sometimes deferred to antitrust enforcement agencies and the courts on issues of antitrust policy. For example, the FCC dismissed a complaint alleging that a licensee unlawfully monopolized the broadcasting of sporting events because, in the Commission's view, the Department of Justice, the Federal Trade Commission, or the courts were better equipped to deal with the antitrust analysis required.[383] Similarly, the FCC dismissed a petition by an association of theater owners to direct a program producer to cease exhibiting motion pictures on pay cable television.[384] The Commission held that the petition was tantamount to a request for interpretation and enforcement of an antitrust consent decree and thus was brought in the wrong forum.[385]

The Commission has historically recognized that it has some antitrust enforcement responsibility and that "competitive considerations are an important element of the 'public interest' standard" that governs its decision making.[386] In affirming the Commission's duty to consider competitive factors in its regulation of broadcasting, the Supreme Court has suggested that "in a given case the Commission might find that antitrust considerations alone would keep the statutory standard from being met."[387]

However, the Commission has discretion to determine the appropriate weight that should be accorded competitive considerations in particular circumstances, and it has demonstrated an increased willingness to rely on case-by-case enforcement by private parties and the antitrust enforcement agencies, as opposed to broad, prophylactic rules and policies that may inhibit otherwise efficient conduct.[388] The Commission has recently reiterated that its "overriding responsibility is not to foster the maximum level of competition in the industry but rather to promote the public interest."[389]

The FCC has considered competitive factors primarily in its regulation of licensing and in certain aspects of its regulation of broadcast industry behavior and structure. The intersection of competition and these regulatory areas is discussed below.

---

381. *Id.* at 350; *see also* United States v. ABC, 1977-2 Trade Cas. (CCH) ¶ 61,580, at 72,371 (C.D. Cal. 1977); United States v. CBS, 1977-1 Trade Cas. (CCH) ¶ 61,327, at 71,139 (C.D. Cal. 1977); United States v. NBC, 1974-1 Trade Cas. (CCH) ¶ 74,885, at 95,922 (C.D. Cal. 1973).

382. *E.g.*, Writers' Guild of Am. v. ABC, 609 F.2d 355 (9th Cir. 1979), *cert. denied*, 449 U.S. 824 (1980); Levitch v. CBS, 495 F. Supp. 649, 658 (S.D.N.Y. 1980), *aff'd*, 697 F.2d 495 (2d Cir. 1983).

383. Cahill & Kaswell, 37 RAD. REG. 2d (P&F) 197, 200-01 (1976).

384. Warner Communs., 51 F.C.C.2d 1079, 1081-82 (1975).

385. *Id.* at 1081.

386. United States v. FCC, 652 F.2d 72, 81-82 (D.C. Cir. 1980) (quoting Northern Natural Gas Co. v. FPC, 399 F.2d 953, 961 (D.C. Cir. 1968)); *see also* NBC v. United States, 319 U.S. 190, 223-24 (1943); United States v. CBS, 1977-1 Trade Cas. (CCH) ¶ 61,327, at 71,135 (C.D. Cal. 1977).

387. United States v. RCA, 358 U.S. 334, 351 (1959).

388. *See* Elimination of Unnecessary Broadcast Regulation, 50 FED. REG. 5583, 5588 n.19 (1985). Regulation of certain types of competitive practices by the Commission was found to be "unnecessary and possibly counterproductive. To the extent the policies cover areas regulated by the antitrust laws, other agencies such as the Department of Justice or the Federal Trade Commission have primary enforcement responsibility." *Id.* at 5588 (footnote omitted).

389. United States Cellular Operating Co., 3 F.C.C. Rcd 5345, 5346 n.3 (1988).

(1) Licensing

Prior to 1986, in considering whether the grant of a particular application for a broadcast license was in the public interest, the FCC weighed, among other factors, whether the applicant had been prosecuted or convicted under the antitrust laws.[390] For example, in *NBC v. United States*,[391] the Supreme Court stated that the Commission " 'might infer from the fact that the applicant had in the past tried to monopolize radio, or had engaged in unfair methods of competition, that the disposition so manifested would continue and that if it did it would make him an unfit licensee.' "[392]

In 1986, however, the FCC radically altered its treatment of competitive factors as part of its function of the regulation of licensing.[393] Instead of considering whether the applicant has been prosecuted or convicted under any antitrust laws,[394] the Commission generally will restrict its inquiry to specific convictions of antitrust laws by licensees or station applicants in broadcast related activities.[395] The FCC will use these criteria primarily in comparative licensing proceedings.

The FCC historically has given less weight to antitrust violations than to other factors.[396] While the FCC will now be giving very little weight to antitrust violations in the licensing context, it is still continuing to enforce those violations that occurred in a case decided prior to the issuance of the *1986 Policy Statement*.[397] In *RKO General, Inc. (WNAC-TV)*, antitrust considerations were important to the Commission's decision to deny RKO's application for renewal of three of its television station licenses and to designate for hearing the licenses of thirteen other RKO stations.[398] The Commission found that RKO and its parent corporation, General Tire and Rubber Company, had engaged in a pattern of misconduct with their broadcast stations that included anticompetitive reciprocal trade practices, falsification of financial statements filed with the FCC, and a lack of candor in its dealings with the FCC.[399] The Commission also found that General

390. FEDERAL COMMUNICATIONS COMMISSION, REPORT ON UNIFORM POLICY AS TO VIOLATION BY APPLICANTS OF LAWS OF UNITED STATES, 42 F.C.C.2d 399 (1951) [hereinafter 1951 REPORT].

391. 319 U.S. 190 (1943).

392. *Id.* at 222 (quoting NBC v. United States, 47 F. Supp. 940, 944 (S.D.N.Y. 1942)).

393. POLICY REGARDING CHARACTER QUALIFICATIONS in BROADCAST LICENSING, 102 F.C.C.2d 1179 (1986), *recon. denied*, 1 F.C.C. Rcd 421 (1986), *appeal dismissed sub nom.* National Ass'n for Better Broadcasting v. FCC, No. 86-1179 (D.C. Cir. June 11, 1987) [hereinafter 1986 POLICY STATEMENT].

394. Factors that previously were relevant to the weight and significance of a given antitrust violation included whether the violation was willful or not, recurring or isolated, and recent or remote in time, and whether the antitrust judgment was final or on appeal. 1951 REPORT, *supra* note 390, at 402-03.

395. If the licensee or applicant allegedly engaged in nonbroadcast related anticompetitive activity, the inquiry will be limited to adjudicated violations of the law involving fraudulent misconduct before a government agency or criminal felony convictions involving false statements or dishonesty. 1986 POLICY STATEMENT, *supra* note 393, at 1200-01.

396. *See* Westinghouse Broadcasting Co., 44 F.C.C. 2778, 2779-81, 2784-85 (1962).

397. *See* RKO Gen., Inc. (KHJ-TV), 2 F.C.C. Rcd 4807 (1987).

398. RKO Gen., Inc. (WNAC-TV), 78 F.C.C.2d 1, 116-18 (1980), *aff'd in part and rev'd in part*, RKO Gen., Inc. v. FCC, 670 F.2d 215 (D.C. Cir. 1981), *cert. denied*, 456 U.S. 927 (1982); *see also* RKO Gen., Inc., 82 F.C.C.2d 291, 318 (1980), *vacated in part and remanded sub nom.* New S. Media Corp. v. FCC, 685 F.2d 708 (D.C. Cir. 1982); RKO Gen., Inc. (KHJ-TV), 78 F.C.C.2d 355 (1980).

399. 78 F.C.C.2d at 3-4.

Tire had engaged in misconduct not directly related to the activities of its broadcast affiliates, including improper domestic political contributions, schemes that defrauded its affiliates, improper foreign payments, and improper secret accounts designed to avoid foreign tax and currency exchange laws.[400]

On appeal, the D.C. Circuit held that the FCC could not disqualify the licensee for reciprocal trade practices ("nonleveraged, mutual patronage agreements") that occurred during the early 1960s, before the illegality of reciprocal dealings was established. The court held, however, that it would be proper to deal severely in the future with anticompetitive reciprocity practices:

> The Commission has laid down the rule that those who induce others to advertise on their stations for reasons unrelated to the station's programming or audience will do so at their peril. We agree that the purposes of the Communications Act are best served by leaving stations to obtain advertising and customers on the basis of their rates and audience, and that even unleveraged reciprocal trading distorts the normal free market process in the broadcast industry by which the demand for advertising time helps ensure that radio and television programming is responsive to public desires. Competition in the broadcast industry means that a broadcaster should "survive or succumb according to his ability to make his programs attractive to the public," and reciprocity injects an extrinsic factor that breaks the link between program quality and revenues.[401]

The court concluded that the FCC's finding that the licensee submitted intentionally false financial reports also was insufficient to support disqualification, but it ruled that the licensee's lack of candor before the agency was sufficiently egregious to support forfeiture of the television license involved in the proceeding.[402]

(2) Licensee Sales Practices

In passing on the qualifications of broadcast license applicants, the FCC has taken into consideration behavior that, although not necessarily violative of the antitrust laws, may nevertheless tend to restrain competition.[403] A variety of sales practices of broadcast licensees have in the past been the subject of scrutiny under this aspect

---

400. *Id.* at 4-5.

401. RKO Gen., Inc. v. FCC, 670 F.2d at 224-25 (quoting *Sanders Bros.*, 309 U.S. at 475).

402. 670 F.2d at 235. The court remanded the case for further proceedings with respect to its other licenses. *Id.* at 237. The proceedings involving RKO's New York license were terminated when RKO agreed to relocate its station to New Jersey. RKO Gen., Inc. (WOR-TV), 92 F.C.C.2d 303 (1983). Subsequently, an Initial Decision was issued that proposed denial of all of RKO's pending license renewal applications. RKO Gen., Inc. (KHJ-TV), 2 F.C.C. Rcd 4807 (1987). However, in 1988, the Commission approved separate settlement agreements whereby RKO would be permitted to sell its facilities and the stations would be placed in the hands of "an unquestionably qualified licensee." RKO Gen., Inc. (KHJ-TV), 3 F.C.C. Rcd 5057, 5060 (1988), *appeal dismissed sub nom.* Los Angeles Television v. FCC, No. 88-1673 (D.C. Cir. Aug. 4, 1989) (settlement of KHJ-TV, Los Angeles proceeding); *see also* RKO Gen., Inc. (WHBQ), 3 F.C.C. Rcd 5055 (1988) (settlement of WHBQ, Memphis proceeding); RKO Gen., Inc. (WGMS), 3 F.C.C. Rcd 5262 (1988) (settlement of WGMS and WGMS-FM, Bethesda proceeding); RKO Gen., Inc. (WRKO), 3 F.C.C. Rcd 6603 (1988) (settlement of WRKO and WROR-FM, Boston proceeding).

403. Metropolitan Television Co. v. FCC, 289 F.2d 874, 876 (D.C. Cir. 1961) ("it is settled that practices which present realistic dangers of competitive restraint are a proper consideration for the Commission in determining the 'public interest, convenience, and necessity'") (citations and footnote omitted); *cf. supra* note 386.

of the Commission's public interest standard.[404] For example, the Commission issued policy statements declaring that joint sales agreements, which combine and discount the advertising rates for separately owned stations serving substantially the same geographic area, raised serious antitrust questions and were not in the public interest.[405] However, the FCC has recently eliminated its rules concerning combination advertising rates and joint sales practices on the basis that they are not anticompetitive; instead, such practices may realize economies of scale, thereby permitting reductions in cost.[406]

The FCC has also regulated the use of a common sales representative by competing stations. A sales representative who does not own a broadcast station may represent any number of stations irrespective of location or type.[407] Formerly, when common ownership existed between the sales representative and a broadcast station, the sales representative could not represent another broadcast station of a similar type in the same area;[408] however, in 1981 the FCC changed this policy upon finding that diversity in programming and service would not be diminished by a sales representative's affiliation with a competitor.[409] The Commission continues to prohibit television networks from representing affiliated stations in the sale of nonnetwork time[410] on the theory that networks, because of their control over affiliation, can influence affiliates in their choice of spot representative and thus restrain competition.[411]

In the past, the FCC also scrutinized licensee use of broadcast facilities to further nonbroadcast activities.[412] It found a licensee's "use of its broadcast facility to

---

404. *See* COMBINATION ADVERTISING RATES and OTHER JOINT SALES PRACTICES, 59 F.C.C.2d 894 (1976) [hereinafter 1976 REPORT]; First Report and Further Notice of Proposed Rule Making, Combination Advertising Rates and Other Joint Sales Practices, 51 F.C.C.2d 679 (1975); Notice of Inquiry and Notice of Proposed Rule Making, Combination Advertising Rates and Other Joint Sales Practices, 41 F.C.C.2d 951 (1973); Public Notice, Combination Advertising Rates, 45 F.C.C. 581 (1963).

405. Eleven Fifty Corp., 42 F.C.C.2d 207 (1973); 1976 REPORT, *supra* note 404; First Report and Further Notice of Proposed Rule Making, Combination Advertising Rates and Other Joint Sales Practices, 51 F.C.C.2d 679 (1975). *But see* Elimination of Unnecessary Broadcast Regulation, 50 FED. REG. 5583 (1985). The Commission interpreted the principle underlying this policy to apply whether or not the independently owned licensees are in the same service area, Subrink Broadcasting, Inc., 42 F.C.C.2d 271 (1973); whether or not a discount is involved in the combination rate, 1976 REPORT, *supra* note 404, at 19; and, except for commonly owned AM and FM broadcast stations, whether or not the licensees are commonly owned, if they are in the same service area, *id.* at 17.

406. Elimination of Unnecessary Broadcast Regulation, 51 FED. REG. 11,914 (1986).

407. *See* Notice of Inquiry, Representation of Stations by Representatives, 45 FED. REG. 55,242 (1980).

408. *Id.*

409. Representation of Stations by Representatives Owned by Competing Stations in the Same Area, 87 F.C.C.2d 668, 682-83 (1981). The Commission recently decided to retain this rule. Amendment of § 73.658(i) of the Commission's Rules, Concerning Network Representation of TV Stations in National Spot Sales. 5 F.C.C. Rcd 7280 (1990).

410. *See* 47 C.F.R. § 73.658(i) (1991). However, a proceeding is pending to determine whether this rule should be amended or eliminated. *See infra* notes 476-80 and accompanying text.

411. Network Representation of Stations in National Spot Sales, 27 F.C.C. 697, 720 (1959), *recon. denied*, 28 F.C.C. 447 (1960), *aff'd sub nom.* Metropolitan Television Co. v. FCC, 289 F.2d 874 (D.C. Cir. 1961).

412. *See, e.g.,* Carolinas Advertising, Inc., 42 F.C.C.2d 1027, 1028 (1973); WFLI, Inc., 13 F.C.C.2d 846, 847 (1968).

advertise its nonbroadcast activities in a manner which forecloses competition or unfairly treats a competitor" to be contrary to the public interest.[413]   Other uses of broadcast facilities that the Commission considered to be anticompetitive included the granting of advertising rate discounts to firms associated with the licensee,[414] the refusal to sell advertising time to competitors of the licensee,[415] and the granting of credits to advertisers in the licensee's wholly-owned newspaper subsidiary to be applied against advertising time on the licensee's stations.[416]

However, the Commission eliminated these policies in its ongoing review of the accumulated "underbrush" of broadcast regulation.[417]   First, the FCC stated, "We see no reason to assume, without more evidence than was adduced by the enacting Commission, that the practice of selling commercial time at a discount to another business owned by the licensee is anticompetitive."[418]   The Commission went on to note that, "[i]f indeed the conduct in issue illegally hurts competitors in a non-broadcast market," the antitrust laws, not Commission oversight, would be the proper recourse.[419]   Second, the Commission determined that regulation of the type fostered in the *Carolinas* case, the *WFLI, Inc.* case, and the *Sarkes Tarzian* case was "unnecessary and possibly counterproductive."[420]   To the extent that these policies covered areas regulated by the antitrust laws, the Commission again deferred to the antitrust enforcement agencies.[421]

In 1982, the Department of Justice brought an antitrust suit against the National Association of Broadcasters in which it alleged that certain advertising standards provisions of the broadcast industry's self-regulatory code violated Section 1 of the Sherman Act because they constituted an agreement among broadcasters to limit the availability of commercial advertising time.[422]   After a partial summary judgment ruling in favor of the government, the case was settled upon the entry of a consent decree that required the abolition of the challenged code provisions.[423]

(3) Ownership of Broadcast Licenses

The FCC has pursued a structural approach to broadcast regulation.   The Commission's multiple and cross-ownership rules are designed to further two basic policies: (1) diversification of programming sources and viewpoints, and (2) prevention of economic concentration in the broadcast industry.[424]   The Supreme Court has upheld both the FCC's power to restrict multiple ownership and the validity of the FCC's policy goals.[425]

---

413.   *Carolinas Advertising*, 42 F.C.C.2d at 1028.

414.   *Id.*

415.   *See* E. Boyd Whitney, 86 F.C.C.2d 1133, 1144 (1981); WFLI, Inc., 13 F.C.C.2d at 847.

416.   Sarkes Tarzian, Inc., 23 F.C.C.2d 221, 222 (1970).

417.   Elimination of Unnecessary Broadcast Regulation, 50 FED. REG. 5583 (1985).

418.   *Id.* at 5587.

419.   *Id.*

420.   *Id.* at 5588.

421.   *Id.*

422.   United States v. National Ass'n of Broadcasters, 536 F. Supp. 149, 153 n.11 (D.D.C. 1982).

423.   *Id.* at 152-53; United States v. National Ass'n of Broadcasters, 1982-83 Trade Cas. (CCH) ¶¶ 65,049-50 (D.D.C. 1982) (consent decree).

424.   *See* Multiple Ownership Rules, 22 F.C.C.2d 306, 307 (1970).

425.   United States v. Storer Broadcasting Co., 351 U.S. 192, 203-05 (1956).

The Commission's multiple ownership rules are intended to promote program diversity and to prevent media concentration at the national, regional, and local levels. The rules limit ownership of broadcast facilities by: (1) setting an overall limit on the number of broadcast licenses a single entity can hold regardless of location,[426] and (2) limiting the extent to which a broadcast licensee can have an interest in other media or media-related entities.

For many years, the Commission had in place a "seven station rule" that limited the number of television and broadcast stations a licensee could own to seven television stations (five VHF, two UHF), seven AM radio stations, and seven FM radio stations.[427] In October 1983, the Commission commenced a rulemaking to determine whether the "seven station rule" should be repealed.[428] The Commission, relying largely on comments of the Antitrust Division, concluded that "elimination of the Seven Station Rules will raise little risk of adverse competitive effects in any market."[429] The FCC expanded the rule from seven to twelve stations.[430]

The Commission reconsidered that decision and stayed implementation of the modified rule as it applied to television after Congress exerted strong pressure on the Commission.[431] This pressure focused principally on questions relating to the ability of broadcast television networks to act anticompetitively through control of a large number of stations. After reconsideration, the FCC refused to promulgate a special rule for network ownership,[432] but it substantially modified its proposed rule to limit ownership by one person to a total of twelve UHF and VHF stations that, in the aggregate, do not reach more than 25% of the national audience[433]

---

426. In May 1984, the FCC repealed the "regional concentration rule," which limited to three the number of broadcast stations that could be owned by a licensee in a single geographic area. Repeal of the "Regional Concentration of Control" Provisions of the Commission's Multiple Ownership Rules, 101 F.C.C.2d 402 (1984), *recon. denied*, 100 F.C.C.2d 1544 (1985).

427. Ownership that exceeded the seven station limit was presumed to constitute concentration of control, contrary to the public interest. 47 C.F.R. §§ 73.235, 73.240, 73.636 (1983); *see* United States v. Storer Broadcasting Co., 351 U.S. 192, 194-97 (1956). The FCC could also prohibit ownership that did not exceed the limit if other factors were present, including the size of the stations owned, the size of the audience served, and the lack of other competition in the areas served by the stations. *See* Clarksburg Pub. Co. v FCC, 225 F.2d 511, 519 (D.C. Cir. 1955).

428. Notice of Proposed Rule Making, 95 F.C.C.2d 360 (1983).

429. Report and Order, 100 F.C.C.2d 17, 38 (1984) (quoting comments of the Department of Justice at 2-3).

430. That is, the Commission will not grant, transfer, or assign a broadcast license to a party if that recipient (including its stockholders, partners, members, officers, and directors) directly or indirectly owns, controls, operates, or has a cognizable interest in more than 12 AM stations and 12 FM stations. If the party is minority-controlled, however, it may hold up to 14 stations in the same service. 47 C.F.R. § 73.3555(d)(1) (1991); 100 F.C.C. 2d at 18.

431. Multiple Ownership (Seven Stations Rule), 56 RAD. REG. 2d (P&F) 887 (1984). Congress also enacted a moratorium on the implementation of the Report and Order. Second Supplemental Appropriations Act, Pub. L. No. 98-396 § 304, 98 Stat. 1969, 1423 (1984).

432. Memorandum Opinion and Order, 100 F.C.C.2d 74, 83-84 (1985), *appeal dismissed sub nom.* National Ass'n of Black Owned Broadcasters, Inc. v. FCC, No. 85-1139 (D.C. Cir. Jan. 4, 1991).

433. If the party is minority controlled, it may own, control, operate or have a cognizable interest in television stations that have an aggregate national audience reach up to 30%. 47 C.F.R. § 73.3555(d)(2) (1991).

according to the ADI market ratings.[434]   The rules applying to radio did not contain a "reach" cap, but the FCC eliminated the automatic sunset of the ownership rules for both radio and television, noting that "it is appropriate to proceed cautiously in relaxing rules that affect such a vital aspect of the broadcasting industry."[435]   In 1992, the twelve station ownership rule was revised to permit ownership of up to thirty AM stations and thirty FM stations nationwide.[436]

The Commission's cross-ownership rules prohibit the ownership of both a broadcast facility and either a daily newspaper[437] or a cable television system[438] in the same community.   The rules also prohibit, subject to waiver,

---

434.   100 F.C.C.2d at 87. ADI stands for area of dominant influence and is based on Arbitron Market Index Guide. *Id.* at 85. The rule also "discounts" the reach of UHF stations, so that owners of UHF stations are attributed only 50% of an ADI market's audience reach. *Id.* at 93.

435.   *Id.* at 96.

436.   Revision of Radio Rules and Policies, MM Docket 91-140 (Report and Order FCC 92-97 Mar. 12, 1992) (from 12 to 30).

437.   47 C.F.R. § 73.3555 (1991). The Supreme Court upheld the Commission's rules restricting colocated newspaper-broadcast cross-ownership in FCC v. National Citizens Committee for Broadcasting, 436 U.S. 755, 802 (1978).

The Commission has, however, granted temporary waivers of the rules upon a showing that the owner will have to sell at a distress price, when separate ownership and operation of the newspaper and station cannot be supported in the locality, or when "for whatever reason" the purposes of the rule will be best served by continued joint ownership. Second Report and Order, 50 F.C.C.2d 1046, 1085 (1975). The FCC recently granted a twenty-four month waiver of this provision where the proposed assignee of the license of a television station, who already owned a newspaper, made a sufficient showing that it would be difficult for him to sell the newspaper at a reasonable price. Metromedia Radio and Television, Inc., 102 F.C.C.2d 1334 (1985), *aff'd sub nom.* Health and Medicine Policy Research Group v. FCC, 807 F.2d 1038 (D.C. Cir. 1986); *see also* Owosso Broadcasting Co., 60 RAD. REG. 2d (P&F) 99 (1986) (denying indefinite stay of the divestiture deadline imposed on newspaper/broadcast cross-owners, but granting temporary waiver of eleven months).

In 1986, the FCC granted Rupert Murdoch an eighteen-month waiver to divest either his Boston UHF television station or The Boston Herald. Twentieth Holdings Corp., 1 F.C.C. Rcd 1201 (1986). On December 22, 1987, Congress passed and the President signed a Continuing Resolution that included the following provision:

Provided, further, that none of the funds appropriated by the Act or any other Act may be used to repeal, to retroactively apply changes in, or begin or continue a re-examination of the rules of the FCC with respect to common ownership of a daily newspaper and a television station where the grade A contour of the television station encompasses the entire community in which the newspaper is published, or to extend the time period of current grant of temporary waivers to achieve compliance with such rules . . . .

Pub. L. No. 100-202, 101 Stat. 1329 (1987). Murdoch nonetheless applied for an extension of the temporary waiver on January 14, 1988, but the FCC denied the request based on the language of Pub. L. No. 100-202. Based on the equal protection clause of the United States Constitution, U.S. CONST. amend. XIV, § 1, the D.C. Circuit struck down that portion of the law that foreclosed FCC consideration of waiver extension because the law "strikes at Murdoch with the precision of a laser beam." News Am. Publishing, Inc. v. FCC, 844 F.2d 800, 814 (D.C. Cir. 1988). The D.C. Circuit, however, refused to rule on the constitutionality of the law's prohibition against the FCC reexamining the television-newspaper cross-ownership rules on the ground that the question was not ripe. *Id.* at 802 n.1.

438.   47 C.F.R. § 76.501 (1991). The rule applies only to colocated cable systems and television stations.

ownership of both a national television network and a cable system,[439] or a telephone company and a cable system.[440]

In addition to its rules restricting multiple ownership of broadcast licenses, the FCC has granted a preference in comparative licensing proceedings to applicants who have no other media interests.[441] For firms with other media interests, however, a substantial broadcast record in the public interest can outweigh the absence of diversification.[442]

The FCC's multiple ownership rules focus on local concentration of ownership and, within the boundaries of the twelve station rule, do not discourage group ownership. Moreover, even those rules against regional and local concentration have recently been relaxed. The Commission's "cross-interest" policy prevents individuals or entities from having "meaningful" cross-interests in two broadcast stations that serve substantially the same area.[443] Such "meaningful" relationships have been found, through case-by-case adjudication, to arise generally (1) where a "key employee" of a station has an attributable interest in another station in the same community or market,[444] (2) where an individual acts as a consultant for two competing stations,[445] (3) where two competing stations propose to enter a joint venture to establish a new station in the market,[446] (4) where a station enters into a "time brokerage" arrangement to buy time for programming and advertising on a competing station in the same market,[447] and (5) where an individual has an interest in both a broadcast station and an advertising agency that purchases advertising time on behalf of its clients on other stations in the same service in the

---

439. 47 C.F.R. § 76.501 (1984) (as amended); Cable Communications Policy Act of 1984, Pub. L. No. 98-549, § 613(a), 98 Stat. 2779 (1984) (codified at 47 U.S.C. § 533 (1988)). The FCC has waived its rule prohibiting a national network from owning a cable system to allow CBS to purchase or build a cable system serving a maximum of 90,000 subscribers. CBS, 87 F.C.C.2d 587, 596 (1981); cf. Whitcom Investment Co., 92 F.C.C.2d 1067 (1983); Teleprompter Corp., 89 F.C.C.2d 417 (1982). These prohibitions are currently the subject of a rulemaking proceeding that is considering their elimination. Further Notice of Proposed Rulemaking, Amendment of Part 76, Subpart J, Section 76.501 of the Commission's Rules and Regulations Relative to Elimination of the Prohibition of Common Ownership of Cable Television Systems and National Television Networks, Ct. Dkt. 82-434 (Aug. 4, 1988); see also NEW TELEVISION NETWORKS: ENTRY, JURISDICTION, OWNERSHIP AND REGULATION (Oct. 1980) (network entry into cable television deemed to increase competition, enhance efficiency, and improve quality of cable service to advertisers and viewers) [hereinafter NEW TELEVISION NETWORKS].
440. See Section D.2.c of this chapter.
441. See Policy Statement on Comparative Broadcast Hearings, 1 F.C.C.2d 393, 394-95 (1965). Compare McClatchy Broadcasting Co. v. FCC, 239 F.2d 15, 18 (D.C. Cir. 1956) (rejecting newspaper owner), cert. denied, 353 U.S. 918 (1957) with Massachusetts Bay Telecasters, Inc. v. FCC, 261 F.2d 55, 63-64 (D.C. Cir. 1958) (newspaper owner preferred), vacated, 295 F.2d 131 (D.C. Cir.), cert. denied, 366 U.S. 918 (1961).
442. See Policy Statement on Comparative Broadcast Hearings, 1 F.C.C.2d 393, 394-99 (1965).
443. See Notice of Inquiry, Reexamination of The Commission's Cross-Interest Policy, 2 F.C.C. Rcd 3699 (1987); Further Notice of Inquiry/Notice of Proposed Rulemaking, Reexamination of the Commission's Cross-Interest Policy, 4 F.C.C. Rcd 2035 (1988); Policy Statement, Reexamination of the Commission's Cross-Interest Policy, 4 F.C.C. Rcd 2208 (1989).
444. See, e.g., Martin Lake Broadcasting Co., 21 F.C.C.2d 180, 181-82 (1970); United Community Enters., 37 F.C.C.2d 953 (1972).
445. See, e.g., Lexington County Broadcasters, Inc., 42 F.C.C.2d 581 (1973); Guy S. Erway, 48 RAD. REG. 2d (P&F) 829 (1980).
446. See, e.g., Macon Television Co., 8 RAD. REG. (P&F) 703 (1952).
447. See, e.g., WCVL, Inc., 55 F.C.C.2d 879 (1975); Station WWSM, 31 F.C.C.2d 584 (1971).

same market.[448] In 1988, however, the FCC abolished the cross-interest policy as it applied to consulting positions, time brokerage agreements, and advertising agencies,[449] and it sought further information regarding the elimination of the remaining prohibitions.[450]

In February 1989, the Commission also issued two orders that substantially relaxed its "duopoly" and "one-to-a-market" rules.[451] The radio duopoly rule, which prohibited common ownership of two or more commercial radio stations in the same broadcast service if their 1 mv/m contours overlapped, was relaxed to prohibit joint ownership only where the stations' "principal city" coverage contours (i.e., 5 mv/m for AM stations and 3.16 mv/m for FM stations) overlap. Based on the increased availability of media outlets throughout local markets of various sizes, the FCC concluded that relaxing the duopoly rule would not adversely affect the viewpoint and diversity of programming at the local level, and the increase of media outlets "virtually eliminated the risk of any reduction in competition that may occur as a result of relaxing the radio duopoly rule."[452]

The one-to-a-market rule, which prohibited a party from owning a commercial radio station (or an AM-FM combination) and a commercial television station in the same market, was relaxed by the adoption of a liberalized waiver policy.[453] The FCC will henceforth look favorably upon requests for waiver of the one-to-a-market rule when (1) cross-ownership will occur in one of the top twenty-five television markets and at least thirty separately owned, operated, and controlled broadcast licensees or "voices" will remain after the proposed merger, or (2) the request involves a "failed" station that has not been operated for a substantial period of time or is involved in bankruptcy proceedings.[454] The FCC will consider other waiver requests on a more rigorous case-by-case basis, placing particular emphasis on the potential benefits of the combination, the types of facilities involved, the number of stations already owned by the applicant, the financial difficulties of the station(s), and the nature of the market in light of the FCC's goals of diversity and competition.[455]

Even prior to the relaxation of its rules, the Commission generally would not in the absence of an allegation of abuse designate for hearing an application for license on the basis that the applicant had a concentration of control; a showing of common ownership structure or market share alone would not suffice.[456] The Commission also has waived its multiple ownership rules on a number of occasions, for such

---

448. *See, e.g.*, Eastern Broadcasting Corp., 30 F.C.C.2d 745 (1971).
449. Reexamination of the Commission's Cross-Interest Policy, 4 F.C.C. Rcd 2208 (1988).
450. Reexamination of the Commission's Cross-Interest Policy, 4 F.C.C. Rcd 2035 (1988).
451. Amendment of Section 73.3555 of the Commission's Rules, the Broadcast Multiple Ownership Rules, First Report and Order, 4 F.C.C. Rcd 1723 (1989); Second Report and Order, 4 F.C.C. Rcd 1741 (1989).
452. 4 F.C.C. Rcd 1723, 1727 (1989).
453. 4 F.C.C. Rcd 1741, 1741 (1989).
454. *Id.* at 1751-53.
455. *Id.* at 1753.
456. Multiple Ownership, 50 F.C.C.2d 1046, 1089 n.49 (1975); *see* KSL, Inc., 39 RAD. REG. 2d (P&F) 249, 253 (1976); Newhouse Broadcasting Corp., 59 F.C.C.2d 218, 237 (1976).

reasons as weakness of the market,[457] peculiar circumstances mitigating anticompetitive effects,[458] furtherance of other diversification policies,[459] and other countervailing factors.[460]

(4) Networks

The FCC has long been concerned with the economic power of the three commercial television networks and has sought to limit the power and influence of the networks over their affiliated stations in order to make the stations more independent.[461] However, because it was uncertain of its jurisdiction, until 1971 the FCC generally did not attempt to regulate them directly;[462] rather, it affected network behavior by regulating the networks' owned and affiliated stations.[463] In 1971, however, the Second Circuit upheld direct regulation of the networks as long as the regulation was "reasonably ancillary" to the Commission's statutory authority to regulate the broadcasting field.[464]

Most regulation designed to reach network practices has resulted from industry studies and rulemaking proceedings conducted by the FCC staff.[465] For example,

---

457.   *E.g.*, Pacific Broadcasting Corp., 66 F.C.C.2d 256, 259 (1977) (assignment of commonly owned Guam AM-FM-TV stations to single entity permitted because the market was small, the number of media serving the market was not insubstantial and, absent waiver, creditors would force station into receivership); KBLU Broadcasting Corp., 42 F.C.C.2d 450 (1973); Combined Communications Corp., 28 F.C.C.2d 16, 17 (1970) (Yuma-El Centro market one of the smallest in the country and significantly penetrated by cable); *cf.* Central Broadcasting Co., 28 F.C.C.2d 229, 229-30 (1971) (one-to-a-market rule waived because market revenues are so small and UHF station might otherwise go under); Marvin L. Rich, 19 RAD. REG. 2d (P&F) 751, 751-52 (1970) (one-to-a-market rule waived because acquisition contract signed long before rule's adoption; divestiture required within one year).

458.   Lady Sarah McKinney-Smith and J. Shelby McCallum, 59 F.C.C.2d 398, 402 (1976) (marriage of owners of two stations in the same service area that had substantial contour overlap; prenuptial agreement would aid in assuring arm's-length transactions between the parties); Washington Star Communs., 57 F.C.C.2d 475, 482-85 (1976).

459.   J.W. Woodruff, Jr., 39 F.C.C.2d 487, 488 (1973) (waiver of one-to-a-market rule in community with other VHF, UHF, AM, and FM facilities to diversify broadcast and print ownership).

460.   Marshall County Broadcasting Co. v. FCC, 42 RAD. REG. 2d (P&F) 605, 606 (D.D.C.) (FCC grant of application for FM station upheld notwithstanding the fact that the principal owner of the applicant was a 50% owner of the local telephone company; court noted that although the Review Board had established a policy disfavoring such cross-ownership, policy was outweighed by the substantial preference accorded the applicant under the standard competitive criteria), *aff'd mem.*, 571 F.2d 674 (D.C. Cir. 1978); *see also* discussion of Commission's cross-ownership rules, *infra* notes 437-40 and accompanying text.

461.   *See generally* FCC NETWORK INQUIRY SPECIAL STAFF, FCC RULES GOVERNING COMMERCIAL TELEVISION PRACTICES (Oct. 1979) [hereinafter cited as FCC RULES REPORT].

462.   *See* FCC NETWORK INQUIRY SPECIAL STAFF, FCC JURISDICTION TO REGULATE COMMERCIAL TELEVISION NETWORK PRACTICES (Oct. 1979).

463.   *Id.*

464.   Mt. Mansfield Television, Inc. v. FCC, 442 F.2d 470, 480-81 (2d Cir. 1971); *see also* CBS v. FCC, 629 F.2d 1, 27 (D.C. Cir. 1980) (Commission's application to the networks of § 312(a)(7) of the Communications Act relating to access by candidates for federal elective office "an exercise of its power 'reasonably ancillary' to the effective enforcement of the provision"), *aff'd*, 453 U.S. 367 (1981).

465.   FCC NETWORK INQUIRY SPECIAL STAFF, AN ANALYSIS OF TELEVISION PROGRAM PRODUCTION, ACQUISITION AND DISTRIBUTION (June 1980) [hereinafter NISS REPORT]; FCC RULES REPORT, *supra* note 461.

pursuant to a rulemaking proceeding in 1970, the Commission adopted "prime time access" and "financial interest and syndication" rules. These rules were intended to reduce television network power in program development[466] and to encourage the growth of alternative sources of programs for network and nonnetwork broadcast.[467] The rules prohibited commercial television stations in the top fifty markets owned or affiliated with a national television network from carrying more than three hours of network programming in prime time and prohibited a network from obtaining certain financial interests in programs not wholly produced by the network.[468] The Second Circuit upheld these rules.[469]

In 1972 the Justice Department instituted three separate antitrust suits against CBS, NBC, and ABC. The suits alleged that each network had violated Sections 1 and 2 of the Sherman Act by engaging in restraints of trade with their affiliates and others that resulted in each network monopolizing a market consisting of its own prime time entertainment programming and a market consisting of all prime time entertainment programming. The court declined to defer to the FCC[470] but nevertheless dismissed the latter claim.[471] Ultimately each of the suits was terminated with the entry of a consent judgment.[472]

In 1980, the FCC's Network Inquiry Special Staff recommended that the network rules be repealed because they were based on a misapprehension of the networks' role in the marketplace, served no useful purpose, and were anticompetitive.[473] The FCC commenced a rulemaking proceeding to determine whether the financial interest and syndication rules (but not the prime time access rule) should be repealed. After receiving comments from the Antitrust Division and the Federal

---

466. Competition and Responsibility in Network Television Broadcasting, 23 F.C.C.2d 382, 384, 397-98 (1970).

467. *Id.* at 394-95, 397.

468. *Id.* at 402; *see* 47 C.F.R. § 73.658(j) (1991) (financial interest and syndication rules); *id.* § 73.658(k) (prime time access rules).

469. Mt. Mansfield Television Inc. v. FCC, 442 F.2d 470, 489 (2d Cir. 1971); *see* CBS, 87 F.C.C.2d 30, 35-38 (1981) (declaratory ruling on § 73.658(j)(1)(ii) of the Commission's rules). The financial interest and syndication rules were modified in 1991 to allow greater network ability to develop program content. Evaluation of the Syndication and Financial Interest Rules, 10 FCC Digest 1589 (1991); 56 FED. REG. 26,242 (1991), *as amended,* 56 FED. REG. 64,207 (1991).

470. United States v. ABC, 1977-2 Trade Cas. (CCH) ¶ 61,580, at 72,371 (C.D. Cal. 1977); United States v. CBS, 1977-1 Trade Cas. (CCH) ¶ 61,327, at 71,139 (C.D. Cal. 1977); United States v. NBC, 1974-1 Trade Cas. (CCH) ¶ 74,885, at 95,922 (C.D. Cal. 1973).

471. United States v. CBS, 459 F. Supp. 832, 835 (C.D. Cal. 1978).

472. United States v. ABC, 1981-1 Trade Cas. (CCH) ¶ 64,150, at 76,895-900 (C.D. Cal. 1980); United States v. CBS, 1980-81 Trade Cas. (CCH) ¶ 63,594, at 77,171-76 (C.D. Cal. 1980); United States v. NBC, 449 F. Supp. 1127, 1131-34, 1145 (C.D. Cal. 1978). The consent judgment entered against NBC was modified in 1984 to conform to the decrees entered against the other networks, pursuant to a "most favored nation" clause contained in the NBC judgment. United States v. NBC, 1986-1 Trade Cas. (CCH) ¶ 66,956 (C.D. Cal. 1984).

473. NISS REPORT, *supra* note 465; *see also* Comments of the United States Department of Justice in BC Dkt. No. 82-345 (Jan. 26, 1983); Reply Comments of the Department of Justice in BC Dkt. No. 82-345 (Apr. 26, 1983); Comments of the Bureaus of Consumer Protection, Economics, and Competition of the Federal Trade Commission in BC Dkt. No. 82-345 (Jan. 26, 1983); Reply Comments of the Bureaus of Consumer Protection, Economics, and Competition of the Federal Trade Commission (Apr. 26, 1983); NEW TELEVISION NETWORKS, *supra* note 439 (network entry into cable television deemed to increase competition, enhance efficiency, and improve quality of cable service to advertisers and viewers).

Trade Commission supporting repeal, the FCC proposed a tentative decision that would delete the financial interest rule and modify the prohibition on syndication; however, subsequently the President directed the Antitrust Division to modify its position, and the FCC's Chairman announced that the Commission would take no action before May 10, 1984.[474]

In 1991, the Commission promulgated final rules that substantially relaxed but did not totally repeal the financial interest and syndication rules.[475]

In 1978, the Commission also initiated a proceeding[476] to determine whether it should alter its "network representation rule,"[477] which prohibits television stations, other than those owned and operated by a network, from being represented by their network in the nonnetwork (spot) sales market. The rule stemmed from the Commission's determination that network involvement would inhibit competition in the national advertising market and interfere "with the licensee's independent duty to operate his station in the public interest."[478] The Commission commenced the proceeding by granting a "temporary" waiver of the rule to the affiliates of the Spanish International Network (SIN) pending resolution of the proceeding. The Commission reopened the record in 1988 to obtain general comments regarding the continued efficacy of the rule.[479] The SIN waiver and other similar waivers granted by the FCC have now been made permanent.[480]

In 1989, the Commission eliminated Section 73.658(c) of its rules,[481] which had imposed a two-year limit on the duration of affiliation agreements between television station licensees and television networks, and had barred networks and stations from entering into affiliation agreements more than six months prior to the time the agreement was to commence.[482] The Commission concluded that, because of changes that have occurred in the television industry and in the mass media marketplace generally since the two-year rule was first applied to television in 1945, the rule is no longer necessary to promote competition among the networks and may

---

474. 45 ANTITRUST & TRADE REG. REP. (BNA) 791 (Nov. 17, 1983); see FCC News, Report No. 17633 (Aug. 4, 1983); Tentative Decision and Request for Further Comments, 94 F.C.C.2d 1019 (1983) (proposed amendment of the financial interest and syndication rules). The proposed amendment of financial interest and syndication rules (48 FED. REG. 38,020 (1983) was terminated effective March 14, 1990, and a new rulemaking proceeding was instituted the same day. 55 FED. REG. 11,222-23 (1990); cf. 47 C.F.R. § 73.658(j) (1991).

475. 56 FED. REG. 26,242 (1991), as amended, 56 FED. REG. 64,207 (1991). The rules permit greater network ability to develop program content.

476. Memorandum Opinion and Order and Notice of Proposed Rulemaking, 43 FED. REG. 45,895 (1978).

477. 47 C.F.R. § 73.658(i) (1991).

478. Network Representation of Stations in National Spot Sales, 27 F.C.C. 697, 720 (1959), recon. denied, 28 F.C.C. 447 (1960), aff'd sub nom. Metropolitan Television Co. v. FCC, 289 F.2d 874 (D.C. Cir. 1961).

479. Further Notice of Proposed Rulemaking, 53 FED. REG. 18,305 (1988). The FCC has proposed three alternative resolutions: (1) modification of the rule to exempt emerging networks, (2) elimination of the rule based on the increase in media voices in the marketplace, or (3) retaining the rule with a waiver policy.

480. 55 FED. REG. 53,152 (1990); see also Order, TV Network Representation Rule, 4 F.C.C. Rcd 4114 (1989) (granting waiver to Seven Hills Television Co., licensee of KTVW-TV, Phoenix, Arizona, subject to final approval of assignment of the station to Hallmark Acquisitions, Inc.).

481. 54 FED. REG. 14,961 (1989).

482. Review of Rules and Policies Concerning Network Broadcasting by Television Stations: Elimination or Modification of Section 73.658(c), 66 RAD. REG. 2d (P&F) 190 (1989).

actually serve to stifle such competition.[483]

(5) Regulatory Efforts to Increase Broadcast Competition

The FCC has largely deregulated the cable television industry, although cable systems are still subject to varying degrees of regulation by state and local authorities.[484] Also, the FCC has authorized direct broadcasting satellite (DBS) systems to provide television service directly to the home[485] and has determined that the service does not constitute "broadcasting" under Title III of the Communications Act, thereby relieving DBS Systems of numerous restrictions and obligations under the Act.[486] The FCC also has relaxed restrictions on subscription television[487] and on multipoint distribution service.[488]

In an effort to increase intraindustry competition, the FCC allocated four new short-spaced VHF television channels (called "drop-ins") and proposed to "drop-in" over one hundred new VHF stations across the United States.[489] Furthermore, the Commission has abolished its prior practice of assessing the impact of new local television outlets on existing stations.[490] Previously, the *Carroll* doctrine[491] and

---

483. *Id.* at 195.

484. *See* Section D.2.c of this chapter.

485. Direct Broadcast Satellites, 45 FED. REG. 72,719 (1980); Action Taken on Eight DBS Applications, FCC Rep. No. 18568 (Nov. 5, 1982); Satellite Television Corp., 91 F.C.C.2d 953 (1982); Direct Broadcast Satellites, 90 F.C.C.2d 676 (1982), *aff'd in part and vacated in part sub nom.* National Ass'n of Broadcasters v. FCC, 740 F.2d 1190 (D.C. Cir. 1984); 47 C.F.R. § 100 (1991).

486. Report and Order, Subscription Video, 2 F.C.C. Rcd 1001 (1987), *aff'd sub nom.* National Ass'n for Better Broadcasting v. FCC, 849 F.2d 665 (D.C. Cir. 1988); *see, e.g.,* 47 U.S.C. §§ 310(b), 312(a)(7), 315, 317, 318, 325, 503(b), 508, 509 (1988).

487. Subscription Television, 15 F.C.C.2d 466, 595-98 (1968), *aff'd sub nom.* National Ass'n of Theatre Owners v. FCC, 420 F.2d 194 (D.C. Cir. 1969), *cert. denied,* 397 U.S. 922 (1970); *see also* Report and Order, Subscription Video, 2 F.C.C. Rcd 1001 (1987), *aff'd sub nom.* National Ass'n for Better Broadcasting v. FCC, 849 F.2d 665 (D.C. Cir. 1988) (upholding FCC determination that subscription television is not "broadcasting" under Title III of the Communications Act); Fourth Report and Order, Subscription Television Service, 95 F.C.C.2d 457 (1983); Third Report and Order, Subscription Television Service, 90 F.C.C.2d 341 (1982); Subscription TV Program Rules, 52 F.C.C.2d 1, 70-72 (1974), 55 F.C.C.2d 187, 192 (1975), 67 F.C.C.2d 202, 205-08 (1977), FCC 79-535 (Oct. 12, 1979), 85 F.C.C.2d 631, 636-37 (1981).

488. Instructional Television Fixed Service (MDS Reallocation), 54 RAD. REG. 2d (P&F) 107 (1983), *recon. denied,* 98 F.C.C.2d 68 (1984); Orth-O-Vision, Inc., 69 F.C.C.2d 657, 669-71 (1978); Midwest Corp., 38 F.C.C.2d 897, 899-900 (1973), *recon. denied,* 53 F.C.C.2d 294 (1975); MultiPoint Distribution Serv., 34 F.C.C.2d 719, 725-29 (1971), 37 F.C.C.2d 444, 444-46 (1972), 45 F.C.C.2d 616, 627-36 (1974), *recon. denied,* 57 F.C.C.2d 301 (1975).

The FCC has allocated eight channels for multichannel MDS from the Instructional Television Fixed Service (ITFS) allowing for two four-channel systems. Multichannel MDS can be viewed, essentially, as "over-the-air" cable. ITFS users have also been allowed to lease excess capacity to MDS operators to enable them to provide additional channels for multichannel MDS. *See* Report and Order, 94 F.C.C.2d 1203 (1983); Memorandum Opinion and Order on Reconsideration, 98 F.C.C.2d 129 (1984). The Commission has decided to use a lottery to select permittees. Second Report and Order, 57 RAD. REG. 2d (P&F) 943 (1985), *stay denied,* FCC 85-229 (released May 7, 1985), *amended in part,* 104 F.C.C.2d 634 (1986), *aff'd on other grounds sub nom.* Pappas v. FCC, 807 F.2d 1019 (D.C. Cir. 1986).

489. VHF TV Top 100 Market, 81 F.C.C.2d 233, 234-35 (1980), *recon. denied,* 90 F.C.C.2d 160 (1982).

490. Policies Regarding Detrimental Effects of Proposed New Broadcast Stations on Existing Stations, 3 F.C.C. Rcd 638 (1988).

the UHF impact policy[492] had permitted an existing licensee to challenge a new entrant to the market on the grounds that the new station threatened adverse economic impact on existing or potential stations, thereby resulting in a net loss of service to the public. Upon reexamination of the policies, the FCC concluded that elimination of the policies would actually foster greater competition and would benefit the public by hastening the introduction of new service.[493] Finally, the Commission stated that the policies conflict with the FCC's "general policy of relying whenever possible on market forces rather than government regulation."

> We have consistently pursued regulatory policies intended to provide opportunities for development of alternative mass media technologies on the basis that an unrestricted, competitive environment generally leads to better service to the public than governmentally mandated market structures and service requirements.[494]

The Commission also authorized a new class of low power television stations.[495]

In regulating radio broadcasting, the FCC commenced a plan to allocate numerous new FM stations[496] and most recently has created an additional class of FM broadcast stations, designated "Class C3," to be available throughout most of the United States.[497] As part of its plan to expand the AM band, the Commission has proposed to liberalize its licensing procedures.[498] The FCC also has approved the institution of AM Stereo but has left it to the marketplace to determine which stereo system broadcasters will adopt.[499]

---

491. *See* Carroll Broadcasting Co. v. FCC, 258 F.2d 440 (D.C. Cir. 1958).
492. *See* Triangle Publications, 29 F.C.C. 315 (1960), *aff'd*, Triangle Publications v. FCC, 291 F.2d 342 (D.C. Cir. 1961).
493. 3 F.C.C. Rcd at 640, 642.
494. *Id.* at 640.
495. Low Power Television Broadcasting, 68 F.C.C.2d 1525, 1535 (1978), 82 F.C.C.2d 47, 54-55 (1980); Inquiry into the Future Role of Low Power Television Broadcasting and Television Translators, Report and Order, 51 RAD. REG. 2d (P&F) 476 (1982), *recon. granted*, 53 RAD. REG. 2d (P&F) 1267 (1983), *stay denied*, FCC 83-447 (released Sept. 28, 1983), *further recon. denied*, FCC 83-486 (released October 27, 1983). The Commission has adopted lottery procedures for the processing of Low Power Television applications. Low Power Television and Television Translator Service, 102 F.C.C.2d 295 (1984).
496. Modification of FM Broadcast Station Rules, 94 F.C.C.2d 152 (1983). Implementation of BC Docket No. 80-90 to Increase the Availability of FM Broadcast Assignments, 100 F.C.C.2d 1332 (1985); *see also* Amendment of Part 73 of the Rules to Provide for an Additional FM Station Class, 3 F.C.C. Rcd 5941 (1988). The FCC has announced procedures for selecting licensees for the additional FM allocations made available in this proceeding. 50 FED. REG. 15,558 (1985), *clarified and recon. denied in part*, 51 FED. REG. 9210 (1986). Under these procedures, certain AM daytime licensees in markets where FM stations are available will be given "special consideration" in comparative hearings to resolve mutually exclusive applications. This special consideration will result in this broadcast experience being upgraded "so that it will be equal to the enhancement value of local residence or minority ownership." 50 FED. REG. at 15,561; Second Report and Order, 101 F.C.C.2d 638 (1985), *aff'd*, National Black Media Coalition v. FCC, 822 F.2d 277 (1987).
497. First Report and Order, 66 RAD. REG. 2d (P&F) 338 (1989) (the FCC determined that the new class of station "will promote a competitive marketplace for the development and use of broadcast facilities and services").
498. 50 FED. REG. 33, 844 (1985); 51 FED. REG. 8706 (1986); Fourth Notice of Inquiry, FCC 82-72 (1988).
499. AM Stereophonic Broadcasting, 84 F.C.C.2d 960 (1981), 51 RAD. REG. 2d (P&F) 1 (1982).

The Commission has eliminated radio and television regulations relating to program content, the ascertainment of community interests, commercial time limits, and requirements to keep logs of programs.[500] Correspondingly, the Commission has refused to consider proposed program format changes as a factor in license renewal cases. The Supreme Court upheld this position upon finding that the FCC could promote the public interest by reliance on unregulated market forces and competition.[501]

Congress also has shown strong interest in the deregulation of radio. Amendments in 1981 and 1982 to the Communications Act permit licensee selection by lottery and authorize longer radio television license terms.[502]

Congress is considering the removal of legal obstacles to the development of High Definition Television (HDTV) technology. The sponsors of the legislation are seeking elimination of certain antitrust restrictions in order to spur the formation of consortiums, to allow companies to spread out the costs of research and development, and to allow the United States to become more competitive in the high-technology trade.[503]

---

500. Deregulation of Radio, 73 F.C.C.2d 457, 538-39 (1979); 46 FED. REG. 13,888 (1981), aff'd in part and remanded in part sub nom. Office of Communication of the Church of Christ v. FCC, 707 F.2d 1413 (D.C. Cir. 1983) (affirming elimination of programming guidelines, ascertainment procedures, and commercial guidelines); Revision of Programming and Commercialization Policies, Ascertainment Requirements, and Program Log Requirements for Commercial Television Stations, 98 F.C.C.2d 1076 (1984), recon. denied, 104 F.C.C.2d 357 (1986), aff'd in part and remanded in part sub nom. Action for Children's Television v. FCC, 821 F.2d 741 (D.C. Cir. 1987); Further Notice of Proposed Rulemaking, 2 F.C.C. Rcd 6822 (1987); see also Ascertainment of Community Problems by Broadcast Applicants: Small Market Exemption, 86 F.C.C.2d 798 (1981), aff'd, National Black Media Coalition v. FCC, No. 80-1758 (D.C. Cir. 1983); Simplified Renewal Application, 87 F.C.C.2d 1127 (1981), aff'd, Black Citizens for a Fair Media v. FCC, 719 F.2d 407 (D.C. Cir. 1983), cert. denied, 467 U.S. 1255 (1984).

501. FCC v. WNCN Listeners Guild, 450 U.S. 582, 604 (1981).

502. 47 U.S.C. § 309(i) (1988). Authority to utilize lotteries for initial licensing was conferred on the FCC by the Communications Amendments Act of 1982, Pub. L. No. 97-259, 96 Stat. 1087 (1982); Omnibus Reconciliation Act of 1981, Pub. L. No. 97-35, 95 Stat. 357 (1981); see S. 2827, 96th Cong., 2d Sess. (1980) (The Communications Act Amendments of 1980); H.R. 6121, 96th Cong., 1st Sess. (1979) (The Telecommunications Act of 1979); The Communications Act of 1979; Hearings on H.R. 333 Before the Subcomm. on Communications of the House Comm. on Interstate and Foreign Commerce, 96th Cong., 1st Sess. 2 (1979).

   The Commission has adopted rules implementing a lottery system to choose among competing applications in various services other than the licensing of AM and FM radio and full-power television stations. See Amendment of the Commission's Rules to Allow the Selection from Among Certain Competing Applications Using Random Selection or Lotteries Instead of Comparative Hearings, 93 F.C.C.2d 952 (1983), recon. granted in part., FCC 84-596 (released Dec. 4, 1984), modified, 49 FED. REG. 49,466 (1984), corrected, 50 FED. REG. 5,583 (1985), recon. denied, 50 FED. REG. 50,167 (1985); Third Report and Order, 102 F.C.C.2d 140 (1985), aff'd, Inquiry on Amendment of Part 74 of the Commission's Rules Concerning FM Translator Stations, 3 F.C.C. Rcd 3664, 3670 (1988).

   On March 20, 1989, the Commission initiated a proceeding "to explore the possibility of improving the system to award licenses for new broadcast facilities" by using random selection or lottery procedures. Notice of Proposed Rulemaking, Amendment of the Commission's Rules for New AM, FM, and Television Stations by Random Selection (Lottery), 4 F.C.C. Rcd 2256 (1989).

503. H.R. 1024, 101st Cong., 1st Sess. (1989) (The National Cooperative Innovation and Commercialization Act of 1989), introduced by Reps. Boucher and Campbell, would relax antitrust restrictions on joint production ventures through an exemption procedure. Several other bills designed to promote joint ventures are also being considered by the Economic and Commercial

b. COMMON CARRIERS

(1) Overview

Telecommunications common carriers, including telephone and telegraph companies, are generally regulated both by state regulatory agencies pursuant to state law and by the FCC pursuant to its authority under the Communications Act of 1934, as amended.[504] Title II of the Act gives the FCC most of the conventional powers of a regulator, including the power to regulate entry, terms and conditions of service, interconnection, construction, systems of accounts, depreciation, and the division of property between state and federal regulatory jurisdictions. The extent to which the FCC has exercised this authority has varied from time to time and among classes of carriers.

The implementation of two antitrust consent decrees secured by the Department of Justice in 1982 and 1984 has significantly shaped the structure of this portion of the communications industry. The 1982 decree in *United States v. American Telephone & Telegraph Co.* resulted in the 1984 spin-off of seven regional telephone holding companies from AT&T.[505] AT&T continues to be in the international, interstate, and intrastate long distance business, as well as the manufacture and provision of telecommunications equipment. In addition, the 1982 decree relieved AT&T of restraints imposed on it under a 1956 consent decree that had limited the other kinds of business in which AT&T could engage.[506] Conversely, the 1982 decree limited the seven regional holding companies spun off by AT&T, the Bell Operating Companies (BOCs), to what the decree defined as exchange and exchange access telecommunications services.[507] The district court suggested, and the parties agreed, however, that the decree, be modified to permit the divested companies also to provide telephone directories and customer premises equipment. In the years since it entered the decree, the court has removed or waived a number of the restrictions. The regional holding companies remain precluded from providing domestically long distance services, from manufacturing or providing telecommunications equipment, and from manufacturing customer premises equipment for the domestic market. In 1991, however, the court removed the restrictions on information services.[508]

Law Subcommittee.

 In addition, the FCC is in the process of deciding the standard for HDTV. First Report and Order, Advanced Television Systems and Their Impact on the Existing Television Broadcast Service, 5 F.C.C. Rcd 5627 (1990).

504. 47 U.S.C. §§ 151-757 (1988).

505. The decision adopting the consent decree is reported at 552 F. Supp. 131 (D.D.C. 1982), *aff'd sub nom.* Maryland v. United States, 460 U.S. 1001 (1983).

506. *Id.* at 226.

507. *See, e.g.,* United States v. Western Elec. Co., 604 F. Supp. 256, 267 (D.D.C. 1984) (granting several waivers of the line of business restrictions of the decree).

508. United States v. Western Elec. Co., 767 F. Supp. 308, 332 (D.D.C. 1991), *stay vacated,* 1991-2 Trade Cas. (CCH) ¶ 69,610 (D.C. Cir. 1991). In removing the restrictions, the district court made clear that it was doing so only to comply with the mandate of the D.C. Circuit. *See* United States v. Western Elec. Co., 900 F.2d 283 (D.C. Cir.), *cert. denied,* 111 S. Ct. 283 (1990).

 Legislation is also being considered in Congress to remove or relax the manufacturing restriction, and to improve safeguards on BOCs' provision of information services. *See, e.g.,* S. 2112, 102d Cong., 1st Sess. (1991) (Information Service Diversity Act of 1991); H.R. 3515, 102d

In 1983 the Department of Justice took a somewhat different approach in approving the acquisition of Sprint, the third largest long distance carrier, by GTE Corporation, which was at the time the second largest telephone holding company. The decree proposed in that case permitted GTE to acquire Sprint but required GTE to separate its telephone operations from its long distance and information services and to agree not to discriminate in interconnection between its affiliates and other providers. In early 1985 the GTE decree was approved by the same district court that approved the AT&T decree.[509] Shortly thereafter GTE completed the acquisition of Sprint. By 1989 GTE had reportedly reduced its ownership interest in Sprint to only 20% with United Telecommunications — another telephone holding company — holding the remaining interest.

Largely as a result of these two consent decrees, common carriers in telecommunications today are described as either local exchange carriers (i.e., local telephone companies) or interexchange carriers (i.e., long distance companies). Local exchange carriers provide both local calling services and "access" services used by interexchange carriers to originate or terminate long distance calls. Interexchange carriers provide interstate and intrastate long distance services.

In the last few years, another significant group of common carriers has arisen to provide a form of radio-based telephone service called cellular telephone service. While only 1 or 2% of the population currently uses cellular telephone service, some observers predict that more than 10% of the households in major urban areas will subscribe to cellular service within the next decade. As they are structured today, cellular carriers permit a significant number of people to make and receive telephone calls by means of radio connections between a grid of transmitters and their cellular radio-telephones. The transmitters permit efficient use of radio frequencies by handing off the call to an adjacent transmitter as the caller moves from the coverage area of one transmitter to the coverage area of another transmitter. Most cellular calls today either originate or terminate with the landline telephone system. Thus, cellular carriers depend heavily on local exchange carriers and interexchange carriers to connect the landline system with the cellular system.

In each major geographic area the FCC has licensed two carriers to provide cellular service and has required those carriers to permit "resellers" to compete with them in providing service at the retail level to the public.[510] Largely because the FCC has licensed cellular systems separately for each geographic area, in most areas the non-wireline[511] cellular "wholesale" carriers are partnerships or corporations owned by several different entities, and many investors have had ownership interests in a large number of different cellular companies. As might be expected, the last few

Cong., 1st Sess. (1991) (Telecommunications Act of 1991).
509. United States v. GTE Corp., 1985-1 Trade Cas. (CCH) ¶ 66,355, at 64,771 (D.D.C. 1985).
510. Cellular Communs. Sys., 86 F.C.C.2d 469 (1981), recon. granted in part, 89 F.C.C.2d 58 (1982), further recon. granted in part, 90 F.C.C.2d 571 (1982), aff'd sub nom. MCI Cellular Tel. Co. v. FCC, 738 F.2d 1322 (D.C. Cir. 1984).
511. One of the two licenses in each area is generally reserved for the "wireline" carrier, i.e., the local exchange carrier, although in rare instances the wireline carrier has not chosen to accept such a license. Under the 1982 consent decree, the BOCs remain generally prohibited from providing interexchange cellular services, however. United States v. Western Elec. Co., 673 F. Supp. 525, 550-52 (D.D.C. 1987), aff'd in part and rev'd in part on other grounds, 900 F.2d 283 (D.C. Cir.), cert. denied, 111 S. Ct. 283 (1990).

years have seen the major investors in cellular systems trading or selling their ownership interests so that the number of investors in most systems has declined. Further, as a result of several mergers between the major investors, only a dozen or so of these investors remain as of January 1992.

(2) Federal Regulation

Although the FCC has the statutory authority to impose traditional public utility regulation on interstate common carriers, in the last two decades it has come to rely more and more on market forces to accomplish its regulatory goals. In doing so, however, the Commission has devised a variety of means to protect the new competition it has sought to authorize.[512] For instance, when the FCC deregulated customer premises equipment, it also precluded the states from regulating that equipment and required the Bell System telephone companies to use separate subsidiaries to provide the equipment.[513] Over the next few years the FCC waived or modified those rules. In 1987 it replaced structural separation with accounting and interconnection rules designed to protect against cross-subsidy of unregulated businesses by regulated businesses.[514] Similarly, the Commission deregulated "inside wire" (the wires inside a customer's home that connect the customer's telephone to the telephone company facilities outside the house). The D.C. Circuit has said the FCC does not have a basis to preempt state regulation of inside wire.[515]

Despite continued concentration in the industry, the FCC has largely forborne from regulating entry or the interstate services of most interexchange carriers. In a string of decisions from 1980 through 1985, the FCC deregulated all interstate carriers except AT&T.[516] In 1989 the FCC adopted a "price cap" plan for regulating AT&T, which, in effect, relieves AT&T from the formalistic approach of rate of return regulation and gives it a large amount of pricing freedom for its interstate services.[517] In 1991, the FCC further relaxed regulation of a wide range of AT&T services. In the same vein, the Commission has never regulated the interstate services of cellular carriers and paging carriers, though many states do regulate the intrastate services offered by such companies. Similarly, the Commission

---

512. For a summary of the FCC's view of the history of its regulation of common carriers, see the discussion in In the Matter of Policy and Rules Concerning Rates for Dominant Carriers, 66 RAD. REG. 2d (P&F) 372 (1989).

513. Second Computer Inquiry, 77 F.C.C.2d 384 (1980), modified on recon., 84 F.C.C.2d 50 (1980), modified on further recon., 88 F.C.C.2d 512 (1981), aff'd sub nom. Computer & Communs. Indus. Ass'n v. FCC, 693 F.2d 198 (D.C. Cir. 1982), cert. denied, 461 U.S. 938 (1983).

514. Furnishing of Customer Premises Equipment by the Bell Operating Telephone Companies and the Independent Telephone Companies, 2 F.C.C. Rcd 143, modified on recon., 3 F.C.C. Rcd 22 (1987), aff'd sub nom. Illinois Bell Tel. Co. v. FCC, 883 F.2d 104 (D.C. Cir. 1989).

515. The FCC's most recent decision is at Detariffing the Installation and Maintenance of Inside Wiring, 3 F.C.C. Rcd 1719 (1988). The D.C. Circuit's decision reversing and remanding the aspects of that decision preempting state regulation is National Association of Regulatory Utility Commissioners v. FCC, 880 F.2d 422 (D.C. Cir. 1989).

516. A summary of the history of these decisions is set forth at Policy and Rules Concerning Rates for Dominant Carriers, 2 F.C.C. Rcd 5208, 5223 nn.9-11 (1987).

517. In the Matter of Policy and Rules Concerning Rates for Dominant Carriers, 66 RAD. REG. 2d (P&F) 372 (1989).

has encouraged new entry in the market for international telecommunications services.

In 1984, the FCC began implementing a new set of rates for local exchange carriers to charge as compensation for providing access services for the origination and termination of interstate interexchange carriers. The Commission was moving toward this structure even before the AT&T and GTE consent decrees, but those decrees created an urgency to its deliberations. In a string of decisions beginning in 1983, the Commission has established rates for local exchange carriers to charge for these services. Because the FCC does not yet consider these services to be subject to sufficient competition, its policy of reduced regulation has not resulted in deregulation of local exchange carriers. Indeed, in the course of the access charge proceedings, the FCC has extended the reach of its tariffing requirements even to small local exchange carriers that traditionally have simply concurred in the interstate tariffs of interexchange carriers. In 1991 the FCC initiated a proceeding to examine the possibility of requiring local exchange carriers (LEC) to offer so-called "alternate access carriers" interconnection to the public switched networks via the LEC's end office.[518]

In late 1988 the FCC approved plans by AT&T and each of the Bell Operating Companies to implement the Commission's Open Network Architecture orders. The purpose of those orders is to assure that the BOCs and AT&T do not impair the ability of other companies to provide enhanced services, which rely on the use of their local exchange and interexchange services. Consequently, the FCC required the telephone companies to establish plans to unbundle services where practical to assure that enhanced-service providers had nondiscriminatory access to those services.[519] The Ninth Circuit subsequently found that the FCC's decision to substitute nonstructural for structural safeguards to protect ratepayers and competitors from the harmful effects of cross-subsidization was arbitrary and capricious.[520]

Generally, FCC regulation does not provide antitrust immunity. Only one section of the Communications Act, Section 221(a),[521] allows the Commission to give express antitrust immunity. That section, which antedates the 1934 Communications Act, provides that the FCC may immunize a merger of two telephone companies from antitrust attack by approving the merger. Otherwise, there is no express antitrust immunity in the Communications Act. The courts have usually refused to

---

518. *See* Third Report and Order, MTS and WATS Market Structure, 93 F.C.C.2d 241 (1983) (Access Order), *modified on recon.*, 97 F.C.C.2d 682 (1983) (Reconsideration Order), *modified on further recon.*, 97 F.C.C.2d 834 (1984), *aff'd in principal part and remanded in part sub nom.* National Ass'n of Regulatory Util. Comm'rs v. FCC, 737 F.2d 1095 (D.C. Cir. 1984), *cert. denied,* 469 U.S. 1227 (1985), *modified on recon.*, 99 F.C.C.2d 708 (1984), *modified on further recon.*, 50 FED. REG. 18,249 (1985) (Third Reconsideration), *modified on further recon.*, 59 RAD. REG. 2d (P&F) 1127 (1986), *aff'd sub nom.* AT&T v. FCC, 832 F.2d 1285 (D.C. Cir. 1987).

    See Notice of Proposed Rulemaking and Notice of Inquiry, Expanded Interconnect with Local Telephone Company Facilities, CC Dkt. No. 91-141, 56 FED. REG. 34,159-201 (1991).

519. Filing and Review of Open Network Architecture Plans, 4 F.C.C. Rcd 1 (1988), *modified on recon.*, 5 F.C.C. Rcd 3084, *further order,* 5 F.C.C. Rcd 3103 (1990).

520. California v. FCC, 905 F.2d 1217, 1238 (9th Cir. 1990). On remand, the Commission claimed to have denied a "strengthened" set of nonstructural safeguards and again removed the structual separation requirement. *See* Computer III Remand Proceedings: Bell Operating Company Safeguards and Tier 1 Local Exchange Company Safeguards, 6 F.C.C. Rcd 7571 (1991).

521. 47 U.S.C. § 221(a) (1988).

find that Congress intended to confer blanket immunity on regulated telecommunications common carriers.[522] The courts have likewise considered and usually rejected claims that the Communications Act effects an implied repeal of the antitrust laws that would give regulated telecommunications common carriers implied immunity.[523] Nevertheless, at least one court has held that consideration of antitrust issues should be deferred because the FCC has primary jurisdiction.[524]

(3) State Regulation

Like the FCC, state regulators have had to adapt quickly to changes in the number and kinds of common carriers operating in their jurisdictions. The states, like the FCC, have developed a series of access charges that local exchange carriers may assess for originating and terminating long distance calls. Likewise, the states are beginning to wrestle with the ratemaking questions posed by the FCC's Open Network Architecture requirements for unbundling of service elements. At the same time, the states are dealing with the realities of a telecommunications marketplace that offers purchasers many more choices than were imagined at the time state regulatory statutes were written. As a result, state regulators are addressing both consumer and competitive issues that arise from alternative operator services, customer-owned coin telephones, and recorded announcements available from every telephone.

Although the states have moved more slowly than the FCC, the trend toward relaxed regulation of telecommunications services is now clear. By now, most states have allowed interexchange carriers a good deal of flexibility in pricing and entry. Iowa was the first state to deregulate these services entirely in June 1989. The majority of states also do not actively regulate the rates of radio common carriers. In addition, several states are presently considering or have already adopted new forms of regulation for the local exchange carriers under their jurisdiction. For the most part, however, these new forms of regulation have not amounted to deregulation in the conventional sense. The local exchange companies generally have retained their tariffing and nondiscrimination obligations. The new regulations continue to limit the ability of local exchange companies to change the price of services and continue to limit their overall profitability.

Unlike FCC regulation, state regulation of common carriers may be found to provide immunity from federal antitrust actions under the state action doctrine first enunciated in *Parker v. Brown*.[525] However, as state regulators change the form

---

522. *See, e.g.,* Phonetele, Inc. v. AT&T, 664 F.2d 716, 729 (9th Cir. 1982), *cert. denied*, 459 U.S. 1145 (1983).

523. *See, e.g.,* Southern Pac. Communs. Co. v. AT&T, 740 F.2d 980, 999-1000 (D.C. Cir. 1984) (no implied immunity because no pervasive regulatory control over rates and interconnection devices so as to conflict with antitrust laws), *cert. denied*, 470 U.S. 1005 (1985); Mid-Texas Communs. Sys. v. AT&T, 615 F.2d 1372, 1379 (immunity implied only if necessary to permit regulatory scheme to function), *cert. denied*, 449 U.S. 912 (1980).

524. *See, e.g.,* Carter v. AT&T, 365 F.2d 486, 498 (5th Cir. 1966), *cert. denied*, 385 U.S. 1008 (1967). *But see* Litton Sys. v. AT&T, 700 F.2d 785 (2d Cir. 1983) (rejecting primary jurisdiction argument), *cert. denied*, 464 U.S. 1073 (1984).

525. 317 U.S. 341 (1943); *see, e.g.,* Capital Tel. Co. v. New York Tel. Co., 750 F.2d 1154 (2d Cir. 1984) (affirming judgment on pleadings on ground of state action immunity), *cert. denied*, 471 U.S. 1101 (1985).

of regulation, the extent to which a state "actively supervises" common carrier conduct may require a specific factual investigation.[526]

c. CABLE TELEVISION

The FCC has deregulated many aspects of the cable television industry,[527] while leaving certain regulation to state and local authorities.[528] The FCC has preempted state and local regulation of "all operational aspects of cable communications, including signal carriage and technical standards."[529] It also has preempted state and local authority to regulate the rates of all but the basic tier of cable service and has affirmed the authority of each cable operator to "add, delete, or realign its service as long as the basic service contains all signals mandated by the Commission's rules."[530]

FCC regulatory oversight does not generally confer antitrust immunity on a regulated industry such as the broadcast or cable industry.[531] As a policy matter,

---

526. See Subpart B.2 of this chapter for a discussion of the state action defense.

527. The cable industry is primarily governed by the Cable Communications Policy Act of 1984, 47 U.S.C. §§ 521-559 (1988) (Cable Act). The major provisions of the Cable Act (1) largely preclude enforcement of programming obligations contained in cable franchises (§ 544), (2) impose substantive and procedural restrictions on the ability of municipalities and other franchising authorities to modify or deny renewal of their cable franchises (§§ 545, 546), (3) preempt all rate regulation of cable television services by the federal government and the states, except where they act as franchising authorities (§ 543), (4) grandfather basic rate regulation provisions of municipal and other cable franchises for a two-year period and thereafter permit rate regulation only of "basic cable service" where, pursuant to Commission-established criteria, "a cable system is not subject to effective competition" (id.), (5) permit enforcement of cable franchise requirements for public, governmental, and educational channel access (§ 531), (6) require cable systems to set aside a portion of their channel capacity for "commercial use" and establish procedures for resolution of disputes arising out of the guarantee of commercial access (§532), (7) codify existing Commission regulations governing broadcast/cable and telephone/cable cross-ownership (§ 553), and (8) protect subscriber privacy and impose criminal penalties for unauthorized reception and cable or satellite communications (§§ 551, 553, 605). The FCC promulgated certain regulations to implement provisions of the Cable Act. Cable Communications Act Rules, 58 RAD. REG. 2d (P&F) 1 (1985), recon. denied, 104 F.C.C.2d 386 (1986), aff'd sub nom. American Civil Liberties Union v. FCC, 823 F.2d 1554 (D.C. Cir. 1987).

528. There has been some recent concern about the cable industry's "apparent lack of accountability" and the suggestion that cable might be reregulated on the federal level. Remarks of House Commerce Comm. Chairman Dingell before INTV Board, Communications Daily, June 14, 1989, at 1. Chairman Dingell also recommended that the FCC begin preparing for its report to Congress on cable rates and services and the effect of competition on the cable marketplace. The report was due in 1990 and is required by the 1984 Cable Act (47 U.S.C. § 543(h)). Rep. Neal has circulated a letter in the House of Representatives urging support for his resolution (H.R. Con. Res. 138), which calls for a comprehensive review of cable industry practices with possible reinstatement of regulation. Communications Daily, Vol. 9, No. 113 (June 13, 1989). In 1991, the Commission modified the rule defining "effective competition" in cable service and adopted new rules for the regulation of basic cable rates in the absence of such competition. 56 FED. REG. 33,387 (1991).

Legislation reregulating the cable industry was passed in the House in 1991, but failed to clear the Senate. In early 1992, the Senate passed an extensive reregulation bill, but at the time of writing the House has not acted on the Senate bill, and the President has threatened to veto the bill. S. 12, 102d Cong., 2d Sess. (1992) (Cable Television Consumer Protection Act of 1992).

529. Capital Cities Cable, Inc. v. Crisp, 467 U.S. 691, 702 (1984).

530. Community Cable TV, Inc., 98 F.C.C.2d 1180, 1190 (1984).

531. United States v. RCA, 358 U.S. 334, 336 (1959).

the FCC usually will not consider an investigation or enforcement of the antitrust laws. In *Character Qualifications in Broadcast Licensing*,[532] the FCC explicitly stated:

> While [broadcast related antitrust and anticompetitive] activity may have a potential bearing on the applicant's character, we do not believe it appropriate or necessary for this agency to engage in the initial investigation or enforcement of the antitrust laws . . . . [W]e are of the view that, for the purposes of a character determination, consideration should be given only to *adjudications involving antitrust or anticompetitive violations* from a court of competent jurisdiction, the Federal Trade Commission, or other governmental unit charged with the responsibility of policing such activity.[533]

The FCC recently reemphasized that adjudicated status is essential to the relevance of a charge of "economic misconduct" under its basic qualifications criteria.[534] *Dubuque TV Limited Partnership* involved the assignment of a television license. CRTV, a rival television station of Dubuque TV Limited Partnership (DTV) contended that DTV had violated federal antitrust laws and the FCC's network program nonduplication rules[535] by conspiring with the Dubuque cable television system operator to black out CRTV's programming on the Dubuque cable system. The FCC found no basis for CRTV's contentions under the FCC's character evaluation standards, because CRTV did not allege that DTV had been *adjudicated* to have violated federal antitrust statutes.

The FCC does not license cable systems, which by statute are subject to franchise by any governmental authority empowered by federal, state, or local law to grant a franchise.[536] However, the FCC does license associated facilities in the cable television relay service (CARS).[537] In doing so, the FCC is often asked to take into account antitrust considerations. In *Tele-Communications, Inc. (TCI)*, the petitioner challenged the transfer of control of CARS stations licensed to Group W Cable, Inc. on the ground that the transfer would "create a combination of large cable systems with both the incentive and the ability to inhibit full and free competition in the cable television industry."[538] The petition also alleged that increased concentration would preclude program suppliers from entering the market if the larger multiple system operators chose not to carry a particular service.[539]

The FCC allowed the transfer, pointing out first the narrow scope of its review as an agency concerned primarily with telecommunications policy and not antitrust enforcement.[540] The FCC quoted its statement from *Teleprompter Corp.*:[541]

> It is not our function to apply the antitrust laws as such. It is our duty, however, to refuse licenses or renewals to any person who engages or proposes to engage in practices which

---

532. 102 F.C.C.2d 1179 (1985), *recon. denied*, 1 F.C.C.Rcd. 421 (1986).
533. 102 F.C.C.2d at 1202 (footnote omitted) (emphasis supplied).
534. Dubuque TV Limited Partnership, 4 F.C.C.Rcd 1999 (1989).
535. 47 C.F.R. § 76.92(g) (1991).
536. 47 U.S.C. § 552(9) (1988).
537. *See* 47 C.F.R. §§ 78.1 *et seq.* (1991).
538. TCI, slip op., ¶ 4 (May 27, 1986).
539. *Id.*
540. *Id.* at ¶ 18.
541. 87 F.C.C. 2d 531 (1981), *aff'd*, 89 F.C.C.2d 417 (1982).

will prevent either himself or other licensees or both from making the fullest use of radio facilities. This is the standard of public interest, convenience or necessity which we must apply to all applications for licenses and renewals.[542]

The FCC then noted that it had previously addressed and rejected contentions that large size per se is an evil in the communications industry.[543] Furthermore, in 1982, the FCC reviewed the ownership patterns in the cable television industry and found nothing to suggest that the industry was not highly competitive, nor that regulatory intervention to redirect development patterns was warranted at the time.[544] As a result, most antitrust and antitrust-related issues are resolved in the courts.

Antitrust issues may arise in situations in which an acquisition results in vertical integration, for example, acquisition by a supplier of an ownership interest in a customer.[545] Operators and program suppliers may desire vertical integration for various reasons: securing channel access, provision of know-how, provision of funding, reduction of transportation costs, expansion of program supply, and spreading of risks.[546] The FCC currently has a rulemaking proceeding that would eliminate its proscription of common ownership of a national television network and a cable system that carries any broadcast signal.[547]

Pricing practices of cable operators also have resulted in antitrust complaints. Alleged unlawful pricing practices may be divided into two groups – discriminatory

---

542.   TCI, slip op., at 18 (quoting *Teleprompter Corp.*, 87 F.C.C.2d at 541) (footnote omitted).

543.   TCI, slip op., at ¶ 21 (citing *Teleprompter Corp.*, 87 F.C.C.2d at 542); Combined Communs. Corp., 72 F.C.C.2d 637 (1979), *aff'd*, 76 F.C.C.2d 445 (1980).

544.   *See* CATV Multiple Ownership, 91 F.C.C.2d 46 (1982). On May 26, 1989, the FCC approved the Time-Warner merger, involving over 700 cable systems. *See* Communications Daily, May 30, 1989 and June 20, 1989.

545.   In a sense, all cable operators are vertically integrated in that they are both signal transporters and programming retailers.

546.   The Department of Justice, in comments filed November 29, 1982, in the FCC's network/cable cross-ownership proceeding (CC Dkt. 82-434), expressed concern that vertical integration could create possible incentives for network-owned cable operators to deny channels to competing networks. In United States v. Columbia Pictures Indus., 507 F. Supp. 412 (S.D.N.Y. 1980), *aff'd without opinion*, 659 F.2d 1063 (2d Cir. 1981), the district court granted a preliminary injunction and held, inter alia, that the existing vertical integration between HBO, Showtime, and Rainbow, and multiple system operators was not such a barrier to entry to justify the proposed ventures' nine-month exclusive window and price-fixing features.

         On August 12, 1983, the Department of Justice approved the merger of Showtime and The Movie Channel, conditioned upon Warner remaining the only studio to own the combined programming sources (MCA and Paramount could not remain co-owners). 45 ANTITRUST & TRADE REG. REP. (BNA) 275 (Aug. 18, 1983).

547.   47 C.F.R. § 76.501(a)(1) (1991); *see* Further Notice of Proposed Rulemaking, BC Dkt. No. 82-434, FCC 88-271 (released Sept. 6, 1988). In a related issue, the FCC eliminated its mandatory signal carriage ("must-carry") rules, which required cable systems to carry the signals of local television stations. The rules were struck down as violating the first amendment rights of cable operators. Quincy Cable TV, Inc. v. FCC, 768 F.2d 1434 (D.C. Cir. 1985), *cert. denied*, 476 U.S. 1169 (1986). The FCC then adopted interim "must-carry" rules applicable for only five years. *See generally* Amendments of part 76, 1 F.C.C.Rcd 864 (1986), *recon.*, 2 F.C.C.Rcd 3593 (1987). The interim rules were again invalidated. Century Communs. Corp. v. FCC, 835 F.2d 292 (D.C. Cir. 1987). As a result, in Amendments of part 76, MM Dkt. 85-349 and Gen. Dkt. 87-107, FCC 89-162 (released May 30, 1989), the FCC's "must-carry" rules were eliminated effective July 14, 1989.

pricing and predatory or below-cost pricing. Discriminatory pricing allegations might arise, for example, when a cable operator lowers its prices in a portion of the franchise area overbuilt by a competing cable company, but not in other portions of the franchise area. Several courts have held that the Robinson-Patman Act does not apply, characterizing cable television as the provision of entertainment – a service rather than a commodity.[548] Cable operators have also been charged with engaging in predatory conduct by reducing rates in order to retain or regain subscribers when a newly franchised second cable operator entered the area.[549]

Allegations of nonprice predation include situations in which the established cable operator allegedly induces the local franchise authority to delay or reject an overbuild franchise to a second cable operator or in which pole attachment overcharges potentially deter entry. Under *Eastern Railroad Presidents Conference v. Noerr Motor Freight, Inc.*[550] and *United Mine Workers v. Pennington*,[551] individual or concerted efforts to influence government action are immune from federal antitrust claims or claims under any federal or state law.[552] In *Video International Production v. Warner-Amex Cable Communications*,[553] a franchised cable operator lobbied the city to interpret zoning laws in a particular way and to send violation notices to customers of the operator's satellite master antenna TV competitors. The Fifth Circuit held that the lobbying was protected because the cable operator's intent was to obtain the legal interpretation it obtained.[554]

---

548. Rankin County Cablevision v. Pearl River Valley Water Supply Dist., 692 F. Supp. 691 (S.D. Miss. 1988). The court used this characterization rather than considering cable the provision of electronic impulses and equipment, which are commodities; *see also* H.R.M., Inc. v. Tele-Communications, Inc., 653 F. Supp. 645 (D. Colo. 1987) (cable television not a commodity as required for a Clayton Act § 2(a) violation); Satellite T Assoc. v. Continental Cablevision, Inc., 586 F. Supp. 973 (E.D. Va. 1982), *aff'd sub nom.* Satellite Television & Associated Resources, Inc. v. Continental Cablevision, Inc., 714 F.2d 351, 358 (4th Cir. 1983), *cert. denied*, 465 U.S. 1027 (1984); TV Signal Co. v. AT&T, 462 F.2d 1256 (8th Cir. 1972) (Clayton Act § 2(a) only applies to commodities, not pole attachment agreements, which are akin to real estate transactions).

549. *See* Resort Satellite Communs. v. Cox Enters., Civ. No. 86 LA 2207 (Va. Cir. Ct. Apr. 1988) (jury awarded $1.37 million against a multiple cable system operator (MSO) for selling cable service below cost and disparaging a satellite master antenna TV (SMATV) operator in order to capture the SMATV operator's hotel/motel business); Aurora Cable Communs. v. Jones Intercable, Inc., No. M87-183CA2 (W.D. Mich. filed June 17, 1987), which alleges that Jones Intercable engaged in predatory pricing to drive out an overbuilder.

550. 365 U.S. 127 (1961).

551. 381 U.S. 657 (1965).

552. The *Noerr-Pennington* doctrine has an exemption for "sham" conduct. *See* California Motor Transport Co. v. Trucking Unlimited, 404 U.S. 508 (1972). See Subpart B.3 of this chapter for a discussion of the *Noerr-Pennington* doctrine.

553. 858 F.2d 1075 (5th Cir. 1988).

554. *Id.; see also* Central Telecommuns. v. TCI Cablevision, Inc., 880 F.2d 711 (8th Cir. 1986) (unlawful threats, intimidation, and coercion in lobbying city for renewal fell into "sham" exception), *cert. denied*, 480 U.S. 910 (1987); Affiliated Capital Corp. v. City of Houston, 735 F.2d 1555 (5th Cir. 1984) (en banc) (unsuccessful franchise applicant claimed one of the successful applicants, the city, and the mayor conspired to divide up city among conspiring applicants; court found that jury could properly infer that plaintiff would have obtained franchise but for the conspiracy), *cert. denied*, 469 U.S. 1205 (1986); Metro Cable Co. v. CATV of Rockford, Inc., 516 F.2d 220 (7th Cir. 1975); Lamb Enters. v. Toledo Blade Co., 461 F.2d 506 (6th Cir. 1972); Aircapital Cablevision, Inc. v. Stanlink Communs. Group, 634 F. Supp. 316 (D. Kan. 1986); Hopkinsville Cable TV, Inc. v. Pennyroyal Cablevision, Inc., 562 F. Supp. 543 (W.D. Ky. 1982).

In *Parker v. Brown*,[555] the Supreme Court held that immunity from the Sherman Act exists to protect anticompetitive conduct of state governments acting through their legislatures.[556] *Parker* does not, however, shelter a municipality from antitrust scrutiny if state legislation is merely neutral as to whether it authorized the municipality to displace competition.[557]

Exclusive distributorships award franchised cable operators the exclusive right to distribute and to select distributors and may also give rise to antitrust claims. Generally, however, the courts have permitted exclusive distributorships as promoting interbrand competition. Additionally, unilateral refusals to deal are permissible under the Sherman Act, but a cable operator's alleged "monopoly" position may lead to claims that the cable system is an essential facility. The operator thus potentially violates the Sherman Act by refusing to carry programming.[558]

Allegations of tying arrangements may arise when, for example, a cable operator offers a premium channel only on the condition that a buyer also subscribe to basic service. Where a cable operator already has "an absolute lawful monopoly," however, the tie has been found legal because it could not be harming competition.[559]

Another major issue is the entry of telephone companies into the cable business. This issue has been debated in several forums. The FCC has proposed a recommendation to Congress to eliminate the telephone company/cable cross-ownership rules[560] that are now codified in the Cable Act, or to loosen the FCC's own standards for waivers of the rules or of prohibited affiliations between

---

555.   317 U.S. 341 (1943).

556.   *Id.* at 350-51. For a discussion of the *Parker* state action defense, see Subpart B.2 of this chapter.

557.   Community Communs. Co. v. City of Boulder, 455 U.S. 40 (1982) (the state constitution had granted "home rule" to the city generally and thus was "neutral" regarding exclusive cable franchising); *see also* Consolidated Television Cable Serv. v. City of Frankfurt, 857 F.2d 354 (6th Cir. 1988), *cert. denied*, 489 U.S. 1082 (1989); Preferred Communs. v. City of Los Angeles, 754 F.2d 1396 (9th Cir. 1985), *aff'd*, 476 U.S. 488 (1986); Catalina Cablevision Assocs. v. City of Tucson, 745 F.2d 1266 (9th Cir. 1984); City Communs. v. City of Detroit, 650 F. Supp. 1570 (E.D. Mich. 1987); Century Federal, Inc. v. City of Palo Alto, 579 F. Supp. 1553 (N.D. Cal. 1984).

558.   *See* Midland Telecasting Co. v. Midessa Television Co., 617 F.2d 1141 (5th Cir. 1980); New York Citizens Committee on Cable TV v. Manhattan Cable TV, Inc., 651 F. Supp. 802 (S.D.N.Y. 1986); *see also* Viacom Int'l, Inc. v. Time, Inc., 89 Civ. 3139 JMW (S.D.N.Y. filed May 9, 1989).

559.   Friedman v. Adams Russell Cable Servs., 624 F. Supp. 1195 (S.D.N.Y. 1986); *see also* Ciminelli v. Cablevision, 583 F. Supp. 158 (E.D.N.Y. 1984) (noting that protection from theft might be justification for otherwise illegal arrangement tying cable accessories to cable services); Florida Cablevision v. Telesat Cablevision, Inc., No. 87-8358 (S.D. Fla. filed May 26, 1987) (antitrust challenge to "bulk rate" contract for allegedly tying the sale or renewal of a multiple dwelling unit to the provision of cable TV service).

560.   The rules state that telephone companies may not provide cable service in the areas in which they provide basic telephone service. *See* 47 C.F.R. §§ 63.54-63.58 (1991). Currently, a waiver may be granted where the cable system "demonstrably could not exist" without telephone company involvement. 47 U.S.C. 533(b)(4) (1988); 47 C.F.R. § 63.56. A waiver may also be granted upon "other showing of good cause," (47 C.F.R. § 63.56), but the FCC has never used this as a grounds for waiver. *See, e.g.,* Sugar Land Tel. Co., 76 F.C.C.2d 19, 230 (1980). However, telephone company construction of leaseback systems for cable operators is allowed. General Tel. Co., 3 F.C.C.Rcd 2371 (1985) (waiver granted on grounds that otherwise cable "demonstrably could not exist").

telephone and cable companies. In August 1987 the FCC issued a Notice of Inquiry[561] proposing to eliminate the rules, stating that the cable industry was "robustly competitive and comparatively mature" and that the 1978 Pole Attachment Act[562] had eliminated the bottleneck monopoly power of telephone companies over cable system access to homes.[563]

The consent decree approved in *United States v. AT&T*[564] also barred the Bell Operating Companies from providing information services, including cable programming.[565] Additionally, the 1984 law deregulating cable rates bars Bell Operating Companies from providing cable programming. As discussed above, in 1991 following the D.C. Circuit's instructions, Judge Greene lifted the information service restriction.

3. Energy

In 1977, Congress vested responsibility for federal energy policy, regulation, and research and development in the Department of Energy (DOE).[566] One of DOE's purposes is "to foster and assure competition among parties engaged in the supply of energy and fuels."[567] The DOE Act also created the Federal Energy Regulatory Commission (FERC) within DOE and transferred to FERC wide-ranging regulatory functions previously exercised by other agencies, principally the Federal Power Commission (FPC).[568] The interplay among the antitrust laws, federal energy laws and regulations, and state regulation of energy industries is discussed below in relation to natural gas, electricity, oil transportation, nuclear power and federal lands.

a. NATURAL GAS

The federal and state regulatory framework for the natural gas industry can be understood with reference to three functions and three corresponding transactions: (1) the production and gathering of natural gas in the field — the step at which the "field price" or "wellhead price" is generally set; (2) the interstate and intrastate transmission of the gas by pipeline from the producing field to consumer markets — the costs of which are included in the "city gate rate"; and (3) the local distribution of the gas to consumers, which is reflected in the "resale rate." While

---

561. 2 F.C.C. Rcd 5092 (1987). In September 1988, the FCC issued a Further Notice of Inquiry/Notice of Proposed Rulemaking which is still pending. *See* 3 F.C.C. Rcd 5849 (1988).

562. 47 U.S.C. § 224 (1988).

563. Telephone companies do not have a specific obligation to give cable companies access to poles. *See* FCC v. Florida Power Corp., 480 U.S. 245 (1987); *see also* Cable Television Ass'n v. Chesapeake & Potomac Tel. Co., File No. PA-88-002 (FCC filed Mar. 10, 1988).

An Indiana cable company challenged the cross-ownership rules after the FCC held in 1985 that family, business, and financial ties between a small telephone company and small cable company violated the rules. Comark Cable Fund III, 100 F.C.C.2d 1244 (1985), *recon. denied*, 103 F.C.C.2d 600 (1985), *remanded sub nom.* Northwestern Ind. Tel. Co. v. FCC, 824 F.2d 1205 (D.C. Cir. 1987). The FCC reaffirmed its affiliation finding. CCI Cablevision v. Northwestern Ind. Tel. Co., 3 F.C.C. Rcd 3096 (1988).

564. United States v. AT&T, 552 F. Supp. 131 (D.D.C. 1983), *aff'd sub nom.* Maryland v. United States, 460 U.S. 1001 (1983).

565. United States v. AT&T, 673 F. Supp. 525 (D.D.C. 1987).

566. The Department of Energy Organization Act, 42 U.S.C. §§ 7101-7375 (1988) (DOE Act).

567. *Id.* § 7112(12).

568. *Id.* §§ 7171-7177.

many natural gas companies are vertically integrated, often some of these functions are performed by separate companies.

(1) Regulatory History

(a) The Natural Gas Act

At the federal level, the natural gas industry is regulated by FERC, formerly the FPC. The scope of FERC's jurisdiction over the industry, and the standards by which it regulates the industry, are set forth in the Natural Gas Act (NGA).[569] The NGA gives FERC the power to establish rates for the interstate transmission of gas and its sale for resale, and to regulate asset acquisitions and changes in facilities and service by natural gas companies.[570]

FERC must consider antitrust policies when it applies the NGA's public interest requirements.[571] As the D.C. Circuit stated in *Northern Natural Gas Co. v. FPC*:[572] "Although the Commission is not bound by the dictates of the antitrust laws, it is clear that antitrust concepts are intimately involved in a determination of what action is in the public interest, and therefore the Commission is obliged to weigh antitrust policy."[573] There, the FPC had approved a plan under which a joint venture of two pipeline companies was to enter a market in which "the half-owner of the joint venture ... was already the dominant force."[574] The petitioners, whose alternative plan had been rejected by the FPC, claimed that the joint venture violated both Section 1 of the Sherman Act and Section 7 of the Clayton Act. The court remanded for findings and conclusions "related to the pertinent antitrust policies,"[575] and concluded:

> [W]e believe that the joint venture substantially lessened competition among suppliers. . . .
> Unless the Commission finds that other important considerations militate in favor of the

---

569.   15 U.S.C. §§ 717-717w (1988). Until 1938, regulation of the natural gas industry was largely a state and local matter. Today, state regulation of the natural gas industry is confined primarily to local distribution. Some states also regulate intrastate transmission of natural gas, and producing states regulate producing properties, including rates of production.

570.   Production, gathering and local distribution are exempted from the NGA, but in Phillips Petroleum Co. v. Wisconsin, 347 U.S. 672 (1954), the Supreme Court held that the Commission had jurisdiction to regulate the wellhead price of natural gas.

   Until 1977, the Commission set the price of gas at the wellhead, and every producer sale to interstate pipelines was subject to regulatory review. Enactment in 1978 of the Natural Gas Policy Act, 15 U.S.C. §§ 3301-3342 (1988) (NGPA), brought about gradual deregulation of the price of gas at the wellhead. The Natural Gas Wellhead Decontrol Act of 1989, Pub. L. No. 101-60, 103 Stat. 157 (1989) (codified at 15 U.S.C. § 3301 (1991 Supp.)), completed the process of the deregulation of the wellhead pricing of natural gas by removing those price and nonprice controls that remain in place pursuant to the NGPA.

571.   Maryland People's Counsel v. FERC, 760 F.2d 318 (D.C. Cir. 1985); Alabama Power Co. v. FPC, 511 F.2d 383, 393 (D.C. Cir. 1974); City of Pittsburgh v. FPC, 237 F.2d 741, 754 (D.C. Cir. 1956) (FERC "has the right to consider a congressional expression of fundamental national policy" such as the Sherman Act).

572.   399 F.2d 953 (D.C. Cir. 1968).

573.   *Id.* at 958.

574.   *Id.* at 968.

575.   *Id.* at 961.

joint venture and that these considerations are more beneficial to the public than additional competition, the antitrust policies should be respected and the joint venture set aside.[576]

(b) The Natural Gas Policy Act of 1978: Competition at the Wellhead

The Natural Gas Policy Act of 1978 (NGPA)[577] was designed to stimulate production of natural gas to alleviate the shortages that had occurred during the early 1970s.[578] The NGPA provided for gradual deregulation of wellhead prices for certain categories of natural gas.[579] The Supreme Court explained this change in regulatory policy as an indication of Congress' belief in the competitive nature of the production segment of the industry:

> The change in regulatory perspective embodied in the [Natural Gas Policy Act] rested in significant part on the belief that direct federal price control exacerbated supply and demand problems by preventing the market from making long-term adjustments.[580]

On July 26, 1989, Congress passed the Natural Gas Wellhead Decontrol Act of 1989, which eliminated all remaining price controls on wellhead sales of natural

---

576. *Id.* at 971.

577. 15 U.S.C. §§ 3301-3432 (1988).

578. The Supreme Court in 1954 determined that the NGA required regulation of the price at which producers sold gas to pipelines (wellhead price) as well as regulation of the price at which pipelines sold gas to local distribution customers (city-gate price). Phillips Petroleum Co. v. Wisconsin, 347 U.S. 672 (1954). At the time of passage of NGPA, it was widely believed that imposition of wellhead price regulation by the *Phillips* decision had contributed to the severe gas shortages of the early 1970s.

579. The NGPA did not change traditional regulation of pipeline sales of gas to local distribution customers, but addressed wellhead sales of gas. It largely eliminated the requirement that wellhead gas be sold at "just and reasonable" rates and created instead several categories of gas, establishing for many a "maximum lawful price," referred to commonly as a ceiling price. 15 U.S.C. §§ 3312-3319 (1988). The ceiling prices for almost all categories of gas other than gas which had been subject to federal regulation at the time of the NGPA's enactment ("old gas") was decontrolled as of January 1, 1985. *Id.*

  The FERC attempted to create a rate mechanism that was responsive to changes in market conditions for the old gas that remained subject to regulation. Order No. 451 established a single alternative ceiling price for categories of old gas and eliminated the various ceiling prices for different "vintages" of old gas that FERC had previously set according to when the gas reserves were produced. The Supreme Court in Mobil Oil Exploration & Producing Southeast, Inc. v. United Distribution Cos., 111 S. Ct. 615 (1991), sustained Order No. 451 and its successor, Order No. 451-A, in their entirety. Virtually all old gas was decontrolled for future purposes by the Wellhead Decontrol Act of 1989.

580. Transcontinental Gas Pipe Line Corp. v. State Oil & Gas Bd., 474 U.S. 409, 424 (1986); *see also* Pennzoil Co. v. FERC, 645 F.2d 360 (5th Cir. 1981) (regulatory change under Natural Gas Policy Act reflected Congress' decision that gas producers do not have "natural" monopoly power, hence the competitive nature of the industry's production segment makes agency regulation unnecessary to protect consumers), *cert. denied*, 454 U.S. 1142 (1982). Since July 1984, the Secretary of Energy must prepare an annual report on natural gas prices, supplies and demand, and the market forces and competitive conditions in the domestic natural gas industry. 15 U.S.C. § 3333 (1988); *see, e.g.*, First Report Requested By Section 123 of the Natural Gas Policy Act of 1978, Report No. DOE/PE-0054 (July 1984); Increasing Competition in the Natural Gas Market: Second Report Required by Section 123 of the Natural Gas Policy Act of 1978, Report No. DOE/PE-0069 (Jan. 1985).

gas.[581] The Wellhead Decontrol Act ends thirty-five years of efforts to regulate the pricing of natural gas supplies. It explicitly chose competition over regulatory control as the best mechanism for pricing natural gas.[582] FERC has implemented the provisions of the Wellhead Decontrol Act by regulations promulgated in Order No. 523, issued on April 18, 1990.[583]

(c) Open Access Transportation

As the price of gas was decontrolled, drilling for new gas increased significantly, resulting in an abundant gas supply by the early 1980s. The unleashing of competition in the gas production market, combined with falling prices of alternative fuels, energy conservation efforts and other factors, led to the growth of a "spot market," in which gas is available under short-term arrangements, generally at lower prices than those offered by pipelines, for purchase by any willing buyer.

Prior to the NGPA, interstate gas pipelines bought gas from producers, and the customers of interstate pipelines (local distribution companies (LDCs) and certain large gas users such as industrial customers) purchased a package of regulated gas and regulated transportation. As gas supplies became more plentiful, and the market prices began to drop, LDCs and large end users sought to purchase natural gas directly from producers as opposed to their traditional pipeline suppliers. These purchasers sought to have their gas supplies transported by pipelines on a nondiscriminatory, "open access" basis.

In response to the demand for transmission of gas other than that owned by the transporting pipeline ("open-access transportation"), FERC issued a number of orders designed to authorize pipelines to "unbundle" transportation and the sale of natural gas, thereby providing transportation as a separate service. During the early period (1978-1980), FERC authorized special programs for transportation of certain regulated categories of gas.[584] Later, FERC implemented some new regulatory programs such as transportation under the blanket certificate program.[585] Then,

---

581. Pub. L. No. 101-60, 103 Stat. 157 (1989) (codified at 15 U.S.C. § 3301 (1991 Supp.)). The Act calls for a relatively quick transition to a completely deregulated market at the wellhead. Any gas supplies still regulated as of Jan. 1, 1993, will be completely decontrolled on that date.

582. The House Report accompanying the bill states:
      [NGPA price] controls are an outdated, inaccurate relic from a period of stringent economic regulation of energy supplies Congress has largely ended and reversed in recent years.
         In retrospect, government regulation induced many of the volatile swings in the gas markets over the past fifteen years. Tight wellhead controls and noncompetitive gas purchasing practices in the 1970s created severe interstate shortages in that period; high incentive prices in the 1978 NGPA and these same purchasing practices created large supply gluts and a costly take-or-pay problem during the 1980s.
      H.R. REP. No. 29, 101st Cong., 1st Sess. 2-3, reprinted in 1989 U.S. CODE CONG. & ADMIN. NEWS 51, 52-53.

583. [Regs. Preamble 1986-1990] F.E.R.C. STATS. & REGS. (CCH) ¶ 30,887 (1990).

584. For example, during the oil crisis of 1979, FERC created a procedure for the issuance of special certificates to interstate pipelines for transportation of gas to displace fuel oil consumption. Transportation Certificates for Natural Gas for the Displacement of Fuel Oil, Order No. 30, [Regs. Preamble 1977-1981] F.E.R.C. STATS. & REGS. (CCH) ¶ 30,054 (1979).

585. Transportation of natural gas requires prior FERC approval through issuance of a "certificate of public convenience and necessity." NGA § 7(c), 15 U.S.C. § 717f(c) (1988). The blanket certificate program permits interstate pipelines to transport gas for other pipelines' supply without prior FERC approval. Interstate Pipeline Transportation on Behalf of Other Interstate Pipelines,

in back-to-back Orders issued in the summer of 1983, FERC created a broad-based category of end-users eligible for transportation (Order No. 234-B)[586] and expanded the categories of activities authorized under the blanket certificate program to include transportation of various types (Order No. 319).[587] FERC also approved various "special marketing programs" (SMPs) whereby pipelines would provide lower priced gas to those customers that had the ability to switch to lower cost alternate fuel (fuel switchable customers), or those customers which can shut down in the absence of lower cost gas (interruptible customers).

The D.C. Circuit vacated these orders in a series of related cases, all styled *Maryland People's Counsel v. FERC*,[588] on the grounds that they discriminated against captive customers (primarily local distribution companies) of interstate pipelines, who were not provided access to transportation equal to that provided to fuel-switchable industrial customers. FERC responded to the directives of *Maryland People's Counsel* by issuing Order No. 436, intended in part to "secure to consumers the benefits of competition in natural gas markets."[589] The Order allowed pipelines to provide transportation services under "blanket certificate" authority, thus avoiding the regulatory process for individual certificates, on the condition that the pipeline provided open-access transportation service to all customers on a nondiscriminatory basis.

On petition for review, the District of Columbia Circuit supported FERC's efforts to end pipeline monopsony power over wellhead purchases.[590] The court affirmed FERC's factual finding that open-access transportation was necessary to increase competition at the wellhead, and held that FERC possessed statutory authority to enforce such a condition. Order No. 436 nevertheless was remanded for its failure to consider the need to resolve problems associated with uneconomic

---

Order No. 60, [Regs. Preamble 1977-1981] F.E.R.C. STATS. & REGS. (CCH) ¶ 30,107 (1979). This program was later expanded to allow wholly intrastate pipelines to obtain similar authority. Order No. 63, Certain Transportation, Sales and Assignments by Pipeline Companies Not Subject to Commission Jurisdiction Under Section 1(c) of the Natural Gas Act, [Regs. Preamble 1977-1981] F.E.R.C. STATS. & REGS. (CCH) ¶ 30,118 (1980).

586. Interstate Pipeline Blanket Certificates for Routine Transactions and Sales and Transportation by Interstate Pipeline and Distributors, Order No. 234-B, [Regs. Preamble 1982-1985] F.E.R.C. STATS. & REGS. (CCH) ¶ 30,476 (1983). Under Order 234-B, "low priority" end users, as defined by FERC, could purchase gas from producers and arrange for transportation by pipelines. By its terms, Order No. 234-B was effective only through June 30, 1985.

587. Sales and Transportation by Interstate Pipelines and Distributors; Expansion of Categories of Activities Authorized Under Blanket Certificate, Order No. 319, [Regs. Preamble 1982-1985] F.E.R.C. STATS. & REGS. (CCH) ¶ 30,477 (1983). Order No. 319 permitted "high priority" end-users, as defined in the order, to purchase natural gas and arrange for transportation. It permitted purchase contracts of up to five years.

588. 760 F.2d 318 (D.C. Cir. 1985) (MPC I); 761 F.2d 780 (D.C. Cir. 1985) (MPC II); 768 F.2d 450 (D.C. Cir. 1985) (MPC III). In *MPC III*, the D.C. Circuit found that SMP orders which permitted certain captive customers to nominate up to 10% of their contractual entitlement to be purchased for system supply under the SMP were "marginally less discriminatory than their predecessors, but they continue to entail identical lapses of logic and evidence." *MPC III*, 768 F.2d at 455.

589. Regulation of Natural Gas Pipelines After Partial Wellhead Decontrol, Order No. 436, [Regs. Preamble 1982-1985] F.E.R.C. STATS. & REGS. (CCH) ¶ 30,665 (1985).

590. Associated Gas Distribs. v. FERC, 824 F.2d 981, 995-96 (D.C. Cir. 1987) (AGD), *cert. denied*, 485 U.S. 1006 (1988).

pipeline-producer take-or-pay contracts.[591] The court noted that pipelines used access to transportation as a negotiating tool with producers to obtain take-or-pay relief and held that FERC's failure seriously to consider the negative impact on pipelines as marketers of natural gas represented an incurable flaw in the Order No. 436 program.[592] Another District of Columbia Circuit decision, *Consolidated Edison Co. v. FERC*,[593] stated even more strongly that FERC could not achieve the desired free market at the wellhead unless it first addressed the mounting take-or-pay problem. In *Consolidated Edison*, the court reviewed orders issued by FERC granting Felmont Oil Corporation limited term abandonment authority to sell on the open, or "spot," market natural gas previously dedicated to Transcontinental Gas Pipe Line Corporation (Transco). Transco had stopped taking the gas and the wells had been shut in. FERC reasoned that the injection of low cost gas to the supply market would benefit consumers as a whole. The court disagreed. In remanding the orders, the court isolated two flaws in FERC's reasoning: (1) the Commission did not explain how the pipeline's captive customers would benefit from the abandonment policy, and (2) by authorizing the abandonment, the Commission crippled the pipeline's ability to renegotiate the take-or-pay contracts.[594]

(d) Bypass: A Consequence of Open Access

Order 436 and its successor orders dramatically increased the opportunities for LDCs to purchase competitively priced natural gas at the wellhead. These same regulatory changes have also increased opportunities for the LDCs' industrial customers to engage in "bypass." "Bypass," as the term has been used in connection

---

591. Traditionally, pipelines had entered into very long-term gas purchase contracts with producers, often with automatic escalator clauses in them that caused the contract price of the gas to rise. These "take-or-pay" contracts obligated the pipelines to take delivery of a specified quantity of gas at the contract price or to pay producers for quantities of gas not taken. Thus, while the producer bore all the risk of exploration and production, the pipeline bore all the market risk, that is, the risk that the gas ultimately could not be sold. When pipelines were the sole suppliers to local distribution companies (LDCs), marketability was not a great risk; however, when FERC's access orders gave LDCs access to lower cost sources of gas, many LDCs stopped purchasing from the pipelines and purchased directly from producers. Pipelines, nevertheless, had to continue to pay producers for gas at previously negotiated (often very high) prices, whether or not that gas could be sold. These costs were, to some extent, passed on to pipeline customers who could not take advantage of open access and were "captive" to the pipeline. To limit exposure to take-or-pay costs, some pipelines refused to transport gas for customers or refused to transport gas from producers who did not agree to release the pipelines from take-or-pay obligations.

592. On remand, the Commission issued an interim transportation order, Order No. 500, which repromulgated most provisions of Order No. 436. Regulation of Natural Gas Pipelines After Partial Wellhead Decontrol, Order No. 500, [Regs. Preamble 1986-1990] F.E.R.C. Stats. & Regs. (CCH) ¶ 30,761 (1987). Since issuing Order No. 500, the Commission has modified it several times and extended various deadlines. *See, e.g.*, Order No. 500-A, [Regs. Preamble 1986-1990] F.E.R.C. Stats. & Regs. (CCH) ¶ 30,770 (1987); Order No. 500-K, III F.E.R.C. Stats. & Regs. (CCH) ¶ 30,917 (1991).

   Order No. 500 went beyond Order No. 436, however, by adopting a "crediting" provision that allows pipelines to condition access to pipeline transportation capacity upon the pipeline's receiving take-or-pay relief from certain gas purchase contracts for the volumes of natural gas transported. Order No. 500 was remanded for further consideration by FERC in American Gas Ass'n v. FERC, 888 F.2d 136 (D.C. Cir. 1989).

593. 823 F.2d 630 (D.C. Cir. 1987).

594. *Id.* at 637, 641.

with regulated industries, is the practice of supplanting all or some part of a regulated supplier's product with products obtained from another source. Often this source is another supplier that is either unregulated or unconstrained by regulation. In the gas industry, the term "bypass" typically is used to describe the situation where an industrial customer terminates its purchases from a LDC and obtains supplies directly from the pipeline supplying the LDC.[595]

Open access transportation on interstate pipelines encouraged industrial customers and LDCs to purchase natural gas directly from producers, foregoing pipeline system supply. Historically, it had been deemed in the public interest to preserve the natural monopoly characteristics of local gas markets and to discourage duplication of pipeline facilities. Under this traditional regime, even when industrial customers could make direct purchases of natural gas, they would turn to the LDC with which they were connected for the last leg of transmission. However, in *Northern Natural Gas Co.*,[596] the FERC made it clear that it will now favor "competition" as its overriding policy concern in bypass cases, and will generally approve applications for transportation service that further that policy even where that results in bypass of local distribution facilities.

FERC explained that open access was the deciding factor that required it to change its bypass policy. Previously it had held a qualified preference for local distribution companies, but "[t]he need to assure access to the workably competitive wellhead market" was found to outweigh the LDCs' concern over potential bypass.[597] This policy "imposes upon the LDC, which often has monopoly power, the need to discipline its costs to maintain its customer base and the incentive to unbundle its services."[598] In response to concerns over the impact on customers unable to obtain bypass, the FERC pointed to state commissions, and stated that through varied approaches to the design of rates, LDCs could be permitted to compete and ratepayers that would otherwise find fixed costs shifted to them could be protected.

FERC defined as its remaining task: "to assure that the competitive process operates fairly pursuant to the powers entrusted to us by Congress."[599] It noted that examples of conditions which could be indicative of unfair competition include: (1) a pipeline refusing to provide sales or transportation to a LDC when the sales are necessary to serve an end-user; and (2) undue discrimination which could be indicated by a pipeline discounting its service only when it seeks to displace an existing LDC. Subsequent to *Northern Natural*, FERC has consistently approved requests for authorization of construction of pipeline facilities or for transportation

---

595. Conceptually, however, it is no less a "bypass" when the LDC reduces its purchases from the pipeline that historically supplied its needs and substitutes products from other suppliers.

596. 48 F.E.R.C. (CCH) ¶ 61,232 (1989).

597. *Id.* at 61,828; *see also id.* at 61,828 n.23 (quoting Order No. 436); Associated Gas Distribs. v. FERC, 824 F.2d 981, 1036 (D.C. Cir. 1987), *cert. denied*, 485 U.S. 1006 (1988). Specifically FERC listed the following reasons for the change in policy regarding LDCs: changes in the industry due to maturation; Congress' decision to deregulate wellhead prices; FERC's policy of open access transportation; the increasingly competitive needs of industrial and commercial users; and the varied approaches available to state commissions to regulate local transportation markets. 48 F.E.R.C. at 61,828.

598. 48 F.E.R.C. at 61,829.

599. *Id.*

certificates to facilitate bypass, absent a showing of unfair competition or undue discrimination, and has characterized the objections of LDCs as arguments against competition.[600]

(2) Litigation Under the Sherman Act

This changing regulatory environment has resulted in a natural gas industry in which gas pipelines operate both in competitive (gas sales) markets and monopolistic (gas transportation) markets. The need for independent sellers and buyers of gas to gain access to pipeline transportation has been a fertile source of litigation under the Sherman Act.[601]

In *Kansas v. Utilicorp United, Inc.*,[602] the Supreme Court resolved a significant threshold issue on which the circuit courts had split — the standing under *Illinois Brick*[603] of consumers who purchase gas from a regulated public utility to sue the utility's gas supplier for alleged overcharges passed on to them by the utility. The Seventh Circuit[604] had held that a suit by the state on behalf of residential consumers fell within the cost-plus exception to *Illinois Brick*'s prohibition of suits by indirect purchasers. The court reasoned that "regulation plus the residential consumers' lack of alternatives" ensured that the whole overcharge was passed on to them by the utility in accordance with the fuel passthrough provision of their contract with the utility.[605] The Tenth Circuit reached the opposite result in *In re Wyoming Tight Sands Antitrust Cases*, and the Supreme Court affirmed.[606] The Supreme Court held that no general exception to the indirect purchaser rule of *Illinois Brick* should be made for cases involving regulated public utilities that pass on all of their costs to consumers.[607] The Court also rejected the argument that regulations and tariffs requiring the utility to pass on its costs to the consumers

---

600. Northwest Pipeline Corp., 52 F.E.R.C. (CCH) ¶ 61,053 (1990); Panhandle E. Pipe Line Co., 52 F.E.R.C. (CCH) ¶ 61,048 (1990); Southern Natural Gas Co., 51 F.E.R.C. (CCH) ¶ 61,186 (1990), *reh'g denied*, 54 F.E.R.C. (CCH) ¶ 61,098 (1991); Northwest Pipeline Corp., 48 F.E.R.C. (CCH) ¶ 61,231 (1989); Northern Natural Gas Co., 48 F.E.R.C. (CCH) ¶ 61,232 (1989); Panhandle E. Pipe Line Co., 48 F.E.R.C. (CCH) ¶ 61,233 (1989); Cascade Natural Gas Corp. v. Northwest Pipeline Corp., 48 F.E.R.C. (CCH) ¶ 61,234 (1989).

601. The pipelines' handling of take-or-pay problems with producers has been raised unsuccessfully in antitrust actions. *See* Cayman Exploration Corp. v. United Gas Pipe Line Co., 873 F.2d 1357 (10th Cir. 1989) (affirming dismissal of claim that pipeline violated § 1 of the Sherman Act by refusing to honor take-or-pay contracts and pressuring producers to renegotiate contract prices when no facts were alleged showing injury to competition); Garshman v. Universal Resources Holding, Inc., 824 F.2d 223 (3d Cir. 1987) (affirming dismissal of claim that pipeline violated § 1 and § 2 of the Sherman Act by refusing to take gas under take-or-pay contracts and pressuring producers to renegotiate contracts; no facts were alleged to show that pipeline had monopoly power or there was an adverse effect on competition in the purchase and sale of natural gas).

602. 110 S. Ct. 2807 (1990).

603. Illinois Brick Co. v. Illinois, 431 U.S. 720 (1977) (holding that indirect purchasers may not maintain a claim for damages against a remote seller for illegal overcharges).

604. Illinois *ex rel.* Hartigan v. Panhandle Eastern Pipe Line Co., 852 F.2d 891 (7th Cir.) (en banc), *cert. denied*, 488 U.S. 986 (1988).

605. *Id.* at 898. The court held, however, that industrial customers lacked standing under *Illinois Brick* to sue for damages. *Id.* at 898-99.

606. 866 F.2d 1286 (10th Cir. 1989), *aff'd sub. nom.* Kansas v. Utilicorp United, Inc., 110 S. Ct. 2807 (1990).

607. 110 S. Ct. at 2812-13.

placed the case within the cost-plus contract exception:

> The utility customers made no commitment to purchase any particular quantity of gas, and the utility itself had no guaranty of any particular profit. Even though the [utility] raised its prices to cover its costs, we cannot ascertain its precise injury because . . . we do not know what might have happened in the absence of an overcharge. In addition, even if the utility customers had a highly inelastic demand for natural gas, the need to inquire into the precise operation of market forces would negate the simplicity and certainty that could justify a cost-plus contract exception. Thus, although we do not alter our observations about the possibility of an exception for cost-plus contracts, we decline to create the general exception for utilities sought [here].[608]

Monopolization claims under Section 2 of the Sherman Act for denial of access to transportation have met with mixed success. In an early case, *Woods Exploration & Producing Co. v. Aluminum Co. of America*,[609] defendants, Alcoa and a wholly owned subsidiary, owned a pipeline which was used to transport gas from the Appling Field to an Alcoa plant and to market gas from the field for third parties. The plaintiffs, leaseholders in the field, requested Alcoa to transport their gas and to "unitize" the field. Alcoa refused both requests, and plaintiffs began construction of a pipeline. The defendants then attempted to thwart the construction of the pipeline by such actions as forcing the plaintiffs to file condemnation proceedings to gain right-of-way. The Fifth Circuit reinstated a jury verdict finding that defendants had engaged in a pattern of conduct that violated Section 2.

In *Consolidated Gas Co. v. City Gas Co.*,[610] a retail distributor of liquid petroleum (LP) gas who had attempted to enter the retail natural gas distribution market in portions of Dade and Broward Counties brought action against a major distributor of natural gas in southern Florida for refusing to transport or sell natural gas to it on reasonable terms. The district court held that the defendant had monopoly power in the wholesale and retail sale of natural gas in the relevant geographic area, and had acquired that power by virtue of a territorial agreement with another natural gas distributor that was not immune from the antitrust laws under the state action doctrine. Moreover, the court held that under either the "essential facilities" or "intent" test for determining whether a monopolist had a duty to deal, the defendant had a duty to deal with the LP distributor. The court held that the plaintiff was entitled to recover both lost profits during the period of antitrust misconduct, and resulting diminution in value of the business,[611] and was entitled to an injunction requiring the distributor to sell or transport gas to the plaintiff at a reasonable price.[612]

---

608. *Id.* at 2818 (citations omitted).
609. 438 F.2d 1286 (5th Cir. 1971), *cert. denied*, 404 U.S. 1047 (1972).
610. 665 F. Supp. 1493 (S.D. Fla. 1987), *aff'd*, 880 F.2d 297 (11th Cir. 1989), *reinstated on reh'g*, 912 F.2d 1262 (11th Cir. 1990) (en banc; per curiam), *vacated as moot*, 111 S. Ct. 1300 (1991).
611. On recoverable damages, see Colorado Interstate Gas Co. v. Natural Gas Pipeline Co., 661 F. Supp. 1448 (D. Wyo. 1987), *aff'd in part and rev'd in part*, 885 F.2d 683 (10th Cir. 1989), *cert. denied*, 111 S. Ct. 441 (1990).
612. Two judges dissented in part from the Eleventh Circuit's en banc decision on the grounds that the territorial agreement between City Gas and another major natural gas distributor was entitled to antitrust immunity under the state action doctrine. 912 F.2d at 1262-1266 (Johnson, J. & Kravitch, J. concurring in part and dissenting in part). Chief Judge Tjoflat dissented on the ground of state action immunity and on the ground that because City Gas was not in the business

Two recent cases have addressed the issue of "legitimate business justifications" for a pipeline's refusal to transport gas purchased by its customers from third parties. In *Illinois ex rel. Hartigan v. Panhandle Eastern Pipe Line Co.*[613] the state, suing on its own behalf and on behalf of a class of residential and industrial natural gas consumers, alleged that Panhandle monopolized the sale of natural gas within central Illinois by refusing to transport gas purchased directly from independent producers by LDCs.[614] The LDCs were full requirements sales customers of Panhandle pursuant to Panhandle's FERC-approved "G-tariff" rate schedule. Panhandle justified its refusal to transport nonsystem gas for these G-tariff customers on the ground that enabling them to obtain gas from other sources would dramatically reduce demand for the expensive gas Panhandle was contractually obligated to purchase and expose it to enormous take-or-pay liability. The district court, after a bench trial, ruled in Panhandle's favor. It found that Panhandle had monopoly power over natural gas sales to LDCs for use by residential and commercial customers within central Illinois, and that FERC regulation did not effectively constrain Panhandle's ability to exercise monopoly power with respect to the practices at issue.[615] The court held, however, that Panhandle's insistence on enforcing its FERC-approved tariff during a period of regulatory turmoil and uncertainty did not constitute willful maintenance of monopoly power, but merely a "lawful refusal to cut its own throat."[616]

In affirming, the Seventh Circuit emphasized that because Panhandle acted with a legitimate business purpose in refusing to permit its customers to avoid their contractual obligations when to do so would be to expose it to enormous take-or-pay obligations, its conduct could not be characterized as anticompetitive.[617] It noted that "measures designed to avoid higher costs are essentially measures designed to lower costs" and thus can support a business justification defense.[618]

The Seventh Circuit also affirmed the district court's dismissal of the state's "essential facilities" claim, on two grounds. First, access to Panhandle's pipeline was not essential for other gas sellers to compete with Panhandle. It was economically feasible for competitors to duplicate much of Panhandle's system within central Illinois by means of interconnections with competing pipelines and the construction

---

of selling natural gas at wholesale, it could not be found to possess monopoly power in the relevant market. 912 F.2d at 1266-1338 (Tjoflat, C.J., dissenting).

613. 730 F. Supp. 826 (C.D. Ill. 1990), *aff'd sub nom.* Illinois *ex rel.* Burris v. Panhandle E. Pipe Line Co., 935 F.2d 1469 (7th Cir. 1991).

614. The complaint, brought under both federal and Illinois antitrust laws, alleged unlawful monopolization, attempted monopolization, monopoly leveraging, an unlawful denial of access to an essential facility, and an unlawful tie of gas transportation to gas purchases.

615. 730 F. Supp. at 871, 876. The court found, however, that Panhandle did not possess monopoly power with respect to industrial end-users capable of using alternate fuels. *Id.* at 874.

616. *Id.* at 882-83, 918.

617. 935 F.2d at 1481, 1484-85. The Seventh Circuit held that the Supreme Court's decision in Kansas v. Utilicorp United, Inc., 110 S. Ct. 2807 (1990), barred the state's indirect purchaser claims under the federal antitrust laws. 935 F.2d at 1479. However it reviewed the merits of the trial court's dismissal of the state's parallel claims under the Illinois antitrust laws, which explicitly permit suits by indirect purchasers.

618. *Id.* at 1483 n.13 (The Seventh Circuit thus rejected the district court's view (730 F. Supp. at 932-33) that Panhandle's concern about take-or-pay liability was insufficient by itself to constitute a defense, because "[i]t is not a legitimate business justification for antitrust purposes that the defendant sought to protect itself from added costs or lost profits.").

of new pipelines.[619] Second, to support liability on an essential facility theory, providing access to the facility must have been feasible for the owner. Refusals to provide access justified by the owner's legitimate business concerns cannot be a basis of liability.[620]

In *City of Chanute v. Williams Natural Gas Co.*,[621] a Kansas federal district court held that a natural gas pipeline had a legitimate business reason for reversing its policy of interim open access "given the uncertainty and chaotic conditions in the natural gas industry at the time and the potential take-or-pay liability it was facing," and thus granted summary judgment against monopolization and attempted monopolization claims brought by various cities seeking access.[622]

Many of Williams' sales customers took advantage of its interim open access policy to buy cheaper natural gas from producers. The customers' conversion from sales service to transportation service resulted in a dramatic increase in Williams' exposure under its take-or-pay contracts with producers. When Williams' efforts to negotiate take-or-pay relief with its producers failed, Williams "closed" its pipeline to transportation of third party gas. The court found that Williams' decision was reasonable, holding: "It is the *potential seriousness* of the take-or-pay exposure which provides Williams with a legitimate business rationale for reversing its policy of open access."[623] It noted that failure to take measures to check such significant exposure "could certainly affect a pipeline's ability to provide reliable services to its customers."[624] The court also granted summary judgment against the cities' essential facility claim. It held that the cities could not show, as required to support their essential facility claim, that they had no feasible alternative to use of Williams' facilities for open-access transportation of third party gas. It found that both the purchase of gas from producers pursuant to FERC Order No. 451 and purchase of Williams' own sales gas, which was reasonably priced, were feasible alternatives for the cities.[625]

Consul, Ltd. v. Transco Energy Co.[626] also addressed an essential facility claim against a natural gas pipeline. In that case, Consul, a natural gas broker, alleged that Transco had violated Section 2 by refusing to transport from the Green Creek Field in Mississippi gas brokered by Consul. The Fourth Circuit rejected Consul's contention that a plaintiff claiming denial of access to an essential facility need not

---

619.   935 F.2d at 1482-83.

620.   *Id.* at 1483.

621.   743 F. Supp. 1437 (D. Kan. 1990).

622.   *Id.* at 1459. Earlier, the Kansas district court had granted a preliminary injunction requiring Williams to keep its pipeline open for transportation of gas purchased by the cities from third parties. *See* City of Chanute v. Williams Natural Gas Co., 678 F. Supp. 1517 (D. Kan. 1988).

623.   743 F. Supp. at 1454 (emphasis in original).

624.   *Id.* at 1460.

625.   743 F. Supp. at 1461; *cf.* Reynolds Metals Co. v. Columbia Gas Sys., No. 87-0446-R (E.D. Va. Aug. 17, 1988) (dismissing essential facility claim by natural gas end-user against pipeline on ground that the essential facilities doctrine is available only to competitors, and not to consumers). The court in *Chanute* also rejected the cities' monopoly leveraging claim. It reasoned that the Tenth Circuit would not recognize monopoly leveraging as a separate offense under Section 2 of the Sherman Act. Thus, since the cities could not establish the "willful maintenance" element of their general monopolization claim, their monopoly leveraging claim also failed. 743 F. Supp. at 1461-62.

626.   805 F.2d 490 (4th Cir. 1986), *cert. denied*, 481 U.S. 1050 (1987).

define a relevant market and establish the defendant's market power in that market.[627] It held that Consul's Section 2 claim was defeated by Consul's inability to show that Transco possessed market power in the market for natural gas at the wellhead or in the nationwide market in which Consul and Transco competed as brokers of natural gas.[628]

(3) Mergers and Acquisitions

FERC has no regulatory authority over acquisitions of voting securities of natural gas companies. FERC does have authority over asset acquisitions by virtue of Section 7(c) of the NGA,[629] which prohibits the operation of acquired assets without a certificate of public convenience and necessity. In *California v. FPC*,[630] the Supreme Court concluded that the authority granted in Section 7(c) does not deprive the federal courts of jurisdiction to enforce the antitrust laws with respect to natural gas industry. Hence, the Antitrust Division, the FTC, and private parties remain free to challenge even FERC-approved acquisitions under the antitrust laws.

In *United States v. El Paso Natural Gas Co.*,[631] the government challenged El Paso's acquisition of a pipeline that was the "only actual supplier of out-of-state gas" to the California market.[632] Because El Paso, although it had never sold gas in the California market, was found to "have been a substantial factor in the California market,"[633] the Supreme Court held that the effect of the merger may be substantially to lessen competition within the meaning of Section 7 of the Clayton Act, and ordered the lower court to require El Paso to divest itself of the acquired pipeline.

The FTC has challenged several mergers involving gas pipelines and has obtained consent decrees.[634] In 1985, the FTC challenged MidCon's acquisition of United Energy Resources on the grounds that the proposed merger of the two pipeline companies would substantially lessen competition in (1) the transportation of natural

---

627.   *Id.* at 494.
628.   *Id.* at 495-96.
629.   15 U.S.C. § 717(c) (1988).
630.   369 U.S. 482 (1962).
631.   376 U.S. 651 (1964).
632.   *Id.* at 658.
633.   *Id.* at 660.
634.   *See* Arkla Inc., 5 TRADE REG. REP. ¶ 22,686 (Oct. 10, 1989) (alleging that Arkla's acquisition of pipeline from TransArk might lessen actual and potential competition in pipeline transportation of gas out of Arkansas portion of Arkoma Basin and transportation of gas into the Conway-Morrilton-Russellville corridor in Arkansas; consent decree required divestiture); Panhandle Eastern Corp., 5 TRADE REG. REP. (CCH) ¶ 22,680 (July 17, 1989) (alleging that Panhandle's acquisition of Texas Eastern might substantially lessen competition in the pipeline transportation of natural gas out of portions of the Gulf of Mexico; consent decree required Panhandle to divest its interest in a pipeline gathering system that competed with a pipeline owned by Texas Eastern); Occidental Petroleum Corp., 109 F.T.C. 167 (1986) (challenging vertical merger between natural gas producer and sole pipeline supplier of gas in St. Louis area on the ground that pipeline could pass on to consumers cost of gas purchased at inflated prices from affiliated producer; consent decree required Occidental to divest pipeline serving St. Louis area); InterNorth, Inc., 106 F.T.C. 312 (1985) (alleging that merger of two gas pipeline companies would lessen competition in purchase and transportation of natural gas from producing areas in the Permian Basin and the Panhandle region, and in transportation and sale of natural gas in the Texas Gulf Coast consuming area; consent decree required divesture of certain pipelines and interests in certain pipelines).

gas from producing fields and basins in certain areas in the Gulf of Mexico off the coasts of Louisiana and Texas, and (2) the transportation and sale of natural gas in the Baton Rouge/New Orleans consuming area.[635] The FTC's charges concerning the Baton Rouge/New Orleans consuming area were settled by a consent decree in which Midcon agreed to divest its interest in the Louisiana portion of the Arcadian pipeline system, which serves markets in Louisiana and Texas.[636] The FTC's charges concerning the offshore producing areas were heard by an Administrative Law Judge, who dismissed the complaint on the ground that the FTC staff had failed to prove a relevant geographic market in which competition would be harmed.[637] The FTC affirmed that decision.[638]

b. ELECTRIC POWER

The electric power industry is regulated by both federal and state authorities. Retail sales of electricity generally are regulated by state public utility commissions, while other aspects of the industry, including interstate sales for resale, are regulated by FERC pursuant to the Federal Power Act.[639]

The "public interest" standard of the Federal Power Act requires FERC to consider antitrust policies.[640] In *Gulf States Utilities Co. v. FPC*,[641] the Supreme Court found that one basis for passage of the Federal Power Act was an intent to control "abusive practices" by public utility companies.[642] The Court held that the power granted the FPC to regulate the industry "clearly carries with it the responsibility to consider, in appropriate circumstances, the anticompetitive effects of regulated aspects of interstate utility operations."[643] The FPC was to serve "the important function of establishing a first line of defense against those competitive practices that might later be the subject of antitrust proceedings."[644]

FERC regulation does not confer a blanket immunity from the antitrust laws. In *Otter Tail Power Co. v. United States*,[645] the Supreme Court rejected the utility's implied immunity claim. The Court found a Congressional intent to reject:

> a pervasive regulatory scheme for controlling the interstate distribution of power in favor of voluntary commercial relationships. When these relationships are governed in the first

---

635. Midcon Corp., 107 F.T.C. 48 (1986).
636. *Id.*
637. Midcon Corp., 5 TRADE REG. REP. (CCH) ¶ 22,510 (Feb. 2, 1988).
638. Midcon Corp., 5 TRADE REG. REP. (CCH) ¶ 22,708 (July 18, 1989).
639. 16 U.S.C. §§ 791a-828c (1988).
640. Gulf States Utils. Co. v. FPC, 411 U.S. 747, 759-60 (1973); *see* Central Power & Light Co. v. FERC, 575 F.2d 937, 938-39 (D.C. Cir.) (per curiam) (remanding to FERC to conduct a hearing considering antitrust issues under its public interest mandate), *cert. denied*, 439 U.S. 981 (1978); *cf.* Northern Cal. Power Agency v. FPC, 514 F.2d 184, 189 (D.C. Cir.) (request for hearing on antitrust issues contained in contracts between a utility and public power agency denied), *cert. denied*, 423 U.S. 863 (1975).
641. 411 U.S. 747 (1973).
642. *Id.* at 758. The Second Circuit has held that FERC has jurisdiction to require modification of contracts containing restrictive resale provisions that FERC found anticompetitive. New York State Elec. & Gas Corp. v. FERC, 638 F.2d 388, 393-98 (2d Cir. 1980), *cert. denied*, 454 U.S. 821 (1981).
643. 411 U.S. at 758-59.
644. *Id.* at 760.
645. 410 U.S. 366 (1973).

instance by business judgment and not regulatory coercion, courts must be hesitant to conclude that Congress had intended to override the fundamental national policy embodied in the antitrust laws.[646]

Early cases applied the antitrust laws to concerted anticompetitive conduct of utilities.[647] More recently, regulatory and antitrust litigation has focused on denial of wheeling access to a utility's transmission lines and on allegations of price squeezes by vertically-integrated utilities. Wheeling, price squeezes, and mergers and acquisitions are discussed below.

(1) Wheeling

Changes in energy policy and in technology have changed the structure of the electric utility industry. Where once a single electric utility often generated electricity and distributed it to a franchised service territory, now large industrial customers and municipally owned distribution companies often seek to purchase electricity from sources other than their local utility. These purchasers then turn to their local utilities for transmission service or "wheeling" to bring the power from the distant generation source to the purchaser. This has created a more competitive market for delivered electricity and created a demand for transmission that previously had been used only to serve the local utility's own power sales customers.

Pursuant to the Public Utility Regulatory Policies Act of 1978 (PURPA),[648] FERC has limited authority to compel wheeling and interconnection where to do so would serve the public interest, and promote efficiency, conservation, and reliability without causing the transmitting utility to suffer uncompensated economic loss or other undue burden.[649] The Second Circuit has held that PURPA applies to existing wheeling arrangements as well as to post-PURPA initial requests for wheeling, and that the elimination of anticompetitive restrictions through involuntary modification of wheeling tariffs already on file at FERC must also meet PURPA's

---

646. *Id.* at 374.
647. *See* Gainesville Utils. Dep't v. Florida Power & Light Co., 573 F.2d 292, 300 (5th Cir.) (holding that agreements between utilities that fix prices or divide territories are per se unlawful; relying on *Otter Tail*, the court "saw no reason to assume an antitrust exemption, nor to defer its decision pending FPC guidance"), *cert. denied*, 439 U.S. 966 (1978); Pennsylvania Water & Power Co. v. Consolidated Gas, Elec. Light & Power Co., 184 F.2d 552 (4th Cir.) (agreement between two utilities that allowed one utility to control the prices at which the second could sell electricity to other customers and the territories in which it could operate violated § 1 of the Sherman Act), *cert. denied*, 340 U.S. 906 (1950); United States v. Florida Power Corp., 1971 Trade Cas. (CCH) ¶ 73,637 (M.D. Fla. 1971) (consent decree prohibiting two utilities from agreeing to allocate territories and customers).
648. Pub. L. No. 95-617, 92 Stat. 3117 (1978) (codified at 16 U.S.C. §§ 2601-2645 (1988)).
649. *Id.* Section 202 of PURPA amended the Federal Power Act by adding § 210, which grants to FERC certain interconnection authority. 16 U.S.C. § 824 (1988). Section 203 of PURPA amends the Federal Power Act by adding § 211, which grants to FERC certain wheeling authority. 16 U.S.C. § 824. Any order issued by FERC under § 210 or §211 of PURPA must meet the requirements of § 212 of the Federal Power Act (a new section added by § 204 of PURPA). 16 U.S.C. § 824k. Section 212 places certain limitations on FERC's authority to ensure that the utility that is subject to the order does not suffer any uncompensated economic loss.

requirements if the result is an expanded wheeling obligation.[650] Several proceedings have been commenced at FERC under the PURPA wheeling provisions.[651]

In *Richmond Power & Light v. FERC*,[652] the District of Columbia Circuit suggested in dictum that its decision to deny FERC the authority effectively to compel wheeling, as a condition to its approval of a proposed rate under the FPA, did not foreclose the possibility that FERC could compel wheeling to prevent or to combat anticompetitive activity in another context.[653] The court also suggested that FERC might be empowered to require the expansion of a voluntary wheeling program upon a showing that a utility's voluntary wheeling program was "the result of anticompetitive intentions or, perhaps [was] at least unreasonable."[654]

The Fifth Circuit denied FERC the authority to compel wheeling in a general rule-making context in *Florida Power & Light Co. v. FERC*.[655] The court, however, left open the issue whether FERC could require wheeling access to combat specific anticompetitive activities resulting from rates or practices.[656]

In *Associated Gas Distributors v. FERC (AGD)*,[657] a case involving natural gas transmission under the Natural Gas Act, the D.C. Circuit implied that it continues to follow the *Richmond*[658] decision's dictum. The court in *AGD* upheld the authority of FERC to implement a voluntary program pursuant to Order No. 436 that effectively mandated open-access transportation on natural gas transmission lines under the Natural Gas Act. In reaching its decision in *AGD*, the court rejected the contention that the *Richmond* and *Florida Power & Light* decisions construing analogous portions of the Federal Power Act had held that FERC could not compel wheeling.[659]

In part because of its limited authority to order wheeling, FERC has sought to use incentives to make voluntary wheeling more attractive. Recognizing that open

---

650. New York State Elec. & Gas Corp. v. FERC, 638 F.2d 388, 393-98 (2d Cir. 1980), *cert. denied*, 454 U.S. 821 (1981).

651. Pacific Power & Light Co., 26 F.E.R.C. (CCH) ¶ 63,048 (1984); Florida Power & Light Co., 29 F.E.R.C. (CCH) ¶ 61,140 (1984); Southeastern Power Admin. v. Kentucky Utils. Co., 25 F.E.R.C. (CCH) ¶ 61,204 (1983) (FERC's authority to order wheeling under PURPA not intended to be tool to control anticompetitive conduct; wheeling would not generally be ordered when the wheeling utility would lose sales to its wholesale customers).

652. 574 F.2d 610 (D.C. Cir. 1978).

653. *Id.* at 623-24 (noting that FERC had the duty to rectify injury resulting from unjustifiable discrimination in rates and practices).

654. *Id.* at 624. The court noted that a unilateral refusal to wheel electricity for one customer but not another is not automatically discriminatory; the complainant has the burden to present a prima facie case that the refusal was the result of anticompetitive actions. *Id.* at 625-26.

655. 660 F.2d 668 (5th Cir. Unit B 1981), *cert. denied*, 459 U.S. 1156 (1983).

656. *Id.* at 679. The court of appeals did not address that issue because FERC had not relied on an anticompetitive rationale. The court stated in dictum, however, that "in the absence of findings of specific anticompetitive activities or antitrust violations, the Commission is without authority under the FPA to compel wheeling." *Id.*

657. 824 F.2d 981 (D.C. Cir. 1987), *cert. denied*, 485 U.S. 1006 (1988).

658. 574 F.2d at 623-24.

659. 824 F.2d at 998-99 (holding that under *Richmond* and *Florida Power & Light*, FERC is not barred from imposing open-access conditions in all circumstances under the Natural Gas Act). The court also noted that the Fifth Circuit had left open, in *Florida Power & Light*, the question whether FERC would be entitled to use open-access conditions as a remedy for anticompetitive conduct. *Id.*

transmission can create more competitive markets for bulk power, FERC has allowed some utilities that will open their transmission systems to others to sell bulk power at market-based rather than strictly regulated rates. FERC has allowed market-based rates in the limited circumstances where (1) the seller is not a dominant firm in the market, and, because of the likely entry of other suppliers, is not likely to become a dominant firm; (2) the buyers have a significant number of other supply options apart from the seller; or (3) if the seller is a dominant firm in the market, its market power can be mitigated by transmission commitments.[660] The practical application of this policy, however, is to require the proponent to voluntarily divest itself of all market power inherent in control of transmission facilities in order to relieve itself of regulatory scrutiny of its electricity sales. These cases are based on regulatory policy and not antitrust requirements, and may require transmission commitments beyond the obligations of regulated firms generally under the antitrust laws.[661]

Wheeling has also been the subject of antitrust litigation under Section 2 of the Sherman Act. In *Otter Tail Power Co. v. United States*,[662] the government challenged under Section 2 Otter Tail's refusal to sell wholesale power or wheel bulk power from another source to municipalities formerly served by Otter Tail at retail that wanted to establish municipally owned distribution systems. The Supreme Court rejected Otter Tail's implied immunity claim, holding that there was "no basis for concluding that the limited authority of the Federal Power Commission to order interconnections was intended to be a substitute for, or to immunize Otter Tail from, antitrust regulation."[663] The Court affirmed the district court's finding that Otter Tail had monopoly power in retail sales of electric power in its service area and held that by refusing to sell at wholesale or wheel power to the municipalities, Otter Tail violated Section 2 by using its strategic dominance in transmission to foreclose potential competition for sales at retail.[664]

Since *Otter Tail*, a number of decisions have addressed Section 2 claims based on refusals to wheel.[665] Two recent decisions have focused on legitimate business

---

660.   *See, e.g.*, Public Serv. Co. of Ind., Inc., Op. No. 349, 51 F.E.R.C. (CCH) ¶ 61,367 (1990); Terra Comfort Corp., 52 F.E.R.C. (CCH) ¶ 61,241 (1990).

661.   *See, e.g.*, Pacific Gas & Elec. Co., 50 F.E.R.C. (CCH) ¶ 61,339 (1990); Pacific Gas & Elec. Co., 47 F.E.R.C. (CCH) ¶ 61,121 (1989); Pacific Gas & Elec. Co., 38 F.E.R.C. (CCH) ¶ 61,242 (1987). Similarly, FERC has attempted to develop regional bulk power markets by allowing rate flexibility to bulk power traders who agree to transmit for others opting into the market programs.

662.   410 U.S. 366 (1973).

663.   *Id.* at 374-75; *see* City of Chanute v. Kansas Gas & Elec. Co., 754 F.2d 310, 312-13 (10th Cir. 1985) (FERC's limited authority under PURPA to order wheeling of power in certain instances does not deprive plaintiffs of a remedy at law for alleged anticompetitive behavior).

664.   410 U.S. at 380-81.

665.   *See* City of Malden v. Union Elec. Co., 887 F.2d 157, 161 (8th Cir. 1989) (upholding jury verdict for defendant where there was only one existing electric transmission line accessible to the city, but the city could have "economically provided for an alternative transmission system to convey electrical power"); Greenwood Utils. Comm'n v. Mississippi Power Co., 751 F.2d 1484 (5th Cir. 1985) (plaintiff's inability to obtain power generated by Southeastern Power Administration and transmitted over lines of defendant was result of activities and relationships between government agency and defendant that were immunized by the Noerr-Pennington doctrine); Borough of Lansdale v. Philadelphia Elec. Co., 692 F.2d 307 (3d Cir. 1982) (utility's refusal to wheel power did not violate Section 2 because utility did not have monopoly power in the relevant market, which included the service areas of other nearby wholesale suppliers); City of Groton v. Connecticut Light & Power Co., 662 F.2d 921 (2d Cir. 1981) (holding utility's policy of evaluating

justifications for a utility's denial or limitation of access to its transmission lines. In *City of Vernon v. Southern California Edison Co.*,[666] the district court held that the antitrust laws do not require that a utility provide a municipal electric system located within its service territory with access to the utility's transmission lines on an equal basis with the utility's native load customers, when to do so would impair the utility's ability to provide lowest cost service to the native load customers. That the utility was fully utilizing its transmission lines for the benefit of all of its customers, including the plaintiff, established a legitimate business justification for the denial of access. In *Cities of Anaheim v. Southern California Edison Co.*,[667] the district court rejected the plaintiffs' essential facility claim both because they failed to show that the denial of access to the particular power line at issue handicapped their overall competitive viability and because the defendant's protection of its other customers constituted a legitimate business justification for the denial of access.

(2) Price Squeeze

Both FERC regulatory proceedings and private antitrust actions have involved allegations of "price squeezes" by vertically integrated utilities that sell electricity at wholesale and also compete with their wholesale customers to supply retail service. The wholesale customer, typically a municipal electric distribution system, alleges that the differential between its supplier's wholesale and retail rates impairs the customer's ability to compete with the supplier at retail.[668]

In *FPC v. Conway Corp.*,[669] the Supreme Court held that FERC must consider the potential anticompetitive effect of an alleged price squeeze in determining whether wholesale rates are just and reasonable and that FERC has the discretion to push wholesale rates to the lower end of a "zone of reasonableness" to remedy a price squeeze. FERC originally adopted a rebuttable presumption of anticompetitive effect in considering price squeeze allegations in rate cases. In *Connecticut Light and Power Co.*,[670] it held that a prima facie case of price squeeze is established by showing a price discrimination (a non-cost justified differential between the supplying utility's wholesale and retail rates) and competition for retail customers between the supplying utility and the wholesale customer.[671] The utility then has the burden to rebut the presumption of anticompetitive effect.

---

wheeling requests on a case-by-case basis represented reasonable behavior); Town of Massena v. Niagara Mohawk Power Corp., 1980-2 Trade Cas. (CCH) ¶ 63,526, at 76,823-24 (N.D.N.Y. 1980) (refusal to wheel based on legitimate business reasons did not violate § 2 of Sherman Act).

666. 1990-1 Trade Cas. (CCH) ¶ 69,032 (C.D. Cal. 1990).

667. 1990-2 Trade Cas. (CCH) ¶ 69,246 (C.D. Cal. 1990).

668. One court has defined a price squeeze for regulatory purposes as "a price differential between [a supplier's] retail and wholesale rates that is not justified by differing costs and which places the wholesale customer at a disadvantage in competing with its own supplier for retail customers." Public Serv. Co. v. FERC, 832 F.2d 1201, 1207 n.6 (10th Cir. 1987).

669. 426 U.S. 271, 278-79 (1976); *see also* Borough of Ellwood City v. FERC, 731 F.2d 959 (D.C. Cir. 1984) (holding that FERC decision not to ameliorate a proven price squeeze ordinarily must be based on a determination that the anticompetitive effects of the price squeeze are outweighed by the effect of a remedy on the supplying utility's financial viability and its ability to serve all its customers).

670. 8 F.E.R.C. (CCH) ¶ 61,187 (1979).

671. *See* Kansas Gas & Elec. Co., 10 F.E.R.C. (CCH) ¶ 61,243 (1980) (failure to establish prima facie case because no evidence that rate disparity was not cost justified).

In *Southern California Edison Co.*,[672] FERC retracted its policy of providing a rebuttable presumption of anticompetitive effect and held that in order to make a prima facie case of price squeeze in future proceedings, parties making price squeeze claims must come forward with evidence "that the alleged price squeeze will have either an actual or a potential anticompetitive effect."[673] Noting that non-cost-justified price discrimination is not always undue, the FERC stated:

> Upon further consideration, we believe that our policy of providing a rebuttable presumption of an anticompetitive effect is no longer valid with respect to our responsibilities under the Federal Power Act to evaluate and remedy price squeeze. Price differences of limited magnitude and duration may not result in an injury to competition, and the Supreme Court's decision in *Conway* makes clear that the anticompetitive effect of utility rates should be our concern.[674]

Although FERC emphasized that price squeeze rate proceedings are not intended to become antitrust suits and FERC did not adopt the standards applied in antitrust cases, it stated that "decisions addressing alleged violations of the antitrust laws may serve as useful guides to parties involved in price squeeze proceedings."[675]

FERC's jurisdiction to consider price squeeze allegations in determining whether a utility's rates are just and reasonable does not preclude antitrust claims based on price squeezing by a regulated utility. Courts have rejected claims that FERC has exclusive or primary jurisdiction based on its regulation of wholesale rates,[676] and have also rejected claims of immunity under the state action doctrine based on state regulation of the utility's retail rates.[677] They have also held that the filed rate doctrine, under which a customer cannot obtain damages based on a claim that rates filed with a regulatory commission are unlawful under the antitrust laws, does not

---

672. 40 F.E.R.C. (CCH) ¶ 61,371 (1987).

673. *Id.* at 62,167.

674. *Id.* at 62,166; *see also* Pennsylvania Power Co., 21 F.E.R.C. (CCH) ¶ 61,313 (1982) (anticompetitive effects depend on the magnitude and duration of the price discrimination); Minnesota Power & Light Co., 11 F.E.R.C. (CCH) ¶ 61,313 (1980) (same).

675. 40 F.E.R.C. at 62,168. On the merits, FERC determined that Edison had engaged in an illegal price squeeze. This determination was reversed on appeal. Cities of Anaheim v. FERC, 941 F.2d 1234 (D.C. Cir. 1991).

676. *See* City of Kirkwood v. Union Elec. Co., 671 F.2d 1173, 1179 (8th Cir. 1982) (neither FERC nor the state regulatory commission had exclusive jurisdiction over price squeeze claim; antitrust courts may consider price squeeze claims without infringing on the regulatory jurisdiction of federal or state regulatory agencies because "the question is not whether the rates themselves are anticompetitive, but whether the defendant utility acted illegally in proposing a certain anticompetitive combination of rates"), *cert. denied*, 459 U.S. 1170 (1983); City of Mishawaka v. Indiana & Mich. Elec. Co., 560 F.2d 1314 (7th Cir. 1977) (holding that FPC did not have exclusive or primary jurisdiction over price squeeze claim against regulated utility), *cert. denied*, 436 U.S. 922 (1978); Borough of Ellwood City v. Pennsylvania Power Co., 570 F. Supp. 553 (W.D. Pa. 1983) (rejecting claim that FERC had exclusive jurisdiction over price squeeze allegations); City of Newark v. Delmarva Power & Light Co., 467 F. Supp. 763, 769, 771-72 (D. Del. 1979) (rejecting exclusive jurisdiction claim, and declining to stay court proceedings pending FERC decision on price squeeze issues).

677. See *City of Kirkwood*, 671 F.2d at 1179-80; *City of Mishawaka*, 560 F.2d at 1319-20.

apply to price squeeze claims.[678]

Courts generally have addressed the merits of price squeeze claims brought under Section 2 of the Sherman Act against regulated utilities by assessing the effect on competition and the reasonableness of the utility's conduct on a case-by-case basis.[679] In *Town of Concord v. Boston Edison Co.*,[680] however, the First Circuit adopted a qualified general rule against antitrust liability for price squeezes in fully regulated industries. It held that, in light of regulatory rules, constraints and practices, a price squeeze by a firm whose prices are regulated at both the wholesale and retail levels is not ordinarily exclusionary, and for that reason does not violate Section 2 of the Sherman Act.[681]

The *Town of Concord* court acknowledged that regulated utilities have no blanket immunity from the antitrust laws. But it emphasized that where regulatory and antitrust regimes coexist, antitrust rules must take account of the distinctive legal and economic setting of the industry to which they apply.[682] The court viewed full price regulation as "dramatically alter[ing] the calculus of antitrust harms and benefits" that justifies imposing price-squeeze liability in unregulated industries,[683] for four reasons: (1) regulation significantly diminishes the likelihood of major antitrust harm from a price squeeze; (2) an antitrust rule making price squeezes in fully regulated industries unlawful may, contrary to antitrust objectives, bring about reduced efficiency and increased consumer prices; (3) an antitrust rule prohibiting price squeezes presents special administrative difficulties in the regulatory context; and (4) a distributor who believes that a price squeeze will harm it has an administrative remedy before FERC.[684] Based on this analysis, the First Circuit concluded that "a price squeeze in a fully regulated industry such as electricity will

---

678. *See City of Kirkwood*, 671 F.2d at 1179 (filed rate doctrine inapplicable because price squeeze allegations are not a direct attack on filed rates, but rather attack the relationship between wholesale and retail rates; and the plaintiff alleges injury as a competitor, not a customer); City of Groton v. Connecticut Light & Power Co., 662 F.2d 921 (2d Cir. 1981) (filed rate doctrine inapplicable because price squeeze plaintiff sues as competitor, not as customer).

679. *See City of Groton*, 662 F.2d at 934-35 (remanding price squeeze claims for determination whether differential between utility's wholesale and retail rates had an anticompetitive effect); Cities of Anaheim v. Southern Cal. Edison Co., 1990-2 Trade Cas. (CCH) ¶ 69,246 (C.D. Cal. 1990) (utility price squeeze did not violate § 2 because no specific intent to monopolize could be inferred when utility had legitimate economic reasons for seeking what it regarded as a reasonable rate of return before regulatory agencies); Ray v. Indiana & Mich. Elec. Co., 606 F. Supp. 757 (N.D. Ill. 1984) (rates that are cost-justified and that would permit efficient competitors to operate profitably did not constitute an unlawful price squeeze), *aff'd*, 758 F.2d 1148 (7th Cir. 1985); City of Mishawaka v. American Elec. Power Co., 616 F.2d 976 (7th Cir. 1980) (affirming § 2 judgment against utility based on price squeeze resulting from unjustified disparity between utility's wholesale and retail rates and on other exclusionary conduct directed at municipal electric systems), *cert. denied*, 449 U.S. 1096 (1981).

680. 915 F.2d 17 (1st Cir. 1990), *cert. denied*, 111 S. Ct. 1337 (1991).

681. *Id.* at 28. The court also held, as an additional ground for reversing the judgment against the utility, that the cities had failed to show that Boston Edison had monopoly power in the relevant power generation market.

682. *Id.* at 22.

683. *Id.* at 25.

684. *Id.* at 25-28.

not normally constitute 'exclusionary conduct' under Sherman Act § 2."[685]

Another type of leveraging claim was raised in *Grason Electric Co. v. Sacramento Municipal Utility District*.[686] Thirteen electrical contractors brought a Sherman Act Case alleging that a municipal electric utility unlawfully used its monopoly power in the retail electrical energy market to "smother competition" for work installing and maintaining street and outdoor lighting systems.[687] The district court denied the contractors' motion for summary judgment, finding that the utility's use of customer contacts for advertising purposes did not constitute an unlawful use of monopoly power under Section 2 of the Sherman Act.[688] The court observed that a monopolist may lawfully use "legitimate competitive advantages" such as size, integration, foresight and business acumen if these advantages are available to all businesses of "similar size and sophistication."[689]

Similar concerns are addressed in the National Energy Conservation Policy Act,[690] which authorizes public utility diversification into energy conservation businesses but requires that utilities take special precautions to avoid injuring competitors that finance, supply, or install energy conservation measures. The Act requires utilities to charge fair prices and interest rates and not to discriminate against lenders, suppliers or contractors.[691] Moreover, utilities may supply and install energy conservation measures only pursuant to contracts between the utility and independent suppliers and contractors.[692] An unreasonably large share of supply and installation contracts may not be placed with any one supplier or contractor.[693]

(3) Mergers and Acquisitions

Under Section 203 of the Federal Power Act, FERC has jurisdiction to authorize proposed mergers and acquisitions of electric utilities subject to its jurisdiction.[694]

---

685. *Id.* at 28. The court emphasized that it had limited its holding by stating that "normally" a price squeeze will not constitute an exclusionary practice in the context of a fully regulated monopoly, thus leaving open the possibility that liability might be found in cases involving "exceptional circumstances." *Id.* at 29. The court also noted that its holding did not apply to the case where a monopolist is regulated only at one level. *Id.*

686. 571 F. Supp. 1504 (E.D. Cal. 1983).

687. *Id.* at 1506. The contractors pointed to four allegedly unlawful uses of monopoly power, including the utility's practice of informing its electric customers that it would construct and maintain street lighting systems at no initial cost. *Id.* at 1528.

688. *Id.* at 1528-29.

689. *Id.* The court concluded that physical access to customers constitutes a competitive advantage when "a monopolist can force its customers to accept a product that they would not otherwise purchase at the price tendered, but any firm can use the regular contact it has with its customers to promote a new product." *Id.*

690. 42 U.S.C. §§ 8201-8287 (1988).

691. *Id.* § 8214.

692. *Id.* § 8217.

693. *Id.*

694. 16 U.S.C. § 824b (1988); *see* Northeast Utils. Serv. Co., 50 F.E.R.C. (CCH) ¶ 61,266 (1990); Southern Cal. Edison Co., 47 F.E.R.C. (CCH) ¶ 61,196 (1989); Tucson Elec. Power Co., 44 F.E.R.C. (CCH) ¶ 61,441 (1988); Utah Power & Light Co., 41 F.E.R.C. (CCH) ¶ 61,283 (1987). Section 203 of the FPA provides that a public utility must acquire FERC approval in order to "sell, lease, or otherwise dispose of the whole of its facilities subject to the jurisdiction of the Commission, . . . or by any means whatsoever, directly or indirectly, merge or consolidate such

FERC is to grant approval of the merger if it finds that the merger "will be consistent with the public interest,"[695] although a positive benefit is not necessary.[696]

In addition to the traditional inquiry into effects on system reliability and effects upon the ratepayers of the merging companies, FERC will consider the competitive effects of a proposed merger in assessing whether the proposed merger is in the public interest.[697] In *Utah Power & Light*, FERC requested that evidence be presented on the following issues in a hearing on the proposed merger: (1) whether the proposed merger would result in a significant increase in concentration of economic power and control over facilities essential to participation in the bulk sales market; (2) the definition of the relevant product and geographic markets in which the merged company would compete; and (3) whether the merged company would be able to foreclose actual or potential competition by virtue of its control over the consolidated transmission system.[698]

In *Northeast Utilities Service Co.*,[699] FERC expanded its examination of the effects a proposed merger may have on competition. It focused on two sources of market power: the ownership and control of generation facilities and the ownership and control of transmission facilities.[700] The inquiry, according to FERC, is whether the merged company will have significantly greater market power than the two companies separately.[701] The parties contesting the merger should

---

facilities or any part thereof with those of any other person." 16 U.S.C. § 824b (1988).

695. *Utah Power & Light*, 41 F.E.R.C. at 61,752 (quoting 16 U.S.C. § 824b(a) (1988)); *see also Northeast Utilities*, 50 F.E.R.C. at 61,833; *Southern California Edison*, 47 F.E.R.C. at 61,671; *Tucson Electric*, 44 F.E.R.C. at 62,394.

696. *Utah Power & Light*, 41 F.E.R.C. at 61,752 (citing Pacific Power & Light Co. v. FPC, 111 F.2d 1014, 1017 (9th Cir. 1940)). FERC has found that the standards set forth in the Public Utility Holding Company Act are relevant but not binding on FERC. *See, e.g., Utah Power & Light*, 41 F.E.R.C. at 61,753 ("the policies proscribed by the SEC for dealing with holding companies are not necessarily applicable to the same degree in dealing with operating companies").

697. *See Utah Power & Light*, 41 F.E.R.C. at 61,752-53 (citing Commonwealth Edison Co., 36 F.P.C. 927, 932 (1966), *aff'd sub nom.* Utility Users League v. FPC, 394 F.2d 16 (7th Cir.), *cert. denied*, 393 U.S. 953 (1968)). In Utah Power & Light Co., 45 F.E.R.C. (CCH) ¶ 61,095, at 61,291-92 (1989), FERC conditioned approval of the merger on agreement by the merged company to wheel power for others.

698. 41 F.E.R.C. at 61,754. FERC stated that barriers to entry should be considered in defining the relevant market and that evidence concerning the practicability of duplicating the facilities should also be introduced at the hearing. *Id.; see also* Southern Cal. Edison Co., 47 F.E.R.C. (CCH) ¶ 61,196, at 61,674-75 (1989) (same); Tucson Elec. Power Co., 44 F.E.R.C. (CCH) ¶ 61,441, at 62,396 (1988) (The parties should address whether the proposed merger will tend to create a monopoly in a relevant market, to what extent alternate pathways exist, whether an increase in concentration and control of essential facilities will result, the feasibility of making facilities available, the feasibility of duplicating such facilities, the definition of the relevant product and geographic markets, whether barriers to entry will result in the relevant market, and the likelihood that actual or potential competition will be lessened.).

699. 50 F.E.R.C. (CCH) ¶ 61,266 (1990).

700. *Id.* at 61,834; *see also* Kansas City Power & Light Co., 53 F.E.R.C. (CCH) ¶ 61,097 at 61,286 (1990).

701. *Northeast Utilities*, 50 F.E.R.C. at 61,834; *Kansas City Power*, 53 F.E.R.C. at 61,286. Indeed, in cases where FERC has found that an intracorporate affiliate consolidation would not affect the competitive status quo, it has applied light scrutiny under Section 203 of the FPA. *See, e.g.*, Union Electric Co., 25 F.E.R.C. (CCH) ¶ 61,394 (1983); Delmarva Power & Light Co., 5 F.E.R.C. (CCH) ¶ 61,201 (1978); Wisconsin Elec. Power Co., 59 F.P.C. 1196 (1977).

define the relevant market, evaluate the market power the merged company will achieve, illustrate how that market power can be exercised, and describe the effects of using such market power.[702]

A second statute relevant to mergers and acquisitions in the electric power industry is the Public Utility Holding Company Act of 1935 (PUHCA).[703] Requirements of the PUHCA, which is administered by the SEC, include registration of public utility holding company systems, regulation of certain types of acquisitions, examination of such systems by the SEC to "simplify" and limit their operations, and divestiture of properties found to be detrimental to the proper functioning of such systems.[704]

The SEC must consider anticompetitive effects in exercising its jurisdiction under Sections 9 and 10 of PUHCA[705] to authorize stock acquisitions by registered holding companies or their subsidiaries. In *Municipal Electric Ass'n v. SEC*[706] the D.C. Circuit remanded a decision to the SEC that authorized certain electric utilities to acquire the stock of two electric generating companies. Municipal electric utilities challenged the proposed acquisition as violative of Section 10(b)(1) of the PUHCA on the ground that the municipal utilities were excluded from participating in the venture through stock ownership or power purchase. Section 10(b)(1) prohibits the approval of stock acquisitions that "tend towards interlocking relations or the concentration of control of public-utility companies, of a kind or to an extent detrimental to the public interest or the interest of investors or consumers."[707] The court held that this standard required the SEC to consider antitrust matters in determining whether to approve stock acquisitions and that the alleged impact on municipal utilities, if proved, would violate Section 10(b)(1). The court also held that the SEC had authority to approve the acquisition subject to conditions that would avoid the exclusionary impact on the municipal utilities.[708]

In *City of Lafayette v. SEC*,[709] however, the D.C. Circuit held that in exercising its jurisdiction under Sections 6 and 7 of PUHCA[710] to approve the issuance of securities by registered holding companies or their subsidiaries, the SEC was not

---

702.   *Northeast Utilities*, 50 F.E.R.C. at 61,834; *Kansas City Power*, 53 F.E.R.C. at 61,286; *see also* Southern Cal. Edison Co., 47 F.E.R.C. (CCH) ¶ 61,196, at 61,674 (1989). In *Northeast Utilities* FERC emphasized additional questions that the parties should address in the hearing, for example: "To what extent is any market power due to the merged company's control of transmission assets? . . . To what extent can the combined company's transmission system be used to prevent competitive entry of new generation facilities or to exclude potential competitors . . . from delivered bulk power markets . . . ? How does this differ from the existing situation?" 50 F.E.R.C. at 61,835.

703.   15 U.S.C. §§ 79-79z-6 (1988).

704.   *Id.* §§ 79e, 79h-79j, 79k.

705.   *Id.* §§ 79i, 79j.

706.   413 F.2d 1052, 1053, 1061 (D.C. Cir. 1969); *see also* Municipal Elec. Ass'n v. SEC, 419 F.2d 757, 759 (D.C. Cir. 1969) (per curiam).

707.   15 U.S.C. § 79j(b)(1) (1988).

708.   413 F.2d at 1060.

709.   454 F.2d 941, 955 (D.C. Cir. 1971), *aff'd sub nom.* Gulf States Utils. Co. v. FPC, 411 U.S. 747 (1973); *cf.* City of Lafayette v. SEC, 481 F.2d 1101, 1104-05 (D.C. Cir. 1973) (denial of petition to reopen hearing on proposed acquisition of a utility when the antitrust claims came 14 months after the close of hearing, were not related to industry structure, and failed to meet the nexus requirement between the complained conduct and the acquisition).

710.   15 U.S.C. §§ 79f, 79g (1988).

required to consider claims by cities that the proceeds of an issue by two utilities would be used to further an unlawful conspiracy to suppress competition. The court reasoned that the SEC need not consider the cities' claims because they related to operations of the utility companies over which the SEC had no jurisdiction.[711] On the other hand, the court held that the FPC, which did have jurisdiction to regulate the operations at issue, was required to consider the antitrust allegations in exercising its authority under Section 204 of the Federal Power Act[712] to approve the issuance of securities by public utilities.[713]

FERC has disclaimed jurisdiction over holding company mergers that do not involve a merger of the holding companies' public utility subsidiaries. In *Missouri Basin Municipal Power Agency v. Midwest Energy Co.*,[714] Midwest Energy Company, an exempt holding company which owned 100% of Iowa Public Service Company (a utility subject to FERC's jurisdiction) agreed to merge with another exempt holding company, Iowa Resources, which owned 100% of Iowa Power, Inc. (also a public utility subject to FERC's jurisdiction under the Federal Power Act). Although the holding companies were to be merged, the parties had no plans to immediately merge or consolidate the jurisdictional facilities of their respective public utility subsidiaries. Despite opposition, FERC disclaimed FPA jurisdiction over the transaction, basing its decision on the fact that the two holding companies

> did not own or operate FERC-jurisdictional facilities. Rather, they owned the common stock of public utility companies which in turn own FERC-jurisdictional facilities. To classify such holding companies as public utilities in these circumstances would be inconsistent with the distinct statutory definitions provided by Congress.
> ... Because the parties to the instant merger were not public utilities, but were only holding companies, the instant merger does not come within the scope of section 203.[715]

The opposition argued that the merged holding company would coordinate the operations of the public utility subsidiaries, and this coordination would constitute a merger of the public utility subsidiaries under Section 203. FERC rejected this argument, holding that the "[c]oordination of operations between and among separate public utilities is common and does not *ipso facto* constitute a merger or consolidation of jurisdictional facilities."[716]

Acquisition by a registered holding company of the stock of a public utility, however, may be subject to both SEC and FERC review. In *Savannah Electric &*

---

711.   454 F.2d at 955. The D.C. Circuit cautioned that there may be § 6 proceedings in which antitrust considerations are relevant, for example where "the operations assailed are of such a nature as to be equivalent, in significance and consequence, to structural affiliation, or if the purpose of the utility's sale of securities is otherwise shown to have a reasonable nexus to matters within the SEC's jurisdiction under other provisions." *Id.* at 956.

712.   16 U.S.C. § 824c (1988).

713.   454 F.2d at 953.

714.   53 F.E.R.C. (CCH) ¶ 61,368 (1990).

715.   53 F.E.R.C. at 62,298-99.

716.   *Id.* at 62,299 (footnote omitted) (emphasis in original). FERC noted, however, that it continued to retain jurisdiction under sections 205 and 206 of the Federal Power Act. Moreover, although it was disclaiming jurisdiction over the holding company merger, the Commission observed that if the two utility subsidiaries merged, "[s]uch a merger or consolidation ... will require Commission approval under section 203." *Id.*

Power Co.,[717] FERC determined that the proposed reorganization under which Southern, a holding company registered under the PUHCA, would acquire all of the outstanding common stock of Savannah was subject to FERC jurisdiction under Section 203 of the FPA.[718] FERC applied the holding of *Central Vermont Public Service Corp.*[719] that "the transfer of ownership and control of [the utility's] jurisdictional facilities, from [the utility's] existing shareholders to . . . [a] holding company, constitutes a disposition of jurisdictional facilities requiring prior Commission approval under section 203."[720] Thus, the proposed transaction was "clearly a jurisdictional disposition of utility property under section 203."[721]

Savannah and Southern argued, in the alternative, that even if the reorganization was subject to Section 203 of the FPA, pursuant to Section 318 of the FPA[722] the exercise of jurisdiction by the SEC deprived the FERC of its jurisdiction. FERC concluded, however, that Section 318 did not apply.[723] It held that a direct conflict between FERC and SEC regulation must exist in order to call into play Section 318.[724] According to the FERC, no conflict existed between the FERC's responsibility to protect ratepayers and guarantee reliable service and the SEC's responsibility under PUHCA.[725]

---

717. 42 F.E.R.C. (CCH) ¶ 61,240 (1988).
718. *Id.* at 61,778. The reorganization had already been approved by the SEC pursuant to its authority under Section 10 of PUHCA to review stock acquisitions by registered holding companies.
719. 39 F.E.R.C. (CCH) ¶ 61,295 (1987).
720. *Savannah*, 42 F.E.R.C. at 61,778 (quoting *Central Vermont*, 39 F.E.R.C. at 61,960)). FERC noted that the holding of *Central Vermont* specifically reversed an earlier line of cases in which it had narrowly construed § 203 to apply only to sales of real and personal property and had rejected jurisdiction over holding company reorganizations. Since *Central Vermont*, the FERC has consistently asserted jurisdiction under § 203 in instances of stock acquisitions or company recapitalizations. See Northern Ind. Pub. Serv. Co., 42 F.E.R.C. (CCH) ¶ 61,245 (1988); Public Serv. Co. of Ind., 42 F.E.R.C. (CCH) ¶ 61,243 (1988); Central Ill. Pub. Serv. Co., 42 F.E.R.C. (CCH) ¶ 61,073 (1988).
721. *Savannah*, 42 F.E.R.C. at 61,778.
722. Section 318 provides:
      If, with respect to the issue, sale, or guaranty of a security, or assumption of obligation or liability in respect of a security . . . or the acquisition or disposition of any security, capital assets, facilities, or any other subject matter, any person is subject both to a requirement of the Public Utility Holding Company Act of 1935 [15 U.S.C. 79 et seq.] or of a rule, regulation, or order thereunder and to a requirement of this chapter or of a rule, regulation, or order thereunder, the requirement of the Public Utility Holding Company Act of 1935 shall apply to such person, and such person shall not be subject to the requirement of this chapter, or of any rule, regulation or order thereunder, with respect to the same subject matter, unless the Securities and Exchange Commission has exempted such person from such requirement of the Public Utility Holding Company Act of 1935, in which case the requirements of this chapter shall apply to such person.
      16 U.S.C. § 825q (1988).
723. *Savannah*, 42 F.E.R.C. at 61,779.
724. *Id.*
725. *Id.* FERC granted approval for the proposed stock acquisition under § 203. The Supreme Court in Arcadia v. Ohio Power Co., 111 S. Ct. 415 (1990), discussed the application of § 318 but did not reach the question whether § 318 bars all FERC regulation of a subject matter regulated by the SEC or only such regulation as imposes a conflicting requirement. The Court interpreted § 318 as applying only when an electric power company is subjected to both a SEC and a FERC requirement with respect to one of the four subject matters specifically enumerated in § 318 and where the SEC and FERC requirements both concern the same such subject matter. It held that § 318 did not apply to the case before it because the SEC's requirements (concerning Ohio

c.   OIL TRANSPORTATION

Regulation of oil transportation is divided principally between FERC, which regulates pipelines, and the Department of Transportation, which regulates offshore oil structures.[726]

While the revised Interstate Commerce Act[727] gives the ICC general jurisdiction over pipeline transportation,[728] FERC has jurisdiction over interstate pipelines[729] when the commodity being transported is oil.[730] There is, however, no express antitrust immunity for FERC-approved acts, and the statutes do not specify the role competition and antitrust policies should play in FERC's regulation of the oil pipeline industry. The D.C. Circuit has concluded, based on examination of the structure of the Interstate Commerce Act, that Congress intended "to allow a freer play of competitive forces among oil pipeline companies than in other common carrier industries."[731] In *Farmers Union Central Exchange v. FERC*[732] (*Farmers Union II*), the D.C. Circuit more clearly delineated the role competition may play in setting oil pipeline rates under the Interstate Commerce Act. The court rejected FERC's view "that oil pipeline rate regulations should serve only as a cap on egregious price exploitation by the regulated pipelines, and that competitive market forces be relied upon in the main to assure proper rate levels."[733] Analogizing to the NGA and the Federal Communications Act, the court discussed "rational or permissible assumptions about the relationship between 'just and reasonable' rates and the market price":

> FERC's methodology [allowed rates which] . . . would exceed the "zone of reasonableness" by definition, unless competition in the oil pipeline market drives the actual prices back down into the zone. But nothing in the regulatory scheme itself acts as a monitor to see if this occurs or to check rates if it does not. That is the fundamental flaw in the Commission's scheme.[734]

In compliance with *Farmers Union II*, FERC began, before implementing

---

Power's acquisition of a coal company or its acquisition of coal from that company) and the FERC's requirements (concerning the portion of its coal costs Ohio Power could recover in its rates) did not both concern one of the enumerated subject matters or did not both concern the same such subject matter.

726.   Transportation over land by motor carriers has been deregulated.

727.   49 U.S.C. §§ 10101-11917 (1988).

728.   *Id.* § 10501.

729.   Intrastate oil pipelines are not subject to FERC jurisdiction. FERC's authority to regulate oil pipelines emanating from the outer continental shelf is less clear, but such lines are in any event covered by certain competitive principles expressed in the Outer Continental Shelf Lands Act Amendments of 1978. *See infra* notes 781-793 and accompanying text.

730.   42 U.S.C. § 7172(b) (1988); *see* 49 U.S.C. § 10501(a)(1)(c) (1988). FERC jurisdiction is under the original, not the recodified, Interstate Commerce Act. Pub. L. No. 95-473, § 4(c), 92 Stat. 1470 (1978).

731.   Farmers Union Cent. Exch. v. FERC, 584 F.2d 408, 413 (D.C. Cir.), *cert. denied*, 439 U.S. 995 (1978) (Farmers Union I).

732.   734 F.2d 1486 (D.C. Cir.) (vacating FERC Opinion No. 154, Williams Pipe Line Co., 21 F.E.R.C. (CCH) ¶ 61,260 (1982)), *cert. denied*, 469 U.S. 1034 (1984).

733.   734 F.2d at 1490.

734.   *Id.* at 1509 (citations omitted). *Farmers Union II* is applicable to all the industries under FERC regulation.

light-handed regulation, to analyze whether sufficient competition exists in a market to ensure that rates remain within the zone of reasonableness. In *Buckeye Pipe Line Co.,*[735] FERC approached its competition inquiry by defining the relevant product and geographic markets. It utilized the Herfindahl-Hirshman Index (HHI) as a preliminary screening device to determine concentration in each market area. In evaluating competitive conditions in the market areas, FERC also considered potential competition, available alternatives, market share, capacity availability, and monopsonistic pressure.

The regulation of oil pipelines has been the continuing subject of Congressional inquiry, and the Department of Justice has published a report outlining a methodology for measuring market power in oil pipeline markets.[736] In the Department's view, regulation is necessary for some, but not all interstate oil pipelines.

Certain offshore structures used as terminals to load and unload oil for transportation to the United States must be licensed by the Department of Transportation as "deepwater ports."[737] Before the Secretary of Transportation may issue a license for a deepwater port, he or she must obtain the opinion of the Attorney General and the FTC as to whether the grant of the license "would adversely affect competition, restrain trade, promote monopolization, or otherwise create a situation in contravention of the antitrust laws."[738] Deepwater port licenses granted by the Secretary of Transportation have incorporated some of the Attorney General's antitrust recommendations with respect to specific license conditions.[739] The Deepwater Port Act Amendments of 1984[740] eliminated the requirements for tariff filing and regulation by the FERC, provided that effective competition exists for the transportation of oil by alternative means and that the licensee sets its rates, fees, charges, and conditions of service competitively.[741]

d.   NUCLEAR POWER

The Nuclear Regulatory Commission (NRC) has jurisdiction to license the

---

735.   53 F.E.R.C. (CCH) ¶ 61,473 (1990).

736.   ANTITRUST DIV., U.S. DEP'T OF JUSTICE, COMPETITION IN THE OIL PIPELINE INDUSTRY: A PRELIMINARY REPORT (MAY 1984); ANTITRUST DIV., U.S. DEP'T OF JUSTICE, OIL PIPELINE DEREGULATION: REPORT OF THE U.S. JUSTICE DEPARTMENT (May 1986).

737.   33 U.S.C. § 1503 (1988).

738.   *Id.* § 1506(a). The Deepwater Port Act Amendments of 1984, Pub. L. 98-419, 98 Stat. 1607 (1984) (codified at 33 U.S.C. §§ 1501-1524 (1988)), eliminated the requirement that the Secretary await the review and opinion of the Attorney General and FTC before amending, transferring or renewing a license. Instead, so long as the petition to amend, transfer or renew a license is transmitted to the Attorney General and the FTC, the Secretary may take such action if it is consistent with the "findings" made at the time the original license was issued. During this review, the Secretary has the power to amend or rescind any license condition no longer necessary or required. Licenses now remain in effect unless suspended or revoked by the Secretary or until surrendered by the licensee. 33 U.S.C. § 1503(e)(1), (h) (1988).

739.   *See, e.g.,* DEPARTMENT OF TRANSPORTATION, DECISION ON THE DEEPWATER PORT LICENSE APPLICATION OF LOOP, INC. AND SEADOCK, INC. (Dec. 17, 1976).

740.   Pub. L. No. 98-419, 98 Stat. 1607 (1984) (codified at 33 U.S.C. §§ 1501-1518 (1988)).

741.   Under 33 U.S.C. § 1507 (1988) if the Secretary has reason to believe that these two preconditions are not being met, the Secretary can request the FERC to initiate an investigation on whether to reimpose tariff regulation; can request the Attorney General to enforce the statutory common carrier obligations; or can suspend or revoke the license.

construction and operation of nuclear power plants to generate electricity. The Atomic Energy Act of 1954 expressly makes the antitrust laws applicable to NRC-approved activities.[742] Thus there is a system of dual regulation: "economic supervision by the [NRC] which is largely prospective, and antitrust enforcement by the Justice Department, which is largely retrospective."[743]

In 1970, Congress amended the Atomic Energy Act to require prelicensing antitrust review for all nuclear facilities to be used for commercial purposes.[744] The Atomic Safety and Licensing Appeal Board, which oversees license grants, suspensions, revocations, and amendments, has stated: "The change reflects congressional recognition that the nuclear industry is in great measure the product of public funds, having originated as a government monopoly, as well as the legislature's concern that the licensing process not encourage private monopolies but assure fair access to nuclear power."[745] Under the prelicensing review procedures, the NRC must determine whether the grant of an application for a construction permit "would create or maintain a situation inconsistent with the antitrust laws."[746]

Upon receipt of an application to construct a nuclear facility, the NRC must solicit the advice of the Attorney General and publish this advice in the Federal Register.[747] If the Attorney General "advises that there may be adverse antitrust aspects and recommends that there be a hearing," the NRC must hold a hearing and permit the Justice Department to participate as a party.[748] If a hearing record demonstrates with "reasonable probability"[749] that anticompetitive effects would flow from the grant of an application, the NRC may issue a license as applied for, refuse to issue a license, or issue one with remedial conditions.[750]

Appeal Board decisions have emphasized that an actual violation of the antitrust laws need not be demonstrated; it is sufficient to show that conditions are inconsistent with the policies underlying the antitrust laws.[751] Furthermore, licensed activities will be deemed to "create or maintain" an anticompetitive situation when there is a "reasonable nexus between the alleged anticompetitive practices and

742. 42 U.S.C. § 2135 (1988); United Nuclear Corp. v. Combustion Eng'g, Inc., 302 F. Supp. 539, 552 (E.D. Pa. 1969).
743. Statement of then Assistant Att'y Gen., Antitrust Div., Thomas E. Kauper, Before the Joint Comm. on Atomic Energy 27 (Aug. 1, 1973).
744. 42 U.S.C. § 2135(c) (1988); see also Fort Pierce Utils. Auth. v. United States, 606 F.2d 986, 994 (D.C. Cir.), cert. denied, 444 U.S. 842 (1979).
745. Toledo Edison Co., 10 N.R.C. 265, 271-72 (1979).
746. 42 U.S.C. § 2135(c)(1), (5) (1988).
747. Id. § 2135(c)(1), (5).
748. Id. § 2135(c)(5).
749. Consumers Power Co., 6 N.R.C. 892, 903, 908 n.33 (1977).
750. 42 U.S.C. § 2135(c)(6) (1988). In several proceedings of this type, the NRC Atomic Safety and Licensing Appeal Board has sustained the Antitrust Division's position that the inquiry should encompass the competitive impact of all the applicant's commercial power market practices. Memorandum and Order, Alabama Power Co., AEC Dkts. 50-348A, 50-364A (Feb. 9, 1973); Prehearing Order No. 2, Georgia Power Co., AEC Dkt. 50-366A (Feb. 7, 1973). The broad scope of this review process has been upheld by Appeal Board decisions. Toledo Edison Co., 10 N.R.C. 265, 283-84 (1979); Consumers Power, 6 N.R.C. at 916.
751. Toledo Edison Co., 10 N.R.C. 265, 272-73 (1979); Consumers Power, 6 N.R.C. at 907-09; see also S. REP. No. 1247, 91st Cong., 2d Sess. 14-15 (1970).

the [licensed] activities."[752]   This nexus requirement is met when the anticompetitive effects are "intertwined with or exacerbated by" the grant of a license.[753] The Appeal Board decisions indicate that the NRC antitrust review process will analyze alleged anticompetitive practices in retail power, wholesale power, and coordination of service markets.[754]

In the only Section 105(c) case that has reached the courts, the Eleventh Circuit affirmed an NRC finding that the grant of an unconditional license to the Alabama Power Company would maintain a situation inconsistent with the antitrust laws.[755] The NRC had found that in conducting its existing electric utility business, Alabama Power had engaged in a variety of anticompetitive acts, including threats of termination of potential competitors, refusals to deal and use of exclusive dealing agreements, and that it "had wrongly wielded monopoly power."[756]   Alabama Power argued that the NRC's antitrust review should be limited to activities arising directly from the proposed construction and operation of the nuclear power plant for which it sought a permit and that under the "inconsistency" standard of Section 105(c), the NRC must confine its antitrust concerns to actual, rather than probable violations.[757] The court disagreed.   It ruled that the NRC had not abused its discretion by considering the antitrust consequences of activities not directly arising from the construction and operation of the proposed nuclear power plant.   The court also ruled that "[t]he NRC is to look only for 'reasonable probability' of violation" of the antitrust laws.[758]

Most antitrust problems revealed during the NRC prelicensing review process have been resolved without a hearing, through negotiated license restrictions.[759]

e.   COMPETITION AND FEDERAL LANDS

Much of the nation's unexploited or unexplored energy reserves lie under lands owned or effectively controlled by the federal government.[760] In the mid-1970s Congress established three programs under which the Department of Justice conducts an antitrust review of proposed sales of leases or production from federal lands. These three programs are described individually below.   Because the three programs

---

752.   Florida Power & Light Co., 15 N.R.C. 22, 30 (1982) (quoting Louisiana Power & Light Co. (Waterford Elec. Generating Station, Unit 3), CLI-73-25, 6 A.E.C. 619, 621 (1973)).
753.   Florida Power & Light, 15 N.R.C. 22 (1982); Consumers Power, 6 N.R.C. at 915-17.
754.   Consumers Power, 6 N.R.C. at 915-17.
755.   Alabama Power Co. v. NRC, 692 F.2d 1362, 1368-69 (11th Cir. 1982), cert. denied, 464 U.S. 816 (1983).
756.   Id. at 1365.
757.   Id. at 1367-68.
758.   Id. at 1368.
759.   See, e.g., Houston Lighting & Power Co., 15 N.R.C. 1143 (1982).
760.   The federal government owns about one-third of the nation's coal resources. In the states west of the Mississippi River, where most federal coal reserves are located, the federal government owns as much as 60% of the total reserve base and controls an additional 20% through its trust responsibility for Indian lands and the inability to mine, legally or economically, much of the non-federal reserve base without obtaining a federal lease, as well. U.S. DEP'T OF INTERIOR, FEDERAL COAL MANAGEMENT REPORT, FISCAL YEAR 1988, at 1 (1989). As much as one-third of the nation's unexplored oil resources lie in federally controlled offshore waters. U.S. Geological Survey, Circular 860. The federal government also owns the eighth largest oil field in the United States from which it produces crude oil and natural gas for its own account, selling the production to third parties. 20 INTERNATIONAL PETROLEUM ENCYCLOPEDIA 238-39 (1987).

employ an identical antitrust review standard whether the proposed lease or sale "would create or maintain a situation inconsistent with the antitrust laws" the origin and the Department's interpretation of that standard are discussed in the following section.

(1) Antitrust Review Framework

(a) Federal Coal Leasing

The federal coal leasing program is managed by the Department of Interior. Coal reserves are leased either through a competitive sealed-bid lease sale[761] or by "application."[762] Under Section 15 of the Federal Coal Leasing Amendments Act of 1976, the Secretary of Interior must notify the Attorney General thirty days prior to the proposed issuance, renewal or readjustment of a federal coal lease and provide the Attorney General with such information as the Attorney General requires to determine whether the proposed lease "would create or maintain a situation inconsistent with the antitrust laws."[763] If the Attorney General advises the Secretary that issuance of the proposed lease would create or maintain such a situation, the Secretary may not issue the lease unless, after conducting a public hearing on the record, the Secretary finds that issuance of the lease "is necessary to effectuate the purposes of the [federal coal leasing laws], that it is consistent with the public interest, and that there are no reasonable alternatives consistent with [the Act], the antitrust laws, and the public interest."[764]

Before being issued leases, successful bidders for federal coal leases must provide information in a form or a format approved by the Department of Justice.[765] The Department requires that a variety of information be reported, including total in-place coal reserves, uncommitted in-place coal reserves, the characteristics of the coal to be leased, and the identity of any affiliates, subsidiaries, and joint ventures, including affiliations or joint ventures with railroads, electric utilities, and nuclear fuel fabricators or converters.[766] The Department of Interior may not issue a lease until thirty days after the Attorney General has received the information required to be submitted by the successful bidder.[767] If the information submitted is

---

761. 43 C.F.R. subpart 3422 (1991).
762. *Id.* subpart 3425. Leasing by application can occur if a tract is outside a designated regional coal production region or if the tract is necessary to maintain production at existing mines, to meet contractual obligations, or to prevent the bypass of federal coal. *Id.*
763. 30 U.S.C. § 184(l)(2) (1988). Regulations promulgated by the Department of Interior require that lease exchanges and transfers also be reviewed by the Department of Justice. 43 C.F.R. §§ 3435.3-7, 3453.2-2(e) (1991).
764. 30 U.S.C. § 184(l)(2) (1988); 43 C.F.R. § 3422.3-4(e)(2) (1991).
765. 43 C.F.R. § 3422.3-4(a)-(d) (1991).
766. Antitrust Div., U.S. Dep't of Justice, OMB No. 1105-0025. The Department of Justice has created two reporting forms, one covering federal coal leases in certain western states (Arizona, Colorado, Montana, New Mexico, North Dakota, South Dakota, and Wyoming) and a second form covering leases in certain eastern states (Texas, Nebraska, Iowa, Kansas, Missouri, Oklahoma, Arkansas, Illinois, Indiana, and western Kentucky). These forms are available from the Department of Interior.
767. 43 C.F.R. § 3422.3-4(c) (1991).

incomplete, however, the thirty-day period is tolled pending the submission of correct or complete data.[768]

In addition to the lease review provisions, the Federal Coal Leasing Amendments Act of 1976 requires that the Attorney General submit an annual report to Congress on "competition in the coal and energy industries" in conjunction with the Department of Interior report on the federal coal management program.[769] The Department of Justice has used the occasion of that report to set forth its policy regarding review of federal coal leases. The Department's initial report, submitted in May 1978, set forth the analytical framework for reviewing federal coal leases and defined the relevant geographic and product markets. The Department found separate markets for metallurgical coal, utility steam coal, spot coal, and long-term contract coal, although the market for long-term contracts for uncommitted utility steam coal predominated.[770] The Department described four geographic markets in which it would evaluate coal leases, the Appalachian market,[771] the Midwest market,[772] the Northern Plains market,[773] and the Southwest market.[774] In a subsequent report, the Department revised its federal coal lease review policies in light of the product and market definition standards announced in the 1982 *Merger Guidelines* and additional information obtained since its initial effort to define relevant markets. As a result, the Department somewhat narrowed its geographic market definition, finding a smaller Powder River Region market within the Northern Plains market.[775]

Although the Department found that the nation's coal markets were currently competitive, it nonetheless announced that it will regard the fact that a lease winner's share of the relevant market, including the leases under review, exceeds 15% of uncommitted nonfederal reserves as prima facie evidence that award of the lease would create or maintain a situation inconsistent with the antitrust laws. The Department also stated that it would consider relevant mitigating evidence that would demonstrate that the lease sale subject to the prima facie rule would not, in fact, be anticompetitive, although the burden of coming forward with such evidence will rest upon the prospective lease holder.[776] The Department also stated that, because coal and nuclear fuel are fairly good substitutes, a 10% prima facie standard will be applied to companies in the conversion and fuel fabrication stages of the nuclear fuel industry.[777] Subsequently, the Department announced that it would give special attention to proposed leases to affiliates of the Burlington Northern Railroad, which it found had market power over coal transportation from the Powder

---

768.   *Id.*

769.   30 U.S.C. § 208-2 (1988).

770.   U.S. DEP'T OF JUSTICE, COMPETITION IN THE COAL INDUSTRY 39-42 (1978).

771.   Maryland, Ohio, Pennsylvania, West Virginia, Alabama, Georgia, eastern Kentucky, North Carolina, eastern Tennessee, Virginia, and Michigan. *Id.* at 47-48.

772.   Illinois, Indiana, western Kentucky, Arkansas, Iowa, Kansas, Louisiana, Missouri, Oklahoma, and Texas. *Id.* at 48-51.

773.   Idaho, Montana, North Dakota, South Dakota, Wyoming, Alaska, Oregon, and Minnesota. *Id.* at 51-52.

774.   Arizona, Colorado, New Mexico, and Utah. *Id.* at 52-53.

775.   U.S. DEP'T OF JUSTICE, COMPETITION IN THE COAL INDUSTRY 47 (1982).

776.   U.S. DEP'T OF JUSTICE, COMPETITION IN THE COAL INDUSTRY 130-131 (1978).

777.   *Id.*

River Region,[778] and to leases to electric utilities, because of the potential for the evasion of rate regulation.[779]   The Department has not, however, applied the Herfindahl-Hirshman Index to its review of federal coal leasing.[780]

(b) Outer Continental Shelf Oil and Gas Leasing

Under the Section 205 of the Outer Continental Shelf Lands Act Amendments of 1978,[781] the Department of Justice reviews proposed new federal offshore oil and gas leases on the outer Continental Shelf.[782]   Lease sales are conducted by the Secretary of Interior by competitive bidding under regulations promulgated by the Secretary.[783]   Before the Secretary may accept any bids at a proposed sale, the Secretary must allow the Attorney General, in consultation with the Federal Trade Commission (FTC), thirty days to review the results of the sale.[784]   The statute grants the Attorney General the discretion to conduct such antitrust review as the Attorney General believes is appropriate, in consultation with the FTC, and the Secretary is required to provide such information as they require in order to conduct their antitrust review.[785]

Under Section 205, the Attorney General, in consultation with the FTC, may make such recommendations to the Secretary as may be appropriate, including the nonacceptance of any bid. If either the Attorney General (in consultation with the FTC) or the Secretary determines that the issuance of the lease "may create or maintain a situation inconsistent with the antitrust laws," the Secretary may refuse to issue the lease even though the bidder is otherwise qualified. Alternatively, he may issue the lease, notifying the Attorney General and the lessee of the reason for the Secretary's decision.[786]   The statute specifically provides that this antitrust review process leaves unaltered the rights and authority of the Department, the FTC, or private parties under the antitrust laws.[787]

The Department has announced that it generally will analyze Outer Continental Shelf lease sales in one of two relevant markets. Leases off the eastern and Gulf

---

778.   U.S. DEP'T OF JUSTICE, COMPETITION IN THE COAL INDUSTRY 79-81, 104-106 (1980). Leasing directly to railroad companies is prohibited by Section 2(c) of the Mineral Lands Leasing Act of 1920, 30 U.S.C. § 202 (1988). *See* National Coal Ass'n v. Hodel, 825 F.2d 523, 526 (D.C. Cir. 1987).

779.   U.S. DEP'T OF JUSTICE, COMPETITION IN THE COAL INDUSTRY 68-69 (1982).

780.   *See* U.S. DEP'T OF JUSTICE, COMPETITION IN THE COAL INDUSTRY 31 (1983) (redefining coal markets in light of the MERGER GUIDELINES, but reaffirming the 15% test for prima facie inconsistency with the antitrust laws).

781.   43 U.S.C. § 1337(c) (1988).

782.   The term "Outer Continental Shelf" is defined as submerged lands subject to the control of the United States lying outside a line three miles from the coastline. *Id.* §§ 1301(a), 1331(a).

783.   *Id.* § 1337.

784.   *Id.* § 1337(c)(1). The statute permits the Attorney General and the FTC to agree to a shorter period. *Id.*

785.   *Id.* § 1337(c)(2).

786.   *Id.* § 1337(c)(3).

787.   *Id.* § 1337(c)(4), (f). Under Department of Interior regulations, the Secretary "shall consult with and give due consideration to the views of the Attorney General" prior to approving a transfer or assignment of a lease. 30 C.F.R. § 265.65 (1991). The Attorney General has thirty days to provide those views. *Id.*

coasts are considered part of a world crude oil market.[788] The Department, however, has defined a separate geographic market consisting of the states of Alaska, California, Washington, Oregon, Nevada, and Arizona, an area known as "PAD District V," for which lower quality crudes, i.e., crude oil of high sulfur content and viscosity, form a separate product.[789] The FTC defined a more narrow market consisting only of crude oil similar to that produced in Alaska, excluding similar crude oil produced in California.[790] The Department has announced that it will recommend that the Secretary reject any joint bid submitted by two or more of the four largest reserve holders in PAD District V.[791] At the time the Department announced its policy, joint ventures among BP, Exxon, and Shell were forbidden by Section 105 of the Energy Policy and Conservation Act.[792] The Department found that the concentration in the relevant market was very high, there were substantial barriers to entry, and the existence of joint ventures made independent action more difficult.[793]

(c) Naval and National Petroleum Reserves

Section 201(11) of the Naval Petroleum Reserves Production Act of 1976[794] makes the sale of petroleum or petroleum leases from the four naval petroleum reserves and the National Petroleum Reserve in Alaska, or the formulation of any leasing or sale plans affecting those reserves, subject to review by the Attorney General "with respect to matters which may affect competition."[795] Before any contract or operating agreement may be issued or executed with respect to any of the naval petroleum reserves, the Secretary of Energy must notify the Attorney General at least fifteen days prior to the issuance or execution of such an agreement or contract. The Secretary of Energy must also provide such information as the Attorney General requires to formulate his advice to the Secretary. If, within the fifteen-day period, the Attorney General advises the Secretary that "a contract or operating agreement may create or maintain a situation inconsistent with the

---

788. U.S. DEP'T OF JUSTICE, ADVICE AND RECOMMENDATIONS OF THE U.S. DEPARTMENT OF JUSTICE TO THE SECRETARY OF INTERIOR PURSUANT TO SECTION 205 OF THE OUTER CONTINENTAL SHELF LANDS ACT AMENDMENTS OF 1978, 30-31 (1980) [hereinafter 1980 DOJ REPORT]. The Department concluded that in the world oil market all crudes are generally substitutes for one another even though they produce different quantities of the various refined petroleum products. *Id.* at 31, n.37.

789. *Id.* at 21-29. The Department of Justice's market definition was based in part on the excess supply of such quality crudes in PAD District V, environmental restrictions, and a legal prohibition on the export of crude oil produced in Alaska. *See* 50 U.S.C. app. § 2403(1) (1988); 30 U.S.C. § 185(u) (1988).

790. 1980 DOJ REPORT, *supra* note 788, at 30-31.

791. Atlantic Richfield Company, British Petroleum, Exxon Corporation, and Shell Oil Company. *Id.* at 67.

792. 42 U.S.C. § 6213 (1988). The Department simply added Atlantic Richfield to the group of firms prohibited from submitting joint bids. It was clear from the Department's report, however, that if Exxon, BP, or Shell were no longer subject to § 105, the Department would nonetheless continue to recommend against the acceptance of any joint bid submitted among them. The Department of Interior regulations implementing § 105 are found at 30 C.F.R. §§ 256.38-46, 260.303 (1991).

793. 1980 DOJ REPORT, *supra* note 788, at 36-47.

794. 10 U.S.C. § 7430(g) (1988).

795. *Id.* § 7430(g)(1).

antitrust laws," the Secretary may not enter into the proposed contract.[796] The National Petroleum Reserve in Alaska, administered by the Secretary of Interior, is subject to the same statutory provisions.[797] In addition, any plans for the exploration, development, and production of the naval and national petroleum reserves must be submitted to Congress and must contain a report by the Attorney General with respect to the anticipated effect of the plans on competition.[798] The Secretary of Interior has published regulations covering competitive leasing of the National Petroleum Reserve in Alaska, extending the time for the Attorney General to review a proposed lease to thirty days,[799] and requiring prospective bidders to submit such information as required by the Attorney General to conduct an antitrust review.[800] Any information submitted must be treated as confidential by the Secretary and the Attorney General.[801]

Although the Department has not announced any policy with respect to leases or sales of production from the National and Naval Petroleum Reserves, the geographic and product market definitions and general policies set out with respect to its role in providing advice pursuant to Section 205 of the Outer Continental Shelf Lands Act Amendments of 1978[802] would appear to be applicable to such leasing and sales.[803]

(2) The Statutory Standard

The standard of antitrust review applicable to each of the three federal energy leasing or sale programs is identical: whether a particular lease or sale "may create or maintain a situation inconsistent with the antitrust laws."[804] The Department has stated that a recommendation against issuing a lease does not require a finding of a prosecutable antitrust violation. Rather, the Department views its role as advising whether there is a "reasonable probability that issuance of a lease will contravene the policies underlying the antitrust laws or will lead to an antitrust violation."[805]

Although the legislative histories of each of the Acts is bereft of any expressed purpose underlying the antitrust review standard, provisions incorporating nearly identical language have appeared in various federal statutes since 1944.[806] The legislative history, as well as judicial and administrative interpretations of the

---

796. *Id.* § 7430(g)(2).

797. 42 U.S.C. § 6506 (1988).

798. *Id.*; 10 U.S.C. § 7431(b)(2) (1988).

799. 43 C.F.R. § 3130.1(c) (1991).

800. *Id.* § 3130.1(b).

801. *Id.* § 3130.1(f).

802. 43 U.S.C. § 1337(c) (1988).

803. *See* Subsection D.3.e (1)(b) of this chapter.

804. 30 U.S.C. § 184(l)(2) (1988); 43 U.S.C. § 1337(c) (1988); 10 U.S.C. § 7430(g)(2) (1988).

805. U.S. DEP'T OF JUSTICE, COMPETITION IN THE COAL INDUSTRY 5-7 (1978); 1980 DOJ REPORT, *supra* note 788, at 8.

806. This standard first appeared in the Surplus Property Act of 1944, *as amended by* Section 207 of the Federal Property and Administrative Services Act of 1949, 40 U.S.C. § 488 (1988); *see also* 1970 Amendments to the Atomic Energy Act of 1954, § 105(c)(5), 42 U.S.C. § 2135(c)(5) (1988); Deep Seabed Hard Mineral Resources Act of 1980, §§ 103(d), 104, 30 U.S.C. § 1413(d) (1988); 1980 Amendments to the Patent and Trademark Laws, 35 U.S.C. § 209(c)(2) (1988); Ocean Thermal Energy Conversion Act of 1980, § 104, 42 U.S.C. § 9114 (1988).

antitrust review standard under one of those statutes, Section 105 of the Atomic Energy Act of 1954,[807] supports the Department's view. In amending Section 105, Congress stated:

> The concept of certainty of contravention of the antitrust laws or the policies clearly underlying these laws is not intended to be implicit in this standard; nor is mere possibility of inconsistency. It is intended that the finding be based on reasonable probability of contravention of the antitrust laws or the policies clearly underlying these laws.[808]

In *Alabama Power Co. v. NRC*,[809] the Eleventh Circuit held that this language was intended to reach "situations which would not, if left to fruition, in fact violate any antitrust law."[810] The court added that the reference to "the policies clearly underlying these laws," means that "a traditional antitrust enforcement scheme is not envisioned, and a wider one is put in place."[811]

The Department and the FTC view Section 7 of the Clayton Act[812] as the appropriate framework in which to analyze lease sales.[813] The Department analogizes the sale of a federal coal or oil lease to a holder of existing, uncommitted reserves to an acquisition of a potential de novo entrant, rather than a conventional horizontal merger.[814] It reasons that, unlike a horizontal merger, where previously independent productive assets are combined under one seller, a lease sale necessarily expands the potential productive assets in the market.[815] The Department has stated, however, that even where award of a lease would not alter the existing market structure, it would nonetheless regard such an award as sufficiently anticompetitive to justify rejection, if the proposed buyer is a leading firm in a concentrated market with high entry barriers and the award could, "eliminate significant possibilities for eventual deconcentration."[816] In applying this standard, however, the Department has considered the effect on concentration of the entire lease sale, not only of those

---

807.   42 U.S.C. § 2135 (1988). Under § 105(c)(5) of the Atomic Energy Act of 1954, the Department reviews each license for a nuclear electric generating facility to determine "whether the activities under the license would create or maintain a situation inconsistent with the antitrust laws." *Id.* § 2135(c)(5).

808.   Report by the Joint Comm. on Atomic Energy, H.R. REP. 1470, 91st Cong., 2d Sess. (1970), *reprinted in* 1970 U.S. CODE CONG. & ADMIN. NEWS 4981, 4994.

809.   692 F.2d 1362 (11th Cir. 1982), *cert. denied*, 464 U.S. 816 (1983).

810.   *Id.* at 1368.

811.   *Id.*; *see* Consumers Power Co., [1975-1978 Transfer Binder] NUCLEAR REG. REP. (CCH) ¶ 30,263 (1977); *see also* Louisiana Power & Light Co., 6 A.E.C. 48, 49 (1973). In practice, the Department has used the "wider" enforcement scheme envisioned by the statutes only to extend to lease sales by the federal government the incipiency standard of § 7 of the Clayton Act, 15 U.S.C. § 18 (1988), which otherwise would not apply to acquisitions of resources from the government. U.S. DEP'T OF JUSTICE, COMPETITION IN THE COAL INDUSTRY 7 (1978); *see also* 1980 DOJ Report, *supra* note 788, at 10.

812.   15 U.S.C. § 18 (1988).

813.   U.S. DEP'T OF JUSTICE, COMPETITION IN THE COAL INDUSTRY 7 (1978); 1980 DOJ Report, *supra* note 788, at 10.

814.   U.S. DEP'T OF JUSTICE, COMPETITION IN THE COAL INDUSTRY 8 (1978).

815.   *Id.*

816.   1980 DOJ REPORT, *supra* note 788, at 13-14. The Department nonetheless concluded that the award of a lease to a leading firm, where there was no other bidder, was preferable to withholding those tracts from the market or delaying their development by requiring that they be reoffered at a later sale. *Id.* at 68-69.

leases won by the leading firm.[817] It has also taken in account long lead times needed to develop leases and the uncertainty that oil would be found in sufficient quantities to be produced economically.[818] Finally, the Department has noted that a variety of factors, other than concentration, may enhance or diminish the likelihood of noncompetitive behavior in a relevant market. These factors include ease of entry, the cost or difficulty of monitoring competitors' actions, the presence of joint ventures, offsetting buyer concentration, the diversity and complexity of products and terms of sale, and the degree to which a firm's market share accurately reflects its competitive significance.[819]

4. *Financial Institutions and Markets*

a. FINANCIAL INSTITUTIONS

Sections 1 and 2 of the Sherman Act[820] and Section 7 of the Clayton Act[821] apply to banking activities. Congress has not granted financial institutions immunity

---

817. *Id.* at 69-71 (concluding that leases could be awarded to a leading firm where the award of other leases offered at the same sale would reduce overall concentration by 3 to 6%).

818. *Id.* at 12, 71.

819. U.S. DEP'T OF JUSTICE, COMPETITION IN THE COAL INDUSTRY 11-14 (1978). Although the Department's principal policy statements on federal leasing predate its MERGER GUIDELINES, the cited factors appear to mirror those set out at §§ 3.2 through 3.4 of the 1984 MERGER GUIDELINES. Moreover, while "efficiencies" are not addressed specifically, various aspects of the Department's analyses, such as its statement that it is preferable to lease a tract to a leading firm rather than to withhold it from development, indicate that it would likely consider efficiencies that could not be achieved, absent award of the lease. *See* 1984 MERGER GUIDELINES § 3.5, *reprinted in* Appendix B of this treatise and 4 TRADE REG. REP. (CCH) ¶ 13,103 (1984).

820. United States v. First Nat'l Bank & Trust Co., 376 U.S. 665, 669-70 (1964); Michaels Bldg. Co. v. Ameritrust Co., N.A., 848 F.2d 674 (6th Cir. 1988) (complaint provided adequate notice of claim of alleged conspiracy to fix interest rate); Sharon Steel Corp. v. Chase Manhattan Bank, 691 F.2d 1039 (2d Cir. 1982) (concerted activity by indenture trustee banks who were faced with a common breach of indenture agreements by liquidating debtor corporation, and their arrival at a common position, did not violate antitrust laws, since there was no anticompetitive purpose or effect), *cert. denied*, 460 U.S. 1012 (1983); Tose v. First Pa. Bank, N.A., 648 F.2d 879, 893 (3d Cir.) (affirming district court's rejection of conspiracy by banks to fix interest rates and engage in group boycott among banks), *cert. denied*, 454 U.S. 893 (1981); Weit v. Continental Ill. Nat'l Bank & Trust Co., 641 F.2d 457 (7th Cir. 1981) (affirming summary judgment for defendants on claim that banks conspired to fix credit card interest rates), *cert. denied*, 455 U.S. 988 (1982); Worthen Bank & Trust Co. v. National BankAmericard, Inc., 485 U.S. 119, 129-30 (8th Cir. 1973) (reversing lower court ruling that ban on dual membership in competing bank credit card systems constituted per se illegal "group boycott," and remanding for consideration under the rule of reason), *cert. denied*, 415 U.S. 918 (1974); United States v. Central State Bank, 621 F. Supp. 1276 (W.D. Mich. 1985) (individual's control of two competing banks did not create unreasonable restraint of trade), *aff'd*, 817 F.2d 22 (6th Cir. 1987); Wilcox Dev. Co. v. First Interstate Bank, NA, 605 F. Supp. 592 (D. Or. 1985) (claim for alleged conspiracy to fix prime rate), *aff'd in part and rev'd in part and remanded*, 815 F.2d 522 (9th Cir. 1987); United States v. Warren Five Cents Sav. Bank, 1980-81 Trade Cas. (CCH) ¶ 63,772 (D. Mass. 1981) (consent decree in suit based on Section 1 violation forbade use of restrictive lease between bank and shopping center); United States v. Northwestern Nat'l Bank, 1964 Trade Cas. (CCH) ¶ 71,022 (D. Minn. 1964) (consent decree prohibited banks from fixing interest rates and exchanging information relating to interest rates); United States v. Hunterdon County Trust Co., 1962 Trade Cas. (CCH) ¶ 70,623 (D.N.J. 1962) (consent decree prohibited banks from fixing uniform service charges and from exchanging information relating to such charges).

821. United States v. Philadelphia Nat'l Bank, 374 U.S. 321, 371-72 (1963).

from the antitrust laws. Congress has, however, enacted several statutes that apply special antitrust rules to financial institutions and that affect the fora in which such issues are decided. For example, the Bank Merger Acts of 1960[822] and 1966[823] incorporate the language and criteria of Section 7 of the Clayton Act but also set unique procedures for bank mergers and acquisitions. In addition, Section 106 of the 1970 Bank Holding Company Act Amendments[824] and Section 331 of the Garn-St Germain Depository Institutions Act of 1982[825] prohibit certain tying arrangements by financial institutions. Of course, many antitrust issues relating to financial institutions have arisen under Sections 1 and 2 of the Sherman Act and have not directly involved the banking regulatory agencies.

(1) Joint Activities Under Sections 1 and 2 of the Sherman Act

Antitrust issues raised by joint ventures among financial institutions, such as automated teller machine networks and bank credit card ventures, have involved fee setting arrangements and exclusivity requirements.[826]

Automated teller machines (ATMs) frequently offer customers access to one or more "networks" of ATMs. Thus, a customer can draw funds from an account at one bank through an ATM of another bank. In most instances, the customer's bank pays an "interchange fee" to the bank that operates the ATM used by the customer.[827] An arbitrator examining a fee setting arrangement under the rule of reason held that when (a) a single interchange fee for an ATM network is set by the joint venture and (b) the joint venture has market power, the network must provide its members the ability to impose surcharges or grant rebates.[828] One district court has held that a regional ATM network may forbid its members from joining other competing regional networks.[829] The Antitrust Division has declined to challenge the admission into an ATM network of an institution that was already a member of a

---

822. Act of May 13, 1960, Pub. L. No. 86-463, 74 Stat. 129 (codified as amended at 12 U.S.C. § 1828(c) (1988)).

823. Bank Merger Act of 1966, Pub. L. No. 89-356, 80 Stat. 7 (codified as amended as 12 U.S.C. § 1828(c) (1988)).

824. Pub. L. No. 91-607, 84 Stat. 1766 (codified as amended at 12 U.S.C. §§ 1971-1978 (1988)).

825. Pub. L. No. 97-320, 96 Stat. 1503 (codified at 12 U.S.C. § 1464(q) (1988)).

826. See Remarks of Charles F. Rule, then Acting Assistant Att'y Gen., Antitrust Div., Before the Federal Bar Ass'n and the Am. Bar Ass'n, Antitrust Analysis of Joint Ventures in the Banking Industry: Evaluating Shared ATMs (May 23, 1985).

827. For descriptions of ATM networks and interchange and processing fees, see Treasurer, Inc. v. Philadelphia Nat'l Bank, 682 F. Supp. 269 (D.N.J.), aff'd mem., 853 F.2d 921 (3d Cir. 1988); In re Arbitration Between First Tex. Sav. Ass'n and Fin. Interchange, Inc., 55 ANTITRUST & TRADE REG. REP. (BNA) 340, 341-42 (1988) (Kauper, Arb.).

828. In re Arbitration Between First Tex. Sav. Ass'n and Fin. Interchange, Inc., 55 ANTITRUST & TRADE REG. REP. (BNA) 340, 349-51, 370-72 (1988) (Kauper, Arb.). The arbitrator's finding of market power rested on findings that, at the time of his decision, no other national, regional or combination of local ATM networks offered coverage comparable to that of the respondent ATM network. Id. at 352-56.

829. Treasurer, Inc. v. Philadelphia Nat'l Bank, 682 F. Supp. 269, 279-80 (D.N.J.), aff'd mem., 853 F.2d 921 (3d Cir. 1988). The district court also held that one regional network lacked standing to challenge a transaction that was, in effect, a merger of two competing regional networks because it failed to make a showing of antitrust injury.

competing ATM network.[830]

Bank credit card joint ventures raise similar issues. Such ventures of large numbers of banks offering bank credit cards enable merchants to offer credit card purchases to much larger numbers of consumers than would otherwise be possible. In a bank credit card transaction, the merchant's bank forwards the card holder's receipt to the card holder's bank for collection. The merchant's bank pays an issuer reimbursement fee (IRF) to the card holder's bank.[831] One district court examined an IRF under the rule of reason because it found that prearranged interchange rules are an inescapable consequence of the integration necessary to achieving the efficiencies of a bank card joint venture.[832] The district court concluded that the IRF was "procompetitive" because a national bank credit card system could not exist without an IRF.[833] The Eighth Circuit has held that a bank card joint venture exclusivity requirement should be analyzed under the rule of reason, because of the novelty and complexity of the antitrust issues.[834] In a business review letter, the Antitrust Division refused to grant clearance to a bank card joint venture's proposed bylaw that would prohibit both card issuing and agency banks from participating in other credit card systems. The Division's decision was based on both insufficient information and a concern that potential entrants could be deterred.[835]

(2) Mergers and Acquisitions[836]

Bank mergers are governed by the same legal principles that apply to mergers in other industries. The procedures and fora, however, differ. The applicable statutes, the Bank Merger Acts of 1960 and 1966 and the Bank Holding Company Act, all incorporate the language and standards of Section 7 of the Clayton Act. After the Supreme Court in 1963 applied the Clayton Act to bank mergers in *United States v. Philadelphia National Bank*,[837] Congress amended the Bank Merger Act of

---

830. Letter from William F. Baxter, then Assistant Att'y Gen., Antitrust Div., to Donald I. Baker (Aug. 3, 1983).

831. For a description of bank credit card joint ventures, see National Bancard Corp. v. VISA USA, Inc., 596 F. Supp. 1231, 1236-38 (S.D. Fla. 1984), *aff'd*, 779 F.2d 592 (11th Cir.), *cert. denied*, 479 U.S. 923 (1986).

832. 596 F. Supp. at 1252-56. The Eleventh Circuit considered the IRF to be "a potentially efficiency creating agreement among members of a joint enterprise." 779 F.2d at 602.

833. 596 F. Supp. at 1259-60. The court's decision was explicitly influenced by its finding that VISA lacked market power in a market the court labeled as a "nationwide market for payment systems." *Id.* at 1258. As a result, the court concluded "VISA lacks the ability to impose any restraint detrimental to competition." *Id.*

834. Worthen Bank & Trust Co. v. National BankAmericard, Inc., 485 F.2d 119, 126 (8th Cir. 1973), *cert. denied*, 415 U.S. 918 (1974).

835. Letter from Thomas E. Kauper, then Assistant Att'y Gen., Antitrust Div., to Francis R. Kirkham and Allan N. Littman (Oct. 7, 1975). Much earlier, the Division obtained a consent decree against the Bank of Virginia ending the bank's practice of allowing merchants to accept its bank card only if the merchants refused to accept all other regional credit cards. United States v. Bank of Va., 1966 Trade Cas. (CCH) ¶ 71,947 (E.D. Va. 1966).

836. This subsection deals largely with the regulatory structure governing bank mergers and acquisitions. For a discussion of substantive issues that have arisen in bank merger cases, such as geographic and product market definition, see Chapter III of this treatise (treating such cases together with other merger cases).

837. 374 U.S. 321 (1963).

1960[838] to establish substantive standards and procedures for bank mergers and acquisitions.[839]   The Bank Merger Act of 1966 incorporated Sherman Act and Clayton Act standards, barring the responsible agency from allowing any transaction "whose effect in any section of the country may be substantially to lessen competition, or to tend to create a monopoly, or which in any other manner would be in restraint of trade."[840]   In addition, the responsible agency may not approve any transactions "which would result in a monopoly, or which would be in furtherance of any combination or conspiracy to monopolize or to attempt to monopolize the business of banking in any part of the United States."[841] "Agencies may approve transactions, even if they are anticompetitive, if they find that the anticompetitive effects of the proposed transaction are clearly outweighed in the public interest by the probable effect of the transaction in meeting the convenience and needs of the community to be served."[842]   Banks have the burden of proving the convenience and needs defense.[843]   That defense was also applied by a district court to a bank merger challenged by the United States under the Sherman Act.[844]

Under the Bank Merger Act of 1966, a court must automatically enter a preliminary injunction against any bank merger challenged by the attorney general within thirty days of banking agency approval.[845]   If such a merger is not challenged within thirty days of such approval, it is immune from attack under any antitrust laws other than Section 2 of the Sherman Act.[846]

Under the Bank Merger Act of 1966, commercial bank mergers are reviewed by three federal banking agencies.   The Comptroller of the Currency reviews transactions where the "acquiring, assuming or resulting bank" is a national bank; the Federal Deposit Insurance Corporation (FDIC) reviews transactions where the acquiring or resulting bank will be a federally insured state chartered bank that is not a member of the Federal Reserve System; and the Board of Governors of the Federal Reserve System reviews transactions where the acquiring or resulting bank will be a

---

838.   Bank Merger Act of 1966, Pub. L. No. 89-356, 80 Stat. 7 (codified as amended at 12 U.S.C. § 1828(c) (1988)). The Bank Merger Act of 1960, Pub. L. No. 86-463, 74 Stat. 129 (codified as amended at 12 U.S.C. § 1828(c) (1988)), had directed the Comptroller of the Currency, the Federal Reserve System and the Federal Deposit Insurance Corporation to take competitive effects into account when evaluating bank mergers and to consider reports on a proposed transaction from the other two bank regulatory agencies and the attorney general.

839.   1966 U.S. CODE CONG. & ADMIN. NEWS 8, 1860.

840.   12 U.S.C. § 1828(c)(5)(B) (1988).

841.   Id. § 1828(c)(5)(A).

842.   Id. For transactions in which the defense was considered by the Federal Reserve System, see First Nat'l Bankshares, 70 Fed. Res. Bull. 832 (1984) (defense satisfied); First Am. Bank Corp., 70 Fed. Res. Bull. 516 (1984) (same, in part). For judicial consideration of the defense, see United States v. Phillipsburg Nat'l Bank and Trust Co., 399 U.S. 350 (1970); United States v. Third Nat'l Bank, 390 U.S. 171 (1968); United States v. First Nat'l Bank, 310 F. Supp. 157 (D. Md. 1970); United States v. Provident Nat'l Bank, 280 F. Supp. 1 (E.D. Pa. 1968).

843.   United States v. First City Nat'l Bank, 386 U.S. 361 (1967).

844.   United States v. Central State Bank, 564 F. Supp. 1478 (W.D. Mich. 1983).

845.   12 U.S.C. § 1828(c)(7)(A) (1988). The automatic stay is to be given full effect unless the government's complaint is "frivolous." United States v. First City Nat'l Bank, 386 U.S. 361, 366 (1967). The automatic stay provision of 12 U.S.C. § 1828(c)(7)(A) does not apply to antitrust actions brought by private parties. Vial v. First Commerce Corp., 564 F.Supp 650, 666-67 (E.D. La. 1983).

846.   12 U.S.C. § 1828(c)(7)(C) (1988).

state-chartered bank that is a member of the Federal Reserve System.[847] Each regulatory agency is required to conduct its own examination of the transaction and to obtain a report from the Department of Justice before approving the transaction.[848] Transactions governed by the Bank Merger Act are exempt from the premerger notification requirements of the Hart-Scott-Rodino Act.[849]

While Congress has directed each agency to evaluate transactions under standards that apply in other antitrust cases, in practice each agency has developed its own approach to examining mergers. The agencies typically refer to the *Merger Guidelines* of the Antitrust Division of the Department of Justice. In evaluating bank mergers, the Antitrust Division applies the standards contained in the *Merger Guidelines*. During the mid-1980s, the Division departed from the usual Herfindahl-Hirschmann Index (HHI) standards and applied a modified test under which it was not likely to oppose a bank acquisition unless the transaction resulted in a postacquisition HHI over 1,800 and the increase is more than 200.[850] The bank regulatory agencies continue to use the Antitrust Division's modified test to analyze transactions.[851] The Federal Reserve Board and the Antitrust Division also have indicated that under certain circumstances, mergers may be challenged on the basis of the potential

---

847. *Id.* § 1828(c)(2).
848. *Id.* § 1828(c)(4).
849. 15 U.S.C. § 18a(c)(7) (1988).
850. Letter from Charles F. Rule, then Acting Assistant Att'y Gen., to C. Todd Conover, Comptroller of the Currency (Feb. 8, 1985) (advising the Comptroller that the Antitrust Division would not oppose the First National Bank of Jackson's acquisition of Brookhaven Bank and Trust Co.). The Department adopted the special standard in order to reflect the possible influence of nonbanking organizations in the relevant product market whose presence is not reflected in market shares calculated on the basis of deposits.

   In more recent cases, where the Department has been able to take the presence of nonbanking organizations into account, it has followed the ordinary standard of the GUIDELINES. Letter from James F. Rill, Assistant Att'y Gen., to Alan Greenspan, Federal Reserve Chairman (Oct. 5, 1990) (relating to the proposed acquisition of First Interstate of Hawaii, Inc. by First Hawaiian, Inc.); *see also* United States v. Society Corp. and Ameritrust Corp., 6 TRADE REG. REP. ¶ 50,737 (N.D. Ohio Mar. 13, 1992) (proposed consent decree); United States v. Fleet/Norstar Financial Group, Inc., Civ. No. 91-0021-P (D. Me. Dec. 3, 1991) (consent decree). Before it announced the modified test, the Antitrust Division challenged two transactions under the standards contained in the MERGER GUIDELINES. In United States v. Virginia National Bankshares, Inc., 1982-2 Trade Cas. (CCH) ¶ 64,871 (W.D. Va. 1982) (oral opinion), the district court rejected the government's alleged geographic market in favor of a service area approach, which eliminated the horizontal overlap between the acquiring and acquired banks. In United States v. National Bank & Trust Co., 1984-2 Trade Cas. (CCH) ¶ 66,074 (N.D.N.Y. 1984), the case was settled during trial and a consent decree entered. The acquisition was consummated after the acquiring bank agreed to divest two of its branches and to take whatever steps were necessary to eliminate "home office protection," a legal barrier that limited entry in the geographic market affected by the acquisition.
851. *See, e.g.*, Fleet/Norstar Financial Group, Inc., 77 Fed. Res. Bull. 750 (1991); First Hawaiian, Inc., 77 Fed. Res. Bull. 52 (1990); Louisiana Bancshares, Inc., 72 Fed. Res. Bull. 154, 155 & n.5 (1985) (approving merger of bank holding companies with respect to market in which postacquisition HHI was 1,703, reflecting increase of 548); First Wis. Corp., 72 Fed. Res. Bull. 50, 51 & n.4 (1985) (approving acquisition with respect to market in which postacquisition HHI was 1,987, reflecting increase of 93); *see also* OCC Quick Check Merger Screen, *printed in* Comptroller's Manual for Corporate Activities (available from Communications Division, Office of the Comptroller of the Currency, Washington, D.C.).

competition.[852]

The FDIC proposed a Statement of Policy on bank mergers in 1988.[853] That policy statement explicitly adopted HHI standards, similar to those the Antitrust Division had already stated it would apply to bank merger transactions. The FDIC proposed that it would not normally challenge transactions where the resulting HHI is under 1,800 or where, if the resulting HHI exceeds 1,800, the change is less than 200. Even where the HHI exceeded those standards, the FDIC proposed considering the numbers, size, financial strength, quality of management and aggressiveness of the various participants in the market, the attractiveness of the market in terms of population, wealth, income levels and economic growth, legal impediments to entry or expansion, and the likelihood of new participants entering the market and creating a significant presence either by establishing an office de novo or generating a substantial volume of business from outside the market through agencies, electronic means, or the mail.[854] The proposed Statement of Policy also set out the FDIC standards for defining geographic and product markets.[855] The Antitrust Division filed comments urging changes in the proposed Statement because, the Division argued, the proposed "Statement is ambiguous with regard to the principles by which relevant product and geographic markets will be defined, and with respect to the relevance and weight that will be accorded to certain factors other than market definition."[856] The Statement has not been officially adopted by the FDIC.

---

852. The Antitrust Division uses the tests contained in the MERGER GUIDELINES and examines entry conditions in the market (particularly branching restrictions), the number and size of potential entrants, and the acquiring firm's entry advantages. In February 1982, the Federal Reserve Board proposed guidelines for analyzing bank transactions under the potential competition doctrine. Proposed Policy Statement of the Board of Governors of the Federal Reserve System for Assessing Competitive Factors Under the Bank Merger Act and the Bank Holding Company Act, 47 FED. REG. 9017 (1982). Although the Policy Statement guidelines have never been formally adopted, the Board purports to use them in assessing the effect of a proposed transaction on future competition. See, e.g., Union Planters Corp., 73 Fed. Res. Bull. 469, 470 & n.5 (1987); United Banks of Colo., Inc., 73 Fed. Res. Bull. 383, 386 & n.12 (1987); Key Bancshares, Inc., 71 Fed. Res. Bull. 965 (1985); Marine Corp., 71 Fed. Res. Bull. 795, 796 n.11 (1985); First Midwest Bancorp, 71 Fed. Res. Bull. 41 n.3 (1984); Mercantile Tex. Corp., 70 Fed. Res. Bull. 595, 597 (1984); Norstar Bancorp, 70 Fed. Res. Bull. 164, 167 (1984); Banc One Corp., 69 Fed. Res. Bull. 379, 381 n.8 (1983). The Department of Justice advised against adoption of the Policy Statement guidelines. Comments of the U.S. Dep't of Justice, In Re Statement of Policy on Bank Acquisitions (Apr. 9, 1982). Since 1980, the Antitrust Division has not challenged any bank mergers on potential competition grounds. Hauberg, Mergers and Acquisitions, Trends in Competitive Analysis, 6 Bank Expansion Rep. No. 13, at 1, 13 (July 6, 1987).

853. 53 FED. REG. 39,803 (1988). The proposed Statement of Policy was a revision of the FDIC's earlier proposed policy statement (50 FED. REG. 40,599 (1985)), designed to reflect more accurately current FDIC policy.

854. 53 FED. REG. at 39,805.

855. Id. at 39,804.

856. Comments of the U.S. Dep't of Justice Before the FDIC, In the Matter of: Statement of Policy, Bank Merger Transactions 3 (Dec. 12, 1988). The Division objected that the FDIC did not make clear if it "will limit its analysis to a single, aggregated service market . . . or if it will analyze competition in individual financial services, treating them as separate service markets where appropriate." Id. at 6. The Division raised a similar objection relating to geographic markets. Id. The Division also recommended that the FDIC state that "the likelihood of entry into a market will be accorded substantial weight" and that the attractiveness of entry be considered a factor in evaluating the likelihood of entry. Id. at 16. The Division also recommended that the FDIC make clear that parties must establish the efficiencies of a transactions, id. at 17, and that

The Comptroller of the Currency has generally applied a more permissive standard than the Federal Reserve Board and the FDIC.[857] In response, in 1973, the Ninth Circuit found that because the main objective of the Bank Merger Act of 1966 was to curtail the unrestrained discretion of the banking agencies in regulatory bank merger transactions, the agencies did not have the authority to impose more rigid competitive standards than those of the antitrust laws.[858] Following the Ninth Circuit's approach, the Fifth Circuit prohibited the regulatory agencies from disapproving transactions on the basis of standards that diverge from the test incorporated in the banking statutes.[859]

Under the Bank Holding Company Act,[860] the Federal Reserve Board must apply the same standards to mergers and acquisitions involving bank holding companies as those set in the Bank Merger Act of 1966.[861] The Bank Holding Company Act does not require the Federal Reserve Board to obtain a report from the Department of Justice before approving a transaction. Nonetheless, such transactions are exempt from the premerger notification procedures of the Hart-Scott-Rodino Act.[862]

The Bank Holding Company Act also requires bank holding companies to obtain Federal Reserve Board approval for any acquisition of a nonbank.[863] To evaluate these transactions, the Federal Reserve Board determines whether the activity in which the bank holding company would be engaged as a result of the acquisition "is a proper incident to banking or managing or controlling banks."[864] To make that determination, it considers whether the "benefits to the public, such as greater convenience, increased competition, or gains in efficiency, outweigh possible adverse effects, such as undue concentration of resources, decreased or unfair competition, conflicts of interest, or unsound bank practices."[865] Copies of bank holding company applications to purchase nonbanks must be filed with the Department of Justice and the Federal Trade Commission at least thirty days before consummation

---

the FDIC offer "a clearer conceptual description" of how it would weigh the costs and benefits of a transaction. *Id.* at 20.

857. *See, e.g.*, United States v. First City Nat'l Bank, 386 U.S. 361, 364-65 (1967) (bank merger application approved by the Comptroller of the Currency despite disapproval by the Federal Reserve Board); GAO, BANK MERGER PROCESS SHOULD BE SIMPLIFIED (GAO) (1982).

858. Washington Mut. Sav. Bank v. FDIC, 482 F.2d 459, 465 (9th Cir. 1973).

859. *See* Republic of Tex. Corp. v. Board of Governors, 649 F.2d 1026, 1043 (5th Cir. 1981); Mercantile Tex. Corp. v. Board of Governors, 638 F.2d 1255, 1263 (5th Cir. 1981).

860. 12 U.S.C. §§ 1841-1850 (1988). The Bank Holding Company Act was amended in 1966 to conform with the Bank Merger Act of 1966. Act of July 1, 1966, Pub. L. No. 89-485, §§ 1-11, 80 Stat. 236-40 (codified as amended at 12 U.S.C. §§ 1841-1859 (1988)). The Bank Holding Company Act applies to all companies that own 25% or more of the stock of a bank, control the election of a majority of a bank's directors, or that the Federal Reserve Board finds exercise a "controlling influence" over a bank. *Id.* § 1841(a).

861. 12 U.S.C. § 1842(c) (1988); *see, e.g.*, County Nat'l Bancorp. v. Board of Governors, 654 F.2d 1253, 1260 (8th Cir. 1981) (Board may not "deny a merger on competitive grounds absent a finding of an antitrust violation"); Mercantile Tex. Corp. v. Board of Governors, 638 F.2d 1255, 1260-63 (5th Cir. 1981) (Board may not employ "convenience and needs" consideration to create a more stringent standard than the Clayton Act).

862. 15 U.S.C. § 18a(c)(7) (1988).

863. 12 U.S.C. § 1843(a) (1988).

864. *Id.* § 1843(c)(8).

865. *Id.*

of the transaction for it to be exempt from regular Hart-Scott-Rodino reporting requirements.[866]

In general, the banking agencies are amenable to partial divestiture solutions in order to permit bank merger transactions that otherwise pose a substantial likelihood to reduce competition.[867]

The Office of Thrift Supervision regulates the formation of and acquisitions by savings and loan holding companies.[868] A savings and loan holding company is any company that directly or indirectly controls a federally insured savings and loan association.[869] The Director of the Office of Thrift Supervision is required to request and to consider a report from the Attorney General "on the competitive factors involved."[870] Finally, the Director of the Office of Thrift Supervision may not approve an acquisition that would violate codified standards similar to those of Section 7 of the Clayton Act unless he finds the anticompetitive effects of the transaction to be in the public interest by "meeting the convenience and needs of the community."[871] No Hart-Scott-Rodino filing is required for these transactions.[872]

The FIRREA authorizes the FDIC to create "bridge banks," institutions that hold assets of one or more banks that are "in default or in danger of default."[873] Bridge bank charters are granted by the Office of the Comptroller of the Currency and expire after two years.[874] The standards and procedures of the Bank Merger Act, including notification of the Department of Justice, apply to mergers and acquisitions involving bridge banks.[875] The responsible agency may allow the transaction to be consummated immediately to prevent failure.[876]

Congress has not addressed the issue of mergers of federally chartered credit unions or of federally chartered credit unions with state chartered credit unions. Pursuant to the general regulatory authority granted to the National Credit Union Administration Board,[877] however, the Board has promulgated regulations

---

866.   15 U.S.C. § 18a(c)(8) (1988).
867.   *See, e.g.*, Wells Fargo & Co., 72 Fed. Res. Bull. 424 n.14 (1986); Brownsville Bancshares Corp., 72 Fed. Res. Bull. 43, 44 (1986); United States v. National Bank & Trust Co., 1984-2 Trade Cas. (CCH) ¶ 66,074, at 65,960-61 (N.D.N.Y. 1984) (injunction lifted on condition that acquiring bank divest two offices); Decision of the Comptroller of the Currency on the Application to Merge Trustmark Nat'l Bank (Aug. 6, 1987) (two offices would be divested simultaneously with merger); Bank of New England Corp., 73 Fed. Res. Bull. 373 (1987).
868.   12 U.S.C. § 1467a(e) (1988). That authority previously resided with the Federal Home Loan Bank Board. The Federal Institutions Reform Recovery Enforcement Act of 1989 (FIRREA) abolished the Federal Home Loan Bank Board and transferred the authority to regulate the formation and acquisition of savings and loan holding companies to the newly-created Director of the Office of Thrift Supervision. Pub. L. No. 101-73, tit. IV, § 401, 103 Stat. 183, 354 (1989).
869.   12 U.S.C. § 1467a(a)(1)(D) (1988).
870.   *Id.* § 1467a(e)(2).
871.   *Id.*
872.   15 U.S.C. § 18a(c)(7) (1988).
873.   Pub. L. No. 101-73, tit. II, § 214, 103 Stat. 183, 246 (1989) (codified at 12 U.S.C. § 1821(n) (1991 Supp.)).
874.   *Id.* § 1821(n)(2).
875.   *Id.* § 1821(n)(8)(A). The Justice Department has challenged an acquisition of a bridge bank. United States v. Fleet/Norstar Fin. Group, Civ. Doc. No. 91-0021-P (D. Me. filed July 5, 1991).
876.   *Id.*
877.   12 U.S.C. § 1766 (1988).

establishing procedures and standards governing consideration of these mergers.[878] Under the regulations, a federal credit union must submit a plan describing a proposed merger to the Administrator. The credit union is not required to include in the merger plan any information regarding the impact on competition of the proposed merger. The plan is limited to information concerning the financial condition of the credit unions.[879] The regulations do not suggest that the Administrator will consider any competitive issues.

In 1984, the Bush Task Group, empaneled by the Reagan Administration and chaired by then Vice President Bush, recommended repeal of the Bank Merger Act and those provisions of the other regulatory statutes that give the bank regulatory agencies authority to consider the competitive aspects of mergers involving banking institutions. The Task Group recommended that the Antitrust Division have exclusive authority in this area except for emergency mergers of failing institutions, which would continue to be within the jurisdiction of the banking agencies, and that it apply the same standards applied to all other mergers and acquisitions.[880] More recently, the President's Commission on Privatization stated that federal agencies created to encourage home ownership through lending and loan insurance programs "may now compete unfairly with the private sector."[881] The Commission recommended that the federal government reduce its lending and loan guarantee activities to those necessary to assist only those citizens who could not achieve home ownership without the assistance of the federal government.[882]

(3) Tie-Ins

In 1970, Congress amended the Bank Holding Company Act to prohibit banks from providing any service on the condition that the customer obtain from or provide to the bank any additional credit, property or service other than one of the four "traditional" banking services — loans, discounts, deposits or trust services.[883] The intent of Congress was to regulate the manner in which banks operate in nonbanking markets.[884] The prohibitions also apply to transactions with bank holding companies of the involved banks and their subsidiaries.[885] In addition, these provisions prohibit a bank from entering into certain exclusive dealing agreements with its customers, that is, conditioning transactions on the customer's agreement not to obtain some other credit, property, or service from the bank's competitor (including a bank holding company or a nonbank affiliate), unless the requirement is one that the bank can "reasonably impose in a credit transaction to assure the soundness of the credit."[886]

---

878.   12 C.F.R. §§ 708.101-.108 (1991).

879.   Id. § 708.104.

880.   BLUEPRINT FOR REFORM: REPORT OF THE TASK GROUP ON REGULATION OF FINANCIAL SERVICES 91 (July 2, 1984).

881.   REPORT OF THE PRESIDENT'S COMMISSION ON PRIVATIZATION, PRIVATIZATION, TOWARD MORE EFFECTIVE GOVERNMENT 27 (Mar. 1988).

882.   Id. at 27-63.

883.   12 U.S.C. §§ 1971-1978 (1988).

884.   See CONF. REP. NO. 1727, 91st Cong., 2d Sess., reprinted in 1970 U.S. CODE CONG. & ADMIN. NEWS 5561, 5579-80.

885.   12 U.S.C. § 1972(1) (1988).

886.   Id. § 1972(1)(D)(E).

The statute has been held to be largely coextensive with the antitying prohibitions of the antitrust laws[887] except that no showing of market power or anticompetitive effect is required,[888] and, according to the Fifth Circuit, no showing of coercion is required.[889] Courts have held that Congress did not intend to interfere with traditional banking practices,[890] attempting to protect investments through means that are not anticompetitive,[891] or conditions normally related to a loan.[892] Some courts have stated, therefore, that for a condition to be barred by the Bank Holding Company Act, it must be of an anticompetitive nature.[893] One district court has stated to the contrary.[894]

The antitying prohibitions of the Bank Holding Company Act are enforced by the Attorney General, who is authorized "to institute proceedings in equity to prevent and restrain" violations of the provision.[895] In addition, private plaintiffs may sue for treble damages, costs, and attorneys' fees, or for injunctive relief.[896] A somewhat broader class of persons than mere customers may have standing to sue as private plaintiffs under the antitying prohibitions of the Act.[897] Actions under the Act may be brought against domestic banks,[898] but not against natural persons or foreign banks.[899]

In 1982, Congress applied similar prohibitions against tying to savings and loan institutions.[900] The ban employs language similar to that of the Bank Holding Company Act.[901] Also, like the Bank Holding Company Act, the 1982

---

887.   The Seventh Circuit has held that the statute is equivalent to § 3 of the Clayton Act. Exchange Nat'l Bank v. Daniels, 768 F.2d 140 (7th Cir. 1985).

888.   Dibidale, Inc. v. American Bank & Trust Co., 916 F.2d 300, 305-06 (5th Cir. 1990); Parsons Steel, Inc. v. First Ala. Bank, 679 F.2d 242, 245 (11th Cir. 1982); Costner v. Blount Nat'l Bank, 578 F.2d 1192, 1196 (6th Cir. 1978).

889.   Dibidale, 916 F.2d at 306-07.

890.   B.C. Recreational Indus. v. First Nat'l Bank, 639 F.2d 828 (1st Cir. 1981).

891.   Parsons Steel, Inc. v. First Ala. Bank, 679 F.2d 242 (11th Cir. 1982).

892.   McCoy v. Franklin Sav. Ass'n, 636 F.2d 172 (7th Cir. 1980).

893.   Parsons Steel, 679 F.2d at 246; Tose v. First Pa. Bank, 648 F.2d 879, 897-98 (3d Cir.), cert. denied, 454 U.S. 893 (1981).

894.   Sharkey v. Security Bank & Trust Co., 651 F. Supp. 1231 (D. Minn. 1987).

895.   12 U.S.C. § 1973 (1988).

896.   Id. §§ 1975-1976.

897.   See Campbell v. Wells Fargo Bank, N.A., 781 F.2d 440 (5th Cir.), cert. denied, 476 U.S. 1159 (1986); Swerdloff v. Miami Nat'l Bank, 584 F.2d 54 (5th Cir. 1978). But see Shulman v. Continental Bank, 513 F. Supp. 979, 984 (E.D. Pa. 1981) (holders of junior participation in loan lacked standing to sue based on bank's conditioning of loan to corporation on holders' purchase of participation); Omega Homes, Inc. v. Citicorp Acceptance Co., 656 F. Supp. 393, 402-03 (W.D. Va. 1987) (mobile home seller that claimed it lost commissions on sale of insurance to buyers when financing companies required purchase of insurance through them lacked standing to challenge alleged tying arrangement under the Act).

898.   12 U.S.C. §§ 1971, 1841(c) (1988).

899.   Nordic Bank, P.L.C. v. Trend Group, 619 F. Supp. 542 (S.D.N.Y. 1985).

900.   Pub. L. No. 97-320, § 331, 96 Stat. 1469, 1503 (codified at 12 U.S.C. § 1464(q) (1988)).

901.   Id. § 1464(q)(1); see Bruce v. First Fed. Sav. & Loan Ass'n of Conroe, Inc., 837 F.2d 712 (5th Cir. 1988) (borrower stated claim under 12 U.S.C. § 1464(q) by alleging that savings and loan association conditioned extension or refinancing of loan on transfer of principal payment made on one loan to interest payment on loan to be extended and on participation in the loan by other lenders); see also Sundance Land Corp. v. Community First Fed. Sav. & Loan Ass'n, 1988-Trade Cas. (CCH) ¶ 67,924 (9th Cir. 1988) (mortgage conditioned on borrower erecting two motels and conveying them to lender).

amendments create a private cause of action for injunctive relief[902] and treble damages,[903] and authorize the Director of the Office of Thrift Supervision to promulgate regulations.[904] The ban on tying also applies to savings and loan holding companies.[905]

(4) Interlocking Directorates

Section 8 of the Clayton Act[906] prohibits, with certain exceptions, any director, officer, or employee of any member bank of the Federal Reserve System from holding a similar position in any other bank.[907] The Depository Institution Management Interlocks Act[908] limits interlocks between depository institutions. It provides that a management official of a depository institution or holding company may not serve in a similar capacity at another nonaffiliated depository institution in either the same primary metropolitan statistical area or the same city, town or village.[909] The Garn-St Germain Depository Institution Act of 1982 gives the Attorney General and the Assistant Attorney General in charge of the Antitrust Division specific enforcement authority for depository institution management interlocks.[910] Furthermore, the Investment Company Act of 1940[911] provides that a registered investment company may not have an investment banker as a director, officer, or employee unless a majority of the company's directors are not investment bankers.[912]

b. THE SECURITIES INDUSTRY

The securities industry, defined broadly, includes all firms engaged in the issuance, distribution, and sale of securities, including firms concerned with brokerage, investment research and advice, trading, market-making, underwriting, and investment banking.

The Securities Exchange Act of 1934 established a system of federal regulation to provide

> fair and honest mechanisms for the pricing of securities, to assure that dealing in securities is fair and without undue preferences or advantages among investors, to ensure that securities can be purchased and sold at economically efficient transaction costs, and to

---

902. 12 U.S.C. § 1464(q)(2)(A) (1988).
903. *Id.* § 1464(q)(3).
904. *Id.* § 1464(q)(4). No regulation issued under § 1464(q) shall constitute a defense to an action brought under the section. *Id.*
905. *Id.* § 1467a(n).
906. 15 U.S.C. § 19 (1988), *amended by* Antitrust Amendments Act of 1990, Pub. L. No. 101-588, 104 Stat. 2879 (1990). For a more extensive discussion of § 8, see Part J of Chapter III of this treatise.
907. In 1983, the Supreme Court ruled that § 8 does not forbid interlocking directorates between banks and insurance companies or other nonbanking companies. BankAmerica Corp. v. United States, 462 U.S. 122 (1983).
908. Pub. L. No. 95-630, §§ 202-207, 209, 92 Stat. 3641, 3672-3675 (codified at 12 U.S.C. §§ 3201-3207 (1988)).
909. 12 U.S.C. § 3202 (1988).
910. Pub. L. No. 97-320, § 426, 96 Stat. 1469, 1524 (codified at 12 U.S.C. § 3208 (1988)).
911. 15 U.S.C. §§ 80a to 80b-21 (1988).
912. *Id.* § 80a-10(b)(3).

provide, to the maximum degree practicable, markets that are open and orderly.[913]

The 1934 Act provides for self-regulation by the national securities exchanges, with oversight by the Securities and Exchange Commission (SEC).[914] In 1938, Congress provided for regulation of the "over-the-counter" market for securities trading by allowing eligible associations of brokers or dealers to register with the SEC as "national securities associations."[915] Subsequently, the SEC was given similar direct regulatory authority over the activities of investment companies[916] and investment advisers.[917]

The 1934 Act, as substantially amended in 1975,[918] now addresses three issues relating to competition: the propriety of fixed brokerage commissions, the development of a competitive national market for trading securities, and the consideration to be given competitive factors under the standards guiding SEC decisions. The 1975 amendment eliminated fixed minimum commission rates effective May 1, 1976,[919] adopted a statutory policy of competitive commissions, and gave the SEC the authority to reimpose fixed rates only after considering the effects such action would have on competition.[920]

Section 11A of the 1934 Act directed the SEC to "facilitate the establishment of a national market system for securities."[921] The goals of this national market are to promote the efficient execution of securities transactions and assure fair competition among a variety of market participants.[922] A national market would link "all markets for qualified securities through communications and data processing facilities," and would increase the availability of quotation and transaction information.[923] Because Congress intended this national market system to evolve in reaction to competitive forces, free of unnecessary regulatory restrictions,[924] it did not impose on the SEC a specific deadline or method for achieving the end result. Although the SEC has taken steps to encourage the evolution of a national market, Congress has expressed disappointment with the pace of SEC action.[925]

---

913.   H.R. REP. No. 229, 94th Cong., 1st Sess. 91-92, *reprinted in* 1975 U.S. CODE CONG. & ADMIN. NEWS 322-23.

914.   *See* Silver v. New York Stock Exch., 373 U.S. 341, 352 (1963).

915.   15 U.S.C. § 78o-3 (1988). This section was held constitutional in Sorrell v. SEC, 679 F.2d 1323 (9th Cir. 1982).

916.   Investment Company Act of 1940, 15 U.S.C. §§ 80a-1 to 80a-52 (1988).

917.   *Id.* §§ 80b-1 to 80b-21.

918.   Securities Acts Amendments of 1975, Pub. L. No. 94-29, 89 Stat. 97 (1975) (codified in scattered sections of 15 U.S.C.).

919.   15 U.S.C. § 78f(e) (1988).

920.   *Id.* The SEC may approve fixed commission rates only if the rates are reasonable in relation to costs and the fixed rates do not impose an unnecessary burden on competition. *Id.*

921.   *Id.* § 78k-1(a)(2).

922.   Securities Exchange Act of 1934, § 11A(a)(1), 15 U.S.C. § 78k-1(a)(1) (1988).

923.   *Id.*

924.   H.R. CONF. REP. No. 229, 94th Cong., 1st Sess. 92, *reprinted in* 1975 U.S. CODE CONG. & ADMIN. NEWS 323.

925.   SUBCOMM. ON OVERSIGHT AND INVESTIGATIONS OF THE HOUSE COMMITTEE ON INTERSTATE AND FOREIGN COMMERCE, 96TH CONG., 2D SESS., NATIONAL MARKET SYSTEM: FIVE YEAR STATUS REPORT (Comm. Print 1980); SUBCOMM. ON OVERSIGHT AND INVESTIGATIONS AND SUBCOMM. ON CONSUMER PROTECTION AND FINANCE OF THE HOUSE COMMITTEE, 95TH CONG., 1ST SESS., OVERSIGHT OF THE FUNCTIONING AND ADMINISTRATION OF THE SECURITIES ACTS AMENDMENTS OF 1975, 3 (Comm. Print 1977).

The Act specifically directs the SEC to consider the competitive impact of its rules and regulations. The Act prohibits adoption of any "rule or regulation which would impose a burden on competition not necessary or appropriate in furtherance of the purposes of this chapter."[926]

The Supreme Court first considered the applicability of the antitrust laws to SEC regulated activities in *Silver v. New York Stock Exchange*.[927] The New York Stock Exchange, pursuant to its rules, had ordered its members to remove private direct wire connections with the offices of nonmembers. The Exchange had not provided nonmembers with notice, the reason for the disconnection, or an opportunity for a hearing prior to disconnection. The plaintiff, a nonmember that had been disconnected as a result of the Exchange order, alleged that the action constituted a violation of Section 1 of the Sherman Act.

The Supreme Court began its analysis by stating that the challenged conduct "would, had it occurred in a context free from other federal regulation, constitute a *per se* violation of § 1 of the Sherman Act. The concerted action of the Exchange and its members here was, in simple terms, a group boycott. . . ."[928] The Court observed that the Securities Exchange Act of 1934 did not expressly contain an exemption from the antitrust laws and wrote that "[r]epeal is to be regarded as implied only if necessary to make the Securities Exchange Act work, and even then only to the minimum extent necessary."[929]

As to whether the 1934 Securities Exchange Act implied that exchange regulations are exempt from the antitrust laws, the Court stated:

> Although, as we have seen the statutory scheme of that Act is not sufficiently pervasive to create a total exemption from the antitrust laws, it is also true that particular instances of exchange self-regulation which fall within the scope and purposes of the Securities Exchange Act may be regarded as justified in answer to the assertion of an antitrust claim.[930]

The Court accordingly framed the issue as "whether the act of self-regulation in this case was so justified," and held that it was not.[931] The Court found that Section 19(b) of the Securities Exchange Act of 1934 contemplated self-regulation, subject to the SEC's power to alter or supplement exchange rules, but it did not provide for SEC review of particular applications of Exchange rules. Because the SEC had no jurisdiction over specific exercises of Exchange power, no conflict existed between the SEC's regulatory responsibility and the power of a court to judge the

---

926.   15 U.S.C. § 78w(a)(2) (1988). The SEC is also directed to assure that no self-regulatory organization's actions or rules "impose any burden on competition not necessary or appropriate in furtherance of the purposes of this chapter." *Id.* § 78f(b)(8). A similar mandate applies to the allowance of fixed commission rates in limited circumstances (*id.* § 78f(e)); approval of the rules of registered securities associations (*id.* § 78o-3(b)(9)); and approval of the rules of a clearing agency (*id.* § 78q-1(b)(3)(I)). In Clement v. SEC, 674 F.2d 641 (7th Cir. 1982), § 78f(b)(8) was cited as requiring reconsideration by the SEC of an exchange's proposed rule changes because of threatened adverse impact on competition among market makers.

927.   373 U.S. 341 (1963).

928.   *Id.* at 347 (emphasis in original).

929.   *Id.* at 357; *see also* Thill Sec. Corp. v. New York Stock Exch., 433 F.2d 264, 273 (7th Cir. 1970) (remanding for determination of necessity of Exchange's antirebate rule to operation of Securities Exchange Act), *cert. denied*, 401 U.S. 944 (1971).

930.   373 U.S. at 360-61 (citation omitted).

931.   *Id.* at 361.

antitrust legality of the Exchange's enforcement of its own rules. The Exchange's failure to accord nonmembers a fair hearing was therefore actionable under Section 1 of the Sherman Act.[932]

Two 1975 Supreme Court decisions clarified the extent to which antitrust immunity may be implied with respect to SEC regulated activities. In *Gordon v. New York Stock Exchange*,[933] a small investor alleged that the commission rate schedule upon which all brokers had agreed pursuant to the rules of the New York Stock Exchange constituted a price-fixing agreement in violation of the Sherman Act. In addressing the issue whether the agreement was immune from antitrust attack because of the SEC's authority to supervise the exchange, the Court stated:

> [W]e are concerned with whether antitrust immunity, as a matter of law, must be implied in order to permit the Exchange Act to function as envisioned by the Congress. The issue of the wisdom of fixed rates becomes relevant only when it is determined that there is no antitrust immunity.[934]

The Court found that, under Section 19(b)(9) of the Securities Exchange Act of 1934, the SEC was empowered to alter or supplement Exchange rules relating to the fixing of reasonable rates of commission. It further found that the SEC had been active in regulating commissions and that Congressional action, beginning in 1934 and continuing through the 1975 amendments, evidenced Congress' approval of the SEC's oversight of the Commission rate structure. On this basis, the Court held that antitrust immunity was "necessary to make the Exchange Act work as it was intended."[935]

The Supreme Court also considered the scope of antitrust immunity in the securities industry in *United States v. National Association of Securities Dealers*.[936] There the Department of Justice challenged vertical price restrictions in the

---

932. The Court did not believe that application of the antitrust laws to exchange actions would defeat the purposes of the Act since "under the aegis of the rule of reason, traditional antitrust concepts are flexible enough to permit the Exchange sufficient breathing space within which to carry out the mandate of the Securities Exchange Act." *Id.* at 360 (citations omitted). However, the Court said, "[s]hould review of exchange self-regulation be provided through a vehicle other than the antitrust laws, a different case as to antitrust exemption would be presented." *Id.* (citation omitted). Lower court opinions finding antitrust immunity following *Silver* include, e.g., Kaplan v. Lehman Bros., 371 F.2d 409, 411 (7th Cir.) (practice of fixed commission rates not subject to private antitrust attack), *cert. denied*, 389 U.S. 954 (1967); Shumate & Co. v. New York Stock Exch., 486 F. Supp. 1333 (N.D. Tex. 1980) (SEC jurisdiction to review NYSE's off-board trading restrictions implies antitrust immunity); Abbott Sec. Corp. v. New York Stock Exch., 384 F. Supp. 668, 670 (D.D.C. 1974) (SEC jurisdiction to review NYSE's competitive restraints on floor access implies antitrust immunity).

933. 422 U.S. 659 (1975).

934. *Id.* at 688.

935. *Id.* at 691; *see also* Austin Mun. Sec., Inc. v. National Ass'n of Sec. Dealers, 757 F.2d 676, 694-96 (5th Cir. 1985) (NASD's self-regulation, needed to make policy of statute work, immune from antitrust attack); Thill Sec. Corp. v. New York Stock Exch., 473 F. Supp. 1364, 1368 (E.D. Wis. 1979) (dismissing challenge to Exchange's antirebate rule in light of *Gordon*), *aff'd*, 633 F.2d 65 (7th Cir. 1980), *cert. denied*, 450 U.S. 998 (1981).

936. 422 U.S. 694, 697 (1975) (NASD).

"secondary market" for mutual fund shares.[937] Section 22(f) of the Investment Company Act of 1940[938] empowered the SEC to promulgate rules and regulations concerning restrictions on transferability and negotiability of mutual fund shares. Contending that the SEC had never actively regulated pursuant to Section 22(f), the government argued that there had been an insufficient regulatory presence to create the inconsistency between Section 22(f) and the antitrust laws that would be required for a finding of implied immunity. The Court, however, concluded that (1) the challenged restrictions were among those Congress contemplated when it enacted Section 22(f); (2) Congress had anticipated that mutual funds would retain the power to impose restrictions on transferability and negotiability; and (3) the SEC's tacit acceptance of those restrictions for three decades constituted an administrative judgment that antitrust courts might frustrate if immunity were not implied.[939] Accordingly, the Court concluded that "[t]here can be no reconciliation of [the SEC's] authority under § 22(f) to permit these and similar restrictive agreements with the Sherman Act's declaration that they are illegal *per se*. In this instance the antitrust laws must give way if the regulatory scheme established by the Investment Company Act is to work."[940]

In *NASD*, the United States also had alleged a conspiracy between the association and its members to prevent the growth of the secondary dealer market. The government based its challenge on unofficial NASD interpretations and extensions of its rules that inhibited active trading in that secondary market. The Court found that the SEC's pervasive regulatory authority over the NASD under the Maloney Act[941] and the Investment Company Act of 1940[942] impliedly immunized the challenged activities.[943] The Court noted that the SEC was obligated by those statutes to review and approve or disapprove proposed rule changes of the NASD, that the Commission had considered competitive factors when exercising its review authority,[944] and that the challenged restriction had been repeatedly approved by the SEC. Thus, the Court concluded that

> maintenance of an antitrust action for activities so directly related to the SEC's responsibilities poses a substantial danger that appellees would be subjected to duplicative and inconsistent standards. . . . We therefore hold that with respect to the activities

---

937. Restrictions in the primary market for mutual fund securities, which includes distribution of securities from mutual funds to underwriters to dealers to investors and redemption of those shares, were not at issue. The challenged restrictions involved "secondary market" transactions–transactions between brokers, between investors, and between brokers and investors. The parties agreed that § 22(d) of the Investment Company Act of 1940 provided an express antitrust exemption with respect to restrictions at the primary level. The Court decided that § 22(d) did not provide an express statutory exemption from the antitrust laws for agreements establishing fixed resale prices for transactions in the secondary market. *Id.* at 720.

938. Section 22(f) of the Investment Company Act of 1940 forbids restrictions on the transfer of mutual fund shares "except in conformity with the statements . . . in its registration statement not in contravention of such rules and regulations as the [Securities and Exchange] Commission may prescribe." 15 U.S.C. § 80a-22(f) (1988).

939. 422 U.S. at 721-29.

940. *Id.* at 729-30 (citation omitted) (emphasis in original).

941. 15 U.S.C. §§ 78o, 78o-3, 78q, 78cc, 78ff (1988).

942. *Id.* §§ 80a-1 to 80a-64.

943. 422 U.S. at 734-35.

944. *Id.* at 730-35.

challenged, . . . the Sherman Act has been displaced by the pervasive regulatory scheme established by the Maloney and Investment Company Acts.[945]

There is, of course, a wide range of securities industry practices over which the SEC has no regulatory authority. As to these, courts have applied the Sherman Act and Clayton Act standards.[946]

c.   COMMODITIES FUTURES

As with securities firms, commodity futures firms, including futures commission merchants, associated persons, floor brokers, commodity trading advisors, introducing brokers, and commodity pool operators, are chartered under state law. They are required to register with the Commodity Futures Trading Commission (CFTC), established in 1974.[947] The CFTC has delegated much of the supervision of these firms or persons to the sole industry self-regulatory organization or "registered futures association," the National Futures Association (NFA).[948]

The CFTC also registers and supervises exchanges as contract markets.[949] A separate designation must be made for each contract.[950] The CFTC has applied the statutory standard that such designation "will not be contrary to the public interest,"[951] to include an "economic purpose" test consisting of showings that any proposed futures contract would be used for commercial hedging, not just speculation, and that prices of the traded commodity can be used as a basis for determining future prices.[952]

Unlike securities exchanges, which do not create new issues of stock for trading, commodity futures exchanges create and market the contracts that are traded. As new financial products have emerged, especially options and indices based on groups of securities, jurisdictional questions between the SEC and the CFTC have arisen.

---

945.   *Id.* at 735. The Second Circuit has held that the antitrust laws do not apply to joint bidding agreements among rival bidders in contested corporate takeovers. Finnegan v. Campeau Corp., 915 F.2d 824 (2d Cir. 1990), *cert. denied*, 111 S. Ct. 1624 (1991). In finding implied antitrust immunity, the court reasoned that because the SEC has the power to regulate such bidders' agreements under § 14(e) of the Williams Act, 15 U.S.C. § 78n(e) (1988), and has impliedly authorized them by requiring their disclosure under Schedule 14D-1 as part of a takeover battle, permitting antitrust suits against joint takeover bidders would conflict with the proper functioning of the securities laws.

946.   *See, e.g.,* Quinonez v. National Ass'n of Sec. Dealers, 540 F.2d 824, 828-29 (5th Cir. 1976) (agreements between brokerage firms not to pirate each other's employees and not to offer employment to applicants who had either been fired or refused employment by the firms not immune from attack); Vandervelde v. Put & Call Brokers & Dealers Ass'n, 344 F. Supp. 118, 136-37 (S.D.N.Y. 1972) (dealers' association rule requiring members to give discounts to other members held violative of the antitrust laws).

947.   7 U.S.C. §§ 6d, 6e, 6k (1988).

948.   The Department of Justice opposed CFTC registration of NFA because of its mandatory membership requirements. *See, e.g.,* Comments of the U.S. Dep't of Justice before the Commodity Futures Trading Comm'n, In the Matter of Petition for Commission Rulemaking; Registered Futures Associations (Jan. 24, 1983).

949.   7 U.S.C. §§ 7, 7a (1988).

950.   *Id.* § 7(a).

951.   *Id.* § 7(g).

952.   Interpretive Statement Regarding Economic and Public Interest Requirements For Contract Market Designation, 17 C.F.R. pt. 5, app. A (1991).

After an interagency accord in 1981, the Securities Acts Amendments of 1982[953] and the Futures Trading Act of 1982[954] codified the resolution of the jurisdictional dispute. Basically, the SEC retains jurisdiction over options on securities and related instruments, including options on exempted securities like options traded on a national securities exchange and options on groups or indices of securities. The CFTC reviews futures contracts on groups or indices of securities and options on such futures contracts if (1) the contracts or options are settled in cash or other than by transfer or receipt of securities, (2) the contracts or options are not susceptible to price manipulation, and (3) any group or index is predominately of securities of unaffiliated issues and is based on substantially all publicly traded securities.[955] The two agencies have jointly issued guidelines for reviewing nondiversified stock index futures contracts.[956]

In its role as designator of contracts markets, the CFTC approves mergers and other affiliations between exchanges. Few contracts overlap between exchanges, however, and therefore innovation in new contracts by exchanges is an important consideration in the competitive analysis of these arrangements.[957]

Mergers of commodity brokers and other participants are reviewed under the Hart-Scott-Rodino Act.[958] The CFTC does not directly approve such mergers but must review the license for the merged entity. Banks and bank holding company subsidiaries have been permitted by the Office of the Comptroller of Currency and the Federal Reserve Board to acquire or act as futures commission merchants.[959]

Section 15 of the Commodity Futures Trading Commission Act[960] requires the CFTC to consider the competitive effect of adopting any CFTC rule or regulation or of approving any bylaw, rule, or regulation of an exchange or a registered futures association. The test is that the CFTC must endeavor to use the "least anticompetitive means" of achieving the objectives of the CFTC Act.[961]

Some rules control competitive aspects of futures contract pricing. The exchanges, subject to CFTC oversight, set both initial and maintenance margins.[962] The exchanges also set daily limits on price movements until the last day(s) of trading in a futures contract.[963]

Antitrust enforcement has centered on price-fixing concerns. In *United States v. Board of Trade of the City of Chicago, Inc.*,[964] the Department of Justice obtained

---

953. Pub. L. No. 97-303, 96 Stat. 1409 (1982).

954. Pub. L. No. 97-444, 96 Stat. 2294 (1982).

955. 7 U.S.C. § 2a(ii) (1988).

956. Designation Criteria for Futures Contracts and Options on Futures Contracts Involving Non-Diversified Stock Indexes of Domestic Issuers, Exchange Act Release No. 34-20578 [1985 Transfer Binder] FED. SEC. L. REP. (CCH) ¶ 22,667 (1984).

957. *See* Letter from Douglas H. Ginsburg, then Assistant Att'y Gen., Antitrust Div., to Alan L. Seifert, Deputy Director, Division of Trading and Markets, CFTC (Feb. 14, 1986) (concerning the proposed affiliation between the Mid America Commodity Exchange and the Chicago Board of Trade).

958. Clayton Act § 7A, 15 U.S.C. § 18a (1988).

959. *See, e.g.*, J.P. Morgan & Co., 68 Fed. Res. Bull. 514 (1982).

960. 7 U.S.C. § 19 (1988).

961. *Id.*

962. *Id.* § 7a(12).

963. *See, e.g.*, Chicago Bd. of Trade Reg. 100 8.01.

964. 1974-1 Trade Cas. (CCH) ¶ 75,071 (N.D. Ill. 1974).

a consent decree enjoining the exchange from fixing brokerage rates or restricting the right of any member or broker to agree with his customer on commissions or fees. Private litigation over fixed exchange commission rates was likewise settled.[965] In *United States v. New York Coffee & Sugar Exchange*,[966] the Antitrust Division obtained a consent decree against posttrading setting of world and domestic spot sugar prices by an exchange committee.

Private litigants have also been active in this area. In *Strobl v. New York Mercantile Exchange*,[967] private litigants established that a conspiracy by shorts, i.e., sellers, to drive down potato prices and default on Maine potato contracts, even though prohibited as price manipulation under the Commodity Exchange Act, can also constitute a cause of action under the Sherman and Clayton Acts. Thus, treble damages for plaintiff longs, i.e., buyers of the futures contracts, were upheld.[968]

As in the securities area, however, questions of agency jurisdiction and antitrust immunity have arisen. In *Ricci v. Chicago Mercantile Exchange*,[969] the Supreme Court held that a broker's antitrust suit against the Exchange should be stayed until the matter was considered by the Commodity Exchange Commission (predecessor to the CFTC), even though the statute provided for neither antitrust review by the agency or express antitrust exemption. The Court reasoned that this step would help in concluding whether implied repeal of antitrust provisions was necessary.[970] Thereafter the Section 15 "least anticompetitive means" test[971] was inserted by Congress in the Commodity Futures Trading Act.

The standards of the Sherman Act, however, have been held irrelevant in cases brought under the commodities statutes alleging manipulation or cornering. To establish manipulation of prices in violation of the Commodity Exchange Act,[972] proof of some form of fraud and an artificial or unreasonable price are required.[973] Likewise, to establish cornering or monopolizing a futures marketing violation of the Commodity Exchange Act, there must be proof of acquiring a dominant portion of

---

965.   Arenson v. Board of Trade, 372 F. Supp. 1349 (N.D. Ill. 1974).

966.   1979-1 Trade Cas. (CCH) ¶ 62,665 (S.D.N.Y. 1979).

967.   768 F.2d 22 (2d Cir.), *cert. denied*, 474 U.S. 1006 (1985).

968.   *See* Apex Oil Co. v. DiMauro, 713 F. Supp. 587 (S.D.N.Y. 1989) (upholding, on summary judgment motion, claim of conspiracy under § 1 of the Sherman Act by longs in the market for heating oil, although dismissing claim alleging conspiracy to monopolize under § 2 of the Sherman Act against same defendants); Minpeco, SA v. Conticommodity Servs., 673 F. Supp. 684 (S.D.N.Y. 1987) (denying defendants' motions for summary judgment to dismiss conspiracy claims alleging manipulation of the price of silver and silver futures brought under, among other statutes, §§ 1 and 2 of the Sherman Act and § 9(b) of the Commodity Exchange Act); Grosser v. Commodity Exch., Inc., 639 F. Supp. 1293 (S.D.N.Y. 1986) (denying motions by certain defendants to dismiss antitrust claims on standing grounds in action brought by holder of long silver futures position alleging conspiracy to manipulate the price of refined silver and silver futures contracts), *aff'd*, 859 F.2d 148 (2d Cir. 1988).

969.   409 U.S. 289 (1973).

970.   *Cf.* Chicago Mercantile Exch. v. Deaktor, 414 U.S. 113 (1973) (staying complaint alleging violation of the Commodity Exchange Act).

971.   7 U.S.C. § 19 (1988).

972.   *Id.* § 13b.

973.   *See, e.g.,* Cargill, Inc. v. Hardin, 452 F.2d 1154 (8th Cir. 1971), *cert. denied*, 406 U.S. 932 (1972); Volkart Bros. v. Freeman, 311 F.2d 52 (5th Cir. 1962); General Foods Corp. v. Brannan, 170 F.2d 220 (7th Cir. 1948).

the commodity "with the purpose of artificially enhancing the price."[974] Proof of an artificial price has been held essential in later cornering cases.[975] Moreover, dominance in both cash and futures markets must be shown.[976]

5. *Government Contracts*

The federal antitrust laws and federal procurement statutes and regulations prohibit anticompetitive agreements and conduct by competitors for government contracts. The federal procurement statutes and regulations require executive agencies to notify the Attorney General of any apparent antitrust violations in the bidding for and proposal of government contracts.[977]

"Full and open competition," pursuant to which "all responsible sources are permitted to compete,"[978] is the express procurement policy of the United States Government. To that end, certain provisions of the Federal Acquisition Regulation (FAR) exist primarily to assist executive agencies in making a determination whether anticompetitive practices have occurred. For example, Section 52.203-2 of FAR requires, in part, that government contract bidders certify that their bids have been independently arrived at and have not been disclosed to other offerors.[979] FAR Section 3.303(c) provides a list of factors that may indicate a possible antitrust violation.[980] FAR Section 9.604 disallows contractor teaming arrangements in

---

974. United States v. Patten, 226 U.S. 525, 539 (1913); *see* Peto v. Howell, 101 F.2d 353 (7th Cir. 1939) (allegation of monopolization under § 2 of Sherman Act upheld).

975. *See* Great Western Food Distribs. v. Brannan, 201 F.2d 476 (7th Cir.), *cert. denied*, 345 U.S. 997 (1953); General Foods Corp. v. Brannan, 170 F.2d 220 (7th Cir. 1948).

976. *See* Chicago Bd. of Trade v. Olsen, 262 U.S. 1 (1923); Cargill, Inc. v. Hardin, 452 F.2d 1154 (8th Cir. 1971), *cert. denied*, 406 U.S. 932 (1972).

977. 10 U.S.C. §§ 2302, 2304-05 (1988); 48 C.F.R. § 3.301(a)-(b) (1991) (Federal Acquisition Regulation (FAR) § 3.3). The provisions of FAR can be found at 48 C.F.R. chs. 1-99 (1991).

For an extensive discussion of the antitrust issues that arise in the context of government procurement, see ABA ANTITRUST SECTION, THE ANTITRUST GOVERNMENT CONTRACTS HANDBOOK (1990).

978. 48 C.F.R. § 6.003 (1991) (FAR § 6.003).

979. FAR § 52.203-2 provides that the offeror must certify the following:

(1) The prices in this offer have been arrived at independently, without, for the purpose of restricting competition, any consultation, communication, or agreement with any other offeror or competitor relating to (i) those prices, (ii) the intention to submit any offer, or (iii) the methods or factors used to calculate the prices offered;

(2) The prices in this offer have not been and will not be knowingly disclosed by the offeror, directly or indirectly, to any other offeror or competitor before bid opening (in the case of a formally advertised solicitation) or contract award (in the case of a negotiated solicitation) unless otherwise required by law; and

(3) No attempt has been made or will be made by the offeror to induce any other concern to submit or not to submit an offer for the purpose of restricting competition.

48 C.F.R. § 52.203-2 (1991).

The Department of Defense certification requirements state that before the issuance of a contract valued at over $100,000, the contractor must warrant that its prices have been independently set and that it has not disclosed its prices to other offerors nor attempted to induce any other firm to submit or not submit an offer "for the purposes of restricting competition." 53 FED. REG. 42,945-49 (1988).

980. The following factors are included:

(1) The existence of an *industry price list* or *price agreement* to which contractors refer in formulating their offers;

violation of antitrust laws.[981]

Enforcement of these provisions can be initiated by the Department of Justice, FTC, or a private individual or corporation. In addition to the monetary fines and jail sentences available under federal law, the United States is authorized to seek suspension and or debarment from bidding on a government contract[982] as well as injunctive relief[983] and damages.

Antitrust issues commonly arise in the context of a bid protest initiated on the grounds that the awarded contract was the product of a bid-rigging scheme. A government contractor also may bring a private action claiming federal and state antitrust violations. Where the collusive bidding resulting in a price below the complaining contractor's offering bid, a private action requires the plaintiff to establish antitrust injury[984] and damages.[985]

Government contract activity which is subject to antitrust scrutiny includes: (a) bid rigging and price fixing; (b) customer and market allocation; (c) group boycotts and concerted refusals to deal; and (d) information exchanges. Courts have routinely found antitrust liability in cases involving direct competitors who have rigged bids in order to allocate government contracts among themselves.[986] Courts have defined bid rigging to include "bid-rotation" schemes in which contractors agree

---

(2)   A sudden change from competitive bidding to identical bidding;

(3)   Simultaneous price increases or follow-the-leader pricing;

(4)   Rotation of bids or proposals, so that each competitor takes a turn in sequence as low bidder, or so that certain competitors bid low only on some sizes of contracts and high on other sizes;

(5)   Division of the market, so that certain competitors bid low only for contracts led by certain agencies, or for contracts in certain geographical areas, or on certain products, and bid high on all other jobs;

(6)   Establishment by competitors of a collusive price estimating scheme;

(7)   The filing of a joint bid by two or more competitors when at least one of the competitors has sufficient technical capacity and productive capacity for contract performance.

48 C.F.R. § 3.303 (1991) (emphasis in original).

981.   *Id.* at § 9.604 (1991). FAR Section 52.203-6 requires that each government contract include a provision expressly prohibiting a prime contractor from preventing a subcontractor from selling directly to the government.

982.   *See* 48 C.F.R. §§ 9.406-2(a)(2), 9.407-2(a)(2).

983.   Under the Competition in Contracting Act of 1984, Pub L. No. 98-369, 98 Stat. 1175 (codified in scattered sections of 10 U.S.C., 31 U.S.C., 40 U.S.C., and 41 U.S.C.), a government contractor may obtain from the General Accounting Office a stay of a contract and request that a contract award be set aside.

984.   *See* Brunswick Corp. v. Pueblo Bowl-O-Mat, Inc., 429 U.S. 477, 489 (1977).

985.   *See* Matsushita Elec. Indus. Co. v. Zenith Radio Corp., 475 U.S. 574 (1986). *But see* Power Conversion, Inc. v. Saft Am., Inc., 672 F. Supp. 224 (D. Md. 1987) (defendant's motion to dismiss plaintiff's complaint was denied because plaintiff had submitted evidence showing that defendants had engaged in a concerted predatory pricing scheme).

Antitrust issues often arise in the context of a bid protest initiated on the grounds that the awarded contract was the product of a bid-rigging scheme. However, the federal agencies consistently have declined to consider alleged antitrust violations in exercising their bid protest functions. *See* THE ANTITRUST GOVERNMENT CONTRACTS HANDBOOK, *supra* note 977, at 16 n.76.

986.   *See, e.g.*, United States v. W.F. Brinkley & Son Constr. Co., 783 F.2d 1157 (4th Cir. 1986); United States v. Koppers Co., 652 F.2d 290 (2d Cir.), *cert. denied*, 454 U.S. 1083 (1981). *See generally* THE ANTITRUST GOVERNMENT CONTRACTS HANDBOOK, *supra* note 977, at 38-39.

to refrain from bidding or to submit bids known to be unrealistically high;[987] agreements to compare bids before submitting them to the purchasing authority;[988] and agreements to forgo independent bidding in favor of a joint bid through which the contractors will allocate work and profits."[989]   Similarly, courts have found unlawful agreements among contractors that allocate governmental customers or territories.[990]

Although market allocations, bid rigging and price fixing are often held per se illegal, rule of reason analysis is usually applied to teaming arrangements.[991]   Such teaming arrangements are more commonly found in highly specialized government contracts. This type of contract has greater costs and is more technically complex than most others. As a result, cooperation among firms is either expressly required by the government or necessitated by the contract's terms.[992]

Information exchanges resulting from government encouraged contract teaming arrangements are not immune from antitrust scrutiny.[993]   As a result, government contractors must exercise care in documenting all instances in which government officials have necessitated any exchange of information among direct competitors.[994]

6. Insurance

Even before the adoption of the Sherman Act, the domestic insurance industry operated in the belief that it was not subject to regulation by Congress, based on the 1868 decision of the Supreme Court in *Paul v. Virginia*[995] in which the Court held that the business of insurance was not interstate commerce, but "local transactions . . . governed by the local law." The Court subsequently reaffirmed[996]

---

987. *See, e.g.*, United States v. Champion Int'l Corp., 557 F.2d 1270 (9th Cir.), *cert. denied*, 434 U.S. 938 (1977).

988. *See, e.g.*, United States v. J.L. Hammett Co., 1964 Trade Cas. (CCH) ¶ 71,178 (E.D. Pa. 1964) (consent judgment).

989. *See* COMPACT v. Metropolitan Gov't, 594 F. Supp. 1567 (M.D. Tenn. 1984).

990. *See* United States v. Koppers Co., 652 F.2d 290 (2d Cir.), *cert. denied*, 454 U.S. 1083 (1981); *COMPACT*, 594 F. Supp. at 1577. *See generally* THE ANTITRUST GOVERNMENT CONTRACTS HANDBOOK, *supra* note 977, at 40.

991. Northrop Corp. v. McDonnell Douglas Corp., 498 F. Supp. 1112 (C.D. Cal. 1980), *rev'd*, 700 F.2d 506 (9th Cir.), *cert. denied*, 464 U.S. 849 (1983). See the discussion of joint ventures in Part I of Chapter III of this treatise for a discussion of the treatment of ancillary restraints.

992. *See* FAR § 9.602, which states:
     (a) Contractor team arrangements may be desirable from both a Government and industry standpoint in order to enable the companies involved to (1) complement each other's unique capabilities and (2) offer the Government the best combination of performance, cost and delivery for the system or product being acquired.
     (b) Contractor team arrangements may be particularly appropriate in complex research and development acquisitions, but may be used in other appropriate acquisitions, including production.
     48 C.F.R. § 9.602 (1991). *See generally* THE ANTITRUST GOVERNMENT CONTRACTS HANDBOOK, *supra* note 977, at 41-44.

993. *See* United States v. Container Corp., 393 U.S. 333 (1969).

994. *See* General Motors Corp., 103 F.T.C. 374 (1984).

995. 75 U.S. 168, 183 (1868).

996. New York Life Ins. Co. v. Deer Lodge County, 231 U.S. 495, 503-04, 510 (1913); Hooper v. California, 155 U.S. 648, 658-59 (1895).

this decision, and many states relied upon it in enacting extensive regulatory and taxing measures applicable to the business of insurance. In 1944, however, the Supreme Court, in *United States v. South-Eastern Underwriters Association*,[997] held that the insurance business was within the regulatory power of Congress under the commerce clause, and upheld a Sherman Act indictment charging that a large group of insurance companies had conspired through a rating organization to fix fire insurance premiums and eliminate competition.

The decision in *South-Eastern Underwriters* threatened many of the traditional practices of the insurance industry and raised the possibility that the power of the states to regulate and tax insurance companies would be declared invalid under the commerce clause.[998] Congress responded in 1945 by enacting the McCarran-Ferguson Act,[999] under which it delegated to the states the power to continue to regulate and tax the business of insurance. The Sherman, Clayton, and Federal Trade Commission Acts were to be applied to the "business of insurance to the extent that such business is not regulated by State Law."[1000] Agreements to boycott, coerce, or intimidate and acts of boycott, coercion, or intimidation were excluded from the exemption and remained subject to antitrust liability under the Sherman Act.[1001] Accordingly, the availability of the McCarran exemption depends on three basic factors: (1) whether the challenged activity is part of "the business of insurance"; (2) whether the activity is "regulated by State Law"; and (3) whether the activity constitutes an agreement to or an act of boycott, coercion, or intimidation.

The scope of the statutory phrase "business of insurance" was considered by the Supreme Court in *Group Life & Health Insurance Co. v. Royal Drug*,[1002] which involved a challenge to a prepaid prescription drug plan regulating the amount of reimbursement that Blue Shield would pay to pharmacies providing drugs to its insureds. In finding that the provider agreements between Blue Shield and participating pharmacies were not the "business of insurance," the Court's five-member majority focused on two elements: (1) the "spreading and underwriting of a policyholder's risk," and (2) a direct connection with the contractual relationship between the insurer and insured.[1003] Prior to *Royal Drug*, the Court had observed in *SEC v. National Securities, Inc.*,[1004] that not all the activities of insurance companies would be protected under the exemption.[1005] There, the Court noted that the business of insurance related to the contract between insurer and insured and emphasized the distinction between the "activities of insurance *companies*" and the "*'business* of insurance.'"[1006] The Court in *Royal Drug* reaffirmed these

---

997.   322 U.S. 533 (1944).

998.   *See id.* at 547-48.

999.   Act of March 9, 1945, ch. 20, §§ 1-5, 59 Stat. 33-34 (codified at 15 U.S.C. §§ 1011-15 (1988)); *see* Joint Hearings on S. 1362, H.R. 3269, H.R. 3270, Before Subcomms. of the Comm. on the Judiciary, 78th Cong., 1st & 2d Sess., pts. 1-6 (1943-44).

1000. 15 U.S.C. § 1012(b) (1988).

1001. *Id.* at § 1013(b).

1002. 440 U.S. 205 (1979).

1003. *Id.* at 211-13, 215-17.

1004. 393 U.S. 453 (1969).

1005. *Id.* at 459-60. Among the protected activities the Court noted were "the fixing of rates," "the selling and advertising of policies," and "the licensing of companies and their agents." *Id.* at 460.

1006. *Id.* at 459 (emphasis in original).

elements of *National Securities*, but substantially restricted the suggestion in that case that the business of insurance included "business of insurance companies" when such activities were closely related to the companies' "status as reliable insurers."[1007] According to the Court in *Royal Drug*, the "reliable insurer" standard, which had been applied primarily to agreements between insurance companies and third parties,[1008] was too broad because every business decision made by an insurance company arguably has some impact on its status as a reliable insurer.[1009]

The Court thus held that agreements between insurance companies and third parties that supply goods or services to claimants, such as pharmacies which deliver drugs to insured persons, generally are not part of the "business of insurance" for purposes of the McCarran Act.[1010] The Court distinguished such provider agreements from contracts of insurance which spread the risk among all insureds, even though the former arrangements might ultimately result in lower premiums by reducing the insurer's costs. The Court also noted other commercial transactions which, although necessary to the functioning of the insurer's business, are not part of the "business of insurance" contemplated by the act.[1011]

The Court next considered the scope of the "business of insurance" in *Union Labor Life Insurance Co. v. Pireno*,[1012] in which it held that a peer review process, by which the reasonableness of health care claims was determined, was outside the "business of insurance." The action had been brought by a doctor whose fees and practices had been criticized by the peer review committee, and who claimed that the procedure amounted to a conspiracy to fix both prices and permissible methods of practice. The Court held that the activities of the peer review committee fell outside the business of insurance. In its analysis, the majority found a third factor in the Court's *Royal Drug* opinion: whether the allegedly anticompetitive practice is

---

1007.   440 U.S. at 217, 230.
1008.   *Id.* at 217; *see, e.g.,* Frankford Hosp. v. Blue Cross, 554 F.2d 1253 (3d Cir. 1977) (per curiam), *aff'g* 417 F. Supp. 1104 (E.D. Pa. 1976), *cert. denied,* 434 U.S. 860 (1977); Nankin Hosp. v. Michigan Hosp. Serv., 361 F. Supp. 1199 (E.D. Mich. 1973); California League of Indep. Ins. Producers v. Aetna Casualty & Sur. Co., 175 F. Supp. 857 (N.D. Cal. 1959).
1009.   440 U.S. at 216-17. *But cf.* Metropolitan Life Ins. Co. v. Massachusetts, 471 U.S. 724, 743-44 (1985) (quoting *National Securities* with approval) (dictum).
1010.   The Court found support for its position in the Act's legislative history. 440 U.S. at 217-30. Lower court decisions in which the *Royal Drug* criteria have been applied to provider contracts include Ratino v. Medical Serv., 718 F.2d 1260 (4th Cir. 1983) (Blue Shield's " 'usual, customary and reasonable' " insurance plan involving provider agreements is not the business of insurance); Klamath-Lake Pharmaceutical Ass'n v. Klamath Medical Serv. Bureau, 701 F.2d 1276 (9th Cir.), *cert. denied,* 464 U.S. 822 (1983); Proctor v. State Farm Mut. Auto. Ins. Co., 675 F.2d 308 (D.C. Cir.) (vertical arrangements between insurers and automobile repair shops that agreed in advance to do repair work at prices fixed by insurers are not within the business of insurance), *cert. denied,* 459 U.S. 839 (1982); Virginia Academy of Clinical Psychologists v. Blue Shield, 624 F.2d 476 (4th Cir. 1980) (refusal of two Blue Cross plans to pay for services rendered by clinical psychologists, unless they are billed through a physician, is not the business of insurance); St. Bernard Gen. Hosp. v. Hospital Serv. Ass'n, 618 F.2d 1140 (5th Cir. 1980); Liberty Glass Co. v. Allstate Ins. Co., 607 F.2d 135 (5th Cir. 1979); Pritt v. Blue Cross & Blue Shield, Inc., 699 F. Supp. 81 (S.D.W. Va. 1988).
1011.   440 U.S. at 213-14 n.9, 215.
1012.   458 U.S. 119 (1982).

"limited to entities within the insurance industry."[1013] The Court found that none of the three elements of the business of insurance were satisfied by the peer review system.

Thus the Supreme Court established a three-part analysis to determine whether practices of insurance companies fall within the "business of insurance": (1) whether the practice has the effect of spreading or transferring a policyholder's risk,[1014] (2) whether the practice is an integral part of the policy relationship between insurer and the insured,[1015] and (3) whether the practice is limited to entities within the

---

1013.   *Id.* at 129. The Court cautioned that neither this factor nor either of the two *Royal Drug* criteria was solely determinative. *Id.* For a discussion of varying interpretations of the Court's "solely determinative" statement, see Ticor Title Ins. Co., 5 TRADE REG. REP. (CCH) ¶ 22,744, at 22,456 (Oct. 19, 1989), *vacated on other grounds*, Ticor Title Ins. Co. v. FTC, 922 F.2d 1122 (3d Cir. 1991), *cert. granted*, 60 U.S.L.W. 3257 (U.S. Oct. 7, 1991) (No. 91-72).

1014.   *See Ticor*, 5 TRADE REG. REP. (CCH) at 22,455, 22,457 (title search and examination services do not qualify as business of insurance because they lack the indispensable element of risk spreading or underwriting; the most significant risk that title insurers face is whatever peril attaches to conducting a competent search and examination of the public records, but this " 'risk' has nothing to do with the notion of risk as it is commonly encountered in casualty insurance . . . that an unforseen or uncontrollable event will affect the insured"); *see also In re* Insurance Antitrust Litig., 723 F. Supp. 464, 473 (N.D. Cal. 1989) ("reinsurance is no less a part of the process of underwriting and spreading risks than primary insurance"), *rev'd and remanded on other grounds*, 938 F.2d 919 (9th Cir. 1991); James M. King & Assocs. v. G.D. Van Wagenen Co., 717 F. Supp. 667 (D. Minn. 1989) (agent-carrier disputes are not per se business of insurance; collateral protection program, which is essentially a collateral monitoring and tracking service unrelated to risk pooling, and which features insurance as an ancillary element, and a payment shaver program, which is not primarily a risk pooling program but is instead a financing package, do not constitute the business of insurance); Reazin v. Blue Cross & Blue Shield, 663 F. Supp. 1360, 1403 (D. Kan. 1987) (functioning as a third-party administrator for self-insured plans was not "the business of insurance" since self-insurance involves no spreading of risk), *aff'd in part and remanded in part*, 899 F.2d 951 (10th Cir.), *cert. denied*, 110 S. Ct. 3241 (1990); Maryland v. Blue Cross and Blue Shield Ass'n, 620 F. Supp. 907, 916-17 (D. Md. 1985) (in order to fall within the definition of "business of insurance" the territorial market division conducted by defendant nonprofit health insurers must be related positively to underwriting and ratemaking, i.e., directly facilitate risk spreading and transfer through the provision of insurance; a "mere relationship" to these aforementioned factors is insufficient). A number of pre-*Royal Drug* cases held that arrangements tying insurance products to noninsurance products (often loans) were within the business of insurance. Dexter v. Equitable Life Assurance Soc'y of the United States, 527 F.2d 233 (2d Cir. 1975) (tying insurance policies to mortgage loans falls within business of insurance); Addrisi v. Equitable Life Assurance Soc'y, 503 F.2d 725 (9th Cir. 1974) (same), *cert. denied*, 420 U.S. 929 (1975); Mathis v. Automobile Club Inter-Ins. Exch., 410 F. Supp. 1037, 1038-39 (W.D. Mo. 1976) (McCarran Act exempts practice of requiring membership in auto club in order to purchase insurance). Other cases, however, have rejected that position. *See* FTC v. Dixie Fin. Co., 695 F.2d 926, 929-30 (5th Cir.) (misrepresenting need to purchase credit insurance to obtain credit not business of insurance), *cert. denied*, 461 U.S. 928 (1983); Cody v. Community Loan Corp., 606 F.2d 499, 503 (5th Cir. 1979) (extension of loans by insurance company to finance payment of insurance premiums not business of insurance), *cert. denied*, 446 U.S. 988 (1980); Perry v. Fidelity Union Life Ins. Co., 606 F.2d 468, 470-71 (5th Cir. 1979) (same), *cert. denied*, 446 U.S. 987 (1980); FTC v. Manufacturers Hanover Consumer Serv., 567 F. Supp. 992 (E.D. Pa. 1983) (misrepresenting need to purchase credit insurance to obtain credit not the business of insurance); Peacock Buick, 86 F.T.C. 1532 (1975) (same), *on reconsideration*, 87 F.T.C. 379 (1976), *aff'd mem.*, 553 F.2d 97 (4th Cir. 1977).

1015.   *See, e.g.*, Maryland v. Blue Cross & Blue Shield Ass'n, 620 F. Supp. 907, 917-19 (D. Md. 1985) (the decision not to market at all in a particular geographic area is not an "integral part of the policy relationship between insurer and insured," but instead precludes any relationship at all;

insurance industry.[1016] The opinions in *Royal Drug, Pireno*, and subsequent lower court decisions reflect a narrowing of the scope of the "business of insurance"[1017] and thus a narrowing of the McCarran Act exemption.[1018] Lower courts, however, have continued to find that many activities of insurance companies fall within the

---

however, the potential impact of territorial division on rates could satisfy the policy relationship criterion).

1016. *See, e.g.* Reazin v. Blue Cross & Blue Shield, 663 F. Supp. 1360, 1404 (D. Kan. 1987) (highly doubtful that plenary state regulation precludes Sherman Act scrutiny of an "unsupervised agreement between an insurance company with others outside that industry"), *aff'd in part and remanded in part*, 899 F.2d 951 (10th Cir.), *cert. denied*, 110 S. Ct. 3241 (1990); Maryland v. Blue Cross and Blue Shield Ass'n, 620 F. Supp. 907, 918-19 (D. Md. 1985) (trade association composed of local Blue Cross and Blue Shield plans is sufficiently related to the insurance company parties to be an entity within the insurance industry).

1017. *See, e.g.* United States v. Title Ins. Rating Bureau, 700 F.2d 1247 (9th Cir. 1983) (the provision of escrow services by title insurers held not to be within the "business of insurance" under *Royal Drug/Pireno* criteria), *cert. denied*, 467 U.S. 1240 (1984); American Standard Life & Accident Ins. Co. v. U.R.L., Inc., 701 F. Supp. 527, 532-33 (M.D. Pa. 1988) (insurance agents' practice of unlawfully using competitors' confidential information and customer lists to induce customers to switch policies to defendants' company is not the business of insurance, failing all three *Royal Drug/Pireno* factors); Reazin v. Blue Cross & Blue Shield, 663 F. Supp. 1360, 1403 (D. Kan. 1987) (private health care financing is not the business of insurance because the activities go beyond traditional indemnity coverage), *aff'd in part and remanded in part*, 899 F.2d 951 (10th Cir.), *cert. denied*, 110 S. Ct. 3241 (1990); Trident Neuro-Imaging Lab. v. Blue Cross & Blue Shield, 568 F. Supp. 1474 (D.S.C. 1983) (Blue Cross' refusal to reimburse for services performed on physician-owned, as opposed to hospital-owned, CAT scanners not business of insurance); Custom Auto Body, Inc. v. Aetna Casualty & Sur. Co., 1983-2 Trade Cas. (CCH) ¶ 65,629, at 69,182-83 (D.R.I. 1983) (agreement whereby insurer recommends repair shops to insured and shops agree to accept insurer's repair estimates did not constitute "business of insurance" under the McCarran Act exemption); Ticor Title Ins. Co., 5 TRADE REG. REP. (CCH) ¶ 22,744 (Oct. 19, 1989) (provision of title search and examination services is not protected by the business of insurance exemption as practice fails all three *Royal Drug* criteria; services offered apart from any concept of insurance risk spreading), *vacated on other grounds*, Ticor Title Co. v. FTC, 922 F.2d 1122 (3d Cir. 1991), *cert. granted*, 60 U.S.L.W. 3257 (U.S. Oct. 7, 1991) (No. 91-72).

1018. Many insurance company activities held not to involve the business of insurance for McCarran Act purposes nonetheless have been found lawful under the antitrust laws, or have been saved by state action immunity. *See, e.g.*, Ticor Title Ins. Co. v. FTC, 922 F.2d 1122 (3rd Cir. 1991) (collective setting of rates for title search and examination services, which the FTC determined did not involve the business of insurance for McCarran purposes, held immune from antitrust scrutiny by virtue of the state action doctrine; court does not reach McCarran issue on appeal), *cert. granted*, 60 U.S.L.W. 3257 (U.S. Oct. 7, 1991) (No. 91-72); Ocean State Physicians Health Plan v. Blue Cross & Blue Shield, 883 F.2d 1101, 1109-13 (1st Cir. 1989) (although Prudent Buyer policy – by which Blue Cross ensured that it did not pay more than its competitors for the same provider services – was not exempt from antitrust scrutiny, court found policy did not violate the Sherman Act as a matter of law), *cert. denied*, 494 U.S. 1027 (1990); Royal Drug Co. v. Group Life and Health Ins. Co., 737 F.2d 1433 (5th Cir. 1984) (on remand from Supreme Court, Fifth Circuit affirms district court holding that Blue Shield's prepaid prescription drug plan does not violate federal antitrust laws), *cert. denied*, 469 U.S. 1160 (1985); Proctor v. State Farm Mut. Auto. Ins. Co., 675 F.2d 308, 337-39 (D.C. Cir.) (vertical arrangements between insurers and automobile repair shops where repair shops agree in advance to do repair work at prices fixed by insurers, in exchange for referrals, are not exempt by McCarran but nonetheless do not violate antitrust laws), *cert. denied*, 459 U.S. 839 (1982).

exemption when the *Royal Drug/Pireno* factors are applied.[1019]

The second prerequisite to the application of the McCarran Act is that the particular challenged activity be "regulated by State Law." The Act does not define the nature or extent of state regulation necessary to confer the exemption from the antitrust laws, and the issue remains unsettled. While some courts have held that to confer exemption under the McCarran Act, the state statute must be directed specifically at the insurance industry,[1020] other courts are of the view that general state statutes can also satisfy the state regulation requirement.[1021] The Supreme

---

1019.   *See, e.g.*, *In re* Insurance Antitrust Litig., 938 F.2d 919 (9th Cir. 1991) (reinsurance is as much the business of insurance as the offering of primary insurance); Ocean State Physicians Health Plan v. Blue Cross & Blue Shield, 883 F.2d 1101, 1107-08 (1st Cir. 1989) (HMO-type health insurance policies, as well as the marketing and pricing of such policies, are within the business of insurance), *cert. denied*, 494 U.S. 1027 (1990); *In re* Workers' Compensation Ins. Antitrust Litig., 867 F.2d 1552, 1556 (8th Cir. 1989) (fixing rates, whether by private or by state-approved rate setting, is integral to the price charged to policy holders, and to the contractual relationship with the insured, and is central to the transferring and spreading of the insurance risk), *cert. denied*, 492 U.S. 920 (1989); Health Care Equalization Comm. v. Iowa Medical Soc'y, 851 F.2d 1020, 1028 (8th Cir. 1988) (plaintiffs' allegation, that insurance companies monopolized the health care insurance business within the state, focuses on the contractual relationship between insurer and insured; these contracts are an integral part of the business of insurance); Mackey v. Nationwide Ins. Cos., 724 F.2d 419, 420 (4th Cir. 1984) (redlining included in business of insurance); Feinstein v. Nettleship Co., 714 F.2d 928, 931-33 (9th Cir. 1983) (agreement between medical association and insurer to offer group medical insurance only to association members was within the business of insurance), *cert. denied*, 466 U.S. 972 (1984); Owens v. Aetna Life & Casualty Co., 654 F.2d 218, 226 (3d Cir.) (authorization of agents to solicit insurance policies and acceptance or rejection of coverage tendered by brokers is business of insurance), *cert. denied*, 454 U.S. 1092 (1981); Grant v. Erie Ins. Exch., 542 F. Supp. 457, 462 (M.D. Pa. 1982) ("Cooperative efforts . . . with respect to the collection of statistical data and ratemaking are unquestionably part of the business of insurance."), *aff'd mem.*, 716 F.2d 890 (3d Cir.), *cert. denied*, 464 U.S. 938 (1983); Weatherby v. RCA Corp., 1988-1 Trade Cas. (CCH) ¶ 68,077, at 58,534 (N.D.N.Y. 1986) (business of insurance includes insurer's refusal to write new policies, refusal to renew policies, and decision to terminate agency agreement); Gribbin v. Southern Farm Bureau Life Ins., 1984-1 Trade Cas. (CCH) ¶ 65,798, at 67,341-42 (W.D. La. 1984) (contractual limitations on insurer's agents fall within business of insurance), *aff'd mem.*, 751 F.2d 1257 (1985); UNR Indus. v. Continental Ins. Co., 607 F. Supp. 855, 862 (N.D. Ill. 1984) ("an agreement to change the type of policy offered is the business of insurance[;] [t]he type of coverage offered directly affects the spreading of risk, is at the very heart of the policy relationship, and the agreement is limited to insurance companies"); Hopping v. Standard Life Ins. Co. 1984-1 Trade Cas. (CCH) ¶ 65,814, at 67,409-10 (N.D. Miss. 1983) (insurance company requirement that agent refrain from replacing medical carrier with other carriers concerned insurance company and its policyholders and was "business of insurance").

1020.   *See* Ohio v. Ohio Medical Indem., Inc., 1976-2 Trade Cas. (CCH) ¶ 61,128, at 70,113 n.1 (S.D. Ohio 1976) (general state antitrust laws are not state regulation of the business of insurance); *see also* Fry v. John Hancock Mut. Life Ins. Co., 355 F. Supp. 1151, 1153-54 (N.D. Tex. 1973) (state statute seeking to regulate the antitrust aspects of insurance company lending is not sufficiently related to the business of insurance).

1021.   *See, e.g.*, Klamath-Lake Pharmaceutical Ass'n v. Klamath Med. Serv. Bureau, 701 F.2d 1276, 1287 (9th Cir.) (court notes that, in addition to regulation under state insurance code, state insurers were subject to state antitrust regulation as well), *cert. denied* 464 U.S. 822 (1983); Maryland v. Blue Cross & Blue Shield Ass'n, 620 F. Supp. 907, 920-21 (D. Md. 1985) (state's antitrust laws are sufficient to meet the state regulation requirement for the McCarran Act exemption); California League of Indep. Ins. Producers v. Aetna Casualty & Sur. Co., 175 F. Supp. 857 (state antitrust statute which applies to insurance companies is sufficient regulation, if the charges in the complaint are covered by the statute), *modified on other grounds*, 179 F. Supp. 65 (N.D. Cal.

Court has determined, however, that the state statute must regulate the insurance company in its relationship with its policyholders, rather than in some other aspect of the company's business, to come "within the sweep of the McCarran-Ferguson Act."[1022]

The courts have consistently held that once a statute that purports to regulate insurance practices has been enacted, the effectiveness of state regulation is not an issue.[1023] In *FTC v. National Casualty Co.*,[1024] the Supreme Court rejected the Federal Trade Commission's argument that the state regulatory provisions were insufficient to support application of the McCarran Act exemption because they had not been effectively elaborated or applied. The Court noted that the Commission did not argue that those provisions "were mere pretense,"[1025] and thus left open the possibility that a regulatory scheme might not satisfy the state regulation requirement if it could be so classified. Subsequent cases, however, have construed the requirement liberally and have declined to deny McCarran Act protection on the basis that state regulation was so ineffective as to be meaningless.[1026] The exemption has been conferred by most courts upon a demonstration of the existence of a general state regulatory scheme with jurisdiction over the challenged practice.[1027]

1959); Professional and Business Men's Life Ins. Co. v. Banker's Life Co., 163 F. Supp. 274 (D. Mont. 1958) (holding, in the alternative, that state antitrust laws applicable to the business of insurance are state regulation for purposes of the McCarran Act).

1022. *See* SEC v. National Sec., Inc., 393 U.S. 453, 457 (1969).

1023. *See, e.g.*, Ohio AFL-CIO v. Insurance Rating Bd., 451 F.2d 1178, 1184 (6th Cir. 1971) ("there is nothing in the language of the McCarran Act or in its legislative history to support the thesis that the Act does not apply when the state's scheme of regulation has not been effectively enforced"), *cert. denied*, 409 U.S. 917 (1972).

1024. 357 U.S. 560 (1958).

1025. *Id.* at 564-65.

1026. *See, e.g.*, Seasongood v. K&K Ins. Agency, 548 F.2d 729 (8th Cir. 1977); Commander Leasing Co. v. Transamerica Title Ins. Co., 477 F.2d 77 (10th Cir. 1973); Ohio AFL-CIO v. Insurance Rating Bd., 451 F.2d 1178, 1184 (6th Cir. 1971), *cert. denied*, 409 U.S. 917 (1972); Schwartz v. Commonwealth Land Title Ins. Co., 374 F. Supp. 564, 575-76 (E.D. Pa.), *opinion supplemented by* 384 F. Supp. 302 (E.D. Pa. 1974); Fleming v. Travelers Indem. Co., 324 F. Supp. 1404, 1406 (D. Mass. 1971); Holly Springs Funeral Home v. United Funeral Serv., 303 F. Supp. 128, 135 (N.D. Miss. 1969).

1027. *See, e.g.*, Ocean State Physicians Health Plan v. Blue Cross & Blue Shield, 883 F.2d 1101, 1108-09 (1st Cir. 1989) (marketing and pricing of health insurance policies to subscribers was regulated by state law where state department of business regulation approved these activities), *cert. denied*, 494 U.S. 1027 (1990); *In re* Workers' Compensation Ins. Antitrust Litig., 867 F.2d 1552, 1557-58 (8th Cir. 1989) (state statutory amendment deregulating insurance rates did not repeal insurance commissioner's supervisory authority over rate setting practices, thus private agreement among workers' compensation insurers to maintain premiums at maximum rate permitted by law, continued to be regulated by state law), *cert. denied*, 492 U.S. 920 (1989); Health Care Equalization Comm. v. Iowa Medical Soc'y, 851 F.2d 1020, 1029 (8th Cir. 1988) (contractual relationship between insurer and insureds, at heart of monopolization claim, is regulated by state law where contracts and rates contained in them are approved by state commissioner of insurance); Mackey v. Nationwide Ins. Cos., 724 F.2d 419, 420-21 (4th Cir. 1984) (defendant's alleged practice of "redlining" – the arbitrary refusal to underwrite risks of persons residing in certain neighborhoods – falls squarely within exemption because insurance business is regulated in North Carolina under an extensive regulatory scheme); Feinstein v. Nettleship Co., 714 F.2d 928, 933 (9th Cir. 1983), *cert. denied*, 466 U.S. 972 (1984); Klamath-Lake Pharmaceutical Ass'n v. Klamath Med. Serv. Bureau, 701 F.2d 1276, 1287 n.10 (9th Cir.), *cert. denied*, 464 U.S. 822

Although the courts have been unwilling to rule that a state's regulatory provisions are so inadequate or ineffective as to preclude application of the McCarran Act exemption, the state must have the power to enforce its regulations. Thus, in *FTC v. Travelers Health Association*,[1028] the Supreme Court defined state regulation for the purposes of the Act as "regulation by the State in which the [challenged activity] is practiced and has its impact";[1029] regulation by a single state of the extraterritorial activities of its domiciliary insurance companies is not sufficient to allow the McCarran Act to displace federal law.[1030]

An activity that is within the business of insurance and regulated by state law for purposes of Section 2(b) of the McCarran Act will not be exempt from the Sherman Act if it constitutes an agreement to or act of boycott, or coercion or intimidation

---

(1983); Dexter v. Equitable Life Assurance Soc'y of the United States, 527 F.2d 233, 236 (2d Cir. 1975); Crawford v. American Title Ins. Co., 518 F.2d 217 (5th Cir. 1975); Addrisi v. Equitable Life Assurance Soc'y, 503 F.2d 725, 727-28 (9th Cir. 1974), *cert. denied*, 420 U.S. 929 (1975); Commander Leasing Co. v. Transamerica Title Ins. Co., 477 F.2d 77, 83 (10th Cir. 1973); Ohio AFL-CIO v. Insurance Rating Bd., 451 F.2d 1178 (6th Cir. 1971), *cert. denied*, 409 U.S. 917 (1972); Maryland v. Blue Cross & Blue Shield Ass'n, 620 F. Supp. 907, 920-21 (D. Md. 1985) (general and pervasive regulation is sufficient, state need not expressly approve a particular practice here, territorial market division by nonprofit health insurers and whether a state regulates a practice through insurance laws or antitrust laws is not controlling for purposes of McCarran-Ferguson); Gribbin v. Southern Farm Bureau Life Ins. Co., 1984-1 Trade Cas. (CCH) ¶ 65,798 (W.D. La. 1984); Hopping v. Standard Life Ins., 1984-1 Trade Cas. (CCH) ¶ 65,814 (N.D. Miss. 1983); Hahn v. Oregon Physicians' Serv., 508 F. Supp. 970, 975 (D. Or. 1981) ("if the state regulates the business of insurance, and the practices challenged are part of the business of insurance, the failure of the state to react to a particular practice does not affect the application of the McCarran-Ferguson Act"), *rev'd and remanded on other grounds*, 689 F.2d 840 (9th Cir. 1982), *cert. denied*, 462 U.S. 1133 (1983). *But see* United States v. Crocker Nat'l Corp., 656 F.2d 428, 452-53 (9th Cir. 1981) (McCarran does not apply because state law does not regulate the specific practices challenged under the federal antitrust laws), *rev'd on other grounds*, 462 U.S. 122 (1983); Reazin v. Blue Cross & Blue Shield, 663 F. Supp. 1360, 1404 (D. Kan. 1987) ("Congress did not intend, through [the McCarran Act] to foreclose all federal antitrust scrutiny of private conspiracies of insurers simply because a state has enacted generally comprehensive regulation."), *aff'd in part and remanded in part*, 899 F.2d 951 (10th Cir.), *cert. denied*, 110 S. Ct. 3241 (1990).

1028. 362 U.S. 293 (1960).

1029. *Id.* at 299; *see, e.g.*, Seasongood v. K&K Ins. Agency, 548 F.2d 729 (8th Cir. 1977); United States v. Chicago Title & Trust Co., 242 F. Supp. 56 (N.D. Ill. 1965). The Court had previously held, in FTC v. National Casualty Co., 357 U.S. 560 (1958), that state regulation prohibiting deceptive advertising by companies within their respective borders was sufficient to exempt the advertising practices governed by such statutes from the jurisdiction of the Federal Trade Commission.

1030. 362 U.S. at 297-99; *see In re* Insurance Antitrust Litig., 938 F.2d 919, 928 (9th Cir. 1991) ("established law blocks regulation by one state of the United States of the insurance business outside the borders of that state"); *see also* American Gen. Ins. Co. v. FTC, 359 F. Supp. 887, 894-96 (S.D. Tex. 1973) (McCarran Act does not preclude federal antitrust scrutiny of insurance company mergers, even when those mergers are regulated by the relevant states, because the territorial limits on the individual state's regulation make that regulation inadequate), *aff'd on other grounds*, 496 F.2d 197 (5th Cir. 1974); *In re* Aviation Ins. Indus., 183 F. Supp. 374 (S.D.N.Y. 1960) (when unlawful activities of insurance companies would be practiced and have impact in all states, one state's "complete" regulation does not warrant exemption); American Gen. Ins. Co., 89 F.T.C. 557, 619-20 (1977) (same), *rev'd and remanded on other grounds*, 589 F.2d 462 (9th Cir. 1979), *complaint dismissed*, 97 F.T.C. 339 (1981); Statesman Life Ins. Co., 74 F.T.C. 1322 (1968) (mail order insurer's deceptive trade practices not effectively "regulated" when the laws of another state must be resorted to for enforcement purposes).

within the meaning of Section 3(b) of the Act.[1031]   Before the Supreme Court's decision in *St. Paul Fire & Marine Insurance Co. v. Barry*,[1032] conflict existed among the circuits as to whether Section 3(b) was limited to boycotts or concerted activity directed against competing insurers or agents, or could apply to boycotts of policyholders as well.[1033]   *Barry* involved a suit by physicians against four malpractice insurers, three of which allegedly had agreed not to offer insurance on any terms to the customers or former customers of the remaining insurer. The Court construed the term "boycott" broadly, holding that it should "be read in light of" the "tradition of meaning" under the Sherman Act,[1034] and rejected the defendants' argument that it reached only activities intended to coerce competitors rather than policyholders. The Court reasoned that "[t]he generic concept of boycott refers to a method of pressuring a party with whom one has a dispute by withholding, or enlisting others to withhold, patronage or services from the target."[1035]

Lower courts, however, have divided over the precise scope of a "boycott" for purposes of the Section 3(b) exemption even after *Barry*.[1036]   Some courts have

---

1031.   Section 3(b) provides that nothing in the McCarran Act shall render the Sherman Act inapplicable to boycotts and other acts of coercion and intimidation. Section 3(b) does not apply to the Clayton and Federal Trade Commission Acts. 15 U.S.C. § 1013(b) (1988).

1032.   438 U.S. 531 (1978).

1033.   *Compare* Meicler v. Aetna Casualty & Sur. Co., 506 F.2d 732, 734 (5th Cir. 1975) (boycott exception was designed to reach insurance company blacklists rather than concerted refusal to deal with the public on other than specified terms) *and* Addrisi v. Equitable Life Assurance Soc'y, 503 F.2d 725, 729 (9th Cir. 1974) (same) *with* Barry v. St. Paul Fire & Marine Ins. Co., 555 F.2d 3, 7-8 (1st Cir. 1977) (concerted refusal by a number of insurance companies to sell policies on certain terms fits within the unambiguous language of McCarran Act boycott exemption), *aff'd*, 438 U.S. 531 (1978); Monarch Life Ins. Co. v. Loyal Protective Life Ins. Co., 326 F.2d 841 (2d Cir. 1963) (same), *cert. denied*, 376 U.S. 952 (1964) *and* Frankford Hosp. v. Blue Cross, 417 F. Supp. 1104, 1111 (E.D. Pa. 1976) (court notes uncertainty in caselaw regarding whether "boycott" extends to boycotts of persons other than insurance companies and insurance agents), *aff'd per curiam*, 554 F.2d 1253 (3d Cir.), *cert. denied*, 434 U.S. 860 (1977).

1034.   438 U.S. at 541 (footnote omitted).

1035.   *Id.*

1036.   *See, e.g.*, In re Insurance Antitrust Litig., 938 F.2d 919, 930 (9th Cir. 1991) (McCarran defense not available where defendants alleged to have engaged in boycott and coercion by agreeing to refuse reinsurance to nonconforming insurers, and by coercing insurers to adopt the terms defendants wanted); *In re* Workers' Compensation Ins. Antitrust Litig., 867 F.2d 1552, 1562-63 (8th Cir. 1989) (question of fact existed whether there was an express agreement to exclude insurers from membership in rate setting bureau if the prescribed rates were not utilized, and whether acts of intimidation and coercion were used to maintain uniform rates by all workers' compensation carriers), *cert. denied*, 492 U.S. 920 (1989); Feinstein v. Nettleship Co., 714 F.2d 928, 933-34 (9th Cir. 1983) (no boycott established), *cert. denied*, 466 U.S. 972 (1984); Blackburn v. Crum & Forster, 611 F.2d 102 (5th Cir.) (same), *cert. denied*, 447 U.S. 906 (1980); Bartholomew v. Virginia Chiropractors Ass'n, 612 F.2d 812 (4th Cir. 1979) (same), *cert. denied*, 446 U.S. 938 (1980); Card v. National Life Ins. Co., 603 F.2d 828 (10th Cir. 1979) (same); Grant v. Erie Ins. Exch., 542 F. Supp. 457 (M.D. Pa. 1982) (no boycott involved when insurers agree to fix terms of coverage and to commonly interpret language in a No Fault statute), *aff'd mem.*, 716 F.2d 890 (3d Cir.), *cert. denied*, 464 U.S. 938 (1983); Quality Auto Body, Inc. v. Allstate Ins. Co., 1980-2 Trade Cas. (CCH) ¶ 63,507 (N.D. Ill. 1980) (no boycott established), *aff'd*, 660 F.2d 1195 (7th Cir. 1981), *cert. denied*, 455 U.S. 1020 (1982); *see also* Malley-Duff & Assocs. v. Crown Life Ins. Co., 734 F.2d 133, 144 (3d Cir.) ("to the extent that . . . appellees' conduct constituted a group boycott, appellees may not use McCarran-Ferguson as a shield"), *cert. denied*, 469 U.S. 1072 (1984); James M. King & Assocs. v. G.D. Van Wagenen Co., 717 F. Supp. 667 (D. Minn. 1989) (refusal to deal with plaintiff insurance agents at behest of defendant competitor of plaintiff was an illicit boycott

extrapolated from the total refusal to deal involved in *Barry* a requirement that a boycott be absolute,[1037] while other courts have held that an absolute refusal to deal on any terms is not required for concerted action to constitute a boycott.[1038] In addition, the Supreme Court's decision in *Barry* left the meaning of Section 3(b)'s other terms — "coercion" and "intimidation" — unresolved.[1039]

---

of coercive nature); Weatherby v. RCA Corp., 1988-1 Trade Cas. (CCH) ¶ 68,078, at 58,543 n.8 (N.D.N.Y. 1986) (plaintiffs' boycott claim fails because plaintiffs failed to show concerted action, among two or more persons, to drive plaintiffs from life insurance market); Maryland v. Blue Cross & Blue Shield Ass'n, 620 F. Supp. 907, 921-22 (D. Md. 1985) (territorial market division by defendant nonprofit health insurers does not constitute a boycott as the term is ordinarily used in antitrust analysis and, therefore, is not within the exception to McCarran-Ferguson); UNR Indus. v. Continental Ins. Co., 607 F. Supp. 855, 862 (N.D. Ill. 1984) (an agreement to refuse to issue an occurrence policy (to change to a new type of policy) "is not a boycott and does not constitute coercion or intimidation"); Hopping v. Standard Life Ins. Co., 1984-1 Trade Cas. (CCH) ¶ 65,814, at 67,413-14 (N.D. Miss. 1983) (no boycott without concert of action; "[t]ermination of agents for violations of 'exclusive agency' provisions, 'covenants not to compete,' and 'nonsolicitation agreements' do not constitute 'boycott' within the § 1013(b) exception to McCarran-Ferguson").

1037.   See, e.g., UNR Indus. v. Continental Ins. Co., 607 F. Supp. 855 (N.D. Ill. 1984); Grant v. Erie Ins. Exch., 542 F. Supp. 457 (N.D. Pa. 1982), aff'd mem., 716 F.2d 890 (3d Cir.), cert. denied, 464 U.S. 438 (1983); Hahn v. Oregon Physicians' Serv., 508 F. Supp. 970, 975 (D. Or. 1981) (to qualify for boycott exemption, concerted activity must foreclose competition anywhere in the relevant market), rev'd and remanded on other grounds, 689 F.2d 840 (9th Cir. 1982), cert. denied, 462 U.S. 1133 (1983); Pireno v. New York State Chiropractic Ass'n, 1979-2 Trade Cas. (CCH) ¶ 62,758 (S.D.N.Y. 1979), rev'd and remanded on other grounds, 650 F.2d 387 (2d Cir. 1981), aff'd sub nom. Union Labor Life Ins. Co. v. Pireno, 458 U.S. 119 (1982).

1038.   See In re Insurance Antitrust Litig., 938 F.2d 919, 930 (9th Cir. 1991) ("[t]he evil of a boycott is not its absolute character but the use of the economic power of a third party to force the boycott victim to agree to the boycott beneficiary's terms"); Nurse Midwifery Assocs. v. Hibbett, 549 F. Supp. 1185, 1191-92 (M.D. Tenn. 1982) (denial of medical malpractice coverage to plaintiffs for the purpose of restraining competition in the maternity services market could be a boycott); Workman v. State Farm Mut. Auto Ins. Co., 520 F. Supp. 610, 623 (N.D. Cal. 1981) (no boycott found, although fact that boycott is not absolute is not dispositive) (quoting Proctor v. State Farm Mut. Auto. Ins. Co., 561 F.2d 262, 267 (D.C. Cir. 1977), vacated and remanded in light of Royal Drug, 440 U.S. 942 (1979), on remand, 1980-81 Trade Cas. (CCH) ¶ 63,591 (D.D.C. 1980), aff'd, 675 F.2d 308 (D.C. Cir.), cert. denied, 459 U.S. 839 (1982)).

1039.   The Court stated that, in light of its holdings that the activity at issue constituted a "boycott," there was no need to reach the issue of whether the conduct amounted to "coercion" or "intimidation" under § 3(b). 438 U.S. at 541 n.10; see Ocean State Physicians Health Plan v. Blue Cross & Blue Shield, 883 F.2d 1101, 1109 (1st Cir. 1989) (plaintiffs' claims do not amount to allegations of "coercion" under the McCarran Act since, although plaintiffs may face higher costs as a result of defendant's policy, no allegation that policy left plaintiffs with no choice in the matter), cert. denied, 494 U.S. 1027 (1990); Travelers Ins. Co. v. Blue Cross, 481 F.2d 80 (3d Cir.) (finding defendant's actions did not amount to coercion), cert. denied, 414 U.S. 1093 (1973); Weatherby v. RCA Corp., 1988-1 Trade Cas. (CCH) ¶ 68,078, at 58,544 (N.D.N.Y. 1986) (unlike boycott claim, coercion and intimidation under McCarran Act do not require showing of concerted action; plaintiffs sufficiently alleged facts which could constitute coercion or intimidation to withstand summary judgment); Hopping v. Standard Life Ins. Co., 1984-1 Trade Cas. (CCH) ¶ 65,814, at 67,413 (N.D. Miss. 1983) (only such coercion and intimidation that would constitute an agreement or act of boycott is within the exception to the exemption; "[t]ermination, or threatened termination, of an agent pursuant to an otherwise lawful exclusive dealing contract or agency agreement is not 'coercion or intimidation' [under] McCarran-Ferguson"); Ray v. United Family Life Ins. Co., 430 F. Supp. 1353 (W.D.N.C. 1977) (finding McCarran-Ferguson Act inapplicable because defendant's actions constituted "coercion" within the meaning of § 3(b)).

7. *Organized Labor*

Certain agreements and activities involving labor are immune from the antitrust laws on the basis of statutory and nonstatutory exemptions. The statutory exemption applies to the right of workers to organize to eliminate competition among themselves and extends only to certain types of activities that workers undertake unilaterally in their own interests. The nonstatutory exemption applies to agreements or concerted action between employees or their labor organizations and employers or other nonlabor entities when the agreement or action is appropriate to achieve the objectives of national labor policy and does not have an unwarranted anticompetitive impact on the business market.

a. THE STATUTORY EXEMPTION

Prior to passage of the Clayton Act in 1914, courts generally held concerted activities by employees aimed at obtaining union recognition to be illegal. In 1908, in *Loewe v. Lawlor* (the Danbury Hatters case),[1040] the Supreme Court held that a union violated the Sherman Act when it organized a nationwide secondary boycott of nonunion-made hats as part of an organizational strike against a hat manufacturer. Congress responded in 1914 by granting, as part of the Clayton Act,[1041] specific exemptions from the antitrust laws for certain conduct arising out of a "labor dispute." Section 6 of the Clayton Act states:

> The labor of a human being is not a commodity or article of commerce. Nothing contained in the antitrust laws shall be construed to forbid the existence and operation of labor . . . organizations, . . . or to forbid or restrain individual members of such organizations from lawfully carrying out the legitimate objects thereof; nor shall such organizations, or the members thereof, be held or construed to be illegal combinations or conspiracies in restraint of trade, under the antitrust laws.[1042]

Section 20 of the Clayton Act prohibits the issuance of federal injunctions against strikes, boycotts, or picketing "in any case between an employer and employees, or between employees, or between persons employed and persons seeking employment, involving, or growing out of, a dispute concerning terms or conditions of employment," and concludes with the broad prohibition that none "of the acts specified in this paragraph be considered or held to be violations of any law of the United States."[1043] Notwithstanding these provisions, however, the Supreme Court in *Duplex Printing Press Co. v. Deering*[1044] upheld an injunction against a secondary boycott conducted by all union members against the goods of an employer. The Court held that the immunity granted by the Clayton Act was limited solely to the collective action by employees of the employer with whom the labor dispute existed.[1045]

Congress responded to *Duplex Printing* and other antitrust decisions narrowly

---

1040.   208 U.S. 274 (1908).

1041.   Act of Oct. 15, 1914, ch. 323, § 6, 38 Stat. 731 (codified at 15 U.S.C. § 17 (1988)).

1042   15 U.S.C. § 17 (1988).

1043.   Act of Oct. 15, 1914, ch. 323, § 20, 38 Stat. 738 (codified at 29 U.S.C. § 52 (1988)).

1044.   254 U.S. 443 (1921).

1045.   *Id.*; *see also* Bedford Cut Stone Co. v. Journeymen Stone Cutters' Ass'n, 274 U.S. 37 (1927).

construing the Clayton Act exemption by enacting the Norris-LaGuardia Act,[1046] which was intended "to restore the broad purpose which Congress thought it had formulated in the Clayton Act but which was frustrated, so Congress believed, by unduly restrictive judicial construction."[1047] The Norris-LaGuardia Act deprives the federal courts of jurisdiction to issue injunctions "in a case involving or growing out of a labor dispute," except where unlawful acts are threatened or committed.[1048] The protection of the Norris-LaGuardia Act extends to all persons "participating or interested" in a labor dispute — including any member of the union whose members are involved in the dispute.[1049]

After Congress passed Section 20 of the Clayton Act and the Norris-LaGuardia Act, the Supreme Court in *United States v. Hutcheson*[1050] articulated the scope of the antitrust exemption in the following terms:

> The Norris-LaGuardia Act reasserted the original purpose of the Clayton Act by infusing into it the immunized trade union activities as redefined by the later Act. In this light § 20 removes all such allowable conduct from the taint of being a "violation of any law of the United States," including the Sherman Law.[1051]

Although the labor exemption is broad, it has not been interpreted to immunize labor or union activity in all circumstances. In *Hutcheson*, the Court suggested that the exemption applied "[s]o long as a union acts in its self-interest and does not combine with non-labor groups."[1052]

In *American Federation of Musicians v. Carroll*,[1053] the Supreme Court held that in determining whether a group is a "labor group," and therefore covered by the exemption, a court must examine the degree of economic interrelationship between that group and the union on matters of legitimate union concern and evaluate the extent to which the challenged union practice relates to those legitimate concerns. The *Carroll* case involved agreements between orchestra leaders and musicians that imposed broad restrictions on orchestra leaders, including restrictions on the hiring and paying of musicians and the use of booking agents. The orchestra leaders sought to invalidate the agreements by arguing that the leaders constituted a nonlabor group and thus were subject to the antitrust laws. The Supreme Court approved the district court's use of an "economic interrelationship" test and sustained its findings that the "orchestra leaders performed work and functions which actually or potentially affected the hours, wages, job security, and working conditions of [the labor union's] members."[1054] These were matters of traditional, legitimate union

---

1046. Act of Mar. 23, 1932, ch. 90, §§ 1-15, 47 Stat. 70-73 (codified at 29 U.S.C. §§ 101-110, 113-115 (1988)).

1047. United States v. Hutcheson, 312 U.S. 219, 236 (1941).

1048. 29 U.S.C. §§ 101, 107 (1988).

1049. *Id.* at §§ 104, 105, 113(b). The Norris-LaGuardia Act has been held to insulate unions from Sherman Act injunctive relief in cases involving labor disputes. *See, e.g.*, Utilities Servs. Eng'g, Inc. v. Colorado Bldg. & Constr. Trades Council, 549 F.2d 173 (10th Cir. 1977).

1050. 312 U.S. 219 (1941).

1051. *Id.* at 236.

1052. *Id.* at 232.

1053. 391 U.S. 99 (1968).

1054. *Id.* at 106. The Supreme Court reaffirmed the "economic interrelationship" test in H.A. Artists & Assocs. v. Actors' Equity Ass'n, 451 U.S. 704 (1981).

concern. Because the orchestra leaders and musicians competed with each other in the same labor market, orchestra leaders constituted a "labor group" subject to union pressures to maintain labor standards among its own membership. The Court also held that the prohibition against dealing with unlicensed booking agents was justified, despite the lack of competition between musicians and booking agents, because of the effect that the higher fees charged by unlicensed agents would have on musicians' wages.[1055]

b. THE NONSTATUTORY EXEMPTION

While the statutory exemption has been limited to the legitimate organizing and other unilateral activities of employees and their labor unions, the courts have developed a "nonstatutory" exemption that applies to concerted activities of and agreements between labor and nonlabor parties. The "nonstatutory" labor exemption is designed to accommodate the national labor policy and the antitrust laws. In most cases in which the exemption is applied, the concerted activities and agreements arise in a collective-bargaining setting, are intimately related to a mandatory subject of bargaining, and do not have "a potential for restraining competition in the business market in ways that would not follow naturally from elimination of competition over wages and working conditions."[1056]

The Supreme Court's most extensive discussion of the nonstatutory exemption is in *Connell Construction Co. v. Plumbers & Steamfitters Local Union No. 100*.[1057] After tracing the history of the labor exemptions through three landmark cases, *Allen Bradley Co. v. Local 3, International Brotherhood of Electrical Workers*,[1058] *United Mine Workers v. Pennington*,[1059] and *Local 189, Amalgamated Meat Cutters v. Jewel Tea Co.*,[1060] the Court explained the rationale for the nonstatutory exemption:

> The nonstatutory exemption has its source in the strong labor policy favoring the association of employees to eliminate competition over wages and working conditions. Union success in organizing workers and standardizing wages ultimately will affect price competition among employers, but the goals of federal labor law never could be achieved if this effect on business competition were held a violation of the antitrust laws. The Court therefore has acknowledged that labor policy requires tolerance for the lessening of business competition based on differences in wages and working conditions.[1061]

As the Court also observed, however, the scope of the exemption is not unlimited:

> Labor policy clearly does not require, however, that a union have freedom to impose direct restraints on competition among those who employ its members. Thus, while the statutory exemption allows unions to accomplish some restraints by acting unilaterally, the

---

1055.   391 U.S. at 113.
1056.   Connell Constr. Co. v. Plumbers & Steamfitters Local Union No. 100, 421 U.S. 616, 635 (1975).
1057.   *Id.*
1058.   325 U.S. 797 (1945).
1059.   381 U.S. 657 (1965).
1060.   381 U.S. 676 (1965).
1061.   421 U.S. at 622.

nonstatutory exemption offers no similar protection when a union and a nonlabor party agree to restrain competition in a business market.[1062]

In *Connell*, a union representing plumbing and mechanical workers picketed Connell, a general contractor, to secure an agreement whereby Connell would subcontract plumbing and mechanical work only to firms that had a current contract with the union. The union did not represent or seek to represent any of Connell's employees. Connell signed the agreement under protest and then brought suit for a declaratory judgment and injunctive relief, alleging violations of Sections 1 and 2 of the Sherman Act and of state antitrust laws. The district court held that the subcontracting agreement was exempt from the antitrust laws because it was authorized by the construction industry proviso in Section 8(e) of the National Labor Relations Act.[1063] The Fifth Circuit affirmed.[1064]

The Supreme Court reversed in a five to four decision, holding that the restrictive subcontracting agreement with a "stranger" contractor was not authorized under the labor laws and was not exempt from antitrust scrutiny.[1065] The Court emphasized the broad anticompetitive effect of the subcontracting agreement, noting that the union had been able to secure such agreements with other general contractors in the area in additional to Connell.[1066] The Court also noted that the effect of these agreements went beyond the elimination of competition in wages, hours, and working conditions by excluding from the bidding process subcontractors whose lower bids might result from cost efficiencies unrelated to the wages they paid to their nonunion employees.[1067] Thus, while the sole purpose of the subcontracting agreement appeared to be to organize as many subcontractor employees as possible,[1068] the effect was to insulate union subcontracting firms from all types of competition — not merely wage competition.[1069] The Court found this to be a substantial anticompetitive effect on the subcontracting business market that did not follow naturally from the collective-bargaining process. The Court concluded, therefore, that "[t]he federal policy favoring collective bargaining" could "offer no shelter" to the union's activities.[1070]

In order to invoke the nonstatutory exemption, the parties must have standing to

---

1062. *Id.* at 622-23 (citations omitted).

1063. *See id.* at 633-35.

1064. 483 F.2d 1154 (5th Cir. 1973).

1065. 421 U.S. at 633-35. In Kaiser Steel Corp. v. Mullins, 455 U.S. 72, 85 (1982), the Court commented that in *Connell* it was necessary to decide the § 8(e) issue first in order "to determine whether the agreement was immune from the antitrust laws." But, as the Ninth Circuit observed in Richards v. Nielsen Freight Lines, 810 F.2d 898, 906 (9th Cir. 1987), "[t]he Supreme Court's consideration [in *Connell*], however, of the actual and potential anticompetitive effects of the agreement independently of the violation of section 158(e) [§ 8(e)] suggests that the presence of a section 158(e) violation may not itself decide the exemption issue."

1066. 421 U.S. at 623.

1067. *Id.* at 624.

1068. *Id.* at 625.

1069. *Id.* at 624.

1070. *Id.* at 626. The Court also rejected the union's argument that Congress intended to make the NLRA remedies exclusive, thereby precluding liability under the antitrust laws. However, the Court did agree that the federal labor law preempts state antitrust claims provided the union activity "is closely related to organizational goals." *Id.* at 637.

sue. In *Associated General Contractors, Inc. v. California State Council of Carpenters*,[1071] the Supreme Court held that a union lacked antitrust standing under Section 4 of the Clayton Act to challenge the efforts of a multiemployer collective bargaining association to encourage and coerce others to use nonunion contractors.[1072] The Court noted that unions acting in their collective bargaining capacity rarely will be appropriate parties under the antitrust laws to sue employers with which they bargain because "[f]ederal policy has since developed . . . a broad labor exemption from the antitrust laws . . . ."[1073]

In *In re Detroit Auto Dealers Association v. FTC*,[1074] the Sixth Circuit held that the nonstatutory exemption did not protect an agreement between auto dealers to restrict automobile showroom hours. In deferring to the FTC's "'informed judgment'" in dealing with alleged unfair and anticompetitive conduct, the court endorsed the Commission's decision that the dealers' agreement to restrict showroom hours, though responsive to salesmen violence and pressure, was not generally "a direct product of employer collective bargaining, nor of arm's length dealing with salespersons."[1075] The court, however, did remand to the Commission for further consideration whether the exemption would apply to the closings by dealers which "may be entitled to claim an exemption under the circumstances of bona fide collective bargaining with a union for shorter showroom hours or as a direct result of *union directed* violence and force for shorter showroom hours."[1076]

Lower courts have interpreted the nonstatutory exemption to protect a wide variety of labor-nonlabor agreements and activities from antitrust scrutiny.[1077] *Powell v. NFL*,[1078] involved a challenge by the NFL Players Association to the provision in the expired collective bargaining agreement with the NFL team owners which restrained a player's ability to sign with other teams, commonly referred to as "free agency." In granting the players' motion for partial summary judgment, the district court held that the nonstatutory exemption did not protect the owners' restraint on players' ability to sell their services when the collective bargaining agreement had expired and the parties had reached an impasse in their negotiations.[1079] On interlocutory appeal, the Eighth Circuit reversed, holding that "the antitrust laws are inapplicable under the circumstances of this case as the nonstatutory labor exemption

---

1071. 459 U.S. 519 (1983).
1072. *Id.* at 535-42. For a discussion of the standing requirements under § 4, see Part C of Chapter VIII of this treatise.
1073. *Id.* at 539.
1074. 1992-1 Trade Cas. (CCH) ¶ 69,696, at 67,158 (8th Cir. 1991).
1075. *Id.* at 67,166.
1076. *Id.* at 67,167 (emphasis in original).
1077. Cannon v. Teamsters & Chauffeurs Union, Local 627, 657 F.2d 173 (7th Cir. 1981); Larry V. Muko, Inc. v. Southwestern Pa. Bldg. & Constr. Trades Council, 609 F.2d 1368 (3d Cir. 1979) (en banc), *appeal after remand*, 670 F.2d 431 (3d Cir.), *cert. denied*, 459 U.S. 916 (1982); Consolidated Express, Inc. v. New York Shipping Ass'n, 602 F.2d 494 (3d Cir. 1979), *vacated sub nom.* International Longshoremen's Ass'n v. Consolidated Express, Inc., 448 U.S. 901 (1980), *modified*, 641 F.2d 90 (3d Cir.), *mandamus denied*, 451 U.S. 905 (1981); Home Box Office, Inc. v. Directors Guild of Am., Inc., 531 F. Supp. 578 (S.D.N.Y. 1982), *aff'd per curiam*, 708 F.2d 95 (2d Cir. 1983).
1078. 888 F.2d 559 (8th Cir. 1989), *cert. denied*, 111 S. Ct. 711 (1991).
1079. Powell v. NFL, 690 F. Supp. 812 (D. Minn. 1988) (Powell II); *see also* Powell v. NFL, 678 F. Supp. 777 (D. Minn. 1988) (Powell I).

extends beyond impasse."[1080]

In *Wood v. NBA*,[1081] a player selected in the first round of the NBA draft challenged under Section 1 of the Sherman Act the collective bargaining agreement between the players' association and the team owners. Wood alleged that the agreement limited his ability to sell his services to the highest bidder of his choice, imposed a cap on his earnings, and applied to him despite the fact that the agreement was executed before he was drafted. Relying primarily on the federal labor law policy favoring collective bargaining agreements, the Second Circuit held that Wood's claim under the antitrust laws "must be rejected out of hand."[1082] The court noted that it was common for unions through collective bargaining agreements to seek the best deal for the greatest number of employees at the expense of some employees who could do better individually, including those not within the bargaining unit at the time the agreement was executed.[1083] After declaring that the player restraints were, as in *Connell*, "intimately related to 'wages, hours, and other terms and conditions of employment,' "[1084] the court distinguished *Connell* by holding that the restraint alleged by Wood affected only the labor market, and therefore the antitrust laws did not apply.[1085]

Section 8(e) of the National Labor Relations Act continues to generate controversies involving the applicability of the nonstatutory exemption.[1086] In

---

1080.   888 F.2d at 568.

1081.   809 F.2d 954 (2d Cir. 1987).

1082.   *Id.* at 959.

1083.   *Id.*

1084.   *Id.* at 962.

1085.   *Id.* at 963. For other cases involving the nonstatutory labor exemption in professional sports, see Powell v. NFL, 690 F. Supp. 812 (D. Minn. 1988); Powell v. NFL, 678 F. Supp. 777 (D. Minn. 1988); Bridgeman v. NBA, 675 F. Supp. 960 (D.N.J. 1987) (restrictions in collective bargaining agreement do not necessarily lose exemption upon expiration of agreement); Zimmerman v. NFL, 632 F. Supp. 398 (D.D.C. 1986).

In Mackey v. NFL, 543 F.2d 606, 614 (8th Cir. 1976), *cert. dismissed*, 434 U.S. 801 (1977), the Eighth Circuit articulated a three-part test and denied the exemption to unilateral agreements by employers because the third requirement was not satisfied. For the exemption to apply under the *Mackey* test: (1) the restraint on trade must affect primarily the parties to the agreement; (2) the employee agreement must concern a mandatory subject of collective bargaining; and (3) the agreement must be the result of bona fide, arm's-length bargaining. The *Mackey* test was not applied by the Eighth Circuit three years later in Amalgamated Meat Cutters, Local 476 v. Wetterau Foods, Inc., 597 F.2d 133 (8th Cir. 1979) (applying the exemption to joint employer activity opposing striking employees of one employer). *Compare* McCourt v. California Sports, Inc., 600 F.2d 1193 (6th Cir. 1979) (*Mackey* test applied to team owners' agreement restraining professional hockey player) *with* Detroit Newspaper Publishers Ass'n v. Detroit Typographical Union No. 18, 471 F.2d 872 (6th Cir. 1972) (applying exemption without adopting *Mackey* test), *cert. denied*, 411 U.S. 967 (1973). The *Mackey* test was relied upon to apply the exemption in Continental Maritime, Inc. v. Pacific Coast Metal Trades Dist. Council, 817 F.2d 1391 (9th Cir. 1987) (summary judgment for union defendants upheld on Sherman Act charge of conspiracy to make wage concessions for defendant shipyards).

1086.   Section 8(e) of the NLRA, 29 U.S.C. § 158(e) (1988), provides in part:

It shall be an unfair labor practice for any labor organization and any employer to enter into any contract or agreement, express or implied, whereby such employer ceases or refrains or agrees to cease or refrain from handling, using, selling, transporting or otherwise dealing in any of the products of any other employer, or to cease doing business with any other person, and any contract or agreement entered into heretofore or hereafter containing such an agreement shall be to such extent unenforceable and void: Provided, That nothing

Local 210, Laborers' International Union v. Labor Relations Division Associated General Contractors, Inc.,[1087] the union filed suit to enforce an arbitration clause against the employer and the employer association of general contractors. The contractor-defendants counterclaimed contending that the collective bargaining agreement clause that prohibited subcontracting work to *or from* the employer violated Sections 1 and 2 of the Sherman Act. The district court granted the union's motion for summary judgment and held that the clause was protected by the construction industry proviso of Section 8(e). The Second Circuit affirmed, but unlike the district court, held that although the clause was legal under the proviso, this did not necessarily mean it was beyond the reach of the antitrust laws, unless the clause was exempted under the nonstatutory exemption. Applying the exemption, the Second Circuit modified the *Mackey* test:

> In assessing whether any particular agreement is protected by the nonstatutory exemption, the " 'crucial determinant is not the form of the agreement . . . but its relative impact on the product market and the interests of union members.' " In essence, the test is one that balances the conflicting policies embodied in the labor and antitrust laws, with the policies inherent in labor law serving as the first point of reference. First, the agreement at issue must further goals that are protected by national labor law and that are within the scope of traditionally mandatory subjects of collective bargaining. Second, the agreement must not impose a "direct restraint on the business market [that] has substantial anticompetitive effects, both actual and potential, that would not follow naturally from the elimination of competition over wages and working conditions [that results from collective bargaining agreements]."[1088]

In *Richards v. Nielsen Freight Lines,*[1089] a local trucking firm named Foothills was targeted for organization by the union. Foothills claimed that the larger, unionized trucking firms conspired to boycott it as a result of coercion by and separate agreements with the union. The Ninth Circuit affirmed summary judgment in favor of the defendant trucking firms on the ground that the plaintiff failed to raise a triable issue of conspiracy.[1090] The court also applied the nonstatutory exemption to the antitrust claims against the union, even though the union agreements with the employers were not part of collective bargaining agreements:

> In *Connell,* before finding that the nonstatutory exemption did not apply, the court made an extensive analysis of the anticompetitive effect of the challenged contract, which was not a collective bargaining agreement. Such analysis would have been unnecessary if the nonstatutory exemptions were limited to restraints imposed by collective bargaining agreements . . . . We understand *Connell* to hold that the nonstatutory exemption is unavailable to shield agreements reached outside the context of collective bargaining where the challenged action imposes direct restraints on a business market, which restraints are

---

in this subsection shall apply to an agreement between a labor organization and an employer in the construction industry relating to the contracting or subcontracting of work to be done at the site of the construction, alteration, painting, or repair of a building, structure, or other work . . . .

1087.   844 F.2d 69 (2d Cir. 1988).
1088.   *Id.* at 79-80 (citations omitted).
1089.   810 F.2d 898 (9th Cir. 1987).
1090.   *Id.* at 902-04.

not related in economics to the elimination of competition over wages and working conditions.[1091]

The court also applied the exemption even though the union-led action may have violated 29 U.S.C. § 158(b)(4)(B), prohibiting secondary boycotts, and 29 U.S.C. § 158(e), prohibiting "hot cargo" contracts. The court held:

> The Supreme Court's consideration, however, of the actual and potential anticompetitive effects of the agreement independently of the violation of Section 158(e) suggests that the presence of a Section 158(e) violation may not itself decide the exemption issue. . . . *Connell* does not suggest that every violation of Section 158(e) gives rise to an antitrust suit. It is not paradoxical that a labor law violation may still be within the antitrust exemption, for the violation will carry its own remedies under the labor laws, although we recognize that in some cases the violation of the labor laws may involve conduct whose consequences are so far-reaching that it falls outside the exemption. Where, as here, there is no showing the alleged agreements posed actual or potential anticompetitive risks other than those related to a reduction in competitive advantages based on differential wages or working conditions, the nonstatutory labor exemption prevents antitrust scrutiny of the union activity.[1092]

In *Sun-Land Nurseries, Inc. v. Southern California District Council of Laborers*,[1093] a landscaping contractor's collective bargaining agreement contained a Section 8(e) provision prohibiting subcontracting with nonunion and "other union" subcontractors. Sun-Land sought to invalidate the clause as illegal under Section 8(e) and under Sections 1 and 2 of the Sherman Act. The district court granted the union's motion for summary judgment. The Ninth Circuit, en banc, affirmed. The court held first that the clause did not violate Section 8(e). In deciding whether the summary judgment based on the nonstatutory exemption was correct, the court held that although the exemption may not protect Section 8(e) clauses if they are instruments of an antitrust conspiracy,[1094] a valid Section 8(e) clause standing alone "cannot serve as the basis of an antitrust claim."[1095]

8. *Transportation*

a. MOTOR CARRIERS

The extent of regulation of the motor carrier industry[1096] by the Interstate

---

1091.   *Id.* at 905.
1092.   *Id.* at 906.
1093.   793 F.2d 1110 (9th Cir. 1986) (en banc), *cert. denied*, 479 U.S. 1090 (1987).
1094.   *Id.* at 1117.
1095.   *Id.* In Altemose Construction Co. v. Building and Construction Trades Council, 751 F.2d 653 (3d Cir. 1985), *cert. denied*, 475 U.S. 1107 (1986), the Third Circuit reversed a summary judgment for the defendant union based upon the nonstatutory exemption because the record raised an issue as to the legality under the labor laws of agreements with union contractors to boycott nonunion contractors and the legality of coercion directed against nonunion contractors in support of those agreements.
1096.   The motor carrier industry consists of private and "for hire" carriers. Private carriers, companies that carry their own goods using their own vehicles, have never been subject to economic regulation. "For hire" carriers that transport agricultural products or perform local pickup and delivery services are also exempt from ICC regulation. Regulated "for hire" motor carriers fall

Commerce Commission (ICC) has changed substantially since 1980. In the first four decades of regulation under the Motor Carrier Act of 1935, competition was extremely limited by regulatory policies that established, in effect, a presumption against new entry or expansion.[1097] In addition, all motor carrier rates were subject to ICC approval and most were established by rate bureaus — associations of motor carriers allowed collectively to set rates with antitrust immunity.[1098]

After the Supreme Court's decision in 1974 in *Bowman Transportation, Inc. v. Arkansas-Best Freight System*[1099] which stressed the importance of competition as a regulatory consideration, the ICC began to ease the requirements for new entry into the industry as well as for expansion by existing carriers. In the Motor Carrier Act of 1980 (1980 Act),[1100] Congress essentially endorsed, codified, and extended the ICC's movement toward deregulation. The 1980 Act did not entirely deregulate motor carriers. Under the 1980 Act an applicant for new or expanded authority must prove it is "fit, willing, and able" to provide the service and the existence of a "public purpose" for the authority.[1101] The 1980 Act, however, amended the national transportation policy specifically to require the ICC "to promote competitive and efficient transportation services,"[1102] and specifically endorsed the ICC's policy that opponents of applications for authority must show not merely that they would be injured by diversion of traffic but that the public interest would be adversely affected by granting the new authority.[1103]

The 1980 Act also changed the ICC's regulation of rates. Motor common carriers still must file their rates with the ICC and adhere to the filed rates.[1104] A rate may become effective on one day's notice for rate reductions and on seven workdays' notice for rate increases.[1105] However, the ICC may not investigate, suspend,

---

into two groups — common carriers and contract carriers. A contract carrier does not file rates and charges with the ICC. Contracts with shippers must be for more than just a single trip. 49 C.F.R. § 1053 (1991). Common carrier rates and charges must be filed at the ICC.

1097. *See, e.g.*, J.H. Rose Truck Lines, 110 M.C.C. 180, 184-85 (1969) ("It has consistently been held that existing carriers should be afforded the opportunity to transport all the traffic which they can handle adequately, economically and efficiently in the territory they serve before a new service is authorized.").

1098. *See* H.R. REP. NO. 1069, 96th Cong., 2d Sess. 27 (1980). Antitrust immunity was conferred by the Reed-Bullwinkle Act of 1948, 49 U.S.C. § 5b(9) (1976), *partially repealed by* Pub. L. No. 95-473, § 4(b), (c), 92 Stat. 1377, 1466-70 (1978) (codified as amended at 49 U.S.C. § 10706(b) (1988)).

1099. 419 U.S. 281, 297-99 (1974).

1100. Pub. L. No. 96-296, 94 Stat. 793 (1980) (codified as amended in scattered sections of 49 U.S.C.).

1101. 49 U.S.C. § 10922(b)(1) (1988).

1102. *Id.* § 10101(a)(2).

1103. *Id.* § 10922(b)(2)(B). The ICC has noted that during the period between October 1988 and June 1989, only one out of 11,968 applications for motor carrier operating authority was denied, and only twenty-seven applications were even opposed. In recognition of this "extremely low protest rate," the ICC completely restructured and streamlined its regulations governing applications for motor carrier operating authority, making it relatively easy to obtain operating authority. *See* Rules Governing Applications for Operating Authority – Revisions of Form OP-1, 6 I.C.C.2d 266, 268 (1989) (amending 49 C.F.R. § 1160).

1104. 49 U.S.C. §§ 10761(a), 10762 (1988). In Maislin Industries, U.S. v. Primary Steel, Inc., 110 S. Ct. 2759 (1990), the Supreme Court overturned the ICC's "Negotiated Rates" policy, which permitted shippers to enforce privately negotiated rates that were lower than a motor common carrier's filed rates. The Court rejected the ICC's argument that its policy was supported by the procompetitive purposes of the 1980 Act. *Id.* at 2769-70.

1105. 49 C.F.R. § 1312.4 (1991).

revise or revoke an independently established rate on the ground it is unreasonably high or low if the rate is filed under the Zone of Ratemaking Freedom (ZORF) provision and is not more than 10% higher or lower than prior rates defined according to specified statutory benchmarks.[1106] The Commission has limited authority to change these percentages after taking into account the state of competition, among other factors.[1107] The ICC may regulate all common carrier rates with respect to reasonableness (except ZORF rates) and predation or discrimination (including ZORF rates).[1108]

As to rate bureaus, the 1980 Act provides that after January 1, 1984, no antitrust immunity exists for the collective discussion and setting of specific single line rates.[1109] Immunity continues, however, for collective discussion and setting of general rate increases or decreases, provided that adequate notice is given to the industry and public, that discussions are limited to industry average carrier costs as opposed to individual markets or particular single line rates, and that the ICC approves the rate change.[1110] Antitrust immunity also continues for commodity classification changes, tariff structure changes, and a variety of nonprice rate bureau activities.[1111]

Freight classification changes by carrier groups not specially relating to rates do not necessarily violate Section 1 of the Sherman Act. For example, in *National Classification Committee v. United States*[1112] the D.C. Circuit held that an ICC order defining the concept of freight classification matters contained in an agreement among motor carriers, and prohibiting member carriers from collectively charging $2.00 per shipment on "order-notify" shipments of ten thousand pounds or less based upon a rule or regulation governing classification matters, could not operate retroactively to impose antitrust liability on parties to the agreement because the ICC had consistently accepted rules and regulations of this type in the past. In *Jays Foods, Inc. v. National Classification Committee*,[1113] a district court held that the

---

1106.   49 U.S.C. § 10708(d)(1) (1988).

1107.   *Id.* § 10708(d)(4).

1108.   *Id.*

1109.   *Id.* § 10706(b)(3)(D). The original January 1 date was automatically extended to July 1, 1984. The 1980 Act places the burden of proof on the plaintiff in an antitrust case to show a violation of these provisions and provides that a mere showing of parallel behavior will not satisfy that burden. *Id.* § 10706(b)(3)(G). The ICC has concluded that the prohibition on collective single-line rate making encompasses any collective action on rates for services that are performed by a single carrier and are not a general rate change. Clark & Reid Co. v. United States, 851 F.2d 1468 (D.C. Cir. 1988); Niagara Frontier Tariff Bureau v. United States, 826 F.2d 1186 (2d Cir. 1987); Niagara Frontier Tariff Bureau v. United States, 1 I.C.C.2d 317 (1984), *aff'd per curiam*, 780 F.2d 109 (D.C. Cir. 1986).

1110.   49 U.S.C. § 10706(b)(3)(D) (1988). In part in response to the motor carrier industry's practice of applying for collectively-set general rate increases at the same time that individual carriers are offering widespread discounts to individual shippers, the ICC initiated a wide-ranging investigation to review the entire motor carrier ratemaking process, rate bureau activities, and rate discounting practices, including the practice of filing parallel independent action general rate increases following rate bureau discussions. *See* Investigation of Motor Carrier Collective Ratemaking and Related Procedures and Practices, Ex Parte No. MC-196 (July 10, 1990). The ICC's report in this proceeding, served May 31, 1991, concluded that there was no need for maximum rate regulation by the ICC. 7 I.C.C. 2d 388 (1991).

1111.   49 U.S.C. § 10706(b)(3)(D) (1988).

1112.   746 F.2d 886 (D.C. Cir. 1984).

1113.   646 F. Supp. 604 (E.D. Va. 1985), *aff'd*, 801 F.2d 394 (4th Cir. 1986).

mere publication by a motor carrier freight classification group of a freight classification (without reference to a rate) for a nonregulated commodity was not a per se violation of Section 1 of the Sherman Act. The court noted that: (1) while the classification was a useful tool in establishing rates, its function, purpose and effect did not operate to set prices; (2) the defendants' conduct of freight classification for commodities was not price fixing, or even an "attempt" to interfere with market forces; (3) the effect on competition of a classification publication cannot be discerned by any "quick look"; and (4) the classification system historically has not been regarded as an antitrust violation.

The 1980 Act also mandates a number of procedural changes in the rate bureau process and limits the scope of permissible rate bureau action.[1114] Rate bureaus must now meet certain conditions in order to qualify for ICC approval.[1115] For example, only carriers with operating authority over a particular route can vote on a rate proposal involving that route,[1116] and rate bureaus cannot protest the published tariff item of any motor carrier.[1117]

In *Southern Motor Carriers Rate Conference, Inc. v. United States*,[1118] the Supreme Court held that rate bureau intrastate collective ratemaking is immunized under the state action doctrine, if such ratemaking is expressly permitted and actively supervised by the state. A clearly articulated state policy permitting such conduct may be evidenced by state statutes[1119] or by a state regulatory program demonstrating that "the State as sovereign clearly intends to displace competition in a particular field with a regulatory structure."[1120]

Antitrust immunity is automatically extended to rate bureau agreements approved by the ICC.[1121] Statutory immunity does not necessarily exist, however, where all of the required procedures have not been followed,[1122] nor does it extend to agreements to eliminate competition by nonmembers of the bureau, or to coercing other bureau members to give up their right of independent action.[1123] In *Square D Co. v. Niagara Frontier Tariff Bureau*,[1124] the Supreme Court reaffirmed its holding in *Keogh v. Chicago & Northwestern Railway*[1125] that a private party may not recover damages based upon a tariff rate filed with the ICC. Private parties are prohibited by Section 16 of the Clayton Act from obtaining an injunction against an

---

1114.   49 U.S.C. § 10706(b)(3)(B) (1988). The rate bureau provisions of the 1980 Act are explained in and implemented by the ICC's decision in Motor Carrier Rate Bureaus – Implementation of Pub. L. No. 96-296, Ex Parte No. 297 (Sub-No. 5) (Dec. 19, 1980).

1115.   49 U.S.C. § 10706(b)(3)(B) (1988).

1116.   *Id.* § 10706(b)(3)(B)(i).

1117.   *Id.* § 10706(b)(3)(B)(iii).

1118.   471 U.S. 48 (1985). For a discussion of *Southern Motor Carriers*, see Section B.2.b of this chapter.

1119.   *Id.* at 63.

1120.   *Id.* at 64.

1121.   49 U.S.C. § 10706(b)(2) (1988).

1122.   *See* Board of Trade v. ICC, 646 F.2d 1187 (7th Cir. 1981).

1123.   *See* Atchison, T. & S.F. Ry. v. Aircoach Transport Ass'n, 253 F.2d 877 (D.C. Cir. 1958), *cert. denied,* 361 U.S. 930 (1960); United States v. Baltimore & O.R.R., 538 F. Supp. 200 (D.D.C. 1982), *aff'd sub nom.* United States v. Bessemer & L.E.R.R., 717 F.2d 593 (D.C. Cir. 1983); United States v. Morgan Drive Away, Inc., 1974-1 Trade Cas. (CCH) ¶ 74,888 (D.D.C. 1974).

1124.   476 U.S. 409 (1986).

1125.   260 U.S. 156 (1922).

ICC regulated carrier concerning any matter subject to the jurisdiction of the ICC.[1126]

Activity conducted in accordance with a pooling agreement approved by the ICC is exempt from the antitrust laws.[1127] In *Rothery Storage & Van Co. v. Atlas Van Lines,*[1128] the D.C. Circuit held that a van line's restriction of its agents from utilizing their own ICC operating authority in competition with the van line was not a violation of the Sherman Act even absent an ICC-approved pooling agreement. In *Three-Way Corp. v. ICC,*[1129] the D.C. Circuit held that a van line's proposed amendments to a pooling agreement with its agents, requiring those agents to tender to the van line any shipments in excess of 1,700 miles, could not constitute an unlawful conspiracy in restraint of trade between the carrier and its agents. Such a restriction would not lessen, but actually promote competition among carriers, and would eliminate the free rider problem of the carrier's agents using the carrier's reputation and services for their sole benefit.[1130]

Motor carrier mergers that are approved or exempted from prior-approval requirements by the ICC are immune from the antitrust laws.[1131] The standard governing ICC review of motor carrier mergers was set forth in *McLean Trucking Co. v. United States.*[1132] In *McLean,* the Supreme Court held that the question presented to the ICC by a proposed trucking merger was not whether the merger would violate the antitrust laws, but rather whether the merger was in the public interest according to the national transportation policy set forth in the Transportation Act of 1940.[1133] The Court held that the effect of a merger on competition is only one of several factors to be considered by the ICC:

> [N]o other inference is possible but that, as a factor in determining the propriety of motor-carrier consolidations the preservation of competition among carriers, although still a value, is significant chiefly as it aids in the attainment of the objectives of the national transportation policy.[1134]

This broad and openended public interest standard was modified by the Staggers Rail Act of 1980, which requires the ICC to approve a proposed carrier merger or consolidation not involving two or more major railroads, unless it finds that the

---

1126.   15 U.S.C. § 26 (1988).

1127.   49 U.S.C. §§ 11341(a), 11342 (1988).

1128.   792 F.2d 210 (D.C. Cir. 1986) (Bork, J.), *cert. denied,* 479 U.S. 1033 (1987).

1129.   792 F.2d 232 (D.C. Cir.), *cert. denied,* 479 U.S. 985 (1986).

1130.   In Richards v. Neilsen Freight Lines, 810 F.2d 898 (9th Cir. 1987), an agreement which had not been submitted to the ICC concerning the sharing of revenue and traffic between motor carriers, wherein one of the carriers performed short haul deliveries, was held not to be a per se violation of the Sherman Act even though the local delivery carrier was forbidden to solicit the customers of the other carriers. The Ninth Circuit held that the mere fact that several carriers had similar restrictions in their agreements with the same local delivery carrier did not constitute a per se violation.

1131.   49 U.S.C. § 11341(a) (1988).

1132.   321 U.S. 67 (1944).

1133.   *Id.* at 83-85.

1134.   *Id.* at 85-86 (footnote omitted); 49 U.S.C. § 10101 (1988). The ICC's jurisdiction to enforce § 7 of the Clayton Act has been held to be primary and obligatory. United States v. Navajo Freight Lines, 339 F. Supp. 554, 565 (D. Colo. 1971); *see also* Denver & Rio Grande W.R.R. v. United States, 387 U.S. 485, 492-93 (1967).

transaction is likely to have a substantial anticompetitive impact and that the anticompetitive effects of the transaction outweigh the public interest in meeting significant transportation needs.[1135]

Pursuant to Section 21 of the Bus Regulatory Reform Act of 1982,[1136] the ICC has exempted from the statutory prior approval requirements all merger and consolidation transactions involving motor property carriers.[1137] Under this class exemption, motor property carriers wishing to carry out a proposed merger or consolidation may file a brief notice of exemption with the ICC describing the proposed transaction and observe a sixty-day waiting period. If the ICC takes no action to revoke the class exemption for the proposed transaction, the parties may consummate it.[1138]

b. RAIL TRANSPORTATION

Since 1887, the railroad industry has been subject to extensive regulation by the ICC. In 1976 Congress passed the Railroad Revitalization and Regulatory Reform Act (4R Act).[1139] The 4R Act was intended to deregulate most rail traffic. In 1980, Congress moved further toward deregulation by passing the Staggers Rail Act.[1140] Together, these amendments to the Interstate Commerce Act substantially alter the role of antitrust in the regulation of entry and exit, rates and related agreements, and mergers and acquisitions of rail carriers.

(1) National Rail Transportation Policy

The Interstate Commerce Act, as amended by the Staggers Rail Act, requires that the ICC determine whether an action requiring Commission approval will further the national rail transportation policy.[1141] In contrast to the more general transportation policy, which emphasizes such general principles as the encouragement of "sound economic conditions in transportation,"[1142] the national rail

---

1135. Pub. L. No. 96-488, § 228, 94 Stat. 1931 (1980) (codified at 49 U.S.C. § 11344(d) (1988)). The ICC applied the competitive impact standards of § 11344(d) in approving the consolidation of the Trailways and Greyhound bus systems in 1988. *See* GLI Acquisition Co.–Purchase–Trailways Lines, No. MC-F-18505, 4 I.C.C.2d 591 (1988). The ICC also relied heavily on the "failing firm" doctrine as justifying the acquisition.

1136. Pub. L. No. 97-261, § 21b, 96 Stat. 1102 (1982) (codified at 49 U.S.C. § 11343(e) (1988)).

1137. Mergers or consolidations involving motor passenger carriers are not subject to this class exemption, and are reviewed by the ICC under the statutory approval standards set forth in 49 U.S.C. § 11344(d) (1988).

1138. *See* 49 C.F.R. § 1186 (1991); Regular Common Carrier Conf. v. United States, 820 F.2d 1323 (D.C. Cir. 1987).

1139. Pub. L. No. 94-210, 90 Stat. 31 (1976) (codified in scattered sections of 49 U.S.C.).

1140. Pub. L. No. 96-448, 94 Stat. 1899, 1900 (1980) (codified in scattered sections of 49 U.S.C.). The constitutionality of §§ 201, 202, 203, and 214 of the Staggers Rail Act, 49 U.S.C. §§ 10701a, 10707a, 10709, 11501 (1988), was upheld in Texas v. United States, 730 F.2d 339 (5th Cir.), *cert. denied,* 469 U.S. 892 (1984). Sections 201-209 and 301-303 have also been upheld against constitutional challenges. Illinois Commerce Comm'n v. ICC, 749 F.2d 875 (D.C. Cir. 1984), *cert. denied,* 474 U.S. 820 (1985).

1141. *See, e.g.,* 49 U.S.C. § 10706(a)(2)(A) (1988) (approval of agreement between rail carriers predicated on determination that "making and carrying out of agreement will further the transportation policy of section 10101a . . . .").

1142. *See* 49 U.S.C. § 10101(a)(1)(C) (1988).

transportation policy includes specific factors that particularize the desirability of competition in the rail transportation system:

> [I]t is the policy of the United States Government –
> (1) to allow, to the maximum extent possible, competition and the demand for services to establish reasonable rates for transportation by rail;
> (2) to minimize the need for Federal regulatory control over the rail transportation system and to require fair and expeditious regulatory decisions when regulation is required;
> . . . .
> (6) to maintain reasonable rates where there is an absence of effective competition and where rail rates provide revenues which exceed the amount necessary to maintain the rail system and to attract capital;
> . . . .
> (7) to reduce regulatory barriers to entry into and exit from the industry;
> . . . .
> (13) to prohibit predatory pricing and practices, to avoid undue concentrations of market power and to prohibit unlawful discrimination . . . .[1143]

(2) ICC Exemption Authority

Among other things, the Staggers Rail Act substantially broadens the ICC's authority to exempt, upon certain findings, railroads, railroad transactions and railroad transportation services from its regulatory jurisdiction.[1144]

The ICC has exercised its rail exemption authority in a wide variety of cases. For example, the ICC has exempted broad categories of railroad traffic from rate regulation.[1145] The ICC has also used its exemption authority to relieve certain

---

1143. *Id.* § 10101a.
1144. As amended by the Staggers Act, the exemption section provides, with certain exceptions, that the ICC "shall" exempt rail carriers, transactions or services from continued regulation when it finds that (1) continued regulation is "not necessary to carry out the [rail] transportation policy" set forth in 49 U.S.C. § 10101a, and (2) either (a) the transaction or service is "of limited scope" or (b) continued regulation is "not needed to protect shippers from the abuse of market power." 49 U.S.C. § 10505(a)(2) (1988). Courts have construed this provision to confer on the ICC "very broad authority" to eliminate all unnecessary regulation of railroads. Coal Exporters Ass'n v. United States, 745 F.2d 76, 82 (D.C. Cir. 1984), *cert. denied*, 471 U.S. 1072 (1985); *see also* Simmons v. ICC, 760 F.2d 126, 132 (7th Cir. 1985) ("Congress wanted the exemption power to be wielded boldly"), *cert. denied*, 474 U.S. 1055 (1986).
1145. *See, e.g.,* Brae Corp. v. United States, 740 F.2d 1023, 1036-44 (D.C. Cir. 1984) (exemption of boxcar traffic from maximum rate regulation), *cert. denied*, 471 U.S. 1069 (1985); American Trucking Ass'ns v. ICC, 656 F.2d 1115 (5th Cir. 1981) (exemption of piggyback traffic from rate regulation); Improvement of TOFC/COFC Regulations (Pickup and Delivery), 6 I.C.C.2d 208 (1989) (ICC expanded piggyback exemption to include motor carrier pickup and delivery portion of certain piggyback movements); Rail General Exemption Authority–Miscellaneous Manufactured Commodities, 6 I.C.C.2d 186 (1989)(ICC exemption of certain miscellaneous manufactured commodities traffic from rate regulation); Improvement of TOFC/COFC Regulations (Railroad-Affiliated Motor Carriers and Other Motor Carriers), 3 I.C.C.2d 869 (1987) (ICC expanded piggyback exemption to include motor carrier portion of certain piggyback movements), *amended* (served July 22, 1987) (not printed), *petition for review sub nom.* Central & S. Motor Freight Tariff Ass'n v. United States, No. 87-8647 (11th Cir.) (dismissed Feb. 8, 1988); Railroad Exemption–International Joint Through Rates, 2 I.C.C.2d 121 (1986) (exemption of ocean/rail international through rates). *But see* Coal Exporters Ass'n v. United States, 745 F.2d 76 (D.C. Cir. 1984) (court vacated ICC's decision exempting export coal rail traffic from rate regulation), *cert.*

classes of rail-related transactions or services from statutory prior approval requirements,[1146] as well as from other statutory requirements.[1147]

A significant issue relating to the ICC's rail exemption authority is whether transactions or services that are otherwise within the ICC's exclusive jurisdiction, and thus immune from the operation of other state and federal laws (including federal antitrust laws), lose that immunity when the ICC exempts them from continued regulation under Section 10505. In a number of decisions exempting certain classes of rail traffic from rate regulation, the ICC has announced that the effect of the exemption is to remove whatever antitrust immunity might otherwise apply to the exempted rates.[1148] The ICC has employed similar reasoning in connection with other types of rail exemptions.[1149]

---

denied, 471 U.S. 1072 (1985).

1146.   *See, e.g.,* Exemption from 49 U.S.C. 11322(a) for Certain Interlocking Directorates, 5 I.C.C.2d 7 (1988) (exemption from statutory prior approval requirements of certain interlocking directorates between rail carriers), *petition for review dismissed sub nom.* United Transp. Union v. ICC, 891 F.2d 908 (D.C. Cir. 1989), *cert. denied,* 110 S. Ct. 3271 (1990); Exemption of Out of Service Rail Line, 2 I.C.C.2d 146 (1986) (exemption from statutory prior-approval requirements of rail line abandonments and service and trackage rights discontinuances where no rail traffic has originated or terminated on rail line during past two years), *on remand from* Illinois Commerce Comm'n v. ICC, 787 F.2d 616 (D.C. Cir. 1986); Class Exemption for the Acquisition and Operation of Rail Lines Under 49 U.S.C. 10901, 1 I.C.C.2d 810 (1985) (exemption from statutory prior-approval requirement of certain sales of railroad lines to new rail operators); Railroad Consolidation Procedures – Trackage Rights Exemption, 1 I.C.C.2d 270 (1985) (exemption from statutory prior-approval requirement of certain trackage rights agreements among rail carriers), *aff'd mem. sub nom.* Illinois Commerce Comm'n v. ICC, Nos. 86-1107, 86-1131 (D.C. Cir. May 12, 1987), *aff'd,* 819 F.2d 311 (D.C. Cir. 1987); Exemption of Railroads From Securities Regulation Under 49 U.S.C. 11301, 1 I.C.C.2d 915 (1985) (exemption of railroad securities transactions).

1147.   *See, e.g.,* Simmons v. ICC, 697 F.2d 326 (D.C. Cir. 1982) (exemption of state-operated rail carriers from statutory certification requirements and other provisions); McGinness v. ICC, 662 F.2d 853 (D.C. Cir. 1981) (exemption of "designated operators" conducting rail operations over portions of bankrupt Penn Central rail system from rail consolidation and interlocking directorate provisions of Interstate Commerce Act).

The courts have upheld the ICC's requirement that state regulatory commissions certified by the ICC to regulate intrastate rail traffic automatically adopt all exemptions granted by the ICC pursuant to its rail exemption authority. Illinois Commerce Comm'n v. ICC, 749 F.2d 875 (D.C. Cir. 1984), *cert. denied,* 474 U.S. 820 (1985); *see also* Wheeling-Pittsburgh Steel Corp. v. ICC, 723 F.2d 346, 354-55 (3d Cir. 1983) (addressing question whether state regulatory agencies must follow ICC rules and decisions); Illinois Cent. Gulf R.R. v. ICC, 702 F.2d 111, 115 (7th Cir. 1983) (same).

1148.   *See, e.g.,* Railroad Exemption – Export Coal, 367 I.C.C. 570, 595 & n.69 (1983), *vacated and remanded on other grounds sub nom.* Coal Exporters Ass'n v. United States, 745 F.2d 76 (D.C. Cir. 1984), *cert. denied,* 471 U.S. 1072 (1985); Exemption From Regulation – Boxcar Traffic, 367 I.C.C. 425, 446 (1983), *aff'd in part sub nom.* Brae Corp. v. United States, 740 F.2d 1023 (D.C. Cir. 1984), *cert. denied,* 471 U.S. 1069 (1985); Improvement of TOFC/COFC Regulation, 364 I.C.C. 731, 736 (1981), *aff'd sub nom.* American Trucking Ass'ns v. ICC, 656 F.2d 1115 (5th Cir. 1981).

1149.   *See, e.g.,* Railroad Consolidation Procedures – Trackage Rights Exemption, 1 I.C.C.2d 270, 279 (1985) (exempted trackage rights agreements between railroads not immune from antitrust laws or other federal and state laws), *aff'd sub nom.* Illinois Commerce Comm'n v. ICC, 819 F.2d 311 (D.C. Cir. 1987); Finance Docket No. 29757, Colorado & S. Ry. – Merger into Burlington N.R.R. – Exemption & Request for Determination of Fairness (served Dec. 31, 1981) (not printed) (exempted rail merger transaction not immune from operation of state corporation laws conferring rights on dissenting shareholders); Finance Docket No. 31035, Merger – Baltimore & O.R.R. and Chesapeake & O. Ry. (decision served Mar. 2, 1988) (reaffirming *Colorado & Southern*).

In more recent decisions, however, the ICC has suggested that the granting of an exemption under Section 10505 neither extinguishes the ICC's exclusive jurisdiction nor permits the application of inconsistent federal or state laws to the exempted transaction or activity.[1150] In *G. & T. Terminal Packaging Co. v. Consolidated Rail Corp.*,[1151] a divided panel of the Third Circuit agreed with the position asserted by the ICC and concluded that the ICC's exemption of the subject traffic did not affect the Interstate Commerce Act's preemption of state common-law rights of action. In *Alliance Shippers v. Southern Pacific Transportation Co.*[1152] the Ninth Circuit concluded that the ICC's exemption of particular traffic did not revive common-law discrimination remedies because these remedies would be inconsistent with the goals of the Staggers Rail Act, that the Staggers Rail Act preempts state statutory remedies, and that federal and state antitrust remedies "unquestionably survived" deregulation and apply to exempted traffic.[1153]

(3) Regulation of Entry and Exit

The Staggers Rail Act amendments to the Interstate Commerce Act permit easier entry.[1154] Before 1980, the ICC could issue a certificate of public convenience and necessity authorizing the construction or extension of a railroad line only if it found that the public convenience and necessity "require or will be enhanced by" the construction or extension.[1155] Section 221 of the Staggers Rail Act reduces the stringency of the requisite finding by substituting the word "permit" for the words "will be enhanced by."[1156]

Section 402 of the Staggers Rail Act amended or repealed provisions of the Interstate Commerce Act to permit easier abandonment of lines. Section 402(c) of the Staggers Act places a time limit of 135 days on abandonment application investigations, as well as time limits on other actions and decisions by the ICC on such applications.[1157] Section 402 also creates a statutory mechanism to permit

---

1150. *See, e.g.,* Exemption of Railroads From Securities Regulation Under 49 U.S.C. § 11301, 1 I.C.C.2d 915, 916-18 (1985) (exemption of railroad securities transactions does not remove ICC's exclusive jurisdiction over, and does not permit federal or state authorities to regulate, such transactions).

1151. 830 F.2d 1230 (3d Cir. 1987), *cert. denied,* 485 U.S. 988 (1988).

1152. 858 F.2d 567 (9th Cir. 1988).

1153. *Id.* at 569-70.

1154. *See* H.R. REP. NO. 1430, 96th Cong., 2d Sess. 115-16, *reprinted in* 1980 U.S. CODE CONG. & ADMIN. NEWS 4110, 4147 (Conference Committee Report on Staggers Act).

The ICC has also held that the Staggers Rail Act permits easier entry of rail carriers into motor carrier operations. *See* Applications for Motor Carrier Operating Authority by Railroads and Rail Affiliates, 132 M.C.C. 978 (1982), *aff'd sub nom.* American Trucking Ass'ns v. ICC, 722 F.2d 1243 (5th Cir.), *cert. denied,* 469 U.S. 930 (1984).

1155. 49 U.S.C. § 10901(a) (Supp. III 1979) (amended 1980).

1156. 49 U.S.C. § 10901(a) (1988); *see* New Mexico Navajo Ranchers Ass'n v. ICC, 702 F.2d 227 (D.C. Cir. 1983) (determination of public convenience or necessity requires consideration of whether line extension would subject communities on route to serious injury).

1157. *See* 49 U.S.C. § 10904(c)(1) (1988). Many cases discuss the standards used by the ICC in reviewing railroad abandonment applications. *See, e.g.,* Southern Pac. Transp. Co. v. ICC, 871 F.2d 838 (9th Cir. 1989); Busboom Grain Co. v. ICC, 856 F.2d 790 (7th Cir. 1988); Baltimore & O.R.R. v. ICC, 826 F.2d 1125 (D.C. Cir. 1987); Simmons v. ICC, 784 F.2d 242 (7th Cir. 1985); Illinois Commerce Comm'n v. ICC, 776 F.2d 355 (D.C. Cir. 1985); Illinois v. ICC, 751 F.2d 903 (7th Cir. 1985); Glazer Steel Corp. v. ICC, 748 F.2d 1006 (5th Cir. 1984); Black v. ICC, 737 F.2d 643 (7th Cir. 1984); Cartersville Elevator, Inc. v. ICC, 724 F.2d 668 (8th Cir.), *aff'd on reh'g en*

parties to make offers of financial assistance to avoid abandonment or discontinuance of a railroad line.[1158]

(4) Regulation of Rates and Agreements

The Staggers Act amendments establish two separate sets of standards to determine what rate a rail carrier may set. To decide which set of standards applies to a particular rate, the ICC must determine whether the carrier that established the rate has "market dominance."[1159] If the ICC determines that the carrier does not have market dominance, the carrier may establish any rate for transportation or other service that it provides,[1160] so long as that rate is not "below a reasonable minimum."[1161] If, however, the ICC determines that the carrier has market dominance, the rate that the carrier establishes must be "reasonable."[1162] Before it may determine that a carrier has "market dominance," the ICC must make two findings. First, the ICC must find that there is an "absence of effective competition from other carriers or modes of transportation for the transportation to which [the] rate applies."[1163] The ICC has adopted a set of evidentiary guidelines to be used in making this determination. Under these guidelines, factors such as the physical characteristics of the route, the amount of product involved, the access of the shipper and the receiver to alternative transportation, the number of such alternatives, and the transportation costs associated with each alternative, will be taken into account with respect to intramodal, intermodal, geographic, and product competition.[1164] Second, the ICC must find that the rate charged results in a revenue-variable cost

---

banc, 735 F.2d 1059 (8th Cir. 1984); Illinois v. United States, 668 F.2d 923 (7th Cir. 1981), cert. denied, 455 U.S. 100 (1982).

1158. 49 U.S.C. § 10905(b) (1988).

1159. Id. § 10709(c).

1160. Id. § 10701a(c); see Bessemer & L.E.R.R. v. ICC, 691 F.2d 1104, 1108 (3d Cir. 1982) (effect of market dominance provision was to end for most rail services ICC control over maximum rates and to permit carriers not having market dominance to set rates in response to their perception of market conditions), cert. denied, 462 U.S. 1110 (1983).

1161. Cost Standards for Railroad Rates, 364 I.C.C. 898 (1981) (approving ICC regulations establishing standards for determining when railroad rates are unreasonably low), aff'd sub nom. Water Transp. Ass'n v. ICC, 684 F.2d 81 (D.C. Cir. 1982).

1162. 49 U.S.C. § 10701a(b)(1) (1988).

1163. Id. § 10709(a).

1164. See Market Dominance Determinations and Consideration of Product Competition, 365 I.C.C. 118 (1981), aff'd sub nom. Western Coal Traffic League v. United States, 719 F.2d 772 (5th Cir. 1983) (en banc) (affirming ICC's decision to allow consideration of product and geographic competition), cert. denied, 466 U.S. 953 (1984); Product and Geographic Competition, 2 I.C.C.2d 1 (1985) (amending market dominance evidentiary guidelines, inter alia, to shift burden of proving product and geographic competition to the railroad defendants in rate complaint cases). Many courts apply the market dominance provisions in rate complaint cases. See General Chem. Corp. v. United States, 817 F.2d 844 (D.C. Cir. 1987) (per curiam); Salt River Project Agric. Improvement & Power Dist. v. United States, 762 F.2d 1053 (D.C. Cir. 1985); Aluminum Co. of Am. v. ICC, 761 F.2d 746 (D.C. Cir. 1985); Arizona Pub. Serv. Co. v. United States, 742 F.2d 644 (D.C. Cir. 1984).

In Union Pacific R.R. v. ICC, 867 F.2d 646 (D.C. Cir. 1989), the D.C. Circuit held that the ICC cannot avoid the market dominance test by challenging rates under 49 U.S.C. § 10701(a) as an "unreasonable practice."

percentage[1165] that exceeds the percentage set forth in the statute.[1166] If these findings cannot be made, i.e., if there is effective competition or if the revenue-variable cost percentage is less than the percentage established by the statute the carrier lacks market dominance, and the ICC lacks jurisdiction to determine whether the rate exceeds a maximum reasonable level.[1167]

Even if the ICC determines that the rail carrier has market dominance, that finding does not establish a presumption that the rate in question is unreasonable.[1168] Instead, the ICC must make a separate determination whether the rate is unreasonable. The test is whether "it exceeds a reasonable maximum" for the transportation to which the rate applies.[1169] Under Section 203 of the Staggers Rail Act, which creates a "zone of rate flexibility," a carrier that is deemed to have market dominance with respect to a particular rate may increase that rate so long as the increased rate does not exceed the "adjusted base rate"[1170] for the transportation involved, plus any rate increases implemented under subsections (c) or (d).[1171] However, any rate increases implemented under subsections (c) and (d) may not exceed a "reasonable maximum" for the transportation involved.[1172]

1165.   " 'Revenue-variable cost percentage' " means "the quotient, expressed as a percentage figure, obtained by dividing the total revenues produced by the transportation of all traffic received by rail carriers for rail transportation by the total variable cost of such transportation." 49 U.S.C. § 10709(d)(1)(B)(ii) (1988). The statute further defines " 'cost recovery percentage' " as

the lowest revenue-variable cost percentage which, if all movements that produced revenues resulting in revenue-variable cost percentages in excess of the cost recovery percentage are deemed to have produced only revenues resulting in the cost recovery percentage, would produce revenues which would be equal, when combined with total revenues produced by all other traffic transported by rail carrier, to the total fixed and variable cost of the transportation of all traffic by rail carrier.

Id. § 10709(d)(1)(B)(i).

1166.   For the period beginning on and after October 1, 1984, the percentage is the cost recovery percentage as determined by the ICC. For purposes of determining the percentage in this period, the cost recovery percentage may not be less than a revenue-variable cost percentage of 170% or more than a revenue-variable cost percentage of 180%. Id. § 10709(d)(2)(C).

1167.   Id. §§ 10709(c), 10709(d)(2).

1168.   See id. § 10709(b).

1169.   Id.

1170.   Section 203 defines "adjusted base rate" as "the base rate for the transportation of a particular commodity multiplied by the latest rail cost adjustment factor published by the [ICC] pursuant to this paragraph." Id. § 10707a(a)(2)(A).

1171.   Id. § 10707a(b)(1). With some exceptions, a rail carrier may increase its rates, in addition to the adjusted base rate, by an annual amount of not more than 4% of the adjusted base rate. Id. § 10707a(d)(1). Even where the Commission has previously prescribed a maximum future rate pursuant to 49 U.S.C. § 10704(a), the carrier may increase the prescribed rate in accordance with the "zone of rate flexibility." CSX Transp. v. United States, 867 F.2d 1439 (D.C. Cir. 1989).

1172.   49 U.S.C. § 10707a(b)(2), (e)(1) (1988). The ICC has promulgated standards for maximum reasonable coal rates where railroads possess market dominance. Coal Rate Guidelines–Nationwide, 1 I.C.C.2d 520 (1985), aff'd sub nom. Consolidated Rail Corp. v. United States, 812 F.2d 1444 (3d Cir. 1987). Under the Guidelines, railroad pricing of market dominant coal traffic is subject to four upward constraints: (1) the achievement of revenue adequacy, (2) certain checks on inefficient management, (3) the cost an efficient hypothesized new entrant would incur in serving the subject traffic, alone or in combination with other traffic ("stand-alone cost"), and (4) phasing of any substantial rate increases. The ICC is presently considering a proposal to extend the ratemaking methodology developed in its Coal Rate Guidelines decision to non-coal rail traffic. Ex Parte No. 347 (Sub-No. 2), Rate Guidelines–Non-Coal Proceedings (served Apr. 8, 1987) (not printed). In Union Pacific Railroad v. ICC, 867 F.2d 646 (D.C. Cir. 1989), a case

With respect to rate discrimination, the Staggers Rail Act amended the Interstate Commerce Act to provide a more lenient standard in determining what constitutes unlawful rate discrimination. Under Section 212, differences between rates do not constitute unlawful discrimination "if such differences result from different services provided by rail carriers."[1173] The House Committee Report on the Act did not define the term "different services," but stated that it was "intended to recognize any differences that would normally be recognized in unregulated service industries as constituting a basis for price differences which would not have an adverse effect on competition."[1174] Section 212 of the Act also exempts contracts between rail carriers and "purchasers of rail services" (i.e., shippers) that the ICC has approved, surcharges or cancellations of joint rates, separate rates for distinct rail services, rail rates applicable to different routes, and certain business entertainment expenses from the general prohibition of rate discrimination.[1175]

The Act added a new provision that clarifies the legal status of contracts for individually negotiated rates between rail carriers and shippers. Section 208(a) provides that a rail carrier "may enter into a contract with one or more purchasers of rail services to provide specified services under specified rates and conditions."[1176] All such contracts must be filed, and within thirty days of filing the ICC must "determine whether the contract unduly impairs the carrier's common carrier function."[1177] Once it has been approved, the contract is not subject to the provisions of Section 208, and may not be subsequently challenged before the ICC or in court on the ground that it violates a provision of the Interstate Commerce Act.[1178] "If anticompetitive behavior is alleged, under this section, the antitrust laws are the appropriate and only remedy available."[1179]

The Railroad Revitalization and Regulatory Reform Act and the Staggers Rail Act also narrow the permissible scope of antitrust exempt collective ratemaking by rail carriers. Under these Acts, members of railroad rate bureaus may not discuss, participate in an agreement related to, or vote on single-line rates (i.e., a rate

---

involving the shipment of nuclear wastes, the D.C. Circuit held that the Commission must either apply the reasonableness standards established in the Coal Rate Guidelines, or explain why application of the Guidelines would be inappropriate.

1173. 49 U.S.C. § 10741(e) (1988); *see* Seaboard Coast Line R.R. v. United States, 724 F.2d 1482 (11th Cir. 1984) (holding that railroad engaged in unlawful discrimination when it permitted Western but not Northeastern connecting rail carriers to use its proportional rates for certain traffic destined for the Southeast); Dresser Indus. v. ICC, 714 F.2d 588 (5th Cir. 1983) (holding that railroad did not engage in unlawful discrimination when it charged a shipper more to ship a commodity between designated origins and destinations than it charged a competing shipper to ship the same commodity a longer distance over the same lines).

1174. H.R. REP. No. 1035, 96th Cong., 2d Sess. 60, *reprinted in* 1980 U.S. CODE CONG. & ADMIN. NEWS 3978, 4005.

1175. 49 U.S.C. § 10741(f) (1988).

1176. *Id.* § 10713(a).

1177. H.R. REP. No. 1035, 96th Cong., 2d Sess. 57, *reprinted in* 1980 U.S. CODE CONG. & ADMIN. NEWS 3978, 4002.

1178. 49 U.S.C. § 10713(i)(1) (1988).

1179. *See* H.R. REP. No. 1035, 96th Cong., 2d Sess. 58, *reprinted in* 1980 U.S. CODE CONG. & ADMIN. NEWS 3978, 4003.

proposed by a single carrier for transportation over its own line),[1180] or on rates for interline movements (i.e., rates for transportation involving more than one railroad) unless each railroad involved in such activities "practicably participates" in such movements.[1181] In addition, where there are multiple interline movements between two end points, members of a rate bureau may not discuss, participate in an agreement related to, or vote on an interline rate, unless that railroad forms part of the particular route that is the subject of the agreement.[1182]

With respect to the establishment of rate agreements, the Staggers Rail Act permits a rail carrier to enter into an agreement for the compilation, publication, and distribution of railroad rates "in effect or to become effective," without submitting it to the ICC for prior approval.[1183] A rail carrier, however, that is a party to an agreement of at least two rail carriers or an agreement with a class of carriers (i.e., pipeline, motor, and water carriers and freight forwarders)[1184] that relates to rates, classifications, divisions, or rules related to them, or procedures for joint consideration, initiation, publication, or establishment of them, must apply to the ICC for approval of the agreement.[1185] Before it can approve such an agreement, the ICC must find that the making and carrying out of the agreement will further the national rail transportation policy.[1186] If the ICC makes this finding and approves the agreement, or if the agreement concerns solely the compilation or publication of

---

1180. 49 U.S.C. § 10706(a)(3)(A)(i) (1988). Rate bureaus are associations of railroads allowed to discuss and set rates under certain circumstances with antitrust immunity. While the Staggers Act does not address the possibility that joint-line contract rates may be within the limited immunity provided for certain rate bureau discussions and agreements, the ICC apparently takes the position that all contract rates are "single-line rates" and are therefore not a permissible subject of rate bureau agreement. *See* Western Railroads–Agreement, 364 I.C.C. 635, 644 (1981).

1181. 49 U.S.C. § 10706(a)(3)(A)(ii) (1988). Congress left the responsibility for defining "practicably participates" to the ICC. S. REP. No. 1430, 96th Cong., 2d Sess. 114 (1980). In *Western Railroads*, the ICC declared that "[p]racticable participants in an interline movement are only those carriers who are direct connectors to a specific joint-line movement." 364 I.C.C. at 651; *see also* Petition to Delay Application of Direct Connector Requirement to Joint Rates in General Increases, 367 I.C.C. 886 (1983).

1182. 49 U.S.C. § 10706(a)(3)(A)(iii) (1988). The Staggers Act also provided that rate bureaus must prepare transcripts or sound recordings of all meetings and keep records of votes. These materials must be provided to the ICC and other relevant federal agencies, but they are exempt from disclosure under the Freedom of Information Act. *Id.* § 10706(a)(3)(D).

1183. *Id.* § 10706(a)(4). The Antitrust Division of the Department of Justice has issued Business Review Letters approving the collection and dissemination of rates where the collection of the rate information is not likely to enhance the possibility of collusion among carriers. *See* Letter from Kenneth G. Starling, then Acting Assistant Att'y Gen., to Edward Wheeler, counsel for the Freight Rate Information Service (June 28, 1988); Letter from Helmut F. Furth, then Acting Assistant Att'y Gen., to J. N. Baker, Chrmn., Western Railroad Traffic Ass'n and Bruce B. Wilson, Vice President, Consolidated Rail Corp. (May 22, 1984); Letter from William F. Baxter, then Assistant Att'y Gen., to Mark M. Levin, Western Railroad Traffic Ass'n (Oct. 28, 1983).

1184. 49 U.S.C. § 10706(d)(1) (1988).

1185. *Id.* § 10706(a)(2)(A). Prior ICC approval, however, is not required for agreements that provide "solely for compilation, publication, and other distribution of rates in effect or to become effective." *Id.* § 10706(a)(4).

1186. *Id.* § 10101a.

rates, the agreement is exempted from the federal antitrust laws.[1187] This exemption, however, is conditioned on compliance with the terms of the agreement and with any additional conditions required by the ICC.[1188] Moreover, the exemption can be withheld or withdrawn if the carrier fails to meet those conditions, or if the ICC finds that the parties to such an agreement have exceeded its scope.[1189] Even it the antitrust exemption is deemed inapplicable to a particular collective rate agreement, a private treble damage remedy under Section 4 of the Clayton Act may be precluded by the *Keogh* doctrine.[1190]

The Staggers Rail Act also specifically assigns burdens of proof and establishes evidentiary standards for challenges to rate agreements. Under the Act, a person who alleges that a rail carrier voted or agreed upon a rate, classification, division, or rule in violation of the Act's provision has the burden of proving that the vote or agreement occurred.[1191] A showing of parallel behavior "does not satisfy this burden by itself."[1192] Moreover, the Act provides that an antitrust conspiracy may not be inferred from the fact that two or more rail carriers acted together on an interline rate and that a party to the action took a similar action on another route.[1193] Evidence of a discussion or agreement between or among carriers, or of a resulting rate or action, is not admissible in court, if the discussion or agreement was either in accordance with an approved rate bureau agreement or concerned a discussion or agreement on an interline movement that in itself did not violate the antitrust laws.[1194] According to the House Committee Report that accompanied the legislation, the justification for this provision was that carriers must talk to competitors about interline movements in which they interchange in order to fulfill the requirement that they concur in changes to joint rates.[1195]

1187.   The Staggers Rail Act specifies that the Sherman Act, the Clayton Act, the FTC Act, §§ 73-74 of the Wilson Tariff Act, and the Act of June 19, 1936, as amended, "do not apply to parties and other persons with respect to making or carrying out the agreement." 49 U.S.C. § 10706(a)(2)(A) (1988).

   The ICC also has authority to approve, and thereby to immunize from the antitrust laws agreements under which regulated common carriers "pool or divide traffic or services or any part of their earnings." *Id* § 11342(a).

1188.   *See* United States v. Bessemer & Lake Erie R.R. Co., 717 F.2d 593, 599-600 (D.C. Cir. 1983); Board of Trade v. ICC, 646 F.2d 1187 (7th Cir. 1981). *But see In re* Wheat Rail Freight Rate Antitrust Litig., 759 F.2d 1305 (7th Cir. 1985) (immunity from treble damage actions attaches even where carrier fails to comply with terms of rate agreement), *cert. denied,* 476 U.S. 1158 (1986).

1189.   49 U.S.C. §§ 10706(a)(2)(A), 10706(a)(4) (1988). In general, the ICC lacks authority to approve rate bureau agreements that contemplate collusion on rates that are not subject to its jurisdiction. *See* Atchison, T. & S.F. Ry. v. United States, 597 F.2d 593, 595-96 (7th Cir. 1979); United States v. Southern Motor Carriers Rate Conference, Inc., 467 F. Supp. 471, 485-86 (N.D. Ga. 1979), *aff'd,* 672 F.2d 469 (5th Cir. Unit B 1982), *rev'd on other grounds,* 471 U.S. 48 (1985); Atchison, T. & S.F. Ry. v. Aircoach Transp. Ass'n, 253 F.2d 877, 884-86 (D.C. Cir. 1958), *cert. denied,* 361 U.S. 930 (1960).

1190.   The *Keogh* doctrine is discussed in Subpart C.3 of this chapter.

1191.   49 U.S.C. § 10706(a)(3)(C)(i) (1988).

1192.   *Id.*

1193.   *Id.* § 10706(a)(3)(C)(ii).

1194.   *Id.*

1195.   H.R. REP. No. 1430, 96th Cong., 2d Sess. 114, *reprinted in* 1980 U.S. CODE CONG. & ADMIN. NEWS 4110, 4146.

(5) Competitive Access and Related Issues

The ICC has several means at its disposal to prescribe "competitive access." The Commission may (1) order railroads to participate in through routes and joint rates,[1196] (2) prohibit the cancellation of an existing through route or joint rate,[1197] (3) order a rail carrier to allow another rail carrier to operate over tracks within the first carrier's terminal facilities (referred to as terminal trackage rights),[1198] and (4) order a railroad to provide switching service between a shipper located on its line and the tracks of another rail carrier (referred to as reciprocal switching).[1199]

The ICC has promulgated rules governing "competitive access" by means of through routes, joint rates and reciprocal switching (the competitive access rules are referred to as CARs).[1200] In *Midtec Paper Corp. v. Chicago and Northwestern Transportation Co.,*[1201] the ICC applied the CARs to requests for terminal trackage rights. Interpreting the CARs, the ICC held that a decision to order trackage rights or reciprocal switching will turn on: (1) whether the railroad has used its market power to extract unreasonable terms on through movements, or (2) whether because of its monopoly position it has shown a disregard for the shipper's needs by rendering inadequate service.[1202] In making the foregoing determinations the ICC will consider evidence of intramodal, intermodal, and geographic competition.[1203]

In *Laurel Sand & Gravel, Inc. v. CSX Transportation, Inc.,*[1204] a shipper and its prospective rail carrier filed suit in federal court to obtain trackage rights from CSX through the application of traditional antitrust principles. The plaintiff carrier alleged that the refusal by CSX to grant the carrier trackage rights, which precluded the carrier from serving the shipper directly (i.e., on a single line rate), violated, inter alia, Section 2 of the Sherman Act as a denial by monopolist of access to an essential facility.[1205] The district court concluded that even if CSX had a monopoly in a

---

1196.   49 U.S.C. § 10705(a) (1988).
1197.   *Id.* § 10705(e).
1198.   *Id.* § 11103(a).
1199.   *Id.* § 11103(c)(1).
1200.   *Ex parte* 445, Intramodal Rail Competition, 1 I.C.C.2d 822 (1985), *aff'd sub nom.* Baltimore Gas & Elec. Co. v. United States, 817 F.2d 108 (D.C. Cir. 1987) (codified at 49 C.F.R. § 1144 (1991)). The CARs provide, inter alia, that (1) the ICC will prescribe through routes and joint rates, and establish switching arrangements, only when necessary to remedy or prevent acts that are contrary to the competition policies of the rail transportation policy (49 U.S.C. § 10101a) or are otherwise anticompetitive; (2) the ICC will set aside proposed cancellations of joint rates and through routes only when a cancellation, or a rate that would remain after the cancellation, is anticompetitive after considering all relevant factors (except product competition); and (3) the ICC will initially suspend any cancellation that eliminates effective railroad competition for the affected traffic between origin and destination, without regard to whether intermodal or other forms of competition might exist.
1201.   3 I.C.C.2d 171 (1986), *aff'd sub nom.* Midtec Paper Corp. v. United States, 857 F.2d 1487 (D.C. Cir. 1988).
1202.   3 I.C.C.2d at 181.
1203.   *Id.; see also* Vista Chem. Co. v. Atchison, T. & S.F. Ry., 5 I.C.C.3d 331 (1989).
1204.   704 F. Supp. 1309 (D. Md. 1989), *aff'd,* 924 F.2d 539 (4th Cir.), *cert. denied,* 112 S. Ct. 64 (1991).
1205.   CSX had proposed a joint rate with the plaintiff rail carrier; however, the joint rate was allegedly too high to allow the plaintiff shipper to compete successfully. The plaintiffs then demanded trackage rights which CSX refused to grant.

relevant market and control of an essential facility, CSX had not violated Section 2 of the Sherman Act because it had offered reasonable access by means of a joint rate proposal[1206] and had no duty to offer trackage rights because CSX was not in the track leasing business.[1207]

In *Delaware & Hudson Railway Co. v. Consolidated Rail Corp.*,[1208] the Delaware & Hudson (D & H) sued Conrail under Section 2 of the Sherman Act alleging monopolization, denial of an essential facility and attempted monopolization. The dispute centered on a "make or buy" policy instituted by Conrail under which Conrail would agree to participate in a joint rate only if it received the same profit contribution on the movement as it would have received if it had been the sole carrier. In reversing the district court's grant of summary judgment to Conrail on the monopolization and attempted monopolization claims, the Second Circuit held that there were genuine issues of material fact as to whether the "make or buy" policy was a legitimate business strategy, or a plan willfully to preserve Conrail's monopoly power.[1209] The fact that the "make or buy" policy was profit-maximizing for Conrail did not shield the policy from Section 2.[1210] Similarly, the court held that there was a genuine issue of fact as to whether Conrail had denied D & H the use of an essential facility insofar as Conrail's rates under the "make or buy" policy may have been so unreasonable as to constitute a denial.[1211] The court contrasted Conrail's rates, which increased eightfold for the shipment in question under the "make or buy" policy, with the CSX rates at issue in *Laurel Sand & Gravel*.[1212]

(6) Mergers and Acquisitions

In addition to its authority to exempt rate bureau agreements from the antitrust laws, the ICC has authority to immunize mergers and consolidations by rail carriers when it finds the transaction to be "consistent with the public interest."[1213] In considering proposed mergers involving major railroads, the ICC must determine whether the transaction would have an adverse effect on competition among rail carriers in the affected region.[1214] And in rail merger proceedings not involving

---

1206. The district court held that the reasonableness of the CSX rate in the joint rate proposal must be viewed from CSX's perspective in the rail transportation business regardless of whether the rate allowed the shipper to be competitive in its business. 704 F. Supp. at 1323-24.

1207. *Id.* at 1324.

1208. 902 F.2d 174 (2d Cir. 1990), *cert. denied*, 111 S. Ct. 2041 (1991).

1209. *Id.* at 178-79. The court also held that there was a genuine issue as to whether Conrail possessed monopoly power in the relevant market. *Id.* at 179.

1210. *Id.* at 178.

1211. *Id.* at 179-80.

1212. *Id.* at 180.

1213. 49 U.S.C. § 11344(c) (1988); *see* United States v. ICC, 396 U.S. 491, 508-13 (1970); Seaboard A.L.R.R. v. United States, 382 U.S. 154, 156-57 (1965) (per curiam); Minneapolis & St. L. Ry. v. United States, 361 U.S. 173, 186-88 (1959).

1214. The Staggers Act added to the list of statutory factors that the ICC must consider in reviewing railroad mergers and consolidations under the "public interest" standard "whether the proposed transaction would have an adverse effect on competition among rail carriers in the affected region." Pub. L. No. 96-448, § 228(a), 94 Stat. 1895, 1931 (1980) (codified at 49 U.S.C. § 11344(b)(1)(E) (1988)); *see* Norfolk & W. Ry.–Purchase–Illinois T.R.R., 363 I.C.C. 882, 886 (1981). The Staggers Rail Act was intended to codify the ICC's prior approach of considering

major railroads, the ICC must grant its approval unless it determines that "the anticompetitive effects of the transaction outweigh the public interest in meeting significant transportation needs."[1215]

Following passage of the Staggers Rail Act, the ICC approved several major railroad mergers and consolidations. In a number of these cases the ICC exercised its statutory authority to condition its approval on the applicant railroads' acceptance of certain measures (such as trackage rights awards to other carriers, line divestitures and others) designed to alleviate the potential adverse competitive effects of the transaction.[1216] In *Santa Fe Southern Pacific Corp.–Control–Southern Pacific Transportation Co.*, the ICC rejected the proposed acquisition, concluding that the merger of the two railroads (whose rail lines paralleled one another to a substantial extent) would have significantly adverse effects on intramodal rail competition, that the potential public benefits of the transaction (including cost savings and other efficiencies as well as service improvements) did not outweigh these anticompetitive effects, and that the poor financial health of one of the merging railroads did not justify approval of the transaction.[1217] The ICC ordered the applicant holding company to divest itself of one of the two railroads, which had been operated separately during the pendency of the ICC's proceedings pursuant to an independent voting trust.[1218]

The ICC has approved several significant carrier consolidation transactions uniting railroads and other transportation modes, such as water carriers and trucking companies. The ICC has concluded that such intermodal consolidations, which are

---

competitive impacts when evaluating railroad mergers. *See* 126 CONG. REC. H8604 (daily ed. Sept. 9, 1980) (statement of Rep. Panetta); Union Pac. Corp., Pac. Rail Sys. & Union Pac. R.R.–Control–Missouri Pac. Corp. & Missouri Pac. R.R., 366 I.C.C. 459, 483 (1982), *aff'd in part and rev'd in part sub nom.* Southern Pac. Transp. Co. v. ICC, 736 F.2d 708 (D.C. Cir. 1984) (per curiam), *cert. denied,* 469 U.S. 1208 (1985). In *Southern Pacific Transportation Co.,* the D.C. Circuit stated that the Staggers Rail Act "modifies but does not basically alter the ICC's traditional approach," and that the ICC "has always, and should continue, to perform a balancing test which takes a myriad of factors – including competition – into consideration and weighs 'the potential benefits to applicants and the public against the potential harm to the public.'" 736 F.2d at 717 (quoting 49 C.F.R. § 1111.10(c) (1981)).

1215. 49 U.S.C. § 11344(d)(2) (1988).

1216. *See, e.g.,* Chicago, M., St. P. & Pac. R.R.–Reorganization–Acquisition by Grand Trunk Corp., 2 I.C.C.2d 161 (1984), *aff'd sub nom.* No. 77-B-8999, *In re* Chicago, M., St. P. & Pac. R.R. (N.D. Ill.) (Bench Order dated Feb. 19, 1985), *aff'd,* 799 F.2d 317 (7th Cir. 1986), *cert. denied,* 481 U.S. 1068 (1987); Union Pacific Corp., 366 I.C.C. 459; Guilford Transp. Indus.–Control–Delaware & H. Ry., 366 I.C.C. 396 (1982), *aff'd in part and rev'd in part sub nom.* Central Vt. Ry. v. ICC, 711 F.2d 331 (D.C. Cir. 1983); Guilford Transp. Indus.–Control–Boston & Main Corp., 366 I.C.C. 292 (1982), *aff'd in part and rev'd in part sub nom.* Lamoille Valley R.R. v. ICC, 711 F.2d 295 (D.C. Cir. 1983); Norfolk S. Corp.–Control–Norfolk & W. Ry. & S. Ry., 366 I.C.C. 171 (1982); CSX Corp.–Control–Chessie Sys. and Seaboard Coast Line Indus., 363 I.C.C. 518 (1980), *aff'd sub nom.* Brotherhood of Maintenance of Way Employees v. ICC, 698 F.2d 315 (7th Cir. 1983); Burlington N., Inc.–Control and Merger–St. Louis-S.F. Ry., 360 I.C.C. 784 (1980), *aff'd sub nom.* Missouri-Kan.-Tex. R.R. v. United States, 632 F.2d 392 (5th Cir. 1980), *cert. denied,* 451 U.S. 1017 (1981).

1217. 2 I.C.C. 2d 709 (1986), *petition to reopen denied,* 3 I.C.C. 2d 926 (1987).

1218. The ICC subsequently approved a plan of divestiture calling for the sale of Southern Pacific to another rail carrier. *See* Rio Grande Indus., SPTC Holding, Inc. & Denver & R.G. W. R.R.–Control–Southern Pac. Transp. Co., 4 I.C.C.2d 834 (1988), *aff'd sub nom.* Kansas City S. Indus. v. ICC, 902 F.2d 423 (5th Cir. 1990).

reviewed under separate statutory criteria, can benefit competition and the public by enhancing the efficiency of service.

In addition to general review under the "public interest" standards of the carrier consolidation provisions of the Interstate Commerce Act, consolidation transactions involving railroads and water carriers are subject to ICC scrutiny under the Panama Canal Act.[1219] This Act generally prohibits a railroad from owning any interest in a water common carrier with which the railroad does or may compete for traffic. However, the statute explicitly authorizes the ICC to approve a railroad interest in a competing water carrier when the ICC finds that railroad ownership will allow the water carrier "to be operated in the public interest advantageously to interstate commerce" and will allow "competition, without reduction, on the water route in question."[1220]

In *Crounse Corp. v. ICC*,[1221] the Sixth Circuit upheld an ICC decision that approved, under the Panama Canal Act, the acquisition of the nation's largest inland barge line by the second largest railroad. The ICC had concluded that the railroad and barge line competed directly with one another for traffic, thus triggering the general prohibition of the statute, but found that the transaction would not reduce competition on affected water routes and would not impair the barge line's ability to provide service to the public. The court, which also rejected the claim that the Panama Canal Act embodies an absolute prohibition of rail/water consolidations, found sufficient evidence to support the ICC's findings that the transaction would not reduce competition due to the intensity of existing and potential barge competition and that the transaction would promote competition by enhancing the efficiency of intermodal rail/barge transportation. In the course of its analysis, the court rejected the suggestion that the elimination of competition between the railroad and barge line could itself constitute an impermissible reduction in competition and sustained the ICC's decision to focus its competitive analysis on the potential effects of the proposed consolidation on barge competition. The court also ruled that harm to individual barge competitors is not harm to competition within the meaning of the statute.[1222]

The standards governing railroad/motor carrier consolidation and acquisition transactions are ambiguous at present. The Interstate Commerce Act provides that the ICC may approve a rail/motor consolidation "only if it finds that the transaction (1) is consistent with the public interest, (2) enables the rail carrier to use motor carrier transportation to public advantage in its operations, and (3) does not

---

1219.   Ch. 337, 37 Stat. 560, 566 (1912) (codified at 49 U.S.C. § 11321(a) (1988)).

1220.   49 U.S.C. § 11321(b) (1988). The provision excludes from the ICC's approval authority railroad interests in competing water carriers that are "operated through the Panama Canal." *Id.*; *see generally* Water Transp. Ass'n v. ICC, 715 F.2d 581 (D.C. Cir. 1983) (discussing Panama Canal Act in context of question whether Act permits railroad to use an independent voting trust to hold stock of acquired water carrier pending ICC decision on application for approval of acquisition), *cert. denied*, 465 U.S. 1006 (1984).

1221.   781 F.2d 1176 (6th Cir.), *cert. denied*, 479 U.S. 890 (1986). The court's decision affirmed the ICC's decision in CSX Corp.–Control–American Commercial Lines, 2 I.C.C.2d 490 (1984).

1222.   The ICC has extended its interpretation of the Panama Canal Act by approving a railroad's acquisition of a major U.S. flagship ocean container shipping line. Joint Application of CSX Corp. and Sea-Land Corp., 3 I.C.C. 2d 512 (1981), *petition for review dismissed*, No. 87-4037 (2d Cir. Aug. 12, 1987), *cert. denied*, 488 U.S. 841 (1988).

unreasonably restrain competition."[1223] The first and third statutory criteria — consistency with the public interest and competitive impact are — essentially the same as those applied by the ICC in other carrier consolidation proceedings. The second statutory criterion the requirement that the ICC find that the acquiring railroad will use the motor carrier advantageously in the railroad's operations imposes an additional restriction on rail/motor consolidations.

Prior to the Staggers Rail Act, the ICC applied a restrictive interpretation of the "in its operations" requirement. The ICC permitted a railroad to acquire a motor carrier only for the performance of operations that were "auxiliary to or supplemental of" the railroad's rail service, unless the acquiring railroad could demonstrate the existence of "special circumstances" warranting unrestricted operating authority.[1224] The ICC and the courts have referred to this interpretation of the "in its operations" requirement as the "special circumstances" doctrine.

Following passage of the Staggers Rail Act, the ICC determined that its restrictive interpretation of the "in its operations" requirement was no longer necessary to maintain effective intermodal competition. In *Ex Parte No. 438, Acquisition of Motor Carriers By Railroads (Ex Parte 438)*,[1225] the ICC held that the "in its operations" requirement would be satisfied by a showing that the acquired motor carrier would be used to public advantage in the railroad's overall transportation operations, rather than in its rail operations specifically, and eliminated the requirement of a showing of "special circumstances."

The ICC subsequently applied this more relaxed interpretation of the "in its operations" requirement in its decision in *Norfolk Southern Corp.—Control—North American Van Lines, Inc. (Norfolk Southern)*,[1226] which approved a railroad's proposed acquisition of a trucking company. On appeal, however, the D.C. Circuit reversed the ICC's decision, holding that the ICC had exceeded its statutory authority in adopting and applying the *Ex Parte 438* interpretation of the "in its operations" requirement.[1227] Congress then passed legislation directing the ICC to apply the *Ex Parte 438* standard to rail/motor carrier consolidations that were initiated between July 20, 1984 and September 30, 1986.[1228]

1223.   49 U.S.C. § 11344(c) (1988).

1224.   *See, e.g.*, Rock Island Motor Transit Co.–Purchase–White Line Motor Freight Co., 40 M.C.C. 457 (1946), *supplemented*, 55 M.C.C. 567 (1949), *aff'd sub nom.* United States v. Rock Island Motor Transit Co., 340 U.S. 419 (1951); Pennsylvania Truck Lines, Acquisition of Control of Baker Motor Freight, Inc., 1 M.C.C. 101 (1936), *supplemented*, 5 M.C.C. 9 (1937), *supplemented*, 5 M.C.C. 49 (1937).

1225.   1 I.C.C.2d 716 (1984).

1226.   1 I.C.C.2d 842 (1985).

1227.   International Bhd. of Teamsters v. ICC, 801 F.2d 1423 (D.C. Cir. 1986), *vacated per curiam*, 818 F.2d 87 (D.C. Cir. 1987). The D.C. Circuit has also held that the ICC may not use its authority under the motor carrier exemption provision of 49 U.S.C. § 11343(e)(1) to exempt rail/motor consolidation transactions from the prior approval requirements of the Interstate Commerce Act. Regular Common Carrier Conf. v. United States, 820 F.2d 1323 (D.C. Cir. 1987) (§ 11343(e) applies only to transactions between motor carriers and not to rail/motor transactions).

1228.   *See* Omnibus Anti-Drug Abuse Act of 1986, Pub. L. No. 99-570, § 3403, 100 Stat. 3207 (1986). The legislation directs the ICC to apply the *Ex Parte 438* standard in reviewing rail/motor consolidation transactions if the applicant rail carrier, between July 20, 1984, and September 30, 1986: (1) filed an application with the ICC to acquire a motor carrier, (2) entered into a contract or signed a letter of intent to acquire a motor carrier, or (3) made a public tender offer to acquire

(7) Section 10 of the Clayton Act

The Antitrust Amendments Act of 1990[1229] repealed Section 10 of the Clayton Act,[1230] which prohibited "dealings in securities, supplies, or other articles of commerce . . . [or] contracts for construction or maintenance" with a common carrier in the aggregate of $50,000 a year or more if the other party to the transaction and the common carrier had interlocking personnel, including common directors, unless there was public bidding. Common carriers, including railroads, are now subject under Section 8 of the Clayton Act[1231] to the same interlock standards as other businesses.

c. AIR TRANSPORTATION

(1) Regulatory History

The domestic air transportation industry, formerly one of the nation's more closely regulated, is today almost entirely free of economic regulation. As of January 1, 1989, the antitrust laws, enforced by the Department of Justice, rather than the regulatory statutes administered by the Department of Transportation, govern virtually all competitive issues in this industry.

From 1938 to 1978, air carriers[1232] were subject to extensive regulation pursuant to the Civil Aeronautics Act of 1938 and the Federal Aviation Act of 1958 (the Act).[1233] The regulatory scheme was administered by the Civil Aeronautics Board (CAB), which had broad powers to regulate, among other things, entry and exit,[1234] rates,[1235] consolidations, mergers and acquisitions of control,[1236] interlocking relationships,[1237] methods of competition,[1238] and agreements among carriers.[1239]

The passage of the Airline Deregulation Act of 1978[1240] set in motion a continuing reduction in the powers of the CAB in various areas, terminating the

---

a motor carrier. *See* International Bhd. of Teamsters v. ICC, 818 F.2d 87, 88-90 (D.C. Cir. 1987) (vacating the court's earlier decision in the *Norfolk Southern* matter in light of the subsequent legislation) (per curiam); Finance Dkt. No. 31000, Union Pac. Corp. & BTMC Corp.–Control–Overnite Transp. Co. (served Sept. 23, 1987) (not printed).

1229. Pub. L. No. 101-588, 104 Stat. 2879 (1990).

1230. 15 U.S.C. § 20 (1988).

1231. 15 U.S.C. § 19 (1988), *as amended by* Antitrust Amendments Act of 1990, Pub. L. No. 101-588, 104 Stat. 2879 (1990); *see* Part J of Chapter III of this treatise.

1232. "Air carrier" means "any citizen of the United States who undertakes, whether directly or indirectly or by a lease or any other arrangement, to engage in air transportation." 49 U.S.C. app. § 1301(3) (1988). "Foreign air carrier" means "any person, not a citizen of the United States, who undertakes, whether directly or indirectly or by lease or any other arrangement, to engage in foreign air transportation." *Id.* § 1301(22).

1233. The Civil Aeronautics Act of 1938, 49 U.S.C. §§ 401-03 was repealed by the Federal Aviation Act, 49 U.S.C. app. §§ 1301-1387 (1988).

1234. 49 U.S.C. app. § 1371 (1988); *see also id.* § 1372 (relating to foreign air carriers).

1235. *Id.* § 1373.

1236. *Id.* § 1378.

1237. *Id.* § 1379.

1238. *Id.* § 1381.

1239. *Id.* § 1382.

1240. Pub. L. No. 95-504, 92 Stat. 1705 (1978).

agency altogether on January 1, 1985.[1241]   At that point, the Department of
Transportation took over the regulatory tasks that remained. The Transportation
Department retained authority, under Sections 408, 409, and 412 of the Act, to
regulate consolidations, mergers and acquisitions of control, interlocking
relationships, and pooling and other agreements in the aviation industry.[1242]   It
also had authority, pursuant to Section 414 of the Act, to grant antitrust
immunity.[1243]

1241.   All remaining functions, powers and duties of the CAB were terminated or transferred effective
         on or before January 1, 1985. *See* 49 U.S.C. app. § 1551 (1988). Statutory and regulatory
         references to the "Board" subsequent to that date should therefore all be read as references to
         Department of Transportation.

1242.   Section 408 of the Act declared unlawful enumerated types of consolidations, mergers, purchases,
         leases, operating contracts and acquisitions of control involving air carriers, foreign air carriers,
         persons controlling air carriers or foreign air carriers, other common carriers, or persons
         "substantially engaged in the business of aeronautics" unless granted prior approval. 49 U.S.C.
         app. § 1378(a)(1)-(7) (1988). Approval for such transactions, however, was required, unless the
         regulators found that the transaction would "not be consistent with the public interest." *Id.*
         § 1378(b)(1). Moreover, the CAB and the Department of Transportation were permitted to
         approve transactions that might lessen competition, tend to create a monopoly, or in any other way
         be tantamount to a "restraint of trade" upon a finding that the "anticompetitive effects" were
         "outweighed in the public interest by the probable effect of the transaction in meeting significant
         transportation conveniences and needs of the public," for which there was not "a reasonably
         available alternative having materially less anticompetitive effects." *Id.* § 1378(b)(1)(B).
             Section 409 prohibited interlocking relationships between air carriers and common carriers or
         persons "substantially engaged in the business of aeronautics." *Id.* § 1379. Again, approval could
         be granted upon a showing that the "public interest" would not be "adversely affected." *Id.*
             Section 412 allowed air carriers and foreign air carriers to request authority to discuss possible
         cooperative working agreements or to file contracts or agreements for approval (*id.* § 1382(a)(1))
         which was to be granted upon a finding that the contract, agreement or request was not "adverse
         to the public interest." (*Id.* § 1382(a)(2)(A). The regulators were specifically directed to
         disapprove any contract, agreement, or request that substantially reduced or eliminated
         competition, absent findings that the contract, agreement, or request is necessary to meet a serious
         transportation need or to secure important public benefits, including international comity or
         foreign policy considerations, and that such need can be met or such benefits can be secured by
         a reasonably available alternative means having materially less anticompetitive effects. *Id.*
         § 1382(a)(2)(A)(i).
             The regulators also had to disapprove any "contract or agreement . . . that limits the level of
         capacity among air carriers in markets in which they compete, that fixes rates, fares, or charges
         between or among air carriers . . . ." *Id.* § 1382(a)(2)(A)(iii).

1243.   49 U.S.C. app. § 1384 (1988). The CAB and Transportation Department were vested with
         discretion to exempt a person affected by a Transportation Department order regarding
         consolidation, merger, acquisition or control (*id.* § 1378), interlocking relationships (*id.* § 1379),
         or pooling and other agreements (*id.* § 1382) from the antitrust laws. The most significant
         decisions in this area had to do with ARC and SATO.
             As of January 1, 1985, ARC, the Airlines Reporting Corporation, took over the various
         functions that had been performed by ATC, an affiliate of the Air Transportation Association
         (ATA). These functions include travel agent accreditation and operation of the Area Settlement
         Plan, an agreement among major domestic and international carriers designed to regulate the sale
         of tickets and the settlement of agents' accounts with the carriers. In 1982, the CAB held that
         certain provisions of the agreements unnecessarily reduced competition, and that the portions of
         the agreements of which it did approve did not require the § 414 antitrust immunity that had
         earlier been afforded them. The 1982 Order set December 31, 1984, as the date for the expiration
         of the § 414 immunity so as to give the participating carriers an opportunity to review and modify
         their agreements accordingly. *See* Order 82-12-85 (1982). In response to that decision, the
         airlines established ARC, arranging for a corporate entity, which the Transportation Department,

As part of the continuing process of deregulation, the Department of Transportation lost the power to approve mergers and interlocking relationships in the aviation industry on January 1, 1989. Airline mergers, acquisitions, and interlocking relationships no longer require Transportation Department approval, and the Justice Department now analyzes them under the antitrust laws using the same standards applied to other industries.[1244] Most of Transportation Department's authority to approve and grant antitrust immunity to agreements among carriers has also expired.[1245]

(2) Civil Aeronautics Board and Department of Transportation Decisions in Merger, Acquisition, and Control Cases

While it had antitrust authority for the airline industry, the CAB decided a number

---

upon revisiting the issue in 1984, described as one that gave it "no reason to believe [it] anticompetitive or otherwise unlawful." Order 84-12-43, at 4 n.3 (1984).

SATO, an airline joint venture also operated under ATC agreements, provides air travel and ticketing services on federal premises to civilian and military government personnel. Although the CAB had approved these agreements under § 412 and afforded them antitrust immunity under § 414, the Transportation Department determined that the immunity should not be extended indefinitely, and set a January 31, 1986, deadline for its expiration. Order 85-9-57 (1985). Antitrust immunity was extended for an additional three months in light of the fact that the member carriers were making good progress with the necessary modifications to the agreements by creating a new corporation and by establishing a new settlement system for ticket sales. Order 86-1-62 (1986). Immunity expired in 1986.

1244. Pursuant to 49 U.S.C. app. § 1551 (1988), §§ 408 and 409 of the Act (49 U.S.C. app. §§ 1378, 1379) expired on January 1, 1989. With the expiration of the Transportation Department's authority to approve mergers, acquisitions, and interlocking relationships in the aviation industry, the antitrust laws now govern all such transactions.

One statutory anomaly, however, remains. The Clayton Act still gives exclusive authority to the Secretary of Transportation, rather than the Federal Trade Commission, to enforce its provisions applicable to "air carriers and foreign air carriers subject to the Federal Aviation Act of 1958." 15 U.S.C. § 21 (1988). Therefore, despite the fact that the Department of Justice and the Federal Trade Commission now receive premerger notification of proposed aviation transactions, only the Justice Department or the Transportation Department can bring an action to challenge a merger. The Deputy General Counsel of the Department of Transportation has stated, however, that while the Department had authority to approve or disapprove mergers under the Federal Aviation Act, "it had never implemented its 15 U.S.C. § 21 authority," and indeed, now that it no longer has § 408 authority, it "has no plans to do so at this time." GENERAL ACCOUNTING OFFICE, AIRLINE COMPETITION: DOT'S IMPLEMENTATION OF AIRLINE REGULATORY AUTHORITY 34 (June 1989). It is the position of the Transportation Department that "airline merger authority should belong to the Department of Justice and Federal Trade Commission." *Id.*

1245. Pursuant to 49 U.S.C. app. § 1551 (1988), § 414 of the Act (49 U.S.C. app. § 1384) expired on January 1, 1989, for all transactions that would have been within Transportation Department's jurisdiction pursuant to §§ 408, 409 and 412(a) and (b) of the Act. The only exception is Mutual Aid Agreements made pursuant to § 412(c) of the Act, for which the Department of Transportation, under § 414, can still, under certain circumstances, grant antitrust immunity. 49 U.S.C. app. §§ 1382(c), 1384 (1988). A mutual aid agreement is any contract or agreement between air carriers which provides that any such air carrier will receive payments from the other air carriers which are parties to such contract or agreement for any period during which such air carrier is not engaging in air transportation, or is providing reduced levels of service in air transportation, due to a labor strike. *Id.* § 1382(c)(3)(a). Previously approved mutual aid agreements in effect on October 24, 1978, are statutorily "deemed disapproved and not in effect on and after October 24, 1978." *Id.* § 1382(c)(1).

of consolidation and merger cases under Section 408.[1246]   In some cases it declined to exercise its discretion to grant antitrust immunity,[1247] and rather than relying exclusively on market share statistics as an indication of the potential effect of the transaction, it analyzed possible barriers to entry to determine whether a proposed acquisition "would substantially inhibit actual competition or the ability of potential entrants to respond to any attempt to exercise market power 'by decreasing service or raising fares above competitive levels in any relevant market.' "[1248]

Once vested with antitrust authority for the airline industry, the Transportation Department also decided several consolidation and merger cases.[1249]   It considered a total of seventeen substantial transactions under Section 408, issuing thirteen final orders approving twelve proposed mergers or acquisitions.[1250] Three applications were withdrawn.[1251]   The Department of Transportation emphasized the competitive impact aspect of its Section 408 jurisdiction, and did not

---

1246. *E.g.*, Texas Int'l-Continental Acquisition Case, Order 81-10-66 (1981); Continental-Western Merger Case, Order 81-6-1/2 (1981); Republic-Airwest Acquisition Case, Order 80-9-65 (1980); Tiger Int'l-Seaboard World Acquisition Case, Order 80-7-20 (1980); Eastern-National Acquisition Case, Order 79-12-163/164/165 (1979); Continental-Western Merger Case, Order 79-9-185 (1979); North Central-Southern Merger Case, Order 79-6-6/8 (1979).

1247. *See, e.g.*, Texas Int'l-Nat'l and Pan American-Nat'l Acquisition Case, Order 79-12-163/164/165, at 75 (1979). In *Pan American-Nat'l*, the CAB declined to transfer National's Miami-London route to Pan American on the grounds that the transfer might substantially lessen competition in the United States-London market and would thus violate § 408(b)(1). At the same time, the CAB issued exemption authority to Pan American to serve the Miami-London route pending the outcome of a separate proceeding for that route. Order 79-12-163/164/165, at 47-54 (1979). Similarly, in *Texas Int'l-Continental*, the CAB deleted Texas International's route between Dallas/Fort Worth and the Yucatan in Mexico but granted it exemption authority to serve the route pending the outcome of a separate proceeding.

1248. *Texas Int'l-Continental*, Order 81-10-66, at 5 (citing *Texas Int'l-Nat'l* and *Pan American-Nat'l*); *Continental-Western*, Order 81-6-1/2, at 3-5. Although these decisions do not use the term "contestability," this formulation of the test for antitrust analysis captures the essence of the contestability theory. *See infra* note 1253, discussing the contestability theory in detail.

1249. Transportation Department review of mergers generally focused on transactions involving two large-aircraft, scheduled passenger air carriers. Section 408 exemptions granted by the Department included approval for USAir's acquisition of Pennsylvania Commuter Airlines (Order 85-5-115 (1985)) and approval for Alaska Air Group's acquisition of Horizon Air (Order 86-12-61 (1986)).

1250. USAir's acquisition of Piedmont, Order 87-10-58 (1987); American Airline's acquisition of AirCal, Order 87-3-80 (1987); USAir's acquisition of Pacific Southwest Airlines, Order 87-3-11 (1987); Texas Air's acquisition of People Express and Frontier, Order 86-10-53 (1986); Texas Air's acquisition of Eastern Air Lines, Order 86-10-2 (1986) (Earlier, in Order 86-8-77, the Transportation Department had found that this proposed merger was likely to substantially reduce competition in the Washington-New York and New York-Boston shuttle markets, but rescinded its initial disapproval when Texas Air agreed to transfer enough additional slots to Pan Am to enable it to provide effective competition in those markets.); Trans World Airlines' acquisition of Ozark Airlines, Order 86-9-29 (1986); Northwest Airlines' acquisition of Republic Airlines, Order 86-7-81 (1986); Horizon's acquisition of Cascade, Order 86-1-67 (1986); Piedmont Aviation's acquisition of Empire Airlines, Order 86-1-45 (1986); United Airlines' acquisition of Pan American World Airways' Int'l Pac. Operations, Order 85-11-67 (1985); Southwest Airline's acquisition of Muse Air, Order 85-6-79 (1985); Midway's acquisition of Air Florida, Order 85-6-33 (1985).

1251. Texas Air's proposed acquisition of Trans World Airlines, Dkt. No. 43224; Texas Air Corp.'s proposed acquisition of Frontier Airlines, Dkt. No. 43413; TWA's proposed acquisition of USAir, Dkt. Nos. 44715, 44722.

approve any proposed merger on the ground that, although anticompetitive, it nevertheless met transportation needs and secured public benefits that could not be met or obtained by any reasonably available, less anticompetitive transaction.[1252]

(3) Merger and Acquisition Decisions After January 1, 1989

In a speech shortly after the expiration of the Transportation Department's authority over mergers and acquisitions, the Justice Department rejected the "contestability" theory on which the Transportation Department based approval of several mergers.[1253] It also announced that because of the limited number of remaining national carriers, it will focus its analysis on the impact of a proposed merger on national concentration levels.[1254] It also stated that:

1252. Nor did the Department of Transportation grant antitrust immunity under § 414 of the Act to any of the transactions it approved under § 408.

1253. "Contestability" theory examines the ease of "entry and exit in city pair markets" and the effect of "incumbents' fear of entry by other carriers" on fare levels. *See* Joint Application of Texas Air Corp. and People Express, Inc., Order 86-10-53, at 14 (1986).

    In a March 1989 speech, the Justice Department's senior antitrust official announced that "[t]oday . . . most airline markets do not appear to be contestable, if they ever were." Remarks of Charles F. Rule, then Assistant Att'y Gen., Antitrust Div., Before the International Aviation Club, Antitrust and Airline Mergers: A New Era, 15 (Mar. 7, 1989) [hereinafter Justice Department Speech]. The Justice Department has also drawn attention to its opposition to the Transportation Department-approved TWA/Ozark and Northwest/Republic mergers, and stated that "in the absence of unusual circumstances . . . the Antitrust Division will seek to block mergers between airlines with overlapping hubs." *Id.* at 19-21. The Assistant Attorney General also noted that "although we ultimately decided that we did not have the evidence to sustain a challenge to the USAir/Piedmont merger in the face of DOT's presumption that airline markets are contestable, mergers like it in the future could face an antitrust challenge." *Id.* at 23-24. The problem with a merger between carriers with hubs concentrated in a particular region "related to competition on one- or two-stop flights over alternative hubs in the region." *Id.* at 24.

    The U.S. General Accounting Office (GAO) criticized the Transportation Department's use of the contestability theory. According to GAO, Transportation continued to use the theory, originally that of the CAB, without taking into consideration "fundamental changes" in the industry that called into question its continuing viability. GAO defines the theory as follows:

> Contestability theory focuses on the role of potential competitors in restraining an incumbent firm's ability to exercise market power and charge monopolistic prices. According to contestability theory, even in a concentrated market where there are few or no other carriers serving the same two cities (city-pair market), incumbent carriers cannot take advantage of their dominant position if it is not costly for other carriers to enter and exit the market.

GENERAL ACCOUNTING OFFICE, AIRLINE COMPETITION: DOT'S IMPLEMENTATION OF AIRLINE REGULATORY AUTHORITY 20 (June 1989). GAO observed that even if CAB's contestability theory was correct, "by 1985, when DOT assumed airline merger responsibility, changes in the operating environment made the presumption of easy market entry less persuasive." *Id.* at 22. GAO also pointed out that several studies of the airline industry showed that the number of airlines actually competing in a market was positively correlated with fares, indicating that potential competition alone was not sufficient to discipline fares. These studies (including a 1982 Staff Report that the CAB did not adopt) and observations made by industry experts about the differences between airline competition immediately after deregulation and airline competition in 1985 called into question the Transportation Department's assumptions that the threat of new entry would prevent merged airlines from exploiting their market power. The Department of Transportation neither tested its assumptions to see if they were valid, nor looked at the effects its merger decisions were having on the industry. *Id.* at 14.

1254. Justice Department Speech, *supra* note 1253, at 25-26.

Perhaps somewhat overlooked by DOT in the course of deregulating the airline industry, the antitrust laws have a valuable role to play to ensure that a competitive environment does not sow the seeds of its own demise.[1255]

The Department of Justice announced that it "will apply the expertise and analytic tools . . . developed by reviewing mergers in all industries for many years," and expressed the opinion that "[t]his institutional knowledge and experience . . . gives [the Department] a significant advantage in airline merger review over agencies — like DOT — of a narrower, industry-specific perspective."[1256]

Since January 1, 1989, the Department announced that it would file suit to oppose three proposed transactions: sale of eight gates at Philadelphia International Airport and route authority between Toronto and Philadelphia by Eastern Air Lines to USAir,[1257] the proposed joint venture of American Airlines SABRE computer reservation system (CRS) with that of Delta's Datas II CRS,[1258] and sale of sixty-seven landing and takeoff slots and five gates at Washington National Airport by Eastern Air Lines to United Air Lines.[1259]

On June 7, 1989, the Department announced that it had advised USAir and Eastern that it would file a civil antitrust suit alleging a violation of Section 1 of the Sherman Act in order to oppose the proposed transaction. It found that USAir "is the largest provider of passenger transportation at Philadelphia, with about 43% of the enplanements and 56% of the departures" there. It also found that USAir controls fifteen of the forty-nine gates at the Philadelphia airport, while Eastern and Continental control twelve, the second largest block of gates.[1260] According to the Department, "[t]he proposed acquisition of the gates poses a significant threat to competition in the provision of passenger air service to and from Philadelphia."[1261] It also stated that "[w]ith USAir's acquisition of Eastern's block of gates it is unlikely that another carrier would be able within a reasonable period to assemble a block of gates sufficiently large to operate a hub in competition with USAir."[1262] On the question of the Toronto-Philadelphia route authority, the Department observed that "Eastern carries about 76 percent of the passengers travelling between Philadelphia and Toronto on its non-stop routes," and that "USAir is Eastern's most significant competitor, and carries about 20 percent on its one-stop service over various gateways," concluding that "[b]ecause entry on Canadian routes is strictly limited, we are concerned that this transfer of authority will significantly impair competition on this route."[1263]

On June 22, 1989, the Department announced that it would challenge the the proposed joint venture of the CRS systems of American Airlines and Delta Air Lines,[1264] alleging that the proposed joint venture "would violate Section 7 of the Clayton Act and Section 1 of the Sherman Act because it would substantially lessen

---

1255.   *Id.* at 32-33.
1256.   *Id.* at 28.
1257.   Department of Justice Press Release, 89-173 (June 7, 1989).
1258.   Department of Justice Press Release, 89-191 (June 22, 1989).
1259.   Department of Justice Press Release, 91-57 (Feb. 14, 1991).
1260.   Department of Justice Press Release, 89-173 (June 7, 1989).
1261.   *Id.*
1262.   *Id.*
1263.   *Id.*
1264.   Department of Justice Press Release, 89-191 (June 22, 1989).

competition both in the sale of CRS services to travel agents and in the provision of scheduled airline passenger service."[1265]   It found that there are only five computer reservation systems in the United States and concluded that the elimination of one of the five competitors "could result in higher charges to travel agents for using CRS services."[1266]   On the question of lessening competition in "the provision of scheduled airline passenger service," the Department of Justice offered the following analysis:

> Travel agents using a particular CRS tend to sell a disproportionately high number of tickets on that CRS owner's airline. Because owner airlines sell more tickets when their CRS is used to book flights than they would if a neutral CRS were used, competing airlines are less able to enter or expand service on city pairs in competition with airlines that also possess high CRS shares on that city pair.
>
> The proposed transaction will increase CRS concentration on many city pairs and will combine high CRS market shares and the air transportation service of Delta or American on those city pairs. In city pair markets that are already highly concentrated, the effect of the joint venture could be both to increase concentration in those markets and make it more difficult for other airlines to enter the markets even if fares go up. As a result, in those city pairs, fares are likely to go up and service quality is likely to fall.[1267]

On February 14, 1991, the Department announced that it had advised United Air Lines and the bankruptcy trustee of Eastern Air Lines that it would file a civil antitrust suit alleging that the proposed sale by Eastern to United of slots and gates at Washington National Airport would violate Section 1 of the Sherman Act by lessening competition in the provision of airline passenger service between Washington, D.C., and other United States cities.[1268]   It observed that after Eastern's shutdown, United, through its hub at Dulles International Airport, and USAir, the largest carrier at Washington National, were the only carriers with nonstop service from Washington to many other cities.   Moreover, "without a sufficiently large number of slots at National, it would be unlikely for another carrier to compete with United and USAir in many of these markets."[1269]   The Department of Justice also stated that "under the antitrust laws, a proposed sale by a failed firm that is anticompetitive cannot proceed if there exists a less anticompetitive purchaser," and that Northwest Airlines, which submitted the second highest bid at the public auction of Eastern's assets, constituted a less anticompetitive purchaser than United.[1270]

Although competitive issues are raised periodically in proceedings before the Department of Transportation under Section 401 of the Act[1271] the Department

---

1265.   *Id.*
1266.   *Id.*
1267.   *Id.* In announcing Justice Department's opposition to the proposed American-Delta CRS deal, the Attorney General noted that the Secretary of Transportation had expressed concern that the transaction might have an adverse effect on competition in the airline industry and said that the Department of Justice was "pleased that the Department of Transportation shares our concern for competition in the industry." *Id.*
1268.   Department of Justice Press Release, 91-57 (Feb. 14, 1991).
1269.   *Id.*
1270.   *Id.*
1271.   49 U.S.C. app. § 1371 (1988).   Section 401 has provisions on transfers of certificates (*id.* § 1371(h)) and continuing fitness. *Id.* § 1371(r).

has indicated that the "primary concern over the antitrust implications of a merger is now the domain of the Department of Justice."[1272]

(4) Preemption

The Airline Deregulation Act prohibits local governments from imposing economic regulations on the industry to replace those of the Department of Transportation. Section 105(a) of the Airline Deregulation Act specifies:

> no State or political subdivision thereof and no interstate agency or other political agency of two or more States shall enact or enforce any law, rule, regulation, standard, or other provision having the force and effect of law relating to rates, routes, or services of any air carrier having authority . . . [49 U.S.C. §§ 1371-1389] to provide air transportation.[1273]

The most significant issue in this area concerns advertisements of airline fares. From 1985 to 1988, Department of Transportation issued a series of orders that modified regulations[1274] on advertisements of airfares promulgated pursuant to Section 411 of the Act.[1275] The regulations, originally designed to prevent deceptive advertising of ground and airfare components of tour packages, require that tour operators and airlines advertise only the total price of the services sold: the "entire price to be paid by the customer to the air carrier, or agent, for . . . air transportation, tour or tour component."[1276] In December 1985, the Department of Transportation issued an order allowing advertisers to separate from the total price a $3 international departure tax if the amount of the tax was clearly stated elsewhere in the advertisement.[1277] In December 1987, the National Association of Attorneys General (NAAG) adopted guidelines that took the position that separate advertising of air travel surcharges was deceptive within the meaning of the consumer protection laws of various states.[1278] In March 1988, the Transportation Department issued another order also exempting from the regulation government-imposed surcharges for the provision of, among others, customs, immigration, and security services, on the condition that they be clearly stated elsewhere in the advertisement.[1279] In August 1988, the Department refused to

---

1272. Joint Application of Federal Express Corp. and Flying Tigers Line, Order 89-3-54, at 2 (1989).

1273. 49 U.S.C. app. § 1305(a)(1) (1988). An exception is made for intrastate air transportation in Alaska. Id. § 1305(a)(2). The statute does not limit the authority of states, political subdivisions of states, and interstate agencies of states that own or operate airports served by certificated air carriers to exercise their proprietary powers and rights. Id. § 1305(b)(2).

1274. 14 C.F.R. §§ 380.30, 399.84 (1991).

1275. 49 U.S.C. app. § 1381 (1988).

1276. 14 C.F.R. § 399.84 (1991).

1277. Order 85-12-68 (1985).

1278. NATIONAL ASSOCIATION OF ATTORNEYS GENERAL, GUIDELINES FOR AIR TRAVEL ADVERTISING (Dec. 12, 1987), *reprinted in* 53 ANTITRUST & TRADE REG. REP. (BNA) No. 1345 (Special Supp. Dec. 17, 1987).

1279. Order 88-3-25 (1988). The Department of Transportation remarked:
   In some international markets, there is a security fee for each flight to and from the United States. In addition, the U.S. government has imposed a $5 customs fee and a $5 immigration fee, and a $1 tourism fee has been proposed for certain international flights. Some States and municipalities have imposed fuel surcharges of varying amounts to ticket charges.
   For advertisers to comply literally with current provisions of sections 380.30 and 399.84,

sanction extensions of the exemption to surcharges not collected by the government on a per-passenger basis.[1280] Twenty-seven states joined together to challenge its 1988 Orders, neither of which had been issued pursuant to Administrative Procedure Act notice-and-comment procedures. The D.C. Circuit rejected the Department of Transportation's assertions that the states lacked standing to bring the suit and held that the orders were "invalid by virtue of the Department's failure to employ notice-and-comment procedures."[1281] The case did not decide the issue whether state action in this area is preempted.

In *TWA v. Mattox*,[1282] TWA, Continental, and British Airways sued the Attorney General of Texas to enjoin his enforcement of Texas consumer protection laws against airlines that followed the Transportation Department's regulations rather than the NAAG Guidelines. The district court issued a preliminary injunction against the State of Texas, holding that the plaintiffs were likely to prevail on their claim that the Federal Aviation Act preempted the states' power to regulate deceptive airline advertising. The court also granted Pan American and ten foreign air carriers the right to intervene in the case and expanded the injunction to cover the attorneys general of thirty-three other states.

(5) Regulation of Unfair Competition

The Department of Transportation retains authority to regulate unfair competition in the air transportation industry under Section 411 of the Federal Aviation Act. Authority to administer Section 411 was transferred from the CAB to the Department on January 1, 1985.[1283] This section, which was not changed by the Airline Deregulation Act, provides:

> The Board may, upon its own initiative or upon complaint by any air carrier, foreign air carrier, or ticket agent, if it considers that such action by it would be in the interest of the public, investigate and determine whether any air carrier, foreign air carrier, or ticket agent has been or is engaged in unfair or deceptive practices or unfair methods of competition in air transportation or the sale thereof.[1284]

If the Transportation Department determines that an air carrier, foreign air carrier, or ticket agent is engaging in unfair or deceptive practices or methods of

---

they are obligated to include the total cost of all such fees and charges in the advertised price. However, security charges do not apply in all international markets, and immigration and customs fees apply only on the return segment of the trip. Fuel surcharges generally apply only on the flight leaving the State or city making such an assessment and not on the return.

As a result of the variety of additional fees and charges imposed on air travelers for a variety of services, advertisers are confused as to how the charges for such services must be presented . . . and in many instances, readers are not receiving the true picture of what their trip will cost.

Id. at 2.

1280. Order 88-8-2 (1988).

1281. Alaska v. United States Dep't of Transp., 868 F.2d 441, 445 (D.C. Cir. 1989).

1282. 712 F. Supp. 99 (W.D. Tex. 1989), *aff'd*, 897 F.2d 773 (5th Cir.), *cert. denied*, 111 S. Ct. 307 (1990).

1283. 49 U.S.C. app. § 1551(b)(1)(C) (1988).

1284. *Id.* § 1381(a).

competition, it may issue a cease and desist order.[1285]

The Supreme Court has twice reviewed determinations under Section 411. In *American Airlines v. North American Airlines*,[1286] the Court considered a CAB order directing North American Airlines to cease and desist from using a name containing the word "American."[1287] The CAB had found that use of "American" caused confusion with American Airlines and was an unfair or deceptive practice or method of competition. The Court, which analogized Section 411 to Section 5 of the Federal Trade Commission Act,[1288] first determined that

> a finding as to the "interest of the public" under both § 411 and § 5 is not a prerequisite to the issuance of a cease and desist order as such. Rather, consideration of the public interest is made a condition upon the assumption of jurisdiction by the agency to investigate trade practices and methods of competition and determine whether or not they are unfair.[1289]

After noting that "it is the Board that speaks in the public interest," the Supreme Court held that judicial review was limited to whether "the Board has stayed within its jurisdiction and applied criteria appropriate to that determination."[1290] The Court explained that "'[u]nfair or deceptive practices or unfair methods of competition,' as used in § 411, are broader concepts than the common-law idea of unfair competition."[1291] As to the CAB's determination, the Court stated:

> The Board found that respondent knowingly adopted a trade name that might well cause confusion. But it made no findings that the use of the name was intentionally deceptive or fraudulent or that the competitor, American Airlines, was injured thereby. Such findings are not required of the Trade Commission under § 5, and there is no reason to require them of the Civil Aeronautics Board under § 411.
>
> The Board had jurisdiction to inquire into the methods of competition presented here, and its evidentiary findings concerned confusion of the type which can support a finding of violation of § 411.[1292]

In *Pan American World Airways (Panagra) v. United States*,[1293] the Supreme Court first considered the relationship between Section 411 and the antitrust laws. In that case, the Court held that the CAB had primary jurisdiction over antitrust matters under Section 411.[1294] The Department of Justice complaint had alleged that Pan American and W.R. Grace & Co. had violated Section 1 of the Sherman

---

1285. *See* Carrier-Owned Computer Reservation Sys., 14 C.F.R. § 255 (1991) (rules prohibiting as anticompetitive practices of airlines that provide computer reservation systems to travel agents and other air carriers, including biased displays of information and discrimination in price and other forms of access). These regulations were upheld in United Air Lines v. CAB, 766 F.2d 1107 (7th Cir. 1985).

1286. 351 U.S. 79 (1956).

1287. *Id.* at 80-81.

1288. 15 U.S.C. § 45 (1988).

1289. 351 U.S. at 83.

1290. *Id.* at 85. The CAB may delegate the authority to make this public interest determination. Aloha Airlines v. CAB, 598 F.2d 250, 256 (D.C. Cir. 1979).

1291. 351 U.S. at 85 (citations omitted).

1292. *Id.* at 86 (citations omitted).

1293. 371 U.S. 296 (1963).

1294. *Id.* at 302, 310.

Act by forming a joint venture (Panagra) with the understanding that Panagra and Pan American would divide the market for air service to South America. A second count alleged that the joint venture constituted a conspiracy to monopolize the markets for such air service.

The Supreme Court held that "the narrow questions presented by this complaint have been entrusted to the Board,"[1295] and ordered the complaint dismissed. The Court found that the agreements and acts in question involved "[l]imitations of routes and division of territories and the relation of common carriers to air carriers" which "are basic in this regulatory scheme,"[1296] and their legality was, therefore, "peculiarly a question for the Board, subject of course to judicial review."[1297] Furthermore, if the CAB believed that a practice was unfair and that the public interest required its termination, it could proceed under the broad terms of Section 411. Thus, the Court concluded that "the Act leaves for the Board under § 411 all questions of injunctive relief against the division of territories or the allocation of routes or against combinations between common carriers and air carriers."[1298]

At the same time, the Court made clear that it was not holding that Section 411 vested all authority with respect to enforcement of the antitrust laws in the CAB:

> While the Board is empowered to deal with numerous aspects of what are normally thought of as antitrust problems, those expressly entrusted to it encompass only a fraction of the total. Apart from orders which give immunity from the antitrust laws by reason of § 414, the whole criminal law enforcement problem remains unaffected by the Act. Moreover, on the civil side, violations of antitrust laws other than those enumerated in the Act might be imagined. We, therefore, refuse to hold that there are no antitrust violations left to the Department of Justice to enforce.[1299]

The CAB's (and now the Department of Transportation's) obligation to initiate an investigation upon receipt of a complaint alleging a violation of Section 411 has been a subject of litigation. It has been recognized that "Congress has committed to the Board's discretion, by the terms of § 411, the questions whether and under what circumstances it will initiate an investigation in response to a formal

---

1295. *Id.* at 313.

1296. *Id.* at 305.

1297. *Id.* at 309. On primary jurisdiction issues, the Ninth Circuit distinguished the *Pan American* case in Foremost International Tours, Inc. v. Qantas Airways Ltd., 525 F.2d 281 (9th Cir. 1975), *cert. denied*, 429 U.S. 816 (1976). In *Foremost*, a tour operator plaintiff brought a Sherman Act § 1 and § 2 action against a foreign air carrier, alleging that the carrier had entered the tour industry with an intent to monopolize, with predatory intent, and with the purpose of eliminating the plaintiff as a competitor. The Ninth Circuit described the *Pan American* rule as one that holds "that when a regulatory agency has pervasive authority and the ability and expertise to exercise coordinated control over an entire industry and over all factors of that industry's industrial behavior [that] agency . . . is in the better position to resolve wholly intra-industry problems," (*id.* at 284) but held that was not the case with Foremost's complaint against Qantas:

> The fact that a regulated industry is involved and that some of the issues in this antitrust case deal with matters within the expertise of the regulatory agency, gives the CAB a substantial interest in this litigation, though not exclusive primary jurisdiction over it, since the matters are not confined to intra-industry effects.

Id. at 286.

1298. 371 U.S. at 310 (footnote and citations omitted).

1299. *Id.* at 305 (citations omitted).

complaint."[1300]   This exercise of discretion, however, is subject to judicial review.[1301] Courts have interpreted Section 411 as being "concerned neither with the punishment of wrongdoing nor with the protection of injured competitors, but rather with protection of the public interest"[1302] and have held that the Board "may not employ its powers to vindicate private rights."[1303]   Thus, in *REA Express*, the Second Circuit found no abuse of discretion in a CAB decision not to investigate public confusion resulting from allegedly confusing names when the complainant did not show "specific and substantial" public confusion.[1304] In that case, the Second Circuit held that "an administrative agency properly exercises its discretionary authority when it refuses to investigate a complaint, which, accepting as true its factual allegations, fails to establish a prima facie claim for relief."[1305]

Some courts have found that Section 411 does not give rise to an implied private right of action.[1306] The D.C. Circuit, however, has stated that it "simply cannot accept the proposition that the existence of the Board's power under Section 411 eliminates all private remedies for common law torts arising from . . . misrepresentation or other forms of unfair or deceptive practices."[1307] A prerequisite for recovery for such torts under the principles of primary jurisdiction is that the CAB first determine the legality of the challenged practice.[1308]

1300.   REA Express, Inc. v. CAB, 507 F.2d 42, 45 (2d Cir. 1974); *see also* Transcontinental Bus Sys. v. CAB, 383 F.2d 466, 478 (5th Cir. 1967); Flying Tigers Line v. CAB, 350 F.2d 462, 465 (D.C. Cir. 1965), *cert. denied,* 385 U.S. 945 (1966). That competitors performed similar deeds is no defense to a CAB finding that a carrier violated § 411. Aloha Airlines v. CAB, 598 F.2d 250, 258 (D.C. Cir. 1979).

1301.   *REA Express,* 507 F.2d at 45; *see also* Trailways v. CAB, 412 F.2d 926, 931 (1st Cir. 1969); *cf.* American Airlines v. North American Airlines, 351 U.S. 79, 85 (1956).

1302.   *REA Express,* 507 F.2d at 46 (citing *American Airlines,* 351 U.S. at 83); *see also* Costantini v. CAB, 706 F.2d 1025 (9th Cir. 1983).

1303.   *REA Express,* 507 F.2d at 46; *see also* Pan Am. World Airways v. United States, 371 U.S. 296, 306 (1963); FTC v. Klesner, 280 U.S. 19, 25-30 (1929); *Aloha Airlines,* 598 F.2d at 255.

1304.   507 F.2d at 46.

1305.   *Id.* at 45-46 (citing Nebraska Dep't of Aeronautics v. CAB, 298 F.2d 286, 295 (8th Cir. 1962), and Flight Eng'rs' Int'l Ass'n v. CAB, 332 F.2d 312, 314-15 (D.C. Cir. 1964)).

1306.   Wolf v. TWA, 544 F.2d 134, 136 (3d Cir.), *cert. dismissed,* 380 U.S. 248 (1976); Polansky v. TWA, 523 F.2d 332, 337 (3d Cir. 1975).

1307.   Nader v. Allegheny Airlines, 512 F.2d 527, 542-43 (D.C. Cir. 1975), *rev'd on other grounds,* 426 U.S. 290 (1976); *see also* Aloha Airlines v. Hawaiian Airlines, 489 F.2d 203, 208 (9th Cir. 1973), *cert. denied,* 417 U.S. 913 (1974); TWA v. Hughes, 332 F.2d 602, 608-09 (2d Cir. 1964), *cert. dismissed,* 380 U.S. 248 (1965).

1308.   *Nader,* 512 F.2d at 544.
        [I]f the Board properly finds that a practice is not deceptive, a common law action for misrepresentation must fail as a matter of law. Given this interpretation, when the allegedly tortious practice is one that has been directly regulated by the Board, or while not directly regulated is so obviously tied to a regulated practice or rate that a change in one would require a change in the other, the Board must determine, in the first instance, whether the practice falls within the ambit of the deceptive practices provision of section 411.
        Even if CAB finds a practice to be deceptive under § 411, a claimant must still prove the other elements of a tort. *Id.* at 544 n.20.

d.   OCEAN SHIPPING

In the foreign commerce of the United States, the activities of ocean common carriers (sometimes referred to as "liner" operators) and the shipping conferences that many of them join are regulated by the Federal Maritime Commission (FMC) pursuant to the Shipping Act of 1984.[1309] Congress, in enacting the Shipping Act of 1984, removed some of the regulatory requirements that had been imposed upon such carriers and conferences by the Shipping Act of 1916[1310] and significantly expanded the scope of antitrust immunity.[1311]

Section 7(a)(2) of the 1984 Act immunizes activity so long as it is "undertaken or entered into with a reasonable basis to conclude" that it is pursuant to a filed agreement or an agreement not required to be filed.[1312] Section 7(c)(2) precludes private parties from suing for treble damages or injunctive relief under the antitrust laws with respect to conduct prohibited by the 1984 Act.[1313] In place of private antitrust action, the 1984 Act establishes an administrative complaint process adjudicated by the FMC.[1314] The FMC is the exclusive forum for claims based on such prohibited conduct.[1315] The 1984 Act also prescribes a regulatory scheme for liner carriers in foreign trade[1316] and limits the jurisdiction of the Shipping

---

1309.   46 U.S.C. app. §§ 1701-1720 (1988). An "ocean common carrier" is defined as "a vessel-operating common carrier." *Id.* § 1702(18). The 1984 Act defines a "common carrier" as:
   a person holding itself out to the general public to provide transportation by water of passengers or cargo between the United States and a foreign country for compensation that –
   (A) assumes responsibility for the transportation from the port or point of receipt to the port or point of destination, and
   (B) utilizes, for all or part of that transportation, a vessel operating on the high seas or the Great Lakes between a port in the United States and a port in a foreign country, except that the term does not include a common carrier engaged in ocean transportation by ferry boat, ocean tramp, or chemical parcel-tanker.
   Id. § 1702(6). A "conference" is defined as:
   an association of ocean common carriers permitted, pursuant to an approved or effective agreement, to engage in concerted activity and to utilize a common tariff; but the term does not include a joint service, consortium, pooling, sailing, or transshipment arrangement.
   Id. § 1702(7).

1310.   46 U.S.C. app. §§ 801-42 (1988).

1311.   There has been controversy over whether the 1984 Act applies to preenactment conduct. *See* Seawinds, Ltd. v. Ned Lloyd Lines, BV, 80 Bankr. 181 (N.D. Cal. 1987) (the 1984 Act applies to conduct occurring prior to its enactment), *aff'd*, 846 F.2d 586 (9th Cir.), *cert. denied*, 488 U.S. 891 (1988). *But see* Johnson Prods. Co. v. M/V La Molinera, 619 F. Supp. 764 (S.D.N.Y. 1985) (the 1984 Act does not apply to such conduct).

1312.   46 U.S.C. app. § 1706(a)(2) (1988).

1313.   *Id.* § 1706(c)(2). The prohibited acts are enumerated in § 1709. Other provisions grant immunity to agreements or activities relating to transportation within or between foreign countries, or relating to wharfage, dock, warehouse or other terminal facilities provided outside the United States. *Id.* § 1706(a)(3), (5).

1314.   *Id.* § 1710(a).

1315.   *See Seawinds*, 80 Bankr. 181.

1316.   The Shipping Act of 1984 gives the FMC authority to regulate only common carriers. 46 U.S.C. app. § 1702(6) (1988). The agency cannot therefore regulate either contract carriers or ocean tramp carriers (i.e., carriers that do not hold themselves out to the general public on fixed routes or schedules). Grace Line, Inc. v. FMB, 280 F.2d 790 (2d Cir. 1960), *cert. denied*, 364 U.S. 933 (1961); Carrier Status of Containerships, Inc., 9 F.M.C. 56 (1965); Philip R. Consolo v. Grace Lines, 4 F.M.C. 293, 300 (1953). Section 7 of the Intercoastal Shipping Act, however, applies the

Act of 1916 to domestic offshore routes.[1317]

While the FMC, through the agreement filing process, has broad authority to confer antitrust immunity upon a wide range of agreements among ocean common carriers and among marine terminal operators,[1318] in other respects the FMC's authority under the 1984 Shipping Act is more limited than it was under the 1916 Act.[1319] This section reviews the FMC's authority to regulate entry and exit, rates, and agreements, including mergers and acquisitions.

(1) Regulation of Entry and Exit

The FMC has no direct authority to regulate entry or exit.[1320] Carriers are free to commence liner operations in the U.S. foreign commerce without agency approval, and they are assured of the right to join conferences by Section 5(b)(2) of the 1984 Act.[1321] This section requires that each conference agreement "provide reasonable and equal terms and conditions for admission and readmission to conference membership for any ocean common carrier willing to serve the particular trade or route."[1322] Further, pursuant to Section 5(b)(3), each conference agreement must also "permit any member to withdraw from conference membership upon reasonable notice without penalty."[1323] In furtherance of this open entry policy, FMC regulations require conference agreements to "specify the terms and conditions for admission, withdrawal, readmission and expulsion to or from membership in the agreement, including membership fees, refundable deposits, and

---

provisions of the Shipping Act in all respects to intercoastal shipping (i.e., common and contract carriers by water that transport passengers or property between any two states of the United States by way of the Panama Canal), except for certain provisions with respect to rates, fares and charges. *See* Intercoastal Shipping Act of 1933, §§ 1, 7, 46 U.S.C. app. §§ 843, 847 (1988).

1317.   The Shipping Act of 1916, while no longer applicable to U.S. foreign trade, continues to apply to activities of common carriers in domestic offshore routes, e.g., between the United States mainland and Puerto Rico.

1318.   A "marine terminal operator" is defined as "a person engaged in the United States in the business of furnishing wharfage, dock, warehouse, or other terminal facilities in connection with a common carrier." 46 U.S.C. app. § 1702(15) (1988).

1319.   Under the 1984 Shipping Act, approval of an agreement by the FMC no longer is required to obtain antitrust immunity. Instead, a new methodology has been created whereby an agreement becomes effective forty-five days from the date of its filing unless the FMC acts to prevent or delay its effectiveness, or on the thirtieth day after notice of the filing is published in the Federal Register, whichever day is later. *See id.* § 1705(c). Any activity undertaken pursuant to such an agreement is immune from the antitrust laws. *Id.* § 1706(a)(2).

1320.   Senator Inouye commented during the floor debate on the 1984 Shipping Act:
        Our liner trades operate on a come one, come all basis, inviting participation of foreign-flag carriers as cross-traders (that is carriers of a nation(s) other than those of our trading partner in a given trade).
        Since we are the largest trading nation in the world, our policy of freedom of access to our liner trades has attracted cross-traders from all over the world.
        129 CONG. REC. 51,678-79 (1983).

1321.   46 U.S.C. app. § 1704(b)(2) (1988); *see also id.* § 814 (carriers in domestic offshore commerce).

1322.   *Id.* § 1704(b)(2); *see also* H.R. REP. No. 600, 98th Cong., 2d Sess. 33 (1984) (any conference agreement must include "provisions that require open membership"); H.R. REP. No. 53, 98th Cong., 1st Sess. 14 (1983) (the Act requires "that conference membership not be restricted").

1323.   46 U.S.C. app. § 1704(b)(3) (1988); H.R. REP. No. 53, 98th Cong., 1st Sess. 14 (1983); *see also* 46 U.S.C. app. § 814 (1988) (carriers in domestic offshore commerce).

other fees or charges associated with membership."[1324]

The open entry policy characteristic of ocean shipping regulation is subject to two qualifications. First, neither "subsidized ships"[1325] nor vessels operating under foreign flags may operate in the U.S. intercoastal trade.[1326] Second, an "ocean freight forwarder"[1327] is required to obtain a license from the FMC.[1328]

(2) Regulation of Rates and Rebates

Each common carrier or conference operating in the U.S. foreign commerce is required to file tariffs with the FMC[1329] showing all of its "rates, charges, classifications, rules and practices between all points or ports on its own route and on any through transportation route that has been established."[1330] However, the FMC has little authority to regulate the level of rates filed by common carriers and conferences in the foreign trades.[1331] No longer may the FMC disapprove

---

1324. 46 C.F.R. § 572.501(b)(7) (1991); see also id. § 560.501(b) (domestic offshore commerce).

1325. Subsidized ships are U.S. flag carriers that receive operating-differential subsidies from the U.S. Maritime Administration, an agency of the Department of Transportation. See 46 U.S.C. app. §§ 1171-1183a (1988).

1326. Id. § 883.

1327. The 1984 Act defines an "ocean freight forwarder" as a person in the United States who dispatches shipments from the United States via common carriers, books or otherwise arranges for space for those shipments on behalf of shippers, and processes the documentation or performs related activities incident to those shipments. Id. § 1702(19).

1328. Id. § 1718; see 46 C.F.R. pt. 510 (1991). The FMC will issue a license to an applicant that:
> (1) the Commission determines to be qualified by experience and character to render forwarding services; and
> (2) furnishes a bond in a form and amount determined by the Commission to insure financial responsibility that is issued by a surety company found acceptable by the Secretary of the Treasury.

46 U.S.C. app. § 1718(a) (1988). The FMC has broad authority to adopt or not adopt rules pertaining to the licensing and regulation of the activities of ocean freight forwarders. National Customs Brokers & Forwarders Ass'n v. United States, 883 F.2d 93, 95 (D.C. Cir. 1989) ("[t]he forwarder is the only entity regulated by the FMC that is required to obtain a license before it can operate lawfully").

1329. 46 U.S.C. app. § 1707(a) (1988). This requirement applies equally to ocean common carriers and to non-vessel operating common carriers. The latter are defined in the 1984 Act as a carrier that does "not operate the vessels by which the ocean transportation is provided, and is a shipper in its relationship with an ocean common carrier." Id. § 1702(17). The 1984 Act exempts bulk cargo, forest products, recycled metal scrap, waste paper, and paper waste from any tariff filing requirement. Id. § 1707(a).

1330. Id. The Shipping Act of 1984 has resolved the dispute over whether the FMC has jurisdiction to grant antitrust immunity to collective action by ocean carriers concerning the entirety of intermodal rates. The legislative history of the Act makes it clear that if ocean carriers engage in such collective action pursuant to an agreement on file with the FMC, there is antitrust immunity. See H.R. CONF. REP. NO. 600, 98th Cong., 2d Sess. 34, reprinted in 1984 U.S. CODE CONG. & ADMIN. NEWS 283, 290.

1331. Although the FMC does not affirmatively approve rates filed in ocean carrier tariffs, ratemaking reflected in tariffs may be protected from antitrust attack by the "filed rate" doctrine enunciated in Keogh v. Chicago & N. Ry., 260 U.S. 156 (1922). The Keogh doctrine was reaffirmed by the Supreme Court in the context of motor carrier rates filed with the Interstate Commerce Commission in Square D Co. v. Niagara Frontier Tariff Bureau, 476 U.S. 409 (1986). The application of the Keogh doctrine in the ocean shipping context is unclear, but private parties are prohibited by the 1984 Act from recovering treble damages under the Clayton Act for conduct prohibited by the 1984 Act, including collective rate making pursuant to unfiled agreements.

any rate that it finds to be unreasonably high or so low as to be detrimental to the commerce of the United States.[1332] Now, it is limited to taking action against unfair or unjustly discriminatory rates[1333] or against any rebate, privilege or concession that is not set forth in a tariff or service contract.[1334] Violations of these provisions are punishable by a civil penalty of up to $5,000 a day for each day the violation continues or, in the case of a violation "willfully and knowingly committed," a civil penalty of up to $25,000 a day and suspension of tariffs filed with the FMC for up to twelve months.[1335] Continued operation while tariffs are suspended is punishable by penalties of up to $50,000 for each shipment.[1336]

Changes in existing tariff rates that result in decreased costs to shippers may become effective immediately, while new or initial rates or changes in existing rates that result in increased costs do not become effective for thirty days.[1337]

Ocean common carriers or conferences are also required to file service contracts.[1338] Service contracts contain rates and terms that have been negotiated with particular shippers.[1339] Service contracts offer shippers an alternative to tendering cargo under standard tariff terms. Although such contracts are filed confidentially with the FMC, their essential terms are required to be revealed to the public and made "available to all shippers similarly situated."[1340] These contracts must be predicated upon a specific volume commitment by the shipper; a commitment to tender a percentage of its total requirements is not permissible.[1341]

Except as provided by treaty and in certain other specified circumstances, a carrier

---

There are also some pre-1984 Act indications that the *Keogh* doctrine would appropriately apply. *See* United States Navigation Co. v. Cunard S.S. Co., 284 U.S. 474, 483 (1932), *cited in* Square D Co. v. Niagara Frontier Tariff Bureau, 760 F.2d 1347, 1356 (2d Cir. 1985), *aff'd*, 476 U.S. 409 (1986); *cf. In re* Ocean Shipping Antitrust Litig., 500 F. Supp. 1235, 1241 (S.D.N.Y. 1980).

1332. The FMC did have such authority with regard to rates in the foreign commerce under the Shipping Act of 1916. 46 U.S.C. app. § 817(b)(5) (1982). However, this authority was revoked by the 1984 Act. *See* 46 U.S.C. app. §§ 1707, 1709 (1988).

1333. 46 U.S.C. app. § 1709(b)(6), (10) (1988).

1334. *Id.* § 1709(b)(1)-(4), (8).

1335. *Id.* § 1712(a), (b)(1).

1336. *Id.* § 1712(b)(3).

1337. *Id.* § 1707(d). Service contracts may become effective upon filing with the FMC. 46 C.F.R. § 581.8(c) (1991).

1338. 46 U.S.C. app. § 1707(c) (1988). Non-vessel operating common carriers are not authorized to enter into service contracts with shippers. *Id.* § 1702(21). The same commodities exempt from tariff filing requirements also are exempt from service contract filing requirements. *Id.* § 1707(c).

1339. A "service contract" is defined as
a contract between a shipper and an ocean common carrier or conference in which the shipper makes a commitment to provide a certain minimum quantity of cargo over a fixed time period, and the ocean common carrier or conference commits to a certain rate or rate schedule as well as a defined service level – such as, assured space, transit time, port rotation, or similar service features; the contract may also specify provisions in the event of nonperformance on the part of either party.
Id. § 1702(21).

1340. *Id.* § 1707(c).

1341. 46 C.F.R. § 581.5(a)(3)(v) (1991). Stating the minimum volume commitment as a percentage of total requirements would, in effect, turn the service contract into a "loyalty contract" which, for all intents and purposes, is prohibited for conferences. 46 U.S.C. app. § 1709(b)(9) (1988); *see also* 52 FED. REG. 23,989, 23,999 (1987); 49 FED. REG. 45,366 (1984).

whose operating assets are controlled by a government under whose registry the vessels of the carrier operate (a controlled carrier) may not "maintain rates or charges in its tariffs filed with Commission that are below a level which is just and reasonable."[1342] The statute specifies the criteria that are to be applied in judging the reasonableness of controlled carrier rates, including whether they are "below a level which is fully compensatory to the controlled carrier based upon that carrier's actual costs or upon its constructive costs [as defined]."[1343] In the absence of special FMC permission, controlled-carrier rates may not be effective until thirty days after filing.[1344] If a controlled carrier's rates appear to be unreasonable, the Commission may issue an order to show cause why the suspect rates should not be disapproved and, pending resolution of the issue, may suspend the proposed rates for up to 180 days.[1345] FMC orders of suspension and disapproval are subject to presidential approval.[1346]

The Interstate Commerce Commission (ICC) continues to be the regulatory agency responsible for water transportation between states in the continental United States,[1347] while the FMC, pursuant to the Shipping Act of 1916, regulates certain types of water transportation between the U.S. mainland and offshore states and territories.[1348] Common carriers by water in interstate commerce are required to establish "just and reasonable rates," and to file statements of those rates with the FMC.[1349] If the FMC finds such a rate to be unjust or unreasonable, it may determine and enforce an appropriate rate.[1350]

(3) Regulation of Agreements

The Shipping Act of 1984 grants the FMC authority to regulate the making and carrying out of a wide variety of agreements in the foreign commerce of the United States that affect competition in the ocean shipping industry. Section 5(a) of the 1984 Act requires that various agreements by or among ocean common carriers, agreements among marine terminal operators, and agreements among one or more marine terminal operators and one or more ocean common carriers be filed with the FMC.[1351] In particular, the agreements subject to this filing requirement include agreements among ocean common carriers to

(1) discuss, fix, or regulate transportation rates, including through rates, cargo space accommodations, and other conditions of service;
(2) pool or apportion traffic, revenues, earnings, or losses;

1342. 46 U.S.C. app. § 1708(a) (1988).
1343. Id. § 1708(b)(1).
1344. Id. § 1708(c).
1345. Id. § 1708(d).
1346. Id. § 1708(e).
1347. 49 U.S.C. § 10541 (1988).
1348. The FMC's regulatory authority extends only to all-water (i.e., port-to-port) movements. The ICC is the applicable regulatory body with respect to intermodal rates between the U.S. mainland and offshore states and territories. Puerto Rico Maritime Shipping Auth. v. Valley Freight Sys., 856 F.2d 546 (3d Cir. 1988); Puerto Rico Maritime Shipping Auth. v. ICC, 645 F.2d 1102 (D.C. Cir. 1981); Trailer Marine Transp. Corp. v. FMC, 602 F.2d 379, 396 (D.C. Cir. 1979).
1349. 46 U.S.C. app. § 817(a) (1988).
1350. Id.
1351. Id. § 1704(a).

(3)   allot ports or restrict or otherwise regulate the number and character of sailings between ports;

(4)   limit or regulate the volume or character of cargo or passenger traffic to be carried;

(5)   engage in exclusive, preferential, or cooperative working arrangements among themselves or with one or more marine terminal operators or non-vessel-operating common carriers;

(6)   control, regulate, or prevent competition in international ocean transportation; and

(7)   regulate or prohibit their use of service contracts.[1352]

Similarly, agreements among marine terminal operators to "(1) discuss, fix, or regulate rates or other conditions of service; and (2) engage in exclusive, preferential, or cooperative working arrangements" must be filed.[1353]

There are, however, two general exceptions to the filing requirement for the agreements described above. First, "agreements related to transportation to be performed within or between foreign countries" need not be filed with the FMC.[1354] Second, an agreement to establish, operate, or maintain a marine terminal in the United States is not subject to filing.[1355] In addition, maritime labor agreements are specifically excluded from any regulation by the FMC.[1356] Section 5(e) of the Shipping Act of 1984 provides that except with regard to rates, charges, regulations, or practices of a common carrier that are required to be filed

---

1352.   *Id.* § 1703(a). A comparable provision requiring the filing and approval of agreements among common carriers in interstate commerce is set forth in § 15 of the Shipping Act of 1916. *Id.* § 814. Section 15 defines the term "agreement" to include "understandings, conferences and other arrangements . . . ." *Id.*

1353.   *Id.* § 1703(b).

1354.   *Id.* § 1704(a). There has been considerable uncertainty and dispute as to whether, even though such "foreign-to-foreign" agreements are not required to be filed under § 5(a), they may be filed voluntarily and thereby receive antitrust immunity under § 7(a)(1). On December 8, 1987, the FMC issued a Notice of Proposed Rulemaking which would have explicitly permitted voluntary filing (and immunity) of foreign-to-foreign agreements "where the parties to the agreement deem it to have a direct, substantial and reasonably foreseeable effect on the commerce of the United States." 52 FED. REG. 46,501, 46,505 (1987). Section 7(a)(3) of the Act excludes agreements having such effects from its general antitrust immunity for foreign-to-foreign agreements. However, the FMC subsequently withdrew the proposed rule, concluding that the agency was "without jurisdiction to regulate agreements among ocean carriers regarding foreign-to-foreign transportation" even if voluntarily filed. 53 FED. REG. 50,264, 50,270 (1988). That ruling was affirmed by the Ninth Circuit in Transpacific Westbound Rate Agreement v. FMC, 938 F.2d 1025 (9th Cir. 1991).

1355.   46 U.S.C. app. § 1704(a) (1988). While such an agreement need not be filed, it has no antitrust immunity. *Id.* § 1706(b)(3).

1356.   A "maritime labor agreement" is defined as:

a collective-bargaining agreement between an employer subject to this Act, or group of such employers, and a labor organization representing employees in the maritime or stevedoring industry, or an agreement preparatory to such a collective-bargaining agreement among members of a multiemployer bargaining group, or an agreement specifically implementing provisions of such a collective-bargaining agreement, or providing for the formation, financing, or administration of a multiemployer bargaining group; but the term does not include an assessment agreement.

Id. § 1702(16).

in a tariff and which may arise out of or be related to a maritime labor agreement,[1357] the 1984 Act, the 1916 Shipping Act, and the 1933 Intercoastal Shipping Act "do not apply to maritime labor agreements."[1358]

Moreover, pursuant to Section 16 of the Shipping Act of 1984, the FMC is authorized to "exempt . . . any class of agreements between persons subject to this [Act] or any specified activity of those persons from any requirement of this [Act] . . . ."[1359] The Supreme Court has acknowledged the FMC's authority "to determine after appropriate administrative proceedings, that some types or classes of agreements . . . are of such a *de minimis* or routine character as not to require formal filing."[1360] The FMC has exercised its authority to exempt from any filing requirement husbanding agreements,[1361] agency agreements,[1362] equipment interchange agreements,[1363] and agreements between or among wholly owned subsidiaries and/or their parent.[1364]

For those agreements that are not of a de minimis nature, and have not been exempted, filing with and processing by the FMC is required before implementation. However, unlike the approval process which had applied to agreements under the regulatory scheme of the 1916 Act, an agreement filed with the FMC under the provisions of the 1984 Act automatically becomes effective unless the Commission

---

1357.   The FMC is authorized under this "tariff matter" provision of the Maritime Labor Agreements Act to regulate labor related activities required to be published in tariffs pursuant to the Shipping Acts. New York Shipping Ass'n v. FMC, 854 F.2d 1338 (D.C. Cir. 1988) (the so-called "50-Mile Container Rules" held to be unjust and unreasonable practices prohibited by the shipping laws, notwithstanding that such rules were the product of a maritime labor agreement), *cert. denied,* 488 U.S. 1041 (1989).

1358.   46 U.S.C. app. § 1704(e) (1988). Although maritime labor agreements were historically not considered subject to the filing requirements of § 15 of the 1916 Shipping Act, certain court decisions, beginning with Volkswagenwerk AG v. FMC, 390 U.S. 261 (1968), extended the FMC's jurisdiction to certain types of maritime labor agreements. As a result, Congress amended § 15 in 1980 to expressly prohibit FMC regulation of maritime labor agreements, stating that:

> Under recent court decisions, however, certain maritime collective bargaining agreements and related agreements among multiemployer bargaining associations which implement such collective bargaining agreements must now be filed with the Commission for approval.

S. REP. NO. 854, 96th Cong., 2d Sess. 1, *reprinted in* 1980 U.S. CODE CONG. & ADMIN. NEWS 2447.

1359.   46 U.S.C. app. § 1715 (1988). The FMC may grant such an exemption if it finds that the exemption will not "substantially impair effective regulation by the Commission, be unjustly discriminatory, result in a substantial reduction in competition, or be detrimental to commerce." *Id.; see also* the 1916 Shipping Act for comparable exemption authority with respect to agreements pertaining to interstate commerce and the domestic offshore trades.

1360.   *Volkswagenwerk,* 390 U.S. at 276. In *Volkswagenwerk,* the Supreme Court observed that an agreement "levying $29,000,000 over five years, binding all principal [common] carriers [by water], stevedoring contractors, and terminal operators on the Pacific Coast, and necessarily resulting in substantially increased stevedoring and terminal charges – was neither *de minimis* or routine" and held that such an agreement was required to be filed under the 1984 Act. 390 U.S. at 277; *see also* Sea-Land Serv. v. FMC, 653 F.2d 544, 551 n.20 (D.C. Cir. 1991).

1361.   46 C.F.R. § 572.303 (1991).

1362.   *Id.* § 572.304.

1363.   *Id.* § 572.305.

1364.   *Id.* § 572.308. Nonexclusive transshipment agreements need not be filed with the FMC if certain conditions and tariff filing obligations are satisfied. *Id.* § 572.306. Marine terminal agreements must be filed with FMC, but are exempt from any waiting period requirements provided for in § 6 of the 1984 Act, 46 U.S.C. app. § 1705 (1988). *See* 46 C.F.R. § 572.307 (1991).

acts to prevent or retard its effectiveness.[1365] Only in very few circumstances may the FMC prevent the effectiveness of an agreement. First, the FMC can reject any agreement that, after preliminary review, it finds does not satisfy certain filing requirements.[1366] These filing requirements include a right of independent action for any member of a conference agreement and a right of independent action for each conference in an interconference agreement.[1367] Further, the FMC may seek an injunction to prevent the operation of an agreement which it determines is likely, by a reduction in competition, to produce an unreasonable reduction in transportation service or an unreasonable increase in transportation cost.[1368] In such a suit, the burden of proof is on the FMC.[1369] Finally, the FMC may delay the effectiveness of an agreement by a request for more information.[1370]

Generally, unless rejected by the FMC, an agreement becomes automatically effective on the forty-fifth day after filing or on the thirtieth day after notice of the filing is published in the FEDERAL REGISTER, whichever is later.[1371] However, if additional information is requested, the agreement becomes effective forty-five days after such information is received by the FMC.[1372]

The 1984 Act seeks to eliminate the widespread confusion with regard to the scope of the antitrust immunity under the 1916 Shipping Act. A Senate Report on an early version of the 1984 Act described the state of antitrust immunity under the 1916 Shipping Act and court decisions construing it as follows:

> The margins of acceptable conduct have been unclear and the protection of the antitrust immunity granted by the Commission tenuous. The chilling effect, the uncertainties, and the inefficiencies forced by antitrust exposure have plagued carriers of all flags serving our foreign trade.[1373]

1365. 46 U.S.C. app. § 1705(c) (1988).

1366. Id. § 1705(b).

1367. Id. § 1704(c).

1368. Id. § 1705(g). This section provides:
   If, at any time after the filing or effective date of an agreement, the Commission determines that the agreement is likely, by a reduction in competition, to produce an unreasonable reduction in transportation service or an unreasonable increase in transportation cost, it may, after notice to the person filing the agreement, seek appropriate injunctive relief under subsection (h) of this section.

1369. Id. § 1705(h).

1370. Id. § 1705(c)-(d).

1371. Id. § 1705(c). An assessment agreement, however, becomes effective immediately upon filing. Id. § 1704(d). An assessment agreement is defined as "an agreement, whether part of a collective-bargaining agreement or negotiated separately, to the extent that it provides for the funding of collectively bargained fringe benefit obligations on other than a uniform man-hour basis, regardless of the cargo handled or type of vessel or equipment utilized." Id. § 1702(3).

1372. Id. § 1705(c).

1373. S. REP. No. 414, 97th Cong., 2d Sess. 7 (1982). Under the 1916 Shipping Act, the antitrust laws were held to apply to any activities engaged in by common carriers under an agreement that had not been approved by the FMC. Carnation Co. v. Pacific Westbound Conference, 383 U.S. 213 (1966); see also Volkswagenwerk AG v. FMC, 390 U.S. 261 (1968); Pacific Seafarers, Inc. v. Pacific Far East Line, 404 F.2d 804 (D.C. Cir. 1968), cert. denied, 393 U.S. 1093 (1969). The 1984 Act sought particularly to eliminate confusion regarding the immunity accorded to agreements and activities undertaken by parties with a good faith belief that they are within the scope of the 1916 Act.

The limited antitrust immunity afforded by the 1916 Shipping Act[1374] was significantly broadened in the 1984 Act. Section 7(a) of the 1984 Act provides that the antitrust laws do not apply to:

(1) any agreement that has been filed under section 1704 of this Appendix and is effective under section 1704(d) or section 1705 of this Appendix, or is exempt under section 1715 of this Appendix from any requirement of this chapter;

(2) any activity or agreement within the scope of this chapter, whether permitted under or prohibited by this chapter, undertaken or entered into with a reasonable basis to conclude that (A) it is pursuant to an agreement on file with the Commission and in effect when the activity took place, or (B) it is exempt under section 1715 of this Appendix from any filing requirement of this chapter;

(3) any agreement or activity that relates to transportation services within or between foreign countries, whether or not via the United States, unless that agreement or activity has a direct, substantial, and reasonably foreseeable effect on the commerce of the United States;

(4) any agreement or activity concerning the foreign inland segment of through transportation that is part of transportation provided in a United States import or export trade;

(5) any agreement or activity to provide or furnish wharfage, dock, warehouse, or other terminal facilities outside the United States; or

(6) subject to section 1719(e)(2) of this Appendix, any agreement, modification, or cancellation approved by the Commission before the effective date of this chapter under section 15 of the Shipping Act, 1916 . . . or permitted under section 14b thereof, and any properly published tariff, rate, fare, or charge, classification, rule, or regulation explanatory thereof implementing that agreement, modification, or cancellation.[1375]

The Act precludes private parties from suing for treble damages or for injunctive relief under the antitrust laws with respect to conduct prohibited by the 1984 Act.[1376]

The intent of the 1984 Act was to eliminate the parallel jurisdiction of the FMC and the federal courts under the antitrust laws with regard to claims by private parties for violations of the 1984 Act.[1377] Those claims must now be presented

---

1374. *See, e.g.,* FMC v. Aktiebolaget Svenska Amerika Linien, 390 U.S. 238 (1968); Carnation Co. v. Pacific Westbound Conference, 383 U.S. 213 (1966); Sabre Shipping Corp. v. American President Lines, 285 F. Supp. 949 (S.D.N.Y. 1968) (imposing substantial restrictions on the antitrust immunity conferred by Section 15 of the 1916 Act), *cert. denied sub nom.* Japan Line v. Sabre Shipping Corp., 407 F.2d 173 (2d Cir.), *cert. denied,* 395 U.S. 922 (1969). *Compare* Far E. Conference v. United States, 342 U.S. 570 (1952) *and* United States Navigation Co. v. Cunard S.S. Co., 284 U.S. 474 (1932) *with* National Ass'n of Recycling Indus. v. American Mail Line, 720 F.2d 618 (9th Cir. 1983) (holding that antitrust immunity for conduct authorized by FMC agreement is not lost even if such conduct were to violate some other Shipping Act provision or other statute), *cert. denied,* 465 U.S. 1109 (1984).

1375. 46 U.S.C. app. §§ 1706(a)(1)-(6) (1988).

1376. *Id.* § 1706(c)(2).

1377. H.R. REP. No. 53(I), 98th Cong., 2d Sess. at 12, *reprinted in* 1984 U.S. CODE CONG. & ADMIN. NEWS, 167, 177 ("[T]he Committee intends that violations of this Act not result in the creation of parallel jurisdiction over persons or matters which are subject to the Shipping Act [of 1984]; the remedies and sanctions provided for in the Shipping Act [of 1984] will be the exclusive remedies and sanctions for violation of the Act.")

to the FMC, and reparations may be awarded pursuant to Section 11(g) of the Act.[1378] The United States can, of course, continue to pursue criminal or civil actions against conduct pursuant to unfiled agreements, and private parties as well can challenge conduct that is not immunized from the antitrust laws and not prohibited by the 1984 Act.[1379]

Finally, the Shipping Act of 1984 expressly provides that voting security or asset acquisitions are not subject to the Act and therefore cannot be immunized from the antitrust laws by the filing of an acquisition agreement with the FMC.[1380] The legislative history also makes it clear that merger agreements are beyond the scope of the 1984 Act.[1381]

1378.   O.N.E. Shipping Ltd. v. Flota Mercante Grancolombiana, SA, 830 F.2d 449 (2d Cir. 1987); Seawinds Ltd., 80 Bankr. 181 (N.D. Cal. 1987). Reparations awarded by the FMC under § 11(g) of the 1984 Act are for actual injury and include interest and reasonable attorney's fees. 46 U.S.C. app. § 1710(g) (1988).

1379.   15 U.S.C. §§ 1-3, 13(a) (1988). The Shipping Act of 1984 does not extend antitrust immunity:
        (1) to any agreement with or among air carriers, rail carriers, motor carriers, or common carriers by water not subject to this chapter with respect to transportation within the United States;
        (2) to any discussion or agreement among common carriers that are subject to this chapter regarding the inland divisions (as opposed to the inland portions) of through rates within the United States; or
        (3) to any agreement among common carriers subject to this chapter to establish, operate, or maintain a marine terminal in the United States.
        46 U.S.C. app. § 1706(b) (1988).

1380.   Id. § 1703(c).

1381.   The Senate Committee on Commerce, Science, and Transportation made this clear in its report on a predecessor of the 1984 Act which contained a subsection identical to the final § 1703(c):
        [This subsection] is intended to make clear that this act does not remove mergers and acquisitions in the maritime area from the normal antitrust oversight which might otherwise be conducted by various agencies of the executive branch.
        S. REP. NO. 3, 98th Cong., 1st Sess. 24 (1983).

APPENDIX A

BASIC ANTITRUST AND TRADE REGULATION STATUTES

Sherman Act

Section 1

Every contract, combination in the form of trust or otherwise, or conspiracy, in restraint of trade or commerce among the several States, or with foreign nations, is declared to be illegal. Every person who shall make any contract or engage in any combination or conspiracy hereby declared to be illegal shall be deemed guilty of a felony, and, on conviction thereof, shall be punished by fine not exceeding $10,000,000 if a corporation, or, if any other person, $350,000, or by imprisonment not exceeding three years, or by both said punishments, in the discretion of the court. [15 U.S.C. § 1]

Section 2

Every person who shall monopolize, or attempt to monopolize, or combine or conspire with any other person or persons, to monopolize any part of the trade or commerce among the several States, or with foreign nations, shall be deemed guilty of a felony, and, on conviction thereof, shall be punished by fine not exceeding $10,000,000 if a corporation, or, if any other person, $350,000, or by imprisonment not exceeding three years, or by both said punishments, in the discretion of the court. [15 U.S.C. § 2]

Section 3

Every contract, combination in form of trust or otherwise, or conspiracy, in restraint of trade or commerce in any Territory of the United States or of the District of Columbia, or in restraint of trade or commerce between any such Territory and another, or between any such Territory or Territories and any State or States or the District of Columbia, or with foreign nations, or between the District of Columbia and any State or States or foreign nations, is declared illegal. Every person who shall make any such contract or engage in any such combination or conspiracy, shall be deemed guilty of a felony, and, on conviction thereof, shall be punished by fine not exceeding $10,000,000 if a corporation, or, if any other person, $350,000, or by imprisonment not exceeding three years, or by both said punishments, in the discretion of the court. [15 U.S.C. § 3]

Section 4

The several district courts of the United States are invested with jurisdiction to prevent and restrain violations of [this Act]; and it shall be the duty of the several United States attorneys, in their respective districts, under the direction of the Attorney General, to institute proceedings in equity to prevent and restrain such violations. Such proceedings may be by way of petition setting forth the case and praying that such violation shall be enjoined or otherwise prohibited. When the parties complained of shall have been duly notified of such petition the court shall proceed, as soon as may be, to the hearing and determination of the case; and pending such petition and before final decree, the court may at any time make such temporary restraining order or prohibition as shall be deemed just in the premises. [15 U.S.C. § 4]

Section 5

Whenever it shall appear to the court before which any proceeding under section 4 of this [Act] may be pending, that the ends of justice require that other parties should be brought before the court, the court may cause them to be summoned, whether they reside in the district in which the court is held or not; and subpoenas to that end may be served in any district by the marshal thereof. [15 U.S.C. § 5]

Section 6

Any property owned under any contract or by any combination, or pursuant to any conspiracy (and being the subject thereof) mentioned in section 1 of this [Act], and being in the course of transportation from one State to another, or to a foreign country, shall be forfeited to the United States, and may be seized and condemned by like proceedings as those provided by law for the forfeiture, seizure, and condemnation of property imported into the United States contrary to law. [15 U.S.C. § 6]

Section 6a[*]

[This Act] shall not apply to conduct involving trade or commerce (other than import trade or import commerce) with foreign nations unless —

(1)   such conduct has a direct, substantial, and reasonably foreseeable effect —
    (A) on trade or commerce which is not trade or commerce with foreign nations, or on import trade or import commerce with foreign nations; or
    (B) on export trade or export commerce with foreign nations, of a person engaged in such trade or commerce in the United States; and
(2)   such effect gives rise to a claim under the provisions of [this Act], other than this section.

If [this Act (15 U.S.C. §§ 1-7) applies] to such conduct only because of the operation

---

[*]   This is the Export Trading Company Act, Pub. L. No. 97-290, 96 Stat. 1246 (Oct. 8, 1982), amendments to § 7 of the Sherman Act.

of paragraph (1)(B), then [this Act (15 U.S.C. §§ 1-7)] shall apply to such conduct only for injury to export business in the United States. [15 U.S.C. § 6a]

Section 7

The word "person," or "persons," whenever used in [this Act] shall be deemed to include corporations and associations existing under or authorized by the laws of either the United States, the laws of any of the Territories, the laws of any State, or the laws of any foreign country. [15 U.S.C. § 7]

Clayton Act

Section 1

(a)   "Antitrust laws," as used herein, includes the Act entitled "An Act to protect trade and commerce against unlawful restraints and monopolies," approved July second, eighteen hundred and ninety; sections seventy-three to seventy-seven, inclusive, of an Act entitled "An Act to reduce taxation, to provide revenue for the Government, and for other purposes," of August twenty-seventh, eighteen hundred and ninety-four; an Act entitled "An Act to amend sections seventy-three and seventy-six of the Act of August twenty-seventh, eighteen hundred and ninety-four, entitled 'An Act to reduce taxation, to provide revenue for the Government, and for other purposes,'" approved February twelfth, nineteen hundred and thirteen; and also this Act.

"Commerce," as used herein, means trade or commerce among the several States and with foreign nations, or between the District of Columbia or any Territory of the United States and any State, Territory, or foreign nation, or between any insular possessions or other places under the jurisdiction of the United States, or between any such possession or place and any State or Territory of the United States or the District of Columbia or any foreign nation, or within the District of Columbia or any Territory or any insular possession or other place under the jurisdiction of the United States: *Provided*, That nothing in this Act contained shall apply to the Philippine Islands.

The word "person" or "persons" wherever used in this Act shall be deemed to include corporations and associations existing under or authorized by the laws of either the United States, the laws of any of the Territories, the laws of any State, or the laws of any foreign country.

(b)   This Act may be cited as the "Clayton Act". [15 U.S.C. § 12]

Section 2*

(a)   It shall be unlawful for any person engaged in commerce, in the course of such commerce, either directly or indirectly, to discriminate in price between different purchasers of commodities of like grade and quality, where either or any of the purchases involved in such discrimination are in commerce, where such commodities are sold for use, consumption, or resale within the United States or any

---

*   Robinson-Patman Act amendments to the Clayton Act.

Territory thereof or the District of Columbia or any insular possession or other place under the jurisdiction of the United States, and where the effect of such discrimination may be substantially to lessen competition or tend to create a monopoly in any line of commerce, or to injure, destroy, or prevent competition with any person who either grants or knowingly receives the benefit of such discrimination, or with customers of either of them: *Provided,* That nothing herein contained shall prevent differentials which make only due allowance for differences in the cost of manufacture, sale, or delivery resulting from the differing methods or quantities in which such commodities are to such purchasers sold or delivered: *Provided, however,* That the Federal Trade Commission may, after due investigation and hearing to all interested parties, fix and establish quantity limits, and revise the same as it finds necessary, as to particular commodities or classes of commodities, where it finds that available purchasers in greater quantities are so few as to render differentials on account thereof unjustly discriminatory or promotive of monopoly in any line of commerce; and the foregoing shall then not be construed to permit differentials based on differences in quantities greater than those so fixed and established: *And provided further,* That nothing herein contained shall prevent persons engaged in selling goods, wares, or merchandise in commerce from selecting their own customers in bona fide transactions and not in restraint of trade: *And provided further,* That nothing herein contained shall prevent price changes from time to time where in response to changing conditions affecting the market for or the marketability of the goods concerned, such as but not limited to actual or imminent deterioration of perishable goods, obsolescence of seasonal goods, distress sales under court process, or sales in good faith in discontinuance of business in the goods concerned. [15 U.S.C. § 13(a)]

(b) Upon proof being made, at any hearing on a complaint under this section, that there has been discrimination in price or services or facilities furnished, the burden of rebutting the prima-facie case thus made by showing justification shall be upon the person charged with a violation of this section, and unless justification shall be affirmatively shown, the Commission is authorized to issue an order terminating the discrimination: *Provided, however,* That nothing herein contained shall prevent a seller rebutting the prima-facie case thus made by showing that his lower price or the furnishing of services or facilities to any purchaser or purchasers was made in good faith to meet an equally low price of a competitor, or the services or facilities furnished by a competitor. [15 U.S.C. § 13(b)]

(c) It shall be unlawful for any person engaged in commerce, in the course of such commerce, to pay or grant, or to receive or accept, anything of value as a commission, brokerage, or other compensation, or any allowance or discount in lieu thereof, except for services rendered in connection with the sale or purchase of goods, wares, or merchandise, either to the other party to such transaction or to an agent, representative, or other intermediary therein where such intermediary is acting in fact for or in behalf, or is subject to the direct or indirect control, of any party to such transaction other than the person by whom such compensation is so granted or paid. [15 U.S.C. § 13(c)]

(d) It shall be unlawful for any person engaged in commerce to pay or contract for the payment of anything of value to or for the benefit of a customer of such person in the course of such commerce as compensation or in consideration for any services or facilities furnished by or through such customer in connection with the processing, handling, sale, or offering for sale of any products or commodities manufactured, sold, or offered for sale by such person, unless such payment or consideration is available on proportionally equal terms to all other customers competing in the distribution of such products or commodities. [15 U.S.C. § 13(d)]

(e)   It shall be unlawful for any person to discriminate in favor of one purchaser against another purchaser or purchasers of a commodity bought for resale, with or without processing, by contracting to furnish or furnishing, or by contributing to the furnishing of, any services or facilities connected with the processing, handling, sale, or offering for sale of such commodity so purchased upon terms not accorded to all purchasers on proportionally equal terms. [15 U.S.C. § 13(e)]

(f)   It shall be unlawful for any person engaged in commerce, in the course of such commerce, knowingly to induce or receive a discrimination in price which is prohibited by this section. [15 U.S.C. § 13(f)]

Section 3

It shall be unlawful for any person engaged in commerce, in the course of such commerce, to lease or make a sale or contract for sale of goods, wares, merchandise, machinery, supplies, or other commodities, whether patented or unpatented, for use, consumption, or resale within the United States or any Territory thereof or the District of Columbia or any insular possession or other place under the jurisdiction of the United States, or fix a price charged therefor, or discount from, or rebate upon, such price, on the condition, agreement, or understanding that the lessee or purchaser thereof shall not use or deal in the goods, wares, merchandise, machinery, supplies, or other commodities of a competitor or competitors of the lessor or seller, where the effect of such lease, sale, or contract for sale or such condition, agreement, or understanding may be to substantially lessen competition or tend to create a monopoly in any line of commerce. [15 U.S.C. § 14]

Section 4

(a)   Except as provided in subsection (b) of this section, any person who shall be injured in his business or property by reason of anything forbidden in the antitrust laws may sue therefor in any district court of the United States in the district in which the defendant resides or is found or has an agent, without respect to the amount in controversy, and shall recover threefold the damages by him sustained, and the cost of suit, including a reasonable attorney's fee. The court may award under this section, pursuant to a motion by such person promptly made, simple interest on actual damages for the period beginning on the date of service of such person's pleading setting forth a claim under the antitrust laws and ending on the date of judgment, or for any shorter period therein, if the court finds that the award of such interest for such period is just in the circumstances. In determining whether an award of interest under this section for any period is just in the circumstances, the court shall consider only —

(1)   whether such person or the opposing party, or either party's representative, made motions or asserted claims or defenses so lacking in merit as to show that such party or representative acted intentionally for delay, or otherwise acted in bad faith;

(2)   whether, in the course of the action involved, such person or the opposing

party, or either party's representative, violated any applicable rule, statute, or court order providing for sanctions for dilatory behavior or otherwise providing for expeditious proceedings; and

(3)   whether such person or the opposing party, or either party's representative, engaged in conduct primarily for the purpose of delaying the litigation or increasing the cost thereof. [15 U.S.C. § 15(a)]

(b)(1)   Except as provided in paragraph (2), any person who is a foreign state may not recover under subsection (a) of this section an amount in excess of the actual damages sustained by it and the cost of suit, including a reasonable attorney's fee.

(2)   Paragraph (1) shall not apply to a foreign state if —

(A)   such foreign state would be denied, under section 1605(a)(2) of Title 28, immunity in a case in which the action is based upon a commercial activity, or an act, that is the subject matter of its claim under this section;

(B)   such foreign state waives all defenses based upon or arising out of its status as a foreign state, to any claims brought against it in the same action;

(C)   such foreign state engages primarily in commercial activities; and

(D)   such foreign state does not function, with respect to the commercial activity, or the act, that is the subject matter of its claim under this section as a procurement entity for itself or for another foreign state. [15 U.S.C. § 15(b)]

(c)   For purposes of this section —

(1)   the term "commercial activity" shall have the meaning given it in section 1603(d) of Title 28, and

(2)   the term "foreign state" shall have the meaning given it in section 1603(a) of Title 28. [15 U.S.C. § 15(c)]

Section 4A

Whenever the United States is hereafter injured in its business or property by reason of anything forbidden in the antitrust laws it may sue therefor in the United States district court for the district in which the defendant resides or is found or has an agent, without respect to the amount in controversy, and shall recover threefold the damages by it sustained and the cost of suit. The court may award under this section, pursuant to a motion by the United States promptly made, simple interest on threefold the damages for the period beginning on the date of service of the pleading of the United States setting forth a claim under the antitrust laws and ending on the date of judgment, or for any shorter period therein, if the court finds that the award of such interest for such period is just in the circumstances. In determining whether an award of interest under this section for any period is just in the circumstances, the court shall consider only —

(1)   whether the United States or the opposing party, or either party's representative, made motions or asserted claims or defenses so lacking in merit as to show that such party or representative acted intentionally for delay or otherwise acted in bad faith;

(2)   whether, in the course of the action involved, the United States or the opposing party, or either party's representative, violated any applicable rule, statute,

or court order providing for sanctions for dilatory behavior or otherwise providing for expeditious proceedings;

(3) whether the United States or the opposing party, or either party's representative, engaged in conduct primarily for the purpose of delaying the litigation or increasing the cost thereof; and

(4) whether the award of such interest is necessary to compensate the United States adequately for the injury sustained by the United States. [15 U.S.C. § 15a]

Section 4B

Any action to enforce any cause of action under sections [4, 4A, or 4C] of this [Act] shall be forever barred unless commenced within four years after the cause of action accrued. No cause of action barred under existing law on the effective date of this Act shall be revived by this Act. [15 U.S.C. § 15b]

Section 4C

(a)(1) Any attorney general of a State may bring a civil action in the name of such State, as parens patriae on behalf of natural persons residing in such State, in any district court of the United States having jurisdiction of the defendant, to secure monetary relief as provided in this section for injury sustained by such natural persons to their property by reason of any violation of [the Sherman Act]. The court shall exclude from the amount of monetary relief awarded in such action any amount of monetary relief (A) which duplicates amounts which have been awarded for the same injury, or (B) which is properly allocable to (i) natural persons who have excluded their claims pursuant to subsection (b)(2) of this section, and (ii) any business entity.

(2) The court shall award the State as monetary relief threefold the total damage sustained as described in paragraph (1) of this subsection, and the cost of suit, including a reasonable attorney's fee. The court may award under this paragraph, pursuant to a motion by such State promptly made, simple interest on the total damage for the period beginning on the date of service of such State's pleading setting forth a claim under the antitrust laws and ending on the date of judgment, or for any shorter period therein, if the court finds that the award of such interest for such period is just in the circumstances. In determining whether an award of interest under this paragraph for any period is just in the circumstances, the court shall consider only —

(A) whether such State or the opposing party, or either party's representative, made motions or asserted claims or defenses so lacking in merit as to show that such party or representative acted intentionally for delay or otherwise acted in bad faith;

(B) whether, in the course of the action involved, such State or the opposing party, or either party's representative, violated any applicable rule, statute, or court order providing for sanctions for dilatory behavior or otherwise providing for expeditious proceedings; and

(C) whether such State or the opposing party, or either party's representative, engaged in conduct primarily for the purpose of delaying the litigation or increasing the cost thereof.

(b)(1) In any action brought under subsection (a)(1) of this section, the State attorney general shall, at such times, in such manner, and with such content as the court may direct, cause notice thereof to be given by publication. If the court finds that notice given solely by publication would deny due process of law to any person or persons, the court may direct further notice to such person or persons according to the circumstances of the case.

(2)   Any person on whose behalf an action is brought under subsection (a)(1) of this section may elect to exclude from adjudication the portion of the State claim for monetary relief attributable to him by filing notice of such election with the court within such time as specified in the notice given pursuant to paragraph (1) of this subsection.

(3)   The final judgement in an action under subsection (a)(1) of this section shall be res judicata as to any claim under section [4 of this Act] by any person on behalf of whom such action was brought and who fails to give such notice within the period specified in the notice given pursuant to paragraph (1) of this subsection.

(c) An action under subsection (a)(1) of this section shall not be dismissed or compromised without the approval of the court, and notice of any proposed dismissal or compromise shall be given in such manner as the court directs.

(d) In any action under subsection (a) of this section —

(1)   the amount of the plaintiffs' attorney's fee, if any, shall be determined by the court; and

(2)   the court may, in its discretion, award a reasonable attorney's fee to a prevailing defendant upon a finding that the State attorney general has acted in bad faith, vexatiously, wantonly, or for oppressive reasons. [15 U.S.C. § 15c]

Section 4D

In any action under section [4C](a)(1) of this [Act], in which there has been a determination that a defendant agreed to fix prices in violation of [the Sherman Act], damages may be proved and assessed in the aggregate by statistical or sampling methods, by the computation of illegal overcharges, or by such other reasonable system of estimating aggregate damages as the court in its discretion may permit without the necessity of separately proving the individual claim of, or amount of damage to, persons on whose behalf the suit was brought. [15 U.S.C. § 15(d)]

Section 4E

Monetary relief recovered in an action under section [4C](a)(1) of this [Act] shall—

(1)   be distributed in such manner as the district court in its discretion may authorize; or

(2)   be deemed a civil penalty by the court and deposited with the State as general revenues;

subject in either case to the requirement that any distribution procedure adopted afford each person a reasonable opportunity to secure his appropriate portion of the net monetary relief. [15 U.S.C. § 15e]

Section 4F

(a)   Whenever the Attorney General of the United States has brought an action under the antitrust laws, and he has reason to believe that any State attorney general would be entitled to bring an action under this Act based substantially on the same alleged violation of the antitrust laws, he shall promptly give written notification thereof to such State attorney general.

(b)   To assist a State attorney general in evaluating the notice or in bringing any action under this Act, the Attorney General of the United States shall, upon request by such State attorney general, make available to him, to the extent permitted by law, any investigative files or other materials which are or may be relevant or material to the actual or potential cause of action under this Act. [15 U.S.C. § 15f]

Section 4G

For the purposes of sections [4C, 4D, 4E, and 4F] of this [Act]:

(1)   The term "State attorney general" means the chief legal officer of a State, or any other person authorized by State law to bring actions under section [4C] of this [Act], and includes the Corporation Counsel of the District of Columbia, except that such term does not include any person employed or retained on —
  (A) a contingency fee based on a percentage of the monetary relief awarded under this section; or
  (B) any other contingency fee basis, unless the amount of the award of a reasonable attorney's fee to a prevailing plaintiff is determined by the court under section [4C](d)(1) of this [Act].
(2)   The term "State" means a State, the District of Columbia, the Commonwealth of Puerto Rico, and any other territory or possession of the United States.
(3)   The term "natural persons" does not include proprietorships or partnerships.
[15 U.S.C. § 15g]

Section 4H

Sections [4C, 4D, 4E, 4F, and 4G] of this [Act] shall apply in any State, unless such State provides by law for its nonapplicability in such State. [15 U.S.C. § 15h]

Section 5

(a) A final judgment or decree heretofore or hereafter rendered in any civil or criminal proceeding brought by or on behalf of the United States under the antitrust laws to the effect that a defendant has violated said laws shall be prima facie evidence against such defendant in any action or proceeding brought by any other party against such defendant under said laws as to all matters respecting which said judgment or decree would be an estoppel as between the parties thereto: *Provided,* That this section shall not apply to consent judgments or decrees entered before any testimony has been taken. Nothing contained in this section shall be construed to impose any limitation on the application of collateral estoppel, except that, in any action or proceeding brought under the antitrust laws, collateral estoppel effect shall not be given to any finding made by the Federal Trade Commission under the antitrust laws or under section [5 of the Federal Trade Commission Act] which could give rise to a claim for relief under the antitrust laws.

(b)   Any proposal for a consent judgment submitted by the United States for entry in any civil proceeding brought by or on behalf of the United States under the antitrust laws shall be filed with the district court before which such proceeding is pending and published by the United States in the Federal Register at least 60 days prior to the effective date of such judgment. Any written comments relating to such proposal and any responses by the United States thereto, shall also be filed with such district court and published by the United States in the Federal Register within such sixty-day period. Copies of such proposal and any other materials and documents which the United States considered determinative in formulating such proposal, shall also be made available to the public at the district court and in such other districts as the court may subsequently direct.   Simultaneously with the filing of such proposal, unless otherwise instructed by the court, the United States shall file with the district court, publish in the Federal Register, and thereafter furnish to any person upon request, a competitive impact statement which shall recite –

(1)   the nature and purpose of the proceeding;
(2)   a description of the practices or events giving rise to the alleged violation of the antitrust laws;
(3)   an explanation of the proposal for a consent judgment, including an explanation of any unusual circumstances giving rise to such proposal or any provision contained therein, relief to be obtained thereby, and the anticipated effects on competition of such relief;
(4)   the remedies available to potential private plaintiffs damaged by the alleged violations in the event that such proposal for the consent judgment is entered in such proceeding;
(5)   a description of the procedures available for modification of such proposal; and
(6)   a description and evaluation of alternatives to such proposal actually considered by the United States.

(c)   The United States shall also cause to be published, commencing at least 60 days prior to the effective date of the judgment described in subsection (b) of this section, for 7 days over a period of 2 weeks in newspapers of general circulation of the district in which the case has been filed, in the District of Columbia, and in such other districts as the court may direct –

(i)   a summary of the terms of the proposal for consent judgment,
(ii)   a summary of the competitive impact statement filed under subsection (b) of this section,
(iii)   and a list of the materials and documents under subsection (b) of this section which the United States shall make available for purposes of meaningful public comment, and the place where such materials and documents are available for public inspection.

(d)   During the 60-day period as specified in subsection (b) of this section, and such additional time as the United States may request and the court may grant, the United States shall receive and consider any written comments relating to the proposal for the consent judgment submitted under subsection (b) of this section. The Attorney General or his designee shall establish procedures to carry out the provisions of this subsection, but such 60-day time period shall not be shortened except by order of the district court upon a showing that (1) extraordinary circumstances require such shortening and (2) such shortening is not adverse to the public interest. At the close of the period during which such comments may be received, the United States shall file with the district court and cause to be published in the Federal Register a response to such comments.

(e)   Before entering any consent judgment proposed by the United States under this section, the court shall determine that the entry of such judgment is in the public interest. For the purpose of such determination, the court may consider —

(1)   the competitive impact of such judgment, including termination of alleged violations, provisions for enforcement and modification, duration or relief sought, anticipated effects of alternative remedies actually considered, and any other considerations bearing upon the adequacy of such judgment;

(2)   the impact of entry of such judgment upon the public generally and individuals alleging specific injury from the violations set forth in the complaint including consideration of the public benefit, if any, to be derived from a determination of the issues at trial.

(f)   In making its determination under subsection (e) of this section, the court may —

(1)   take testimony of Government officials or experts or such other expert witnesses, upon motion of any party or participant or upon its own motion, as the court may deem appropriate;

(2)   appoint a special master and such outside consultants or expert witnesses as the court may deem appropriate; and request and obtain the views, evaluations, or advice of any individual, group or agency of government with respect to any aspects of the proposed judgment or the effect of such judgment, in such manner as the court deems appropriate;

(3)   authorize full or limited participation in proceedings before the court by interested persons or agencies, including appearance amicus curiae, intervention as a party pursuant to the Federal Rules of Civil Procedure, examination of witnesses or documentary materials, or participation in any other manner and extent which serves the public interest as the court may deem appropriate;

(4)   review any comments including any objections filed with the United States under subsection (d) of this section concerning the proposed judgment and the responses of the United States to such comments and objections; and

(5)   take such other action in the public interest as the court may deem appropriate.

(g)   Not later than 10 days following the date of the filing of any proposal for a consent judgment under subsection (b) of this section, each defendant shall file with the district court a description of any and all written or oral communications by or on behalf of such defendant, including any and all written or oral communications on behalf of such defendant, or other person, with any officer or employee of the United States concerning or relevant to such proposal, except that any such communications made by counsel of record alone with the Attorney General or the employees of the Department of Justice alone shall be excluded from the requirements of this subsection. Prior to the entry of any consent judgment pursuant to the antitrust laws, each defendant shall certify to the district court that the requirements of this subsection have been complied with and that such filing is a true and complete description of such communications known to the defendant or which the defendant reasonably should have known.

(h) Proceedings before the district court under subsections (e) and (f) of this section, and the competitive impact statement filed under subsection (b) of this section, shall not be admissible against any defendant in any action or proceeding brought by any other party against such defendant under the antitrust laws or by the United States under section [4A] of this [Act] nor constitute a basis for the introduction of the consent judgment as prima facie evidence against such defendant in any such action or proceeding.

(i)   Whenever any civil or criminal proceeding is instituted by the United States to prevent, restrain, or punish violations of any of the antitrust laws, but not including an action under section [4A] of this [Act], the running of the statute of limitations in respect to every private or State right of action arising under said laws and based in whole or in part on any matter complained of in said proceeding shall be suspended during the pendency thereof and for one year thereafter: *Provided, however,* That whenever the running of the statute of limitations in respect of a cause of action arising under section [4] or [4C] of this [Act] is suspended hereunder, any action to enforce such cause of action shall be forever barred unless commenced either within the period of suspension or within four years after the cause of action accrued. [15 U.S.C. § 16]

Section 6

The labor of a human being is not a commodity or article of commerce. Nothing contained in the antitrust laws shall be construed to forbid the existence and operation of labor, agricultural, or horticultural organizations, instituted for the purposes of mutual help, and not having capital stock or conducted for profit, or to forbid or restrain individual members of such organizations from lawfully carrying out the legitimate objects thereof; nor shall such organizations, or the members thereof, be held or construed to be illegal combinations or conspiracies in restraint of trade, under the antitrust laws. [15 U.S.C. § 17]

Section 7

No person engaged in commerce or in any activity affecting commerce shall acquire, directly or indirectly, the whole or any part of the stock or other share capital and no person subject to the jurisdiction of the Federal Trade Commission shall acquire the whole or any part of the assets of another person engaged also in commerce or in any activity affecting commerce, where in any line of commerce or in any activity affecting commerce in any section of the country, the effect of such acquisition may be substantially to lessen competition, or to tend to create a monopoly.

No person shall acquire, directly or indirectly, the whole or any part of the stock or other share capital and no person subject to the jurisdiction of the Federal Trade Commission shall acquire the whole or any part of the assets of one or more persons engaged in commerce or in any activity affecting commerce, where in any line of commerce or in any activity affecting commerce in any section of the country, the effect of such acquisition, of such stocks or assets, or of the use of such stock by the voting or granting of proxies or otherwise, may be substantially to lessen competition, or to tend to create a monopoly.

This section shall not apply to persons purchasing such stock solely for investment and not using the same by voting or otherwise to bring about, or in attempting to bring about, the substantial lessening of competition. Nor shall anything contained in this section prevent a corporation engaged in commerce or in any activity affecting commerce from causing the formation of subsidiary corporations for the actual carrying on of their immediate lawful business, or the natural and legitimate branches or extensions thereof, or from owning and holding all or a part of the stock of such subsidiary corporations, when the effect of such formation is not to substantially lessen competition.

Nor shall anything herein contained be construed to prohibit any common carrier subject to the laws to regulate commerce from aiding in the construction of branches or short lines so located as to become feeders to the main line of the company so aiding in such construction or from acquiring or owning all or any part of the stock of such branch lines, nor to prevent any such common carrier from acquiring and owning all or any part of the stock of a branch or short line constructed by an independent company where there is no substantial competition between the company owning the branch line so constructed and the company owning the main line acquiring the property or an interest therein, nor to prevent such common carrier from extending any of its lines through the medium of the acquisition of stock or otherwise of any other common carrier where there is no substantial competition between the company extending its lines and the company whose stock, property, or an interest therein is so acquired.

Nothing contained in this section shall be held to affect or impair any right heretofore legally acquired: *Provided,* That nothing in this section shall be held or construed to authorize or make lawful anything heretofore prohibited or made illegal by the antitrust laws, nor to exempt any person from the penal provisions thereof or the civil remedies therein provided.

Nothing contained in this section shall apply to transactions duly consummated pursuant to authority given by the Secretary of Transportation, Federal Communications Commission, Federal Power Commission, Interstate Commerce Commission, the Securities and Exchange Commission in the exercise of its jurisdiction under section [10 of the Public Utility Holding Company Act of 1955], the United States Maritime Commission, or the Secretary of Agriculture under any statutory provision vesting such power in such Commission or Secretary. [15 U.S.C. § 18]

Section 7A[*]

(a)   Except as exempted pursuant to subsection (c) of this section, no person shall acquire, directly or indirectly, any voting securities or assets of any other person, unless both persons (or in the case of a tender offer, the acquiring person) file notification pursuant to rules under subsection (d)(1) of this section and the waiting period described in subsection (b)(1) of this section has expired, if —

(1)   the acquiring person, or the person whose voting securities or assets are being acquired, is engaged in commerce or in any activity affecting commerce;

(2)(A)   any voting securities or assets of a person engaged in manufacturing which has annual net sales or total assets of $10,000,000 or more are being acquired by any person which has total assets or annual net sales of $100,000,000 or more;

(B)   any voting securities or assets of a person not engaged in manufacturing which has total assets of $10,000,000 or more are being acquired by any person which has total assets or annual net sales of $100,000,000 or more; or

(C)   any voting securities or assets of a person with annual net sales or total assets of $100,000,000 or more are being acquired by any person with total assets or annual net sales of $10,000,000 or more; and

(3)   as a result of such acquisition, the acquiring person would hold —

(A)   15 per centum or more of the voting securities or assets of the acquired person, or

(B)   an aggregate total amount of the voting securities and assets of the acquired person in excess of $15,000,000.

In the case of a tender offer, the person whose voting securities are sought to be acquired by a person required to file notification under this subsection shall file notification pursuant to rules under subsection (d) of this section.

(b)(1)   The waiting period required under subsection (a) of this section shall —

(A)   begin on the date of the receipt by the Federal Trade Commission and the Assistant Attorney General in charge of the Antitrust Division of the Department of Justice (hereinafter referred to in this section as the "Assistant Attorney General") of —

(i)   the completed notification required under subsection (a) of this section, or

(ii)   if such notification is not completed, the notification to the extent completed and a statement of the reasons for such noncompliance, from both persons, or, in the case of a tender offer, the acquiring person; and

(B)   end on the thirtieth day after the date of such receipt (or in the case of a cash tender offer, the fifteenth day), or on such later date as may be set under subsection (e)(2) or (g)(2) of this section.

(2)   The Federal Trade Commission and the Assistant Attorney General may, in individual cases, terminate the waiting period specified in paragraph (1) and allow any person to proceed with any acquisition subject to this section, and promptly shall

---

[*]   Hart-Scott-Rodino Antitrust Improvements Act amendments to the Clayton Act.

cause to be published in the Federal Register a notice that neither intends to take any action within such period with respect to such acquisition.

(3)   As used in this section —

(A) The term "voting securities" means any securities which at present or upon conversion entitle the owner or holder thereof to vote for the election of directors of the issuer or, with respect to unincorporated issuers, persons exercising similar functions.

(B) The amount of percentage of voting securities or assets of a person which are acquired or held by another person shall be determined by aggregating the amount or percentage of such voting securities or assets held or acquired by such other person and each affiliate thereof.

(c) The following classes of transactions are exempt from the requirements of this section —

(1)   acquisitions of goods or realty transferred in the ordinary course of business;

(2)   acquisitions of bonds, mortgages, deeds of trust, or other obligations which are not voting securities;

(3)   acquisitions of voting securities of an issuer at least 50 per centum of the voting securities of which are owned by the acquiring person prior to such acquisition;

(4)   transfers to or from a Federal agency or a State or political subdivision thereof;

(5)   transactions specifically exempted from the antitrust laws by Federal statute;

(6)   transactions specifically exempted from the antitrust laws by Federal statutes if approved by a Federal agency, if copies of all information and documentary material filed with such agency are contemporaneously filed with the Federal Trade Commission and the Assistant Attorney General;

(7)   transactions which require agency approval under section [18(c) of the federal Deposit Insurance Act (12 U.S.C. § 1828(c)), or Section 3 of the Bank Holding Company Act of 1956 (12 U.S.C. § 1842)];

(8)   transactions which require agency approval under section [4 of the Bank Holding Company Act of 1956 (12 U.S.C. § 1843), Section 403 or 408(e) of the National Housing Act (12 U.S.C. § 1726 and § 1730(a), or Section 5 of the Home Owners' Loan Act of 1933 (12 U.S.C. § 1464)], if copies of all information and documentary material filed with any such agency are contemporaneously filed with the Federal Trade Commission and the Assistant Attorney General at least 30 days prior to consummation of the proposed transaction;

(9)   acquisitions, solely for the purpose of investment, of voting securities, if, as a result of such acquisition, the securities acquired or held do not exceed 10 per centum of the outstanding voting securities of the issuer;

(10) acquisitions of voting securities, if, as a result of such acquisition, the voting securities acquired do not increase, directly or indirectly, the acquiring person's per centum share of outstanding voting securities of the issuer;

(11) acquisitions, solely for the purpose of investment, by any bank, banking association, trust company, investment company, or insurance company, of

(A) voting securities pursuant to a plan of reorganization or dissolution; or

(B) assets in the ordinary course of its business; and

(12) such other acquisitions, transfers, or transactions, as may be exempted under

subsection (d)(2)(B) of this section.

(d) The Federal Trade Commission, with the concurrence of the Assistant Attorney General and by rule in accordance with section 553 of Title 5, consistent with the purposes of this section —

(1)   shall require that the notification required under subsection (a) of this section be in such form and contain such documentary material and information relevant to a proposed acquisition as is necessary and appropriate to enable the Federal Trade Commission and the Assistant Attorney General to determine whether such acquisition may, if consummated, violate the antitrust laws; and

(2)   may —

(A) define the terms used in this section;

(B) exempt, from the requirements of this section, classes of persons, acquisitions, transfers, or transactions which are not likely to violate the antitrust laws; and

(C) prescribe such other rules as may be necessary and appropriate to carry out the purposes of this section.

(e)(1)   The Federal Trade Commission or the Assistant Attorney General may, prior to the expiration of the 30-day waiting period (or in the case of a cash tender offer, the 15-day waiting period) specified in subsection (b)(1) of this section, require the submission of additional information or documentary material relevant to the proposed acquisition, from a person required to file notification with respect to such acquisition under subsection (a) of this section prior to the expiration of the waiting period specified in subsection (b)(1) of this section, or from any officer, director, partner, agent, or employee of such person.

(2)   The Federal Trade Commission or the Assistant Attorney General, in its or his discretion, may extend the 30-day waiting period (or in the case of a cash tender offer, the 15-day waiting period) specified in subsection (b)(1) of this section for an additional period of not more than 20 days (or in the case of a cash tender offer, 10 days) after the date on which the Federal Trade Commission or the Assistant Attorney General, as the case may be, receives from any person to whom a request is made under paragraph (1), or in the case of tender offers, the acquiring person, (A) all the information and documentary material required to be submitted pursuant to such a request, or (B) if such request is not fully complied with, the information and documentary material submitted and a statement of the reasons for such noncompliance. Such additional period may be further extended only by the United States district court, upon an application by the Federal Trade Commission or the Assistant Attorney General pursuant to subsection (g)(2) of this section.

(f)   If a proceeding is instituted or an action is filed by the Federal Trade Commission, alleging that a proposed acquisition violates section 18 of this title, or section [7] of this [Act] [or Section 5 of the Federal Trade Commission Act], or an action is filed by the United States, alleging that a proposed acquisition violates such section [7] of this [the Sherman Act], or section 1 or 2 of this [Act], and the Federal Trade Commission or the Assistant Attorney General (1) files a motion for a preliminary injunction against consummation of such acquisition pendente lite, and (2) certifies the United States district court for the judicial district within which the respondent resides or carries on business, or in which the action is brought, that it or he believes that the public interest requires relief pendente lite pursuant to this subsection, then upon the filing of such motion and certification, the chief judge of such district court shall immediately notify the chief judge of the United States court of appeals for the circuit in which such district court is located, who shall designate a United States district judge to whom such action shall be assigned for all purposes.

(g)(1)   Any person, or any officer, director, or partner thereof, who fails to comply with any provision of this section shall be liable to the United States for a civil penalty of not more than $10,000 for each day during which such person is in violation of this section. Such penalty may be recovered in a civil action brought by the United States.

(2)   If any person, or any officer, director, partner, agent, or employee thereof, fails substantially to comply with the notification requirement under subsection (a) of this section or any request for the submission of additional information or documentary material under subsection (e)(1) of this section within the waiting period specified in subsection (b)(1) of this section and as may be extended under subsection (e)(2) of this section, the United States district court —

(A) may order compliance;

(B) shall extend the waiting period specified in subsection (b)(1) of this section and as may have been extended under subsection (e)(2) of this section until there has been substantial compliance, except that, in the case of a tender offer, the court may not extend such waiting period on the basis of a failure, by the person whose stock is sought to be acquired, to comply substantially with such notification requirement or any such request; and

(C) may grant such other equitable relief as the court in its discretion determines necessary or appropriate,

upon application of the Federal Trade Commission or the Assistant Attorney General.

(h)   Any information or documentary material filed with the Assistant Attorney General or the Federal Trade Commission pursuant to this section shall be exempt from disclosure under section 552 of Title 5 [U.S. Code], and no such information or documentary material may be made public, except as may be relevant to any administrative or judicial action or proceeding. Nothing in this section is intended to prevent disclosure to either body of Congress or to any duly authorized committee or subcommittee of the Congress.

(i)(1)   Any action taken by the Federal Trade Commission or the Assistant Attorney General or any failure of the Federal Trade Commission or the Assistant Attorney General to take any action under this section shall not bar any proceeding or any action with respect to such acquisition at any time under any other section of this Act or any other provision of law.

(2)   Nothing contained in this section shall limit the authority of the Assistant Attorney General or the Federal Trade Commission to secure at any time from any person documentary material, oral testimony, or other information under the Antitrust Civil Process Act [15 U.S.C. §§ 1311 et seq.], the Federal Trade Commission Act [15 U.S.C. §§ 41 et seq.], or any other provision of law.

(j)   Beginning not later than January 1, 1978, the Federal Trade Commission, with the concurrence of the Assistant Attorney General, shall annually report to the Congress on the operation of this section. Such report shall include an assessment of the effects of this section, of the effects, purpose, and need for any rules promulgated pursuant thereto, and any recommendations for revisions of this section. [15 U.S.C. § 18a]

Section 8

(a)(1)   No person shall, at the same time, serve as a director or officer in any two corporations (other than banks, banking associations, and trust companies) that are-
    (A)   engaged in whole or in part in commerce; and
    (B)   by virtue of their business and location of operation, competitors, so that the elimination of competition by agreement between them would constitute a violation of any of the antitrust laws;
if each of the corporations has capital, surplus, and undivided profits aggregating more than $10,000,000 as adjusted pursuant to paragraph (5) of this subsection.
    (2)   Notwithstanding the provisions of paragraph (1), simultaneous service as a director or officer in any two corporations shall not be prohibited by this section if-
    (A)   the competitive sales of either corporation are less than $1,000,000, as adjusted pursuant to paragraph (5) of this subsection;
    (B)   the competitive sales of either corporation are less than 2 per centum of that corporation's total sales; or
    (C)   the competitive sales of each corporation are less than 4 per centum of that corporation's total sales.
For purposes of this paragraph, "competitive sales" means the gross revenues for all products and services sold by one corporation in competition with the other, determined on the basis of annual gross revenues for such products and services in that corporation's last completed fiscal year. For the purposes of this paragraph, "total sales" means the gross revenues for all products and services sold by one corporation over that corporation's last completed fiscal year.
    (3)   The eligibility of a director or officer under the provisions of paragraph (1) shall be determined by the capital, surplus and undivided profits, exclusive of dividends declared but not paid to stockholders, of each corporation at the end of that corporation's last completed fiscal year.
    (4)   For purposes of this section, the term "officer" means an officer elected or chosen by the Board of Directors.
    (5)   For each fiscal year commencing after September 30, 1990, the $10,000,000 and $1,000,000 thresholds in this subsection shall be increased (or decreased) as of October 1 each year by an amount equal to the percentage increase (or decrease) in the gross national product, as determined by the Department of Commerce or its successor, for the year then ended over the level so established for the year ending September 30, 1989. As soon as practicable, but not later than October 30 of each year, the Federal Trade Commission shall publish the adjusted amounts required by this paragraph.

(b)   when any person elected or chosen as a director or officer of any corporatoin subject to the provisions hereof is eligible at the time of his election or selection to act for such corportaion in such capacity, his eligibilty to act in such capacity shall not be affected by any of the provisions hereof by reason of any change in the capital, surplus and undivided profits, or affairs of such corporation from whatever cause, until the expiration of one year from the date on which the event causing ineligibility occurred.

[15 U.S.C. § 19, as amended Oct. 17, 1978, Pub. L. 95-473, § 3(b), 92 Stat. 1466; Nov. 16, 1990, Pub. L. No. 101-588, § 2, 104 Stat. 2879]

Section 11

(a) Authority to enforce compliance with sections [2, 3, 7, and 8] of this [Act] by the persons respectively subject thereto is vested in the Interstate Commerce Commission where applicable to common carriers subject to subtitle IV of Title 49; in the Federal Communications Commission where applicable to common carriers engaged in wire or radio communication or radio transmission of energy; in the Secretary of Transportation where applicable to air carriers and foreign air carriers subject to the Federal Aviation Act of 1958 [49 App. U.S.C.A. §§ 1301 et seq.]; in the Board of Governors of the Federal Reserve System where applicable to banks, banking associations, and trust companies; and in the Federal Trade Commission where applicable to all other character of commerce to be exercised as follows:

(b) Whenever the Commission, Board, or Secretary vested with jurisdiction thereof shall have reason to believe that any person is violating or has violated any of the provisions of sections [2, 3, 7, and 8] of this [Act], it shall issue and serve upon such person and the Attorney General a complaint stating its charges in that respect, and containing a notice of a hearing upon a day and at a place therein fixed at least thirty days after the service of said complaint. The person so complained of shall have the right to appear at the place and time so fixed and show cause why an order should not be entered by the Commission, Board, or Secretary requiring such person to cease and desist from the violation of the law so charged in said complaint. The Attorney General shall have the right to intervene and appear in said proceeding and any person may make application, and upon good cause shown may be allowed by the Commission, Board, or Secretary, to intervene and appear in said proceeding by counsel or in person. The testimony in any such proceeding shall be reduced to writing and filed in the office of the Commission, Board, or Secretary. If upon such hearing the Commission, Board, or Secretary, as the case may be, shall be of the opinion that any of the provisions of said sections have been or are being violated, it shall make a report in writing, in which it shall state its findings as to the facts, and shall issue and cause to be served on such person an order requiring such person to cease and desist from such violations, and divest itself of the stock, or other share capital, or assets, held or rid itself of the directors chosen contrary to the provisions of sections [7 and 8] of this [Act], if any there be, in the manner and within the time fixed by said order. Until the expiration of the time allowed for filing a petition for review, if no such petition has been duly filed within such time, or, if a petition for review has been filed within such time then until the record in the proceeding has been filed in a court of appeals of the United States, as hereinafter provided, the Commission, Board, or Secretary may at any time, upon such notice and in such manner as it shall deem proper, modify or set aside, in whole or in part, any report or any order made or issued by it under this section. After the expiration of the time allowed for filing a petition for review, if no such petition has been duly filed within such time, the Commission, Board, or Secretary may at any time, after notice and opportunity for hearing, reopen and alter, modify, or set aside, in whole or in part, any report or order made or issued by it under this section, whenever in the opinion of the Commission, Board, or Secretary conditions of fact or of law have so changed as to require such action or if the public interest shall so require: *Provided however,* That the said person may, within sixty days after service upon him or it of said report or order entered after such a reopening, obtain a review thereof in the appropriate court of appeals of the United States, in the manner provided in subsection (c) of this section.

(c)   Any person required by such order of the commission, board or Secretary to cease and desist from any such violation may obtain a review of such order in the court of appeals of the United States for any circuit within which such violation occurred or within which such person resides or carries on business, by filing in the court, within sixty days after the date of the service of such order, a written petition praying that the order of the commission, board, or Secretary be set aside. A copy of such petition shall be forthwith transmitted by the clerk of the court to the commission, board, or Secretary, and thereupon the commission, board, or Secretary shall file in the court the record in the proceeding, as provided in section 2112 of Title 28, [of the U.S. Code]. Upon such filing of the petition the court shall have jurisdiction of the proceeding and of the question determined therein concurrently with the commission, board, or Secretary until the filing of the record, and shall have power to make and enter a decree affirming, modifying, or setting aside the order of the commission, board, or Secretary, and enforcing the same to the extent that such order is affirmed, and to issue such writs as are ancillary to its jurisdiction or are necessary in its judgment to prevent injury to the public or to competitors pendente lite. The findings of the commission, board, or Secretary as to the facts, if supported by substantial evidence, shall be conclusive. To the extent that the order of the commission, board, or Secretary is affirmed, the court shall issue its own order commanding obedience to the terms of such order of the commission, board, or Secretary. If either party shall apply to the court for leave to adduce additional evidence, and shall show to the satisfaction of the court that such additional evidence is material and that there were reasonable grounds for the failure to adduce such evidence in the proceeding before the commission, board, or Secretary, the court may order such additional evidence to be taken before the commission, board, or Secretary, and to be adduced upon the hearing in such manner and upon such terms and conditions as to the court may seem proper. The commission, board, or Secretary may modify its findings as to the facts, or make new findings, by reason of the additional evidence so taken, and shall file such modified or new findings, which if supported by substantial evidence, shall be conclusive, and its recommendation, if any, for the modification or setting aside of its original order, with the return of such additional evidence. The judgment and decree of the court shall be final, except that the same shall be subject to review by the Supreme Court upon certiorari, as provided in section 1254 of Title 28 [of the U.S. Code].

(d)   Upon the filing of the record with its jurisdiction of the court of appeals to affirm, enforce, modify, or set aside orders of the commission, board, or Secretary shall be exclusive.

(e) No order of the commission, board, or Secretary or judgment of the court to enforce the same shall in anyway relieve or absolve any person from any liability under the antitrust laws.

(f) Complaints, orders, and other processes of the commission, board, or Secretary under this section may be serviced by anyone duly authorized by the commission, board, or Secretary, either (1) by delivering a copy thereof to the person to be served, or to a member of the partnership to be served, or to the president, secretary, or other executive officer or a director of the corporation to be served; or (2) by leaving a copy thereof at the residence or the principal office or place of business of such person; or (3) by mailing by registered or certified mail a copy thereof addressed to such person at his or its residence or principal office or place of business. The verified return by the person so serving said complaint, order, or other process setting forth the manner of said service shall be proof of the same, and the return post office receipt for said complaint, order, or other process mailed by registered or certified mail as aforesaid shall be proof of the service of the same.

(g) Any order issued under subsection (b) of this section shall become final —
   (1) upon the expiration of the time allowed for filing a petition for review, if no such petition has been duly filed within such time; but the commission, board, or Secretary may thereafter modify or set aside its order to the extent provided in the last sentence of subsection (b) of this section; or
   (2) upon the expiration of the time allowed for filing a petition for certiorari, if the order of the commission, board, or Secretary has been affirmed, or the petition for review has been dismissed by the court of appeals, and no petition for certiorari has been duly filed; or
   (3) upon the denial of a petition for certiorari, if the order of the commission, board, or Secretary has been affirmed or the petition for review has been dismissed by the court of appeals; or
   (4) upon the expiration of thirty days from the date of issuance of the mandate of the Supreme Court, if such Court directs that the order of the commission, board, or Secretary be affirmed or the petition for review be dismissed.

(h) If the Supreme Court directs that the order of the commission, board, or Secretary be modified or set aside, the order of the commission, board, or Secretary rendered in accordance with the mandate of the Supreme Court shall become final upon the expiration of thirty days from the time it was rendered, unless within such thirty days either party has instituted proceedings to have such order corrected to accord with the mandate, in which event the order of the commission, board, or Secretary shall become final when so corrected.

(i) If the order of the commission, board, or Secretary is modified or set aside by the court of appeals, and if (1) the time allowed for filing a petition for certiorari has expired and no such petition has been duly filed, or (2) the petition for certiorari has been denied, or (3) the decision of the court has been affirmed by the Supreme Court, then the order of the commission, board, or Secretary rendered in accordance with the mandate of the court of appeals shall become final on the expiration of thirty days from the time such order of the commission, board, or Secretary was rendered, unless within such thirty days either party has instituted proceedings to have such order corrected so that it will accord with the mandate, in which event the order of the commission, board, or Secretary shall become final when so corrected.

(j)   If the Supreme Court orders a rehearing; or if the case is remanded by the court of appeals to the commission, board, or Secretary for a rehearing, and if (1) the time allowed for filing a petition for certiorari has expired, and no such petition has been duly filed, or (2) the petition for certiorari has been denied, or (3) the decision of the court has been affirmed by the Supreme Court, then the order of the commission, board, or Secretary rendered upon such rehearing shall become final in the same manner as though no prior order of the commission, board, or Secretary had been rendered.

(k)   As used in this section the term "mandate," in case a mandate has been recalled prior to the expiration of thirty days from the date of issuance thereof, means the final mandate.

(l)   Any person who violates any order issued by the commission, board, or Secretary under subsection (b) of this section after such order has become final, and while such order is in effect, shall forfeit and pay to the United States a civil penalty of not more than $5,000 for each violation, which shall accrue to the United States and may be recovered in a civil action brought by the United States. Each separate violation of any such order shall be a separate offense, except that in the case of a violation through continuing failure or neglect to obey a final order of the commission, board, or Secretary each day of continuance of such failure or neglect shall be deemed a separate offense. [15 U.S.C. § 21(a)-(l)]

Section 12

Any suit, action, or proceeding under the antitrust laws against a corporation may be brought not only in the judicial district whereof it is an inhabitant, but also in any district wherein it may be found or transacts business; and all process in such cases may be served in the district of which it is an inhabitant, or wherever it may be found. [15 U.S.C. § 22]

Section 13

In any suit, action, or proceeding brought by or on behalf of the United States subpoenas for witnesses who are required to attend a court of the United States in any judicial district in any case, civil or criminal, arising under the antitrust laws may run into any other district: *Provided,* That in civil cases no writ of subpoena shall issue for witnesses living out of the district in which the court is held at a greater distance than one hundred miles from the place of holding the same without the permission of the trial court being first had upon proper application and cause shown. [15 U.S.C. § 23]

Section 14

Whenever a corporation shall violate any of the penal provisions of the antitrust laws, such violation shall be deemed to be also that of the individual directors, officers, or agents of such corporation who shall have authorized, ordered, or done any of the acts constituting in whole or part such violation, and such violation shall be deemed a misdemeanor, and upon conviction therefor of any such director, officer, or agent he shall be punished by a fine of not exceeding $5,000 or by imprisonment for not exceeding one year, or by both, in the discretion of the court. [15 U.S.C. § 24]

Section 15

The several district courts of the United States are invested with jurisdiction to prevent and restrain violations of this Act, and it shall be the duty of the several United States attorneys, in their respective districts, under the direction of the Attorney General, to institute proceedings in equity to prevent and restrain such violations. Such proceedings may be by way of petition setting forth the case and praying that such violation shall be enjoined or otherwise prohibited. When the parties complained of shall have been duly notified of such petition, the court shall proceed, as soon as may be, to the hearing and determination of the case; and pending such petition, and before final decree, the court may at any time make such temporary restraining order or prohibition as shall be deemed just in the premises. Whenever it shall appear to the court before which any such proceeding may be pending that the ends of justice require that other parties should be brought before the court, the court may cause them to be summoned whether they reside in the district in which the court is held or not, and subpoenas to that end may be served in any district by the marshal thereof. [15 U.S.C. § 25]

Section 16

Any person, firm, corporation, or association shall be entitled to sue for and have injunctive relief, in any court of the United States having jurisdiction over the parties, against threatened loss or damage by a violation of the antitrust laws, including sections [2, 3, 7, and 8] of this [Act], when and under the same conditions and principles as injunctive relief against threatened conduct that will cause loss or damage is granted by courts of equity, under the rules governing such proceedings, and upon the execution of proper bond against damages for an injunction improvidently granted and a showing that the danger of irreparable loss or damage is immediate, a preliminary injunction may issue: *Provided,* That nothing herein contained shall be construed to entitle any person, firm, corporation, or association, except the United States, to bring suit in equity for injunctive relief against any common carrier subject to the provisions of subtitle IV of Title 49, in respect of any matter subject to the regulation, supervision, or other jurisdiction of the Interstate Commerce Commission. In any action under this section in which the plaintiff substantially prevails, the court shall award the cost of suit, including a reasonable attorney's fee, to such plaintiff. [15 U.S.C. § 26]

Robinson-Patman Act

(Excerpt)

Section 3

It shall be unlawful for any person engaged in commerce, in the course of such commerce, to be a party to, or assist in, any transaction of sale, or contract to sell, which discriminates to his knowledge against competitors of the purchaser, in that, any discount, rebate, allowance, or advertising service charge is granted to the purchaser over and above any discount, rebate, allowance, or advertising service charge available at the time of such transaction to said competitors in respect of a sale of goods of like grade, quality, and quantity; to sell, or contract to sell, goods in any way part of the United States at prices lower than those exacted by said person elsewhere in the United States for the purpose of destroying competition, or eliminating a competitor in such part of the United States; or, to sell, or contract to sell, goods at unreasonably low prices for the purpose of destroying competition or eliminating a competitor.

Any person violating any part of the provisions of this section shall, upon conviction thereof, be fined not more than $5,000 or imprisoned not more than one year, or both.

[15 U.S.C. § 13a. Unlike Section 1, this section of the Robinson-Patman Act is not part of the Clayton Act. Robinson-Patman Act Sections 2 and 4 are not reprinted herein.]

Federal Trade Commission Act

(Excerpts)

Section 5

(a)(1) Unfair methods of competition in or affecting commerce, and unfair or deceptive acts or practices in or affecting commerce, are declared unlawful.

(2) The Commission is empowered and directed to prevent persons, partnerships, or corporations, except banks, savings and loan institutions described in section 57a(f)(3) of this title, Federal credit unions described in section 57a(f)(4) of this title, common carriers subject to the Acts to regulate commerce, air carriers and foreign air carriers subject to the Federal Aviation Act of 1958 [49 App. U.S.C. §§ 1301 et seq.], and persons, partnerships, or corporations insofar as they are subject to the Packers and Stockyards Act, 1921, as amended [7 U.S.C. §§ 181 et seq.], except as provided in section 406(b) of said Act [7 U.S.C. § 227(b)], from using unfair methods of competition in or affecting commerce and unfair or deceptive acts or practices in or affecting commerce.

(3) This subsection shall not apply to unfair methods of competition involving commerce with foreign nations (other than import commerce) unless —

(A) such methods of competition have a direct, substantial, and reasonably foreseeable effect —

(i) on commerce which is not commerce with foreign nations, or on import commerce with foreign nations; or

      (ii) on export commerce with foreign nations, of a person engaged in such commerce in the United States; and

    (B) such effect gives rise to a claim under the provisions of this subsection, other than this paragraph.

If this subsection applies to such methods of competition only because of the operation of subparagraph (A)(ii), this subsection shall apply to such conduct only for injury to export business in the United States.

(b) Whenever the Commission shall have reason to believe that any such person, partnership, or corporation has been or is using any unfair method of competition or unfair or deceptive act or practice in or affecting commerce, and if it shall appear to the Commission that a proceeding by it in respect thereof would be to the interest of the public, it shall issue and serve upon such persons, partnership, or corporation a complaint stating its charges in that respect and containing a notice of a hearing upon a day and at a place therein fixed at least thirty days after the service of said complaint. The person, partnership, or corporation so complained of shall have the right to appear at the place and time so fixed and show cause why an order should not be entered by the Commission requiring such person, partnership, or corporation to cease and desist from the violation of the law so charged in said complaint. Any person, partnership, or corporation may make application, and upon good cause shown may be allowed by the Commission to intervene and appear in said proceeding by counsel or in person. The testimony in any such proceeding shall be reduced to writing and filed in the office of the Commission. If upon such hearing the Commission shall be of the opinion that the method of competition or the act or practice in question is prohibited by this subchapter, it shall make a report in writing in which it shall state its findings as to the facts and shall issue and cause to be served on such person, partnership, or corporation an order requiring such person, partnership, or corporation to cease and desist from using such method of competition or such act or practice. Until the expiration of the time allowed for filing a petition for review, if no such petition has been duly filed within such time, or, if a petition for review has been filed within such time then until the record in the proceeding has been filed in a court of appeals of the United States, as hereinafter provided, the Commission may at any time, upon such notice and in such manner as it shall deem proper, modify or set aside, in whole or in part, any report or any order made or issued by it under this section. After the expiration of the time allowed for filing a petition for review, if no such petition has been duly filed within such time, the Commission may at any time, after notice, and opportunity for hearing, reopen and alter, modify, or set aside, in whole or in part, any report or order made or issued by it under this section, whenever in the opinion of the Commission conditions of fact or of law have so changed as to require such action or if the public interest shall so require, except that (1) the said person, partnership, or corporation may, within sixty days after service upon him or it of said report or order entered after such a reopening, obtain a review thereof in the appropriate court of appeals in the United States, in the manner provided in subsection (c) of this section; and (2) in the case of an order, the Commission shall reopen any such order to consider whether such order (including any affirmative relief provision contained in such order) should be altered, modified, or set aside, in whole or in part, if the person, partnership, or corporation involved files a request with the Commission which makes a satisfactory showing that changed conditions of law or fact require such order to be altered, modified, or set aside, in whole or in part. The Commission shall determine whether to alter, modify, or set aside any order of the Commission in response to a request made by a person, partnership, or corporation under paragraph[1] (2) not later than 120 days after the date of the filing of such request.

(c) Any person, partnership, or corporation required by an order of the Commission to cease and desist from using any method of competition or act or practice may obtain a review of such order in the court of appeals of the United States, within any circuit where the method of competition or the act or practice in question was used or where such person, partnership, or corporation resides or carries on business, by filing in the court, within sixty days from the date of the service of such order, a written petition praying that the order of the Commission be set aside. A copy of such petition shall be forthwith transmitted by the clerk of the court to the Commission, and thereupon the Commission shall file in the court the record in the proceeding, as provided in section 2112 of Title 28 [the U.S. Code]. Upon such filing of the petition the court shall have jurisdiction of the proceeding and of the question determined therein concurrently with the Commission until the filing of the record and shall have the power to make and enter a decree affirming, modifying, or setting aside the order of the Commission, and enforcing the same to the extent that such order is affirmed and to issue such writs as are ancillary to its jurisdiction or are necessary in its judgment to prevent injury to the public or to competitors pendente lite. The findings of the Commission as to the facts, if supported by evidence, shall be conclusive. To the extent that the order of the Commission is affirmed, the court shall thereupon issue its own order commending obedience to the terms of such order of the Commission. If either party shall apply to the court for leave to adduce additional evidence, and shall show to the satisfaction of the court that such additional evidence is material and that there were reasonable grounds for the failure to adduce such evidence in the proceeding before the Commission, the court may order such additional evidence to be taken before the Commission and to be adduced upon the hearing in such manner and upon such terms and conditions as to the court may seem proper. The Commission may modify its findings as to the facts, or make new findings, by reason of the additional evidence so taken, and it shall file such modified or new findings, which, if supported by evidence, shall be conclusive, and its recommendation, if any, for the modification or setting aside of its original order, with the return of such additional evidence. The judgment and decree of the court shall be final, except that the same shall be subject to review by the Supreme Court upon certiorari, as provided in section 347 of Title 28 [of the U.S. Code].

(d) Upon the filing of the record with it the jurisdiction of the court of appeals of the United States to affirm, enforce, modify, or set aside orders of the Commission shall be exclusive.

---

1.   So in original. Probably should be "clause."

(e) No order of the Commission or judgment of court to enforce the same shall be anywise relieve or absolve any person, partnership, or corporation from any liability under the Antitrust Acts.

(f) Complaints, orders, and other processes of the Commission under this section may be served by anyone duly authorized by the Commission, either (a) by delivering a copy thereof to the person to be served, or to a member of the partnership to be served, or the president, secretary, or other executive officer or a director of the corporation to be served; or (b) by leaving a copy thereof at the residence or the principal office or place of business of such person, partnership, or corporation; or (c) by mailing a copy thereof by registered mail or by certified mail addressed to such person, partnership, or corporation at his or its residence or principal office or place of business. The verified return by the person so serving said complaint, order, or other process setting forth the manner of said service shall be proof of the same, and the return post office receipt of said complaint, order, or other process mailed by registered mail or by certified mail as aforesaid shall be proof of the service of the same.

(g) An order of the Commission to cease and desist shall become final —

(1) Upon the expiration of the time allowed for filing a petition for review, if no such petition has been duly filed within such time; but the Commission may thereafter modify or set aside its order to the extent provided in the last sentence of subsection (b); or
(2) Upon the expiration of the time allowed for filing a petition for certiorari, if the order of the Commission has been affirmed, or the petition for review dismissed by the court of appeals, and no petition for certiorari has been duly filed; or
(3) Upon the denial of a petition for certiorari, if the order of the Commission has been affirmed or the petition for review dismissed by the court of appeals; or
(4) Upon the expiration of thirty days from the date of issuance of the mandate of the Supreme Court, if such Court directs that the order of the Commission be affirmed or the petition for review dismissed.

(h) If the Supreme Court directs that the order of the Commission be modified or set aside, the order of the Commission rendered in accordance with the mandate of the Supreme Court shall become final upon the expiration of thirty days from the time it was rendered, unless within such thirty days either party has instituted proceedings to have such order corrected to accord with the mandate, in which event the order of the Commission shall become final when so corrected.

(i) If the order of the Commission is modified or set aside by the court of appeals, and if (1) the time allowed for filing a petition for certiorari has expired and no such petition has been duly filed, or (2) the petition for certiorari has been denied, or (3) the decision of the court has been affirmed by the Supreme Court, then the order of the Commission rendered in accordance with the mandate of the court of appeals shall become final on the expiration of thirty days from the time such order of the Commission was rendered, unless within such thirty days either party has instituted proceedings to have such order corrected so that it will accord with the mandate, in which event the order of the Commission shall become final when so corrected.

(j)   If the Supreme Court orders a rehearing; or if the case is remanded by the court of appeals to the Commission for a rehearing; and if (1) the time allowed for filing a petition for certiorari has expired, and no such petition has been duly filed, or (2) the petition for certiorari has been denied, or (3) the decision of the court has been affirmed by the Supreme Court, then the order of the Commission rendered upon such rehearing shall become final in the same manner as though no prior order of the Commission had been rendered.

(k)   As used in this section the term "mandate", in case a mandate has been recalled prior to the expiration of thirty days from the date of issuance thereof, means the final mandate.

(l)   Any person, partnership, or corporation who violates an order of the Commission after it has become final, and while such order is in effect, shall forfeit and pay to the United States a civil penalty of not more than $10,000 for each violation, which shall accrue to the United States and may be recovered in a civil action brought by the Attorney General of the United States.   Each separate violation of such an order shall be a separate offense, except that in a case of a violation through continuing failure to obey or neglect to obey a final order of the Commission, each day of continuance of such failure or neglect shall be deemed a separate offense.   In such actions, the United States district courts are empowered to grant mandatory injunctions and such other and further equitable relief as they deem appropriate in the enforcement of such final orders of the Commission.

(m)(1)(A) The Commission may commence a civil action to recover a civil penalty in a district court of the United States against any person, partnership, or corporation which violates any rule under this chapter respecting unfair or deceptive acts or practices (other than an interpretive rule or a rule violation of which the Commission has provided is not an unfair or deceptive act or practice in violation of subsection (a)(1) of this section) with actual knowledge or knowledge fairly implied on the basis of objective circumstances that such act is unfair or deceptive and is prohibited by such rule.   In such action, such person, partnership, or corporation shall be liable for a civil penalty of not more then $10,000 for each violation.

   (B)   If the Commission determines in a proceeding under subsection (b) of this section that any act or practice is unfair or deceptive, and issues a final cease and desist order with respect to such act or practice, then the Commission may commence a civil action to obtain a civil penalty in a district court of the United States against any person, partnership, or corporation which engages in such act or practice —

      (1)   after such cease and desist order becomes final (whether or not such person, partnership, or corporation was subject to such cease and desist order), and

      (2)   with actual knowledge that such act or practice is unfair or deceptive and is unlawful under subsection (a)(1) of this section.

In such action, such person, partnership, or corporation shall be liable for a civil penalty of not more than $10,000 for each violation.

(C) In the case of a violation through continuing failure to comply with a rule or with subsection (a)(1) of this section, each day of continuance of such failure shall be treated as a separate violation, for purposes of subparagraph (A) and (B). In determining the amount of such a civil penalty, the court shall take into account the degree of culpability, any history of prior such conduct, ability to pay, effect on ability to continue to do business, and such other matters as justice may require.

(2) If the cease and desist order establishing that the act or practice is unfair or deceptive was not issued against the defendant in a civil penalty action under paragraph (1)(B) the issues of fact in such action against such defendant shall be tried de novo.

(3) The Commission may compromise or settle any action for a civil penalty if such compromise or settlement is accompanied by public statement of its reasons and is approved by the court. [15 U.S.C. § 45]

Section 13(b)

(b) Whenever the Commission has reason to believe –

(1) that any person, partnership, or corporation is violating, or is about to violate, any provision of law enforced by the Federal Trade Commission, and

(2) that the enjoining thereof pending the issuance of a complaint by the Commission and until such complaint is dismissed by the Commission or set aside by the court on review, or until the order of the Commission made thereon has become final, would be in the interest of the public –

the Commission by any of its attorneys designated by it for such purpose may bring suit in a district court of the United States to enjoin any such act or practice. Upon a proper showing that, weighing the equities and considering the Commission's likelihood of ultimate success, such action would be in the public interest, and after notice to the defendant, a temporary restraining order or a preliminary injunction may be granted without bond: *Provided, however,* That if a complaint is not filed within such period (not exceeding 20 days) as may be specified by the court after issuance of the temporary restraining order or preliminary injunction, the order or injunction shall be dissolved by the court and be of no further force and effect: *Provided, further,* That in proper cases the Commission may seek, and after proper proof, the court may issue, a permanent injunction. Any such suit shall be brought in the district in which such person, partnership, or corporation resides or transacts business. [15 U.S.C. § 53]

Section 18

(a)(1) Except as provided in subsection (i) of this section, the Commission may prescribe –

(A) interpretive rules and general statements of policy with respect to unfair or deceptive acts or practices in or affecting commerce (within the meaning of section [5(a)(1) of this Act]), and

(B) rules which define with specificity acts or practices which are unfair or deceptive acts or practices in or affecting commerce (within the meaning of section

[5(a)(1) of this Act]), except that the Commission shall not develop or promulgate any trade rule or regulation with regard to the regulation of the development and utilization of the standards and certification activities pursuant to this section. Rules under this subparagraph may include requirements prescribed for the purpose of preventing such acts or practices.

(2)   The Commission shall have no authority under [this Act], other than its authority under this section, to prescribe any rule with respect to unfair or deceptive acts or practices in or affecting commerce (within the meaning of section [5(a)(1) of this Act]). The preceding sentence shall not affect any authority of the Commission to prescribe rules (including interpretive rules), and general statements of policy, with respect to unfair methods of competition in or affecting commerce.

(b)(1)   When prescribing a rule under subsection (a)(1)(B) of this section, the Commission shall proceed in accordance with section 553 of Title 5 (without regard to any reference in such section to sections 556 and 557 of such title), and shall also (A) publish a notice of proposed rulemaking stating with particularity the text of the rule, including any alternatives, which the Commission proposes to promulgate, and the reason for the proposed rule; (B) allow interested persons to submit written data, views, and arguments, and make all such submissions publicly available; (C) provide an opportunity for an informal hearing in accordance with subsection (c) of this section; and (D) promulgate, if appropriate, a final rule based on the matter in the rulemaking record (as defined in subsection (e)(1)(B) of this section), together with a statement of basis and purpose.

(2)(A)   Prior to the publication of any notice of proposed rulemaking pursuant to paragraph (1)(A), the Commission shall publish an advance notice of proposed rulemaking in the Federal Register. Such advance notice shall –

(i) contain a brief description of the area of inquiry under consideration, the objectives which the Commission seeks to achieve, and possible regulatory alternatives under consideration by the Commission; and

(ii) invite the response of interested parties with respect to such proposed rulemaking, including any suggestions or alternative methods for achieving such objectives.

(B) The Commission shall submit such advance notice of proposed rulemaking to the Committee on Commerce, Science, and Transportation of the Senate and to the Committee on Energy and Commerce of the House of Representatives. The Commission may use such additional mechanisms as the Commission considers useful to obtain suggestions regarding the content of the area of inquiry before the publication of a general notice of proposed rulemaking under paragraph (1)(A).

(C) The Commission shall, 30 days before the publication of a notice of proposed rulemaking pursuant to paragraph (1)(A), submit such notice to the Committee on Commerce, Science, and Transportation of the Senate and to the Committee on Energy and Commerce of the House of Representatives.

(c)   The Commission shall conduct any informal hearings required by subsection (b)(1)(C) of this section in accordance with the following procedure:

(1)(A)   The Commission shall provide for the conduct of proceedings under this subsection by hearing officers who shall perform their functions in accordance with the requirements of this subsection.

(B) The officer who presides over the rulemaking proceedings shall be responsible to a chief presiding officer who shall not be responsible to any other officer or employee of the Commission. The officer who presides over the rulemaking proceeding shall make a recommended decision based upon the findings and conclusions of such officer as to all relevant and material evidence, except that such recommended decision may be made by another officer if the officer who presided over the proceeding is no longer available to the Commission.

(C) Except as required for the disposition of ex parte matters as authorized by law, no presiding officer shall consult any person or party with respect to any fact in issue unless such officer gives notice and opportunity for all parties to participate.

(2) Subject to paragraph (3) of this subsection, an interested person is entitled –

(A) to present his position orally or by documentary submissions (or both), and

(B) if the Commission determines that there are disputed issues of material fact it is necessary to resolve, to present such rebuttal submissions and to conduct (or have conducted under paragraph (3)(B)) such cross-examination of persons as the Commission determines (i) to be appropriate, and (ii) to be required for a full and true disclosure with respect to such issues.

(3) The Commission may prescribe such rules and make such rulings concerning proceedings in such hearings as may tend to avoid unnecessary costs or delay. Such rules or rulings may included (A) imposition of reasonable time limits on each interested person's oral presentations, and (B) requirements that any cross-examination to which a person may be entitled under paragraph (2) be conducted by the Commission on behalf of that person in such manner as the Commission determines (i) to be appropriate, and (ii) to be required for a full and true disclosure with respect to disputed issues of material fact.

(4)(A) Except as provided in subparagraph (B), if a group of persons each of whom under paragraphs (2) and (3) would be entitled to conduct (or have conducted) cross-examination and who are determined by the Commission to have the same or similar interests in the proceeding cannot agree upon a single representative of such interests for purposes of cross-examination, the Commission may make rules and rulings (i) limiting the representation of such interest, for such purposes, and (ii) governing the manner in which such cross-examination shall be limited.

(B) When any person who is a member of a group with respect to which the Commission has made a determination under subparagraph (A) is unable to agree upon group representation with the other members of the group, then such person shall not be denied under the authority of subparagraph (A) the opportunity to conduct (or have conducted) cross-examination as to issues affecting his particular interests if (i) he satisfies the Commission that he has made a reasonable and good faith effort to reach agreement upon group representation with the other members of the group and (ii) the Commission determines that there are substantial and relevant issues which are not adequately presented by the group representative.

(5) A verbatim transcript shall be taken of any oral presentation, and cross-examination, in an informal hearing to which this subsection applies. Such transcript

shall be available to the public.

(d)(1) The Commission's statement of basis and purpose to accompany a rule promulgated under subsection (a)(1)(B) of this section shall include (A) a statement as to the prevalence of the acts or practices treated by the rule; (B) a statement as to the manner and context in which such acts or practices are unfair or deceptive; and (C) a statement as to the economic effect of the rule, taking into account the effect on small business and consumers.

(2)(A) The term "Commission" as used in this subsection and subsections (b) and (c) of this section includes any person authorized to act in behalf of the Commission in any part of the rulemaking proceeding.

(B) A substantive amendment to, or repeal of, a rule promulgated under subsection (a)(1)(B) of this section shall be prescribed, and subject to judicial review, in the same manner as a rule prescribed under such subsection. An exemption under subsection (g) of this section shall not be treated as an amendment or repeal of a rule.

(3)   When any rule under subsection (a)(1)(B) of this section takes effect a subsequent violation thereof shall constitute an unfair or deceptive act or practice in violation of section [5(a)(1) of this Act], unless the Commission otherwise expressly provides in such rule.

(e)(1)(A) Not later than 60 days after a rule is promulgated under subsection (a)(1)(B) of this section by the Commission, any interested person (including a consumer or consumer organization) may file a petition, in the United States Court of Appeals for the District of Columbia circuit or for the circuit in which such person resides or has his principal place of business, for judicial review of such rule. Copies of the petition shall be forthwith transmitted by the clerk of the court to the Commission or other officer designated by it for that purpose. The provisions of section 2112 of Title 28 shall apply to the filing of the rulemaking record of proceedings on which the Commission based its rule and to the transfer of proceedings in the courts of appeals.

(B) For purpose of this section, the term "rulemaking record" means the rule, its statement of basis and purpose, the transcript required by subsection (c)(5) of this section, any written submissions, and any other information which the Commission considers relevant to such rule.

(2) If the petitioner or the Commission applies to the court for leave to make additional oral submissions or written presentations and shows to the satisfaction of the court that such submissions and presentations would be material and that there were reasonable grounds for the submissions and failure to make such submissions and presentations in the proceeding before the Commission, the court may order the Commission to provide additional opportunity to make such submissions and presentations. The Commission may modify or set aside its rule or make a new rule by reason of the additional submissions and presentations and shall file such modified or new rule, and the rule's statement of basis of purpose, with the return of such submissions and presentations. The court shall thereafter review such new or modified rule.

(3) Upon the filing of the petition under paragraph (1) of this subsection, the court shall have jurisdiction to review the rule in accordance with chapter 7 of Title 5 and to grant appropriate relief, including interim relief, as provided in such

chapter. The court shall hold unlawful and set aside the rule on any ground specified in subparagraphs (A),(B),(C), or (D) of section 706(2) of Title 5 (taking due account of the rule of prejudicial error), or if —

 (A) the court finds that the Commission's action is not supported by substantial evidence in the rulemaking record (as defined in paragraph (1)(B) of this subsection) taken as a whole, or

 (B) the court finds that —

  (i) a Commission determination under subsection (c) of this section that the petitioner is not entitled to conduct cross-examination or make rebuttal submissions, or

  (ii) a Commission rule or ruling under subsection (c) of this section limiting the petitioner's cross-examination or rebuttal submissions, has precluded disclosure of disputed material facts which was necessary for fair determination by the Commission of the rulemaking proceeding taken as a whole.

The term "evidence", as used in this paragraph, means any matter in the rulemaking record.

 (4) The judgment of the court affirming or setting aside, in whole or in part, any such rule shall be final, subject to review by the Supreme Court of the United States upon certiorari or certification, as provided in section 1254 of Title 28.

 (5)(A) Remedies under the preceding paragraphs of this subsection are in addition to and not in lieu of any other remedies provided by law.

 (B) The United States Courts of Appeal shall have exclusive jurisdiction of any action to obtain judicial review (other than in an enforcement proceeding) of a rule prescribed under subsection (a)(1)(B) of this section, if any district court of the United States would have had jurisdiction of such action but for this subparagraph. Any such action shall be brought in the United States Court of Appeals for the District of Columbia circuit, or for any circuit which includes a judicial district in which the action could have been brought but for this subparagraph.

 (C) A determination, rule, or ruling of the Commission described in paragraph (3)(B)(i) or (ii) may be reviewed only in a proceeding under this subsection and only in accordance with paragraph (3)(B). Section 706(2)(E) of Title 5 shall not apply to any rule promulgated under subsection (a)(1)(B) of this section. The contents and adequacy of any statement required by subsection (b)(1)(D) of this section shall not be subject to judicial review in any respect.

 (f)(1) In order to prevent unfair or deceptive acts or practices in or affecting commerce (including acts or practices which are unfair or deceptive to consumers) by banks or savings and loan institutions described in paragraph (3), each agency specified in paragraph (2) or (3) of this subsection shall establish a separate division of consumer affairs which shall receive and take appropriate action upon complaints with respect to such acts or practices by banks or savings and loan institutions described in paragraph (3) subject to its jurisdiction. The Board of Governors of the Federal Reserve System (with respect to banks) and the Federal Home Loan Bank Board (with respect to savings and loan institutions described in paragraph (3)) and the National Credit Union Administration Board (with respect to Federal credit unions described in paragraph (4)) shall prescribe regulations to carry out the purposes of this section, including regulations defining with specificity such unfair or deceptive acts or practices, and containing requirements prescribed for the purpose of preventing such acts or practices. Whenever the Commission prescribes a rule under subsection (a)(1)(B) of this section, then within 60 days after such rule takes effect each such Board shall promulgate substantially similar regulations prohibiting acts or practices of banks or savings and loan institutions described in paragraph (3), or Federal credit unions described in paragraph (4), as the case may be, which are substantially similar to those prohibited by rules of the Commission and which impose substantially similar requirements, unless (A) any such Board finds that such acts or practices of banks or savings and loan institutions described in paragraph (3), or Federal credit unions described in paragraph (4), as the case may be, are not unfair or deceptive, or (B) the Board of Governors of the Federal Reserve System finds that implementation of similar regulations with respect to banks, savings and loan institutions or Federal credit unions would seriously conflict with essential monetary and payments systems policies of such Board, and publishes any such finding, and the reasons therefor, in the Federal Register.

(2)   Compliance with regulations prescribed under this subsection shall be enforced [under Section 8 of the Federal Deposit Insurance Act] [12 U.S.C.A. § 1818], in the case of —

(A) national banks and banks operating under the code of law for the District of Columbia, and Federal branches and Federal agencies of foreign banks, by the division of consumer affairs established by the Office of the Comptroller of the Currency;

(B) member banks of the Federal Reserve System (other than national banks and banks operating under the code of law for the District of Columbia), branches and agencies of foreign banks (other than Federal branches, Federal agencies, and insured State branches of foreign banks), commercial lending companies owned or controlled by foreign banks, and organizations operating under section 25 or 25(a) of the Federal Reserve Act [12 U.S.C.A. §§ 601 et seq., 611 et seq.], by the division of consumer affairs established by the Board of Governors of the Federal Reserve System; and

(C) banks insured by the Federal Deposit Insurance Corporation (other than banks[1] referred to in subparagraph (A) or (B)) and insured State branches of foreign banks, by the division of consumer affairs established by the Board of Directors of the Federal Deposit Insurance Corporation.

(3)   Compliance with regulations prescribed under this subsection shall be enforced under section [8 of the Federal Deposit Insurance Act] [12 U.S.C.A. § 1818] with respect to savings associations as defined in section [3 of the Federal Deposit Insurance Act] [12 U.S.C.A. § 1813].

(4)   Compliance with regulations prescribed under this subsection shall be enforced with respect to Federal credit unions under sections 120 and 206 of the Federal Credit Union Act (12 U.S.C. §§ 1766 and 1786).

(5)   For the purpose of the exercise by any agency referred to paragraph (2) of its powers under any Act referred to in that paragraph, a violation of any regulation prescribed under this subsection shall be deemed to be a violation of a requirement imposed under that Act. In addition to its powers under any provision of law specifically referred to in paragraph (2), each of the agencies referred to in that

---

1.   So in original. Probably should be "other than banks".

paragraph may exercise, for the purpose of enforcing compliance with any regulation prescribed under this subsection, any other authority conferred on it by law.

(6)   The authority of the Board of Governors of the Federal Reserve System to issue regulations under this subsection does not impair the authority of any other agency designated in this subsection to make rules respecting its own procedures in enforcing compliance with regulations prescribed under this subsection.

(7)   Each agency exercising authority under this subsection shall transmit to the Congress each year a detailed report on its activities under this paragraph during the preceding calendar year.

(g)(1)   Any person to whom a rule under subsection (a)(1)(B) of this section applies may petition the Commission for an exemption from such rule.

(2)   If, on its own motion or on the basis of a petition under paragraph (1), the Commission finds that the application of a rule prescribed under subsection (a)(1)(B) of this section to any person or class or[2] persons is not necessary to prevent the unfair or deceptive act or practice to which the rule relates, the Commission may exempt such person or class from all or part of such rule. Section 553 of Title 5 shall apply to action under this paragraph.

(3)   Neither the pendency of a proceeding under this subsection respecting an exemption from a rule, nor the pendency of judicial proceedings to review the Commission's action or failure to act under this subsection, shall stay the applicability of such rule under subsection (a)(1)(B) of this section.

(h)(1) The Commission may, pursuant to rules prescribed by it, provide compensation for reasonable attorneys, fees, expert witness fees, and other costs of participating in a rulemaking proceeding under this section to any person (A) who has, or represents, an interest (i) which would not otherwise be adequately represented in such proceeding, and (ii) representation of which is necessary for a fair determination of the rulemaking proceeding taken as a whole, and (B) who is unable effectively to participate in such proceeding because such person cannot afford to pay costs of making oral presentations, conducting cross-examination, and making rebuttal submissions in such proceeding.

(2)   The Commission shall reserve an amount equal to 25 percent of the amount appropriated for the payment of compensation under this subsection for any fiscal year for use in accordance with this paragraph. Such reserved amount shall be available solely for the payment of compensation to persons who either (A) would be regulated by the proposed rule involved; or (B) represent persons who would be so regulated. Any portion of such reserved amount which is not used for the payment of compensation to such persons under this paragraph shall revert to the Treasury of the United States.

(3)   The aggregate amount of compensation paid to all persons in any fiscal year under this subsection may not exceed $1,000,000.

(4)   The Commission, in connection with the administration of this subsection pursuant to rules prescribed by the Commission under paragraph (1), shall establish a small business outreach program. Such program shall —

(A) solicit public comment from small businesses whose views otherwise

---

2.   So in original. Probably should be "of".

would not be adequately represented, in order to ensure a fair determination in rulemaking proceedings under this section; and

(B) encourage the participation of small businesses in the compensation program administered by the Commission under this subsection by disseminating to small businesses information which explains the procedures and requirements applicable to the receipt of compensation under such program.

(i) The Commission shall not have any authority to promulgate any rule in the children's advertising proceeding pending on May 28, 1980, or in any substantially similar proceeding on the basis of a determination by the Commission that such advertising constitutes an unfair act or practice in or affecting commerce.

(j)(1) For purposes of this subsection, the term "outside party" means any person other than (A) a Commissioner; (B) an officer or employee of the Commission; or (C) any person who has entered into a contract or any other agreement or arrangement with the Commission to provide any goods or services (including consulting services) to the Commission.

(2) Not later than 60 days after May 28, 1980, the Commission shall publish a proposed rule, and not later than 180 days after May 28, 1980, the Commission shall promulgate a final rule, which shall authorize the Commission or any Commissioner to meet with any outside party concerning any rulemaking proceeding of the Commission. Such rule shall provide that —

(A) notice of any such meeting shall be included in any weekly calendar prepared by the Commission, and

(B) a verbatim record or a summary of any such meeting, or of any communication relating to any such meeting, shall be kept, made available to the public, and included in the rulemaking record.

(k) Not later than 60 days after May 28, 1980, the Commission shall publish a proposed rule, and not later than 180 days after May 28, 1980, the Commission shall promulgate a final rule, which shall prohibit any officer, employee, or agent of the Commission with any investigative responsibility or other responsibility relating to any rulemaking proceeding within any operating bureau of the Commission, from communicating or causing to be communicated to any Commissioner or to the personal staff of any Commissioner any fact which is relevant to the merits of such proceeding and which is not on the rulemaking record of such proceeding, unless such communications is made available to the public and is included in the rulemaking record. The provisions of this subsection shall not apply to any communication to the extent such communication is required for the disposition of ex parte matters as authorized by law. [15 U.S.C. § 57a]

Section 19

(a)(1) If any person, partnership, or corporation violates any rule under this chapter respecting unfair or deceptive acts or practices (other than an interpretive rule, or a rule violation of which the Commission has provided is not an unfair or deceptive act or practice in violation of [section 5(a)]), then the Commission may commence a civil action against such person, partnership, or corporation for relief under subsection (b) of this section in a United States district court or in any court of competent jurisdiction of a State.

(2)   If any person, partnership, or corporation engages in any unfair or deceptive act or practice (within the meaning of section [5(a)(1)] of this title) with respect to which the Commission has issued a final cease and desist order which is applicable to such person, partnership, or corporation, then the Commission may commence a civil action against such person, partnership, or corporation in a United States district court or in any court of competent jurisdiction of a State. If the Commission satisfies the court that the act or practice to which the cease and desist order relates is one which a reasonable man would have known under the circumstances was dishonest or fraudulent, the court may grant relief under subsection (b) of this section.

(b) The court in an action under subsection (a) of this section shall have jurisdiction to grant such relief as the court finds necessary to redress injury to consumers or other persons, partnerships, and corporations resulting from the rule violation or the unfair or deceptive act or practice, as the case may be. Such relief may include, but shall not be limited to, rescission or reformation of contracts, the refund of money or return of property, the payment of damages, and public notification respecting the rule violation or the unfair or deceptive act or practice, as the case may be; except that nothing in this subsection is intended to authorize the imposition of any exemplary or punitive damages.

(c)(1)   If (A) a cease and desist order issued under [section 5(b)] has become final under [section 5(g)] with respect to any person's, partnership's, or corporation's rule violation or unfair or deceptive act or practice, and (B) an action under this section is brought with respect to such person's, partnership's, or corporation's rule violation or act or practice, then the findings of the Commission as to the material facts in the proceeding under [section 5(b)] with respect to such person's, partnership's, or corporation's rule violation or act or practice, shall be conclusive until (i) the terms of such cease and desist order expressly provide that the Commission's findings shall not be conclusive, or (ii) the order becomes final by reason of [section 5(g)(1)], in which case such finding shall be conclusive if supported by evidence.

(2)   The court shall cause notice of an action under this section to be given in a manner which is reasonably calculated, under all of the circumstances, to apprise the persons, partnerships, and corporations allegedly injured by the defendant's rule violation or act or practice of the pendency of such action. Such notice may, in the discretion of the court, be given by publication.

(d) No action may be brought by the Commission under this section more than 3 years after the rule violation by which an action under subsection (a)(1) of this section relates, or the unfair or deceptive act or practice to which an action under subsection (a)(2) of this section relates; except that if a cease and desist order with respect to any person's, partnership's, or corporation's rule violation or unfair or deceptive act or practice has become final and such order was issued in a proceeding under [section 5(b)] which was commenced not later than 3 years after the rule violation or act or practice occurred, a civil action may be commenced under this section against such person, partnership, or corporation at any time before the expiration of one year after such order becomes final.

(e)   Remedies provided in this section are in addition to, and not in lieu of, any other remedy or right of action provided by State or Federal law. Nothing in this section shall be construed to affect any authority of the Commission under any other provision of law. [15 U.S.C. § 57b]

1984 U.S. DEPARTMENT OF JUSTICE MERGER GUIDELINES

1. Purpose and Underlying Policy Assumptions

1.0 These Guidelines state in outline form the present enforcement of the U.S. Department of Justice ("Department") concerning acquisition and mergers ("mergers") subject to section 7 of the Clayton Act[1] or to section 1 of the Sherman Act.[2] They describe the general principles and specific standards normally used by the Department in analyzing mergers.[3] By stating its policy as simply and clearly as possible, the Department hopes to reduce the uncertainty associated with enforcement of the antitrust laws in this area.

Although the Guidelines should improve the predictability of the Department's merger enforcement policy, it is not possible to remove the exercise of judgment from the evaluation of mergers under the antitrust laws. Because the specific standards set forth in the Guidelines must be applied to a broad range of possible factual circumstances, strict application of those standards may provide misleading answers to the economic questions raised under the antitrust laws. Moreover, the picture of competitive conditions that develops from historical evidence may provide an incomplete answer to the forward-looking inquiry of the Guidelines. Therefore, the Department will apply the standards of the Guidelines reasonably and flexibly to the particular facts and circumstances of each proposed merger.

The Guidelines are designed primarily to indicate when the Department is likely to challenge mergers, not how it will conduct the litigation of cases that it decides to bring. Although relevant in the latter context, the factors contemplated in the standards do not exhaust the range of evidence that the Department may introduce in court.[4]

The unifying theme of the Guidelines is that mergers should not be permitted to create or enhance "market power" or to facilitate its exercise. A sole seller (a "monopolist") of a product with no good substitutes can maintain a selling price that

---

1. 15 U.S.C. § 18 (1982). Mergers subject to section 7 are prohibited if their effect "may be substantially to lessen competition, or to tend to create a monopoly."
2. 15 U.S.C. § 1 (1982). Mergers subject to section 1 are prohibited if they constitute a "contract, combination . . . , or conspiracy in restraint of trade."
3. They update the Guidelines issued by the Department in 1982. The Department may from time to time revise the Merger Guidelines as necessary to reflect any significant changes in enforcement policy or to clarify aspects of existing policy.
4. Parties seeking more specific advance guidance concerning the Department's enforcement intentions with respect to any particular merger should consider using the Business Review Procedure, 28 [C.F.R. § 50.6].

is above the level that would prevail if the market were competitive. Where only a few firms account for most of the sales of a product, those firms can in some circumstances either explicitly or implicitly coordinate their actions in order to approximate the performance of a monopolist. This ability of one or more firms profitably to maintain prices above competitive levels for a significant period of time is termed "market power." Sellers with market power also may eliminate rivalry on variables other than price. In either case, the result is a transfer of wealth from buyers to sellers and a misallocation of resources.

"Market power" also encompasses the ability of a single buyer or group of buyers to depress the price paid for a product to a level that is below the competitive price. The exercise of market power by buyers has wealth transfer and resource misallocation effects analogous to those associated with the exercise of market power by sellers.

Although they sometimes harm competition, mergers generally play an important role in a free enterprise economy. They can penalize ineffective management and facilitate the efficient flow of investment capital and the redeployment of existing productive assets. While challenging competitively harmful mergers, the Department seeks to avoid unnecessary interference with that larger universe of mergers that are either competitively beneficial or neutral. In attempting to mediate between these dual concerns, however, the Guidelines reflect the congressional intent that merger enforcement should interdict competitive problems in their incipiency.

2. Market Definition and Measurement

2.0 Using the standards stated below, the Department will define and measure the market for each product or service (hereinafter "product") of each of the merging firms. The standards in the Guidelines are designed to ensure that the Department analyzes the likely competitive impact of a merger within economically meaningful markets – i.e., markets that could be subject to the exercise of market power. Accordingly, for each product of each merging firm, the Department seeks to define a market in which firms could effectively exercise market power if they were able to coordinate their actions. Formally, a market is defined as a product or group of products and a geographic area in which it is sold such that a hypothetical, profit-maximizing firm, not subject to price regulation, that was the only present and future seller of those products in that area would impose a "small but significant and nontransitory" increase in price above prevailing or likely future levels. The group of products and geographic area that comprise a market will be referred to respectively as the "product market" and the "geographic market."

In determining whether one or more firms would be in a position to exercise market power, it is necessary to evaluate both the probable demand responses of consumers and the probable supply responses of other firms. A price increase could be made unprofitable by any of four types of demand or supply responses: (1) Consumers switching to other products; (2) consumers switching to the same product produced by firms in other areas; (3) producers of other products switching existing facilities to the production of the product; or (4) producers entering into the production of the product by substantially modifying existing facilities or by constructing new facilities. Each type of response is considered under the Guidelines.

In determining whether any of these responses are probable, the Department usually must rely on historical market information as the best, and sometimes the only, indicator of how the market will function in the future. It is important to note, however, that the Guidelines are fundamentally concerned with probable future demand or supply responses.

Sections 2.1 through 2.4 described how product and geographic markets will be defined under these Guidelines and how market shares will be calculated.

2.1 Product Market Definition

2.11 GENERAL APPROACH

The Department will first determine the relevant product market with respect to each of the products of each of the merging firms. In general, the Department will include in the product market a group of products such that a hypothetical firm that was the only present and future seller of those products (a "monopolist") could profitably impose a "small but significant and nontransitory" increase in price. That is, assuming that buyers could respond to an increase in price for a tentatively identified product group only by shifting to other products, what would happen? If readily available alternatives were, in the aggregate, sufficiently attractive to enough buyers, an attempt to raise price would not prove profitable, and the tentatively identified product group would prove to be too narrow.

Specifically, the Department will begin with each product (narrowly defined) produced or sold by each merging firm and ask what would happen if a hypothetical monopolist of that product imposed a "small but significant ad nontransitory" increase in price.[5] If the price increase would cause so many buyers to shift to other products that a hypothetical monopolist would not find it profitable to impose such an increase in price, then the Department will add to the product group the product that is the next-best substitute for the merging firm's product and ask the same question again. This process will continue until a group of products is identified for which a hypothetical monopolist could profitably impose a "small but significant and nontransitory" increase in price. The Department generally will consider the relevant product market to be the smallest group of products that satisfies this test.

In the above analysis, the Department will use prevailing prices of the products of the merging firms and possible substitutes for such products. However, the Department may use likely future prices when changes in the prevailing prices can be predicted with reasonable reliability. Changes in price may be predicted on the basis of, for example, expected changes in regulations that directly affect price.

In general, the price for which an increase will be postulated will be whatever is considered to be the price of the product at the stage of the industry being examined.[6] In attempting to determine objectively the effect of a "small but

---

5.   Although discussed separately, product market definition and geographic market definition are interrelated. In particular, the extent to which buyers of a particular product would shift to other products in the event of a "small but significant and nontransitory" increase in price must be evaluated in the context of the relevant geographic market.

6.   For example, in a merger between retailers, the relevant price would be the retail price of a product to consumers. In the case of a merger among all pipelines, the relevant price would be the tariff – the price of the transportation service.

significant and nontransitory" increase in price, the Department in most contexts will use price increase of five percent lasting one year. However, what constitutes a "small but significant and nontransitory" increase in price will depend on the nature of the industry, and the Department at times may use a price increase that is larger or smaller than five percent.[7] For the purposes of its analysis, the Department will assume that the buyers and sellers immediately become aware of the price increase.

2.12 RELEVANT EVIDENCE

Although direct evidence of the likely effect of a future price increase may sometimes be available, it usually will be necessary for the Department to infer the likely effects of a price increase from various types of reliable, circumstantial evidence. The postulated "small but significant and nontransitory" price increase provides an objective standard by which to analyze the available evidence. Thus, in evaluating product substitutability, the Department will consider all relevant evidence but will give particular weight to the following factors:

(1)   Evidence of buyers' perceptions that the products are or are not substitutes, particularly if those buyers have actually considered shifting purchases between the products in response to changes in relative price or other competitive variables;

(2)   Differences in the price movements of the products or similarities in price movements over a period of years that are not explainable by common or parallel changes in factors such as costs of inputs, income, or other variables;

(3)   Similarities or differences between the products in customary usage, design, physical composition, and other technical characteristics; and

(4)   Evidence of sellers' perceptions that the products are or are not substitutes, particularly if business decisions have been based on those perceptions.

2.13 PRICE DISCRIMINATION

The analysis of the product market definition to this point has assumed that price discrimination − charging different buyers different prices for products having the same cost, for example − would not be possible after the merger. Existing buyers sometimes will differ significantly in their assessment of the adequacy of a particular substitute and the ease with which they could substitute it for the product of the merging firm. Even though a general increase in price might cause such significant substitution that it would not be profitable, sellers who can price discriminate could raise price only to groups of buyers who cannot easily substitute away.[8] If such price discrimination is possible, the Department will consider defining additional, narrower relevant product markets consisting of particular uses of the product for which a hypothetical monopolist could profitably impose a "small but significant and nontransitory" increase in price.

---

7.   For example, a larger increase may be appropriate if the "price" to be increased is a tariff or commission that constitutes a small fraction of the price of the product being transported or sold.

8.   Price discrimination requires that sellers be able to identify those buyers and that other buyers be unable profitably to purchase and resell to them.

2.2 *Identification of Firms That Produce the Relevant Product*

In most cases, the Department's evaluation of a merger will focus primarily on firms that currently produce and sell the relevant product. In addition, the Department may include other firms in the market if their inclusion would more accurately reflect probable supply responses. The following are examples of circumstances in which such additional firms would be included in the market.

2.21 PRODUCTION SUBSTITUTION

The same productive and distributive facilities can sometimes be used to produce and sell two or more products that buyers do not regard as good substitutes. Production substitution refers to the shift by a firm in the use of facilities from producing and selling one product to producing and selling another. Depending upon the cost and speed of that shift, production substitution may allow firms that do not currently product the relevant product to respond effectively to an increase in the price of that product.[9]

If a firm has existing productive and distributive facilities that could easily and economically be used to produce and sell the relevant product within one year in response to a "small but significant and nontransitory" increase in price, the Department will include that firm in the market.[10] In this context, a "small but significant and nontransitory" increase in price will be determined in the same way in which it is determined in product market definition. In many cases, a firm that could readily convert its facilities from the production of one product to another would have significant difficulty distributing or marketing the new product or for some other reason would find the substitution unprofitable. Such firms will not be included in the market. The competitive significance of such firms, as well as those that will not be included in the market because they must construct significant new productive and distributive facilities, will be considered in evaluating entry conditions generally. *See* Section 3.3. (Ease of Entry).

2.22 DURABLE PRODUCTS

Some long-lived products may continue to exert competitive influence after the time of original sale. If, under the standards stated in Section 2.1, recycled or reconditioned products represent good substitutes for new products, the Department will include in the market firms that recycle or recondition those products.

---

9.   Under other analytical approaches, production substitution sometimes has been reflected in the description of the product market. For example, the product market for stamped metal products such as automobile hub caps might be described as "light metal stamping," a production process rather than a product. The Department believes that the approach described in the text provides a more clearly focused method of incorporating this factor in merger analysis. If production substitution among a group of products is nearly universal among the firms selling one or more of those products, however, the Department may use an aggregate description of those markets as a matter of convenience.

10.   The amount of sales or capacity to be included in the market is a separate question discussed in Section 2.4, below.

2.23 INTERNAL CONSUMPTION

Captive production and consumption of the relevant product by vertically integrated firms are part of the overall market supply and demand. Such firms may respond to an increase in the price of the relevant product in either of two ways. They may begin selling the relevant product, or alternatively, they may continue to consume all of their production but increase their production of both the relevant product and products in which the relevant product is embodied. Either kind of supply response could frustrate collusion by firms currently selling the relevant product. If a firm would be likely to respond either way to a "small but significant and nontransitory" increase in price, the Department will include that firm in the market. In this context, a "small but significant and nontransitory" increase in price will be determined in product market definition.

2.3 *Geographic Market Definition*

2.31 GENERAL APPROACH

For each product market of each merging firm, the Department will determine the geographic market or markets in which that firm sells. The purpose of geographic market definition is to establish a geographic boundary that roughly separates firms that are important factors in the competitive analysis of a merger from those that are not. Depending on the nature of the product and the competitive circumstances, the geographic market may be as small as part of a city or as large as the entire world. Also, a single firm may operate in a number of economically discrete geographic markets.

In general, the Department seeks to identify a geographic area such that a hypothetical firm that was the only present or future producer *or seller* of the relevant product in that area could profitably impose a "small but significant and nontransitory" increase in price. That is, assuming that buyers could respond to a price increase within a tentatively identified area only by shifting to firms located outside the areas, what would happen? If firms located elsewhere readily could provide the relevant product to the hypothetical firm's buyers in sufficient quantity at a comparable price, an attempt to raise price would not prove profitable, and the tentatively identified geographic area would prove to be too narrow.

In defining the geographic market or markets affected by a merger, the Department will begin with the location of each merging firm (or each plant of a multiplant firm) and ask what would happen if a hypothetical monopolist of the relevant product at that point imposed a "small but significant and nontransitory" increase in price. If this increase in price would cause so many buyers to shift to products produced in other areas that a hypothetical monopolist producing or selling the relevant product at the merging firm's location would not find it profitable to impose such an increase in price, then the department will add the location from which production is next-best substitute for production at the merging firm's location and ask the same question again. This process will be repeated until the Department identifies an area in which a hypothetical monopolist could profitably impose a "small but significant and nontransitory" increase in price. The "smallest market" principle will be applied as it is in product market definition. Both the price in which an increase will be postulated and what constitutes a "small but significant and nontransitory" increase in price will be determined in the same way in which it is determined in product market definition.

2.32 RELEVANT EVIDENCE

Although direct evidence of the likely effect of a future price increase may sometimes be available, it usually will be necessary for the Department to infer the likely effects of a price increase from various types of reliable, circumstantial evidence. The postulated "small but significant and nontransitory" increase in price provides an objective standard by which to analyze the available evidence. Thus, in evaluating geographic substitutability, the Department will consider all relevant evidence that will give particular weight to the following factors:

1)   The shipment patterns of the merging firm and of those firms with which it actually competes for sales;

2)   Evidence of buyers having actually considered shifting their purchases among sellers at different geographic locations, especially if the shifts corresponded to changes in relative price or other competitive variables;

3)   Differences in the price movements of the relevant product or similarities in price movements over a period of years that are not explainable by common or parallel changes in factors such as the cost of inputs, income, or other variables in different geographic areas;

4)   Transportation costs;

5)   Costs of local distribution; and

6)   Excess capacity of firms outside the location of the merging firm.

2.33 PRICE DISCRIMINATION

The analysis of geographic market definition to this point has assumed that geographic price discrimination — charging different prices net of transportation costs for the same product to buyers in different locations, for example — would not be possible after the merger. As in the case of product market definition, however, where price discrimination is possible,[11] the Department will consider defining additional, narrower geographic markets consisting of particular locations in which a hypothetical monopolist could profitably impose a "small but significant and nontransitory" increase in price.

2.34 FOREIGN COMPETITION

In general, the foregoing standards will govern market definition, whether domestic or international. Although voluntary or involuntary quotas may prevent foreign competitors from increasing their imports into the United States in response to a domestic price increase, the Department will not exclude foreign competitors from the relevant market solely on the basis of the quotas. This is primarily because it frequently is difficult to determine and measure the effectiveness and longevity of a particular quota or any offsetting supply response from firms in countries not subject to the quota. The Department will consider the effects of a quota as a separate

---

11.   Geographic price discrimination against a group of buyers is more likely when other buyers cannot easily purchase and resell the relevant product to them. Such arbitrage is particularly difficult where the product is sold on a delivered basis and where transportation costs are a significant percentage of the final cost.

factor in interpreting the significant of market shares and market concentration. *See* Section 3.23 (Special Factors Affecting Foreign Firms).

2.4 Calculating Market Shares

The Department normally will include in the market the total sales of capacity of all domestic firms (or plants) that are identified as being in the market under Sections 2.2 and 2.3. Market shares can be expressed either in dollar terms through measurement of sales, shipments, or production, or in physical terms through measurement of sales, shipments, production, capacity, or reserves. As a practical matter, the availability of data often will determine the measurement basis. When the availability of data allows a choice, dollars sales or shipments generally will be used if branded or relatively differentiated products are involved, and physical capacity, reserves, or dollar production generally will be used if relatively homogeneous, undifferentiated products are involved.

In some cases, however, total sales or capacity may overstate the competitive significance of a firm. The Department will include only those sales likely to be made or capacity likely to be used in the market in response to a "small but significant and nontransitory" increase in price, for example, with respect to firms included in the market under Sections 2.21 (Production Substitution) and 2.23 (Internal Consumption). Similarly, a firm's capacity may be so committed elsewhere that it would not be available to respond to an increase in price in the market. In such cases, the Department also may include a small part of the firm's sales or capacity.

To the extent available information permits, market shares will be assigned to foreign competitors in the same way in which they are assigned to domestic competitors. If dollar sales or shipments are used to measure shares of domestic firms, the market shares of foreign firms will be measured using dollar sales in, or shipments to, the relevant market.[12] If physical capacity, reserves, or dollar production is used for domestic firms, the shares of foreign firms will be measured in terms of the capacity or reserves likely to be used to supply, or production that is likely to be shipped to, the relevant market in response to a "small but significant and nontransitory" price increase. If shipments from a particular country to the United States are subject to a quota, the market shares assigned to firms in that country will not exceed the amount of shipments by such firms allowed under the quota. Current shipments rather than capacity or reserves may be used for foreign firms if it is impossible reliably to quantify the proportion of the firms' capacity, reserves, or production that would be devoted to the relevant market in response to a "small but significant and nontransitory" increase in price because of, for example, the lack of available data regarding foreign capacity or the commitment of such capacity to other markets. Finally, a single market share may be assigned to a country or group of countries if firms in that country or group of countries act in coordination or if necessitated by data limitations.

12.		If exchange rates fluctuate significantly, making comparable dollar calculations for different firms difficult, then the volume of unit sales may be a better measure of market share than dollar sales and may be used instead.

3. Horizontal Mergers

3.0 Where the merging firms are in the same product and geographic market, the merger is horizontal. In such cases, the Department will focus first on the post-merger concentration of the market and the increase in concentration caused by the merger. For mergers that result in low market concentration or a relatively slight increase in concentration, the Department will be able to determine without a detailed examination of other factors that the merger poses no significant threat to competition. In other cases, however, the Department will proceed to examine a variety of other factors relevant to that question.

3.1 Concentration and Market Shares

Market concentration is a function of the number of firms in a market and their respective market shares.[13] Other things being equal, concentration affects the likelihood that one firm, or a small group of firms, could successfully exercise market power. The smaller the percentage of total supply that a firm controls, the more severely it must restrict it own output in order to produce a given price increase, and the less likely it is that an output restriction will be profitable. If collective action is necessary, an additional constraint applies. As the number of firms necessary to control a given percentage of total supply increases, the difficulties and costs of reaching and enforcing consensus with respect to the control of that supply also increase.

As an aid to the interpretation of market data, the Department will use the Herfindahl-Hirschman Index ("HHI") of market concentration. The HHI is calculated by summing the squares of the individual market shares of all the firms included in the market under the standards in Section 2 of these Guidelines.[14] Unlike the traditional four-firm concentration ratio, the HHI reflects both the distribution of the market shares of the top four firms and the composition of the market outside the top four firms. It also gives proportionately greater weight to the market shares of the larger firms, which probably accords with their relative importance in any collusive interaction.

The Department divides the spectrum of market concentration as measured by the HHI into three regions that can be broadly characterized as unconcentrated (HHI below 1000), moderately concentrated (HHI between 1000 and 1800), and highly concentrated (HHI above 1800). An empirical study by the Department of the size dispersion of firms within markets indicates that the critical HHI thresholds at 1000 and 1800 correspond roughly to four-firm concentration ratios of 50 percent and 70

---

13.   Markets can range from atomistic, where very large numbers of firms that are small relative to the overall size of the market compete with one another, to monopolistic, where one firm controls the entire market. Far more common, and more difficult analytically, is the large middle range of instances where a relatively small number of firms accounts for most of the sales in the market.

14.   For example, a market consisting of four firms with market shares of 30 percent, 30 percent, 20 percent and 20 percent has an HHI of 2600 $(30^2+30^2+20^2+20^2=2600)$. The HHI ranges from 10,000 (in the case of a pure monopoly) to a number approaching zero (in the case of an atomistic market). Although it is desirable to include all firms in the calculation, lack of information about small fringe firms is not critical because such firms do not affect the HHI significantly.

percent, respectively. Although the resulting regions provide a useful format for merger analysis, the numerical divisions suggest greater precision than is possible with the available economic tools and information. Other things being equal, cases falling just above and just below a threshold present comparable competitive concerns. Moreover, because concentration and market share data present a historical picture of the market, the Department must interpret such data in light of the relevant circumstances and the forward-looking objective of the Guidelines — to determine likely future effects of a given merger.

3.11 GENERAL STANDARDS

In evaluating horizontal mergers, the Department will consider both the post-merger market concentration and the increase in concentration resulting from the merger.[15] The link between concentration and market power is explained above. The increase in concentration is relevant to several key issues. Although mergers among small firms increase concentration, they are less likely to have anticompetitive consequences. Moreover, even in concentrated markets, it is desirable to allow firms some scope for merger activity in order to achieve economics of scale and to permit exit from the market. However, market share and concentration data provide only the starting point for analyzing the competitive impact of a merger. Before determining whether to challenge a merger, the Department will consider all other relevant factors that pertain to its competitive impact.

The general standards for horizontal mergers are as follows:

(a) Post-Merger HHI Below 1000. Markets in this region generally would be considered to be unconcentrated. Because implicit coordination among firms is likely to be difficult and because the prohibitions of section 1 of the Sherman Act are usually an adequate response to any explicit collusion that might occur, the Department will not challenge mergers falling in this region, except in extraordinary circumstances.

(b) Post-Merger HHI Between 1000 and 1800. Because this region extends from the point at which the competitive concerns associated with concentration are raised to the point at which they become quite serious, generalization is particularly difficult. The Department, however, is unlikely to challenge a merger producing an increase in the HHI of less than 100 points.[16] The Department is likely to challenge mergers in this region that produce an increase in the HHI or more than 100 points, unless the Department concludes, on the basis of the post-merger HHI, the increase in the HHI, and the presence or absence of the factors discussed in Sections 3.2, 3.3, 3.4, and 3.5 that the merger is not likely substantially to lessen

---

15.   The increase in concentration as measured by the HHI can be calculated independently of the overall market concentration by doubling the product of the market shares of the merging firms. For example, the merger of firms with shares of 5 percent and 10 percent of the market would increase the HHI by 100 (5x10x2=100). The explanation for this technique is as follows: In calculating the HHI before the merger, the market shares of the merging firms are squared individually: $(a)^2+(b)^2$. After the merger, the sum of those shares would be squared: $(a+b)^2$, which equals $a^2+2ab+b^2$. The increase in the HHI therefore is represented by 2ab.

16.   Mergers producing increases in concentration close to the 100 point threshold include those between firms with market shares of 25 percent and 2 percent, 16 percent and 3 percent, 12 percent and 4 percent, 10 percent and 5 percent, 8 percent and 6 percent, and 7 percent and 7 percent.

competition.

(c)   Post-Merger HHI Above 1800.   Markets in this region generally are considered to be highly concentrated.   Additional concentration resulting from mergers is a matter of significant competitive concern.   The Department is unlikely, however, to challenge mergers producing an increase in the HHI of less than 50 points.[17]   The Department is likely to challenge mergers in this region that produce an increase in the HHI of more than 50 points, unless the Department concludes, on the basis of the post-merger HHI, the increase in the HHI, and the presence or absence of the factors discussed in Sections 3.2, 3.3, 3.4, and 3.5, that the merger is not likely substantially to lessen competition.   However, if the increase in the HHI exceeds 100 and the post-merger HHI substantially exceeds 1800, only in extraordinary cases will such factors establish that the merger is not likely substantially to lessen competition.

3.12 LEADING FIRM PROVISO

In some cases, typically where one of the merging firms is small, mergers that may create or enhance the market power of a single dominant firm could pass scrutiny under the standards stated in Section 3.11.   Notwithstanding those standards, the Department is likely to challenge the merger of any firm with a market share of at least one percent with the leading firm in the market, provided the leading firm has a market share that is at least 35 percent.   Because the ease and profitability of collusion are of little relevance to the ability of a single dominant firm to exercise market power, the Department will not consider the presence or absence of the factors discussed in Section 3.4 because they relate to the likelihood of collusion. The Department will consider, however, the factors in Sections 3.2, 3.3, and 3.5 because they are relevant to the competitive concerns associated with a leading-firm merger.

3.2 Factors Affecting the Significance of Market Shares and Concentration

In a variety of situations, market share and market concentration data may either understate or overstate the likely future competitive significance of a firm or firms in the market.   The following are examples of such situations.

3.21 CHANGING MARKET CONDITIONS

Market concentration and market share data of necessity are based on historical evidence.   However, recent or on-going changes in the market may indicate that the current market share of a particular firm either understates or overstates the firm's future competitive significance.   For example, if a new technology that is important to long-term competitive viability is not available to a particular firm, the Department may conclude that the historical market share of the firm overstates the firm's future competitive significance.   The Department will consider reasonably predictable effects of recent or on-going changes in market conditions in interpreting

---

17.   Mergers producing increases in concentration close to the 50 point threshold include those between firms with market shares of 12 percent and 2 percent, 8 percent and 3 percent, 6 percent and 4 percent, and 5 percent and 5 percent.

market concentration and market share data.

3.22 FINANCIAL CONDITION OF FIRMS IN THE RELEVANT MARKET

The Department will consider the financial condition of a merging firm or any firm in the relevant market, to the extent that it is relevant to an analysis of the firm's likely future competitive significance.[18] If the financial difficulties of a firm cannot be explained as phenomena of, for example, the business cycle, but clearly reflect an underlying structural weakness of the firm, the firm's current market share may overstate its likely future competitive significance. For example, a firm's current market share may overstate its future competitive significance if that firm has chronic financial difficulties resulting from obsolete productive facilities in a market experiencing a long-term decline in demand.

3.23 SPECIAL FACTORS AFFECTING FOREIGN FIRMS

Actual import sales, shipment data, or capacity in some cases may tend to overstate the relative competitive significance of foreign firms. This will be the case, for example, if foreign firms are subject to quotas (imposed either by the United States or by their own country) that effectively limit the volume of their imports into this country. Foreign firms that are subject to such quotas generally cannot increase imports into the United States in response to a domestic price increase. In the case of restraints that limit imports to some percentage of the total amount of the product sold in the United States (i.e., percentage quotas), a domestic price increase that reduces domestic consumption would actually reduce the volume of imports into the United States. Thus, actual import sales and shipment data will tend to overstate the competitive significance of firms in countries subject to binding quotas.[19] Less significant, but still important factors, such as other types of trade restraints and changes in exchange rates, also may cause actual import sales and shipment data to overstate the future competitive significance of foreign firms. To the extent that the relative competitive significance of imports is overstated by the current market shares of foreign firms, the relative competitive significance of domestic firms concomitantly will be understated.

In addition, limitations on available data concerning the amount of foreign capacity that could be devoted to the United States in response to a "small but significance and nontransitory" increase in price may require the Department to use market share data that understate the true competitive significance of foreign competitors. Despite the inability to obtain data to quantify precisely the supply response of foreign competitors, the Department will consider strong qualitative evidence that, for example, there is significant worldwide excess capacity that could readily be devoted to the United States. To the extent market shares based on the best available evidence tend to understate the competitive significance of foreign

---

18.   This factor is distinguished from the failing company doctrine, which is an affirmative defense to an otherwise unlawful merger and which, as noted in Section 5.1, the Department will construe strictly.

19.   For example, in the extreme situation where there is an effective trade restraint that places a fixed or percentage limitation on the quantity of goods that can be imported into the United States from all or almost all foreign sources, market shares of foreign sources would usually be accorded little, if any, weight.

competitors, the relative competitive significance of domestic firms may be overstated.

In all cases addressed by Section 3.23 of the Guidelines, the Department will make appropriate adjustment in its analysis of the available data to reflect more accurately actual competitive concerns.

3.3 Ease of Entry

If entry into a market is so easy that existing competitors could not succeed in raising price for any significant period of time, the Department is unlikely to challenge mergers in that market. Under the standards in Section 2.21, firms that do not currently sell the relevant product, but that could easily and economically sell it using existing facilities, are included in the market and are assigned a market share. This section considers the additional competitive effects of (1) production substitution requiring significant modifications of existing facilities and (2) entry through the construction of new facilities.[20]

In assessing the ease of entry into a market, the Department will consider the likelihood and probable magnitude of entry in response to a "small but significant and nontransitory" increase in price.[21] Both the price to be increased and what constitutes a "small but significant and nontransitory" increase in price will be determined as they are in product market definition, except that a two-year time period generally will be used.[22] The more difficult entry into the market is, the more likely the Department is to challenge the merger.

3.4 Other Factors

A variety of other factors affect the likelihood that a merger will create, enhance, or facilitate the exercise of market power. In evaluating mergers, the Department will consider the following factors, among others, as they relate to the ease and profitability of collusion. Where relevant, the factors are most likely to be important where the Department's decision whether to challenge a merger is otherwise close.

3.41 NATURE OF THE PRODUCT AND TERMS OF SALE

3.411   Homogeneity-Heterogeneity of the Relevant Product Generally

In a market with a homogeneous and undifferentiated product, a cartel need

---

20.   "Entry" may occur as firms outside the market enter for the first time or as fringe firms currently in the market greatly expand their current capacity.

21.   In general, entry is likely to occur when the additional assets necessary to produce the relevant product are short-lived or widely used outside the particular market. Entry is generally facilitated by the growth of the market and hindered by its stagnation or decline. Entry also is hindered by the need for scarce special skills or resources, or the need to achieve a substantial market share in order to realize important economics of scale. See also Section 4.212 (Increased Difficulty of Simultaneous Entry to Both Markets).

22.   Although this type of supply response may take longer to materialize than those considered under Section 2.21, its prospect may have a greater deterrent effect on the exercise of market power by present sellers. Where new entry involves the dedication of long-lived assets to a market, the resulting capacity and its adverse effects on profitability will be present in the market until those assets are economically depreciated.

establish only a single price — a circumstance that facilitates reaching consensus and detecting deviation. As the products which constitute the relevant product market become more numerous, heterogeneous, or differentiated, however, the problems facing a cartel become more complex. Instead of a single price, it may be necessary to establish and enforce a complex schedule of prices corresponding to gradations in actual or perceived quality attributes among the competing products.[23]

Product variation is arguably relevant in all cases, but practical considerations dictate a more limited use of the factor. There is neither an objective index of product variation nor an empirical basis for its use in drawing fine distinctions among cases. As a result, this factor will be taken into account only in relatively extreme cases where both identification and effect are more certain. For example, when the relevant product is completely homogeneous and undifferentiated, the Department is more likely to challenge the merge. Conversely, when the relevant product is very heterogeneous or sold subject to complex configuration options or customized production, the Department is less likely to challenge the merger.[24] Over a significant middle range of the spectrum of product variation, this factor is less likely to affect the Department's analysis.

3.412 Degree of Difference Between the Products and Locations in the Market and the Next-Best Substitutes

The market definition standards stated in Section 2 of these Guidelines require drawing relatively bright lines in order to determine the products and sellers to be considered in evaluating a merger. For example, in defining the relevant product, all "good substitutes" in demand are included. The profitability of any collusion that might occur will depend in part, however, on the quality of the next-best substitute. That is, it matters whether the next-best substitute is only slightly or significantly inferior to the last product included in the relevant product. Similarly, it matters whether the next-most-distant seller is only slightly or significantly farther away than the last seller included in the geographic market. The larger the "gap" at the edge of the product and geographic markets, the more likely the Department is to challenge the merger.

3.413 Similarities and Differences in the Products and Locations of the Merging Firms

There also may be relevant comparisons among the products or sellers included in the market. Where products in a relevant market are differentiated or sellers are spatially dispersed, individual sellers usually compete more directly with some rivals than with others. In markets with highly differentiated products, the Department will consider the extent to which consumers perceive the products of the merging firms to be relatively better or worse substitutes for one another than for other products in the market. In markets with spatially dispersed sellers and significant transportation costs, the Department will consider the relative proximity of the merging firms. If

---

23. A similar situation may exist where there is rapid technological change or where supply arrangements consist of many complicated terms in addition to price.

24. This conclusion would not apply, however, where the significance of heterogeneity is substantially reduced through detailed specifications that are provided by the buyer and that form the basis for all firms' bids.

the products or plants of the merging firms are particularly good substitutes for one another, the Department is more likely to challenge the merger.

3.42 INFORMATION ABOUT SPECIFIC TRANSACTIONS AND BUYER MARKET CHARACTERISTICS

Collusive agreements are more likely to persist if participating firms can quickly detect and retaliate against deviations from the agreed prices or other conditions. Such deviations are easiest to detect, and therefore least likely to occur, in markets where detailed information about specific transactions or individual price or output levels is readily available to competitors. The Department is more likely to challenge a merger if such detailed information is available to competitors, whether the information comes from an exchange among sellers, public disclosure by buyers, reporting by the press or a government agency, or some other source.

Certain buyer market characteristics also may facilitate detection of deviation from collusive agreements. If orders for the relevant product are frequent, regular and small relative to the total output of a typical firm in the market, collusion is more likely to succeed because the benefits of departing from the collusive agreement in any single transaction are likely to be small relative to the potential costs. In order to increase its sales significantly in such circumstances, a seller would have to depart from the collusive agreement on a large number of orders. Each such sale takes customers away from other parties to the agreement, a fact that is particularly evident when demand is stable or declining. As a result, the chances of detection and effective response by other sellers increase with the number of such sales. The Department is more likely to challenge a merger where such buyer market characteristics exist.

3.43 ABILITY OF SMALL OR FRINGE SELLERS TO INCREASE SALES

Collusion is less likely to occur if small or fringe sellers in the market are able profitably to increase output substantially in response to a "small but significance and nontransitory" increase in price and, thus, to undermine a cartel. The Department is less likely to challenge a merger if small or fringe firms currently are able to expand significantly their sales at incremental costs that are approximately equal to their incremental costs experienced at current levels of output.

3.44 CONDUCT OF FIRMS IN THE MARKET

The Department is more likely to challenge a merger in the following circumstances:

a)   Firms in the market previously have been found to have engaged in horizontal collusion regarding price, territories, or customers, and the characteristics of the market have not changed appreciably since the most recent finding. The additional concentration resulting from the merger could make explicit collusion more difficult to detect or tacit collusions more feasible.

b)   One or more of the following types of practices are adopted by substantially all of the firms in the market: (1) mandatory delivered pricing; (2) exchange of price or output information in a form that could assist firms in setting or enforcing an agreed price; (3) collective standardization of product variables on which the firms could compete; and (4) price protection clauses. Although not objectionable under all circumstances, these types of practices tend to make collusion easier, and their widespread adoption by the firms in the market raises some concern that collusion may already exist.

c)   The firm to be acquired has been an unusually disruptive and competitive influence in the market. Before invoking this factor, the Department will determine whether the market is one in which performance might plausibly deteriorate because of the elimination of one disruptive firm.

3.45 MARKET PERFORMANCE

When the market in which the proposed merger would occur is currently performing noncompetitively, the Department is more likely to challenge the merger. Noncompetitive performance suggests that the firms in the market already have succeeded in overcoming, at least to some extent, the obstacles to effective collusion. Increased concentration of such a market through merger could further facilitate the collusion that already exists. When the market in which the proposed merger would occur is currently performing competitively, however, the Department will apply its ordinary standards of review. The fact that the market is currently competitive casts little light on the likely effect of the merger.

In evaluating the performance of [the] market, the Department will consider any relevant evidence, but will give particular weight to the following evidence of possible noncompetitive performance when the facts are found in conjunction:

a)   Stable relative market shares of the leading firms in recent years;

b)   Declining combined market share of the leading firms in recent years; and

c)   Profitability of the leading firms over substantial periods of time that significantly exceeds that of firms in industries comparable in capital intensity and risk.

3.5 Efficiencies

The primary benefit of mergers to the economy is their efficiency-enhancing potential, which can increase the competitiveness of firms and result in lower prices to consumers. Because the antitrust laws and, thus, the standards of the Guidelines, are designed to proscribe only mergers that present a significant danger to competition, they do not present an obstacle to most mergers. As a consequence, in the majority of cases, the Guidelines will allow firms to achieve available efficiencies through mergers without interference from the Department.

Some mergers that the Department otherwise might challenge may be reasonably necessary to achieve significant net efficiencies. If the parties to the merger establish by clear and convincing evidence that a merger will achieve such efficiencies, the Department will consider those efficiencies in deciding whether to challenge the merger.

Cognizable efficiencies include, but are not limited to, achieving economies of scale, better integration of production facilities, plant specialization, lower transportation costs, and similar efficiencies relating to specific manufacturing, servicing, or distribution operations of the merging firms. The Department may also consider claimed efficiencies resulting from reductions in general selling, administrative, and overhead expenses, or that otherwise do not relate to specific manufacturing, servicing, or distribution operations of the merging firms, although, as a practical matter, these types of efficiencies may be difficult to demonstrate. In addition, the Department will reject claims of efficiencies if equivalent or comparable savings can reasonably be achieved by the parties through other means. The parties must establish a greater level of expected net efficiencies the more significant are the competitive risks identified in Section 3.

4.   Horizontal Effect From Non-Horizontal Mergers

4.0   By definition, non-horizontal mergers involve firms that do not operate in the same market. It necessarily follows that such mergers produce no immediate change in the level of concentration in any relevant market as defined in Section 2 of these Guidelines. Although non-horizontal mergers are less likely than horizontal mergers to create competitive problems, they are invariably innocuous. This section describes the principal theories under which the Department is likely to challenge non-horizontal mergers.

4.1 Elimination of Specific Potential Entrants

4.11 THE THEORY OF POTENTIAL COMPETITION

In some circumstances, the non-horizontal merger[25] of a firm already in a market (the "acquired firm") with a potential entrant to that market (the "acquiring firm")[26] may adversely affect competition in the market. If the merger effectively removes the acquiring firm from the edge of the market, it could have either of the following effects.

4.111   Harm to "Perceived Potential Competition"

By eliminating a significant present competitive threat that constrains the behavior of the firms already in the market, the merger could result in an immediate deterioration in market performance. The economic theory of limiting pricing suggests that monopolists and groups of colluding firms may find it profitable to restrain their pricing in order to deter new entry that is likely to push prices even lower by adding capacity to the market. If the acquiring firm had unique advantages in entering the market, the firms in the market might be able to set a new and higher price after the threat of entry by the acquiring firm was eliminated by the merger.

4.112   Harm to "Actual Potential Competition"

By eliminating the possibility of entry by the acquiring firm in a more procompetitive manner, the merger could result in a lost opportunity for improvement in market performance resulting from the addition of a significant competitor. The more procompetitive alternatives include both new entry and entry through a "toehold" acquisition of a present small competitor.

---

25.   Under traditional usage, such a merger could be characterized as either "vertical" or "conglomerate," but the label adds nothing to the analysis.

26.   The terms "acquired" and "acquiring" refer to the relationship of the firms to the market of interest, not to the way the particular transaction is formally structured.

4.12 RELATION BETWEEN PERCEIVED AND ACTUAL POTENTIAL COMPETITION

If it were always profit-maximizing for incumbent firms to set price in such a way that all entry was deterred and if information and coordination were sufficient to implement this strategy, harm to perceived potential competition would be the only competitive problem to address. In practice, however, actual potential competition has independent importance. Firms already in the market may not find it optimal to set price low enough to deter all entry; moreover, those firms may misjudge the entry advantages of a particular firm and, therefore, the price necessary to deter its entry.[27]

4.13 ENFORCEMENT STANDARDS

Because of the close relationship between perceived potential competition and actual potential competition, the Department will evaluate mergers that raise either type of potential competition concern under a single structural analysis analogous to that applied to horizontal mergers. The Department first will consider a set of objective factors designed to identify cases in which harmful effects are plausible. In such cases, the Department then will conduct a more focused inquiry to determine whether the likelihood and magnitude of the possible harm justify a challenge to the merger. In this context, the Department will consider any specific evidence presented by the merging parties to show that the inferences of competitive harm drawn from the objective factors are unreliable.

The factors that the Department will consider are as follows:

4.131 Market Concentration

Barriers to entry are unlikely to affect market performance if the structure of the market is otherwise not conducive to monopolization or collusion. Adverse competitive effects are likely only if overall concentration, or the largest firm's market share, is high. The Department is unlikely to challenge a potential competition merger unless overall concentration of the acquired firm's market is above 1800 HHI (a somewhat lower concentration will suffice if one or more of the factors discussed in Section 3.4 indicate that effective collusion in the market is particularly likely). Other things being equal, the Department is increasingly likely to challenge a merger as this threshold is exceeded.

4.132 Conditions of Entry Generally

If entry to the market is generally easy, the fact that entry is marginally easier for one or more firms is unlikely to affect the behavior of the firms in the market. The Department is unlikely to challenge a potential competition merger when new entry into the acquiring firm's market can be accomplished by firms without any specific entry advantages under the conditions stated in Section 3.3. Other things being

---

27.   When collusion is only tacit, the problem of arriving at and enforcing the correct limit price is likely to be particularly difficult.

equal, the Department is increasingly likely to challenge a merger as the difficulty of entry increases above that threshold.

4.133   The Acquiring Firm's Entry Advantage

If more than a few firms have the same or a comparable advantage in entering the acquired firm's market, the elimination of one firm is unlikely to have any adverse competitive effect. The other similarly situated firm or firms would continue to exert a present restraining influence, or, if entry would be profitable, would recognize the opportunity and enter. The Department is unlikely to challenge a potential competition merger if the entry advantage ascribed to the acquiring firm (or another advantage of comparable importance) is also possessed by three or more other firms. Other things being equal, the Department is increasingly likely to challenge a merger as the number of other similarly situated firms decreases below three and as the extent of the entry advantage over non-advantaged firms increases.

If the evidence of likely actual entry by the acquiring firm is particularly strong,[28] however, the Department may challenge a potential competition merger, notwithstanding the presence of three or more firms that are objectively similarly situated. In such cases, the Department will determine the likely scale of entry, using either the firm's own documents or the minimum efficient scale in the industry. The Department will then evaluate the merger much as it would a horizontal merger between a firm the size of the likely scale of entry and the acquired firm.

4.134   The Market Share of the Acquired Firm

Entry through the acquisition of a relatively small firm in the market may have a competitive effect comparable to new entry. Small firms frequently play peripheral roles in collusive interactions, and the particular advantages of the acquiring firm may convert a fringe firm into a significant factor in the market.[29] The Department is unlikely to challenge a potential competition merger when the acquired firm has a market share of five percent or less. Other things being equal, the Department is increasingly likely to challenge a merger as the market share of the acquired firm increases above that threshold. The Department is likely to challenge any merger satisfying the other conditions in which the acquired firm has a market share of 20 percent or more.

4.135   Efficiencies

As in the case of horizontal mergers, the Department will consider expected efficiencies in determining whether to challenge a potential competition merger. See Section 3.5 (Efficiencies).

---

28.   For example, the firm already may have moved beyond the stage of consideration and have made significant investments demonstrating an actual decision to enter.

29.   Although a similar effect is possible with the acquisition of larger firms, there is an increased danger that the acquiring firm will choose to acquiesce in monopolization or collusion because of the enhanced profits that would result from its own disappearance from the edge of the market.

4.2 Competitive Problems From Vertical Mergers

4.21 BARRIERS TO ENTRY FROM VERTICAL MERGERS

In certain circumstances, the vertical integration resulting from vertical mergers could create competitively objectionable barriers to entry. Stated generally, three conditions are necessary (but not sufficient) for this problem to exist. First, the degree of vertical integration between the two markets must be so extensive that entrants to one market (the "primary market") also would have to enter the other market (the "secondary market")[30] simultaneously. Second, the requirement of entry at the secondary level must make entry at the primary level significantly more difficult and less likely to occur. Finally, the structure and other characteristics of the primary market must be otherwise so conducive to noncompetitive performance that the increased difficulty of entry is likely to affect its performance. The following standards state the criteria by which the Department will determine whether these conditions are satisfied.

4.211 Need for Two-Level Entry

If there is sufficient unintegrated capacity[31] in the secondary market, new entrants to the primary market would not have to enter both markets simultaneously. The Department is unlikely to challenge a merger on this ground where post-merger sales (or purchases) by unintegrated firms in the secondary market would be sufficient to service two minimum-efficient-scale plants in the primary market. When the other conditions are satisfied, the Department is increasingly likely to challenge a merger as the unintegrated capacity declines below this level.

4.212 Increased Difficulty of Simultaneous Entry of Both Markets

The relevant question is whether the need for simultaneous entry to the secondary market gives rise to a substantial incremental difficulty as compared to entry into the primary market alone. If entry at the secondary level is easy in absolute terms, the requirement of simultaneous entry to that market is unlikely adversely to affect entry to the primary market. Whatever the difficulties of entry into the primary market may be, the Department is unlikely to challenge a merger on this ground if new entry into the secondary market can be accomplished under the conditions stated in

---

30.   This competitive problem could result from either upstream or downstream integration, and could affect competition in either the upstream market or the downstream market. In the text, the term "primary market" refers to the market in which the competitive concerns are being considered, and the term "secondary market" refers to the adjacent market.

31.   Ownership integration does not necessarily mandate two-level entry by new entrants to the primary market. Such entry is most likely to be necessary where the primary and secondary markets are completely integrated by ownership and each firm in the primary market uses all of the capacity of its associated firm in the secondary market. In many cases of ownership integration, however, the functional fit between vertically integrated firms is not perfect, and an outside market exists for the sales (purchases) of the firms in the secondary market. If that market is sufficiently large and diverse, new entrants to the primary market may be able to participate without simultaneous entry to the secondary market. In considering the adequacy of this alternative, the Department will consider the likelihood of predatory price or supply "squeezes" by the integrated firms against their unintegrated rivals.

Section 3.3.[32] When entry is not possible under those conditions, the Department is increasingly concerned about vertical mergers as the difficulty of entering the secondary market increases. The Department, however, will invoke this theory only where the need for secondary market entry significantly increases the costs (which may take the form of risks) of primary market entry.

More capital is necessary to enter two markets than to enter one. Standing alone, however, this additional capital requirement does not constitute a barrier to entry to the primary market. If the necessary funds were available at a cost commensurate with the level of risk in the secondary market, there would be no adverse effect. In some cases, however, lenders may doubt that would-be entrants to the primary market have the necessary skills and knowledge to succeed in the secondary market and, therefore, in the primary market. In order to compensate for this risk of failure, lenders might charge a higher rate for the necessary capital. This problem becomes increasingly significant as a higher percentage of the capital assets in the secondary market are long-lived and specialized to that market and, therefore, difficult to recover in the event of failure. In evaluating the likelihood of increased barriers to entry resulting from increased cost of capital, therefore, the Department will consider both the degree of similarity in the essential skills in the primary and secondary markets and the economic life and degree of specialization of the capital assets in the secondary market.

Economies of scale in the secondary market may constitute an additional barrier to entry to the primary market in some situations requiring two-level entry. The problem could arise if the capacities of minimum-efficient-scale plants in the primary and secondary markets differ significantly. For example, if the capacity of a minimum-efficient-scale plant in the secondary market were significantly greater than the needs of a minimum-efficient-scale plant in the primary market, entrants would have to choose between inefficient operation at the secondary level (because of operating an efficient plant at an inefficient output or because of operating an inefficiently small plant) or a larger than necessary scale at the primary level. Either of these effects could cause a significant increase in the operating costs of the entering firm.[33]

4.213   Structure and Performance of the Primary Market

Barriers to entry are unlikely to affect performance if the structure of the primary market is otherwise not conducive to monopolization or collusion.[34] The Department is unlikely to challenge a merger on this ground unless overall concentration of the primary market is above 1800 HHI (a somewhat lower concentration will suffice if one or more of the factors discussed in Section 3.4 indicate that effective collusion is particularly likely). Above that threshold, the

---

32.   Entry into the secondary market may be greatly facilitated in that an assured supplier (customer) is provided by the primary market entry.

33.   It is important to note, however, that this problem would not exist if a significant outside market exists at the secondary level. In that case, entrants could enter with the appropriately scaled plants at both levels, and sell or buy in the market as necessary.

34.   For example, a market with 100 firms of equal size would perform competitively despite a significant increase in entry barriers.

Department is increasingly likely to challenge a merger that meets the other criteria set forth above as the concentration increases.

4.22 FACILITATING COLLUSION THROUGH VERTICAL MERGERS

4.221   Vertical Integration to the Retail Level

A high level of vertical integration by upstream firms into the associated retail market may facilitate collusion in the upstream market by making it easier to monitor price. Retail prices are generally more visible than prices in upstream markets, and vertical mergers may increase the level of vertical integration to the point at which the monitoring effect becomes significant. Adverse competitive consequences are unlikely unless the upstream market is generally conducive to collusion and a larger percentage of the products produced there are sold through vertically integrated retail outlets.

The Department is unlikely to challenge a merger on this ground unless (1) overall concentration of the upstream market is above 1800 HHI (a somewhat lower concentration will suffice if one or more of the factors discussed in Section 3.4 indicate that effective collusion is particularly likely), and (2) a large percentage of the upstream product would be sold through vertically-integrated retail outlets after the merger. Where the stated thresholds are met or exceeded, the Department's decision whether to challenge a merger on this ground will depend upon an individual evaluation of its likely competitive effect.

4.222   Elimination of a Disruptive Buyer

The elimination by vertical merger of a particularly disruptive buyer in a downstream market may facilitate collusion in the upstream market. If upstream firms view sales to a particular buyer as sufficiently important, they may deviate from the terms of a collusive agreement in an effort to secure that business, thereby disrupting the operation of the agreement. The merger of such a buyer with an upstream firm may eliminate that rivalry, making it easier for the upstream firms to collude effectively. Adverse competitive consequences are unlikely unless the upstream market is generally conducive to collusion and the disruptive firm is significantly more attractive to sellers than the other firms in its market.

The Department is unlikely to challenge a merger on this ground unless (1) overall concentration of the upstream market is 1800 HHI or above (a somewhat lower concentration will suffice if one or more of the factors discussed in Section 3.4 indicate that effective collusion is particularly likely), and (2) the allegedly disruptive firm differs substantially in volume of purchases or other relevant characteristics from the other firms in its market. Where the stated thresholds are met or exceeded, the Department's decision whether to challenge a merger on this ground will depend upon an individual evaluation of its likely competitive effect.

4.23 EVASION OF RATE REGULATION

Non-horizontal mergers may be used by monopoly public utilities subject to rate regulation as a tool for circumventing that regulation. The clearest example is the acquisition by a regulated utility of a supplier of its fixed or variable inputs. After the merger, the utility would be selling to itself and might be able arbitrarily to inflate the prices of internal transactions. Regulators may have great difficulty in policing these practices, particularly if there is no independent market for the product (or service) purchased from the affiliate.[35] As a result, inflated prices could be passed along to consumers as "legitimate" costs. In extreme cases, the regulated firm may effectively preempt the adjacent market, perhaps for the purpose of suppressing observable market transactions, and may distort resource allocation in that adjacent market as well as in the regulated market. In such cases, however, the Department recognizes that genuine economies of integration may be involved. The Department will consider challenging mergers that create substantial opportunities for such abuses.[36]

4.24 EFFICIENCIES

As in the case of horizontal mergers, the Department will consider expected efficiencies in determining whether to challenge a vertical merger. *See* Section 3.5 (Efficiencies). An extensive pattern of vertical integration may constitute evidence that substantial economies are afforded by vertical integration. Therefore, the Department will give relatively more weight to expected efficiencies in determining whether to challenge a vertical merger than in determining whether to challenge a horizontal merger.

5. Defenses

5.1 Failing Firm

The "failing firm defense" is a long-established, but ambiguous, doctrine under which an anticompetitive merger may be allowed because one of the merging firms is "failing." Because the defense can immunize significantly anticompetitive mergers, the Department will construe its element strictly.

The Department is unlikely to challenge an anticompetitive merger in which one of the merging firms is allegedly failing when: (1) the allegedly failing firm probably would be unable to meet its financial obligations in the near future; (2) it probably would not be able to reorganize successfully under Chapter 11 of the Bankruptcy Act;[37] and (3) it has made alternative offers of acquisition of the failing firm[38] that would keep it in the market and pose a less severe danger to competition than does the proposed merger.

5.2 Failing Division

A similar argument can be made for "failing" divisions as for "failing" firms. A multidivisional firm may decide to leave a particular line of business by selling or

---

35.   A less severe, but nevertheless serious, problem can arise when a regulated utility acquires a firm that is not vertically related. The use of common facilities and managers may create an insoluable cost allocation problem and provide the opportunity to charge utility customers for non-utility costs, consequently distorting resource allocation in the adjacent as well as the regulated market.

36.   Where a regulatory agency has the responsibility for approving such mergers, the Department may express its concerns to that agency in its role as competition advocate.

37.   11 U.S.C. §§ 1101-1174 (1982).

38.   The fact that an offer is less than the proposed transaction does not make it unreasonable.

liquidating a division.   If the specific conditions set out below are met, the Department will consider the "failure" of the division as an important factor affecting the likely competitive effect of the merger.   First, the proponents of a merger involving a "failing" division must establish, not based solely on management plans, which could be prepared simply for the purpose of creating evidence of intent, that the division would be liquidated in the near future if not sold.   Second, the proponents of the merger also must demonstrate compliance with the competitively preferable purchaser requirement of the "failing firm defense".

APPENDIX C

STATEMENT OF FEDERAL TRADE COMMISSION CONCERNING HORIZONTAL MERGERS

(June 14, 1982)[*]

I. Background

The Federal Trade Commission ("Commission") and the Antitrust Division of the Department of Justice ("Antitrust Division") have been reexamining the legal and economic basis for horizontal merger policy. In light of enforcement experience and more recent economic research, the two agencies have both concluded that continued reliance on the Department of Justice's Merger Guidelines, promulgated in 1968 ("1968 Guidelines"), is no longer appropriate. In order to revise the 1968 Guidelines and incorporate new factors that are relevant to current horizontal merger analysis, the Commission and the Antitrust Division formed working groups of lawyers and economists to evaluate past experience under the 1968 Guidelines and to recommend specific modifications. The staffs of both agencies have worked closely in this endeavor. In addition to their research and analytical work, they have also solicited and carefully examined the views of the private bar, the academic and business communities, as well as the public at large.

The Commission is issuing this Statement to express its collective judgment of the reasons why it supports changes in the 1968 Guidelines and to highlight the principal considerations that will guide its horizontal merger enforcement. However, the Department of Justice's 1982 revisions to the 1968 Guidelines will be given considerable weight by the Commission and its staff in their evaluation of horizontal mergers and in the development of the Commission's overall approach to horizontal mergers.[1]

II. Market Share Considerations

Congress enacted Section 7 of the Clayton Act to prevent the corporate

---

[*] As officially revised by FTC to correct errors in the first printing. Typefaces in citations in footnotes have been edited to conform in style to the body of this Treatise. Additional modifications are bracketed.

1. While the Commission supports the Department of Justice's decision to revise the 1968 Guidelines, individual Commissioners, however, may not endorse each specific revision that has been proposed.

accumulation of market power through mergers.[2] The subsequent amendment to the Clayton Act,[3] while primarily focusing on competitive considerations,[4] also reflected Congress' concern about the overall social and political ramifications of economic concentration attributable to merger activity.[5] Legal analysis of horizontal mergers, however, has focused on the extent to which these mergers confer market power on the acquiring firm or enhance the ability of firms to collude, either expressly or tacitly.

In measuring these market power effects, the courts, the Commission and the Antitrust Division have traditionally looked to market share data and derivative concentration ratios as the principal indicators of market power. Their reliance on such evidence was founded on early empirical economic literature indicating a significant positive relationship between concentration levels, industry performance and profits.[6] In addition, market share data provided an easily ascertainable and relatively objective benchmark to evaluate the potential effects of horizontal mergers.

More recent empirical economic research[7] and well over a decade of practical experience in analyzing and evaluating horizontal mergers, however, have led the Commission to conclude that proper consideration of market realities justifies some revision of market share benchmarks and greater consideration of evidence beyond mere market shares when such evidence is available and in a reliable form. Whether utilizing the Herfindahl-Hirschman index or other concentration measures, the Commission believes that an increase in the threshold market shares is clearly justified on at least three bases. First, current economic analysis suggests that the low combined market share thresholds contained in the 1968 Guidelines, e.g., 8 percent and 10 percent, are unlikely to contribute to oligopolistic behavior or market dominance.[8] Second, the threshold levels in the 1968 Guidelines do not capture as fully as possible economies of scale achieved through merger.[9] Third, the relationship between the number and relative size of firms in the relevant market was not taken into account in the 1968 Guidelines. Recent studies also suggest that poor market performance may be partly a function of firm size disparity. Thus, although far from definitive, this research suggests that particular attention should be given to disparity in market shares between the top one or two firms and the remaining

---

2.   Clayton Act, Pub. L. No. 63-212, 38 Stat. 730 (1914) (codified at 15 U.S.C. § 18 (1976)).

3.   Celler-Kefauver Act, Pub. L. No. 81-899, 64 Stat. 1125 (1950) (codified at 15 U.S.C. §§ 18, 21 (1976)).

4.   See IV P. AREEDA & D. TURNER, ANTITRUST LAW 8-14 (1980).

5.   For a discussion of Congress' interest in the noneconomic aspects of mergers, see Bok, Section 7 of the Clayton Act and the Merging of Law and Economics, 74 HARV. L. REV. 226, 233-49, 306-07 (1960). See also Pitofsky, The Political Content of Antitrust, 127 U. Pa. L. Rev. 1051 (1979).

6.   See IV P. AREEDA & D. TURNER, supra note 4, at 52-54. For a discussion of the relevant literature, see generally Pautler, A Review of the Economic Basis for Broad-Based Horizontal Merger Policy, [28 ANTITRUST BULL. 571, 587-96 (1983)].

7.   See literature survey contained in Pautler, supra note 6, at [596-98, 624-37].

8.   Id.

9.   See II P. AREEDA & D. TURNER, supra note 4, at 291-98; R. POSNER, ANTITRUST LAW 112-13 (1976); Fisher & Lande, Efficiency Considerations in Merger Enforcement, [71 CALIF. L. REV. 1580], at Section III [(1983)]. In certain circumstances, an increase in threshold levels will enhance the ability of small firms to exit from the market, thereby facilitating entry. See Pillsbury Co., 93 F.T.C. 966, 1041-42 (1979).

firms in an industry.[10]

For these reasons, while the Commission will continue to look to market share data as an important indicium of the likely competitive effects of a merger, a more refined treatment of that data is in order.

III. Nonmarket Share Considerations

Current statistical information helps to provide a good snapshot of an industry, but consideration of additional market characteristics, entry barriers being the major example, may provide a clearer and more accurate picture of the competitive dynamics of that industry. Such an inquiry may reveal whether any market power conferred by the merger is likely to persist over time and whether market conditions are conducive either to the exercise of individual firm market power or to collusive-type behavior.

The Commission recognizes, of course, that any type of market analysis, including reliance on market shares, inevitably carries with it an element of imprecision. For example, relevant evidence may be difficult to obtain or, where it is available, may be fragmentary and inconsistent. Further, evidence peculiarly within the control of the parties to the proceeding may be subject to bias and be difficult to verify. Nevertheless, the Commission believes that consideration of factors other than market shares, including qualitative factors, can be useful and desirable. If proper allowance is given to the evidentiary limitations, a balance can be struck that achieves the twin objectives of maintaining reasonable predictability in merger policy while enhancing the quality of the analysis and the correctness of the ultimate outcome.

The following discussion of non-market share factors will serve to define the scope of the merger inquiry and to prevent the analysis from becoming a limitless search for any evidence of possible relevance, since an open-ended examination may prevent the Commission and the courts from providing meaningful and timely guidance to business.

A. Market Power/Duration Factors

As we have noted, market share data can serve as an important preliminary surrogate measure of market power. For a variety of reasons, however, that indicator may not always accurately measure the market power of merging firms. The critical task, then, is to isolate and evaluate those additional factors that are also relevant to the assessment of market power effects.

(1) MARKETWIDE CONDITIONS

Ideally, if we could measure all relevant demand and supply elasticities, we could arrive at relatively precise estimates of market power.[11] Such evidence, however, is rarely, if ever, available and is not readily susceptible to direct measurement. Therefore, other criteria must be utilized to determine the probable impact of a merger. The most probative criteria include: entry barriers; concentration trends (including the volatility of market shares); technological change; demand trends; and

---

10.   For a detailed discussion of this research, see Pautler, *supra* note 6, at [641-48].
11.   Landes & Posner, *Market Power in Antitrust Cases*, 94 HARV. L. REV. 937, 939-43 (1981).

market definition. These factors are interrelated and primarily address industrywide conditions rather than firm specific characteristics.

The issue of entry barriers is perhaps the most important qualitative factor, for if entry barriers are very low it is unlikely that market power, whether individually or collectively exercised, will persist for long.[12] Conversely, if entry barriers are quite high, the effect may be to exacerbate any market power conferred by the merger. Of course, the evidence relating to entry barriers may not always point clearly to the conclusion that a merger should or should not be allowed. On the other hand, evidence of actual entry, especially recent and frequent new entry, is highly probative, as is evidence of failed entry or the absence of entry over long periods of time. Besides mere entry, effective competition might also depend upon a firm's achieving a certain scale of operation. Evidence of substantial expansion by firms already in an industry, especially nondominant firms, may persuasively indicate that barriers to larger scale are not high. Conversely, evidence of frequent entry, but on a small scale, without significant expansion by fringe firms, may also suggest the existence of barriers to larger scale.

Market power also may be harder to exercise or less likely to endure in the face of rapid technological change or significant upward shifts in demand. Moreover, this kind of evidence may shed light on questions of market definition and the market's propensity towards collusive interdependence. New technology, for example, may signal that the market is being transformed and that traditional boundaries do not accurately measure the degree of product substitutability which actually exists. If these trends are strong, they are likely to result in new entry, declining concentration or unstable market shares. These issues are closely intertwined. Market share fluctuations may represent overt manifestations of underlying market forces and, as such, provide a very useful picture of market dynamics. Of course, like other evidence, the value of such data depends upon the magnitude and likely duration of the shifts that are occurring. Small deviations in market shares, even if they recur on a frequent basis, may be of little significance.

Additionally, the issue of market definition is relevant in determining whether market power exists and can be exercised successfully. The more carefully the lines are drawn, the more confidence can be placed in the predictive value of market share data; but market boundaries cannot always be drawn with fine precision. Where the boundaries are highly blurred, it may be appropriate to take that fact into account, especially at the margin where the market shares are not particularly high.[13]

These factors are important in revealing whether the market shares overstate or understate the competitive impact of a merger. The weight to be assigned this evidence is a critical issue since, as noted above, it will often be impossible to make fine distinctions based on the quantity and quality of the non-statistical information. For instance, the fact that demand is increasing or new products are being introduced does not necessarily mean that the market share data should automatically be discounted by some factor. Rather, it is important to look at overall trends to see

---

12.   See F. SCHERER, INDUSTRIAL MARKET STRUCTURE AND ECONOMIC PERFORMANCE 5, 11, 236 (2d ed. 1980); G. STIGLER, THE THEORY OF PRICE 220-27 (3d ed. 1966); Demsetz, *Barriers to Entry*, 72 Am. Econ. Rev. 47 (1982).

13.   See Coca-Cola Bottling Co., 93 F.T.C. 110 (1979); SKF Industries, Inc., 94 F.T.C. 6, 86-87 (1979).

where the market is heading and at what rate.

Where all of the non-market share evidence consistently points in the same direction, its value will be high. Such evidence will be of even greater significance where the market shares are in the low to moderate range. On the other hand, if the anti-competitive potential of a merger is large, as predicted by the combined market shares of the merging parties, other non-market share factors may appropriately be given less weight, even if the adverse effects are relatively shortlived. To be sure, merger analysis properly focuses primarily on long-term competitive implications, but short-term effects should not be ignored, particularly if they are substantial.

(2) FIRM-SPECIFIC CHARACTERISTICS

So far, we have focused on marketwide conditions that may bear on the competitive effects of a merger. Factors peculiar to the merging parties can also be of relevance, although some caution should be exercised since this kind of evidence is harder to verify.[14] The most important type of evidence is that which relates to the failing company doctrine, about which we will say more later. However, it is frequently argued by parties to a merger that financial weakness should be considered as a defense by the enforcement agencies. While not endorsing this approach in all its dimensions,[15] the Commission does believe that evidence of individual firm performance can be of use in evaluating the probable effects of a merger, primarily if it indicates that a firm's market share overstates its competitive significance. For example, poor financial performance may accompany new entry or technological change, which itself may be evidence of the firm's declining competitive significance and its lack of prospects for future success or it may be indicative of other changes taking place in the market.[16]

Another issue related to individual company performance concerns the acquisition of firms with small market shares whose competitive potential is unique.[17] Like the previous discussion, the issue here is not so much whether the firm is performing well *per se*, but whether its presence in the market is having some discernible impact on competition. For example, is the firm a disruptive force in an industry that is otherwise susceptible to oligopolistic behavior? Does it have a unique technological capability that can be capitalized to advantage? Obviously, these considerations have more force in markets that are highly concentrated and where the acquiring firm is one of the industry leaders. Thus, there may be situations where the market shares of acquired firms clearly understate their competitive significance. This kind of inquiry most likely will involve combined market shares above the Guidelines, but it could, on occasion, involve acquisitions where the combined market shares fall slightly below the triggering threshold levels.

---

14.   *See* United States v. General Dynamics Corp., 415 U.S. 486, 506-08 (1974); Kaiser Aluminum & Chem. Corp. v. FTC, 652 F.2d 1324, 1338-39 (7th Cir. 1981); Pillsbury Co., 93 F.T.C. 966, 1038-39 (1979).

15.   The courts and the Commission have held that evidence of poor financial performance alone is insufficient, as a matter of law, to sanction a merger. *See* United States v. General Dynamics Corp., 415 U.S. 486 (1974); Kaiser Aluminum & Chem. Corp. v. FTC, 652 F.2d 1324, 1338-39 (7th Cir. 1981); Pillsbury Co., 93 F.T.C. 966, 1036-39 (1979).

16.   *See* Pillsbury Co., 93 F.T.C. 966 (1979).

17.   *See* United States v. Aluminum Co. of America, 377 U.S. 271, 280-81 (1964); Stanley Works v. FTC, 469 F.2d 498 (2d Cir. 1972), *cert. denied*, 412 U.S. 928 (1973).

B. *Factors Facilitating Collusion*

In the preceding section, market conditions that may facilitate or hinder the exercise of market power were discussed. This section focuses on market characteristics that may enhance or detract from the ability of firms to collude or to raise prices and restrict output by interdependent behavior. The oligopolistic markets, or at least markets with few substantial firms, are more conducive to interdependent behavior than a market without such characteristics. However, the number and size of the firms may not reveal the full picture. Other factors may affect the relative ease or difficulty of achieving or maintaining inter-firm coordination. Thus, the Commission believes that it is appropriate to take some account of these considerations, particularly at the pre-complaint stage. The most relevant factors appear to be: the homogeneity (or fungibility) of products in the market; the number of buyers (as well as sellers); the similarity of producers' costs; the history of interfirm behavior, including any evidence of previous price fixing by the firms at issue; and the stability of market shares over time.

The Commission recognizes, of course, that knowledge of the dynamics of collusion or price coordination is far from complete. Moreover, in mergers where individual market power concerns predominate, issues of collusion will be of less importance. Nevertheless, some consideration of these issues should, at the very least, help the courts and enforcement agencies to sort out those cases where there appears to be little, if any, likelihood that an acquisition will contribute significantly to oligopolistic interdependence. Conversely, where the evidence of these factors points strongly in the opposite direction, we will want to examine a merger more closely, even if the market shares are relatively low.

IV. Efficiency Considerations

Mergers may enhance the efficiency of the combining firms in such diverse areas as management, distribution and production. The difficult issue is whether such efficiency gains should be considered, at least as a partial offset to the potential anti-competitive effects of a merger, given the inherent difficulty of accurately predicting and measuring certain efficiencies.[18] Unlike the issues discussed previously, the question here is not whether efficiency considerations reduce or enhance the market power effects of a merger, but whether efficiencies should be treated as an independent countervailing factor in merger analysis.

There are two ways merger guidelines might take efficiencies into account. One way is by raising the market share thresholds so that economies of scale generally can be realized to the fullest extent possible. The Commission supports an adjustment in the numerical criteria, in part, for this reason. Such an approach, however, may not account for all possible efficiencies. To accomplish the latter objective, an efficiencies defense could be allowed in individual cases. Of necessity, such a defense would require an assessment of both the magnitude of the efficiencies anticipated from the merger and the relative weight to accord this evidence vis-a-vis the potential market power effects of the merger.

To minimize measurement difficulties, it has been suggested that an efficiencies

---

18.   *See* IV P. AREEDA & D. TURNER, *supra* note 4, at 146-99; Fisher & Lande, *supra* note 9.

defense could be limited to measurable operating efficiencies, such as production or plant economies of scale.[19] These efficiencies are also more likely to be of the kind that may eventually represent an improved state of the art available to all producers.[20] While such evidence is appropriate for consideration by the agency in the exercise of its prosecutorial discretion at the pre-complaint stage,[21] the Commission believes that there are too many analytical ambiguities associated with the issue of efficiencies to treat it as a legally cognizable defense.[22] To the extent that efficiencies are considered by the Commission as a policy matter, the party or parties raising this issue must provide the Commission with substantial evidence that the resulting cost savings could not have been obtained without the merger and clearly outweigh any increase in market power.

V. Failing Company Defense and Related Arguments

The failing company defense recognizes a general preference for having assets productively utilized rather than withdrawn from a market. Whether assets will in fact be withdrawn is a difficult question and depends heavily on evidence under the control of the affected firm. For this reason, the failing company doctrine imposes rigorous requirements on firms seeking to invoke it.[23] In addition, the restrictions contained in the doctrine reflect the fact that the defense is absolute, regardless of any increased market power accruing to the acquiring firm by virtue of its purchase of the failing company's assets.

Because of proof burdens and general competitive considerations, the suggestion has been made that the doctrine should be relaxed to allow greater latitude for a troubled company to sell its assets to the highest bidder. For example, the doctrine could be liberalized to allow for a failing division defense or to permit a sale to the least objectionable purchaser available, where the technical requirements relating to business failure are otherwise not met, but a substantial risk exists that operations will cease if a merger is not consummated.

An increasing number of mergers evaluated by the Commission involve diversified firms seeking to divest a division or subsidiary. To require subsidization of a division or continuation of unprofitable operations carries its own costs to competition,

---

19. *See* IV [P.] AREEDA & [D.] TURNER, *supra* note 4, at 175-96. For a discussion of operating efficiencies and methods of proof, *see* Fisher & Lande, *supra* note 9, at Sections III(A), V(A) and Muris, *The Efficiency Defense Under Section 7 of the Clayton Act*, 30 CASE W. RES. L. REV. 381 (1980).

20. Where efficiencies flow from factors peculiar to the merged firms, such as improved quality of management, their contribution to the economy as a whole is more problematic.

21. This procedural approach has been suggested by Williamson, *Economies As An Antitrust Defense Revisited*, 125 U. PA. L. REV. 699, 734-35 (1977), and by the Section 7 Clayton Act Committee Task Force of the American Bar Association Antitrust Section, "Proposed Revision to the Justice Department's Merger Guidelines," at 71 (1982).

22. Chairman Miller disagrees with this conclusion and believes that scale-type efficiencies should be considered as part of the legal analysis, consistent with the statutory scheme underlying Section 7 of the Clayton Act, *see* Muris, *supra* note 19.

23. *See, e.g.,* United States v. General Dynamics Corp., 415 U.S. 486 (1974); United States v. Greater Buffalo Press, Inc., 402 U.S. 549, 555-56 (1971); Citizens Publishing Co. v. United States, 394 U.S. 131, 136-39 (1969); Pillsbury Co., 93 F.T.C. 966, 1031-33, 1036-39 (1979); Reichhold Chems., Inc., 91 F.T.C. 246, 288-91 (1978), *aff'd*, 598 F.2d 616 (4th Cir. 1979).

including diminished efficiency and innovation. Such a result encourages firms to make unsound investments and leads to the inefficient use of capital.[24] The Commission's past reluctance to give legal status to a less-than-failing company defense stems from the difficulty of determining whether the costs of continued operation (until another acceptable purchaser, if any, is found) outweigh the market effects of the proposed merger. For example, with respect to the failing division argument, because of the potential facility to shift overhead and losses among divisions, an individual unit can be made to appear in worse fiscal condition by its parent than in fact is the case.[25]

In light of these considerations, the Commission will take into account evidence of a failing division or other similar evidence that falls short of the technical requirements of the failing company defense. However, due to the difficulties of proof, consideration of this evidence will be limited to the Commission's exercise of its prosecutorial discretion.[26] With respect to any such analysis, the Commission will look closely at the following factors: the extent and history of a firm's financial difficulties; whether established accounting procedures have been followed; whether a good faith effort to find another purchaser for the firm or division has been made; and whether the proposed purchaser is the least anti-competitive purchaser willing to acquire the firm or division.

VI. Market Definition

The predictive value of evidence concerning competitive effects is directly affected by the manner in which the relevant product and geographic markets are defined. Thus, issues of market definition are critically important to sound merger analysis.

A. Product Market

The purpose of product market analysis is to ascertain what grouping of products or services should be included in a single relevant market. Where the cross-elasticity of demand for separate products or services is high, they normally will be within the same product market. Similarly, a high cross-elasticity of supply tends to suggest the

---

24.   Refusal to consider evidence of a failing division has been characterized as unfair in that it requires diversified firms "to absorb losses that independent companies can avoid, or to take risks that the independent lenders would deem improvident." IV P. AREEDA & D. TURNER, *supra* note 4, at 112.

25.   *See* Dean Foods Co., 70 F.T.C. 1146, 1285 (1966); Farm Journal, Inc., 53 F.T.C. 26, 47-48 (1956). The lower courts, however, are clearly divided on the issue of the failing division. *Compare* FTC v. Great Lakes Chem. Corp., 1981-2 Trade Cas. (CCH) ¶ 64,175 at 73,592 (N.D. Ill., 1981); United States v. Reed Roller Bit Co., 274 F. Supp. 573, 584 n.1 (W.D. Okla. 1967); *and* United States v. Lever Bros. Co., 216 F. Supp. 887 (S.D.N.Y. 1963), *with* United States v. Blue Bell, Inc., 395 F. Supp. 538, 550 (M.D. Tenn. 1975), *and* United States v. Phillips Petroleum Co., 367 F. Supp. 1226, 1259-60 (C.D. Cal. 1973), *aff'd per curiam*, 418 U.S. 906 (1974). For a discussion of the problems associated with accurately assessing failing division evidence, see generally *Conglomerate Mergers – Their Effects on Small Business and Local Communities: Hearings Before the Subcommittee on Antitrust and Restraint of Trade Activities Affecting Small Business of the House Committee on Small Business*, 96th Cong., 2d Sess. 49-57, 91-130, 368-435 (1980).

26.   Chairman Miller would permit evidence of a failing division to be raised as a legal defense in a merger proceeding.

existence of a common product market. Therefore, the issue of whether related products or services place a significant constraint on the ability of merging firms to raise prices, limit supply or lower quality is central to evaluating the competitive effects of a horizontal merger.

Cross-elasticity of demand (or supply) is best measured by the change in the quantity of another product induced by a price rise in the merged firm's product, either over time or in different geographic markets. Since direct evidence of cross-elasticities is generally unavailable, the courts and enforcement agencies look to other, less direct market indicia. For example, the existence of separate product markets may be evidenced by: the persistence of sizeable price disparities for equivalent amounts of different products; the presence of sufficiently distinctive characteristics which render a product suitable only for a specialized use; the preference of a number of purchasers who traditionally use only a particular kind of product for a distinct use; or the judgment of purchasers or sellers as to whether products are, in fact, competitive. In addition, where firms routinely study the business decisions of other firms, including their pricing decisions, such evidence may reflect a single product market. These secondary indicia, however, will be closely scrutinized because of the inherently imprecise and sometimes self-serving nature of this type of evidence. Finally, investment, marketing and production plans may also evidence whether a firm may competitively enter into the production and sale of another good. Particularly where such information is detailed and provides the basis for a firm's decision, it will be considered in the product market analysis.

B. Geographic Market

This component of market definition focuses on the extent to which different geographic areas should be combined into a single relevant market. The issue is whether producers of the merged firm's product in other geographic areas place a significant constraint on the ability of the merged firm to raise price or restrict output. As a general proposition, an area is a separate geographic market if a change in the price of the product in that area does not, within a relevant period of time, induce substantial changes in the quantity of the product sold in other areas.

The Commission will consider the following factors relevant to this determination: the relationship between price and quantity (or, if evidence of such relationship is shown not to be available, evidence of independent price movement, collusive pricing or price discrimination within a single area); barriers to trade flows, *e.g.*, high transportation costs, time required to make deliveries or municipal, state or federal regulation; and shipping patterns (absence of shipments, however, does not necessarily indicate separate geographic markets because, in some circumstances, a slight price rise in one area could precipitate shipments from other areas). Evidence of shipments may be particularly probative when it reflects long-held patterns of trade and industry perceptions.

An additional consideration relevant to geographic market definition concerns the extent to which foreign markets should be included in the analysis. There is increasing evidence that national boundaries may not fully reflect trade patterns or competitive realities in certain instances. At the same time, evidence relating to foreign markets may be very difficult to obtain. Nevertheless, while these limitations may preclude the delineation of larger-than-domestic markets, some consideration should be given to this issue in determining the competitive significance of domestic market share data.

1987 HORIZONTAL MERGER GUIDELINES OF THE NATIONAL ASSOCIATION OF ATTORNEYS GENERAL

1. Purpose and Scope of the Guidelines

These Guidelines explain the general enforcement policy of the fifty-five state and territorial attorneys general ("the Attorneys General") who comprise the National Association of Attorneys General[1] ("NAAG") concerning horizontal[2] acquisitions and mergers (mergers) subject to section 7 of the Clayton Act,[3] sections 1 and 2 of the Sherman Act[4] and analogous provisions of the antitrust laws of those states which have enacted them.[5]

The state attorney general is the primary or exclusive public enforcer of the antitrust law in most states. The Attorneys General also represent their states and the natural person citizens of their states in federal antitrust litigation.[6]

These Guidelines embody the general enforcement policy of NAAG and its members. Individual attorneys general may vary or supplement this general policy in recognition of variations in precedents among the federal circuits and differences in state antitrust laws and in the exercise of their individual prosecutorial discretion.

These Guidelines serve three primary purposes. First, they provide a uniform framework for the states to evaluate the facts of a particular horizontal merger and the dynamic conditions of an industry. Second, they inform the business community of the substantive standards used by the Attorneys General to review, and when appropriate, challenge specific mergers. This will allow the business community to assess potential transactions under these standards and therefore be useful as a risk assessment and business planning tool. Third, the Guidelines put forward a

---

1. The Attorneys General of American Samoa, Guam, The Commonwealth of Northern Mariana Islands, The Commonwealth of Puerto Rico and the Virgin Islands are members of the NAAG. The Attorney General of New Mexico has not adopted these Guidelines.

2. A horizontal merger involves firms that are actually or potentially in both the same product and geographic markets, as those markets are defined in Section 3 of these Guidelines.

3. Section 7 of the Clayton Act, 15 U.S.C. § 18 prohibits mergers if their effect "may be substantially to lessen competition or to tend to create a monopoly."

4. Section 1 of the Sherman Act, 15 U.S.C. § 1 prohibits mergers which constitute an unreasonable "restraint of trade." Section 2 of the Sherman Act, 15 U.S.C. § 2 prohibits mergers which create a monopoly or constitute an attempt, combination or conspiracy to monopolize.

5. [Citations to the antitrust laws of the States are set forth in Appendix A.]

6. The authority of the Attorneys General to invoke section 7 of the Clayton Act to enjoin a merger injurious to the general welfare and economy of the State is confirmed in Georgia v. Pennsylvania Railroad Co., 324 U.S. 439 (1945).

framework for the analysis of horizontal mergers which relies upon market realities and which is grounded in and consistent with the purposes and meaning of section 7 of the Clayton Act, as amended by the Celler-Kefauver Act of 1950 ("section 7"), and as reflected in its clear legislative history and consistent interpretation by the United States Supreme Court.[7]

The organizing principle of the Guidelines is the application of facts concerning the marketplace and widely accepted economic theory to these authoritative sources of the law's meaning.

2. Policies Underlying These Guidelines

The federal antitrust law provisions relevant to horizontal mergers, most specifically section 7 and analogous state law provisions,[8] have one primary and several subsidiary purposes. The central purpose of the law is to prevent firms from attaining market or monopoly power,[9] because firms possessing such power can raise prices to consumers above competitive levels, thereby effecting a transfer of wealth from consumers to such firms.[10]

Congress determined that highly concentrated industries were characterized by and conducive to the exercise of market power and prohibited mergers which may substantially lessen competition. Such mergers were prohibited even prior to the actual attainment or exercise of market power, that is, when the trend to harmful concentration was incipient.

Other goals of the law were the prevention of excessive levels of industrial concentration because of the political and social effects of concentrated economic power and the fostering of productive efficiency, organizational diversity, technological innovation and the maintenance of opportunities for small and regional businesses to compete.[11]

Goals such as productive efficiency, though subsidiary to the central goal of preventing wealth transfers from consumers to firms possessing market power, are often consistent with this primary purpose. When the productive efficiency of a firm increases, (its cost of production is lowered) the firm may pass on some of the savings to consumers in the form of lower prices. However, there is little likelihood

---

7. This orientation recognizes a basic principle which should properly guide governmental enforcement of the law. It is the legislative function to make basic policy choices, whether or not those choices coincide with the beliefs of a particular administration, enforcement agency, or a particular school of economic theory.

8. For example, see statutes of Hawaii, Maine, Mississippi, Nebraska, New Jersey, Ohio, Oklahoma, Texas, Washington and Puerto Rico for provisions analogous to section 7. [Appendix B contains citations to state anti-merger provisions.] However, all states with a provision analogous to Sherman Act § 1 may also challenge mergers under such authority. *See* note 6 concerning state enforcement of section 7.

9. Market power is the ability of one or more firms to maintain prices above a competitive level, or to prevent prices from decreasing to a lower competitive level, for a significant period of time.

10. A buyer or group of buyers may similarly attain and exercise the power to drive prices below a competitive level for a significant period of time. This is usually termed an exercise of "monopsony power." When the terms "buyer(s)" or "groups of buyers" are used herein they are deemed to include "seller(s)" or "groups of sellers" adversely affected by the exercise of market or monopsony power.

11. Brown Shoe Co. v. United States, 370 U.S. 294, 315-16 (1962).

that a productively efficient firm with market power would pass along savings to consumers. To the limited extent that Congress was concerned with productive efficiency in enacting these laws, it prescribed the prevention of high levels of market concentration as the means to this end.[12] Furthermore, the Supreme Court has clearly ruled that any conflict between the goal of preventing anticompetitive mergers and that of increasing efficiency must be resolved in favor of the former explicit and predominant concern of the Congress.[13]

The Congress evidenced little or no concern for allocative efficiency when it enacted section 7 and the other antitrust laws.[14] Nevertheless, preserving allocative efficiency is generally considered an additional benefit realized by the prevention of market power, because the misallocative act of restricting output has the concomitant effect of raising prices to consumers. It is counterintuitive, however, to primarily base merger policy on the analysis of these efficiency effects, which are inconsequential in the statutory scheme, and are insignificant in relation to the wealth transfers associated with the exercise of market power.[15]

---

12.   There is vigorous debate whether firms in industries with high concentrations are on average more or less efficient than those in industries with moderate or low levels of concentration.

      The theory of "x-inefficiency" predicts that firms constrained by vigorous competition have lower production costs than firms in an industry with little or no competition. Various economists have attempted to quantify production cost increases due to x-inefficiency and the theory is the subject of ongoing debate.

      Regardless of such debate, Congress had the prerogative to make a choice, opting for less concentration, and did so with little regard for efficiency. The primary concern was wealth transfers from consumers to firms exercising market power.

13.   In FTC v. Procter & Gamble Co., 386 U.S. 568, 580 (1967), the Court stated:

      Possible economies cannot be used as a defense to illegality. Congress was aware that some mergers which lessen competition may also result in economies but it struck the balance in favor of protecting competition.

In United States v. Philadelphia National Bank, 374 U.S. 321, 371 (1963), the Court stated:

      We are clear, however, that a merger the effect of which "may be substantially to lessen competition" is not saved because, on some ultimate reckoning of social or economic debits and credits, it may be deemed beneficial. A value choice of such magnitude is beyond the ordinary limits of judicial competence, and in any event has been made for us already, by Congress when it enacted the amended § 7. Congress determined to preserve our traditionally competitive economy. It therefore proscribed anticompetitive mergers, the benign and malignant alike, fully aware, we must assume, that some price might have to be paid.

14.   Perfect "allocative efficiency" or "Pareto optimality" is a state of equilibrium on the so-called "utility-possibility frontier" in which no person can be made better off without making someone else worse off. Allocative efficiency can be achieved in an economy with massive inequalities of income and distribution, e.g., 1% of the population can receive 99% of the economy's wealth and 99% of the population can receive 1%. A massive transfer of wealth from consumers to a monopolist does not of itself decrease allocative efficiency. However, when a monopolist restricts its output, the total wealth of society is diminished, thereby reducing allocative efficiency. Economists term this loss of society's wealth the "deadweight loss."

15.   In most mergers creating market power, the effect of the wealth transfer from consumers will be many times as great quantitatively as the effect on allocative efficiency (dead-weight loss). See note 14. It is important to re-emphasize that wealth transfer is irrelevant to the issue of allocative efficiency. The term of art "consumer welfare," often used when discussing the efficiency effects of mergers and restraints of trade, refers to the concept of allocative efficiency. A transfer of wealth from consumers to firms with market power does not diminish "consumer welfare." For the unwary Judge or practitioner stumbling upon this term it is important to understand this fact and to further understand that "consumer welfare," when used in this

2.1 The Competitive Effects of Mergers

Mergers may have negative or positive competitive consequences. The following is a summary description of the most common competitive effects of mergers relevant to enforcement of section 7.[16]

2.11 ACQUISITION OF MARKET POWER AND WEALTH TRANSFERS

When two firms, neither possessing market power, cease competing and merge, the inevitable consequence is the elimination of the competition between them. More significantly, however, the merged entity may now possess market power, an unambiguously anticompetitive outcome.

A merger may also increase the concentration level in an industry to a point at which the few remaining firms can effectively engage in active collusion or implicitly coordinate their actions and thus collectively exercise market power.

When a firm or firms exercise market power by profitably maintaining prices above competitive levels for a significant period of time, a transfer of wealth from consumers to those firms occurs.[17] This transfer of wealth is the major evil sought to be addressed by section 7.[18]

The wealth transfer orientation of section 7 is the same as that of the Sherman Act. The major difference and reason for the enactment of section 7 of the Clayton Act was the "incipiency" standard, which permits antitrust intervention at a point when the anticompetitive consequences of a merger are not manifest but are likely to occur absent intervention. The Celler-Kefauver amendments retained and strengthened the "incipiency" standard by extending the coverage of the law to acquisitions of assets. In Section 4 of these Guidelines the Attorneys General specifically attempt to give expression to the statutory concern of "incipiency."

2.12 PRODUCTIVE EFFICIENCY

A merger may increase or decrease the costs of the parties to the merger and thus

---

manner, has nothing to do with the welfare of consumers.

16. These Guidelines deal only with these competitive consequences of horizontal mergers. Mergers may have many other consequences, beneficial or detrimental, not relevant to the enforcement of section 7. The penalization of ineffective management and the distortion of cash flow and capital flow patterns are two frequent results of mergers not substantially related to the purposes of section 7. More important, mergers may also have other consequences that are relevant to the objectives of section 7. These implicate concerns that are primarily social and political in nature, such as the effect upon opportunities for small and regional business to survive and compete. These consequences are especially significant in the analysis of conglomerate mergers, which are beyond the scope of these Guidelines.

17. Tacit or active collusion on terms of trade other than price also produces wealth transfer effects. This would include, for example, an agreement to eliminate rivalry on service features or to limit the choices otherwise available to consumers.

18. The predominant concern with wealth transfers was evidenced in the statements of both supporters and opponents of the Celler-Kefauver amendments. See, e.g., 95 Cong. Rec. 11,506 (1949) (remarks of Rep. Bennett); Id. at 11,492 (remarks of Rep. Carroll); Id. at 11,506 (remarks of Rep. Byrne); Hearings before the Subcomm. on the Judiciary, 81st Cong., 1st and 2d Sess., note 260, at 180 (remarks of Sen. Kilgore); 95 Cong. Rec. 11,493 (1949) (remarks of Rep. Yates); Id. at 11,490-91 (remarks of Rep. Goodwin); 95 Cong. Rec. 16,490 (1949) (colloquy of Sen. Kefauver and Sen. Wiley).

increase or decrease productive efficiency. A merger which increases productive efficiency and does not produce a firm or firms capable of exercising market power should lower prices paid by consumers. An inefficient merger in an unconcentrated industry is generally of no competitive concern. The efficiency effects of mergers are easy to speculate about but hard to accurately predict. There is much disagreement among economists as to whether merged firms usually perform well and whether, on average, mergers have been shown to produce significant efficiencies. However, most efficiencies and those most quantitatively significant will be realized in mergers involving small firms. Such mergers do not raise any concern under the enforcement standards adopted in Section 4 of these Guidelines. Furthermore, the concentration thresholds adopted in Section 4 are more than high enough to enable firms to obtain the most significant efficiencies likely to result from growth through merger as opposed to growth through internal expansion.

2.13 ALLOCATIVE EFFICIENCY

A merger which facilitates the exercise of market power results in a decrease in allocative efficiency. When firms with market power restrict their output, the total wealth of society diminishes. This effect is universally condemned by economists, and its prevention, while not a significant concern of the Congress which enacted section 7, is a goal consistent with the purposes of the antitrust laws.

2.14 RAISING RIVALS' COSTS

In certain circumstances a merger may raise the costs of the competitors of the parties to the merger. For example, a merger could increase the power of a firm to effect the price that rivals must pay for inputs or the conditions under which they must operate, in a manner that creates a relative disadvantage for the rivals. If the market structure is such that these increased costs will be passed on to consumers, then the prevention of this effect is consistent with the goals of the antitrust laws. Preventing such effect will also prevent a decrease in allocative efficiency.

3. Market Definition

These Guidelines are concerned with horizontal mergers, that is, mergers involving firms that are actual or potential competitors in the same product and geographic markets.

The primary analytical tool utilized in the Guidelines is the measurement of concentration in a particular market and increase in concentration in that market resulting from a merger. The market shares used to compute these concentration factors will depend upon the market definition adopted.[19] The reasonable delineation of these market boundaries is critical to realizing the objectives of the Guidelines and the antitrust laws. If the market boundaries chosen are seriously distorted in relation to the actual workings of the marketplace, an enforcement error

---

19.   For example, consider the proposed merger of two firms producing the same product. Each has a 50% share of the sales of this product in a certain state but only 1% of national sales. If the proper geographic market is the state, then the competitive consequences of the merger will be far different than if the geographic market is the entire country.

is likely.[20] An overly restricted product or geographic market definition may trigger antitrust intervention when the merger would not significantly harm competition or in other circumstances result in the failure to challenge an anticompetitive merger. An overly expansive market definition also may result in the failure to challenge a merger with serious anticompetitive consequences.[21] Markets should be defined from the perspective of those interests section 7 was primarily enacted to protect, *i.e.,* the classes of consumers (or suppliers) who may be adversely affected by an anticompetitive merger. The Attorneys General will utilize historical data to identify these classes of consumers ("the protected interest group") their sources of supply, suitable substitutes for the product and alternative sources of the product and its substitutes. The market thus defined will be presumed correct unless rebutted by hard evidence that supply responses within a reasonable period of time will render unprofitable an attempted exercise of market power.[22]

The following sections detail how these general principles will be applied to define product and geographic markets and to calculate the market shares of firms determined to be within the relevant market.

3.1 Product Market Definition

The Attorneys General will determine the customers who purchase the products or services ("products") of the merging firms. Each product produced in common by the merging parties will constitute a provisional product market. The provisional product market will be expanded to include suitable substitutes for the product which

---

20.   Governmental challenge of a merger which is not likely to lessen competition substantially is frequently termed "Type I error." The failure to challenge a merger which is likely to lessen competition substantially is termed "Type II error." Type I error should be corrected by the Court which determines the validity of the challenge. Type II error will most likely go uncorrected, since the vast majority of merger challenges are mounted by the government. In other areas of antitrust law, private actions predominate and can correct Type II error. Consumers, whose interests were paramount in the enactment of section 7 and section 1 of the Sherman Act, suffer the damage of Type II error.

21.   Consider, for example, the market(s) for flexible wrapping materials. These materials include clear plastic, metallic foils, waxed paper and others. Firms A and B each produce 30% of the clear plastic wrap and 5% of all flexible wrapping material in a relevant geographic market. Firm C produces 70% of the metallic foil and 60% of all flexible wrap. If the proper market definition is all flexible wrapping materials, then treating clear plastic and metallic foils as separate markets may lead to an unwarranted challenge to a merger between firms A and B. The same incorrect market definition may also result in the failure to challenge a merger between Firm C and either Firm A or Firm B because of the incorrect assumption that metallic foil and clear plastic wrap do not compete. However, if the correct market definition is clear plastic wrap but the more expansive market definition of all flexible materials is chosen, this may result in the failure to challenge an anticompetitive merger of Firms A and B.

22.   Hard evidence, as contrasted with speculation, is generally grounded in historical fact. Hard evidence of a probable supply response would include a factual showing that this response had occurred in the past when prices increased significantly. A mere prediction that a manufacturer will shift his production from one product to another to capitalize on a price increase, when unsupported by evidence of a previous similar response or other information of similarly probative nature, is not considered "hard evidence."

are comparably priced.[23] A comparably priced substitute will be deemed suitable and thereby expand the product market definition if, and only if, considered suitable by at least 75% of the customers.

Actual substitution by customers in the past will presumptively establish that a product is considered a suitable substitute for the provisionally defined product. However, other evidence probative of the assertion that customers deem a product to be a suitable substitute offered by the parties to the merger will also be considered.[24]

3.11 PRODUCT SUBMARKETS

Notwithstanding the determination in Section 3.1 that a product is a suitable substitute for the provisional product pursuant to application of the 75% rule, there may be small but significant groups of consumers who cannot substitute or can do so only with great difficulty. These consumers may be subject to price discrimination and be particularly adversely affected by a merger. In such instances, the Attorneys General may define additional narrower product submarkets.

Evidence of the commercial reality of such a submarket includes price discrimination, inelasticity of demand and industry or public recognition of a distinct submarket.

3.2 Geographic Market Definition

Utilizing the product market(s) defined in Section 3.1, the Attorneys General will define the relevant geographic market.

First, the Attorneys General will determine the sources and locations where the customers of the merging parties readily turn for their supply of the relevant product. These will include the merging parties and other sources of supply. To this group of suppliers and their locations will be added suppliers of buyers closely proximate to the customers of the merging parties. In determining those suppliers to whom the protected interest group readily turn for supply of the relevant product, the Attorneys General will include all sources of supply within the past two years still present in the market.

---

23.   The existence of a functionally suitable substitute which is significantly more expensive than the relevant product will not discipline an exercise of market power until the price of the relevant product has been raised to a level comparable to the substitute. The Attorneys General will also seek to ascertain whether current price comparability of two products resulted from an exercise of market power. For example, suppose that the provisionally defined product recently cost 20% less than a possible substitute, but its price has recently risen 20% as a result of the exercise of market power. Rather than serving as a basis for broadening the product market to include the possible substitute, this finding will provide compelling evidence that any further concentration through merger will only exacerbate the market power which already exists. To ascertain whether the price comparability of two possibly interchangeable products was the result of an exercise of market power over one product, the appropriate question to ask may be "what would happen if the price of the product in question dropped?" If a significant price decrease does not substantially increase sales, then a previous exercise of market power has likely been detected, and the two products should probably be considered to be in separate product markets. *See,* United States v. E.I. duPont de Nemours & Co., 351 U.S. 377, 399-400 (1956).

24.   Recycled or reconditioned goods will be considered suitable substitutes if they meet the requirements of this Section.

Utilizing the locations from which supplies of the relevant product are obtained by members of the protected interest group, the geographic market will be defined as the area encompassing the production locations from which this group purchases 75% of their supplies of the relevant product.

The product and geographic markets as defined above will be utilized in calculating market shares and concentration levels unless additional sources of supply are recognized by application of the procedures specified in Section 3.3.

3.22 GEOGRAPHIC SUBMARKETS

The Attorneys General may define additional narrower geographic markets when there is strong evidence that sellers are able to discriminate among buyers in separate locations within the geographic market(s) defined in Section 3.2. The Attorneys General will evaluate evidence concerning discrimination on price, terms of credit and delivery and priority of shipment.[25]

3.3 Principles for Recognizing Potential Competition

The firms identified as being in the markets defined by the procedures outlined in Sections 3.1 and 3.2 will be utilized in calculating market shares and measuring concentration unless the parties to the merger produce relevant hard evidence of profitable supply and demand responses which will be likely to occur within one year of any attempted exercise of market power. When such potential competition is proven to be likely to emerge within a year, the Attorneys General will calculate market shares and concentration levels after incorporating such sources of potential supply.

The Attorneys General will evaluate hard evidence produced by the parties to a merger of the following sources of potential competition:

1) That firms will divert supplies of the product not currently sold in the relevant geographic market into that market.

2) That current suppliers of the product will produce additional supplies for the relevant market by utilizing excess capacity or adding new productive capacity.

3) That new sources of the product will be readily available from firms with production flexibility, firms who will build new capacity and firms engaging in arbitrage.

3.31 DIVERSION OF EXISTING SUPPLIES INTO THE MARKET

The parties to a merger may produce evidence that firms will divert supplies of the product into the market in response to a price increase or restriction of output. The Attorneys General will analyze proof concerning such probable diversions of supplies currently exported from the relevant market, supplies internally consumed by vertically integrated firms in the market and additional supplies from firms currently shipping part of their production into the market.

---

25.   The Attorneys General welcome submissions by buyers concerning such discrimination or any other hard evidence that a proposed merger will adversely effect them because it is likely substantially to lessen competition.

3.31A   Exports

A firm currently exporting the product from the relevant market may divert the supply back into the market in response to a price increase or restriction of output.

This response is unlikely from an exporter who is a party to the merger, since it is unlikely to discipline its own attempted exercise of market power. It is also unlikely if the exporter is an oligopolist likely to benefit from the collective exercise of market power.

Although parties wishing to prove this supply response are free to produce any hard evidence, the most persuasive proof will be historical shipping patterns showing past diversion of exports in response to price increases or restricted supply. In addition the parties should, at a minimum, address the following questions: Are the exports contractually committed and for what term? Are the exports otherwise obligated to current buyers?

3.31B   Internal Consumption

A vertically integrated firm producing the product for internal consumption may divert this supply to the open market. Diversion is unlikely if there are no suitable and economical substitutes for the product and/or the firm has contractual or other obligations for the goods utilizing the relevant product. The most persuasive proof of such diversion will be evidence that a vertically integrated firm already sells some of the product on the open market and has a history of transferring production intended for internal consumption to the open market.

3.31C   Increased Importation

A firm shipping part of its output of the product into the relevant market may respond to an attempted exercise of market power by diverting additional production into the relevant market. Parties seeking to prove the likelihood of this supply response should, at a minimum, address the factual issues of whether and for what terms these additional supplies are contractually or otherwise obligated to buyers outside the relevant market, the percentage of the suppliers' production now sent into the market and their historical shipping patterns.

3.32 EXPANSION OF OUTPUT

The parties to a merger may produce evidence that current suppliers of the product will expand their output by utilization of excess capacity or the addition of new capacity within one year of any attempted exercise of market power. Parties attempting to prove probable utilization of excess capacity should at a minimum address the issues of (i) the cost of bringing the excess capacity on line; (ii) the amount of excess capacity; (iii) for a firm not currently supplying the relevant market, prior history of supplying this market or present intention to do so; and (iv) how much prices would have to rise to likely induce this supply response.

3.33 NEW PRODUCTION SOURCES OF ADDITIONAL SUPPLY

The parties to a merger may produce evidence that firms not currently supplying the product will do so within one year of any attempted exercise of market power.

This might be shown for firms with production flexibility, firms who will erect new production facilities and firms engaging in arbitrage.

3.33A   Production Flexibility

The Attorneys General will evaluate proof concerning firms with flexible production facilities who are capable of switching to the production of the relevant product within one year and are likely to do so. A history of such switching in the past will be the most persuasive evidence that this response is probable.

3.33B   Construction of New Facilities

A party may attempt to demonstrate that firms not presently supplying the product will erect new plant facilities (or establish new service facilities) within one year of an attempted exercise of market power.

3.33C   Arbitrage

Firms proximate to the relevant market may respond to an exercise of market power by buying the product outside the market and reselling it inside the market. This potential source of supply is unlikely if the relevant product is a service or combined product and service. A history of arbitrage in the industry will be most probative that this potential response is probable.

3.4   Calculating Market Shares

Using the product and geographic markets defined in Sections 3.1 and 3.2, the firms supplying the market and any additional sources of supply recognized under Section 3.3, the shares of all firms determined to be in the market will be calculated.

The market shares of firms presently supplying the market shall be based upon actual sales within the relevant market. If there has been a demonstration of a probable supply response as defined in Section 3.3, the market shares of firms already selling in the market will be adjusted to account for the proven probable supply response. Similarly, market shares will be assigned to firms not currently supplying the market who have been shown to be likely to enter the market in response to an attempted exercise of market power. The assigned market shares of such firms will be based upon the amount of the product these firms would supply in response to an attempted exercise of market power. The Attorneys General will utilize dollar sales, unit sales or other appropriate sales measurements to quantify actual sales. Expected dollar or unit sales will be used when proven supply responses have expanded the market definition.

3.41   FOREIGN FIRMS

Foreign firms presently supplying the relevant market will be assigned market shares in the same manner as domestic firms, according to their actual current sales in the relevant market. Foreign firms and their productive capacity are inherently a less reliable check on market power by domestic firms because foreign firms face a variety of barriers to continuing sales or increasing their sales. These barriers include import quotas, voluntary quantitative restrictions, tariffs and fluctuations in exchange rates. When such barriers exist, market share based upon historical sales data will be reduced.

A single market share will be assigned to the firms of any foreign country or group of countries which in fact coordinate their sales.[26]

4. Measurement of Concentration

The primary tool utilized by the Attorneys General to determine whether a specific horizontal merger is likely to substantially harm competition is a measurement of the level of concentration in each market defined in Section 3. Concentration is a measurement of the number of firms in a market and their market shares. The Guidelines employ the Herfindahl-Hirschman Index ("HHI") to calculate the level of concentration in an industry before and after a merger and, therefore, the increase in concentration which would result from the merger.[27] Basing merger policy on measurements of market concentration furthers the goals of both section 7 and these Guidelines.

Unlike the traditional four firm concentration ratio ("CR4") which was formerly used by enforcement agencies and courts to measure market concentration,[28] the HHI reflects both the distribution of the market shares of all the leading firms in the market and the composition of the market beyond the leading firms.[29]

The predominant concern of the Congress in enacting section 7 was the prevention of high levels of industrial concentration because of the likely anticompetitive consequences. Foremost among these likely anticompetitive effects of high concentration is the exercise of market power by one or more firms through monopolization, collusion or interdependent behavior in an oligopolistic market. Section 7 militates that the HHI levels which trigger an action to block a merger be

---

26.   For example, an import quota may be established for a foreign country and the foreign government may then apportion the quota among firms engaged in the import of the relevant product.

27.   The HHI is computed by summing the numerical squares of the market shares of all the firms in the market. For example, a market with four firms each having a market share of 25% has an HHI of 2500 calculated as follows: $25^2 + 25^2 + 25^2 + 25^2 = 2500$. A market with a pure monopolist, i.e., a firm with 100% of the market, has an HHI of 10,000 calculated as $100^2 = 10,000$. If the market has four firms, each having a market share of 25% and two of these four firms merge, the increase in the HHI is computed as follows: Pre-merger $25^2 + 25^2 + 25^2 + 25^2 = 2500$. Post-merger $50^2 + 25^2 + 25^2 = 3750$. The increase in the HHI due to the merger is 1250, i.e., 3750 - 2500 = 1250. The increase is also equivalent to twice the product of the market shares of the merging firms, i.e., 25 x 25 x 2 = 1250.

28.   The CR4 is the sum of the market shares of the top four firms in the market. A CR4 cannot be converted into any single HHI but rather includes a possible range of HHI levels. For example, consider two markets with CR4 of 100%. The first is comprised of 4 firms; each with a market share of 25%. This yields an HHI of 2500, i.e., $25^2 + 25^2 + 25^2 + 25^2 = 2500$. The second market is comprised of four firms with market shares of 70%, 10%, 10% and 10%. This yields an HHI of 5200, i.e., $70^2 + 10^2 + 10^2 + 10^2 = 5200$.

29.   The HHI also gives significantly greater weight to the market shares of the largest firms, which properly reflects the leading roles which such firms are likely to play in a collusive agreement or other exercise of market power. A single dominant firm's likely role as the price leader in an oligopolistic market is also reflected in the HHI. For these reasons, the HHI is now the generally preferred measure of concentration.

set at the concentration levels likely to prevent these anticompetitive actions and interactions.

The objective of preventing future likely anticompetitive effects should be based primarily upon the historical picture of the market rendered by concentration levels, since industrial and economic concentration were the primary concerns of the framers of Section 7. Furthermore, the predominant focus of scholarly economic inquiry into the competitive consequences of mergers has been the correlation of concentration levels with various indicia of competition. Other theories which predict the competitive effects of mergers based upon factors other than market concentration, though valuable, have not nearly reached the level of precision which is necessary for them to form the basis for responsible policy decisions. The facts of recent history are a far more reliable gauge of future consequences than such theories.[30]

The Attorneys General divide the spectrum of market concentration into the same three numerical regions utilized by the United States Department of Justice.[31] They are characterized in these Guidelines as "acceptable concentration" (HHI below 1000), "moderate to high concentration" (HHI between 1000 and 1800) and "very high concentration" (HHI above 1800).[32]

4.1 General Standards

The Attorneys General will calculate the post-merger concentration level in the market and the increase in concentration due to the merger. In certain cases, increases in concentration during the 36 months prior to the merger will also be assessed.

While it may be justifiable to challenge any merger above the threshold of market concentration where collusion and interdependent behavior are significantly facilitated (HHI 1000) the Attorneys General are unlikely to challenge mergers which do not significantly increase concentration. This policy recognizes section 7's prohibition of mergers whose effect "may be substantially to lessen competition."

---

30.   There may be instances where clear evidence compels the conclusion that concentration levels and market shares inaccurately portray the competitive significance of a particular merger. In accordance with the doctrine of United States v. General Dynamics Corp., 415 U.S. 486 (1974), such situations will require case by case analysis.

31.   Although these Guidelines and those of the Department of Justice are generally consistent in their adoption of the HHI thresholds which will likely trigger an enforcement action, the market definition principles employed are different. See Section 3 herein and Section 2 of the Justice Department Guidelines; U.S. Dep't of Justice Merger Guidelines (June 14, 1984) reprinted in Antitrust & Trade Reg. Rep. (BNA) No. 1169 (June 14, 1984); Trade Reg. Rep. (CCH) No. 655 at 25 (June 18, 1984). The different market definition principles will often produce differing market shares which are then utilized to calculate the HHI. This is so because the process of market definition in the Justice Department's Guidelines will, in many respects, overstate the bounds of both the geographic and product markets in relation to the actual workings of the marketplace. This will result in the systematic understatement of market shares used in calculating market concentration.

32.   The Attorneys General are unlikely to challenge any merger in an industry with a post-merger HHI of less than 1000. An HHI of 1000, the level at which enforcement actions start to become probable under these Guidelines, can be found in a market with ten firms each with a 10% market share. Collusion and/or oligopolistic behavior are plausible in a market comprised of ten or fewer firms of roughly equal size.

When the threshold of very high concentration is traversed (HHI 1800) the likelihood of anticompetitive effects are greatly increased and the increase in concentration likely to substantially lessen competition concomitantly reduced. The concentration increases which are likely to trigger an enforcement action under these Guidelines have been adopted in reasonable accommodation of both the "substantiality" requirement of Section 7 and the need to objectively factor in the dynamic conditions in an industry. The latter concern is addressed by measuring increases in market concentration during the 36 months prior to a merger.

4.2 Post-Merger HHI Between 1000 and 1800

An action to challenge a merger is likely if the merger
(a)   increases the HHI by more than 100 points or
(b)   increases the HHI by more than 50 points and during the 36 months prior to the proposed merger the HHI has increased by more than 100 points. Notwithstanding the foregoing, a challenge is unlikely in either case if assessment of the factors discussed in Sections 5.1 and/or 5.3 clearly compel the conclusion that the merger is not likely substantially to lessen competition.

4.3 Post-Merger HHI Above 1800

An action to challenge a merger is likely if the merger
(a)   increases the HHI by more than 50 points or
(b)   increases the HHI by more than 25 points and during the 36 months prior to the proposed merger the HHI has increased by more than 50 points. Notwithstanding the foregoing, a challenge is unlikely in either case if assessment of the factor discussed in Section 5.1 clearly compels the conclusion that the merger is not likely substantially to lessen competition.

4.4 Mergers Involving the Leading Firm or a New Innovative Firm in a Market

The merger of a dominant firm with a small firm in the market may create or increase the market power of the dominant firm yet increase the HHI by an amount less than the levels set forth in Sections 4.2 and 4.3. Similarly, the merger of a new, innovative firm with an existing significant competitor in the market may substantially reduce competition yet increase the HHI by an amount less than the levels set forth in Sections 4.2 and 4.3. Therefore, an action to challenge a merger will also be likely if the proposed merger involves either a leading firm with a market share of at least 35 percent and firm with a market share of 1 percent or more, or a firm with a market share of 20 percent or more and a new, innovative firm in a market with moderate to high concentration or very high concentration, unless assessment of the factor discussed in Section 5.1 clearly compels the conclusion that the merger is not likely substantially to lessen competition. In addition, in a market with moderate to high concentration the factor discussed in Section 5.3 will also be assessed.

5. Additional Factors Which May Be Considered in Determining Whether to Challenge a Merger

There are numerous factors aside from market share and market concentration which may make a merger more or less likely substantially to lessen competition. While the assessment of most or many of these factors would increase the flexibility of these Guidelines, this would also significantly vitiate the predictability of their application and the consistency of enforcement under the Guidelines and would greatly reduce their value as a planning and risk assessment tool for the business community.

While maintaining primary reliance on the concentration and market share analysis discussed in Section 4, the Attorneys General will, under the limited circumstances specified herein, assess three additional factors. These are "ease of entry," collusive behavior and efficiencies.

5.1 Ease of Entry

If meaningful entry into the market can be easily and speedily accomplished, any attempted exercise of market power is likely to fail. For entry to be meaningful it must contribute enough additional product to discipline a price increase or supply restriction. Entry must also be economical so that there is sufficient incentive to make it likely to occur.[33] Financial, informational, technological and regulatory barriers to entry and those posed by excess capacity will also be assessed. Finally, entry must be likely to occur within one year. While entry requiring longer than this period of time can eventually discipline the exercise of market power, during a year consumers will suffer significant harm of the precise nature which the law was primarily enacted to prevent.

If under the foregoing standards the Attorneys General find that easy and meaningful entry can be accomplished within one year, action to block a merger is unlikely.

5.2 Collusion and Oligopolistic Behavior

If the market has a history of collusion or if there is evidence of current collusion or oligopolistic behavior,[34] the Attorneys General are more likely than otherwise to challenge a merger below one of the numerical thresholds set forth in Section 4[35] and very likely to challenge a merger exceeding any of the numerical thresholds set forth in Section 4.

---

33.   Even a significant increase in prices following a merger might not elicit entry since the potential entrants may conclude that their entry into the market could cause prices to drop substantially.

34.   An oligopolistic market will usually be moderately to highly concentrated or very highly concentrated and prone to one or more of the following practices: (1) price leadership; (2) pre-announced price changes; (3) price rigidity in response to excess capacity or diminished demand; (4) public pronouncements and discussions of "the right price" for the industry; and (5) systematic price discrimination.

35.   An oligopolistic market is unlikely to fall below the numerical concentration threshold of HHI 1000. However, a merger affecting such a market may not increase the HHI enough to make a challenge to the merger likely under the standards set forth in Section 4.

The absence of collusion or oligopolistic behavior will not diminish the probability of a challenge otherwise likely under the standards set forth in Section 4.

5.3 *Efficiencies*

To the limited extent that efficiency was a concern of the Congress in enacting section 7, that concern focused on productive efficiency and was expressed in the legislative finding that less industrial concentration would further that goal.[36]

The Attorneys General find that there is no substantial empirical support for the assertion that mergers involving firms of sufficient size to raise concerns under the standards set forth in Section 4, usually or on average result in substantial efficiencies. Furthermore, the concentration thresholds adopted in Section 4 are more than high enough to enable firms to obtain the most significant efficiencies likely to result from growth through merger.

Even in those rare situations where significant efficiencies can be demonstrated, rather than merely predicted, this showing cannot constitute a defense to an otherwise unlawful merger.[37] Accordingly, efficiencies will only be considered when the post-merger HHI is 1800 points or below. When the post-merger HHI is 1800 or below, the Attorneys General will evaluate any hard evidence offered by the parties that a merger will produce significant efficiencies, such as clearly proven savings on transportation costs or scale economies. In general, proven cost savings of 5%, for both firms using a weighted average, will make a challenge to a merger "unlikely" notwithstanding the standards set forth in Sections 4.2 and 4.4.[38] There may, however, be instances where proven cost savings of a lower magnitude may significantly reduce prices to consumers or where the Attorneys General will require evidence of cost reductions in excess of 5%.[39] The Attorneys General will evaluate such claims on a case by case basis.[40]

6.   Failing Firm Defense

The failing firm doctrine, which has been recognized by the United States Supreme

---

36.   For example, see 95 Cong. Rec. 11,487 (1949) statement of Rep. Celler (co-author of legislation) "Bigness does not mean efficiency, a better product, or lower prices"; 95 Cong. Rec. 11,495-98 (1949) (statement of Rep. Boggs); Corporate Mergers and Acquisitions: Hearings on H.R. 2734 before a Subcomm. of the Senate Comm. on the Judiciary, 81st Cong. 1st & 2nd Sess. 206, 308 (1950) (statement of James L. Donnelly).

37.   *See* Note 13.

38.   In a merger involving the leading firm and innovative firm proviso set forth in Section 4.4, proven cost savings will only be considered if the post-merger HHI is 1800 or below.

39.   Example: In an industry with a 1% profit margin, proven cost savings of 3% would be significant.

40.   If a merger which produces cost savings of the magnitude specified does not simultaneously facilitate the exercise of market power, these savings should reduce consumer prices, an effect complementary to the purposes of section 7. However, if the merger simultaneously produces these efficiencies and creates or enhances market power, there is no likelihood that consumer prices will be reduced. In such circumstances consumer prices will probably rise as a result of the exercise of market power.

Court, will be a defense to an otherwise unlawful merger.[41] Because it may therefore allow anticompetitive mergers, the defense will be strictly construed.

The Attorneys General are unlikely to challenge an anticompetitive merger when one of the merging firms is a failing company and satisfies its burden of showing the following three elements: (1) that the resources of the allegedly failing firm are so depleted and the prospect of rehabilitation is so remote that the firm faces the grave probability of a business failure; (2) that it had made reasonable good faith efforts and had failed to find another reasonable prospective purchaser; and (3) that there is no less anticompetitive alternative available.[42]

---

41.   U.S. v. General Dynamics Corp., 415 U.S. 486, 507 (1974); U.S. v. Greater Buffalo Press, Inc., 402 U.S. 549, 555 (1971).

42.   The Attorneys General may exercise their prosecutorial discretion by declining to challenge a merger which will sustain a failing division of an otherwise viable firm. Since the failing division claim is highly susceptible to manipulation and abuse, the Attorneys General will view such claims with the utmost skepticism and in such cases require the three elements of the "failing firm" defense to be proven by clear and convincing evidence.

APPENDIX E

1988 ANTITRUST GUIDELINES FOR INTERNATIONAL OPERATIONS

Part I

1. Introduction
2. Relevant Antitrust Laws Enforced by the Department
   2.1   Sherman Act
   2.2   Clayton Act
   2.3   Hart-Scott-Rodino Antitrust Improvements Act of 1976
   2.4   National Cooperative Research Act of 1984
   2.5   Webb-Pomerene Act
   2.6   Export Trading Company Act of 1982
3. Enforcement Policy
   3.1   Criminal Violations of the Sherman Act
   3.2   Monopolization
   3.4   Joint Ventures
   3.5   Vertical Nonprice Distribution Restraints
   3.6   Intellectual Property Licensing Arrangements
4. Jurisdictional Considerations
   4.1   Foreign Trade Antitrust Improvement Act
   4.2   Foreign Sovereign Immunities Act
5. Factors Affecting the Department's Exercise of Discretion in Asserting Jurisdiction
6. Foreign Sovereign Compulsion
7. International Trade Friction and the U.S. Trade Laws
8. Conclusion

Part II.   Illustrative Cases

Case 1:   Merger of a U.S. Firm and a Foreign Firm
Case 2:   Merger Analysis Involving Trade Restraints
Case 3:   Acquisition of a Foreign Potential Competitor
Case 4:   Merger of Two Foreign Firms
Case 5:   Joint Bidding
Case 6:   Research and Development Joint Venture
Case 7:   Distributing a Foreign Competitor's Product
Case 8:   Exclusive Vertical Distribution Arrangements
Case 9:   A Multinational Operation
Case 10:   Vertical Restraints in a Patent License

Case 11: Exclusive Patent Cross Licenses with Grantbacks
Case 12: Know-How Technology Transfer Agreement with Exclusive Territories
Case 13: Anticompetitive Use of Section 337
Case 14: International Cartel Activities
Case 15: Government-Imposed Export Restraint
Case 16: Voluntary Export Restraint
Case 17: Settling a Trade Case
Case 18: Information Exchange in Connection with a Proceeding Under U.S. Trade Law

1. Introduction

The U.S. antitrust laws are the legal embodiment of our nation's commitment to a free market economy. The competitive process, unimpeded by privately and governmentally imposed barriers, ensures the most efficient allocation of resources and the maximization of consumer welfare. In enforcing the U.S. antitrust laws, the U.S. Department of Justice ("Department") focuses its efforts on protecting U.S. consumers from anticompetitive conduct. The Department does not seek to reach anticompetitive conduct that has no effect, or only a remote effect, on U.S. consumer welfare. To protect U.S. consumer welfare, however, the Department's enforcement efforts must sometimes reach foreign defendants and conduct that arguably occurs outside the territorial limits of the United States. For example, an international cartel of private producers cannot agree to impose higher prices on U.S. consumers with impunity simply by holding its cartel meetings outside the United States. On the other hand, in some cases, considerations of international comity may require the Department to take into account the interests of other nations that also may have jurisdiction over international conduct in determining whether to challenge that conduct.

These Guidelines are intended to provide businesses engaged in international operations with practical guidance concerning the Department's internal antitrust enforcement policies and procedures. The remainder of Part I of these Guidelines describes the most relevant applicable antitrust laws enforced by the Department (Section 2); the analysis the Department uses for enforcement purposes to assess the likely competitive effects of certain types of business conduct under those laws (Section 3); the jurisdictional rules that govern the Department's enforcement efforts (Section 4); factors that may affect the Department's decision whether to assert jurisdiction in a particular case (Section 5); circumstances under which alleged compulsion of private conduct by a foreign government will lead the Department not to prosecute anticompetitive conduct (Section 6); and the analysis the Department employs in assessing certain antitrust issues that may arise in the context of international trade frictions or disputes under the U.S. trade laws (Section 7). Part II of these Guidelines consists of eighteen hypothetical cases that illustrate the enforcement policies described in Part I.

These Guidelines are intended only to provide general guidance as to how the Department analyzes certain commonly occurring issues affecting its own enforcement decisions. Several caveats therefore apply to use of the Guidelines. First, these Guidelines are not intended to be a restatement of the law as it has developed in the courts.[1] Readers should separately evaluate the risk of private litigation by competitors, consumers, and suppliers, as well as the risk of enforcement by state prosecutors under state and federal antitrust laws. Second, these Guidelines do not express any view regarding the applicability of the laws of other nations. U.S. businesses engaged in or contemplating activities abroad or transactions with foreign partners should consider the applicability of foreign competition laws relating to

---

[1].   The Department may undertake a more extensive market power analysis under the rule of reason for enforcement purposes than some courts would require in litigation. The essential inquiry of both the Department and the courts under the antitrust laws remains the same, however – that is, whether a restraint would be anticompetitive.

business activities affecting commerce in those nations. Third, these Guidelines are not intended to substitute for the advice of experienced private antitrust counsel or for formal guidance under the Department's Business Review Procedure. Persons seeking more specific advance guidance concerning the Department's enforcement intentions with respect to a particular transaction should consider using the Business Review Procedure.[2] In addition, persons engaged in U.S. export trade can seek to obtain an export trade certificate of review conferring a limited immunity from suit under the U.S. federal and state antitrust laws for activities that meet the competition standards of the Export Trading Company Act of 1982.[3] Finally, although these Guidelines should improve the predictability of the Department's enforcement policy with respect to many common types of international business transactions, it is not possible to remove the exercise of judgment from the evaluation of conduct under the antitrust laws and the determination whether to assert jurisdiction in a given case. The standards set forth in these Guidelines will be applied reasonably and flexibly in each case.

2.   Relevant Antitrust Laws Enforced by the Department

2.0. The following is a brief summary of antitrust laws enforced by the Department that are likely to have the greatest significance in the planning of international business transactions.[4]

2.1. Sherman Act

Section 1 of the Sherman Act sets forth the basic antitrust prohibition against contracts, combinations, and conspiracies "in restraint of trade or commerce among the several States, or with foreign nations."[5] Section 2 of the Sherman Act prohibits monopolization, attempts to monopolize, and conspiracies to monopolize "any part of trade or commerce among the several States, or with foreign nations."[6] Section 6a of the Sherman Act defines the jurisdictional reach of the Sherman Act with respect to non-import foreign commerce.[7]

Violations of the Sherman Act may be prosecuted as civil or criminal offenses, depending on the nature of the violation.[8] Criminal violations of the Sherman Act

---

2.   28 C.F.R. § 50.6 (1987).

3.   See discussion at Section 2.6, *infra*.

4.   The Federal Trade Commission ("FTC") may proceed in a civil action under section 5 of the Federal Trade Commission Act ("FTC Act") (15 U.S.C. §§ 41-57c) against conduct that violates the Sherman Act and the Clayton Act as well as directly under the Clayton Act. The FTC has exclusive authority to enforce the FTC Act's prohibition against "unfair methods of competition" and "unfair or deceptive acts or practices" (15 U.S.C. § 45). Historically, the FTC, rather than the Department, has enforced the Robinson-Patman Act (15 U.S.C. §§ 13-13b, 21a). Only the Department, however, is authorized to prosecute criminal violations of the antitrust laws.

5.   15 U.S.C. § 1 (1982). The Wilson Tariff Act (15 U.S.C. §§ 8-11), which essentially parallels and is coextensive with section 1 of the Sherman Act, specifically prohibits conspiracies in restraint of U.S. import trade.

6.   15 U.S.C. § 2.

7.   15 U.S.C. § 6a (1982). *See* discussion at Section 4.1, *infra*.

8.   See discussion at Section 3.1, *infra*, concerning when conduct that violates the Sherman Act will be subject to criminal prosecution by the Department.

are punishable by fines and imprisonment. The Sherman Act provides that corporate defendants may be fined up to $1 million and individual defendants may be fined up to $100,000 and sentenced to up to three years of imprisonment. Under the Criminal Fine Enforcement Act of 1984[9] and the Sentencing Reform Act of 1984,[10] however, for felony violations continuing or committed after December 31, 1984, a corporate defendant may be fined up to $1 million, twice the gross pecuniary loss by victims, or twice the corporation's gross pecuniary gain from the violation, whichever is greatest. An individual defendant may be fined up to $250,000, twice the gross pecuniary loss by victims, or twice the defendant's gross pecuniary gain from the violation, whichever is greatest.[11] For antitrust felony violations committed or continuing on or after November 1, 1987, the U.S. Sentencing Commission's Sentencing Guidelines require convicted corporate defendants to be fined a minimum of $100,000 and require convicted individuals to be fined a minimum of $20,000.[12] The Sentencing Guidelines also generally require sentencing of individuals to a minimum of four months incarceration, with substantially longer sentences required as the amount of commerce involved in the conspiracy increases.[13] In a civil proceeding, the Department may obtain injunctive relief or actual damages where the U.S. Government is the purchaser of affected goods or services.[14]

2.2. *Clayton Act*

Section 7 of the Clayton Act expands on the general prohibitions of the Sherman Act by prohibiting a merger or acquisition of stock or assets "where in any line of commerce or in any activity affecting commerce in any section of the country, the effect of such acquisition may be substantially to lessen competition, or to tend to create a monopoly."[15] Section 15 of the Clayton Act empowers the Attorney General to seek a court order enjoining consummation of a merger that would violate Section 7.[16]

---

9.   Pub. L. 98-596, 18 U.S.C. § 3623 (repealed eff. Nov. 1, 1987, by the Sentencing Reform Act of 1984).

10.   Chapter II of the Comprehensive Crime Control Act of 1984, Pub. L. 98-473, as amended by § 6 of the Criminal Fine Improvements Act of 1987, Pub. L. 100-185, 18 U.S.C. § 3571.

11.   Although the Criminal Fine Enforcement Act was repealed by the Sentencing Reform Act as of November 1, 1987, it continues to govern fines for offenses continuing or committed after December 31, 1984 and before November 1, 1987. The Sentencing Reform Act applies to offenses continuing or committed on or after November 1, 1987. The Criminal Fine Improvements Act, which amended the Sentencing Reform Act to include alternative fines of the greater of twice the gain or twice the loss, was approved on December 11, 1987.

12.   Sentencing Guidelines and Policy Statement, United States Sentencing Commission (April 13, 1987) (hereinafter "Sentencing Guidelines"). The U.S. Sentencing Commission was created by Congress to establish sentencing policies and practices for the federal criminal justice system to ensure that the purposes of sentencing (e.g., deterrence and punishment) are met and to provide certainty and fairness in sentencing by avoiding unwarranted disparities among similarly situated offenders while permitting individualized sentences when justified by mitigating or aggravating circumstances. Federal Sentencing Guidelines Manual 1.1 (1988).

13.   *See* Sentencing Guidelines § 2R1.1.

14.   *See* 15 U.S.C. § 4 (injunctive relief); 15 U.S.C. § 15a (damages).

15.   15 U.S.C. § 18 (1982).

16.   15 U.S.C. § 25.

Section 3 of the Clayton Act prohibits any person engaged in commerce from leasing or selling patented or unpatented products for use, consumption, or resale within the United States or from in any way fixing the price of such products on a condition, agreement, or understanding that the lessee or purchaser will not use or deal in the products of any competitor of the lessor or seller if the effect may be "to substantially lessen competition or to tend to create a monopoly in any line of commerce."[17]

Under the Clayton Act, "commerce" includes "trade or commerce among the several States and with foreign nations." "Persons" include corporations and associations existing under or authorized either by the laws of the United States or any of its states or territories or by the laws of any foreign country.[18]

2.3. Hart-Scott-Rodino Antitrust Improvements Act of 1976

The Hart-Scott-Rodino Antitrust Improvements Act of 1976 ("H-S-R Act") provides the Department and the FTC with several procedural devices to facilitate enforcement of the antitrust laws with respect to anticompetitive mergers and acquisitions.[19] The H-S-R Act requires persons engaged in commerce or in any activity affecting commerce to notify the Department and the FTC of proposed mergers or acquisitions that would exceed certain size-of-parties and size-of-transaction thresholds,[20] to provide certain information relating to reportable transactions,[21] and to wait for a prescribed period — 15 days for cash tender offers and 30 days for all other transactions — before consummating the transaction.[22] The Department or the FTC may request additional information concerning a transaction and thereby extend the waiting period beyond the receipt of the requested information by 10 days in the case of cash tender offers and 20 days for all other transactions.[23]

The H-S-R Act and the FTC rules implementing the H-S-R Act exempt from the premerger notification requirements certain international transactions (typically those having little nexus to U.S. commerce) that otherwise meet the thresholds set forth in the Act.[24] Failure substantially to comply with the H-S-R Act is punishable by civil penalties of up to $10,000 for each day a violation continues.[25] The Department may also obtain injunctive relief to remedy a failure to comply with the H-S-R

---

17.   15 U.S.C. § 14.
18.   15 U.S.C. § 12.
19.   15 U.S.C. § 18a (1982).
20.   15 U.S.C. § 18a(a). Whether or not the H-S-R Act premerger notification thresholds are satisfied, the Department may request the parties to a merger affecting U.S. commerce voluntarily to provide information concerning the transaction or may issue Civil Investigative Demands ("CIDs") (15 U.S.C. §§ 1311-1314).
21.   15 U.S.C. § 18a(a), (d); 16 C.F.R. § 803.1 (1988).
22.   15 U.S.C. § 18a(b).
23.   15 U.S.C. § 18a(e).
24.   16 C.F.R. §§ 801.1(e), 801.1(k), 802.50-802.52. Circumstances under which the acquisition by one foreign corporation of the stock of another foreign corporation would be exempt from the premerger notification requirements of the H-S-R Act are explained and illustrated in Case 4 of these Guidelines.
25.   15 U.S.C. § 18a(g)(1).

Act.[26] Businesses may seek an interpretation of their obligations under the H-S-R Act from the FTC.[27]

2.4. National Cooperative Research Act of 1984

The National Cooperative Research Act of 1984 ("NCRA") clarifies substantive application of the U.S. antitrust laws to joint research and development ("R&D") activities.[28] The NCRA requires U.S. courts to judge the competitive effects of joint R&D in properly defined, relevant technology markets under a rule-of-reason standard that balances the procompetitive benefits of joint R&D against any potential anticompetitive effects.[29] The NCRA also limits the monetary relief that may be obtained in civil suits against participants in joint R&D to actual, rather than treble, damages where the challenged conduct is within the scope of notification filed by the joint R&D venture with the Attorney General and the FTC.[30]

2.5. Webb-Pomerene Act

The Webb-Pomerene Act provides a limited antitrust exemption for the formation and operation of associations of otherwise competing businesses to engage in collective export sales.[31] The exemption applies only to the export of "goods, wares, or merchandise."[32] It does not apply to conduct that has an anticompetitive effect in the United States or that injures domestic competitors of the members of an export association.[33] Associations seeking an exemption under the Webb-Pomerene Act must file their articles of agreement and annual reports with the FTC, but pre-formation approval from the FTC is not required.[34]

2.6. Export Trading Company Act of 1982

The Export Trading Company Act of 1982 (the "ETC Act") is designed to increase U.S. exports of goods and services by encouraging more efficient provision of export trade services to U.S. producers and suppliers, by reducing restrictions on trade financing provided by financial institutions, and by reducing uncertainty concerning application of the U.S. antitrust laws to U.S. export trade.[35] Title III of the ETC Act establishes a procedure by which persons engaged in U.S. export trade can obtain an export trade certificate of review. Persons named in the certificate obtain limited immunity from suit under state and federal antitrust laws for activities that are specified in and comply with the terms of the certificate.[36]

Certificates are issued by the Secretary of Commerce with the concurrence of the

---

26.   15 U.S.C. § 18a(g)(2).
27.   See 16 C.F.R. § 803.30.
28.   15 U.S.C. §§ 4301-4305 (Supp. II 1984).
29.   15 U.S.C. § 4302.
30.   15 U.S.C. § 4303(a).
31.   15 U.S.C. §§ 61-65(1982).
32.   15 U.S.C. § 61.
33.   15 U.S.C. § 62.
34.   15 U.S.C. § 65.
35.   15 U.S.C. §§ 4001-4053 (1982).
36.   15 U.S.C. §§ 4011-4021.

Attorney General. To obtain a certificate, an applicant must show that proposed export conduct will:

(1) result in neither a substantial lessening of competition or restraint of trade within the United States nor a substantial restraint of the export trade of any competitor of the applicant;

(2) not unreasonably enhance, stabilize, or depress prices in the United States of the class of goods or services covered by the application;

(3) not constitute unfair methods of competition against competitors engaged in the export of the class of goods or services exported by the applicant; and

(4) not include any act that may reasonably be expected to result in the sale for consumption or resale in the United States of such goods or services.[37]

Although an export trade certificate of review provides significant protection under the antitrust laws, it does have limitations. First, conduct that falls outside the scope of a certificate remains fully subject to private and governmental enforcement actions. Second, a certificate that is obtained by fraud is void from the outset and thus offers no protection under the antitrust laws. Third, any person that has been injured by certified conduct may recover actual (rather than treble) damages if that conduct is found to violate any of the statutory criteria described above. In any such action, certified conduct enjoys a presumption of legality, and the prevailing party is entitled to recover costs and attorneys' fees.[38] Fourth, a certificate confers no protection from prosecution under foreign laws.

The Secretary of Commerce may revoke or modify a certificate if the Secretary or the Attorney General determines that the applicant's export activities have ceased to comply with the statutory criteria for obtaining a certificate.[39] The Attorney General may also bring suit under section 15 of the Clayton Act to enjoin conduct that threatens "a clear and irreparable harm to the national interest."[40]

The Commerce Department, in consultation with the Justice Department, has issued guidelines setting forth the standards used in reviewing certificate applications.[41] The ETC Guidelines contain several examples illustrating application of the certification standards to specific export trade conduct, including the use of vertical and horizontal restraints and technology licensing arrangements. In addition, the Commerce Department's Export Trading Company Guidebook[42] provides information on the functions and advantages of establishing or using an export trading company, including factors to consider in applying for a certificate of review. The Commerce Department Office of Export Trading Company Affairs provides advice and information on the formation of export trading companies and facilitates

---

37.   15 U.S.C. § 4013(a).

38.   15 U.S.C. § 4016(b)(1), (b)(4).

39.   15 U.S.C. § 4014(b)(2).

40.   15 U.S.C. § 40l6(b)(5).

41.   See Department of Commerce, International Trade Administration, Guidelines for the Issuance of Export Trade Certificates of Review (2d ed.), 50 Fed. Reg. 1786 (Jan. 11, 1985) (hereinafter "ETC Guidelines").

42.   The Export Trading Company Guidebook, U.S. Department of Commerce, International Trade Administration (March 1984).

contacts between producers of exportable goods and services and firms offering export trade services.

Title IV of the ETC Act (the "Foreign Trade Antitrust Improvement Act of 1984") clarifies the jurisdictional reach of the Sherman Act and the FTC Act with respect to non-import foreign commerce. Title IV of the ETC Act is discussed further in Section 4.1 of these Guidelines.

3.   Enforcement Policy

3.0.   Unlike many of the legal rules that businesses encounter in their international dealings, the U.S. antitrust laws do not provide a checklist of detailed regulatory requirements.   Instead, the U.S. antitrust laws establish broad principles of competition that are designed to preserve an unrestrained interaction of competitive forces that will yield the best allocation of resources, the lowest prices, and the highest quality products and services for consumers. These Guidelines set forth the principles and standards the Department employs in enforcing the broad competition mandate embodied in those laws.[43]

Despite the literal terms of section 1 of the Sherman Act, which condemns "[e]very contract [or] combination . . . in restraint of trade," it has long been recognized that section 1 prohibits only unreasonable restraints of trade.   Nearly all productive activity involves cooperation that limits the independent commercial decision making of the parties and that therefore literally could be said to restrain trade.   Such cooperation, however, more often than not increases productive efficiency and thereby increases consumer welfare.[44] For enforcement purposes, the Department views as "unreasonable" restraints of trade that would create, enhance, or facilitate the exercise of market power where the risk of anticompetitive effect is not outweighed by the potential for procompetitive integrative efficiencies.   "Market power" for this purpose is the power profitably to restrict output or raise (or depress) price in a relevant market for a significant period of time.[45]

As a general matter, the Department uses two modes of analysis: per se condemnation and case-by-case examination under a "rule of reason."   The Department condemns as per se unlawful "naked" restraints of trade that are so inherently anticompetitive and so rarely beneficial that extensive analysis of their precise competitive effects is unnecessary. The Department considers a restraint to be naked if it is a type of restraint that is inherently likely to restrict output or raise

---

43.   As stated at n.l and accompanying text, *supra*, these Guidelines are not a restatement of the law as it has been developed and continues to evolve in the courts.   Rather, these Guidelines describe the analysis the Department employs in determining whether to challenge conduct or transactions under the U.S. antitrust laws because of their anticompetitive effect in the United States. These Guidelines thus are not intended to provide guidance as to whether a particular transaction or course of conduct is likely to be challenged by state prosecutors or private litigants.

44.   *See, e.g.,* Business Electronics Corp. v. Sharp Electronics Corp., 108 S. Ct. 1515 (1988).

45.   When a firm or a combination of firms is able artificially to restrict output and maintain price above a competitive level, the result is a transfer of wealth from buyers to sellers and a misallocation of society's resources. The exercise of market power by buyers has wealth transfer and resource misallocation effects analogous to those associated with the exercise of market power by sellers. All references in these Guidelines to raising price should be read to include depressing price where the concern is with the exercise of market power by buyers.

price and is not plausibly related to some form of economic integration (by contract or otherwise) of the parties' operations that in general may generate procompetitive efficiencies. The most common examples of naked restraints of trade are price-fixing and bid-rigging schemes among competitors. The Department prosecutes naked restraints of trade among competitors as criminal violations under the Sherman Act.[46]

On the other hand, the Department applies a rule-of-reason analysis to agreements that involve some form of economic integration that goes beyond the mere coordination of the parties' decisions on price or output and that in general may generate procompetitive efficiencies.[47] Examples of such integrative efficiencies include those that would enable the parties to produce greater output at the same or less cost, to produce new products or services that otherwise would not be produced, or to undertake research and development that would not be undertaken without such cooperation. Such efficiencies typically result if the parties possess complementary skills and assets or if the arrangement would allow them to take advantage of significant economies of scale or scope in production, distribution, or R&D. On the other hand, an agreement among competitors to set a minimum price, for example, would not be saved from per se condemnation simply because the defendants claimed that the agreement eliminated the transaction costs that consumers would otherwise incur in searching out the lowest price. It similarly would be no defense that a cartel agreement was necessary to restrain ruinous competition that made it difficult to maintain quality levels or that created confusion for consumers. Examples of conduct that the Department analyzes under a rule of reason include legitimate joint ventures for R&D, production, or distribution; vertical nonprice distribution arrangements; and intellectual property licensing arrangements.

Once the Department concludes that a particular transaction or course of conduct should be analyzed under a rule of reason, the Department's first question is whether the transaction or conduct would likely create, enhance, or facilitate the exercise of market power in any relevant market.[48] A number of different factors are relevant

---

46.   *See* discussion at Section 3.1, *infra*.

47.   The Department does not attempt to determine at this initial characterization stage whether the economic integration involved in a particular transaction actually would generate efficiencies. It is enough if the form of integration involved in general generates efficiencies. Thus, for example, because integration in the form of standards setting or technology licensing in general often generates efficiencies, particular transactions or conduct involving such integration is not condemned per se, but is evaluated under a rule of reason. The Department considers whether a specific transaction involving such integration actually would generate efficiencies only if a rule-of-reason analysis indicates that, under the circumstances, the transaction would likely create, enhance, or facilitate the exercise of market power.

48.   The Department does not require the parties to a transaction to demonstrate the necessity of particular restrictions associated with a legitimate joint venture, distribution arrangement, or intellectual property licensing arrangement. Instead, as discussed *infra*, if the Department determines that a transaction would likely create, enhance, or facilitate the exercise of market power in one or more markets, then the Department may consider whether particular restrictions are necessary to achieve offsetting efficiency benefits claimed by the parties. Of course, restraints associated with a joint venture or other arrangement that is merely a sham disguising naked price fixing, and restraints that themselves are naked agreements to fix price or output unrelated to any integration involved in the underlying transaction, would likely be prosecuted as criminal violations of the Sherman Act. For example, the Department would likely

to answering this question, depending upon the conduct involved. For example, in analyzing a merger or joint venture among competitors, the Department considers, among other factors, the level of concentration in affected markets, the ability of existing and new competitors (including foreign firms) to frustrate any attempted exercise of market power, and characteristics of the relevant product or products that would make successful collusion more or less likely.

If the Department concludes that a particular transaction or course of conduct would not be anticompetitive, then the Department will not challenge it, regardless of whether the transaction or conduct actually would result in significant procompetitive efficiencies. The Department examines the procompetitive justifications for a transaction or course of conduct only if the Department concludes that the transaction or conduct would likely create, enhance, or facilitate the exercise of market power in some market or markets.

If the Department does conclude that the transaction or conduct would likely create, enhance, or facilitate the exercise of market power, then the Department considers whether the risk of anticompetitive harm is outweighed by procompetitive efficiencies that the parties claim will result from the transaction or conduct. The Department's comparison of anticompetitive risks and procompetitive efficiencies is necessarily a qualitative one, rather than one based on precise measures of welfare effects. The risk of anticompetitive effects in a particular case may be insignificant compared to the expected benefits, or vice versa. The parties must establish a greater level of expected net efficiencies the more significant are the competitive risks.

Of course, if it is clear that equivalent efficiencies can be achieved by means that involve no anticompetitive effect, then the Department will not recognize the parties' efficiencies claim. In addition, although the Department in general considers the cumulative effects of restrictions associated with a transaction or course of conduct, if a restriction that would have an anticompetitive effect does not contribute to (i.e., is not related to) achieving the claimed efficiencies, then the Department will likely require the restriction to be stricken before approving the transaction or course of conduct.

In applying the foregoing analysis, the Department does not discriminate against foreign firms. Nor is the Department concerned with conduct that solely affects foreign consumers. Rather, the Department is concerned about transactions and conduct that, under the analysis described above, would likely result in reduced output and increased prices to U.S. consumers. In addition, in enforcing U.S. antitrust laws, the Department is concerned about effects on competition, rather than on competitors.

* * *

The remaining part of this section describes in general how the Department analyzes the competitive effects of six types of conduct: criminal violations

---

prosecute as a violation of the Sherman Act an agreement in a joint venture to produce pocket calculators that fixed the price of ball point pens. The Department will not treat as a sham, however, any restraint that is plausibly related to the economic integration entailed in the underlying transaction.

of section 1 of the Sherman Act; monopolization; mergers; joint ventures; vertical nonprice distribution arrangements; and intellectual property licensing arrangements.

3.1. Criminal Violations of the Sherman Act

The Department prosecutes naked agreements among competitors to restrict output or raise price as criminal violations of section 1 of the Sherman Act.[49] Conduct prosecuted as a criminal violation typically possesses four characteristics: (1) (except for monopolization involving independently illegal acts, such as bribery or physical violence) the conduct involves agreement among actual, potential, or apparent competitors; (2) that agreement is inherently likely to restrict output and raise (or, in the case of monopsony, to lower) price without the promise of any significant integrative efficiency benefit; (3) the agreement is generally covert or fraudulent; and (4) the conspirators generally are aware of the probable anticompetitive consequences of their conduct.[50]

Neither an express agreement nor an overt act pursuant to an agreement is necessary to warrant criminal prosecution. Nor is it necessary that conspirators agree to charge exactly the same price for a product or service. For example, naked agreements among competitors to raise their individual prices by a specified amount, to maintain a specified profit margin, to adopt a standard formula for computing price, or to notify one another before reducing price are also criminal violations of section 1 of the Sherman Act. It is also not necessary that a particular agreement be successful, or that it have an actual, demonstrable anticompetitive effect.

The Department's analysis of various substantive and jurisdictional issues that may arise with respect to international price and output agreements among competitors is illustrated in Case 14 (International Cartel Activities), Case 15 (Government-Imposed Export Restraint), Case 16 (Voluntary Export Restraint), Case 17 (Settling a Trade Case), and Case 18 (Information Exchange in Connection With a Proceeding Under U.S. Trade Law).

3.2. Monopolization

The offense of unlawful monopolization under section 2 of the Sherman Act has two elements: (i) the possession of monopoly power in a relevant market and (ii) willful acquisition or maintenance of that power through anticompetitive or

---

49.   See discussion of naked restraints of trade at Section 3.0, *supra*. In addition to prosecuting such naked restraints of trade under the Sherman Act, in appropriate circumstances the Department may add charges under other federal statutes, including the Racketeer Influenced and Corrupt Organization ("RICO") law (18 U.S.C. §§ 1961-1964) and statutes prohibiting mail and wire fraud (18 U.S.C. §§ 1341, 1343); conspiracy to defraud the government (18 U.S.C. § 371); making false statements to a government agency (18 U.S.C. § 1001); and tax offenses (26 U.S.C. § 7201). In addition to fines and imprisonment available for Sherman Act violations, in appropriate cases the Department may also seek civil damages under the Clayton Act (15 U.S.C. § 15a) for injury to the United States and damages or civil penalties under the False Claims Act (31 U.S.C. § 3729).

50.   These characteristics are not, however, legal constraints on the cases that may be prosecuted as criminal violations. See "Criminal Enforcement of the Antitrust Laws: Targeting Naked Cartel Restraints," Remarks by Charles F. Rule, Assistant Attorney General, Antitrust Division, Department of Justice, before the 36th Annual ABA Antitrust Section Spring Meeting (March 24, 1988), *reprinted in* 57 Antitrust L.J. 257 (1988).

predatory acts, as opposed to growth or development as a consequence of superior product, business acumen, or "historic accident."[51] The offense of unlawful attempt to monopolize has three elements: (i) a specific intent to monopolize; (ii) the use of anticompetitive or predatory means to that end; and (iii) a dangerous probability that the attempt will succeed.

If it appears that there is no dangerous probability of achieving or sustaining monopoly power, then the Department will not inquire further. In assessing the probability of successful monopolization, the Department considers the market share of the firm, concentration in the market, and the probability that new competitors would enter the market in response to an anticompetitive price increase.

Where market conditions indicate a dangerous probability of monopolization, the Department proceeds to assess whether the conduct in question is predatory (that is, whether it is inefficient and aimed at achieving or maintaining market power).[52] In making this assessment, the Department is sensitive to the inherent difficulty of distinguishing between efficient forms of vigorous competition and inefficient forms of predation. The same type of conduct that plausibly could be part of a predatory monopolization strategy may actually be a legitimate effort to win customers. For example, what might be labelled as predatory pricing may actually be promotional pricing that benefits consumers. The Department therefore exercises considerable caution to ensure that its enforcement with respect to unilateral conduct will not punish or deter procompetitive activity that the antitrust laws are designed to preserve.

In the international context, claims of anticompetitive single-firm conduct most frequently arise in two situations. First, when a foreign firm sells a product or service in the United States more cheaply than it sells that product or service abroad, U.S. competitors may allege that the pricing is predatory, aimed at achieving sustainable market power by driving U.S. firms out of the market. Second, when U.S. firms prosecute actions under the U.S. trade laws, those actions may be alleged to be part of a predatory attempt to disadvantage foreign competitors by forcing them to bear significant litigation costs.[53]

As a general matter, the Department considers pricing and other conduct to be

---

51.   United States v. Grinnell Corp., 384 U.S. 563, 570-71 (1966).

52.   Predatory conduct that is likely to create or sustain monopoly power is often economically implausible. For predation to succeed, the firm pursuing the predatory strategy must be able first to acquire market power by disadvantaging competitors and then to collect sufficiently large profits through the exercise of that market power to earn least at the market rate of return on its investment in (that is, the cost of) the predatory conduct without giving rise to new entry that competes away any monopoly profits. In some cases, particularly where the predatory activity involves underpricing competitors until they are forced to exit the market, the costs that must be recouped will far outweigh the increased profits available from an increase in market power. See, e.g., Matsushita Electric Industrial Co. v. Zenith Radio Corp., 475 U.S. 574, 588-90 (1986) (discussing implausibility of predatory pricing strategies). In general, the Department will not be concerned with unilateral conduct if a firm has a market share of less than 35 percent. Cf. U.S. Department of Justice Merger Guidelines (June 14, 1984) (hereinafter "Merger Guidelines") (analysis of vertical mergers), reprinted in 4 Trade Reg. Rep. (CCH) ¶ 13,103.

53.   In addition, parties to a naked agreement to restrain trade might use predation against firms outside the agreement (to prevent them from underselling the cartel) or against parties to the agreement (to punish them for cheating on the cartel). The Department normally would challenge such conduct along with the underlying naked agreement to restrain trade as a criminal violation of section 1 of the Sherman Act.

predatory only when, judged objectively, it appears to be consistent only with an anticompetitive purpose. In particular, with respect to alleged predatory pricing, the Department seeks to ascertain the relationship between a firm's prices and its costs of providing the good or service. If its price covers those costs, then the Department concludes that the conduct is consistent with procompetitive, profit-maximizing behavior.[54] The cost standard that the Department uses may vary depending on the nature of the industry and information available to the Department. The Department may use average variable cost, marginal cost, or incremental (out-of-pocket) cost, whichever available measure is closest to the firm's additional cost of providing the last unit of output.[55] As a general rule, however, the Department will not challenge pricing as predatory where prices are not below marginal cost or some reasonable approximation of marginal cost.[56]

The use of governmental processes to disadvantage a competitor and thus to increase market power is in general a more plausible anticompetitive strategy than is pricing below cost because a firm may be able to trigger significant litigation costs and other administrative burdens at little cost to itself. Application of the antitrust laws in these contexts is limited, however, by the First Amendment to the U.S. Constitution, which protects the right to petition the government, and by government's need to receive information to assist it in its governing functions.[57] Indeed, many governmental processes are designed precisely to allow firms to attempt to exclude existing or potential competitors (for example, because a competitor has engaged in unlawful dumping or because a licensing authority determines that the market is already adequately served). The need to protect legitimate petitioning activity is not raised, however, when governmental processes are used solely as a means of imposing direct costs on competitors, rather than as part of a genuine effort to solicit government action. In appropriate circumstances, therefore, the Department may challenge the abuse of governmental processes to disadvantage a competitor. Case 13 illustrates the Department's analysis in the context of the filing of an action under the U.S. trade laws to exclude a competitor's product from the United States.

3.3. Mergers

The Department recognizes that mergers and acquisitions generally play a crucial

---

54.   *See, e.g.*, Letter to William C. Clarke, Esq., Counsel for British Airways PLC, from J. Paul McGrath, Assistant Attorney General, Antitrust Division, Dec. 20, 1984.

55.   For example, in the case of products characterized by costs that decline as firms gain experience in the industry (or move along the learning curve), the appropriate measure of marginal cost may be the last unit of projected output. *See* "Claims of Predation in a Competitive Marketplace: When is an Antitrust Response Appropriate?," Remarks by Charles F. Rule, Assistant Attorney General, Antitrust Division, Department of Justice, before the 1988 ABA Annual Meeting (Aug. 9, 1988), *reprinted in* 57 Antitrust L.J. 421 (1988).

56.   Even if the Department would not challenge pricing as predatory under the antitrust laws, however, such pricing by foreign firms selling into the United States may violate U.S. antidumping law. The purpose of the U.S. antidumping law is different from the purpose of the antitrust laws; by its terms, U.S. antidumping law may condemn pricing that is above a firm's marginal cost. The U.S. Department of Commerce and the U.S. International Trade Commission, rather than the Department of Justice, enforce U.S. antidumping law.

57.   *See* discussion of *Noerr-Pennington* doctrine at Section 7, *infra*.

and beneficial role in our economy. They can discipline ineffective management and facilitate the movement of investment capital and productive assets through the economy to more highly valued uses. They may also enable industries to undertake restructuring that is necessary to remain competitive in changing markets, allow the realization of significant joint-operating efficiencies, and enable the combined firm to provide new products or better products than either firm could provide separately. While challenging competitively harmful mergers, the Department seeks to avoid unnecessary interference with the larger universe of mergers that are either competitively beneficial or neutral.

The standards and principles the Department applies in analyzing mergers are set forth in detail in the Department's Merger Guidelines.[58] The Department's merger enforcement policy is targeted at those mergers that would create, enhance, or facilitate the exercise of market power in the United States.[59] Where only a few firms account for most of the sales of a product or service for which there are no good substitutes, those firms in some circumstances might be able tacitly or explicitly to coordinate their actions to restrict output and raise price. Other things being equal, where collusion among firms is necessary to exercise market power, such collusion is more likely to occur and to be successful among a small group of firms in a highly concentrated market.[60]   Reaching and enforcing an agreement concerning output or price would be difficult and costly — and would be more likely to be detected by criminal prosecutors — if many firms would have to be included in an agreement to make a collusive price increase successful. Therefore, a merger that would reduce the number of sellers of a product or service in a market to only a few might substantially lessen competition unless other factors, such as the threat of entry by new sellers or expansion by fringe firms, would frustrate any attempted exercise of market power.

The ease and profitability of collusion is less relevant where a merger involves an acquisition by a single dominant firm (a firm that has a market share of at least 35 percent) of another firm in the market. In that case, the dominant firm might itself be able to exercise market power by restricting its own output and raising price. The Department is likely to challenge a merger between any firm with a significant market share and a dominant firm unless changing market conditions,[61] the financial condition of the firms,[62] ease of entry into the market,[63] or significant efficiencies that would result from the merger[64] indicate that on balance the merger would not likely be anticompetitive.[65]

In determining whether one or more firms would be able to exercise market power, the Department evaluates both the probable demand responses of consumers and the probable supply responses of other firms. An attempt to exercise market power could be made unprofitable by any of four types of demand or supply responses: (1) consumers switching to other products; (2) consumers switching to the same product

---

58.   Merger Guidelines, *supra* note 52.
59.   Merger Guidelines § 1.
60.   *Id.*
61.   *Id.* § 3.21.
62.   *Id.* § 3.22.
63.   *Id.* § 3.3.
64.   *Id.* § 3.5.
65.   *Id.* § 3.12.

produced by firms in other areas; (3) producers of other products switching existing facilities to production of the product; or (4) producers entering into the production of the product by substantially modifying existing facilities or by constructing new facilities.[66]   Each type of response is considered in the Department's merger analysis, which is summarized below.

3.31.   MARKET DEFINITION

The first step in the Department's merger analysis is to identify the relevant market or markets that would be affected by the merger and the competitors in that market or those markets.[67] The Merger Guidelines provide a paradigm for defining the relevant product and geographic markets that is based on the likely demand response of consumers to an anticompetitive price increase. The result of applying this paradigm is to identify a group of products (the "product market") and a geographic area (the "geographic market") with respect to which sellers could exercise market power if they were able perfectly to coordinate their actions so as to act like a monopolist.[68]   Stated another way, market definition identifies which sellers would have to coordinate their pricing and/or output decisions to exercise market power.[69] Market definition is illustrated in Case 1 of these Guidelines.

3.32.   COMPETITIVE ANALYSIS

If merging firms compete in the same product and geographic market, the Department next determines whether the elimination of competition between them would likely create, enhance, or facilitate the exercise of market power. To make this determination, the Department focuses first on the level of and increase in concentration in the market that would result from the merger.[70]

The Department divides the spectrum of market concentration as measured by the HHI (which ranges from near zero in an atomistic market to 10,000 in the case of a pure monopoly) into three regions that can be broadly characterized as unconcentrated (post-merger HHI below 1000), moderately concentrated (post-merger HHI between 1000 and 1800), and highly concentrated (post-merger

---

66.   *Id.* § 2.0.

67.   *Id.*

68.   *Id.* § 2.1 (product market definition) and § 2.3 (geographic market definition). Under some analytical approaches, production substitution (that is, the ability of a seller to shift the use of production and distribution assets from producing and selling one product to producing and selling another) is reflected in the description of the relevant product market. The Department, however, defines the relevant product market by reference to demand substitution and accounts for production substitution when it identifies firms competing in the relevant market. Merger Guidelines § 2.21 & n.9.

69.   The Department also uses this paradigm whenever it defines a market in examining the competitive effects of conduct such as joint ventures, nonprice vertical distribution restraints, and intellectual property licensing arrangements.

70.   Market concentration is a function of the number of firms in a market and their respective market shares.   To assist in interpreting market data, the Department uses the Herfindahl-Hirschman Index ("HHI") of concentration. The HHI is calculated by summing the squares of the market shares of individual firms in the market. The HHI gives proportionately greater weight to larger firms to reflect their relatively greater importance in collusive interaction. Merger Guidelines § 3.1.

HHI above 1800).[71] The Department will not challenge a merger that would result in an HHI of less than 1000 because the structure of the market itself indicates that the successful exercise of market power by one or more firms is unlikely. The Department also will not challenge a merger that would result in moderate concentration if the level of concentration would increase by 100 HHI points or less, or a merger that would result in high concentration if the level of concentration would increase by 50 HHI points or less.

The HHI concentration thresholds set forth in the Department's Merger Guidelines are, however, not bright line tests except to the extent that they define "safe harbors." Where a merger does not fall within an HHI "safe harbor," the Department proceeds to consider the merger's effect on concentration along with all other relevant factors bearing on whether the merger would likely create, enhance, or facilitate the exercise of market power.[72] A merger in a highly concentrated market may result in no ability to exercise market power, for example, if any attempt to restrict output or raise price would be frustrated by new entry or by expansion by fringe firms, or if other factors (such as the heterogeneous nature of the product) would make successful collusion unlikely.[73] In addition, efficiencies that could only be achieved through the merger may be so significant that, despite its anticompetitive potential, the merger's net effect would not be anticompetitive.

3.321. Special Factors Affecting the Significance of Market Share and Market Concentration Data

In evaluating market concentration data, the Department considers a number of factors that may indicate that the current market shares of individual firms either overstate or understate their competitive significance. One such factor is recent or ongoing changes in market conditions. For example, if a technology that is important to long-term competitive viability is not available to a particular firm, the Department may conclude that the historical market share of that firm overstates its future competitive significance.[74]

Another factor that may affect the significance of current market share data is a firm's financial condition, to the extent that condition will likely decrease the firm's future competitive significance and is caused by an underlying structural weakness of the firm. For example, a firm's current market share may overstate its competitive significance if the firm suffers chronic financial difficulties resulting from obsolete production facilities in a market that is experiencing a long-term decline in demand.[75] The Department also considers special factors that may affect the

---

71.   *Id.*
72.   Merger Guidelines § 3.0. Conclusions as to the competitive threat posed by a merger that are based solely on concentration data may be flawed for two reasons. First, factors other than concentration may be more determinative of whether a merger would likely create, enhance, or facilitate the exercise of market power. *See id.* § 3.4; *see also* discussion below and at Section 3.322, *infra.* Second, current market shares (particularly if based on current sales) may not accurately reflect the future competitive significance of firms in the market. *See* Merger Guidelines § 3.2; Sections 3.321, 3.323, *infra.*
73.   Merger Guidelines §§ 1.3, 3.4.
74.   *Id.* § 3.21.
75.   *Id.* § 3.22. The Merger Guidelines also contain a "defense" applicable where one of the merging firms qualifies as a failing firm under standards set forth in the Merger Guidelines. *Id.* § 5.1.

competitive significance of foreign firms, such as U.S. government restrictions on imports or foreign export restrictions.[76] The Department's analysis of such trade restraints in evaluating the likely competitive effects of a merger is discussed in greater detail at Section 3.323, *infra,* and is illustrated in Case 2.

3.322. Other Relevant Competitive Factors

In addition to factors that may affect the future competitive significance of individual firms, the Department also considers the likelihood, timing, and scope of substantial new entry into the relevant market,[77] the likelihood of expansion by fringe firms,[78] and other factors (such as the nature of the relevant product and historical market performance) bearing on the ease and profitability of collusion in the relevant market.[79]

3.3221. Entry

Ease of entry is often the most significant of these factors. The Department is unlikely to challenge a merger if entry into the relevant market is so easy that existing competitors could not successfully raise price for any significant period of time (i.e., two years).[80] In analyzing entry conditions, the Department focuses on the practical, rather than the theoretical, ease of entry. The Department asks whether new firms actually would enter the market and counteract the merger's effect on price. For the purpose of the Department's analysis, the time it would take to enter the relevant market at an efficient scale of operation and the level of expected entry in response to a price increase are at least as important as the fact that entry can occur. Entry may be hindered, for example, by the need for scarce or specialized resources, the need to acquire a substantial share of the market in order to realize important economies of scale, or stagnation or decline in the relevant market that would make new entry unlikely to occur. The Department is more likely to challenge a merger that would result in a high degree of concentration in the relevant market as the difficulty of entry into the market increases.[81]

3.3222. Efficiencies

The Department generally will not challenge a merger if the parties can establish by clear and convincing evidence that the merger would result in significant procompetitive efficiencies that could not be achieved except through the merger and that the merger would therefore not likely result in a net decrease in consumer welfare.[82] The parties must establish a proportionately greater level of expected net efficiencies as the competitive risks of the merger increase.[83]

---

76.   *Id.* § 3.23.
77   *Id.* § 3.3 & n.21.
78.   *Id.* §§ 3.33 n.20; 3.43.
79.   *Id.* § 3.4.
80.   *Id.* § 3.3.
81.   *Id.*
82.   *Id.* § 3.5.
83.   *Id.*

3.323. *Foreign Competition*

Nothing in the U.S. antitrust laws restricts the acquisition of assets in the United States on the basis of the national origin of the investment.[84] The Department's competitive analysis therefore does not discriminate against or in favor of firms on the basis of their citizenship.

The existence of foreign competition, however, is relevant to the Department's analysis of any merger, whether or not one of the parties is foreign. Competition by foreign firms that are not involved in a merger may make the exercise of market power in the United States following a merger impossible if those foreign firms would increase their sales in the United States significantly in response to a significant and nontransitory price increase. On the other hand, constraints on foreign supply, such as U.S. import quotas and foreign export restraints, may prevent or limit a response by foreign producers to an anticompetitive price increase in the United States.

Existing foreign competitors are not excluded from a relevant market solely because their sales in the United States are subject to quotas or other governmentally-imposed trade restrictions. That is because it is difficult to assess the effectiveness or longevity of such restraints and to measure the likely offsetting supply responses of producers that are not subject to restraints. A quota that applied only to shipments from one country, for example, might have little or no impact on the overall level of foreign supply in response to a price increase in the United States if shipments could readily be shifted to the United States from other countries not subject to the quota or if firms in countries not subject to the quota could purchase the product from firms in countries subject to the quota and resell the product in the United States.

Nevertheless, any such constraint on the ability of foreign firms to respond to a price increase – and thus to frustrate an attempt to exercise market power in the United States – is an important fact that the Department considers in assessing a merger's likely competitive effects. Foreign firms that are subject to an effective, binding restraint[85] that limits the volume of their sales in the United States would be unable to constrain a domestic price increase. In fact, in the case of an effective, binding percentage quota, a reduction in domestic production would actually lead to reduced imports by foreign firms subject to the quota, making successful collusion in the United States even more likely.[86] In the extreme situation in which there were an effective, binding trade restraint that placed a fixed or percentage limitation

---

84.   Although foreign investment is not generally subject to special restrictions (exceptions include airline acquisitions and acquisitions of U.S. broadcasting stations), section 5021 of the Omnibus Trade and Competitiveness Act of 1988, Pub. L. No. 100-418 (Aug. 23, 1988) (hereinafter "1988 Trade Act"), authorizes the President to take action to suspend or prohibit mergers or acquisitions that would result in foreign control of persons engaged in U.S. interstate commerce if the President determines that doing so is necessary to protect U.S. national security interests. This authority is wholly separate from the Department's review of mergers and acquisitions under the U.S. antitrust laws as described in these Guidelines.

85.   An "effective" trade restraint is one that cannot be substantially avoided through diversion and arbitrage. A trade restraint is "binding" if firms would sell more than the restraint ceiling if the restraint did not exist.

86.   Merger Guidelines § 3.23.

on imports from all or virtually all foreign sources of supply, foreign firms would be accorded little, if any, competitive significance in the Department's analysis.[87]

Thus, while the Department's analysis under the Merger Guidelines expressly recognizes the significant competitive impact of foreign competition, the Department also recognizes that trade restraints can serve to insulate U.S. firms from foreign competition. The Department's analysis of special factors affecting the competitive significance of foreign firms is illustrated in Case 2 of these Guidelines.

The Department's analysis of a merger between a domestic and a foreign firm (including issues relating to market definition and the impact of trade restraints) is illustrated in Cases 1 and 2. Case 3 illustrates the Department's analysis of a merger involving a foreign potential competitor. Case 4 illustrates the circumstances in which the Department might challenge a merger between two foreign firms.

3.4. Joint Ventures

A joint venture is essentially any collaborative effort among firms, short of a merger, with respect to R&D, production, distribution, and/or the marketing of products or services. Joint ventures may be created for a variety of good business reasons. For example, joint ventures may be created to take advantage of complementary skills or economies of scale in production, marketing, or R&D, or to spread risk. In foreign markets in particular, joint ventures may be politically and commercially more practical than either merger or independent operation. Because joint ventures typically achieve integrative efficiencies, the Department judges the likely competitive effects of joint ventures under a rule of reason.

Simply labelling an arrangement a "joint venture," of course, will not protect what is actually a naked agreement on price or output among competitors. The nature of a putative joint venture's conduct — and not merely its designation as a joint venture by the parties — is determinative. The Department would not hesitate to prosecute an arrangement among competitors that was not plausibly related to some form of economic integration of the parties' operations, but rather was simply a device to restrict output or raise price. Similarly, a restraint associated with a joint venture must not be a naked agreement unrelated to any economic integration of the parties' operations, and designed instead simply to restrict output or raise price in a market other than one in which the joint venture integration occurs.[88]

3.41. RULE-OF-REASON ANALYSIS

The Department's rule-of-reason analysis of joint ventures involves four steps.[89]

---

87.   *Id.* § 3.23 & n.19.
88.   *See* Section 3.0, *supra.*
89.   The four-step analysis is a paradigm designed to ensure that the Department considers every possible anticompetitive effect (as well as, where necessary, the procompetitive efficiencies) before reaching a conclusion about the likely competitive effect of a joint venture. Few cases should actually require extensive analysis under each of the four steps. For example, if the joint venturers do not compete in any market, the Department would likely analyze the joint venture at most under steps 3 and 4. For a given joint venture, it may be quickly evident without extensive analysis (for example, based on the size of the firms involved or market concentration) that there is no competitive concern under one or more of the first three steps. In addition, it would not matter to the Department's analysis whether a joint venture's likely competitive effect in particular markets were analyzed under either step 1 or step 2, since the substantive analysis

First, the Department determines whether the joint venture would likely have anticompetitive effect in the market or markets in which the joint venture proposes to operate or in which the economic integration of the parties' operation occurs (the "joint venture markets").[90] Second, the Department determines whether the joint venture or any of its restraints would likely have an anticompetitive effect in any other market or markets ("spill-over markets") in which the joint venture members are actual or potential competitors outside of the joint venture. Third, using the analysis described in Section 3.5 of these Guidelines, the Department analyzes the likely competitive effects of any nonprice vertical restraints imposed in connection with the joint venture.[91] The Department will not challenge a joint venture if under the first three steps, the Department concludes that the joint venture would not likely have any significant anticompetitive effects. If, however, the Department's analysis under the first three steps reveals significant anticompetitive risks, then, under step 4, the Department considers whether any procompetitive efficiencies that the parties claim would be achieved by the joint venture would outweigh the risk of anticompetitive harm. Each of these four steps is discussed further below.

3.42.   STEP 1 – THE JOINT VENTURE MARKET OR MARKETS

The Department first determines whether the joint venture or any of its restraints restrict the independent decision making of competitors in the joint venture market (or markets) with respect to price or output. If the joint venture participants do not compete in the joint venture market and are not likely to begin doing so in the near future independently of the joint venture, then the Department can conclude that the joint venture poses no significant threat to competition in that market. In that case, the joint venture would not eliminate competition, but would increase production capacity in the joint venture market.

If a joint venture or any of its restraints restricts competition between or among participants in a joint venture market, then the Department determines whether the joint venture would likely create, enhance, or facilitate the exercise of market power in that market. As it does in analyzing mergers, after defining the relevant markets, the Department first focuses with respect to each market on the level of and increase in concentration that would result if the parties merged.[92] If, based on market concentration, the Department would not challenge a merger of the joint venture participants in a relevant market, then the Department concludes without detailed examination of other factors that the joint venture and its individual restraints would not likely have any anticompetitive effects in that market, and the Department would proceed to step 2. If concentration in the relevant market indicates that a merger of the joint venture participants could be anticompetitive, however, then the Department proceeds to examine other factors that bear on whether the joint venture would likely create, enhance, or facilitate the exercise of market power, including ease of entry into the relevant market and characteristics of the relevant product or

---

under both steps is identical.

90.   If a joint venture involved R&D, production and distribution, then the economic integration would occur at each of those three levels of the market.

91.   *See also* Section 3.6 (Intellectual Property Licensing Arrangements) and Case 6, *infra*.

92.   The Department applies the same market definition principles and analysis of market share and market concentration data as it applies in analyzing mergers. *See* Sections 3.31, 3.32, *supra.*

service that may make successful collusion more or less likely.

Depending on its structure, a joint venture may have a less restrictive effect on the independent decision making of joint venture participants with respect to price and output than would an outright merger. As a result, a joint venture may be substantially less likely than a merger to result in either the "unilateral" exercise of market power by the joint venture or successful tacit or explicit collusion between the joint venture (or its members) and other competitors in the relevant market.[93] For example, a joint venture may operate for only a limited period of time, or it may reserve substantial independent pricing, output, or marketing discretion to the individual venture members.[94] In such instances, the anticompetitive risks posed by a joint venture may be substantially less significant than if the parties merged.

As is implicit in this analysis, the Department in general is concerned about the anticompetitive effects of a joint venture when it is overinclusive — that is, when it restricts competition among competitors that account for a large portion of sales (or capacity) in the market, thereby creating, enhancing, or facilitating the exercise of market power. In fact, selectivity in the membership of a joint venture often enhances a joint venture's procompetitive potential. Forcing joint ventures to open membership to all competitors (or to license the product of an R&D joint venture to all who seek licenses) would decrease the incentives to form joint ventures, particularly those that are formed to undertake risky endeavors such as research and development and innovative manufacturing. For example, the inability to exclude those who would bring little or nothing to the joint venture, or those who would fail to share fully in the risks, would decrease the efficiency of the joint venture and reduce the expected reward from successfully accomplishing the joint venture's mission. An enforcement policy that denied a joint venture the ability to select its members might also encourage firms to forego risky endeavors in the hope of being able to gain access through antitrust litigation to the fruits of the successful endeavors of others. Thus, the department generally will be concerned about a joint venture's policy of excluding others only if (i) an excluded firm cannot compete in a related market or markets (that is, a market or markets with respect to which the joint venture product or service is a complement or an input) in which the joint venture members are currently exercising market power without having access to the joint venture and (ii) there is no reasonable basis related to the efficient operation of the joint venture for excluding other firms.[95]

---

93.   The joint venture may be unable to act with sufficient cohesion to exercise market power in concert with competitors outside the joint venture if its members can readily cheat on price or output restrictions agreed to by the cartel or if the joint venture reserves independent pricing or output discretion to its members.

94.   *See, e.g.,* Letter from Charles F. Rule, Assistant Attorney General, Antitrust Division, to Jerome J.C. Ingels, Petroleum Independents Cooperative, Inc., Mar. 9, 1988 (indicating no present intention to challenge proposed association of natural gas producers to negotiate and market services that individual members are too small to provide alone, where several safeguards against anticompetitive conduct are in place).

95.   The mere fact that it is more costly for excluded firms to enter the joint venture market or markets on their own rather than through the joint venture does not by itself make access to the joint venture essential. In addition, a decision to impose different conditions on firms that join the venture after it has been in existence for some time (as opposed to those that join early) may simply reflect the greater risk assumed by the initial members of the joint venture.

3.43. STEP 2 – OTHER MARKETS

The Department next determines whether the joint venture or any of its restraints would likely have an anticompetitive effect in other markets in which joint venture integration does not occur and in which the joint venture members are actual or potential competitors. For example, information exchanges that are designed to enhance the efficient operation of a joint venture might also serve to facilitate collusion in markets outside of the joint venture market or markets; an association of manufacturers formed to purchase joint transportation services may possess no monopsony power with respect to purchasing such services, but may be able to use the association to coordinate the price and output of the product they manufacture in the United States; or a joint venture of U.S. firms to bid on an overseas project not funded by the U.S. Government would have no adverse effect on U.S. consumer welfare with respect to that project, but may facilitate collusion in bidding on projects in the United States.[96]

In performing its rule-of-reason analysis under step 2, the Department first considers whether a theoretical anticompetitive "spill-over" effect in markets other than the joint venture market or market is actually likely. A joint venture may, for example, include operational or procedural safeguards that substantially eliminate any risk of anticompetitive spill-over effects.[97] Examples of such safeguards include a requirement that certain types of competitively sensitive business information be aggregated or disclosed only to neutral third parties, a requirement that meetings involving representatives of the joint venture members be monitored by knowledgeable counsel, or a requirement that accurate and complete records of discussions of such meetings be maintained.[98] The use of effective safeguards may eliminate the need to conduct an elaborate structural analysis of the spill-over market.

If safeguards are not used by the joint venture (or if the safeguards are not likely

---

96. As discussed at n.48, *supra,* any restraint that is merely, a naked agreement to fix price or output that is unrelated to any integration involved in the joint venture would likely be prosecuted under Section 1 of the Sherman Act. The Department will not treat as a naked price-fixing agreement any restraint that is plausibly related to some economic integration entailed in the joint venture.

97. *See, e.g.,* Letter from Charles F. Rule, Assistant Attorney General, Antitrust Division, to Carl W. Mullis, III, Esq., Counsel for the Georgia Bankers Association Information Exchange, Sept. 8, 1988. While safeguards may ameliorate the risk of anticompetitive spill-over effects, safeguards are not necessary where the joint venture would not likely create or facilitate the exercise of market power in any spill-over market. On the other hand, the Department will take appropriate enforcement action if collusion does occur in any spill-over market, despite the presence of safeguards (perhaps because the safeguards were ignored or circumvented).

98. With respect to shipping associations, for example, the Department has suggested two safeguards against anticompetitive spill-over effects. First, negotiations between an association and a carrier or shipping conference could be conducted on a confidential basis by an officer or employee of the association who is not also an employee of an association member. Second, all communications between association and individual members could be kept confidential. *See* "The Antitrust Division's Approach to Shippers' Associations," Remarks by Charles F. Rule, Deputy Assistant Attorney General, Antitrust Division, Department of Justice, Before the Chemical Manufacturers Association, Oct. 21, 1985 (setting forth guidelines for assessing the competitive effects of shipping associations) (hereinafter "Shippers Speech"); *see also* ETC Guidelines, *supra* note 41, 50 Fed. Reg. at 1794-1798 (discussing, *inter alia*, conditions of certification relating to exchange of competitively sensitive information).

to be effective), then the Department examines market concentration and other relevant factors to determine whether the joint venture would likely create, enhance, or facilitate the exercise of market power in any relevant spill-over market. This market power analysis is the same as that described under step 1 above. In some cases, it will be clear that the joint venture members could not exercise market power in a relevant spill-over market. For example, the joint venture members may account for only a small percentage of sales (or capacity) in that market, entry into that market may be easy, or there may be strong disincentives for the joint venture members to collude in that market.[99]

3.44.   STEP 3 — VERTICAL RESTRAINTS ANALYSIS

Next, the Department seeks to determine whether vertical nonprice restraints in a joint venture agreement would likely have any anticompetitive effects.[100] This analysis is necessary because even though a joint venture might not sufficiently restrict competition among members of the joint venture to raise a competitive concern under the first two steps, the use of vertical nonprice restraints in some circumstances conceivably could facilitate marketwide collusion in or exclude competitors from a relevant market. The Department's method of analyzing the competitive effects of vertical nonprice restraints in general is set forth in Section 3.5 of these Guidelines.

3.45.   STEP 4 — OFFSETTING EFFICIENCY BENEFITS

If, after applying the first three steps of this analysis, the Department concludes that the joint venture is not likely to have any significant anticompetitive effect, the joint venture and its restraints will not be challenged regardless of whether the joint venture actually generates efficiencies. If the joint venture would likely have significant anticompetitive effects, however, then the Department proceeds to determine whether, considered cumulatively, those anticompetitive effects are outweighed by procompetitive efficiency benefits that the parties claim would be achieved by the joint venture and its restrictions.[101] The parties bear the burden of proving such offsetting procompetitive efficiencies on the basis of clear and convincing evidence. The burden increases in direct proportion to the magnitude of the likely anticompetitive harm.

---

99.   *See, e.g.,* Letter from William F. Baxter, Assistant Attorney General, Antitrust Division, to Irving B. Yoskowitz, Vice President and General Counsel, United Technologies Corp., Oct. 27, 1983 (identifying disincentives to collusion among joint venture participants in spill-over markets).

100.   As explained in Section 3.5, *infra,* vertical nonprice restraints are arrangements between firms operating at different levels of the manufacturing or distribution chain, for example, between a manufacturer and a wholesaler or between the owner of technology (licensor) and a licensee who neither owns nor controls access to competing technology, that restrict the conditions under which firms may purchase, sell, or resell goods. Examples of vertical nonprice restraints that may occur in a joint venture context include exclusive dealing arrangements and restrictions on the territories in which, or customers to whom, a product of the joint venture may be sold by joint venture members.

101.   *See* discussion at Section 3.0, *supra.* It may be very difficult to isolate and measure the effects and/or the efficiencies associated with each individual restriction in a joint venture arrangement; the anticompetitive risks and/or efficiencies may result from the interaction of several or all of the restrictions in a joint venture agreement.

The Department will not recognize claimed efficiencies if it is clear that equivalent efficiencies can be achieved by means that involve no anticompetitive effect.   In addition, although the Department in general considers the cumulative effects of restrictions associated with a joint venture, if a restriction that would have an anticompetitive effect did not contribute to (that is, if it were not related to) the claimed efficiencies, then the Department would likely require the restriction to be stricken before approving the joint venture.

The Department's analysis of production, R&D, and distribution joint ventures is illustrated in Case 5 (Joint Bidding), Case 6 (Research and Development Joint Venture), and Case 7 (Distributing a Foreign Competitor's Product), respectively.

3.5. Vertical Nonprice Distribution Restraints[102]

Vertical nonprice distribution restraints are arrangements between firms operating at different levels of the manufacturing or distribution chain (for example, between a manufacturer and a wholesaler or between a wholesaler and a retailer) that restrict the conditions under which firms may purchase, sell, or resell goods.[103]   As the Supreme Court recognized in *Continental T.V., Inc. v. GTE Sylvania, Inc.,*[104] vertical nonprice distribution restraints are often procompetitive. They can promote competition by allowing a manufacturer to achieve efficiencies in the distribution of its products and by permitting firms to compete through different methods of distribution.[105]   For example, firms entering a market can use distribution restraints "to induce competent and aggressive retailers to make the kind of investment in capital and labor that is often required in the distribution of products

---

102.   An agreement between a manufacturer and one or more distributors setting the resale price of the manufacturer's product is per se illegal. However, a vertical distribution arrangement is per se illegal only if it includes some agreement on price or price levels; a distribution restraint that may only incidentally affect price is analyzed under the rule of reason. *See Sharp,* 108 S. Ct. at 1521.

103.   Another way to describe a vertical arrangement is as an arrangement that involves the owners of complementary inputs, such that use of one input makes use of the other more valuable. In these terms, a horizontal arrangement is one that involves the owners of substitute goods or services, such that use of one good or service eliminates or substantially diminishes demand for the other. A given transaction may involve restraints on the sale of both complementary goods or services and substitute goods or services. The analysis set forth in this Section applies restrictions that affect complementary inputs. Restrictions that affect substitute inputs are analyzed in steps 1 and 2 of the joint venture analysis as described in Section 3.4, unless they are naked restraints of trade (*see* Sections 3.0 and 3.1, *supra*). The Department's analysis of intellectual property licensing arrangements, which might in given cases involve restrictions affecting both complementary and substitute products, is described in Section 3.6, *infra.*

104.   433 U.S. 36, 54-57 (1977).

105.   A manufacturer, as a consumer of distribution services, generally desires the lowest cost, most efficient distribution of its products possible. A manufacturer generally maximizes its profits by maximizing demand for its product. Moreover, since any profit earned by a manufacturer's distributors reduces the return to the manufacturer, the manufacturer generally deals with its distributors in a way that allows them to earn no more than a competitive return on the manufacturer's product. Therefore, when manufacturer-imposed distribution restraints such as exclusive territories allow distributors to earn a greater return on the manufacturer's product, those restraints typically are designed to induce the distributors to undertake efforts that achieve greater distributional efficiency, which in turn benefits consumers.

unknown to the consumer."[106]   Manufacturers may also use such restraints to protect dealers who make investments in service and promotion relating to the manufacturer's brands from dealers who do not make such investments but cut their prices in order to take advantage of the full-service dealers' investments (the so-called "free-rider" problem). Eliminating the free-rider problem is only one way in which vertical restraints can enhance competition.[107] Because vertical nonprice restraints hold significant potential for generating procompetitive efficiencies, the Department analyzes such restraints under a rule of reason.

Nevertheless, under certain market conditions, vertical nonprice restraints conceivably might serve to facilitate collusion among the dealers of competing manufacturers or directly among competing manufacturers themselves with respect to the price or output of their products.[108]   For example, dealers theoretically might induce all or almost all suppliers of a product to grant exclusive territories or exclusive dealerships in order to facilitate a cartel at the dealer level. The exclusive territories or dealerships conceivably could facilitate a dealer cartel by reducing the number of dealers that must collude and by facilitating policing of the dealer cartel. Conversely, under certain conditions it is conceivable that competing suppliers might attempt to facilitate collusion through their dealers where a dealer cartel would be more practical or less costly than direct collusion among the suppliers and where the suppliers could share in the resulting monopoly profits.[109]   Of course, if the Department has evidence that a vertical nonprice restraint is part of a broader horizontal price-fixing agreement, then the Department will prosecute that horizontal agreement as a criminal violation of section 1 of the Sherman Act.

In the absence of a direct agreement among competitors, vertical nonprice restraints conceivably could facilitate collusion only if each of three necessary (but not sufficient) market conditions exists: (i) the market at the level of the manufacturing or distribution chain with respect to which collusion might be facilitated (referred to as the "primary market") must be highly concentrated at the time the restraint becomes effective; (ii) firms in the other market (or level of the manufacturing or distribution chain) (referred to as the "secondary market") using or subject to the restraints or to restraints having the same effect must account for most sales in that market;[110] and (iii) entry into the primary market must be difficult.[111]   Thus, for example, if the restraint were serving to coordinate and

---

106.   *GTE Sylvania*, 433 U.S. at 52 n.19.

107.   Additional procompetitive uses of nonprice vertical restraints are described in the Department's Vertical Restraints Guidelines. U.S. Department of Justice Vertical Restraints Guidelines (Jan. 23. 1985) § 3.1, *reprinted in* 4 Trade Reg. Rep. (CCH) ¶ 13,105.

108.   The Supreme Court noted in *Sharp*, 108 S. Ct. at 1520, however, that "support for the cartel-facilitating effect of vertical nonprice restraints was and remains lacking."

109.   *But see id.*

110.   For this purpose, the Department considers the sales of firms that are vertically integrated into both the primary and secondary levels to be subject to "restraints having the same effect." *See* Case 8.

111.   If a restraint is used to facilitate collusion among dealers of competing suppliers, then the dealer market is the "primary" market, and the supplier market is the "secondary" market. Conversely, if the restraint is used to facilitate collusion among suppliers, then the supplier market is the primary market, and the dealer market is the secondary market. Where it is not clear whether suppliers or dealers are instigating use of a restraint to facilitate collusion, the Department analyzes the likely competitive effects of a restraint from both perspectives.

police a cartel among dealers, the Department would expect to find that the dealer market was highly concentrated, that new entry into the dealer market was difficult, and that the dealers had convinced suppliers accounting for most sales in the relevant market for supply of the product to use the same restraint or restraints having the same effect. Conversely, if the restraint were serving to coordinate and police a cartel among suppliers, the Department would expect to find that the supplier market was highly concentrated, that new entry into the supplier market was difficult, and that the restraint or restraints having the same effect covered most sales made in the dealer market.

It is implausible that vertical nonprice restraints would serve to coordinate and police the collective exercise of market power in the absence of a horizontal agreement (that is, through tacit collusion) in any market unless that market were highly concentrated at the time the restraints became effective. In addition, to prevent cheating on the cartel, firms in the other market that use or are subject to the same restraint or restraints having the same effect must account for most of the sales in that market. Otherwise, the substantial sales not subject to (and thus uncoordinated by) the restraints would frustrate tacit collusion. Finally, unless entry into the primary market is difficult, new competitors would quickly enter and undercut attempted collusion.

Under certain market conditions, a vertical nonprice restraint conceivably could also result in the anticompetitive exclusion of competitors from the market by denying them access to an essential input or essential distribution facilities.[112] For example, if most or all of the outlets capable of distributing competing products were subject to exclusive dealing arrangements, a new entrant in the sale of such a product might have to enter into both the manufacture and distribution of the product. Under certain circumstances, the need to enter at both levels could significantly delay, if not completely prohibit, new entry into a product market that was not performing competitively.[113] For any anticompetitive exclusion scenario to be plausible, however, the restraint, (considered together with similar restraints operating in the market) must significantly increase the cost to new entrants attempting to gain access to essential inputs or distribution facilities. In addition, the firm (or firms) imposing the restraint must be able to collect a sufficiently large return from using the restraint to offset the increased costs that that firm (or those firms) had to incur to impose the restraint.[114]

A vertical nonprice restraint could conceivably have an anticompetitive exclusionary effect only if each of three necessary (but not sufficient) market conditions exists: (i) the market in which firms imposing the restraint operate (and

---

112.   All contracts between two parties in some sense exclude non-contracting parties. The Department is concerned, however, only with exclusion that will result in the ability to exercise power over price or output in a relevant market. In addition, the Department does not penalize firms that develop efficient distribution systems that make distribution less costly (perhaps because of superior management). Thus, the fact that a particular firm has a more efficient distribution system than other systems that are available or that could be developed is not sufficient to prohibit that firm from continuing to use its distribution system or to require it to make its distribution system available to its competitors.

113.   See Merger Guidelines § 4.212. Although vertical restraints may only delay entry, and not block it entirely, in some cases the period of delay may be sufficiently long to affect consumer welfare significantly.

114.   See n.52, supra.

which is supposed not to be performing competitively) (referred to as the "nonforeclosed" market) must be very highly concentrated, and leading firms in the market must use the restraint or restraints having the same effect;[115]   (ii) the restraints must cover most of the capacity of the market for the input or distribution facilities being foreclosed to competitors (referred to as the "foreclosed" market); and (iii) entry into the "foreclosed" market must be difficult.[116]

Unless the firms imposing the restraints are very few in number, control most or all of the foreclosed market, and are currently earning monopoly profits, they will have neither the incentive nor the ability effectively to exclude other competitors from the nonforeclosed market. In addition, unless the restraint applies to all or a very large portion of firms in the foreclosed market, competitors could simply use remaining available capacity to enter or expand in the market. Thus, for example, competitors are unlikely to be foreclosed if only one firm signs all of its dealers to exclusive dealing contracts, as long as its dealers represent only a small proportion of dealers in the relevant market. Finally, foreclosing inputs or distribution facilities would not inhibit new entry or expansion in the nonforeclosed market if competitors could easily enter into the foreclosed market themselves or could count on entry by other firms in response to the increased demand for input production or distribution facilities.[117]

If the minimum necessary market conditions for successful collusion or anticompetitive exclusion are not met, or if entry is easy into both the primary and secondary markets (or the foreclosed and nonforeclosed markets), then the Department can quickly determine that use of a restraint is not anticompetitive. In addition, even without determining whether the three minimum necessary conditions exist, if the firm instigating or imposing a restraint has a small market share (e.g., ten percent or less), the Department normally will not challenge that firm's use of the restraint.[118]   Firms with such small market shares do not possess market power individually, and are unlikely to be important to any cartel or agreement to facilitate a cartel or to any exclusionary scheme.[119]   In fact, vertical nonprice restraints may be used by such firms to facilitate their entry into a highly concentrated market. Of course, if the Department has evidence that a fringe firm employing restraints is part of an unlawful cartel among competitors, the Department will not hesitate to investigate and, if appropriate, to prosecute any unlawful cartel activities.

If the three minimum necessary conditions for collusion or anticompetitive exclusion are present, then the Department considers other relevant factors bearing on whether a particular nonprice vertical restraint would likely have an anticompetitive effect. The factors the Department considers include whether the restraint actually has had an exclusionary effect; the duration and restrictiveness of the restraint; direct evidence of anticompetitive intent; and whether market

---

115.   In general, the Department is concerned about the exclusionary effect of a vertical nonprice restraint when the restraint is imposed by a firm possessing market (or monopoly) power.

116.   For example, when a manufacturer exclusively licenses a dealer to distribute the manufacturer's product, the dealer market is the foreclosed market and the manufacturing market is the nonforeclosed market.

117.   Vertical Restraints Guidelines § 3.22.

118.   Id. § 4.1.

119.   See Merger Guidelines § 4.134.

conditions are conducive to collusion or anticompetitive exclusion.[120]   If vertical restraints have been used in a market for a sufficient length of time to make it possible to evaluate their actual competitive effects, the Department will look primarily to direct evidence of market performance.[121]   If it appears after an examination of these and other relevant factors that a vertical nonprice restraint could have an anticompetitive effect, then the Department considers whether the risk of anticompetitive harm is outweighed by the procompetitive efficiency benefits of using the restraint.[122]

Case 8 of these Guidelines illustrates the Department's analysis of a foreign firm's use of an exclusive distribution arrangement in the United States. The Department's analysis of various types of vertical intellectual property licensing arrangements is discussed below and illustrated in Cases 10, 11, and 12.

3.6. Intellectual Property Licensing Arrangements[123]

For the purpose of antitrust analysis, the Department regards intellectual property (e.g., patents, copyrights, trade secrets, and know-how) as being essentially comparable to any other form of tangible or intangible property that is created, transferred, or used in the production of goods or services.   At one time, the Department's enforcement policy proceeded on the assumption that intellectual property rights and certain practices in the licensing of those rights conflicted with the goals of the antitrust laws because intellectual property rights were thought to create "monopolies." Today, however, the Department recognizes that intellectual property — even a patent — does not necessarily confer a monopoly or market power in any relevant market.[124]   A patent, for example, is merely the right to exclude others from making, using, or reselling the product or process covered by the patent claims.   The patented product or process remains subject to competition from products or processes outside the scope of the patent that are economic substitutes. As a result, the owner of a patented technology may earn little more than a nominal rate of return on its investment in producing the patented product or process.[125]

---

120.   See Merger Guidelines § 3.4 (collusion), § 4.21 (exclusion).
121.   All other things being equal, the Department is more likely to challenge a restraint that may facilitate collusion if there is a history of collusion by firms at either level of the market.
122.   See Section 3.0, supra (discussing the balancing of the risk of anticompetitive harm and procompetitive efficiencies).
123.   This discussion does not deal with the judicially-created doctrine of patent misuse. That doctrine, which provides a defense to a patent infringement suit if the patent owner is found to have engaged in "misuse" of its patent, is not an antitrust doctrine (although an antitrust violation may form the basis for a finding of misuse). But see Title II of the Patent and Trademark Office Authorization Act, Pub. L. No. 100-703 (1988) (patent misuse cannot be found on the basis of an alleged tie-in arrangement unless the patent owner has market power in the relevant market for the "tying" patent or patented product and any anticompetitive effect of the tie-in is not outweighed by the benefits of the arrangement, including procompetitive benefits and other business justifications).
124.   See also Title II of the Patent and Trademark Office Authorization Act, supra note 123, (requiring a preliminary showing of market power to support a claim of patent misuse based on an alleged tie-in).
125.   For example, if two patented pharmaceuticals were economic substitutes for the same medical indication, any attempt by one patent owner to raise the price of its pharmaceutical would result in substitution to the other pharmaceutical.

Even when a patent or other form of intellectual property does confer a significant competitive advantage on its owner (even to the extent of conferring monopoly power), it is no more in conflict with the antitrust laws than any tangible asset, such as an exceptionally low-cost factory, that enables its owner to earn significantly supranormal profits. Market power or even a monopoly that is the result of superior effort, acumen, foresight, or luck does not violate the antitrust laws.[126] The owner of intellectual property is entitled to enjoy whatever market power the property itself may confer. Indeed, respecting the rights of the creator of intellectual property to enjoy the full value of that property provides incentive for the innovative effort required to create the property. And the results of that innovative effort both increase productive efficiency and expand society's knowledge and wealth.

3.61. LICENSING BENEFITS

Licenses of patents and other forms of intellectual property are contracts transferring to the licensees a right to use intellectual property.[127] The licensing of intellectual property generally benefits consumers by expanding access to technology and bringing it to the marketplace in the quickest and most efficient manner. Licensing permits the technology owner, in effect, to combine its assets with the manufacturing and distribution assets of its licensees. By enabling the technology owner to exploit its intellectual property as efficiently and effectively as possible, licensing also increases the expected economic returns from intellectual property and thereby increases the incentive to invest in creating such property in the first place.

Restraints in an intellectual property license can play an important role in ensuring that new technology realizes its maximum return and benefits consumers as quickly and efficiently as possible. For example, license restrictions such as tie-ins, package licenses, and similar restrictions, can be used to differentiate among licensees that value the technology differently, allowing the licensor to charge prices that more closely approximate the value that individual licensees place on the technology (this practice is sometimes referred to as "metering"). In addition to increasing the return to the technology owner, metering can also lead to greater dissemination of the technology by reducing the price to licensees that would have been unable or unwilling to pay the higher uniform price that the technology owner would have charged in the absence of metering.

In addition, restrictions such as exclusive fields of use and exclusive territories may be used to encourage the licensee to make investments that are necessary to develop and promote the licensed technology by protecting the licensee against free-riding on those investments by other licensees or perhaps even by the licensor. Allowing the owner of intellectual property to use license restrictions to reserve some exclusive use of the licensed property to itself similarly may encourage efficient licensing of

---

126.   *See* United States v. Grinnell Corp., 384 U.S. at 570-75.
127.   A patent license is in effect a waiver granted to the licensee by the patentee of the patentee's exclusive rights under the patent. A license provides the licensee with immunity from a suit for infringement of the patent.

technology where the owner of intellectual property otherwise might choose not to license its property at all.[128]

An exhaustive listing of the integrative efficiency benefits that may be generated by individual licensing restrictions is beyond the scope and purpose of these Guidelines. As is the case in general with respect to transactions subject to rule-of-reason analysis, the Department does not inquire as to the precise procompetitive benefits of a restraint unless and until the restraint is determined to be likely to create, enhance, or facilitate the exercise of market power in some relevant market beyond that which is inherent in the intellectual property being licensed.[129] The Department has no list of approved or disapproved license restrictions or of expected benefits from such restrictions. Instead, when the Department's analysis indicates that restrictions in a license would likely create, enhance, or facilitate the exercise of market power beyond that which is inherent in the intellectual property itself, the Department considers whether that risk is outweighed by procompetitive efficiency benefits.[130]

3.62. RULE-OF-REASON ANALYSIS

Because they hold significant procompetitive potential, the Department analyzes restrictions in an intellectual property license under a rule of reason unless the underlying transfer of technology is a sham.[131] That analysis is conducted with two fundamental principles in mind. First, the Department will not challenge licensing arrangements that represent simply an effort by the creator of intellectual property to appropriate the full inherent value of that property. The potential for appropriating that value provides the economic incentive to engage in risky and costly research and development in the first place. Second, the Department will not require the owner of technology to create competition in its own technology.

The Department's rule-of-reason analysis of intellectual property licensing arrangements involves four steps. Step 1 is designed to determine whether the license restrains independent competition between the licensor and its licensee (or licensees) in a relevant market for technology and, if it does, whether it would likely create, enhance, or facilitate the exercise of market power. Step 2 is designed to determine whether the license expressly or implicitly restrains competition in any other market in which the licensor and its licensee do or would compete in the absence of the license. Step 2 covers both express restrictions in a license relating to competition in some product market that incorporates the licensed technology and

---

128.   *See* "The Antitrust Implications of International Licensing: After the Nine No-No's," Remarks by Charles F. Rule before the Legal Conference sponsored by the World Trade Association and the Cincinnati Patent Law Association (Oct. 21, 1986), *reprinted in* 4 Trade Reg. Rep. (CCH) ¶ 13,131; *see also* the discussion of the procompetitive potential of the specific technology license restrictions employed in Cases 10 through 12, *infra.*

129.   *See* n.47, *supra.*

130.   *See* Section 3.66, *infra.*

131.   A license is regarded as a sham if the parties demonstrably are not interested in transferring intellectual property rights, but rather are using the license to disguise their effort to restrict output or raise price in some market other than the market for the intellectual property.

"spill-over" effects.[132] Step 3 is a vertical analysis designed to determine (i) whether a license (or licenses) would result in anticompetitive exclusion (beyond exclusion inherent in the intellectual property rights themselves); and (ii) whether, even if a license does not restrain competition between the licensor and its licensee, it would likely serve to facilitate collusion in a technology market or some other market. In step 4, the Department determines whether any risk of anticompetitive effects revealed under the first three steps is outweighed by the procompetitive efficiencies generated by the license restrictions.[133]

3.63.   STEP 1 – THE TECHNOLOGY LICENSING MARKET

The Department employs step 1 if the licensor and its licensee own or control access to competing technologies and the license either implicitly or explicitly restricts their independent decision making with respect to the price or output of those technologies. The Department seeks to determine whether such restrictions would likely create, enhance, or facilitate the exercise of market power beyond that which is conferred unilaterally by each parties' intellectual property in a relevant market for technology.[134]

The Department first identifies all technologies with which the technology or technologies covered by the license compete.[135] This process is analogous to the

---

132.   The first two steps of this analysis are analogous to the first two steps of the joint venture analysis described in Section 3.4, *supra.* In the Department's joint venture analysis, however, step 1 is designed to detect anticompetitive effects resulting from express restrictions in the joint venture agreement in any market in which integration of the parties' activities pursuant to the joint venture occurs. Step 2 of the joint venture analysis is designed to detect anticompetitive "spill-over" effects in markets where there is no joint venture integration, but in which the parties compete. The Department's paradigm for analyzing intellectual property licenses deviates slightly in form from the joint venture paradigm: step 1 of the intellectual property licensing analysis is designed to detect anticompetitive effects in markets in which the intellectual property covered by a license competes; step 2, is designed to detect anticompetitive effects in other markets in which the license achieves some integration, as well as in markets in which no license integration occurs, but in which the licensor and licensee compete. This difference is one of form only, however. The Department's conclusions would be the same whether competitive effects in markets other than the technology licensing market were analyzed under step 1 or step 2, since the analysis in both steps is substantively the same. Indeed, where the technology and a product produced using the technology are largely coextensive, the Department's step 1 analysis would subsume the step 2 analysis. Two steps are used only to ensure that the Department examines competitive effects in all affected relevant markets.

133.   In many cases, it will not be necessary to use each step. For example, if the licensor and licensee do not compete in any market at the time the license becomes effective, or if the license does not expressly or implicitly restrict competition in such markets, then steps 1 and 2 would not apply. In addition, in analyzing license restrictions under steps 1, 2, or 3, the Department may be able quickly to conclude that there is no significant threat to competition. Finally, step 4 applies only if the Department first concludes under any of the previous three steps that license restrictions raise a significant risk of anticompetitive harm. The four steps are thus a kind of checklist to ensure that every conceivable anticompetitive risk is examined.

134.   In general, step 1 is designed to analyze the competitive effects of cross licenses and patent pools involving competing technologies.

135.   Technologies compete if consumers regard them as substitutes. As a practical matter, it often is difficult to determine whether particular technologies are substitutes or complements. Technologies are complements if they are used together, such that an increase in the use of one technology increases, rather than decreases, use of the other technology. The same technology, however, may be both a complement and a substitute. For example, while consumers may view

process the Department uses to define markets for purposes of its merger analysis.[136] The relevant market includes all technologies to which users would turn if the price of the licensed technology (e.g., the license royalty) increased by five to ten percent. The relevant market includes both functional substitutes for a particular technology as well as technologies used to manufacture substitute products. In defining the relevant technology market, the Department does not assume that a patent or other piece of intellectual property delimits the relevant market. As explained above, there may be economic substitutes for that property which would make any attempt to exercise unilateral market power impossible.[137]

The geographic scope of the relevant technology market typically will be international. Except where there are governmental restrictions on the export of technology, technologies generally can readily cross borders and be employed in the United States (although the owners must often apply for legal recognition and protection of their intellectual property in each country).

After identifying the relevant technology market or markets, the Department seeks to determine whether the complete elimination of competition by merger between the licensor and its licensees would likely lead to the unilateral or collective exercise of market power with respect to the licensing of technologies in that market or those markets.[138] The Department's analysis of technology markets focuses on the apparent relative efficiencies of competing technologies. In assigning market shares to competing technologies, the Department uses the best available evidence of the relative efficiencies of the technologies, including royalty revenues or market shares in downstream product markets that incorporate the competing technologies. In cases that involve emerging technologies, the Department bases its assessment on the best available evidence of the likely future strength of those technologies in the market. If it appears that competing technologies are all comparably efficient, then the Department assigns equal market shares to each technology.[139]

If combining the technologies of the licensor and licensee through merger would be anticompetitive, then the Department proceeds to consider other factors bearing on the ability to exercise market power that the Department normally considers in merger analysis.[140] Those factors include evidence of active R&D that is reasonably expected to produce comparably efficient technologies within two years

---

a product produced using either of two technologies to be substitutes, that product might be produced more efficiently by combining both technologies, rather than by using either of them alone.

136.   *See* Section 3.31, *supra.*
137.   Although in Jefferson Parish Hospital Dist. No. 2 v. Hyde, 466 U.S. 2, 16 (1984), the majority of the court noted in dicta that market power could fairly be presumed from a patent, the Department does not employ such a presumption in its internal analysis. *See also* 466 U.S. at 37 n.7 (O'Connor, J., concurring) (noting that a patent may confer no market power if there are close substitutes for the patented product); Digidyne Corp. v. Data General Corp., 473 U.S. 908, 909 (1985) (White and Blackmun, JJ., dissenting from denial of certiorari). *Cf.* Title II of the Patent and Trademark Office Authorization Act, *supra* note 123.
138.   *See* Merger Guidelines §§ 3.1-3.4; Sections 3.32, 3.42, *supra.*
139.   Thus, for example, if there are five comparably efficient competing technologies in the market, the Department assigns each a market share of 20 percent (resulting in an HHI of 2000).
140.   *See* Section 3.32, *supra.*

and the ability of fringe technologies to expand output and frustrate any attempt to exercise market power.[141]

The Department recognizes that, because of the heterogeneous nature of intellectual property, collusion with respect to technology licensing may be impractical.[142] Consumers may place different values on competing technologies depending on the particular efficiencies they perceive from their use of those technologies. The perceived efficiency of a technology may depend on factors that are not known to the technology owner, such as a licensee's ability to adapt the technology to the licensee's existing machinery or the level of expertise that the licensee's employees have in using the technology. As a result, collusion may be impossible without an express agreement on price and output among most or all of the technology owners in the market; it may be impossible tacitly to collude to exercise market power when the responses of technology consumers to price differentials cannot be predicted.[143]

Finally, even if a merger of the licensee and licensor would be anticompetitive, a particular license may not restrict competition in the relevant market or markets as completely as would the total economic integration entailed by a merger. The Department therefore examines the precise nature and extent of the elimination of independent price and output decision making that would result from the license restriction.[144]

Since competitive problems in the technology licensing market typically arise from the elimination of competition among technologies, the Department in general is concerned about the anticompetitive effects of a licensing agreement (or license pool) when it is overinclusive, rather than when it is underinclusive.[145] Thus, for example, "open" patent pools are in general more likely to create competitive problems than are "closed" patent pools that leave some competing technologies outside the pool. Moreover, as explained above, the ability to exclude others is the essence of an intellectual property rights system; exclusion enables the owners of intellectual property to realize the return from their investment in creating the property. Selective exclusion may often represent the most efficient means of disseminating and developing technology.

In general, the Department is likely to be concerned about limitations on participation in license pools only if (i) the pool (or other licensing arrangement)

---

141.   In some cases, technologies that currently represent a small share of the market may be viewed by consumers as being only marginally less efficient than a technology or technologies that have dominant market shares. In those cases, owners of fringe technologies may be able to expand their technology outputs in response to a price increase and thus to defeat any attempted exercise of market power.

142.   *See* Merger Guidelines § 3.411 (regarding the likelihood of collusion with respect to heterogeneous products).

143.   *See id.* § 3.43; *see also* Andewelt, *Analysis of Patent Pools Under the Antitrust Laws*, 54 Antitrust L.J. 611 (1985). In addition, it has been argued that where patented technology is involved, the price to the cartel members of cheating may be even greater than where technology is not involved. Because patent licenses normally are for the full 17-year life of the patent, a "sale" of technology made by a cheating cartel member may effectively preclude other cartel members from ever licensing their technology to the licensee, or "customer," of the cheater. *Id.*

144.   *See* Section 3.42 and text accompanying nn.93-94, *supra* (applying a similar analysis to joint ventures).

145.   *See* discussion with respect to joint ventures generally at text accompanying n.88, *supra*.

involves the cross licensing of competing technologies; (ii) without access to the pool, an excluded firm cannot compete in a product market that incorporates the licensed technologies and in which the pool members or licensees have market power; and (iii) there is no reasonable basis relating to the efficient development and dissemination of the pooled technologies for excluding other firms.[146]   The Department will challenge limitations on the ability of competing technology owners to license their technologies to others only where those limitations would result in market power in a relevant technology licensing market or in some other market (see step 2).

3.64.   STEP 2 — OTHER MARKETS

Next, the Department seeks to determine whether the license would likely create, enhance, or facilitate the exercise of market power in any other market in which the licensor and its licensees compete or would compete in the absence of the license. Under step 2, the Department focuses both on license restrictions that restrict competition between the licensor and licensees in a market other than the technology licensing market that incorporates the licensed technology and on restrictions or other aspects of the license (for example, information exchanges) that, while not directly restricting competition between the licensee and licensor, may have an anticompetitive "spill-over" effect.[147]

The Department begins its analysis by determining whether the complete integration through merger of the parties' price and output decisions in the affected market or markets would likely create, enhance, or facilitate the exercise of market power. After defining the relevant market or markets, with respect to each market the Department first looks at the level of concentration and increase in concentration that would result from a merger of the parties.   If it appears on the basis of concentration at the time the license becomes effective that a merger of the licensor and its licensee would not be anticompetitive (i.e., that it would fall within a Merger Guidelines safe harbor), then the Department concludes that the license raises no significant competitive concerns. If it appears on the basis of concentration that a merger could be anticompetitive, however, then the Department proceeds to consider other factors normally considered in merger analysis bearing on the ability to exercise market power. Those factors include the likelihood of new entry into the relevant market that would frustrate any attempt to exercise market power and characteristics of the relevant product that make collusion more or less likely.

---

146.   *See* discussion of exclusion from joint ventures at Section 3.42, *supra*. Where a license pool does not involve the cross licensing of competing technologies, any limitation on access to the licensed technologies is unlikely to raise any competitive problems in a relevant technology market.

147.   In some cases, competitive effects in the technology markets and product markets that incorporate relevant technology will be identical. An example is a license by one pharmaceutical manufacturer to another of a pharmaceutical product patent. In other cases, however, license restrictions conceivably could have distinct effects in the technology and other related markets. An example is a license by one automobile manufacturer to another of know-how relating to the manufacture of pollution control devices for automobiles. In such a case, even if the technology market were unconcentrated (that is, there were many competing technologies for manufacturing pollution control devices), the automobile market (hypothetically) might be highly concentrated and characterized by significant barriers to entry. A restriction in the know-how license might have no anticompetitive effect in the technology market, but conceivably could facilitate collusion between the licensor and licensee in the automobile market.

In performing this market power analysis, the Department is guided by two principles. First, the Department is concerned only about the elimination of actual or potential competition between the licensor and its licensees that would occur in the absence of the license. In general, the Department is not concerned about competition that could only occur if a licensee had access to the licensor's technology. Second, where access to the licensed technology is essential to compete in a relevant market, the Department discounts the market shares of licensees that, prior to the license, had access only to clearly inferior technologies.[148]

3.65.   STEP 3 — VERTICAL RESTRAINTS ANALYSIS

The Department next seeks to determine whether vertical restraints in a license would likely have any anticompetitive effects. This step is designed to detect three types of anticompetitive harm that would not be detected under steps 1 and 2: (i) the use of vertical restraints by all or most owners of competing technologies to facilitate collusion among themselves; (ii) the use of vertical restraints by the licensees of competing technologies to facilitate collusion among themselves in markets that incorporate the licensed technology; and (iii) vertical restraints that result in anticompetitive exclusion by "tying up" some essential input.[149] The Department is likely to challenge purely vertical restraints in intellectual property licenses only in exceptional circumstances. An exclusive license to a single licensee, for example, would normally raise little, if any, risk of collusion; in many cases, it would be procompetitive by allowing a technology to be brought to the market.

Under certain market conditions, however, vertical restraints in an intellectual property license might facilitate collusion among owners of competing technologies or among the licensees of competing technologies in other markets. The owners of competing technologies conceivably might be able tacitly to collude through restrictions imposed on their licensees where a cartel among the licensees would be more practical or less costly than direct collusion among the technology owners themselves. Alternatively, firms that use the licensed technology as an input or complement in producing some product conceivably might induce one or more licensors to facilitate collusion in the market for that product. In the absence of an express horizontal agreement, however, a license restriction could plausibly serve to facilitate such collusion only if three necessary (but not sufficient) market conditions exist: (i) the market with respect to which collusion might be facilitated (the "primary market") must be very highly concentrated at the time the restraint or restraints become effective; (ii) firms in the other market (the "secondary market") using or subject to the restraint (or restraints having the same effect) must account

---

148.   *See* Merger Guidelines § 3.21 (treatment of firms that would not be significant competitors in the future because they lack access to significant new technology); Section 3.321, *supra*.

149.   If the licensor and its licensees compete in the relevant technology market as well as in any other market affected by restrictions in the license, such that the Department analyzes the license under both steps 1 and 2, then a step 3 analysis is unnecessary; any collusion or anticompetitive exclusion concern would be adequately addressed in steps 1 and 2. If a license restriction affects a market in which the licensor does not compete with its licensees, then a step 3 analysis of any vertical license restraints affecting such a market would be necessary.

for most sales in that market; and (iii) entry into the primary market must be difficult.[150]

Under certain market conditions, vertical restraints in an intellectual property license also conceivably might result in the anticompetitive exclusion of competitors from a relevant market by denying firms that compete with the licensees access to an essential technology input, or by denying firms that compete with the licensor access to production or distribution assets that are needed to exploit a competing technology. Thus, for example, if a product market that incorporated the licensed technology were very highly concentrated, and firms accounting for a large share of that market obtained exclusive licenses to all available competing technologies, those firms might be able to exercise market power without the fear of new entry. Alternatively, the owner or owners of leading technologies might grant exclusive licenses to the only firms capable of exploiting competing technologies. Anticompetitive exclusion is plausible, however, only if three necessary (but not sufficient) conditions exist: (i) the market in which the firm or firms imposing the restraint operate (and which is supposed not to be performing competitively) (the "nonforeclosed market") must be very highly concentrated and leading firms in that market must use the same or similar restraints; (ii) the same or similar restraints must cover most of the capacity in the market being foreclosed to competitors (the "foreclosed market"); and (iii) entry into the foreclosed market must be difficult.[151]

If the minimum necessary market conditions for collusion or anticompetitive exclusion are not met, then the Department can quickly determine that the use of a vertical restraint is not anticompetitive. In addition, even without determining whether the three minimum necessary conditions exist, if the firm imposing the restraint has a small market share (e.g., ten percent or less), the Department normally will not challenge that firm's use of the restraint.[152]

If the minimum necessary conditions do exist, then the Department considers other factors that bear on whether the license would likely create, enhance, or facilitate the exercise of market power. Those factors include whether the restraint actually has had an exclusionary effect, the duration and restrictiveness of the restraint, direct evidence of anticompetitive intent, and whether market conditions are conducive to collusion or anticompetitive exclusion. If the restraints have been used for a

---

150. *See* the discussion of the three minimum necessary conditions for a nonprice vertical restraint to facilitate collusion at Section 3.5, *supra*. Vertical restrictions in a license of technology that has no substitutes obviously would not facilitate collusion in a technology market. The use of vertical restraints by a licensor to facilitate naked collusion in other markets also would be implausible (in the absence of an explicit horizontal agreement among the licensees that would be subject to criminal prosecution), since such collusion would reduce the technology owner's profits.

151. *See* the discussion of the three minimum necessary conditions for a nonprice vertical restraint to have an anticompetitive exclusionary effect at Section 3.5, *supra*. In general, where the technology being licensed has no substitutes, the technology market will not be deemed to be a "foreclosed" market. Any exclusion would then be inherent in the intellectual property itself, and the owner of intellectual property has no obligation to create competition in its technology. The technology owner, moreover, will have an incentive to structure its licenses in a way that ensures that all potential "nonforeclosed" markets operate as competitively as is efficiently possible (that is, that they operate as close to marginal cost as possible). *See also* n.105, *supra*.

152. *See* text accompanying nn.118-119, *supra*.

sufficient period of time to make it possible to evaluate their actual competitive effects, then the Department will look primarily to direct evidence of market performance.[153]

3.66.   STEP 4 – OFFSETTING EFFICIENCY BENEFITS

If, after applying the first three steps of this analysis, the Department concludes that a licensing arrangement would have no significant anticompetitive effects, then the Department will not challenge the license, regardless of whether it actually will generate procompetitive efficiencies. If, however, a license does create a significant risk of anticompetitive effects, then the Department proceeds to determine whether the risk of anticompetitive effects is outweighed by procompetitive efficiency benefits that the parties claim would be achieved by the license and its restrictions.[154] The parties bear the burden of proving such offsetting efficiencies on the basis of clear and convincing evidence. The burden increases in direct relationship to the magnitude of the likely anticompetitive harms.[155]

The Department will not recognize an efficiencies claim if it is clear that equivalent efficiencies can be achieved by means that involve no anticompetitive effect. In addition, although the Department in general considers the cumulative effects of restrictions in an intellectual property license, if a restriction that would have an anticompetitive effect did not contribute to (that is, if it were not related to) achieving the claimed efficiencies, then the Department would likely require the restriction to be stricken before approving the licensing arrangement.

The Department's analysis of various common types of intellectual property licensing arrangements is illustrated in Cases 10, 11, and 12 of these Guidelines. Case 10 illustrates the Department's analysis of vertical restrictions in a patent license. Case 11 illustrates the Department's analysis of an exclusive patent cross-license with grantbacks. Case 12 illustrates the Department's analysis of a know-how technology transfer agreement with exclusive territories.

4.   Jurisdictional Considerations

4.0. Just as the acts of U.S. citizens in a foreign nation ordinarily are subject to the law of the country in which they occur, the acts of foreign citizens in the United States ordinarily are subject to U.S. law. The reach of the U.S. antitrust laws is not limited solely to conduct and transactions that occur within the United States, however. Conduct relating to U.S. import trade that harms consumers in the United States may be subject to the jurisdiction of the U.S. antitrust laws regardless of where such conduct occurs or the nationality of the parties involved. Thus, for example, applying the Sherman Act to restrain or punish a private international cartel the purpose and effect of which is to restrict output and raise prices to U.S. consumers

---

153.   *See* Section 3.5, *supra.*

154.   *See* discussion of the procompetitive benefits of technology licensing restrictions at Section 3.61, *supra.*

155.   *See* discussion of the balancing of the risk of anticompetitive harm and procompetitive efficiencies at Section 3.0, *supra.*

may be both appropriate and necessary to effective enforcement of that Act.[156] On the other hand, the Sherman Act does not reach the activities of U.S. or foreign firms in foreign markets if those activities have no direct, substantial, and reasonably foreseeable effect on U.S. interstate commerce, on import trade or commerce, or on the export trade or commerce of a person engaged in trade or commerce in the United States.[157]

The jurisdictional limits of the Sherman Act as it applies to conduct involving non-import foreign commerce are described in the Foreign Trade Antitrust Improvement Act ("FTAIA").[158]

4.1. Foreign Trade Antitrust Improvement Act

The FTAIA provides that the Sherman Act:

shall not apply to conduct involving trade or commerce (other than import trade or import commerce) with foreign nations unless –

(1)   such conduct has a direct, substantial, and reasonably foreseeable effect –
       (A)   on trade or commerce which is not trade or commerce with foreign nations, or on import trade or import commerce with foreign nations; or
       (B)   on export trade or export commerce with foreign nations, of a person engaged in such trade or commerce in the United States; and

(2)   such effect gives rise to a claim under the provisions of [the Sherman Act], other than this section.

If [the Sherman Act] appl[ies] to such conduct only because of the operation of paragraph (1)(B), then [the Sherman Act] shall apply to such conduct only for injury to export business in the United States.

The FTAIA thus confers subject matter jurisdiction over the anticompetitive export conduct of U.S. firms only when that conduct would have a direct, substantial, and reasonably foreseeable effect on trade or commerce within the United States or on import trade or commerce.[159] The export conduct of U.S. firms conceivably could have such an effect under two circumstances. First, it could have such an effect if supply in the relevant U.S. and foreign export markets were fixed or highly inelastic and U.S. firms accounting for a substantial share of the domestic market

---

156.   The European Court of Justice has adopted a similar interpretation of the competition laws of the European Economic Community. *See* A. Ahlstrom Osakeytio v. EC Commission, Case No. 89/85 (Ct. of Just. of the Eur. Communities Sept. 27, 1988) (Wood Pulp Case).

157.   *See* 15 U.S.C. § 6a (1982), discussed more fully below. Of course, not all conduct that falls within the jurisdictional reach of the federal antitrust laws constitutes a substantive violation of those laws (*see* discussion at Section 3, *supra*). In addition, the Department may decline to assert jurisdiction granted under the antitrust law if the anticompetitive conduct was compelled by a foreign sovereign or for comity-related reasons (*see* discussion at Section 5, *infra*).

158.   15 U.S.C. § 6a.

159.   Although the FTAIA extends jurisdiction under the Sherman Act to conduct that has a direct, substantial, and reasonably foreseeable effect on the export trade or export commerce of a person engaged in such commerce in the United States, the Department is concerned only with adverse effects on competition that would harm U.S. consumers by reducing output or raising prices. *See* Section 3.0, *supra*.

agreed on the level of their exports in order to reduce supply and raise prices in the United States. Second, it could have such an effect if conduct that ostensibly involved exports were actually designed to affect the price of products that were to be sold or resold in the United States.[160]

The Department is also concerned about the export conduct of U.S. firms when the U.S. Government is the purchaser of, or substantially funds the purchase of, those goods or services. The effect of anticompetitive conduct with respect to the sale of those goods or services falls primarily on U.S. taxpayers who are deprived of the benefits of competition guaranteed by the federal antitrust laws, rather than on the nominal foreign purchaser. The foreign elements of such a sale are by comparison insignificant. Such sales should therefore not be considered to be "exports," but rather should be treated as sales to the U.S. Government. There is no reason to believe that in enacting the FTAIA Congress intended to immunize anticompetitive conduct with respect to sales to the U.S. Government. To do so would have been to place the burden of anticompetitive pricing squarely on the shoulders of U.S. taxpayers, something that the Department will not assume that Congress intended. Rather, the Department will assume that Congress intended to preserve for U.S. taxpayers the main benefits of competition among U.S. firms.[161] As a general matter, the Department considers there to be a sufficient effect on U.S. interests to support the assertion of jurisdiction where, as a result of its payment or financing, the U.S. Government bears more than half the cost of the transaction.[162]

By its terms, the FTAIA applies only to non-import trade or commerce with foreign nations. Enforcement actions against conduct involving import commerce and mergers and acquisitions under section 7 of the Clayton Act remain subject to

---

160.   This would be the case, for example, if U.S. firms fixed the price of an input used to manufacture a product overseas for sale in the United States and if fixing the price of the input served to facilitate collusion among the U.S. firms with respect to the product sold in the United States.

161.   *See, e.g.,* United States v. Concentrated Phosphate Export Ass'n, 393 U.S. 199, 208 (1968) ("[A]lthough the fertilizer shipments were consigned to Korea and although in most cases Korea formally let the contracts, American participation was the overwhelmingly dominant feature. The burden of noncompetitive pricing fell, not on any foreign purchaser, but on the American taxpayer. The United States was, in essence, furnishing fertilizer to Korea. . . . The foreign elements in the transaction were, by comparison, insignificant."); United States v. Standard Tallow Corp., 1988-1 Trade Cas. (CCH) ¶ 67,913 (S.D.N.Y. Jan. 28, 1988) (consent decree) (barring suppliers from fixing prices or rigging bids for the sale of tallow financed in whole or in part through grants or loans by the U.S. Government); United States v. Anthracite Export Ass'n, 1970 Trade Cas. (CCH) ¶ 73,348 (M.D. Pa. Nov. 12, 1970) (consent decree) (barring price fixing, bid rigging, and market allocation on Army foreign aid program).

162.   For the purpose of determining when more than half of the cost of a transaction is borne by the U.S. Government, the Department applies the standards used in certifying export conduct under the Export Trading Company Act of 1982, 15 U.S.C. §§ 4011-4021 (1982). *See* ETC Guidelines, *supra* note 41, 50 Fed. Reg. at 1799-1800. The requisite U.S. Government involvement could include the actual purchase of goods by the U.S. Government for shipment abroad, a U.S. Government grant to a foreign government that is specifically earmarked for the transaction, or a U.S. Government loan specifically earmarked for the transaction that is made on such generous terms that it amounts to a grant. U.S. Government interests would not be considered to be sufficiently implicated with respect to a transaction that is funded by an international agency for which the U.S. Government does not supply a major portion of funding or a transaction in which the foreign government receives non-earmarked funds from the United States as part of a general government-to-government aid program.

the jurisdictional thresholds of sections 1 and 2 of the Sherman Act and section 7 of the Clayton Act, respectively. For its own enforcement purposes, however, the Department also applies the "direct, substantial, and reasonably foreseeable" standard to import commerce and to mergers and acquisitions.

4.2. Foreign Sovereign Immunities Act

Under the Foreign Sovereign Immunities Act, foreign sovereigns and their instrumentalities are immune from suit in U.S. courts, except under specifically delineated circumstances.[163] The most commonly applied exception in antitrust cases is the so-called "commercial acts" exception. Under that exception, foreign sovereigns and their agencies and instrumentalities may be sued for their commercial activities if those activities otherwise satisfy the jurisdictional tests of the U.S. antitrust laws.[164] The Foreign Sovereign Immunities Act defines "commercial activity" as "either a regular course of conduct or a particular commercial transaction or act. The commercial character of an activity shall be determined by reference to the nature of the course of conduct or particular transaction or act, rather than by reference to its purpose."[165] Application of this exception to the Foreign Sovereign Immunities Act is illustrated in Case 14 of these Guidelines.

5. Factors Affecting the Department's Exercise of Discretion in Asserting Jurisdiction

In enforcing the antitrust laws, the Department recognizes that considerations of comity among nations — the notion that foreign nations are due deference when acting within their legitimate spheres of authority — properly play a role in determining "the recognition which one nation allows within its territory to the legislative, executive or judicial acts of another nation."[166] Thus, in determining whether it would be reasonable to assert jurisdiction or to seek particular remedies in a given case, the Department considers whether significant interests of any foreign sovereign would be affected and asserts jurisdiction only when the Department concludes that it would be reasonable to do so.[167] The Department has in fact

---

163.   28 U.S.C. §§ 1330, 1602-1611 (1982).

164.   See id. § 1605(a)(2); see, e.g., Laker Airways Ltd. v. Sabena, Belgian World Airlines, 731 F.2d 909, 925 (D.C. Cir. 1984).

165.   28 U.S.C. § 1603(d).

166.   Hilton v. Guyot, 159 U.S. 113, 164 (1895).

167.   In lieu of bringing an enforcement action, of course, the Department may consult with interested foreign sovereigns through appropriate diplomatic channels to attempt to eliminate or substantially reduce anticompetitive effects in the United States.

          In the Department's view, antitrust suits prosecuted by the U.S. Government should not be subject to dismissal by U.S. courts on the basis of comity. A decision by the Department to prosecute an antitrust action amounts to a determination by the Executive Branch that the interests of the United States supercede the interests of any foreign sovereign and that the challenged conduct is more harmful to the United States than any injury to foreign relations that might result from the antitrust action. In addition, government suits do not create the same risk as that raised by private actions that a judicial finding of liability will intrude on the legitimate interests of foreign sovereigns because, unlike a private plaintiff, the U.S. Government will have considered those interests before bringing suit.

committed itself to consider the legitimate interests of other nations in accordance with recommendations of the Organization for Economic Cooperation and Development (OECD) and with bilateral agreements with several foreign governments.[168]

In performing a comity analysis, the Department first asks what laws or policies of the arguably interested foreign jurisdictions are implicated by the conduct in question. In many cases, there will be no actual conflict between the antitrust enforcement interests of the United States and the laws or policies of the foreign sovereign. For example, the anticompetitive conduct in question may also be prohibited under the laws of the foreign sovereign. If that is true, then there should be no conflict with the laws of the foreign sovereign resulting from application of the U.S. antitrust laws. The same is true when the anticompetitive conduct is neither encouraged nor prohibited under the national laws or policies of a foreign sovereign. Thus, for example, while the U.S. Webb-Pomerene Act and Export Trading Company Act exempt certain U.S. export conduct from the prohibitions of the Sherman Act, those statutes do not require the formation of export cartels, and the U.S. Government does not actively supervise export cartels under those laws as instruments of national policy. The U.S. Government therefore would not view those statutes as conflicting with another country's nondiscriminatory enforcement action against export cartel activity that affects foreign markets. The Department considers it to be appropriate to prosecute foreign cartels formed privately under similar circumstances that affect the U.S. marketplace.

A true conflict may arise, however, if anticompetitive conduct within the jurisdiction of the U.S. antitrust laws is encouraged or promoted by the law or policy of a foreign sovereign. Where the private anticompetitive conduct is actually compelled by the foreign sovereign, the defense of foreign sovereign compulsion may prevent challenge under the U.S. antitrust laws.[169] Where the defense of foreign

---

168.   *See* Revised Recommendation of the [OECD] Council Concerning Cooperation Between Member Countries on Restrictive Business Practices Affecting International Trade, OECD Doc. No. C(86)44(Final) (May 21, 1986); Memorandum of Understanding as to Notification, Consultation and Cooperation with respect to the Application of National Antitrust Laws, Mar. 9, 1984, United States-Canada, *reprinted in* 4 Trade Reg. Rep. (CCH) ¶ 13,503; Agreement Relating to Cooperation on Antitrust Matters, June 29, 1982, United States-Australia, T.I.A.S. No. 10365, *reprinted in* 4 Trade Reg. Rep. (CCH) ¶ 13,502; Agreement Relating to Mutual Cooperation Regarding Restrictive Business Practices, June 23, 1976, United States-Federal Republic of Germany, 27 U.S.T. 1956, T.I.A.S. No. 8291, *reprinted in* 4 Trade Reg. Rep. (CCH) ¶ 13,501.

169.   *See* Section 6, *infra*. The foreign sovereign compulsion defense should be distinguished from the act of state doctrine. The act of state doctrine is a doctrine of judicial abstention based on considerations of international comity and separation of powers. In the Department's view, that doctrine applies only if the specific conduct complained of is a public act of the foreign sovereign within its territorial jurisdiction on matters pertaining to its governmental sovereignty. In that case, the act of state doctrine generally requires that the foreign sovereign's action be accepted by U.S. courts as a rule of law for their decision. The act of state doctrine generally has no application, however, unless resolution of issues presented in the suit would call into question the validity of a specific foreign sovereign act. *See* Brief for the United States as Amicus Curiae, O.N.E. Shipping, Ltd. v. Flota Mercante Grancolombiana, S.A., No. 87-1350 (U.S. filed Sept. 1988) (on petition for writ of certiorari); Brief for the United States as Amicus Curiae at 32-33, Republic of the Philippines v. Marcos, Nos. 86-6091, 86-6093 (9th Cir. filed January 1988).

sovereign compulsion does not apply, the Department attempts to balance the interests of the U.S. Government in preserving competitive markets and protecting U.S. consumers and the interests of the affected foreign sovereign in promoting its laws and policies.[170]

In addition, the Department may, in extraordinary circumstances, take into account possible effects on the United States' conduct of foreign relations.[171]

6. Foreign Sovereign Compulsion

In some cases, foreign sovereign authorities may compel private parties to engage in conduct that has an anticompetitive effect on U.S. commerce. A sensible approach to the antitrust laws that accommodates notions of comity and fairness supports the reading of an implied defense to application of the U.S. antitrust laws based on foreign sovereign compulsion. As discussed above, Congress enacted our antitrust laws against the background of well-recognized principles of international comity among nations which give due deference to the lawful acts of foreign sovereigns acting within their legitimate spheres of authority.[172] That deference is most acutely called for when a foreign sovereign has compelled the conduct in question. Indeed, in a system of international trade where the United States occasionally negotiates to have certain export restraints imposed by foreign governments, it would be anomalous not to recognize the existence of foreign sovereign compulsion as a defense. Recognizing this defense also ensures that U.S. and foreign firms will not be unfairly subjected to prosecution under the U.S.

---

170. In making this determination, the Department may consider a number of factors, including:
    (1) the relative significance, to the violation alleged, of conduct within the United States as compared to conduct abroad;
    (2) the nationality of the persons involved in or affected by the conduct;
    (3) the presence or absence of a purpose to affect United States consumers or competitors;
    (4) the relative significance and foreseeability of the effects of the conduct on the United States as compared to the effects abroad;
    (5) the existence of reasonable expectations that would be furthered or defeated by the action; and
    (6) the degree of conflict with foreign law or articulated foreign economic policies.
    These factors have been included in proposed legislation that would govern the exercise of jurisdiction by U.S. courts in private antitrust litigation that arises out of disputes involving foreign or transnational conduct. S. 539, 100th Cong., 1st Sess. (1987); S. 397, 99th Cong., 2d Sess. (1986). It should be noted that several of these factors – for example, the relative significance and foreseeability of the effects of the conduct in the United States as compared to the effects abroad – will also be relevant to determining whether there is a sufficiently "direct, substantial, and reasonably foreseeable effect" on U.S. trade or commerce to justify the exercise of jurisdiction under the U.S. antitrust laws in the first place. See Section 4, supra.

171. See U.S. Department of Justice Press Release dated Nov. 19, 1984, announcing termination, based on foreign policy concerns, of a grand jury investigation into passenger air travel between the United States and the United Kingdom. The Department does not believe, however, that this factor should properly be considered by courts in either private or government litigation, since the conduct of foreign relations is constitutionally reserved to the Executive Branch.

172. See text accompanying n.167, supra.

antitrust laws for activities that were not voluntary, but that were the result of governmental compulsion.[173]

The Department will not prosecute anticompetitive conduct that has been compelled by a foreign sovereign under the following circumstances. First, a foreign sovereign must have compelled the anticompetitive conduct in circumstances in which a refusal to comply with the foreign sovereign's command would give rise to the imposition of significant penalties or to the denial of specific substantial benefits.[174] As a general matter, the Department regards a foreign government's formal representation that refusal to comply with its command would have such a result as being sufficient to establish that the conduct in question has been compelled.[175] It is not enough, however, that private anticompetitive conduct is merely encouraged by, permitted by, or consistent with the laws or policies of the foreign sovereign. While such foreign government encouragement or permission may be taken into account in a general comity analysis, it will not have the determinative effect of actual compulsion.

Second, although territorial tests are often difficult to apply and are therefore not always useful, the Department generally will not recognize foreign sovereign compulsion as a defense when the compelled conduct plainly has occurred wholly or primarily in the United States. For example, the Department would not recognize the defense where a foreign government required the U.S. subsidiary of a foreign firm to organize a cartel in the United States to fix the price at which products would be sold in the U.S. marketplace.

The Department believes that the defense of foreign sovereign compulsion must be distinguished from the federalism-based state action doctrine. The state action doctrine applies to private anticompetitive conduct that is taken pursuant to clearly articulated state policies and is subject to active state supervision, as well as to conduct that actually is compelled by a state.[176] The doctrine embodies the notion that the U.S. Congress should not be presumed to have intended to interfere with the authority of the states constitutionally "to regulate their domestic commerce."[177] Because our federal structure of government is designed to secure to the states a wide range of regulatory alternatives, the U.S. Supreme Court has held that compulsion is too strict a standard to employ in state action cases.[178] At the same time, the federal government retains authority under the Supremacy Clause to void any state program that has a noxious effect on interstate commerce. In contrast, the sovereign compulsion defense serves the quite different purposes of

---

173. For an example of an arrangement as to which the Department concluded that the defense of sovereign compulsion would apply, see Exchange of letters between William French Smith, United States Attorney General, and Yoshio Okawara, Ambassador of Japan, May 7, 1981, *reprinted in* U.S. Import Weekly (BNA), May 13, 1981, at M-1 to M-2.

174. This does not include, however, the denial of benefits that may flow directly from participation in the anticompetitive conduct (for example, sharing in monopoly profits generated by an export cartel).

175. The Department may not regard as dispositive, however, a statement that is ambiguous or that on its face appears to be internally inconsistent. In such a case, the Department may inquire into the circumstances underlying the statement.

176. *See* Southern Motor Carriers Rate Conference, Inc. v. United States, 471 U.S. 48 (1985); Parker v. Brown, 317 U.S. 341 (1943).

177. *Southern Motor Carriers*, 471 U.S. at 56.

178. *Id.* at 61.

preventing direct clashes with the most significant interests of foreign sovereigns and of protecting parties whose actions are compelled by a foreign sovereign from being unfairly condemned under the U.S. antitrust laws. These purposes are advanced most directly when the foreign government has actually compelled the challenged conduct.[179] Case 14 of these Guidelines addresses the issue of foreign sovereign compulsion in the context of a cartel governing sales made in the United States.

Difficult legal and policy issues nevertheless may arise when anticompetitive conduct is not strictly compelled by a foreign sovereign, but has clearly arisen from the decision and actions of the foreign sovereign and is intended to promote significant national economic interests of the sovereign. In such cases, considerations of international comity may lead the Department not to challenge the conduct in question. This is especially likely to be true if the foreign government has instigated the conduct in question at the request of the U.S. Government. The Department's analysis of this kind of situation is illustrated in Case 16, which deals with a voluntary export restraint.

Businesses may obtain greater certainty concerning their liability for anticompetitive conduct conforming to the order of a foreign government by seeking to obtain an opinion of the Department under its Business Review Procedure.[180]

7. International Trade Friction and the U.S. Trade Laws

Governmental and private conduct undertaken pursuant to the U.S. trade laws, or to resolve disputes causing international trade friction, often affects competition in markets serving U.S. consumers. This may occur, for example, when an antidumping or countervailing duty case leads to the imposition of additional duties or to resolution under provisions in the law that allow for restrictions on the prices or quantities of imported products. Foreign imports may also be limited by voluntary export restraints unilaterally adopted by a foreign government at the request of the U.S. Government.

The individual or joint conduct of U.S. firms in petitioning the U.S. Government for protection from foreign competition generally is immune from prosecution under the U.S. antitrust laws. Under the *Noerr-Pennington* doctrine, the courts have construed the Sherman Act not to apply to individual or collective petitioning of the U.S. federal or state governments, even when the government action sought would have an anticompetitive effect.[181]

---

179.   In addition, a standard like that of the state action doctrine would be difficult to apply in the international context. Given the complexity and novelty of foreign legal systems and the difficulty of obtaining foreign-located evidence, defendants would have many opportunities to attempt to evade legitimate application of the U.S. antitrust laws wherever there was an arguable foreign national policy underlying anticompetitive conduct. The use of an active supervision standard of the sort applied in state action cases would also require difficult inquiries into the foreign sovereign's conduct of its own affairs.

180.   28 C.F.R. § 50.6 (1987).

181.   *See* Eastern Railroad Presidents Conference v. Noerr Motor Freight, Inc. 365 U.S. 127 (1961); United Mine Workers of America v. Pennington, 381 U.S. 657 (1965); California Motor Transport Co. v. Trucking Unlimited, 404 U.S. 508 (1972) (extending protection to petitioning before "all departments of Government," including the courts). The doctrine that has developed out of these cases is known as the *Noerr-Pennington* doctrine.

The *Noerr-Pennington* doctrine rests on a construction of the Sherman Act that is rooted in two different rationales — one concerning the First Amendment right to petition government and the other concerning the right of a government to take actions that operate to restrain trade and the concomitant need to receive communications with respect to those actions.

Ostensible petitioning conduct is not immune, however, when it is in fact a mere sham concealing a direct restraint by the parties. Examples of petitioning that is not protected by *Noerr-Pennington* immunity include the meritless invocation of administrative procedures to delay a competitor's entry or to deny its access to governmental processes and the deliberate misleading of the government during such administrative proceedings.[182] The threat to consumer welfare from such abuse may be substantial. Although most litigated findings of sham petitioning have involved a pattern of abuse, a single anticompetitive abuse of governmental processes may suffice in appropriate circumstances. Application of the sham exception to the *Noerr-Pennington* doctrine is illustrated in Case 13, which deals with the filing of a patent claim under section 337 of the 1930 Tariff Act in order to exclude imports.

The Supreme Court has not ruled on whether the *Noerr-Pennington* doctrine applies to the petitioning of foreign governments by U.S. and foreign firms.[183] The Department's policy, however, is not to prosecute the legitimate petitioning of foreign governments by foreign or U.S. firms in circumstances in which the United States protects such activities by its own citizens. This point is illustrated in Case 15, which deals with a foreign government-imposed export restraint.

Of course, the mere involvement of U.S. or foreign government officials, allegations of U.S. trade law violations, or an alleged intention to resolve international trade frictions, will not protect naked agreements among competitors to restrict output or fix prices. The U.S. trade laws, for example, set forth specific procedures for settling disputes under those laws. Any agreement among competitors that does not comply with those procedures may be prosecuted in appropriate cases, perhaps even as a criminal violation. The Department's analysis of agreements made in the context of trade disputes is illustrated in Case 17. The Department's analysis of the exchange of information among competitors in connection with the bringing of a trade action under the U.S. trade laws is illustrated in Case 18.

8. Conclusion

Like most domestic transactions, the vast majority of international business transactions do not raise antitrust concerns. One of the purposes of these Guidelines is to ensure that uncertainty about the Department's enforcement policy does not cause businesses to limit unobjectionable transactions or to avoid efficient and productive arrangements that benefit consumers. At the same time, these Guidelines make plain the Department's commitment to prosecute naked restraints of trade,

---

182.   *See California Motor Transport*, 404 U.S. at 515-16.
183.   *Compare* Coastal States Marketing, Inc. v. Hunt, 694 F.2d 1358, 1364-67 (5th Cir. 1983) (applying doctrine) *with* Occidental Petroleum Corp. v. Buttes Oil & Gas Co., 331 F. Supp. 92, 107-08 (C.D. Cal. 1971) (refusing to apply doctrine), *aff'd per curiam*, 461 F.2d 1261 (9th Cir.), *cert. denied*, 409 U.S. 950 (1972).

such as horizontal price fixing, bid rigging, and market allocation, which by their nature have no plausible connection to achieving significant integrative efficiencies that benefit U.S. consumers and that almost certainly reduce output and/or raise prices to the detriment of U.S. consumers.

PART II. ILLUSTRATIVE CASES

The following hypothetical case discussions illustrate how the Department would apply the foregoing analysis in eighteen fact situations. In each case, of course, the outcome of the Department's analysis would depend on the specific facts and circumstances of the case. These hypothetical case discussions therefore do not provide determinative answers to the factual and economic questions the Department would ask in analyzing particular conduct and transactions under the antitrust laws. Rather, they are intended to provide and illustrate application of a coherent framework for that analysis. By providing this analytical framework, the Department hopes to provide U.S. and foreign businesses and their counsel a better understanding of when and why the Department is likely to take antitrust enforcement action with respect to particular conduct.

Case 1 – Merger of a U.S. Firm and a Foreign Firm

Alpha Corporation, a Japanese firm that exports product X to the United States, proposes to acquire all of the stock of Beta Corporation, a U.S. firm that manufactures and sells X in the United States. X is a piece of high technology hardware that is used in several military and civil aerospace applications. There are no known substitutes for X for those applications, and no other known applications for X. Alpha and Beta sell no product other than X.

Alpha is the world's leading producer of X. It supplies approximately ten percent of U.S. consumption of X. Beta is the largest supplier of X in the United States. It supplies approximately 25 percent of all U.S. consumption of X. Imports of X from Japan, the European Economic Community ("EEC"), and Brazil collectively account for approximately 40 percent of current U.S. consumption. Although U.S. producers at one time supplied almost all U.S. consumption of X, their share of the market has fallen to imports. Some smaller, less efficient U.S. producers of X have left the market. There are no quotas or any other kind of governmentally-imposed trade restraints limiting the volume of X imports into the United States.

Discussion

Because Alpha and Beta are both engaged in commerce in the United States, the proposed acquisition clearly is subject to section 7 of the Clayton Act. Section 7 prohibits mergers and acquisitions that may substantially lessen competition or tend to create a monopoly "in any line of commerce . . . in any section" of the United States.[184]

---

184.   15 U.S.C § 18 (1982). Section 7 of the Clayton Act applies to a merger if the parties are engaged "in commerce or in any activity affecting commerce." *Id.* The Department may also challenge a merger under section 1 of the Sherman Act (15 U.S.C. § 1), which prohibits

In analyzing this merger, the Department would focus on the merger's likely competitive effects in the United States. The Department would seek to determine whether the merged firm would have the ability, alone or in coordination with other firms in the market, to restrict output or raise prices to U.S. consumers. The fact that Alpha is a foreign firm would not cause the Department to apply any different competitive standard.[185]

The Department's first step in analyzing this merger would be to define the market or markets that would be affected by the merger. Because a firm can compete at the see time in a number of economically discrete geographic markets, it is possible that Alpha and Beta compete in markets outside the United States. The Department would be concerned only about this merger's effect on U.S. consumer welfare, however, and would not be concerned about the merger's competitive effects in foreign markets.

PRODUCT MARKET

To define the relevant product market or markets that would be affected by this merger, the Department would begin by considering separately each product (narrowly defined) sold by Alpha and Beta in the United States. With respect to each such product, the Department would ask what would happen if a hypothetical monopolist of that product imposed a significant and nontransitory increase in price (usually five percent for one year). If so many buyers would shift to other products that the price increase would be unprofitable, then the Department would add to the product group the product that was the next best substitute for consumers. The Department would repeat this process until it had identified a group of products with respect to which a hypothetical monopolist could profitably raise price. Ultimately, this process would identify all products with which the products sold by Alpha and Beta do or would compete in response to a significant and nontransitory increase in

---

contracts, combinations, and conspiracies "in restraint of trade or commerce among the several States, or with foreign nations." The Department's substantive analysis of a merger is the same under both section 7 and section 1. Merger Guidelines § 1.

185. As noted at n.84, *supra*, the 1988 Trade Act authorizes the President to direct the Attorney General to seek appropriate judicial relief against any merger, acquisition, or takeover that could result in foreign control of a firm engaged in U.S. interstate commerce if the President finds credible evidence that the foreign controlling entity might take action that threatens to impair the national security and that no other law provides adequate and appropriate authority to protect the national security. The Department's competition analysis under the antitrust laws is completely separate from considerations under the 1988 Trade Act.

price.[186]   The Department generally will consider the relevant product market to be the smallest group of products that satisfies this test.[187]

Under the facts of this case, X is the only product sold by Alpha and Beta in the United States, and there are no known substitutes for X for any group of buyers. The Department would therefore conclude that X comprises the relevant product market.

GEOGRAPHIC MARKET

Next, the Department would define the relevant geographic market. The purpose of defining a relevant geographic market is to establish a geographic boundary that roughly separates producers that are important factors in the competitive analysis (that is, that would frustrate an attempt by a firm or firms to exercise market power) from those that are not.

To define the relevant geographic market in this case, the Department would begin by considering Beta's locations (or the location of each of its plants) in the United States. With respect to each location, the Department would ask what would happen if a hypothetical monopolist of X imposed a significant and nontransitory increase in price. If so many buyers would shift to X produced in other areas that the price increase would be unprofitable, then the Department would add the location from which production of X would be the next best substitute and ask the same question again.[188]   Ultimately, this process would identify all areas, foreign and domestic, in which producers do compete or would compete with Beta for sales in the United States in response to a significant and nontransitory increase in the price of X. As with respect to product market definition, the Department generally will consider the relevant geographic market to be the smallest area that satisfies this test.[189]

Although direct evidence of the likely effect of a price increase (such as historical evidence of consumer response to previous price increases) might sometimes be available, the Department normally would infer the likely effect of a price increase from reliable circumstantial evidence. The Department would give particular weight to shipment patterns, evidence that U.S. consumers had actually considered shifting their purchases of X to producers located in other areas in response to changes in competitive variables, differences or similarities in price movements over a period of years that are not explainable by parallel changes in factors such as the cost of

---

186.	Merger Guidelines § 2.11. Existing buyers may differ in their ability to use particular substitute products and the ease with which they could substitute those products for the product of the merging firms. Therefore, even though an across-the-board price increase might cause such significant substitution that the price increase would not be profitable, if sellers could discriminate in the prices they charged to different groups of buyers, then sellers might be able to raise price to only those buyers who could not easily substitute away. Price discrimination requires that sellers be able to identify those buyers. It also requires that other buyers not be able profitably to purchase and resell the product to them (that is, arbitrage must not occur). If price discrimination were possible, the Department would consider defining additional, narrower product markets consisting of particular uses of the product. *See* Merger Guidelines § 2.13 & n.8.

187.	*Id.* § 2.11. This is known as the "smallest market" principle.

188.	*See* Merger Guidelines § 2.31.

189.	*Id.*

inputs, transportation and local distribution costs, and excess capacity of producers outside Beta's locations.[190]

The facts that Alpha and other producers in Japan, the EEC, and Brazil currently account for approximately 40 percent of X consumption in the United States and that X imports from those countries have been rising suggest that U.S. consumers would shift to X produced by firms in those areas in response to a price increase in the United States. This would not necessarily be true, however. For example, a U.S. Department of Defense requirement that contractors use X produced in the United States would preclude foreign producers of X from increasing their sales of X in the United States in response to a price increase for X used for military applications.[191] X imports might still be an alternative for civilian aerospace applications. The Department would likely define a national market for the sale of X for U.S. military applications that would exclude foreign producers of X (including Alpha) and a second market for the sale of X for civilian applications that would include those foreign competitors that currently sell in the United States or to which consumers would turn in response to a price increase.

IDENTIFYING FIRMS IN THE RELEVANT MARKET

After defining the relevant market, the Department would then identify and assign shares to competitors in the market. The Department would include in the market all firms that currently sell X in the market plus all firms that could easily and economically begin selling X in the market using existing production and distribution facilities within one year of a price increase.[192] Of course, firms that could readily convert their facilities to produce X within one year might nevertheless find it difficult to market or distribute X in the United States, or for some other reason might find the substitution to be unprofitable. The Department would not include those firms in the relevant market but, if appropriate, would consider their competitive significance in evaluating the likelihood of new entry within two years of a domestic price increase.[193]

ASSIGNING MARKET SHARES

The Department would count in the market the total sales or total capacity of all domestic firms (or plants) in the market, unless the facts indicated that total sales or capacity would overstate the competitive significance of a particular firm or group of firms.[194] If some portion of a firm's output would not be used to respond to a price increase (for example, because it was already contractually committed

---

190.   *Id.* § 2.32.
191.   The competitive significance of foreign firms might also be significantly constrained by governmentally-imposed trade restraints, such as import quotas or voluntary export restraints. Although foreign firms would not be excluded from the relevant market on the basis of such trade restraints, the constraint on their responses to a post-merger price increase would be reflected in the market share assigned to them.
192.   *See* Merger Guidelines §§ 2.2, 2.21. Firms that would need to construct new facilities or significantly to modify existing facilities in order to produce and sell X would not be included in the relevant market. Instead, the role of those firms in constraining an anticompetitive price increase would be considered in evaluating ease of entry into the relevant market. *Id.* § 3.3.
193.   *See id.* §§ 2.21, 3.3
194.   *Id.* § 2.4.

elsewhere), then the Department might exclude that portion of the firm's output from the market.[195] Whether and to what extent the Department would exclude such output from the market would depend on the extent to which that output could either be resold to buyers in the relevant market or would free up the output of other producers to be sold in the relevant market.

Market shares would be expressed either in dollar terms (through the measurement of sales, shipments, or production), or in physical terms (through the measurement of sales, shipments, production, capacity, or reserves). As a practical matter, in each case, the availability of data would determine which measurement base the Department used. If it had a choice, however, the Department would use dollar sales or shipments if X were a branded or relatively differentiated product. It would use capacity, production, or reserves if X were a relatively homogeneous and undifferentiated product.[196]

As to foreign firms, if market shares generally were to be assigned on the basis of dollar sales or shipments, the Department would count a foreign firm's sales in, or shipments to, the relevant market. If varying exchange rates made comparable dollar calculations for firms in different countries difficult, the Department might use unit volume sales instead of dollar sales.[197] If market shares generally were to be assigned on the basis of capacity, reserves, or production, the Department would count a foreign firm's capacity, reserves, or production likely to be devoted to the relevant market in response to a price increase. The total capacity of a foreign firm would not be counted in the market if the firm lacked specialized distribution facilities needed to supply additional demand in the United States and could not develop such facilities within one year. In addition, the Department might use current shipments for foreign firms if the Department were unable to obtain adequate data to quantify reliably the amount of capacity, reserves, or production that would be devoted to the United States in response to a price increase.[198] Finally, the Department generally would assign a single, aggregate market share to firms in a country or group of countries if there were insufficient data available to allocate shares between individual firms or if firms in a country or group of countries coordinated their production or sales into the United States.[199]

In some circumstances, current market shares calculated as described above might either overstate or understate the competitive significance of firms in the market.[200] For example, if the Department lacked data concerning foreign capacity, it might be forced to use market share data that understated the true competitive significance of foreign competitors. If current market share data would give a distorted view of the market, the Department would consider that fact in interpreting the significance of that data.[201] Thus, for example, despite the inability to quantify precisely the supply response of foreign competitors, the

---

195.   *Id.*
196.   *Id.*
197.   *Id.* § 2.4 & n.12.
198.   *Id.* § 2.4.
199.   *Id.*
200.   The Department's analysis of quotas and other governmentally-imposed trade restraints that constrain the ability of foreign producers to increase their sales in the United States is illustrated in Case 2.
201.   *See* Merger Guidelines § 3.23.

Department would consider strong qualitative evidence that there was significant worldwide excess capacity that could readily be devoted to the United States in response to a post-merger price increase.[202]

COMPETITIVE ANALYSIS

After defining the relevant market, identifying firms competing in that market, and assigning market shares, the Department would determine the level of post-merger concentration in the market and the increase in concentration that would result from the merger.[203] If concentration in the relevant market for X would remain low after the merger, or if concentration would increase only slightly, then the Department would conclude without further examination that the merger in this case would pose no significant threat to competition.[204] Otherwise, the Department would proceed to examine other factors bearing on whether the merger would likely result in market power.

Even if a merger of Alpha and Beta would result in a highly concentrated market, it would not likely create, enhance, or facilitate the exercise of market power in the United States if any attempt to restrict output or raise price after the merger would be frustrated by new entry or by expansion of fringe firms or if other factors would make the successful exercise of market power unlikely.[205] In addition, efficiencies that could only be achieved through the merger may be so great that, despite its anticompetitive potential, the merger's net effect would be to benefit U.S. consumer welfare.

In considering whether efficiencies would offset the threat of anticompetitive harm, the Department would compare the estimated cost savings from the claimed efficiencies (less the estimated cost of consolidating the operations of the merging firms) with the threat of harm to competition resulting from the merger. The Department would consider efficiencies such as economies of scale, better integration of production facilities, plant specialization, and lower transportation costs. The Department would also consider the reduction of general selling and administrative and overhead expenses, although these types of efficiencies alone would be less likely to offset any significant threat of anticompetitive harm. The Department would require the parties to demonstrate a greater level of expected efficiencies the greater was the level of anticompetitive risks posed by the merger. The parties would bear the burden of establishing offsetting efficiencies on the basis of clear and convincing evidence.

In this hypothetical case, the relevant market for X would likely at least moderately concentrated following the merger, and concentration would increase by 500 HHI points (25 x 10 x 2). Alpha and Beta have a combined share of 35 percent of current U.S. sales of X. The process of defining the relevant market, identifying competitors in that market, and assigning market shares might reveal, however, that

---

202.   *Id.*
203.   As explained at Section 3.32 of these Guidelines, the Department measures market concentration using the Herfindahl-Hirschman Index ("HHI"). The HHI is calculated by summing the squares of the individual market shares of all firms included in the relevant market. *See* Merger Guidelines § 3.1 & n.14.
204.   *Id.* § 3.11. *See also* discussion at Section 3.32, *supra*.
205.   *See* Merger Guidelines §§ 3.3, 3.4; Section 3.322, *supra*.

a more accurate calculation of the combined market share of Alpha and Beta is something less that 35 percent (or more if, for example, market shares are measured based on capacity). The Department's ultimate conclusion whether to challenge Alpha's acquisition of Beta would turn on a careful examination of other factors, including the likelihood and extent of new entry in response to a price increase and procompetitive efficiencies that would result from the acquisition.

Case 2 – Merger Analysis Involving Trade Restraints

The facts of this case are the same as those in Case 1, plus the following facts. Japanese producers of X are subject to a voluntary export restraint ("VER") limiting the quantity of their X exports to the United States. Shipments from the EEC are subject to binding U.S. import quotas, some of which limit imports of X from the EEC to a fixed quantity (fixed quotas), and some of which limit X imports to a percentage of U.S. production (percentage quotas). Imports of X from Brazil are subject to a tariff that was imposed as a result of a countervailing duty proceeding under the U.S. trade laws.

Discussion

The Department would not exclude foreign competitors from the relevant market solely because their sales in the United States are subject to quotas or VERs. It often is impossible to quantify the precise effect of such restraints on the overall level of foreign supply. A quota that applied only to the EEC, for example, might have only a limited effect on the extent of foreign competition faced by domestic firms in the event of a price increase if non-EEC firms could readily shift shipments to the United States from countries that do not limit EEC imports or if non-EEC firms could purchase X from EEC firms and resell it in the United States.

Nevertheless, the Department would consider the supply-restraining effect of the EEC quotas and the Japanese VER both in assigning market shares and in interpreting market share data. To the extent that actual sales or shipments by EEC and Japanese firms would overstate their future competitive significance (because the quotas and the VER limited the ability of those firms to expand shipments to the United States in response to a price increase), concentration data based on those sales or shipments may understate the threat of harm to competition. If a cartel of domestic producers restricted their output of X in order to drive up prices in the United States, for example, EEC firms bound by the percentage quota would be forced to reduce their U.S. shipments along with the domestic cartel. The competitive significance of those firms would therefore be heavily, if not completely, discounted in the Department's analysis. Similarly, if the VER in this case would prevent Japanese firms from expanding their shipments to the United States, current U.S. sales by Japanese firms might tend to overstate their ability to inhibit the post-merger exercise of market power.

Because Beta is subject to the VER, the Department would count only Beta's current sales in the United States in assigning it a market share. The Department would not further discount Beta's market share, however, even if it would do so with respect to other Japanese firms. A merger between Alpha and Beta conceivably could increase the likelihood of collusion because, following the merger, a domestic cartel would control a greater share of the market. On the other hand, the merger may be designed to avoid the effect of the VER and to expand output in the United States. In that case, the merger would be procompetitive.[206]

If Brazilian firms have been shipping X to the United States subject to the tariff, then the tariff by itself would not likely inhibit Brazilian producers in responding to a significant and nontransitory price increase in the United States. If the tariff were prohibitive, however, such that Brazilian firms were not currently selling in the United States, then those firms would be included in the relevant market only if a price increase would make shipments to the United States under the tariff profitable.[207]

Case 3 – Acquisition of a Foreign Potential Competitor

Beta Corporation, a U.S. firm that manufactures and sells product X in the United States, and Alpha Corporation, a Japanese firm that manufactures and sells product X in Japan, plan to merge. Beta Corporation is the largest supplier of X in the United States, supplying approximately 25 percent of all X consumed in the United States. Alpha Corporation does not currently sell X in the United States. It would take Alpha at least 18 months to establish sufficient distribution facilities to begin selling X in the United States, if it chose to do so. It is assumed for the purpose of this case that X comprises the relevant product market.

Discussion

Because Alpha does not currently compete with Beta in the sale of X in the United States,[208] this merger could have an anticompetitive effect in the relevant market for X only if (i) Alpha would enter the market independently in the near future if it did not merge with Beta; (ii) the market were very highly concentrated; and (iii) Alpha were one of only a very few other firms capable of entering the market in response to an anticompetitive price increase (for example, because few or no other firms possessed the technology needed to enter the market).[209] Even if the relevant market were very highly concentrated, eliminating Alpha would not have any significant anticompetitive effect if there were several other potential entrants in addition to Alpha.

In determining whether Alpha actually would enter the U.S. market independently (or through a "toe-hold" acquisition) but for this merger, the Department would consider evidence that Alpha actually intended to enter the market (including, for example, internal management studies, expansion plans, actual investments, and other

---

206.   *Cf.* General Motors Corp., 103 F.T.C. 374, 387-88 (1984) (statement of Chairman Miller) (discussing procompetitive benefits of a joint venture of General Motors Corporation and Toyota Corporation, including expanding the supply of small automobiles available in the United States despite restrictions on Japanese imports).

207.   *See* discussion of geographic market definition at Case 1.

208.   If Alpha could easily and economically begin selling X in the United States within one year of a significant and nontransitory price increase, then the Department would regard Alpha as an actual competitor. *See* Merger Guidelines § 2.21; Case 1.

209.   Applying a more speculative test would insulate inefficient management from the threat of takeover without necessarily inducing independent entry and would thus lead to decreased consumer welfare.

steps taken toward entry), any past attempts by Alpha to enter the market, and the profitability of independent entry.[210]

If these three necessary conditions existed, then the Department would proceed to consider other factors it normally considers in determining whether a merger would likely create, enhance, or facilitate the exercise of market power. Those factors include whether the market for X currently was performing anticompetitively and whether characteristics of X would make successful collusion more or less difficult.[211] If, after considering these factors, the Department concluded that the merger would likely result in the ability to exercise market power, then the Department would consider whether any procompetitive efficiencies the parties claim would result from the merger would outweigh the threat of anticompetitive harm to U.S. consumers.[212]

Case 4 – Merger of Two Foreign Firms

Beta Corporation and Delta Corporation are among the leading diversified electronics companies in Country A. They are the two most significant producers outside the United States of product X, a highly advanced and complex electronic device possessing important and unique capabilities. Beta and Delta together supply approximately 60 percent of all X consumed in the United States, accounting for more than $110 million in annual sales. Each company has at least $15 million (book value) in assets located in the United States, although none of those assets are used to produce or sell X. Both companies' facilities for producing X are located in Country A. Beta and Delta each make sales of X in the United States through agreements with independent distributors. There are no quotas or other governmentally-imposed trade restraints constraining sales by Beta and Delta in the United States.

Beta has announced that it intends to purchase all of the stock of Delta. After conducting a preliminary investigation, the Department has determined that the relevant market for the sale of X in which Beta and Delta compete is highly concentrated and that concentration will increase substantially as a result of the merger. It therefore appears that the merger could have an anticompetitive effect in the United States unless other factors, such as significant likely entry into the market in response to a price increase, would make the post-merger exercise of market power unlikely or unless procompetitive efficiencies that would result from the merger outweigh any threat of anticompetitive harm to U.S. consumers. Although both Beta and Delta sell products other than X in the United States, it does not appear based on concentration data that the merger could have an anticompetitive effect with respect to any of those other products.

---

210.   The Department would not likely challenge the merger if Beta had a market share of five percent or less. Given the insignificant role that small firms usually play in collusive interactions, a merger between a potential entrant and a firm with only five percent of the market may have the same competitive effect as new entry and could be procompetitive by, in effect, converting a fringe firm into a more significant competitive factor in the market. *See* Merger Guidelines § 4.134.

211.   *See* Section 3.322, *supra*, and Case 1.

212.   *Id*. § 3.5. *See* discussion of efficiencies at Section 3.3222, *supra*.

Discussion

Because Beta and Delta both sell X in the United States, this merger clearly would be subject to section 7 of the Clayton Act.[213] The Department's Merger Guidelines explain when the Department ordinarily will challenge a merger or acquisition under section 7. That analysis is also described in Section 3 of these Guidelines and illustrated in Cases 1, 2, and 3.

The U.S. antitrust laws represent a fundamental and important national policy that generally must be protected when U.S. commerce is significantly affected, even when doing so would require bringing an enforcement action against conduct or transactions that occur outside the United States. Nevertheless, enforcing the U.S. antitrust laws with respect to such conduct or transactions can sometimes conflict with the legitimate interests of other nations. Therefore, as a matter of comity and in the exercise of its prosecutorial discretion, the Department would consider such interests in deciding whether to challenge the transaction in this case.

The Department would not challenge the merger in this case notwithstanding any possible anticompetitive effect the merger might have on U.S. commerce. Since both of the merging firms are foreign and all of their assets involved in producing and distributing X are located outside the United States, it would be difficult, if not practically impossible, to obtain effective relief that would preserve competition in the United States.

This does not mean, however, that the Department would never challenge a merger between foreign firms that would have a substantial anticompetitive effect in the United States. For example, the Department might reach a different conclusion in this case if either Beta or Delta had production facilities or substantial distribution assets used to produce or distribute X located in the United States. In that case, the Department would probably request additional information concerning the likely competitive effects of the merger, using procedures under the Hart-Scott-Rodino Act,[214] Civil Investigative Demands,[215] or informal requests, as appropriate. The Department would likely challenge the merger if it concluded after reviewing such information that the merger would likely result in reduced output and higher prices to U.S. consumers without offsetting efficiency benefits. If assets used to produce X belonging to Beta or Delta and located in the United States would constitute a viable business standing alone or if acquired by another company (or if assets used to distribute X belonging to Beta or Delta would enable a firm that acquired those facilities to enter or expand its sales in the relevant market), then the merger might be permitted to go forward conditioned on the divestiture of all or a portion of those assets to a suitable buyer approved by the Department. The Department might seek the views of the government of Country A concerning the impact of various alternative remedies on that country's national interests.

HART-SCOTT-RODINO PREMERGER NOTIFICATION REQUIREMENT

Foreign firms that have all of their assets used to produce and sell the relevant product located outside the United States (and the merger of which therefore would

---

213. See n.183, *supra*.
214. See Section 2.3, *supra*.
215. See n.20, *supra*.

not be subject to challenge by the Department) might still be required by the Hart-Scott-Rodino Act to file premerger notification with the Department and the FTC. Although meeting the general thresholds of the H-S-R Act, the acquisition in this case would be exempt from the premerger notification requirements of the Act as an acquisition by a foreign person if (i) the acquisition would not confer control of a U.S. issuer having annual net sales or total assets of $25 million or more, or of any issuer with assets located in the United States having a book value of $15 million or more; or (ii) aggregate annual net sales of the merging firms in the United States were less than $110 million and the aggregate book value of their assets in the United States was less than $110 million.[216] Neither exception is satisfied in this case. Beta's acquisition of Delta's stock would give Beta control over Delta's assets in the United States, which have a book value of more than $15 million. In addition, the combined sales of Beta and Delta in the United States exceed $110 million. In the absence of some other exemption under the Hart-Scott-Rodino Act, the parties would therefore be required to file premerger notification under the Act, and failure to do so would subject them to, *inter alia*, civil penalties of $10,000 a day.

Case 5 – Joint Bidding

Several U.S. electrical equipment manufacturers and engineering firms have established a consortium to submit a bid to develop a nationwide system of hydroelectric power plants in Country A. The consortium includes three of the ten largest U.S. equipment manufacturers and three of the ten largest U.S. engineering firms. No other U.S. or foreign firms have been invited to join the consortium. Four similar consortia supported by the Japanese, British, Korean, and German Governments, respectively, are also preparing bids.

Country A is financing the entire project through a 30-year loan from the U.S. Government. The interest rate on the loan is substantially below the current commercial rate of lending and payments on the loan do not come due until the fifteenth year. As a result, the present value of the expected future repayment of principal and interest on the loan is less than half of the value of the loan.

Because of the importance of this project, several senior U.S. Government officials have been strong supporters of the U.S. consortium.

Discussion

This case involves issues of joint venture analysis. As discussed in Section 3.4 of these Guidelines, joint ventures often play an important role in promoting the growth and international competitiveness of U.S. industry by generating significant integrative efficiencies and adding new capacity to the market. The Department judges legitimate joint ventures – those that involve some economic integration of the venture members' operations beyond the mere coordination of their pricing and output decisions – under a rule of reason. The Department will challenge a joint venture only when on balance the joint venture would likely result in reduced output or higher prices to U.S. consumers.

In the absence of U.S. Government funding, the Department will not challenge a

---

216.   *See* 16 C.F.R. § 802.51 (1988).

joint venture — or even outright bid rigging — by U.S. firms on the basis of competitive effects in a foreign market.[217]   In this case, however, the U.S. Government is substantially funding the project through a noncommercial-rate loan. As a general matter, the Department considers there to be a sufficient effect on U.S. interests to support the assertion of jurisdiction under the antitrust laws where, as a result of its payment or financing, the U.S. Government bears more than half of the cost of a transaction affected by anticompetitive conduct.[218] Anticompetitive conduct with respect to the transaction would then have the primary effect of harming U.S. taxpayers. In this hypothetical case, since the present value of the expected future repayment of the loan is less than half the value of the transaction, more than half of the cost of the transaction will be borne by the U.S. Government.

The initial question in this case is therefore whether the bidding consortium is a legitimate joint venture that should be analyzed under a rule of reason, or a naked restraint of trade that should be treated as per se unlawful.[219] The Department would treat the consortium in this case as per se unlawful if it were merely a sham designed to disguise naked bid rigging.   The Department would regard the consortium to be a sham if, for example, the consortium members secretly agree to allow one pair of engineering firm and equipment manufacturer to perform the entire contract in exchange for some quid pro quo paid to the consortium's other members. The true intention of the parties in that case would be covert, and the consortium would be merely diversionary. The consortium's goal would be to eliminate competition among the bidders, rather than to achieve efficiencies from the economic integration of the parties' operations.

It does not appear from the facts of this case that the U.S. consortium is a sham. The facts suggest that the consortium may be intended to achieve integrative efficiencies by combining the complementary assets of joint venture members and by spreading risk among them. The consortium appears to be intended not merely to eliminate competition among consortium members, but rather to enable them to compete more effectively against other bidders. Assuming that the consortium is a legitimate joint venture, the Department would analyze its likely competitive effects under the four-step rule of reason described in Section 3.4 of these Guidelines.[220] The Department would challenge the consortium if that analysis revealed that on balance the consortium would be anticompetitive.

STEP 1 — THE JOINT VENTURE MARKET

The Department would first determine whether the consortium would have an anticompetitive effect in any market or markets in which the economic integration of the parties' operations occurs (the "joint venture markets"). If it appeared from the facts of this case that some smaller group of consortium members would have the same probability of winning the bid as would other bidders such that the consortium effectively reduces the number of independent bidders in the market, then the

---

217.   *But see* discussion of potential "spill-over" effects in markets in which U.S. consumers participate, *infra*.

218.   *See* Section 4.1, *supra*.

219.   *See* Section 3.0, *supra*.

220.   If it were not a legitimate joint venture, the Department would prosecute it as criminal bid rigging, which is punishable by substantial fines as well as imprisonment. *See* Section 2.1, *supra*.

Department would seek to determine whether the elimination of that competition would likely have an anticompetitive effect.[221] The relevant joint venture market in this case would be the bidding market to perform the foreign project. The market would include all individual firms and consortia, foreign and domestic, that were willing and able to bid on and perform the project.

In conducting its analysis, the Department would focus first on the level of and increase in bidder concentration after the U.S. consortium is formed. If each of the other bidders in the market were equally capable of submitting competitive bids, the Department would consider each bidder to be of equal competitive significance.[222] The Department would measure concentration in the bidder market by dividing the number of bidders into one and multiplying the result by 10,000 (the HHI of a single-firm market). Thus, for example, if there would have been seven bidders in the market before the U.S. consortium was formed (e.g., three U.S. consortia and four foreign consortia), the U.S. consortium would reduce the number of bidders in the market to five. Concentration would be increased from approximately 1428 (1/7 x 10,000) to 2000 (1/5 x 10,000). Since the bidder market would be highly concentrated and the consortium would result in a substantial increase in concentration, the Department would proceed to consider other factors bearing on whether the U.S. consortium would likely have an anticompetitive effect.[223]

In particular, the Department would consider whether, given the magnitude of the project being bid and the uncertainty surrounding the costs of each of the bidders, the numbers of actual (and potential) bidders on the project will be sufficiently large to ensure a competitive outcome despite the consortium. Depending on the manner in which bids were received and contracts were let, if there were a large pool of potential bidders, a bid market might be operating competitively even if there were only two actual bidders. The number of actual bidders on a project might be limited by the costs of bidding (e.g., the cost of forming the consortium, formulating the bid, or qualifying to bid). As a general rule, all other things being equal, fewer bidders

---

221. Otherwise, the consortium would not eliminate competition among actual, potential, or apparent bidders and this case would raise no antitrust concern with respect to competition for the project (although, depending on the facts, the Department still might be concerned about anticompetitive spillover effects in U.S. markets).

222. This assumes that the joint venture members would be bidding only on this project. If, instead, a series of bid opportunities were involved, then, depending on the facts, the Department's analysis might have to reflect the fact that the capacity of some bidders would become constrained in the course of the bidding.

In addition, if it appeared that the separate bids of one or more groups of firms in the U.S. consortium would have been the two lowest (or most efficient) bids on the project, then the Department would expect the consortium to increase bid prices, regardless of its impact on the likelihood of collusion. Conversely, if there would be at least two other bidders that would have been as efficient as (or more efficient than) the U.S. firms, then the consortium would have no direct effect on the bid price, since the bid price would be no lower than what would be bid by the second most efficient bidder. In that case. the consortium conceivably would have a procompetitive effect by making the U.S. firms more competitive. Of course, it often is difficult to assess the relative efficiencies of bidders *ex ante*. Therefore, unless there is evidence to the contrary,.the Department will likely assume that each bidder is comparably efficient.

223. *See* Section 3.32, *supra*.

would be expected to bid on a given project the higher were the costs of bidding.[224]

STEP 2 – OTHER MARKETS

Next, the Department would determine whether the U.S. consortium would likely have any anticompetitive spill-over effects in markets affecting U.S. consumers in which the consortium members do or would compete. Under certain circumstances, the consortium in this case conceivably might serve to facilitate collusion among its members on the price or output of electrical equipment or engineering services or on bidding for projects in the United States.

In formulating the consortium's bid, for example, consortium members might exchange sensitive business information that could be used to coordinate prices or output in the United States. Such spill-over effects may be of no concern if none of the information the consortium members might share about the foreign project would be relevant to competition among consortium members in the United States, if the consortium adopted adequate safeguards against anticompetitive spill-over effects resulting from the exchange of sensitive information,[225] or if the spill-over markets were not conducive to successful collusion (for example, because they were not concentrated, the consortium members represented a small share of the markets, or entry into the markets was easy).[226]

STEP 3 – VERTICAL RESTRAINTS ANALYSIS

Next, the Department would determine whether any nonprice vertical restraints associated with the bidding consortium would likely have any anticompetitive effects. There do not appear to be any such restraints in this case. If there were, they would be analyzed as described in Section 3.5 of these Guidelines.

STEP 4 – OFFSETTING EFFICIENCY BENEFITS

If after applying the first three steps of this analysis the Department concluded that the bidding consortium would not be anticompetitive, then the Department would not challenge it regardless of whether it actually generated procompetitive benefits. If the consortium or any of its restraints did raise a significant risk of anticompetitive effects, however, then the Department would consider whether that risk would be outweighed by procompetitive efficiency benefits that the parties claimed would be achieved by the consortium and its restraints.[227] The parties to

---

224.   Another way of looking at this issue would be to suppose that the four foreign consortia in this case knew that there would be three U.S. bidders instead of one. If, as a result, two of the foreign bidders would not bid, then a market with five bidders would be competitive. Although the Department may not be able to answer this question *ex ante* in all cases, in some cases reliable historical evidence may indicate that no more than a certain number of bidders tend to bid on a particular type of project.

225.   *See* text accompanying nn.97-98, *supra*. The Department, of course, would not be precluded from prosecuting any unlawful agreement made despite the existence of safeguards.

226.   *See* Section 3.322, *supra*. Of course, if the consortium members actually rigged bids on U.S. projects, then the Department would not hesitate to prosecute them for such bid rigging, even in the presence of these factors. *See* Section 3.1, *supra*.

227.   The Department would not, of course, consider any claimed efficiencies defense to per se offenses such as naked bid rigging and price fixing.

the consortium would bear the burden of proving such offsetting efficiency benefits on the basis of clear and convincing evidence. Their burden would increase in direct proportion to the magnitude of the risk of anticompetitive harm.[228]

If it were clear that equivalent efficiencies could be achieved by means that involved no anticompetitive effect, then the Department would not recognize the efficiencies claim. In addition, although the Department would consider the cumulative effects of restraints associated with the consortium, if some aspect of the consortium's operation (for example, the exchange of competitively sensitive information) would have a significant anticompetitive effect and would not contribute to the claimed efficiencies, then the Department would likely require that that aspect of the consortium's operations be modified or eliminated before approving the consortium.

If the consortium did raise significant antitrust concern, the informal encouragement given to the consortium or its members by U.S. Government officials would not confer any kind of antitrust immunity. If bidding consortia and other joint ventures engaged in exporting goods or services desire greater certainty about their potential antitrust liability, they can seek to obtain a business review from the Department or a certificate of review under the Export Trading Company Act.[229]

Case 6 – Research and Development Joint Venture

Three of the largest producers of X-metal in the United States, which collectively supply 50 percent of domestic consumption of X-metal, have entered into an agreement with Beta Corporation, a British company that is one of the largest X-metal producers in the EEC. Beta currently supplies approximately 10 percent of the X-metal consumed in the United States. The parties plan to engage in joint research and development ("R&D") to develop a process for producing X-metal from sources other than X-ore, which currently is the only source of X-metal. X is found in a variety of shales located throughout the world, but no one has found an economical way to produce X-metal from these shales. Beta and several X-metal producers, including each of the U.S. parties to the joint R&D agreement, are independently engaged in laboratory research activities.

The parties will form a British company to conduct the joint R&D. Each party will own one-fourth of the shares of this company, and each will designate one-fourth of the members of the board of directors. Each of the parties has agreed to conduct all of its R&D activities devoted to seeking processes for producing X-metal from shale through this new company. They each have also agreed to provide the company with past and projected price and cost data relating to their production and sale of X-metal from X-ore.

The new British company will seek to obtain patents on any new process it develops. It will grant to the U.S. joint venture partners (but to no one else) licenses to all patent rights and use of know-how in North America. The U.S. venture partners have agreed not to market X-metal produced using licensed technology in territory reserved to Beta. Beta will be given similar rights to patents and know-how in the United Kingdom, other EEC countries, and all the British Commonwealth

---

228. *See* Section 3.45, *supra.*
229. *See* Section 2.6, *supra.*

countries except Canada. Beta has also agreed not to sell X-metal produced using licensed technology in North America.

For the purpose of this hypothetical case, it is assumed that none of the parties sells products other than X-metal. There are no restraints associated with the joint venture or intellectual property licenses other than those noted above.

Discussion

As is true with respect to all international transactions, the Department's review of the R&D joint venture and technology licensing arrangement in this case would focus on their likely competitive effects in the United States. Although the joint venture's activities will be conducted overseas by the new British company, the agreement would directly affect R&D competition among firms that do or could produce and sell X-metal in the United States, as well as the sale of X-metal in the United States by Beta.[230]

The National Cooperative Research Act of 1984 ("NCRA")[231] prohibits courts from condemning a joint R&D venture on antitrust grounds unless the joint venture is proven to have anticompetitive effects in a properly defined, relevant market that outweigh the joint venture's procompetitive benefits.[232] The NCRA includes in the definition of joint R&D the patenting and licensing of the results of an R&D joint venture. It excludes (i) any exchange of competitively sensitive information among competitors "that is not reasonably required to conduct the research and development that is the purpose" of the venture; (ii) any agreement or conduct restricting competition among venture members with respect to producing or marketing products, processes, or services other than the intellectual property (e.g., patents or know-how) developed through the joint venture; and (iii) any agreement or conduct restricting the sale, licensing, or sharing of intellectual property developed outside the joint venture or restricting or requiring participation in other R&D activities that is "not reasonably required to prevent misappropriation of proprietary information" that is contributed by any joint venture member or that results from the joint venture.[233]

Conduct excluded from application of the NCRA is not necessarily unlawful. Nor, in the Department's opinion, would the fact that some excluded conduct was part of the joint venture agreement result in the denial of benefits under the NCRA with respect to the remainder of the joint venture's activities that do fall within the Act's definition of R&D activity.

---

230.   Both section 7 of the Clayton Act and section 1 of the Sherman Act would apply to the formation of this joint R&D venture because of the acquisition of shares of the new British company, a person whose activities "affect" U.S. commerce. 15 U.S.C. § 18. That acquisition may also be subject to the premerger notification requirements of the Hart-Scott-Rodino Act. See 16 C.F.R. § 801.40. In addition, the licensing of technology produced by the joint venture to U.S. firms would occur "in commerce."

231.   15 U.S.C. §§ 4301-4305. See Section 2.4, supra.

232.   15 U.S.C. § 4303; H.R. Conf. Rep. No. 1044, 98th Cong., 2d Sess. 11-12, reprinted in 1984 U.S. Code Cong. & Admin. News 3105, 3135-36 (hereinafter "NCRA House Conf. Rep.").

233.   15 U.S.C. § 4301(b).

RULE-OF-REASON ANALYSIS

The Department would analyze the likely competitive effects of the joint venture in this case using the four-step joint venture analysis described in Section 3.4 of these Guidelines.[234] The joint venture also involves the licensing of intellectual property, which the Department in general analyzes as described in Section 3.6 of these Guidelines. As the discussion in Part I of these Guidelines suggests, the Department's analysis of intellectual property licensing arrangements is a derivative of the Department's joint venture analysis. Because the intellectual property licensing provisions of this joint venture agreement affect markets that are related to the R&D market and are part of the integration of the joint venture, the Department would analyze those licensing provisions in the context of the overall joint venture agreement.

STEP 1 − JOINT VENTURE MARKETS

Under step 1, the Department would determine whether restrictions in the joint venture or intellectual property licensing agreement would have any anticompetitive effects in a relevant market for R&D or for any technology resulting from that R&D.

R&D MARKET

The Department would begin its analysis by defining the relevant R&D market and identifying firms that compete in that market.[235] The relevant R&D market would include all firms that, judged objectively, appeared to have the incentive and ability, alone or cooperatively, to undertake R&D comparable to the R&D proposed to be undertaken by the joint venture in this case. The Department would consider, among other things, such firms' business objectives, facilities, existing technologies and technologies under development, and other relevant available assets. Firms would not have to be competitors in producing or selling X-metal to be included in the relevant R&D market. In addition, because there normally are no geographic barriers to the free movement of information, foreign R&D competitors in most cases would be significant competitive factors in the R&D market, even if they could not sell products incorporating the technology in the United States.

Unless the facts in this case indicated otherwise, the Department would regard all possible comparable R&D efforts in the market to be of equal competitive significance. As a general matter (and consistent with the legislative history of the NCRA), the Department believes that an anticompetitive effect in an R&D market is unlikely where there are at least four other comparable R&D efforts underway or

---

234. This assumes, of course, that the joint venture represents a legitimate integration of efforts to produce valuable R&D. An R&D "joint venture" that was not formed to pursue R&D, but was formed merely to disguise a naked agreement to fix prices or allocate territories or customers for the sale of some product or service would be viewed as a sham, and would probably be prosecuted as a criminal violation of the Sherman Act. *See* Section 3.0 *supra.*

235. *See* Merger Guidelines § 2 and Cases 1, 2, and 3 of these Guidelines. It is intrinsically more difficult to define markets and to assign market shares for R&D than it is to define markets and assign market shares in connection with products and services for which capacity and sales (the typical measures of output) can easily be identified, measured, and compared. The process of defining R&D markets is thus necessarily less precise and more qualitative (as opposed to quantifiable) in nature than normally is the case under the Merger Guidelines.

where there is a substantial potential for such efforts by firms or groups of firms included in the market.[236] The fact that there were fewer than four other actual or potential R&D competitors would not necessarily mean that an R&D joint venture would be anticompetitive, however. Fewer R&D competitors might provide adequate competition.[237] Even a joint venture that included a large portion or even all of the competitors in an R&D market might be necessary in a particular case for successful R&D.

From the facts of this case, it is not possible to conclude whether the joint venture would be anticompetitive. Although the joint venture members account for a substantial share of X-metal sales in the United States, they would not necessarily account for a large share of the relevant R&D market. If they did, the Department would consider whether, given the nature of the specific R&D in this case, the joint venture would actually be likely to result in a reduction of R&D output. That analysis would include a consideration of the incentives of a firm with market power to innovate under the circumstances.[238]

TECHNOLOGY MARKET

Depending on the results of the joint R&D efforts, the joint venture (as licensor) may control access to technologies that compete with technologies owned or controlled by individual joint venture members (as licensees). The Department would therefore seek to determine whether the licenses in this case would implicitly or explicitly restrict the independent pricing and output decisions of the joint venture members with respect to competing technologies and, if so, whether the result would likely be anticompetitive. It is necessary separately to analyze effects in the relevant R&D market and effects in the relevant market for technology resulting from the R&D. Even if the relevant market for R&D were highly atomistic, there may be few suppliers of technologies that compete with the technologies produced by the R&D, such that owners of those technologies could exercise market power for some

---

236. In enacting the NCRA, Congress indicated that the existence of four or more comparable R&D ventures would generally be sufficient to insulate an R&D joint venture from antitrust condemnation. *See* NCRA House Conf. Rep., *supra* note 232, at 10, 1984 U.S. Code Cong. & Admin. News at 3134-35. The HHI of a market with five comparably situated firms would be 2000. This is slightly higher than the 1800 HHI that demarcates a highly concentrated market under the Department's Merger Guidelines; however, a higher threshold screen is supported by the facts that it is more difficult accurately to define R&D markets and assign shares in those markets and that collusion with respect to R&D is in general significantly less likely than with respect to products and services. *Cf.* Letter from Charles F. Rule, Assistant Attorney General, Antitrust Division, to Paul A. Volcker, Chairman, Board of Governors of the Federal Reserve System, Aug. 7, 1985 (applying higher HHI screen for mergers involving depository institutions).

237. *See* NCRA House Conf. Rep., *supra* note 232, at 10, 1984 U.S. Cong. & Admin. News at 3135.

238. It has been suggested that a monopolist will choose the optimal level of R&D because it cannot earn further supranormal profits by restricting the output of R&D. *Cf.* Pazner, *Quality Choice and Monopoly Regulation*, in Regulating the Product: Quality and Variety 3, 15 (R. Caves & M. Roberts eds. 1975) (quality same under monopoly or competition). The major exception to this result would occur where the innovation that is the object of the R&D is mandated by government (for example, automobile pollution control) and will raise costs to the industry. In that case, the industry may have an incentive to act collectively to forestall the development of the new technology. See United States v. Automobile Manufacturers Ass'n, 1969 Trade Cas. (CCH) ¶ 72,907 (C.D. Cal. 1969) (consent decree), *modified*, 1982-83 Trade Cas. (CCH) ¶ 65,088 (C.D. Cal. 1982).

significant period of time. In this case, the only restraint on the use of technology among the members of the joint venture relates to the technology developed by the joint venture (i.e., the joint venture members have agreed not to license anyone outside the joint venture),[239] and the agreement does not restrict the individual members' use of any preexisting technology. The Department, therefore, would probably conclude that there are no anticompetitive effects likely in the technology market.[240]

STEP 2 – OTHER MARKETS

Next, the Department would analyze other markets in which competition among the joint venture members might be restricted. The joint venture agreement in this case conceivably could also affect competition in the sale of X-metal in the United States. First, Beta has agreed not to sell X-metal produced using the licensed technology in the United States. Second, the parties' agreement to provide the joint venture company with past and projected price and cost data relating to their production and sale of X-metal from X-ore could facilitate collusion among the parties with respect to their price or output of X-metal produced using existing technology.

RESTRICTION ON BETA'S SALES OF X-METAL

As a general matter, the Department will treat the licensing of technology owned and developed by multiple parties no more harshly than it treats technology owned and developed by a single entity. Joint venture partners who have created a new technology may desire to control the processes and products that incorporate or are a complement to that technology in order to recover as quickly and fully as possible the value of their inventive efforts. Without such joint coordination, the value of the parties' R&D might be dissipated through competition in the product market. As a result, firms might avoid efficient joint R&D altogether, which at best might result in the costly duplication of R&D efforts. Coordination in markets using the technology output of the joint venture is therefore often essential to beneficial R&D.

The Department would, however, seek to determine whether the elimination of competition by Beta would likely create, enhance, or facilitate the exercise of market power in the relevant market for the sale of X-metal in the United States. Because the joint venture members may account for a substantial share of sales in the relevant market for X-metal, it is conceivable that the license would be used, not to convey valuable technology produced by the joint venture, but to disguise a naked agreement to restrict competition in the sale of X-metal (that is, that the joint venture would be used as the "hub" of a conspiracy among its members). Assuming that the Department was satisfied that the licensing arrangement was not a sham, the Department would seek to determine the likely competitive effects of the license restrictions in the relevant X-metal market, focusing on the elimination of the

---

239.   As indicated under step 2, the Department will not treat the licensing of technology created jointly any less favorably than it treats the licensing of technology created by a single firm. In both cases, the owner or owners of the technology are entitled to earn the maximum value inherent in the technology itself.

240.   The Department's analysis of effects in a technology market is described in Section 3.63 of these Guidelines.

competition that would have occurred in that market without the joint venture and licensing arrangement.[241]

After defining the relevant market and identifying firms competing in that market, the Department would look at the level of and increase in concentration that would occur in that market if Beta exited the market.[242]   If a merger having the same effect would not fall within a Merger Guidelines "safe harbor," then the Department would proceed to consider other factors bearing on the ability to exercise market power, including the likelihood that sufficient new entry would occur to frustrate any attempted exercise of market power by the joint venture members.

INFORMATION EXCHANGE

Under certain conditions, the joint venture members' exchange of competitively sensitive price and cost data relating to their current X-metal production using existing technology conceivably might serve to facilitate collusion in a relevant market for the sale of X-metal. Adequate safeguards, however, might be implemented to prevent anticompetitive use of the information by the joint venture members. The fact that the joint venture's activities are to be carried out through a separately incorporated entity is one such safeguard, which might be supplemented by independent staffing of that entity and other steps to ensure that competitively sensitive information does not flow back to the joint venture members. Because it appears from the facts of this case that the X-metal market may be highly concentrated, unless entry into the market were easy or other factors would make collusion unlikely, the joint venture might pose a significant risk of anticompetitive spill-over effects in the absence of such safeguards.

STEP 3 — VERTICAL RESTRAINTS ANALYSIS

Even if the elimination of competition among the joint venture members in any market would not be anticompetitive, under certain market conditions, vertical restraints of the type employed by the joint venture in this case conceivably might serve to facilitate collusion among the joint venture members and other competitors in those markets. In this case, however, the only restraint on the joint venture members' use of the technology (other than that on Beta, the effect of which is analyzed under step 2) prohibits the licensing of nonmembers; the restraint, therefore, could not plausibly have the effect of facilitating collusion.

Under certain conditions, restraints on the ability of members to market the joint venture technology conceivably might also result in the anticompetitive exclusion of competitors to the joint venture from the relevant technology market or the relevant market for X-metal. Under the facts of this case, however, the joint venture members are not prohibited from using competing technologies for the production of X-metal from alternative sources. There is thus no reason to believe that the licensing arrangement would likely have an anticompetitive exclusionary effect in the

---

241.   *See* Section 3.64, *supra.*
242.   Under the facts of this case, although Beta has agreed not to compete in the United States, there is no restriction on competition among the U.S. joint venture members. If there were, then the Department would begin to analyze the likely competitive effects of such a restriction by supposing that all of the parties had merged.

relevant technology market (i.e., where X-metal production is the foreclosed market and X-metal technology is the nonforeclosed market).

Nor would the Department be concerned about anticompetitive exclusion of competing suppliers of X-metal that do not possess access to the technology produced by the joint venture. First, the joint venture does not foreclose the access of other firms to existing technology necessary to produce X-metal. Second, as discussed in Part I of these Guidelines, even if the technology developed by the joint venture were to make existing X-metal technology obsolete, the Department would not be concerned where, as in this case, only a single technology — that for producing X-metal from shale — is subject to the exclusive license in what would otherwise would be the "foreclosed" market. In that case, the exclusion is inherent in the nature of the property rights of the technology owner.[243]

STEP 4 — OFFSETTING EFFICIENCY BENEFITS

If after applying the first three steps of this analysis, it appeared that no anticompetitive effects were likely, the Department would not challenge the joint venture or licensing arrangement regardless of whether they would actually produce procompetitive efficiency benefits. On the other hand, the possibility of anticompetitive effects would not lead the Department automatically to condemn the joint venture. The Department would consider whether the threat of anticompetitive effects would be outweighed by procompetitive efficiencies that the parties claimed would result from the joint venture.

As a general matter, joint R&D activities can have substantial procompetitive effects. They can promote the development of new technologies, products, and processes that otherwise would not be available and that could substantially improve the efficiency of firms serving U.S. consumers. The specific benefits that can be derived from joint R&D include sharing the substantial economic risks involved in R&D; increasing the efficiency of R&D efforts by exploiting economies of scale or scope beyond what individual firms could realize, or by pooling important information or complementary skills; and overcoming the "free rider" disincentive to invest in R&D by including likely end users of the R&D in undertaking the research efforts and sharing the costs. An R&D joint venture can also provide a low-cost means of transmitting information created by the venture, thus minimizing transactions costs and allowing venture members to use information at its actual zero marginal cost. As a general matter, the procompetitive benefits of joint R&D are more likely to outweigh the risk of anticompetitive harm the greater is the cost of R&D relative to a single firm's budgetary limits or the greater are the economies of scale that would be achieved through the jointly conducted R&D.[244]

A restriction on the venturers' ability to engage in competing R&D may be reasonably necessary to the successful operation of the venture. Such a restriction probably would be designed to avoid the threat that a venture member would "free ride" on the venturers' efforts. Such free-riding could occur if a member used information provided by other members to the joint venture in that member's own private R&D efforts and did not share the benefits of its R&D with other venture

---

243.   *See* n.151, *supra*.

244.   *See* NCRA House Conf. Rep., *supra* note 232, at 11, 1984 U.S. Code Cong. & Admin. News at 3136.

members. Without the restriction, firms might be reluctant to disclose information to the venture, thus significantly impeding the success of the venture.

The license restrictions also could produce substantial efficiency benefits by maximizing the incentive to invest in the joint R&D in the first place. Indeed, the parties may not have entered into the joint R&D venture unless they were able to determine in advance how the product of the joint venture would be exploited.

Case 7 – Distributing a Foreign Competitor's Product

Alpha Corporation and Beta Corporation are significant, but not dominant, manufacturers of machine tools in the United States and the Federal Republic of Germany, respectively. Neither company makes substantial sales in the other company's home country. Alpha has agreed to appoint Beta as its exclusive distributor in the EEC, and Beta has agreed to appoint Alpha as its exclusive distributor in North America. Both appointments will be for a period of five years.

Some of Alpha's and Beta's products are directly interchangeable in use. Most, however, are either complementary (that is, they can be used in conjunction with each other) or have special features that substantially differentiate them. Alpha and Beta recognize that neither company is likely to promote imports of the other that are directly interchangeable with its own products. They each believe, however, that their total exports under this arrangement will be significantly greater than if an independent distributor were used. In addition, Alpha reasonably believes that the ability to offer a full line of machine tools by handling Beta's products will enable Alpha to compete more effectively against competing machine tool manufacturers in the United States.

Alpha and Beta will each pay a predetermined price (based on factory costs) under the proposed distribution arrangement. They each will be free to resell the imported machine tools at whatever price they choose. Alpha and Beta have agreed that each will prohibit distributors of its machine tools in other countries from re-exporting its machine tools into either the EEC or North America.

Discussion

The appointment of an exclusive foreign distributor by a U.S. firm does not by itself raise concern under the U.S. antitrust laws. Such an arrangement normally would not affect consumers in the United States. Where the parties are actual or potential competitors, however, a reciprocal distribution arrangement such as the one in this case raises at least the possibility that the Department will challenge it as an unlawful scheme to allocate markets between the parties or as an agreement that otherwise might adversely affect competition in a relevant market affecting U.S. consumers.

This case initially raises a question of characterization: should the distribution arrangement between Alpha and Beta be treated as per se unlawful market allocation between horizontal competitors, or should it be examined under a rule-of-reason analysis that recognizes the arrangement's potential procompetitive benefits? The arrangement in this case does not appear to be a naked agreement to restrict output or raise price. Rather, it appears to involve a form of economic integration of the parties' operations beyond simply the coordination of price and output that may increase productivity.[245]   Moreover, although Alpha and Beta both produce machine tools, some of which are directly interchangeable, their product lines appear to be largely complementary. Further, Alpha reasonably believes that its ability to offer a full line of machine tools under the distribution arrangement will enable it to compete more effectively against other machine tool manufacturers in the United States. The fact that this arrangement is open and notorious also makes it less likely (though not impossible) that the arrangement is designed to facilitate naked price fixing.

The Department would therefore analyze the distribution arrangement under the rule of reason using the four-step joint venture analysis described in Section 3.4 of these Guidelines. First, the Department would determine whether the distribution arrangement would likely have any anticompetitive effect in a relevant market or markets for the sale of machine tools (the market or markets in which the economic integration of the parties' operations occurs, or the "joint venture" markets). Second, the Department would determine whether the distribution arrangement would likely have any anticompetitive effect in any other markets ("spill-over" markets) in which Alpha and Beta are actual or potential competitors. Third, the Department would analyze the likely competitive effects of any nonprice vertical restraints imposed in connection with the distribution arrangements. Finally, if the Department concluded under any of the first three steps that the distribution arrangement would likely have an anticompetitive effect, then the Department would consider whether the procompetitive efficiencies that the parties claim would be achieved by the arrangement would outweigh the risk of anticompetitive harm.

STEP 1 — THE JOINT VENTURE MARKET OR MARKETS

The joint distribution arrangement eliminates competition between Alpha and Beta (and their distributors) in the sale of machine tools in the United States. Since no Beta products will be sold in the United States except through Alpha, the effect of this restriction is essentially the same as would result from a merger between Alpha and Beta. After defining the relevant market or markets affected by the restriction, the Department would first focus on the level of and increase in concentration in each such market that would result from a merger of Alpha and Beta.[246]   The facts that Beta currently makes insubstantial sales in the United States and that Alpha is not a dominant supplier of machine tools in the United States suggest that a merger between them might fall within a Merger Guidelines concentration "safe harbor." In that case, the Department would not challenge the distribution arrangement.

If a merger between Alpha and Beta would not fall within a safe harbor, however, then the Department would proceed to consider other factors bearing on the ability to exercise market power.   Those factors would include whether new entry in response to a price increase would frustrate any attempted exercise of market power and characteristics of the relevant product or products that would make successful collusion more or less likely. If there were no restriction against transshipping by Beta's worldwide distributors, then the arrangement would be significantly less

---

245.   *See* Section 3.0, *supra*.
246.   *See* Section 3.32, *supra*.

restrictive than a merger; any attempt by Alpha to exercise market power (unilaterally, or in collusion with other machine tool manufacturers) in the United States might be undercut by competition from Beta's distributors.

STEP 2 – OTHER MARKETS

Next, the Department would seek to determine whether the distribution arrangement would be likely to have any significant anticompetitive effect in other markets in which Alpha and Beta are actual or potential competitors. The facts of the case do not indicate that Alpha and Beta compete in anything but the sale of machine tools. In that case, the Department would not need to apply a step 2 analysis.

STEP 3 – VERTICAL RESTRAINTS ANALYSIS

Next, the Department would seek to determine whether Beta's appointment of Alpha as Beta's exclusive distributor in North America would likely serve to facilitate collusion in or result in anticompetitive exclusion of competitors from any relevant market. Since, as discussed above, the effect of the distribution arrangement in this case is the same as though Alpha and Beta had merged, any threat of collusion created by the arrangement would have been detected by the Department's analysis under step 1. Nor would there be any concern about anticompetitive exclusion. Alpha is not precluded by its agreement with Beta from distributing the machine tools of other suppliers. But even if it were, Alpha is not obligated to make its distribution facilities open to competitors.

STEP 4 – OFFSETTING EFFICIENCY BENEFITS

If the Department concluded that the distribution arrangement would have no significant anticompetitive effect, then the Department would not challenge the arrangement, regardless of whether it actually generated procompetitive efficiencies. If the distribution arrangement did present a significant threat of an anticompetitive effect, however, then the Department would proceed to determine whether that risk were outweighed by procompetitive efficiencies that the parties claimed would be achieved by the arrangement.

In this case, Alpha believes that the joint distribution arrangement will allow it to compete more effectively against other machine tool manufacturers in the United States. The parties also believe that Beta's sales of machines tools in the United States would be greater with this distribution arrangement than if Beta used an independent distributor. The transshipping prohibition supports Beta's underlying agreement not to market its machine tools in the United States in competition with Alpha; the restriction may be necessary to encourage Alpha to invest in promotional and post-sale services with respect to Beta's products, which Alpha might not do if transshippers could "free ride" on its efforts. Assuming that the parties could substantiate these claims through clear and convincing evidence, these claims may well outweigh the risk to competition presented by the arrangement. If the parties' claims were true, the net effect of the arrangement would be to expand, rather than reduce, the supply of machine tools in the United States.

Case 8 – Exclusive Vertical Distribution Arrangements

As in Case 7, Alpha Corporation and Beta Corporation are significant, but not dominant, manufacturers of machine tools in the United States and the Federal Republic of Germany, respectively. The relevant market for the sale of machine tools is unconcentrated (the HHI is below 1000). Alpha sells machine tools in the United States exclusively through Delta Distribution, Inc. Alpha chose Delta to distribute Alpha's products because of Delta's substantial experience and expertise in the promotion and sale of machine tools. Alpha prohibits its other worldwide distributors from selling its machine tools in the United States or to firms that intend to transship Alpha's machine tools to the United States.

For a number of years, Beta has been selling machine tools in the United States through a number of non-exclusive independent distributors, selling to any distributor that sent in an order. Beta's market share has been declining. To halt this decline, Beta recently selected Delta to be Beta's exclusive distributor in the United States. Beta believes that Delta will more effectively distribute Beta's machine tools because of Delta's expertise. In addition, the fact that Delta will have the exclusive right to distribute Beta's products will result in better promotion and servicing of Beta's machine tools. Beta initially was concerned that Delta might be less aggressive in promoting Beta's line of machine tools because Delta also distributed Alpha's line. Beta ultimately concluded, however, that, since Alpha's line of machine tools largely complemented Beta's line, both product lines would benefit if Delta could market both. Delta has agreed to distribute only machine tools supplied by Beta and Alpha. In selecting Delta, Beta chose among several competing distributors. Entry into and expansion at the distribution level of the market is easy.

Discussion

This case illustrates the use of two types of vertical nonprice restraints: a requirement that a distributor deal exclusively with the products of a limited number of manufacturers and the grant of an exclusive territory to a distributor. A manufacturer's appointment of an exclusive distributor in the United States (or its appointment of a group of U.S. distributors, each with an exclusive territory) ordinarily raises no concern under the U.S. antitrust laws. Indeed, such arrangements can often enhance interbrand competition. For example, by preventing other distributors from "free riding," the use of exclusive territories may encourage distributors to provide substantial promotional or post-sale services that are necessary to gain recognition for, or build up good will in, the manufacturer's brand. A U.S. manufacturer may prevent foreign distributors from selling in the United States in order to encourage those distributors to devote their full efforts to developing foreign markets. Under the rule of reason, the Department would challenge such restraints only if they would pose significant anticompetitive threat in some relevant market that included at least part of the United States, regardless of whether the particular vertical restraint actually generated procompetitive benefits.

Under certain market conditions, in the absence of direct agreement among competitors, widespread use of exclusive distribution arrangements and/or exclusive territories by leading manufacturers conceivably might facilitate collusion among the dealers of different manufacturers or among the manufacturers themselves with respect to the price or output of their products. Such collusion would be plausible, however, only if, at a minimum: (i) the relevant market in which collusion is to be facilitated is very highly concentrated; (ii) firms in the other market that are subject to or use exclusive territories or distributorships (or that are vertically integrated) represent most sales in that market; and (iii) entry into the primary market is difficult.[247]

In this case, it is clear that the appointment of Delta as exclusive U.S. distributor by both Alpha and Beta would pose no significant risk of collusion. Because both the manufacturing and distribution markets are unconcentrated, coordinating and policing the pricing and output activities in either market would be difficult, if not impossible, without an explicit agreement. Competing manufacturers, for example, would have an incentive to cheat by selling directly to consumers or by dealing with non-colluding distributors. Therefore, even if each of the other machine tool manufacturers in the relevant market were vertically integrated into distribution or its products were distributed through exclusive distributors, it would be extremely unlikely that the manufacturers could successfully develop, police, and benefit from a scheme to facilitate collusion either among themselves or among their dealers.

Under certain market conditions, a restraint that requires a distributor to deal exclusively in the product of one or a limited number of manufacturers also conceivably might have the effect of excluding competing manufacturers from the market by denying them access to essential distribution facilities.[248] In this case, however, it appears that there are a number of distributors other than Delta with which competing machine tool manufacturers could deal. (Indeed, the Department would be more likely to be concerned if many competing machine tool manufacturers used the same exclusive distributor.) Moreover, the relevant machine tool market is not highly concentrated. Therefore, even if all existing distributors were subject to exclusive dealing arrangements (so that machine tool manufacturers seeking to enter the market would have to integrate into distribution or establish a new distributor), there could be no anticompetitive effect in the relevant machine tool market.

Case 9 – A Multinational Operation

Alpha Corporation is a large multinational corporation headquartered in New York City. Alpha manufactures printing machines in New Jersey. It exports its printing machines only to Latin American countries. It uses non-U.S. subsidiaries to manufacture and sell its products throughout the rest of the world. Although Alpha's patents on its printing machines expired years ago, Alpha and its subsidiaries collectively have retained a dominant position in most markets because of their superior sales and service organizations, know-how, and low manufacturing costs.

Alpha's system of management involves a strong "profit center" concept. Individual subsidiaries are judged by their ability to make sales in their assigned territories. Normally, when an order comes in to one Alpha subsidiary from the assigned territory of another, the recipient sends it on, or suggests that the customer contact directly the subsidiary assigned to that territory.

---

247.   *See* Section 3.5, *supra.*
248.   *See* Section 3.5, *supra.*

Alpha has three subsidiaries. Alpha (U.K.) Limited manufactures Alpha products and sells them throughout the United Kingdom, Ireland, and the Commonwealth, except Canada. Alpha (U.K.) was a wholly-owned subsidiary of Alpha when it was formed in 1954, but 40 percent of its stock is now publicly held as a result of a 1964 public stock offering. Beta Corporation is a wholly-owned Canadian subsidiary of Alpha that manufactures and sells Alpha products in Canada. Alpha G.m.b.H. is a German subsidiary that manufactures and sells Alpha products in the Common Market countries other than the United Kingdom and Ireland and in all other countries except the Commonwealth, Canada, the United States, and Latin America. Alpha acquired Alpha G.m.b.H. in 1951 from four large individual investors. Alpha now holds 56 percent of the stock of Alpha G.m.b.H. The remaining 44 percent is evenly divided among the four original investors.

Alpha plans to sell an additional seven percent of its stock holdings in Alpha G.m.b.H., which would leave Alpha with 49 percent of the stock of Alpha G.m.b.H., but effective working control. Alpha is also negotiating to sell 50 percent of the stock of Beta Corporation to a Canadian corporation that purchases the stock of Canadian companies for investment purposes.

Discussion

This case involves the issue of intra-enterprise conspiracy. In *Copperweld Corp. v. Independence Tube Corp.*,[249] the Supreme Court held that, because a parent corporation and its wholly-owned subsidiary have a "complete unity" of economic interests, they are not independent actors capable of conspiring to restrain trade within the meaning of section 1 of the Sherman Act.[250] The Court declined to decide whether the same result would apply where a subsidiary is less than wholly-owned.[251] In the Department's view, however, the policies underlying the Sherman Act (as discussed in *Copperweld*) support the conclusion that a parent corporation and any subsidiary corporation of which the parent owns more than 50 percent of the voting stock are a single economic unit under common control and are thus legally incapable of conspiring with one another within the meaning of section 1.[252] If a parent company controlled a significant, but less than majority, share of the voting stock of a subsidiary, the Department would make a factual inquiry to determine whether the parent corporation actually had effective working control of the subsidiary. In this case, prior to any stock divestitures, the Department would view Alpha and its subsidiaries as a single economic entity incapable of conspiring among themselves because Alpha holds a majority voting stock interest (100 percent, 60 percent, and 56 percent, respectively) in each of them. Alpha's sale of its majority

---

249.   467 U.S. 752 (1984).
250.   *Id.* at 771, 777.
251.   *Id.* at 767.
252.   This standard is consistent with the Department's longstanding practice under section 7 of the Clayton Act of treating as a merger any stock acquisition that would facilitate coordination of the price and output decisions of the acquiring and acquired firms. For example, the acquisition of more than 50 percent of the stock of another firm is always treated as a merger despite the continued existence of a significant minority interest. In such cases, the Department presumes that the acquired and acquiring firms will coordinate their behavior. The Department may also challenge under section 7 stock acquisitions that involve less than 50 percent of the stock of the acquired company.

interests in the German and Canadian subsidiaries would probably not change that conclusion. Alpha would retain nearly a majority stock interest and apparent effective working control of both subsidiaries. It appears that the remaining stock interests in both subsidiaries would be held by investors that do not represent any independent competitive interests. As a practical matter, Alpha and the subsidiaries should continue to function as a single economic entity, and there would be no change in the essential competitive situation. If it appeared that Alpha relinquished effective working control over either subsidiary, however, then Alpha and that subsidiary would not be viewed as a single economic entity, and any agreement between them would be subject to normal antitrust rules under section 1 of the Sherman Act.[253]

Case 10 – Vertical Restraints in a Patent License

AutoGlass Corporation is a leading U.S. producer of windshields and other automobile glass. It markets these products to automobile manufacturers and in the automotive aftermarket throughout the world. AutoGlass has no other business.

AutoGlass invents a new, scratch-resistant transparent coating for automobile glass applications. It obtains U.S. and foreign product patent protection for this material, which it calls AGPLEX. AutoGlass discovers broad interest in AGPLEX by safety eyeglass manufacturers, who believe that AGPLEX-coated safety eyeglasses would be superior to the currently available uncoated safety eyeglasses, which are prone to scratching and breaking.

Amer-Eye Company is one of several safety eyeglass manufacturers in the United States. It obtains an exclusive, field-of-use license under AutoGlass's U.S. patent to make and sell safety eyeglasses coated with AGPLEX in the United States. Amer-Eye's AGPLEX license forbids Amer-Eye from manufacturing and selling safety eyeglasses coated with any other material that might be developed, but Amer-Eye may continue to manufacture and sell uncoated safety eyeglasses anywhere in the world. The license requires Amer-Eye to pay royalties based on its total unit sales of safety eyeglasses, coated and uncoated. British Optics Corporation is one of several British safety eyeglass manufacturers. It obtains an exclusive license from AutoGlass to make and sell safety eyeglasses coated with AGPLEX in the United Kingdom and in all other member countries of the EEC. British Optics is subject to the same manufacturing restriction and royalties payment provisions that are contained in Amer-Eye's license.

British Optics currently supplies five percent of all U.S. consumption of safety eyeglasses. It requested, but did not receive, a license under AutoGlass's U.S. patent as well. Without such a license, British Optics cannot sell AGPLEX-coated safety eyeglasses in the United States.

It is assumed for the purpose of this hypothetical case that the relevant market for the sale of safety eyeglasses (coated and uncoated) in the United States is not concentrated.

---

253. *See* Sections 3.0 and 3.1, *supra*.

Discussion

As is true with respect to international transactions in general, the Department's consideration of the patent licenses in this case would be limited to their effects on U.S. commerce. Otherwise, the Department's substantive analysis of the licenses would be identical to its analysis of similar licensing arrangements arising in a purely domestic context.

RULE-OF-REASON ANALYSIS

Unless the underlying transfer of technology is a sham, the Department analyzes restrictions in an intellectual property license under a rule of reason. Since the licenses in this case appear to be of significant value to the licensees, and there is no evidence that the licenses are mere shams, the Department would analyze their likely competitive effects using the rule-of-reason analysis set forth in Section 3.6 of these Guidelines.

Applying that analysis, the Department would quickly determine that the licenses in this case would not restrict horizontal competition between Autoglass and its licensees. With respect to technology, neither Amer-Eye nor British Optics owns or controls access to technology that competes with AGPLEX. AGPLEX appears to be a complementary input into the production of coated safety eyeglasses. Nor would the Department be concerned that the licenses would discourage Amer-Eye and British Optics from engaging in developing competing coating technologies. It does not appear from the facts of this case that Amer-Eye or British Optics are uniquely able to develop such technology. In addition to the several remaining safety eyeglass manufacturers that are not licensed by AutoGlass, the facts provide no indication that there are no (or only a very few) other persons that could engage in research and development of alternatives to AGPLEX (AutoGlass itself, for example, is not engaged in the manufacture of safety eyeglasses).

With respect to other markets, AutoGlass does not compete with Amer-Eye or British Optics in the manufacture and sale of safety eyeglasses or any other product. Nor would the Department be concerned about the loss of potential competition from AutoGlass in the safety eyeglass market since there is no indication that AutoGlass would enter the safety eyeglass market in the absence of this licensing arrangement or that it is uniquely capable of doing so. The license therefore does not restrain actual or significant competition between AutoGlass and its licensees in the sale of technology, safety eyeglasses, or any other product.

Under a vertical restraints analysis, the Department would challenge the license restrictions in this case only if their use would likely (i) facilitate collusion in a relevant market for the sale of safety eyeglasses or in the licensing of technologies that compete with AGPLEX; or (ii) result in the anticompetitive exclusion of firms from either the relevant market for the sale of safety eyeglasses or the relevant technology market. With respect to collusion, because there are no substitutes for AGPLEX in the coating of safety eyeglasses, vertical license restrictions obviously would not serve to facilitate collusion among competing technologies.[254] Nor

---

254. Even if competing coating technologies were developed in the future, AutoGlass's prior decision to grant an exclusive license to Amer-Eye would not appear to make collusion between AutoGlass and any other competing technology owner any more likely than if AutoGlass had

would vertical license restrictions be likely to facilitate collusion in the relevant market for safety eyeglasses, which under the facts of this case is not concentrated. The grant of an exclusive U.S. license to Amer-Eye would neither enable AutoGlass to help police a cartel among Amer-Eye and other safety eyeglass manufacturers in the market nor make it easier for those manufacturers to reach agreement.[255]

Nor would the Department be concerned about exclusion. Since there are no substitute technologies for AGPLEX, the Department would not treat the relevant technology market as the "foreclosed" market. Any exclusion would be inherent in the patent itself; AutoGlass has no obligation to create competition in its own technology.

In addition, the license restrictions are not likely to exclude new technologies that would compete with AGPLEX from entering the market by "tying-up" safety eyeglass manufacturing capacity. Although the licenses prohibit Amer-Eye and British Optics from manufacturing and selling in the United States safety eyeglasses coated with any material other than AGPLEX, there are many other safety eyeglass manufacturers that presumably could market competing coating technologies. Moreover, there is no indication on the facts of this case that entry into the manufacture and sale of safety eyeglasses would be difficult.

The Department would not be concerned about the ability of manufacturers of non-coated safety eyeglasses to continue to compete with Amer-Eye in the United States. The antitrust laws do not condemn even monopolies that are obtained through the offering of superior products. Nor do they require patent holders to make their technology open to all. Others are free to attempt to develop technologies that would compete with AGPLEX. In the meantime, AutoGlass and its licensees are entitled under the U.S. patent laws to enjoy whatever competitive advantages may result from AutoGlass's innovation, even if AGPLEX-coated safety eyeglasses dominate or monopolize the safety eyeglass market because of the superior desirability of AGPLEX-coated safety eyeglasses to consumers.

Because it is clear that the license arrangements in this case are not anticompetitive, the Department would not need to inquire as to whether those restrictions are efficient. If it did appear that the licenses would likely have an anticompetitive effect, however, then the Department would consider whether the procompetitive efficiency benefits of the licenses outweighed the risk of anticompetitive harm.[256] The following are some of the potential efficiency benefits of the types of restrictions presented in this case.

EXCLUSIVE LICENSES

The principal value of a patent is the right to its exclusive use. A licensor may properly seek to transfer this right to another person in the form of an exclusive license to practice the patent generally or for a specific purpose. Licensing the

---

tried to exploit the safety eyeglass field on its own.

255.   Even if AGPLEX-coated safety eyeglasses proved to be so superior to uncoated safety eyeglasses that AGPLEX-coated safety eyeglasses truly monopolized the relevant market, AutoGlass's decision not to grant British Optics a license to make and sell AGPLEX-coated safety eyeglasses in the United States would not raise any antitrust concern. The owner of a patented technology is not required to create competition in its own technology.

256.   *See* discussion at Sections 3.0 and 3.6, *supra*, discussing the balancing of the risk of anticompetitive harm and procompetitive efficiency benefits.

patent in this way may maximize the return on the patentee's investment in innovation. The grant of an exclusive license also may encourage more efficient development and promotion of the patent by the licensee by removing the risk that other licensees, or even the patentee, will benefit from those investments. It may encourage the licensee to develop innovations which, although they may not be patentable, would nevertheless make the technology more valuable to consumers. While this case involves an exclusive field-of-use license, other forms of exclusive licenses — for example, granting the licensee the exclusive rights to sell the patented product in some area of the United States or to some class of customers — can provide similar benefits.

RESTRICTION ON THE USE OF COMPETING TECHNOLOGIES

AutoGlass's requirement that Amer-Eye not use competing technologies to coat its safety eyeglasses may be used to give Amer-Eye a strong incentive to develop and aggressively market the AutoGlass technology. Thus, the restriction can generate economic benefits, particularly in a case where it stimulates competition among technologies.

ROYALTIES BASED ON TOTAL SALES

The Department generally is not concerned with the amount of license royalties or the basis upon which license royalties are measured.[257] As a general matter, licensees will pay for the licensed technology no more than what they think the technology is worth. Moreover, various types of royalty payment provisions (for example, package licensing and royalties paid on sales of products made from a patented process), can encourage licensees to develop and promote the licensed technology efficiently by enabling the licensee to use the technology in combination with other inputs in order to produce the final product at the lowest possible cost. In particular, a royalty provision based on total unit sales of a product regardless of whether it is made using the licensed technology may save licensors the costs of determining the extent to which its licensees' production utilizes the licensed technology. Finally, calculating a royalty on the basis of a licensee's use of some complementary input or inputs or on the basis of the sales of some downstream product can be used to meter differences in demand for the technology among

---

257. In the past, various types of royalty arrangements have been found by the courts to be unlawful under the doctrine of patent misuse as well as under the Sherman Act. *See, e.g.,* Zenith Radio Corp. v. Hazeltine Research, Inc., 395 U.S. 100, 135, 138 (1969) ("conditioning the grant of a patent license upon payment of royalties on products which do not use the teaching of the patent" is unlawful as patent misuse except where the "convenience of the parties rather than patent power dictates the total-sales royalty provision"). The Department believes, however, that for its enforcement purposes, it is appropriate to focus the Department's analysis on whether a restraint would likely create, enhance, or facilitate the exercise of market power in some relevant market.

different licensees. In this way, the licensor may be able to disseminate its technology more widely than if it had to charge a fixed royalty.[258]

Case 11 – Exclusive Patent Cross Licenses with Grantbacks

Alpha Corporation, a U.S. firm, is the second largest seller of product X in the United States. Beta Corporation, a Japanese firm, is the largest seller of X in Japan. Alpha and Beta each possess both U.S. and Japanese process patents covering certain technologies they use in manufacturing X. Beta currently does not sell significant amounts of X in the United States, and Alpha does not currently sell significant amounts of X in Japan. Alpha and Beta produce no product other than X.

Alpha and Beta agree to cross-license one another to practice their foreign patents. Alpha grants to Beta the exclusive right to practice Alpha's Japanese patents, and Beta grants to Alpha the exclusive right to practice Beta's U.S. patents. Each license contains an exclusive grantback clause: If Beta makes patented improvements on Alpha's technology, Beta agrees to assign the U.S. rights to practice those improvements to Alpha; if Alpha makes patented improvements on Beta's technology, Alpha agrees to assign the Japanese rights to practice those improvements to Beta. Alpha and Beta also agree that if either of them develops patented improvements on its own patent, they will grant an exclusive license to the other party to practice the improvements in that party's home country. Finally, Alpha and Beta agree that they will not sell X produced with licensed technology in the home country of the other party. The effect of this licensing arrangement is to give Alpha the exclusive right to practice both its own technology and Beta's technology and all improvements thereon in the United States and to give Beta comparable rights in Japan.

Discussion

As is true with respect to international transactions in general, the Department's consideration of the process patent licenses in this case would be limited to their effects on U.S. commerce. Otherwise, the Department's substantive analysis of the licenses would be identical to its analysis of similar licensing arrangements arising in a purely domestic context.

RULE-OF-REASON ANALYSIS

In general, except in very highly concentrated markets involving homogeneous products, the cross-licensing of competing (or potentially competing) process patents alone is unlikely to be anticompetitive; rather, it generally is the restrictions that are used in connection with the cross-licensing that may raise antitrust concern. In fact, cross-licensing by itself is generally procompetitive because it expands access to technology. In this case, for example, the cross license allows Alpha and Beta to use an alternative technology for producing X to which they otherwise would not have access. Similarly, if Alpha's and Beta's technologies are complementary (that is, if in at least some circumstances they are more efficient when used together), then the cross license might enable Alpha and Beta to compete more effectively against the

---

258.   *See* Section 3.61, *supra.*

owners of other competing technologies. The cross license may also allow Alpha and Beta to avoid protracted and expensive good-faith litigation over the validity and infringement of their respective patents. Assuming that the underlying transfer of technology in this case is not a sham, the Department would analyze its likely competitive effects using the rule-of-reason analysis set forth in Section 3.6 of these Guidelines.

STEP 1 – TECHNOLOGY MARKET

The Department would first determine whether the licenses in this case would likely have an anticompetitive effect in a relevant technology market or markets. The cumulative effect of the license restrictions, which in this case give Alpha the exclusive right in the United States to practice Beta's technology and any improvements thereon, is competitively indistinguishable from the outright acquisition by Alpha of Beta's technology.

The Department would begin its analysis by defining the relevant market in which the technologies of Alpha and Beta compete and identifying all other technologies that compete in that market.[259] The relevant technology market would include all other technologies that appear to be functional substitutes for the licensed technologies in producing X and all technologies used to produce products that are reasonable substitutes for X to which consumers would switch if the price of X were increased significantly. After identifying the technologies in the market (which is likely to be international in scope), the Department would assign market shares to those technologies based on their apparent relative efficiency.[260]

An acquisition by Alpha of Beta's technology might be anticompetitive if there were only a very few close substitutes for the licensed technologies in the production of X and substitutes for X. If that were the case, then the Department would consider other factors that are relevant to whether the licensing scheme would create, enhance, or facilitate the exercise of market power, including whether existing R&D efforts are reasonably expected to result in competing technologies within a two-year period and whether fringe technologies would be able to defeat any attempted exercise of market power.[261]

---

259.   For the purpose of this case, it is assumed that the technologies owned by Alpha and Beta are substitutes. As a practical matter, however, it often may be difficult to determine whether particular technologies are substitutes, complements, or both. *See* n.135, *supra*.

260.   *See* Section 3.63, *supra*. Patents, of course, grant exclusive rights to the use of the underlying technology only to the geographic extent of the granting authority's jurisdictional reach. For example, a patent granted by the U.S. Patent and Trademark Office provides only the exclusive right to make, use, or sell the patented invention and products made using the patented invention in the United States. Technologies typically are granted intellectual property protection in various national markets. And, as a general matter, a technology developed and patented in Japan can readily be patented and transferred to compete in the United States.

261.   *See* n.141, *supra* (fringe technologies).

STEP 2 – OTHER MARKETS[262]

Beta has agreed not to sell in the United States X produced with its own technology.[263] Although the license does not by its terms prevent Beta from selling X produced with technology owned by third parties, the practical effect of the restriction may be to eliminate all competition between Alpha and Beta in the sale of X in the United States that would have occurred if not for the license arrangement. The Department would therefore determine whether eliminating actual or potential competition by Beta in the sale of X in the United States would give Alpha (alone or in conjunction with other sellers of X in the United States) the ability to reduce output and increase the price of X to U.S. consumers.

As in merger analysis, after defining the relevant market for the sale of X in the United States, the Department would first focus on the level of concentration and increase in concentration that would result from a merger of Alpha and Beta. The facts of this case do not provide sufficient information to determine the level of concentration in the relevant market for X or the extent to which a merger between Alpha and Beta would increase concentration in that market. Given that Beta sells very little X in the United States, and that Alpha is not the leading seller of X in the United States, however, it is likely that a merger between Alpha and Beta would fall within a Merger Guidelines concentration "safe harbor." If a merger between Alpha and Beta would fall within a safe harbor, the Department would conclude that the cross licenses are not likely to be anticompetitive.

If, however, a merger of Alpha and Beta would not fall within a safe harbor, then the Department would consider the other relevant market factors it normally considers in evaluating the likely competitive effects of a merger. Those factors would include ease of entry into the relevant market for X and characteristics of X that would make collusion more or less likely.[264]

Finally, the Department would consider whether Alpha's and Beta's agreement not to license their respective technologies to anyone else would likely result in market power in the relevant market for X. The Department would be concerned about the agreement only if (i) without access to the licensed technologies, an excluded firm could not compete in a relevant market (e.g., the relevant market for X) and in which Alpha and Beta possess market power; and (ii) there were no reasonable basis relating to the efficient development and dissemination of the licensed technologies

---

262. If the relevant technology were largely coextensive with the relevant market for X (as might be true if a competing technology were necessary to manufacture X and if the market shares assigned to the technologies were equal to the sales of or capacity for producing X), then the Department's analysis under step 1 would subsume its analysis under step 2. The fact that Alpha and Beta compete in a relevant market for X would likely be relevant only because a new entrant into the technology market might also be required simultaneously to enter the market for X, thus making entry in response to a price increase less likely. *See* discussion of step 3, *infra*.

263. Since Beta is not licensed under Alpha's U.S. patent, it also cannot sell in the United States X that is produced using Alpha's technology. *See* Section 1342 of the 1988 Trade Act, *supra* note 84, which extends protection to products made using patented processes. One purpose of Section 1342 is to enable the holder of a U.S. process patent to exploit its technology more effectively in other countries without the fear that such licensing will disrupt its own exploitation of the technology in the United States.

264. *See* Section 3.64, *supra*.

for excluding other firms from access. It is not clear from the facts of this case that competing sellers of X require access to the process patents owned by Alpha and Beta. Since Alpha is the second largest seller of X in the United States, there obviously is at least one competing process technology being used to produce X sold in the United States, and there may be others as well. Nor is it clear that Alpha and Beta possess market power in the sale of X in the United States. Although Alpha is the second largest seller of X in the United States, Beta currently does not make significant sales of X in the United States.

STEP 3 — VERTICAL RESTRAINTS ANALYSIS

Step 3 is designed to determine whether vertical restraints associated with an intellectual property licensing arrangement would either facilitate collusion in some technology or other market or result in the anticompetitive exclusion of competitors from any such market. Since the cross-licensing arrangement in this case is tantamount to a merger of Alpha and Beta in the technology market and the relevant market for X, any threat of collusion would have been detected in steps 1 and 2. Any threat of anticompetitive exclusion resulting from Alpha's and Beta's agreement not to license others to their technology would have been detected under step 2.

STEP 4 — OFFSETTING EFFICIENCY BENEFITS

If, under the first three steps, the Department concluded that the licenses posed no significant threat to competition, the Department would not challenge the licenses, regardless of whether they would actually generate procompetitive efficiencies. If the Department concluded that the licenses would likely create, enhance, or facilitate the exercise of market power beyond that conveyed by the intellectual property itself, however, then the Department would consider whether the threat of anticompetitive harm is outweighed by procompetitive efficiency benefits that the parties claim would result from the licenses.

The Department would consider the cumulative anticompetitive risks and benefits of the licensing arrangement in this case, and would not attempt to assign and balance the threats and benefits of particular features of the licenses.[265] Nevertheless, since these restrictions would not necessarily occur together in a license, it might be helpful to consider some of the potentially procompetitive benefits that each in general might generate.[266]

GRANTBACKS

A grantback feature in a patent license can be procompetitive, especially if it is nonexclusive. Where practicing a patent is likely to lead to further innovations in a patented technology (whether or not such innovations are patentable), a grantback may enable a patentee to avoid the possibility that such innovations by the licensee

---

265.   *See* Section 3.66, *supra*.
266.   *See also* Section 3.61, *supra*.

will either make obsolete the patentee's own technology or effectively prevent the patentee from itself developing further improvements in its technology.

A grantback also can serve to compensate the patentee for improvements developed by the licensee that the licensee could not have developed without having access to the patentee's technology. In this case, for example, if Beta's ability to develop improvements on Alpha's technology depended on the actual practice of Alpha's patents, Alpha would be entitled to be compensated for conferring this benefit on Beta. A grantback of any U.S. rights to such improvements is a logical choice for such compensation.

A grantback can also increase the efficiency of bargaining for a license. The grantback might function as consideration to the patentee in a contract to exploit the licensed technology. In that case, the price would be determined ex ante (in the form of a grantback), rather than ex post (after the improvements exist), when bargaining would be complicated by the parties' bilateral monopolies. Using a grantback to facilitate bargaining would directly benefit the parties and ultimately would also benefit consumers.

CONVEYANCE OF RIGHTS TO FUTURE IMPROVEMENTS BY LICENSOR

The fundamental purpose of a patent license or any other technology is to allow the licensee to use the technology efficiently to his and the licensor's mutual benefit, as well as to the benefit of consumers. Such use often will require significant investment by the licensee. Licensees may be reluctant to make such investments, however, if there is a significant risk that the patentee will improve the underlying technology and make the originally-licensed technology obsolete. Thus, just as a grantback may protect a licensor from adverse effects deriving from improvements on the licensed technology by the licensee, an agreement allowing the licensee to use any improvements in the technology developed by the licensor can protect the licensee's investment in the technology.

EXCLUSIVITY

Exclusivity is inherent in the patent grant itself; the patent laws do not require a patentee to create competition in the manufacture, use, or sale of the technology. Exclusive licensing provisions may also encourage licensees to maximize their promotion and utilization of the licensed technology without free-rider concerns and allow a patent owner to maximize the return on its investment in R&D efforts to acquire the patent.

Case 12 – Know-How Technology Transfer Agreement with Exclusive Territories

Alpha Corporation is a small, but growing, Massachusetts corporation. It possesses valuable unpatented know-how that it uses to produce product X. Alpha has not been successful in exporting X to other countries. Alpha proposes to enter into a twenty-year technology transfer agreement with Beta Corporation, a German firm, under which Alpha will convey its know-how to Beta. Beta is a large, well-financed multinational corporation. Beta does not currently produce X, but it produces closely related products, and it wishes to produce and sell X in the EEC.

As part of the technology transfer agreement, Beta will agree not to sell X in the United States, whether it is manufactured using Alpha's know-how or any other technology, for the duration of the technology transfer agreement.

Alpha is negotiating a similar agreement with Epsilon Corporation. Epsilon is a large Japanese conglomerate that currently produces X. Epsilon's technology has permitted it to obtain only a small share of the Japanese market. It makes even more limited sales in the United States. Epsilon believes that Alpha's technology will increase Epsilon's production efficiency and improve the quality of the X it produces. Epsilon insists that Beta be barred from selling X in Japan, Australia, and East Asia. The prohibition would apply to all X produced by Beta, whether or not it was produced using Alpha's know-how.

Discussion

As is true with respect to international transactions in general, the Department's consideration of the know-how transfer agreements in this case would be limited to their effects on U.S. commerce. Otherwise, the Department's substantive analysis of the agreements would be identical to its analysis of similar agreements arising in a purely domestic context.

KNOW-HOW

Know-how is useful technical information concerning productive activity that is not generally known or accessible but is not protected by a patent.[267] Like patented technology, know-how represents the fruits of inventive activity that is stimulated by the ability to exclude others from using those fruits without the owner's permission. Because of the essentially similar roles that transfers of know-how and patent licensing play in the competitive process, the Department generally analyzes them in the same way. In fact, precisely because know-how is not statutorily defined and protected by a government grant, restrictions in agreements transferring know-how may be even more essential to protecting procompetitive investment in valuable technology. Because know-how is not necessarily susceptible to precise definition, however, in some cases it may be more difficult to distinguish a transfer of know-how from a sham arrangement shielding a naked cartel. In appropriate cases, therefore, the Department may be required to determine whether the know-how that is transferred is of nontrivial economic value. If the know-how in this case were of trivial importance to the efficient production of X, then the agreement might be merely a sham intended to restrict output and raise the price of X. The fact that Epsilon will be able to improve the efficiency of its production of X by using Alpha's know-how, however, suggests that the economic value of Alpha's know-how is nontrivial.

---

267.   *See, e.g.*, Kirkpatrick and Mahinka, *Antitrust and the International Licensing of Trade Secrets and Know-how: A Need for Guidelines*, 9 Law & Pol'y in Int'l Bus. 725, 728 (1977) ("know-how consists of technological information concerning manufacturing processes not protected by patent, not generally known or accessible, and of competitive value to its owner").

RULE-OF-REASON ANALYSIS

The proposed agreements in this case involve several restrictions that may be used in international technology licensing arrangements. First, Beta and Epsilon will be restricted from using Alpha's know-how to compete with Alpha in selling X in the United States. Second, Beta and Epsilon will be restricted from selling X manufactured using other technologies in the United States. Third, Beta will be restricted from selling X manufactured using any technology in foreign markets reserved to Epsilon. Assuming that the licenses in this case do not constitute a mere sham hiding a naked cartel among Alpha, Beta, and Epsilon, the Department would analyze their competitive effect under the four-step rule-of-reason analysis set forth in Section 3.6 of these Guidelines.

STEP 1 – TECHNOLOGY MARKET

The licenses in this case do not by their terms restrict competition in the licensing of technologies. Nevertheless, under certain circumstances, the provision restricting Epsilon from selling X made using its technology in the United States could have the effect of excluding Epsilon's technology from the United States. This would be the case if Epsilon could not readily transfer its know-how to third parties or if the license provisions otherwise removed its incentive to do so, such that Epsilon's technology could reach the U.S. marketplace only through Epsilon's sale of X.

The exclusion of Epsilon's technology from the U.S. marketplace could raise competitive concern if, for example, there was only one other technology available in the United States besides Alpha's technology. If consumers viewed Epsilon's technology as being only marginally less efficient than the other two technologies, then, in the absence of the license restriction, Epsilon might be able to defeat any attempted exercise of market power by them. In that case, the effect of excluding Epsilon's technology would be to reduce the number of available technologies in the United States from three to two. The effective exclusion of Epsilon's technology from the market would not be anticompetitive, however, if there were many other competing technologies that would similarly constrain any attempt to exercise market power or if, as the facts of this case suggest, Epsilon's technology is very much inferior to other technologies in the market.[268]

STEP 2 – OTHER MARKETS

Next, the Department would determine whether the licenses in this case would have an anticompetitive effect in any other markets, including markets in which the licensed technology is an input or for which it is a complement. Under the facts of

---

268.   On the facts of this case, the Department would not likely be concerned about the elimination of potential competition by Beta in the relevant technology market since there is no indication that Beta would sell X in the United States at all without having access to Alpha's technology. The minimum conditions necessary for an anticompetitive effect resulting from the elimination of significant potential competition do not appear to be present here (*see also* Case 3).

this case, only Epsilon competes with Alpha for the sale of X in the United States.[269]

As to Alpha's agreement with Epsilon, the Department would begin its analysis by determining whether a merger between Alpha and Epsilon prior to entering into the license would likely have had an anticompetitive effect in a relevant market for the sale of X. This analysis would be essentially the same as the analysis under step 1.[270]

In measuring Epsilon's share of the relevant market, the Department would consider only sales that Epsilon would have made without having access to Alpha's technology.[271] The Department would not be concerned about market power in the relevant market for X that reflected merely the inherent superiority of Alpha's technology. As stated in Section 3.6 of these Guidelines, market power that is attributable to the superior quality or efficiency of a product is not unlawful. Moreover, technology owners are free to appropriate the full inherent value of their property, and are not required to create competition in that property. The Department therefore would not be concerned if it appeared that any market power possessed by Alpha in the relevant market for X resulted from the superiority of its technology.

If, with respect to the relevant market for X, a merger between Alpha and Epsilon would not fall within a Merger Guidelines concentration "safe harbor," then the Department would consider other relevant evidence bearing on whether the license would likely create, enhance, or facilitate the exercise of market power. Those factors would include ease of entry into the relevant market for X using competing know-how and characteristics of X that would make successful collusion with respect to the sale of X more or less likely.

The territorial restriction on competition between Beta and Epsilon would not appear to have any direct, substantial, or reasonably foreseeable effect on U.S. commerce and would therefore not fall within the subject matter jurisdiction of the U.S. antitrust laws.[272]

STEP 3 — VERTICAL RESTRAINTS ANALYSIS

Next, the Department would seek to determine whether vertical restraints associated with the licenses in this case would facilitate collusion in a relevant technology market or other market or would result in the anticompetitive exclusion

---

269. On the facts of this case, the Department would not likely conclude that the agreement between Alpha and Beta eliminated competition in a relevant market for X. The agreement would be anticompetitive only if it eliminated important potential competition provided by Beta in the market for X. The minimum necessary conditions for such an anticompetitive effect do not appear to be present here (*see also* Case 3).

270. Indeed, as discussed in Case 11, if the technology and product markets are coextensive, the analysis of anticompetitive effects in the two markets would be the same. In some circumstances, there may be differences in the markets (e.g., the know-how may be a small part of the value of the final product) that make it appropriate to analyze possible competitive effects in both markets separately.

271. As explained in Section 3.321, *supra*, the Department discounts a firm's market share based on current sales or shipments if it appears that the firm would be a less significant competitor in the future because it does not own or control access to a technology needed to remain competitive. *See* Merger Guidelines § 3.21.

272. *See* Section 4.1, *supra*; *see also* Foreign Trade Antitrust Improvement Act, 15 U.S.C. § 6a (1982).

of competitors from a relevant market. In this case, any threat of collusion would already have been detected under steps 1 and 2, in which the Department focuses on whether the elimination of competition between Beta and Epsilon would create, enhance, or facilitate the exercise of unilateral or collusive market power in the United States.

The Department would also seek to determine whether, by prohibiting Beta and Epsilon from selling X in the United States, the licenses in this case would result in the anticompetitive exclusion of competitors from the relevant technology market (by denying them access to production or distribution assets in the United States needed to exploit a competing technology) or from the relevant market for X (by "tying up" competing technologies). Anticompetitive exclusion is highly implausible in this case. First, Beta and Epsilon do not appear to be the only firms capable of exploiting in the United States competing technologies for the manufacture of X. In fact, Beta does not currently produce X (though it produces closely related products) and Epsilon apparently is only one of many other firms selling X in Japan. Moreover, neither Beta nor Epsilon appears to be a significant competitive factor in the United States for any product. It therefore seems likely that there is substantial other existing capacity available to exploit competing technologies. Nor, as explained in step 1, would the licenses likely result in anticompetitive exclusion from the relevant market for the sale of X in the United States by "tying up" access to technologies.

STEP 4 − OFFSETTING EFFICIENCY BENEFITS

If the Department's analysis under the first three steps indicated that the licenses would not likely have any anticompetitive effect, then the Department would not challenge the licenses, regardless of whether they actually generated procompetitive efficiencies. If it appeared that the licenses would likely result in the ability to restrict output or raise prices to U.S. consumers in any market, however, then the parties would bear the burden of showing by clear and convincing evidence that procompetitive efficiency benefits generated by the licenses would outweigh the threat of anticompetitive harm.[273]

In this case, the restriction on sales of X by Epsilon in the United States could encourage the transfer of know-how in the first place. As is true with respect to all forms of intellectual property, the creator of know-how is not required to transfer the know-how; it may in fact choose not to do so if the result would be to reduce the value of the know-how. Prohibiting Epsilon from selling any X in the United States, regardless of whether it is produced using the licensed know-how, could save Alpha, and probably Epsilon and consumers as well, the costs of monitoring compliance with a narrower restriction. It might be difficult, for example, for Alpha to discover and prove that a particular product was made using know-how very similar to its own; there might be significant resources expended in litigation to resolve whether the transferee's know-how was developed independently.

In this case, of course, it could be argued that U.S. consumers would not be the primary beneficiaries of the transfer of Alpha's know-how to Beta and Epsilon. On the other hand, enabling Alpha to exploit its technology in foreign markets serves to stimulate the production of technology that ultimately benefits U.S. consumers.

---

273.   *See* Section 3.66, *supra*.

Therefore, the Department would consider efficiencies unless they could be achieved without threatening U.S. consumers with anticompetitive harm.

Case 13 – Anticompetitive Use of Section 337

Alpha Corporation, a major U.S. chemical company, is the sole U.S. producer of product X, an artificial fiber possessing unique and valuable properties. Alpha owns a U.S. process patent covering its technology for producing X.

Beta Corporation, a small Italian specialty chemical producer, has developed a new, substantially less costly process to produce X. Although Beta has never sold X outside of Italy, it decides to explore marketing opportunities in the United States. Beta's new process would enable it to sell X profitably in the United States at a lower price than Alpha can profitably offer. Alpha believes that Beta's imports would significantly threaten Alpha's X sales in the United States.

Alpha files an action under section 337 of the 1930 Tariff Act[274] to prohibit the importation of Beta's X into the United States, alleging that Beta's process is covered by Alpha's U.S. process patent. Alpha's technical staff has advised Alpha's management that Beta's process is substantially different from, and outside the scope of, Alpha's patent. Alpha's management nevertheless files the action hoping that the cost, delay, and uncertainty resulting to Beta from having to defend the proceeding will deter Beta, and perhaps ultimately others, from attempting to compete in the United States.

Discussion

Section 337 of the 1930 Tariff Act permits the U.S. International Trade Commission, *inter alia*, to order the exclusion of imported products that infringe domestic intellectual property rights or that are made abroad using a process that is protected by a U.S. process patent. Like other laws that protect rights in intellectual property, when properly used, section 337 helps to preserve incentives for the procompetitive creation and efficient exploitation of innovative technology.[275]

The Supreme Court has held that a firm's efforts to obtain action by the U.S. Government or any state government does not violate the Sherman Act even when the result of that action would be anticompetitive.[276] That protection does not extend, however, to petitioning activity that is in fact a "mere sham to cover what is actually nothing more than an attempt to interfere directly with the business relationships of a competitor."[277] If Alpha lacked a reasonable basis for believing that its claim had merit, the Department would treat Alpha's filing of a 337 action as a "sham" filing. Where such misuse of governmental processes is part of a scheme to monopolize a relevant market, it might violate section 2 of the Sherman Act.[278] In this case, however, it appears that Alpha may not have a reasonable basis to believe that its process patent is infringed by Beta's technology. Alpha's purpose in filing the action may be not to protect its process patent rights, but to exclude a

---

274.   19 U.S.C. § 1337, *as amended by* § 1342 of the 1988 Trade Act, *supra* note 84.
275.   *See generally* discussion at Section 3.60, *supra*.
276.   *See* text accompanying nn.181-183, *supra* (discussing *Noerr-Pennington* doctrine).
277.   *Noerr*, 365 U.S. at 144.
278.   *See* Section 3.2 (monopolization).

competitor's noninfringing product from the United States by imposing prohibitive additional costs on its sales into the United States.

If, judged objectively, Alpha did have a reasonable basis to believe that Beta's process infringed its patent, then Alpha's filing of the 337 action would not be considered to be a sham even if Alpha ultimately did not prevail in court. Because the very nature of an action under section 337 is to attempt to exclude a competitor's products, the Department will not consider the filing of such an action to be a sham unless there was no reasonable basis for the petitioner to believe that the action had merit (or unless the Department had evidence that the petitioner believed the claim to be baseless). Only then would it be possible to conclude that the petitioner's sole motivation was to interfere directly with the legitimate business relationships of a competitor.

Case 14 – International Cartel Activities

Alpha Corporation, a large multinational corporation incorporated in Delaware, mines X-ore abroad and processes it into X-product, which it sells in the United States and other countries. Alpha owns 75 percent of a subsidiary which it organized in Country A to operate a large X-ore mine there.

Beta Corporation, which is headquartered in Country A, mines X-ore in five overseas countries and sells X-ore and X-product in a number of countries, including the United States. A majority of the common stock of Beta is owned by the Delta Investment Corporation, a diversified investment company which in turn is majority owned and controlled by the government of Country A.

Epsilon Corporation is a European-based fruit company that sells large quantities of fruit juices through its own retail outlets located in the United States. Epsilon recently discovered a very large X-ore deposit on one of its overseas fruit plantations, and has been selling X-ore abroad.

Beta, Epsilon, and the four other foreign X-ore producers (but not Alpha) recently attended a secret meeting in Country A at which they agreed on quotas and prices for all of their X-ore production. Beta is the only one of these foreign X-ore producers that sells X-ore or X-product directly to purchasers in the United States, but the others all sell substantial amounts of X-ore to foreign brokers, which in turn sell substantial quantities in the United States. The cartel members collectively account for a large portion of the world's X-ore production. With Alpha, they would account for substantially all world X-ore production. More than 25 percent of world X-ore production is consumed in the United States. A representative of the government of Country A has notified Alpha that it wants Alpha to pledge to the cartel members that it will abide by the quotas and prices set by the cartel.

Discussion

This case involves a naked, private cartel agreement among horizontal competitors to fix the price and quantity of a product sold to U.S. consumers. The only possible effect of the agreement would be to reduce output and raise the price of X-ore; the agreement is unrelated to any integration of the parties' assets or operations that might generate efficiencies. Moreover, the parties have entered into the agreement secretly in an attempt to conceal the true nature of their activities and to defraud consumers into believing that they are benefiting from active competition among X-ore producers.

In view of the large percentage of world X-ore production that is sold in the United States, it seems clear that the cartel would have a direct, substantial, and reasonably forseeable effect on U.S. import trade. The Department thus would likely prosecute the agreement as a clear violation of the U.S. antitrust laws unless particular defendants were protected by foreign sovereign immunity or foreign sovereign compulsion, or unless considerations of comity counseled otherwise with respect to particular defendants.[279]

For reasons explained in Section 6 of these Guidelines, the Department would not seek to prosecute anticompetitive conduct that a foreign sovereign actually has compelled unless the conduct occurred wholly or primarily in the United States. In this case, however, the fact that the government of Country A has requested Alpha to abide by the cartel agreement would not excuse Alpha's participation. Although the government of Country A has made it clear that it wishes Alpha to join the cartel, it has not attempted to compel Alpha to do so.

For reasons of comity, the Department might refrain from prosecuting anticompetitive conduct that clearly has arisen from the decision and action of a foreign sovereign even in the absence of strict legal compulsion.[280] It does not appear that considerations of comity would cause the Department to refrain from prosecuting the cartel in this case, however. The cartel does not appear to be either required or contemplated by any law or articulated economic policy of the government of Country A. The cartel also covers X-ore production and sales that occur substantially outside of Country A. Indeed, it appears that the cartel's purpose and effect is not primarily to regulate the economy of Country A, but rather to raise prices to consumers in the United States and other markets. Given the substantial adverse effect that the cartel would have on U.S. consumers and the lack of any apparent connection to regulation by Country A of its economy, there does not appear to be any reason to defer to the jurisdiction of Country A and refrain from prosecuting this cartel.

The facts in this case do raise questions of personal jurisdiction with respect to some of the cartel members.[281] Alpha, which is a U.S. corporation, and Epsilon, which has extensive (although unrelated) business operations in the United States, clearly are subject to the jurisdiction of the U.S. courts. Beta sells X-ore and X-product directly in the United States and is therefore likely to have sufficient contacts with the United States to subject it to the jurisdiction of the U.S. courts. The fact that Beta is indirectly controlled by the government of Country A would not immunize Beta for its participation in the cartel. Immunity from suit under the Foreign Sovereign Immunities Act does not extend to the commercial activities of an entity controlled by a foreign government.[282]

Whether there is personal jurisdiction over the remaining foreign cartel members is less clear. Even if a potential defendant in a criminal antitrust action is outside

---

279.   *See* Section 3.1, *supra* (discussing criminal enforcement under the Sherman Act).
280.   *See* Section 5, *supra*.
281.   For a discussion of the exercise of personal jurisdiction by U.S. courts, see Asahi Metal Industry Co. v. Superior Court of California, 480 U.S. 102 (1987).
282.   28 U.S.C. § 1605(a)(2). *See* discussion at Section 4.1, *supra*.

the jurisdiction of the United States, however, the Department may file indictments or other process against that individual or firm and hold the indictments or other process outstanding until the jurisdictional requirements are met. In addition, if defendants possess property in the United States, under certain circumstances that property may be seized to induce consent to the jurisdiction of a U.S. court.[283]

Case 15 – Government-Imposed Export Restraint

Alpha Corporation, which is organized under the laws of Country A, is a wholly-owned subsidiary of Beta Corporation, a U.S. company. Alpha manufactures product X in Country A and exports X to the United States. The other five producers of X in Country A, which also sell X in the United States, are all locally owned.

The sales and profits of U.S. producers of X have fallen because of increased imports of X from Country A. U.S. producers of X have been seeking U.S. legislation that would substantially curtail X imports from Country A. The government of Country A is concerned that these legislative efforts might succeed. It asks producers of X in Country A to form an advisory council to advise the government of Country A on how to counter the threat of U.S. import restraints. Alpha joins the other producers of X in Country A in advising the government of Country A to issue an order limiting the amount of X that may be exported to the United States and allocating the export quota among the producers of X in Country A in proportion to their current U.S. sales. The government of Country A does so. Violations of the quota allocations are subject to significant sanctions by the government of Country A.

Discussion

The export restraint in this case has been imposed by the government of Country A. A foreign government's imposition of controls over exports by its own producers is considered to be a sovereign function of the state. Compliance with those controls would not normally be viewed as constituting agreement among private producers; if such an agreement were found in this case, however, it would likely be protected from challenge under the U.S. antitrust laws by the doctrine of foreign sovereign compulsion, which is discussed at Section 6 and Case 14 of these Guidelines.[284]

Nor would the Department challenge Alpha's conduct in joining with the X producers of Country A in recommending export restraints to the government of Country A. The collective petitioning of government by competitors is not unlawful even if the desired government action would have an anticompetitive effect, so long as that collective activity is not a mere sham concealing a direct restraint of trade by the parties.[285] As explained in Section 7 of these Guidelines, the Department will not prosecute the legitimate petitioning of foreign governments by foreign or

---

283.   *See* 15 U.S.C. §§ 6, 11.
284.   *See* Exchange of letters between William F. Baxter, Assistant Attorney General, Antitrust Division, Department of Justice, and Sir Roy Denman, Head of Delegation to the United States, Commission of the European Communities, Oct. 21, 1982, and attachments (steel export restraints); Exchange of letters between William French Smith, U.S. Attorney General, and Yoshio Okawara, Ambassador of Japan, May 7, 1981 (automobile export restraints).
285.   *See also* Case 13 (the filing of sham cases under Section 337).

domestic firms in circumstances in which the *Noerr-Pennington* doctrine would protect such activities in the United States.

On the facts of this case, the petitioning does not appear to be a sham. The fact that the petitioning activity occurred in the context of an advisory council appointed by the government of Country A supports this conclusion. The conclusion would be the same, however, even if Alpha and the other producers of X had proposed the restraints to the government of Country A on their own initiative.

Case 16 – Voluntary Export Restraint

The Association of American X Manufacturers (the "Association"), whose members are suffering from overcapacity, slack demand, and the impact of increased imports of X from Country A, has been seeking legislated import quotas. The Association has publicly announced that its members may also invoke provisions of the U.S. trade laws that could lead to the restriction of imports. U.S. Government trade officials have informed officials of the government of Country A about the problem. They have suggested that Country A take action to ease trade relations between the two countries.

In an effort to forestall the imposition of U.S. import quotas and to respond to the concern of the U.S. Government, Country A's Minister of Trade holds separate meetings with the top representatives of each of Country A's five X producers. The Minister asks each producer to reduce its exports to the United States during the coming year by ten percent. The Minister makes it clear that the government of Country A views the reduction of exports to be crucial to Country A's overall trade relationship with the United States.

Each of the five producers of X agrees to reduce its exports to the United States. The Minister advises U.S. trade officials of this fact and publicly announces the voluntary restraint program. Each of the five producers of X has a U.S. sales subsidiary.

Discussion

This case raises two questions. First, is there an agreement among the producers of X in Country A? Second, would a U.S. antitrust enforcement action be appropriate in view of the involvement of the government of Country A and the request by U.S. Government officials that the government of A act to resolve the trade friction?

As discussed at Section 3.1 of these Guidelines, an unlawful conspiracy to restrain trade under section 1 of the Sherman Act does not require an express agreement; a meeting of the minds is sufficient. As a general matter, however, mere parallel conduct, without more, is not enough to establish agreement. Parallel conduct by competitors in some cases can be equally consistent both with agreement and with independent decision making. A conspiracy may be inferred from parallel conduct, however, where the parties appear to have a rational economic motive for engaging in the conspiracy (e.g., to restrict output and raise price) and it would not be in the economic self-interest of individual firms to engage in the conduct alone.

If it appeared that the Minister of Trade were simply acting as the coordinator for a private conspiracy among Country A's producers of X to restrict exports to the United States, the Department might seek to prosecute this arrangement as an unlawful cartel. The fact that the Minister served as the "hub" of the conspiracy would not insulate the private-party "spokes".

Mere foreign government acquiescence would not shield privately-imposed anticompetitive restraints clearly designed to raise prices to U.S. consumers. For reasons of comity, however, the Department likely would not challenge a voluntary export restraint that clearly arose from the decision and official action of the government of Country A in response to specific trade concerns officially expressed by the U.S. Government. As a matter of prosecutorial discretion, in deciding whether to challenge such conduct, the Department would consider the potential impact of a U.S. antitrust enforcement action on Country A's national interests as well as on the U.S. government's relationship with the government of Country A. The Department's action in a particular case would depend on the totality of the circumstances.[286]

Case 17 – Settling a Trade Case

The three largest American producers of product X, which together account for 85 percent of domestic X production, have filed a petition under the U.S. trade laws seeking the imposition of antidumping duties on X imported from producers in Country A. Country A is the largest foreign source of X sold in the United States. The U.S. Department of Commerce has preliminarily found weighted-average dumping margins for the various respondents ranging from three to 40 percent.[287] Petitioners have continued to argue that the margins are substantially greater.

The producers of X in Country A meet and decide to offer to settle the case with the U.S. producers of X. A representative of the X producers' association in Country A informs counsel for the U.S. petitioners that each producer of X in Country A will raise its U.S. prices by an agreed amount if the U.S. firms agree to withdraw their petition.

Discussion

An agreement among domestic and foreign competitors to raise the price of products imported into the United States would be per se unlawful under the U.S. antitrust laws.[288] The fact that the agreement purported to settle a dumping case would not constitute a defense.

An agreement by foreign competitors to restrict output or raise price in response to an antidumping investigation is exempt from application of the U.S. antitrust laws

---

286. In the Department's view, if the Department (in consultation with other Executive Branch agencies) did decide that an antitrust action was appropriate under all of the circumstances, that action would not be subject to dismissal in the U.S. courts on comity-related grounds. Since the Constitution charges the Executive Branch with responsibility for conducting the foreign relations of the United States, the Department believes that it would be improper for a court to review the constitutional actions of the Executive Branch in such a case. *See* n.167, *supra*.

287. Generally speaking, a dumping margin is the amount by which a foreign firm's domestic or third-country prices exceed the price of its exports to the United States. If a significant portion of the foreign firm's domestic prices are below its fully-allocated cost of production, the dumping margin is the amount by which the firm's fully-allocated cost exceeds the price of its exports to the United States.

288. *See* Section 3.0, *supra*.

only to the extent that the agreement is reached and carried out in accordance with the suspension agreement provisions of the antidumping law.[289] Congress has enacted detailed rules governing the effects of a suspension on the rights and obligations of affected domestic and foreign industries. Under those rules, the Commerce Department may suspend an antidumping investigation when foreign firms that account for substantially all of the relevant imports agree with the Commerce Department that they will (i) cease exports of the relevant product to the United States; (ii) eliminate sales made at less than fair value; or (iii) eliminate the injurious effects of the exports by raising their prices to a level that eliminates at least 85 percent of the dumping margin.[290] The Commerce Department must find the suspension agreement to be in the public interest following notice and comment by interested parties.[291] If exporters or interested parties so request, the Commerce Department must continue the investigation even after it is suspended; if it ultimately is determined that the antidumping laws have not been violated, the suspension agreement is voided and the investigation is terminated.[292]

An agreement by exporters with respect to the price of their exports that met all of the relevant statutory criteria for suspension agreements and was accepted by the Commerce Department would enjoy an implied immunity under the antitrust laws. The Commerce Department will not accept provisions in a proposed suspension agreement that do not appear to be necessary to comply with the antidumping law.[293] And, of course, no exemption would extend to an agreement that was made outside or beyond the scope of the provisions of the antidumping law. In this case, the agreement proposed by the X producers of Country A to the U.S. petitioners to raise their prices would not qualify for exemption under the antidumping law. There is no implied immunity under the U.S. antidumping laws for private anticompetitive agreements between or among U.S. and foreign producers in connection with the withdrawal of an antidumping petition. If the U.S. producers of X agreed to withdraw their petition on the basis of a promise by their foreign competitors to raise the price of exports to the United States, both the U.S. and foreign producers would be subject to action under the antitrust laws. The additional fact that certain officials of the government of Country A suggested that X producers in Country A settle the U.S. trade case would provide no protection since compliance with this suggestion would not require the X producers to act outside the provisions of the antidumping law.

A detailed discussion of the provisions in various U.S. trade laws that allow agreements or other measures to restrict import competition is beyond the scope of these Guidelines. It is important to bear in mind, however, that private

---

289.   19 U.S.C. § 1673c(b)-(j) (1982).
290.   19 U.S.C. § 1673c(b)-(c).
291.   19 U.S.C. § 1673c(d)-(e); 19 C.F.R. § 353.42(h).
292.   19 U.S.C. § 1673c(f)(3), (g).
293.   *See, e.g.*, Letter from Charles F. Rule, Acting Assistant Attorney General, Antitrust Division, Department of Justice, to Mr. Makoto Kuroda, Vice-Minister for International Affairs, Japanese Ministry of International Trade and Industry, July 30, 1986 (concluding that a suspension agreement did not violate U.S. antitrust laws on the basis of factual representations that the agreement applied only to products under investigation, that it did not require pricing above levels needed to eliminate sales below foreign market value, and that assigning weighted-average foreign market values to exporters who were not respondents in the investigation was necessary to achieve the purpose of the antidumping law).

anticompetitive agreements entered into outside the specific framework of U.S. trade law provisions allowing for such agreements enjoy no exemption from the antitrust laws merely because they arise in the context of a trade dispute.

Case 18 – Information Exchange in Connection with a Proceeding Under U.S. Trade Law

Country B is the largest foreign source of X sold in the United States. The U.S. industry has become concerned that Country B's producers are selling X at "unfairly" low prices in the United States. The three largest U.S. producers of product X, which together account for 85 percent of domestic production of X, decide to bring an antidumping case against Country B's X producers for selling X in the United States at "less than fair value."[294] U.S. producers of X have lost significant U.S. market share to producers of X from Country B.

In the course of preparing their antidumping case, the three U.S. producers of X collect and study historical data about the pricing and volume of imported X in the United States. This information is necessary to support their claim that X imports from Country B have depressed or suppressed prices in the United States. The three U.S. producers also exchange detailed cost and price data concerning domestic sales of X, including information about specific transactions. All of this information is exchanged directly among the X producers themselves (rather than through a third party) in a disaggregated form that clearly identifies the producer that submitted particular data. The antidumping case is successful.

Discussion

This case illustrates how the Department analyzes information exchanges among private firms in the context of seeking government action under the U.S. trade laws. The Department would first determine whether the conduct in this case was immune under the *Noerr-Pennington* doctrine; if it were not immune, the Department would proceed to determine whether on balance it was anticompetitive.

As discussed at Section 7 of these Guidelines, the *Noerr-Pennington* doctrine protects the collective petitioning of government from antitrust condemnation even if the resulting government action would itself have an anticompetitive effect. The *Noerr-Pennington* doctrine does not, however, protect private anticompetitive conduct that is not "'incidental' to a valid effort to influence governmental action."[295] Thus, although the *Noerr-Pennington* doctrine extends to preliminary, organizational, and preparatory steps to petitioning a government entity, the doctrine does not shield conduct that is illegal for reasons wholly independent of any restraint of trade that would result from the government action and that, given the "context and nature" of the petitioning activity, goes beyond what is reasonably necessary to convince the government to act.[296] Thus, for example, an agreement among competitors on price or output that has an anticompetitive effect wholly independent of the government action sought would not be protected from antitrust scrutiny by the

---

294.   *See* 19 U.S.C. §§ 1673, *et seq.; see also* Case 17 (discussing U.S. antidumping law).
295.   Allied Tube & Conduit Corp. v. Indian Head, Inc., 108 S.Ct. 1931, 1936 (1988).
296.   *Id.* at 1936, 1939.

Noerr-Pennington doctrine merely because it was reached during the course of organizing the joint petitioning activity. An exchange of competitively sensitive information used to coordinate such an anticompetitive agreement (rather than as an incident to obtaining valid government action) also would not be protected.

In this case, the outcome of a *Noerr-Pennington* analysis is unclear. Depending on the facts, the Department might conclude that the direct exchange of sensitive price and cost data on domestic sales was not incidental to prosecuting the antidumping case and was thus not protected by the *Noerr-Pennington* doctrine. If the facts indicated that the information exchange was designed to implement a naked price-fixing agreement, of course, the *Noerr-Pennington* doctrine obviously would not shield that agreement, regardless of whether it was reached in the course of the producers' collaboration in the antidumping proceeding.[297] If the Department concluded that the information exchange in this case was not protected under the *Noerr-Pennington* doctrine, it would determine whether on balance the exchange was likely to be anticompetitive. An exchange of information among competitors often may generate procompetitive benefits by increasing the amount of information about the market, by enabling domestic producers to meet foreign competition, or (as in this case) by enabling domestic producers to prepare an antidumping or countervailing duty action. Therefore, unless an exchange of information among competitors were simply a device to implement a naked agreement to raise price or restrict output, the Department would analyze it under a rule of reason.[298]

If the parties to an information exchange collectively do not possess market power, or if the relevant market or markets are not concentrated or are subject to easy entry, then an exchange of information by itself would not likely harm competition. On the other hand, if the market is highly concentrated and the parties account for most or all of the sales in that market, then an exchange of competitively sensitive information among them might be anticompetitive. In this case, the U.S. producers of X account for 85 percent of domestic production of X. However, that does not necessarily represent their share of any relevant market. Moreover, even if U.S. producers had a significant market share, they may not possess market power if new entry into the market or expanded import sales, for example, would frustrate any attempted exercise of market power. In this case, it appears that Country B's X producers may be a significant competitive factor in the market. The antidumping relief may change that if X from Country B would be significantly less attractive to U.S. consumers at higher prices.

If it appeared that the three U.S. producers of X did account for a large share of sales in a highly concentrated market for X, then the Department would also consider other relevant factors, including the nature of the information being exchanged, factors (such as the degree of product homogeneity) that would make collusion in the relevant market more or less likely, and whether the information exchange would generate significant procompetitive efficiencies. The way in which the information is exchanged in this case would be particularly significant. The parties likely could adopt safeguards to eliminate any anticompetitive effects from the information exchange. For example, sensitive competitive information ordinarily

---

297.   *See* Case 17.
298.   In appropriate cases, the Department may infer an agreement to fix prices from the agreement to exchange information.

does not have to be exchanged directly among competitors. Instead, information can be provided to an independent accounting firm, counsel, or some other appropriate intermediary; that independent entity could then aggregate and develop the information for the firms' use as needed without divulging each firm's individual data to its competitors.[299]

---

299.   *See* Letter from Douglas H. Ginsburg, Acting Assistant Attorney General, Antitrust Division, to Alan M. Frey, Esq., counsel for PQ Corporation, July 6, 1984 (indicating no present intention to challenge a proposed import information exchange where participating firms would not exchange information on their own prices or sales; the information would be provided to an independent accounting firm on a confidential basis; and information reported back to firms in the information exchange would be aggregated, would be at least 30 days old, and would not be broken down by geographic area).

DEPARTMENT OF JUSTICE AND FEDERAL TRADE COMMISSION HORIZONTAL MERGER GUIDELINES

- Commentary

- Statement Accompanying Release of Revised Merger Guidelines

- Department of Justice and Federal Trade Commission Horizontal Merger Guidelines, Issued April 2, 1992

- Dissenting Statement of Commissioner Mary L. Azcuenaga on the Issuance of Horizontal Merger Guidelines

---

Commentary[*]

On April 2, 1992, as this treatise was going to press, the Department of Justice and the Federal Trade Commission issued new, joint *1992 Horizontal Merger Guidelines* (*1992 Guidelines*). The *1992 Guidelines*, reprinted as part of this appendix, represent the first set of joint guidelines issued by the Department and the Commission. They supersede the *1982 Statement of the Federal Trade Commission Concerning Horizontal Mergers* (*1982 FTC Statement*, set forth in Appendix C of this treatise) and the *1984 Department of Justice Merger Guidelines* (*1984 Guidelines*, set forth in Appendix B) discussed in the text of Chapter III of this treatise, except for Section 4 of the Department's *1984 Guidelines* (Horizontal Effects From Non-Horizontal Mergers, addressing elimination of specific potential entrants and competitive problems from vertical mergers). The joint press release accompanying the *1992 Guidelines* states that "[n]either agency has changed its policy with respect to non-horizontal mergers" and that "[s]pecific guidance on non-horizontal mergers" is provided in Section 4 of the *1984 Guidelines* as "read in the context of today's [the 1992] revisions to the treatment of horizontal mergers."[1]

---

[*]   This commentary was prepared by a group of attorneys assisting the Editorial Board. Although it was reviewed by officials of the Department of Justice and the Federal Trade Commission, the Commentary does not necessarily represent the views either of these agencies. The Commentary is provided as a preliminary analysis of the 1992 GUIDELINES to highlight the differences between the 1992 and 1984 statements of merger enforcement policy by the Department of Justice and Federal Trade Commission.

1.   U.S. Department of Justice and Federal Trade Commission Statement Accompanying Release

The Department and FTC consulted with the National Association of Attorneys General (NAAG) and received useful input from NAAG representatives in an effort to harmonize federal and state enforcement agency merger standards.[2] As of the time this treatise went to press, it remained unclear whether NAAG would revise its *1987 Horizontal Merger Guidelines* (set forth in Appendix D) to bring them into greater harmony with the *1992 Guidelines* or instead will follow different enforcement standards for horizontal mergers.

The *1992 Guidelines* represent the evolution of the federal enforcement agencies' standards for reviewing horizontal mergers, reflecting refinements in and clarifications of the analytical approaches, both legal and economic, that were articulated in 1984. Some of the changes between the *1984* and the *1992 Guidelines* were foreshadowed in speeches by various agency officials during the intervening years. This discussion cites a number of those speeches. The reader should exercise caution, however, in relying on those earlier speeches, some of which may no longer reflect the policy of the agency involved or of its sister agency.

In announcing the revised *Guidelines*, the agencies emphasized the observations in both the *1992* and *1984 Guidelines* that the "specific standards set forth . . . must be applied to a broad range of possible factual circumstances," that "mechanical application" of the standards could produce "misleading answers," and that the agencies "will apply the standards of the Guidelines reasonably and flexibly to the particular facts and circumstances of each proposed merger."[3]

Like prior guidelines, the *1992 Guidelines* are designed primarily to articulate the analytical framework the federal enforcement agencies use in assessing the competitive effects of a merger. They state that they do not "describe how the agencies will conduct litigation" and "neither dictate nor exhaust the range of evidence" the agencies "must or may introduce in litigation."[4]

The *1992 Guidelines* are divided into six parts. Following this discussion, the *1992 Guidelines* are reprinted in their entirety.

---

of Revised Merger Guidelines, Apr. 2, 1992, at 3. (Joint Release).

2.   *Id.* at 3.

3.   1992 GUIDELINES § 0. *See also* Remarks of K. Arquit, Director, Bureau of Competition, FTC, "Perspectives on the 1992 U.S. Government Horizontal Merger Guidelines," Before the ABA Antitrust Section, Spring Meeting (Apr. 2, 1992), at 3.

4.   1992 GUIDELINES § 0.1. Some courts, however, have held the enforcement agencies to the analysis set forth in the agencies' various guidelines. *See* United States v. Baker Hughes, Inc., 908 F.2d 981, 988, 992 n.13 (D.C. Cir. 1990); *cf.* Allis-Chalmers Mfg. Co. v. White Consol. Indus., Inc., 414 F.2d 506, 524 (3d Cir. 1969) (in private case, court stated that Justice Department's position, as expressed in the GUIDELINES, "is entitled to some consideration"), *cert. denied*, 396 U.S. 1009 (1970); Crane Co. v. Harsco Corp., 509 F. Supp. 115, 124-25 (D. Del. 1969) (GUIDELINES, while not binding on courts, "are often paid some deference"). *But see* Monfort of Colo., Inc. v. Cargill, Inc., 591 F. Supp. 683, 695 (D. Colo. 1981) (Department of Justice "not necessarily bound"), *aff'd*, 761 F.2d 570 (10th Cir. 1985), *rev'd on other grounds*, 479 U.S. 104 (1986); United States v. Atlantic Richfield Co., 297 F. Supp. 1061, 1073 (S.D.N.Y. 1969) ("in no way binding on the Department"), *aff'd*, 401 U.S. 986 (1971); *see also* Marathon Oil Co. v. Mobil Corp., 530 F. Supp. 315, 325 (N.D. Ohio 1981) (in dictum, quoting *Atlantic Richfield* with approval), *aff'd*, 669 F.2d 378 (6th Cir. 1981), *cert. denied*, 455 U.S. 982 (1982).

0. Purpose, Underlying Policy Assumptions and Overview

In concept, structure and content, the *1992 Guidelines* resemble the *1984 Guidelines*. Although there is a number of significant changes, in many areas the approach of the *1984 Guidelines* is simply imported into the new version with relatively minor clarifying or editorial changes.

New Part 0, "Purpose, Underlying Policy Assumptions and Overview," is similar to Section 1 of the *1984 Guidelines* although it is now emphasized that the *Guidelines* articulate the "analytical framework" for merger analysis by the enforcement agencies and do not assign or adjust burdens of proof or burdens of coming forward with evidence in context of the agencies' analysis. Rather, the *Guidelines* describe the methodology for analyzing mergers once the relevant evidence is available.[5]

Like that of the *1984 Guidelines*, the "unifying theme" of the *1992 Guidelines* is that "mergers should not be permitted to create or enhance market power or to facilitate its exercise."[6] New Section 0.2 lays out the five key steps in the analytical process designed to identify such transactions: (1) does the merger significantly increase concentration and result in a concentrated market; (2) does it raise concern about potential adverse competitive effects; (3) would entry sufficient either to deter or to counteract the competitive effects of concern be both timely and likely to occur; (4) would the merger create any efficiency gains that reasonably could not be achieved by the parties through other means; and (5) would either party be likely to fail, in the absence of the merger, and would its assets exit the market as a result?[7]

Under the *1992 Guidelines*, the agencies analyze competitive behavior on the basis of the parties' incentives: "whether consumers or producers 'likely would' take certain actions, that is, whether the action is in the actor's economic interest."[8]

1. Market Definition, Measurement and Concentration

Part 1, "Market Definition, Measurement and Concentration," combines Section 2 and part of Section 3 of the *1984 Guidelines* dealing with the same subjects. The new *Guidelines* make clearer that market definition focuses solely on demand substitution factors, and that supply substitution factors are relevant to identifying present and possible prospective participants in a market once that market has been defined.[9]

The General Standards for Product Market Definition[10] and Geographic Market

---

5.   1992 GUIDELINES § 0.1.
6.   *Id.* at § 0.1 first introduces the concept that a merger may be challenged because it creates the opportunity for unilateral (i.e., non-coordinated) exercise of market power, a concept that was implicit in the "Leading Firm Proviso," contained in § 3.12 of the 1984 GUIDELINES.
7.   The GUIDELINES note that these steps are analytical tools aimed at answering the ultimate question of whether the merger is likely to create or enhance market power or to facilitate its exercise. 1992 GUIDELINES § 0.2.
8.   *Id.* at § 0.1. In assessing the profitability of various actions in determining whether they "likely would" occur, the 1992 GUIDELINES make clear that the focus is on "economic profits" rather than "accounting profits," that is the "excess of revenues over costs where costs include the opportunity costs of invested capital." *Id.*
9.   *Id.* at § 1.0.
10.   *Id.* at § 1.11.

Definition[11] are essentially unchanged from the *1984 Guidelines*. Some of the examples of relevant evidence contained in Sections 1.11 and 1.21 differ somewhat from those in old Sections 2.12 and 2.32. Unlike the earlier version, the *Guidelines* state that product market definition methodology will use prevailing prices of the products of the merging firms and possible substitutes, unless there is evidence that those prices reflect "coordinated interaction." This recognition of the "Cellophane trap" from the Supreme Court's *duPont* case[12] allows use of a lower price "more reflective of the competitive price,"[13] where the premerger price already reflects the effects of collusion. Use of such a "competitive price" could narrow the market.

The "small but significant and nontransitory" price increase used to test demand substitution responses is now described as normally being an increase of 5% lasting for the foreseeable future.[14] The *1984 Guidelines* had postulated a similar increase lasting for one year. The *1992 Guidelines*, like their predecessor, also indicate that, depending on "the nature of the industry," the enforcement agencies may at times use a price increase "that is larger or smaller than five percent,"[15] but the new *Guidelines* do not explain under what circumstances such use would be appropriate.[16]

Finally, the *1992 Guidelines* indicate that in performing successive iterations of the "small but significant nontransitory price increase" test, the ability to maintain a price increase need not be uniform. The *1992 Guidelines* thus state that "the hypothetical monopolist will be assumed to pursue maximum profits in deciding whether to raise the prices of *any or all* of the additional products under its control."[17]

The *1992 Guidelines* continue to recognize the possibility that product and geographic market definition may reflect the ability of a hypothetical monopolist to engage in price discrimination among buyers. According to Sections 1.12 and 1.22, the market may in such circumstances be confined to a particular use or uses by buyers upon whom a price increase could profitably be imposed.[18]

There are a number of differences between Section 1.3 of the *1992 Guidelines*, which covers "Identification of Firms that Participate in the Relevant Market," and the corresponding provisions in the *1984 Guidelines*. Old Section 2.2 focused primarily on "firms that currently produce and sell the relevant product." New Section 1.31 includes in the analysis "all firms that currently produce *or* sell in the relevant market" (emphasis added). The substantive significance of the change, if any, is not known. Old Section 2.23 included vertically integrated firms that, in response to a price increase, would likely either begin selling a portion of their

---

11.   *Id.* at § 1.21.

12.   United States v. E.I. du Pont de Nemours & Co., 351 U.S. 377 (1956).

13.   1992 GUIDELINES § 1.11.

14.   *Id.* The 1992 GUIDELINES note that the 5% standard is simply a "methodological tool" for market definition analysis, and "not a tolerance level for price increase." *Id.* at § 1.0.

15.   *Id.* at § 1.11.

16.   Footnote 7 of the 1984 GUIDELINES, which stated that a larger increase might be appropriate if the price to be increased is a tariff or commission that is a small fraction of the price of the final product, has been eliminated.

17.   1992 GUIDELINES § 1.11 (emphasis added).

18.   Theoretically, a single purchaser who could be discriminated against and who purchases in a market with a limited number of suppliers could itself comprise a market under this standard.

production to third parties or increase their production of the relevant product and downstream products. New Section 1.31 somewhat cryptically includes all vertically integrated firms "to the extent that such inclusion accurately reflects their competitive significance in the relevant market prior to the merger." That qualification is not explained.[19]

Additional participants in the relevant market are identified from firms that are not currently producing or selling in that market but, in response to a price increase, could do so within one year "without the expenditure of significant sunk costs of entry and exit."[20] Sunk costs are defined as "the acquisition costs of tangible and intangible assets that cannot be recovered through the redeployment of those assets outside the relevant market, i.e., costs uniquely incurred to supply the relevant product and geographic market."[21] "Significant" sunk costs are those that would not be recovered within one year, assuming a small but significant and nontransitory price increase in the relevant market lasting for one year.

Calculation of market shares based on total sales or capacity of all market participants is essentially the same as in the *1984 Guidelines*. Market concentration and the amount by which a proposed merger will increase that concentration are stated in terms of the Herfindahl-Hirschman Index (HHI). However, the general standards for agency enforcement actions have been restated somewhat.

As under the old *Guidelines*, transactions resulting in a postmerger HHI of less than 1000 (i.e., an unconcentrated market) will ordinarily not be further analyzed.[22] Similarly, where the merger would increase concentration by less than one hundred

---

19. A speech by the Assistant Attorney General for Antitrust the day after issuance of the GUIDELINES states that "the Guidelines now include *all* current producers or sellers of the relevant product, even if the firm is vertically integrated and produces only for its own internal consumption." J. Rill, "60 Minutes With the Honorable James F. Rill," Before the American Bar Association's 40th Annual Antitrust Spring Meeting, at 8 (Apr. 3, 1992); *see also* C. James, Deputy Assistant Att'y Gen., Antitrust Div., Remarks before the Manufacturer's Alliance on Productivity and Innovation, at 12 (Apr. 10, 1992) ("[i]nternal production by vertically integrated firms is given full credit in market measurement under the new Guidelines"). However, a speech by the Director of the FTC's Bureau of Competition states that little or no substantive change from the 1984 GUIDELINES was intended, and that the issue is "whether, and to what extent, captive producers are likely to exert a competitive impact on the relevant market, either by selling the relevant product or by increasing production of both the relevant product and downstream products." K. Arquit, Further Thoughts on the 1992 U.S. Government Horizontal Merger Guidelines, Before the State Bar of Texas, at 7-8 (Apr. 24, 1992). Arquit notes that "an integrated producer may compete in downstream product or geographic markets different from these occupied by customers of other producers of the relevant product, so that any increase in its production both upstream and downstream would not exert competitive pressure on the relevant market." *Id.* at 8; *cf.* 1992 GUIDELINES § 1.41 ("In measuring a firm's market share, the Agency will not include its sales or capacity to the extent that the firm's capacity is committed or so profitably employed outside the relevant market that it would not be available to respond to an increase in price in the market.").

20. 1992 GUIDELINES § 1.32. Participants able to enter and exit the relevant market without incurring significant sunk costs are termed "uncommitted entrants," in that they can enter (and exit) without being economically "committed" to remain in the market. The 1992 GUIDELINES do not make clear how the market shares of "uncommitted entrants" would be calculated. Supply responses requiring more time or requiring expenditure of significant sunk costs of entry and exit (i.e., by "committed entrants") are treated in the entry analysis discussion in Part 3 of the GUIDELINES.

21. *Id.* at § 1.32.

22. *Id.* at § 1.51(a).

points and result in an HHI between 1000 and 1800 (i.e., a moderately concentrated market), the transaction will ordinarily require no further analysis.[23] Nor will a transaction increasing the HHI by less than fifty points and resulting in an HHI of more than 1800 (i.e., a highly concentrated market) normally require additional analysis.[24]

However, in the *1992 Guidelines*, a merger which increases the HHI by more than one hundred points and results in a moderately concentrated market may "potentially raise significant competitive concerns," depending upon analysis of other factors.[25] This appears to soften somewhat the position in Section 3.11(b) of the *1984 Guidelines*, which predicted that a Department challenge to such a merger was "likely" in the absence of a determination that the merger would not substantially diminish competition.

Similarly, under Section 1.51(c) of the *1992 Guidelines*, a transaction raising the HHI by more than fifty points to a figure above 1800 (i.e., a highly concentrated market) is now described as "potentially [raising] significant competitive concerns," while one that increases the HHI by more than one hundred points is "presumed" likely to create or enhance market power or facilitate its exercise. That presumption may be overcome by a showing that other *Guidelines* factors make such an anticompetitive result unlikely. This too appears to soften the *1984 Guidelines* position that the Department would likely challenge mergers increasing the HHI by more than fifty points in concentrated markets and that only in "extraordinary cases" would transactions in such markets increasing the HHI by more than one hundred points not be challenged.[26] These changes appear to bring the *1992 Guidelines* into closer harmony with actual enforcement practice over the past decade.

Part 1 of the *1992 Guidelines* concludes with a discussion in Section 1.52 of "Factors Affecting the Significance of Market Shares and Concentration." This discussion differs from the *1984 Guidelines* in three respects. First, it omits old Section 3.22, which suggested that the weak financial condition of any firm in the relevant market could justify discounting its present market share, on the theory that its current share overstated its likely long term competitive significance. While the *1992 Guidelines* retain the so-called "failing firm" defense, they dispense with any explicit notion of adjusting the shares of market participants to reflect their financial strength or weakness.[27]

Second, new Section 1.52 omits old Section 3.23, which had been one of three

---

23.   *Id.* at § 1.51(b).
24.   *Id.* at § 1.51(c).
25.   *Id.* at § 1.51(b).
26.   1984 GUIDELINES § 3.11(c).
27.   The Chairman of the Federal Trade Commission, in discussing the change, noted that the language of the 1984 GUIDELINES had sometimes been misapplied by people attempting to turn it into a "flailing firm" defense. Remarks of J. Steiger Before the American Bar Association Section of Antitrust Law, at 6 (Apr. 3, 1992). The Director of the FTC's Bureau of Competition has made similar statements, Arquit, *supra* note 19, at 15-16 (elimination of 1984 GUIDELINES language "should dispel any notion . . . that a firm's financial weakness, standing alone and short of imminent failure, is likely to be a 'changing market condition' . . ."; while noting that "[s]erious and sustained financial difficulties may be a *symptom* of a firm's more fundamental, structural disadvantages . . . and they will be relied upon as such."). A Department of Justice spokesman has stated that the "changing market conditions" provision of § 1.521 should be read to include the stricken section. James, *supra* note 19, at 12.

sections in the *1984 Guidelines* that addressed the treatment of foreign firms.[28] Under the *1992 Guidelines*, the various strands relating to foreign firms are revised and combined in Section 1.43, which addresses the "Special Factors Affecting Foreign Firms" in connection with the calculation of market shares. The *Guidelines* continue to provide that market shares will be assigned to foreign competitors in the same way as to domestic competitors, subject to specified adjustments (revised somewhat from the *1984 Guidelines*) to account for exchange rate fluctuations, quotas and other trade restraints, and foreign coordination.

Third, Section 1.52 includes a new subsection providing that the magnitude of potential competitive harm from a merger may depend on the degree of difference between the products and locations in the market and the substitutes outside the market.[29] A similar concept had been expressed in the *1984 Guidelines*[30] as one of the "other factors" that would be evaluated when relevant.[31] The discussion has now been relocated to the discussion of factors affecting the significance of market shares and concentration.

2. The Potential Adverse Competitive Effects of Mergers

While recognizing that it is easier for firms to exercise market power in concentrated markets, the *1992 Guidelines* deem concentration and market share data only a starting point for merger analysis.[32] The Section 2.0 Overview identifies and

---

28.   The other sections were the old § 2.34, which discussed "Foreign Competition" in the context of the broader treatment of "Geographic Market Definition," and the third paragraph of old § 2.4, which discussed "Calculating Market Shares."

29.   1992 GUIDELINES § 1.522.

30.   *See* 1984 GUIDELINES § 3.412.

31.   Under the 1984 GUIDELINES, these other factors, where relevant, were "most likely to be important where the Department's decision whether to challenge a merger is otherwise close." 1984 GUIDELINES, § 3.4. That language no longer appears in the 1992 GUIDELINES.

32.   The 1992 GUIDELINES, however, do not specify how concentration and the increase in concentration resulting from the merger continue to be relevant in the assessment of competitive effects once a transaction exceeds the various thresholds of § 1.51. The GUIDELINES do state that competitive effects are assessed "in light of market concentration and other factors that characterize the market." *Id.* § 0.2; *see also* § 1.51(c). The precise role played by concentration and market shares at that stage, however, is not explained.

       The Assistant Attorney General for Antitrust has stated that the "weight accorded to concentration data does not increase with the level of post-merger concentration or the change in concentration." J. Rill, "60 Minutes with the Honorable James F. Rill," Before the American Bar Association's 40th Annual Antitrust Spring Meeting (Apr. 3, 1992), at 13; *see* James, *supra* note 19, at 5; *cf. id.* at 4 ("Concentration and market shares can provide useful information, but only when they are considered in light of the specific conditions in the market under examination.")

       The Director of the FTC's Bureau of Competition has emphasized, however, that "high concentration is cause for more concern than low concentration," and that "the level of these concerns and the evidence needed to rebut them does not artificially plateau at 1800." Arquit, *supra* note 19, at 5. This is in accord with a prior Commission decision indicating that the strength of the evidence required to overcome a presumption of anticompetitive effect increases with concentration. *See* B.F. Goodrich Co., 110 F.T.C. 207, 305, 338-39 (1988); *cf.* United States v. Baker Hughes, Inc., 908 F.2d 981, 991 (D.C. Cir. 1990) (judicial decision to same effect) ("The more compelling the prima facie case, the more evidence the defendant must present to rebut it successfully.").

describes two types of potential anticompetitive effects of mergers — effects of coordinated interaction and effects of unilateral activity — and factors relevant in the analysis of them.

The *1992 Guidelines* differ from the *1984 Guidelines* in that the 1984 version contained no distinct section devoted to the potential anticompetitive effects of a merger. The potential effects of mergers were discussed throughout the *1984 Guidelines* in the context of specific factors that could cause or prevent such effects. For the first time, the *1992 Guidelines* attempt to articulate the ways in which mergers may harm competition.

Coordinated Interaction. Section 2.1 of the *1992 Guidelines* recognizes that a merger may enable competing firms in a market to engage in coordinated interaction that harms consumers. Coordinated interaction is defined as tacit or express conduct, whether lawful or unlawful, that is profitable for each participant only because the other participants accommodate its conduct.

The *1984 Guidelines* focused on the possibility that firms in a highly concentrated market could collude so as to approximate the performance of a monopolist and thereby exercise market power. In the *1992 Guidelines*, the term "collude" has been replaced with the term "coordinated interaction" in order to make clear that the focus of concern is on economic conditions that enhance the possibility of mutually accommodating group action, not just collusion.

The *1992 Guidelines* do not attempt to delineate all of the factors that could affect whether a given market is conducive to coordination. In assessing whether conditions in the anticipated post-merger market are conducive to coordination, the reviewing agency will consider all relevant factors including information availability, product homogeneity or heterogeneity, and common pricing and marketing practices. Prior express collusion among firms in a market whose characteristics have not changed significantly is considered to increase the likelihood that present market conditions are conducive to coordinated interaction.

This approach broadens the arguably more limiting language of Section 3.44(b) of the *1984 Guidelines*, which sets forth specific practices that could tend to foster collusion. The *1992 Guidelines* set forth a three-step inquiry in which all relevant facts can be evaluated: (1) can terms of coordination be reached that are profitable for each participant only because the other participants accomodate its conduct, (2) do the participating firms have the ability to detect deviations from those terms, and (3) do the participating firms have the ability to punish deviations from those terms? Market conditions relevant to each element will be examined, and the inquiry will focus on whether market conditions, on the whole, are conducive to reaching terms of coordination and detecting and punishing deviations from those terms. Section 2.1 of the *1992 Guidelines* states that certain market conditions that are conducive to reaching terms of coordination also may be conducive to detecting and punishing deviations from those terms.

Terms of Coordination. The *1992 Guidelines* recognize that coordination does not require all-encompassing terms nor achievement of a monopoly; the terms may be limited or incomplete and still significantly harm consumers. However, too many imperfections will make coordination unprofitable and therefore unlikely.

Clarifying the *1984 Guidelines*, the *1992 Guidelines* recognize that it is impossible to demonstrate with certainty that coordinated interaction will occur in the postmerger market. Accordingly, the *1992 Guidelines* ask whether, given current and anticipated postmerger market conditions, coordination is made easier as the result of the merger. This is a highly fact-specific analysis and the *1992 Guidelines* recognize that the nature of the coordination and conditions of the market can be of infinite variety.[33] This approach gives the agencies more freedom than was available under the arguably more limiting Sections 3.411, 3.412, and 3.45 of the *1984 Guidelines*.

Detecting and Punishing Deviations. Expanding on the *1984 Guidelines*, the *1992 Guidelines* emphasize that successful coordinated interaction requires the ability to detect and punish deviation. While the *1984 Guidelines* arguably considered the availability of information to be the critical factor in detection and punishment,[34] Section 2.12 of the *1992 Guidelines* makes clear that a variety of market conditions may affect a firm's incentive to deviate and the ability of others to detect and punish deviation.

While recognizing that buyer and purchasing process characteristics may affect incentives to deviate, the *1992 Guidelines*, with one exception, do not attempt to limit those characteristics as Section 3.42 of the *1984 Guidelines* may be read to have done. The exception relates to large buyers (which were not discussed in the *1984 Guidelines*); the *1992 Guidelines* set forth limited circumstances in which large buyers might be considered to affect incentives to deviate. The mere fact that buyers are large is not sufficient. The *1992 Guidelines* require that buyers be large, contracts with them be long term, the contracts cover sufficient portions of a firm's output, and buyers be willing to switch to the deviator.[35]

The *1992 Guidelines* also clarify the concept in Section 3.43 of the *1984 Guidelines* that firms with excess or divertable capacity and low opportunity costs may prevent or limit coordination.[36] The *1984 Guidelines* emphasized behavioral characteristics in identifying maverick firms as opposed to the *1992 Guidelines'* reliance on more objective economic incentives. The *1992 Guidelines* retain the conclusion that the acquisition of a maverick firm may enhance the likelihood of coordination.

Unilateral Effects. The *1992 Guidelines* introduce the concept that a merger may result in lessened competition through unilateral effects, even where the merger does not increase the likelihood of successful coordinated interaction.[37] The *1992*

---

33. *See* P. Denis, Acting Deputy Assistant Att'y Gen., Antitrust Div., Market Power in Antitrust Merger Analysis: Refining the Collusion Hypothesis, Remarks at ABA Antitrust Section CLE Inst., The Cutting Edge of Antitrust: Market Power, at 4-5 (Oct. 17, 1991) (recognizing that Assistant Attorney General of Antitrust Division embraces broad view of collusion hypothesis); J. Rill, *Report from Official Washington: Merger Enforcement at the Department of Justice*, 59 ANTITRUST L. J. 45, 51-53 (1990) (discusses the wide variety of factors bearing on competitive impact).

34. *See* 1984 GUIDELINES § 3.42.

35. *But see* United States v. Baker Hughes, Inc., 908 F.2d 981, 986-87 (D.C. Cir. 1990); United States v. Archer-Daniels-Midland Co., 1991-2 Trade Cas. (CCH) ¶ 69,647, at 69,918-19, 69,922 (S.D. Iowa 1991); FTC v. R.R. Donnelley & Sons, Co., 1990-2 Trade Cas. (CCH) ¶ 69,239, at 64,852, 64,855 (D.D.C. 1990); United States v. Country Lake Foods, Inc., 754 F. Supp. 669, 679-80 (D. Minn. 1990). The GUIDELINES appear to recognize, however, that large buyers can also be relevant to entry. *See infra* note 57 and accompanying text.

36. *See* J. Rill, Assistant Att'y Gen., Antitrust Div., Antitrust Enforcement at the Department of Justice, Remarks Before the 24th New England Antitrust Conference, at 6-7 (Nov. 2, 1990) (recognizing potential of maverick firms in replacement tire market to make collusion difficult).

37. The 1984 GUIDELINES did not address the unilateral effects theory except for a brief discussion of the "Leading Firm Proviso" in § 3.12.

Guidelines specify two theories under which such unilateral effects may arise.

First, the *1992 Guidelines* contemplate that unilateral effects may arise in some markets where products are *differentiated*. Under this theory, when the products sold by different producers are not perfect substitutes and vary in their degree of substitutability, competition may be nonuniform so that individual sellers compete more directly with rivals selling closer substitutes.[38] For a substantial unilateral price increase to occur in this setting, a significant share of sales must be accounted for by consumers who regard the merged firms' products as their first and second choices,[39] and repositioning of nonparties' product lines must be unlikely.[40]

According to the *1992 Guidelines*, market concentration measures may help assess the extent of the likely competitive effect from a unilateral price increase. Where (1) each product's market share reflects not only its relative appeal as a first choice to consumers of the merging firms' products but also its relative appeal as a second choice, (2) market concentration data fall outside the *Guidelines'* safe-harbor regions, and (3) the merging firms have a combined market share of at least 35%, the enforcement agencies will presume that a significant share of sales in the market are to consumers who regard the merging firms' products as their first and second choices.[41] The *Guidelines* do not indicate why these factors necessarily make unilateral effects more likely or reveal whether the enforcement agencies will analyze unilateral effects absent such market concentration.

Second, the *Guidelines* contemplate that unilateral effects may arise in markets for relatively undifferentiated products when firms are distinguished by their capacity. Under this theory, a merger provides a larger sales base on which to enjoy a price increase and eliminates a competitor to which sales otherwise would be diverted. The *Guidelines* state that when the merging firms have a combined market share of at least 35%, they may find it profitable to raise price and reduce output because the lost markups on the forgone sales may be outweighed by the resulting price increase on the merged sales base.[42]

The *Guidelines* recognize that such a unilateral effect is unlikely unless a sufficiently large number of the merged firm's customers would not be able to find economical alternative sources of supply. Nonparty expansion is unlikely if binding capacity constraints could not be economically relaxed within two years or if existing excess capacity is significantly more costly to operate than capacity currently in use.[43]

---

38.   1992 GUIDELINES § 2.21.
39.   *Id.* at § 2.211. *See* Rill, *supra* note 33, at 52.
40.   1992 GUIDELINES § 2.212.
41.   *Id.* at § 2.211. The combined 35% is at the same level as the single dominant firm share used in the 1984 GUIDELINES' leading firm proviso (Section 3.12). The leading firm proviso was rarely used, and was described by an FTC official as being largely redundant of the general standards for challenging a merger based on increases in concentration. *See* K. Arquit, Director, Bureau of Competition, FTC, Perspectives on the 1992 U.S. Government Horizontal Merger Guidelines, Prepared Remarks Before the ABA Antitrust Section (Apr. 2, 1992). The proviso has been eliminated from the 1992 GUIDELINES.
42.   *Id.* at § 2.22.
43.   *Id.*

3.   Entry Analysis

The *1992 Guidelines*, like the *1984* and *1982 Guidelines* and the *1982 FTC Statement*, observe that market power cannot be created or its exercise facilitated when entry into the market is sufficiently easy.[44] If entry is easy, that fact is likely to deter acquisitions from being undertaken solely for anticompetitive purposes and to counteract any anticompetitive effects of such transactions if consummated. Part 3 of the *1992 Guidelines* provides that a demonstration of easy entry can rebut a presumption from market share distributions under Section 1.5 or an inference from other evidence of competitive effect under Part 2 that a merger or acquisition is likely to be anticompetitive. The *1992 Guidelines* "ease of entry" defense, however, differs from its predecessors in the prior guidelines as well as the caselaw both in its conception and in the evidence required for its demonstration.[45]

The *1984* and *1982 Guidelines* assessed ease of entry by considering "the likelihood and probable magnitude of entry in response to a 'small but significant and nontransitory' increase in price" continuing over a period of two years.[46] Like the courts, the Department and the FTC in the mid-1980s focused primarily on the conditions of entry, from which they inferred both the likelihood and probable magnitude of entry.[47] Although the *1982* and *1984 Guidelines* clearly posed the questions of the incentives to enter and the sufficiency of entry, the agencies during this time were willing to assume, without additional proof, that if the structural barriers to entry were low, new firms in fact would enter to take advantage of any supracompetitive margins resulting from an anticompetitive merger and that this competition would return prices to their previously competitive levels. The *1982* and *1984 Guidelines* did refine the analysis by specifying that the anticompetitive price increase usually would be assumed to be 5% and that entry must occur within two years to be cognizable under the defense, but overall the inquiry remained focused on the absence of structural barriers to entry.

In contrast, the *1992 Guidelines* view the structural conditions of entry as only the starting point of the analysis. Beginning in the late 1980s, both the Antitrust Division and the FTC became increasingly skeptical that the conditions of entry alone could provide sufficient basis for concluding that an anticompetitive price increase is not sustainable in the market. The agencies concluded that a more detailed examination of the actual incentives to enter and the sufficiency of entry is required.[48] As a result, the emphasis in the agencies' ease of entry analysis changed from whether effective entry *could* occur given the conditions of entry to whether it

---

44.   *Id.* at § 3.0; 1984 GUIDELINES § 3.3; 1982 FTC STATEMENT § III(A)(1).
45.   *See, e.g.,* United States v. Baker Hughes Inc., 908 F.2d 981 (D.C. Cir. 1990); United States v. Syufy Enters., 903 F.2d 659 (9th Cir. 1990); United States v. Waste Mgmt., Inc., 743 F.2d 976 (2d Cir. 1984); United States v. Country Lake Foods, Inc., 754 F. Supp. 669 (D. Minn. 1990); United States v. Calmar Inc., 612 F. Supp. 1298 (D.N.J. 1985), and the discussion in Chapter III of this treatise, at pp. 307-11.
46.   1984 GUIDELINES § 3.3.
47.   *E.g.,* Echlin Mfg. Co., 105 F.T.C. 410 (1985).
48.   *See, e.g.,* Statement of K. Arquit, Director, Bureau of Competition, FTC, Before the ABA Antitrust Section, Spring Meeting (Mar. 22, 1990), *reprinted in* 7 TRADE REG. REP. (CCH) ¶ 50,030; Statement of J. Whalley, former Deputy Assistant Att'y Gen., Antitrust Division, Before the 29th Annual Antitrust Seminar, Practicing Law Institute (Dec. 1, 1989), *reprinted in* 7 TRADE REG. REP. (CCH) ¶ 50,029.

would occur given the alternative profit opportunities facing possible potential entrants. This change in emphasis is reflected in the *1992 Guidelines*, which separately address in detail questions of the timeliness, likelihood and sufficiency of entry to deter or counteract the anticompetitive effects of a merger or acquisition.

Part 3 of the *Guidelines* considers the importance of committed entry — supply responses that require the commitment of significant sunk costs. As discussed above in the analysis of Part 1, uncommitted entrants — whose supply responses do not require the commitment of significant sunk costs — are deemed to be market participants even when they are not actually selling the relevant product.

Timeliness. The *1992 Guidelines* retain the two-year window for entry to be cognizable under the defense. The two-year period is measured from the inception of planning to the time when the entry has a significant market impact.[49] Structural barriers to entry are a significant factor in assessing the timeliness of entry under the *1992 Guidelines*, but they are not the only considerations. All phases of the entry process necessary to achieve a significant market impact are included in this two-year period, including, where relevant, planning, design, and management; permitting, licensing, and other government approvals; construction, debugging, and operation of production facilities; and promotion, marketing, distribution, and satisfaction of customer testing and qualification requirements.[50] The *Guidelines* recognize that recent examples of entry, whether or not successful, may be probative in identifying the necessary actions, time requirements, and characteristics of entry. Firms that have committed to entering the market prior to the merger generally will be included as participants in the market and will not count as new entrants for the purposes of the ease of entry defense.[51]

The *Guidelines* accord special treatment to markets with durable goods. If in response to a significant commitment to entry consumers are likely to defer purchases of a durable product by making additional investment to extend the useful life of a previously purchased good, the anticompetitive effects of a merger may be temporarily lessened or postponed. In these circumstances, the *Guidelines* consider entry to be timely "so long as it would deter or counteract the competitive effects of concern within the two year period and subsequently."[52]

Likelihood of entry. The price assumed to exist in the postmerger marketplace is a critical determinant of the likelihood of entry. The change in the price assumption is perhaps the most significant modification of the entry analysis in the *1992 Guidelines*. Unlike the *1984 Guidelines*, which assessed the likelihood of entry in a market in which a 5% price increase would prevail for a period of two years, the *1992 Guidelines* find entry likely only if it is profitable at *premerger prices*.[53] The premise is that if entry is to counteract any anticompetitive effects of a merger, it must return the market to the premerger price levels. Failure to do so leaves the postmerger market with a supracompetitive price, and so negates the ease of entry defense. According to the *Guidelines*, firms considering entry that entails significant sunk costs must evaluate the profitability of entry on the basis of a long-term

---

49.   1992 GUIDELINES § 3.2.
50.   *Id.* at § 3.1.
51.   *Id.* at § 3.2 n.27.
52.   *Id.* at § 3.2.
53.   *Id.* at § 3.3.

participation in the market, since the underlying assets representing the sunk costs will be committed to the market until they are economically depreciated to their salvage value. Since the ease of entry defense requires that prices in the long-term return to premerger levels, a committed entrant's participation in the market must be viable at those levels. Consequently, only entry that envisions a return to premerger prices or lower should be considered under the ease of entry defense.

Rather than posit a postmerger price increase to finance the new entry as did the *1984 Guidelines*, the *1992 Guidelines* assume that an anticompetitive merger will create a structural change in the market that reduces the aggregate output of the existing market participants and would result in higher prices in the absence of new entry. This creates a "sales opportunity" at the premerger prices for new entrants. The *1992 Guidelines* then test the likelihood of entry by comparing this sales opportunity to the new entrants' "minimum viable scale" at premerger prices.[54] If entry could be profitable long-term at a scale not exceeding the available sales opportunity, the *Guidelines* consider such entry likely. If profitable entry requires a scale larger than the sales opportunity, then entry is not likely. The *Guidelines* state that minimum viable scale for entry will be large when fixed costs of entry are high or largely sunk, when the marginal costs of production are high at low levels of output (reflecting significant economies of scale), and when a new facility is underutilized for a long time because of delays in achieving market acceptance.[55]

The *1992 Guidelines* assume that the output reduction associated with the merger typically will be 5% of the aggregate premerger sales.[56] The available sales opportunity within the meaning of the *Guidelines* will be the result of the output reduction associated with the merger, the entrants' ability to capture a share of reasonably expected growth in market demand, the entrants' ability to divert sales from incumbents, for example, through vertical integration or forward contracting,[57] and any additional expected reduction in the incumbents' aggregate output in response to entry. The converse of these factors will decrease the available sales opportunity.

Sufficiency of entry. In principle, the sufficiency of entry should be measured against the likelihood that the new entry, whether one firm or multiple firms collectively, will restore the output originally reduced by the merger.[58] The *1992 Guidelines* assume that in most cases committed entry that satisfies the requirements of timeliness and likelihood also will be sufficient without the need for further proof. Under the *Guidelines*, there are at least two situations where additional evidence of sufficiency will be necessary: (1) where, as a result of incumbent control, the tangible and intangible assets required for entry are not adequately available for entrants to take full advantage of their available sales opportunities, and (2) where, in differentiated products markets, the anticompetitive effect is likely to be localized,

---

54. *Id.* Minimum viable scale is the smallest average annual level of sales that the firm must persistently achieve to be profitable. It is a function of expected revenues at the prevailing market prices and of all costs associated with entry and operation, including an appropriate rate of return on capital adjusted for the risk of failure and the loss of sunk cost investments. Minimum viable scale generally will be less than minimum efficient scale. *Id.*

55. *Id.* at § 3.3 n.31.

56. *Id.* at § 3.3 n.32. This reflects a unit elasticity if prices increase 5%.

57. This is one respect in which large buyers can affect the competitive analysis.

58. 1992 GUIDELINES § 3.4.

so that to return the market to the premerger competitive status quo, entry must occur in the local area of competitive concern.

4. Efficiencies

The *1992 Guidelines'* treatment of efficiencies provides that the Agency will consider whether an otherwise objectionable merger may be necessary to achieve certain types of significant net efficiencies.[59] In 1989, a Department official advanced the proposition that efficiencies would only be considered to the extent their benefits were passed on to consumers over time.[60] The *1992 Guidelines*, like their 1984 predecessor, is silent on the subject.[61] The efficiencies recognized in this category include, without limitation, economies of scale, better integration of production facilities, plant specialization, lower transportation costs, and similar efficiencies relating to specific manufacturing, servicing, or distribution operations.[62] The *Guidelines* also acknowledge the possibility of efficiencies resulting more generally from reductions in selling, administrative, and overhead expenses, although they state that such efficiencies may be difficult to demonstrate in practice.[63] Furthermore, the *Guidelines* provide that the claimed efficiencies must not be capable of achievement through other means that do not pose the anticompetitive risks of the merger; and, the higher those risks, the more substantial must be the offsetting efficiencies.[64]

The *1992 Guidelines* differ materially from the *1984 Guidelines* only in that a sentence in the *1984 Guidelines* requiring "clear and convincing evidence" has been eliminated. However, reference should be made to footnote five of the *1992 Guidelines*, which states that the burden of proof with respect to efficiency resides

---

59.   1992 GUIDELINES § 4.0; *see* Memorandum in Support of Plaintiff's Motion In Limine Relating to Efficiencies, at 4 (May 4, 1987); United States v. Archer-Daniels-Midland Co., 1991-2 Trade Cas. ¶ 69,647 (S.D. Iowa 1991); *see generally* K. Arquit, Director, Bureau of Competition, FTC, Remarks on Efficiency Considerations and Horizontal Restraints, Before the National Health Care Lawyers Association (Feb. 14, 1991).

60.   J. Whalley, former Deputy Assistant Att'y Gen., Antitrust Div., Remarks on Entry and Efficiencies in Merger Enforcement, Before the 29th Annual Antitrust Seminar, Practising Law Institute, at 10-20 (Dec. 1, 1989).

61.   The Assistant Attorney General for Antitrust has stated that efficiencies are recognized "even though they may not in every case inure to the benefit of consumers in the short term." Rill, *supra* note 19, at 27. The Director of the FTC's Bureau of Competition, commenting on that statement, has accepted the possibility that "a short-term price increase may at least hypothetically be tolerated as necessary to achieve efficiencies, [where] such efficiencies are expected to lead to price declines in the future." Arquit, *supra* note 19, at 14. As a general matter, however, he emphasized that the Commission may challenge mergers that allow supracompetitive pricing if the benefits of efficiencies will not be passed on to consumers. *Id.* at 11.

62.   *Cf.* Arquit, *supra* note 59, at 6 (efficiencies that would improve the product, lower its cost, or increase its output); *see also* Whalley, *supra* note 60 at 18-22.

63.   1992 GUIDELINES § 4.0; K. Arquit, Director, Bureau of Competition, FTC, Remarks Before the Cleveland Chapter of the Federal Bar Association, at 5 (Dec. 14, 1989); Whalley, *supra* note 60, at 21-22.

64.   1992 GUIDELINES § 4; *see generally* Whalley, *supra* note 60, at 22.

with the proponents of the merger.[65]

5. Failure and Exiting Assets

The *1992 Guidelines'* treatment of the failing firm and failing division defense provides that a merger is not likely to create unacceptable anticompetitive effects (that is, the relevant market would be no worse off because of the merger), if imminent failure would cause the assets of one of the merging firms to exit the relevant market in the absence of the merger. The *1992 Guidelines* clarify that four conditions must be met to establish the failing firm portion of the defense. The failing firm must be unable to (1) meet its financial obligations; (2) reorganize in bankruptcy; or (3) find a more competitively neutral, alternative purchaser;[66] with the result that (4) its assets would exit the relevant market absent the merger. The *1992 Guidelines* provide in footnote 36 that any offer above the liquidation value of the assets (liquidation would send the assets outside the relevant market) will be regarded as a reasonable offer.[67] As with efficiency, it is the proponent's burden to establish the failing company defense.[68]

The *1992 Guidelines'* treatment of the failing division portion of the defense requires that the division have a negative cash flow on an operating basis, that the assets would exit the relevant market in the near future if not sold, and that the competitively-preferable purchaser requirement of the failing firm defense be met. The *1992 Guidelines* also caution that because of the ability of the parent company to allocate costs, revenues and other intra-company elements of transactions, evidence will be required that is not based solely on management plans demonstrating the negative cash flow and the prospect of exit elements of the defense.

The *1992 Guidelines* differ from the *1984 Guidelines*, both with respect to the addition of the points of clarification and caution described above, and in that the *1992 Guidelines* do not expressly acknowledge that the doctrine is a judicially-created and legislatively recognized[69] affirmative defense to liability. In this respect, the failing firm and failing division affirmative defense is unlike the efficiencies "defense." Efficiencies, to the extent taken into account by the courts and agencies,

---

65. *Cf.* Dissenting Statement of Commissioner Azcuenaga on the Issuance of the Horizontal Merger Guidelines, at 4-5 (Apr. 2, 1992) (deletion of "clear and convincing" language signals no change in policy); Arquit, *supra* note 19, at 8-9 (same; change is simply consistent with 1992 GUIDELINES' disavowal in § 0.1 of any intention to assign or change burdens of proof). *But cf.* Rill, *supra* note 19, at 27 ("clear and convincing" standard had been interpreted by some as suggesting hostility to efficiency-enhancing mergers; under the new GUIDELINES, "all elements of the analysis are treated the same"); James, *supra* note 19, at 13 ("unwarranted evidentiary 'tilt[ ]' " eliminated).
66. 1992 GUIDELINES § 5.1; *see* Remarks of K. Arquit, Director, Bureau of Competition, FTC, on the Failing Firm Defense and Related Issues, Before the American Bar Association, Antitrust Section (Apr. 12, 1991). ABA ANTITRUST SECTION, MONOGRAPH NO. 12, HORIZONTAL MERGERS: LAW and POLICY, 237-38 (1986).
67. 1992 GUIDELINES § 5.1 n.36; *see* FTC v. Harbour Group Investments, 1990-2 Trade Cas. ¶ 69,247, at 64,917 (D.D.C. 1990).
68. *1992 Guidelines* § 0.1, n.5.
69. *See* S. Rep. No. 1775, 81st Cong., 2d Sess. 7 (1950); H.R. Rep. No. 1191, 81st Cong., 1st Sess. 6 (1949).

are balanced against the competitive risks of the merger.[70] The failing firm and failing division defense assumes a prima facie case for liability, but presents the counterpoint of imminent failure as a complete defense.[71] The status of the doctrine as an immunizing defense was recognized in Section 5 of the *1984 Guidelines*. It is not so recognized in the 1992 revisions.

---

70. *See* Chapter III of this treatise, *supra* at 319-22; 1992 GUIDELINES, § 4.
71. *See* Chapter III of this treatise, *supra* at 313-18; *see also* Dissenting Statement of Commissioner Azcuenaga on the Issuance of the Horizontal Merger Guidelines, at 5 (Apr. 2, 1992); FTC v. Harbour Group Investments, 1990-2 Trade Cas. ¶ 69,247 (D.D.C. 1990); Remarks of K. Arquit, *supra* note 66.

U.S. Department of Justice and Federal Trade Commission Statement Accompanying Release of Revised Merger Guidelines

April 2, 1992

The U.S. Department of Justice (Department) and Federal Trade Commission (Commission) today jointly issued Horizontal Merger Guidelines revising the Department's *1984 Merger Guidelines* and the Commission's *1982 Statement Concerning Horizontal Merger Guidelines*. The release marks the first time that two federal agencies that share antitrust enforcement jurisdiction have issued joint guidelines.

Central to the 1992 Department of Justice and Federal Trade Commission Horizontal Merger Guidelines is a recognition that sound merger enforcement is an essential component of our free enterprise system benefitting the competitiveness of American firms and the welfare of American consumers. Sound merger enforcement must prevent anticompetitive mergers yet avoid deterring the larger universe of procompetitive or competitively neutral mergers. The 1992 Horizontal Merger Guidelines implement this objective by describing the analytical foundations of merger enforcement and providing guidance enabling the business community to avoid antitrust problems when planning mergers.

The Department first released *Merger Guidelines* in 1968 in order to inform the business community of the analysis applied by the Department to mergers under the federal antitrust laws. The *1968 Merger Guidelines* eventually fell into disuse, both internally and externally, as they were eclipsed by developments in legal and economic thinking about mergers.

In 1982, the Department released revised *Merger Guidelines* which, reflecting those developments, departed dramatically from the 1968 version. Relative to the Department's actual practice, however, the *1982 Merger Guidelines* represented an evolutionary not revolutionary change. On the same date, the Commission released its *Statement Concerning Horizontal Mergers* highlighting the principal considerations guiding the Commission's horizontal merger enforcement and noting the "considerable weight" given by the Commission to the Department's *1982 Merger Guidelines*.

The Department's current *Merger Guidelines*, released in 1984, refined and clarified the analytical framework of the *1982 Merger Guidelines*. Although the agencies' experience with the *1982 Merger Guidelines* reaffirmed the soundness of its underlying principles, the Department concluded that there remained room for improvement.

The revisions embodied in the 1992 Horizontal Merger Guidelines reflect the next logical step in the development of the agencies' analysis of mergers. They reflect the Department's experience in applying the *1982* and *1984 Merger Guidelines* as well as the Commission's experience in applying those *Guidelines* and the Commission's *1982 Statement*. Both the Department and the Commission believed that their respective *Guidelines* and *Statement* presented sound frameworks for antitrust analysis of mergers, but that improvements could be made to reflect advances in legal and economic thinking. The 1992 Horizontal Merger Guidelines accomplish this objective and also clarify certain aspects of the *Merger Guidelines* that proved to be ambiguous or were interpreted by observers in ways that were inconsistent with the actual policy of the agencies.

The 1992 Horizontal Merger Guidelines do not include a discussion of horizontal effects from non-horizontal mergers (e.g., elimination of specific potential entrants and competitive problems from vertical mergers). Neither agency has changed its policy with respect to non-horizontal mergers. Specific guidance on non-horizontal mergers is provided in Section 4 of the Department's *1984 Merger Guidelines*, read in the context of today's revisions to the treatment of horizontal mergers.

A number of today's revisions are largely technical or stylistic. One major objective of the revisions is to strengthen the document as an analytical road map for the evaluation of mergers. The language, therefore, is intended to be burden-neutral, without altering the burdens of proof or burdens of coming forward as those standards have been established by the courts. In addition, the revisions principally address two areas.

The most significant revision to the *Merger Guidelines* is to explain more clearly how mergers may lead to adverse competitive effects and how particular market factors relate to the analysis of those effects. These revisions are found in Section 2 of the 1992 Horizontal Merger Guidelines. The second principal revision is to sharpen the distinction between the treatment of various types of supply responses and to articulate the framework for analyzing the timeliness, likelihood and sufficiency of entry. These revisions are found in Sections 1.3 and 3.

The 1992 Horizontal Merger Guidelines observe, as did the *1984 Guidelines*, that because the specific standards they set out must be applied in widely varied factual circumstances, mechanical application of those standards could produce misleading results. Thus, the *Guidelines* state that the agencies will apply those standards reasonably and flexibly to the particular facts and circumstances of each proposed merger.

**Department of Justice and Federal Trade Commission
Horizontal Merger Guidelines, Issued April 2, 1992**

0.   Purpose, Underlying Policy Assumptions, and Overview
     0.1   Purpose and Underlying Policy Assumptions of the Guidelines
     0.2   Overview
1.   Market Definition, Measurement and Concentration
     1.0   Overview
     1.1   Product Market Definition
     1.2   Geographic Market Definition
     1.3   Identification of Firms That Participate in the Relevant Market
     1.4   Calculating Market Shares
     1.5   Concentration and Market Shares
2.   The Potential Adverse Competitive Effects of Mergers
     2.0   Overview
     2.1   Lessening of Competition Through Coordinated Interaction
     2.2   Lessening of Competition Through Unilateral Effects
3.   Entry Analysis
     3.0   Overview
     3.1   Entry Alternatives
     3.2   Timeliness of Entry
     3.3   Likelihood of Entry
     3.4   Sufficiency of Entry
4.   Efficiencies
5.   Failure and Exiting Assets
     5.0   Overview
     5.1   Failing Firm
     5.2   Failing Division

0.   Purpose, Underlying Policy Assumptions and Overview

These Guidelines outline the present enforcement policy of the Department of Justice and the Federal Trade Commission (the Agency) concerning horizontal acquisitions and mergers (mergers) subject to section 7 of the Clayton Act,[1] to section 1 of the Sherman Act,[2] or to section 5 of the FTC Act.[3] They describe the analytical framework and specific standards normally used by the Agency in analyzing mergers.[4] By stating its policy as simply and clearly as possible, the Agency hopes to reduce the uncertainty associated with enforcement of the antitrust laws in this

---

1.   15 U.S.C. § 18 (1988).   Mergers subject to section 7 are prohibited if their effect "may be substantially to lessen competition, or to tend to create a monopoly."

2.   15 U.S.C. § 1 (1988).   Mergers subject to section 1 are prohibited if they constitute a "contract, combination . . . , or conspiracy in restraint of trade."

3.   15 U.S.C. § 45 (1988).   Mergers subject to section 5 are prohibited if they constitute an "unfair method of competition."

4.   These Guidelines update the Merger Guidelines issued by the U.S. Department of Justice in 1984 and the Statement of Federal Trade Commission Concerning Horizontal Mergers issued in 1982. The Merger Guidelines may be revised from time to time as necessary to reflect any significant changes in enforcement policy or to clarify aspects of existing policy.

area.

Although the Guidelines should improve the predictability of the Agency's merger enforcement policy, it is not possible to remove the exercise of judgment from the evaluation of mergers under the antitrust laws. Because the specific standards set forth in the Guidelines must be applied to a broad range of possible factual circumstances, mechanical application of those standards may provide misleading answers to the economic questions raised under the antitrust laws. Moreover, information is often incomplete and the picture of competitive conditions that develops from historical evidence may provide an incomplete answer to the forward-looking inquiry of the Guidelines. Therefore, the Agency will apply the standards of the Guidelines reasonably and flexibly to the particular facts and circumstances of each proposed merger.

0.1 Purpose and Underlying Policy Assumptions of the Guidelines

The Guidelines are designed primarily to articulate the analytical framework the Agency applies in determining whether a merger is likely substantially to lessen competition, not to describe how the Agency will conduct the litigation of cases that it decides to bring. Although relevant in the latter context, the factors contemplated in the Guidelines neither dictate nor exhaust the range of evidence that the Agency must or may introduce in litigation. Consistent with their objective, the Guidelines do not attempt to assign the burden of proof, or the burden of coming forward with evidence, on any particular issue. Nor do the Guidelines attempt to adjust or reapportion burdens of proof or burdens of coming forward as those standards have been established by the courts.[5] Instead, the Guidelines set forth a methodology for analyzing issues once the necessary facts are available. The necessary facts may be derived from the documents and statements of both the merging firms and other sources.

Throughout the Guidelines, the analysis is focused on whether consumers or producers "likely would" take certain actions, that is, whether the action is in the actor's economic interest. References to the profitability of certain actions focus on economic profits rather than accounting profits. Economic profits may be defined as the excess of revenues over costs where costs include the opportunity cost of invested capital.

Mergers are motivated by the prospect of financial gains. The possible sources of the financial gains from mergers are many, and the Guidelines do not attempt to identify all possible sources of gain in every merger. Instead, the Guidelines focus on the one potential source of gain that is of concern under the antitrust laws: market power.

The unifying theme of the Guidelines is that mergers should not be permitted to create or enhance market power or to facilitate its exercise. Market power to a seller is the ability profitably to maintain prices above competitive levels for a significant period of time.[6] In some circumstances, a sole seller (a monopolist) of a product with no good substitutes can maintain a selling price that is above the level that

---

5.   For example, the burden with respect to efficiency and failure continues to reside with the proponents of the merger.

6.   Sellers with market power also may lessen competition on dimensions other than price, such as product quality, service, or innovation.

would prevail if the market were competitive. Similarly, in some circumstances, where only a few firms account for most of the sales of a product, those firms can exercise market power, perhaps even approximating the performance of a monopolist, by either explicitly or implicitly coordinating their actions. Circumstances also may permit a single firm, not a monopolist, to exercise market power through unilateral or non-coordinated conduct — conduct the success of which does not rely on the concurrence of other firms in the market or on coordinated responses by those firms. In any case, the result of the exercise of market power is a transfer of wealth from buyers to sellers or a misallocation of resources.

Market power also encompasses the ability of a single buyer (a "monopsonist"), a coordinating group of buyers, or a single buyer, not a monopsonist, to depress the price paid for a product to a level that is below the competitive price and thereby depress output. The exercise of market power by buyers ("monopsony power") has adverse effects comparable to those associated with the exercise of market power by sellers. In order to assess potential monopsony concerns, the Agency will apply an analytical framework analogous to the framework of these Guidelines.

While challenging competitively harmful mergers, the Agency seeks to avoid unnecessary interference with the larger universe of mergers that are either competitively beneficial or neutral. In implementing this objective, however, the Guidelines reflect the congressional intent that merger enforcement should interdict competitive problems in their incipiency.

0.2 Overview

The Guidelines describe the analytical process that the Agency will employ in determining whether to challenge a horizontal merger. First, the Agency assesses whether the merger would significantly increase concentration and result in a concentrated market, properly defined and measured. Second, the Agency assesses whether the merger, in light of market concentration and other factors that characterize the market, raises concern about potential adverse competitive effects. Third, the Agency assesses whether entry would be timely, likely and sufficient either to deter or to counteract the competitive effects of concern. Fourth, the Agency assesses any efficiency gains that reasonably cannot be achieved by the parties through other means. Finally the Agency assesses whether, but for the merger, either party to the transaction would be likely to fail, causing its assets to exit the market. The process of assessing market concentration, potential adverse competitive effects, entry, efficiency and failure is a tool that allows the Agency to answer the ultimate inquiry in merger analysis: whether the merger is likely to create or enhance market power or to facilitate its exercise.

1. Market Definition, Measurement and Concentration

1.0 Overview

A merger is unlikely to create or enhance market power or to facilitate its exercise unless it significantly increases concentration and results in a concentrated market, properly defined and measured. Mergers that either do not significantly increase concentration or do not result in a concentrated market ordinarily require no further analysis.

The analytic process described in this section ensures that the Agency evaluates the likely competitive impact of a merger within the context of economically meaningful markets — i.e., markets that could be subject to the exercise of market power. Accordingly, for each product or service (hereafter product) of each merging firm, the Agency seeks to define a market in which firms could effectively exercise market power if they were able to coordinate their actions.

Market definition focuses solely on demand substitution factors — i.e., possible consumer responses. Supply substitution factors — i.e., possible production responses — are considered elsewhere in the Guidelines in the identification of firms that participate in the relevant market and the analysis of entry. See Sections 1.3 and 3. A market is defined as a product or group of products and a geographic area in which it is produced or sold such that a hypothetical profit-maximizing firm, not subject to price regulation, that was the only present and future producer or seller of those products in that area likely would impose at least a "small but significant and nontransitory" increase in price, assuming the terms of sale of all other products are held constant. A relevant market is a group of products and a geographic area that is no bigger than necessary to satisfy this test. The "small but significant and non-transitory" increase in price is employed solely as a methodological tool for the analysis of mergers: it is not a tolerance level for price increases.

Absent price discrimination, a relevant market is described by a product or group of products and a geographic area. In determining whether a hypothetical monopolist would be in a position to exercise market power, it is necessary to evaluate the likely demand responses of consumers to a price increase. A price increase could be made unprofitable by consumers either switching to other products or switching to the same product produced by firms at other locations. The nature and magnitude of these two types of demand responses respectively determine the scope of the product market and the geographic market.

In contrast, where a hypothetical monopolist likely would discriminate in prices charged to different groups of buyers, distinguished, for example, by their uses or locations, the Agency may delineate different relevant markets corresponding to each such buyer group. Competition for sales to each such group may be affected differently by a particular merger and markets are delineated by evaluating the demand response of each such buyer group. A relevant market of this kind is described by a collection of products for sale to a given group of buyers.

Once defined, a relevant market must be measured in terms of its participants and concentration. Participants include firms currently producing or selling the market's products in the market's geographic area. In addition, participants may include other firms depending on their likely supply responses to a "small but significant and nontransitory" price increase. A firm is viewed as a participant if, in response to a "small but significant and nontransitory" price increase, it likely would enter rapidly into production or sale of a market product in the market's area, without incurring significant sunk costs of entry and exit. Firms likely to make any of these supply responses are considered to be "uncommitted" entrants because their supply response would create new production or sale in the relevant market and because that production or sale could be quickly terminated without significant loss.[7] Uncommitted entrants are capable of making such quick and uncommitted supply responses that they likely influenced the market premerger, would influence it post-merger, and accordingly are considered as market participants at both times. This analysis of market definition and market measurement applies equally to foreign and domestic firms.

If the process of market definition and market measurement identifies one or more relevant markets in which the merging firms are both participants, then the merger is considered to be horizontal. Sections 1.1 through 1.5 describe in greater detail how product and geographic markets will be defined, how market shares will be calculated and how market concentration will be assessed.

1.1 Product Market Definition

The Agency will first define the relevant product market with respect to each of the products of each of the merging firms.[8]

1.11 GENERAL STANDARDS

Absent price discrimination, the Agency will delineate the product market to be a product or group of products such that a hypothetical profit-maximizing firm that was the only present and future seller of those products (monopolist) likely would impose at least a "small but significant and nontransitory" increase in price. That is, assuming that buyers likely would respond to an increase in price for a tentatively identified product group only by shifting to other products, what would happen? If the alternatives were, in the aggregate, sufficiently attractive at their existing terms of sale, an attempt to raise prices would result in a reduction of sales large enough that the price increase would not prove profitable, and the tentatively identified product group would prove to be too narrow.

Specifically, the Agency will begin with each product (narrowly defined) produced or sold by each merging firm and ask what would happen if a hypothetical monopolist of that product imposed at least a "small but significant and nontransitory" increase in price, but the terms of sale of all other products remained constant. If, in response to the price increase, the reduction in sales of the product would be large enough that a hypothetical monopolist would not find it profitable to impose such an increase in price, then the Agency will add to the product group the product that is the next-best substitute for the merging firm's product.[9]

---

7.   Probable supply responses that require the entrant to incur significant sunk costs of entry and exit are not part of market measurement, but are included in the analysis of the significance of entry. *See* Section 3. Entrants that must commit substantial sunk costs are regarded as "committed" entrants because those sunk costs make entry irreversible in the short term without foregoing that investment; thus the likelihood of their entry must be evaluated with regard to their long-term profitability.

8.   Although discussed separately, product market definition and geographic market definition are interrelated. In particular, the extent to which buyers of a particular product would shift to other products in the event of a "small but significant and nontransitory" increase in price must be evaluated in the context of the relevant geographic market.

9.   Throughout the Guidelines, the term "next best substitute" refers to the alternative which, if available in unlimited quantities at constant prices, would account for the greatest value of diversion of demand in response to a "small but significant and nontransitory" price increase.

In considering the likely reaction of buyers to a price increase, the Agency will take into account all relevant evidence, including, but not limited to, the following:

(1) evidence that buyers have shifted or have considered shifting purchases between products in response to relative changes in price or other competitive variables;

(2) evidence that sellers base business decisions on the prospect of buyer substitution between products in response to relative changes in price or other competitive variables;

(3) the influence of downstream competition faced by buyers in their output markets; and

(4) the timing and costs of switching products.

The price increase question is then asked for a hypothetical monopolist controlling the expanded product group. In performing successive iterations of the price increase test, the hypothetical monopolist will be assumed to pursue maximum profits in deciding whether to raise the prices of any or all of the additional products under its control. This process will continue until a group of products is identified such that a hypothetical monopolist over that group of products would profitably impose at least a "small but significant and nontransitory" increase, including the price of a product of one of the merging firms. The Agency generally will consider the relevant product market to be the smallest group of products that satisfies this test.

In the above analysis, the Agency will use prevailing prices of the products of the merging firms and possible substitutes for such products, unless premerger circumstances are strongly suggestive of coordinated interaction, in which case the Agency will use a price more reflective of the competitive price.[10] However, the Agency may use likely future prices, absent the merger, when changes in the prevailing prices can be predicted with reasonable reliability. Changes in price may be predicted on the basis of, for example, changes in regulation which affect price either directly or indirectly by affecting costs or demand.

In general, the price for which an increase will be postulated will be whatever is considered to be the price of the product at the stage of the industry being examined.[11] In attempting to determine objectively the effect of a "small but significant and nontransitory" increase in price, the Agency, in most contexts, will use a price increase of five percent lasting for the foreseeable future. However, what constitutes a "small but significant and nontransitory" increase in price will depend on the nature of the industry, and the Agency at times may use a price increase that is larger or smaller than five percent.

1.12 PRODUCT MARKET DEFINITION IN THE PRESENCE OF PRICE DISCRIMINATION

The analysis of product market definition to this point has assumed that price discrimination — charging different buyers different prices for the same product, for

---

10.   The terms of sale of all other products are held constant in order to focus market definition on the behavior of consumers. Movements in the terms of sale for other products, as may result from the behavior of producers of those products, are accounted for in the analysis of competitive effects and entry. *See* Sections 2 and 3.

11.   For example, in a merger between retailers, the relevant price would be the retail price of a product to consumers. In the case of a merger among oil pipelines, the relevant price would be the tariff — the price of the transportation service.

example — would not be profitable for a hypothetical monopolist. A different analysis applies where price discrimination would be profitable for a hypothetical monopolist.

Existing buyers sometimes will differ significantly in their likelihood of switching to other products in response to a "small but significant and nontransitory" price increase. If a hypothetical monopolist can identify and price differently to those buyers (targeted buyers) who would not defeat the targeted price increase by substituting to other products in response to a "small but significant and nontransitory" price increase for the relevant product, and if other buyers likely would not purchase the relevant product and resell to targeted buyers, then a hypothetical monopolist would profitably impose a discriminatory price increase on sales to targeted buyers. This is true regardless of whether a general increase in price would cause such significant substitution that the price increase would not be profitable. The Agency will consider additional relevant product markets consisting of a particular use or uses by groups of buyers of the product for which a hypothetical monopolist would profitably and separately impose at least a "small but significant and nontransitory" increase in price.

1.2 Geographic Market Definition

For each product market in which both merging firms participate, the Agency will determine the geographic market or markets in which the firms produce or sell. A single firm may operate in a number of different geographic markets.

1.21 GENERAL STANDARDS

Absent price discrimination, the Agency will delineate the geographic market to be a region such that a hypothetical monopolist that was the only present or future producer of the relevant product at locations in that region would profitably impose at least a "small but significant and nontransitory" increase in price, holding constant the terms of sale for all products produced elsewhere. That is, assuming that buyers likely would respond to a price increase on products produced within the tentatively identified region only by shifting to products produced at locations of production outside the region, what would happen? If those locations of production outside the region were, in the aggregate, sufficiently attractive at their existing terms of sale, an attempt to raise price would result in a reduction in sales large enough that the price increase would not prove profitable, and the tentatively identified geographic area would prove to be too narrow.

In defining the geographic market or markets affected by a merger, the Agency will begin with the location of each merging firm (or each plant of a multiplant firm) and ask what would happen if a hypothetical monopolist of the relevant product at that point imposed at least a "small but significant and nontransitory" increase in price, but the terms of sale at all other locations remained constant. If, in response to the price increase, the reduction in sales of the product at that location would be large enough that a hypothetical monopolist producing or selling the relevant product at the merging firm's location would not find it profitable to impose such an increase in price, then the Agency will add the location from which production is the next-best substitute for production at the merging firm's location.

In considering the likely reaction of buyers to a price increase, the Agency will take into account all relevant evidence, including, but not limited to, the following:

(1)   evidence that buyers have shifted or have considered shifting purchases between different geographic locations in response to relative changes in price or other competitive variables;

(2)   evidence that sellers base business decisions on the prospect of buyer substitution between geographic locations in response to relative changes in price or other competitive variables;

(3)   the influence of downstream competition faced by buyers in their output markets; and

(4)   the timing and costs of switching suppliers.

The price increase question is then asked for a hypothetical monopolist controlling the expanded group of locations. In performing successive iterations of the price increase test, the hypothetical monopolist will be assumed to pursue maximum profits in deciding whether to raise the price at any or all of the additional locations under its control. This process will continue until a group of locations is identified such that a hypothetical monopolist over that group of locations would profitably impose at least a "small but significant and nontransitory" increase, including the price charged at a location of one of the merging firms.

The "smallest market" principle will be applied as it is in product market definition. The price for which an increase will be postulated, what constitutes a "small but significant and nontransitory" increase in price, and the substitution decisions of consumers all will be determined in the same way in which they are determined in product market definition.

1.22 GEOGRAPHIC MARKET DEFINITION IN THE PRESENCE OF PRICE
      DISCRIMINATION

The analysis of geographic market definition to this point has assumed that geographic price discrimination — charging different prices net of transportation costs for the same product to buyers in different areas, for example — would not be profitable for a hypothetical monopolist. However, if a hypothetical monopolist can identify and price differently to buyers in certain areas ("targeted buyers") who would not defeat the targeted price increase by substituting to more distant sellers in response to a "small but significant and nontransitory" price increase for the relevant product, and if other buyers likely would not purchase the relevant product and resell to targeted buyers,[12] then a hypothetical monopolist would profitably impose a discriminatory price increase. This is true even where a general price increase would cause such significant substitution that the price increase would not be profitable. The Agency will consider additional geographic markets consisting of particular locations of buyers for which a hypothetical monopolist would profitably and separately impose at least a "small but significant and nontransitory" increase in price.

---

12.   This arbitrage is inherently impossible for many services and is particularly difficult where the product is sold on a delivered basis and where transportation costs are a significant percentage of the final cost.

1.3 Identification of Firms That Participate in the Relevant Market

1.31 CURRENT PRODUCERS OR SELLERS

The Agency's identification of firms that participate in the relevant market begins with all firms that currently produce or sell in the relevant market. This includes vertically integrated firms to the extent that such inclusion accurately reflects their competitive significance in the relevant market prior to the merger. To the extent that the analysis under Section 1.1 indicates that used, reconditioned or recycled goods are included in the relevant market, market participants will include firms that produce or sell such goods and that likely would offer those goods in competition with other relevant products.

1.32 FIRMS THAT PARTICIPATE THROUGH SUPPLY RESPONSE

In addition, the Agency will identify other firms not currently producing or selling the relevant product in the relevant area as participating in the relevant market if their inclusion would more accurately reflect probable supply responses. These firms are termed "uncommitted entrants." These supply responses must be likely to occur within one year and without the expenditure of significant sunk costs of entry and exit, in response to a "small but significant and nontransitory" price increase. If a firm has the technological capability to achieve such an uncommitted supply response, but likely would not (e.g., because difficulties in achieving product acceptance, distribution, or production would render such a response unprofitable), that firm will not be considered to be a market participant. The competitive significance of supply responses that require more time or that require firms to incur significant sunk costs of entry and exit will be considered in entry analysis. See Section 3.[13]

Sunk costs are the acquisition costs of tangible and intangible assets that cannot be recovered through the redeployment of these assets outside the relevant market, i.e., costs uniquely incurred to supply the relevant product and geographic market. Examples of sunk costs may include market-specific investments in production facilities, technologies, marketing (including product acceptance), research and development, regulatory approvals, and testing. A significant sunk cost is one which would not be recouped within one year of the commencement of the supply response, assuming a "small but significant and nontransitory" price increase in the relevant market. In this context, a "small but significant and nontransitory" price increase will be determined in the same way in which it is determined in product market definition, except the price increase will be assumed to last one year. In some instances, it may be difficult to calculate sunk costs with precision. Accordingly, when necessary, the Agency will make an overall assessment of the extent of sunk costs for firms likely to participate through supply responses.

These supply responses may give rise to new production of products in the relevant product market or new sources of supply in the relevant geographic market.

---

13.   If uncommitted entrants likely would also remain in the market and would meet the entry tests of timeliness, likelihood and sufficiency, and thus would likely deter anticompetitive mergers or deter or counteract the competitive effects of concern (*see* Section 3, *infra*), the Agency will consider the impact of those firms in the entry analysis.

Alternatively, where price discrimination is likely so that the relevant market is defined in terms of a targeted group of buyers, these supply responses serve to identify new sellers to the targeted buyers. Uncommitted supply responses may occur in several different ways: by the switching or extension of existing assets to production or sale in the relevant market; or by the construction or acquisition of assets that enable production or sale in the relevant market.

1.321   Production Substitution and Extension: The Switching or Extension of Existing Assets to Production or Sale in the Relevant Market

The productive and distributive assets of a firm sometimes can be used to produce and sell either the relevant products or products that buyers do not regard as good substitutes. Production substitution refers to the shift by a firm in the use of assets from producing and selling one product to producing and selling another. Production extension refers to the use of those assets, for example, existing brand names and reputation, both for their current production and for production of the relevant product. Depending upon the speed of that shift and the extent of sunk costs incurred in the shift or extension, the potential for production substitution or extension may necessitate treating as market participants firms that do not currently produce the relevant product.[14]

If a firm has existing assets that likely would be shifted or extended into production and sale of the relevant product within one year, and without incurring significant sunk costs of entry and exit, in response to a "small but significant and nontransitory" increase in price for only the relevant product, the Agency will treat that firm as a market participant. In assessing whether a firm is such a market participant, the Agency will take into account the costs of substitution or extension relative to the profitability of sales at the elevated price, and whether the firm's capacity is elsewhere committed or elsewhere so profitably employed that such capacity likely would not be available to respond to an increase in price in the market.

1.322   Obtaining New Assets for Production or Sale of the Relevant Product

A firm may also be able to enter into production or sale in the relevant market within one year and without the expenditure of significant sunk costs of entry and exit, in response to a "small but significant and nontransitory" increase in price for only the relevant product, even if the firm is newly organized or is an existing firm without products or productive assets closely related to the relevant market. If new firms, or existing firms without closely related products or productive assets, likely would enter into production or sale in the relevant market within one year without the expenditure of significant sunk costs of entry and exit, the Agency will treat those

---

14.   Under other analytical approaches, production substitution sometimes has been reflected in the description of the product market. For example, the product market for stamped metal products such as automobile hub caps might be described as "light metal stamping," a production process rather than a product. The Agency believes that the approach described in the text provides a more clearly focused method of incorporating this factor in merger analysis. If production substitution among a group of products is nearly universal among the firms selling one or more of those products, however, the Agency may use an aggregate description of those markets as a matter of convenience.

firms as market participants.

1.4 Calculating Market Shares

1.41 GENERAL APPROACH

The Agency normally will calculate market shares for all firms (or plants) identified as market participants in Section 1.3 based on the total sales or capacity currently devoted to the relevant market together with that which likely would be devoted to the relevant market in response to a "small but significant and nontransitory" price increase. Market shares can be expressed either in dollar terms through measurement of sales, shipments, or production, or in physical terms through measurement of sales, shipments, production, capacity, or reserves.

Market shares will be calculated using the best indicator of firms' future competitive significance. Dollar sales or shipments generally will be used if firms are distinguished primarily by differentiation of their products. Unit sales generally will be used if firms are distinguished primarily on the basis of their relative advantages in serving different buyers or groups of buyers. Physical capacity or reserves generally will be used if it is these measures that most effectively distinguish firms.[15] Typically, annual data are used, but where individual sales are large and infrequent so that annual data may be unrepresentative, the Agency may measure market shares over a longer period of time.

In measuring a firm's market share, the Agency will not include its sales or capacity to the extent that the firm's capacity is committed or so profitably employed outside the relevant market that it would not be available to respond to an increase in price in the market.

1.42 PRICE DISCRIMINATION MARKETS

When markets are defined on the basis of price discrimination (Sections 1.12 and 1.22), the Agency will include only sales likely to be made into, or capacity likely to be used to supply, the relevant market in response to a "small but significant and nontransitory" price increase.

1.43 SPECIAL FACTORS AFFECTING FOREIGN FIRMS

Market shares will be assigned to foreign competitors in the same way in which they are assigned to domestic competitors. However, if exchange rates fluctuate significantly, so that comparable dollar calculations on an annual basis may be unrepresentative, the Agency may measure market shares over a period longer than one year.

If shipments from a particular country to the United States are subject to a quota, the market shares assigned to firms in that country will not exceed the amount of shipments by such firms allowed under the quota.[16] In the case of restraints that limit imports to some percentage of the total amount of the product sold in the

---

15. Where all firms have, on a forward-looking basis, an equal likelihood of securing sales, the Agency will assign firms equal shares.

16. The constraining effect of the quota on the importer's ability to expand sales is relevant to the evaluation of potential adverse competitive effects. *See* Section 2.

United States (i.e., percentage quotas), a domestic price increase that reduced domestic consumption also would reduce the volume of imports into the United States. Accordingly, actual import sales and capacity data will be reduced for purposes of calculating market shares. Finally, a single market share may be assigned to a country or group of countries if firms in that country or group of countries act in coordination.

1.5 Concentration and Market Shares

Market concentration is a function of the number of firms in a market and their respective market shares. As an aid to the interpretation of market data, the Agency will use the Herfindahl-Hirschman Index ("HHI") of market concentration. The HHI is calculated by summing the squares of the individual market shares of all the participants.[17] Unlike the four-firm concentration ratio, the HHI reflects both the distribution of the market shares of the top four firms and the composition of the market outside the top four firms. It also gives proportionately greater weight to the market shares of the larger firms, in accord with their relative importance in competitive interactions.

The Agency divides the spectrum of market concentration as measured by the HHI into three regions that can be broadly characterized as unconcentrated (HHI below 1000), moderately concentrated (HHI between 1000 and 1800), and highly concentrated (HHI above 1800). Although the resulting regions provide a useful framework for merger analysis, the numerical divisions suggest greater precision than is possible with the available economic tools and information. Other things being equal, cases falling just above and just below a threshold present comparable competitive issues.

1.51 GENERAL STANDARDS

In evaluating horizontal mergers, the Agency will consider both the post-merger market concentration and the increase in concentration resulting from the merger.[18] Market concentration is a useful indicator of the likely potential competitive effect of a merger. The general standards for horizontal mergers are as follows:

a) *Post-Merger HHI Below 1000.* The Agency regards markets in this region to be unconcentrated. Mergers resulting in unconcentrated markets are unlikely to have adverse competitive effects and ordinarily require no further analysis.

b) *Post-Merger HHI Between 1000 and 1800.* The Agency regards markets in this

---

17.   For example, a market consisting of four firms with market shares of 30 percent, 30 percent, 20 percent and 20 percent has an HHI of 2600 ($30^2 + 30^2 + 20^2 + 20^2 = 2600$). The HHI ranges from 10,000 (in the case of a pure monopoly) to a number approaching zero (in the case of an atomistic market). Although it is desirable to include all firms in the calculation, lack of information about small firms is not critical because such firms do not affect the HHI significantly.

18.   The increase in concentration as measured by the HHI can be calculated independently of the overall market concentration by doubling the product of the market shares of the merging firms. For example, the merger of firms with shares of 5 percent and 10 percent of the market would increase the HHI by 100 ($5 \times 10 \times 2 = 100$). The explanation for this technique is as follows: In calculating the HHI before the merger, the market shares of the merging firms are squared individually: $(a)^2 + (b)^2$. After the merger, the sum of those shares would be squared: $(a + b)^2$, which equals $a^2 + 2ab + b^2$. The increase in the HHI therefore is represented by $2ab$.

region to be moderately concentrated. Mergers producing an increase in the HHI of less than 100 points in moderately concentrated markets post-merger are unlikely to have adverse competitive consequences and ordinarily require no further analysis. Mergers producing an increase in the HHI of more than 100 points in moderately concentrated markets post-merger potentially raise significant competitive concerns depending on the factors set forth in Sections 2-5 of the Guidelines.

c) *Post-Merger HHI Above 1800.* The Agency regards markets in this region to be highly concentrated. Mergers producing an increase in the HHI of less than 50 points, even in highly concentrated markets post-merger, are unlikely to have adverse competitive consequences and ordinarily require no further analysis. Mergers producing an increase in the HHI of more than 50 points in highly concentrated markets post-merger potentially raise significant competitive concerns, depending on the factors set forth in Sections 2-5 of the Guidelines. Where the post-merger HHI exceeds 1800, it will be presumed that mergers producing an increase in the HHI of more than 100 points are likely to create or enhance market power or facilitate its exercise. The presumption may be overcome by a showing that factors set forth in Sections 2-5 of the Guidelines make it unlikely that the merger will create or enhance market power or facilitate its exercise, in light of market concentration and market shares.

1.52 FACTORS AFFECTING THE SIGNIFICANCE OF MARKET SHARES AND CONCENTRATION

The post-merger level of market concentration and the change in concentration resulting from a merger affect the degree to which a merger raises competitive concerns. However, in some situations, market share and market concentration data may either understate or overstate the likely future competitive significance of a firm or firms in the market or the impact of a merger. The following are examples of such situations.

1.521 Changing Market Conditions

Market concentration and market share data of necessity are based on historical evidence. However, recent or ongoing changes in the market may indicate that the current market share of a particular firm either understates or overstates the firm's future competitive significance. For example, if a new technology that is important to long-term competitive viability is available to other firms in the market, but is not available to a particular firm, the Agency may conclude that the historical market share of that firm overstates its future competitive significance. The Agency will consider reasonably predictable effects of recent or ongoing changes in market conditions in interpreting market concentration and market share data.

1.522 Degree of Difference Between the Products and Locations in the Market and Substitutes Outside the Market

All else equal, the magnitude of potential competitive harm from a merger is greater if a hypothetical monopolist would raise price within the relevant market by substantially more than a "small but significant and nontransitory" amount. This may occur when the demand substitutes outside the relevant market, as a group, are not close substitutes for the products and locations within the relevant market.

There thus may be a wide gap in the chain of demand substitutes at the edge of the product and geographic market. Under such circumstances, more market power is at stake in the relevant market than in a market in which a hypothetical monopolist would raise price by exactly five percent.

2. The Potential Adverse Competitive Effects of Mergers

2.0 Overview

Other things being equal, market concentration affects the likelihood that one firm, or a small group of firms, could successfully exercise market power. The smaller the percentage of total supply that a firm controls, the more severely it must restrict its own output in order to produce a given price increase, and the less likely it is that an output restriction will be profitable. If collective action is necessary for the exercise of market power, as the number of firms necessary to control a given percentage of total supply decreases, the difficulties and costs of reaching and enforcing an understanding with respect to the control of that supply might be reduced. However, market share and concentration data provide only the starting point for analyzing the competitive impact of a merger. Before determining whether to challenge a merger, the Agency also will assess the other market factors that pertain to competitive effects, as well as entry, efficiencies and failure.

This section considers some of the potential adverse competitive effects of mergers and the factors in addition to market concentration relevant to each. Because an individual merger may threaten to harm competition through more than one of these effects, mergers will be analyzed in terms of as many potential adverse competitive effects as are appropriate. Entry, efficiencies, and failure are treated in Sections 3-5.

2.1 Lessening of Competition Through Coordinated Interaction

A merger may diminish competition by enabling the firms selling in the relevant market more likely, more successfully, or more completely to engage in coordinated interaction that harms consumers. Coordinated interaction is comprised of actions by a group of firms that are profitable for each of them only as a result of the accommodating reactions of the others. This behavior includes tacit or express collusion, and may or may not be lawful in and of itself.

Successful coordinated interaction entails reaching terms of coordination that are profitable to the firms involved and an ability to detect and punish deviations that would undermine the coordinated interaction. Detection and punishment of deviations ensure that coordinating firms will find it more profitable to adhere to the terms of coordination than to pursue short-term profits from deviating, given the costs of reprisal. In this phase of the analysis, the Agency will examine the extent to which post-merger market conditions are conducive to reaching terms of coordination, detecting deviations from those terms, and punishing such deviations. Depending upon the circumstances, the following market factors, among others, may be relevant: the availability of key information concerning market conditions, transactions and individual competitors; the extent of firm and product heterogeneity; pricing or marketing practices typically employed by firms in the market; the characteristics of buyers and sellers; and the characteristics of typical transactions.

Certain market conditions that are conducive to reaching terms of coordination also may be conducive to detecting or punishing deviations from those terms. For example, the extent of information available to firms in the market, or the extent of homogeneity, may be relevant to both the ability to reach terms of coordination and to detect or punish deviations from those terms. The extent to which any specific market condition will be relevant to one or more of the conditions necessary to coordinated interaction will depend on the circumstances of the particular case.

It is likely that market conditions are conducive to coordinated interaction when the firms in the market previously have engaged in express collusion and when the salient characteristics of the market have not changed appreciably since the most recent such incident. Previous express collusion in another geographic market will have the same weight when the salient characteristics of that other market at the time of the collusion are comparable to those in the relevant market.

In analyzing the effect of a particular merger on coordinated interaction, the Agency is mindful of the difficulties of predicting likely future behavior based on the types of incomplete and sometimes contradictory information typically generated in merger investigations. Whether a merger is likely to diminish competition by enabling firms more likely, more successfully or more completely to engage in coordinated interaction depends on whether market conditions, on the whole, are conducive to reaching terms of coordination and detecting and punishing deviations from those terms.

2.11 CONDITIONS CONDUCIVE TO REACHING TERMS OF COORDINATION

Firms coordinating their interactions need not reach complex terms concerning the allocation of the market output across firms or the level of the market prices but may, instead, follow simple terms such as a common price, fixed price differentials, stable market shares, or customer or territorial restrictions. Terms of coordination need not perfectly achieve the monopoly outcome in order to be harmful to consumers. Instead, the terms of coordination may be imperfect and incomplete — inasmuch as they omit some market participants, omit some dimensions of competition, omit some customers, yield elevated prices short of monopoly levels, or lapse into episodic price wars — and still result in significant competitive harm. At some point, however, imperfections cause the profitability of abiding by the terms of coordination to decrease and, depending on their extent, may make coordinated interaction unlikely in the first instance.

Market conditions may be conducive to or hinder reaching terms of coordination. For example, reaching terms of coordination may be facilitated by product or firm homogeneity and by existing practices among firms, practices not necessarily themselves antitrust violations, such as standardization of pricing or product variables on which firms could compete. Key information about rival firms and the market may also facilitate reaching terms of coordination. Conversely, reaching terms of coordination may be limited or impeded by product heterogeneity or by firms having substantially incomplete information about the conditions and prospects of their rivals' businesses, perhaps because of important differences among their current business operations. In addition, reaching terms of coordination may be limited or impeded by firm heterogeneity, for example, differences in vertical integration or the production of another product that tends to be used together with the relevant product.

2.12 CONDITIONS CONDUCIVE TO DETECTING AND PUNISHING DEVIATIONS

Where market conditions are conducive to timely detection and punishment of significant deviations, a firm will find it more profitable to abide by the terms of coordination than to deviate from them. Deviation from the terms of coordination will be deterred where the threat of punishment is credible. Credible punishment, however, may not need to be any more complex than temporary abandonment of the terms of coordination by other firms in the market.

Where detection and punishment likely would be rapid, incentives to deviate are diminished and coordination is likely to be successful. The detection and punishment of deviations may be facilitated by existing practices among firms, themselves not necessarily antitrust violations, and by the characteristics of typical transactions. For example, if key information about specific transactions or individual price or output levels is available routinely to competitors, it may be difficult for a firm to deviate secretly. If orders for the relevant product are frequent, regular and small relative to the total output of a firm in a market, it may be difficult for the firm to deviate in a substantial way without the knowledge of rivals and without the opportunity for rivals to react. If demand or cost fluctuations are relatively infrequent and small, deviations may be relatively easy to deter.

By contrast, where detection or punishment is likely to be slow, incentives to deviate are enhanced and coordinated interaction is unlikely to be successful. If demand or cost fluctuations are relatively frequent and large, deviations may be relatively difficult to distinguish from these other sources of market price fluctuations, and, in consequence, deviations may be relatively difficult to deter.

In certain circumstances, buyer characteristics and the nature of the procurement process may affect the incentives to deviate from terms of coordination. Buyer size alone is not the determining characteristic. Where large buyers likely would engage in long-term contracting, so that the sales covered by such contracts can be large relative to the total output of a firm in the market, firms may have the incentive to deviate. However, this only can be accomplished where the duration, volume and profitability of the business covered by such contracts are sufficiently large as to make deviation more profitable in the long term than honoring the terms of coordination, and buyers likely would switch suppliers.

In some circumstances, coordinated interaction can be effectively prevented or limited by maverick firms — firms that have a greater economic incentive to deviate from the terms of coordination than do most of their rivals (e.g., firms that are unusually disruptive and competitive influences in the market). Consequently, acquisition of a maverick firm is one way in which a merger may make coordinated interaction more likely, more successful, or more complete. For example, in a market where capacity constraints are significant for many competitors, a firm is more likely to be a maverick the greater is its excess or divertable capacity in relation to its sales or its total capacity, and the lower are its direct and opportunity costs of expanding sales in the relevant market.[19] This is so because a firm's incentive to deviate from price-elevating and output-limiting terms of coordination is greater the more the firm is able profitably to expand its output as a proportion of the sales it

---

19. But excess capacity in the hands of non-maverick firms may be a potent weapon with which to punish deviations from the terms of coordination.

would obtain if it adhered to the terms of coordination and the smaller is the base of sales on which it enjoys elevated profits prior to the price cutting deviation.[20] A firm also may be a maverick if it has an unusual ability secretly to expand its sales in relation to the sales it would obtain if it adhered to the terms of coordination. This ability might arise from opportunities to expand captive production for a downstream affiliate.

2.2 Lessening of Competition Through Unilateral Effects

A merger may diminish competition even if it does not lead to increased likelihood of successful coordinated interaction, because merging firms may find it profitable to alter their behavior unilaterally following the acquisition by elevating price and suppressing output. Unilateral competitive effects can arise in a variety of different settings. In each setting, particular other factors describing the relevant market affect the likelihood of unilateral competitive effects. The settings differ by the primary characteristics that distinguish firms and shape the nature of their competition.

2.21 FIRMS DISTINGUISHED PRIMARILY BY DIFFERENTIATED PRODUCTS

In some markets the products are differentiated, so that products sold by different participants in the market are not perfect substitutes for one another. Moreover, different products in the market may vary in the degree of their substitutability for one another. In this setting, competition may be non-uniform (i.e., localized), so that individual sellers compete more directly with those rivals selling closer substitutes.[21]

A merger between firms in a market for differentiated products may diminish competition by enabling the merged firm to profit by unilaterally raising the price of one or both products above the premerger level. Some of the sales loss due to the price rise merely will be diverted to the product of the merger partner and, depending on relative margins, capturing such sales loss through merger may make the price increase profitable even though it would not have been profitable premerger. Substantial unilateral price elevation in a market for differentiated products requires that there be a significant share of sales in the market accounted for by consumers who regard the products of the merging firms as their first and second choices, and that repositioning of the non-parties' product lines to replace the

---

20.   Similarly, in a market where product design or quality is significant, a firm is more likely to be an effective maverick the greater is the sales potential of its products among customers of its rivals, in relation to the sales it would obtain if it adhered to the terms of coordination. The likelihood of expansion responses by a maverick will be analyzed in the same fashion as uncommitted entry or committed entry (*see* Sections 1.3 and 3) depending on the significance of the sunk costs entailed in expansion.

21.   Similarly, in some markets sellers are primarily distinguished by their relative advantages in serving different buyers or groups of buyers, and buyers negotiate individually with sellers. Here, for example, sellers may formally bid against one another for the business of a buyer, or each buyer may elicit individual price quotes from multiple sellers. A seller may find it relatively inexpensive to meet the demands of particular buyers or types of buyers, and relatively expensive to meet others' demands. Competition, again, may be localized: sellers compete more directly with those rivals having similar relative advantages in serving particular buyers or groups of buyers. For example, in open outcry auctions, price is determined by the cost of the second lowest-cost seller. A merger involving the first and second lowest-cost sellers could cause prices to rise to the constraining level of the next lowest-cost seller.

localized competition lost through the merger be unlikely. The price rise will be greater the closer substitutes are the products of the merging firms, i.e., the more the buyers of one product consider the other product to be their next choice.

2.211 Closeness of the Products of the Merging Firms

The market concentration measures articulated in Section 1 may help assess the extent of the likely competitive effect from a unilateral price elevation by the merged firm notwithstanding the fact that the affected products are differentiated. The market concentration measures provide a measure of this effect if each product's market share is reflective of not only its relative appeal as a first choice to consumers of the merging firms' products but also its relative appeal as a second choice, and hence as a competitive constraint to the first choice.[22] Where this circumstance holds, market concentration data fall outside the safeharbor regions of Section 1.5, and the merging firms have a combined market share of at least thirty-five percent, the Agency will presume that a significant share of sales in the market are accounted for by consumers who regard the products of the merging firms as their first and second choices.

Purchasers of one of the merging firms' products may be more or less likely to make the other their second choice than market shares alone would indicate. The market shares of the merging firms' products may understate the competitive effect of concern, when, for example, the products of the merging firms are relatively more similar in their various attributes to one another than to other products in the relevant market. On the other hand, the market shares alone may overstate the competitive effects of concern when, for example, the relevant products are less similar in their attributes to one another than to other products in the relevant market.

Where market concentration data fall outside the safeharbor regions of Section 1.5, the merging firms have a combined market share of at least thirty-five percent, and where data on product attributes and relative product appeal show that a significant share of purchasers of one merging firm's product regard the other as their second choice, then market share data may be relied upon to demonstrate that there is a significant share of sales in the market accounted for by consumers who would be adversely affected by the merger.

2.212 Ability of Rival Sellers to Replace Lost Competition

A merger is not likely to lead to unilateral elevation of prices of differentiated products if, in response to such an effect, rival sellers likely would replace any localized competition lost through the merger by repositioning their product lines.[23]

In markets where it is costly for buyers to evaluate product quality, buyers who consider purchasing from both merging parties may limit the total number of sellers they consider. If either of the merging firms would be replaced in such buyers'

---

22. Information about consumers' actual first and second product choices may be provided by marketing surveys, information from bidding structures, or normal course of business documents from industry participants.

23. The timeliness and likelihood of repositioning responses will be analyzed using the same methodology as used in analyzing uncommitted entry or committed entry (see Sections 1.3 and 3), depending on the significance of the sunk costs entailed in repositioning.

consideration by an equally competitive seller not formerly considered, then the merger is not likely to lead to a unilateral elevation of prices.

2.22 FIRMS DISTINGUISHED PRIMARILY BY THEIR CAPACITIES

Where products are relatively undifferentiated and capacity primarily distinguishes firms and shapes the nature of their competition, the merged firm may find it profitable unilaterally to raise price and suppress output. The merger provides the merged firm a larger base of sales on which to enjoy the resulting price rise and also eliminates a competitor to which customers otherwise would have diverted their sales. Where the merging firms have a combined market share of at least thirty-five percent, merged firms may find it profitable to raise price and reduce joint output below the sum of their premerger outputs because the lost markups on the foregone sales may be outweighed by the resulting price increase on the merged base of sales.

This unilateral effect is unlikely unless a sufficiently large number of the merged firm's customers would not be able to find economical alternative sources of supply, i.e., competitors of the merged firm likely would not respond to the price increase and output reduction by the merged firm with increases in their own outputs sufficient in the aggregate to make the unilateral action of the merged firm unprofitable. Such non-party expansion is unlikely if those firms face binding capacity constraints that could not be economically relaxed within two years or if existing excess capacity is significantly more costly to operate than capacity currently in use.[24]

3. Entry Analysis

3.0 Overview

A merger is not likely to create or enhance market power or to facilitate its exercise, if entry into the market is so easy that market participants, after the merger, either collectively or unilaterally could not profitably maintain a price increase above premerger levels. Such entry likely will deter an anticompetitive merger in its incipiency, or deter or counteract the competitive effects of concern.

Entry is that easy if entry would be timely, likely, and sufficient in its magnitude, character and scope to deter or counteract the competitive effects of concern. In markets where entry is that easy (i.e., where entry passes these tests of timeliness, likelihood, and sufficiency), the merger raises no antitrust concern and ordinarily requires no further analysis.

The committed entry treated in this Section is defined as new competition that requires expenditure of significant sunk costs of entry and exit.[25] The Agency employs a three step methodology to assess whether committed entry would deter or counteract a competitive effect of concern.

The first step assesses whether entry can achieve significant market impact within

---

24.   The timeliness and likelihood of non-party expansion will be analyzed using the same methodology as used in analyzing uncommitted or committed entry (*see* Sections 1.3 and 3) depending on the significance of the sunk costs entailed in expansion.

25.   Supply responses that require less than one year and insignificant sunk costs to effectuate are analyzed as uncommitted entry in Section 1.3.

a timely period. If significant market impact would require a longer period, entry will not deter or counteract the competitive effect of concern.

The second step assesses whether committed entry would be a profitable and, hence, a likely response to a merger having competitive effects of concern. Firms considering entry that requires significant sunk costs must evaluate the profitability of the entry on the basis of long term participation in the market, because the underlying assets will be committed to the market until they are economically depreciated. Entry that is sufficient to counteract the competitive effects of concern will cause prices to fall to their premerger levels or lower. Thus, the profitability of such committed entry must be determined on the basis of premerger market prices over the long-term.

A merger having anticompetitive effects can attract committed entry, profitable at premerger prices, that would not have occurred premerger at these same prices. But following the merger, the reduction in industry output and increase in prices associated with the competitive effect of concern may allow the same entry to occur without driving market prices below premerger levels. After a merger that results in decreased output and increased prices, the likely sales opportunities available to entrants at premerger prices will be larger than they were premerger, larger by the output reduction caused by the merger. If entry could be profitable at premerger prices without exceeding the likely sales opportunities — opportunities that include pre-existing pertinent factors as well as the merger-induced output reduction — then such entry is likely in response to the merger.

The third step assesses whether timely and likely entry would be sufficient to return market prices to their premerger levels. This end may be accomplished either through multiple entry or individual entry at a sufficient scale. Entry may not be sufficient, even though timely and likely, where the constraints on availability of essential assets, due to incumbent control, make it impossible for entry profitably to achieve the necessary level of sales. Also, the character and scope of entrants' products might not be fully responsive to the localized sales opportunities created by the removal of direct competition among sellers of differentiated products. In assessing whether entry will be timely, likely, and sufficient, the Agency recognizes that precise and detailed information may be difficult or impossible to obtain. In such instances, the Agency will rely on all available evidence bearing on whether entry will satisfy the conditions of timeliness, likelihood, and sufficiency.

3.1 Entry Alternatives

The Agency will examine the timeliness, likelihood, and sufficiency of the means of entry (entry alternatives) a potential entrant might practically employ, without attempting to identify who might be potential entrants. An entry alternative is defined by the actions the firm must take in order to produce and sell in the market. All phases of the entry effort will be considered, including, where relevant, planning, design, and management; permitting, licensing, and other approvals; construction, debugging, and operation of production facilities; and promotion (including necessary introductory discounts), marketing, distribution, and satisfaction of customer testing and qualification requirements.[26] Recent examples of entry, whether successful or

---

26.   Many of these phases may be undertaken simultaneously.

unsuccessful, may provide a useful starting point for identifying the necessary actions, time requirements, and characteristics of possible entry alternatives.

3.2 Timeliness of Entry

In order to deter or counteract the competitive effects of concern, entrants quickly must achieve a significant impact on price in the relevant market. The Agency generally will consider timely only those committed entry alternatives that can be achieved within two years from initial planning to significant market impact.[27] Where the relevant product is a durable good, consumers, in response to a significant commitment to entry, may defer purchases by making additional investments to extend the useful life of previously purchased goods and in this way deter or counteract for a time the competitive effects of concern. In these circumstances, if entry only can occur outside of the two year period, the Agency will consider entry to be timely so long as it would deter or counteract the competitive effects of concern within the two year period and subsequently.

3.3 Likelihood of Entry

An entry alternative is likely if it would be profitable at premerger prices, and if such prices could be secured by the entrant.[28] The committed entrant will be unable to secure prices at premerger levels if its output is too large for the market to absorb without depressing prices further. Thus, entry is unlikely if the minimum viable scale is larger than the likely sales opportunity available to entrants.

Minimum viable scale is the smallest average annual level of sales that the committed entrant must persistently achieve for profitability at premerger prices.[29] Minimum viable scale is a function of expected revenues, based upon premerger prices,[30] and all categories of costs associated with the entry alternative, including an appropriate rate of return on invested capital given that entry could fail and sunk costs, if any, will be lost.[31]

Sources of sales opportunities available to entrants include: (a) the output reduction associated with the competitive effect of concern,[32] (b) entrants' ability

---

27. Firms which have committed to entering the market prior to the merger generally will be included in the measurement of the market. Only committed entry or adjustments to pre-existing entry plans that are induced by the merger will be considered as possibly deterring or counteracting the competitive effects of concern.

28. Where conditions indicate that entry may be profitable at prices below premerger levels, the Agency will assess the likelihood of entry at the lowest price at which such entry would be profitable.

29. The concept of minimum viable scale (MVS) differs from the concept of minimum efficient scale (MES). While MES is the smallest scale at which average costs are minimized, MVS is the smallest scale at which average costs equal the premerger price.

30. The expected path of future prices, absent the merger, may be used if future price changes can be predicted with reasonable reliability.

31. The minimum viable scale of an entry alternative will be relatively large when the fixed costs of entry are large, when the fixed costs of entry are largely sunk, when the marginal costs of production are high at low levels of output, and when a plant is underutilized for a long time because of delays in achieving market acceptance.

32. Five percent of total market sales typically is used because where a monopolist profitably would raise price by five percent or more across the entire relevant market, it is likely that the accompanying reduction in sales would be no less than five percent.

to capture a share of reasonably expected growth in market demand,[33] (c) entrants' ability securely to divert sales from incumbents, for example, through vertical integration or through forward contracting, and (d) any additional anticipated contraction in incumbents' output in response to entry.[34] Factors that reduce the sales opportunities available to entrants include: (a) the prospect that an entrant will share in a reasonably expected decline in market demand, (b) the exclusion of an entrant from a portion of the market over the long term because of vertical integration or forward contracting by incumbents, and (c) any anticipated sales expansion by incumbents in reaction to entry, either generalized or targeted at customers approached by the entrant, that utilizes prior irreversible investments in excess production capacity. Demand growth or decline will be viewed as relevant only if total market demand is projected to experience long-lasting change during at least the two year period following the competitive effect of concern.

3.4 Sufficiency of Entry

Inasmuch as multiple entry generally is possible and individual entrants may flexibly choose their scale, committed entry generally will be sufficient to deter or counteract the competitive effects of concern whenever entry is likely under the analysis of Section 3.3. However, entry, although likely, will not be sufficient if, as a result of incumbent control, the tangible and intangible assets required for entry are not adequately available for entrants to respond fully to their sales opportunities. In addition, where the competitive effect of concern is not uniform across the relevant market, in order for entry to be sufficient, the character and scope of entrants' products must be responsive to the localized sales opportunities that include the output reduction associated with the competitive effect of concern. For example, where the concern is unilateral price elevation as a result of a merger between producers of differentiated products, entry, in order to be sufficient, must involve a product so close to the products of the merging firms that the merged firm will be unable to internalize enough of the sales loss due to the price rise, rendering the price increase unprofitable.

4. Efficiencies

The primary benefit of mergers to the economy is their efficiency-enhancing potential, which can increase the competitiveness of firms and result in lower prices to consumers. Because the antitrust laws, and thus the standards of the Guidelines, are designed to proscribe only mergers that present a significant danger to competition, they do not present an obstacle to most mergers. As a consequence, in the majority of cases, the Guidelines will allow firms to achieve available efficiencies through mergers without interference from the Agency.

Some mergers that the Agency otherwise might challenge may be reasonably necessary to achieve significant net efficiencies. Cognizable efficiencies include, but

---

33.   Entrants' anticipated share of growth in demand depends on incumbents' capacity constraints and irreversible investments in capacity expansion, as well as on the relative appeal, acceptability and reputation of incumbents' and entrants' products to the new demand.

34.   For example, in a bidding market where all bidders are on equal footing, the market share of incumbents will contract as a result of entry.

are not limited to, achieving economies of scale, better integration of production facilities, plant specialization, lower transportation costs, and similar efficiencies relating to specific manufacturing, servicing, or distribution operations of the merging firms. The Agency may also consider claimed efficiencies resulting from reductions in general selling, administrative, and overhead expenses, or that otherwise do not relate to specific manufacturing, servicing, or distribution operations of the merging firms, although, as a practical matter, these types of efficiencies may be difficult to demonstrate. In addition, the Agency will reject claims of efficiencies if equivalent or comparable savings can reasonably be achieved by the parties through other means. The expected net efficiencies must be greater the more significant are the competitive risks identified in Section 1-3.

5.   Failure and Exiting Assets

5.0 Overview

Notwithstanding the analysis of Sections 1-4 of the Guidelines, a merger is not likely to create or enhance market power or to facilitate its exercise, if imminent failure, as defined below, of one of the merging firms would cause the assets of that firm to exit the relevant market. In such circumstances, post-merger performance in the relevant market may be no worse than market performance had the merger been blocked and the assets left the market.

5.1 Failing Firm

A merger is not likely to create or enhance market power or facilitate its exercise if the following circumstances are met: (1) the allegedly failing firm would be unable to meet its financial obligations in the near future; (2) it would not be able to reorganize successfully under Chapter 11 of the Bankruptcy Act;[35] (3) it has made unsuccessful good-faith efforts to elicit reasonable alternative offers of acquisition of the assets of the failing firm[36] that would both keep its tangible and intangible assets in the relevant market and pose a less severe danger to competition than does the proposed merger; and (4) absent the acquisition, the assets of the failing firm would exit the relevant market.

5.2 Failing Division

A similar argument can be made for "failing" divisions as for failing firms. First, upon applying appropriate cost allocation rules, the division must have a negative cash flow on an operating basis. Second, absent the acquisition, it must be that the assets of the division would exit the relevant market in the near future if not sold. Due to the ability of the parent firm to allocate costs, revenues, and intracompany transactions among itself and its subsidiaries and divisions, the Agency will require evidence, not based solely on management plans that could be prepared solely for the

---

35.   11 U.S.C. §§ 1101-1174 (1988).
36.   Any offer to purchase the assets of the failing firm for a price above the liquidation value of
         those assets – the highest valued use outside the relevant market or equivalent offer to purchase
         the stock of the failing firm – will be regarded as a reasonable alternative offer.

purpose of demonstrating negative cash flow or the prospect of exit from the relevant market. Third, the owner of the failing division also must have complied with the competitively-preferable purchaser requirement of Section 5.1.

Dissenting Statement of Commissioner Mary L. Azcuenaga on the Issuance of Horizontal Merger Guidelines

April 2, 1992

Today the Department of Justice and the Federal Trade Commission issue new Horizontal Merger Guidelines. These new Guidelines, which generally follow the analytic approach of the 1984 Guidelines, improve the explanation in several respects of the way in which mergers are analyzed by the federal agencies. For example, the Guidelines now explain that the likelihood of entry will defeat the exercise of market power only if entry would be timely, likely and sufficient. They clarify that all phases of entry, from planning and design through distribution and sales, will be considered. Recognition of the possibility of certain unilateral effects from single firm conduct, although present in the 1984 Guidelines, is now made more explicit. The new Guidelines explain more fully some of the analysis the agencies employ. All these efforts are positive.

Despite the substantial additive contribution of the new Guidelines, I have reservations about endorsing them. Merger guidelines are useful to the extent they help predict whether government prosecutors will challenge a particular transaction. To have a predictive value, enforcement guidelines must accurately reflect how the agencies analyze mergers and how they respond to different sets of facts. I question whether the new Guidelines accurately express what the Commission does now or is likely to do in analyzing mergers, and I am reluctant to subscribe to them on the pretext that they do.

The new Guidelines may not be "wrong" insofar as they are grounded in sound, even if untested, economic theory, but they may still lead to misunderstandings. The 1984 Guidelines, the FTC Horizontal Merger Statement and Commission case law provide good overall guidance and a reliable basis for predicting the enforcement policies of the Commission. In my view, the new Guidelines do not provide as much guidance to what we do in fact.

To the extent that merger guidelines do not provide guidance concerning government enforcement policy, they may in some situations encourage mergers that are likely to be challenged and, in others, discourage efficient mergers. This will impose costs and, to some extent, distort the free functioning of the market for corporate control.

Much will be written in full exegesis of the numerous issues the new Guidelines pose. It is not my purpose to provide an exhaustive list of concerns nor to explore those concerns in detail. Rather, I will highlight a few examples in which, in my view, the new Guidelines are not predictive of the Commission's analysis and could even mislead.

Simplicity and clarity are virtues in writing guidelines. The new Guidelines are opaque on a number of points and ambiguous on issues of critical importance. The opacity is a short term problem. Members of the bar and the business community, perhaps with some effort, no doubt will master the underlying concepts. The ambiguities are more serious, because they promote uncertainty and reduce the instructive value of the document.

Although the new Guidelines purport to "outline the present enforcement policy" of the government, they generally abandon the useful statements of enforcement intentions contained in the 1984 Guidelines. Where the 1984 Guidelines identified the characteristics that were more likely to weigh in favor of enforcement action, the new Guidelines offer instead a more academic discussion of an "analytical framework." The new Guidelines identify conditions or factors or characteristics to be considered in the analysis but do not tell us what weight they will carry in a decision to challenge a merger. This change in focus may significantly limit the usefulness of the new Guidelines, although perhaps only for the uninitiated.

The extended discussion in the new Guidelines of some facets of merger analysis may be misunderstood as creating new elements of a Section 7 case and, to that extent, may tend to undercut the incipiency standard of Section 7. For example, the new Guidelines may suggest, erroneously and perhaps unintentionally, that the government will challenge a proposed merger only if it can establish with some degree of objective certainty how a cartel, yet to be created following a merger, would work. That will rarely be possible, and it is not what the Commission has required.

The new Guidelines omit some discussion that was in the 1984 Guidelines, such as, for example, market performance (§ 3.45). The implications of these omissions, if any, are not clear. To the extent that industry performance is relevant in assessing the likely competitive effects of a merger, the deletion may diminish the predictive value of the new Guidelines. Other aspects of the analysis receive less attention than may seem warranted. For example, the new Guidelines explain that large buyers may encourage non-collusive pricing if they seek large volume, longterm purchase contracts, but only if the contracts would be more profitable for the seller than maintaining the cartel price and only if the buyers "likely would switch suppliers." There may be situations that do not fit this description in which power buyers will be able to defeat collusion. Although the power buyer defense tends to be overused and requires careful analysis, the sole example in the new Guidelines seems unduly narrow and may have the potential to mislead.

The new Guidelines employ the concept of sunk costs in various places, notably to distinguish between production substitution and entry. Although the new Guidelines permit "an overall assessment" of sunk costs when precise calculations "may be difficult," the prominence accorded sunk costs nevertheless may have the unfortunate effect of imposing expensive new burdens on the government and on the business community. Determining the nature and magnitude of sunk costs can be a major undertaking, and determining the payback period for recovery of those costs could be even more problematic. Sunk costs were relevant under the 1984 Guidelines but did not need to be measured if the issues could be resolved by easier means. It is unclear from the four corners of the document whether this degree of flexibility will continue under the new Guidelines.

The test used to identify the relevant market seems changed in a way that may be difficult to implement and may make market definition less predictable. The 1984 Guidelines hypothesized a uniform price increase to identify the market. Under the new Guidelines, the price increase is not necessarily uniform. Instead, the hypothetical monopolist, "to pursue maximum profits," may increase prices for some products and for some locales more than for others (as long as he "would profitably impose at least a 'small but significant and nontransitory' increase, including the price of a product of one of the merging firms"). Requiring a determination of the pricing policy of the hypothetical monopolist raises the level of complexity in market analysis. With even a moderate number of products and locales, the analysis may prove to be a daunting task. Various assumptions about factors influencing the monopolist's decision may lead to different pricing policies and, thus, different definitions of relevant markets. While the approach may be appropriate in theory, it is unclear how we might choose among the myriad of plausible price choices that the hypothetical profit-maximizing monopolist might make. The relatively "crude" test of the 1984 Guidelines has the saving grace of simplicity, feasibility and predictability.

The explicit statement that entry must be timely, likely and sufficient to defeat the exercise of market power is welcome. To the extent that placing the discussion of entry after the extended discussion of competitive effects may tend to suggest that entry is less relevant to exploring market conditions than to establishing a defense, the new Guidelines may be unrealistic. Other changes in the discussion of entry introduce new elements of uncertainty not just for the public but for the government as well. They may not change the agencies' enforcement decisions, or they may portend fundamental change.

For example, the new Guidelines propose to measure the likelihood of entry by comparing the minimum viable scale of entry (as defined) at the premerger price against a hypothetical 5% reduction in output. If the identified scale of entry is greater than the 5% "gap" (adjusted as appropriate to reflect "sales opportunities"), then entry is deemed unlikely. By implication, if the gap and the identified scale of entry are commensurate, then entry is deemed likely and, in most cases, sufficient. The Commission has in the past examined the effects on entry of minimum scale requirements as one element in a multi-faceted analysis. The new Guidelines make the relationship between the estimated scale of entry and the hypothetical reduction in output more formal and more important.

The degree of precision that the new Guidelines seem to contemplate in measuring minimum viable scale may be unattainable in practice. The process is likely to involve a range of estimates and considerable exercise of judgment, and more subjective assessments may continue to be important in defining the "entry alternatives" and "sales opportunities" and in assessing the amount of time that entry is likely to take.

Even assuming the availability of exact information, however, the new test may not provide meaningful answers. The 5% standard is an untested assumption, and we do not know whether we will ever find ease of entry or will always find it. There is an uncertainty here that may turn out to be important. Until the usefulness of the approach has been established, it may be premature to incorporate it into enforcement policy.

The new Guidelines omit the statement contained in the 1984 Guidelines that efficiencies will be considered in deciding whether to challenge a merger provided that the parties to the merger show by "clear and convincing evidence" that a merger will achieve such efficiencies. This omission does not, as far as I am aware, signal any change in policy but nevertheless may send a message that little will be required to support an efficiency claim. That perception will not be helpful to the government, to the parties or to the state of competition in the market. In my experience, the Commission always has been receptive to efficiencies in its merger analysis, but, as a practical matter, merger-specific efficiencies are infrequently demonstrated.

The requirement that the parties present clear and convincing evidence of efficiencies helps winnow out those relatively few cases in which merger-specific efficiencies are worth extensive examination. This filter is advantageous to the government and, because it does not raise false hopes in the vast majority of cases, to the parties. We should not encourage parties to undertake futile and wasteful efforts to persuade the agencies of proposed efficiencies, and we should not mislead them into thinking that an unsubstantiated claim of efficiencies is likely to protect an anticompetitive merger.

If I had seen any evidence whatsoever that the clear and convincing requirement had been responsible for making it more difficult for mergers with genuine merger-specific efficiencies to clear the enforcement agencies, then I might favor a relaxation of the standard. Here I see no reason to relax the standard and every reason to retain it. It seems highly unlikely that the Commission intends to permit a greater number of anticompetitive mergers to go unchallenged because of asserted efficiencies than it has in the past. If this perception is correct, and I think it is, then the new Guidelines may be misleading.

The 1984 Guidelines, recognizing that the failing firm defense can immunize otherwise anticompetitive mergers, warned that the elements of the defense would be strictly construed. The new Guidelines appear more hospitable to the defense and abandon the warning without comment. The Commission has construed the defense strictly and has argued this position in court, most recently in *Harbour Group Investments, L.P.*, 1990-2 Trade Cas. (CCH) ¶ 69,247 (D.D.C. 1990). To the best of my knowledge, the Commission has not affirmatively changed its position concerning the failing firm defense, and, to the extent that adopting the revised language may suggest otherwise, the new Guidelines are less predictive of the Commission's enforcement intentions.

For many years, antitrust enforcement policy has paralleled but lagged behind developments in microeconomics. In some respects, the new Guidelines appear to be an attempt to eliminate or reduce the size of the lag. This may or may not be advisable. The lagging parallel has the advantage that the theories, rigorous in themselves, can be tested for their practical value in the law enforcement process before they are adopted as enforcement policy. To the extent that the testing period has been reduced, the value of the new Guidelines as predictors of future enforcement also may be diminished.

Unlike the Department of Justice, the Commission is quasi-judicial. Because we bind ourselves institutionally through our adjudicative opinions, the policies of the two agencies, although consistent, are likely never to be expressed in a completely identical fashion. As a matter of law, the new Guidelines would bind the Commission only if the Commission adopts them as standards in a contested, adjudicative proceeding. Nevertheless, court decisions suggest that the government embraces some risk of losing if it brings cases in federal court that do not fit within its own guidelines.

Although we are not legally bound by guidelines, I am reluctant in a policy statement to stray too far from what we actually do. I am particularly reluctant to suggest any departure from the incipiency standard embodied in Section 7 and the case law. It is possible to read the new Guidelines in a manner that makes them consistent with current Commission policy, and that is what I intend to do. It is my hope that the matters about which I am concerned soon will be clarified through the speeches and interpretations that no doubt will follow. Indeed, if I am correct about the Commission's enforcement policy, explanations that my fears are unfounded should begin to appear almost immediately.

The reason for revising guidelines presumably is to improve their predictive value and to promote understanding of agency enforcement intentions. In important respects, I cannot agree that the new Guidelines accomplish this goal. Perhaps I am wrong about this, but in that event, I have substantive objections. For now, my obligation is simply to indicate whether the new Guidelines on their face reflect what I think the Commission's enforcement policy is or should be. Having made the judgment that they do not, it would not be responsible for me to subscribe to a document that does not appear to explain enforcement policy as it is, should be or likely will be.

With regret, I have voted not to adopt the new Guidelines.

TABLE OF CASES

A

AAA Liquors, Inc. v. Joseph E. Seagram & Sons, 705 F.2d 1203 (10th cir. 1982), *cert. denied*, 461 U.S. 919 (1983), 111, 112, 114

Aamco Automatic Transmissions, Inc. v. Tayloe, 67 F.R.D. 440 (E.D. Pa. 1975), 718, 720, 733

Aamco Automatic Transmissions, Inc. v. Tayloe, 82 F.R.D. 405 (E.D. Pa. 1979), 784

AAMCO Automatic Transmissions, Inc. v. Tayloe, 368 F. Supp. 1283 (E.D. Pa. 1973), 141

AAMCO Automatic Transmissions, Inc. v. Tayloe, 407 F. Supp. 430 (E.D. Pa. 1976), 157, 158

A. & E. Plastik Pak Co. v. Monsanto Co., 396 F.2d 710 (9th Cir. 1968), 842, 850

A&M Records, Inc. v. A.L.W., Ltd., 855 F.2d 368 (7th Cir. 1988), 6, 706

A.A. Poultry Farms v. Rose Acre Farms, 683 F. Supp. 680 (S.D. Ind. 1988) *aff'd on other grounds*, 881 F.2d 1396 (7th Cir. 1989), *cert. denied*, 110 S. Ct. 1326 (1990), 427

A.A. Poultry Farms v. Rose Acre Farms, 881 F.2d 1396 (7th Cir. 1989), *cert. denied*, 110 S. Ct. 1326 (1990), 208, 210, 211, 226, 228, 234, 235, 237, 263, 406, 413, 415

Aaron E. Levine & Co. v. Calkraft Paper Co., 429 F. Supp. 1039 (E.D. Mich. 1976), 187

ABA Distribs. v. Adolph Coors Co., 661 F.2d 712 (8th Cir. 1981), 676, 678

ABA Players Ass'n v. NBA, 404 F. Supp. 832 (S.D.N.Y. 1975), 91

Abadir v. First Miss. Corp., 651 F.2d 422 (5th Cir. 1981), 35, 37, 38, 39, 123, 128

Abbate v. United States, 359 U.S. 187 (1959), 619, 629

Abbott Labs. v. Brennan, 952 F.2d 1346 (Fed. Cir. 1991), 831

Abbott Labs. v. Gardner, 387 U.S. 136 (1967), 524

Abbott Labs. v. Portland Retail Druggists Ass'n, 425 U.S. 1 (1976), 448

Abbott Sec. Corp. v. New York Stock Exch., 384 F. Supp. 668 (D.D.C. 1974), 1102

ABC Great States, Inc. v. Globe Ticket Co., 310 F. Supp. 739 (N.D. Ill. 1970), 869

ABC Great Stores v. Globe Ticket Co., 309 F. Supp. 181 (E.D. Pa. 1970), 598

Abcor Corp. v. AM Int'l, Inc., 916 F.2d 924 (4th Cir. 1990), 222, 223, 225, 226, 227, 244, 259, 260

Abercrombie v. Lum's, Inc., 345 F. Supp. 387 (S.D. Fla. 1972), 720

Abernathy v. Bausch & Lomb, Inc., 97 F.R.D. 470 (N.D. Tex. 1983), 728

Abex Corp. v. FTC, 420 F.2d 928 (6th Cir.), *cert. denied*, 400 U.S. 865 (1970), 287

ABG-Oil Cos., 20 O.J. EUR. COMM. (No. L 117) 1 (1977), [1976-1978 Transfer Binder] COMMON MKT. REP. (CCH) ¶ 9944, *rev'd sub nom.* BP v. Commission, Case 77/77, [1978] E.C.R. 1513, [1977-1978 Transfer Binder] COMMON MKT. REP. (CCH) ¶ 8465, 951, 953, 954

ABI, 29 O.J. EUR. COMM. (No. L 43) 51 (1986), [1985-1988 Transfer Binder] COMMON MKT. REP. (CCH) ¶ 10,846, 936

Abrams v. Interco, Inc., 1980-2 Trade Cas. (CCH) ¶ 63,292 (S.D.N.Y. 1980), 657

Abrams v. Interco, Inc., 719 F.2d 23 (2d Cir. 1983), 728, 733

AB Volvo v. Eric Veng (UK) Ltd., Case 238/87, [1988] E.C.R. 6211, [1987-1988 Transfer Binder] COMMON MKT. REP. (CCH) ¶ 14,498, 953, 955

Ace Beer Distribs. v. Kohn, Inc., 318 F.2d 283 (6th Cir.), *cert. denied*, 375 U.S. 922 (1963), 50, 188, 193

Ackerman-Chillingworth v. Pacific Elec. Contractors Ass'n, 579 F.2d 484 (9th Cir. 1978), *cert. denied*, 439 U.S. 1089 (1979), 47

Acme Precision Prods., Inc. v. American Alloys Corp., 484 F.2d 1237 (8th Cir. 1973), 205

Acme Refrigeration, Inc. v. Whirlpool Corp., 785 F.2d 1240 (5th Cir.), *cert. denied*, 479 U.S. 848 (1986), 408

A. Copeland Enters. v. Guste, 1989-2 Trade Cas. (CCH) ¶ 68,713 (E.D. La. 1988), 364, 663

ACS Enters. v. Sylvania Commercial Elecs. Corp., 1979-2 Trade Cas. (CCH) ¶ 62,765 (E.D. Pa. 1979), 427, 438

Action for Children's Television v. FCC, 821 F.2d 741 (D.C. Cir. 1987), 1029, 1044

A.D.M. Corp. v. Sigma Instruments Inc., 628 F.2d 753 (1st Cir. 1980), 364, 663

Adams Tire Co. v. Dunlop Tire & Rubber Corp., 1984-1 Trade Cas. (CCH) ¶ 65,871 (N.D. Tex. 1984), 184

Adams v. Burke, 84 U.S. (17 Wall.) 453 (1873), 826

Adams v. FTC, 296 F.2d 861 (8th Cir. 1961), *cert. denied*, 369 U.S. 864 (1962), 507

Adams v. Pan Am. World Airways, 828 F.2d 24 (D.C. Cir. 1987), *cert. denied*, 485 U.S. 961 (1988), 647, 662, 663

Addino v. Genesee Valley Medical Care, Inc., 593 F. Supp. 892 (W.D.N.Y. 1984), 70, 71

Addrisi v. Equitable Life Assurance Soc'y, 503 F.2d 725 (9th Cir. 1974), *cert. denied*, 420 U.S. 929 (1975), 1113, 1116, 1117

Addyston Pipe & Steel Co. v. United States, 175 U.S. 211 (1899), 3, 74, 117

Adjusters Replace-a-Car, Inc. v. Agency Rent-A-Car, Inc., 735 F.2d 884 (5th Cir. 1984), *cert. denied*, 469 U.S. 1160 (1985), 97, 222, 228, 229, 235, 414

Admiral Theatre Corp. v. Douglas Theatre Co., 585 F.2d 877 (8th Cir. 1978), 6, 196

Adolph Coors Co., 83 F.T.C. 32 (1973), *aff'd*, 497 F.2d 1178 (10th Cir. 1974), *cert. denied*, 419 U.S. 1105 (1975), 119, 164

Adolph Coors Co. v. A & S Wholesalers, 561 F.2d 807 (10th Cir. 1977), 124

Adolph Coors Co. v. FTC, 497 F.2d 1178 (10th Cir. 1974), *cert. denied*, 419 U.S. 1105 (1975), 107, 110, 121, 174, 521, 522

Adolph Coors Co. v. Wallace, 1984-1 Trade Cas. (CCH) ¶ 65,931 (N.D. Cal. 1984), 94

Adria Labs., 103 F.T.C. 512 (1984), 474

Advance Bus. Sys. & Supply Co. v. SCM Corp., 415 F.2d 55 (4th Cir. 1969), *cert. denied*, 397 U.S. 920 (1970), 133, 143, 146, 147, 157, 162, 673

Advanced Health-Care Servs. v. Radford Community Hosp., 910 F.2d 139 (4th Cir. 1990), 19, 45, 173, 178, 222, 223, 252, 271

Advanced Micro Devices v. CAB, 742 F.2d 1520 (D.C. Cir. 1984), 1017

Advanced Office Sys. v. Accounting Sys. Co., 442 F. Supp. 418 (D.S.C. 1977), 409, 410

Ad-Vantage Tel. Directory Consultants v. GTE Directories Corp., 849 F.2d 1336 (11th Cir. 1987), 199, 201, 202, 248

Adventist Health Sys./West, 5 TRADE REG. REP. (CCH) ¶ 22,658 (Mar. 15, 1989), 507

Adventist Health Sys./West, 5 TRADE REG. REP. (CCH) ¶ 23,038 (Aug. 2, 1991), 279

Advertising Checking Bureau, 93 F.T.C. 4 (1979), 113

Advertising Checking Bureau, 109 F.T.C. 146 (1987), 113

Ad Visor, Inc. v. Commissioner, 37 T.C.M. (CCH) 606 (1978), 794

Ad Visor, Inc. v. Pacific Tel. & Tel. Co., 640 F.2d 1107 (9th Cir. 1981), 1001

Advocaat Zwarte Kip, 17 O.J. EUR. COMM. (No. L 237) 12 (1974), [1973-1975 Transfer Binder] COMMON MKT. REP. (CCH) ¶ 9669, 944, 946

AEG-Telefunken, 25 O.J. EUR. COMM. (No. L 117) 15 (1982), [1982-1985 Transfer Binder] COMMON MKT. REP. (CCH) ¶ 10,366, 940, 942

AEG-Telefunken AG v. Commission, Case 107/82, [1983] E.C.R. 3151, [1983-1985 Transfer Binder] COMMON MKT. REP. (CCH) ¶ 14,018, 940

Aerojet-General Corp. v. Machine Tool Works, Oerlikon-Buehrle Ltd., No. 88-1351 (Fed. Cir. Oct. 5, 1989), 851

Affanto v. Merrill Bros., 547 F.2d 138 (1st Cir. 1971), 768

Affiliated Capital Corp. v. City of Houston, 1982-1 Trade. Cas. (CCH) ¶ 64,627 (S.D. Tex. 1981), 679

Affiliated Capital Corp. v. City of Houston, 700 F.2d 226 (5th Cir. 1983), *aff'd on other grounds*, 735 F.2d 1555 (5th Cir. 1984), *cert. denied*, 474 U.S. 1053 (1986), 77

Affiliated Capital Corp. v. City of Houston, 735 F.2d 1555 (5th Cir. 1984), *cert. denied*, 474 U.S. 1053 (1986), 666, 987, 997, 1053

AG Bliss Co. v. United Carr Fastener Co. of Can., 116 F. Supp. 291 (D. Mass. 1953), *aff'd*, 213 F.2d 541 (1st Cir. 1954), 869

Agostine v. Sidcon Corp., 69 F.R.D. 437 (E.D. Pa. 1975), 695, 697

Agrashell, Inc. v. Hammons Prods. Co., 479 F.2d 269 (8th Cir.), *cert. denied*, 414 U.S. 1022 (1973), 262, 672

AHC Pharmacal, Inc., 101 F.T.C. 40 (1983), 516

A.G.S. Elec., Ltd. v. B.S.R., Ltd., 460 F. Supp. 707 (S.D.N.Y.), *aff'd without opinion*, 591 F.2d 1329 (2d Cir. 1978), 364

A.G. Spalding & Bros., 56 F.T.C. 1125 (1960), *aff'd*, 301 F.2d 585 (3d Cir. 1962), 290

A.G. Spalding & Bros. v. FTC, 301 F.2d 585 (3d Cir. 1962), 284, 286

A.H. Belo Corp., 43 F.C.C.2d 336, (1973), 1029

A.H. Cox & Co. v. Star Mach. Co., 653 F.2d 1302 (9th Cir. 1981), 54, 97, 118, 183, 188

ACH Pharmacal, Inc., 101 F.T.C. 40 (1983), 515

Ahlström v. Commission (Wood Pulp), 28 O.J. EUR. COMM. (No. L 85) 1 (1985), [1982-1985 Transfer Binder] COMMON MKT. REP. (CCH) ¶ 10,654, 928

Ahlström v. Commission (Wood Pulp), Joined Cases 89/85, 104, 114, 116, 117 and 125-129/85, [1988] E.C.R. 5193, [1987-1988 Transfer Binder] COMMON MKT. REP. (CCH) ¶ 14,491, 928

Ahmed Saeed Flugreisen v. Zentrale, Case 66/86, [1989] E.C.R. 803, [1989] 2 CEC (CCH) 654, 961

Aircapital Cablevision, Inc. v. Starlink Communs. Group, 634 F. Supp. 316 (D. Kan. 1986), 1001, 1054

Air Freight Haulage Co. v. Ryd-Air, Inc., 1978-2 Trade Cas. (CCH) ¶ 62,231 (S.D.N.Y. 1978), *aff'd*, 603 F.2d 1 (2d Cir.), *cert. denied*, 444 U.S. 864 (1979), 185

A.I. Root Co. v. Computer/Dynamics, Inc., 806 F.2d 673 (6th Cir. 1986), 151, 152, 155, 831

Airweld, Inc. v. Airco, Inc., 742 F.2d 1184 (9th Cir. 1984), *cert. denied*, 469 U.S. 1213 (1985), 135, 148, 409, 682

Akron Presform Mold Co. v. McNeil Corp., 496 F.2d 230 (6th Cir.), *cert. denied*, 419 U.S. 997 (1974), 681, 689, 693

Akzo Chemie BV v. Commission, Case C-62/86, (Eur. Comm. Ct. J. 1991), 956

Akzo v. United States Int'l Trade Comm'n, 808 F.2d 1471 (Fed. Cir. 1986), *cert. denied*, 482 U.S. 909 (1987), 824

Alabama Homeowners, Inc. v. Findahome Corp., 640 F.2d 670 (5th Cir. 1981), 29

Alabama Power Co. v. Alabama Elec. Coop., 394 F.2d 672 (5th Cir. 1968), *cert. denied*, 404 U.S. 1047 (1972), 964, 965

Alabama Power Co. v. FPC, 511 F.2d 383 (D.C. Cir. 1974), 1056

Alabama Power Co. v. NRC, 692 F.2d 1362 (11th Cir. 1982), *cert. denied*, 464 U.S. 816 (1983), 1082, 1088

Alabama v. Blue Bird Body Co., 573 F.2d 309 (5th Cir. 1978), 604, 712, 726, 728

Aladdin Oil Co. v. Texaco, Inc., 603 F.2d 1107 (5th Cir. 1979), 118, 180, 181, 192, 702, 703

Alamo Rent-A-Car, Inc., 111 F.T.C. 644 (1989), 475

Alan's of Atlanta, Inc. v. Minolta Corp., 903 F.2d 1414 (11th Cir. 1990), 413, 417, 438, 444, 451

Alaska Airlines v. United Airlines, 948 F.2d 536 (9th Cir. 1991), 249, 252

Alaska Sleeping Bag Co., 80 F.T.C. 665 (1972), 479

Alaska v. Chevron Chem. Co., 669 F.2d 1299 (9th Cir. 1982), 604

Alaska v. U.S. Dep't of Transp., 868 F.2d 441 (D.C. Cir. 1989), 1153

Al Barnett & Son v. Outboard Marine Corp., 64 F.R.D. 43 (D. Del. 1974), 719, 724

Alberta Gas Chems. Ltd. v. E.I. du Pont de Nemours & Co., 826 F.2d 1235 (3d Cir. 1987), *cert. denied*, 486 U.S. 1059 (1988), 322, 331, 332, 363, 364, 706

Alberto-Culver Co. v. Andrea Dumon, Inc., 295 F. Supp. 1155 (N.D. Ill. 1969), *aff'd in part and rev'd in part*, 466 F.2d 705 (7th Cir. 1972), 848

Alberto-Culver Co. v. Andrea Dumon, Inc., 466 F.2d 705 (7th Cir. 1972), 847

Albert Pick-Barth Co. v. Mitchell Woodbury Corp., 57 F.2d 96 (1st Cir.), *cert. denied*, 286 U.S. 552 (1932), 95

Albertson's Inc., 110 F.T.C. 1 (1987), 357, 516

Albertson's, Inc. v. Amalgamated Sugar Co., 62 F.R.D. 43 (D. Utah 1973), *aff'd in relevant part*, 503 F.2d 459 (10th Cir. 1974), 719

Albertson's, Inc. v. Amalgamated Sugar Co., 503 F.2d 459 (10th Cir. 1974), 712, 719, 736

Alberty v. FTC, 182 F.2d 36 (D.C. Cir.), *cert. denied*, 340 U.S. 818 (1950), 491

Albrecht v. Herald Co., 367 F.2d 517 (8th Cir. 1966), *rev'd*, 390 U.S. 145 (1968), 104

Albrecht v. Herald Co., 390 U.S. 145 (1968), 11, 15, 16, 17, 22, 101, 103, 104, 109, 652

Albrecht v. Herald Co., 452 F.2d 124 (8th Cir. 1971), 670, 671

Alcatel/Telettra, 34 O.J. Eur. Comm. (No. L 122) 48 (1991), 960

Alcon Labs., Inc., [1983-1987 Complaints & Orders Transfer Binder] Trade Reg. Rep. (CCH) ¶ 22,175 (July 27, 1984), 352

Aldens, Inc., 92 F.T.C. 901 (1978), 538

Alders v. AFA Corp., 353 F. Supp. 654 (S.D. Fla. 1973), *aff'd*, 490 F.2d 990 (5th Cir. 1974), 99

Alexander's, Inc., 89 F.T.C. 531 (1977), 537

Alexander v. National Farmers Org., 637 F. Supp. 1487 (W.D. Mo. 1986), 767, 781

Alexander v. National Farmers Org., 687 F.2d 1173 (8th Cir. 1982), *cert. denied*, 416 U.S. 937 (1983), 272, 667, 776, 998, 1001, 1005, 1015, 1026, 1027

Alexander v. National Farmers Org., 696 F.2d 1210 (8th Cir. 1982), *cert. denied*, 461 U.S. 938 (1983), 785

Alfred Bell & Co. v. Catalda Fine Arts, Inc., 74 F. Supp. 973 (S.D.N.Y. 1947), *interlocutory decree aff'd*, 86 F. Supp. 399 (S.D.N.Y. 1949), *modified*, 191 F.2d 99 (2d Cir. 1951), 896

Alfred Dunhill, Ltd. v. Interstate Cigar Co., 499 F.2d 232 (2d Cir. 1974), 645

Alfred Dunhill of London, Inc. v. Republic of Cuba, 425 U.S. 682 (1976), 900, 903, 907, 908

Al George, Inc. v. Envirotech Corp., 939 F.2d 1271 (5th Cir. 1991), 682

Alhambra Motor Parts, 57 F.T.C. 1007 (1960), *rev'd and remanded*, 309 F.2d 213 (9th Cir. 1962), *on remand*, 68 F.T.C. 1039 (1965), 430

Alhambra Motor Parts, 68 F.T.C. 1039 (1965), 424, 425, 448

Alimenta, Inc. v. Anheuser-Busch Co., 99 F.R.D. 309 (N.D. Ga. 1983), 752

Alioto & Alioto v. E.F. Hutton & Co., 484 U.S. 823 (1987), 789

Allegheny Pepsi-Cola Bottling Co. v. Mid-Atlantic Coca-Cola Bottling Co., 690 F.2d 411 (4th Cir. 1982), 669, 671, 672

Allen Bradley Co. v. Local 3, IBEW, 325 U.S. 797 (1945), 1025

Allen-Myland, Inc. v. IBM, 693 F. Supp. 262 (E.D. Pa. 1988), 144, 151, 152, 153, 154, 155, 158, 163

Allen-Myland, Inc. v. IBM, 746 F. Supp. 520 (E.D. Pa. 1990), 575

Allen Pen Co. v. Springfield Photo Mount Co., 653 F.2d 17 (1st Cir. 1981), 431, 434, 437

Allgeyer v. Louisiana, 165 U.S. 578 (1897), 628

Alliance Shippers v. Southern Pac. Transp. Co., 673 F. Supp. 1005 (C.D. Cal. 1986), *aff'd*, 858 F.2d 567 (9th Cir. 1988), 409

Alliance Shippers, Inc. v. Southern Pac. Transp. Co., 858 F.2d 567 (9th Cir. 1988), 42, 114, 1134

Allied Accessories & Auto Parts Co. v. General Motors Corp., 825 F.2d 971 (6th Cir. 1987), 422, 423, 424, 450

Allied Bank Int'l v. Banco Credito Agricola de Cartago, 757 F.2d 516 (2d Cir.), *cert. dismissed*, 473 U.S. 934 (1985), 903

Allied Int'l, Inc. v. International Longshoreman's Ass'n, 640 F.2d 1368 (1st Cir. 1981), *aff'd*, 456 U.S. 212 (1982), 78, 94

Allied Research Prods., Inc. v. Heatbath Corp., 300 F. Supp. 656 (N.D. Ill. 1969), 824

Allied Tube & Conduit Corp. v. Indian Head, Inc., 486 U.S. 492 (1988), 40, 84, 87, 88, 993, 994, 997, 1002, 1004, 1006, 1007, 1009, 1010, 1013

Allis-Chalmers Mfg. Co. v. White Consol. Indus., 414 F.2d 506 (3d Cir. 1969), *cert. denied*, 396 U.S. 1009 (1970), 167, 334, 336

Allis-Chalmers Mfg. v. Commonwealth Edison Co., 315 F.2d 558 (7th Cir. 1963), 688

Alloy Int'l Co. v. Hoover-NSK Bearings Co., 635 F.2d 1222 (7th Cir. 1980), 40, 180

All-State Indus. v. FTC, 423 F.2d 423 (4th Cir.), *cert. denied*, 400 U.S. 828 (1970), 491

Ally Gargano/MCA Advertising, Ltd. v. Cooke Properties, Inc., 1989-2 Trade Cas. (CCH) ¶ 68,817 (S.D.N.Y. 1989), 103

Almeda Mall, Inc. v. Houston Lighting & Power Co., 615 F.2d 343 (5th Cir.), *cert. denied*, 449 U.S. 870 (1980), 188, 218

Aloha Airlines v. CAB, 598 F.2d 250 (D.C. Cir. 1979), 1156, 1158

Aloha Airlines v. Hawaiian Airlines, 349 F. Supp. 1064 (D. Haw. 1972), *aff'd*, 489 F.2d 203 (9th Cir. 1973), *cert. denied*, 417 U.S. 913 (1974), 1024

Aloha Airlines v. Hawaiian Airlines, 489 F.2d 203 (9th Cir. 1973), *cert. denied*, 417 U.S. 913 (1974), 1156

Alpert's Newspaper Delivery, Inc. v. New York Times Co., 1988-2 Trade Cas. (CCH) ¶ 68,220 (E.D.N.Y. 1988), *aff'd*, 876 F.2d 266 (2d. Cir. 1989), 108, 776

Alpert's Newspaper Delivery Inc. v. New York Times Co., 876 F.2d 266 (2d Cir. 1989), 733

Alpha Distrib. Co. v. Jack Daniels Distillery, 454 F.2d 442 (9th Cir. 1972), *cert. denied*, 419 U.S. 842 (1974), 50,118

Alpha Shoe Serv. v. Fleming Cos., 849 F.2d 352 (8th Cir.), *cert. denied*, 488 U.S. 942 (1988), 663

Altemose Constr. Co. v. Building and Constr. Trades Council, 751 F.2d 653 (3d Cir. 1985), *cert. denied*, 475 U.S. 1107 (1986), 1126

Alterman Foods, Inc. v. FTC, 497 F.2d 993 (5th Cir. 1974), 438, 442, 445, 459, 522

Althoff's, Inc. v. Sterling Faucet Co., 1972 Trade Cas. (CCH) ¶ 74,066 (N.D. Ill. 1972), 684

Aluminum, 28 O.J. Eur. Comm. (No. L 92) 1 (1985), [1982-1985 Transfer Binder] COMMON MKT. REP. (CCH) ¶ 10,658, 932

Aluminum Co. of Am. v. ICC, 761 F.2d 746 (D.C. Cir. 1985), 1135

Aluminum Co. of Am. v. Tandet, 235 F. Supp. 111 (D. Conn. 1964), 408

Aluminum Co. of Am. v. United States Dep't of Justice, 444 F. Supp. 1342 (D.D.C. 1978), 560

Aluminum Shapes, Inc. v. K-A Liquidating Co., 290 F. Supp. 356 (W.D. Pa. 1968), 170

ALW, Inc. v. United Air Lines, 510 F.2d 52 (9th Cir. 1975), 205

Alyeska Pipeline Serv. v. Wilderness Soc'y, 421 U.S. 240 (1975), 781

Amalgamated Meat Cutters, Local 476 v. Wetterau Foods, Inc., 597 F.2d 133 (8th Cir. 1979), 1124

Amalgamated Util. Workers v. Consolidated Edison Co., 309 U.S. 261 (1940), 542

AM&S Europe v. Commission, Case 155/79, [1982] E.C.R. 1575, [1979-1981 Transfer Binder] COMMON MKT. REP. (CCH) ¶ 8757, 919

Ambook Enters. v. Time, Inc., 464 F. Supp. 1127, (S.D.N.Y.), *aff'd in part and rev'd in part*, 612 F.2d 604 (2d Cir. 1979), *cert. dismissed*, 448 U.S. 914 (1980), 646

Ambook Enters. v. Time, Inc., 612 F.2d 604 (2d Cir. 1979), *cert. dismissed*, 448 U.S. 914 (1980), 410, 722, 779

Ambulance Serv. v. Nevada Ambulance Servs., 819 F.2d 910 (9th Cir. 1987), 986

AM/COMM Sys. v. AT&T, 101 F.R.D. 317 (E.D. Pa. 1984), 714, 717, 718, 731

American Academic Suppliers v. Beckley-Cardy, Inc., 699 F. Supp. 152 (N.D. Ill. 1988), 448

American Academic Suppliers v. Beckley-Cardy, Inc., 922 F.2d 1317 (7th Cir. 1991), 215, 227, 228, 229, 233, 237, 263

American Airlines v. North American Airlines, 351 U.S. 79 (1956), 1154, 1156

American Bakeries Co. v. Gourmet Bakers, Inc., 515 F. Supp. 977 (D. Md. 1981), 395

American Banana Co. v. United Fruit Co., 213 U.S. 347 (1909), 856, 902, 903, 905

American Bankers Club v. American Express Co., 1977-1 Trade Cas. (CCH) ¶ 61,247 (D.D.C. 1977), 408, 409

American Bearing Co. v. Litton Indus., 540 F. Supp. 1163 (E.D. Pa. 1982), 674

American Bonded Warehouse Corp. v. Compagnie Nationale Air France, 653 F. Supp. 861 (N.D. Ill. 1987), 901

American Brake Shoe Co., 67 F.T.C. 1387 (1965), 511

American Bus. Sys. v. Panasonic Indus. Co., 1989-1 Trade Cas. (CCH) ¶ 68,631 (E.D.La. 1988), *aff'd without published opinion*, 867 F.2d 1426 (5th Cir. 1989), 124, 126, 184

American Can Co. v. A.B. Dick Co., 1983-2 Trade Cas. (CCH) ¶ 65,751 (S.D.N.Y. 1983), 191, 245

American Candle Co., 78 F.T.C. 1158 (1971), 438

American Civil Liberties Union v. FCC, 823 F.2d 1554 (D.C. Cir. 1987), 1050

American Column & Lumber Co. v. United States, 257 U.S. 377 (1921), 67, 71, 74

American Computer Trust Leasing v. Jack Farrell Implement Co., 1991-1 Trade Cas. (CCH) ¶ 69,488 (D. Minn. 1991), 132, 143, 144, 147

American Crystal Sugar Co. v. Cuban-Am. Sugar Co., 152 F. Supp. 387 (S.D.N.Y. 1957), *aff'd*, 259 F.2d 524 (2d Cir. 1958), 198, 280, 281, 293

American Cyanamid Co. v. FTC, 363 F.2d 757 (6th Cir. 1966) *on remand*, 72 F.T.C. 618 (1967), *aff'd sub nom.* Charles Pfizer & Co. v. FTC, 401 F.2d 574 (6th Cir. 1968), *cert. denied*, 394 U.S. 920 (1969), 491, 521, 522, 807, 854

American Dairy Ass'n, 83 F.T.C. 518 (1973), 473

American Dermatologists' Medical Group v. Collagen Corp., 595 F. Supp. 79 (N.D. Ill. 1984), 704

American Fed of Musicians v. Carroll, 391 U.S. 99 (1968), 1120, 1121

American Fin. Servs. Ass'n v. FTC, 767 F.2d 957 (D.C. Cir. 1985), *cert. denied*, 475 U.S. 1011 (1986), 487, 529, 530

American Floral Servs. v. Florists' Transworld Delivery Ass'n, 633 F. Supp. 201 (N.D. Ill. 1986), 39, 53, 84, 87, 186, 380, 381, 383

American Football League v. NFL, 323 F.2d 124 (4th Cir. 1963), 209

American Gas Ass'n v. FERC, 888 F.2d 136 (D.C. Cir. 1989), 1060

American Gen. Ins. Co., 89 F.T.C. 557 (1977), *rev'd and remanded*, 589 F.2d 462 (9th Cir. 1979), *complaint dismissed*, 97 F.T.C. 339 (1981), 1116

American Gen. Ins. Co. v. FTC, 359 F. Supp. 887 (S.D. Tex. 1973), *aff'd on other grounds*, 496 F.2d 197 (5th Cir. 1974), 1116

American Gen. Ins. Co. v. FTC, 496 F.2d 197 (5th Cir. 1974), 523

American Gen. Ins. Co. v. FTC, 589 F.2d 462 (9th Cir. 1979), 510

American Hoechst Corp., 110 F.T.C. 4 (1988), 345, 347, 348, 349

American Hoist & Derrick Co. v. Sowa & Sons, 725 F.2d 1350, (Fed. Cir.), *cert. denied*, 469 U.S. 821 (1984), 801, 802, 808, 809, 810, 851

American Home Assurance Co. v. Insurance Corp. of Ireland, 603 F. Supp. 636 (S.D.N.Y 1984), 879

American Home Prods. Corp., 98 F.T.C. 136 (1981), *enforced as modified*, 695 F.2d 681 (3d Cir. 1982), 465, 492

American Home Prods. Corp. v. FTC, 402 F.2d 232 (6th Cir. 1968), 494

American Home Prods. Corp. v. FTC, 695 F.2d 681 (3d Cir. 1982), 465, 474, 480, 489, 492, 521, 522

American Hosp. Supply Corp. v. Hospital Prods. Ltd., 780 F.2d 589 (7th Cir. 1986), 367, 677

American Indus. Contracting, Inc. v. Johns-Manville Corp., 326 F. Supp. 879 (W.D. Pa. 1971), 753, 887, 906

American Infra-Red Radiant Co. v. Lambert Indus., 360 F.2d 977 (8th Cir.), *cert. denied*, 385 U.S. 920 (1966), 813

American Key Corp. v. Cole Nat'l Corp., 762 F.2d 1569 (11th Cir. 1985), 208, 210, 749

American Medical Ass'n, 94 F.T.C. 701 (1979), *enforced as modified*, 638 F.2d 443 (2d Cir. 1980), *aff'd per curiam by an equally divided court*, 455 U.S. 676 (1982), 455, 456, 489, 494, 512

American Medical Ass'n v. FTC, 638 F.2d 443 (2d Cir. 1980), *aff'd per curiam by an equally divided court*, 455 U.S. 676 (1982), 456, 489, 493

American Medical Ass'n v. United States, 317 U.S. 519 (1943), 79

American Medical Int'l, 104 F.T.C. 1 (1984),276, 290, 294, 306, 321, 322, 361

American Medical Int'l, 107 F.T.C. 310 (1986), 346

American Medicinal Prods., Inc. v. FTC, 136 F.2d 426 (9th Cir. 1943), 468

American Medicorp, Inc. v. Humana, Inc., 445 F. Supp. 589 (E.D. Pa. 1977), 290, 300, 365

American Medicorp, Inc. v. Humana, Inc., 445 F. Supp. 573 (E.D. Pa. 1977), 398

American Metal Prods. Co., 60 F.T.C. 1667, *vacated as moot*, 60 F.T.C. 1667 (1962), 424

American Mfrs. Mut. Ins. Co. v. American Broadcasting-Paramount Theatres, 221 F. Supp. 848 (S.D.N.Y. 1963), 138

American Mfrs. Mut. Ins. Co. v. American Broadcasting-Paramount Theatres, 388 F.2d 272 (2d Cir. 1967), 136, 137, 138, 703

American Mfrs. Mut. Ins. Co. v. American Broadcasting-Paramount Theatres, 446 F.2d 1131 (2d Cir. 1971), cert. denied, 404 U.S. 1063 (1972), 144, 146

American Motor Inns v. Holiday Inns, 521 F.2d 1230 (3d Cir. 1975), 45, 48, 49, 55, 56, 77, 121, 128, 169, 172, 177, 700

American Motors Corp. v. FTC, 384 F.2d 247 (6th Cir. 1967) *rev'g* 68 F.T.C. 87 (1965), *cert. denied*, 390 U.S. 1012 (1968), 423, 424, 490

American Motor Specialties Co., 55 F.T.C. 1430 (1959), *aff'd*, 278 F.2d 225 (2d Cir.), *cert. denied*, 364 U.S. 884 (1960), 424, 427, 429, 445, 447

American Motor Specialties Co. v. FTC, 278 F.2d 225 (2d Cir.), *cert. denied*, 364 U.S. 884 (1960), 448

American News Co. v. FTC, 300 F.2d 104 (2d Cir.), *cert. denied*, 371 U.S. 824 (1962), 429, 457, 459

American Oil Co., 60 F.T.C. 1786 (1962), *rev'd*, 325 F.2d 101 (7th Cir. 1963), *cert. denied*, 377 U.S. 954 (1964), 427

American Oil Co. v. McMullin, 508 F.2d 1345 (10th Cir. 1975), 103, 408

American Optometric Ass'n v. FTC, 626 F.2d 896 (D.C. Cir. 1980), 485, 522, 527, 529, 530

American Photocopy Equip. Co. v. Rovico, Inc., 359 F.2d 745 (7th Cir.), *on remand*, 257 F. Supp. 192 (N.D. Ill. 1966), *aff'd*, 384 F.2d 813 (7th Cir. 1967), *cert. denied*, 390 U.S. 945 (1968), 823

American Pipe & Const. Co. v. Utah, 414 U.S. 538 (1974), 693, 695, 697

American Safety Equip. Corp. v. J.P. Maguire & Co., 391 F.2d 821 (2d Cir. 1968), 787, 896

American Securit Co. v. Hamilton Glass Co., 254 F.2d 889 (7th Cir. 1958), 575

American Securit Co. v. Shatterproof Glass Corp., 268 F.2d 769 (3d Cir.), *cert. denied*, 361 U.S. 902 (1959), 575, 814, 835

American Serv. Bureau, 92 F.T.C. 330 (1978), 536

American Soc'y of Internal Medicine, 105 F.T.C. 505 (1985), 64

American Soc'y of Mechanical Eng'rs v. Hydrolevel Corp., 456 U.S. 556 (1982), 87, 795

American Standard, Inc. v. Bendix Corp., 487 F. Supp. 265 (W.D. Mo. 1980), 212, 216

American Standard Life & Accident Ins. Co. v. U.R.L., Inc., 701 F. Supp. 527 (M.D. Pa. 1988), 97, 1113

American Tobacco Co. v. United States, 328 U.S. 781 (1946), 3, 6, 9, 18, 195, 197, 212, 220, 262, 263, 264, 270, 271, 272

American Trucking Ass'ns v. ICC, 656 F.2d 1115 (5th Cir. 1981) 1133, 1134

American Trucking Ass'ns v. ICC, 722 F.2d 1243 (5th Cir.), *cert. denied*, 469 U.S. 930 (1984), 1134

American Vision Centers, Inc. v. Cohen, 711 F. Supp. 721 (E.D.N.Y. 1989), 663

America's Best Cinema Corp. v. Fort Wayne Newspapers, 347 F. Supp. 328 (N.D. Ind. 1972), 94, 184, 191

America West Airlines v. GPA Group, 877 F.2d 793 (9th Cir. 1989), 900

Amernational Indus. v. Action-Tungsram, Inc., 925 F.2d 970 (6th Cir. 1991), 770

Amersham Buchler, 25 O.J. EUR. COMM. (No. L 314) 34 (1982), [1982-1985 Transfer Binder] COMMON MKT. REP. (CCH) ¶ 10,431, 938

Amey, Inc. v. Gulf Abstract & Title, Inc., 758 F.2d 1486 (11th Cir. 1985), *cert. denied*, 475 U.S. 1107 (1986), 73, 136, 139, 158, 159, 163, 172, 173, 176, 660, 681

AMF, Inc., 95 F.T.C. 310 (1980), 485

Amplex of Maryland, Inc. v. Outboard Marine Corp., 380 F.2d 112 (4th Cir. 1967), *cert. denied*, 389 U.S. 1036 (1968), 147, 182, 188

AMREP Corp. v. FTC, 768 F.2d 1171 (10th Cir. 1985), *cert. denied*, 475 U.S. 1034 (1986), 471, 492, 521, 531

Amstar Corp., 83 F.T.C. 659 (1973), 474

AM Stereophonic Broadcasting, 84 F.C.C.2d 960 (1981), 1043

Amtrol, Inc. v. Vent-Rite Valve Corp., 646 F. Supp. 1168 (D. Mass. 1986), 648, 876

Amway Corp., 86 F.T.C. 653 (1975), 514

Amway Corp., 93 F.T.C. 618 (1979), 124, 126, 129

Anaconda Co. v. Crane Co., 411 F. Supp. 1210 (S.D.N.Y.), 281

Anaya v. Las Cruces Sun News, 455 F.2d 670 (10th Cir. 1972), 184, 186

Anaya v. United States, 815 F.2d 1373 (10th Cir. 1987), 754

An Bord Bainne v. Milk Mktg. Bd., [1984] 1 COMMON MKT. L. R. 519 (Q.B.), *aff'd*, [1984] 2 COMMON MKT. L. R. 584 (Eng. C.A.), 920

Andersen v. American Auto Ass'n, 454 F.2d 1240 (9th Cir. 1972), 121

Anderson Foreign Motors, Inc. v. New England Toyota Distribs., 475 F. Supp. 973 (D. Mass. 1979), 131, 137, 138, 146, 157, 161

Anderson Foreign Motors v. New England Toyota Distribs., 492 F. Supp. 1383 (D. Mass. 1980), 405

Anderson v. Home Style Stores, 381 F. Supp. 402 (E.D. Pa. 1974), 133

Anderson v. Home Style Stores, 58 F.R.D. 125 (E.D. Pa. 1972), 713

Anderson v. Liberty Lobby, Inc., 477 U.S. 242 (1986), 702, 704

Anesthesia Advantage, Inc. v. Metz Group, 912 F.2d 397 (10th Cir. 1990), 25

Anheuser-Busch, Inc., 54 F.T.C. 277 (1957), *set aside*, 265 F.2d 677 (7th Cir. 1959), *rev'd*, 363 U.S. 536 (1960), 420

Anheuser-Busch, Inc. v. FTC, 359 F.2d 487 (8th Cir. 1966), 508

Anheuser-Busch, Inc. v. Goodman, 745 F. Supp. 1048 (M.D. Pa. 1990), 973, 980, 984

Ansac, Decision 91/301, 34 O.J. EUR. COMM (No. L 152) 54 (1991), [1991] 2 CEC (CCH) 2071, 933

Ansell, Inc. v. Schmid Labs., 757 F. Supp. 467 (D.N.J.), *aff'd without published opinion*, 941 F.2d 1200 (3d Cir. 1991), 284, 285, 286, 287, 288, 289, 292, 363

Ansul Co. v. Uniroyal, Inc., 306 F. Supp. 541 (S.D.N.Y. 1969), *aff'd in part and rev'd in part and remanded*, 448 F.2d 872 (2d Cir. 1971), *cert. denied*, 404 U.S. 1018 (1972), 119, 121, 821, 833

Ansul Co. v. Uniroyal, Inc., 448 F.2d 872 (2d Cir. 1971), *cert. denied*, 404 U.S. 1018 (1972), 813, 814, 816, 847

Anthony v. Texaco, Inc., 803 F.2d 593 (10th Cir. 1986), 336

AOIP/Beyrard, 19 O.J. EUR. COMM. (No. L 6) 8 (1976), [1976-1978 Transfer Binder] COMMON MKT. REP. (CCH) ¶ 9801, 948

A.O. Smith Corp. v. FTC, 530 F.2d 515 (3d Cir. 1976), 508

Apanewicz v. General Motors Corp., 80 F.R.D. 672 (E.D. Pa. 1978), 721, 722

Apex Elec. Mfg. Co. v. Altorfer Bros., 238 F.2d 867 (7th Cir. 1956), 835, 837

Apex Hosiery Co. v. Leader, 310 U.S. 469 (1940), 1, 30, 46, 47, 54, 62

Apex Oil Co. v. DiMauro, 713 F. Supp. 587 (S.D.N.Y. 1989), 32, 37, 39, 197, 212, 701, 1106

Apex Oil Co. v. DiMauro, 822 F.2d 246 (2d Cir.), *cert. denied*, 484 U.S. 977 (1987), 3, 4, 6, 7, 8, 9, 706

A.P. Hopkins Corp. v. Studebaker Corp., 355 F. Supp. 816 (E.D. Mich. 1972), *aff'd*, 496 F.2d 969 (6th Cir. 1974), 121, 130

Appalachian Coals, Inc. v. United States, 288 U.S. 344 (1933), 18, 56, 390

Appalachian Power Co. v. General Elec. Co., 1976-2 Trade Cas. (CCH) ¶ 61,228 (S.D.N.Y. 1976), 749

Appeal of Starkey, 600 F.2d 1043 (8th Cir. 1979), 771

Application of Chase Manhattan Bank, 297 F.2d 611 (2d Cir. 1962), 887

Application of Linen Supply Cos., 15 F.R.D. 115 (S.D.N.Y. 1953), 563

Arcadia v. Ohio Power Co., 111 S. Ct. 415 (1990), 1078

Arden-Mayfair, Inc., 77 F.T.C. 705 (1970), 432

Arenson v. Board of Trade, 372 F. Supp. 1349 (N.D. Ill. 1974), 1106

Arey v. Lemons, 232 N.C. 531, 61 S.E.2d 596 (1950), 635

ARG/Rover/Unipart, 31 O.J. EUR. COMM. (No. L 45) 34 (1988), [1985-1988 Transfer Binder] COMMON MKT. REP. (CCH) ¶ 10,968, 943

Argus Chem. Corp. v. Fibre Glass-Evercoat Co., 645 F. Supp. 15 (C.D. Cal. 1986), aff'd, 812 F.2d 1381 (Fed. Cir. 1987), 811

Argus Chem. Corp. v. Fibre Glass-Evercoat Co., 759 F.2d 10 (Fed. Cir.), cert. denied, 474 U.S. 903 (1985), 810

Argus Chem. Corp. v. Fibre Glass-Evercoat Co., 812 F.2d 1381 (Fed. Cir. 1987), 258, 809, 810, 851

Argus, Inc. v. Eastman Kodak Co., 552 F. Supp. 589 (S.D.N.Y. 1982), 681, 777

Arizona Pub. Serv. Co. v. United States, 742 F.2d 644 (D.C. Cir. 1984), 1017, 1135

Arizona v. Cook Paint & Varnish Co., 391 F. Supp. 962 (D. Ariz. 1975), aff'd per curiam, 541 F.2d 226 (9th Cir. 1976), cert. denied, 430 U.S. 915 (1977), 73

Arizona v. Maricopa County Medical Soc'y, 457 U.S. 332 (1982), 31, 33, 35, 36, 37, 39, 43, 62, 66, 70, 71, 80, 94, 101, 103, 373, 374, 379, 390

Arizona v. Maricopa County Medical Soc'y, 578 F. Supp. 1262 (D. Ariz. 1984), 608, 783, 785, 786

Arkansas La. Gas Co. v. Hall, 453 U.S. 571 (1981), 239

Ark Dental Supply Co. v. Cavitron Corp., 323 F. Supp. 1145 (E.D. Pa. 1971), aff'd per curiam, 461 F.2d 1093 (3d Cir. 1972), 118

Ark Dental Supply Co. v. Cavitron Corp., 461 F.2d 1093 (3d Cir. 1972), 191, 193

Arkla Inc., No. C-3265 (FTC Oct. 10, 1989), 1067

Arkla Inc., 5 Trade Reg. Rep. ¶ 22,686 (Oct. 10, 1989), 1066

Armco Steel Corp. v. North Dakota, 376 F.2d 206 (8th Cir. 1967), 603, 671, 778

Armstrong Cork, 104 F.T.C. 540 (1984), 110

Armstrong v. Board of School Directors, 616 F.2d 305 (7th Cir. 1980), 741, 742, 743

Arneil v. Ramsey, 550 F.2d 774 (2d Cir. 1977), 696

Arnett v. Gerber Scientific Inc., 566 F. Supp. 1270 (S.D.N.Y. 1983), 363, 644

Arnold Pontiac-GMC, Inc. v. Budd Baer, Inc., 826 F.2d 1335 (3d Cir. 1987), 7, 8, 707

Arnold Pontiac-GMC, Inc. v. General Motors Corp., 700 F. Supp. 838 (W.D. Pa. 1988), 14

Arnold Pontiac-GMC, Inc. v. General Motors Corp., 786 F.2d 564 (3d Cir. 1986), 13, 14, 18, 54, 127

Arnott v. American Oil Co., 609 F.2d 873 (8th Cir. 1979), cert. denied, 446 U.S. 918 (1980), 16, 104, 109, 181

Aronberg v. FTC, 132 F.2d 165 (7th Cir. 1942), 465

Aronson v. Quick Point Pencil Co., 440 U.S. 257 (1979), 826, 850

AROW/BNIC, 25 O.J. EUR. COMM. (No. L 397) 1 (1982), [1982-1985 Transfer Binder] COMMON MKT. REP. (CCH) ¶ 10,458, 931, 932

Arthur Andersen & Co. v. Finesilver, 546 F.2d 338 (10th Cir. 1976), cert denied, 429 U.S. 1096 (1977), 863, 887

Arthur Murray, Inc. v. Reserve Plan, Inc., 406 F.2d 1138 (8th Cir. 1969), 132

Arthur Murray Studio, Inc. v. FTC, 458 F.2d 622 (5th Cir. 1972), 478, 486, 490

Arthur S. Langenderfer, Inc. v. S.E. Johnson Co., 729 F.2d 1050 (6th Cir.), cert. denied, 469 U.S. 1036 (1984), 223, 230, 231, 235, 676, 680

Arthur S. Langenderfer, Inc. v. S.E. Johnson Co., 917 F.2d 1413 (6th Cir. 1990), cert. denied, 112 S. Ct. 51 (1991), 214, 226, 238, 264, 265

Ar-Tik Sys. v. Dairy Queen, Inc., 302 F.2d 496 (3d Cir. 1962), 825

Asahi Metal Ind. Co. v. Superior Court of Cal., 480 U.S. 102 (1987), 872, 873, 875

A.S.B.L., 13 J.O. COMM. EUR. (No. L 153) 14 (1970), [1970-1972 Transfer Binder] COMMON MKT. REP. (CCH) ¶ 9380, 935

Ash Grove Cement Co., 81 F.T.C. 1021 (1972), aff'd sub nom. Ash Grove Cement Co. v. FTC, 577 F.2d 1368 (9th Cir.), cert. denied, 439 U.S. 982 (1978), 531

Ash Grove Cement Co. v. FTC, 577 F.2d 1368 (9th Cir.), cert. denied, 439 U.S. 982 (1978), 330, 359, 521, 522, 531

Ashkanazy v. I. Rokeach & Sons, 757 F. Supp. 1527 (N.D. Ill. 1991), 237, 260

Ashley Meadows Farm v. American Horse Shows Ass'n, 609 F. Supp. 677 (S.D.N.Y. 1985), 38

Aspen Highlands Skiing Corp. v. Aspen Skiing Co., 738 F.2d 1509 (10th Cir. 1984), aff'd, 472 U.S. 585 (1985), 241, 242, 246, 247, 249-50, 666, 673

Aspen Skiing Co. v. Aspen Highlands Skiing Corp., 472 U.S. 585 (1985), 195, 224, 225, 242, 243

Aspen Title & Escrow, Inc. v. Jeld-Wen, Inc., 677 F. Supp. 1477 (D. Or. 1987), 18, 19, 20, 158, 332

Aspinwall Mfg. Co. v. Gill, 32 F. 697 (C.C.D.N.J. 1887), 823

Assam Drug Co. v. Miller Brewing Co., 798 F.2d 311 (8th Cir. 1986), 50, 55, 123, 124, 125, 126, 708

Associated Container Transp. (Austl.) v. United States, 502 F. Supp. 505 (S.D.N.Y. 1980), rev'd, 705 F.2d 53 (2d Cir. 1983), 559

Associated Container Transp. (Austl.) Ltd. v. United States, 705 F.2d 53 (2d Cir. 1983), 558, 902, 903, 904, 908, 912, 914, 1014

Associated Dry Goods Corp., 105 F.T.C. 310 (1985), 536

Associated Elec. Coop. v. Sachs Elec. Co., 1987-1 Trade Cas. (CCH) ¶ 67,567 (W.D. Mo. 1987), 690

Associated Gas Distribs. v. FERC, 824 F.2d 981 (D.C. Cir. 1987), cert. denied, 485 U.S. 1006 (1988), 1059, 1061, 1069

Associated Gen. Contractors, Inc. v. California State Council of Carpenters, 459 U.S. 519 (1983), 659, 660, 661, 668, 1123

Associated Gen. Contractors v. Otter Tail Power Co., 611 F.2d 684 (8th Cir. 1979), 644

Associated Press v. Taft-Ingalls Corp., 340 F.2d 753 (6th Cir.), cert. denied, 382 U.S. 820 (1965), 136, 137

Associated Press v. United States, 326 U.S. 1 (1945), 79, 88, 384, 385

Associated Radio Serv. Co. v. Page Airways, 624 F.2d 1342 (5th Cir. 1980), cert. denied, 450 U.S. 1030 (1981), 97, 672

Association for Intercollegiate Athletics for Women v. NCAA, 735 F.2d 577 (D.C. Cir. 1984), 55, 252, 260, 270, 271

Association of Indep. Dentists, 100 F.T.C. 518 (1982), 69

Association of Indep. Television Stations, Inc. v. College Football Ass'n, 637 F. Supp. 1289 (W.D. Okla. 1986), 39, 41, 52, 86, 390

Association of Nat'l Advertisers, Inc. v. FTC, 627 F.2d 1151 (D.C. Cir. 1979), cert. denied, 447 U.S. 921 (1980), 510

Association of Retail Travel Agents v. Air Transport Ass'n, 1987-1 Trade Cas. (CCH) ¶ 67,449 (D.D.C. 1987), 42, 390

Association of Retail Travel Agents v. Air Transport Ass'n, 635 F. Supp. 534 (D.D.C. 1986), 49, 50

Atalanta Trading Corp. v. FTC, 258 F.2d 365 (2d Cir. 1958), 406, 412, 436, 442

AT&T v. Delta Communs. Corp., 408 F. Supp. 1075 (S.D. Miss. 1976), aff'd, 579 F.2d 972 (5th Cir. 1978), modified, 590 F.2d 100 (5th Cir.), cert. denied, 444 U.S. 926 (1979), 214, 409

AT&T v. Delta Communs. Corp., 590 F.2d 100 (5th Cir.), cert. denied, 444 U.S. 926 (1979), 704

AT&T v. FCC, 832 F.2d 1285 (D.C. Cir. 1987), 1048, 1049

AT&T v. Grady, 594 F.2d 594 (7th Cir. 1978), cert. denied, 440 U.S. 971 (1979), 560

Atari Games Corp. v. Nintendo of Am., Inc., 897 F.2d 1572 (Fed. Cir. 1990), 676, 677, 678, 811, 823, 827

Atari, Inc. v. JS&A Group, 747 F.2d 1422 (Fed. Cir. 1984), 851

Atchison, T. & S.F. Ry. v. Aircoach Transp. Ass'n, 253 F.2d 877 (D.C. Cir. 1958), *cert. denied,* 361 U.S. 930 (1960), 1129, 1139

Atchison, T. & S.F. Ry. v. United States, 597 F.2d 593 (7th Cir. 1979), 1139

ATD Catalogs, Inc., 65 F.T.C. 71 (1964), 440

Athlete's Foot of Delaware, Inc. v. Ralph Libonati Co., 445 F. Supp. 35 (D. Del. 1977), 191, 869

Atlantic City Elec. Co. v. A.B. Chance Co., 313 F.2d 431 (2d Cir. 1963), 757

Atlantic Heel Co. v. Allied Heel Co., 284 F.2d 879 (1st Cir. 1960), 95

Atlantic Prods. Corp., 63 F.T.C. 2237 (1963), 443

Atlantic Ref. Co. v. FTC, 381 U.S. 357 (1965), 132, 458, 522

Atlantic Richfield Co., 89 F.T.C. 330 (1977), 480

Atlantic Richfield Co., 94 F.T.C. 1054 (1979), 324, 349

Atlantic Richfield Co., 5 TRADE REG. REP. (CCH) ¶ 22,878 (Nov. 26, 1990), 324, 349

Atlantic Richfield Co. v. U.S.A. Petroleum Co., 110 S. Ct. 1884 (1990), 66, 105, 223, 227, 363, 650, 651, 652

Atlas Chem. Indus. v. Moraine Prods., 509 F.2d 1 (6th Cir. 1974), 836

Auburn News Co. v. Providence Journal Co., 504 F. Supp. 292 (D.R.I. 1980), *rev'd,* 659 F.2d 273 (1st Cir. 1981), *cert. denied,* 455 U.S. 921 (1982), 203

Auburn News Co. v. Providence Journal Co., 659 F.2d 273 (1st Cir. 1981), *cert. denied,* 455 U.S. 921 (1982), 40, 51, 81, 104, 185, 191, 192, 676, 678

Audubon Life Ins. Co. v. FTC, 543 F. Supp. 1362 (M.D. La. 1982), 507, 508

Aunyx Corp. v. Canon USA, Inc., 1990-2 Trade Cas. (CCH) ¶ 69,201 (D. Mass. 1990), 14, 62, 127

Aurora Cable Communs. v. Jones Intercable, Inc., No. M87-183CA2 (W.D. Mich., complaint filed June 17, 1987), 1053

Aurora Cable Communs. v. Jones Intercable, Inc., 720 F. Supp. 600 (W.D. Mich. 1989), 1007

Aurora Enters. v. NBC, 688 F.2d 689 (9th Cir. 1982), *aff'g* 524 F. Supp. 655 (C.D. Cal. 1981), 661, 686, 691

Austin Mun. Sec., Inc. v. National Ass'n of Sec. Dealers, 757 F.2d 676 (5th Cir. 1985) 1103

Austin v. Blue Cross & Blue Shield, 903 F.2d 1385, (11th Cir. 1990), 660

Australia/Eastern U.S.A. Shipping Conference v. United States, 537 F. Supp. 807 (D.D.C. 1982), *modifying,* 1982-1 Trade Cas. (CCH) ¶ 64,721 (D.D.C. 1981), 913, 1014

Australia/Eastern USA Shipping Conference v. United States, 1981-1 Trade Cas. (CCH) ¶ 63,943 (D.D.C. 1981), *modified,* 537 F. Supp. 807 (D.D.C. 1982), 558, 559

Automatic Canteen Co. of Am. v. FTC, 346 U.S. 61 (1953), 401, 445

Automatic Radio Mfg. Co. v. Ford Motor Co., 272 F. Supp. 744 (D. Mass. 1967), *aff'd,* 390 F.2d 113 (1st Cir.), *cert. denied,* 391 U.S. 914 (1968), 143

Automatic Radio Mfg. Co. v. Ford Motor Co., 390 F.2d 113 (1st Cir.), *cert. denied,* 391 U.S. 914 (1968), 678

Automatic Radio Mfg. Co. v. Hazeltine Research, Inc., 176 F.2d 799 (1st Cir. 1949), *aff'd,* 339 U.S. 827 (1950), 829

Automatic Radio Mfg. Co. v. Hazeltine Research Inc., 339 U.S. 827 (1950), 803, 824, 834, 835

Automobile Importers of Am., Inc. v. Minnesota, 871 F.2d 717 (8th Cir.), *cert. denied,* 493 U.S. 872 (1989), 623

Auton v. Dade City, 783 F.2d 1009 (11th Cir. 1986), 984

Autowest, Inc. v. Peugeot, Inc., 434 F.2d 556 (2d Cir. 1970), 673

Auwood v. Harry Brandt Booking Office, Inc., 850 F.2d 884 (2d Cir. 1988), 673

Avco Fin. Servs., 104 F.T.C. 485 (1984), 532

Aviation Specialties, Inc. v. United Technologies Corp., 568 F.2d 1186 (5th Cir. 1978), 179, 181, 410

Avnet, Inc., 77 F.T.C. 1686 (1970), 511

Avnet, Inc., 82 F.T.C. 391 (1973), *enforced,* 511 F.2d 70 (7th Cir.), *cert. denied* 423 U.S. 833 (1975), 308

Avnet, Inc. v. FTC, 511 F.2d 70 (7th Cir.), *cert. denied,* 423 U.S. 833 (1975), 284, 285

Axelrod v. Saks & Co., 77 F.R.D. 441 (E.D. Pa. 1978), 731, 733
Axis, SpA v. Micafil, Inc., 870 F.2d 1105 (6th Cir. 1989), 551
Aydin Corp. v. Loral Corp., 718 F.2d 897 (9th Cir. 1983), 98, 1001
Aztec Steel Co. v. Florida Steel Corp., 691 F.2d 480 (11th Cir. 1982), *cert. denied*, 460 U.S. 1040
   (1983), 769

B

Babcock & Wilcox Co. v. United Technologies Corp., 435 F. Supp. 1249 (N.D. Ohio 1977), 286,
   335, 363, 663
Bacon v. Texaco, Inc., 503 F.2d 946 (5th Cir. 1974), *cert. denied*, 420 U.S. 1005 (1975), 402, 403
Bailey's Bakery v. Continental Baking Co., 235 F. Supp. 705 (D. Haw. 1964), *aff'd*, 401 F.2d 182
   (9th Cir. 1968), *cert. denied*, 393 U.S. 1086 (1969), 108
Baim & Blank, Inc. v. Philco Corp., 148 F. Supp. 541 (E.D.N.Y. 1957), 408
Bain v. Henderson, 621 F.2d 959 (9th Cir. 1980), 29
Baker-Cammack Hosiery Mills, Inc. v. Davis Co., 181 F.2d 550 (4th Cir.), *cert. denied*, 340 U.S.
   824 (1950), 837
Baker's Aid v. Hussman Foodservice Co., 1988 WL 138254 (E.D.N.Y. Dec. 19, 1988), 764
Baker's Aid v. Hussmann Foodservice Co., 730 F. Supp. 1209 (E.D.N.Y. 1990), 265
Bakers Franchise Corp. v. FTC, 302 F.2d 258 (3d Cir. 1962), 473, 491
Baker v. Carr, 369 U.S. 186 (1962), 902
Baker v. Chagrin Valley Medical Corp., 1985-1 Trade Cas. (CCH) ¶ 66,622 (N.D. Ohio), *appeal
   dismissed*, 719 F.2d 49 (6th Cir. 1985), 682
Baker v. F&F Inv., 420 F.2d 1191 (7th Cir.), *cert. denied*, 400 U.S. 821 (1970), 690, 691, 692
Baker v. Simmons Co., 307 F.2d 458 (1st Cir. 1962), *cert. denied*, 382 U.S. 820 (1965), 160
Baldwin-Lima-Hamilton Corp. v. Tatnall Measuring Sys., 169 F. Supp. 1 (E.D. Pa. 1958), *aff'd
   per curiam*, 268 F.2d 395 (3d Cir.), *cert. denied*, 361 U.S. 894 (1959), 829, 834, 837
Baldwin v. Loew's, Inc., 312 F.2d 387 (7th Cir. 1963), 687
Balian Ice Cream Co. v. Arden Farms Co., 231 F.2d 356 (9th Cir. 1955), *cert. denied*, 350 U.S.
   991 (1956), 419, 427
Ballard v. Blue Shield, 543 F.2d 1075 (4th Cir. 1976), *cert. denied*, 430 U.S. 922 (1977), 27, 28
Ball Memorial Hosp. v. Mutual Hosp. Ins., 603 F. Supp. 1077 (S.D. Ind. 1985), *aff'd*, 784 F.2d
   1325 (7th Cir. 1986), 115
Ball Memorial Hosp. v. Mutual Hosp. Ins., 784 F.2d 1325 (7th Cir. 1986), 51, 215, 217, 224,
   225, 226, 409
Ball v. Paramount Pictures, 4 F.R.D. 194 (W.D. Pa. 1944), 749
Balmoral Cinema, Inc. v. Allied Artists Pictures Corp., 885 F.2d 313 (6th Cir. 1989), 35, 36, 37,
   38, 39, 85
Baltic Int'l Freight Futures Exch., 30 O.J. EUR. COMM. (No. L 222) 24 (1987), [1985-1988
   Transfer Binder] COMMON MKT. REP. (CCH) ¶ 10,908, 936
Baltimore & O.R.R. v. ICC, 826 F.2d 1125 (D.C. Cir. 1987), 1134
Baltimore Gas & Elec. Co. v. United States, 817 F.2d 108 (D.C. Cir. 1987), 1140
Bamford v. Hobbs, 569 F. Supp. 160 (S.D. Tex. 1983), 875, 876
Banana Distrib. v. United Fruit Co., 19 F.R.D. 244 (S.D.N.Y. 1956), 747
Banana Distribs. v. United Fruit Co., 27 F.R.D. 403 (S.D.N.Y. 1961), 793
Banana Serv. Co. v. United Fruit Co., 15 F.R.D. 106 (D. Mass. 1953), 751, 752, 754
Banco Nacional de Cuba v. Sabbatino, 376 U.S. 298 (1964), 902, 903, 907, 908
Banc One Corp., 69 Fed. Res. Bull. 379 (1983), 1094
Bandag, Inc. v. Al Bolser's Tire Stores, 750 F.2d 903 (Fed. Cir. 1984), 851
BankAmerica Corp. v. United States, 462 U.S. 122 (1983), 396, 397, 1099
Bankers Life & Casualty Co. v. Crenshaw, 486 U.S. 71 (1988), 630

Bank of New England Corp., 73 Fed. Res. Bull. 373 (1987), 1096

Banks v. NCAA, 746 F. Supp. 850 (N.D. Ind. 1990), 51, 91

Bantam Books, Inc. v. FTC, 275 F.2d 680 (2d Cir.), *cert. denied*, 364 U.S. 819 (1960), 468

Bantolina v. Aloha Motors, Inc., 75 F.R.D. 26 (D. Haw. 1977), 740

Barber & Ross Co. v. Lifetime Doors, Inc., 810 F.2d 1276 (4th Cir.), *cert. denied*, 484 U.S. 823 (1987), 140, 151, 153, 159, 164, 182, 190

Barber Asphalt Corp. v. La Fera Grecco Contracting Co., 116 F.2d 211 (3d Cir. 1940), 825, 833

Barber-Colman Co. v. National Tool Co., 136 F.2d 339 (6th Cir. 1943), 822

Barber v. Kimbrell's, Inc., 577 F.2d 216 (4th Cir.), *cert. denied*, 439 U.S. 934 (1978), 782

Barkanic v. CAAC, 822 F.2d 11 (2d Cir.), *cert. denied*, 484 U.S. 964 (1987), 900

Barnes Coal Corp. v. Retail Coal Merchants Ass'n, 128 F.2d 645 (4th Cir. l942), 793

Barnosky Oils, Inc. v. Union Oil Co., 582 F. Supp. 1332 (E.D. Mich. 1984), 173, 178

Barnosky Oils, Inc. v. Union Oil Co., 1979-1 Trade Cas. (CCH) ¶ 62,668 (E.D. Mich. 1979), *aff'd*, 665 F.2d 74 (6th Cir. 1981), 430

Barnosky Oils, Inc. v. Union Oil Co., 665 F.2d 74 (6th Cir. 1981), 429, 681

Barnsdall Ref. Corp. v. Birnamwood Oil Co., 32 F. Supp. 308 (E.D. Wis. 1940), 779

Barq's v. Barq's Beverages, Inc., 677 F. Supp. 449 (E.D. La. 1987), 1003

Barr Labs. v. Abbott Labs., 1989-1 Trade Cas. (CCH) ¶ 68,647 (D.N.J. 1989), 176

Barr Rubber Prods. Co. v. Sun Rubber Co., 277 F. Supp. 484, (S.D.N.Y. 1967), *aff'd in part and rev'd in part*, 425 F.2d 1114 (2d Cir.), *cert. denied*, 400 U.S. 878 (1970), 805

Barr v. National Right to Life Comm., 1981-2 Trade Cas. (CCH) ¶ 64,315 (M.D. Fla. 1981), 94

Barry v. Blue Cross, 805 F.2d 866 (9th Cir. 1986), 9, 53, 54, 56, 70

Barry v. St. Paul Fire & Marine Ins. Co., 555 F.2d 3 (1st Cir. 1977), *aff'd*, 438 U.S. 531 (1978), 1117

Barry Wright Corp. v. ITT Grinnell Corp., 724 F.2d 227 (1st Cir. 1983), 55, 176, 177, 231, 235

Bartholomew v. Virginia Chiropractors Ass'n., 612 F.2d 812 (4th Cir. 1979), *cert. denied*, 446 U.S. 938 (1980), 1118

Bartkus v. Illinois, 359 U.S. 121 (1959), 619, 629

Barton's Disposal Serv. v. Tiger Corp., 886 F.2d 1430 (5th Cir. 1989), 991

Bascom Food Prods. Corp. v. Reese Finer Foods, Inc., 715 F. Supp. 616 (D.N.J. 1989), 40, 41, 75, 76, 77, 125, 127, 376, 382, 384

BASF Wyandotte Corp., 100 F.T.C. 261 (1982), 313

Bass Bros. Enters., 107 F.T.C. 303 (1986), 349

Bass Bros. Enters., 108 F.T.C. 51 (1986), 352

Bass v. Gulf Oil, 1970 Trade Cas. (CCH) ¶ 73,039 (S.D. Miss. 1969), 747

BAT Cirgaretten-Fabriken GmbH, Case 35/83, [1985] E.C.R. 363, [1983-1985 Transfer Binder] COMMON MKT. REP. (CCH) ¶ 14,151, 945

Bateman Eichler, Hill Richards, Inc. v. Berner, 472 U.S. 299 (1985), 697

Bateman v. Ford Motor Co., 302 F.2d 63 (3d Cir. 1962), 646

Bates v. State Bar of Ariz., 433 U.S. 350 (1977), 485, 492, 529, 967

B.A.T. Indus., 104 F.T.C. 852 (1984), 283, 284, 288, 292, 294, 306, 323, 325, 326, 327

Battle v. Liberty Nat'l Life Ins. Co., 493 F.2d 39 (5th Cir. 1974), *cert. denied*, 419 U.S. 1110 (1975), 169

Battle v. Lubrizol Corp., 513 F. Supp. 995 (E.D. Mo. 1981), *aff'd by an equally divided court upon reh'g en banc sub nom.* Battle v. Watson, 712 F.2d 1238 (8th Cir. 1983), *cert. denied*, 466 U.S. 931 (1984), 55

Baudes v. Harlow & Jones, Inc., 852 F.2d 661 (2d Cir. 1988), 907

Bauer & Cie v. O'Donnell, 229 U.S. 1 (1913), 813

Baughman v. Cooper-Jarrett, Inc., 530 F.2d 529 (3d Cir.), *cert. denied*, 429 U.S. 825 (1976), 781

Baughman v. Wilson Freight Forwarding, 583 F.2d 1208 (3d Cir. 1978), 783, 784

Baum v. Investors Diversified Servs., 409 F.2d 872 (7th Cir. 1969), 409, 410

Baxley-DeLamar Monuments, Inc. v. American Cemetery Ass'n, 843 F.2d 1154 (8th Cir. 1988), 152, 154, 270

Baxley-DeLamar Monuments, Inc. v. American Cemetery Ass'n, 938 F.2d 846 (8th Cir. 1991), 153, 154

Baxter Travenol Labs. v. LeMay, 514 F. Supp. 1156 (S.D. Ohio 1981), *appeal dismissed*, 708 F.2d 721 (6th Cir. 1982), 761

Baxter Travenol Labs. v. LeMay, 536 F. Supp. 247 (S.D. Ohio 1982), 774, 1004

Bay City-Abrahams Bros. v. Estee Lauder, Inc., 375 F. Supp. 1206 (S.D.N.Y. 1974), 439

Bayer AG, 95 F.T.C. 254 (1980), 349

Bayer/Gist-Brocades, 19 O.J. Eur. Comm. (No. L 30) 13 (1976), [1976-1978 Transfer Binder] Common Mkt. Rep. (CCH) ¶ 9814, 934

Bayerische Motoren Werke AG, 18 O.J. Eur. Comm. (No. L 29) 1 (1974), [1973-1975 Transfer Binder] Common Mkt. Rep. (CCH) ¶ 9701, 941

Bayo-n-ox, Decision 90/38, 33 O.J. Eur. Comm. (No. L 21) 71 (1990), [1990] 1 CEC (CCH) 2066, *appeal dismissed*, Bayer AG v. Commission, Case T-12/90, (Ct. First Instance 1991), 938

Bayou Bottling, Inc. v. Dr. Pepper Co., 725 F.2d 300 (5th Cir.), *cert. denied*, 469 U.S. 833 (1984), 233, 667

Baysoy v. Jessop Steel Co.,90 F. Supp. 303 (W.D. Pa. 1950), 449, 865

BBC Brown Boveri, Decision 88/541, 31 O.J. Eur. Comm. (No. L 301) 68 (1988), [1989] 1 CEC (CCH) 2234, 929

B. B. Chem. Co. v. Ellis, 117 F.2d 829 (1st Cir. 1941), *aff'd*, 314 U.S. 495 (1942), 832, 833

B. B. Chem. Co. v. Ellis, 314 U.S. 495 (1942), 813, 814, 816, 832, 833

BBC v. Commission, Case T-70/89 (Ct. First Instance 1991), 944, 952, 953, 956

BBD Transp. Co. v. U.S. Steel Corp., 1976-2 Trade Cas. (CCH) ¶ 61,079 (N.D. Cal. 1976), 132

BBI/Boosey & Hawkes, 30 O.J. Eur. Comm. (No. L 286) 36 (1987), [1985-1988 Transfer Binder] Common Mkt. Rep. (CCH) ¶ 10,920, 920

B.C. Recreational Indus. v. First Nat'l Bank, 639 F.2d 828 (1st Cir. 1981), 1098

Beach v. Viking Sewing Mach. Co., 784 F.2d 746 (6th Cir. 1986), 123, 126, 187

Beard v. Parkview Hosp., 912 F.2d 138 (6th Cir. 1990), 131, 173

Bear Mill Mfg. Co. v. FTC, 98 F.2d 67 (2d Cir. 1938), 477

Beatrice Foods Co., 67 F.T.C. 473 (1965), *modified*, 1967 Trade Cas. (CCH) ¶ 72,124 (9th Cir. 1967), 276, 308, 460

Beatrice Foods Co., 76 F.T.C. 719 (1969), *aff'd sub nom*. Kroger Co. v. FTC, 438 F.2d 1372 (6th Cir.), *cert. denied*, 404 U.S. 871 (1971), 411, 416, 425

Beatrice Foods Co., 86 F.T.C. 1 (1975), *aff'd*, 540 F.2d 303 (7th Cir. 1976), 283, 324, 335

Beatrice Foods Co., 101 F.T.C. 733 (1983), 352

Beatrice Foods Co. v. FTC, 1966 Trade Cas. (CCH) ¶71,733 (D.C. Cir. 1966), 508

Beatrice Foods Co. v. FTC, 540 F.2d 303 (7th Cir. 1976), 283, 284, 285, 286

Beauford v. Helmsley, 740 F. Supp. 201 (S.D.N.Y. 1990), 132, 144

Beau Prods. v. Permagrain Prods., 97 F.R.D. 50 (M.D. Pa. 1983), 768, 769, 770

Becker v. Egypt News Co., 713 F.2d 363 (8th Cir. 1983), 223, 241

Beckman Instruments, Inc. v. Technical Dev. Corp., 433 F.2d 55 (7th Cir. 1970), *cert. denied*, 401 U.S. 976 (1971), 835

Bedford Cut Stone Co. v. Journeymen Stone Cutters' Ass'n, 274 U.S. 37 (1927), 1119

Beecham/Parke-Davis, 22 O.J. Eur. Comm. (No. L 70) 11 (1979), [1978-1981 Transfer Binder] Common Mkt. Rep. (CCH) ¶ 10,121, 934, 935

Beech Cinema v. Twentieth Century Fox Film Corp., 480 F. Supp. 1195 (S.D.N.Y. 1979), *aff'd*, 622 F.2d 1106 (2d Cir. 1980), 783

Béguelin Import Co. v. G.L. Import Export SA, Case 22/71, [1971] E.C.R. 949, [1971-1973 Transfer Binder] Common Mkt. Rep. (CCH) ¶ 8149, 928, 931

Behagen v. Amateur Basketball Ass'n, 744 F.2d 731 (10th Cir. 1984), *cert. denied,* 471 U.S. 1010 (1985), 873

Behagen v. Amateur Basketball Ass'n, 884 F.2d 524 (10th Cir. 1989), *cert. denied*, 110 S. Ct. 1947 (1990), 1019

Beineman v. City of Chicago, 838 F.2d 962 (7th Cir. 1988), *cert. denied*, 490 U.S. 1080 (1989), 737

Beker Indus. Corp. v. Transammonia, Inc., 1975-2 Trade Cas. (CCH) ¶ 60,503 (N.Y. Sup. Ct. 1975), 634

Bela Seating Co. v. Poloron Prods., Inc., 297 F. Supp. 489 (N.D. Ill. 1968), *aff'd*, 438 F.2d 733 (7th Cir.), *cert. denied*, 403 U.S. 922 (1971), 824, 829

Bela Seating Co. v. Poloron Prods., Inc., 438 F.2d 733 (7th Cir.), *cert. denied*, 403 U.S. 922 (1971), 824, 825

Belasco v. Commission, Case 246/86, [1989] E.C.R. 2117, [1990] 2 CEC (CCH) 912, 929

Belfiore v. New York Times Co., 654 F. Supp. 842 (D. Conn. 1986), *aff'd*, 826 F.2d 177 (2d Cir. 1987), *cert. denied*, 484 U.S. 1067 (1988), 16

Belfiore v. New York Times Co., 826 F.2d 177 (2d Cir. 1987), *cert. denied*, 484 U.S. 1067 (1988), 13, 22, 108, 110, 199, 707

Belgian Banking Ass'n, 30 O.J. EUR. COMM. (No. L 7) 27 (1987), [1985-1988 Transfer Binder] COMMON MKT. REP. (CCH) ¶ 10,847, 936

Belgische Radio en Tèlèvisie v. SABAM, Case 127/73, [1974] E.C.R. 51, [1974 Transfer Binder] COMMON MKT. REP. (CCH) ¶ 8269, 922, 957

Belk-Avery, Inc. v. Henry I. Siegel Co., 457 F. Supp. 1330 (M.D. Ala. 1978), 108

Bellam v. Clayton County Hosp. Auth., 758 F. Supp. 1488 (N.D. Ga. 1990), 92, 173

Bell & Howell Co., 95 F.T.C. 761 (1980), 499

Belliston v. Texaco, Inc., 455 F.2d 175 (10th Cir.), *cert. denied*, 408 U.S. 928 (1972), 72, 146, 403, 418

Bellsouth Advertising & Publishing Corp. v. Donnelley Information Publishing, 719 F. Supp. 1551 (S.D. Fla. 1988), *aff'd*, 933 F.2d 952 (11th Cir. 1991), 247, 248

Bellsouth Advertising & Publishing Corp. v. Donnelley Information Publishing, 933 F.2d 952 (11th Cir. 1991), 846

Bell v. Cherokee Aviation Corp., 660 F.2d 1123 (6th Cir. 1981), 139, 145, 146, 152, 153, 154, 669

Beltone Elecs. Corp., 100 F.T.C. 68 (1982), 124, 125, 126, 172, 175, 177, 178, 179

Beltronics, Inc. v. Eberline Instrument Corp., 509 F.2d 1316 (10th Cir. 1974), *cert. denied*, 421 U.S. 1000 (1975), 179

Bement v. National Harrow Co., 186 U.S. 70 (1902), 801, 821, 827

Bender v. Hearst Corp., 152 F. Supp. 569, (D. Conn. 1957), *aff'd*, 263 F.2d 360 (2d Cir. 1959), 279

Bender v. Southland Corp., 749 F.2d 1205 (6th Cir. 1984), 17, 108, 109

Bendix Corp., 77 F.T.C. 731 (1970), *remanded*, 450 F.2d 534 (6th Cir. 1971), *consent order entered*, 84 F.T.C. 1291 (1974) 286, 328

Bendix Corp., 84 F.T.C. 1291 (1974), 344

Bendix Corp., 107 F.T.C. 60 (1986), 351

Bendix Corp. v. Balax, Inc., 471 F.2d 149 (7th Cir. 1972), *cert. denied*, 414 U.S. 819 (1973), 811, 836

Beneficial Corp., 86 F.T.C. 119 (1975), *modified and enforced*, 542 F.2d 611 (3d Cir. 1976), *cert. denied*, 430 U.S. 983 (1977), 486

Beneficial Corp. v. FTC, 542 F.2d 611 (3d Cir. 1976), *cert. denied*, 430 U.S. 983 (1977), 464, 465, 470, 486, 491, 493, 494, 520

Benger Laboratories v. R.K. Laros Co., 209 F. Supp. 639 (E.D. Pa. 1962), *aff'd per curiam*, 317 F.2d 455 (3d Cir.), *cert. denied*, 375 U.S. 833 (1963), 829

Ben Hur Coal Co. v. Wells, 242 F.2d 481 (10th Cir.), *cert. denied*, 354 U.S. 910 (1957), 451

Bennett v. Behring Corp., 629 F.2d 393 (5th Cir. 1980), 738

Bennett v. Behring Corp., 737 F.2d 982 (11th Cir. 1984), 742, 743

Bennett v. FTC, 200 F.2d 362 (D.C. Cir. 1952), 465

Benrus Watch Co. v. FTC, 352 F.2d 313 (8th Cir. 1965), *cert. denied*, 384 U.S. 939 (1966), 471, 475, 489, 521

Benson and Ford, Inc. v. Wanda Petroleum Co., 833 F.2d 1172 (5th Cir. 1987), 777

Benton & Bowles, Inc., 88 F.T.C. 1 (1976), 481

Benton, Benton & Benton v. Louisiana Pub. Facilities Auth., 897 F.2d 198 (5th Cir. 1990), *cert. denied*, 111 S. Ct. 1619 (1991), 980, 986

Bergen Drug Co. v. Parke, Davis & Co.,307 F.2d 725 (3d Cir. 1962), 678

Bergjans Farm Dairy Co. v. Sanitary Milk Producers, 241 F. Supp. 476 (E.D. Mo. 1965), *aff'd*, 368 F.2d 679 (8th Cir. 1966), 1026

Berkey Photo, Inc. v. Eastman Kodak Co., 603 F.2d 263 (2d Cir. 1979), *cert. denied*, 444 U.S. 1093 (1980), 191, 195, 196, 215, 220, 221, 245, 251, 252, 253, 254, 255, 256, 669, 674, 676

Berlenbach v. Anderson & Thompson Ski Co., 329 F.2d 782 (9th Cir.), *cert. denied*, 379 U.S. 830 (1964), 814, 816, 828

Berman's Inc. v. Great Scott Super Markets, Inc., 433 F. Supp. 343 (E.D. Mich. 1975), 172

Berman v. IBM, 1991-2 Trade Cas. (CCH) ¶ 69,585 (S.D.N.Y. 1991), 133, 661

Berning v. Gooding, 820 F.2d 1550 (9th Cir. 1987), 1025

Bernstein v. NV Nederlandsche-Amerikaansche Stoomvaart-Maatschappij, 210 F.2d 375 (2d Cir. 1954), 908

Bernstein v. Universal Pictures, 79 F.R.D. 59 (S.D.N.Y. 1978), 773

Bernstein v. Van Heyghen Frères, SA, 163 F.2d 246 (2d Cir.), *cert. denied*, 332 U.S. 772 (1947), 906, 907

Bessemer & L.E.R.R. v. ICC, 691 F.2d 1104 (3d Cir. 1982), *cert. denied*, 462 U.S. 1110 (1983), 1135

Best Brands Beverage, Inc. v. Falstaff Brewing Corp., 842 F.2d 578 (2d Cir. 1987), 413, 416

Betaseed, Inc. v. U & I Inc., 681 F.2d 1203 (9th Cir. 1982), 135, 144, 167, 168, 336

Bethlehem Steel Corp. v. Fishbach & Moore, Inc., 641 F. Supp. 271 (E.D. Pa. 1986), 690

Beutler Sheetmetal Works v. McMorgan & Co., 616 F. Supp. 453 (N.D. Cal. 1985), 15

Beverage Distribs. v. Olympia Brewing Co., 440 F.2d 21 (9th Cir. 1971), 188

Beverage Mgmt. v. Coca-Cola Bottling Corp., 653 F. Supp. 1144 (S.D. Ohio 1986), 176, 246

Beverly v. United States, 468 F.2d 732 (5th Cir. 1972), 567

Beyer Farms v. Brown, 721 F. Supp. 644 (D.N.J. 1989), 636

B.F. Goodrich Co., 110 F.T.C. 207 (1988), 292, 306, 309, 310, 313

B.F. Goodrich Co., 50 F.T.C. 622 (1954), 421, 424

Bhan v. NME Hosps., 669 F. Supp. 998 (E.D. Cal. 1987), *aff'd*, 929 F.2d 1404 (9th Cir.), *cert. denied*, 112 S. Ct. 617 (1991), 24, 199

Bhan v. NME Hosps., 772 F.2d 1467 (9th Cir. 1985), 648

Bhan v. NME Hosps., 929 F.2d 1404 (9th Cir.), *cert. denied*, 112 S. Ct. 617 (1991), 38, 45, 46, 49, 56

Bichel Optical Labs v. Marquette Nat'l Bank, 336 F. Supp. 1368 (D. Minn. 1971), *aff'd*, 487 F.2d 906 (8th Cir. 1973), 408

Bieter Co. v. Blomquist, 1990-1 Trade Cas. (CCH) ¶ 69,083 (D. Minn. 1990), 1008

Big Apple Concrete Corp. v. Abrams, 103 A.D.2d 609, 481 N.Y.S.2d 335 (N.Y. App. Div. 1984), 563

Bigelow v. RKO Radio Pictures, 327 U.S. 251 (1946), 668, 671

Bill Johnson's Restaurants v. NLRB, 461 U.S. 731 (1983), 992, 1004

Billy & Ruth Promotion, Inc., 65 F.T.C. 243 (1964), 440

Binderup v. Pathe Exch., 263 U.S. 291 (1923), 79

Binks Mfg. Co. v. Ransburg Electro-Coating Corp., 122 U.S.P.Q. (BNA) 74 (S.D. Ind. 1959), *aff'd in part and rev'd in part*, 281 F.2d 252 (7th Cir. 1960), *cert. dismissed*, 366 U.S. 211 (1961), 834

Binks Mfg. Co. v. Ransburg Electro-Coating Corp., 281 F.2d 252 (7th Cir. 1960), *cert. dismissed*, 366 U.S. 211 (1961), 805, 814, 832

Binon & Cie SA v. Agence et Messageries de SA, Case 243/83, [1985] E.C.R. 2015, [1985-1986 Transfer Binder] COMMON MKT. REP. (CCH) ¶ 14,218, 940

Biochemic Research Found., 83 F.T.C. 1096 (1973), 473

Bird & Son, 25 F.T.C. 548 (1937), 421

Bi-Rite Oil Co. v. Indiana Farm Bureau Coop. Ass'n, 720 F. Supp. 1363 (S.D. Ind. 1989), aff'd, 908 F.2d 200 (7th Cir. 1990), 106, 189, 272

Bi-Rite Oil Co. v. Indiana Farm Bureau Coop. Ass'n, 908 F.2d 200 (7th Cir. 1990), 45, 125, 184

B.J.L.M. Liquor Store v. Block Distrib. Co., 1987-2 Trade Cas. (CCH) ¶ 67,710 (S.D. Tex. 1987), 148

Black Citizens for a Fair Media v. FCC, 719 F.2d 407 (D.C. Cir. 1983), cert. denied, 467 U.S. 1255 (1984), 1029, 1044

Black Gold, Ltd. v. Rockwool Indus., 729 F.2d 676 (10th Cir.), aff'd on reh'g, 732 F.2d 779 (10th Cir.), cert. denied, 469 U.S. 854 (1984), 114, 134, 182, 405, 417, 450

Blackburn v. Crum & Forster, 611 F.2d 102 (5th Cir.), cert. denied, 447 U.S. 906 (1980), 1118

Blackledge v. Perry, 417 U.S. 21 (1974), 581

Blackmon v. Wainwright, 608 F.2d 183 (5th Cir. 1979), 581

Black v. Acme Mkts., 564 F.2d 681 (5th Cir. 1977), 868, 877

Black v. ICC, 737 F.2d 643 (7th Cir. 1984), 1134

Blackwelder Furniture Co. v. Seilig Mfg. Co., 550 F.2d 189 (4th Cir. 1977), 366, 677

Blackwell v. Power Test Corp., 540 F. Supp 802 (D.N.J.), aff'd, 688 F.2d 818 (3d Cir. 1982), 152

Blaine v. Meineke Discount Muffler Shops, 670 F. Supp. 1107 (D. Conn. 1987), 42, 118, 187

Blair Foods, Inc. v. Ranchers Cotton Oil, 610 F.2d 665 (9th Cir. 1980), 270

Blalock v. Ladies Professional Golf Ass'n, 359 F. Supp. 1260 (N.D. Ga. 1963), 90

Blankenship v. Hearst Corp., 519 F.2d 418 (9th Cir. 1975), 119, 181

Blank v. Kirwan, 1985-2 Trade Cas. (CCH) ¶ 66,741 (Cal. 1985), 637

Blank v. Kirwan, 39 Cal.3d 311, 216 Cal. Rptr. 718, 703 P.2d 58 (1985), 1005

Blank v. Talley Indus., 54 F.R.D. 627 (S.D.N.Y. 1972), 766

Blanton Enters. v. Burger King Corp., 680 F. Supp. 753 (D.S.C. 1988), 119, 124, 125

Blanton v. Mobil Oil Corp., 721 F.2d 1207 (9th Cir. 1983), cert. denied, 471 U.S. 1007 (1985), 104, 270, 671

Blatt v. Lorenz-Schneider Co., 1981-1 Trade Cas. (CCH) ¶ 63,982 (S.D.N.Y. 1981), 152, 154

Bloch v. SmithKline Beckman Corp., 1988 U.S. DIST. LEXIS 12397 (E.D. Pa. 1988), 222, 244, 271

Blonder-Tongue Labs. v. University of Ill. Found., 402 U.S. 313 (1971), 776

Bloomer v. McQuewan, 55 U.S. (14 How.) 539 (1852), 826

Blount Fin. Serv. v. Walter E. Heller & Co., 632 F. Supp. 240 (E.D. Tenn. 1986), aff'd, 819 F.2d 151 (1987), 408

Blount Mfg. Co. v. Yale & Towne Mfg. Co., 166 F. 555 (C.C.D. Mass. 1909), 819

Blue Chip Stamps v. Manor Drug Stores, 421 U.S. 723 (1975), 574

Blue Cross & Blue Shield v. Michigan Ass'n of Psychotherapy Clinics, 1980-2 Trade Cas. (CCH) ¶ 63,351 (E.D. Mich. 1980), 115

Blue Cross v. Commonwealth, 211 Va. 180, 176 S.E.2d 439 (1970), 550

Blue Shield v. McCready, 457 U.S. 465 (1982), 658, 659

BMW-Importe, BGH WuW 1643, GRUR 1980, 130, 920

Board of County Comm'rs v. Wilshire Oil Co., 1973-1 Trade Cas. (CCH) ¶ 74,458 (W.D. Okla. 1973), aff'd sub nom. Monarch Asphalt Sales Co. v. Wilshire Oil Co., 511 F.2d 1073 (10th Cir. 1975), 738

Board of Educ. v. Admiral Heating & Ventilation, Inc., 94 F.R.D. 300 (N.D. Ill. 1982), 682

Board of Educ. v. Admiral Heating & Ventilation, Inc., 104 F.R.D. 23 (N.D. Ill. 1984), 747

Board of Governors of Univ. of N.C. v. Helpingstine, 714 F. Supp. 167 (M.D.N.C. 1989), 980

Board of Regents v. NCAA, 546 F. Supp. 1276 (W.D. Okla. 1982), aff'd in relevant part, remanded in part, 707 F.2d 1147 (10th Cir. 1983), aff'd, 468 U.S. 85 (1984), 675, 699

Board of Regents v. NCAA, 707 F.2d 1147 (10th Cir. 1983), aff'd, 468 U.S. 85 (1984), 40, 197, 664

Board of Trade v. ICC, 646 F.2d 1187 (7th Cir. 1981), 1129, 1139

Bobbs-Merrill Co. v. Straus, 210 U.S. 339 (1908), 845

Bob Maxfield, Inc. v. American Motors Corp., 637 F.2d 1033 (5th Cir.), *cert. denied*, 454 U.S. 860 (1981), 144, 146, 158, 172

Bob Rice Ford, Inc., 96 F.T.C. 18 (1980), 540

BOC Int'l, Ltd. v. FTC, 557 F.2d 24 (2d Cir. 1977), 325, 328, 523

Boddicker v. Arizona State Dental Ass'n, 680 F.2d 66 (9th Cir.), *cert. denied*, 434 U.S. 825 (1982), 158, 159

Bodker Dairy Co. v. Michigan Milk Producers Ass'n, Civil No. 23638 (E.D. Mich. 1963), 1026

Boeing Co. v. Sierracin Corp., 108 Wash. 2d 38, 738 P.2d 665 (1987), 811, 850

Boggild v. Kenner Prods., 776 F.2d 1315 (6th Cir. 1985), *cert. denied*, 477 U.S. 908 (1986), 825

Bogosian v. Gulf Oil Corp., 1983-2 Trade Cas. (CCH) ¶ 65,530 (E.D. Pa. 1983), 761

Bogosian v. Gulf Oil Corp., 1985-1 Trade Cas. (CCH) ¶ 66,510 (E.D. Pa. 1985), 742

Bogosian v. Gulf Oil Corp., 596 F. Supp. 62 (E.D. Pa. 1984), 157

Bogosian v. Gulf Oil Corp., 561 F.2d 434 (3d Cir. 1977), *cert. denied*, 434 U.S. 1086 (1978), 143, 145, 146, 154, 171, 238, 715, 723, 725, 727, 737, 738, 849

Bogus v. American Speech & Hearing Ass'n, 582 F.2d 277 (3d Cir. 1978), 88, 146, 649, 729, 730, 736

Boise Cascade Corp., 107 F.T.C. 76 (1986), *rev'd*, 837 F.2d 1127 (D.C. Cir. 1988), *on remand*, 5 TRADE REG. REP. (CCH) ¶ 22,902 (Nov. 1, 1990), 406, 407, 422, 429, 445, 446, 447

Boise Cascade Corp. v. FTC, 498 F. Supp. 772 (D. Del. 1980), 522, 523

Boise Cascade Corp. v. FTC, 637 F.2d 573 (9th Cir. 1980), 460, 522, 523

Boise Cascade Corp. v. FTC, 837 F.2d 1127 (D.C. Cir. 1988), *on remand*, 5 TRADE REG. REP. (CCH) ¶ 22,902 (Nov. 1, 1990), 406, 407, 416, 417, 422, 429, 445, 446, 447

Boise Cascade Int'l, Inc. v. Northern Minn. Pulpwood Producers Ass'n, 294 F. Supp. 1015 (D. Minn. 1968), 1026

Boisjoly v. Morton Thiokol, Inc., 706 F. Supp. 795 (D. Utah 1988), 662

Bolt v. Halifax Hosp. Medical Center, 851 F.2d 1273, (11th Cir. 1988) *vacated en banc per curiam*, 874 F.2d 755 (11th Cir. 1989), *cert. denied*, 110 S. Ct. 1960 (1990), 974

Bolt v. Halifax Hosp. Medical Center, 891 F.2d 810 (11th Cir.), *cert. denied*, 110 S. Ct. 1960 (1990), 7, 8, 21, 980

Bonito Boats, Inc. v. Thunder Craft Boats, Inc., 489 U.S. 141 (1989), 799, 850

Bonjorno v. Kaiser Aluminum & Chem. Corp., 752 F.2d 802 (3d Cir. 1984), *cert. denied*, 477 U.S. 908 (1986), 238, 239, 675

Bonus Oil Co. v. American Petrofina Co., 1975-1 Trade Cas. (CCH) ¶ 60,267 (D. Neb. 1975), 748, 752, 753

Boone v. Redevelopment Agency, 841 F.2d 886 (9th Cir.), *cert. denied*, 488 U.S. 965 (1989), 978, 983, 985, 1007, 1008

Boosey & Hawkes, 30 O.J. EUR. COMM. (No. L 286) 36 (1987), [1985-1988 Transfer Binder] COMMON MKT. REP. (CCH) ¶ 10,920, 955

Borden Co., 62 F.T.C. 130 (1963), *rev'd*, 339 F.2d 133 (5th Cir. 1964), *rev'd*, 383 U.S. 637 (1966), 424, 425

Borden Co. v. FTC, 339 F.2d 133 (5th Cir. 1964), *rev'd*, 383 U.S. 637 (1966), 411

Borden Co. v. FTC, 381 F.2d 175 (5th Cir. 1967), 406, 411, 417

Borden Co. v. Sylk, 289 F. Supp. 847 (E.D. Pa. 1968), *aff'd*, 1969 Trade Cas. (CCH) ¶ 72,799 (3d Cir. 1969), 752, 753

Borden, Inc., 78 F.T.C. 686 (1971), 482

Borden, Inc. v. FTC, 674 F.2d 498 (6th Cir. 1981), *vacated and remanded for entry of consent judgment*, 461 U.S. 940 (1983), 198, 203, 213, 215, 216

Bordenkircher v. Hayes, 434 U.S. 357 (1978), 581

Bordonaro Bros. Theatres v. Loew's, Inc., 7 F.R.D. 210 (W.D.N.Y. 1947), 749

Borger v. Yamaha Int'l Corp., 625 F.2d 390 (2d Cir. 1980), 55, 118, 127, 187, 188, 192

Borg-Warner Corp., 101 F.T.C. 863, *modified*, 102 F.T.C. 1164 (1983), *rev'd on other grounds*, 746 F.2d 108 (2d Cir. 1984), 393, 394, 395, 397, 399, 457

Boris v. United States Football League, 1984-1 Trade Cas. (CCH) ¶ 66,012 (C.D. Cal. 1984), 81

Boris v. United States Football League, 1984-2 Trade Cas. (CCH) ¶ 66,179 (C.D. Cal. 1984), 794

Boro Hall Corp. v. General Motors Corp., 124 F.2d 822 (2d Cir.), *cert. denied*, 317 U.S. 695 (1942), 129

Boro Hall v. Metropolitan Tobacco Co., 74 F.R.D. 142 (E.D.N.Y. 1977), 713, 717, 728

Borough of Ellwood City v. FERC, 731 F.2d 959 (D.C. Cir. 1984), 1071

Borough of Ellwood City v. Pennsylvania Power Co., 462 F. Supp. 1343 (W.D. Pa. 1979), 238

Borough of Ellwood City v. Pennsylvania Power Co., 570 F. Supp. 553 (W.D. Pa. 1983), 410, 1072

Borough of Lansdale v. Philadelphia Elec. Co., 517 F. Supp. 218 (E.D. Pa. 1981), 240

Borough of Lansdale v. Philadelphia Elec. Co., 692 F.2d 307 (3d Cir. 1982), 196, 199, 238, 1015, 1070-71

Boshes v. General Motors Corp., 59 F.R.D. 589 (N.D. Ill. 1973), 724, 732

Boss Mfg. Co. v. Payne Glove Co., 71 F.2d 768 (8th Cir.), *cert. denied*, 293 U.S. 590 (1934), 410

Bostick Oil Co. v. Michelin Tire Corp., 702 F.2d 1207 (4th Cir.), *cert. denied*, 464 U.S. 894 (1983), 113, 631

Bott v. Holiday Universal, Inc., 1976-2 Trade Cas. (CCH) ¶ 60,973 (D.D.C. 1976), 543

Bouldis v. U.S. Suzuki Motor Corp., 711 F.2d 1319 (6th Cir. 1983), 139, 143, 405, 406, 409, 437, 438

Bourjaily v. United States, 483 U.S. 171 (1987), 593

Boussois/Interpane, 30 O.J. EUR. COMM. (No. L 50) 30 (1987), [1985-1988 Transfer Binder] COMMON MKT. REP. (CCH) ¶ 10,859, 949

Bowen v. News, 1969 Trade Cas. (CCH) ¶ 72,768 (S.D.N.Y 1969), 746

Bowen v. New York News, Inc., 366 F. Supp. 651 (S.D.N.Y. 1973), *aff'd*, 522 F.2d 1242 (2d Cir. 1975), *cert. denied*, 425 U.S. 936 (1976), 173, 175, 178

Bowen v. New York News, Inc., 522 F.2d 1242 (2d Cir. 1975), *cert. denied*, 425 U.S. 936 (1976), 15, 81, 109, 118, 271, 272, 273

Bowman v. NFL, 402 F. Supp. 754 (D. Minn. 1975), 91, 713

Boyertown Burial Casket Co. v. Amedco, Inc., 407 F. Supp. 811 (E.D. Pa. 1976), 366

BPB Indus. (British gypsum), Decision 89/22, 32 O.J. EUR. COMM. (No. L 10) 50 (1989), [1989] 1 CEC (CCH) 2008, 956

BPCL/ICI, 27 O.J. EUR. COMM. (No. L 212) 1 (1984), [1982-1985 Transfer Binder] COMMON MKT. REP. (CCH) ¶ 10,611, 937

BP Kemi/DDSF, 22 O.J. EUR. COMM. (No. L 286) 32 (1979), [1978-1981 Transfer Binder] COMMON MKT. REP. (CCH) ¶ 10,165, 932, 942

Bradford v. New York Times Co., 501 F.2d 51 (2d Cir. 1974), 98, 99

Brady v. Maryland, 373 U.S. 83 (1963), 589

Brady v. United States, 397 U.S. 742 (1970), 581

Brae Corp. v. United States, 740 F.2d 1023 (D.C. Cir. 1984), *cert. denied*, 471 U.S. 1069 (1985), 1017, 1133, 1134

Brager & Co. v. Leumi Sec. Corp., 429 F. Supp. 1341 (S.D.N.Y. 1977), *aff'd*, 646 F.2d 559 (2d Cir. 1980), *cert. denied*, 451 U.S. 987 (1981), 273

Branch v. FTC, 141 F.2d 31 (7th Cir. 1944), 477, 864

Brandeis Mach. v. Barber Greene Co., 1973-2 Trade Cas. (CCH) ¶ 74,672 (W.D. Ky. 1973), 164, 166

Brant v. United States, 210 F.2d 470 (5th Cir. 1954), 599

Brant v. United States Polo Ass'n, 631 F. Supp. 71 (S.D. Fla. 1986), 41, 89

Brasserie de Haecht v. Wilkin (No. 1), Case 23/67, [1967] E.C.R. 407, [1967-1970 Transfer Binder] COMMON MKT. REP. (CCH) ¶ 8053, 929

Brattleboro Auto Sales, Inc. v. Subaru of New England, Inc., 633 F.2d 649 (2d Cir. 1980), 182

Brauerei A. Bilger Söhne GmbH v. Jehle, Case 43/69, [1970] E.C.R. 127, [1967-1970 Transfer Binder] COMMON MKT. REP. (CCH) ¶ 8076, 926

Bravman v. Bassett Furniture Indus., 552 F.2d 90 (3d Cir.), *cert. denied*, 434 U.S. 823 (1977), 172, 662

Bray v. Safeway Stores, 392 F. Supp. 851 (N.D. Cal.), *vacated as settled sub nom.* Bray v. Great Atl. & Pac. Tea Co., 1975-2 Trade Cas. (CCH) ¶ 60,533 (9th Cir.), *dismissed*, 403 F. Supp. 412 (N.D. Cal. 1975), 73

Brazil v. Arkansas Bd. of Dental Examiners, 759 F.2d 674 (8th Cir. 1985), 986

Breeders' Rights-Maize Seed, 21 O.J. EUR. COMM. (No. L 286) 23 (1978), [1978-1981 Transfer Binder] COMMON MKT. REP. (CCH) ¶ 10,083, 947

Breen Air Freight, Ltd. v. Air Cargo, Inc., 470 F.2d 767 (2d Cir. 1972), cert. denied, 411 U.S. 932 (1973), 1023

Brennan v. Midwestern United Life Ins. Co., 450 F.2d 999 (7th Cir. 1971), *cert. denied*, 405 U.S. 921 (1972), 735

Brenner v. World Boxing Council, 675 F.2d 445 (2d Cir.), *cert. denied*, 459 U.S. 835 (1982), 87

Brett v. First Fed. Sav. & Loan Ass'n, 461 F.2d 1155 (5th Cir. 1972), 29

Brewer v. Southern Union Co., 1985-2 Trade Cas. (CCH) ¶ 66,802 (D. Colo. 1984), 741, 742

Brian Clewer, Inc. v. Pan Am. World Airways, 674 F. Supp. 782 (C.D. Cal. 1986), 662

Bridgeman v. NBA, 675 F. Supp. 960 (D.N.J. 1987), 91, 1124

Brierwood Shoe Corp. v. Sears, Roebuck & Co., 501 F. Supp. 144 (S.D.N.Y. 1980), 168

Briggs Mfg. Co. v. Crane Co., 185 F. Supp. 177 (E.D. Mich.), *aff'd*, 280 F.2d 747 (6th Cir. 1960), 363

Bright v. Moss Ambulance Serv., 824 F.2d 819 (10th Cir. 1987), 195, 197, 215, 260, 1015

Brillhart v. Mutual Medical Ins., Inc., 768 F.2d 196 (7th Cir. 1985), 115

Brillo Mfg. Co., 64 F.T.C. 245 (1964), *modified*, 75 F.T.C. 811 (1969), 283, 359

Bristol Locknut Co. v. SPS Technologies, Inc., 677 F.2d 1277 (9th Cir. 1982), 836

Bristol-Myers Co., 85 F.T.C. 688 (1975), 471, 482, 489

Bristol-Myers Co., 102 F.T.C. 21 (1983), *aff'd*, 738 F.2d 554 (2d Cir. 1984), *cert. denied*, 469 U.S. 1189 (1985), 467, 473, 474

Bristol-Myers Co. v. FTC, 738 F.2d 554 (2d Cir. 1984), *cert. denied*, 469 U.S. 1189 (1985), 488, 489, 522

British Airways Bd. v. Laker Airways (C.A. July 26, 1983), *reported in* 45 ANTITRUST & TRADE REG. REP. (BNA) 248 (Aug. 18, 1983), 879

British Airways Bd. v. Laker Airways Ltd., [1984] 3 W.L.R. 413, *reprinted in* 23 I.L.M. 727 (July 19, 1984), 879

British-American Tobacco Co. and R.J. Reynolds Indus. v. Commission, Joined Cases 142 and 156/84, [1987] E.C.R. 4487, [1987-1988 Transfer Binder] COMMON MKT. REP. (CCH) ¶ 14,405, 921, 958, 959, 960

British Leyland, 27 O.J. EUR. COMM. (No. L 207) 11 (1984), [1982-1985 Transfer Binder] COMMON MKT. REP. (CCH) ¶ 10,601, *aff'd sub nom.* British Leyland v. Commission, Case 226/84, [1986] E.C.R. 3263, [1985-1986 Transfer Binder] COMMON MKT. REP. (CCH) ¶ 14,336, 954

British Nylon Spinners Ltd. v. Imperial Chem. Indus., [1953] 1 Ch. 19 (C.A. 1952), *made permanent*, [1954] 1 Ch. 37, 893

British Oxygen Co., 86 F.T.C. 1241 (1975), *rev'd sub nom.* BOC Int'l, Ltd v. FTC, 557 F.2d 24 (2d Cir. 1977), 290, 865

British Sugar/Napier Brown, 31 O.J. EUR. COMM. (No. L 284) 41 (1988), [1985-1988 Transfer Binder] COMMON MKT. REP. (CCH) ¶ 11,015, 954

British Telecommuns., 25 O.J. EUR. COMM. (No. L 360) 36 (1982), [1982-1985 Transfer Binder] COMMON MKT. REP. (CCH) ¶ 10,443, *aff'd sub nom.* Italy v. Commission, Case 41/83, [1985] E.C.R. 873, [1983-1985 Transfer Binder] COMMON MKT. REP. (CCH) ¶ 14,168, 957

Broadcast Music, Inc. v. CBS, 441 U.S. 1 (1979), 31, 32, 33, 35, 36, 39, 40, 41, 42, 43, 62, 67, 373, 374, 375, 379, 390, 834, 845

Broadway & Ninety-Sixth Street Realty v. Loew's Inc., 21 F.R.D. 347 (S.D.N.Y. 1958), 748
Broadway Delivery Corp. v. United Parcel Serv., 74 F.R.D. 438 (S.D.N.Y. 1977), 774
Broadway Delivery Corp. v. United Parcel Serv., 651 F.2d 122 (2d Cir.), *cert. denied*, 454 U.S. 968 (1981), 214, 265
Brokers' Assistant, Inc. v. Williams Real Estate Co., 646 F. Supp. 1110 (S.D.N.Y. 1986), 8, 10
Broker's Title, Inc. v. Main, 806 F.2d 257 (4th Cir. 1986), 648, 795
Brotherhood of Maintenance of Way Employees v. ICC, 698 F.2d 315 (7th Cir. 1983), 1211
Broussard v. Socony Mobil Oil Co., 350 F.2d 346 (5th Cir. 1965), 104, 110, 703
Brown & Williamson Tobacco Corp., 56 F.T.C. 956 (1960), 482
Brown & Williamson Tobacco Corp. v. FTC, 710 F.2d 1165 (6th Cir. 1983), *cert. denied*, 465 U.S. 1100 (1984), 524
Brownell v. Ketcham Wire & Mfg. Co., 211 F.2d 121 (9th Cir. 1954), 827, 828
Browning-Ferris Indus. v. Kelco Disposal, Inc., 492 U.S. 257 (1989), 630
Brownlee v. Applied Biosystems Inc., 1989-1 Trade Cas. (CCH) ¶ 68,425 (N.D. Cal. 1989), 207, 222, 270, 1001
Brown Shoe Co., 62 F.T.C. 679 (1963), *rev'd sub nom.* Brown Shoe Co. v. FTC, 339 F.2d 45 (8th Cir. 1964), *rev'd*, 384 U.S. 316 (1966), 174
Brown Shoe Co., 104 F.T.C. 266 (1984), 172, 175, 178
Brown Shoe Co. v. FTC, 339 F.2d 45 (8th Cir. 1964), *rev'd*, 384 U.S. 316 (1966), 522
Brown Shoe Co. v. United States, 370 U.S. 294 (1962), 49, 198, 199, 204, 208, 279, 282, 283, 287, 288, 293, 294, 296, 298, 299, 300, 303, 304, 319, 330, 750
Brownsville Bancshares Corp., 72 Fed. Res. Bull. 43 (1986), 1096
Brown v. Cameron Brown Co., 92 F.R.D. 32 (E.D. Va. 1981), 714, 716, 717, 721, 726, 734
Brown v. Carr, 1980-2 Trade Cas. (CCH) ¶ 63,303 (D.D.C. 1980), 649
Brown v. Donco Enters., 783 F.2d 644 (6th Cir. 1986), 22
Brown v. Hansen Publications, 556 F.2d 969 (9th Cir. 1977), 170, 408
Brown v. Indianapolis Bd. of Realtors, 1977-1 Trade Cas. (CCH) ¶ 61,435 (S.D. Ind. 1977), 88
Brown v. Pro Football, Inc., 1991-2 Trade Cas. (CCH) ¶ 69,545 (D.D.C. 1991), 724
Brown v. Providence Gas Co., 445 F. Supp. 459 (D.R.I. 1976), 534
Bruce Drug, Inc. v. Hollister, Inc., 688 F.2d 853 (1st Cir. 1982), 11, 678
Bruce's Juices, Inc. v. American Can Co., 87 F. Supp. 985 (S.D. Fla. 1949), *aff'd*, 187 F.2d 919 (5th Cir.), *cert. dismissed*, 342 U.S. 875 (1951), 412
Bruce's Juices, Inc. v. American Can Co., 330 U.S. 743 (1947), 406, 407, 645, 791
Bruce v. First Fed. Sav. & Loan Ass'n of Conroe, Inc., 837 F.2d 712 (5th Cir. 1988), 1098
Brulotte v. Thys Co., 379 U.S. 29 (1964), 800, 801, 823, 825, 826
Brunette Machine Works, Ltd. v. Kockum Indus., 406 U.S. 706 (1973), 869-70
Brunswick Corp., 94 F.T.C. 1174 (1979), *aff'd as modified sub nom.* Yamaha Motor Co. v. FTC, 657 F.2d 971 (8th Cir. 1981), *cert. denied*, 456 U.S. 915 (1982), 322, 326, 329, 373, 378, 379, 382, 383, 865, 896
Brunswick Corp. v. Pueblo Bowl-O-Mat, Inc., 429 U.S. 477 (1977), 49, 362, 365, 371, 650, 651, 652, 667, 1108
Brunswick Corp. v. Riegel Textile Corp., 578 F. Supp. 893 (N.D. Ill. 1983), *aff'd*, 752 F.2d 261 (7th Cir. 1984), *cert. denied*, 472 U.S. 1018 (1985), 690, 691, 692, 695
Brunswick Corp. v. Riegel Textile Corp., 752 F.2d 261 (7th Cir. 1984), *cert. denied*, 472 U.S. 1018 (1985), 681, 802, 806, 808, 811, 1022
Bryant Heating and Air Conditioning Corp. v. Carrier Corp., 597 F. Supp. 1045 (S.D. Fla. 1984), 111
Bryan v. Pittsburgh Plate Glass Co., 494 F.2d 799 (3d Cir.), *cert. denied*, 419 U.S. 900 (1974), 742
Bubar v. Ampco Foods, Inc., 752 F.2d 445 (9th Cir.), *cert. denied*, 472 U.S. 1018 (1985), 648
Bubis v. Blanton, 885 F.2d 317 (6th Cir. 1989), 649
Buckeye Assocs. v. Fila Sports, Inc., 616 F. Supp. 1484 (D. Mass. 1985), 868, 871

Buckhead Theatre Corp. v. Atlanta Enters., 327 F.2d 365 (5th Cir.), *cert. denied*, 379 U.S. 888 (1964), 778, 780

Buckley Constr., Inc. v. Shawnee Civic & Cultural Dev. Auth., 933 F.2d 853 (10th Cir. 1991), 978

Buck v. Cecere, 45 F. Supp. 441 (W.D.N.Y. 1942), 846

Buck v. Newsreel, Inc., 25 F. Supp. 787 (D. Mass. 1938), 846

Budd Co., 86 F.T.C. 518 (1975), 288, 323, 328

Buffalo Broadcasting Co. v. American Soc'y of Composers, Authors & Publishers, 744 F.2d 917 (2d Cir. 1984), *cert. denied*, 469 U.S. 1211 (1985), 39-40, 56, 374, 380, 834

Buffalo Courier-Express, Inc. v. Buffalo Evening News, Inc., 601 F.2d 48 (2d Cir. 1979), 228, 261, 679

Bulkferts, Inc. v. Salatin Inc., 1983-1 Trade Cas. (CCH) ¶ 65,272 (S.D.N.Y. 1983), 913

Bulkferts, Inc. v. Salatin, Inc., 574 F. Supp. 6 (S.D.N.Y. 1983), 1015

Bulk Oil (ZUG) AG v. Sun Co., 583 F. Supp. 1134 (S.D.N.Y. 1983), *aff'd without pub. op.*, 742 F.2d 1431 (2d Cir.), *cert. denied*, 469 U.S. 835 (1984), 860

Bulova Watch Co., 111 F.T.C. 766 (1989), 515

Bunker Ramo Corp. v. Cywan, 511 F. Supp. 531 (N.D. Ill. 1981), 431

Bunker Ramo Corp. v. United Bus. Forms, 713 F.2d 1272 (7th Cir. 1983), 29

Bunty v. Shell Oil Co., 1972 Trade Cas. (CCH) ¶ 74,252 (D. Nev. 1972), 184, 185

Burch v. Goodyear Tire & Rubber Co., 420 F. Supp. 82 (D. Md. 1976), *aff'd*, 554 F.2d 633 (4th Cir. 1977), 435

Burch v. Goodyear Tire & Rubber Co., 554 F.2d 633 (4th Cir. 1977), 606

Burdett Sound, Inc. v. Altec Corp., 515 F.2d 1245 (5th Cir. 1975), 118, 184, 188, 193

Bureau Nat'l Interprofessionnel du Cognac v. Clair, Case 123/83, [1985] E.C.R. 391, [1983-1985 Transfer Binder] COMMON MKT. REP. (CCH) ¶ 14,160, 929

Burger King Corp. v. Rudzewicz, 471 U.S. 462 (1985), 872, 874

Burge v. Bryant Pub. School Dist., 520 F. Supp. 328 (E.D. Ark. 1980), *aff'd per curiam*, 658 F.2d 611 (8th Cir. 1981), 435, 436

Burkett v. Shell Oil Co., 487 F.2d 1308 (5th Cir. 1973), 644

Burke v. Ford, 389 U.S. 320 (1967), 23, 31

Burkhalter Travel Agency v. MacFarms Int'l, Inc., 1992-1 Trade Cas. (CCH) ¶ 69,720 (9th Cir. 1992), 458, 491

Burks v. United States, 437 U.S. 1 (1978), 598, 599

Burlington Coat Factory Warehouse Corp. v. Esprit de Corp., 769 F.2d 919 (2d Cir. 1985), 13, 790

Burlington Coat Factory Warehouse v. Belk Bros., 621 F. Supp. 224 (S.D.N.Y. 1985), 789

Burlington Indus. v. Edelman, 666 F. Supp. 799 (M.D.N.C.), *aff'd*, [1987 Transfer Binder] FED. SEC. L. REP. (CCH) ¶ 93,339 (4th Cir. 1987), 364, 663

Burlington Indus. v. Milliken & Co., 690 F.2d 380 (4th Cir. 1982), *cert. denied*, 461 U.S. 914 (1983), 669, 698, 699

Burnup & Sims, Inc. v. Posner, 688 F. Supp. 1532 (S.D. Fla. 1988), 364, 369, 395, 663

Burroughs-Delplanque, 15 O.J. EUR. COMM. (No. L 13) 50 (1972), [1970-1972 Transfer Binder] COMMON MKT. REP. (CCH) ¶ 9485, 947, 949

Burroughs/Geha-Werke, 15 J.O. COMM. EUR. (No. L 13) 53 (1972), [1970-1972 Transfer Binder] COMMON MKT. REP. (CCH) ¶ 9486, 947, 948

Bursey v. United States, 466 F.2d 1059 (9th Cir. 1972), 566, 592

Burton Supply Co. v. Wheel Horse Prods., 1974-2 Trade Cas. (CCH) ¶ 75,224 (N.D. Ohio 1974), 109

Busboom Grain Co. v. ICC, 856 F.2d 790 (7th Cir. 1988), 1134

Bushie v. Stenocord Corp., 460 F.2d 116 (9th Cir. 1972), 118, 188, 191

Business Elecs. Corp. v. Sharp Elecs. Corp., 780 F.2d 1212 (5th Cir. 1986), *aff'd*, 485 U.S. 717 (1988), 106, 107, 672

Business Elecs. Corp. v. Sharp Elecs. Corp., 485 U.S. 717 (1988), 2, 5, 30, 31, 42, 60, 61, 62, 77, 98, 100, 101, 105, 106, 116, 117, 181, 189, 379, 382, 613, 614, 616, 635

Business Equip. Center Ltd. v. DeJurAmsco Corp., 465 F. Supp. 775 (D.D.C. 1978), 184

Business Guides, Inc. v. Chromatic Communs. Enters., 111 S. Ct. 922 (1991), 790, 791

BusTop Shelters, Inc. v. Convenience & Safety Corp., 521 F. Supp. 989 (S.D.N.Y. 1981), 1011

Butera v. Sun Oil Co., 496 F.2d 434 (1st Cir. 1974), 107, 108, 111

Butkus v. Chicken Unlimited Enters., 1971 Trade Cas. (CCH) ¶ 73,780 (N.D. Ill. 1971), 713

Butler Aviation Co. v. Civil Aeronautics Bd., 389 F.2d 517 (2d Cir. 1968), 335

Butt v. Allegheny Pepsi-Cola Bottling Co., 116 F.R.D. 486 (E.D. Va. 1987), 712, 714, 716, 720, 722, 723, 726, 727, 729, 730, 733, 736

B.W.I. Custom Kitchen v. Owens-Illinois, Inc., 191 Cal. App. 3d 1341, 235 Cal. Rptr. 228 (Cal. Ct. App. 1987), 714, 716, 725, 728

Byars v. Bluff City News Co., 609 F.2d 843 (6th Cir. 1979), 179, 212, 216, 241, 242

Byars v. Bluff City News Co., 683 F.2d 981 (6th Cir. 1982), 213

Byers Theaters v. Murphy, 1 F.R.D. 286 (W.D. Va. 1940), 746

Byram Concretanks, Inc. v. Warren Concrete Prods., 374 F.2d 649 (3d Cir. 1967), 782

Byre v. City of Chamberlain, 362 N.W.2d 69 (S.D. 1985), 637

Bywater v. Matsushita Elec. Indus. Co., 1971 Trade Cas. (CCH) ¶ 73,759 (S.D.N.Y. 1971), 898

C

Cable Holdings v. Home Video, Inc., 572 F. Supp. 482 (N.D. Ga. 1983), aff'd, 825 F.2d 1559 (11th Cir. 1987), 297

Cable Holdings v. Home Video, Inc., 825 F.2d 1559 (11th Cir. 1987), 287, 648, 667

Cable Television Ass'n v. Chesapeake & Potomac Tel. Co., File No. PA-88-002 (FCC Complaint filed March 10, 1988), 1055

Cackling Acres, Inc. v. Olson Farms, 541 F.2d 242 (10th Cir. 1976), cert. denied, 429 U.S. 1122 (1977), 209, 211

Cahill & Kaswell, 37 Rad. Reg. 2d (P&F) 197 (1976), 1030

C. Albert Sauter Co. v. Richard S. Sauter Co., 368 F. Supp. 501 (E.D. Pa. 1973), 96

Calculators Haw., Inc. v. Brandt, Inc., 724 F.2d 1332 (9th Cir. 1983), 50, 118

Calderone Enters. v. United Artists Theatre Circuit, Inc., 454 F.2d 1292 (2d Cir. 1971), cert. denied, 406 U.S. 930 (1972), 661

Calder v. Jones, 465 U.S. 783 (1984), 873, 874, 875

Califano v. Yamasaki, 442 U.S. 682 (1979), 737

California Aviation, Inc. v. City of Santa Monica, 806 F.2d 905 (9th Cir. 1986), 972

California Computer Prods., Inc. v. IBM, 613 F.2d 727 (9th Cir. 1979), cert. denied, 464 U.S. 955 (1983) , 223, 225, 227, 230, 245, 253, 254, 255, 257, 268, 269

California Dental Ass'n v. California Dental Hygienists' Ass'n, No. B040189 (Cal. Dist. Ct. App. July 16, 1990), 638

California ex rel. Van de Kamp v. Texaco, Inc., 46 Cal. 3d 1147, 762 P.2d 385, 252 Cal. Rptr. 221 (Cal. 1988), 278

California Glazed Prods. v. Burns & Russell Co., 708 F.2d 1423 (9th Cir.), cert. denied, 464 U.S. 938 (1983), 141, 142

California League of Indep. Ins. Producers v. Aetna Casualty & Sur. Co., 175 F. Supp. 857 (N.D. Cal. 1959), 1111, 1114, 1115

California Motor Transp. Co. v. Trucking Unlimited, 404 U.S. 508 (1972), 259, 494, 812, 899, 913, 992, 993, 998, 1005, 1009, 1053

California Retail Liquor Dealers Ass'n v. Midcal Aluminum, Inc., 445 U.S. 97 (1980), 101, 969, 973, 985, 986

California State Bd. of Optometry v. FTC, 910 F.2d 976 (D.C. Cir. 1990), 485, 526, 529, 967

California Steel & Tube v. Kaiser Steel Corp., 650 F.2d 1001 (9th Cir. 1981), 238

California v. American Stores Co., 697 F. Supp. 1125 (C.D. Cal. 1988), *aff'd in part and rev'd in part*, 872 F.2d 837 (9th Cir. 1989), *rev'd*, 110 S. Ct. 1853 (1990), 278, 290, 307, 309, 367, 369

California v. American Stores Co., 872 F.2d 837 (9th Cir. 1989), *rev'd*, 110 S. Ct. 1853 (1990), 606, 614

California v. American Stores Co., 872 F.2d 837 (9th Cir. 1989), *rev'd on other grounds*, 110 S. Ct. 1853 (1990), 307, 366

California v. American Stores Co., 110 S. Ct. 1853 (1990), 361, 370, 371, 606, 612, 680

California v. ARC America Corp., 490 U.S. 93 (1989), 622, 623, 625, 626, 630, 641, 658

California v. FCC, 905 F.2d 1217 (9th Cir. 1990), 1048

California v. FPC, 369 U.S. 482 (1962), 964, 1066

California v. Frito-Lay, Inc., 474 F.2d 774 (9th Cir.), *cert. denied*, 412 U.S. 908 (1973), 606

California v. Levi Strauss & Co., 41 Cal. 3d 460, 224 Cal. Rptr. 605 (1986), 742

California v. Zook, 336 U.S. 725 (1949), 621

Callaway Mills Co. v. FTC, 362 F.2d 435 (5th Cir. 1966), 418, 419, 420

Call Carl, Inc. v. B.P. Oil Corp., 391 F. Supp. 367 (D. Md. 1975), *aff'd in part and rev'd in part*, 554 F.2d 623 (4th Cir.), *cert. denied*, 434 U.S. 923 (1977), 873

Call Carl, Inc. v. BP Oil Corp., 403 F. Supp. 568 (D. Md. 1975), *modified on other grounds*, 554 F.2d 623 (4th Cir.), *cert. denied*, 434 U.S. 923 (1977), 774

Call Carl, Inc. v. BP Oil Corp., 554 F.2d 623 (4th Cir.), *cert. denied*, 434 U.S. 923 (1977), 103, 182, 191, 192

Calnetics Corp. v. Volkswagen of Am., Inc., 348 F. Supp. 606 (C.D. Cal. 1972), 320

Calnetics Corp. v. Volkswagen of Am., Inc., 532 F.2d 674 (9th Cir.), *cert. denied*, 429 U.S. 940 (1976), 203, 287, 360, 435, 680, 698, 701

Camellia City Telecasters v. Tribune Broadcasting Co., 1984-2 Trade Cas. (CCH) ¶ 66,114 (D. Colo. 1984), 873

Camellia City Telecasters, Inc. v. Tribune Broadcasting Co., 1991-1 Trade Cas. (CCH) ¶ 69,439 (D. Colo. 1991), 143, 163

Cameo Convalescent Center, Inc. v. Senn, 738 F.2d 836 (7th Cir. 1984), *cert. denied*, 469 U.S. 1106 (1985), 786

Camera Care Ltd. v. Commission, Case 792/79R, [1980] E.C.R. 119, [1979-1981 Transfer Binder] COMMON MKT. REP. (CCH) ¶ 8645, 920

Camotex S.R.L. v. Hunt, 1990-2 Trade Cas. (CCH) ¶ 69,100 (S.D.N.Y. 1990), 681, 683, 696, 697

Campari, 21 O.J. EUR. COMM. (No. L 70) 69 (1978), [1978-1981 Transfer Binder] COMMON MKT. REP. (CCH) ¶ 10,035, 947

Campbell Soup Co., 77 F.T.C. 664 (1970), 481, 513

Campbell Soup Co., 5 TRADE REG. REP. (CCH) ¶ 22,967 (Apr. 8, 1991), 469

Campbell Taggart Associated Bakeries, 71 F.T.C. 509 (1967), 511

Campbell v. City of Chicago, 577 F. Supp. 1166 (N.D. Ill. 1983), 27

Campbell v. City of Chicago, 1984-2 Trade Cas. (CCH) ¶ 66,180 (N.D. Ill. 1984), *aff'd*, 823 F.2d 1182 (7th Cir. 1987), 712

Campbell v. City of Chicago, 639 F. Supp. 1501 (N.D. Ill. 1986), *aff'd*, 823 F.2d 1182 (7th Cir. 1987), 1005

Campbell v. City of Chicago, 823 F.2d 1182 (7th Cir. 1987), 972, 983

Campbell v. Mueller, 159 F.2d 803 (6th Cir. 1947), 816

Campbell v. Wells Fargo Bank, N.A., 781 F.2d 440 (5th Cir.), *cert. denied*, 476 U.S. 1159 (1986), 1098

Canadian Ace Brewing Co. v. Jos. Schlitz Brewing Co., 629 F.2d 1183 (7th Cir. 1980), 644

Canadian Ingersoll-Rand Co. v. D. Loveman & Sons, 227 F. Supp. 829 (N.D. Ohio 1964), 435, 448-49, 865

C & W Constr. Co. v. Brotherhood of Carpenters & Joiners, 687 F. Supp. 1453 (D. Haw. 1988), 17, 776

Cannon Mfg. Co. v. Cudahy Packing Co., 267 U.S. 333 (1925), 868

Cannon v. Teamsters & Chauffeurs Union, Local 627, 657 F.2d 173 (7th Cir. 1981), 1123

Cantor v. Detroit Edison Co., 428 U.S. 579 (1976), 968

Cantor v. Multiple Listing Serv., 568 F. Supp. 424 (S.D.N.Y. 1983), 28

Capax, Inc., 91 F.T.C. 1048 (1978), 532

Cape Cod Food Prods. v. National Cranberry Ass'n, 119 F. Supp. 900 (D. Mass. 1954), 1026

Capital Builders, 92 F.T.C. 274 (1978), 534

Capital Cities Cable, Inc. v. Crisp, 467 U.S. 691 (1984), 1050

Capital Imaging Assocs. v. Mohawk Valley Medical Assocs., 725 F. Supp. 669 (N.D.N.Y. 1989), 44, 263

Capital Tel. Co. v. New York Tel. Co., 750 F.2d 1154 (2d Cir. 1984), *cert. denied*, 471 U.S. 1101 (1985), 1049

Capital Temporaries, Inc. v. Olsten Corp., 506 F.2d 658 (2d Cir. 1974), 144, 145, 146, 156, 849

Capitol Ice Cream Wholesalers v. Mid-Atlantic Coca-Cola Bottling Co., 1982-83 Trade Cas. (CCH) ¶ 65,068 (D.D.C. 1982), 407

Capitol Indem. Co. v. First Minn. Constr., 405 F. Supp. 929 (D. Mass. 1975), 758

Caplan v. American Baby, Inc., 582 F. Supp. 869 (S.D.N.Y. 1984), 1002

Carbice Corp. of Am. v. American Patents Dev. Corp., 283 U.S. 27 (1931), 817

Carbon Black Export, Inc., 46 F.T.C. 1245 (1949), 915

Carbon Steel Prods. Corp. v. Alan Wood Steel Co., 289 F. Supp. 584 (S.D.N.Y. 1968), 182

Car Carriers, Inc. v. Ford Motor Co., 745 F.2d 1101 (7th Cir. 1984), *cert. denied*, 470 U.S. 1054 (1985), 37, 38, 48, 49, 85, 183, 185

Cardio-Medical Assocs. v. Crozer-Chester Medical Center, 721 F.2d 68 (3d Cir. 1983), 22, 25, 26, 28

Card v. National Life Ins. Co., 603 F.2d 828 (10th Cir. 1979), 1117

Caremark Homecare, Inc., v. New England Critical Care, Inc., 700 F. Supp. 1033 (D. Minn. 1988), 199

Carey v. Daniel Freeman Memorial Hosp., 1984-1 Trade Cas. (CCH) ¶ 65,831 (C.D. Cal. 1983), 24, 28

Carey v. National Oil Corp., 592 F.2d 673 (2d Cir. 1979), 900

Car-Freshner Corp. v. Auto Aid Mfg. Corp., 438 F. Supp. 82 (N.D.N.Y. 1977), 847

Cargill, Inc. v. Hardin, 452 F.2d 1154 (8th Cir. 1971), *cert. denied*, 406 U.S. 932 (1972), 1106, 1107

Cargill, Inc. v. Monfort of Colo., Inc., 479 U.S. 104 (1986), 49, 223, 227, 236, 265, 299, 304, 362, 415, 643, 650, 651, 652, 664

Cargill, Inc. v. Montfort of Colo., Inc., 872 F.2d 837 (1989), 606

Carib Aviation & Marine Consultants v. Mitsubishi Aircraft Int'l, 640 F. Supp. 582 (S.D. Fla. 1986), 51, 55, 60, 126

Caribe Trailer Sys. v. Puerto Rico Maritime Shipping Auth., 475 F. Supp. 711 (D.D.C. 1979), *aff'd per curiam* (D.C. Cir. 1980), *cert. denied*, 450 U.S. 914 (1981), 870

Carl Hizel & Sons v. Browning-Ferris Indus., 600 F. Supp. 161 (D. Col. 1985), 240

Carlo C. Gelardi Corp. v. Miller Brewing Co., 421 F. Supp. 237 (D.N.J. 1976), 273

Carlo C. Gelardi Corp. v. Miller Brewing Co., 421 F. Supp. 237 (D.N.J. 1976), 502 F. Supp. 637 (D.N.J. 1980), *aff'd without published opinion*, No. 82-5217 (3d Cir. June 15, 1983), 409

Carlo C. Gelardi Corp. v. Miller Brewing Co., 502 F. Supp. 637 (D.N.J. 1980), *aff'd without published opinion*, No. 82-5217 (3d Cir. June 15, 1983), 405, 438

Carlock v. Pillsbury Co., 719 F. Supp. 791 (D. Minn. 1989), 206

Carl Sandburg Village Condominium Ass'n v. First Condominium Dev. Co., 586 F. Supp. 155 (N.D. Ill. 1984), *aff'd*, 758 F.2d 203 (7th Cir. 1985), 131, 132

Carl Sandburg Village Condominium Ass'n v. First Condominium Dev. Co., 758 F.2d 203 (7th Cir. 1985), 158, 159

Carlson Cos. v. Sperry & Hutchinson Co., 374 F.Supp. 1080 (D. Minn. 1974), 747

Carlson Mach. Tools, Inc. v. American Tool, Inc., 630 F.2d 46 (5th Cir. 1982), 109

Carlson Mach. Tools, Inc. v. American Tool, Inc., 678 F.2d 1253 (5th Cir. 1982), 107, 125

Carlson v. Coca-Cola, Co., 483 F.2d 279 (9th Cir. 1973), 542, 645

Carl Wagner & Sons v. Appendagez, Inc., 485 F. Supp. 762 (S.D.N.Y. 1980), 634

Carl Zeiss Stiftung v. V.E.B. Carl Zeiss, Jena, 298 F. Supp. 1309 (S.D.N.Y. 1969), *modified*, 433 F.2d 686 (2d Cir. 1970), *cert. denied*, 403 U.S. 905 (1971), 847, 848

Carnation Co. v. Pacific Westbound Conference, 383 U.S. 213 (1966), 1017, 1019, 1164, 1165

Carolina Furniture Co. v. Rhodes, Inc., 603 F. Supp. 69 (S.D. Ga. 1984), 78, 184

Carolinas Advertising, Inc., 42 F.C.C.2d 1027 (1973), 1033, 1034

Carpa, Inc. v. Ward Foods, Inc., 536 F.2d 39 (5th Cir. 1976), 141, 156, 157, 160, 161, 671

Carpenter v. Central Ark. Milk Producers Ass'n, 1966 Trade Cas. (CCH) ¶ 71,817 (W.D. Ark. 1966), 779

Carpet Seaming Tape Licensing Corp. v. Best Seam, Inc., 616 F.2d 1133 (9th Cir. 1980), *aff'd in part and rev'd in part*, 694 F.2d 570 (9th Cir. 1982), *cert. denied*, 464 U.S. 818 (1983), 837

Carpet Seaming Tape Licensing Corp. v. Best Seam, Inc., 694 F.2d 570 (9th Cir. 1982), *cert. denied*, 464 U.S. 818 (1983), 838

Carpets "R" Us, Inc., 87 F.T.C. 303 (1976), 475

Carrier Corp. v. United Technologies Corp., 1978-2 Trade Cas. (CCH) ¶ 62,393 (N.D.N.Y.), *aff'd*, 1978-2 Trade Cas. (CCH) ¶ 62,405 (2d Cir. 1978), 332, 335, 336, 369

Carroll Broadcasting Co. v. FCC, 258 F.2d 440 (D.C. Cir. 1958), 1043

Carroll v. Greenwich Ins. Co., 199 U.S. 401 (1905), 627

Carsalve Corp. v. Texaco, Inc., 1978-2 Trade Cas. (CCH) ¶ 62,370 (D.N.J. 1978), 405

Carson v. American Brands, Inc., 450 U.S. 79 (1981), 741

Carte Blanche Corp., 89 F.T.C. 305 (1977), 480

Carter Hawley Hale Stores, 85 F.T.C. 1116 (1975), 480

Carter Hawley Hale Stores v. Limited, Inc., 587 F. Supp. 246 (C.D. Cal. 1984), 288, 293, 364

Carter Prods., Inc. v. Colgate-Palmolive Co., 164 F. Supp. 503 (D. Md. 1958), *aff'd*, 269 F.2d 299 (4th Cir. 1959), 835

Carter Prods., Inc. v. FTC, 268 F.2d 461 (9th Cir.), *cert. denied*, 361 U.S. 884 (1959), 473, 513

Carter Prods., Inc. v. FTC, 323 F.2d 523 (5th Cir. 1963), 489

Cartersville Elevator, Inc. v. ICC, 724 F.2d 668 (8th Cir.), *aff'd on reh'g en banc*, 735 F.2d 1059 (8th Cir. 1984), 1134

Carter v. AT&T, 365 F.2d 486 (5th Cir. 1966), cert. denied, 385 U.S. 1008 (1967), 1049

Carter v. Trafalgar Tours Ltd., 704 F. Supp. 673 (W.D. Va. 1989), 872

Carter-Wallace, Inc. v. Hartz Mountain Indus., 1983-1 Trade Cas. (CCH) ¶ 65,332 (S.D.N.Y. 1983), 780

Carter-Wallace, Inc. v. Hartz Mountain Indus., 92 F.R.D. 67 (S.D.N.Y. 1981), 746, 747, 751, 753

Carter-Wallace, Inc. v. United States, 167 U.S.P.Q. (BNA) 667 (Ct. Cl. 1970), 825

Carter-Wallace, Inc. v. United States, 449 F.2d 1374 (Ct. Cl. 1971), 815, 824

Cartrade, Inc. v. Ford Dealers Advertising Ass'n, 446 F.2d 289 (9th Cir. 1971), *cert. denied*, 405 U.S. 997 (1972), 118, 180, 185, 188, 193, 390

Cartwright v. Board of Chiropractic Examiners, 129 Cal. Rptr. 462, 548 P.2d 1134 (Cal. 1976), 582

Cascade Cabinet Co. v. Western Cabinet & Millwork, Inc., 710 F.2d 1366 (9th Cir. 1983), 37, 38, 50, 52, 55, 181, 268, 269

Cascade Natural Gas Corp. v. El Paso Natural Gas Co., 386 U.S. 129 (1967), 360, 578

Cascade Natural Gas Corp. v. Northwest Pipeline Corp., 48 F.E.R.C. (CCH) ¶ 61,234 (1989), 1062

Cascade Steel Rolling Mills, Inc. v. C. Itoh & Co. (Am.), 499 F. Supp. 829 (D. Or. 1980), 866

Case-Swayne Co. v. Sunkist Growers, 369 F.2d 449 (9th Cir. 1966), *rev'd*, 389 U.S. 384 (1967), 198, 209, 211

Case-Swayne Co. v. Sunkist Growers, 389 U.S. 384 (1967), 1027

Casey v. Diet Center, 590 F. Supp. 1561 (N.D. Cal. 1984), 143, 145, 146, 151, 155, 156, 159, 670

Cash v. Arctic Circle, Inc., 85 F.R.D. 618 (E.D. Wash. 1979), 728, 732

Cass Student Advertising, Inc. v. National Educ. Advertising Serv., 516 F.2d 1092 (7th Cir.), *cert. denied*, 423 U.S. 986 (1975), 204

Castelli v. Meadville Medical Center, 702 F. Supp. 1201 (W.D. Pa.), *aff'd without published opinion*, 872 F.2d 411 (3d Cir. 1989), 132, 173

Castillo v. St. Paul Fire & Marine Ins. Co., 938 F.2d 776 (7th Cir. 1991), 769

Castoe v. Amerada Hess Corp., 1976-2 Trade Cas. (CCH) ¶ 61,054 (S.D.N.Y. 1976), 189

Catalano v. Target Sales, Inc., 446 U.S. 643 (1980), 31, 34, 35, 37, 64, 65, 66

Catalina Cablevision Assocs. v. City of Tucson, 745 F.2d 1266 (9th Cir. 1984), 1054

Cataphote Corp. v. DeSoto Chem. Coatings, Inc., 450 F.2d 769, (9th Cir. 1971), *cert. denied*, 408 U.S. 929 (1972), 809, 819

Cate v. Oldham, 450 So. 2d 224 (Fla. 1984), 638

C.A.T. Indus. Disposal v. Browning-Ferris Indus., 704 F. Supp. 120 (W.D. Tex.), *aff'd*, 884 F.2d 209 (5th Cir. 1989), 265

C.A.T. Indus. Disposal v. Browning-Ferris Indus., 884 F.2d 209 (5th Cir. 1989), 266

Catlin v. Washington Energy Co., 791 F.2d 1343 (9th Cir. 1986), 196, 252, 268, 667

Catrone v. Ogden Suffolk Downs, Inc., 683 F. Supp. 302 (D. Mass. 1988), 35, 39, 50, 52

Cayman Exploration Corp. v. United Gas Pipe Line Corp., 1987-1 Trade Cas. (CCH) ¶ 67,482 (N.D. Okla. 1987), 115

Cayman Exploration Corp. v. United Gas Pipe Line Co., 873 F.2d 1357 (10th Cir. 1989), 4, 7, 9, 1062

CBS, 87 F.C.C.2d 30 (1981), 1040

CBS, 87 F.C.C.2d 587 (1981), 1037

CBS v. Amana Refrigeration, Inc., 295 F.2d 375 (7th Cir. 1961), *cert. denied*, 369 U.S. 812 (1962), 169, 410

CBS v. American Soc'y of Composers, Authors & Publishers, 562 F.2d 130 (2d Cir. 1977), *rev'd sub nom.* Broadcast Music, Inc. v. CBS, 441 U.S. 1 (1979), 845

CBS v. American Soc'y of Composers, Authors & Publishers, 607 F.2d 543 (2d Cir. 1979), 845

CBS v. American Soc'y of Composers, Authors and Publishers, 620 F.2d 930 (2d Cir. 1980), *cert. denied*, 450 U.S. 970 (1981), 380, 834

CBS v. FCC, 629 F.2d 1 (D.C.Cir. 1980), aff'd, 453 U.S. 367 (1981), 1039

CBS v. Scorpio Music Distribs., 569 F. Supp. 47 (E.D. Pa. 1983), *aff'd mem.*, 738 F.2d 424 (3d Cir. 1984), 842

CCI Cablevision v. Northwestern Ind. Tel. Co., 3 F.C.C.Rcd 3096 (1988), 1055

C.C.P. Corp. v. Wynn Oil Co., 354 F. Supp. 1275 (N.D. Ill. 1973), 869, 877

Cecil Corley Motor Co. v. General Motors Corp., 380 F. Supp. 819 (M.D. Tenn. 1974), 438, 668

C.E.D. Mobilephone Communs. v. Harris Corp., 1985-1 Trade Cas. (CCH) ¶ 66,386 (S.D.N.Y. 1985), 865

Cekacan, Decision 90/535, 33 O.J. EUR. COMM. (No. L 299) 64 (1990), [1990] 2 CEC (CCH) 2,099, 931

Celanese Corp. v. E.I. duPont de Nemours & Co., 58 F.R.D. 606 (D. Del. 1973), 766

Cellar Door Prods. v. Kay, 897 F.2d 1375 (6th Cir. 1990), 789

Cellular Communs. Sys., 86 F.C.C.2d 469 (1981), *recon. granted in part*, 89 F.C.C.2d 58 (1982), *further recon. granted in part*, 90 F.C.C.2d 571 (1982), *aff'd sub nom.* MCI Cellular Tel. Co. v. FCC, 738 F.2d 1322 (D.C. Cir. 1984), 1046

Celotex Corp. v. Catrett, 477 U.S. 317 (1986), 702, 704

Celtic Constr. Co., 59 F.T.C. 1321 (1961), 477

Cemar, Inc. v. Nissan Motor Corp., 678 F. Supp. 1091 (D. Del. 1988), 159, 163, 408

Cement Mfrs. Protective Ass'n v. United States, 268 U.S. 588 (1925), 64, 67, 71, 72, 405

C.E. Niehoff & Co., 51 F.T.C. 1114 (1955), *aff'd*, 241 F.2d 37 (7th Cir. 1957), *vacated and remanded sub nom.* Moog Indus. v. FTC 355 U.S. 411 (1958)., 412, 424

Centanni v. T. Smith & Son, 216 F. Supp. 330 (E.D. La.), aff'd, 323 F.2d 363 (5th Cir. 1963), 133

Centeno Supermarkets v. H.E. Butt Grocery Co., 1987-2 Trade Cas. (CCH) ¶ 67,753 (W.D. Tex. 1987), 746, 747, 761, 762

Centex-Winston Corp. v. Edward Hines Lumber Co., 447 F.2d 585 (7th Cir. 1971), cert. denied, 405 U.S. 921 (1972), 438

Centrafarm BV v. American Home Prods. Corp., Case 3/78, [1978] E.C.R. 1823, [1977-1978 Transfer Binder] COMMON MKT. REP. (CCH) ¶ 8475, 944

Centrafarm BV v. Sterling Drug Inc., Case 15/74, [1974] E.C.R. 1823, [1974 Transfer Binder] Common Mkt. Rep. (CCH) 8246, 931, 946

Centrafarm BV v. Winthrop BV, Case 16/74, [1974] E.C.R. 1183, [1974 Transfer Binder] Common MKT. Rep. (CCH) ¶ 8247, 944

Central Bank v. Clayton Bank, 424 F. Supp. 163 (E.D. Mo. 1976), aff'd mem., 553 F.2d 102 (8th Cir.), cert. denied, 433 U.S. 910 (1977), 1000, 1006

Central Broadcasting Co., 28 F.C.C.2d 229 (1971), 1039

Central Cal. Lettuce Producers Coop., 90 F.T.C. 18 (1977), 1027

Central Hudson Gas & Elec. Corp. v. Public Serv. Comm'n, 447 U.S. 557 (1980), 492

Central Ice Cream Co. v. Golden Rod Ice Cream Co., 287 F.2d 265 (7th Cir.), cert. denied, 368 U.S. 829 (1961), 403

Central Ice Cream Co. v. Golden Rod Ice Cream Co., 184 F. Supp. 312 (N.D. Ill. 1960), aff'd, 287 F.2d 265 (7th Cir.), cert. denied, 368 U.S. 829 (1961), 412

Central Ill. Pub. Serv. Co., 42 F.E.R.C. (CCH) ¶ 61,073 (1988), 1078

Central Iowa Refuse Sys. v. Des Moines Metro. Solid Waste Agency, 715 F.2d 419 (8th Cir. 1983), cert. denied, 471 U.S. 1003 (1985), 972, 982

Central Nat'l Bank v. Rainbolt, 720 F.2d 1183 (10th Cir. 1983), 364, 661, 663

Central Power & Light Co. v. F.E.R.C., 575 F.2d 937 (D.C. Cir.), cert. denied, 439 U.S. 981 (1978), 1067

Central Retailer-Owned Grocers v. FTC, 319 F.2d 410 (7th Cir. 1963), 433

Central Stikstof Verkoopkantoor, 21 O.J. EUR. COMM. (No. L 242) 15 (1978), [1978-1981 Transfer Binder] COMMON MKT. REP. (CCH) ¶ 10,076, 933

Central Telecommuns. v. City of Jefferson City, 589 F. Supp. 85 (W.D. Mo. 1984), 981

Central Telecommuns. v. TCI Cablevision, Inc., 800 F.2d 711 (8th Cir. 1986), cert. denied, 480 U.S. 910 (1987), 218, 648, 649, 670, 995, 1008, 1034

Central Vt. Pub. Serv. Corp., 39 F.E.R.C. (CCH) ¶ 61,295 (1987), 1078

Central Vt. Ry. v. ICC, 711 F.2d 331 (D.C. Cir. 1983), 1142

Centronics Data Computer Corp. v. Mannesmann, AG, 432 F. Supp. 659 (D.N.H. 1977), 870, 876, 879

Century Communs. Corp. v. FCC, 835 F.2d 292 (D.C. Cir. 1987), 1052

Century Federal, Inc. v. City of Palo Alto, 579 F. Supp. 1553 (N.D. Cal. 1984), 982, 1054

Century Hardware Corp. v. Acme United Corp., 467 F. Supp. 350 (E.D. Wis. 1979), 407, 782

Century Hardware Corp. v. Powernail Corp., 282 F. Supp. 223 (E.D. Wis. 1968), 687

Century Oil Tool, Inc. v. Production Specialties, Inc., 737 F.2d 1316 (5th Cir. 1984), 18, 19

Cernuto, Inc. v. United Cabinet Corp., 595 F.2d 164 (3d Cir. 1979), 40, 45, 60, 168, 189

C.E. Servs. v. Control Data Corp., 759 F.2d 1241 (5th Cir.), cert. denied, 474 U.S. 1037 (1985), 199, 234, 264

Cesnik v. Chrysler Corp., 490 F. Supp. 859 (M.D. Tenn. 1980), 648

Cezar, Ltd., 89 F.T.C. 169 (1977), 541

CHA-Car, Inc. v. Calder Race Course, Inc., 752 F.2d 609 (11th Cir. 1985), 37, 38, 79, 84

Chain Inst., Inc. v. FTC, 246 F.2d 231 (8th Cir.), cert. denied, 355 U.S. 895 (1957), 489

Chambers & Barber, Inc. v. General Adjustment Bureau, 60 F.R.D. 455 (S.D.N.Y. 1973), 691

Chambers Dev. Co. v. Browning-Ferris Indus., 590 F. Supp. 1528 (W.D. Pa. 1984), 30

Champaign Urbana News Agency v. J.L. Cummins News Co., 632 F.2d 680 (7th Cir. 1980), 449

Champion Spark Plug Co., 50 F.T.C. 30 (1953), 429

Champion Spark Plug Co., 103 F.T.C. 546 (1984), 323

Chandler Supply Co. v. GAF Corp., 650 F.2d 983 (9th Cir. 1980), 180, 184

Chandler Trailer Convoy, Inc. v. Morgan Drive-Away, Inc., 1981-2 Trade Cas. (CCH) ¶ 64,418 (W.D. Ark. 1981), 683, 687, 688, 691

Chandler v. Barclays Bank PLC, 898 F.2d 1148 (6th Cir. 1990), 872

Chapiewsky v. G. Heileman Brewing Co., 297 F. Supp. 33 (E.D. Wis. 1968), 119

Chapman v. Rudd Paint & Varnish Co., 409 F.2d 635 (9th Cir. 1969), 407

Charles Jourdan, Decision 89/94, 32 O.J. EUR. COMM. (No. L 35) 31 (1989), [1989] 1 CEC (CCH) 2003, 941

Charles of the Ritz Distrib. Corp. v. FTC, 143 F.2d 676 (2d Cir. 1944), 465, 469, 473

Charles Pfizer & Co. v. FTC, 401 F.2d 574 (6th Cir. 1968), *cert. denied*, 394 U.S. 920 (1969), 807, 854

Charley's Taxi Radio Dispatch Corp. v. SIDA of Haw., 810 F.2d 869 (9th Cir. 1987), 83, 84, 85, 86, 87, 385, 980

Charley's Tour & Transp., Inc. v. InterIsland Resorts, Ltd., 618 F. Supp. 84 (D. Haw. 1985), 686

Charlotte Telecasters, Inc. v. Jefferson-Pilot Corp., 546 F.2d 570 (4th Cir. 1976), 682, 689, 692, 693

Charnita, Inc., 80 F.T.C. 892 (1972), *enforced*, 479 F.2d 684 (3d Cir. 1973), 534

Chase Parkway Garage, Inc. v. Subaru, Inc., 94 F.R.D. 330 (D. Mass. 1982), 712, 728

Chateau De Ville Prods., Inc. v. Tams-Witmark Music Library, Inc., 474 F. Supp. 223 (S.D.N.Y. 1979), 734

Chateau de Ville Prods., Inc. v. Tams-Witmark Music Library, Inc., 586 F.2d 962 (2d Cir. 1978), 723

Chatham Brass Co. v. Honeywell, Inc., 512 F. Supp. 108 (S.D.N.Y. 1981), 654

Chattanooga Foundry & Pipe Works v. City of Atlanta, 203 U.S. 390 (1906), 603, 649, 669

Cheatham's Furniture Co. v. La-Z-Boy Chair Co., 728 F. Supp. 569 (E.D. Mo. 1989), *aff'd without published opinion,* 923 F.2d 858 (8th Cir. 1990), 106, 189

Checker Motors Corp. v. Chrysler Corp., 283 F. Supp. 876 (S.D.N.Y. 1968), *aff'd*, 405 F.2d 319 (2d Cir.), *cert. denied*, 394 U.S. 999 (1969), 110, 412, 429

Checker Motors Corp. v. Chrysler Corp., 405 F.2d 319 (2d Cir.), *cert. denied*, 394 U.S. 999 (1969), 108, 677

Chemagro Corp. v. Universal Chem. Co., 244 F. Supp. 486 (E.D. Tex. 1965), 829

Chemetron Corp. v. Crane Co., 1977-2 Trade Cas. (CCH) ¶ 61,717 (N.D. Ill. 1977), 368, 369, 370

Chemway Corp., 78 F.T.C. 1250 (1971), 474

Chest Hill Co. v. Guttman, 1981-2 Trade Cas. (CCH) ¶ 64,417 (S.D. Ohio 1981), 1004

Chestnut Farms Chevy Chase Dairy, 53 F.T.C. 1050 (1957), 442

Chestnut Fleet Rentals, Inc. v. Hertz Corp., 72 F.R.D. 541 (E.D. Pa. 1976), 718

Chevalier v. Baird Sav. Ass'n, 72 F.R.D. 140 (E.D. Pa. 1976), 733

Chevron Corp. & Gulf Corp., 104 F.T.C. 597 (1984), 368, 369, 370

Chicago Bd. of Trade v. Olsen, 262 U.S. 1 (1923), 1107

Chicago Bd. of Trade v. United States, 246 U.S. 231 (1918), 2, 42, 56, 62, 69, 379

Chicago Mercantile Exch. v. Deaktor, 414 U.S. 113 (1973), 1106

Chicago Professional Sports Ltd. Partnership v. NBA, 754 F. Supp. 1336 (N.D. Ill. 1991), 39, 46, 48, 50, 52, 56, 69, 85, 381

Chicago Seating Co. v. S. Karpen & Bros., 177 F.2d 863, 866 (7th Cir. 1949), 439

Chicago Spring Prods. Co. v. United States Steel Corp., 254 F. Supp. 83, 84 (N.D. Ill.), *aff'd*, 371 F.2d 428 (7th Cir. 1966), 425

Chicago Spring Prods. Co. v. United States Steel Corp., 371 F.2d 428 (7th Cir. 1966), 438

Chicago Title Ins. Co. v. Great Western Fin. Corp., 69 Cal. 2d 305, 70 Cal. Rptr. 849, 444 P.2d 481 (1968), 639

Chicken Delight, Inc. v. Harris, 412 F.2d 830 (9th Cir. 1969), 728, 736

Chick's Auto Body v. State Farm Mut. Auto Ins. Co., 168 N.J. Super. 68, 401 A.2d 722 (1979), *aff'd*, 176 N.J. Super. 320, 423 A.2d 311 (1980), 638

Chiglades Farm v. Butz, 485 F.2d 1125 (5th Cir. 1973), *cert. denied*, 417 U.S. 968 (1974), 1025

Chillicothe Sand & Gravel Co. v. Martin Marietta Corp., 615 F.2d 427 (7th Cir. 1980), 228, 415

Chipanno v. Champion Int'l Corp., 702 F.2d 627 (9th Cir. 1983), 684, 685

Chirikos v. Yellow Cab Co., 1980-2 Trade Cas. (CCH) ¶ 63,557 (Ill. App. Ct. 1980), 637

Chiropractic Coop. Ass'n v. American Medical Ass'n, 617 F. Supp. 264 (E.D. Mich. 1985), 92

Chiropractic Coop. Ass'n v. American Medical Ass'n, 1986-2 Trade Cas. (CCH) ¶ 67,294 (E.D. Mich. 1986), *aff'd in part and reversed in part*, 867 F.2d 270 (6th Cir. 1989), 682

Chisholm Bros. Farm Equip. Co. v. International Harvester Co., 498 F.2d 1137 (9th Cir.), *cert. denied*, 419 U.S. 1023 (1974), 108, 109

Chisholm-Ryder Co. v. Mecca Bros., 1983-1 Trade Cas. (CCH) ¶ 65,406 (W.D.N.Y. 1982), 803, 819

Chlorine & Caustic Soda Antitrust Litig., 116 F.R.D. 622 (E.D. Pa. 1987), 714

Chmieleski v. City Prods. Corp., 71 F.R.D. 118 (W.D. Mo. 1976), 713, 718, 719, 724, 728, 734

Chmieleski v. City Prods. Corp., 522 F. Supp. 917 (W.D. Mo. 1981), 676

Chmieleski v. City Prods. Corp., 1983-1 Trade Cas. (CCH) ¶ 65,446 (W.D. Mo. 1983), 434, 435

Chock Full O'Nuts Corp., 82 F.T.C. 747 (1973), 511

Choy v. Charytan, 1987-2 Trade Cas. (CCH) ¶ 67,708 (E.D.N.Y. 1987), 25

Chrapliwy v. Uniroyal, Inc., 71 F.R.D. 461 (N.D. Ind.) 1976, 744

Christiani & Nielsen, 12 J.O. COMM. EUR. (No. L 165) 12 (1969), [1965-1969 Transfer Binder] COMMON MKT. REP. (CCH) ¶ 9308, 931

Christian Schmidt Brewing Co. v. G. Heileman Brewing Co., 600 F. Supp. 1326 (E.D. Mich.), *aff'd*, 753 F.2d 1354 (6th Cir.), *cert. dismissed*, 469 U.S. 1200 (1985), 294, 317, 362, 367, 368, 369

Christian Schmidt Brewing Co. v. G. Heileman Brewing Co., 753 F.2d 1354 (6th Cir.), *cert. dismissed*, 469 U.S. 1200 (1985), 365, 366, 664, 676, 678

Christiansen v. Mechanical Contractors Bid Depository, 230 F. Supp. 186 (D. Utah 1964), *aff'd*, 352 F.2d 817 (10th Cir. 1965), *cert. denied*, 384 U.S. 918 (1966), 70

Christianson v. Colt Indus. Operating Corp., 1991-1 Trade Cas. (CCH) ¶ 69,415 (C.D. Ill. 1991), 37, 38

Christianson v. Colt Indus. Operating Corp., 766 F. Supp. 670 (C.D. Ill. 1991), 1001

Christianson v. Colt Indus. Operating Corp., 486 U.S. 800 (1988), 851, 852

Christofferson Dairy v. MMM Sales, Inc., 849 F.2d 1168 (9th Cir. 1988), 268, 269, 272

Chromalloy Am. Corp. v. Fischmann, 716 F.2d 683 (9th Cir. 1983), 825

Chronister v. Atlantic Richfield Co., 653 F. Supp. 1573 (M.D. Pa. 1987), 50

Chrysler Corp. v. Fedders Corp., 643 F.2d 1229 (6th Cir.), *cert. denied*, 454 U.S. 893 (1981), 365, 870, 876

Chrysler Corp., 87 F.T.C. 719 (1976), *enforced as modified*, 561 F.2d 357 (D.C. Cir. 1977), 466

Chrysler Corp. v. FTC, 561 F.2d 357 (D.C. Cir. 1977), 464, 466, 494

Chrysler Corp. v. General Motors Corp., 1985-1 Trade Cas. (CCH) ¶ 66,391 (D.D.C. 1985), 701

Chrysler Corp. v. General Motors Corp., 589 F. Supp. 1182 (D.D.C. 1984), 664, 868, 869, 876, 877

Chrysler Corp. v. General Motors Corp., 596 F. Supp. 416 (D.D.C. 1984), 701

Chrysler Corp. v. Texas Motor Vehicle Comm'n, 755 F.2d 1192 (5th Cir. 1985), 623

Chrysler Corp. v. United States, 316 U.S. 556 (1942), 571, 576, 577

Chrysler Credit Crop. v. J. Truett Payne, Inc., 670 F.2d 575 (5th Cir. 1982), *cert. denied*, 459 U.S. 908 (1983), 416

Chuck's Feed & Seed Co. v. Ralston Purina Co., 810 F.2d 1289 (4th Cir.), *cert. denied*, 484 U.S. 827 (1987), 52, 173, 176, 179, 182

Cia. Petrolera Caribe, Inc. v. Arco Caribbean, Inc., 754 F.2d 404 (1st Cir. 1985), 348, 351, 362, 370, 398, 643, 664, 680

Cia. Petrolera Caribe, Inc. v. Avis Rental Car Corp., 576 F. Supp. 1011 (D.P.R. 1983), *aff'd*, 735 F.2d 636 (1st Cir. 1984), 137

Cia. Petrolera Caribe, Inc. v. Avis Rental Car Corp., 735 F.2d 636 (1st Cir. 1984), 146

CICCE v. Commission, Case 298/83, [1985] E.C.R. 1105, [1983-1985 Transfer Binder] COMMON MKT. REP. (CCH) ¶ 14,157, 921

Ciminelli v. Cablevision, 583 F. Supp. 158 (E.D.N.Y. 1984), 1055

Cincinnati Milk Sales Ass'n v. National Farmers' Org., 1967 Trade Cas. (CCH) ¶ 72,092 (S.D. Ohio 1967), 1026

Cinderella Career & Finishing Schools, Inc. v. FTC, 425 F.2d 583 (D.C. Cir. 1970), 470, 510

Cine Forty-Second Street Theatre Corp. v. Allied Artists Pictures Corp., 602 F.2d 1062 (2d Cir. 1979), 768, 770

Cine 42nd Street Theater Corp. v. Nederlander Organization, 790 F.2d 1032 (2d Cir. 1986), 966, 980, 986

Cinema Amusements, Inc. v. Loew's, Inc., 7 F.R.D. 318 (D. Del. 1947), 747

Cinema Serv. Corp. v. Twentieth Century-Fox Film Corp., 477 F. Supp. 174 (W.D. Pa. 1979), 574, 646, 746, 778

Cinnamon v. Abner A. Wolf, Inc., 215 F. Supp. 833 (E.D. Mich. 1963), 793

Cipollone v. Liggett Group, 668 F. Supp. 408 (D.N.J. 1987), 1015

Cities of Anaheim v. FERC, 941 F.2d 1234 (D.C. Cir. 1991), 1072

Cities of Anaheim v. Southern Cal. Edison Co., 1990-2 Trade Cas. (CCH) ¶ 69,246 (C.D. Cal. 1990), 210, 238, 239, 247, 250, 1071, 1073

Cities Serv. Oil Co. v. Coleman Oil Co., 470 F.2d 925 (1st Cir. 1972), *cert. denied*, 411 U.S. 967 (1973), 54, 143

Citizen Publishing Co. v. United States, 394 U.S. 131 (1969), 314, 315, 376

City Communs. v. City of Detroit, 650 F. Supp. 1570 (E.D. Mich. 1987), 1054

City Communs. v. City of Detroit, 660 F. Supp. 932 (E.D. Mich. 1987), 988

City Communs., v. City of Detroit, 888 F.2d 1081 (6th Cir. 1989), 706

City of Atlanta v. Ashland-Warren, Inc., 1982-1 Trade Cas. (CCH) ¶ 64,527 (N.D. Ga. 1981), 1010

City of Batavia v. Commonwealth Edison Co., No. 76 C 4388 (N.D. Ill. Jan. 16, 1984), 415, 421

City of Batavia v. F.E.R.C., 672 F.2d 64 (D.C. Cir. 1982), 239

City of Burbank v. General Elec. Co., 329 F.2d 825 (9th Cir. 1964), 778

City of Chanute v. Kansas Gas & Elec. Co., 754 F.2d 310 (10th Cir. 1985), 1073

City of Chanute v. Williams Natural Gas Co., 678 F. Supp. 1517 (D. Kan. 1988), 208, 210, 211, 1065

City of Chanute v. Williams Natural Gas Co., 743 F. Supp. 1437 (D. Kan. 1990), 246, 248, 605, 1065

City of Chanute v. Williams Natural Gas Co., 1990-1 Trade Cas. (CCH) ¶ 68,967 (D. Kan. 1990), 144

City of Cleveland v. Cleveland Elec. Illuminating Co., 538 F. Supp. 1280 (N.D. Ohio 1980), 685

City of Cleveland v. Cleveland Elec. Illuminating Co., 734 F.2d 1157 (6th Cir.), *cert. denied*, 469 U.S. 884 (1984), 1000, 1015

City of Columbia v. Omni Outdoor Advertising, Inc., 111 S. Ct. 1344 (1991), 189, 240, 244, 255, 258, 966, 977, 978, 979, 984, 990, 996, 1006, 1009, 1010

City of Denver v. American Oil Co., 53 F.R.D. 620 (D. Colo. 1971), 729

City of Detroit v. Grinnell Corp., 495 F.2d 448 (2d Cir. 1974), 682, 693, 741, 742, 743, 782

City of El Paso v. Darbyshire Steel Co., 575 F.2d 521 (5th Cir. 1978), *cert. denied*, 439 U.S. 1121 (1979), 691

City of Gainesville v. Florida Power & Light Co., 488 F. Supp. 1258 (S.D. Fla. 1980), 410, 1003

City of Groton v. Connecticut Light & Power Co., 497 F. Supp. 1040 (D. Conn. 1980), *aff'd in part and rev'd in part*, 662 F.2d 921 (2d Cir. 1981), 410

City of Groton v. Connecticut Light & Power Co., 662 F.2d 921 (2d Cir. 1981), 225, 238, 239, 240, 1020, 1021, 1070, 1073

City of Kansas City v. Federal Pac. Elec. Co., 310 F.2d 271 (8th Cir.), *cert. denied*, 371 U.S. 912 (1962) and 373 U.S. 914 (1963), 688, 689

City of Kirkwood v. Union Elec. Co., 671 F.2d 1173 (8th Cir. 1982), *cert. denied*, 459 U.S. 1170 (1983), 238, 239, 240, 241, 410, 999, 1011, 1018, 1020, 1072

City of Lafayette v. Louisiana Power & Light Co., 435 U.S. 389 (1978), 43,981, 983

City of Lafayette v. SEC, 454 F.2d 941 (D.C. Cir. 1971), *aff'd sub nom.* Gulf States Utils. Co. v. FPC, 411 U.S. 747 (1973), 1076

City of Lafayette v. SEC, 481 F.2d 1101, (D.C. Cir. 1973), 1076

City of Long Beach v. Standard Oil Co., 872 F.2d 1401 (9th Cir. 1989), *cert. denied*, 110 S. Ct. 1126 (1990), 7, 10, 666, 707, 1019

City of Malden v. Union Elec. Co., 887 F.2d 157 (8th Cir. 1989), 197, 246, 1070

City of Mishawaka v. American Elec. Power Co., 465 F. Supp. 1320 (N.D. Ind. 1979), *aff'd in part, vacated in part*, 616 F.2d 976 (7th Cir. 1980), *cert. denied*, 449 U.S. 1096 (1981), 225, 238, 239, 240

City of Mishawaka v. American Elec. Power Co., 616 F.2d 976 (7th Cir. 1980), *cert. denied*, 449 U.S. 1096 (1981), 225, 240, 241, 676, 678, 1022, 1073

City of Mishawaka v. Indiana & Mich. Elec. Co., 560 F.2d 1314 (7th Cir. 1977), *cert. denied*, 436 U.S. 922 (1978), 240, 1023, 1072

City of Mt. Pleasant v. Associated Elec. Coop., 838 F.2d 268 (8th Cir. 1988), 20, 706, 708

City of Newark v. Delmarva Power & Light Co., 467 F. Supp. 763 (D. Del. 1979), 238, 240, 410, 1072

City of Newark v. Delmarva Power & Light Co., 497 F. Supp. 323 (D. Del. 1980), 1002

City of New Orleans v. Dukes, 427 U.S. 297 (1976), 626, 627

City of New York v. Darling-Delaware, 440 F. Supp. 1132 (S.D.N.Y. 1977), 786

City of New York v. General Motors, 60 F.R.D. 393 (S.D.N.Y. 1973), *appeal dismissed*, 501 F.2d 639 (2d Cir. 1974), 715

City of New York v. Pullman, Inc., 662 F.2d 910 (2d Cir. 1981), *cert. denied*, 454 U.S. 1164 (1982), 773

City of Philadelphia v. New Jersey, 437 U.S. 617 (1978), 621

City of Philadelphia v. Westinghouse Elec. Co., 210 F. Supp. 483 (E.D. Pa), *mandamus denied sub nom.* General Elec. Co. v. Kirkpatrick, 312 F.2d 742 (3d Cir. 1962), *cert. denied*, 372 U.S. 943 (1963), 760

City of Pittsburgh v. FPC, 237 F.2d 741 (D.C. Cir. 1956), 1056, 1057

City of Pittsburgh v. May Dep't Stores Co., 1986-2 Trade Cas. (CCH) ¶ 67,304 (W.D. Pa. 1986), 378, 604, 612

City of Riverside v. Rivera, 477 U.S. 560 (1986), 782, 784

City of Rohnert Park v. Harris, 601 F.2d 1040 (9th Cir. 1979) *cert. denied*, 445 U.S. 961 (1980), 649, 665

City of Vernon v. Southern Cal. Edison Co., 1990-1 Trade Cas. (CCH) ¶ 69,032 (C.D. Cal. 1990), 225, 1071

City of Vernon v. Southern Cal. Edison Co., 1992-1 Trade Cas. (CCH) ¶ 69,717 (9th Cir. 1992), 674

City Stores Co., 89 F.T.C. 322 (1977), 480

Clairol, Inc., 69 F.T.C. 1009 (1966), *aff'd*, 410 F.2d 647 (9th Cir. 1969), 439, 440, 441

Clairol, Inc. v. Asaro, 1975-1 Trade Cas. (CCH) ¶ 60,350 (E.D. Mich. 1975), 121

Clairol, Inc. v. Boston Discount Center, 1976-2 Trade Cas. (CCH) ¶ 61,108 (E.D. Mich. 1976), *aff'd*, 608 F.2d 1114 (6th Cir. 1979), 121

Clairol, Inc. v. Boston Discount Centers, Inc., 608 F.2d 1114 (6th Cir. 1979), 124, 126

Clamp-All Corp. v. Cast-Iron Soil Pipe Inst., 851 F.2d 478 (1st Cir. 1988), *cert. denied*, 488 U.S. 1007 (1989), 6, 86, 993

Clark & Reid Co. v. United States, 851 F.2d 1468 (D.C. Cir. 1988), 1128

Clarksburg Pub. Co. v FCC, 225 F.2d 511 (D.C. Cir. 1955), 1035

Clark v. H.P. Hood, Inc., 1985-2 Trade Cas. (CCH) ¶ 66,780 (D. Mass. 1985), 728

Clark v. United Bank of Denver Nat'l Ass'n, 480 F.2d 235 (10th Cir.), *cert. denied*, 414 U.S. 1004 (1973), 184, 185

Clark v. United States, 289 U.S. 1 (1933), 762, 763, 764

Clausen & Sons v. Theo Hamm Brewing Co., 284 F. Supp. 148 (D. Minn. 1967), *rev'd*, 395 F.2d 388 (8th Cir. 1968), 404

Clayco Petroleum Corp. v. Occidental Petroleum Corp., 712 F.2d 404 (9th Cir. 1983) (per curiam), *cert. denied*, 464 U.S. 1040 (1984), 903, 904

Clayton Mfg. Co. v. Cline, 427 F. Supp. 78 (C.D. Cal. 1976), 826

Cleland v. Anderson, 66 Neb. 252, 92 N.W. 306 (1902), 627

Clement v. SEC, 674 F.2d 641 (7th Cir. 1982), 1101

Cliffdale Associates, 103 F.T.C. 110 (1984), 471, 472

Cliff Food Stores v. Kroger, Inc., 417 F.2d 203 (5th Cir. 1969), 214, 403

Clift v. United Auto Workers, 818 F.2d 623 (7th Cir. 1987), *vacated*, 488 U.S. 1025 (1988), 737

Cline v. Frink Dairy Co., 274 U.S. 445 (1927), 628

Clinique Labs., 96 F.T.C. 51 (1980), 107

Clinton Watch Co. v. FTC, 291 F.2d 838 (7th Cir. 1961), *cert. denied*, 368 U.S. 952 (1962), 476

Clipper Exxpress, Inc. v. Rocky Mountain Motor Tariff Bureau, 690 F.2d 1240 (9th Cir. 1982), *cert. denied*, 459 U.S. 1227 (1983), 258, 259, 666, 998, 999, 1001, 1004, 1006, 1007, 1008, 1012, 1014

Coal Exporters Ass'n of U.S. v. United States, 745 F.2d 76 (D.C. Cir. 1984), *cert. denied*, 471 U.S. 1072 (1985), 1017, 1132, 1133, 1134

Coalition to Preserve The Integrity of Am. Trademarks v. United States, 790 F.2d 903 (D.C. Cir. 1986), *aff'd in part and rev'd in part sub nom.* K-Mart Corp. v. Cartier, Inc.,486 U.S. 281 (1988), 843

Coastal Neuro-Psychiatric Assocs. v. Onslow Memorial Hosp., 795 F.2d 340 (4th Cir. 1986), 976, 984

Coastal States Marketing, Inc. v. Hunt, 694 F.2d 1358 (5th Cir. 1983), 912, 1001, 1003, 1014, 1015

Coastal Transfer Co. v. Toyota Motor Sales, 833 F.2d 208 (9th Cir. 1987), 789

Coast v. Hunt Oil Co., 195 F.2d 870 (5th Cir.), *cert. denied*, 344 U.S. 836 (1952), 644

COBELPA/VNP, 20 O.J. EUR. COMM. (No. L 242) 10 (1977), [1976-1978 Transfer Binder] COMMON MKT. REP. (CCH) ¶ 9980, 933

Coblenz GMC/Freightliner v. General Motors Corp., 724 F. Supp. 1364 (M.D. Ala. 1989), *aff'd without pub. op.*, 932 F.2d 977 and 932 F.2d 978 (11th Cir. 1991), 872

Coca-Cola Bottling Co., 93 F.T.C. 110 (1979), 288, 293

Coca-Cola Bottling Co. v. Coca-Cola Co., 696 F. Supp. 97 (D. Del. 1988), 206

Coca-Cola Co., 83 F.T.C. 746 (1973), 471, 473

Coca-Cola Co., 91 F.T.C. 517 (1978), *remanded for dismissal*, 642 F.2d 1387 (D.C. Cir. 1981), 124, 125, 127, 129

Coca-Cola Co., 5 TRADE REG. REP. ¶ 22,584 (Aug. 9, 1988), 352

Coca-Cola Co. v. FTC, 475 F.2d 299 (5th Cir.), *cert. denied*, 414 U.S. 877 (1973), 523, 524

Coca-Cola Co. v. Howard Johnson Co., 386 F. Supp. 330 (N.D. Ga. 1974), 847, 848

Codex Corp. v. Racal-Milgo, Inc., 1984-1 Trade Cas. (CCH) ¶ 65,853 (D. Mass. 1984), 868, 1008

Cody v. Community Loan Corp., 606 F.2d 499 (5th Cir. 1979), *cert. denied*, 446 U.S. 988 (1980), 1112

Cofinco, Inc. v. Angola Coffee Co., 1975-2 Trade Cas. (CCH) ¶ 60,456 (S.D.N.Y. 1975), 909

Cohen v. Beneficial Indus. Loan Corp., 337 U.S. 541 (1949), 754

Cohen v. Primerica Corp., 709 F. Supp. 63 (E.D.N.Y. 1989), 264, 265

Cohn v. Compax Corp., 87 A.D.2d 364, 451 N.Y.S.2d 171 (2d Dep't 1982), 826

Colburn v. Roto-Rooter Corp., 78 F.R.D. 679 (N.D. Cal. 1978), 736

Cold Metal Process Co. v. McLouth Steel Corp., 41 F. Supp. 487 (E.D. Mich. 1931), *aff'd*, 170 F.2d 369 (6th Cir. 1948), 826

Coleman Motor Co. v. Chrysler Corp., 525 F.2d 1338 (3d Cir.), *cert. denied*, 419 U.S. 869 (1975), 49, 189, 672, 674, 675

Cole v. Hughes Tool Co., 215 F.2d 924 (10th Cir.), *cert. denied*, 348 U.S. 927 (1954), 803

Colgate-Palmolive Co., 77 F.T.C. 150 (1970), 481

Collins & Aikman Corp. v. Stratton Indus., 728 F. Supp. 1570 (N.D. Ga. 1989), 1001

Collins v. Associated Pathologists, Ltd., 676 F. Supp. 1388 (C.D. Ill. 1987), *aff'd*, 844 F.2d 473 (7th Cir.), *cert. denied*, 488 U.S. 852 (1988), 50, 79, 85, 173

Collins v. Associated Pathologists, Ltd., 844 F.2d 473 (7th Cir.), *cert. denied*, 488 U.S. 852 (1988), 47, 133, 140, 172, 173, 178, 210, 705, 706, 708

Colonial Ford, Inc. v. Ford Motor Co., 1975-2 Trade Cas. (CCH) ¶ 60,472 (D. Utah 1975), *aff'd*, 577 F.2d 106 (10th Cir. 1978), *cert. denied*, 444 U.S. 837 (1979), 677

Colonial Penn Group v. American Ass'n of Retired Persons, 698 F. Supp. 69 (E.D. Pa. 1988), 247

Colonial Stores, 77 F.T.C. 554 (1970), 446

Colonial Stores v. FTC, 450 F.2d 733 (5th Cir. 1971), 443, 444, 446, 521, 522

Colorado Chiropractic Council v. Porter Memorial Hosp., 650 F. Supp. 231 (D. Colo. 1986), 789

Colorado *ex rel.* Woodard v. Asphalt Paving Co., 1987-1 Trade Cas. (CCH) ¶ 67,473 (D. Colo. 1987), 611

Colorado *ex rel.* Woodard v. Colorado Union of Physicians and Surgeons, 1990-1 Trade Cas. (CCH) ¶ 68,968 (D. Colo. 1990), 618

Colorado *ex rel.* Woodard v. Goodell Bros., 1986-2 Trade Cas. (CCH) ¶ 67,236 (D. Colo. 1986), 681

Colorado *ex rel.* Woodard v. Peter Kiewit Sons Co., 1987-2 Trade Cas. (CCH) ¶ 67,791 (D. Colo. 1987), 611

Colorado *ex rel.* Woodard v. Western Paving Co., 630 F. Supp. 206 (D. Colo. 1986), *aff'd en banc by equally divided court*, 841 F.2d 1025 (10th Cir.), *cert. denied*, 488 U.S. 870 (1988), 688, 689, 690, 691

Colorado Interstate Gas Co. v. Natural Gas Pipeline Co., 661 F. Supp. 1448 (D. Wyo. 1987), *aff'd in part and rev'd in part*, 885 F.2d 683 (10th Cir. 1989), *cert. denied*, 111 S. Ct. 441 (1990), 1063

Colorado Interstate Gas Co. v. Natural Gas Pipeline Co., 885 F.2d 683 (10th Cir. 1989), *cert. denied*, 111 S. Ct. 441 (1990), 212, 214, 259, 261, 264, 266

Colorado Pump & Supply Co. v. Febco, Inc., 472 F.2d 637 (10th Cir.), *cert. denied*, 411 U.S. 987 (1973), 121, 130, 164, 165

Colorado v. Cowan, 1989-1 Trade Cas. (CCH) ¶ 68,395 (D. Colo. 1989), 611

Colorado v. Goodell Bros., 1987-1 Trade Cas. (CCH) ¶ 67,476 (D.C. Colo), 789

Colortronic Reinhard & Co. v. Plastic Controls, Inc., 668 F.2d 1 (1st Cir. 1981), 811

Columbia Metal Culvert Co. v. Kaiser Aluminum & Chem. Corp., 579 F.2d 20 (3d Cir.), *cert. denied*, 439 U.S. 876 (1978), 17, 45, 46, 47, 49, 203, 264, 265

Columbia Metal Culvert v. Kaiser Indus. Corp., 526 F.2d 724 (3d Cir. 1975), 875

Columbia Nitrogen Co. v. Royster Co., 451 F.2d 3 (4th Cir. 1971), 699, 700

Columbia Pictures Indus. v. ABC, 501 F.2d 894 (2d Cir. 1974), 678

Columbia Pictures Indus. v. Professional Real Estate Investors, Inc., 1990-1 Trade Cas. (CCH) ¶ 68,971 (C.D. Cal. 1990) *aff'd*, 944 F.2d 1525 (9th Cir. 1991), *petition for cert. filed*, 60 U.S.L.W. 3482 (U.S. Dec. 23, 1991) (No. 91-1043), 1000

Columbia Pictures Indus. v. Redd Horne, Inc., 749 F.2d 154 (3d Cir. 1984), 258, 847, 1004

Comark Cable Fund III, 100 F.C.C.2d 1244 (1985), *recon. denied*, 103 F.C.C.2d 600 (1985), *remanded sub nom.* Northwestern Indiana Tel. Co. v. FCC, 824 F.2d 1205 (D.C. Cir. 1987), 1055

Combined Communs. Corp., 28 F.C.C.2d 16 (1970), 1039

Combined Communs. Corp., 72 F.C.C.2d 637 (1979), *aff'd*, 76 F.C.C.2d 445 (1980), 1052

Comcoa, Inc. v. NEC Tel., 931 F.2d 655 (10th Cir. 1991), 427, 770

Commander Leasing Co. v. Transamerica Title Ins. Co., 477 F.2d 77 (10th Cir. 1973), 1115, 1116

Commercial Programming Unlimited, Inc., 88 F.T.C. 913 (1976), 492

Commissioner v. Glenshaw Glass Co., 348 U.S. 426 (1955), 794

Committee for an Indep. P-I v. Hearst Corp., 704 F.2d 467 (9th Cir.), *cert. denied*, 464 U.S. 892 (1983), 318

Commodity Elec. Serv. of Los Angeles v. National Elec. Contractors Ass'n, 869 F.2d 1235 (9th Cir.), *cert. denied*, 483 U.S. 891, 790

Commodity Futures Trading Comm'n v. Nahas, 738 F.2d 487 (D.C. Cir. 1984), 880

Commodore Business Machs., Inc., 105 F.T.C. 230 (1985), 468

Commonwealth Edison Co., 36 F.P.C. 927 (1966), *aff'd sub nom.* Utility Users League v. FPC, 394 F.2d 16 (7th Cir.), *cert. denied*, 393 U.S. 953 (1968), 1075

Commonwealth Edison Co. v. Allis-Chalmers Mfg. Co., 323 F.2d 412 (7th Cir. 1963), *cert. denied*, 376 U.S. 939 (1964), 583, 778

Commonwealth Life Ins. Co. v. Neal, 669 F.2d 300 (5th Cir. 1982), 99

Commonwealth of Pennsylvania v. Budget Fuel Co., 1988-2 Trade Cas. (CCH) ¶ 68,229 (E.D. Pa. 1988), 731

Commonwealth v. Budget Fuel Co., 122 F.R.D. 184 (E.D. Pa. 1988), 729

Commonwealth v. McHugh, 326 Mass. 249, 93 N.E.2d 751 (1950), 622, 624

Commonwealth v. Norwood Hosp., No. 90-2284 (Mass. Super. Ct. filed Apr. 23, 1990), 633

Commonwealth v. Winslow, 1987-1 Trade Cas. (CCH) ¶ 67,458 (Va. Ch. Ct. 1987), 616, 640

Communications Brokers of Am. v. Chesapeake & Potomac Tel. Co., 370 F. Supp. 967 (W.D. Va. 1974), 1022

Community Blood Bank of the Kansas City Area, Inc., 70 F.T.C. 728 (1966), 92

Community Blood Bank v. FTC, 405 F.2d 1011 (8th Cir. 1969), 456

Community Builders v. City of Phoenix, 652 F.2d 823 (9th Cir. 1981), 27, 158, 159, 982

Community Cable TV, Inc., 98 F.C.C.2d 1180 (1984), 1050

Community Communs. Co. v. City of Boulder, 660 F.2d 1370 (10th Cir. 1981), *cert. dismissed*, 456 U.S. 1001 (1982), 366, 677

Community Communs. Co. v. City of Boulder, 455 U.S. 40 (1982), 43, 981, 986, 987, 1054

Community Elec. Serv. v. National Elec. Contractors Ass'n, 869 F.2d 1235 (9th Cir.), *cert. denied*, 493 U.S. 891 (1989), 644, 694, 789, 790, 1022

Community Hosp. v. Tomberlin, 712 F. Supp. 170 (M.D. Ala. 1989), 178

Commuter Transp. Sys. v. Hillsborough County Aviation Auth., 801 F.2d 1286 (11th Cir. 1986), 707, 970, 981

COMPACT v. Metropolitan Gov't, 594 F. Supp. 1567 (M.D. Tenn. 1984), 40, 63, 76, 372, 376, 381, 384, 1010

Compagnie Francaise d'Assurance Pour le Commerce Exterieur v. Phillips Petroleum Co., No. 81 Civ. 4463-CLB, *slip op.* at 13-14 (S.D.N.Y. Jan. 23, 1983), 888

Compagnie Francaise d'Assurance Pour le Commerce Exterieur v. Phillips Petroleum Co., 105 F.R.D. 16 (S.D.N.Y. 1984), 880, 884, 888

Compco Corp. v. Day-Brite Lighting, Inc., 376 U.S. 234 (1964), 850

Components, Inc. v. Western Elec. Co., 318 F. Supp. 959 (D. Me. 1970), 854

Compton v. Metal Prods., 453 F.2d 38 (4th Cir. 1971), *cert. denied*, 405 U.S. 968 (1972), 98, 99

Computer & Communs. Indus. Ass'n v. FCC, 693 F.2d 198 (D.C. Cir. 1982), *cert. denied*, 461 U.S. 938 (1983), 1047

Computer Connection, Inc. v. Apple Computer Corp., 621 F. Supp. 569 (E.D. La. 1985), 126, 182, 183

Computer Identics Corp. v. Southern Pac. Co., 756 F.2d 200 (1st Cir. 1985), 20

Computerland, 30 O.J. Eur. Comm. (No. L 222) 12 (1987), [1985-1988 Transfer Binder] Common Mkt. Rep. (CCH) ¶ 10,906, 941

Computer Place, Inc. v. Hewlett-Packard Co., 607 F. Supp. 822 (N.D. Cal. 1984), *aff'd mem.*, 779 F.2d 56 (9th Cir. 1985), 270

Computer Statistics, Inc. v. Blair, 418 F. Supp. 1339 (S.D. Tex. 1976), 431, 435, 783, 786, 787

Computronics, Inc. v. Apple Computer, Inc., 600 F. Supp. 809 (W.D. Wis. 1985), 448

Com-Tel, Inc. v. Du Kane Corp., 669 F.2d 404 (6th Cir. 1982), 81

Conceptual Eng'g Assocs. v. Aelectronic Bonding, Inc., 714 F. Supp. 1262 (D.R.I. 1989), 258, 265, 807, 998

Concordato Incendio, Decision 90/25, 33 O.J. EUR. COMM. (No. L 15) 25 (1990), [1990] 1 CEC (CCH) 2053, 936

Concrete Materials Corp. v. FTC, 189 F.2d 359 (7th Cir. 1951), 513

Congoleum Corp. v. DLW Aktiengesellschaft, 729 F.2d 1240 (9th Cir. 1984), 872

Congoleum Indus. v. Armstrong Cork Co., 366 F. Supp. 220 (E.D. Pa. 1973), aff'd, 510 F.2d 334 (3d Cir.), cert. denied, 421 U.S. 988 (1975), 824, 826, 827, 833, 836

Congress Building Corp. v. Loew's, Inc., 246 F.2d 587 (7th Cir. 1957), 661

Coniglio v. Highwood Serv., Inc., 60 F.R.D. 359 (W.D.N.Y. 1972), 731

Coniglio v. Highwood Servs., 495 F.2d 1286 (2d Cir.), cert. denied, 419 U.S. 1022 (1974), 45, 159

Conley v. Gibson, 355 U.S. 41 (1957), 29

Conmar Corp. v. Mitsui & Co. (U.S.A.), 858 F.2d 499 (9th Cir. 1989), cert. denied, 488 U.S. 1010 (1989), 684, 689, 690, 693

Connecticut ex rel. Riddle v. Wyco New Haven, Inc., 1990-1 Trade Cas. (CCH) ¶ 69,024 (D. Conn. 1990), 612

Connecticut Light and Power Co., 8 F.E.R.C. (CCH) ¶ 61,187 (1979), 1071

Connecticut v. Levi Strauss & Co., 471 F. Supp. 363 (D. Conn. 1979), 625

Connecticut v. Sandoz Pharmaceutical Co., 90-CV 8062 (JFK) (S.D.N.Y. filed Dec. 18, 1990), 611

Connecticut v. Wyco New Haven, Inc., 1990-1 Trade Cas. (CCH) ¶ 69,024 (D. Conn. 1990), 278, 345

Connell Const. Co. v. Plumbers & Steamfitters Local Union No. 100, 421 U.S. 616 (1975), 622, 638, 1121, 1122, 1123

Connolly v. Union Sewer Pipe Co., 184 U.S. 540 (1902), 791

Conoco Inc. v. Inman Oil Co., 774 F.2d 895 (8th Cir. 1985), 260, 261, 264, 405, 414, 415, 431

Consolidated Aluminum Corp. v. Foseco Int'l, Ltd., 716 F. Supp. 316 (N.D. Ill. 1989), aff'd, 910 F.2d 804 (Fed. Cir. 1990), 802, 998

Consolidated Aluminum Corp. v. Foseco Int'l, Ltd., 910 F.2d 804 (Fed. Cir. 1990), 813

Consolidated Edison Co. v. FERC, 823 F.2d 630 (D.C. Cir. 1987), 1060

Consolidated Express, Inc. v. New York Shipping Ass'n, 602 F.2d 494 (3d Cir. 1979), vacated sub nom. International Longshoremen's Ass'n v. Consolidated Express, Inc., 448 U.S. 901 (1980), modified, 641 F.2d 90 (3d Cir.), mandamus denied, 451 U.S. 905 (1981), 81, 1123

Consolidated Farmers Mut. Ins. Co. v. Anchor Sav. Ass'n, 480 F. Supp. 640 (D. Kan. 1979), aff'd, 1980-2 Trade Cas. (CCH) ¶ 63,530 (10th Cir. 1980), 2, 79, 88, 190

Consolidated Gas Co. v. City Gas Co., 623 F. Supp. 1357 (S.D. Fla. 1985), 199

Consolidated Gas Co. v. City Gas Co., 665 F. Supp. 1493 (S.D. Fla. 1987), aff'd, 880 F.2d 297 (11th Cir. 1989), reinstated on reh'g, 912 F.2d 1262 (11th Cir. 1990), vacated as moot, 111 S. Ct. 1300 (1991), 202, 246, 984, 1063

Consolidated Gas Co. v. City Gas Co., 880 F.2d 297 (11th Cir. 1989), reinstated on reh'g, 912 F.2d 1262 (11th Cir. 1990), vacated as moot, 111 S. Ct. 1300 (1991), 219

Consolidated Gold Fields, PLC v. Anglo Am. Corp., 698 F. Supp. 487 (S.D.N.Y. 1988), aff'd in part and rev'd in part sub nom. Consolidated Gold Fields, PLC v. Minorco, SA, 871 F.2d 252 (2d Cir.), cert. dismissed, 492 U.S. 939 (1989), 292, 307, 308, 312, 366, 367, 368, 369, 875

Consolidated Gold Fields, PLC v. Minorco, SA, 871 F.2d 252 (2d Cir.), cert. dismissed, 492 U.S. 939 (1989), 364, 366, 368, 369, 663, 677, 678, 895

Consolidated Metal Prods. v. American Petroleum Inst., 846 F.2d 284 (5th Cir. 1988), 10, 30, 38, 54, 86, 87, 89, 90, 702

Consolidated Rail Corp. v. United States, 812 F.2d 1444 (3d Cir. 1987), 1136

Consolidated Television Cable Serv. v. City of Frankfort, 857 F.2d 354 (6th Cir. 1988), *cert. denied*, 489 U.S. 1082 (1989), 972, 978, 1057

Consolidated Terminal Sys. v. ITT World Communs., 535 F. Supp. 225 (S.D.N.Y. 1982), 195

Consortium, Inc. v. Knoxville Int'l Energy Exposition, 563 F. Supp. 56 (E.D. Tenn. 1983), 39

Consorzio Italiano della Componentistica di Ricambio per Auto Veicoli (Consorzio) and Maxicar SpA v. Renault, Case 53/87, [1988] E.C.R. 6039, [1990] 1 CEC (CCH) 267, 953

Consten & Grundig v. Commission, Cases 56 and 58/64, [1966] E.C.R. 299, [1961-1966 Transfer Binder] COMMON MKT. REP. (CCH) ¶ 8046, 929, 939, 946

Construction Aggregate Transp., Inc. v. Florida Rock Indus., 710 F.2d 752 (11th Cir. 1983), 22, 24, 26, 27, 61, 62

Consul, Ltd. v. Transco Energy Co., 805 F.2d 490 (4th Cir. 1986), *cert. denied*, 481 U.S. 1050 (1987), 1066

Consultants & Designers, Inc. v. Butler Serv. Group, 720 F.2d 1553 (11th Cir. 1983), 37, 53, 55, 99

Consumers Power Co., 6 N.R.C. 892 (1977), 1081

Consumers Power Co., NUCLEAR REG. REP. (CCH) ¶ 30,263 (1977), 1088

Consumers Union v. FTC, 691 F.2d 575 (D.C. Cir. 1982), *aff'd*, 463 U.S. 1216 (1983), 529

Consumers Union v. FTC, 801 F.2d 417 (D.C. Cir. 1986), 478

Consumers Union v. Kissinger, 506 F.2d 136 (D.C. Cir. 1974), *cert. denied*, 421 U.S. 1004 (1975), 911, 912

Consumers Union v. Rogers, 352 F. Supp. 1319 (D.D.C. 1973), *modified and aff'd sub nom.*

Consumers Union v. Kissinger, 506 F.2d 136 (D.C. Cir. 1974), *cert. denied*, 421 U.S. 1004 (1975), 911, 964

Container Co. v. Carpenter Container Corp., 9 F.R.D. 89 (D. Del. 1949), 854

Continental Baking Co., 63 F.T.C. 2071 (1963), 417, 437

Continental Baking Co. v. Dixon, 283 F. Supp. 285 (D. Del. 1968), 508

Continental Baking Co. v. Old Homestead Bread Co., 476 F.2d 97 (10th Cir.), *cert. denied*, 414 U.S. 975 (1973), 407, 414, 670

Continental Baking Co. v. United States, 281 F.2d 137 (6th Cir. 1960), 34

Continental Cablevision, Inc. v. American Elec. Power Co., 715 F.2d 1115 (6th Cir. 1983), 73, 197

Continental Can Co., 15 J.O. COMM. EUR. (No. L 7) 25 (1972), [1970-1972 Transfer Binder] COMMON MKT. REP. (CCH) ¶ 9481, *rev'd*, Europemballage Corp. and Continental Can Co. v. Commission, Case 6/72, [1973] E.C.R. 215, [1971-1973 Transfer Binder] COMMON MKT. REP. (CCH) ¶ 8171, 957

Continental Maritime, Inc. v. Pacific Coast Metal Trades Dist. Council, 817 F.2d 1391 (9th Cir. 1987), 1124

Continental Oil Co. v. United States, 330 F.2d 347 (9th Cir. 1964), 565

Continental Ore v. Union Carbide & Carbon Corp., 289 F.2d 86 (9th Cir. 1961), *vacated and remanded*, 370 U.S. 690 (1962), 912, 913

Continental Ore Co. v. Union Carbide & Carbon Corp., 370 U.S. 690 (1962), 7, 647, 665, 666, 675, 745, 903, 909, 910, 991, 993, 1012

Continental Paper Bag Co. v. Eastern Paper Bag Co., 210 U.S. 405 (1908), 801, 818

Continental T.V., Inc. v. GTE Sylvania Inc., 461 F. Supp. 1046 (N.D. Cal. 1978), *aff'd*, 694 F.2d 1132 (9th Cir. 1982), 48

Continental T.V., Inc. v. GTE Sylvania Inc., 433 U.S. 36 (1977), 2, 30, 31, 33, 35, 36, 37, 42, 43, 45, 46, 52, 53, 60, 100, 101, 106, 115, 116, 117, 119, 121, 122, 123, 127, 181, 182, 331, 635, 828, 830, 896

Continental Wall Paper Co. v. Louis Voight & Sons, 212 U.S. 227 (1909), 791

Continental Wax Corp. v. FTC, 330 F.2d 475 (2d Cir. 1964), 473

Continental Zummi-Werke AG/Compagnie Générale des Etablissements Michelin, Decision 88/555, 31 O.J. EUR. COMM. (No. L 305) 33 (1988), [1989] 1 CEC (CCH) 2241, 935

Contractor Util. Sales Co. v. Certain-teed Prods. Corp., 638 F.2d 1061 (7th Cir. 1981), *cert. denied*, 470 U.S. 1029 (1985), 15

Control Data Corp. v. IBM, 306 F. Supp. 839 (D. Minn. 1969), *aff'd sub nom.* Data Processing Fin. and Gen. Corp. v. IBM, 430 F.2d 1277 (8th Cir. 1970), 574, 780

Conway v. Bulk Petroleum Corp. 545 F. Supp. 398 (N.D. Ill. 1982), 691

Cooga Mooga, Inc., 98 F.T.C. 814 (1981), 474

Cook v. Ralston Purina Co., 366 F. Supp. 999 (M.D. Ga. 1973), 121, 438

Cooley v. Board of Wardens, 53 U.S. (12 How.) 299 (1851), 621

Cooney v. American Horse Shows Ass'n, 495 F. Supp. 424 (S.D.N.Y. 1980), 88, 90

Coöperatieve Vereniging "Suiker Unie" UA v. Commission, Joined Cases 40-48, 50, 54-56, 111, 113 and 114/73, [1975] E.C.R. 1663, [1975 Transfer Binder] COMMON MKT. REP. (CCH) ¶ 8334, 924, 931, 943, 951, 956

Cooper Indus., 93 F.T.C. 1051 (1979), 345

Cooper Indus. v. British Aerospace, Inc., 102 F.R.D. 918 (S.D.N.Y. 1984), 753, 880

Cooper v. Fidelity-Philadelphia Trust Co., 201 F. Supp. 168 (E.D. Pa. 1962), 693

Cooper v. Forsyth County Hosp. Auth., 789 F.2d 278 (4th Cir.), *cert. denied*, 479 U.S. 972 (1986), 8, 10, 93

Cooter & Gell v. Hartmarx Corp., 110 S. Ct. 2447 (1990), 790

Copper Liquor, Inc. v. Adolph Coors Co., 506 F.2d 934 (5th Cir. 1975), 28, 114, 119, 181, 793

Copper Liquor, Inc. v. Adolph Coors Co., 624 F.2d 575 (5th Cir. 1980), 665, 668, 670, 674

Copper Liquor, Inc. v. Adolph Coors Co., 701 F.2d 542 (5th Cir. 1983), 785

Copperweld Corp. v. Imetal, 403 F. Supp. 579 (W.D. Pa. 1975), 363

Copperweld Corp. v. Independence Tube Corp., 467 U.S. 752 (1984), 3, 18, 19, 20, 21, 44, 66, 75, 97, 261, 271, 395, 1027

Copy-Data Sys. v. Toshiba Am., Inc., 663 F.2d 405 (2d Cir. 1981), 37, 38, 123, 125, 128

Cordova & Simonpietri Ins. Agency v. Chase Manhattan Bank, 649 F.2d 36 (1st Cir. 1981), 25, 29

Corey v. Look, 641 F.2d 32 (1st Cir. 1981), 28, 982, 986

Corn Prods. Ref. Co. v. FTC, 324 U.S. 726 (1945), 405, 418, 438, 439

Cornwell Quality Tools Co. v. C.T.S. Co., 446 F.2d 825 (9th Cir. 1971), *cert. denied*, 404 U.S. 1049 (1972), 177, 414

Coro, Inc. v. FTC, 338 F.2d 149 (1st Cir. 1964), *cert. denied*, 380 U.S. 954 (1965), 476, 489, 490

Corporation of Lloyd's v. Lloyd's U.S., 831 F.2d 33 (2d Cir. 1987), 767

Corrosion Resistant Materials Co. v. Steelite, Inc., 692 F. Supp. 407 (D.N.J. 1988), 106, 189

Cosentino v. Carver-Greenfield Corp., 433 F.2d 1274 (8th Cir. 1970), 644

Costal Plastics, Inc. v. Morgan, Olmstead, Kennedy & Gardner, Inc., 72 F.R.D. 601 (W.D. Pa. 1976), 771

Costantini v. CAB, 706 F.2d 1025 (9th Cir. 1983), 1314

Costner v. Blount Nat'l Bank, 578 F.2d 1192 (6th Cir. 1978), 157, 666, 1098

Cotchett v. Avis Rent A Car Sys., 56 F.R.D. 549 (S.D.N.Y. 1972), 731, 733

Cotten v. Witco Chem. Corp., 651 F.2d 274 (5th Cir. 1981), *cert. denied*, 455 U.S. 909 (1982), 773

Cotton v. Hinton, 559 F.2d 1326 (5th Cir. 1977), *reh'g denied*, 861 F.2d 1281 (11th Cir. 1988), 742

Cottonwood Mall Shopping Center v. Utah Power & Light Co., 440 F.2d 36 (10th Cir.), *cert. denied*, 404 U.S. 857 (1971), 649

C-O-Two Fire Equip. Co. v. United States, 197 F.2d 489 (9th Cir.), *cert. denied*, 344 U.S. 892 (1952), 9, 65

Country Maid, Inc. v. Haseotes, 324 F. Supp. 875 (E.D. Pa. 1971), 403

Country Theatre Co. v. Paramount Film Distrib. Corp., 146 F. Supp. 933 (E.D. Pa. 1956), 408

Country Tweeds, Inc. v. FTC, 326 F.2d 144 (2d Cir. 1964), 494

County Nat'l Bancorp. v. Board of Governors, 654 F.2d 1253 (8th Cir. 1981), 1095

County of Orange v. Sullivan Highway Prods., Inc., No. 88-CV 8583 (JFK) (S.D.N.Y. Dec. 21, 1989), 605

County of Suffolk v. Long Island Lighting Co., 710 F. Supp. 1387 (E.D.N.Y. 1989), aff'd in part and rev'd in part, 907 F.2d 1295 (2d Cir. 1990), 991

Court Degraw Theatre v. Loew's, Inc., 20 F.R.D. 85 (E.D.N.Y. 1957), 746

Courtesy Chevrolet, Inc. v. Tennessee Walking Horse Breeders & Exhibitors' Ass'n of Am., 344 F.2d 860 (9th Cir. 1965), 875

Cowan v. Corley, 814 F.2d 223 (5th Cir 1987), 23, 25, 28

Cowles Commun., 80 F.T.C. 997 (1972), 511

Cowley v. Braden Indus., 613 F.2d 751 (9th Cir.), 41, 45, 47, 124, 125, 126, 127

C. Pappas Co. v. E. & J. Gallo Winery, 610 F. Supp. 662 (E.D. Cal. 1985), 188

Craig v. Sun Oil Co., 515 F.2d 221 (10th Cir. 1975), cert. denied, 429 U.S. 829 (1976), 95, 405, 438

Crane & Shovel Sales Corp. v. Bucyrus-Erie Co., 854 F.2d 802 (6th Cir. 1988), 37, 38, 48, 49, 53, 61, 118, 119, 123, 124, 126, 180, 183, 188, 191, 193

Crane Co., 93 F.T.C. 459 (1979), 345

Crane Co. v. Briggs Mfg., 280 F.2d 747 (6th Cir. 1950), 368

Crane Co. v. Harsco Corp., 509 F. Supp. 115 (D. Del. 1981), 280, 281, 300

Crane v. Intermountain Health Care, Inc., 637 F.2d 715 (10th Cir. 1980), 24, 26

Crawford Fitting Co. v. J.T. Gibbons, Inc., 482 U.S. 437 (1987), 780, 786

Crawford Trans. Co. v. Chrysler Corp., 338 F.2d 934 (6th Cir. 1964), cert. denied, 380 U.S. 954 (1965), 132

Crawford v. American Title Ins. Co., 518 F.2d 217 (5th Cir. 1975), 1116

C.R. Bard, Inc. v. Medical Elecs. Corp., 529 F. Supp. 1382 (D. Mass. 1982), 192

C.R. Bard, Inc. v. Schwartz, 716 F.2d 874 (Fed. Cir. 1983), 836

Credit Bureau Assocs., 92 F.T.C. 837 (1978), 536

Credit Bureau Reports, Inc. v. Retail Credit Co., 358 F. Supp. 780 (S.D. Tex. 1971), aff'd, 476 F.2d 989 (5th Cir. 1973), 114, 701, 702

Crest Auto Supplies v. Ero Mfg. Co., 360 F.2d 896 (7th Cir. 1966), 703

Crimmins v. American Stock Exch., 346 F. Supp. 1256 (S.D.N.Y. 1972), 89

Crossland v. Canteen Corp., 711 F.2d 714 (5th Cir. 1983), 136, 144, 158

Crounse Corp v. ICC, 781 F.2d 1176 (6th Cir.), cert. denied, 479 U.S. 890 (1986), 1143, 1216

Crouse-Hinds Co. v. InterNorth, Inc., 518 F. Supp. 416 (N.D.N.Y. 1980), 336

Crown Beverage Co. v. Cerveceria Moctezuma, SA, 663 F.2d 886 (9th Cir. 1982), 180, 191

Crown Cent. Petroleum Corp., 84 F.T.C. 1493 (1974), aff'd mem., 530 F.2d 1093 (D.C. Cir. 1976), 473, 484

Crown Cork & Seal Co. v. Parker, 462 U.S. 345 (1982), 696, 697

Crown Zellerbach Corp., 54 F.T.C. 769 (1957), aff'd, 296 F.2d 800 (9th Cir. 1961), cert. denied, 370 U.S. 937 (1962), 359

Crown Zellerbach Corp. v. FTC, 296 F.2d 800 (9th Cir. 1961), cert. denied, 370 U.S. 937 (1962), 204, 286, 295, 307, 319

C.R. Swaney Co. v. Atlas Copco N. Am., Inc., 1987 WL 33025 at 10 (D. Mass. 1987), 164

Crucible, Inc. v. Stora Kopparbergs Bergslags AB, 701 F. Supp. 1157 (W.D. Pa. 1988), 201, 802, 804, 808

Crummer Co. v. du Pont, 255 F.2d 425 (5th Cir.), cert. denied, 358 U.S. 884 (1958), 689

CSX Transp. v. United States, 867 F.2d 1439 (D.C. Cir. 1989), 1136

CTS Corp. v. Dynamics Corp. of Am., 481 U.S. 69 (1987), 621

Culberson, Inc. v. Interstate Elec. Co., 821 F.2d 1092 (5th Cir. 1987), 14

Culbro Corp., 1978-2 Trade Cas. (CCH) ¶ 62,274, 349

Cullum Elec. & Mech., Inc. v. Mechanical Contractors Ass'n, 436 F. Supp. 418 (D.S.C. 1976), aff'd, 569 F.2d 821 (4th Cir.), cert. denied, 439 U.S. 910 (1978), 79, 270

Cumberland Farms, Inc. v. Browning Ferris Indus., 120 F.R.D. 642 (E.D. Pa. 1988), 716

Cummer-Graham Co. v. Straight Side Basket Corp., 142 F.2d 646 (5th Cir.), *cert. denied*, 323 U.S. 726 (1944), 822

Curly's Dairy v. Dairy Coop. Ass'n, 202 F. Supp. 481 (D. Or. 1962), 171

Curry v. Steve's Franchise Co., 1985-2 Trade Cas. (CCH) ¶ 66,877 (D. Mass. 1985), 17, 110

Curtis Publishing Co., 78 F.T.C. 1472 (1971), 498

Curtis v. Campbell-Taggart, Inc., 687 F.3d 336 (10th Cir.), *cert. denied*, 459 U.S. 1090 (1982), 649

Cusick v. N.V. Nederlandsche Combinatie Voor Chemische Industrie, 317 F. Supp. 1022 (E.D. Pa. 1970), 739

Custom Auto Body, Inc. v. Aetna Casualty & Sur. Co., 1983-2 Trade Cas. (CCH) ¶ 65,629 (D.R.I. 1983), 48, 1113

Cutler v. Lewiston Daily Sun, 105 F.R.D. 137 (D. Me. 1985), 756

Cutler v. Lewiston Daily Sun, 611 F. Supp. 746 (D. Me. 1985), 143, 656, 712, 720, 730

Cutsforth, Trading as for Amusement Only (Hull) v. Mansfield Inn Ltd., [1986] 1 W.L.R. 558, [1986] 1 COMMON MKT. L.R. 1 (Q.B.), 920

Cutter Labs. v. Lyophile-Cryochem Corp., 179 F.2d 80 (9th Cir. 1949), 837

Cutters Exch. v. Durkoppwerke GmbH, 1986-1 Trade Cas. (CCH) ¶ 67,039 (M.D. Tenn. 1986), 16, 97, 98, 188, 207

Cuyler v. Sullivan, 446 U.S. 335 (1980), 602

CVD, Inc. v. Raytheon Co., 769 F.2d 842 (1st Cir. 1985), *cert. denied*, 475 U.S. 1016 (1986), 222, 259, 811, 850, 998, 1001, 1005

Cyborg Sys. v. Management Science Am., Inc., 1978-1 Trade Cas. (CCH) ¶ 61,927 (N.D. Ill. 1978), 1001

D

Dahl, Inc. v. Roy Cooper Co., 448 F.2d 17 (9th Cir. 1971), 646

Daily Press, Inc. v. United Press Int'l, 412 F.2d 126 (6th Cir.), 186

Dairy King v. Kraft, 645 F. Supp. 126 (D. Md. 1986), *aff'd without published opinion*, 851 F.2d 356 (4th Cir. 1988), 416, 417

Dairymen, Inc. v. FTC, 684 F.2d 376 (6th Cir, 1982) *cert. denied*, 462 U.S. 1106 (1983), 523

Daishowa Int'l v. North Coast Export Co., 1982-2 Trade Cas. (CCH) ¶ 64,774 (N.D. Cal. 1982), 678

Dakota Wholesale Liquor, Inc. v. Minnesota, 584 F.2d 847 (8th Cir. 1978), 677

Dale Elec., Inc. v. R.C.L. Elecs., Inc., 53 F.R.D. 531 (D.N.H. 1971), 713

Dalmo Sales Co. v. Tysons Corner Regional Shopping Center, 308 F. Supp. 988 (D.D.C.), 184

Dalweld Co. v. Westinghouse Elec. Corp., 252 F. Supp. 939 (S.D.N.Y. 1966), 779

Damiani v. Rhode Island Hosp., 704 F.2d 12 (1st Cir. 1983), 769

Damon Corp. v. Geheb, 1982-83 Trade Cas. (CCH) ¶ 65,117 (N.D. Ill. 1982), 778

Damon Corp., [1979-1983 Transfer Binder] TRADE REG. REP. (CCH) ¶ 22,007 (Mar. 29, 1983), 515

D & M Distribs., Inc. v. Texaco, Inc., 1970 Trade Cas. (CCH) ¶ 73,099 (C. D. Cal. 1970), 184

D & N Auto Parts Co., 55 F.T.C. 1279 (1959), *aff'd sub nom.* Mid-South Distribs. v. FTC, 287 F.2d 512 (5th Cir.), *cert. denied*, 368 U.S. 838 (1961), 427, 445, 447

D & R Distrib. Co. v. Chambers Corp., 608 F. Supp. 1290 (E.D. Cal. 1984), 188

D & S Redi-Mix v. Sierra Redi-Mix & Contracting Co., 692 F.2d 1245 (9th Cir. 1982), 667, 668, 670

Daniels v. All Steel Equip., Inc., 590 F.2d 111 (5th Cir. 1979), 50, 118

Daniels v. Amerco, 1982-2 Trade Cas. (CCH) ¶ 64,794 (S.D.N.Y. 1982), 734, 736

Daniels v. Amerco, 1983-1 Trade Cas. (CCH) ¶ 65,274 (S.D.N.Y. 1983), 690, 713, 715, 717, 726, 728, 732

Danko v. Shell Oil Co., 115 F. Supp. 886 (E.D.N.Y. 1953), 408

Danny Kresky Enters. Corp. v. Magid, 716 F.2d 206 (3d Cir. 1983), 671

Dan Purvis Drugs, Inc. v. Aetna Life Ins. Co., 1980-81 Trade Cas. (CCH) ¶ 63,628 (Ind. App. 1980), 639

Darda, Inc. USA v. Majorette Toys (U.S.) Inc., 627 F. Supp. 1121 (S.D. Fla. 1986), aff'd in part and rev'd in part, 824 F.2d 976 (Fed. Cir. 1987), 812

D.A. Rickards v. Canine Eye Registration Found., 783 F.2d 1329 (9th Cir.), cert. denied, 479 U.S. 851 (1986), 83, 85

Dart Drug Corp. v. Corning Glass Works, 480 F. Supp. 1091 (D. Md. 1979), 654, 664, 747

Dart Drug Corp. v. Parke, Davis & Co., 344 F.2d 173 (D.C. Cir. 1965), 55, 780

Dart Indus. v. Plunkett Co., 704 F.2d 496 (10th Cir. 1983), 126, 128, 430

Data Gen. Corp. v. Digidyne Corp., 473 U.S. 908 (1985), 152, 831

Data Gen. Corp. v. Grumman Sys. Support Corp., 1991-1 Trade Cas. (CCH) ¶ 69,487 (D. Mass. 1991), 140, 161

Dataphase Sys. v. CL Sys., 640 F.2d 109 (8th Cir. 1981), 366, 677

Data Processing Fin. & Gen. Corp. v. IBM, 430 F.2d 1277 (8th Cir. 1970), aff'g Control Data Corp. v. IBM, 306 F. Supp. 839 (D. Minn. 1969), 574, 780

Daugherty v. Pall, 43 F.R.D. 329 (C.D. Cal. 1967), 740

Davenport Grain Co. v. J. Lynch & Co., 109 F.R.D. 256 (D. Neb. 1985), 768, 771

David R. McGeorge Car Co. v. Leyland Motor Sales, Inc., 504 F.2d 52 (4th Cir. 1974), cert. denied, 420 U.S. 992 (1975), 438

Davidson Rubber Co., 15 J.O. COMM. EUR. (No. 143) 31 (1972), [1970-1972 Transfer Binder] COMMON MKT. REP. (CCH) ¶ 9512, 948

Davis & Cox v. Summa Corp., 751 F.2d 1507 (9th Cir. 1985), 773

Davison v. Crown Cent. Petroleum Corp., 1977-1 Trade Cas. (CCH) ¶ 61,277 (D. Md. 1976), 161

Davis v. American Meter Co., 85 Pa. D. & C. 502, 36 Erie 109 (Penn. County Ct. 1952), 627

Davis v. Marathon Oil Co., 528 F.2d 395 (6th Cir. 1975), cert. denied, 429 U.S. 823 (1976), 146, 158, 184

Davis v. Northside Realty Assoc., 95 F.R.D. 39 (N.D. Ga. 1982), 712, 714, 715, 716, 717, 725, 726, 730, 731, 734, 735

Davis v. Sebring Forest Indus., 588 F. Supp. 688 (S.D. Ohio 1984), 118

Davis v. Southern Bell Tel. & Tel. Co., 755 F. Supp. 1532 (S.D. Fla. 1991), 971, 972, 975, 985

Davis-Watkins Co. v. Service Merchandise Co., 686 F.2d 1190 (6th Cir. 1982), cert. denied, 466 U.S. 931 (1984), 11, 45, 55, 60, 123, 124, 125, 126, 128, 186

Dawson Chem. Co. v. Rohm & Haas Co., 448 U.S. 176 (1980), 801, 817, 818, 833

Day-Brite Lighting, Inc. v. Missouri, 342 U.S. 421 (1952), 627

Dayco Corp. v. Firestone Tire & Rubber Co., 386 F. Supp. 546 (N.D. Ohio 1974), aff'd sub nom. Dayco Corp. v. Goodyear Tire & Rubber Co., 523 F.2d 389 (6th Cir. 1975), 681, 689, 690

Dayco Corp. v. Goodyear Tire & Rubber Co., 523 F.2d 389 (6th Cir. 1975), 665, 679, 688, 689, 692

Dayton Rubber Co., 66 F.T.C. 423, 463-64 (1964), vacated in part and remanded sub nom. Dayco Corp. v. FTC, 362 F.2d 180 (6th Cir. 1966), 430

De Atucha v. Commodity Exch., Inc., 608 F. Supp. 510 (S.D.N.Y. 1985), 660, 858

Deak-Perera Hawaii, Inc. v. Department of Transp., 745 F.2d 1281 (9th Cir. 1984), cert. denied, 470 U.S. 1053 (1985), 980

Deaktor v. Fox Grocery Co., 475 F.2d 1112 (3d Cir.), cert. denied, 414 U.S. 867 (1973), 670, 674

Dealers Wholesale Supply v. Pacific Steel & Supply Co., 1984-2 Trade Cas. (CCH) ¶ 66,109 (N.D. Cal. 1984), 406

Dean Foods Co., 70 F.T.C. 1146 (1966) modified by consent, aff'd and enforced, 1967 Trade Cas. (CCH) ¶ 72,086 (7th Cir. 1967), 276, 314, 459

Dean Milk Co. v. FTC, 395 F.2d 696 (7th Cir. 1968), 403, 404, 414

Deauville Corp. v. Federated Dep't Stores, 1983-2 Trade Cas. (CCH) ¶ 65,599 (S.D. Tex. 1983), *aff'd in part, rev'd in part*, 756 F.2d 1183 (5th Cir. 1985), 199

Deauville Corp. v. Federated Dept. Stores, 756 F.2d 1183 (5th Cir. 1985), 55, 97, 196, 217

Deep South Pepsi-Cola Bottling Co. v. PepsiCo, Inc., 1989-1 Trade Cas. (CCH) ¶ 68,560 (S.D.N.Y. 1989), 206

Deering, Milliken & Co. v. Temp-Resisto Corp., 160 F. Supp. 463 (S.D.N.Y. 1958), *aff'd in part and rev'd in part*, 274 F.2d 626 (2d Cir. 1960), 828

De Forest Radio Tel. Co. v. United States, 273 U.S. 236 (1927), *aff'd on reh'g*, 305 U.S. 124 (1938), 820

Dehydrating Process Co. v. A. O. Smith Corp, 292 F.2d 653 (1st Cir.), *cert. denied*, 368 U.S. 931 (1961), 160, 257

Dehydrators, Ltd. v. Petrolite Corp., 117 F.2d 183 (9th Cir. 1941), 833

DeJong Packing Co. v. USDA, 618 F.2d 1329 (9th Cir.), *cert. denied*, 499 U.S. 1061 (1980), 8

De Laval-Stork, 20 O.J. EUR. COMM. (No. L 215) 11 (1977), [1976-1978 Transfer Binder] COMMON MKT. REP. (CCH) ¶ 9972, 930, 938

Delaware & Hudson Ry. Co. v. Consolidated Rail Corp., 902 F.2d 174 (2d Cir. 1990), *cert. denied*, 111 S. Ct. 2041 (1991), 223, 226, 248, 1141

Delaware Tool Steel Corp. v. Brunner & Lay, Inc., 19 F.R.D. 375 (D. Del. 1956), 746

Dellums v. Powell, 566 F.2d 167 (D.C. Cir. 1977), *cert. denied*, 438 U.S. 916 (1978), 735

Delmarva Power & Light Co., 5 F.E.R.C. (CCH) ¶ 61,201 (1978), 1075

DeLong Equip. Co. v. Washington Mills Abrasive Co., 887 F.2d 1499 (11th Cir. 1989), *cert. denied*, 494 U.S. 1081 (1990), 14, 15, 33, 38, 42, 45, 46, 55, 181, 184, 407, 411, 705, 706, 707, 708

Del Rio Distrib. v. Adolph Coors Co., 589 F.2d 176 (5th Cir.), 124, 125, 126

Delta Chemie-DDD, Decision 88/563, 31 O.J. EUR. COMM. (No. L 309) 34 (1988), [1989] 1 CEC (CCH) 2254, 949

Demaco Corp. v. F. Von Langsdorff Licensing Ltd., 851 F.2d 1387 (Fed. Cir.), *cert. denied*, 488 U.S. 956 (1988), 810

De Modena v. Kaiser Found. Health Plan, Inc., 743 F.2d 1388 (9th Cir. 1984), *cert. denied*, 469 U.S. 1229 (1985), 448

Denison Mattress Factory v. Spring-Air Co., 308 F.2d 403 (5th Cir. 1962), 107, 108, 178

Denman v. City of Idaho Falls, 51 Idaho 118, 4 P.2d 361 (1931), 637

Dennis v. Saks & Co., 1975-2 Trade Cas. (CCH) ¶ 60,396 (S.D.N.Y. 1975), 733, 738

Dennis v. United States, 384 U.S. 855 (1966), 755, 757

Denver & Rio Grande Western R.R. Co. v. United States, 387 U.S. 485 (1967), 280, 281, 1131

Denver Rockets v. All-Pro Mgmt., Inc., 325 F. Supp. 1049 (C.D. Cal. 1971), 81, 91

Deposit Guar. Nat'l Bank v. Roper, 445 U.S. 326 (1980), 736

D.E. Rogers Assocs. v. Gardner-Denver Co., 718 F.2d 1431 (6th Cir. 1983), *cert. denied*, 467 U.S. 1242 (1984), 227, 231, 414

Descent Control, Inc., 105 F.T.C. 280 (1985), 474

Determined Prods. v. R. Dakin & Co., 514 F. Supp. 645 (N.D. Cal. 1979), 187

Detroit Auto Dealer's Ass'n, 111 F.T.C. 417 (1989), *aff'd in part and rev'd in part*, 1992-1 Trade Cas. (CCH) ¶ 69,696 (6th Cir. 1992), 57, 58, 69

Detroit City Dairy v. Kowalski Sausage Co., 393 F. Supp. 453 (E.D. Mich. 1975), 141, 156, 157, 158, 161, 162

Detroit Newspaper Publishers Ass'n v. Detroit Typographical Union No. 18, 471 F.2d 872 (6th Cir. 1972), 1124

Deutsche Grammophon Gesellschaft GmbH v. Metro-SB-Grossmarket GmbH, Case 78/70, [1971] E.C.R. 487, [1971-1973 Transfer Binder] COMMON MKT. REP. (CCH) ¶ 8106, 946, 952

Deutsche Philips GmbH, 16 O.J. EUR. COMM. (No. L 293) 40 (1973), [1973-1975 Transfer Binder] COMMON MKT. REP. (CCH) ¶ 9606, 942

DeVoto v. Pacific Fidelity Life Ins. Co., 618 F.2d 1340 (9th Cir.), *cert. denied*, 449 U.S. 869 (1980), 38, 45, 46, 47, 48, 50, 55, 168, 187, 188

Dexter v. Equitable Life Assurance Soc'y of the United States, 527 F.2d 233 (2d Cir. 1975), 1112, 1116

DFW Metro Line Serv. v. Southwestern Bell Tel. Co., 901 F.2d 1267 (5th Cir. 1990), 676, 678

Diamond Shamrock Corp., 5 TRADE REG. REP. (CCH) ¶ 22,825 (FTC May 11, 1990), 167

Dibidale, Inc. v. American Bank & Trust Co., 916 F.2d 300 (5th Cir. 1990), 1098

Di Costanzo v. Hertz Corp., 63 F.R.D. 150 (D. Mass. 1974), 718

Diehl & Sons v. International Harvester Co., 426 F. Supp. 110 (E.D.N.Y. 1976), 189, 438

Diehl & Sons v. International Harvester Co., 445 F. Supp. 282 (E.D.N.Y. 1978), 405, 429, 430

Diener's, Inc., 81 F.T.C. 945 (1972), *modified and enforced*, 494 F.2d 1132 (D.C. Cir. 1974), 475

DiFilippo v. Morizio, 759 F.2d 231 (2d Cir. 1985), 781

Digidyne Corp. v. Data Gen. Corp., 734 F.2d 1336 (9th Cir. 1984) *cert. denied*, 473, U.S. 908 (1985), 135, 136, 138, 152, 153, 154, 155

Digital Equip. Corp. v. System Indus., 1990-1 Trade Cas. (CCH) ¶68,901 (D. Mass. 1990), 138, 140

Dillon Materials Handling, Inc. v. Albion Indus., 567 F.2d 1299 (5th Cir.), *cert. denied*, 439 U.S. 832 (1978), 170, 182

Dimidowich v. Bell & Howell, 803 F.2d 1473 (9th Cir. 1986), 9, 13, 15, 17, 36, 38, 52, 53, 61, 78, 123, 126, 128, 182

Dimmitt Agri Indus. v. CPC Int'l Inc., 679 F.2d 516 (5th Cir. 1982), *cert. denied*, 460 U.S. 1082 (1983), 197, 214, 227

Diners' Club, Inc., 89 F.T.C. 298 (1977), 480, 532

Dino DeLaurentiis Cinematografica, SpA v. D-150, Inc., 366 F.2d 373 (2d Cir. 1966), 678

D'Ippolito v. American Oil Co., 272 F. Supp. 310 (S.D.N.Y. 1967), 600

Directory Sales Mgmt. Corp. v. Ohio Bell Tel. Co., 833 F.2d 606 (6th Cir. 1987), 19, 131, 138, 143, 233, 249, 271

Disenos Artisticos Industr. S.A. v. Work, 676 F. Supp. 1254 (E.D.N.Y. 1987), 1003

Disher v. Information Resources, 691 F. Supp. 75 (N.D. Ill. 1988), *aff'd*, 873 F.2d 136 (7th Cir. 1989), 662

Distillers, 28 O.J. EUR. COMM. (No. L 369) 19 (1985), [1985-1988 Transfer Binder] COMMON MKT. REP. (CCH) ¶ 10,750, 940

Distillers Co. v. Commission, Case 30/78, [1980] E.C.R. 2229, [1979-81 Transfer Binder] COMMON MKT. REP. (CCH) ¶ 8613, *aff'g* 21 O.J. EUR. COMM. (No. L 50) 16 (1978), [1976-1978 Transfer Binder] COMMON MKT. REP. (CCH) ¶ 10,011, 941

Distilling & Cattle Feeding Co. v. People, 156 Ill. 448, 41 N.E. 188 (1895), 619

DiVerniero v. Murphy, 635 F. Supp. 1531 (D. Conn. 1986), 977

Diversified Brokerage Serv. v. Greater Des Moines Bd. of Realtors, 521 F.2d 1343 (8th Cir. 1975), 29

Diversified Indus. v. Meredith, 572 F.2d 596 (8th Cir. 1978), 761

D. L. Auld Co. v. Park Electrochem. Corp., 1986-2 Trade Cas. (CCH) ¶ 67,309 (E.D.N.Y. 1986), 808

Dobbins v. Kawasaki Motors Corp., U.S.A., 362 F. Supp. 54 (D. Or. 1973), 121

Doctors, Inc. v. Blue Cross, 490 F.2d 48 (3d Cir. 1973), 27

Doe v. St. Joseph's Hosp., 788 F.2d 411 (7th Cir. 1986), 25, 28, 29, 30

Dole Valve Co. v. Perfection Bar Equip., Inc., 311 F. Supp. 459 (N.D. Ill. 1970), 804

Dolgow v. Anderson, 53 F.R.D. 661 (E.D.N.Y. 1971), 711

Dolphin Tours, Inc. v. Pacifico Creative Serv., 773 F.2d 1506 (9th Cir. 1985), 647, 673

D.O. McComb & Sons v. Memory Gardens Mgmt. Corp., 736 F. Supp. 952 (N.D. Ind. 1990), 158

Domed Stadium Hotel v. Holiday Inns, 732 F.2d 480 (5th Cir. 1984), 197, 206, 265

Domestic Air Transportation Antitrust Litig., 1991-2 Trade Cas. (CCH) ¶ 69,518 (N.D. Ga. 1991), 732

Dominicus Americana Bohio v. Gulf & W. Indus., 473 F. Supp. 680 (S.D.N.Y. 1979), 859, 906, 913

Donahue v. Pendleton Woolen Mills, Inc., 633 F. Supp. 1423 (S.D.N.Y. 1986), 662, 681, 682, 683, 684, 689, 692

Donald B. Rice Tire Co. v. Michelin Tire Co., 483 F. Supp. 750 (D. Md. 1980), *aff'd per curiam*, 638 F.2d 15 (4th Cir.), *cert. denied*, 454 U.S. 864 (1981), 45, 124, 125, 126, 129, 182, 203

Donald B. Rice Tire Co. v. Michelin Tire Corp., 638 F.2d 15 (4th Cir.), *cert. denied*, 454 U.S. 864 (1981), 126

Donson Stores v. American Bakeries Co., 58 F.R.D. 485 (S.D.N.Y. 1973), 657, 733, 735

Dos Santos v. Columbus-Cuneo-Cabrini Medical Center, 684 F.2d 1346 (7th Cir. 1982), 677, 679

Doubleday & Co., 52 F.T.C. 169 (1955), 428

Double H Plastics, Inc. v. Sonoco Prods. Co., 732 F.2d 351 (3d Cir.), *cert. denied*, 469 U.S. 900 (1984), 415

Dougherty v. Continental Oil Co., 579 F.2d 954 (5th Cir. 1978), *vacated and dismissed by stipulation*, 591 F.2d 1206 (5th Cir. 1979), 41, 47, 128, 182

Douglas Oil Co. v. Petrol Stops N.W., 441 U.S. 211 (1979), 565, 597, 755, 756, 757, 759

Dovberg v. Dow Chem. Co., 195 F. Supp. 337 (E.D. Pa. 1960), 692

Dow Benelux NV v. Commission, Case 85/87, [1989] E.C.R. 3137 and Dow Chemical Ibérica v. Commission, Joined Cases 97-99/87, [1989] E.C.R. 3165, 919

Doyle v. FTC, 356 F.2d 381 (5th Cir. 1966), 494

Drabbant Enters. v. Great Atl. & Pac. Tea Co., 688 F. Supp. 1567 (D. Del. 1988), 198, 211

Dreibus v. Wilson, 529 F.2d 170 (9th Cir. 1975), 193

Dreiling v. Peugeot Motors of Am., 768 F.2d 1159 (10th Cir. 1985), 789

Dreiling v. Peugeot Motors of Am., Inc., 850 F.2d 1373 (10th Cir. 1988), 38, 49, 54, 184, 193, 270, 706, 708

Dreisbach v. Murphy, 658 F.2d 720 (9th Cir. 1981), 542

Dresser Indus. v. ICC, 714 F.2d 588 (5th Cir. 1983), 1137

Dresser Indus. v. Sandvick, 732 F.2d 783 (10th Cir. 1984), 99

Drinkwine v. Federated Publications, 780 F.2d 735 (9th Cir. 1985), *cert. denied*, 475 U.S. 1087 (1986), 200, 230, 245

Driscoll v. City of New York, 650 F. Supp. 1522 (S.D.N.Y. 1987), 247, 988

Driskill v. Dallas Cowboys Football Club, 498 F.2d 321 (5th Cir. 1974), 159

Dr. Miles Medical Co. v. John D. Park & Sons, 220 U.S. 373 (1911), 100, 101, 849

Drs. Steuer & Latham, P.A. v. National Medical Enters., 672 F. Supp. 1489 (D.S.C. 1987), *aff'd*, 846 F.2d 70 (4th Cir. 1988), 47, 50, 55, 132, 140, 173

Drumm v. Sizeler Realty Co., 817 F.2d 1195 (5th Cir. 1987), 683, 695

Drury Inn - Colorado Springs v. Olive Co., 878 F.2d 340 (10th Cir. 1989), 33, 37, 39, 99, 791, 792

D.R. Wilder Mfg. v. Corn Prods. Ref. Co., 236 U.S. 165 (1915), 791

Dubuque Communs. Corp. v. ABC, 432 F. Supp. 543 (N.D. Ill.), *aff'd*, 547 F.2d 1170 (7th Cir. 1976), *cert. denied*, 430 U.S. 985 (1977), 145

Dubuque TV Ltd., 4 F.C.C.Rcd 1999 (1989), 1051

Duffel v. United States, 221 F.2d 523 (D.C. Cir. 1954), 567

Duff v. Kansas City Star Co., 299 F.2d 320 (8th Cir. 1962), 648

Duke & Co. v. Foerster, 521 F.2d 1277 (3d Cir. 1975), 982, 997

Dunafon v. Delaware McDonald's Corp., 691 F. Supp. 1232 (W.D. Mo. 1988), 51, 98

Dungan v. Morgan Drive-Away, Inc., 570 F.2d 867 (9th Cir.), *cert. denied*, 439 U.S. 829 (1978), 684

Dunham's, Inc. v. National Buying Syndicate, 614 F. Supp. 616 (E.D. Mich. 1985), 866, 868, 871, 876

Dunlop Co. v. Kelsey-Hayes Co., 484 F.2d 407 (6th Cir. 1973), *cert. denied*, 415 U.S. 917 (1974), 121, 841

Dunlop Tire & Rubber Corp. v. PepsiCo, Inc., 591 F. Supp. 88 (N.D. Ill. 1984), 873

Dunn & Mavis, Inc. v. Nu-Car Driveaway, Inc., 691 F.2d 241 (6th Cir. 1982), 180, 188, 652

Dunnivant v. Bi-State Auto Parts, 851 F.2d 1575 (11th Cir. 1988), 7, 14, 123, 124, 182, 184, 186, 706, 707

Dunn v. Phoenix Newspapers, 735 F.2d 1184 (9th Cir. 1984), 48, 108

Duplan Corp. v. Deering Milliken, Inc., 397 F. Supp. 1146 (D.S.C. 1974), 762

Duplan Corp. v. Deering Milliken, Inc., 444 F. Supp. 648 (D.S.C. 1977), *aff'd in part and rev'd in part*, 594 F.2d 979 (4th Cir. 1979), *cert. denied*, 444 U.S. 1015 (1980), 806, 811, 826, 831, 838, 844, 854

Duplan Corp. v. Deering Milliken, Inc., 540 F.2d 1215 (4th Cir. 1976), 762, 764, 766, 837, 838, 854

Duplex Printing Press Co. v. Deering, 254 U.S. 443 (1921), 1119, 1120

du Pont Glore Forgan, Inc. v. AT&T, 69 F.R.D. 481 (S.D.N.Y. 1975), 723

DuPont Walston, Inc. v. E.F. Hutton & Co., 368 F. Supp. 306 (S.D. Fla. 1973), 96

Duran v. City of Yuma, 93 F.R.D. 607 (D. Ariz. 1982), 695

Durbin v. United States, 221 F.2d 520 (D.C. Cir. 1954), 566

Durkee v. Commissioner, 162 F.2d 184 (6th Cir. 1947), 794

Dutch Bankers' Ass'n, Decision 89/512, 32 O.J. EUR. COMM. (No. L 253) (1989), [1989] 2 CEC (CCH) 2,033, 936

Dutch Cheese-Makers, 23 O.J. EUR. COMM. (No. L 51) 19 (1979), [1978-1981 Transfer Binder] COMMON MKT. REP. (CCH) ¶ 10,188, 942

Dutch Engineers & Contractors Ass'n, 7 J.O. COMM. EUR 2761 (1964), [1965] COMMON MKT. L.R. 50, 930

Dutch Express Delivery Servs., Decision 90/16, 33 O.J. EUR. COMM. (No. L 10) 47 (1990), [1990] 1 CEC (CCH) 2038, 924

Dyestuffs, 12 J.O. COMM. EUR. (No. L 195) 11 (1969), [1965-1969 Transfer Binder] COMMON MKT. REP. (CCH) ¶ 9314, *aff'd sub nom.* Imperial Chem. Indus. v. Commission, Case 48/69, [1972] E.C.R. 619, [1971-1973 Transfer Binder] COMMON MKT. REP. (CCH) ¶ 8161, 927

E

Eagle v. Star-Kist Foods, 812 F.2d 538 (9th Cir. 1987), 662

E & J Gallo Winery, 101 F.T.C. 727 (1983), 175, 178

Earley Ford Tractor, Inc. v. Hesston Corp., 556 F. Supp. 544 (W.D. Mo. 1983), 164, 166

Eastern Air Lines v. Atlantic Richfield Co., 609 F.2d 497 (Temp. Emer. Ct. App. 1979), 656

Eastern Auto Distrib. v. Peugeot Motors of Am., Inc., 795 F.2d 329 (4th Cir. 1986), 442

Eastern Broadcasting Corp., 30 F.C.C.2d 745 (1971), 1038

Eastern Publishing & Advertising, Inc. v. Chesapeake Publishing & Advertising, Inc., 831 F.2d 488 (4th Cir. 1987), *vacated*, 492 U.S. 913 (1989), 846

Eastern R.R. Presidents Conference v. Noerr Motor Freight, Inc., 365 U.S. 127 (1961), 257, 638, 899, 912, 990, 991, 992, 1007, 1012, 1053

Eastern Scientific Co. v. Wild Heerbrugg Instruments, Inc., 572 F.2d 883 (1st Cir.), *cert. denied*, 439 U.S. 833 (1978), 38, 114, 119, 124

Eastern States Retail Lumber Dealers' Ass'n v. United States, 234 U.S. 600 (1914), 71, 79

Eastern Venetian Blind Co. v. Acme Steel Co., 188 F.2d 247 (4th Cir.), *cert. denied*, 342 U.S. 824 (1951), 816

Eastex Aviation, Inc. v. Sperry & Hutchison Co., 367 F. Supp. 868 (E.D. Tex. 1973), *aff'd*, 522 F.2d 1299 (5th Cir. 1975), 121, 192

Eastman Kodak Co. v. Southern Photo Materials Co., 273 U.S. 359 (1927), 179, 242, 670, 671, 867, 868

Eastway Constr. Corp. v. City of New York, 637 F. Supp. 558 (E.D.N.Y. 1986), *modified*, 821 F.2d 121 (2d Cir.), *cert. denied*, 484 U.S. 918 (1987), 789

Eastway Constr. Corp. v. City of New York, 762 F.2d 243 (2d Cir. 1985), 789

Eaton Yale & Towne, Inc., 79 F.T.C. 998 (1971), 511, 518

Eaton, Yale & Towne, Inc. v. Sherman Indus. Equip. Co., 316 F. Supp. 435 (E.D. Mo. 1970), 184

E.B.E., Inc. v. Dunkin' Donuts, 387 F. Supp. 737 (E.D. Mich. 1974), 147

E.B. Muller & Co. v. FTC, 142 F.2d 511 (6th Cir. 1944), 477

E. Boyd Whitney, 86 F.C.C.2d 1133 (1981), 1034

Echlin Mfg. Co., 105 F.T.C. 410 (1985), 214, 216, 307, 310

Ecology Corp. of Am., 80 F.T.C. 448 (1972), 473

ECS/AKZO, 26 O.J. EUR. COMM. (No. L 252) 13 (1983), [1982-1985 Transfer Binder] COMMON MKT. REP. (CCH) ¶ 10,517, 920

Eden Hannon & Co. v. Sumitomo Trust & Banking Co., 914 F.2d 556 (4th Cir. 1990), *cert. denied*, 111 S. Ct. 1414 (1991), 258, 1004

Edgar v. MITE Corp., 457 U.S. 624 (1982), 621

Edison Co. v. FERC, 823 F.2d 630 (D.C. Cir. 1987), 1060

Edward B. Marks Music Corp. v. Colorado Magnetics, Inc., 497 F.2d 285 (10th Cir. 1974), *cert. denied*, 419 U.S. 1120 (1975), 846

Edward J. Moriarity & Co. v. General Tire & Rubber Co., 289 F. Supp. 381 (S.D. Ohio 1967), 869, 870, 876

Edward J. Sweeney & Sons v. Texaco, Inc., 478 F. Supp. 243 (E.D. Pa. 1979), *aff'd*, 637 F.2d 105 (3d Cir. 1980), *cert. denied*, 451 U.S. 911 (1981), 181

Edward J. Sweeney & Sons v. Texaco, Inc., 637 F.2d 105 (3d Cir. 1980), *cert. denied*, 451 U.S. 911 (1981), 180, 200, 262, 405, 406, 655

Edward Joseph Hruby, 61 F.T.C. 1437 (1962), 433

E. Edelmann & Co., 51 F.T.C. 978 (1955), *aff'd*, 239 F.2d 152 (7th Cir. 1956), *cert. denied*, 355 U.S. 941 (1958), 410, 430

E. Edelmann & Co. v. FTC, 239 F.2d 152 (7th Cir. 1956), *cert. denied*, 355 U.S. 941 (1958), 412, 489

EGH, Inc. v. Blue Cross and Blue Shield, 1991-2 Trade Cas. (CCH) ¶ 69,642 (D. Or. 1991), 753

Eiberger v. Sony Corp., 622 F.2d 1068 (2d Cir. 1980), 123, 124, 125, 126, 127, 130, 671, 674

Eiberger v. Sony Corp., 659 F. Supp. 1276 (S.D.N.Y. 1978), *aff'd*, 622 F.2d 1068 (2d Cir. 1980), 56

Eichman v. Fotomat Corp., 880 F.2d 149 (9th Cir. 1989), 272, 695, 706

E.I. du Pont de Nemours & Co., 81 F.T.C. 169 (1972), 747

E.I. duPont de Nemours & Co., 96 F.T.C. 653 (1980), *aff'd*, 698 F.2d 1377 (9th Cir.), *cert. denied*, 464 U.S. 955 (1983), 216, 220, 224, 245

E.I. du Pont de Nemours & Co., 96 F.T.C. 705 (1980), 819

E.I. du Pont de Nemours & Co. v. FTC, 488 F. Supp. 747 (D. Del. 1980), 523

E.I. du Pont de Nemours & Co. v. FTC, 729 F.2d 128 (2d Cir. 1984), 10, 73, 462, 463, 522

E.I. du Pont de Nemours & Co. v. Berkley & Co., 620 F.2d 1247 (8th Cir. 1980), 808

Eisel v. Columbia Packing Co., 181 F. Supp. 298 (D. Mass. 1960), 776

Eisen v. Carlisle & Jacquelin, 370 F.2d 119 (2d Cir. 1966), *cert. denied*, 386 U.S. 1035 (1967), 733

Eisen v Carlisle & Jacquelin, 391 F.2d 555 (2d Cir. 1968), 723, 724, 735

Eisen v. Carlisle & Jacquelin, 479 F.2d 1005 (2d Cir. 1973), *vacated and class action dismissed*, 417 U.S. 156 (1974), 732, 733, 735

Eisen v. Carlisle & Jacquelin, 417 U.S. 156 (1974), 695, 696, 697, 734, 738, 739

E. J. Delaney Corp. v. Bonne Bell, Inc., 525 F.2d 296 (10th Cir. 1975), *cert. denied*, 425 U.S. 907 (1976), 196, 262

Ekco Prods. Co., 65 F.T.C. 1163 (1964), *aff'd*, 347 F.2d 745 (7th Cir. 1965), 308, 490

Ekco Prods. Co. v. FTC, 347 F.2d 745 (7th Cir. 1965), 334

El Cid, Ltd. v. New Jersey Zinc Co., 444 F. Supp. 845 (S.D.N.Y. 1977), 866

Elco Corp. v. Microdot, Inc., 360 F. Supp. 741 (D. Del. 1973), 284, 363, 368

Elder-Beerman Stores v. Federated Dep't Stores, 459 F.2d 138 (6th Cir. 1972), 118, 119, 187

Electrical Bid Registration Serv., 107 F.T.C. 240 (1986), 70

Electronic Computer Programming Inst., Inc., 86 F.T.C. 1093 (1975), 512

Electronic Data Sys. Corp., No. 912-3096 (Aug. 21, 1991), 537

Eleven Fifty Corp., 42 F.C.C.2d 207 (1973), 1033

Eliason Corp. v. National Sanitation Found., 614 F.2d 126 (6th Cir.), *cert. denied*, 449 U.S. 826 (1980), 78, 88

Elias v. National Car Rental Sys., 59 F.R.D. 276 (D. Minn. 1973), 740

Elizabeth Arden, Inc. v. FTC, 156 F.2d 132 (2d Cir. 1946), *cert. denied*, 331 U.S. 806 (1947), 402

Elizabeth Arden Sales Corp. v. Gus Blass Co., 150 F.2d 988 (8th Cir.), *cert. denied*, 326 U.S. 773 (1945), 402

Elliot & Frantz, Inc. v. RayGo, Inc., 379 F. Supp. 498 (E.D. Pa. 1974), 183

Elopak/Metal Box-Odin, Decision 90/410, 33 O.J. EUR. COMM. (No. L 209) 15 (1990), [1990] 2 CEC (CCH) 2051, 937

El Salto, S.A. v. PSG Co., 444 F.2d 477 (9th Cir.), *cert. denied*, 404 U.S. 940 (1971), 434

Emerick v. Fenick Indus., 539 F.2d 1379 (5th Cir. 1976), 769

Emhart Corp. v. USM Corp., 527 F.2d 177 (1st Cir. 1975), 335

Emich Motors Corp. v. General Motors Corp., 340 U.S. 558 (1951), 778, 779, 780

EMI Records Ltd. v. CBS Grammofon AS, Case 86/75, [1976] E.C.R. 871, [1976 Transfer Binder] COMMON MKT. REP. (CCH) ¶ 8351, 945, 946

Empire Rayon Co. v. American Viscose Corp., 354 F.2d 182, *adopted as the interpretation of the court en banc*, 364 F.2d 491 (2d Cir. 1965), *cert. denied*, 385 U.S. 1002 (1967), 433

Empire State Pharmaceutical Soc'y v. Empire Blue Cross, 1991-2 Trade Cas. (CCH) ¶ 69,636 (S.D.N.Y. 1991), 791

Empire Volkswagen, Inc. v. World-Wide Volkswagen Corp., 95 F.R.D. 398 (S.D.N.Y. 1982), 745, 746, 752

Empire Volkswagen, Inc. v. World Wide Volkswagen Corp., 627 F. Supp. 1202 (S.D.N.Y. 1986), *aff'd*, 814 F.2d 90 (2d Cir. 1987), 109, 183

Empire Volkswagen, Inc. v. World-Wide Volkswagen Corp., 814 F.2d 90 (2d Cir. 1987), 169, 176

Encyclopaedia Britannica, Inc. v. FTC, 605 F.2d 964 (7th Cir. 1979), *cert. denied*, 445 U.S. 934 (1980), *modified*, 100 F.T.C. 500 (1982), 480, 491

Endicott Johnson Corp. v. Perkins, 317 U.S. 501 (1943), 506

Energex Lighting Indus. v. North Am. Philips, 1990-1 Trade Cas. (CCH) ¶ 69,057 (S.D.N.Y. 1990), 199, 265

Energex Lighting Indus. v. North Am. Philips Lighting Corp., 656 F. Supp. 914 (S.D.N.Y. 1987), 217

Energy Conservation, Inc. v. Heliodyne, Inc., 698 F.2d 386 (9th Cir. 1983), 999, 1001

Engbrecht v. Dairy Queen Co., 203 F. Supp. 714 (D. Kan. 1962), 107, 108

Engine Specialties, Inc. v. Bombardier Ltd., 454 F. 2d 527 (1st Cir. 1972), 877

Engine Specialties, Inc. v. Bombardier Ltd., 605 F.2d 1 (1st Cir. 1979), *modified on reh'g*, 615 F.2d 575 (1st Cir.), *cert. denied*, 446 U.S. 983 (1980), 77, 373, 384, 667

England v. Chrysler Corp., 493 F.2d 269 (9th Cir.), *cert. denied*, 419 U.S. 869 (1974), 439, 442

Englert v. City of McKeesport, 637 F. Supp. 930 (W.D. Pa. 1986), 989

Englert v. City of McKeesport, 736 F.2d 96 (3d Cir. 1984), 28

Englert v. City of McKeesport, 872 F.2d 1144 (3d Cir. 1989), 54

English v. 21st Phoenix Corp., 590 F.2d 723 (8th Cir.), *cert. denied*, 444 U.S. 832 (1979), 874

Enichem/ICI, 31 O.J. EUR. COMM. (No. L 50) 18 (1988), [1985-1988 Transfer Binder] COMMON MKT. REP. (CCH) ¶ 10,962, 937

ENI/Montedison, 30 O.J. EUR. COMM. (No. L 5) 13 (1987), [1985-1988 Transfer Binder] COMMON MKT. REP. (CCH) ¶ 10,860, 934

Entek Corp. v. Southwest Pipe & Supply Co., 683 F. Supp. 1092 (E.D. Tex. 1988), 876

Environmental Tectonics Corp. v. W. S. Kirkpatrick & Co., 659 F. Supp. 1381 (D.N.J. 1987), *aff'd*, 847 F.2d 1052 (3d Cir. 1988), *aff'd*, 493 U.S. 400 (1990), 435

Environmental Tectonics Corp. v. W.S. Kirkpatrick & Co., 847 F.2d 1052 (3d Cir. 1988), *aff'd*, 493 U.S. 400 (1990), 902, 908

Equifax Inc., 96 F.T.C. 844 (1980), *rev'd in part*, 678 F.2d 1047 (11th Cir. 1982), 532, 536

Equifax, Inc. v. FTC, 618 F.2d 63 (9th Cir. 1980), 276, 290, 521

Equifax Inc. v. FTC, 678 F.2d 1047 (11th Cir. 1982), 522

Erewhon, Inc. v. Northeast Health Food Merchants, 428 F. Supp. 551 (D. Mass. 1977), 81

Erie Sand & Gravel Co. v. FTC, 291 F.2d 279 (3d Cir. 1961), 295, 315

Erie Technological Prods. v. JFD Elec. Components Corp., 198 U.S.P.Q. (BNA), 179, 186 (E.D.N.Y. 1978), 808, 809

Ernest W. Hahn, Inc. v. Codding, 615 F.2d 830 (9th Cir. 1980), 1006

Erone Corp. v. Skouras Theatres, 22 F.R.D. 494 (S.D.N.Y. 1958), 747, 752

Esco Corp. v. United States, 340 F.2d 1000 (9th Cir. 1965), 3

ES Dev., Inc. v. RWM Enters., 939 F.2d 547 (8th Cir. 1991), *cert. denied*, 60 U.S.L.W. 3481 (U.S. Feb. 24, 1992), 3, 4, 7, 11, 61, 77, 84

Esplin v. Hirschi, 402 F.2d 94 (10th Cir. 1968), *cert. denied*, 394 U.S. 928 (1969), 695

Esposito v. Mister Softee, Inc., 1976-2 Trade Cas. (CCH) ¶ 61,202 (E.D.N.Y. 1976), 156

Essential Communs. Sys. v. AT&T, 610 F.2d 1114 (3d Cir. 1979), 1020, 1021

E.T. Barwick Indus. v. Walter E. Heller & Co., 692 F. Supp. 1331 (N.D. Ga. 1987), 167

Ethyl Corp., 101 F.T.C. 425 (1983), *vacated sub nom.* E.I. du Pont de Nemours & Co. v. FTC, 729 F.2d 128 (2d Cir. 1984), 10, 462, 463

Ethyl Corp. v. Hercules Powder Co., 232 F. Supp. 453 (D. Del. 1963), 823

Ethyl Gasoline Corp. v. United States, 309 U.S. 436 (1940), 822, 827, 828, 834, 852

Eugene Dietzgen Co. v. FTC, 142 F.2d 321 (7th Cir.), *cert. denied*, 323 U.S. 730 (1944), 964

Euramca Ecosystems, Inc. v. Roediger Pittsburgh, Inc., 581 F. Supp. 415 (N.D. Ill. 1984), 431

Eureka Urethane, Inc. v. PBA, Inc., 746 F. Supp. 915 (E.D. Mo. 1990), *aff'd*, 935 F.2d 990 (8th Cir. 1991), 222, 223, 248

Eurim-Pharm GmbH v. Pfizer Inc., 593 F. Supp. 1102 (S.D.N.Y. 1984), 840, 857, 858

Eurofix Bauco/Hilti, 31 O.J. EUR. COMM. (No. L. 65) 19 (1988), [1985-1988 Transfer Binder] COMMON MKT. REP. (CCH) ¶ 10,976, 957

Europemballage Corp. and Continental Can Co. v. Commission, Case 6/72, [1973] E.C.R. 215, [1971-1973 Transfer Binder] COMMON MKT. REP. (CCH) ¶ 8171, 951, 952, 953, 958

Euster v. Eagle Downs Racing Ass'n, 677 F.2d 992 (3d Cir.), *cert. denied*, 459 U.S. 1022 (1982), 972

Evans Prods. Co., [1983-1987 Transfer Binder] TRADE REG. REP. (CCH) ¶ 22,372 (W.D. Wash. June 17, 1986), 500

Evanston Motor Co. v. Mid-Southern Toyota Distribs., 436 F. Supp. 1370 (N.D. Ill. 1977), 634

Evans v. S.S. Kresge Co., 544 F.2d 1184 (3d Cir. 1976), *cert. denied*, 433 U.S. 908 (1977), 27, 28, 37, 38, 41

Evening News Publishing Co. v. Allied Newspapers Carriers, 263 F.2d 715 (3d Cir.), *cert. denied*, 360 U.S. 929 (1959), 81

Everseal Waterproofing Corp., 89 F.T.C. 110 (1977), 491

Eversharp, Inc., 77 F.T.C. 686 (1970), 482

Eversharp, Inc. v. Fisher Pen Co., 204 F. Supp. 649 (N.D. Ill. 1961), 835

E.W. French & Sons v. General Portland, Inc., 885 F.2d 1392 (9th Cir. 1989), 688

Ex-Cell-O Corp., 82 F.T.C. 36 (1973), 473

Excel Handbag Co. v. Edison Bros. Stores, 630 F.2d 379 (5th Cir. 1980), 435

Exchange Nat'l Bank v. Daniels, 768 F.2d 140 (7th Cir. 1985), 1098

Exhibitors Poster Exch. v. National Screen Serv. Corp., 441 F.2d 560 (5th Cir. 1971), 678

Exhibitors' Serv. v. American Multi-Cinema, Inc., 583 F. Supp. 1186 (C.D. Cal. 1984), *rev'd*, 788 F.2d 574 (9th Cir. 1986), 783, 786

Exhibitors' Serv. v. American Multi-Cinema, Inc., 788 F.2d 574 (9th Cir. 1986), 662

Eximco v. Trane Co., 737 F.2d 505 (5th Cir. 1984), 408

Ex parte Peru, 318 U.S. 578 (1943), 899

Export Liquor Sales, Inc. v. Ammex Warehouse Co., 426 F.2d 251 (6th Cir. 1970), *cert. denied*, 400 U.S. 1000 (1971), 408

Export Screw Ass'n, 43 F.T.C. 980 (1947), 915

Exquisite Form Brassiere, Inc. v. FTC, 301 F.2d 499 (D.C. Cir. 1961), *cert. denied*, 369 U.S. 888 (1962), 437

Extractol Process, Ltd. v. Hiram Walker & Sons, 153 F.2d 264 (7th Cir. 1946), 818, 826, 827, 828

Exxon Corp., 85 F.T.C. 404 (1975), 509

Exxon Corp., 98 F.T.C. 107 (1981), 505, 510, 511

Exxon Corp., 98 FTC 453 (1981), 463

Exxon Corp. v. FTC, 411 F. Supp. 1362 (D. Del. 1976), 523

Exxon Corp. v. FTC, 665 F.2d 1274 (D.C. Cir. 1981), 508

Exxon Corp. v. Governor of Maryland, 437 U.S. 117 (1978), 420, 621, 623, 624, 626, 969

Ezpelata v. Sisters of Mercy Health Corp., 621 F. Supp. 1262 (N.D. Ind. 1985), *aff'd*, 800 F.2d 119 (7th Cir. 1986), 151

Ezpeleta v. Sisters of Mercy Health Corp., 800 F.2d 119 (7th Cir. 1986), 173

F

Fabbrica Pisana and Fabbrica Lastre di Vetro Pietro Sciarra, 23 O.J. EUR. COMM. (No. L 75) 30 (1979), [1978-1981 Transfer Binder] COMMON MKT. REP. (CCH) ¶ 10,209, 918

Fairdale Farms v. Yankee Milk, Inc., 635 F.2d 1037 (2d Cir. 1980), *cert. denied*, 454 U.S. 818 (1981), 1024, 1026, 1027

Fairdale Farms v. Yankee Milk, Inc., 715 F.2d 30 (2d Cir. 1983), *cert. denied*, 464 U.S. 1043 (1984), 1026

Fairfield County Beverage Distrib. v. Narragansett Brewing Co., 378 F. Supp. 376 (D. Conn. 1974), 121

Falk v. City of Chicago, 1986-1 Trade Cas. (CCH) ¶ 67,128 (N.D. Ill. 1986), 971

Fallis v. Pendleton Woolen Mills, Inc., 866 F.2d 209 (6th Cir. 1989), 662

Falls Chase Special Taxing Dist. v. City of Tallahassee, 788 F.2d 711 (11th Cir. 1986), 985

Falls Church Bratwursthaus, Inc. v. Bratwursthaus Mgmt. Corp., 354 F. Supp. 1237 (E.D. Va. 1973), 155, 158, 160

Falls City Indus. v. Vanco Beverage, Inc., 460 U.S. 428 (1983), 405, 413, 416, 417, 418, 665

Falstaff Brewing Co. v. Stroh Brewery Co., 628 F. Supp. 822 (N.D. Cal 1986), *aff'd*, 914 F.2d 1256 (9th Cir. 1990), 222, 270

Falstaff Brewing Corp. v. Philip Morris, Inc., 1979-2 Trade Cas. (CCH) ¶ 62,814 (N.D. Cal. 1979), 690, 691, 692, 693

Famous Brands, Inc. v. David Sherman Corp., 814 F.2d 517 (8th Cir. 1987), 50, 144, 147, 164, 185

F & A Ice Cream Co. v. Arden Farms Co., 98 F. Supp. 180 (S.D. Cal. 1951), 451

F. & M. Schaefer Corp. v. C. Schmidt & Sons, 476 F. Supp. 203 (S.D.N.Y.), *aff'd*, 597 F.2d 814 (2d Cir. 1979), 361, 781

F. & M. Schaefer Corp. v. C. Schmidt & Sons, 597 F.2d 814 (2d Cir. 1979), 281, 293, 295, 296, 314, 366, 368, 369, 678

Farbenfabriken Bayer A.G. v. Sterling Drug, Inc., 197 F. Supp. 627 (D.N.J. 1961), aff'd, 307 F.2d 210 (3d Cir. 1962), cert. denied, 372 U.S. 929 (1963), 681

Far E. Conference v. United States, 342 U.S. 570 (1952), 1017, 1165

Farley Transp. Co. v. Santa Fe Trail Transp. Co., 786 F.2d 1342 (9th Cir. 1985), 115, 222, 668, 674, 675

Farmers Union Cent. Exch. v. FERC, 584 F.2d 408 (D.C. Cir.), cert. denied, 439 U.S. 995 (1978), 1079

Farmers Union Cent. Exch. v. FERC, 734 F.2d 1486 (D.C. Cir.), cert. denied, 469 U.S. 1034 (1984), 1079

Farmington Dowel Prods. Co. v. Forster Mfg., 421 F.2d 61 (1st Cir. 1969), 671, 672, 777, 786

Farm Journal, Inc., 53 F.T.C. 26 (1956), 316

Farnell v. Albuquerque Publishing Co., 589 F.2d 497 (10th Cir. 1978), 647

Fashion Originators' Guild v. FTC, 312 U.S. 457 (1941), 2, 57, 79, 465, 477

Fatty Acids, 30 O.J. EUR. COMM. (No. L 3) 17 (1987), [1985-1988 Transfer Binder] COMMON MKT. REP. (CCH) ¶ 10,841, 932

F. Buddie Contracting, Inc. v. Seawright, 595 F. Supp. 422 (N.D. Ohio 1984), 96, 660, 690, 692, 693, 1012

FCC v. Florida Power Corp., 480 U.S. 245 (1987), 1055

FCC v. League of Women Voters, 468 U.S. 364 (1984), 1028

FCC v. National Citizens Comm. for Broadcasting, 436 U.S. 755 (1978), 1036

FCC v. Sanders Bros. Radio Station, 309 U.S. 470 (1940), 370, 1028

FCC v. WNCN Listeners Guild, 450 U.S. 582 (1981), 1044

F. C. Russell Co. v. Comfort Equip. Corp., 194 F.2d 592 (7th Cir. 1952), 814

F. C. Russell Co. v. Consumers Insulation Co., 226 F.2d 373 (3d Cir. 1955), 814

FDIC v. British-American Corp., 726 F. Supp. 622 (E.D.N.C. 1989), 878

Fedders Corp., 85 F.T.C. 38 (1975), aff'd, 529 F.2d 1398 (2d Cir.), cert. denied, 429 U.S. 818 (1976), 474, 484

Fedders Corp. v. FTC, 529 F.2d 1398 (2d Cir.), cert. denied, 429 U.S. 818 (1976), 489

Federal Crop Ins. Corp. v. Merrill, 332 U.S. 380 (1947), 964

Federal Maritime Bd. v. Isbrandtsen Co., 356 U.S. 481 (1958), 1023

Federal Maritime Comm'n v. Aktiebolaget Svenska Amerika Linien, 390 U.S. 238 (1968), 80

Federal Paper Bd. Co. v. Amata, 693 F. Supp. 1376 (D. Conn. 1988), 32

Federal Paper Bd. Co. v. Commissioner, 90 T.C. 1011 (1988), 796, 797

Federal Prescription Serv. v. American Pharmaceutical Ass'n, 484 F. Supp. 1195 (D.D.C. 1980), aff'd in part and rev'd in part, 663 F.2d 253 (D.C. Cir. 1981), cert. denied, 455 U.S. 928 (1982), 69, 81

Federal Prescription Serv. v. American Pharmaceutical Ass'n, 663 F.2d 253 (D.C. Cir. 1981), cert. denied, 455 U.S. 928 (1982), 665, 1008, 1010

Federal Sign & Signal Corp. v. Bangor Punta Operations, Inc., 357 F. Supp. 1222 (S.D.N.Y. 1973), 833

Federated Dept. Stores, 89 F.T.C. 313 (1977), 480

Federated Dept. Stores, 106 F.T.C. 615 (1985), 536

Federated Dep't Stores v. Grinnell Corp., 287 F. Supp. 744 (S.D.N.Y. 1968), 778

Federated Dep't Stores v. Moitie, 452 U.S. 394 (1981), 631

Federated Nationwide Wholesalers Serv. v. FTC, 398 F.2d 253 (2d Cir. 1968), 477

FEDETAB v. Commission, Joined Cases 209-15 and 218/78, [1980] E.C.R. 3125, [1979-1981 Transfer Binder] COMMON MKT. REP. (CCH) ¶ 8687, 929, 931

Feeney v. Chamberlain Mfg. Corp., 831 F.2d 93 (5th Cir. 1987), 662

Feil v. FTC, 285 F.2d 879 (9th Cir. 1960), 469, 491

Feinstein v. Nettleship Co., 714 F.2d 928 (9th Cir. 1983), cert. denied, 466 U.S. 972 (1984), 1114, 1116, 1117

Feist Publications v. Rural Tel. Serv. Co., 111 S. Ct. 1282 (1991), 248

Feldman v. Gardner, 661 F.2d 1295 (D.C. Cir. 1981), 967

F.E.L. Publications v. Catholic Bishop, 1982-1 Trade Cas. (CCH) ¶ 64,632 (7th Cir.), *rev'g* 506 F. Supp 1127 (N.D. Ill. 1981), *cert. denied*, 459 U.S. 859 (1982), 139, 846

Feminist Women's Health Center, Inc. v. Mohammad, 586 F.2d 530 (5th Cir. 1978), *cert. denied*, 444 U.S. 924 (1979) 92, 1001, 1014, 1015

Ferguson v. Ford Motor Co., 77 F. Supp. 425 (S.D.N.Y. 1948), 866

Ferguson v. Greater Pocatello Chamber of Commerce, 848 F.2d 976 (9th Cir. 1988), 14, 49, 177, 246, 248, 249, 706

Ferguson v. Skrupa, 372 U.S. 726 (1963), 627

Ferrara Imports, Ltd., 91 F.T.C. 510 (1978), 541

Fertig v. Blue Cross, 68 F.R.D. 53 (N.D. Iowa 1974), 732

Fiberglass Insulators, Inc. v. Dupuy, 1986-2 Trade Cas. (CCH), 19

Fields Prods., Inc. v. United Artists Corp., 318 F. Supp. 87 (S.D.N.Y. 1969), *aff'd on opinion below*, 432 F.2d 1010 (2d Cir. 1970), *cert. denied*, 401 U.S. 949 (1971), 661

Fifth Moorings Condominium, Inc. v. Shere, 81 F.R.D. 712 (S.D. Fla. 1979), 713, 727

Figgie Int'l Inc. v. FTC, 107 F.T.C. 313 (1986), *aff'd mem.*, 817 F.2d 102 (4th Cir. 1987), *reprinted in* 1987-1 Trade Cas. (CCH) ¶ 67,546 (4th Cir. 1987), 468

Figgie Int'l Inc. v. FTC, 817 F.2d 102 (4th Cir. 1987), *reprinted in* 1987-1 Trade Cas. (CCH) ¶ 67,546 (4th Cir. 1987), 492, 521

Filartiga v. Pena-Irala, 630 F.2d 876 (2d Cir. 1980), 908

Filco v. Amana Refrigeration, Inc., 709 F.2d 1257 (9th Cir.), *cert. dismissed*, 464 U.S. 956 (1983), 109

Filmdex Chex Sys. v. Telecheck Washington, Inc., 1979-2 Trade Cas. (CCH) ¶ 62,976 (D.D.C. 1979), 185

Filter Queen of the Virginias, Inc. v. Health-Mor, Inc., 1990-1 Trade Cas. (CCH) ¶ 69,086 (N.D. Ill. 1990), 652

Fimex Corp. v. Barmatic Prods. Co., 429 F. Supp. 978 (E.D.N.Y.), *aff'd*, 573 F.2d 1289 (2d Cir. 1977), 448, 865

Fine v. Barry & Enright Prods., 731 F.2d 1394 (9th Cir.), *cert. denied*, 469 U.S. 881 (1984), 45, 50, 85, 188, 648, 649

Finley v. Music Corp., 66 F. Supp. 569 (S.D. Cal. 1946), 787

Finnegan v. Campeau Corp., 915 F.2d 824 (2d Cir. 1990), *cert. denied*, 111 S. Ct. 1624 (1991), 661, 1104

Finnell v. United States, 535 F. Supp. 410 (D. Kan. 1982), 558

Finnpap, 32 O.J. EUR. COMM. (No. C 45) 4 (1989), 929

Fiore v. Kelly Run Sanitation, Inc., 609 F. Supp. 909 (W.D. Pa. 1985), 431

Firestone Tire & Rubber Co., 77 F.T.C. 1666 (1970), 513

Firestone Tire & Rubber Co., 81 F.T.C. 398 (1972), *aff'd*, 481 F.2d 246 (6th Cir.), *cert. denied*, 414 U.S. 1112 (1973), 474, 490

Firestone Tire & Rubber Co. v. FTC, 481 F.2d 246 (6th Cir.), *cert. denied*, 414 U.S. 1112 (1973), 467, 471

First & First, Inc. v. Dunkin' Donuts, Inc., 1990-1 Trade Cas. (CCH) ¶ 68,989 (E.D. Pa. 1990), 364, 678

First Am. Bank Corp., 70 Fed. Res. Bull. 516 (1984), 1092

First Am. Title Co. v. South Dakota Land Title Ass'n, 714 F.2d 1439 (8th Cir. 1983), *cert. denied*, 464 U.S. 1042 (1984), 986, 1005, 1007

First Beverages, Inc. v. Royal Crown Cola Co., 612 F.2d 1164 (9th Cir.), *cert. denied*, 447 U.S. 924 (1980), 124, 126, 698

First Comics, Inc. v. World Color Press, Inc., 672 F. Supp. 1064 (N.D. Ill. 1987), *rev'd*, 884 F.2d 1033 (7th Cir. 1989), *cert. denied*, 493 U.S. 1075 (1990), 406, 417

First Comics, Inc. v. World Color Press, Inc., 884 F.2d 1033 (7th Cir. 1989), *cert. denied*, 493 U.S. 1075 (1990), 410, 413

First Flight Co. v. National Carloading Corp., 209 F. Supp. 730 (E.D. Tenn. 1962), 871, 875

First Hawaiian, Inc., 77 Fed. Res. Bull. 52 (1990), 1093

First Midwest Bancorp, 71 Fed. Res. Bull. 41 (1984), 1094

First Nat. City Bank v. Banco Nacional de Cuba, 406 U.S. 759 (1972), 902, 908

First Nat'l Bankshares, 70 Fed. Res. Bull. 832 (1984), 1092

First Nat'l Bank v. Cities Serv. Co., 391 U.S. 253 (1968), 5, 702, 703, 704

First Nat'l Bank v. Marquette Nat'l Bank, 482 F. Supp. 514 (D. Minn. 1979),aff'd, 636 F.2d 195
    (8th Cir. 1980), cert. denied, 450 U.S. 1042 (1981), 1005

First Wis. Corp., 72 Fed. Res. Bull. 50 (1985), 1093

Fischer & Porter Co. v. Sheffield Corp., 31 F.R.D. 534 (D. Del. 1962), 854

Fischer v. NWA, 883 F.2d 594 (8th Cir. 1989), cert. denied, 110 S. Ct. 2205 (1990), 652

Fisher Baking Co. v. Continental Baking Corp., 238 F. Supp. 332 (D. Utah 1965), 868

Fisher Bros. v. Mueller Brass Co., 102 F.R.D. 570 (E.D. Pa. 1984), 712, 714, 716, 725, 729

Fisher Bros. v. Phelps Dodge Indus., 1985-1 Trade Cas. (CCH) ¶ 66,536 (E.D. Pa. 1984), 744

Fisher Bros. v. Phelps Dodge Indus., 604 F. Supp. 446 (E.D. Pa. 1985), 741

Fisher Cos. v. Commissioner, 84 T.C. 1319 (1985), Acq. in part and non-acq. in part, 1990-2 C.B.
    1, aff'd without opinion, 806 F.2d 263 (9th Cir. 1986), 795, 796

Fisher v. City of Berkeley, 37 Cal. 3d 644, 693 P.2d 261 (Cal. 1984), aff'd on other grounds, 475
    U.S. 260 (1986), 43, 44

Fisher v. City of Berkeley, 475 U.S. 260 (1986), 17, 969

Fisher v. Coca-Cola Bottling Co., 1979-1 Trade Cas. (CCH) ¶ 62,514 (C.D. Cal. 1979), 364

Fishman v. Estate of Wirtz, 1981-2 Trade Cas. (CCH) ¶ 64,378 (N.D. Ill. 1981), aff'd, 807 F.2d
    520 (7th Cir. 1986), 54, 81, 649

Fishman v. Estate of Wirtz, 807 F.2d 520 (7th Cir. 1986), 1, 19, 248, 249, 646, 668, 671, 675 793

Fisichelli v. Town of Methuen, 653 F. Supp. 1494 (D. Mass. 1987), 977, 987, 989

Fisons Ltd. v. United States, 458 F.2d 1241 (7th Cir.), cert. denied, 405 U.S. 1041 (1972), 877

Fitch v. Kentucky-Tennessee Light & Power Co., 136 F.2d 12 (6th Cir. 1943), 435

Flair Zipper Corp. v. Textron, Inc., 1980-2 Trade Cas. (CCH) ¶ 63,555 (S.D.N.Y. 1980), 412

Flank Oil Co. v. Continental Oil Co., 277 F. Supp. 357 (D. Colo. 1967), 866

Flav-O-Rich, Inc. v. North Carolina Milk Comm'n, 593 F. Supp. 13 (E.D.N.C. 1983), aff'd
    without published opinion, 734 F.2d 11 (4th Cir.), cert. denied, 469 U.S. 853 (1984), 73

Fleet/Norstar Financial Group, Inc., 77 Fed. Res. Bull. 750 (1991), 1093

Fleer Corp. v. Topps Chewing Gum, Inc., 415 F. Supp. 176 (E.D. Pa. 1976), 777

Fleer Corp. v. Topps Chewing Gum, Inc., 658 F.2d 139 (3d Cir. 1981), cert. denied, 455 U.S.
    1019 (1982), 45, 55, 102, 109

Fleischmann Distilling Corp. v. Distillers Co., 395 F. Supp. 221 (S.D.N.Y. 1975), 857

Fleming v. Travelers Indem. Co., 324 F. Supp. 1404 (D. Mass. 1971), 1115

Flight Engr's Int'l Ass'n v. CAB, 332 F.2d 312 (D.C. Cir. 1964), 1156

Flinn v. FMC Corp., 528 F.2d 1169 (4th Cir. 1975), cert. denied, 424 U.S. 967 (1976), 741, 742,
    743

Flintkote Co. v. United States, 1991-2 U.S.T.C. (CCH) ¶ 50,435 (N.D. Cal. 1991), 947, 949

Flip Side Prods. v. Jam Prods., 843 F.2d 1024 (7th Cir.), cert. denied, 488 U.S. 909 (1988), 247,
    249, 789

FLM Collision Parts, Inc. v. Ford Motor Co., 543 F.2d 1019 (2d Cir. 1976), cert. denied, 429
    U.S. 1097 (1977), 110, 262, 406, 407, 429, 440

Floersheim v. FTC, 411 F.2d 874 (9th Cir. 1969), cert. denied, 396 U.S. 1002 (1970), 465, 477

Floersheim v. Weinberger, 346 F. Supp. 950 (D.D.C. 1972), aff'd in part, rev'd in part and
    remanded sub nom. Floersheim v. Engman, 494 F.2d 949 (D.C. Cir. 1973), 530

Flood v. Kuhn, 443 F.2d 264 (2d Cir. 1971), aff'd, 407 U.S. 258 (1972), 622

Floral, 22 O.J. EUR. COMM. (No. L 39) 51 (1979), [1978-1981 Transfer Binder] COMMON MKT.
    REP. (CCH) ¶ 10,184, 933

Florida Bar v. Evans, 94 So. 2d 730 (Fla. 1957), 582

Florida Cablevision v. Telesat Cablevision, Inc., No. 87-8358 (S.D. Fla., filed May 26, 1987), 1054

Florida Citrus Mut., 50 F.T.C. 959 (1954), 455

Florida Cities v. Florida Power & Light, 525 F. Supp. 1000 (S.D. Fla. 1981), 249

Florida *ex rel.* Shevin v. Exxon Corp., 526 F.2d 266 (5th Cir.), *cert. denied*, 429 U.S. 829 (1976), 604

Florida *ex. rel.* Smith v. Cargo Gasoline Co., 1986-1 Trade Cas. (CCH) ¶ 66,928 (M.D. Fla. 1986), 608

Florida Fuels, Inc. v. Belcher Oil Co., 717 F. Supp. 1528 (S.D. Fla. 1989), 249

Florida Hard Rock Phosphate Export Ass'n, 42 F.T.C. 843 (1945), 915

Florida Harvestore, Inc. v. A. O. Smith Harvestore Prods., 561 F.2d 631 (5th Cir. 1977), *cert. denied*, 436 U.S. 919 (1978), 124

Florida Lime & Avocado Growers v. Paul, 373 U.S. 132 (1963), 624

Florida Power & Light Co., 15 N.R.C. 22 (1982), 1082

Florida Power & Light Co., 29 F.E.R.C. (CCH) ¶ 61,140 (1984), 1069

Florida Power & Light Co. v. FERC, 660 F.2d 668 (5th Cir. 1981), *cert. denied*, 459 U.S. 1156 (1983), 1069

Florida Power Corp. v. Granlund, 78 F.R.D. 441 (M.D. Fla. 1978), 657

Florida v. Abbott Labs., No. TCA 91-40002 MMP (N.D. Fla. filed Jan. 5, 1991), 605

Florists' Nationwide Tel. Delivery Network v. Florists' Tel. Delivery Ass'n, 371 F.2d 263 (7th Cir.), *cert. denied*, 387 U.S. 909 (1967), 78, 79

Flotill Prods., Inc. v. FTC, 358 F.2d 224 (9th Cir. 1966), *rev'd in part and remanded*, 389 U.S. 179 (1967), 434, 442

Flotken's West, Inc. v. National Food Stores, 312 F. Supp. 136 (E.D. Mo. 1970), 403, 404

Flowers Indus. v. FTC, 1987-2 Trade Cas. (CCH) ¶ 67,797 (11th Cir. 1987), 520

Flowers Indus. v. FTC, 1988-1 Trade Cas. (CCH) ¶ 67,950 (M.D. Ga.), *vacated and remanded*, 849 F.2d 551 (11th Cir. 1988), 347

Flying Tigers Line v. CAB, 350 F.2d 462 (D.C. Cir. 1965), *cert. denied*, 385 U.S. 945 (1966), 1156

FMC Corp. v. Glouster Eng'g, 830 F.2d 770 (7th Cir. 1987), 711

FMC Corp. v. Manitowoc Co., 835 F.2d 1411 (Fed. Cir. 1987), 806, 810

FMC Corp. v. Varonos, 892 F.2d 1308 (7th Cir. 1990), 872

FMC v. Aktiebolaget Svenska Amerika Linien, 390 U.S. 238 (1968), 1165

FMC v. Seatrain Lines, 411 U.S. 726 (1973), 1017

FN-CF, 14 (No. L 134) 6 (1971), [1970-1972 Transfer Binder] COMMON MKT. REP. (CCH) ¶ 9439, 934

Folding Cartons, Inc. v. American Can Co., 79 F.R.D. 698 (N.D. Ill. 1978), 721, 734

Foley v. Alabama State Bar, 481 F. Supp. 1308 (N.D. Ala. 1979), 967

Folmer Graflex Corp. v. Graphic Photo Serv., 41 F. Supp. 319 (D. Mass. 1941), 847

Fonderies Roubaix v. Fonderies A. Roux, Case 63/75, [1976] E.C.R. 111, [1976 Transfer Binder] COMMON MKT. REP. (CCH) ¶ 8341, 926

Fontana Aviation, Inc. v. Beech Aircraft Corp., 432 F.2d 1080 (7th Cir. 1970), *cert. denied*, 401 U.S. 923 (1971), 128

Fontana Aviation, Inc. v. Cessna Aircraft Co., 617 F.2d 478 (7th Cir. 1980), 655, 657

Food Basket, Inc. v. Albertson's, Inc., 383 F.2d 785 (10th Cir. 1967), 403, 404

Food Fair Stores, 83 F.T.C. 1213 (1974), 434

Fooshee v. Interstate Vending Co., 234 F. Supp. 44 (D. Kan. 1964), 867

Forbes v. Greater Minneapolis Bd. of Realtors, 1973-2 Trade Cas. (CCH) ¶ 74,696 (D. Minn. 1973), 746, 747

Ford Motor Co., 94 F.T.C. 564 (1979), *rev'd*, 673 F.2d 1008 (9th Cir. 1981), *cert. denied*, 459 U.S. 999 (1982), 486, 498

Ford Motor Co., 96 F.T.C. 362 (1980), 468, 540

Ford Motor Co., 102 F.T.C. 1732 (1983), 443

Ford Motor Co. v. FTC, 547 F.2d 954 (6th Cir. 1976), *cert. denied*, 431 U.S. 915 (1977), 515

Ford Motor Co. v. FTC, 673 F.2d 1008 (9th Cir. 1981), *cert. denied*, 459 U.S. 999 (1982), 486, 494, 495

Ford Motor Co. v. United States, 335 U.S. 303 (1948), 571, 576, 577

Ford Motor Co. v. United States, 405 U.S. 562 (1972), 319, 330, 331, 358, 360, 569

Ford Motor Co. v. Webster's Auto Sales, Inc., 361 F.2d 874 (1st Cir. 1966), 81, 670

Ford Motor Credit Co. v. Milhollin, 444 U.S. 555 (1980), 534

Ford of Europe Inc. v. Commission, Cases 228 and 229/82, [1984] E.C.R. 1129, [1983-1985 Transfer Binder] COMMON MKT. REP. (CCH) ¶ 14,025, 920

Ford Werke AG, 25 O. J. EUR. COMM. (No. L 256) 20 (1982), [1982-1985 Transfer Binder] COMMON MKT. REP. (CCH) ¶ 10,419, 942

Foreign Car Parts, Inc. v. Auto World, Inc., 366 F. Supp. 977 (M.D. Pa. 1973), 846

Foremost Dairies, 60 F.T.C. 944 (1962), *modified*, 67 F.T.C. 282 (1965), 276, 296, 460

Foremost Dairies, 62 F.T.C. 1344 (1963), *aff'd*, 348 F.2d 674 (5th Cir.), *cert. denied*, 382 U.S. 959 (1965), 422

Foremost Dairies v. FTC, 348 F.2d 674 (5th Cir.), *cert. denied*, 382 U.S. 959 (1965), 403

Foremost Int'l Tours, Inc. v. Qantas Airways Ltd., 379 F. Supp. 88 (D. Haw. 1974), *aff'd*, 525 F.2d 281 (9th Cir. 1975), *cert. denied*, 429 U.S. 816 (1976), 1021

Foremost Int'l Tours, Inc. v. Qantas Airways Ltd., 525 F.2d 281 (9th Cir. 1975), *cert. denied*, 429 U.S. 816 (1976), 1155

Foremost-McKesson, Inc., 109 F.T.C. 127 (1987), 445, 462

Foremost-McKesson, Inc., [1983-1987 Transfer Binder] TRADE REG. REP. (CCH) ¶ 22,445 (Apr. 29, 1987), 437

Foremost-McKesson, Inc. v. Instrumentation Lab., 527 F.2d 417 (5th Cir. 1976), 666

Foremost Pro Color, Inc. v. Eastman Kodak Co., 703 F.2d 534 (9th Cir. 1983), *cert. denied*, 465 U.S. 1038 (1984), 143, 144, 438

Forever Living Prods. v. Blatter, 1986-1 Trade Cas. (CCH) ¶ 67,163 (D. Ariz. 1986), 48

Forno's Continental Motors v. Subaru Distrib. Corp., 649 F. Supp. 746 (N.D.N.Y 1986), 50

Forrest v. Capital Bldg. & Loan Ass'n, 385 F. Supp. 831 (M.D. La. 1973), *aff'd*, 504 F.2d 891 (5th Cir. 1974), *cert. denied*, 421 U.S. 978 (1975), 132, 139

Forro Precision, Inc. v. IBM, 673 F.2d 1045 (9th Cir. 1982), *appeal after remand*, 745 F.2d 1283 (9th Cir. 1984), *cert. denied*, 471 U.S. 1130 (1985), 992

Fortner Enters. v. United States Steel Corp., 394 U.S. 495 (1969), 134, 136, 137, 149, 157, 163

Fort Pierce Utils. Auth. v. United States, 606 F.2d 986 (D.C. Cir.), *cert. denied*, 444 U.S. 842 (1979), 1081

Fort Wayne Telstat v. Entertainment & Sports Programming Network, 753 F. Supp. 109 (S.D.N.Y. 1990), 271

49er Chevrolet, Inc. v. General Motors Corp., 803 F.2d 1463 (9th Cir. 1986), *cert. denied*, 480 U.S. 947 (1987), 15, 115, 131

Foster v. American Mach. & Foundry Co., 492 F.2d 1317 (2d Cir.), *cert. denied*, 419 U.S. 833 (1974), 819

Foster v. Maryland State Savings & Loan Ass'n, 590 F.2d 928 (D.C. Cir. 1978), *cert. denied*, 439 U.S. 1071 (1979), 139

Foundry Servs. v. Beneflux Corp., 110 F. Supp. 857 (S.D.N.Y.), *rev'd on other grounds*, 206 F.2d 214 (2d Cir. 1953), 842, 850

Fount-Wip, Inc. v. Reddi-Wip, Inc., 578 F.2d 1296 (9th Cir. 1978), 180

Fox Motors, Inc. v. Mazda Distribs. (Gulf), 806 F.2d 953 (10th Cir. 1986), 136, 159

Fox Valley Harvestore, Inc. v. A.O. Smith Harvestore Prods., Inc., 545 F.2d 1096 (7th Cir. 1976), 677

Fox v. Comprehensive Accounting Corp., 1984-1 Trade Cas. (CCH) ¶ 65,993 (N.D. Ill. 1984), 134, 143, 144, 145, 206

FPC v. Conway Corp., 426 U.S. 271 (1976), 1071

Fradette v. American Serv. Corp., 1980-2 Trade Cas. (CCH) ¶ 63,403 (S.D. Fla. 1979), 716, 738, 775

Fragale & Sons Beverage Co. v. Dill, 760 F.2d 469 (3d Cir. 1985), 9, 14

Fraley v. Chesapeake & Ohio Ry., 397 F.2d 1 (3d Cir. 1968), 875

France v. Commission, Case C-202/88, (Eur. Comm. Ct. J. 1991), 924

Franchise Realty Interstate Corp. v. San Francisco Local Joint Exec. Bd., 542 F.2d 1076 (9th Cir. 1976), *cert. denied*, 430 U.S. 940 (1977), 1002, 1005

Franchise Tax Bd. v. Construction Laborers Vacation Trust, 463 U.S. 1 (1983), 851

Franco-Japanese Ballbearings Agreement, 17 O.J. EUR. COMM. (No. L 343) 19 (1974), [1973-1975 Transfer Binder] COMMON MKT. REP. (CCH) ¶ 9697, 927

Frank Chevrolet Co. v. General Motors Corp., 419 F.2d 1054 (6th Cir. 1969), 130, 184

Frankford Hosp. v. Blue Cross, 417 F. Supp. 1104 (E.D. Pa. 1976), *aff'd per curiam*, 554 F.2d 1253 (3d Cir.), *cert. denied*, 434 U.S. 860 (1977), 1117

Frankford Hosp. v. Blue Cross, 554 F.2d 1253 (3d Cir. 1977) (per curiam), *aff'g* 417 F. Supp. 1104 (E.D. Pa. 1976), *cert. denied*, 434 U.S. 860 (1977), 1111

Frankford Hosp. v. Blue Cross, 67 F.R.D. 643 (E.D. Pa. 1975), 713, 715, 729

Franklin Container Corp. v. International Paper Co., 1983-2 Trade Cas. (CCH) ¶ 65,727 (E.D. Pa. 1982), 718

Frank Saltz & Sons v. Hart Schaffner & Marx, 1985-2 Trade Cas. (CCH) ¶ 66,768, (S.D.N.Y. 1985), 203, 275, 283, 285, 287, 288, 302, 307, 364

Fran Welch Real Estate Sales, Inc. v. Seabrook Island Co., 809 F.2d 1030 (4th Cir. 1987), 380

Fray Chevrolet Sales, Inc. v. General Motors Corp., 536 F.2d 683 (6th Cir. 1976), 118, 188

Frazier v. Consolidated Rail Corp., 851 F.2d 1447 (D.C. Cir. 1988), 713

Frecker v. City of Dayton, 153 Ohio St. 14, 90 N.E.2d 851 (1950), 627

Fred Bonner Corp., 57 F.T.C. 771 (1960), 416

Frederick Chusid & Co. v. Marshall Leeman & Co., 326 F. Supp. 1043 (S.D.N.Y. 1971), 96

Fred Meyer, Inc., 63 F.T.C. 1 (1963), *modified and aff'd*, 359 F.2d 351 (9th Cir. 1966), *cert. denied*, 386 U.S. 907 (1967), 427

Fred Meyer, Inc., 87 F.T.C. 112 (1976), 480, 496

Fred Meyer, Inc., 96 F.T.C. 60 (1980) *modified*, 100 F.T.C. 510 (1982), 532

Fred Meyer, Inc. v. FTC, 359 F.2d 351 (9th Cir. 1966), *rev'd*, 390 U.S. 341 (1968), 406, 427, 439, 440, 442, 445, 446, 494

Fred Meyer, Inc. v. FTC, 390 U.S. 341 (1968), 440

Freedman v. Meldy's Inc., 587 F. Supp. 658, 660-62 (E.D. Pa. 1984), 543

Freed Oil Co. v. Quaker State Oil Ref. Co., 419 F. Supp. 479 (W.D. Pa. 1976), *vacated per stipulation*, 1977-2 Trade Cas. (CCH) ¶ 61,758 (W.D. Pa. 1977), 186, 686, 687

Freehill v. Lewis, 355 F.2d 46 (4th Cir. 1966), 711

Freeman v. Bee Mach. Co., 319 U.S. 448 (1943), 867

Freeman v. Chicago Title & Trust Co., 505 F.2d 527 (7th Cir. 1974), 409, 410

Free World Foreign Cars, Inc. v. Alfa Romeo, SpA, 55 F.R.D. 26 (S.D.N.Y. 1972), 718, 720, 729

Frey & Son v. Cudahy Packing Co., 256 U.S. 208 (1921), 101

Friedman v. Adams Russell Cable Servs., 624 F. Supp. 1195 (S.D.N.Y. 1986), 159, 1054

Friedman v. Delaware County Memorial Hosp., 672 F. Supp. 171 (E.D. Pa. 1987), 56

Friedman v. Rogers, 440 U.S. 1 (1979), 492

Friendship Materials, Inc. v. Michigan Brick, Inc., 679 F.2d 100 (6th Cir. 1982), 366, 676, 677, 678

Frito-Lay, Inc., 66 F.T.C. 1533 (1964), 511

Frito-Lay, Inc. v. Bachman Co., 659 F. Supp. 1129 (S.D.N.Y. 1986), 437

Frontier Enters. v. Amador Stage Lines, 624 F. Supp. 137 (E.D. Cal. 1985), 240

Fruehauf Corp., 91 F.T.C. 132 (1978), *rev'd*, 603 F.2d 345 (2d Cir. 1979), 335

Fruehauf Corp. v. FTC, 603 F.2d 345 (2d Cir. 1979), 331, 521, 522

Fry v. John Hancock Mut. Life Ins. Co., 355 F. Supp. 1151 (N.D. Tex. 1973), 1114

FTC Line of Business Report Litig., 595 F.2d 685 (D.C. Cir.), *cert. denied*, 439 U.S. 958 (1978), 506, 512

FTC v. Action Credit Sys., No. C-88-1322-EAL (N.D. Cal. Apr. 6, 1988), 532

FTC v. Action Credit Sys., No. C-88-1322 EFL (N.D. Cal. Mar. 1, 1989), 489

FTC v. A.E. Staley Mfg. Co., 324 U.S. 746 (1945), 405, 417, 419

FTC v. Alaska Land Leasing, Inc., 1985-2 Trade Cas. (CCH) ¶ 66,881 (D. Colo. 1985), 512

FTC v. Alaska Land Leasing Inc., 5 TRADE REG. REP. (CCH) ¶ 22,459 (C.D. Cal. July 14, 1987), 214, 479

FTC v. Algoma Lumber Co., 291 U.S. 67 (1934), 464, 465, 473, 482, 486, 496

FTC v. American Nat'l Cellular, Inc., 810 F.2d 1511 (9th Cir. 1987), 510

FTC v. American Nat'l Cellular, Inc., 868 F.2d 315 (9th Cir. 1989), 502

FTC v. American Tobacco Co., 264 U.S. 298, 306 (1924), 506

FTC v. AMREP Corp., 705 F. Supp. 119 (S.D.N.Y. 1988), 498

FTC v. Amy Travel Serv., 5 TRADE REG. REP. (CCH) ¶ 22,546 (N.D. Ill. May 4, 1988), aff'd, 875 F.2d 564 (7th Cir.), cert. denied, 493 U.S. 954 (1989), 479

FTC v. Amy Travel Serv., 875 F.2d 564 (7th Cir.), cert. denied, 493 U.S. 954 (1989), 486, 500

FTC v. Anheuser-Busch, Inc., 363 U.S. 536 (1960), 405, 414, 488

FTC v. Army & Navy Trading Co., 88 F.2d 776 (D.C. Cir. 1937), 477

FTC v. Atlantex Assocs., 1987-2 Trade Cas. (CCH) ¶ 67,788 (S.D. Fla. 1987), aff'd, 872 F.2d 966 (11th Cir. 1989), 480

FTC v. Atlantex Assocs., 872 F.2d 966 (11th Cir. 1989), 479, 500, 501

FTC v. Atlantic Richfield Co., 549 F.2d 289 (4th Cir. 1977), 323, 325, 354, 459, 503

FTC v. Atlantic Richfield Co., 567 F.2d 96 (D.C. Cir. 1977), 509, 511

FTC v. Baltimore Grain Co., 284 F. 886 (D. Md. 1922), aff'd sub nom. FTC v. Hammond Snyder & Co., 267 U.S. 586 (1925), 506

FTC v. Bass Bros. Enters., 1984-1 Trade Cas. (CCH) ¶ 66,041 (N.D. Ohio 1989), 294, 300, 302, 303, 312, 314, 354, 355

FTC v. Beatrice Foods Co., 587 F.2d 1225 (D.C. Cir. 1978), 354, 503

FTC v. Beech-Nut Packing Co., 257 U.S. 441 (1922), 11, 101, 109, 110, 181, 522

FTC v. B.F. Goodrich Co., 242 F.2d 31 (D.C. Cir. 1957), aff'g 134 F. Supp. 39 (D.D.C. 1955), 426

FTC v. Borden Co., 383 U.S. 637 (1966), 410

FTC v. Brigadier Indus. Corp., 613 F.2d 1110 (D.C. Cir. 1979), 527

FTC v. British Oxygen Co., 437 F. Supp. 79 (D. Del. 1977), 354

FTC v. British Oxygen Co., 529 F.2d 196 (3d Cir. 1976), 503, 504

FTC v. Brown & Williamson Tobacco Corp., 778 F.2d 35 (D.C. Cir. 1985), 470, 492

FTC v. Browning, 435 F.2d 96 (D.C. Cir. 1970), 508

FTC v. Brown Shoe Co., 384 U.S. 316 (1966), 2, 163, 164, 174, 276, 458, 459

FTC v. Carter, 636 F.2d 781 (D.C. Cir. 1980), 506

FTC v. Cement Inst., 333 U.S. 683 (1948), 57, 65, 67, 405, 419, 456, 457, 513, 522, 545

FTC v. Citicorp, 1979-1 Trade Cas. (CCH) ¶ 62,671 (S.D.N.Y. 1979), 507

FTC v. Claire Furnace Co., 274 U.S. 160 (1927), 508

FTC v. Coca-Cola Co., 641 F. Supp. 1128 (D.D.C. 1986), vacated mem., 829 F.2d 191 (D.C. Cir. 1987), 285, 289, 294, 304, 305, 308, 309, 319, 354

FTC v. Cockrell, 431 F. Supp. 561 (D.D.C. 1977), 456, 507, 508

FTC v. Colgate-Palmolive Co., 380 U.S. 374 (1965), 464, 465, 466, 470, 481, 482, 489, 503, 522

FTC v. Compagnie de Saint-Gobain-Pont-a-Mousson, 636 F.2d 1300 (D.C. Cir. 1980), 864

FTC v. Consolidated Foods Corp., 396 F.Supp. 1353 (S.D.N.Y. 1975), 496

FTC v. Consolidated Foods Corp., 380 U.S. 592 (1964), 166, 167, 336

FTC v. Creative Advertising Specialty House, 5 TRADE REG. REP. (CCH) ¶ 22,740 (C.D. Cal. Oct. 11, 1989), 533

FTC v. Creditcard Travel Servs., 5 TRADE REG. REP. (CCH) ¶ 22,483 (N.D. Ill. Nov. 2, 1987), 479, 533

FTC v. Creditcard Travel Servs., ANTITRUST & TRUST REG. REP. (BNA) No. 1412 (N.D. Ill. Apr. 14, 1989), 500

FTC v. Credit Rite, Inc., No. 88-1206 (D.N.J. Mar. 7, 1988), 532

FTC v. Dean Foods Co., 384 U.S. 597 (1966), 338, 501

FTC v. Dixie Fin. Co., 695 F.2d 926 (5th Cir.), *cert. denied*, 461 U.S. 928 (1983), 507, 1112

FTC v. Elders Grain, Inc., 868 F.2d 901 (7th Cir. 1989), 294, 311, 312, 355, 357, 358, 504

FTC v. Encore House, No. 85-7385 (S.D.N.Y. Sept. 24, 1985), 489

FTC v. Engage-A-Car Servs., [1983-1987 Transfer Binder] TRADE REG. REP. (CCH) ¶ 22,398 (D.N.J. Sept. 23, 1986), 480

FTC v. Ernstthal, 607 F.2d 488 (D.C. Cir. 1979), 456, 507

FTC v. Evans Prods. Co., 775 F.2d 1084 (9th Cir. 1985), 501, 502

FTC v. Exxon Corp., 1979-2 Trade Cas. (CCH) ¶ 62,763 (D.D.C. 1979), 503

FTC v. Exxon Corp., 1979-2 Trade Cas. (CCH) ¶ 62,972 (D.D.C. 1979), *modified*, 1980-2 Trade Cas. (CCH) ¶ 63,478 (D.D.C.), *aff'd in part and rev'd in part*, 636 F.2d 1336 (D.C. Cir. 1980), 355, 357

FTC v. Exxon Corp., 636 F.2d 1336 (D.C. Cir. 1980), 356, 518, 557

FTC v. Federal Sterling Galleries, 5 TRADE REG. REP. (CCH) ¶ 22,493 (D. Ariz. 1987), 479

FTC v. First Capital Fin., No. AR-90-2007 (D. Md. Jul. 25, 1990), 533

FTC v. Flotill Prods., 389 U.S. 179 (1967), 453

FTC v. Food Town Stores, 539 F.2d 1339 (4th Cir. 1976), *vacated*, 547 F.2d 247 (4th Cir. 1977), 352, 354, 356, 502, 503

FTC v. Gibson Prods., Inc., 569 F.2d 900 (5th Cir. 1978), 511

FTC v. Glenn W. Turner Enters., 446 F. Supp. 1113 (M.D. Fla.1978), 499, 500

FTC v. Go For It, CV-S-90-114-LDG (D. Nev. June 12, 1990), 489

FTC v. Gratz, 253 U.S. 421 (1920), 522

FTC v. Great Lakes Chem. Corp., 1981-2 Trade Cas. (CCH) ¶ 64,175 (N.D. Ill. 1981), 352

FTC v. Great Lakes Chem. Corp., 528 F. Supp. 84 (N.D. Ill. 1981), 313, 315, 316

FTC v. Green, 252 F. Supp. 153 (S.D.N.Y. 1966), 508

FTC v. GTP Marketing, Inc., 1990-1 Trade Cas. (CCH) ¶ 68,959 (N.D. Tex. 1990), 504

FTC v. Harbour Group Investments, L.P., 1990-2 Trade Cas. (CCH) ¶ 69,247 (D.D.C. 1990), 314, 316, 376, 387

FTC v. Henry Broch & Co., 363 U.S. 166 (1960), 425, 431, 432, 436

FTC v. Henry Eldon Stricker, No. 90-5866-AWT (C.D. Cal. filed Oct. 31, 1990), 618

FTC v. H.N. Singer, Inc., 1982-83 Trade Cas. (CCH) ¶ 65,011 (N.D. Cal.), *aff'd*, 668 F.2d 1107 (9th Cir. 1982), 480

FTC v. H.N. Singer, Inc., 668 F.2d 1107 (9th Cir. 1982), 479, 499, 500, 501

FTC v. Hughes, 710 F.Supp. 1524 (N.D. Tx. 1989), 497

FTC v. Hunt Foods & Indus., 178 F. Supp. 448 (S.D. Cal. 1959), *aff'd*, 286 F.2d 803 (9th Cir. 1960), *cert. denied*, 365 U.S. 877 (1961), 507

FTC v. Illinois Cereal Mills, Inc., 691 F. Supp. 1131 (N.D. Ill. 1988), *aff'd*, 868 F.2d 901 (7th Cir. 1989), 287, 298, 302, 307, 309

FTC v. Indiana Fed'n of Dentists, 476 U.S. 447 (1986), 31, 32, 35, 36, 39, 44, 46, 51, 52, 68, 78, 82, 83, 84, 92, 93, 94, 212, 457, 520, 521

FTC v. International Diamond Corp., 1983-2 Trade Cas. (CCH) ¶ 65,725 (N.D. Cal. 1983), 479, 480, 500

FTC v. Investment Devs., Inc., No. Civ. A. 89-642, 1989 WL 62564 (E.D. La. June 8, 1989), 478, 479, 499, 500

FTC v. Jacobson, ANTITRUST & TRADE REG. REP. (BNA) No. 1417 (E.D. Va. May 18, 1989), 500

FTC v. J&R Mktg. Corp., [1983-1987 Transfer Binder] TRADE REG. REP. (CCH) ¶ 22,252 (S.D. Fla. May 10, 1985), 480

FTC v. Jim Walter Corp., 651 F.2d 251 (5th Cir. 1981), 508

FTC v. Kimberly Int'l Gem Corp., [1983-1987 Transfer Binder] TRADE REG. REP. (CCH) ¶ 22,061 (C.D. Cal. Aug. 16, 1983), 479

FTC v. Klesner, 280 U.S. 19 (1929), 455, 1156

FTC v. Lady Venus Centers, Inc., No. 3-84-0158 (M.D. Tenn. Feb. 16, 1984), 489-490

FTC v. Lancaster Colony Corp., 434 F. Supp. 1088 (S.D.N.Y. 1977), 354, 357, 504

FTC v. Las Animas Ranch, Inc., [July-Dec.] ANTITRUST & TRADE REG. REP. (BNA) No. 986, at A-24 (D. Colo. Oct. 6, 1980), 515

FTC v. Leland Indus., [1983-1987 Transfer Binder] TRADE REG. REP. (CCH) ¶ 22,297 (C.D. Cal. Oct. 11, 1985), 479, 500

FTC v. Liberto, No. 86-4237 (E.D.N.Y. Dec. 18, 1986), 532

FTC v. Lukens Steel Co., 444 F. Supp. 803 (D.D.C. 1977), 746, 747, 748

FTC v. Lukens Steel Co., 454 F.Supp. 182 (D.D.C. 1978), 488

FTC v. MacArthur, 532 F.2d 1135 (7th Cir. 1976), 507, 508

FTC v. Macmillan, Inc., 1983-2 Trade Cas. (CCH) ¶ 65,553 (N.D. Ill. 1983), 499

FTC v. Mandel Bros., 359 U.S. 385 (1959), 489

FTC v. Manufacturers Hanover Consumer Servs., 1982-2 Trade Cas. (CCH) ¶ 64,903 (E.D. Pa. 1982), 508

FTC v. Manufacturers Hanover Consumer Serv., 567 F. Supp. 992 (E.D. Pa. 1983), 1112

FTC v. Mary Carter Point Co., 382 U.S. 46 (1965), 475

FTC v. McCormick & Co., 1988-1 Trade Cas. (CCH) ¶ 67,976 (D.D.C. 1988), 343

FTC v. Menzies, 145 F. Supp. 164 (D. Md. 1956), aff'd, 242 F.2d 81 (4th Cir.), cert. denied, 353 U.S. 957 (1957), 507

FTC v. Michael Kaplan, No. CV-S-85-161-LDG (D. Nev. Oct. 28, 1989 and Mar. 20, 1989), 489

FTC v. Miller, 549 F.2d 452 (7th Cir. 1977), 507

FTC v. Monahan, 832 F.2d 688 (1st Cir. 1987), cert. denied, 485 U.S. 987 (1988), 507, 980

FTC v. Morton Salt Co., 334 U.S. 37 (1948), 406, 407, 408, 416, 423, 428, 430

FTC v. Motion Picture Advertising Serv. Co., 344 U.S. 392 (1953), 2, 177, 457, 459

FTC v. Mytel Int'l, Inc., 5 TRADE REG. REP. (CCH) ¶ 22,481 (C.D. Cal. Oct. 30, 1987), 480

FTC v. National Cas. Co., 357 U.S. 560 (1958), 1115, 1116

FTC v. National Comm'n on Egg Nutrition, 517 F.2d 485 (7th Cir. 1975), cert. denied, 426 U.S. 919 (1976), 456, 502

FTC v. Nat'l Health Aids, Inc., 108 F. Supp. 340 (D. Md. 1952), 502

FTC v. National Lead Co., 352 U.S. 419 (1957), 65, 419, 490

FTC v. National Tea Co., 603 F.2d 694 (8th Cir. 1979), 317, 354, 503

FTC v. New England Rare Coin Galleries, [1983-1987 Transfer Binder] TRADE REG. REP. (CCH) ¶ 22,431 (D. Mass. Feb. 13, 1987), 479, 500

FTC v. Occidental Petroleum Corp., 1986-1 Trade Cas. (CCH) ¶ 67,071 (D.D.C. 1986), 288, 292, 301, 354, 355, 356

FTC v. Owens-Corning Fiberglass Corp., 1987-1 Trade Cas. (CCH) ¶ 67,463 (N.D. Ohio 1987), appeal dismissed, 853 F.2d 458 (6th Cir. 1988), cert. denied, 489 U.S. 1015 (1989), 347

FTC v. Owens-Corning Fiberglass Corp., 853 F.2d 458 (6th Cir. 1988), cert. denied, 489 U.S. 1015 (1989), 496

FTC v. Owens-Illinois, Inc., 681 F. Supp. 27 (D.D.C.), vacated as moot, 850 F.2d 694 (D.C. Cir. 1988), 284, 287, 289, 292, 298, 302, 309, 311, 312, 320

FTC v. Pacific States Paper Trade Ass'n, 273 U.S. 52 (1927), 456

FTC v. Page, 378 F. Supp. 1052 (N.D. Ga. 1974), 507

FTC v. Paradise Palms Vacation Club, [1983-1987 Transfer Binder] TRADE REG. REP. (CCH) ¶ 22,402 (W.D. Wash. Oct. 17, 1986), 480

FTC v. Paradise Palms Vacation Club, No. C86-1160V (W.D. Wash. Aug. 9, 1988), 489

FTC v. Pat Clark Pontiac, Misc. No. 77-0093 (D.D.C. 1977), 508

FTC v. PepsiCo, Inc., 477 F.2d 24 (2d Cir. 1973), 304, 308, 355, 356, 357, 501

FTC v. Pillsbury Co., 1976-2 Trade Cas. (CCH) ¶ 61,200 (N.D. Ill. 1976), 355

FTC v. PPG Indus., 628 F. Supp. 881 (D.D.C.), aff'd in part and rev'd in part, 798 F.2d 1500 (D.C. Cir. 1986), 309

FTC v. PPG Indus., 798 F.2d 1500 (D.C. Cir. 1986), 283, 286, 287, 292, 302, 303, 305, 356

FTC v. Procter & Gamble Co., 386 U.S. 568 (1967), 295, 296, 319, 322, 323, 329, 333, 334

FTC v. Promotion Specialists, No. 90-479-CIV-ORL-19 (M. D. Fla. June 26, 1990), 533

FTC v. Rainbow Enzymes Inc., 5 TRADE REG. REP. (CCH) ¶ 22,475 (D. Ariz. Sept. 28, 1987), 479

FTC v. Raladam Co., 283 U.S. 643 (1931), 464

FTC v. Rare Coin Galleries of Am., Inc., 1986-2 Trade Cas. (CCH) ¶ 67,338 (D. Mass. 1986), 479

FTC v. Rare Coin Galleries of Am., Inc., No. 86-2683-C (D. Mass. May 19, 1987), 489

FTC v. Rare Coins of Ga., Inc., 5 TRADE REG. REP. (CCH) ¶ 22,497 (N.D. Ga. Dec. 28, 1987), 479

FTC v. R.A. Walker & Assocs., [1983-1987 Transfer Binder] TRADE REG. REP. (CCH) ¶ 22,080 (D.D.C. Oct. 6, 1983), 480

FTC v. Real Prods. Corp., 90 F.2d 617 (2d Cir. 1937), 478

FTC v. R.F. Keppel & Bro., Inc., 291 U.S. 304 (1934), 453, 482

FTC v. Rhinechem Corp., 459 F. Supp. 785 (N.D. Ill. 1978), 352, 354, 503

FTC v. Rhodes Pharmacal Co., 191 F.2d 24 (2d Cir. 1973), 502

FTC v. Rockefeller, 591 F.2d 182 (2d Cir. 1979), 507

FTC v. Rocky Mountain Circulation, Inc., 5 Trade Reg Rep. (CCH) ¶22,479 (D. Colo. Oct. 20, 1987), 497

FTC v. Ronby Corp., ANTITRUST & TRADE REG. REP. (BNA) No. 1401 (S.D. Fla. Feb. 2, 1989), 496

FTC v. Royal Milling Co., 288 U.S. 212 (1933), 477

FTC v. R.R. Donnelley & Sons Co., 1990-2 Trade Cas. (CCH) ¶ 69,239 (D.D.C. 1990), 284, 292, 311

FTC v. R.R. Donnelley & Sons Co., 931 F.2d 430 (7th Cir. 1991), 524

FTC v. Ruberoid Co., 343 U.S. 470 (1952), 489, 490, 494

FTC v. Samuel Silverman, 5 F.T.C. 294 (1922), 477

FTC v. Schoolhouse Coins, Inc., 5 TRADE REG. REP. (CCH) ¶ 22,602 (C.D. Cal. Sept. 14, 1988), 479

FTC v. Sears, Roebuck & Co., [1983-1987 Transfer Binder] TRADE REG. REP. (CCH) ¶ 22,436 (D. Colo. Mar. 17, 1987), 473

FTC v. Security Rare Coin & Bullion Corp., 931 F.2d 1312 (8th Cir. 1991), 500

FTC v. Serap, 5 TRADE REG. REP. (CCH) ¶ 23,043 (C.D. Cal. Aug. 22, 1991), 502

FTC v. Shaffner, 626 F.2d 32 (7th Cir. 1980), 507

FTC v. Sherry, 1969 Trade Cas. (CCH) ¶ 72,906 (D.D.C. 1969), 508

FTC v. Simeon Mgmt. Corp., 532 F.2d 708 (9th Cir. 1976), 502

FTC v. Simplicity Pattern Co., 360 U.S. 55 (1959), 425, 431, 436, 440, 443, 444

FTC v. Sinclair Ref. Co., 261 U.S. 463 (1923), 160

FTC v. Skaife, No. 900148G(M) (S.D. Cal. July 25, 1990), 489

FTC v. Solar Michigan, Inc., 1988-2 Trade Cas. (CCH) ¶ 68,339 (E.D. Mich. 1988), 480, 501

FTC v. Southland Corp., 471 F. Supp. 1 (D.D.C. 1979), 354, 355, 356, 357, 503

FTC v. Southwest Sunsites, Inc., 665 F.2d 711 (5th Cir.), cert. denied, 456 U.S. 973 (1982), 500

FTC v. Sperry & Hutchinson Co., 405 U.S. 233 (1972), 453, 457, 483

FTC v. Standard Educ. Soc'y, 302 U.S. 112 (1937), 469

FTC v. Standard Motor Prods., Inc., 371 F.2d 613 (2d Cir. 1967), 423, 424

FTC v. Standard Oil Co., 355 U.S. 396 (1958), 521

FTC v. Standard Oil Co., 449 U.S. 232 (1980), 455, 524

FTC v. Sterling Drug, 317 F.2d 669 (2d Cir. 1963), 464, 465, 502

FTC v. Sunkist Growers, [1983-1987 Transfer Binder] TRADE REG. REP. (CCH) ¶ 22,393 (D.D.C. Aug. 28, 1986), 496

FTC v. Sun Oil Co., 371 U.S. 505 (1963), 416, 420

FTC v. Superior Court Trial Lawyers Ass'n, 493 U.S. 411 (1990), 30, 34, 35, 37, 43, 44, 62, 83-84, 85, 86, 95, 613-14, 996, 1013

FTC v. Swanson, 560 F.2d 1 (1st Cir. 1977), 507

FTC v. Tenneco, Inc., 433 F. Supp. 105 (D.D.C. 1977), 357, 503

FTC v. Texaco, Inc., 555 F.2d 862 (D.C. Cir.), *cert. denied*, 431 U.S. 974 (1977), 506, 507, 511

FTC v. Texaco, Inc., 393 U.S. 223 (1968), 132

FTC v. Thomsen-King & Co., 109 F.2d 516 (7th Cir. 1940), 502

FTC v. Thor Enter., No. 3-84-0159 (M.D. Tenn. Feb. 16, 1984), 490

FTC v. Trans-Alaska Energy Corp., [1983-1987 Transfer Binder] TRADE REG. REP. (CCH) ¶ 22,296 (C.D. Cal. Oct. 8, 1985), 502

FTC v. Trans-Alaska Energy Corp., [1983-1987 Transfer Binder] TRADE REG. REP. (CCH) ¶ 22,381 (C.D. Cal. July 22, 1986), 502

FTC v. Trans-Alaska Energy Corp., [1983-1987 Transfer Binder] TRADE REG. REP. (CCH) ¶ 22,446 (C.D. Cal. May 4, 1987), 500

FTC v. Travelers Health Associations, 362 U.S. 293 (1960), 1116

FTC v. TS Indus., [1983-1987 Transfer Binder] TRADE REG. REP. (CCH) ¶22,429 (D. Colo. Feb. 10, 1987), 497

FTC v. Turner, 609 F.2d 743 (5th Cir. 1980), 513

FTC v. Union Carbide Corp., ANTITRUST & TRADE REG. REP. (BNA) No. 1374, (S.D.N.Y. July 7, 1988), 496

FTC v. Universal-Rundle Corp., 387 U.S. 244 (1967), 489, 494

FTC v. University Health, Inc., 938 F.2d 1206 (11th Cir. 1991), 279, 290, 308, 309, 317, 320, 354, 456

FTC v. U.S. Oil & Gas Corp., 748 F.2d 1431 (11th Cir. 1984), 479, 500, 504

FTC v. Virginia Homes Mfg. Corp., 509 F. Supp. 51, 53 (D. Md.), *aff'd mem.*, 661 F.2d 920 (4th Cir. 1981), 540

FTC v. Warner Communs., 742 F.2d 1156 (9th Cir. 1984), 283, 284, 286, 287, 305, 308, 317, 354, 355, 367, 503, 504

FTC v. Washington Fish & Oyster Co., 271 F.2d 39 (9th Cir. 1959), 431

FTC v. Washington Fish & Oyster Co., 282 F.2d 595 (9th Cir. 1960), 436

FTC v. Weyerhaeuser Co., 648 F.2d 739 (D.C. Cir.) (per curiam), *vacated*, 665 F.2d 1072 (D.C. Cir. 1981), 357, 358

FTC v. Weyerhaeuser Co., 665 F.2d 1072 (D.C. Cir. 1981), 276, 355, 356, 357, 503

FTC v. Winsted Hosiery Co., 258 U.S. 483 (1922), 463, 469, 473

FTC v. World Travel Vacation Brokers, Inc., 5 TRADE REG. REP. (CCH) ¶ 22,476 (N.D. Ill. Sept. 28, 1987), *aff'd*, 861 F.2d 1020 (7th Cir. 1988), 479

FTC v. World Travel Vacation Brokers, No. 87 Civ. 8449 (N.D. Ill. Mar. 26, 1990), 533

FTC v. World Travel Vacation Brokers, 861 F.2d 1020 (7th Cir. 1988), 500, 501, 503, 532

FTC v. World Wide Factors, Ltd., 882 F.2d 344 (9th Cir. 1989), 503

Fuchs Sugars & Syrups, Inc. v. Amstar Corp., 447 F. Supp. 867 (S.D.N.Y. 1978), *rev'd*, 602 F.2d 1025 (2d Cir.), *cert. denied*, 444 U.S. 917 (1979), 662

Fuchs Sugars & Syrups, Inc. v. Amstar Corp., 602 F.2d 1025 (2d Cir.), *cert. denied*, 444 U.S. 917 (1979), 15, 16, 118, 181, 191, 193

Fuchs v. Rural Elec. Convenience Coop., 858 F.2d 1210, (7th Cir. 1988), *cert. denied*, 490 U.S. 1020 (1989), 976, 981

Fulton v. Hecht, 580 F.2d 1243 (5th Cir. 1978), *cert. denied*, 440 U.S. 981 (1979), 542, 645

Fund for Constitutional Gov't v. National Archives, 656 F.2d 856 (D.C. Cir. 1981), 754

Furlong v. Long Island College Hosp., 710 F.2d 922 (2d Cir. 1983), 25, 29

Fusco v. Xerox Corp., 676 F.2d 332 (8th Cir. 1982), 407, 408

G

Gaetzi v. Carling Brewing Co., 205 F. Supp. 615 (E.D. Mich. 1962), 690, 692

GAF Corp. v. Circle Floor Co., 329 F. Supp. 823 (S.D.N.Y. 1971), *aff'd*, 463 F.2d 752 (2d Cir. 1972), *cert. denied*, 413 U.S. 901 (1973), 186

GAF Corp. v. Eastman Kodak Co., 519 F. Supp. 1203 (S.D.N.Y. 1981), 255, 775, 777, 819

GAFTA Soya Bean Meal Futures Ass'n, 30 O.J. EUR. COMM. (No. L 19) 18 (1987), [1985-1988 Transfer Binder] COMMON MKT. REP. (CCH) ¶ 10,850, 936

Gaines v. Budget Rent-A-Car Corp., 1972-1 Trade Cas. (CCH) ¶ 73,860 (N.D. Ill. 1972), 718

Gaines v. NCAA, 746 F. Supp. 738 (M.D. Tenn. 1990), 223

Gainesville Utils. Dep't v. Florida Power & Light Co., 573 F.2d 292 (5th Cir.), *cert. denied*, 439 U.S. 966 (1978), 3, 77, 1068

Galloway v. American Brands, Inc., 81 F.R.D. 580 (E.D.N.C. 1978), 695

G&T Terminal Packaging Co. v. Consolidated Rail Corp., 830 F.2d 1230 (3d Cir. 1987), *cert. denied*, 485 U.S. 988 (1988), 1134

Garcia v. San Antonio Metro Transit Auth., 469 U.S. 528 (1985), 979

Gardco Mfg., Inc. v. Herst Lighting Co., 820 F.2d 1209 (Fed. Cir. 1987), 852

Garden Cottage Foods Ltd. v. Milk Mktg. Bd. [1984] App. Cas. 130, [1983] 3 COMMON MKT. L.R. 43, 920

Gardner v. Westinghouse Broadcasting Co., 437 U.S. 478 (1978), 736

Garment Dist. v. Belk Stores Servs., 617 F. Supp. 944 (W.D.N.C. 1985), *aff'd*, 799 F.2d 905 (4th Cir. 1986), *cert. denied*, 486 U.S. 1005 (1988), 187

Garment Dist. v. Belk Stores Servs., 799 F.2d 905 (4th Cir. 1986), *cert. denied*, 486 U.S. 1005 (1988), 13, 14, 184, 189

Garpeg Ltd. v. United States, 583 F. Supp. 789 (S.D.N.Y. 1984), 887, 889

Garpeg Ltd. v. United States, 588 F. Supp. 1237 (S.D.N.Y. 1984), 887, 888

Garrison v. Louisiana, 379 U.S. 64 (1964), 1008

Garshman v. University Resources Holding, Inc., 625 F. Supp. 737 (D.N.J. 1986), *aff'd*, 824 F.2d 223 (3d Cir. 1987), 115

Garshman v. Universal Resources Holding, Inc., 824 F.2d 223 (3d Cir. 1987), 19, 1062

Gas-a-Tron of Ariz. v. American Oil Co., 1977-2 Trade Cas. (CCH) ¶ 61,789 (D. Ariz. 1977), 655, 657

Gas Light Co. v. Georgia Power Co., 313 F. Supp. 860 (M.D. Ga. 1970), *aff'd*, 440 F.2d 1135 (5th Cir. 1971), *cert. denied*, 404 U.S. 1062 (1972), 139

Gates Rubber Co., [1970-1973 Complaints & Orders Transfer Binder] TRADE REG. REP. (CCH) ¶ 19,657 (1971), 360

Gavron v. Blinder Robinson & Co., 115 F.R.D. 318 (E.D. Pa. 1987), 716

Gaylord Shops, Inc. v. Pittsburgh Miracle Mile Town & Country Shopping Center, Inc., 219 F. Supp. 400 (W.D. Pa. 1963), 408

G.D. Searle & Co. v. Institutional Drug Distribs., 151 F. Supp. 715 (S.D. Cal. 1957), 848

Gearhart Indus. v. Smith Int'l, Inc., 592 F. Supp. 203 (N.D. Tex.), *aff'd in part, modified in part and vacated in part*, 741 F.2d 707 (5th Cir. 1984), 286, 294, 300, 323, 363, 368

GEC-ANT-Telettra-SAT, 31 O.J. EUR. COMM. (No. C 180) 3 (1988), [1985-1988 Transfer Binder] COMMON MKT. REP. ¶ 11,005, 935

GEC Weir (Sodium Circulators), 20 O.J. EUR. COMM. (No. L 327) 26 (1977), [1976-1978 Transfer Binder] COMMON MKT. REP. (CCH) ¶ 10,000, 938

Gelb v. FTC, 144 F.2d 580 (2d Cir. 1944), 470

GEMA, 14 O.J. COMM. EUR. (No. L 134) 15 (1971), [1970-1972 Transfer Binder] COMMON MKT. REP. (CCH) ¶ 9438, 954, 957

GEMA Statutes, 25 O.J. EUR. COMM. (No. L 94) 12 (1982), [1978-1981 Transfer Binder] COMMON MKT. REP. (CCH) ¶ 10,357, 957

GEMA v. Commission, Case 125/78, [1979] E.C.R. 3173, [1978-1979 Transfer Binder] COMMON MKT. REP. (CCH) ¶ 8568 (July 11, 1979), 921

Gemco Latinoamerica, Inc. v. Seiko Time Corp., 671 F. Supp. 972 (S.D.N.Y. 1987), 788

Gemini Concerts v. Triple-A Baseball Club Ass'n, 664 F. Supp. 24 (D. Me. 1987), *aff'd*, 884 F.2d 707 (2d Cir. 1989), *cert. denied*, 110 S. Ct. 1169 (1990), 45, 53, 170

Gemini Supply Corp. v. Zeitlin, 590 F. Supp. 153 (E.D.N.Y. 1984), 414, 415

General Aircraft Corp. v. Air Am., Inc., 482 F. Supp. 3 (D.D.C. 1979), 688, 690, 692, 904

General Atomic Co. v. Exxon Nuclear Co., 90 F.R.D. 290 (S.D. Cal. 1981), 888

General Auto Supplies, Inc. v. FTC, 346 F.2d 311 (7th Cir.), *cert. dismissed*, 382 U.S. 923 (1965), 424, 430, 446, 447

General Aviation, Inc. v. Garrett Corp., 743 F. Supp. 515 (W.D. Mich. 1990), 38, 39, 124, 126, 128

General Beverage Sales Co. v. East Side Winery, 396 F. Supp. 590 (E.D. Wis. 1975), *rev'd*, 568 F.2d 1147 (7th Cir. 1978), 444

General Beverages Sales Co. v. East-Side Winery, 568 F.2d 1147 (7th Cir. 1978), 119, 124

General Chem. Corp. v. United States, 817 F.2d 844 (D.C. Cir. 1987), 1135

General Chem. Inc. v. Exxon Chem. Co., USA, 625 F.2d 1231 (5th Cir. 1980), 448, 449, 865

General Cinema Corp. v. Buena Vista Distrib. Co., 532 F. Supp. 1244 (C.D. Cal. 1982), 40, 64

General Cinema Corp. v. Buena Vista Distrib. Co., 681 F.2d 594 (9th Cir. 1982), 107

General Elec. Co. v. Bucyrus-Erie Co., 550 F. Supp. 1037 (S.D.N.Y. 1982), 870, 876, 877

General Elec. Co. v. City of San Antonio, 334 F.2d 480 (5th Cir. 1964), 583, 688, 778

General Fin. Corp. v. FTC, 700 F.2d 366 (7th Cir. 1983), 507, 508

General Foods Corp., 52 F.T.C. 798 (1956), 410, 437, 438

General Foods Corp., 86 F.T.C. 831 (1975), 481, 485

General Foods Corp., 95 F.T.C. 306 (1980), 518

General Foods Corp., 103 F.T.C. 204 (1984), 210, 211, 212, 215, 216, 233, 260, 261, 263, 266, 461

General Foods Corp. v. Brannan, 170 F.2d 220 (7th Cir. 1948), 1106, 1107

General Foods Corp. v. FTC, 386 F.2d 936 (3d Cir. 1967), *cert. denied*, 391 U.S. 919 (1968), 334

General Glass Co. v. Globe Glass & Trim Co., 1978-2 Trade Cas. (CCH) ¶ 62,231 (N.D. Ill. 1978), 410

General Indus. Corp. v. Hartz Mountain Corp., 810 F.2d 795 (8th Cir. 1987), 169, 181, 196, 207, 223, 264, 662

General Inv. Co. v. Lake Shore & M.S.R. Co., 260 U.S. 261 (1922), 632

General Leaseways, Inc. v. National Truck Leasing Ass'n, 744 F.2d 588 (7th Cir. 1984), 39, 40, 43, 51, 53, 74, 76, 77, 647, 667, 699

General Leaseways, Inc. v. National Truck Leasing Ass'n, 830 F.2d 716 (7th Cir. 1987), 669, 672, 673, 700

General Milk Co., 44 F.T.C. 1355 (1947), 915

General Motors Continental NV v. Commission, Case 26/75, [1975] E.C.R. 1367, [1975 Transfer Binder] COMMON MKT. REP. (CCH) ¶ 8320, 951, 954, 956

General Motors Corp., 93 F.T.C. 860 (1979), 477

General Motors Corp., 99 F.T.C. 464 (1982), 462

General Motors Corp., 102 F.T.C. 1741 (1983), 468

General Motors Corp., 103 F.T.C. 374 (1984), 350, 377, 387, 1109

General Motors Corp., 103 F.T.C. 641 (1984), 437, 439, 461

General Motors Corp. v. FTC, 114 F.2d 33 (2d Cir. 1940), *cert. denied*, 312 U.S. 682 (1941), 469, 470

General Motors Corp. v. Gibson Chem. & Oil Corp., 661 F. Supp. 567 (E.D.N.Y. 1987), 143, 159

General Shoe Corp., 1956 Trade Cas. (CCH) ¶ 68,271, 349

General Talking Pictures Corp. v. Western Electric Co., 304 U.S. 175, *aff'd on reh'g*, 305 U.S. 124 (1938), 820, 826, 829

General Tel. Co., 3 F.C.C.Rcd 2371 (1985), 1054

General Tire & Rubber Co. v. Firestone Tire & Rubber Co., 349 F. Supp. 333 (N.D. Ohio 1972), 835

General United Co. v. American Honda Motor Co., 618 F. Supp. 1452 (W.D.N.C. 1985), 407

Genesco, Inc., 89 F.T.C. 451 (1977), 480, 486

Genesco, Inc. v. T. Kakiuchi & Co., 815 F.2d 840 (2d Cir. 1987), 788

Genetic Sys. Corp. v. Abbott Labs., 691 F. Supp. 407 (D.D.C. 1988), 169, 272

Genna v. Lady Foot Int'l, Inc., 1986-2 Trade Cas. (CCH) ¶ 67,317 (E.D. Pa. 1986), 141, 142, 158, 788

Gentry v. C&D Oil Co., 102 F.R.D. 490 (W.D. Ark. 1984), 712, 718, 721, 727

Genuine Parts Co. v. FTC, 445 F.2d 1382 (5th Cir. 1971), 507, 508, 511

George C. Frey Ready-Mixed Concrete, Inc. v. Pine Hill Concrete Mix Corp., 554 F.2d 551 (2d Cir. 1977), 238

George Hantscho Co. v. Miehle-Goss-Dexter, Inc., 33 F.R.D. 332 (S.D.N.Y. 1963), 752

George R. Whitten, Jr., Inc. v. Paddock Pool Builders, 424 F.2d 25 (1st Cir.), *cert. denied*, 404 U.S. 850 (1970), 966, 1010

George R. Whitten, Jr., Inc. v. Paddock Pool Builders, 508 F.2d 547 (1st Cir. 1974), *cert. denied*, 421 U.S. 1004 (1975), 44, 96, 203, 262, 264

George's Radio & Television Co., 94 F.T.C. 1135 (1979), 540

George Van Camp & Sons v. American Can Co., 278 U.S. 245 (1929), 401

Georgia-Pac. Corp., 103 F.T.C. 203 (1984), 167

Georgia v. Pennsylvania R.R., 324 U.S. 439 (1945), 603, 606

GERO-Fabriek, 20 O.J. Eur. Comm. (No. L 16) 8 (1977), [1976-1978 Transfer Binder] Common Mkt. Rep. (CCH) ¶ 9914, 929, 942

Ger-Ro-Mar, Inc., 84 F.T.C. 95 (1974), *modified*, 518 F.2d 33 (2d Cir. 1975), 121

Ger-Ro-Mar, Inc. v. FTC, 518 F.2d 33 (2d Cir. 1975), 489, 522

Gertz v. Robert Welch, Inc., 418 U.S. 323 (1974), 1008

G. Heileman Brewing Co. v. Anheuser-Busch Inc., 676 F. Supp. 1436 (E.D. Wis. 1987), *aff'd*, 873 F.2d 985 (7th Cir. 1989), 848, 1003, 1004

Gianna Enters. v. Miss World (Jersey) Ltd., 551 F. Supp. 1348 (S.D.N.Y. 1982), 713

Giant Food, Inc. v. FTC, 307 F.2d 184 (D.C. Cir. 1962), *cert. denied*, 372 U.S. 910 (1963), 445, 446, 459

Giant Food Inc. v. FTC, 322 F.2d 977 (D.C. Cir. 1963), *cert. dismissed per stipulation*, 376 U.S. 967 (1964), 475

Giant Paper & Film Corp. v Albemarle Paper Co., 430 F. Supp. 981 (S.D.N.Y. 1977), 172, 214, 272

Gibbons v. Udaras na Gaeltachta, 549 F. Supp. 1094 (S.D.N.Y. 1982), 901

Giboney v. Empire Storage & Ice Co., 336 U.S. 490 (1949), 624

Gibson v. Greater Park City Co., 818 F.2d 722 (10th Cir. 1987), 4, 707

Gilchrist Mach. Co. v. Komatsu Am. Corp., 601 F. Supp. 1192 (S.D. Miss. 1984), 53

Gilder v. PGA Tour, Inc., 936 F.2d 417 (9th Cir. 1991), 90, 677

Gillam v. A. Shyman, Inc., 205 F. Supp. 534 (D. Alaska 1962), 782

Gillespie & Co. v. Weyerhaeuser Co., 533 F.2d 51 (2d Cir. 1976), 678

Gillette Co., 102 F.T.C. 1351 (1983), 443

Gillette Tire Jobbers, Inc. v. Appliance Indus., 596 F. Supp. 1277 (E.D. La. 1984), 407

Gilligan, Will & Co. v. SEC, 267 F.2d 461 (2d Cir.), *cert. denied*, 361 U.S. 896 (1959), 510

Girardi v. Gates Rubber Co., 325 F.2d 196 (9th Cir. 1963), 109

Girsh v. Jepson, 521 F.2d 153 (3d Cir. 1975), 742, 743

Giusti v. Pyrotechnic Indus., 156 F.2d 351 (9th Cir.), *cert. denied*, 329 U.S. 787 (1946), 867

G-K Properties v. Redevelopment Agency, 577 F.2d 645 (9th Cir. 1978), 769

Glasofer Motors v. Osterlund, Inc., 1981-2 Trade Cas. (CCH) ¶ 64,241 (N.J. Super. Ct. App. Div. 1981), 639

Glasser v. United States, 315 U.S. 60 (1942), 602

Glazer Steel Corp. v. ICC, 748 F.2d 1006 (5th Cir. 1984), 1134

Glazer Steel Corp. v. Toyomenka, Inc., 392 F. Supp. 500 (S.D.N.Y. 1974), 689, 692

Glen Eden Hosp. v. Blue Cross & Blue Shield, 740 F.2d 423 (6th Cir. 1984), 40, 70

Glick v. Empire Box Corp., 119 F. Supp. 224 (S.D.N.Y. 1954), 874

Glictronix Corp. v. AT&T, 603 F. Supp. 552 (D.N.J. 1984), 716, 718, 734

Glowacki v. Borden, Inc., 420 F. Supp. 348 (N.D. Ill. 1976), 403, 427, 438

Goguen v. Smith, 471 F.2d 88 (1st Cir. 1972), aff'd, 415 U.S. 566 (1974), 628

Gold Bullion Int'l, Ltd., 92 F.T.C. 196 (1978), 469, 542

Gold Cross Ambulance and Transfer v. City of Kansas City, 705 F.2d 1005 (8th Cir. 1983), 982, 986

Golden Gate Acceptance Corp. v. General Motors Corp., 597 F.2d 676 (9th Cir. 1979), 129, 180, 193

Golden Grain Macaroni Co., 78 F.T.C. 63, 172-73 (1971), aff'd, 472 F.2d 882 (9th Cir. 1972), cert. denied, 412 U.S. 918 (1973), 334

Golden Grain Macaroni Co. v. FTC, 472 F.2d 882 (9th Cir. 1972), cert. denied, 412 U.S. 918 (1973), 276, 316, 490

Golden Quality Ice Cream Co. v. Deerfield Specialty Papers, Inc., 87 F.R.D. 53 (E.D. Pa. 1980), 600

Golden State Transit Corp. v. City of Los Angeles, 726 F. 2d 1430 (9th Cir. 1984), cert. denied, 471 U.S. 1003 (1985), 972

Golden v. National Finance Adjusters, 555 F. Supp. 42 (E.D. Mich. 1982), 646

Goldfarb v. Virginia State Bar, 421 U.S. 773 (1975), 23, 43, 63, 967

Goldinger v. Boron Oil, 60 F.R.D. 562 (W.D. Pa. 1973), 747

Goldinger v. Boron Oil Co., 375 F. Supp. 400 (W.D. Pa. 1974), aff'd without published opinion, 511 F.2d 1393 (3d. Cir.), cert. denied, 423 U.S. 834 (1975), 103

Goldlawr, Inc. v. Heiman, 288 F.2d 579 (2d Cir. 1961), rev'd, 369 U.S. 463 (1963), 877

Goldlawr, Inc. v. Shubert, 169 F. Supp. 677 (E.D. Pa. 1958), aff'd, 276 F.2d 614 (3d Cir. 1960), 867, 877

Gold Star Ice Cream Co. v. Haagen-Dazs Ice Cream, Inc., 1981-2 Trade Cas. (CCH) ¶ 64,313 (N.Y. Sup. Ct. 1981), 641

Goldstein v. California, 412 U.S. 546 (1973), 621

Goldstein v. Regal Crest, Inc., 62 F.R.D. 571 (E.D. Pa. 1974), 695

Gold Strike Stamp Co. v. Christensen, 436 F.2d 791 (10th Cir. 1970), 728

Goldwater v. Alston & Bird, 116 F.R.D. 342 (S.D. Ill. 1987), 731

Goldwater v. Carter, 444 U.S. 996 (1979), 902

Golf City, Inc. v. Wilson Sporting Goods Co., 555 F.2d 426 (5th Cir. 1977), 184

Gomez v. Illinois State Board of Education, 811 F.2d 1030 (7th Cir. 1987), 737

Gonzales v. Insignares, 1985-2 Trade Cas. (CCH) ¶ 66,701 (N.D. Ga. 1985), 174, 177

Gonzales v. St. Margaret's House Housing Dev. Fund Corp., 880 F.2d 1514 (2d Cir. 1989), 132

Good Inv. Promotions, Inc. v. Corning Glass Works, 493 F.2d 891 (6th Cir. 1974), 121, 702

Goodsons and Co. v. National Am. Corp., 78 F.R.D. 721 (S.D.N.Y. 1978), 771

Goodyear Italiana-Euram, 18 O.J. EUR. COMM. (No. L 38) 10 (1975), [1973-1975 Transfer Binder] COMMON MKT. REP. (CCH) ¶ 9708, 940

Goodyear Tire & Rubber Co., 22 F.T.C. 232 (1936), order set aside and remanded, 92 F.2d 677 (6th Cir. 1937), rev'd and remanded per curiam, 304 U.S. 257 (1938), order set aside, 101 F.2d 620 (6th Cir.), cert. denied, 308 U.S. 557 (1939), 411

Gordon v. Crown Cent. Petroleum Corp., 423 F. Supp. 58 (N.D. Ga. 1976), aff'd without published opinion, 564 F.2d 413 (5th Cir., 1977) 131

Gordon v. New York Stock Exch., 498 F.2d 1303 (2d Cir. 1974), aff'd, 422 U.S. 659 (1975), 409

Gordon v. New York Stock Exch., 422 U.S. 659 (1975), 1018, 1102

Gorin v. United States, 313 F.2d 641 (1st Cir. 1963), aff'd after remand sub nom. Grillo v. United States, 336 F.2d 211 (1st Cir. 1964), cert. denied, 379 U.S. 971 (1965), 567

Goss v. Memorial Hosp. Sys., 789 F.2d 353 (5th Cir. 1986), 51, 83, 92

Gottesman v. General Motors Corp., 436 F.2d 1205 (2d Cir.), cert. denied, 403 U.S. 911 (1971), 778, 779

Gough v. Rossmoor Corp., 487 F.2d 373 (9th Cir. 1973), cert. denied, 429 U.S. 857 (1976), 27

Gough v. Rossmoor Corp., 585 F.2d 381 (9th Cir. 1978), *cert. denied*, 440 U.S. 936 (1979), 38, 41, 45, 47, 48, 50, 52, 268

Gould, Inc. v. Pechiney Ugine Kuhlmann, 853 F.2d 445 (6th Cir. 1988), 900

Gould v. Control Lazer Corp., 462 F. Supp. 685 (M.D. Fla. 1978), *aff'd in part and appeal dismissed in part*, 650 F.2d 617 (5th Cir. 1981), 839

Gould v. Sacred Heart Hosp., 1990-1 Trade Cas. (CCH) ¶ 68,993 (N.D. Fla. 1990), 144, 159, 173

Government of the Virgin Islands v. Scotland, 614 F.2d 360 (3d Cir. 1980), 582

Government of the Virgin Islands v. Smith, 615 F.2d 964 (3d Cir. 1980), 592, 593

Go-Video, Inc. v. Akai Elec. Co., 885 F.2d 1406 (9th Cir. 1989), 876, 877

Gowdish v. Eaton Corp., 1981-1 Trade Cas. (CCH) ¶ 63,913 (M.D.N.C. 1981), 145, 152

Grace Line, Inc. v. FMB, 280 F.2d 790 (2d Cir. 1960), *cert. denied*, 364 U.S. 933 (1961), 1157

Grace v. E.J. Kozin Co., 538 F.2d 170 (7th Cir. 1976), 432, 435, 436

Graco, Inc. v. Kremlin, Inc., 101 F.R.D. 503 (N.D. Ill. 1984), 887, 888

Graham v. Triangle Publications, 233 F. Supp. 825 (E.D. Pa. 1964), *aff'd per curiam*, 344 F.2d 775 (3d Cir. 1965), 701

Grams v. Boss, 1980-2 Trade Cas. (CCH) ¶ 63,410 (Wis. 1980), 639

Granader v. Public Bank, 281 F. Supp. 120 (E.D. Mich. 1967), *aff'd*, 417 F.2d 75 (6th Cir. 1969), *cert. denied*, 397 U.S. 1065 (1970), 313

Grand Caillou Packing Co., 65 F.T.C. 799 (1964), *aff'd in part and rev'd in part*, 366 F.2d 117 (5th Cir. 1966), 825

Grand Jury Proceedings, 1983-2 Trade Cas. (CCH) ¶ 65,566 (5th Cir. 1983), 757

Grand Spaulding Dodge, Inc., 90 F.T.C. 406 (1977), 492

Grandstaff v. Mobil Oil Corp., 1979-1 Trade Cas. (CCH) ¶ 62,421 (E.D. Va. 1978), 147

Grand Union Co., 57 F.T.C. 382 (1960), *modified and aff'd*, 300 F.2d 92 (2d Cir. 1962), *cert. denied*, 372 U.S. 910 (1963), 445

Grand Union Co., 102 F.T.C. 812 (1983), 276, 290, 302, 306, 322, 323, 324, 326, 512

Grand Union Co. v. FTC, 300 F.2d 92 (2d Cir. 1962), *cert. denied*, 372 U.S. 910 (1963), 459, 461, 494

Grant v. Erie Ins. Exch., 542 F. Supp. 457 (M.D. Pa. 1982), *aff'd mem.*, 716 F.2d 890 (3d Cir.), *cert. denied*, 464 U.S. 938 (1983), 1114, 1117, 1118

Graphic Prods. Distribs. v. Itek Corp., 717 F.2d 1560 (11th Cir. 1983), 45, 51, 125, 126, 127, 128, 670, 675

Grappone, Inc. v. Subaru of New England, Inc., 858 F.2d 792 (1st Cir. 1988), 133, 135, 148, 150, 151, 156, 159

Grason Elec. Co. v. Sacramento Mun. Util. Dist., 571 F. Supp. 1504 (E.D. Cal. 1983), 252, 1074

Grasty v. Amalgamated Cloth. & Textile Wkrs. Union, 828 F.2d 123 (3d Cir. 1987), *cert. denied*, 484 U.S. 1042 (1988), 717

Graybeal v. American Sav. & Loan Ass'n, 59 F.R.D. 7 (D.D.C. 1973), 774

Gray v. Shell Oil Co., 469 F.2d 742 (9th Cir. 1972), *cert. denied*, 412 U.S. 943 (1973), 108, 669

Great Atl. & Pac. Tea Co., 85 F.T.C. 601 (1975), 480

Great Atl. & Pac. Tea Co., 87 F.T.C. 962 (1976), *aff'd*, 557 F.2d 971 (2d Cir. 1977), *rev'd*, 440 U.S. 69 (1979), 418, 425, 446

Great Atl. & Pac. Tea Co. v. FTC, 106 F.2d 667 (3d Cir. 1939), *cert. denied*, 308 U.S. 625 (1940), 431, 436

Great Atl. & Pac. Tea Co. v. FTC, 557 F.2d 971 (2d Cir. 1977), *rev'd on other grounds*, 440 U.S. 69 (1979), 403, 404, 446, 447

Great Atl. & Pac. Tea Co. v. FTC, 440 U.S. 69 (1979), 417, 444, 447, 865

Great Escape, Inc. v. Union City Body Co., 791 F.2d 532 (7th Cir. 1986), 55, 144, 151, 163, 167, 168, 205, 260, 270, 271, 652

Great Lakes Carbon Corp., 82 F.T.C. 1529 (1973), 177

Great Lakes Chem. Corp., 103 F.T.C. 467 (1984), 279

Great Western Food Distribs. v. Brannan, 201 F.2d 476 (7th Cir.), *cert. denied*, 345 U.S. 997 (1953), 1107

Greek Ins. and Banks, 28 O.J. EUR. COMM. (No. L 152) 25 (1985), 924

Green Bay Packaging, Inc. v. Hoganson & Assoc., 362 F. Supp. 78 (N.D. Ill. 1973), 434

Greenberg v. Michigan Optometric Ass'n, 483 F. Supp. 142 (E.D. Mich. 1980), 542, 645

Greenbie v. Noble, 18 F.R.D. 414 (S.D.N.Y. 1955), 752

Greenbrier Cinemas, Inc. v. Attorney General of the United States, 511 F. Supp. 1046 (W.D. Va. 1981), 556

Greene v. Commissioner, 47 T.C.M. 190 (1983), 794

Greene v. General Foods Corp., 517 F.2d 635 (5th Cir. 1975), *cert. denied*, 424 U.S. 942 (1976), 102, 103, 109, 113, 114, 668, 672, 699, 700

Greenfield v. Villager Indus., 483 F.2d 824 (3d Cir. 1973), 743

Greenhaw v. Lubbock County Beverage Ass'n, 721 F.2d 1019 (5th Cir. 1983), *reh'g denied*, 726 F.2d 752 (5th Cir. 1984), 731, 774

Greensboro Lumber Co. v. Georgia Power Co., 643 F. Supp. 1345 (N.D. Ga. 1986), *aff'd*, 844 F.2d 1538 (11th Cir. 1988), 20, 965, 987

Greenspun v. Bogan, 492 F.2d 375 (1st Cir. 1974), 741

Green v. Kleindienst, 378 F. Supp. 1397 (D.D.C. 1974), 549, 550

Greenville Publishing Co. v. Daily Reflector, Inc., 496 F.2d 391 (4th Cir. 1974), 21, 147

Greenwich Film Production v. SACEM, Case 22/79, [1979] E.C.R. 3275, [1978-1979 Transfer Binder] COMMON MKT. REP. (CCH) ¶ 8567, 929

Greenwood Utils. Comm'n v. Mississippi Power Co., 751 F.2d 1484 (5th Cir. 1985), 19, 990, 999, 1002, 1011, 1015, 1070

Gregg Communs. Sys. v. AT&T, 98 F.R.D. 715 (N.D. Ill. 1983), 687

Gregoris Motors v. Nissan Motor Corp. in USA, 630 F. Supp. 902 (E.D.N.Y. 1986), 35, 431

Gregory Mktg. Corp. v. Wakefern Food Corp., 787 F.2d 92 (3d Cir.), *cert. denied*, 479 U.S. 821 (1986), 662

Greyhound Computer Corp. v. IBM, 559 F.2d 488 (9th Cir. 1977), *cert. denied*, 434 U.S. 1040 (1978), 204, 205, 215, 223, 257, 267

Greyhound Corp. v. Mt. Hood Stages, Inc., 437 U.S. 322 (1978), 685, 693

Greyhound Lines v. Miller, 402 F.2d 134 (8th Cir. 1968), 711

Gribbin v. Southern Farm Bureau Life Ins., 1984-1 Trade Cas. (CCH) ¶ 65,798, (W.D. La. 1984), *aff'd mem.*, 751 F.2d 1257 (1985), 1114, 1116

Grid Sys. Corp. v. Texas Instruments Inc., 1991-1 Trade Cas. (CCH) ¶ 69,446 (N.D. Cal. 1991), 140

Griffing v. Lucius O. Crosby Memorial Hosp., 1984-1 Trade Cas. (CCH) ¶ 65,854 (S.D. Miss. 1984), 132

Grillo v. United States, 336 F.2d 211 (1st Cir. 1964), *cert. denied*, 379 U.S. 971 (1965), 567

Grip-Pak, Inc. v. Illinois Tool Works, Inc., 651 F. Supp. 1482 (N.D. Ill. 1986), 648, 808, 812, 1001

Grip-Pak, Inc. v. Illinois Tool Works, Inc., 694 F.2d 466 (7th Cir. 1982), *cert. denied*, 461 U.S. 958 (1983), 258, 648, 776, 999, 1000, 1002

Grochal v. Aeration Processes, Inc., 797 F.2d 1093 (D.C. Cir. 1986), 770

Grolier, Inc., 91 F.T.C. 315 (1978), *remanded*, 615 F.2d 1215 (9th Cir. 1980), *after remand*, 699 F.2d 983 (9th Cir.), *cert. denied*, 464 U.S. 891 (1983), 480

Grolier, Inc. v. FTC, 615 F.2d 1215 (9th Cir. 1980), *after remand*, 699 F.2d 983 (9th Cir.), *cert. denied*, 464 U.S. 891 (1983), 510

Grosser v. Commodity Exch., Inc., 639 F. Supp. 1293 (S.D.N.Y. 1986), *aff'd*, 859 F.2d 148 (2d Cir. 1988), 1106

Grossman & Sons v. Commissioner, 48 T.C. 15 (1967), 795

Grossman Dev. Co. v. Detroit Lions, Inc., 1973-2 Trade Cas. (CCH) ¶ 74,790 (E.D. Mich. 1973), *aff'd without published opinion*, 503 F.2d 1404 (6th Cir. 1974), 139, 159

Grossman v. Automobile Mfrs. Ass'n, 397 U.S. 248 (1970), 839

Groupement des Fabricants de Papiers Peints de Belgique v. Commission, Case 73/74, [1975] E.C.R. 1491, [1976 Transfer Binder] COMMON MKT. REP. (CCH) ¶ 8335, 929

Group Life & Health Ins. Co. v. Royal Drug, 440 U.S. 205 (1979), 1110, 1111

Grove Labs. v. FTC, 418 F.2d 489 (5th Cir. 1969), 489, 494

Growers v. Winckler & Smith Citrus Prods. Co., 370 U.S. 19 (1962), 1027

Grumman Aerospace Corp. v. Titanium Metals Corp., 1984-1 Trade Cas. (CCH) ¶ 65,890 (E.D.N.Y. 1984), 756

Grumman Corp. v. LTV Corp., 527 F. Supp. 86 (E.D.N.Y.), aff'd, 665 F.2d 10 (2d Cir. 1981), 283, 286, 369

Grumman Corp. v. LTV Corp., 533 F. Supp. 1385 (E.D.N.Y. 1982), 361, 781

Grumman Corp. v. LTV Corp., 665 F.2d 10 (2d Cir. 1981), 363, 368, 369

Grunin v. International House of Pancakes, 513 F.2d 114 (8th Cir.), cert. denied, 423 U.S. 864 (1975), 741, 742, 743, 744, 782

GTE Data Servs. v. Electronic Data Sys. Corp., 717 F. Supp. 1487 (M.D. Fla. 1989), 24, 1003

GTE Sylvania Inc. v. Continental T.V., Inc., 537 F.2d 980 (9th Cir. 1976), aff'd, 433 U.S. 36 (1977), 118, 122, 129, 193

Gucci v. Gucci Shops, Inc., 651 F. Supp. 194 (S.D.N.Y. 1986), 19

Guerine v. J&W Invs., 544 F.2d 863 (5th Cir. 1977), 723

Guernsey v. Rich Plan of the Midwest, 408 F. Supp. 582 (N.D. Ind. 1976), 542, 646

Guidry v. Continental Oil Co., 350 F.2d 342 (5th Cir. 1965), 181

Guild Mortgage Co., FTC No. C-3320 (Dec. 31, 1990), 534

Gulf & W. Indus. v. Great Atl. & Pac. Tea Co., 476 F.2d 687 (2d Cir. 1973), 280, 281, 368, 369, 677

Gulf Coast Shrimpers and Oystermans Ass'n v. United States, 236 F.2d 658 (5th Cir.), cert. denied, 352 U.S. 927 (1956), 1026

Gulf Oil Corp. v. Copp Paving Co., 419 U.S. 186 (1974), 22, 23, 402

Gulf Oil Corp. v. Gulf Can. Ltd., [1980] 2 S.C.R. 39, 1980-1 Trade Cas. (CCH) ¶ 63,285, 884

Gulf States Utils. Co. v. FPC, 411 U.S. 747 (1973), 1067, 1076

Gulf Wandes Corp. v. General Elec. Co., 62 F.R.D. 377 (E.D. La. 1974), 728

Gundlach v. United States, 262 F.2d 72 (4th Cir. 1958), cert. denied, 360 U.S. 904 (1959), 580

Gunter Harz Sports, Inc. v. United States Tennis Ass'n, 511 F. Supp. 1103 (D. Neb.), aff'd per curiam, 665 F.2d 222 (8th Cir. 1981), 85, 90

Gupta v. Penn Jersey Corp., 582 F. Supp. 1058 (E.D. Pa. 1984), 739, 740

Guyott Co. v. Texaco, Inc., 261 F. Supp. 942 (D. Conn. 1966), 405, 406, 431

Guy S. Erway, 48 RAD. REG. 2d (P&F) 829 (1980), 1037

GVF Cannery, Inc. v. California Tomato Growers Ass'n, 511 F. Supp. 711 (N.D. Cal. 1981), 1026

GVL, 24 O.J. EUR. COMM. (No. L 370) 49 (1981), [1978-1981 Transfer Binder] COMMON MKT. REP. (CCH) ¶ 10,345, aff'd sub nom. Gesellschaft zur Verwertung von Leistungsschutzrechten (GVL) v. Commission, Case 7/82, [1983] E.C.R. 483, [1981-1983 Transfer Binder] COMMON MKT. REP. (CCH) ¶ 8910, 954

H

H.A. Artists & Assocs. v. Actors' Equity Ass'n., 451 U.S. 704 (1981), 1120

Haas v. Pittsburgh Nat'l Bank, 526 F.2d 1083 (3d Cir. 1975), 696

Haft v. Jewelment Corp., 594 F. Supp. 1468 (N.D. Cal. 1984), 662

Hahn v. Oregon Physicians' Serv., 508 F. Supp. 970 (D. Or. 1981), rev'd and remanded, 689 F.2d 840 (9th Cir. 1982), cert. denied, 462 U.S. 1133 (1983), 1116, 1118

Hahn v. Oregon Physicians' Serv., 689 F.2d 840 (9th Cir. 1982), cert. denied, 462 U.S. 1133 (1983), 24

Hahn v. Oregon Physicians' Serv., 868 F.2d 1022 (9th Cir. 1988), *cert. denied*, 493 U.S. 846 (1989), 36, 41, 55, 70, 78, 83, 94, 707, 708

Hale v. Henkel, 201 U.S. 43 (1906), 564

Hallmark Indus. v. Reynolds Metals Co., 489 F.2d 8 (9th Cir. 1973), *cert. denied*, 417 U.S. 932 (1974), 184

Hall v. Cole, 412 U.S. 1 (1973), 781, 787

Hall v. E.I. du Pont de Nemours & Co., 312 F. Supp. 358 (E.D.N.Y. 1970), 690

Halverson v. Convenient Food Mart, Inc., 69 F.R.D. 331 (N.D. Ill. 1974), 727

Halverson v. Convenient Food Mart, Inc., 458 F.2d 927 (7th Cir. 1972), 723

Hamburg Bros., 54 F.T.C. 1450 (1958), 424

Hamilton Watch Co. v. Benrus Watch Co., 114 F. Supp. 307 (D. Conn.), *aff'd*, 206 F.2d 738 (2d Cir. 1953), 280, 281, 363, 368

Hamilton Watch Co. v. Benrus Watch Co., 206 F.2d 738 (2d Cir. 1953), 366

Hamling v. United States, 418 U.S. 87 (1974), 584

Hammill v. Heister Co., 42 F.R.D. 173 (E.D. Wisc. 1967), 747

Hamner v. Rios, 769 F.2d 1404 (9th Cir. 1985), 787

Hampton v. Graff Vending Co., 516 F.2d 100 (5th Cir. 1975), 424

Hamro v. Shell Oil Co., 674 F.2d 784 (9th Cir. 1982), 849

Hancock Indus. v. Schaeffer, 811 F.2d 225 (3d Cir. 1987), 971, 978

H & B Equip. Co. v. International Harvester Co., 577 F.2d 239 (5th Cir. 1978), 17, 21, 47, 48, 50, 55, 124, 128, 181, 192, 206

H & S Distribs. v. Cott Corp., 1980-2 Trade Cas. (CCH) ¶ 63,358 (D. Conn. 1980), 869

Handgards, Inc. v. Ethicon, Inc., 552 F. Supp. 820 (N.D. Cal. 1982), *aff'd*, 743 F.2d 1282 (9th Cir. 1984), *cert. denied*, 469 U.S. 1190 (1985), 783

Handgards, Inc. v. Ethicon, Inc., 601 F.2d 986 (9th Cir. 1979), *cert. denied*, 444 U.S. 1025 (1980), 258, 802, 808, 809, 811, 812, 813

Handgards, Inc. v. Ethicon, Inc., 743 F.2d 1282 (9th Cir. 1984), *cert. denied*, 469 U.S. 1190 (1985), 269, 802, 808, 811, 812, 813, 851, 998

H & R Block, Inc., 80 F.T.C. 304 (1972), 478

Hand v. Central Transp., Inc., 779 F.2d 8 (6th Cir. 1985), *cert. denied*, 475 U.S. 1129 (1986), 151, 158, 163

Hanks v. Ross, 200 F. Supp. 605 (D. Md. 1961), 825

Hanover Shoe, Inc. v. United Shoe Mach. Corp., 392 U.S. 481 (1968), 653-58, 669, 682, 778, 859

Hanover Star Milling Co. v. Metcalf, 240 U.S. 403 (1916), 847

Hanson v. Denckla, 357 U.S. 235 (1958), 872

Hanson v. Pittsburgh Plate Glass Indus., 482 F.2d 220 (5th Cir. 1973), *cert. denied*, 414 U.S. 1136 (1974), 406, 422, 424

Hanson v. Shell Oil Co., 541 F.2d 1352 (9th Cir. 1976), *cert. denied*, 429 U.S. 1074 (1977), 108, 111, 228

Hanzly v. Blue Cross, 1989-1 Trade Cas. (CCH) ¶ 68,604 (W.D.N.Y. 1989), 713, 720

Harbor Banana Distribs. v. FTC, 499 F.2d 395 (5th Cir. 1974), 448

Hardin v. Houston Chronicle Publishing Co., 572 F.2d 1106 (5th Cir. 1978), 678

Hardy Salt Co. v. Illinois, 377 F.2d 768 (8th Cir.), *cert. denied*, 389 U.S. 912 (1967), 778, 779

Haring v. Prosise, 462 U.S. 306 (1983), 583

Harkins Amusement Enters. v. General Cinema Corp., 748 F. Supp. 1399 (D. Ariz. 1990), 668, 673

Harkins Amusement Enters. v. General Cinema Corp., 850 F.2d 477 (9th Cir. 1988), *cert. denied*, 488 U.S. 1019 (1989), 36, 40, 63, 85, 183, 195

Harkins Amusement Enters. v. Harry Nace Co., 648 F. Supp. 1212 (D. Ariz. 1986), *aff'd in part, rev'd in part*, 850 F.2d 477 (9th Cir. 1988), *cert. denied*, 488 U.S. 1019 (1989), 776

Harman v. Valley Nat'l Bank, 339 F.2d 564 (9th Cir. 1964), 259, 993

Harms, Inc. v. Sansom House Enters., 162 F. Supp. 129 (E.D. Pa. 1958), aff'd sub nom. Leo Feist, Inc. v. Lew Tender Tavern, Inc., 267 F.2d 494 (3d Cir. 1959), 846

Harms v. Cohen, 279 F. 276 (E.D. Pa. 1922), 846

Harnischfeger Corp. v. Paccar, Inc., 474 F. Supp. 1151 (E.D. Wis.), aff'd mem., 624 F.2d 1103 (7th Cir. 1979), 330, 385, 678

Harnischfeger Corp. v. Paccar, Inc., 503 F. Supp. 102 (E.D. Wis. 1980), 781

Harold Friedman, Inc. v. Thorofare Markets, Inc., 587 F.2d 127 (3d Cir. 1978), 27, 28, 78

Harper & Row Publishers v. Decker, 423 F.2d 487 (7th Cir. 1970), aff'd by an equally divided court, 400 U.S. 348 (1971), 760, 761

Harper Plastics, Inc. v. Amoco Chems. Corp., 617 F.2d 468 (7th Cir. 1980), 407, 439

Harran Transp. Co. v. National Trailways Bus Sys., 1985-2 Trade Cas. (CCH) ¶ 66,723 (D.D.C. 1985), 873

Harris Corp. v. National Iranian Radio & Television, 691 F.2d 1344 (11th Cir. 1982), 900

Harriss v. Pan Am. World Airways, 74 F.R.D. 24 (N.D. Cal. 1977), 713

Harris v. Atlantic Richfield Co., 469 F. Supp. 759 (E.D.N.C. 1978), 190

Harris v. Browning-Ferris Indus., Chem. Servs., 100 F.R.D. 775 (M.D. La. 1984), 877, 878

Harron v. United Hosp. Center, 522 F.2d 1133 (4th Cir. 1975), cert. denied, 424 U.S. 916 (1976), 29

Harry and Bryant Co. v. FTC, 726 F.2d 993 (4th Cir.), cert. denied, 469 U.S. 820 (1984), 527, 528, 529

Harry Greenberg, 39 F.T.C. 188 (1944), 473

Hart-Carter Co. v. J.P. Burroughs & Son, 605 F. Supp. 1327 (E.D. Mich. 1985), 811, 813

Hartford-Empire Co. v. United States, 323 U.S. 386 (1945), clarified, 324 U.S. 570 (1945), 69, 803, 804, 819, 823, 838, 852, 853, 854

Hartley & Parker, Inc. v. Florida Beverage Co., 307 F.2d 916 (5th Cir. 1962), 406, 412

Harwick v. Nu-Way Oil Co., 589 F.2d 806 (5th Cir.), cert. denied, 444 U.S. 836 (1979), 103

Hasbrouck v. Texaco, 631 F. Supp. 258 (E.D. Wash. 1986), 784, 787

Hasbrouck v. Texaco, Inc., 830 F.2d 1513 (9th Cir.), amended, 842 F.2d 1034 (9th Cir. 1987), aff'd, 110 S. Ct. 2535 (1990), 416, 423, 450

Hasbrouck v. Texaco, Inc., 842 F.2d 1034 (9th Cir. 1987), aff'd, 110 S. Ct. 2535 (1990), 413, 614, 665, 666, 667

Haskell v. Perkins, 28 F.2d 222 (D.N.J. 1928), rev'd, 31 F.2d 53 (3d Cir.), cert. denied, 279 U.S. 872 (1929), 793

Haskins v. Montgomery Ward & Co., 73 F.R.D. 499 (S.D. Tex. 1977), 734

Hassan v. Independent Practice Assocs., 698 F. Supp. 679 (E.D. Mich. 1988), 33, 35, 39, 41, 48, 51, 83, 93, 376, 385

Hasselblad (GB) Ltd. v. Commission, Case 86/82, [1984] E.C.R. 883, [1983-1985 Transfer Binder] COMMON MKT. REP. (CCH) ¶ 14,014, 930, 941

Hasselblad, 25 O.J. EUR. COMM. (No. L 161) 18 (1982), [1982-1985 Transfer Binder] COMMON MKT. REP. (CCH) ¶ 10,401, aff'd sub nom. Hasselblad (GB) Ltd. v. Commission, Case 86/82, [1984] E.C.R. 883, [1983-1985 Transfer Binder] COMMON MKT. REP. (CCH) ¶ 14,014, 939

Hass v. Oregon State Bar, 883 F.2d 1453 (9th Cir. 1989), cert. denied, 110 S. Ct. 1812 (1990), 980, 983, 986

Hastings Mfg. Co., 95 F.T.C. 345 (1980), 515

Hatley v. American Quarter Horse Ass'n, 552 F.2d 646 (5th Cir. 1977), 78, 85, 88, 91

Havoco v. Shell Oil Co., 626 F.2d 549 (7th Cir. 1980), 97

Hawaii v. Standard Oil Co., 405 U.S. 251 (1972), 605, 606, 643, 644, 647, 649, 650, 658, 664

Hawkins v. Holiday Inns, 734 F.2d 342 (6th Cir. 1980), cert. denied, 451 U.S. 987 (1981), 192

Hayden Publishing Co. v. Cox Broadcasting Corp., 730 F.2d 64 (2d Cir. 1984), 202, 214

Hayden v. Bardes Corp., 1989-1 Trade Cas. (CCH) ¶ 68,477 (W.D. Ky. 1989), 364, 663

Hayden v. Bracy, 744 F.2d 1338 (8th Cir. 1984), 25, 29

Hayes v. Solomon, 597 F.2d 958 (5th Cir. 1979), cert. denied, 444 U.S. 1078 (1980), 647, 649, 661

Hazel-Atlas Glass Co. v. Hartford-Empire Co., 322 U.S. 238 (1944), 809, 810

Hazeltine Research, Inc. v. Zenith Radio Corp., 388 F.2d 25 (7th Cir. 1967), *aff'd in part and rev'd in part*, 395 U.S. 100 (1969), 814, 835

Health and Medicine Policy Research Group v. FCC, 807 F.2d 1038 (D.C. Cir. 1986), 1036

Health Care Equalization Comm. v. Iowa Medical Soc'y, 851 F.2d 1020 (8th Cir. 1988), 705, 707, 708, 975, 1113, 1114

Healthco Int'l, Inc. v. A-dec, Inc., 1989-2 Trade Cas. (CCH) ¶ 68,703 (D.C. Mass. 1989), 241, 245

Hearst Corp., 79 F.T.C. 989 (1971), 512

Hearst Corp. v. Stark, 639 F. Supp. 970 (N.D. Cal. 1986), 843

Heater v. FTC, 503 F.2d 321 (9th Cir. 1974), 478, 490, 499, 511

Heatransfer Corp. v. Volkswagenwerk, AG, 553 F.2d 964 (5th Cir. 1977), *cert. denied*, 434 U.S. 1087 (1978), 135, 146, 148, 157, 204, 206, 213, 315, 330, 371, 650, 666

Hecht v. Pro-Football, Inc., 444 F.2d 931 (D.C. Cir. 1971), *cert. denied*, 404 U.S. 1047 (1972), 964, 1010

Hecht v. Pro-Football, Inc., 570 F.2d 982 (D.C. Cir. 1977), *cert. denied*, 436 U.S. 956 (1978), 210, 211, 246, 649

Hedges Enters. v. Continental Group, 81 F.R.D. 461 (E.D. Pa. 1979), 715, 723, 734

Heilig-Meyers Co., FTC No. C-3269 (Nov. 20, 1989), 534

Heille v. City of St. Paul, 671 F.2d 1134 (8th Cir. 1982), 29

Heinz W. Kirchner, 63 F.T.C. 1282 (1963), *aff'd*, 337 F.2d 751 (9th Cir. 1964), 470

Helbros Watch Co. v. FTC, 310 F.2d 868 (D.C. Cir. 1962), *cert. denied*, 372 U.S. 976 (1963), 469

Heldman v. United States Lawn Tennis Ass'n, 354 F. Supp. 1241 (S.D.N.Y. 1973), 701

Helene Curtis Indus. v. Church & Dwight Co., 560 F.2d 1325 (7th Cir. 1977), *cert. denied*, 434 U.S. 1070 (1978), 854

Helicopteros Nacionales de Colombia, SA v. Hall, 466 U.S. 408 (1984), 873, 874

Helicopter Support Sys. v. Hughes Helicopter, Inc., 818 F.2d 1530 (11th Cir. 1987), 13, 15, 707

Hellerstein v. Mather, 360 F. Supp. 473 (D. Colo. 1973), 695

Hemstreet v. Burroughs Corp., 666 F. Supp. 1096 (N.D. Ill. 1987), *rev'd on other grounds in part and dismissed in part mem.*, 861 F.2d 728 (Fed. Cir. 1988), 852

Henan Oil Tools, Inc. v. Engineering Enters., 262 F. Supp. 629 (S.D. Tex. 1966), 854

Hendricks Music Co. v. Steinway, Inc., 1988-2 Trade Cas. (CCH) ¶ 68,338 (N.D. Ill. 1988), 199

Henkel/Colgate, 15 J.O. COMM. EUR. (No. L 14) 14 (1972), [1970-1972 Transfer Binder] COMMON MKT. REP. (CCH) ¶ 9491, 934, 935

Hennegan v. Pacifico Creative Serv., 787 F.2d 1299 (9th Cir.), *cert. denied*, 479 U.S. 886 (1986), 682, 689

Hennessy-Henkell, 23 O. J. EUR. COMM. (No. L 383) 11 (1980), [1978-1981 Transfer Binder] COMMON MKT. REP. (CCH) ¶ 10,283, 943

Hennessy Indus. v. FMC Corp., 779 F.2d 402 (7th Cir. 1985), 183, 802, 808, 824, 827

Hennessey v. NCAA, 564 F.2d 1136 (5th Cir. 1977), 41, 90, 648

Henry Rosenfeld, Inc., 52 F.T.C. 1535 (1956), 437

Henry v. A. B. Dick Co., 224 U.S. 1 (1912), 817

Henry v. Chloride, Inc., 809 F.2d 1334 (8th Cir. 1987), 231, 232, 414

Hensley Equip. Co. v. Esco Corp., 383 F.2d 252 (5th Cir.), *modified per curiam*, 386 F.2d 442 (5th Cir. 1967), 816, 829, 835

Hensley v. Eckerhart, 461 U.S. 424 (1983), 782, 783, 784

Henson v. East Lincoln Township., 814 F.2d 410 (7th Cir. 1987), 715

Herbert R. Gibson, Sr., 95 F.T.C. 553, *modified*, 96 F.T.C. 126 (1980), *aff'd*, 682 F.2d 554 (5th Cir. 1982), *cert. denied*, 460 U.S. 1068 (1983), 432, 435, 436, 437, 438

Hercules, Inc., 84 F.T.C. 605 (1974), *modified*, 86 F.T.C. 1236 (1975), 474

Hercules Inc., 100 F.T.C. 531 (1982), 515

Herman Schwabe, Inc. v. United Shoe Mach. Corp., 297 F.2d 906 (2d Cir.), *cert. denied*, 369 U.S. 865 (1962), 673, 674

Hershel Cal. Fruit Prods. Co. v. Hunt Foods Co., 111 F. Supp. 732 (N.D. Cal. 1953), *appeal dismissed per curiam*, 221 F.2d 797 (9th Cir. 1955), 451

Herzfeld v. FTC, 140 F.2d 207 (2d Cir. 1944), 477

Heublein, Inc., 96 F.T.C. 385 (1980), 288, 293, 309, 322, 323, 324, 326, 328, 335

Hew Corp. v. Tandy Corp., 480 F. Supp. 758 (D. Mass. 1979), 784

Hewitt v. Joyce Beverages, Inc., 721 F.2d 625 (7th Cir. 1983), 728, 734, 736

Hewlett-Packard Co. v. Bausch & Lomb, Inc., 882 F.2d 1556 (Fed. Cir. 1989), *cert. denied*, 493 U.S. 1076 (1990), 807

Hickman v. Taylor, 329 U.S. 495 (1946), 513, 763

Hicks v. Bekins Moving & Storage Co., 87 F.2d 583 (9th Cir. 1937), 793

Hi-Co Enters., Inc. v. Conagra, Inc., 75 F.R.D. 628 (S.D. Ga. 1976), 713, 727, 733

Higgins v. New York Stock Exch., 942 F.2d 829 (2d Cir. 1991), 694, 695, 1022

Highspire, Inc. v. UKF Am., Inc., 469 F. Supp. 1009 (S.D.N.Y. 1979), 407

High Strength Steel, Inc. v. Svenskt Stal Aktiebolag, 1985-2 Trade Cas. (CCH) ¶ 66,884 (N.D. Ill. 1985), 896

Hiland Dairy v. Kroger Co., 402 F.2d 968 (8th Cir. 1968), *cert. denied*, 395 U.S. 961 (1969), 214

Hill Aircraft & Leasing Corp. v. Fulton County, 561 F. Supp. 667 (N.D. Ga. 1982), *aff'd mem.*, 729 F.2d 1467 (11th Cir. 1984), 270, 1010

Hillman Flying Serv. v. City of Roanoke, 652 F. Supp. 1142 (W.D. Va. 1987), *aff'd mem.*, 846 F.2d 71 (4th Cir. 1988), 984

Hillsborough County v. Automated Medical Labs., 471 U.S. 707 (1985), 625

Hillside Amusement Co. v. Warner Bros. Pictures, 7 F.R.D. 260 (S.D.N.Y. 1944), 745

Hillside Amusement Co. v. Warner Bros. Pictures Distrib. Corp., 1952-1953 Trade Cas. (CCH) ¶ 67,306 (S.D.N.Y. 1952), *aff'd*, 224 F.2d 629 (2d Cir. 1955), 408

Hill v. Art Rice Realty, 66 F.R.D. 449 (N.D. Ala. 1974), *aff'd mem.*, 511 F.2d 1400 (5th Cir. 1975), 741

Hill v. A-T-O, Inc., 535 F.2d 1349 (2d Cir. 1976), 147, 156

Hilton v. Guyot, 159 U.S. 113 (1895), 858

Hines v. Davidowitz, 312 U.S. 52 (1941), 623, 624

Hinshaw v. Beatrice Foods, Inc., 1980-81 Trade Cas. (CCH) ¶ 63,584 (D. Mont. 1980), 969

Hiram Walker, Inc. v. A & S Tropical, Inc., 407 F.2d 4 (5th Cir.), *cert. denied*, 396 U.S. 901 (1969), 404, 408, 429

Hirsh v. Martindale-Hubbell, Inc., 674 F.2d 1343, *cert. denied*, 459 U.S. 973 (1982), 135, 136, 139

Hittman Nuclear & Dev. Corp. v. ChemNuclear Sys., 1980-1 Trade Cas. (CCH) ¶ 63,140 (D. Md. 1979), 208

H.J. Inc. v. Flygt Corp., 925 F.2d 257 (8th Cir. 1991), 782, 783

H.J., Inc. v. ITT, 867 F.2d 1531 (8th Cir. 1989), 15, 144, 198, 201, 202, 205, 260, 262, 265, 670, 673

H.L. Hayden Co. v. Siemens Medical Sys., 672 F. Supp. 724 (S.D.N.Y. 1987), *aff'd*, 879 F.2d 1005 (2d Cir. 1989), 195

H.L. Hayden Co. v. Siemens Medical Sys., 879 F.2d 1005 (2d Cir. 1989), 53, 182, 186, 259, 265, 272, 450, 705, 706

H.L. Moore Drug Exch. v. Eli Lilly & Co., 662 F.2d 935 (2d Cir. 1981), *cert. denied*, 459 U.S. 880 (1982), 4, 11

HMC Mgmt. Corp. v. New Orleans Basketball Club, 375 So. 2d 700 (La. Ct. App. 1979), *cert. denied*, 379 So. 2d 11 (La. 1980), 622

Hobart Bros. v. Malcolm T. Gilliland, Inc., 471 F.2d 894 (5th Cir.), *cert. denied*, 412 U.S. 923 (1973), 62, 76, 128, 130, 673

Hobson v. Wilson, 737 F.2d 1 (D.C. Cir. 1984), 688

Hodge v. Villages of Homestead Homeowners Ass'n, 726 F. Supp. 297 (S.D. Fla. 1989), 138, 140

Hoechst AG v. Commission, Joined Cases 46/87 and 227/88, [1989] E.C.R. 2859, [1991] 1 CEC (CCH) 280, 919

Hoffman Motors Corp. v. Alfa Romeo, SpA, 244 F. Supp. 70 (S.D.N.Y. 1965), 644, 869, 870, 877, 878

Hoffmann-La Roche & Co. AG v. Commission, Case 85/76, [1979] E.C.R. 461, [1978-1979 Transfer Binder] COMMON MKT. REP. (CCH) ¶ 8527, 950, 952, 954, 956

Hoffmann-La Roche & Co. v. Centrafarm Vertriebsgesellschaft Pharmazeutischer Erzeugnisse GmbH, Case 102/77, [1978] E.C.R. 1139, [1977-1978 Transfer Binder] COMMON MKT. REP. (CCH) ¶ 8466, 944, 945

Holiday Magic, Inc., 84 F.T.C. 748 (1974), 119, 121

Holland Furnace Co. v. FTC, 295 F.2d 302 (7th Cir. 1961), 483

Holland v. Goodyear Tire & Rubber Co., 75 F.R.D. 743 (N.D. Ohio 1975), 731

Holleb & Co. v. Produce Terminal Cold Storage Co., 532 F.2d 29 (7th Cir. 1976), 214, 422

Holloway v. Arkansas, 435 U.S. 475 (1978), 602

Holloway v. Bristol-Myers Corp., 485 F.2d 986 (D.C. Cir. 1973), 543, 645

Holly Farms Poultry Indus. v. Kleindienst, 1973-1 Trade Cas. (CCH) ¶ 74,535 (M.D.N.C. 1973), 549

Holly Springs Funeral Home v. United Funeral Serv., 303 F. Supp. 128 (N.D. Miss. 1969), 1114

Holly Sugar Corp. v. Goshen County Coop. Beet Growers Ass'n, 725 F.2d 564 (10th Cir. 1984), 1028

Holmberg v. Armbrecht, 327 U.S. 392 (1946), 688

Holmes v. Penn Sec. Bank & Trust Co., 1982-1 Trade Cas. (CCH) ¶ 64,553 (M.D. Pa. 1981), 717, 719, 722, 731

Home Box Office, Inc. v. Directors Guild of Am., Inc., 531 F. Supp. 578 (S.D.N.Y. 1982), aff'd per curiam, 708 F.2d 95 (2d Cir. 1983), 1123

Homefinders of Am., Inc. v. Providence Journal Co., 621 F.2d 441 (1st Cir. 1980), 191, 245

Home Ins. Co. v. Dick, 281 U.S. 397 (1930), 628

Home Placement Serv. v. Providence Journal Co., 682 F.2d 274 (1st Cir. 1982), cert. denied, 460 U.S. 1028 (1983), 16, 179, 189

Home Placement Serv. v. Providence Journal Co., 819 F.2d 1199 (1st Cir. 1987), 668, 671, 672, 781, 782, 783

Homeware, Inc. v. Rexair, Inc., 1988-1 Trade Cas. (CCH) ¶ 68,085 (E.D. Mich. 1988), 151

Honeywell, Inc. v. Sperry Rand Corp., 180 U.S.P.Q. (BNA) 673 (D. Minn. 1973), 824, 825

Honeywell, Inc. v. Sperry Rand Corp., 1974-1 Trade Cas. (CCH) ¶ 74,874, (D. Minn. 1973), 279, 838

Hood v. Tenneco Texas Life Ins. Co., 739 F.2d 1012 (5th Cir. 1984), 45, 187

Hooper Holmes, Inc., 95 F.T.C. 854 (1980), 536

Hooper v. California, 155 U.S. 648 (1895), 1109

Hoover v. Ronwin, 466 U.S. 558 (1984), 968, 970, 976

Hopkinson Theatre v. RKO Radio Pictures, 18 F.R.D. 379 (S.D.N.Y. 1956), 748

Hopkinsville Cable TV, Inc. v. Pennyroyal Cablevision, Inc., 562 F. Supp. 543 (W.D. Ky. 1982), 1053

Hopping v. Standard Life Ins., 1984-1 Trade Cas. (CCH) ¶ 65,814 (N.D. Miss. 1983), 1113, 1114, 1116, 1118

Horizon Corp., 88 F.T.C. 208 (1976), 512

Horizon Corp., 97 F.T.C. 464 (1981), 466, 486, 491, 499

Horizons Int'l, Inc. v. Baldridge, 811 F.2d 154 (3d Cir. 1987), 917

Hornsby Oil Co. v. Champion Spark Plug Co., 714 F.2d 1384 (5th Cir. 1983), 45, 124, 198, 295

Hospital and Health Servs. Credit Union, 104 F.T.C. 589 (1984), 536

Hospital Bldg. Co. v. Trustees of Rex Hosp., 691 F.2d 678 (4th Cir. 1982), cert. denied, 464 U.S. 904 (1984), 258, 999, 1000, 1015

Hospital Bldg. Co. v. Trustees of Rex Hosp., 425 U.S. 738 (1976), 23

Hospital Corp. of Am., 106 F.T.C. 361 (1985), *aff'd*, 807 F.2d 1381 (7th Cir. 1986), *cert. denied*, 481 U.S. 1038 (1987), 290, 294, 295, 306, 309, 313, 350, 361, 463

Hospital Corp. of Am. v. FTC, 807 F.2d 1381 (7th Cir. 1986), *cert. denied*, 481 U.S. 1038 (1987), 304, 305, 312, 521, 522

Household Goods Carriers' Bureau v. Terrell, 452 F.2d 152 (5th Cir. 1971), 1015

House of Lord's, Inc., 69 F.T.C. 44 (1966), 433

House of Materials, Inc. v. Simplicity Pattern Co., 298 F.2d 867 (2d Cir. 1962), 185

Houser v. Fox Theatres Mgmt. Corp., 845 F.2d 1225 (3d Cir. 1988), 9, 14, 185, 196, 210, 211, 226, 707

Houston Lighting & Power Co., 15 N.R.C. 1143 (1982), 1082

Howard Enters., 93 F.T.C. 909 (1979), 536

Howell Indus. v. Sharon Steel Corp., 532 F. Supp. 400 (E.D. Mich. 1981), 431, 432, 433, 438

Howerton v. Grace Hosp., 1991-1 Trade Cas. (CCH) ¶ 69,430 (W.D.N.C. 1991), 679

H.P. Hood & Sons, 58 F.T.C. 1184 (1961), 519

H.R.M., Inc. v. Tele-Communications, Inc., 653 F. Supp. 645 (D. Colo. 1987), 271, 409, 1053

Hubbard v. Rubbermaid, Inc., 78 F.R.D. 631 (D. Md. 1978), 752

Hudson Pharmaceutical Corp., 89 F.T.C. 82 (1977), 481, 485

Hudson Sales Corp. v. Waldrip, 211 F.2d 268 (5th Cir.), *cert. denied*, 348 U.S. 821 (1954), 182, 184

Hudson's Bay Co. Fur Sales, Inc. v. American Legend Coop., 651 F. Supp. 819 (D.N.J. 1986), 39, 51, 152, 154, 155, 156, 158, 163, 380, 383, 390

Hudson Valley Asbestos Corp. v. Tougher Heating & Plumbing Co., 510 F.2d 1140 (2d Cir.), *cert. denied*, 421 U.S. 1011 (1975), 169, 272, 273, 279

Hudson v. Hermann Pfauter GmbH & Co., 117 F.R.D. 33 (N.D.N.Y. 1987), 885

Hudson v. United States, 272 U.S. 451 (1926), 580

Huelsman v. Civic Center Corp., 873 F.2d 1171 (8th Cir. 1989), 25

Hu-Friedy Mfg. Co. v. Peerless Int'l, Inc., 1986-2 Trade Cas. (CCH) ¶ 67,197 (N.D. Ill. 1986), 808

Hufsmith v. Weaver, 817 F.2d 455 (8th Cir. 1987), 998

Hughes v. United States, 342 U.S. 353 (1952), 575, 577

Hugin Kassaregister AB v. Commission, Case 22/78, [1979] E.C.R. 1869, [1978-1979 Transfer Binder] COMMON MKT. REP. (CCH) ¶ 8524, 928, 930, 951

Hugin/Liptons, 21 O.J. EUR. COMM. (No. L 22) 23 (1978), [1976-1978 Transfer Binder] COMMON MKT. REP. (CCH) ¶ 10,007, *rev'd sub nom.* Hugin Kassaregister AB v. Commission, Case 22/78, [1979] E.C.R. 1869, [1978-1979 Transfer Binder] COMMON MKT. REP. (CCH) ¶ 8524, 954

Hull v. Brunswick Corp., 704 F.2d 1195 (10th Cir. 1983), 826

Hulshizer v. Global Credit Servs., 728 F.2d 1037, (8th Cir. 1984), 531, 538

Humana of Illinois, Inc. v. Board of Trustees of S. Ill. Univ., 1986-1 Trade Cas. (CCH) ¶ 67,127 (C.D. Ill. 1986), 987

Humboldt Bay Mun. Water Dist. v. Louisiana-Pac. Corp., 608 F. Supp. 562 (N.D. Cal. 1985), *aff'd* mem., 787 F.2d 597 (9th Cir.), *cert. denied*, 479 U.S. 884 (1986), 115, 271

Humid-Aire Corp. v. J. Levitt, Inc., 1978-1 Trade Cas. (CCH) ¶ 61,846 (N.D. Ill. 1977), 866, 875

Hunt v. Armour & Co., 185 F.2d 722 (7th Cir. 1950), 820

Hunt v. Mobil Oil Corp., 410 F. Supp. 4 (S.D.N.Y. 1975), *aff'd*, 550 F.2d 68 (2d Cir.), *cert. denied*, 434 U.S. 984 (1977), 868

Hunt v. Mobil Oil Corp., 550 F.2d 68 (2d Cir.), *cert. denied*, 434 U.S. 984 (1977), 903, 904, 907

Hunt v. Washington State Apple Advertising Comm'n, 432 U.S. 333 (1977), 644

Hunt-Wesson Foods, Inc. v. Ragu Foods, Inc., 627 F.2d 919 (9th Cir. 1980), *cert. denied*, 450 U.S. 921 (1981), 214, 215, 269, 272, 273

Hunydee v. United States, 355 F.2d 183 (9th Cir. 1965), 565

Huron Portland Cement Co. v. City of Detroit, 362 U.S. 440 (1960), 621
Huron Valley Hosp. v. City of Pontiac, 612 F. Supp. 654 (E.D. Mich. 1985), *aff'd in part, dismissed in part*, 792 F.2d 563 (6th Cir.), *cert. denied*, 479 U.S. 885 (1986), 989
Huron Valley Hosp. v. City of Pontiac, 666 F.2d 1029 (6th Cir. 1981), 648, 649
Husain v. Helene Fuld Medical Center, 1990-1 Trade Cas. (CCH) ¶ 68,905 (D.N.J. 1989), 93
Hustler Magazine, Inc. v. Falwell, 485 U.S. 46 (1988), 1008
Hutchinson Chem. Corp., 55 F.T.C. 1942 (1959), 482
Hutzler Bros. v. Sales Affiliates, Inc., 164 F.2d 260 (4th Cir. 1947), 854
Hybud Equip. Corp. v. City of Akron, 654 F.2d 1187 (6th Cir. 1981), *vacated mem.*, 455 U.S. 931 (1982), *on remand*, 1983-1 Trade Cas. (CCH) ¶ 65,356 (N.D. Ohio 1983), *cert. denied*, 471 U.S. 1004 (1985), 983
Hydro Air, Inc. v. Versa Technologies, Inc., 599 F. Supp. 1119 (D. Conn. 1984), 118, 189
Hydro-Tech Corp. v. Sundstrand Corp., 673 F.2d 1171 (10th Cir. 1982), 1000, 1005

I

IAZ Int'l v. Commission, (ANSEAU-NAVEWA), Joined Cases 96-102, 104, 105, 108 and 110/82, [1983] E.C.R. 3369, [1983-1985 Transfer Binder] COMMON MKT. REP. (CCH) ¶ 14,023, 932
IBM Personal Computer, 27 O.J. EUR. COMM. (No. L 118) 24 (1984), [1982-1985 Transfer Binder] COMMON MKT. REP. (CCH) ¶ 10,585, 940
IBM v. United States, 471 F.2d 507 (2d Cir. 1972), *vacated*, 480 F.2d 293 (2d Cir. 1973), *cert. denied*, 416 U.S. 979 (1974), 762
IBM v. United States, 493 F.2d 112 (2d Cir. 1973), *cert. denied*, 416 U.S. 995 (1974), 770
IBM v. United States, 298 U.S. 131 (1936), 134, 148, 155, 160, 161, 162, 831, 834
ICI & Commercial Solvents Corp. v. Commission, Joined Cases 6 and 7/73, [1974] E.C.R. 223, [1974 Transfer Binder] COMMON MKT. REP. (CCH) ¶ 8209, 953, 954
Ideal Plumbing Co. v. Benco, Inc., 382 F. Supp. 1161 (W.D. Ark. 1974), *aff'd*, 529 F.2d 972 (8th Cir. 1976), 410
Ideal Plumbing Co. v. Benco, Inc., 529 F.2d 972 (8th Cir. 1976), 431, 433
Ideal-Standard, 28 O.J. EUR. COMM. (No. L 20) 38 (1985), [1982-1985 Transfer Binder] COMMON MKT. REP. (CCH) ¶ 10,662, 940
Ideal Toy Corp., 64 F.T.C. 297 (1964), 482
I. Haas Trucking Corp. v. New York Fruit Auction Corp., 364 F. Supp. 868 (S.D.N.Y. 1973), 158
IIP v. Commission, Case T-76/89, (Ct. First Instance 1991) *appeal filed*, 944
ILC Peripherals Leasing Corp. v. IBM, 458 F. Supp. 423 (N.D. Cal. 1978), *aff'd per curiam sub nom.* Memorex Corp. v. IBM, 636 F.2d 1188 (9th Cir. 1980), *cert. denied*, 452 U.S. 972 (1981), 143, 230, 245, 253, 254, 255, 257, 668, 773
Illinois Bell Tel. Co. v. FCC, 883 F.2d 104 (D.C. Cir. 1989), 1047
Illinois Bell Tel. Co. v. Haines & Co., 905 F.2d 1081 (7th Cir. 1990), *vacated*, 111 S. Ct. 1408 (1991), 250
Illinois Brick Co. v. Illinois, 431 U.S. 720 (1977), 607, 614, 625, 626, 646, 647, 653-60, 664, 1062
Illinois Cent. Gulf R.R. v. ICC, 702 F.2d 111 (7th Cir. 1983), 1131
Illinois Cities of Bethany v. F.E.R.C., 670 F.2d 187 (D.C. Cir. 1981), *aff'd*, 758 F.2d 1148 (7th Cir. 1985), 239
Illinois Commerce Comm'n v. ICC, 749 F.2d 875 (D.C. Cir. 1984), *cert. denied*, 474 U.S. 820 (1985), 1129, 1131
Illinois Commerce Comm'n v. ICC, 776 F.2d 355 (D.C. Cir. 1985), 1133
Illinois Commerce Comm'n v. ICC, 787 F.2d 616 (D.C. Cir. 1986), 1131
Illinois Commerce Comm'n v. ICC, 819 F.2d 311 (D.C. Cir. 1987), 1133, 1134

Illinois Corporate Travel, Inc. v. American Airlines, 700 F. Supp. 1485 (N.D. Ill. 1988), aff'd, 889 F.2d 751 (7th Cir. 1989), cert. denied, 110 S. Ct. 1948 (1990), 42

Illinois Corporate Travel, Inc. v. American Airlines, 806 F.2d 722 (7th Cir. 1986), 9, 49, 53, 78, 103, 129

Illinois Corporate Travel, Inc. v. American Airlines, 889 F.2d 751 (7th Cir. 1989), cert. denied, 110 S. Ct. 1948 (1990), 103, 128, 623

Illinois ex rel. Hartigan v. Panhandle E. Pipe Line Co., 730 F. Supp. 826 (C.D. Ill. 1990), aff'd sub nom. Illinois ex rel. Burris v. Panhandle E. Pipe Line Co., 935 F.2d 1469 (7th Cir. 1991), 158, 197, 198, 210, 211, 213, 218, 219, 223, 225, 251, 1064, 1065

Illinois ex rel. Hartigan v. Panhandle E. Pipeline Co., 852 F.2d 891 (7th Cir. 1988), 656, 1062

Illinois ex rel. Burris v. Panhandle E. Pipe Line Co., 935 F.2d 1469 (7th Cir. 1991), 226, 247, 250

Illinois v. Abbott & Assocs., 460 U.S. 557 (1983), 757

Illinois v. Ampress Brick Co., 67 F.R.D. 461 (N.D. 111. 1975), 654

Illinois v. Ampress Brick Co., 536 F.2d 1163 (7th Cir. 1976), 654

Illinois v. Borg, Inc., 548 F. Supp. 972 (N.D. Ill. 1982), 655, 656

Illinois v. Borg, Inc., 564 F. Supp. 96 (N.D. Ill. 1983), 756, 758

Illinois v. Bristol-Myers Co., 470 F.2d 1276 (D.C. Cir. 1972), 604

Illinois v. Brunswick Corp., 32 F.R.D. 453 (N.D. Ill. 1963), 604

Illinois v. F.E. Moran, Inc., 740 F.2d 533 (7th Cir. 1984), 662, 756, 758

Illinois v. General Paving Co., 590 F.2d 680 (7th Cir.), cert. denied, 444 U.S. 879 (1979), 775, 778

Illinois v. Huckaba & Sons Constr. Co., 442 F. Supp. 56 (S.D. Ill. 1977), 570

Illinois v. ICC, 751 F.2d 903 (7th Cir. 1985), 1134

Illinois v. Ralph Vancil, Inc., 1976-2 Trade Cas. (CCH) ¶ 61,025 (S.D. Ill. 1976), 690, 700

Illinois v. Sangamo Constr., 657 F.2d 855 (7th Cir. 1981), 781, 786

Illinois v. Sarbaugh, 552 F.2d 768 (7th Cir.), cert. denied, 434 U.S. 889 (1977), 590, 597, 756, 758

Illinois v. Sperry Rand Corp., 237 F. Supp. 520 (N.D. Ill. 1965), 691, 777

Illinois v. United States, 668 F.2d 923 (7th Cir. 1981), cert. denied, 455 U.S. 100 (1982), 1133

Image Technical Serv. v. Eastman Kodak Co., 903 F.2d 612 (9th Cir. 1990), cert. granted, 111 S. Ct. 2823 (1991), 140, 151, 152, 162, 268

IMA Rules (Dutch Plywood Imports), 23 O.J. EUR. COMM. (No. L 318) 1 (1980), [1978-1981 Transfer Binder] COMMON MKT. REP. (CCH) ¶ 10,264, 932

Imperial Chem. Indus. v. Commission, Case 48/69, [1972] E.C.R. 619, [1971-1973 Transfer Binder] COMMON MKT. REP. (CCH) ¶ 8161, 928, 931

Imperial Chem. Indus. v. National Distillers & Chem. Corp., 342 F.2d 737 (2d Cir. 1965), 853

Imperial Constr. Mgmt. Corp. v. Laborers Int'l, 1990-1 Trade Cas. (CCH) ¶ 68,927 (D. Kan. 1990), 682

Impervious Paint Indus. v. Ashland Oil, Inc., 1980-1 Trade Cas. (CCH) ¶ 63,138 (W.D. Ky. 1980), 713, 716

Impervious Paint Indus. v. Ashland Oil, Inc., 1981-1 Trade Cas. (CCH) ¶ 63,919 (W.D. Ky. 1981), 737

Implementation of BC Docket No. 80-90 to Increase the Availability of FM Broadcast Assignments, 100 F.C.C.2d 1332 (1985), 1043

In re "Agent Orange" Product Liability Litig., 818 F.2d 146 (2d Cir. 1987), cert. denied, 484 U.S. 1004 (1988), 738, 744

In re Air Passenger Computer Reservation Sys. Antitrust Litig., 694 F. Supp. 1443 (C.D. Cal. 1988), 247, 252, 269

In re Airport Car Rental Antitrust Litig., 521 F. Supp. 568 (N.D. Cal. 1981), aff'd, 693 F.2d 84 (9th Cir. 1982), cert. denied, 462 U.S. 1133 (1983), 994

In re Airport Car Rental Antitrust Litig., 693 F.2d 84 (9th Cir. 1982), cert. denied, 462 U.S. 1133 (1983), 1010

In re Alcoholic Beverages Litig., 95 F.R.D. 321 (E.D.N.Y. 1982), 466, 473, 474, 477, 478, 490, 493, 506, 511, 524, 714, 716, 717, 718, 721, 722, 725, 727, 729

In re Amerada Hess Corp. Antitrust Litig., 395 F. Supp. 1404 (J.P.M.D.L. 1975), 710

In re Ampicillin Antitrust Litig., 315 F. Supp. 317 (J.P.M.D.L. 1970), 709

In re Ampicillin Antitrust Litig., 55 F.R.D. 269 (D.D.C. 1972), 731, 732

In re Ampicillin Antitrust Litig., 81 F.R.D. 377 (D.D.C. 1978), 761

In re Ampicillin Antitrust Litig., 81 F.R.D. 395 (D.D.C. 1978), 784

In re Ampicillin Antitrust Litig., 88 F.R.D. 174 (D.D.C. 1980), 774

In re Amtorg Trading Corp., 75 F.2d 826 (C.C.P.A.), *cert. denied*, 296 U.S. 576 (1935), 827

In re Anschuetz & Co., GmbH, 754 F.2d 602 (5th Cir. 1985), *vacated*, Anschuetz & Co., GmbH v. Mississippi River Bridge Auth., 483 U.S. 1002 (1987), 884

In re Anthracite Coal Antitrust Litig., 436 F. Supp. 402 (J.P.M.D.L. 1977), 710

In re Anthracite Coal Antitrust Litig., 78 F.R.D. 709 (M.D. Pa. 1978), 604, 713, 717, 726, 729, 730, 734

In re Antibiotic Antitrust Actions, 333 F. Supp. 278 (S.D.N.Y. 1971), 604, 620

In re Antibiotic Antitrust Actions, 333 F. Supp. 317 (S.D.N.Y. 1971), 684, 685, 686, 731, 738

In re Antibiotic Antitrust Actions, 410 F. Supp. 680 (D. Minn. 1975), 787

In re Antitrust Grand Jury, 805 F.2d 155 (6th Cir. 1986), 755, 762, 763, 764

In re Arbitration Between First Tex. Sav. Ass'n and Fin. Interchange, Inc., 55 ANTITRUST & TRADE REG. REP. (BNA) 340 (1988), 380, 1090

In re Arizona Dairy Prods. Litig., 1979-1 Trade Cas. (CCH) ¶ 62,605 (D. Ariz. 1978), 604

In re Arizona Dairy Prods. Litig., 1984-2 Trade Cas. (CCH) ¶ 66,284 (D. Ariz. 1984), 685, 686

In re Arizona Dairy Prods. Litig., 627 F. Supp. 233 (D. Ariz. 1985), 661

In re Arizona Escrow Fee Antitrust Litig., 1982-83 Trade Cas. (CCH) ¶ 65,198 (D. Ariz. 1982), 783

In re Armored Car Antitrust Litig., 472 F. Supp. 1357 (N.D. Ga. 1979), 784

In re Armored Car Antitrust Litig., 645 F.2d 488 (5th Cir. 1981), 604

In re Art Materials Antitrust Litig., 100 F.R.D. 367 (N.D. Ohio 1983), 741, 743

In re Art Materials Antitrust Litig., 1983-1 Trade Cas. (CCH) ¶ 65,315 (N.D. Ohio 1983), 714, 716, 718, 725, 731, 732, 735

In re Aviation Ins. Indus., 183 F. Supp. 374 (S.D.N.Y. 1960), 1115

In re Beef Indus. Antitrust Litig., 1986-2 Trade Cas. (CCH) ¶ 67,277 (S.D. Tex. 1986), 712, 726, 727, 733, 736

In re Beef Indus. Antitrust Litig., 419 F. Supp. 720 (J.P.M.D.L. 1976), 710

In re Beef Indus. Antitrust Litig., 713 F. Supp. 971 (N.D. Tex. 1988), *aff'd*, 907 F.2d 510 (5th Cir. 1990), 263

In re Beef Indus. Antitrust Litig., 600 F.2d 1148 (5th Cir. 1979), *cert. denied*, 449 U.S. 905 (1980), 654, 656, 657, 661, 664, 688, 692, 693

In re Beef Indus. Antitrust Litig., 607 F.2d 167 (5th Cir. 1979), *cert. denied*, 452 U.S. 905 (1981), 741, 742

In re Beef Indus. Antitrust Litig., 907 F.2d 510 (5th Cir. 1990), 6, 7, 9, 74, 196, 227

In re Berkley & Co., 629 F.2d 548 (8th Cir. 1980), 566

In re Boise Cascade Sec. Litig., 420 F.Supp. 99 (W.D. Wash. 1976), 773

In re Borden, Inc., 92 F.T.C. 669 (1978) *aff'd*, 674 F.2d 498 (6th Cir. 1982), 848

In re Bristol Bay, Alaska, Salmon Fishery Antitrust Litig., 78 F.R.D. 622 (W.D. Wash. 1978), 719, 720, 721, 724, 731, 733

In re Bristol Bay, Alaska, Salmon Fishery Antitrust Litig., 424 F. Supp. 504 (J.P.M.D.L. 1976), 709, 710

In re Bristol Bay, Alaska, Salmon Fishery Antitrust Litig., 530 F. Supp. 36 (W.D. Wash. 1981), 662

In re Brogna, 589 F.2d 24 (1st Cir. 1978), 566

In re Burlington Northern, Inc., 822 F.2d 518 (5th Cir. 1987), *cert. denied*, 484 U.S. 1007 (1988), 258, 762, 766, 990, 1003, 1004, 1005, 1014

In re California, 195 F. Supp. 37 (E.D. Pa. 1961), 759

In re Career Academy Antitrust Litig., 342 F. Supp. 753 (J.P.M.D.L. 1972), 710

In re Career Academy Antitrust Litig., 60 F.R.D. 378 (E.D. Wis. 1973), 719

In re CBS Licensing Antitrust Litig., 328 F. Supp. 511 (J.P.M.D.L. 1971), 437

In re Cement & Concrete Antitrust Litig., 465 F. Supp. 1299 (J.P.M.D.L. 1979), 709

In re Cement & Concrete Antitrust Litig., 817 F.2d 1435 (9th Cir. 1987), *rev'd on other grounds sub nom.* California v. ARC America Corp., 490 U.S. 93 (1990), 658, 737, 741, 743, 744, 746

In re Chicago, M., St. P. & Pac. R.R. (N.D. Ill.) (Bench Order dated February 19, 1985), *aff'd,* 799 F.2d 317 (7th Cir. 1986), *cert. denied,* 481 U.S. 1068 (1987), 1140

In re Chicken Antitrust Litig., 407 F. Supp. 1285 (N.D. Ga. 1975), 867, 869

In re Chicken Antitrust Litig., 669 F.2d 228 (5th Cir. 1982), 657, 742, 744

In re Chicken Antitrust Litig., 810 F.2d 1017 (11th Cir. 1987), 744

In re Chiropractic Antitrust Litig., 483 F. Supp. (J.P.M.D.L. 1980), 709, 710

In re Chlorine & Caustic Soda Antitrust Litig., 116 F.R.D. 622 (E.D. Pa. 1987), 712, 714, 716, 723, 725, 727, 729, 731, 737

In re Civil Investigative Demand Nos. 5077, 5247, and 5515, 1985-1 Trade Cas. (CCH) ¶ 66,380 (N.D. Ill. 1984), 762

In re Civil Investigative Demand Nos. 5077, 5247, and 5515, 1985-1 Trade Cas. (CCH) ¶ 66,381 (N.D. Ill. 1984), 560

In re Clark Oil & Ref. Corp. Antitrust Litig., 1974-1 Trade Cas. (CCH) ¶ 74,880 (E.D. Wis. 1974), 735

In re Clark Oil & Ref. Corp. Antitrust Litig., 422 F. Supp. 503 (E.D. Wis. 1976), 782

In re Cleveland Trust Co., 1972 Trade Cas. (CCH) ¶ 73,991 (N.D. Ohio 1969), 559

In re Clozapine Antitrust Litig., MDL No. 874, No. 91 C 2431 (N.D. Ill. filed Apr. 16, 1991), 611

In re Commercial Gen. Liab. Ins. Antitrust Litig., MDL No. 767 (N.D. Cal. filed Mar. 22, 1988), 612

In re Commercial Lighting Prods., Inc. Contract Litig., 415 F. Supp. 392 (J.P.M.D.L. 1969), 709

In re Continental Illinois Sec. Litig., 572 F. Supp. 931 (N.D. Ill. 1983), 785

In re Coordinated Pretrial Proceedings in Petroleum Prods. Antitrust Litig., 1978-1 Trade Cas. (CCH) ¶ 61,839 (C.D. Cal. 1978), 605

In re Coordinated Pretrial Proceedings in Petroleum Prods. Antitrust Litig., 1991-2 Trade Cas. (CCH) ¶ 69,669 (C.D. Cal. 1991), 691, 692

In re Coordinated Pretrial Proceedings in Petroleum Prods. Antitrust Litig., 906 F.2d 432 (9th Cir. 1990), *cert. denied,* 111 S. Ct. 2274 (1991), 4, 5, 7, 72, 608

In re Corn Derivatives Antitrust Litig., 486 F. Supp. 929 (J.P.M.D.L. 1980), 710

In re Corrugated Container Antitrust Litig. (Appeal of Conboy), 661 F.2d 1145 (7th Cir. 1981), *aff'd sub nom* Pillsbury v. Comboy, 459 U.S. 248 (1983), 771

In re Corrugated Container Antitrust Litig. (Appeal of Fleischacker), 644 F.2d 70 (2nd Cir. 1981), 771, 772

In re Corrugated Container Antitrust Litig., 441 F. Supp. 921 (J.P.M.D.L. 1977), 710

In re Corrugated Container Antitrust Litig., 611 F.2d 86 (5th Cir. 1980), 738

In re Corrugated Container Antitrust Litig. (Appeal of Franey), 620 F.2d 1086 (5th Cir. 1980), *cert. denied,* 449 U.S. 1102 (1981), 771

In re Corrugated Container Antitrust Litig., 643 F.2d 195 (5th Cir. 1981), 719, 720, 741, 742, 743, 745

In re Corrugated Container Antitrust Litig., 655 F.2d 748 (7th Cir. 1981), *aff'd sub nom.* Pillsbury v. Conboy, 459 U.S. 248 (1983), 592

In re Corrugated Container Antitrust Litig., 659 F.2d 1332 (5th Cir. 1981), *cert. denied,* 456 U.S. 998 (1982), 734, 741

In re Corrugated Container Antitrust Litig., 661 F.2d 1145 (7th Cir. 1981), 592

In re Corrugated Container Antitrust Litig., 687 F.2d 52 (5th Cir. 1982), 757

In re Corrugated Container Antitrust Litig., M.D.L. 310, slip op. (S.D. Tex. Oct. 1987), 745

In re Corrugated Container Antitrust Litig., 80 F.R.D. 244 (S.D. Tex. 1978), 732, 734

In re Cuisinart Food Processor Antitrust Litig., 506 F. Supp. 651, (J.P.M.D.L. 1981), 709, 710

In re Daley, 549 F.2d 469 (7th Cir.), *cert. denied*, 434 U.S. 829 (1977), 592

In re Data Gen. Corp. Antitrust Litig., 490 F. Supp. 1089 (N.D. Cal. 1980) and 529 F. Supp. 801 (N.D. Cal. 1981), *aff'd in part and rev'd in part sub nom.* Digidyne Corp. v. Data Gen. Corp., 734 F.2d 1336 (9th Cir. 1984), *cert. denied*, 473 U.S. 908 (1985), 135, 137, 138, 148, 152, 153, 851

In re Dennis Greenman Sec. Litig., 829 F.2d 1539 (11th Cir. 1987), 736, 737

In re Detroit Auto Dealers Assn, v. FTC, 1992-1, Trade Cas. (CCH) ¶ 69,696 (8th Cir. 1991), 1121

In re Doe, 662 F.2d 1073 (4th Cir. 1981), *cert. denied*, 455 U.S. 1000 (1982), 763

In re Domestic Air Transportation Antitrust Litig., 1991-2 Trade Cas. (CCH) ¶ 69,518 (N.D. Ga. 1991), 712, 714, 720, 724, 725, 726, 731, 732

In re Dun & Bradstreet Credit Servs. Customer Litig., 130 F.R.D. 366 (S.D. Ohio 1990), 741, 742

In re Electrical Serv., 102 N.M. 529, 697 P.2d 948 (1985), 637

In re Electric Weld Steel Tubing Antitrust Litig., 1980-1 Trade Cas. (CCH) ¶ 63,783 (E.D. Pa. 1980), 727

In re Emprise Corp., 344 F. Supp. 319 (W.D.N.Y. 1971), 559

In re Equity Funding Corp. of Am. Secs. Litig., 603 F.2d 1353 (9th Cir. 1979), 745

In re Evans Prods. Co., 1986-1 Trade Cas. (CCH) ¶ 67,113 (S.D. Fla. 1986), 480

In re Fertilizer Antitrust Litig., 1979-2 Trade Cas. (CCH) ¶ 62,894 (E.D. Wash. 1979), 690, 691, 738, 746, 749

In re Fine Paper Antitrust Litig., 446 F. Supp. 759 (J.P.M.D.L. 1978), 710

In re Fine Paper Antitrust Litig., 82 F.R.D. 143 (E.D. Pa. 1979), *aff'd on other grounds*, 685 F.2d 810 (3d Cir. 1982), *cert. denied*, 459 U.S. 1156 (1983), 604, 714, 719, 726, 728, 732, 735

In re Fine Paper Antitrust Litig., 617 F.2d 22 (3d Cir. 1980), 723

In re Fine Paper Antitrust Litig., 685 F.2d 810 (3d Cir. 1982), *cert. denied*, 459 U.S. 1156 (1983), 603, 604, 711, 768, 770

In re Fine Paper Antitrust Litig., 98 F.R.D. 48 (E.D. Pa. 1983), *aff'd in part and rev'd in part*, 751 F.2d 562 (3rd Cir. 1984), 784, 785

In re Fine Paper Litig. State of Wash., 632 F.2d 1081 (3d Cir. 1980), 655

In re First Commodity Corp. of Boston Customer Accts. Litig., 119 F.R.D. 301 (D. Mass. 1987), 741

In re Folding Carton Antitrust Litig., 1980-2 Trade Cas. (CCH) 63,439 (N.D. Ill. 1980), 700

In re Folding Carton Antitrust Litig., 415 F. Supp. 384 (J.P.M.D.L. 1976), 710

In re Folding Carton Antitrust Litig., 75 F.R.D. 727 (N.D. Ill. 1977), 725, 731

In re Folding Carton Antitrust Litig., 83 F.R.D. 251 (N.D. Ill. 1978), 747

In re Folding Carton Antitrust Litig., 83 F.R.D. 260 (N.D. Ill. 1979), 735, 746

In re Folding Carton Antitrust Litig., 84 F.R.D. 245 (N.D. Ill. 1979), 783

In re Folding Carton Antitrust Litig., 88 F.R.D. 211 (N.D. Ill. 1980), 721, 732

In re Folding Carton Antitrust Litig., 609 F.2d 867 (7th Cir. 1979), 771

In re Folding Carton Antitrust Litig., 744 F.2d 1252 (7th Cir. 1984), 745

In re Folding Carton Antitrust Litig., 881 F.2d 494 (7th Cir.), *reh'g denied*, 1989 U.S. APP. LEXIS 14161 (7th Cir. Sept. 15, 1989), *cert. denied*, 494 U.S. 1026 (1990), 745

In re FTC Line of Business Report Litig., 432 F. Supp. 274 (D.D.C. 1977), *aff'd*, 595 F.2d 685 (D.C. Cir.), *cert. denied*, 439 U.S. 958 (1978), 507, 509, 512

In re General Motors Corp. Engine Interchange Litig., 594 F.2d 1106 (7th Cir.), *cert. denied*, 444 U.S. 870 (1979), 604, 719, 741, 742, 743, 744

In re Glassine & Greaseproof Paper Antitrust Litig., 88 F.R.D. 302 (E.D. Pa. 1980), 716, 721, 723

In re Gold Bond Stamp Co., 221 F. Supp. 391 (D. Minn. 1963), *aff'd per curiam sub nom.* Gold Bond Stamp Co. v. United States, 325 F.2d 1018 (8th Cir. 1964), 556, 557

In re Gopman, 531 F.2d 262 (5th Cir. 1976), 602

In re Grand Jury, 446 F. Supp. 1132 (N.D. Tex. 1978), 601, 602

In re Grand Jury, 469 F. Supp. 666 (M.D. Pa. 1978), 758, 759

In re Grand Jury Empaneled January 21, 1975, 536 F.2d 1009 (3d Cir. 1976), 601, 602

In re Grand Jury in the Matter of Fine, 641 F.2d 199 (5th Cir. 1981), 764

In re Grand Jury Investigation (General Motors), 1960 Trade Cas. (CCH) ¶ 69,796 (S.D.N.Y. 1960), 562

In re Grand Jury Investigation (General Motors), 174 F. Supp. 393 (S.D.N.Y. 1959), 564

In re Grand Jury Investigation, 425 F. Supp. 717 (S.D. Fla. 1977), 563, 564

In re Grand Jury Investigation, 436 F. Supp. 818 (W.D. Pa. 1977), 601

In re Grand Jury Investigation, 459 F. Supp. 1335 (E.D. Pa. 1978), 766

In re Grand Jury Investigation, 599 F.2d 1224 (3d Cir. 1979), 763

In re Grand Jury Investigation, 769 F.2d 1485 (11th Cir. 1985), 563

In re Grand Jury Investigation, 774 F.2d 34 (2d Cir. 1985), *rev'd sub nom.* United States v. John Doe, Inc., 481 U.S. 102 (1987), 755

In re Grand Jury Investigation, John Doe, 599 F. Supp. 746 (S.D. Tex. 1984), *aff'd*, 812 F.2d 1404 (5th Cir. 1987), *aff'd sub nom.* Doe v. United States, 487 U.S. 201 (1988), 889

In re Grand Jury Investigation of Cuisinarts, Inc., 665 F.2d 24 (2d Cir. 1981), 560

In re Grand Jury Investigation of the Shipping Indus., 186 F. Supp. 298 (D.D.C. 1960), 899

In re Grand Jury Investigation of Uranium Indus., 1978-2 Trade Cas. (CCH) ¶ 62,329 (D.D.C. 1978), 758

In re Grand Jury Investigation of Ven-Fuel, 441 F. Supp. 1299 (M.D. Fla. 1977), 758

In re Grand Jury Proceedings (PHE, Inc.), 640 F. Supp. 149 (E.D.N.C. 1986), 565

In re Grand Jury Proceedings, 1979-2 Trade Cas. (CCH) ¶ 62,856 (N.D. Ga. 1979), 602

In re Grand Jury Proceedings, 1979-2 Trade Cas. (CCH) ¶ 62,857 (N.D. Ga. 1979), 601, 602

In re Grand Jury Proceedings, 428 F. Supp. 273 (E.D. Mich. 1976), 601

In re Grand Jury Proceedings, 309 F.2d 440 (3d Cir. 1962), 759

In re Grand Jury Proceedings, 473 F.2d 840 (8th Cir. 1973), 566

In re Grand Jury Proceedings, 486 F.2d 85 (3d Cir. 1973), 564

In re Grand Jury Proceedings, 507 F.2d 963 (3d Cir.), *cert. denied*, 421 U.S. 1015 (1975), 563, 564

In re Grand Jury Proceedings, 613 F.2d 501 (5th Cir. 1980), 553, 590

In re Grand Jury Proceedings, 686 F.2d 135 (3d Cir.), *cert. denied*, 459 U.S. 1020 (1982), 564

In re Grand Jury Proceedings, 691 F.2d 1384 (11th Cir. 1982), *cert. denied*, 462 U.S. 1119 (1983), 888

In re Grand Jury Proceedings, 785 F.2d 593 (8th Cir. 1986), 754

In re Grand Jury Proceedings, 791 F.2d 663 (8th Cir. 1986), 563, 564

In re Grand Jury Proceedings, 797 F.2d 1377 (6th Cir. 1986), *cert. denied*, 479 U.S. 1031 (1987), 586

In re Grand Jury Proceedings, 841 F.2d 1264 (6th Cir. 1988), 755, 756, 759

In re Grand Jury Proceedings, 851 F.2d 860 (6th Cir. 1988), 759

In re Grand Jury Proceedings, 867 F.2d 539 (9th Cir. 1989), 763

In re Grand Jury Proceedings Bank of Nova Scotia, 740 F.2d 817 (11th Cir. 1984), *cert. denied*, 469 U.S. 1106 (1985), 863, 880, 887, 888, 908

In re Grand Jury Proceedings Relative to Perl, 838 F.2d 304 (8th Cir. 1988), 758

In re Grand Jury Proceedings, United States v. Field, 532 F.2d 404 (5th Cir.), *cert. denied*, 429 U.S. 940 (1976), 888

In re Grand Jury Subpoena (Legal Services Center), 615 F. Supp. 958 (D. Mass. 1985), 563

In re Grand Jury Subpoena, 405 F. Supp. 1192 (N.D. Ga. 1975), 767

In re Grand Jury Subpoena, 436 F. Supp. 46 (D. Md. 1977), 766

In re Grand Jury Subpoena Duces Tecum, 731 F.2d 1032 (2d Cir. 1984), 764

In re Grand Jury Subpoenas Duces Tecum, 798 F.2d 32 (2d Cir. 1986), 764

In re Grand Jury Subpoena Duces Tecum Addressed to Canadian Int'l Paper Co., 72 F. Supp. 1013 (S.D.N.Y. 1947), 878, 880

In re Grand Jury Subpoena Duces Tecum dated November 16, 1974, 406 F. Supp. 381 (S.D.N.Y. 1975), 565

In re Grand Jury Subpoenas Duces Tecum Issued to Southern Motor Carriers Rate Conference, 405 F. Supp. 1192 (N.D. Ga. 1975), 563

In re Grand Jury Subpoenas to Midland Asphalt Corp., 616 F. Supp. 223 (W.D.N.Y. 1985), 563, 564, 766

In re Grand Jury Subpoena Served Upon Doe, 759 F.2d 968 (2d Cir. 1985), *cert. denied*, 475 U.S. 1108 (1986), 563

In re Grand Jury Subpoena Served Upon Doe, 781 F.2d 238 (2d Cir. 1985), *cert. denied*, 475 U.S. 1108 (1986), 563

In re Grand Jury Transcripts, 309 F. Supp. 1050 (S.D. Ohio 1970), 757

In re Grocery Prods. Grand Jury Proceedings of 1983, 637 F. Supp. 1171 (D. Conn. 1986), 755, 756, 757, 758

In re Gypsum Antitrust Cases, 565 F.2d 1123 (9th Cir. 1977), 739

In re Gypsum Cases, 386 F. Supp. 959 (N.D. Cal. 1974), *aff'd sub nom. In re* Gypsum Antitrust Cases, 565 F.2d 1123 (9th Cir. 1977), 729, 745

In re Gypsum Wallboard, 297 F. Supp. 1350 (J.P.M.D.L. 1969), 710

In re Harry Alexander, Inc., 8 F.R.D. 559 (S.D.N.Y. 1949), 564

In re Hawaii Beer Antitrust Litig., 1978-2 Trade Cas. (CCH) ¶ 62,199 (D. Haw. 1978), 721

In re Hops Antitrust Litig., 832 F.2d 470 (8th Cir. 1987), 896

In re Hotel Tel. Charges, 500 F.2d 86 (9th Cir. 1974), 731, 732, 736

In re IBM Peripheral EDP Devices Antitrust Litig., 481 F. Supp. 965 (N.D. Cal. 1979), *aff'd sub nom.* Transamerica Computer Co. v. IBM, 698 F.2d 1377 (9th Cir.), *cert. denied*, 464 U.S. 955 (1983), 203, 215, 216, 253, 254, 257

In re Independent Gasoline Antitrust Litig., 79 F.R.D. 552 (D. Md. 1978), 715, 733, 775

In re Independent Gasoline Antitrust Litig., 1979-2 Trade Cas. (CCH) ¶ 62,863 (D. Md. 1979), 739

In re Industrial Gas Antitrust Litig., 681 F.2d 514 (7th Cir. 1982), *cert. denied*, 460 U.S. 1016 (1983), 662

In re Innotron Diagnostics, 1986-2 Trade Cas. (CCH) ¶ 67,273 (Fed. Cir. 1986), 774

In re Innotron Diagnostics, 800 F.2d 1077 (Fed. Cir. 1986), 851, 852

In re Insulin Mfg. Antitrust Litig., 487 F. Supp. 1359 (J.P.M.D.L. 1980), 709, 710

In re Insurance Antitrust Litig., 723 F. Supp. 464 (N.D. Cal. 1989), *rev'd*, 938 F.2d 919 (9th Cir. 1991), 612, 1112

In re Insurance Antitrust Litig., 938 F.2d 919 (9th Cir. 1991), 612, 629, 861, 971

In re International House of Pancakes Franchise Litig., 331 F. Supp. 556 (J.P.M.D.L. 1971), 710

In re International House of Pancakes Franchise Litig., 1972 Trade Cas. (CCH) ¶ 73,864 (W.D. Mo. 1972), 743

In re International Sys. & Controls Corp., 693 F.2d 1235 (5th Cir. 1982), 764

In re Investigation Before the February, 1977, Lynchburg Grand Jury, 563 F.2d 652 (4th Cir. 1977), 601, 602

In re Investigation of World Arrangements with Relation to the Prod., Transp., Ref. & Distrib. of Petroleum, 13 F.R.D. 280 (D.D.C. 1952), 880, 899, 909

In re Investigative Grand Jury Proceedings on April 10, 1979 and Continuing, 480 F. Supp. 162 (N.D. Ohio 1979), *appeal dismissed*, 621 F.2d 813 (6th Cir. 1980), *cert. denied*, 449 U.S. 1124 (1981), 601, 602

In re Japanese Elec. Prods. Antitrust Litig., 631 F.2d 1069 (3d Cir. 1980), 773

In re Japanese Elec. Prods. Antitrust Litig., 723 F.2d 238 (3d Cir. 1983), *rev'd on other grounds sub nom.* Matsushita Elec. Indus. v. Zenith Radio Corp., 475 U.S. 574 (1986), 448, 892

In re John Doe Corp., 675 F.2d 482 (2d Cir. 1982), 764

In re Kauffman Mutual Fund Actions, 337 F. Supp. 1337 (J.P.M.D.L. 1972), 710

In re Kilgo, 484 F.2d 1215 (4th Cir. 1973), 592

In re King Resources Co. Sec. Litig., 420 F. Supp. 610 (D. Colo. 1976), 783

In re LTV Sec. Litig., 89 F.R.D. 595 (N.D. Tex. 1981), 565

In re Mack Truck, Inc. Antitrust Litig., 383 F. Supp. 503 (J.P.M.D.L. 1974), 710

In re Marc Rich & Co., 707 F.2d 663 (2d Cir.), *cert. denied*, 463 U.S. 1215 (1983), 876, 880

In re Marc Rich & Co., 736 F.2d 864 (2d Cir. 1984), 888

In re Marine Constr. Antitrust Litig., 487 F. Supp. 1355 (J.P.M.D.L. 1980), 709, 710

In re Master Key Antitrust Litig., 70 F.R.D. 23 (D. Conn.), *appeal dismissed*, 528 F.2d 5 (2d Cir. 1975), 711, 728, 732

In re Master Key Antitrust Litig., 70 F.R.D. 29 (D. Conn. 1976), 682, 697

In re Melvin, 546 F.2d 1 (1st Cir. 1976), 566

In re Messerschmitt Bolkow Blohm GmbH, 757 F.2d 729 (5th Cir. 1985), *cert. granted sub nom.* Messerschmitt Bolkow Blohm GmbH v. Walker, 475 U.S. 1118 (1986), *cert. granted and decision vacated*, 483 U.S. 1002 (1987), 880

In re Mid-Atlantic Toyota Antitrust Litig., 516 F. Supp. 1287 (D. Md. 1981), *aff'd*, 730 F.2d 528 (8th Cir.), *cert. denied*, 469 U.S. 924 (1984), 607, 656, 657, 699

In re Mid-Atlantic Toyota Antitrust Litig., 525 F. Supp. 1265 (D. Md. 1981), *aff'd sub nom.* Pennsylvania v. Mid-Atlantic Toyota Distribs., 704 F.2d 125 (4th Cir. 1983), 607, 608

In re Mid-Atlantic Toyota Antitrust Litig., 560 F. Supp. 760 (D. Md. 1983), 608

In re Mid-Atlantic Toyota Antitrust Litig., 564 F. Supp. 1379 (D. Md. 1983), 608, 741

In re Mid-Atlantic Toyota Antitrust Litig., 585 F. Supp. 1553 (D. Md. 1984), 744

In re Mid-Atlantic Toyota Antitrust Litig., 605 F. Supp. 440 (D. Md. 1984), 611

In re Mid-Atlantic Toyota Antitrust Litig., 93 F.R.D. 485 (D. Md. 1982), 723

In re Midwest Milk Monopolization Litig., 529 F. Supp. 1326 (W.D. Mo. 1982), *aff'd*, 730 F.2d 528 (8th Cir.), *cert. denied*, 469 U.S. 924 (1984), 656, 657, 652

In re Minolta Camera Prods. Antitrust Litig., 668 F. Supp. 456 (D. Md. 1987), 101, 608, 610

In re Montgomery County Real Estate Antitrust Litig., 1988-2 Trade Cas. (CCH) ¶ 68,230 (D. Md. 1988), 608

In re Montgomery County Real Estate Antitrust Litig., 83 F.R.D. 305 (D. Md. 1979), 608

In re Multidistrict Vehicle Air Pollution, 367 F. Supp. 1298 (C.D. Cal.1973), *aff'd*, 538 F.2d 231 (9th Cir. 1976), 839

In re Multidistrict Vehicle Air Pollution, 481 F.2d 122 (9th Cir.), *cert. denied*, 414 U.S. 1045 (1973), 606, 659

In re Multidistrict Vehicle Air Pollution, 591 F.2d 68 (9th Cir.), *cert. denied*, 444 U.S. 900 (1979), 681

In re Murphy, 560 F.2d 326 (8th Cir. 1977), 764

In re National Student Mktg. Litig., 68 F.R.D. 151 (D.D.C. 1974), 742

In re NEC Home Elec. (USA), Inc., ANTITRUST & TRADE REG. REP. (BNA) No. 1355 (Mar. 1, 1988), 500

In re New Mexico Natural Gas Antitrust Litig., 1982-1 Trade Cas. (CCH) ¶ 64,685 (D.N.M. 1982), 656, 657

In re New Mexico Natural Gas Antitrust Litig., 482 F. Supp. 333 (J.P.M.D.L. 1979), 710

In re Nintendo of Am., Inc., No. 91 Civ. 3428 (S.D.N.Y. April 10, 1991), 101

In re Nissan Antitrust Litig., 577 F.2d 910 (5th Cir. 1978), *cert. denied*, 439 U.S. 1072 (1979), 107, 112

In re Nissan Motor Corp. Antitrust Litig., 552 F.2d 1088 (5th Cir. 1977), 733, 738, 739

In re Ocean Shipping Antitrust Litig., 500 F. Supp. 1235 (S.D.N.Y. 1980), 1160

In re Olympia Brewing Co. Antitrust Litig., 415 F. Supp. 398 (J.P.M.D.L. 1976), 710

In re Osterhoudt, 722 F.2d 591 (9th Cir. 1983), 564

In re Panasonic Consumer Elecs. Antitrust Litig., No. 89-CV 0368 (SWK) (S.D.N.Y. filed Jan. 18, 1989), 101, 610

In re Passsenger Computer Reservation Sys. Antitrust Litig., 694 F. Supp. 1443 (C.D. Cal. 1988), 203, 207

In re Petroleum Prods. Antitrust Litig., 407 F. Supp. 249 (J.P.M.D.L. 1976), 711

In re Petroleum Prods. Antitrust Litig., 497 F. Supp. 218 (C.D. Cal. 1980), *aff'd on other grounds*, 691 F.2d 1335 (9th Cir. 1982), *cert. denied*, 464 U.S. 1068 (1984), 661, 664

In re Petroleum Prods. Antitrust Litig., 523 F. Supp. 1116 (C.D. Cal. 1981), *aff'd*, 691 F.2d 1335 (9th Cir. 1982), *cert. denied*, 464 U.S. 1068 (1984), 728

In re Petroleum Prods. Antitrust Litig., 658 F.2d 1355 (9th Cir. 1981), *cert. denied*, 455 U.S. 990 (1982), 761

In re Petroleum Prods. Antitrust Litig., 669 F.2d 620 (10th Cir. 1982), 766

In re Petroleum Prods. Antitrust Litig., 691 F.2d 1335 (9th Cir. 1982), *cert. denied*, 464 U.S. 1068 (1984), 657, 661, 736

In re Petroleum Prods. Antitrust Litig., 906 F.2d 432, (9th Cir. 1990), *cert. denied*, 111 S. Ct. 2274 (1991), 707

In re Plastic Bag Prod. Patent & Antitrust Litig., 1987-1 Trade Cas. (CCH) ¶ 67,561 (D. Mass. 1987), 876

In re Plumbing Fixture Cases, 298 F. Supp. 484, (J.P.M.D.L. 1968), 709

In re Plumbing Fixtures, 311 F. Supp. 349 (J.P.M.D.L. 1971), 709

In re Plywood Antitrust Litig., 655 F.2d 627 (5th Cir. 1981), *cert. granted sub nom.* Weyerhaeuser Co. v. Lyman Lamb Co., 456 U.S. 971 (1982), *cert. dismissed as moot following settlement*, 462 U.S. 1125 (1983), 7, 65, 665

In re Plywood Antitrust Litig., 76 F.R.D. 570 (E.D. La. 1976), 692, 714, 719, 724, 725, 730, 732, 735

In re Ray Dobbins Lincoln Mercury, Inc., 604 F. Supp. 203 (W.D. Va. 1984), *aff'd mem.*, 813 F.2d 402 (4th Cir. 1985), 19

In re Real Estate Title and Settlement Servs. Antitrust Litig., 869 F.2d 760 (3d Cir.), *cert. denied*, 493 U.S. 821 (1989), 734

In re Reclosable Plastic Bags, 192 U.S.P.Q. (BNA) 674 (U.S. Int'l Trade Comm'n 1977), 829

In re Refrigerant Gas Antitrust Litig., 334 F. Supp. 996 (J.P.M.D.L. 1971), 710

In re Republic National-Realty Equities Sec. Litig., 382 F. Supp. 1403 (J.P.M.D.L. 1974), 711

In re Richardson-Merrell, Inc. "Bendectin" Prods. Liability Litig., 624 F. Supp. 1212 (S.D. Ohio 1985), 752, 753

In re Russo, 53 F.R.D. 564 (D. Cal. 1971), 565

In re School Asbestos Litig., 789 F.2d 996 (2d Cir. 1986), 737

In re Scotch Whiskey, 299 F. Supp. 543 (J.P.M.D.L. 1969), 709

In re Screws Antitrust Litig., 91 F.R.D. 52 (D. Mass. 1981), 714, 716, 725, 726, 727, 729, 731, 757, 758

In re Sealed Case, 676 F.2d 793 (D.C. Cir. 1982), 763, 764

In re Sealed Case, 754 F.2d 395 (D.C. Cir. 1985), 764

In re Sealed Case, 801 F.2d 1379 (D.C. Cir. 1986), 759

In re Sealed Case, 825 F.2d 494 (D.C. Cir.), *cert. denied*, 484 U.S. 963 (1987), 888

In re 7-Eleven Franchise Antitrust Litig., 1974-2 Trade Cas. (CCH) ¶ 75,429 (N.D. Cal. 1974), 132, 133, 134, 141

In re Shipowners Litig., 361 N.W.2d 112 (Minn. Ct. App. 1985), 873

In re Shopping Cart Antitrust Litig., 1982-1 Trade Cas. (CCH) ¶ 64,612 (S.D.N.Y. 1982), 692

In re Shopping Cart Antitrust Litig., 1982-2 Trade Cas. (CCH) ¶ 64,946 (S.D.N.Y. 1982), 756

In re Shopping Cart Antitrust Litig., 95 F.R.D. 299 (S.D.N.Y. 1982), 747

In re Siemens & Halske AG, 155 F. Supp. 897 (S.D.N.Y. 1957), 878

In re South Cent. States Bakery Prods. Antitrust Litig., 86 F.R.D. 407 (M.D. La. 1980), 716, 717, 722, 732, 735

In re Southern Minnesota Ready Mix, Inc., 1989-2 Trade Cas. (CCH) ¶ 68,873 (Minn. Dist. Ct. 1989), 612

In re Special February, 1975 Grand Jury, 662 F.2d 1232 (7th Cir. 1981), *aff'd sub nom.* United States v. Baggot, 463 U.S. 476 (1982), 754

In re Special February 1977 Grand Jury, 581 F.2d 1262 (7th Cir. 1978), 601, 602

In re Special Grand Jury, 480 F. Supp. 174 (E.D. Wis. 1979), 602

In re Special Grand Jury No. 81-1 (Harvey), 676 F.2d 1005 (4th Cir.), *vacated on other grounds*, 697 F.2d 112 (4th Cir. 1982), 563

In re Special September 1978 Grand Jury, 640 F.2d 49 (7th Cir. 1980), 763

In re Sugar Indus. Antitrust Litig. (East Coast), 471 F. Supp. 1089 (J.P.M.D.L. 1978), 709

In re Sugar Indus. Antitrust Litig., 1977-1 Trade Cas. (CCH) ¶ 61,373 (N.D. Cal. 1976), 604, 719, 720, 730, 732

In re Sugar Indus. Antitrust Litig., 1977-2 Trade Cas. (CCH) ¶ 61,808 (N.D. Cal. 1977), 757

In re Sugar Indus. Antitrust Litig., 559 F.2d 481 (9th Cir. 1977), 736

In re Sugar Indus. Antitrust Litig., 579 F.2d 13 (3d Cir. 1978), 657

In re Sugar Indus. Antitrust Litig., 73 F.R.D. 322 (E.D. Pa. 1976), 719, 732, 733

In re Super Premium Ice Cream Distrib. Antitrust Litig., 691 F. Supp. 1262 (N.D. Cal. 1988), *aff'd without published opinion sub. nom.* Haagen-Dazs Co. v. Double Rainbow Gourmet Ice Creams, Inc., 895 F.2d 1417 (9th Cir. 1990), 119, 182, 186, 201

In re Toilet Seat Antitrust Litig., 387 F. Supp. 1342 (J.P.M.D.L. 1975), 709

In re Transit Co. Tire Antitrust Litig., 67 F.R.D. 59 (W.D. Mo. 1975), 727

In re United States Grand Jury Proceedings, 767 F.2d 1131 (5th Cir. 1985), 889

In re Uranium Antitrust Litig., 1980-81 Trade Cas. (CCH) ¶ 63,678 (N.D. Ill. 1980), 869

In re Uranium Antitrust Litig., 473 F. Supp. 382 (N.D. Ill. 1979), 893

In re Uranium Antitrust Litig., 480 F. Supp. 1138 (N.D. Ill. 1979), 880, 887

In re Uranium Antitrust Litig., 552 F. Supp. 518 (N.D. Ill. 1982), 662

In re Uranium Antitrust Litig., 617 F.2d 1248 (7th Cir. 1980), 677, 860, 893

In re Uranium Indus. Antitrust Litig., 458 F. Supp. 1223 (J.P.M.D.L. 1978), 645, 709

In re U.S. Fin. Securities Litig., 609 F.2d 411 (9th Cir. 1979), *cert. denied*, 446 U.S. 929 (1980), 773

In re Water Meters, 304 F. Supp. 873 (J.P.M.D.L. 1969), 710

In re Westinghouse Elec. Corp., 16 Ont. 2d 273 (Sup. Ct. 1977), 884

In re Westinghouse Elec. Corp. Uranium Contracts Litig., 563 F.2d 992 (10th Cir. 1977), 888

In re Wheat Rail Freight Rate Antitrust Litig., 579 F. Supp. 510 (N.D. Ill. 1983), *aff'd*, 759 F.2d 1305 (7th Cir. 1985), *cert. denied*, 476 U.S. 1158 (1986), 1011

In re Wheat Rail Freight Rate Antitrust Litig., 759 F.2d 1305 (7th Cir. 1985), *cert. denied sub nom.* Little Crow Milling Co. v. Baltimore & RR., 476 U.S. 1158 (1986), 1018, 1139

In re Willingham Patent Litig., 322 F. Supp. 1019 (J.P.M.D.L. 1971), 709

In re Wirebound Boxes Antitrust Litig., 128 F.R.D. 268 (D. Minn. 1989), 712, 715, 717, 725, 726

In re Wirebound Boxes Antitrust Litig., 1989-1 Trade Cas. (CCH) ¶ 68,609 (D. Minn. 1989), 711

In re Wirebound Boxes Antitrust Litig., 1990-1 Trade Cas. (CCH) ¶ 69,011 (D. Minn. 1990), 687, 693

In re Wiring Device Antitrust Litig., 444 F. Supp. 1348 (J.P.M.D.L. 1978), 710

In re Women's Clothing Antitrust Litig., 455 F. Supp. 1388 (J.P.M.D.L. 1978), 710

In re Workers Compensation Ins. Antitrust Litig., 771 F. Supp. 284 (D. Minn. 1991), 782

In re Workers Compensation Ins. Antitrust Litig., 867 F.2d 1552 (8th Cir.), *cert. denied*, 492 U.S. 920 (1989), 7, 706, 707, 708, 1112, 1114, 1116

In re Wyoming Tight Sands Antitrust Cases, 866 F.2d 1286 (10th Cir. 1989), *aff'd sub. nom.* Kansas v. Utilicorp United, Inc., 110 S. Ct. 2807 (1990), 614, 1062

In re Yarn Process Patent Validity & Anti-trust Litig., 398 F. Supp. 31 (S.D. Fla. 1974), *aff'd in part and rev'd in part*, 541 F.2d 1127 (5th Cir. 1976), *cert. denied*, 433 U.S. 910 (1977), 804

In re Yarn Processing Patent Validity Litig., 541 F.2d 1127 (5th Cir. 1976), *cert. denied*, 433 U.S. 910 (1977), 821, 826, 828

Independence Tube Corp. v. Copperweld Corp., 543 F. Supp. 706 (N.D. Ill.), *aff'd*, 691 F.2d 310 (7th Cir. 1982), *rev'd*, 467 U.S. 752 (1984), 785

Independence Tube Corp. v. Copperweld Corp., 691 F.2d 310 (7th Cir. 1982), *rev'd*, 467 U.S. 752 (1984), 670, 672

Independent Investor Protective League v. Touche Ross & Co., 607 F.2d 530 (2d Cir.), *cert. denied*, 439 U.S. 895 (1978), 771

Independent School Dist. No. 89 v. Bolain Equip., Inc., 90 F.R.D. 245 (W.D. Okla. 1980), 713

Independent Taxicab Drivers' Employees v. Greater Houston Transp. Co., 760 F.2d 607 (5th Cir.), *cert. denied*, 474 U.S. 903 (1985), 972, 1010

Indiana Fed'n of Dentists, 101 F.T.C. 57 (1983), *order vacated*, 745 F.2d 1124 (7th Cir. 1984), *rev'd*, 476 U.S. 447 (1986), 454

Indiana Fed'n of Dentists v. FTC, 745 F.2d 1124 (7th Cir. 1984), *rev'd*, 476 U.S. 447 (1986), 93

Indiana Grocery Co. v. Super Valu Stores, 647 F. Supp 254 (S.D. Ind. 1986), 404

Indiana Grocery Co. v. Super Valu Stores, 684 F. Supp. 561 (S.D. Ind. 1988), *aff'd*, 864 F.2d 1409 (7th Cir. 1989), 224

Indiana Grocery v. Super Valu Stores, 864 F.2d 1409 (7th Cir. 1989), 105, 217, 236, 261, 265, 266, 706

Indiana Manufactured Hous. Ass'n v. FTC, 641 F.2d 481 (7th Cir. 1981), 523, 527

Indian Coffee Corp. v. Procter & Gamble Co., 752 F.2d 891 (3d Cir.), *cert. denied*, 474 U.S. 863 (1985), 235, 405, 667

Indian Head, Inc. v. Allied Tube & Conduit Corp., 817 F.2d 938 (2d Cir. 1987), *aff'd*, 486 U.S. 492 (1988), 44, 63, 994

Indium Corp. of Am. v. Semi-Alloys, Inc., 566 F. Supp. 1344 (N.D.N.Y. 1983), 660

Indium Corp. of Am. v. Semi-Alloys, Inc., 611 F. Supp. 379 (N.D.N.Y.), *aff'd*, 781 F.2d 879 (Fed. Cir. 1985), *cert. denied*, 479 U.S. 820 (1986), 649, 808

Indium Corp. of Am. v. Semi-Alloys, Inc., 781 F.2d 879 (Fed. Cir. 1985), *cert. denied*, 479 U.S. 820 (1986), 808

Individualized Catalogues, Inc., 65 F.T.C. 48 (1964), *rescinded*, 76 F.T.C. 80 (1969), 440

Industrial Bldg. Materials, Inc. v. Interchemical Corp., 437 F.2d 1336 (9th Cir. 1970), 119, 189, 703

Industrial Communs. Sys. v. Pacific Tel. & Tel. Co., 505 F.2d 152 (9th Cir. 1974), 1022

Industrial Inv. Dev. Corp. v. Mitsui & Co., 594 F.2d 48 (5th Cir. 1979), *cert. denied*, 445 U.S. 903 (1980), 902, 904

Industrial Inv. Dev. Corp. v. Mitsui & Co., 671 F.2d 876 (5th Cir. 1982), *vacated on other grounds, and remanded*, 460 U.S. 1007, *reaff'd*, 704 F.2d 785 (5th Cir.), *cert. denied*, 464 U.S. 961 (1983), 859, 860, 866

Industrial Inv. Dev. Corp. v. Mitsui & Co., 704 F.2d 785 (5th Cir.), *cert. denied*, 464 U.S. 961 (1983), 660

Industria Siciliana Asfalti, Bitumi SpA v. Exxon Research & Eng'g Co., 1977-1 Trade Cas. (CCH) ¶ 61,256 (S.D.N.Y. 1977), 168, 866

Industrieverband Solnhofener Natursteinplatten, 23 O.J. EUR. COMM. (No. L 318) 32 (1980), [1978-1981 Transfer Binder] COMMON MKT. REP. (CCH) ¶ 10,268, 932

Ingraham v. Wright, 430 U.S. 651 (1977), 630

Ingram Corp. v. J. Ray McDermott & Co., 1980-1 Trade Cas. (CCH) ¶ 63,277 (E.D. La. 1980), *rev'd on ther grounds*, 698 F.2d 1295 (5th Cir. 1983), 690

Ings v. Ferguson, 282 F.2d 149 (2d Cir. 1960), 881, 887

Instant Delivery Corp. v. City Stores Co., 284 F. Supp. 941 (E.D. Pa. 1968), 391

Institut Merieux SA, 5 TRADE REG. REP. (CCH) ¶ 22,779 (Aug. 6, 1990), 324

Instituto Chemioterapico Italiano SpA and Commercial Sovents Corp. v. Commission, Joined Cases 76 and 7/73, [1974] E.C.R. 223, 252, [1974 transfer binder] COMMON MKT. REP. (CCH) ¶ 8,209, 928

Instructional Sys. Dev. Corp. v. Aetna Casualty & Sur. Co., 787 F.2d 1395 (10th Cir. 1986), *modified*, 817 F.2d 639 (10th Cir. 1987), 847

Instructional Sys. Dev. Corp. v. Aetna Casualty & Sur. Co., 817 F.2d 639 (10th Cir. 1987), 10, 222, 232, 665, 707, 708, 1088

Instructional Television Fixed Service (MDS Reallocation), 54 RAD. REG. 2d (P&F) 107 (1983), *recon. denied*, 98 F.C.C.2d 68 (1984), 1042

Insurance Corp. of Ireland v. Compagnie des Bauxites de Guinee, 456 U.S. 694 (1982), 768, 874, 875

Interamerican Ref. Corp. v. Texaco Maracaibo, Inc., 307 F. Supp. 1291, (D. Del. 1970), 892, 909, 910, 911

Interborough News Co. v. Curtis Publishing Co., 225 F.2d 289 (2d Cir. 1955), 188, 271

Inter-City Tire & Auto Center, Inc. v. Uniroyal, Inc., 701 F. Supp. 1120 (D.N.J. 1988), *aff'd mem.*, 888 F.2d 1380 (3d Cir. 1989), 118, 119, 183, 372

Interco, Inc., 108 F.T.C. 133 (1986), 175

Interface Group v. Massachusetts Port Auth., 816 F.2d 9 (1st Cir. 1987), 42, 49, 170, 172, 175, 178, 217, 246, 248, 985, 986

Intergroup, 18 O.J. Eur. Comm. (No. L 212) 23 (1975), [1973-1975 Transfer Binder] Common Mkt. Rep. (CCH) ¶ 9759, 933

Intermar, Inc. v. Atlantic Richfield Co., 364 F. Supp. 82 (E.D. Pa. 1973), 190

Intermountain Ford Tractor Sales Co. v. Massey-Ferguson, Ltd., 210 F. Supp. 930 (D. Utah 1962), *aff'd per curiam*, 325 F.2d 713 (10th Cir. 1963), *cert. denied*, 377 U.S. 931 (1964), 877

International Air Indus. v. American Excelsior Co., 517 F.2d 714 (5th Cir. 1975), *cert. denied*, 424 U.S. 943 (1976), 228, 229, 413, 414, 415, 419

International Ass'n of Heat & Frost Insulators v. United Contractors Ass'n, 483 F.2d 384 (3d Cir. 1973), *modified*, 494 F.2d 1353 (3d Cir. 1974), 648

International Ass'n of Machinists & Aerospace Workers (IAM) v. Organization of Petroleum Exporting Countries (OPEC), 477 F. Supp. 553 (C.D. Cal. 1979), *aff'd*, 649 F.2d 1354 (9th Cir. 1981), *cert. denied*, 454 U.S. 1163 (1982), 901

International Ass'n of Machinists & Aerospace Workers (IAM) v. Organization of Petroleum Exporting Countries (OPEC), 649 F.2d 1354 (9th Cir. 1981), *cert. denied*, 454 U.S. 1163 (1982), 902, 903, 904, 907, 908

International Bd. of Teamsters v. ICC, 801 F.2d 1423 (D.C. Cir. 1986), *vacated per curiam*, 818 F.2d 87 (D.C. Cir. 1987), 1144

International Bd. of Teamsters v. ICC, 818 F.2d 87 (D.C. Cir. 1987), 1145

International Boxing Club v. United States, 178 F. Supp. 469 (S.D.N.Y. 1959), 577

International Boxing Club v. United States, 358 U.S. 242 (1959), 169, 199, 205, 213

International Distrib. Centers, Inc. v. Walsh Trucking Co., 812 F.2d 786 (2d Cir.), *cert. denied*, 482 U.S. 915 (1987), 8, 97, 270

International Energy Agency, 26 O.J. Eur. Comm. (No. L 376) 30 (1983), [1982-1985 Transfer Binder] Common Mkt. Rep. (CCH) ¶ 10,563, 937

International Harvester Co., 104 F.T.C. 949 (1984), 469, 472, 484, 487

International Harvester Co. of Am. v. Kentucky, 234 U.S. 216 (1914), 627, 628

International Harvester Co. of Am. v. Missouri, 234 U.S. 199 (1914), 627

International Housing Ltd. v. Rafidain Bank Iraq, 893 F.2d 8 (2d Cir. 1989), 900

International Logistics Group v. Chrysler Corp., 884 F.2d 904 (6th Cir. 1989), *cert. denied*, 110 S. Ct. 1783 (1990), 16-17, 123, 126, 128, 182, 206, 210, 614

International Mfg. Co. v. Landon, Inc., 336 F.2d 723 (9th Cir. 1964), *cert. denied*, 379 U.S. 988 (1965), 137, 834, 837

International Nickel Co. v. Ford Motor Co., 166 F. Supp. 551 (S.D.N.Y. 1958), 805, 837

International Raw Materials, Ltd. v. Stauffer Chem. Co., 716 F. Supp. 188 (E.D. Pa. 1989), *reversed*, 898 F.2d 946 (3d Cir. 1990), 914, 915

International Rys. of Cent. Am. v. United Brands Co., 532 F.2d 231 (2d Cir.), *cert. denied*, 429 U.S. 835 (1976), 190, 245

International Rys. of Cent. Am. v. United Fruit Co., 373 F.2d 408 (2d Cir.), *cert. denied*, 387 U.S. 921 (1967), 702

International Salt Co. v. Ohio Turnpike Comm'n, 392 F.2d 579 (8th Cir.), *cert. dismissed per stipulation*, 393 U.S. 947 (1968), 779

International Salt Co. v. United States, 332 U.S. 392 (1947), 134, 148, 155, 157, 160, 161, 569, 831, 852

International Serv. Indus., 84 F.T.C. 408 (1974), 478

International Shoe Co. v. FTC, 280 U.S. 291 (1930), 313

International Shoe Co. v. Washington, 326 U.S. 310 (1945), 871, 873, 876

International Shoe Mach. Corp. v. United Shoe Mach. Corp., 315 F.2d 449 (1st Cir.), *cert. denied*, 375 U.S. 820 (1963), 777, 779, 780

International Travel Arrangers, Inc. v. Western Airlines, 623 F.2d 1255 (8th Cir.), *cert. denied*, 449 U.S. 1063 (1980), 16, 22, 222, 668, 700, 782, 783, 1023

International Travel Arrangers v. NWA, 723 F. Supp. 141 (D. Minn. 1989), 663

International Travel Arrangers v. NWA, 1990-2 Trade Cas. (CCH) ¶ 69,112 (D. Minn. 1990), 680

International Union, United Auto. Aerospace & Agric. Implement Workers v. Brock, 477 U.S. 274 (1986), 644

International Wood Processors v. Power Dry, Inc., 792 F.2d 416 (4th Cir. 1986), 13, 647, 673, 828, 835

InterNorth, Inc., 106 F.T.C. 312 (1985), 1066

Interphoto Corp. v. Minolta Corp., 295 F. Supp. 711 (S.D.N.Y.), *aff'd per curiam*, 417 F.2d 621 (2d Cir. 1969), 16, 109, 119, 121, 128

Interstate Camera Stores v. E.I. du Pont de Nemours & Co., 1970 Trade Cas. (CCH) ¶ 73,077 (E.D.N.Y., 1970), 191, 192

Interstate Cigar Co. v. Sterling Drug, Inc., 655 F.2d 29 (2d Cir. 1981), 417, 437

Interstate Circuit, Inc. v. United States, 306 U.S. 208 (1939), 5, 6, 9

Interstate Commerce Comm'n v. Big Sky Farmers & Ranchers Mktg. Coop., 451 F.2d 511 (9th Cir. 1971), 1023

Interstate Home Equip. Co., 40 F.T.C. 260 (1945), 483

Interstate Properties v. Pyramid Co., 586 F. Supp. 1160 (S.D.N.Y. 1984), 1008

Iowa v. Scott & Fetzer Co., 1982-2 Trade Cas. (CCH) ¶ 64,873 (S.D. Iowa 1982), 608

Irish Banks' Standing Committee, 29 O.J. EUR. COMM. (No. L 295) 28 (1986), [1985-1988 Transfer Binder] COMMON MKT. REP. (CCH) ¶ 10,829, 936

Irving E. Miller, 94 F.T.C. 1122 (1979), 491

Isaac v. Shell Oil, 83 F.R.D. 428 (E.D. Mich. 1979), 752

Isaksen v. Vermont Castings, Inc., 825 F.2d 1158 (7th Cir. 1987), *cert. denied*, 486 U.S. 1005 (1988), 13, 14, 17, 101, 107, 109, 110, 671, 674, 675

Island Tobacco Co. v. R.J. Reynolds Indus., 513 F. Supp. 726 (D. Haw. 1981), 208, 209, 215, 408

Israel v. Baxter Labs., 466 F.2d 272 (D.C. Cir. 1972), 259, 1006, 1007, 1010

Isra Fruit Ltd. v. Agrexco Agricultural Export Co., 631 F. Supp. 984 (S.D.N.Y. 1986), 898

Istituto Chemioterapico Italiano SpA and Commercial Solvents Corp. v. Commission, Joined Cases 6 and 7/73, [1974] E.C.R. 223, [1974 Transfer Binder] COMMON MKT. REP. (CCH) ¶ 8209, 928, 930

Italian Cast Glass, 23 O.J. EUR. COMM. (No. L 383) 19 (1980), [1978-1981 Transfer Binder] COMMON MKT. REP. (CCH) ¶ 10,285, 932

Italian Flat Glass, Decision 89/93, 32 O.J. EUR. COMM. (No. L 33) 44 (1989), [1989] 1 CEC (CCH) 2077, 951

ITP v. Commission, Case T-76/89 (Ct. First Instance 1991), *appeal filed*, 952, 954

ITT, 104 F.T.C. 280 (1984), 203, 233, 261, 263, 264, 265, 402, 411, 414, 417

ITT Continental Baking Co., 83 F.T.C. 865, *modified*, 83 F.T.C. 1105 (1973), *enforced as modified*, 532 F.2d 207 (2d Cir. 1976), 471, 473

ITT Continental Baking Co. v. FTC, 532 F.2d 207 (2d Cir. 1976), 469, 470, 495

ITT v. AT&T, 444 F. Supp. 1148 (S.D.N.Y. 1978), 776

ITT v. GTE, 449 F. Supp. 1158 (D. Haw. 1978), 276

ITT v. GTE Corp., 351 F. Supp. 1153 (D. Hawaii 1972), *rev'd*, 518 F.2d 913 (9th Cir. 1975), 550

ITT v. GTE Corp., 518 F.2d 913 (9th Cir. 1975), 286, 319, 675, 680, 681

ITT v. United Tel. Co., 60 F.R.D. 177 (M.D. Fla. 1973), 763, 766
ITT v. United Tel. Co., 550 F.2d 287 (5th Cir. 1977), 259
IU Int'l Corp. v. NX Acquisition Corp., 840 F.2d 220 (4th Cir. 1988), 367
Iveco/Ford, 31 O.J. EUR. COMM. (No. L 230) 39 (1988), [1985-1988 Transfer Binder] COMMON
   MKT. REP. (CCH) ¶ 11,013, 937

J

Jack Faucett Assocs. v. AT&T, 1983-1 Trade Cas. (CCH) ¶ 65,285 (D.D.C. 1983), 722, 725
Jack Faucett Assoc. v. AT&T, 1986-1 Trade Cas. (CCH) ¶ 66,904 (D.D.C. 1985), 741, 742
Jack Faucett Assocs. v. AT&T, 744 F.2d 118 (D.C. Cir. 1984), *cert. denied*, 469 U.S. 1196
   (1985), 1011
Jack Kahn Music Co. v. Baldwin Piano & Organ Co., 604 F.2d 755 (2d Cir. 1979), 129, 677, 678
Jack La Lanne Mgmt. Corp., 84 F.T.C. 1139 (1974), 478
Jackshaw Pontiac, Inc. v. Cleveland Press Publishing Co., 102 F.R.D. 183 (N.D. Ohio 1984), 712,
   713, 714, 717, 721, 723
Jackson Dairy v. H.P. Hood & Sons, 596 F.2d 70 (2d Cir. 1979), 366
Jack Walters & Sons Corp. v. Morton Bldg., Inc., 737 F.2d 698 (7th Cir.), *cert. denied*, 469 U.S
   1018 (1984), 51, 105, 108, 111, 137, 138, 142, 156, 163, 849
Jack Winter, Inc. v. Koratron Co., 375 F. Supp. 1 (N.D. Cal. 1974), 809, 814
Jacob Siegel Co. v. FTC, 327 U.S. 608 (1946), 488, 489, 491, 523
Jacobson & Co. v. Armstrong Cork Co., 433 F. Supp. 1210 (S.D.N.Y.), *aff'd*, 548 F.2d 438 (2d
   Cir. 1977), 185
Jacobson & Co. v. Armstrong Cork Co., 548 F.2d 438 (2d Cir. 1977), 677, 678
Jacobs, Visconsi & Jacobs Co. v. City of Lawrence, 927 F.2d 1111 (10th Cir. 1991), 983
Jade Aircraft Sales v. City of Bridgeport, 1990-2 Trade Cas. CCH ¶ 69,225 (D. Conn. 1990), 648
Jaffee v. Horton Memorial Hosp., 680 F. Supp. 125 (S.D.N.Y. 1988), 25
Jamesbury Corp. v. Kitamura Valve Mfg. Co., 484 F. Supp. 533 (S.D. Tex. 1980), 873
James F. Herndon, Jr., 107 F.T.C. 468 (1986), 532
James M. King & Assocs. v. G.D. Van Wagenen Co., 1987-1 Trade Cas. (CCH) ¶ 67,534 (D.
   Minn. 1987), 364
James M. King & Assocs. v. G.D. Van Wagenen Co., 717 F. Supp. 667 (D. Minn. 1989), 1111,
   1117, 1118
James R. Snyder Co. v. Associated Gen. Contractors, 677 F.2d 1111 (6th Cir.), *cert. denied*, 459
   U.S. 1015 (1982), 27
Janel Sales Corp. v. Lanvin Parfums, Inc., 396 F.2d 398 (2d. Cir.), *cert. denied*, 393 U.S. 938
   (1968), 114, 119, 121
Janich Bros. v. American Distilling Co., 570 F.2d 848 (9th Cir. 1977), *cert. denied*, 439 U.S. 829
   (1978), 228, 230, 233, 267, 268
Japan Gas Lighter Ass'n v. Ronson Corp., 257 F. Supp. 219 (D.N.J. 1966), 871
Javelin Corp. v. Uniroyal Corp., 546 F.2d 276 (9th Cir. 1976), *cert. denied*, 431 U.S. 938 (1977),
   700
Jayco Sys. v. Savin Bus. Machs. Corp., 777 F.2d 306 (5th Cir. 1985), *cert. denied*, 479 U.S. 816
   (1986), 123, 210, 648
Jay Norris, Inc., 91 F.T.C. 751 (1978), *enforced as modified*, 598 F.2d 1244 (2d Cir.), *cert.
   denied*, 444 U.S. 980 (1979), 472, 479, 486
Jay Norris, Inc. v. FTC, 598 F.2d 1244 (2d Cir.), *cert. denied*, 444 U.S. 980 (1979), 489, 493
Jays Foods, Inc. v. National Classification Comm., 646 F. Supp. 604 (E.D. Va. 1985), *aff'd*, 801
   F.2d 394 (4th Cir. 1986), 69, 1128

Jaz-Peter, 12 J.O. COMM. EUR. (No. L 195) 5 (1969), [1965-1969 Transfer Binder] COMMON MKT. REP. (CCH) ¶ 9317, *exemption renewed*, 20 O.J. EUR. COMM. (No. L 61) 17 (1977), [1976-1978 Transfer Binder] COMMON MKT. REP. (CCH) ¶ 10,013, 934

JBL Enters. v. Jhirmack Enters., 509 F. Supp. 357 (N.D. Cal. 1981), *aff'd*, 698 F.2d 1011 (9th Cir.), *cert. denied*, 464 U.S. 829 (1983), 152

JBL Enters. v. Jhirmack Enters., 519 F. Supp. 1084 (N.D. Cal. 1981), *aff'd*, 698 F.2d 1011 (9th Cir.), *cert. denied*, 464 U.S. 829 (1983), 135, 141, 154

JBL Enters. v. Jhirmack Enters., 698 F.2d 1011 (9th Cir.), *cert. denied*, 464 U.S. 829 (1983), 123, 124, 125, 126, 207

J.B. Lippincott Co. v. FTC, 137 F.2d 490 (3d Cir. 1943), 522

J.B. Williams Co., 81 F.T.C. 238 (1972), 474

J.B. Williams Co. v. FTC, 381 F.2d 884 (6th Cir. 1967), 491

J.C. Penney Co., 109 F.T.C. 54 (1987), 532, 533

Jeanery, Inc. v. James Jeans, Inc., 849 F.2d 1148 (9th Cir. 1988), 15, 33, 54, 106, 107, 109, 181, 189

Jefferson County Pharmaceutical Ass'n v. Abbott Labs, 460 U.S. 150 (1983), 449

Jefferson Disposal Co. v. Parish of Jefferson, 603 F. Supp. 1125 (E.D. La. 1985), 35, 988

Jefferson Parish Hosp. Dist. No. 2 v. Hyde, 466 U.S. 2 (1984), 33, 34, 35, 37, 44, 50, 56, 93, 133, 134, 135, 136, 137, 143, 145, 150, 151, 154, 155, 157, 161, 163, 170, 171, 172, 173, 177, 214, 331, 801, 802, 813, 815, 830, 831, 832

Jefferson v. H.K. Porter Co., 485 F. Supp. 356 (N.D. Ala. 1980), *aff'd on other grounds*, 648 F.2d 337 (5th Cir. 1981), 697

Jenco v. Martech Int'l, Inc., Civ. No. 86-4229 (E.D. La. May 20, 1988), 885

Jennings Oil Co. v. Mobil Oil Corp., 80 F.R.D. 124 (S.D.N.Y. 1978), 715, 728, 735

Jerome Milton, Inc., 110 F.T.C. 104 (1987), 473

Jerrold Elecs. Corp. v. Westcoast Broadcasting Co., 341 F.2d 653 (9th Cir.), *cert. denied*, 382 U.S. 817 (1965), 160, 179

Jeter v. Credit Bureau, 754 F.2d 907 (11th Cir.), *on rehearing,* 760 F.2d 1168, (11th Cir. 1985), 533

Jewish Hosp. Ass'n v. Stewart Mech. Enters., 628 F.2d 971 (6th Cir. 1980), *cert. denied*, 450 U.S. 966 (1981), 656, 657

J.F. Feeser, Inc. v. Serv-A-Portion, Inc., 909 F.2d 1524 (3d Cir. 1990), *cert. denied*, 111 S. Ct. 1313 (1991), 413, 416

J.H. Filbert, 54 F.T.C. 359 (1957), 404

J.H. Rose Truck Lines, 110 M.C.C. 180 (1969), 1127

J.H. Westerbeke Corp. v. Onan Corp., 580 F. Supp. 1173 (D. Mass. 1984), 179, 184, 203, 245

Jicarilla Apache Tribe v. Supron Energy Corp., 728 F.2d 1555 (10th Cir. 1984), *aff'd in part and rev'd in part per curiam*, 782 F.2d 855 (10th Cir.) (en banc), *supplemented*, 793 F.2d 1171 (10th Cir.) (en banc), *cert. denied*, 479 U.S. 970 (1986), 393, 395, 398

Jim Walter Corp., 90 F.T.C. 671 (1977), *vacated and remanded*, 625 F.2d 676 (5th Cir. 1980), 309

Jim Walter Corp. v. FTC, 625 F.2d 676 (5th Cir. 1980), 211, 293

Jiminez v. Aristequieta, 311 F.2d 547 (5th Cir. 1962), *cert. denied*, 373 U.S. 914 (1963), 906

Jiricko v. Coffeyville Mem. Hosp. Medical Center, 628 F. Supp. 329 (D. Kan. 1985), 971

Jiricko v. Coffeyville Mem. Hosp. Medical Center, 700 F. Supp. 1559 (D. Kan. 1988), 974

J. Merrell Redding, 14 F.T.C. 32 (1930), 477

J.M. Sanders Jewelry Co., 85 F.T.C. 250 (1975), 534

J.M. Woodhull, Inc. v. Addressograph-Multigraph Corp., 62 F.R.D. 58 (S.D. Ohio 1974), 718, 723, 732, 733

Joe Regueira, Inc. v. American Distilling Co., 642 F.2d 826 (5th Cir. 1981), 130, 184

Joe Westbrook v. Chrysler Corp., 419 F. Supp. 824 (N.D. Ga. 1976), 141

John B. Hull, Inc. v. Waterbury Petroleum Prods., 588 F.2d 24 (2d Cir.), *cert. denied*, 440 U.S. 960 (1979), 676

John B. Hull, Inc. v. Waterbury Petroleum Prods., 845 F.2d 1172 (2d Cir. 1988), 769, 720

John Lenore & Co. v. Olympia Brewing Co., 550 F.2d 495 (9th Cir. 1977), 364

John Peterson Motors, Inc. v. General Motors Corp., 613 F. Supp. 887 (D. Minn. 1985), 438

Johnson & Johnson, 23 O.J. EUR. COMM. (No. L 377) 16 (1980), [1978-1981 Transfer Binder] COMMON MKT. REP. (CCH) ¶ 10,277, 922

Johnson Prods. Co., 87 F.T.C. 206 (1976), *modified*, 91 F.T.C. 506 (1978), 491

Johnson Prods. Co. v. FTC, 549 F.2d 35 (7th Cir. 1977), 515

Johnson Prods. Co. v. M/V La Molinera, 619 F. Supp. 764 (S.D.N.Y. 1985), 1157

Johnson v. Blue Cross/Blue Shield, 677 F. Supp. 1112 (D.N.M. 1987), 50

Johnson v. Georgia Highway Express, 488 F.2d 714 (5th Cir. 1974), 782, 784

Johnson v. Nationwide Indus., 715 F.2d 1233 (7th Cir. 1983), 138

Johnson v. United States, 32 F.2d 127 (8th Cir. 1929), 599

John Surrey, Ltd., 67 F.T.C. 299 (1965), 475

John Wright & Assocs. v. Ullrich, 328 F.2d 474 (8th Cir. 1964), 220

Jones Knitting Corp. v. Morgan, 244 F. Supp. 235 (E.D. Pa. 1965), *rev'd*, 361 F.2d 451 (3d Cir. 1966), 81

Jones Knitting Corp. v. Morgan, 361 F.2d 451 (3d Cir. 1966), 839

Jones v. 247 East Chestnut Properties, 1975-2 Trade Cas. (CCH) ¶ 60,491 (N.D. Ill. 1974), 133, 138

Jones v. Borden Co., 430 F.2d 568 (5th Cir. 1970), 418

Jones v. Central Soya Co., 748 F.2d 586 (11th Cir. 1984), 784

Jones v. Holy Cross Hosp., 64 F.R.D. 586 (D. Md. 1974), 695

Jones v. Metzger Dairies, 334 F.2d 914 (9th Cir. 1964), *cert. denied*, 379 U.S. 965 (1965), 430

Joseph A. Kaplan & Sons, 63 F.T.C. 1308 (1963), *aff'd and modified*, 347 F.2d 785 (D.C. Cir. 1965), 427, 438

Joseph A. Kaplan & Sons v. FTC, 347 F.2d 785 (D.C. Cir. 1965), 489, 494

Joseph Ciccone & Sons v. Eastern Indus., 537 F. Supp. 623 (E.D. Pa. 1982), 316

Joseph E. Seagram & Sons v. Hawaiian Oke & Liquors, Ltd., 416 F.2d 71 (9th Cir. 1969), *cert. denied*, 396 U.S. 1062 (1970), 118, 188, 193, 674

Joseph E. Seagram & Sons v. Hostetter, 384 U.S. 35 (1966), 628

Joseph Muller Corp. Zurich v. Societe Anonyme de Gerance et D'Armement, 451 F.2d 727 (2d Cir. 1971), *cert. denied*, 406 U.S. 906 (1972), 860

Joyce Beverages, Inc. v. Royal Crown Cola Co., 555 F. Supp. 271 (S.D.N.Y. 1983), 179

J.P. Mascaro & Sons v. William J. O'Hara, Inc., 565 F.2d 264 (3d Cir. 1977), 27, 28

J.P. Morgan & Co., 68 Fed. Res. Bull. 514 (1982), 1105

J.P. Stevens & Co. v. Lex Tex Ltd., 747 F.2d 1553, (Fed. Cir. 1984) *cert. denied*, 474 U.S. 822 (1985), 807, 809, 810

J. Truett Payne Co. v. Chrysler Motors Corp., 451 U.S. 557 (1981), 449, 450, 665, 667, 668

Judd v. First Fed. Sav. & Loan Ass'n, 599 F.2d 820 (7th Cir. 1979), 738

Julius Nasso Concrete Corp. v. DIC Concrete Corp., 467 F. Supp. 1016 (S.D.N.Y. 1979), 655

Juneau Square Corp. v. First Wis. Nat'l Bank, 435 F. Supp. 1307 (E.D. Wis. 1977), *aff'd*, 624 F.2d 798 (7th Cir.), *cert. denied*, 449 U.S. 1013 (1980), 782

Juneau Square Corp. v. First Wis. Nat'l Bank, 624 F.2d 798 (7th Cir.), *cert. denied*, 449 U.S. 1013 (1980), 38, 97, 188, 215

Junghans, 20 O.J. EUR. COMM. (No. L 30) 10 (1977), [1976-1978 Transfer Binder] COMMON MKT. REP. (CCH) ¶ 9912, 930, 941, 942

Justice v. NCAA, 577 F. Supp. 356 (D. Ariz. 1983), 24, 87, 90

Juvenile Shoe Co. v. FTC, 289 F. 57 (9th Cir.), *cert. denied*, 263 U.S. 705 (1923), 477

J.W. Burress, Inc. v. JLG Indus., 491 F. Supp. 15 (W.D. Va. 1980), 407

J. Weingarten, Inc., 62 F.T.C. 1521 (1963), 442

J.W. Woodruff, Jr., 39 F.C.C.2d 487 (1973), 1039

K

Kabelmetal-Luchaire, 18 O.J. Eur. Comm. (No. L 222) 34 (1975), [1973-1975 Transfer Binder] Common Mkt. Rep. (CCH) ¶ 9761, 929, 930, 949

Kadwell v. United States, 315 F.2d 667 (9th Cir. 1963), 582

Kaiser Aluminum & Chem. Corp., 93 F.T.C. 764 (1979), *vacated and remanded on other grounds*, 652 F.2d 1324 (7th Cir. 1981), 209, 211

Kaiser Aluminum & Chem. Corp. v. FTC, 652 F.2d 1324 (7th Cir. 1981), 203, 283, 288, 317

Kaiser Aluminum. & Chem. Sales, Inc. v. Avondale Shipyards, 677 F.2d 1045 (5th Cir. 1982), *cert. denied*, 459 U.S. 1105 (1983), 681, 693, 791

Kaiser Cement Corp. v. Fishbach & Moore, Inc., 793 F.2d 1100 (9th Cir.), *cert. denied*, 479 U.S. 949 (1986), 647

Kaiser Indus. v. Jones & Laughlin Steel Corp., 181 U.S.P.Q. (BNA) 193 (W.D. Pa. 1974), *rev'd*, 515 F.2d 964 (3d Cir.), *cert. denied*, 423 U.S. 876 (1975), 838

Kaiser Steel Corp. v. Mullins, 455 U.S. 72 (1982), 791, 792, 1122

Kaiser v. Dialist Co., 603 F. Supp. 110 (W.D. Pa. 1984), 542

Kaiser v. General Motors Corp., 396 F. Supp. 33 (E.D. Pa. 1975), *aff'd per curiam*, 530 F.2d 964 (3d Cir. 1976), 129, 130

Kalamanovitz v. G. Heileman Brewing Co., 769 F.2d 152 (3d Cir. 1985), 30

Kalamazoo Spice Extraction Co. v. Provisional Military Gov't of Socialist Ethiopia, 616 F. Supp. 660 (W.D. Mich. 1985), 871, 873, 876

Kali und Salz AG v. Commission, Joined Cases 19 and 20/74, [1975] E.C.R. 499, [1975 Transfer Binder] Common Mkt. Rep. (CCH) ¶ 8284, 933

Kallen v. Nexus Corp., 353 F. Supp. 33 (N.D. Ill. 1973), 29

Kalmanovitz v. G. Heileman Brewing Co., 595 F. Supp. 1385 (D. Del. 1984), *aff'd*, 769 F.2d 152 (3d Cir. 1985), 365

Kamm v. California City Dev. Co., 509 F.2d 205 (9th Cir. 1975), 729, 731

K & R Leasing Corp. v. General Motors Corp., 551 F. Supp. 842 (N.D. Ill. 1982), 655

Kane v. Martin Paint Stores, 1974-2 Trade Cas. (CCH) ¶ 75,296 (S.D.N.Y. 1974), 402, 403

Kane v. Martin Paint Stores, 439 F. Supp. 1054 (S.D.N.Y. 1977), *aff'd*, 578 F.2d 1368 (2d Cir. 1978), 783

Kansas City Power & Light Co., 53 F.E.R.C. (CCH) ¶ 61,097 (1990), 1975, 1076

Kansas City S. Indus. v. ICC, 902 F.2d 423 (5th Cir. 1990), 1142

Kansas City Star Co. v. United States, 240 F.2d 643 (8th Cir.), *cert. denied*, 354 U.S. 923 (1957), 201, 584, 585

Kansas City v. Federal Pac. Elec. Co., 310 F.2d 271 (8th Cir.), *cert. denied*, 371 U.S. 912 (1962) and 373 U.S. 914 (1963), 688, 689

Kansas *ex rel.* Stephan v. Lamb, 1987-1 Trade Cas. (CCH) ¶ 67,521 (D. Kan. 1987), 973

Kansas Gas & Elec. Co., 10 F.E.R.C. (CCH) ¶ 61,243 (1980), 1071

Kansas v. Utilicorp United, Inc., 110 S. Ct. 2807 (1990), 607, 656, 1062, 1063, 1064

Kaplan v. Burroughs Corp., 611 F.2d 286 (9th Cir. 1979), *cert. denied*, 447 U.S. 924 (1980), 45, 50, 55

Kaplan v. Clear Lake City Water Auth., 794 F.2d 1059 (5th Cir. 1986), 988

Kaplan v. Lehman Bros., 371 F.2d 409 (7th Cir.), *cert. denied*, 389 U.S. 954 (1967), 1102

Kapp v. NFL, 390 F. Supp. 73 (N.D. Cal. 1974), *vacated in part*, 1975-2 Trade Cas. (CCH) ¶ 60,543 (N.D. Cal. 1975), *aff'd*, 586 F.2d 644 (9th Cir. 1978), *cert. denied*, 441 U.S. 907 (1979), 91, 92, 702

Karlinsky v. New York Racing Ass'n, 517 F.2d 1010 (2d Cir. 1975), 209

Karsten Manufacturing Corp. v. United States Golf Ass'n, 1990-1 Trade Cas. (CCH) ¶ 68,965 (D. Ariz. 1990), 874

Kartell v. Blue Shield, 749 F.2d 922 (1st Cir. 1984), *cert. denied*, 471 U.S. 1029 (1985), 39, 48, 53, 115, 659

Kaspar Wire Works, Inc. v. Leco Eng'g & Mach., Inc., 575 F.2d 530 (5th Cir. 1978), 836

Kastigar v. United States, 406 U.S. 441 (1972), 591, 771

Katherine Gibbs School, Inc. v. FTC, 612 F.2d 658 (2d Cir.), reh'g denied, 628 F.2d 755 (2d Cir. 1979), 530

Katt v. Village of Sturtevant, 269 Wis. 638, 70 N.W.2d 188 (1955), 627

Katz v. Carte Blanche Corp., 496 F.2d 747 (3d Cir.), cert. denied, 419 U.S. 885 (1974), 725, 729

Kauffman v. Dreyfus Fund, Inc., 434 F.2d 727 (3d Cir. 1970), cert. denied, 401 U.S. 974 (1971), 644

Kaw Valley Elec. Coop. Co. v. Kansas Elec. Power Coop., 872 F.2d 931 (10th Cir. 1989), 681

KBLU Broadcasting Corp., 42 F.C.C.2d 450 (1973), 1039

Kearney & Trecker Corp. v. Cincinnati Milacron, Inc., 562 F.2d 365 (6th Cir. 1977), 809, 811, 813

Kearney & Trecker Corp. v. Giddings & Lewis, Inc., 306 F. Supp. 189 (E.D. Wis. 1969), rev'd, 452 F.2d 579 (7th Cir. 1971), cert. denied, 405 U.S. 1066 (1972), 824

Kearney & Trecker Corp. v. Giddings & Lewis, Inc., 452 F.2d 579 (7th Cir. 1971), cert. denied, 405 U.S. 1066 (1972), 813

Kearuth Theatres Corp. v. Paramount Pictures, Inc., 1956 Trade Cas. (CCH) ¶ 68,574 (S.D.N.Y. 1956), 408

Keele Hair & Scalp Specialists, Inc. v. FTC, 275 F.2d 18 (5th Cir. 1960), 491

Keener v. Sizzler Family Steak Houses, 597 F.2d 453 (5th Cir. 1979), 132, 674

Keeton v. Hustler Magazine, Inc., 465 U.S. 770 (1984), 873, 874, 875

Kelco Disposal, Inc. v. Browning-Ferris Indus., 845 F.2d 404 (2d Cir. 1988), aff'd on other grounds, 492 U.S. 257 (1989), 228, 229, 234, 235, 264, 266

Kelcor Corp., 93 F.T.C. 9 (1979), 534

Kellam Energy, Inc. v. Duncan, 616 F. Supp. 215 (D. Del. 1985), 282, 745, 748

Kellam Energy, Inc. v. Duncan, 668 F. Supp. 861 (D. Del. 1987), 103, 109, 144, 145, 147, 169, 172, 208

Kellogg Co., 92 F.T.C. 351 (1978), modified, No. 8883, slip. op. (FTC Nov. 16, 1979), 513

Kellogg Co., 99 F.T.C. 8 (1982), 463

Kellogg Co. v. FTC, 1980-81 Trade Cas. (CCH) ¶ 63,811 (D.D.C. 1981), 523

Kellogg Co. v. National Biscuit Co., 71 F.2d 662 (2d Cir. 1934), 811, 812, 848

Kelly v. General Motors Corp., 425. Supp. 13 (E.D. Pa. 1976), 728

Kelly v. Kosuga, 358 U.S. 516 (1959), 791, 816

Kem-Tech, Inc. v. Mobil Corp., 1986-1 Trade Cas. (CCH) ¶ 66,947 (E.D. Pa. 1985), 408, 435, 437

Kendall Elevator Co. v. LBC&W Assocs., 350 F. Supp. 75 (D.S.C. 1972), 185, 192

Kendler v. Federated Dep't Stores, 88 F.R.D. 688 (S.D.N.Y. 1981), 717, 721, 726

Kenett Corp. v. Massachusetts Furn. & Piano Movers Ass'n, 101 F.R.D. 313 (D. Mass. 1984), 725, 727

Kennecott Copper Corp. v. Curtiss-Wright Corp., 449 F. Supp. 951 (S.D.N.Y.), aff'd in part and rev'd in part and remanded in part, 584 F.2d 1195 (2d Cir. 1978), 359, 363

Kennecott Copper Corp. v. Curtiss-Wright Corp., 584 F.2d 1195 (2d Cir. 1978), 363, 397, 398

Kennecott Copper Corp. v. FTC, 467 F.2d 67 (10th Cir. 1972), cert. denied, 416 U.S. 909 (1974), 284, 289, 334

Kennedy Theater Ticket Serv. v. Ticketron, Inc., 342 F. Supp. 922 (E.D. Pa. 1972), 408

Kentucky Fried Chicken Corp. v. Diversified Packaging Corp., 376 F. Supp. 1136 (S.D. Fla. 1974), aff'd, 549 F.2d 368 (5th Cir. 1977), 146, 161

Kentucky Fried Chicken Corp. v. Diversified Packaging Corp., 549 F.2d 368 (5th Cir. 1977), 35, 41, 132, 160

Kentucky Rural Elec. Coop. Corp. v. Moloney Elec. Co., 232 F.2d 481 (6th Cir. 1960), cert. denied, 365 U.S. 812 (1961), 448

Kentucky v. Southern Belle Dairy Co., No. 90-46 (E. D. Ky. filed Mar. 19, 1990), 605

Kentucky-Tennessee Light & Power & Co. v. Nashville Coal Co., 37 F. Supp. 728 (W.D. Ky. 1941), aff'd sub nom. Fitch v. Kentucky-Tennessee Light & Power Co., 136 F.2d 12 (6th Cir. 1943), 404, 435

Kenworth of Boston, Inc. v. Paccar Fin. Corp., 735 F.2d 622 (1st Cir. 1984), 151, 676, 678

Keogh v. Chicago & Northwestern Ry, 260 U.S. 156 (1922), 239, 1019-20, 1129, 1160

Kerasotes Mich. Theatres v. National Amusements, Inc., 854 F.2d 135 (6th Cir. 1988), cert. dismissed sub nom. G.K.C. Mich. Theatres v. National Amusements, Inc., 490 U.S. 1087 (1989), 251

Kern-Tulare Water Dist. v. City of Bakersfield, 828 F.2d 514 (9th Cir. 1987), cert. denied, 486 U.S. 1015 (1988), 985

Kern-Tulare Water Dist. v. City of Bakersfield, 486 U.S. 1015 (1988), 985

Kerran v. FTC, 265 F.2d 246 (10th Cir.), cert. denied, 361 U.S. 818 (1959), 465, 473

Kestenbaum v. Falstaff Brewing Corp., 514 F.2d 690 (5th Cir. 1975), cert. denied, 424 U.S. 943 (1976), 109, 671, 698, 700

Kestenbaum v. Falstaff Brewing Corp., 575 F.2d 564 (5th Cir.), cert. denied, 440 U.S. 909 (1978), 47, 48, 49, 53, 104, 130, 131, 670, 672, 674

Kewanee Oil Co. v. Bicron Corp., 416 U.S. 470 (1974), 621, 799, 844, 849

Key Bancshares, Inc., 71 Fed. Res. Bull. 965 (1985), 1094

Key Enters. v. Venice Hosp., 919 F.2d 1550 (11th Cir. 1990), 3, 4, 7, 168, 223, 252, 263, 266, 272

Key Fin. Planning Corp. v. ITT Life Ins. Corp., 828 F.2d 635 (10th Cir. 1987), 37, 49, 180, 197, 199, 206, 706, 707

Keystone Driller Co. v. General Excavator Co., 290 U.S. 240 (1933), 813

Keystone Resources v. AT&T, 646 F. Supp. 1355 (W.D. Pa. 1986), aff'd, 826 F.2d 1056 (3d Cir. 1987), 687

Key v. Gillette Co., 782 F.2d 5 (1st Cir. 1986), 737

KFC Corp. v. Marion-Kay Co., 620 F. Supp. 1160 (S.D. Ind. 1985), 142, 682

Kian v. Mirro Alum. Co., 88 F.R.D. 351 (E.D. Mich. 1980), 773

Kiefer-Stewart Co. v. Joseph E. Seagram & Sons, 340 U.S. 211 (1951), 18, 66, 103, 104, 701

Kimberly-Clark Corp. v. Johnson & Johnson, 745 F.2d 1437 (Fed. Cir. 1984), 807, 810

Kimmelman v. Henkels & McCoy, Inc., 1987-2 Trade Cas. (CCH) ¶ 67,674 (N.J. Super. Ct. 1987), 611

King & King Enters. v. Champlin Petroleum Co., 446 F. Supp. 906 (E.D. Okla. 1978), 689, 690

King & King Enters. v. Champlin Petroleum Co., 657 F.2d 1147 (10th Cir. 1981), cert. denied, 454 U.S. 1164 (1982), 72, 692

Kingsdown Medical Consultants v. Hollister Inc., 863 F.2d 867 (Fed. Cir. 1988), cert. denied, 490 U.S. 1067 (1989), 807

Kingsland v. Dorsey, 338 U.S. 318 (1949), 810

King v. Gulf Oil Co., 581 F.2d 1184 (5th Cir. 1978), 735

King v. Idaho Funeral Serv. Ass'n, 862 F.2d 744 (9th Cir. 1988), 992

Kinnett Dairies v. Dairymen, Inc., 512 F. Supp. 608 (M.D. Ga. 1981), aff'd per curiam, 715 F.2d 520 (11th Cir. 1983), cert. denied, 465 U.S. 1051 (1984), 1026

Kipperman v. Academy Life Ins. Co., 554 F.2d 377 (9th Cir. 1977), 542

Kirby v. P. R. Mallory & Co., 489 F.2d 904 (7th Cir. 1973), cert. denied, 417 U.S. 911 (1974), 437, 441

Kirkpatrick v. J.C. Bradford & Co., 827 F.2d 718 (11th Cir. 1987), 716

Kistler Instrumente, AG v. PCB Piezotronics, Inc., 1983-1 Trade Cas. (CCH) ¶ 65,449 (W.D.N.Y. 1983), 774

Kitsap Physicians Serv. v. Washington Dental Serv., 671 F. Supp. 1267 (W.D. Wash. 1987), 93

Klamath-Lake Pharmaceutical Ass'n v. Klamath Medical Serv. Bureau, 701 F.2d 1276 (9th Cir.), cert. denied, 464 U.S. 822 (1983), 444, 1110, 1113, 1115

Klaus Höfner and Fritz Elser v. Macrotron, GmbH, Case C-41/90, (Eur. Comm. Ct. J. 1991), 924

Klein v. American Luggage Works, 323 F.2d 787 (3d Cir. 1963), 107, 108

Klein v. Henry S. Miller Residential Serv., 94 F.R.D. 651 (N.D. Tex. 1982), 715, 716, 722, 724, 725, 727, 734, 735

Klein v. Lionel Corp., 138 F. Supp. 560 (D. Del.), *aff'd*, 237 F.2d 13 (3d Cir. 1956), 430

Kline v. Coldwell, Banker & Co., 508 F.2d 226 (9th Cir. 1974), *cert. denied*, 421 U.S. 963 (1975), 715, 726, 732, 736

Klinger Volkswagen, Inc. v. Chrysler Corp., 583 F.2d 910 (7th Cir.), *cert. denied*, 439 U.S. 1004 (1978), 45

Kling v. St. Paul Fire & Marine Ins. Co., 626 F. Supp. 1285 (C.D. Ill. 1986), 25, 30

Klor's, Inc. v. Broadway-Hale Stores, 359 U.S. 207 (1959), 61, 78, 79, 80

Klo-Zik Co. v. General Motors Corp., 677 F. Supp. 499 (E.D. Tex. 1987), 135, 136, 139, 145, 148, 154, 155, 159, 163

K-Mart Corp. v. Cartier, Inc., 486 U.S. 281 (1988), 843

K-91, Inc. v. Gershwin Publishing Corp., 372 F.2d 1 (9th Cir. 1967), *cert. denied*, 389 U.S. 1045 (1968), 846

Knoll Assocs., 70 F.T.C. 311 (1966), *vacated and remanded*, 397 F.2d 530 (7th Cir. 1968), 441

Knoll Assocs. v. FTC, 397 F.2d 530 (7th Cir. 1968), 506

Knudsen Corp. v. Nevada State Dairy Comm'n, 676 F.2d 374 (9th Cir. 1982), 678

Knuth v. Erie-Crawford Dairy Coop., 395 F.2d 420 (3d Cir. 1968), *appeal after remand*, 463 F.2d 470 (3d Cir. 1972), *cert. denied*, 410 U.S. 913 (1973), 1026

Knutson v. Daily Review, Inc., 468 F. Supp. 226 (N.D. Cal. 1979), *aff'd*, 664 F.2d 1120 (9th Cir. 1981), 104, 784

Knutson v. Daily Review, 479 F. Supp. 1263 (N.D. Cal. 1979), 783, 785

Knutson v. Daily Review, Inc., 548 F.2d 795 (9th Cir 1976), *cert. denied*, 433 U.S. 910 (1977), 45, 49, 104, 107, 109, 118, 130, 188, 191, 647, 672

Kobe, Inc. v. Dempsey Pump Co., 198 F.2d 416 (10th Cir.), *cert. denied*, 344 U.S. 837 (1952), 803, 812

Koblar Constrs. & Engs. v. G.H. Dacy Assocs., 1987-2 Trade Cas. (CCH) ¶ 67,665, (N.D. Fla. 1987), 407

Kodak, 13 J.O. COMM. EUR. (No. L 147) 24 (1970), [1970-1972 Transfer Binder] COMMON MKT. REP. (CCH) ¶ 9378, 940

Koefoot v. American College of Surgeons, 652 F. Supp. 882 (N.D. Ill. 1987), 93

Koerner & Assocs. v. Aspen Labs, 492 F. Supp. 294 (S.D. Tex. 1980), *aff'd without published opinion*, No. 80-1852 (5th Cir. 1982), 439

Kohler Co. v. Briggs & Stratton Corp., 1986-1 Trade Cas. (CCH) ¶ 67,047 (E.D. Wis. 1986), 125, 177, 242

Kolene Corp. v. Motor City Metal Treating, Inc., 440 F.2d 77 (6th Cir.), *cert. denied*, 404 U.S. 886 (1971), 814

Koratron Co. v. Lion Uniform, Inc., 409 F. Supp. 1019 (N.D. Cal. 1976), 787, 816

Korber Hats, Inc. v. FTC, 311 F.2d 358 (1st Cir. 1962), 494

Korody-Colyer Corp. v. General Motors Corp., 828 F.2d 1572 (Fed. Cir. 1987), 785, 809, 810, 851

Korwec v. Hunt, 646 F. Supp. 953 (S.D.N.Y. 1986), *aff'd*, 827 F.2d 874 (2d Cir. 1987), 696

Koscot Interplanetary Inc., 86 F.T.C. 1106 (1975), *modified*, 87 F.T.C. 75 (1976), 478

Koufakis v. Carvel, 425 F.2d 892 (2d Cir. 1970), 854

Kowalski v. Chicago Tribune Co., 854 F.2d 168 (7th Cir. 1988), 103, 191, 677, 678

Kraftco Corp., 89 F.T.C. 46, *remanded sub nom.* SCM Corp. v. FTC, 565 F.2d 807 (2d Cir. 1977), cert. denied, 449 U.S. 821 (1980), 393, 396

Kraft, Inc., 5 TRADE REG. REP. (CCH) ¶ 22,937 (Jan. 31, 1991), 470, 471, 472

Kraft-Phenix Cheese Corp., 25 F.T.C. 537 (1937), 429

Kramer Motors, Inc. v. British Leyland, Ltd., 628 F.2d 1175 (9th Cir. 1980), *cert. denied*, 449 U.S. 1062 (1981), 873

Krampe v. Ideal Indus., 347 F. Supp. 1384 (N.D. Ill. 1972), 828

Krause v. General Motors Corp., 1988-2 Trade Cas. (CCH) ¶ 68,163 (E.D. Mich. 1988), 139, 408

Kreepy Krauly U.S.A., Inc., FTC File No. 901-0089 (Jan. 10, 1991), 101, 107

Krehl v. Baskin-Robbins Ice Cream Co., 78 F.R.D. 108 (C.D. Cal. 1978), 717, 728, 727, 730

Krehl v. Baskin-Robbins Ice Cream Co., 664 F.2d 1348 (9th Cir. 1982), 38, 73, 123, 124, 126, 128, 129, 136, 141, 144, 161, 849

Kremp v. Dobbs, 775 F.2d 1319 (5th Cir. 1985), 647

Kresl Power Equip. v. Acco Indus., 1980-2 Trade Cas. (CCH) ¶ 63,554 (N.D. Ill. 1980), 191

Kreuzer v. American Academy of Periodontology, 735 F.2d 1479 (D.C. Cir. 1984), 7, 35, 40, 55, 56, 78, 85, 86, 92

Kroger Co. v. FTC, 438 F.2d 1372 (6th Cir.), cert. denied, 404 U.S. 871 (1971), 416, 448

Krug v. ITT, 142 F. Supp. 230 (D.N.J. 1956), 430

KSB/Goulds/Lowara/ITT, Decision 91/38, 34 O.J. EUR. COMM. (No. L 19) 25 (1991), [1991] 1 CEC (CCH) 2009, 935

KSL, Inc., 39 RAD. REG. 2d (P&F) 249 (1976), 1038

Kuck v. Bensen, 647 F. Supp. 743 (D. Me. 1986), 173

Kugler v. AAMCO Automatic Transmissions, Inc., 337 F. Supp. 872 (D. Minn. 1971), aff'd, 460 F.2d 1214 (8th Cir. 1972), 137

Kugler v. AAMCO Automatic Transmissions, Inc., 460 F.2d 1214 (8th Cir. 1972), 131, 141

Kunc v. ARA Servs., 414 F. Supp. 809 (W.D. Okla. 1976), 779

Kurek v. Pleasure Driveway & Park Dist., 557 F.2d 580 (7th Cir. 1977), vacated, 435 U.S. 992 (1978), 982

Kusan, Inc. v. Puritan Mills, Inc., 693 F. Supp. 1118 (N.D. Ga. 1987), 792

KWF Indus. v. AT&T, 592 F. Supp. 795 (D.D.C. 1984), 687

Kypta v. McDonald's Corp., 671 F.2d 1282 (11th Cir.), cert. denied, 459 U.S. 857 (1982), 670

L

L.A. Draper & Son v. Wheelabrator-Frye, Inc., 735 F.2d 414 (11th Cir. 1984), 45, 49, 97, 98

Lady Sarah McKinney-Smith and J. Shelby McCallum, 59 F.C.C.2d 398 (1976), 1039

Lafayette Steel Co. v. National Steel Corp., 87 F.R.D. 612 (E. Mich. 1980), 181

Laidlaw Acquisition Corp. v. Mayflower Group, 636 F. Supp. 1513 (S.D. Ind. 1986), 289, 292, 294, 297, 305, 308, 309, 363, 365, 367, 368, 369

Laidlaw Waste Sys. v. City of Fort Smith, 742 F. Supp. 540 (W.D. Ark. 1990), 984

Laing v. Minnesota Vikings Football Club, 372 F. Supp. 59 (D. Minn. 1973), aff'd, 492 F.2d 1381 (8th Cir.), cert. denied, 419 U.S. 832 (1974), 139

L'Air Liquide, SA, 110 F.T.C. 19 (1988), 345, 347, 348

Laitram Corp. v. Deep South Packing Co., 279 F. Supp. 883 (E.D. La. 1968), 684

Laitram Corp. v. Depoe Bay Fish Co., 549 F. Supp. 29 (D. Or. 1982), 825

Laitram Corp. v. King Crab, Inc., 244 F. Supp. 9 (D. Ala.), modified, 245 F. Supp. 1019 (D. Ala. 1965), 825

Laker Airways v. Pan Am. World Airways, 559 F. Supp. 1124 (D.D.C. 1983), aff'd sub nom.

Laker Airways v. Sabena, Belgian World Airlines, 731 F.2d 909 (D.C. Cir. 1984), 863, 879, 893

Laker Airways v. Pan Am. World Airways, 568 F. Supp. 811 (D.D.C. 1983), 866

Laker Airways v. Pan Am. World Airways, 596 F. Supp. 202 (D.D.C. 1984), 913

Laker Airways v. Pan Am. World Airways, 604 F. Supp. 280 (D.D.C. 1984), 913, 1015

Laker Airways v. Pan Am. World Airways, 607 F. Supp. 324 (S.D.N.Y. 1985), 880

Laker Airways v. Sabena, Belgian World Airlines, 731 F.2d 909 (D.C. Cir. 1984), 861, 863

LaMarca v. Miami Herald Publishing Co., 395 F. Supp. 324 (S.D. Fla.), aff'd without published opinion, 524 F.2d 1230 (5th Cir. 1975), 192

LaMar Printing, Inc. v. Minuteman Press Int'l, Inc., 1981-1 Trade Cas. (CCH) ¶ 64,034 (N.D. Ga. 1981), 407

Lamb Enters. v. Toledo Blade Co., 461 F.2d 506 (6th Cir. 1972), 1053

Lambert Pharmacal Co., 38 F.T.C. 726 (1944), 468

Lamb's Patio Theatre v. Universal Film Exch., 582 F.2d 1068 (7th Cir. 1978), 9, 55, 181

Lamb v. Phillip Morris, Inc., 915 F.2d 1024 (6th Cir. 1990), cert. denied, 111 S. Ct. 961 (1991), 905, 908

Lamb v. Volkswagenwerk Aktiengesellschaft, 104 F.R.D. 95 (S.D. Fla. 1985), 878

Lamoille Valley R.R. v. ICC, 711 F.2d 295 (D.C. Cir. 1983), 1212

Lamp Liquors, Inc. v. Adolph Coors Co., 563 F.2d 425 (10th Cir. 1977), 124, 699

Lancaster Community Hosp. v. Antelope Valley Hosp. Dist., 940 F.2d 397 (9th Cir. 1991), 984, 988

L. & C. Mayers Co. v. FTC, 97 F.2d 365 (2d Cir. 1938), 477

L. & L. Howell, Inc. v. Cincinnati Coop. Milk Sales Ass'n, 1983-2 Trade Cas. (CCH) ¶ 65,595 (6th Cir. 1983), cert. denied, 466 U.S. 904 (1984), 1026, 1027

L & L Oil Co., Inc. v. Murphy Oil Corp., 674 F.2d 1113 (5th Cir. 1982), 403, 404, 407, 438

Landmarks Holding Corp. v. Bermant, 664 F.2d 891 (2d Cir. 1981), 999, 1001

Lang's Bowlarama, Inc. v. AMF, Inc., 1974-2 Trade Cas. (CCH) ¶ 75,158 (D.R.I. 1974), 439

Lang's Bowlarama, Inc. v. AMF, Inc., 377 F. Supp. 405 (D.R.I. 1974), 436

Langston Corp. v. Standard Register Co., 553 F. Supp. 632 (N.D. Ga. 1982), 391

Lanier v. American Bd. of Endodontics, 843 F.2d 901 (6th Cir.), cert. denied, 488 U.S. 926 (1988), 874

Lanzetta v. New Jersey, 306 U.S. 451 (1939), 628

LaPeyre v. FTC, 366 F.2d 117 (5th Cir. 1966), aff'g in part and setting aside in part, Grand Caillou Packing Co., 65 F.T.C. 799 (1964), 815

Larkin Gen. Hosp. v. AT&T, 93 F.R.D. 497 (E.D. Pa. 1982), 739, 740

Larry R. George Sales Co. v. Cool Attic Corp., 587 F.2d 266 (5th Cir. 1979), 431

Larry V. Muko, Inc. v. Southwestern Pa. Bldg. & Constr. Trades Council, 609 F.2d 1368 (3d Cir. 1979), appeal after remand, 670 F.2d 431 (3d Cir.), cert. denied, 459 U.S. 916 (1982), 1121

Larry V. Muko, Inc. v. Southwestern Pa. Bldg. & Constr. Trades Council, 670 F.2d 421 (3d Cir.), cert. denied, 459 U.S. 916 (1982), 35, 38, 85, 86

La Salle Extension Univ., 78 F.T.C. 1272 (1971), 477, 478

La Salle St. Press, Inc. v. McCormick & Henderson, Inc., 293 F. Supp. 1004 (N.D. Ill. 1968), modified, 445 F.2d 84 (7th Cir. 1971), 408, 409, 825

La Salle St. Press, Inc. v. McCormick & Henderson, Inc., 445 F.2d 84 (7th Cir. 1971), 824

LaSalvia v. United Dairymen, 804 F.2d 1113 (9th Cir. 1986), cert. denied, 482 U.S. 928 (1987), 682, 1026

Las Animas Ranch, Inc., 9 F.T.C. 255 (1977), 515

Las Vegas Merchant Plumbers Ass'n v. United States, 210 F.2d 732 (9th Cir.), cert. denied, 348 U.S. 817 (1954), 63, 67

Las Vegas Sun, Inc. v. Summa Corp., 610 F.2d 614 (9th Cir. 1979), cert. denied, 447 U.S. 906 (1980), 17, 185, 385, 398

Lasercomb Am., Inc. v. Reynolds, 911 F.2d 970 (4th Cir. 1990), 816, 845

Lasky v. Continental Prods. Corp., 569 F. Supp. 1227 (E.D. Pa. 1983), 887

Latimer v. S/A Industrias Reunidas F. Matarazzo, 175 F.2d 184 (2d Cir. 1949), cert. denied, 338 U.S. 867 (1949), 874

Laughlin v. Wells, 446 F. Supp. 48 (C.D. Cal. 1978), 661

Laundry Equip. Sales Corp. v. Borg-Warner Corp., 334 F.2d 788 (7th Cir. 1964), 689, 693

Laurel Sand & Gravel, Inc. v. CSX Transp., 704 F. Supp. 1309 (D. Md. 1989), aff'd, 924 F.2d 539 (4th Cir.), cert. denied, 112 S. Ct. 64 (1991), 1140, 1141

Laurel Sand & Gravel, Inc. v. CSX Transp., 924 F.2d 539 (4th Cir.), cert. denied, 112 S. Ct. 64 (1991), 249, 250

Lawson Prods. v. Avnet, Inc., 782 F.2d 1429 (7th Cir. 1986), 677

L.C.L. Theatres v. Columbia Pictures, 421 F. Supp. 1090 (N.D. Tex. 1976), *rev'd in part*, 566 F.2d 494 (5th Cir. 1978), 73

LDPE/PVC, Decision 89/191, 31 O.J. EUR. COMM. (No. L 74) 2 (1989), [1989] 1 CEC (CCH) 2193, 932

Lear, Inc. v. Adkins, 395 U.S. 653 (1969), 835, 845

Leasco Data Processing Equip. Corp. v. Maxwell, 468 F.2d 1326 (2d Cir. 1972), 875

Lease Lights, Inc. v. Public Serv. Co., 849 F.2d 1330 (10th Cir. 1988), *cert. denied*, 488 U.S. 1019 (1989), 972, 975

Lease Lights, Inc. v. Public Serv. Co., 701 F.2d 794 (10th Cir. 1983), 27

Leedom v. Kyne, 358 U.S. 184 (1958), 523

Lee-Moore Oil Co. v. Union Oil Co., 599 F.2d 1299 (4th Cir. 1979), 670

Lee's Prescription Shops, Inc. v. Glaxo Group Ltd., 1977-1 Trade Cas. (CCH) ¶ 61,500 (D.D.C. 1977), 721

Lee v. Lee Custom Eng'g, Inc., 476 F. Supp. 361 (E.D. Wis. 1979), 836

Lee v. Venice Work Vessels, Inc. 512 F.2d 85 (5th Cir. 1975), *cert. denied*, 423 U.S. 1056 (1976), 686, 793

Lefrak v. Arabian Am. Oil Co., 487 F. Supp. 808 (E.D.N.Y. 1980), 656

Legal Clinic of Green & Logan v. Gannett Co., 1984-1 Trade Cas. (CCH) ¶ 65,783 (D. Or. 1983), 731

Lehigh Portland Cement Co., 77 F.T.C. 1638 (1970), 518

Lehrman v. Gulf Oil Corp., 464 F.2d 26 (5th Cir.), *cert. denied*, 409 U.S. 1077 (1972), 27, 28, 109, 111, 402

Lehrman v. Gulf Oil Corp., 500 F.2d 659 (5th Cir. 1974), *cert. denied*, 420 U.S. 929 (1975), 671, 673

Leh v. General Petroleum Corp., 382 U.S. 54 (1965), 684, 685

Leitch Mfg. Co. v. Barber Co., 302 U.S. 458 (1939), 817, 832

Lektro-Vend Corp. v. Vendo Corp., 500 F. Supp. 332 (N.D. Ill. 1980), *aff'd*, 660 F.2d 255 (7th Cir. 1981), *cert. denied*, 455 U.S. 921 (1982), 700

Lektro-Vend Corp. v. Vendo Co., 660 F.2d 255 (7th Cir. 1981) *cert. denied*, 455 U.S. 921 (1992), 39, 45, 98, 99, 265, 305

Lemelson v. Bendix Corp., 104 F.R.D. 13 (D. Del. 1984), 763, 764

Lemelson v. Bendix Corp., 621 F. Supp. 1122 (D. Del. 1985), 4, 81, 84, 839

Lender's Serv. v. Dayton Bar Ass'n, 758 F. Supp. 429 (S.D. Ohio 1991), 974, 980, 1004

Lenox, Inc. v. FTC, 17 F.2d 126 (2d Cir. 1969), 490, 491

Leonard F. Porter, Inc., 88 F.T.C. 546 (1976), 470, 476, 489

Leon A. Tashof, 74 F.T.C. 1361 (1968), *enforced*, 437 F.2d 707 (D.C. Cir. 1970), 469

Leonia Amusement Corp. v. Loew's, Inc., 16 F.R.D. 583 (S.D.N.Y. 1954), 748

Lepore v. New York News, Inc., 346 F. Supp. 755 (S.D.N.Y. 1972), 121

Les Shockley Racing, Inc. v. National Hot Rod Ass'n, 884 F.2d 504 (9th Cir. 1989), 43, 45, 46, 49

Lessig v. Tidewater Oil Co., 327 F.2d 459 (9th Cir.), *cert. denied*, 377 U.S. 993 (1964), 111, 267, 674

Letelier v. Republic of Chile, 488 F. Supp. 665 (D.D.C. 1980), 908

Lever Bros., 50 F.T.C. 494 (1953), 444

Levinson v. Maison Grande, Inc., 517 F. Supp. 963 (S.D. Fla. 1981), 139

Levin v. IBM, 319 F. Supp. 51 (S.D.N.Y. 1970), 679

Levin v. Joint Comm'n on Accreditation of Hosps., 354 F.2d 515 (D.C. Cir. 1965), 703

Levitch v. CBS, 495 F. Supp. 649 (S.D.N.Y. 1980), *aff'd*, 697 F.2d 495 (2d Cir. 1983), 1030

Lewis Serv. Center, Inc. v. Mack Trucks, Inc., 714 F.2d 842 (8th Cir. 1983), 38, 111

Lewis Serv. Center, Inc. v. Mack Trucks, Inc., 466 U.S. 902 (1984), 101

Lewis v. Anderson, 81 F.R.D. 436 (S.D.N.Y. 1978), 787

Lexington County Broadcasters, Inc., 42 F.C.C.2d 581 (1973), 1037

Leybold-Heraeus Tech. v. Midwest Instrument Co., 118 F.R.D. 609 (E.D. Wis. 1987), 764

L.G. Balfour Co. v. FTC, 442 F.2d 1 (7th Cir. 1971), 174, 490

L. Heller & Son v. FTC, 191 F.2d 954 (7th Cir. 1951), 491

Liang v. Hunt, 477 F. Supp. 891 (N.D. Ill. 1979), 661

Libbey-Owens-Ford Glass Co. v. FTC, 352 F.2d 415 (6th Cir. 1965), 482, 489

Liberty Glass Co. v. Allstate Ins. Co., 607 F.2d 135 (5th Cir. 1979), 1110

Lieberman v. FTC, 771 F.2d 32 (2d Cir. 1985), 343, 519, 615

Liebig, 21 O.J. EUR. COMM. (No. L 53) 20 (1978), [1976-1978 Transfer Binder] COMMON MKT. REP. (CCH) ¶ 10,017, 942

Liggett & Myers, Inc., 87 F.T.C. 1074 (1976), aff'd, 567 F.2d 1273 (4th Cir. 1977), 283, 284, 285, 287, 288, 308

Liggett Group v. Brown & Williamson Tobacco Corp., 1990-2 Trade Cas. (CCH) ¶ 69,182 (M.D.N.C. 1990), 415

Lighthouse Rug Co. v. FTC, 35 F.2d 163 (7th Cir. 1929), 477

Lightweight Papers, 15 O.J. EUR. COMM. (No. L 182) 24 (1972), [1970-1972 Transfer Binder] COMMON MKT. REP. (CCH) ¶ 9523, 934

Limeco, Inc. v. Division of Lime of Miss. Dep't of Agric. & Commerce, 778 F.2d 1086 (5th Cir. 1985), 979

Lindsley v. Natural Carbonic Gas Co., 220 U.S. 61 (1911), 626

Lindy Bros. Builders v. American Radiator & Standard Sanitary Corp., 487 F.2d 161 (3d Cir. 1973), 782

Lindy Bros. Builders v. American Radiator & Standard Sanitary Corp., 540 F.2d 102 (3d Cir. 1976), 783, 784

Link v. Mercedes-Benz of N. Am., Inc., 550 F.2d 860 (3d Cir.), cert. denied, 431 U.S. 933 (1977), 736

Link v. Mercedes-Benz of N. Am., Inc., 788 F.2d 918 (3d Cir. 1986), 654, 657

Linseman v. World Hockey Ass'n, 439 F. Supp. 1315 (D. Conn. 1977), 902, 908

L'Invincible, 14 U.S. (1 Wheat.) 238 (1816), 899

L. Knife & Son v. Banfi Prods. Corp., 1987-1 Trade Cas. (CCH) ¶ 67,486 (D. Mass. 1987), 670

Lippa & Co. v. Lenox, Inc., 305 F. Supp. 175 (D. Vt. 1969), 868

Lippa's, Inc. v. Lenox, Inc., 305 F. Supp. 182 (D. Vt. 1969), 684

Liquilux Gas Servs. v. Tropical Gas Co., 303 F. Supp. 414 (D.P.R. 1969), 402

Litman v. A. Barton Hepburn Hosp., 679 F. Supp. 196 (N.D.N.Y. 1988), 25

Little Rock School Dist. v. Borden, Inc., 632 F.2d 700 (8th Cir. 1980), 771, 772

Littlejohn v. Shell Oil Co., 483 F.2d 1140 (5th Cir.), cert. denied, 414 U.S. 1116 (1973), 402

Litton Indus., 82 F.T.C. 793 (1973), 302

Litton Indus., 97 F.T.C. 1 (1981), enforced as modified, 676 F.2d 364 (9th Cir. 1982), 466

Litton Indus. Prods. v. Solid State Sys., 755 F.2d 158 (Fed. Cir. 1985), 809

Litton Indus. v. FTC, 676 F.2d 364 (9th Cir. 1982), 489, 493, 494, 521, 522

Litton Sys. v. AT&T, 91 F.R.D. 574 (S.D.N.Y. 1981), aff'd, 700 F.2d 785 (2d Cir. 1983), cert. denied, 464 U.S. 1073 (1984), 771, 781

Litton Sys. v. AT&T, 613 F. Supp. 824 (S.D.N.Y. 1985), 785

Litton Sys. v. AT&T, 700 F.2d 785 (2d Cir. 1983), cert. denied, 464 U.S. 1073 (1984), 258, 259 667, 673, 675, 770, 999, 1006, 1011, 1020, 1049

Litton Sys. v. Southwestern Bell Tel. Co., 539 F.2d 418 (5th Cir. 1976), 1022

Liu v. Republic of China, 892 F.2d 1419 (9th Cir. 1989), cert. dismissed, 111 S. Ct. 27 (1990), 908

Livezey v. American Contract Bridge League, 1985-2 Trade Cas. (CCH) ¶ 66,875 (E.D. Pa. 1985), 87

L.J. Dreiling Motor Co. v. Peugeot Motors of Am., 605 F. Supp. 597 (D. Colo.), aff'd, 768 F.2d 1159 (10th Cir. 1985), 54, 55

L. Knife & Son v. Banfi Prods. Corp., 1987-1 Trade Cas. (CCH) ¶ 67,486 (D. Mass. 1987), 670

Llewellyn v. Crothers, 765 F.2d 769 (9th Cir. 1985), 971, 978, 985, 1005

L.M.I., Inc. v. House of Sobel, 1979-2 Trade Cas. (CCH) ¶ 62,817 (N.D. Cal. 1979), 403

Loan Store v. Independent Food Stamps Assocs., 671 F. Supp. 844 (D. Mass. 1987), aff'd, 843 F.2d 1384 (1st Cir. 1988), 25

Local 189, Amalgamated Meat Cutters v. Jewel Tea Co., 381 U.S. 676 (1965), 4, 1121, 1122

Local 36 of Int'l Fishermen & Allied Workers v. United States, 177 F.2d 320 (9th Cir. 1949), cert. denied, 339 U.S. 947 (1950), 34

Local 210, Laborers' Int'l Union v. Labor Relations Div. Assoc. Gen. Contractors, Inc., 844 F.2d 69 (2d Cir. 1988), 1123

Local Beauty Supply v. Lamaur Inc., 787 F.2d 1197 (7th Cir. 1986), 667, 706

Lochner v. New York, 198 U.S. 45 (1905), 627

LoCicero v. Humble Oil & Refining Co., 52 F.R.D. 28 (E.D. La. 1971), 774

Lockheed Corp., 92 F.T.C. 968 (1978), 435

Locklin v. Day-Glo Color Corp., 378 F. Supp. 423 (N.D. Ill. 1974), 781, 784, 787

Locklin v. Day-Glo Color Corp., 429 F.2d 873 (7th Cir. 1970), cert. denied, 400 U.S. 1020 (1971), 673

Loctite Corp. v. Fel-Pro, Inc., 1978-2 Trade Cas. (CCH) ¶ 62,204 (N.D. Ill. 1978), 1000

Loctite Corp. v. Ultraseal Ltd., 781 F.2d 861 (Fed. Cir. 1985), 258, 801, 807, 811, 851

Loeb v. Eastman Kodak Co., 183 F. 704 (3d Cir. 1910), 659, 662

Loewe v. Lawlor, 208 U.S. 274 (1908), 1117

Loew's, Inc. v. Cinema Amusements, Inc., 210 F.2d 86 (10th Cir.), cert. denied, 347 U.S. 976 (1954), 780

Logan Lanes, Inc. v. Brunswick Corp., 378 F.2d 212 (9th Cir. 1966), cert. denied, 389 U.S. 898 (1967), 448

Lomar Wholesale Grocery v. Dieter's Gourmet Foods, 824 F.2d 582 (8th Cir. 1987), cert. denied, 484 U.S. 1010 (1988), 13, 183, 189, 192, 234, 415, 706, 708

Lombard v. Marcera, 442 U.S. 915 (1979), 715, 736

Lombino & Sons v. Standard Fruit & S.S. Co., 1975-2 Trade Cas. (CCH) ¶ 60,527 (S.D.N.Y. 1975), 413, 427

London European-SABENA, 31 O.J. EUR. COMM. (No. L 317) 47 (1988), (Decision 88/589) [1989] 1 CEC (CCH) 2278, 954

London Grain Futures Mkt., 29 O.J. EUR. COMM. (No. L 19) 22 (1986), [1985-1988 Transfer Binder] COMMON MKT. REP. (CCH) ¶ 10,850, 936

London Meat Futures Exch., 29 O.J. EUR. COMM. (No. L 19) 30 (1986), [1985-1988 Transfer Binder] COMMON MKT. REP. (CCH) ¶ 10,850, 936

London Potato Futures Ass'n, 29 O.J. EUR. COMM. (No. L 19) 26 (1986), [1985-1988 Transfer Binder] COMMON MKT. REP. (CCH) ¶ 10,850, 936

Long Lake Energy Corp. v. Niagara Mohawk Power Corp., 700 F. Supp. 186 (S.D.N.Y. 1988), 1023

Loom Crafters, Inc. v. New Cent. Jute Mills Co., 1971 Trade Cas. (CCH) ¶ 73,734 (S.D.N.Y. 1971), 103

Lorain Journal Co. v. United States, 342 U.S. 143 (1951), 169, 179, 242

Loren Specialty Mfg. Co. v. Clark Mfg. Co., 360 F.2d 913 (7th Cir.), cert. denied, 385 U.S. 957 (1966), 408

Lorillard, 80 F.T.C. 455 (1972), 474

Lorillard Co. v. FTC, 186 F.2d 52 (4th Cir. 1950), 465, 466

Lorillard Co. v. FTC, 267 F.2d 439 (3d Cir.), cert. denied, 361 U.S. 923 (1959), 437, 440

Los Angeles Memorial Coliseum Comm'n v. NFL, 634 F.2d 1197 (9th Cir. 1980), 676, 677, 678, 679

Los Angeles Memorial Coliseum Comm'n v. NFL, 726 F.2d 1381 (9th Cir.), cert. denied, 469 U.S. 990 (1984), 45, 52, 55, 56, 91, 127, 199, 384, 671

Louisiana Bancshares, Inc., 72 Fed. Res. Bull. 154 (1985), 1093

Louisiana Petroleum Retail Dealers, Inc. v. Texas Co., 148 F. Supp. 334 (W.D. La. 1956), 701

Louisiana Power & Light Co., 6 A.E.C. 48 (1973), 1088

Louisiana Pub. Serv. Comm'n v. FCC, 476 U.S. 355 (1986), 623

Lovett v. General Motors Corp., 769 F. Supp. 1506 (D. Minn. 1991), 14, 61, 62, 127, 181

Lowe v. Safeway Stores, 1975-2 Trade Cas. (CCH) ¶ 60,659 (N.D. Iowa 1975), 692

L.S. Amster & Co., Inc. v. McNeil Labs., 504 F. Supp. 617 (S.D.N.Y. 1980), 408, 443

Lubbock Glass & Mirror Co. v. Pittsburgh Plate Glass Co., 313 F. Supp. 1184 (N.D. Tex. 1970), 413

Lucas v. Bechtel Corp., 800 F.2d 839 (9th Cir. 1986), 677, 678

Luckenbach S.S. Co. v. United States, 179 F.Supp. 605 (D. Del. 1959), aff'd in part, vacated in part per curiam, 364 U.S. 280 (1960), 1022

Ludwig v. American Greetings Corp., 264 F.2d 286 (6th Cir. 1959), 409

Lupia v. Stella D'Oro Biscuit Co., 586 F.2d 1163 (7th Cir. 1978), cert. denied, 440 U.S. 982 (1979), 170, 415, 434

Luria Bros. & Co., 62 F.T.C. 243 (1963), aff'd, 389 F.2d 847 (3d Cir.), cert. denied, 393 U.S. 829 (1968), 285

Luria Bros. & Co., 105 F.T.C. 192 (1985), 175

Luria Bros. & Co. v. FTC, 389 F.2d 847 (3d Cir.), cert. denied, 393 U.S. 829 (1968), 169, 459

Luria Steel & Trading Corp. v. Ogden Corp., 327 F. Supp. 1345 (E.D. Pa. 1971), 877

Luria Steel & Trading Corp. v. Ogden Corp., 336 F. Supp. 1238 (E.D. Pa. 1972), aff'd, 484 F.2d 1016 (3d Cir. 1973), cert. denied, 414 U.S. 1158 (1974), 687

Luria Steel & Trading Corp. v. Ogden Corp., 484 F.2d 1016 (3d Cir. 1973), cert. denied, 414 U.S. 1158 (1974), 677, 678

Luxor Ltd., 31 F.T.C. 658 (1940), 429, 437

Lynch Business Machs., Inc. v. A.B. Dick Co., 594 F. Supp. 59 (N.D. Ohio 1984), 184, 206, 296

M

Mabry v. Johnson, 467 U.S. 504 (1984), 581

Mac Adjustment, Inc. v. General Adjustment Bureau, 597 F.2d 1318 (10th Cir.), cert. denied, 444 U.S. 929 (1979), 29

MacGregor v. Westinghouse Elec. & Mfg. Co., 329 U.S. 402 (1947), 837

MacHovec v. Council for Nat'l Register of Health Serv. Providers in Psychology, 616 F. Supp. 258 (E.D. Va. 1985), 88, 92

Mac Inv. Co. v. United States, 350 U.S. 960 (1956), 805

Mackey v. Nationwide Ins. Cos., 724 F.2d 419 (4th Cir. 1984), 1113, 1114

Mackey v. NFL, 543 F.2d 606 (8th Cir. 1976), cert. dismissed, 434 U.S. 801 (1977), 91, 1124

Macon Television Co., 8 Rad. Reg. (P&F) 703 (1952), 1037

Magid Mfg. Co. v. U.S.D. Corp., 654 F. Supp. 325 (N.D. Ill. 1987), 53, 186

Magnaleasing, Inc. v. Staten Island Mall, 76 F.R.D. 559 (S.D.N.Y. 1977), 565

Magna Pictures Corp. v. Paramount Pictures Corp., 265 F. Supp. 144 (C.D. Cal. 1967), 701

Magnavox Co., FTC Dkt. No. 8822, Slip Op. (Mar. 12, 1966), 108, 110, 113

Magnavox Co., 78 F.T.C. 1183 (1971), 166

Magnavox Co., 102 F.T.C. 807 (1983), 172

Magneti Marelli/CEAc, Decision 91/403, 34 O.J. EUR. COMM. (No. L 222) 38 (1991), [1991] 2 CEC 2,146, 959

Magnus Petroleum Co. v. Skelly Oil Co., 446 F. Supp. 874 (E.D. Wis. 1978), rev'd, 599 F.2d 196 (7th Cir.), cert. denied, 444 U.S. 916 (1979), 54

Magnus Petroleum Co. v. Skelly Oil Co., 599 F.2d 196 (7th Cir.), cert. denied, 444 U.S. 916 (1979), 170, 172, 173, 176

Maico Co., 50 F.T.C. 485 (1953), 174

Mailand v. Burckle, 1978-1 Trade Cas. (CCH) ¶ 61,818 (Cal. 1978), 639

Maislin Indus., U.S. v. Primary Steel, Inc., 110 S. Ct. 2759 (1990), 1020, 1127

Malamud v. Sinclair Oil Corp., 521 F.2d 1142 (6th Cir. 1975), 659

Malchman v. Davis, 706 F.2d 426 (2d Cir. 1983), 742, 743

Malchman v. Davis, 761 F.2d 893 (2d Cir. 1985), *cert. denied*, 475 U.S. 1143 (1986), 673

Malcolm v. Cities Serv. Co., 2 F.R.D. 405 (D. Del. 1942), 740

Malcolm v. Marathon Oil Co., 642 F.2d 845 (5th Cir. Unit B), *cert. denied*, 454 U.S. 1125 (1981), 184, 667, 675

Malden v. Union Elec. Co., 887 F.2d 157 (8th Cir. 1989), 246

Malley-Duff & Assoc. v. Crown Life Ins. Co., 734 F.2d 133 (3d Cir.), *cert. denied*, 469 U.S. 1072 (1984), 60, 81, 673, 1116, 1117

Mallinckrodt Chem. Works v. Goldman Sachs & Co., 58 F.R.D. 348 (S.D.N.Y. 1973), 747

Mamakos v. Huntington Hosp., 653 F. Supp. 1447 (E.D.N.Y. 1987), 25, 29

Manasen v. California Dental Serv., 638 F.2d 1152 (9th Cir. 1979), 738

Manco Watch Strap Co., 60 F.T.C. 495, (1962), 476

Mandeville Island Farms v. American Crystal Sugar Co., 334 U.S. 219 (1948), 23, 391

M & H Tire Co. v. Hoosier Racing Tire Corp., 560 F. Supp. 591 (D. Mass. 1983), *rev'd*, 733 F.2d 973 (1st Cir. 1984), 81, 676

M & H Tire Co. v. Hoosier Racing Tire Corp., 733 F.2d 973 (1st Cir. 1984), 35, 37, 38, 39, 56, 78, 85, 86, 90, 91

M & M Medical Supplies & Serv. v. Pleasant Valley Hosp., 738 F. Supp. 1017 (S.D. W.Va. 1990), 178

Mandujano v. Basic Vegetable Prods., Inc., 541 F.2d 832 (9th Cir. 1976), 742, 743

Manildra Milling Corp. v. Ogilvie Mills, Inc., 717 F. Supp. 759 (D. Kan. 1989), 789

Manildra Milling Corp. v. Ogilvie Mills, Inc., 1990-1 Trade Cas. (CCH) ¶ 68,926 (D. Kan. 1990), 682

Mannington Mills, Inc. v. Congoleum Corp., 595 F.2d 1287 (3d Cir. 1979), 843, 859-60, 906, 909

Mannington Mills, Inc. v. Congoleum Indus., 610 F.2d 1059 (3d Cir. 1979), 828, 835

Manok v. Southeast Dist. Bowling Ass'n, 306 F. Supp. 1215 (C.D. Cal. 1969), 90

Manufacturers Supply Co. v. Minnesota Mining & Mfg. Co., 688 F. Supp. 303 (W.D. Mich. 1988), 51, 124, 125, 126, 129, 182, 184

Manufacturing Research Corp. v. Greenlee Tool Co., 693 F.2d 1037 (11th Cir. 1982), 97, 751

Maple Flooring Mfrs. Ass'n v. United States, 268 U.S. 563 (1925), 67, 71, 74, 405

M.A.P. Oil Co. v. Texaco, Inc., 691 F.2d 1303 (9th Cir. 1982), 199, 205, 269

Marathon Oil Co. v. Mobil Corp., 530 F. Supp. 315 (N.D. Ohio), *aff'd*, 669 F.2d 378 (6th Cir. 1981), *cert. denied*, 455 U.S. 982 (1982), 292, 294, 302, 305, 363, 368, 369

Marathon Oil Co. v. Mobil Corp., 669 F.2d 378 (6th Cir. 1981), *cert. denied*, 455 U.S. 982 (1982), 308, 363, 370, 663, 678

Marcera v. Chinlund, 595 F.2d 1231 (2d Cir.), *vacated sub nom.* Lombard v. Marcera, 442 U.S. 915 (1979), 715, 736

Marcor, Inc., 90 F.T.C. 183 (1977) *refiled sub nom.* United States v. Montgomery Ward & Co., FTC No. 70-1412 (D.D.C. May 29, 1979), 537

Marco Sales Co. v. FTC, 453 F.2d 1 (2d Cir. 1971), 482, 489, 494

Marcus v. FTC, 354 F.2d 85 (2d Cir. 1965), 522

Marcus v. Textile Banking Co., 38 F.R.D. 185 (S.D.N.Y. 1965), 740

Mardirosian v. American Inst. of Architects, 474 F. Supp. 628 (D.D.C. 1979), 2, 68, 87

Maremont Corp., 75 F.T.C. 1067 (1969), 507

Margoles v. Johns, 587 F.2d 885 (7th Cir. 1978), 769

Maricopa County v. American Pipe & Constr. Co., 303 F. Supp. 77 (D. Ariz. 1969), *aff'd per curiam*, 431 F.2d 1145 (9th Cir. 1970), *cert. denied*, 401 U.S. 937 (1971), 683, 684, 686, 687

Marine Corp., 71 Fed. Res. Bull. 795 (1985), 1094

Marine Firemen's Union v. Owens-Corning Fiberglass Corp., 503 F.2d 246 (9th Cir. 1974), 686, 687

Marin v. Citizens Memorial Hosp., 700 F. Supp. 354 (S.D. Tex. 1988), 89

Maritime Cinema Serv. Corp. v. Movies En Route, 60 F.R.D. 587 (S.D.N.Y. 1973), 745, 746, 748

Marjorie Webster Junior College v. Middle States Ass'n of Colleges & Secondary Schools, 432 F.2d 650 (D.C. Cir.), *cert. denied*, 400 U.S. 965 (1970), 88, 89

Mark Aero, Inc. v. TWA, 580 F.2d 288 (8th Cir. 1978), 1007

Market Dev. Corp., 95 F.T.C. 100 (1980), 512

Market Force Inc. v. Wauwatosa Realty Co., 906 F.2d 1167 (7th Cir. 1990), 6, 7, 8, 9

Marketing Assistance Plan, Inc. v. Associated Milk Producers, Inc., 338 F. Supp. 1019 (S.D. Tex. 1972), 1026

Marks v. San Francisco Real Estate Bd., 69 F.R.D. 353 (N.D. Cal. 1975), *appeal dismissed*, 549 F.2d 643 (9th Cir. 1977), 736

Marks v. San Francisco Real Estate Bd., 627 F.2d 947 (9th Cir. 1980), 732

Marnell v. United Parcel Serv., 260 F. Supp. 391 (N.D. Cal. 1966), 1023

Marquis v. Chrysler Corp., 577 F.2d 624 (9th Cir. 1978), 54, 193

Marquis v. United States Sugar Corp., 652 F. Supp. 598 (S.D. Fla. 1987), 682, 1018

Marrese v. American Academy of Orthopaedic Surgeons, 1991-1 Trade Cas. (CCH) ¶ 69,398 (N.D. Ill. 1991), 36, 48, 51, 83

Marrese v. American Academy of Orthopaedic Surgeons, 706 F.2d 1488 (7th Cir. 1983), 85

Marrese v. American Academy of Orthopaedic Surgeons, 470 U.S. 373 (1985), 631, 632

Marrese v. Interqual, Inc., 748 F.2d 373 (7th Cir. 1984), *cert. denied*, 472 U.S. 1027 (1985), 26, 28, 29

Marsann Co. v. Brammall, Inc., 788 F.2d 611 (9th Cir. 1986), 230, 234, 268, 706

Marshall County Broadcasting Co. v. FCC, 42 RAD. REG. 2d (P&F) 605 (D.D.C.), *aff'd mem.*, 571 F.2d 674 (D.C. Cir. 1978), 1039

Marshall v. Holiday Magic, Inc., 550 F.2d 1173 (9th Cir. 1977), 741, 742, 743

Marshall v. Segona, 621 F.2d 763 (5th Cir. 1980), 768

Mars Steel Corp. v. Continental Illinois Nat'l Bank & Trust Co., 834 F.2d 677 (7th Cir. 1987), 734, 741, 742

Marston v. Ann Arbor Property Managers Ass'n, 422 F.2d 836 (6th Cir.), *cert. denied*, 399 U.S. 929 (1970), 29

Martin B. Glauser Dodge Co. v. Chrysler Corp., 570 F.2d 72 (3d Cir. 1977), *cert. denied*, 436 U.S. 913 (1978), 45

Martindell v. News Group Publications, 621 F. Supp. 672 (E.D.N.Y. 1985), 108, 111, 112

Martin Ice Cream Co. v. Chipwich, Inc., 554 F. Supp. 933 (S.D.N.Y. 1983), 408

Martin Lake Broadcasting Co., 21 F.C.C.2d 180 (1970), 1037

Martin Motor Sales v. Saab-Scania of Am., 452 F. Supp. 1047 (S.D.N.Y. 1978), *aff'd mem.*, 595 F.2d 1209 (2d Cir. 1979), 669

Martino v. McDonald's Sys., 81 F.R.D. 81 (N.D. Ill. 1979), *modified*, 86 F.R.D. 145 (N.D. Ill. 1980), 714, 720

Martino v. McDonald's Sys., 86 F.R.D. 145 (N.D. Ill. 1980), 725, 726, 727, 735

Martino v. McDonald's Sys., 625 F. Supp. 356 (N.D. Ill. 1985), 131

Martin v. American Kennel Club, 697 F. Supp. 997 (N.D. Ill. 1988), 42, 43, 48, 90

Marty's Floor Covering Co. v. GAF Corp., 604 F.2d 266 (4th Cir. 1979), *cert. denied*, 444 U.S. 1017 (1980), 103, 427, 441

Marvin L. Rich, 19 RAD. REG. 2d (P&F) 751 (1970), 1039

Mary Ann Pensiero, Inc. v. Lingle, 847 F.2d 90 (3d Cir. 1988), 789

Maryland & Virginia Milk Producers Ass'n v. United States, 362 U.S. 458 (1960), 1024

Maryland Carpet Outlet, Inc., 85 F.T.C. 754 (1975), 475

Maryland *ex rel.* Curran v. Mitsubishi Elecs. of Am., Civ. No. S-91-815 (D. Md. Mar. 27, 1991), 101, 610

Maryland People's Counsel v. FERC, 760 F.2d 318 (D.C. Cir. 1985), 1056

Maryland v. Blue Cross & Blue Shield Ass'n, 620 F. Supp. 907 (D. Md. 1985), 1111, 1112, 1113, 1114, 1116

Maryland v. Giant Food, Inc., No. JH-90-2428 (D. Md. filed Sept. 17, 1990), 605

Maryland v. Prescription Network of Md., Inc., No. JH-90-2425 (D. Md. filed Sept. 17, 1990), 605

Maryland v. United States, 460 U.S. 1001 (1983), 1045

Mashburn v. National Healthcare, Inc., 684 F. Supp. 660 (M.D. Ala. 1988), 738

Mason City Tent & Awning Co. v. Clapper, 144 F. Supp. 754 (W.D. Mo. 1956), 838

Massachusetts Bay Telecasters, Inc. v. FCC, 261 F.2d 55 (D.C. Cir. 1958), *vacated*, 295 F.2d 131 (D.C. Cir.), *cert. denied*, 366 U.S. 918 (1961), 1037

Massachusetts Bd. of Registration in Optometry, 110 F.T.C. 549 (1988), 57, 386, 387, 489, 985

Massachusetts Brewer's Ass'n v. P. Ballantine & Sons Co., 129 F. Supp. 736 (D. Mass. 1955), 404

Massachusetts Furniture & Piano Movers Ass'n, 102 F.T.C. 1176, *rev'd in part*, 773 F.2d 391 (1st Cir. 1985), 490

Massachusetts v. Ashland Warren, Inc., 1983-2 Trade Cas. (CCH) ¶ 65,682 (D. Mass. 1983), 604, 691

Massachusetts v. Campeau Corp., 1988-1 Trade Cas. (CCH) ¶ 68,093, (D. Mass. 1988), 278, 345, 612

Matarazzo v. Friendly Ice Cream Corp., 62 F.R.D. 65 (E.D.N.Y. 1974), 718, 720

Material Handling Inst., Inc. v. McLaren, 426 F.2d 90 (3d Cir.), *cert. denied*, 400 U.S. 826 (1970), 506, 557

Mathews Conveyer Co. v. Palmer-Bee Co., 135 F.2d 73 (6th Cir. 1943), 622

Mathis v. Automobile Club Inter-Ins. Exch., 410 F. Supp. 1037 (W.D. Mo. 1976), 1111

Matsushita Elec. Indus. Co. v. Zenith Radio Corp., 475 U.S. 574 (1986), 4, 5, 9, 10, 181, 196, 216, 227, 236, 362, 415, 652, 702, 704, 705, 708, 862-63, 1108

Mattel, Inc., 79 F.T.C. 667 (1971), *modified*, 104 F.T.C. 555 (1984), 482

Mattox v. FTC, 752 F.2d 116 (5th Cir. 1985), 343, 519, 615

Max Daetwyler Corp. v. R. Meyer, 762 F.2d 290 (3d Cir.), *cert. denied*, 474 U.S. 462 (1985), 876

Max Factor & Co., 108 F.T.C. 135 (1986), 443, 444

May Dep't Store v. Graphic Process Co., 637 F.2d 1211 (9th Cir. 1980), 410, 431

May Dep't Stores v. First Nat'l Supermarkets, 1984-1 Trade Cas. (CCH) ¶ 66,010 (N.D. Ohio 1984), 758, 759

Mayer Bros. Poultry Farms v. Meltzer, 274 A.D. 169, 80 N.Y.S.2d 874, *appeal denied*, 274 A.D. 877, 83 N.Y.S.2d 228 (1948), 624

Mayer Paving & Asphalt Co. v. General Dynamics Corp., 486 F.2d 763 (7th Cir. 1973), *cert. denied*, 414 U.S. 1146 (1974), 402

Mayfair Super Markets, Inc., 87 F.T.C. 286 (1976), 480

Maykuth v. Adolph Coors Co., 690 F.2d 689 (9th Cir. 1982), 123, 126, 182

Mays v. Hospital Auth., 596 F. Supp. 120 (N.D. Ga. 1984), 174

Mays v. Massey-Ferguson, Inc., 1990-1 Trade Cas. (CCH) ¶ 69,028 (S.D. Ga. 1990), 406

Mazer v. Stein, 347 U.S. 201 (1954), 844

Mazzola v. Southern New England Tel. Co., 169 Conn. 344, 363 A.2d 170 (1975), 637, 638

M. Berenson Co. v. Faneuil Hall Marketplace, Inc., 103 F.R.D. 635 (D. Mass. 1984), 735

McAlpine v. AAMCO Automatic Transmissions, Inc., 1977-1 Trade Cas. (CCH) ¶ 61,359 (E.D. Mich. 1977), 697

McAlpine v. AAMCO Automatic Transmissions, Inc., 461 F. Supp. 1232 (E.D. Mich. 1978), 146, 155

McBeath v. Inter-American Citizens for Decency Comm., 374 F.2d 359 (5th Cir.), *cert. denied*, 389 U.S. 896 (1967), 29-30, 81

McCabe's Furniture, Inc. v. La-Z-Boy Chair Co., 798 F.2d 323 (8th Cir. 1986), *cert. denied*, 486 U.S. 1005 (1988), 13, 15, 110, 181, 189

McCarthy v. Arndstein, 266 U.S. 34 (1924), 771

McCarthy v. Benton, 13 F.R.D. 454 (D.D.C. 1952), 747

McCarthy v. Kleindienst, 562 F.2d 1269 (D.C. Cir. 1977), 696

McCaw Personal Communs. v. Pacific Telesis Group, 645 F. Supp. 1166 (N.D. Cal. 1986), 376, 362, 648

McClatchy Broadcasting Co. v. FCC, 239 F.2d 15 (D.C. Cir. 1956), *cert. denied*, 353 U.S. 918 (1957), 1037

McCormack v. NCAA, 845 F.2d 1338 (5th Cir. 1988), 42, 90, 648

McCourt v. California Sports, Inc., 600 F.2d 1193 (6th Cir. 1979), 91, 1124

McCoy v. Convenient Food Mart, Inc., 69 F.R.D. 337 (N.D. Ill. 1975), 728

McCoy v. Franklin Sav. Ass'n, 636 F.2d 172 (7th Cir. 1980), 1098

McCready v. Blue Shield, 649 F.2d 228 (4th Cir. 1981), *aff'd*, 457 U.S. 465 (1982), 649, 660

McCreery Angus Farms v. American Angus Ass'n, 379 F. Supp. 1008 (S.D. Ill.), *aff'd without opinion*, 506 F.2d 1404 (7th Cir. 1974), 88, 89

McCrory Corp. v. Cloth World, Inc., 378 F. Supp. 322 (S.D.N.Y. 1974), 869

McCullough Tool Co. v. Well Surveys, Inc., 343 F.2d 381 (10th Cir. 1965), *cert. denied*, 383 U.S. 933 (1966), 835

McCullough Tool Co. v. Well Surveys, Inc., 395 F.2d 230 (10th Cir.), *cert. denied*, 393 U.S. 925 (1968), 814

McCullough v. Kammerer Corp., 166 F.2d 759 (9th Cir.), *cert. denied*, 335 U.S. 813 (1948), 828, 835

McDaniel v. General Motors Corp., 480 F. Supp. 666 (E.D.N.Y. 1979), *aff'd without published opinion*, 628 F.2d 1345 (2d Cir. 1980), 185, 193

McDaniel v. Greensboro News, 1984-1 Trade Cas. (CCH) ¶ 65,792 (M.D.N.C. 1983), 173, 178, 181, 182, 188, 189, 192

McDermott v. FTC, 1981-1 Trade Cas. (CCH) ¶ 63,964 (D.D.C. 1981), 517

McDonald v. Johnson & Johnson, 546 F. Supp. 324 (D. Minn. 1982), *vacated*, 722 F.2d 1370 (8th Cir. 1983), *cert. denied*, 469 U.S. 870 (1984), 786

McDonald v. Johnson & Johnson, 722 F.2d 1370 (8th Cir. 1983), *cert. denied*, 469 U.S. 870 (1984), 365, 660

McDonald v. Smith, 472 U.S. 479 (1985), 1008

McDonald v. St. Joseph's Hosp., 574 F. Supp. 123 (N.D. Ga. 1983), 874

McDonald's Corp. v. Robert A. Makin, Inc., 653 F. Supp. 401 (W.D.N.Y. 1986), 184, 792

McDonnell v. Michigan Chapter #10, American Inst. of Real Estate Appraisers, 587 F.2d 7 (6th Cir. 1978), 89

McElderry v. Cathay Pac. Airways, 678 F. Supp. 1071 (S.D.N.Y. 1988), 857, 858, 861

McElhenney Co. v. Western Auto Supply Store, 269 F.2d 332 (4th Cir. 1959), 164, 165, 182, 183

McElhinney v. Medical Protective Co., 738 F.2d 439 (6th Cir. 1984), 25, 29

McGahee v. Northern Propane Gas Co., 858 F.2d 1487 (11th Cir. 1988), *cert. denied*, 490 U.S. 1084 (1989), 216, 217, 228, 231, 235, 236, 263, 264, 414, 706, 707, 708

McGee v. International Life Ins. Co., 355 U.S. 220 (1957), 872

McGinness v. ICC, 662 F.2d 853 (D.C. Cir. 1981), 1133

McGlinchy v. Shell Chem. Co., 1985-2 Trade Cas. (CCH) ¶ 66,672 (N.D. Cal. 1984), 873

McGlinchy v. Shell Chem. Co., 845 F.2d 802 (9th Cir. 1988), 49, 668, 672, 674, 857

McGuire v. CBS, 399 F.2d 902 (9th Cir. 1968), 169

McGuire v. Times Mirror Co., 405 F. Supp. 57 (C.D. Cal. 1975), 186, 192

MCI Communs. Corp. v. AT&T, 1983-2 Trade Cas. (CCH) ¶ 65,652 (D.D.C. 1983), 868

MCI Communs. Corp. v. AT&T, 708 F.2d 1081 (7th Cir. 1983), *cert. denied*, 464 U.S. 891 (1983), 218, 225, 232, 233, 246, 247, 250, 256, 674, 675, 699, 999, 1001, 1012, 1014

McInerney v. Wm. P. McDonald Constr., 28 F. Supp. 557 (E.D.N.Y. 1939), 747

McKenzie v. Mercy Hosp., 854 F.2d 365 (10th Cir. 1988), 133, 247

McKeon Constr. v. McClatchy Newspapers, 1970 Trade Cas. (CCH) ¶ 73,212 (N.D. Cal. 1969), 680, 751

McLain v. Real Estate Bd., 444 U.S. 232 (1980), 23, 24, 25, 26, 29, 54

McLean Trucking Co. v. United States, 321 U.S. 67 (1944), 1130

McMahon v. Prentice-Hall, Inc., 486 F. Supp. 1296 (E.D. Mo. 1980), 773

McMahon v. Shearson/American Express, Inc., 788 F.2d 94 (2d Cir. 1986), 788

M.C. Mfg. Co. v. Texas Foundries, 517 F.2d 1059 (5th Cir. 1975), *cert. denied*, 424 U.S. 968 (1976), 407, 415

McMillan v. Pennsylvania, 477 U.S. 79 (1986), 595

McTamney v. Stolt Tankers & Terminals, S.A., 678 F. Supp. 118 (E.D. Pa. 1987), 280

Meaamaile v. American Samoa, 550 F. Supp. 1227 (D. Haw. 1982), 877

Meat Sys. Corp. v. Ben Langel-Mol, Inc., 410 F. Supp. 231 (S.D.N.Y. 1976), 877

Mechean Trucking Co. v. United States, 321 U.S. 67 (1944), 1130

Medic Air Corp. v. Air Ambulance Auth., 843 F.2d 1187 (9th Cir. 1988), 971

Medical Arts Pharmacy v. Blue Cross & Blue Shield, 518 F. Supp. 1100 (D. Conn. 1981), *aff'd*, 675 F.2d 502 (2d Cir. 1982), 391

Medical Arts Pharmacy v. Blue Cross & Blue Shield, 675 F.2d 502 (2d Cir. 1982), 115

Medical Ass'n v. Schweiker, 554 F. Supp. 955 (M.D. Ala. 1983), *aff'd*, 714 F.2d 107 (11th Cir. 1983), 964

Meditech Int'l Co. v. Minigrip, Inc., 648 F. Supp. 1488 (N.D. Ill. 1986), 1022

Meehan v. PPG Indus., 802 F.2d 881 (7th Cir. 1986), *cert. denied*, 479 U.S. 1091 (1987), 825

Meeker v. Lehigh Valley R. Co., 236 U.S. 412 (1915), 778

Meenan Oil Co. v. Long Island Lighting Co., 1970 Trade Cas. (CCH) ¶ 73,365 (N.Y. Sup. Ct. 1970), *rev'd*, 1972 Trade Cas. (CCH) ¶ 74,048 (N.Y. App. Div. 1972), 641

Meetinghouse Assocs. v. Warwick Township, 1984-1 Trade Cas. (CCH) ¶ 66,045 (E.D. Pa. 1984), 681

Mego Int'l Inc., 92 F.T.C. 186 (1978), 485

Meicler v. Aetna Casualty & Sur. Co., 506 F.2d 732 (5th Cir. 1975), 1117

Mekani v. Miller Brewing Co., 93 F.R.D. 506 (E.D. Mich. 1982), 728

MELDOC, 29 O.J. EUR. COMM. (No. L 348) 50 (1986), [1985-1988 Transfer Binder] COMMON MKT. REP. (CCH) ¶ 10,853, 932

Melrose Realty Co. v. Loew's, Inc., 234 F.2d 518 (3d Cir. 1956), *cert. denied*, 355 U.S. 900 (1957), 661

Melso v. Texaco, Inc., 532 F. Supp. 1280 (E.D. Pa. 1982), 143

Memorex Corp. v. IBM, 555 F.2d 1379 (9th Cir. 1977), 697, 698, 701

Mendelovitz v. Adolph Coors Co., 693 F.2d 570 (5th Cir. 1982), 123, 126, 127, 182, 776

Mennon Co., 58 F.T.C. 676 (1961), 482

Menominee Rubber Co. v. Gould, Inc., 657 F.2d 164 (7th Cir. 1988), 165, 676

Mercantile Tex. Corp. v. Board of Governors, 638 F.2d 1255 (5th Cir. 1981), 322, 323, 324, 325, 326, 327, 328, 1095

Mercantile Tex. Corp., 70 Fed. Res. Bull. 595 (1984), 1093

Merck & Co., 1980-81 Trade Cas. (CCH) ¶ 63,682, 349

Merck & Co. v. Danbury Pharmacal, Inc., 873 F.2d 1418 (Fed. Cir. 1989), 810

Merck & Co. v. Stephar BV, Case 187/80, [1981] E.C.R. 2063, [1979-1981 Transfer Binder] COMMON MKT. REP. (CCH) ¶ 8707, 946

Mercoid Corp. v. Mid-Continent Inv. Co., 320 U.S. 661 (1944), 801, 817, 832, 853

Mercoid Corp. v. Minneapolis-Honeywell Regulator Co., 320 U.S. 680 (1944), 801, 817, 832

Mercy-Peninsula Ambulance, Inc. v. County of San Mateo, 791 F.2d 755 (9th Cir. 1986), 198, 972

Meredith v. Mid-Atlantic Coca Cola Bottling Co., 129 F.R.D. 130 (E.D. Va. 1989), 714, 716, 721

Merican, Inc. v. Caterpillar Tractor Co., 713 F.2d 958 (3d Cir. 1983), *cert. denied*, 465 U.S. 1024 (1984), 655, 660

Merit Motors, Inc. v. Chrysler Corp., 417 F. Supp. 263 (D.D.C. 1976), *aff'd*, 569 F.2d 666 (D.C. Cir. 1977), 110

Merit Motors, Inc. v. Chrysler Corp., 569 F.2d 666 (D.C. Cir. 1977), 674

Merkle Press, Inc. v. Merkle, 519 F. Supp. 50 (D. Md. 1981), 97, 222

Merola v. Atlantic Richfield Co., 515 F.2d 165 (3d Cir. 1975), 784

Mesirow v. Pepperidge Farm, 1981-2 Trade Cas. (CCH) ¶ 64,292 (N.D. Cal. 1981), aff'd, 703 F.2d 339 (9th Cir.), cert. denied, 464 U.S. 820 (1983), 108

Mesirow v. Pepperidge Farm, 703 F.2d 339 (9th Cir.), cert. denied, 464 U.S. 820 (1983), 103, 114, 123, 126

Metal Lubricants Co. v. Engineered Lubricants Co., 411 F.2d 426 (8th Cir. 1969), 96

Metals Disintegrating Co. v. Reynolds Metals Co., 228 F.2d 885 (3d Cir. 1956), 816

Metrix Warehouse, Inc. v. Daimler-Benz Aktiengesellschaft, 1982-2 Trade Cas. (CCH) ¶ 64,861 (D. Md. 1982), rev'd in part, 716 F.2d 245 (4th Cir. 1983), 137, 146

Metrix Warehouse, Inc. v. Daimler-Benz Aktiengesellschaft, 1984-1 Trade Cas. (CCH) ¶ 65,768 (D. Md. 1983), aff'd, 828 F.2d 1033 (4th Cir. 1987), cert. denied, 486 U.S. 1017 (1988), 156

Metrix Warehouse, Inc. v. Daimler-Benz Aktiengesellschaft, 1984-2 Trade Cas. (CCH) ¶ 66,129 (D. Md. 1984), aff'd, 828 F.2d 1033 (4th Cir. 1987), cert. denied, 486 U.S. 1017 (1988), 872

Metrix Warehouse, Inc. v. Daimler-Benz Aktiengesellschaft, 716 F.2d 245 (4th Cir. 1983), 431

Metrix Warehouse, Inc. v. Daimler-Benz Aktiengesellschaft, 828 F.2d 1033 (4th Cir. 1987), cert. denied, 486 U.S. 1017 (1988), 161, 162, 449, 450, 666, 668, 671, 674

Metro Cable Co. v. CATV of Rockford, Inc., 516 F.2d 220 (7th Cir. 1975), 998, 1005, 1007, 1009, 1053

Metro-Goldwyn-Mayer, Inc. v. Transamerica Corp., 303 F. Supp. 1344 (S.D.N.Y. 1969), 281

Metromedia Broadcasting Corp. v. MGM/UA Entertainment Co., 611 F. Supp. 415 (C.D. Cal. 1985), 138, 140, 149

Metromedia Radio and Television, Inc., 102 F.C.C.2d 1334 (1985), aff'd sub nom. Health and Medicine Policy Research Group v. FCC, 807 F.2d 1038 (D.C. Cir. 1986), 1036

Metro Mobile CTS, Inc. v. New Vector Communs., 661 F. Supp. 1504 (D. Ariz. 1987), aff'd, 892 F.2d 62 (9th Cir. 1989), 197, 217, 240, 971

Metro Mobile CTS, Inc. v. New Vector Communs., 892 F.2d 62 (9th Cir. 1989), 216, 217, 219, 238

Metropolitan Life Ins. Co. v. Adler, 1988-1 Trade Cas. (CCH) ¶ 67,907 (S.D.N.Y. 1988), 206

Metropolitan Life Ins. Co. v. Massachusetts, 471 U.S. 724 (1985), 1111

Metropolitan Life Ins. Co. v. Merchant, 1984-2 Trade Cas. (CCH) ¶ 66,130 (N.D. Fla. 1984), 711

Metropolitan Television Co. v. FCC, 289 F.2d 874 (D.C. Cir. 1961), 1032, 1033, 1041

Metro SB-Grossmarket GmbH & Co. KG v. Commission, Case 75/84, [1986] E.C.R. 3021, [1985-1986 Transfer Binder] COMMON MKT. REP. (CCH) ¶ 14,326, 940

Metro SB-Grossmärkte v. Commission, Case 26/76, [1977] E.C.R. 1875, [1977-1978 Transfer Binder] COMMON MKT. REP. (CCH) ¶ 8435, 940

Metro Video Dist., Inc. v. Vestron Video, Inc., 1990-1 Trade Cas. (CCH) ¶ 68,986 (D.P.R. 1990), 405

Mexico v. Hoffman, 324 U.S. 30 (1945), 899

Meyer Goldberg, Inc. v. Goldberg, 717 F.2d 290 (6th Cir. 1983), 661

Meyer v. Bell & Howell Co., 453 F. Supp. 801 (E.D. Mo.), appeal dismissed, 584 F.2d 291 (8th Cir. 1978), 542, 645

Miami Int'l Realty Co. v. Town of Mt. Crested Butte, 579 F. Supp. 68 (D. Colo. 1984), 28, 30

Miami Int'l Realty Co. v. Town of Mt. Crested Butte, 607 F. Supp. 448 (D. Colo. 1985), 988

Michael Halebian N.J., Inc. v. Roppe Rubber Corp., 718 F. Supp. 348 (D.N.J. 1989), 14, 198

Michaels Bldg. Co. v. Ameritrust Co., N.A., 848 F.2d 674 (6th Cir. 1988), 1089

Michaelson v. Merrill Lynch Pierce Fenner & Smith, Inc., 619 F. Supp. 727 (S.D.N.Y. 1985), 409

Michelman v. Clark-Schwebel Fiber Glass Corp., 1975-2 Trade Cas. (CCH) ¶ 60,551 (S.D.N.Y. 1975), appeal dismissed as moot, 534 F.2d 1036 (2d Cir.), cert. denied, 429 U.S. 885 (1976), 786

Michelman v. Clark-Schwebel Fiber Glass Corp., 534 F.2d 1036 (2d Cir.), cert. denied, 429 U.S. 885 (1976), 64

Michigan Canners & Freezers Ass'n v. Agricultural Mktg. & Bargaining Bd., 467 U.S. 461 (1984), 623, 1025

Michigan Citizens for an Indep. Press v. Thornburgh, 868 F.2d 1285 (D.C. Cir.), aff'd, 493 U.S. 38 (1989), 318

Michigan State Medical Soc'y, 101 F.T.C. 191 (1983), 43, 93, 456, 1013

Michigan State Podiatry Ass'n v. Blue Cross & Blue Shield, 671 F. Supp. 1139 (E.D. Mich. 1987), 25, 29, 659

Michigan v. Morton Salt Co., 259 F. Supp. 35 (D. Minn. 1966), aff'd sub nom. Hardy Salt Co. v. Illinois, 377 F.2d 768 (8th Cir.), cert. denied, 389 U.S. 912 (1967), 682, 683, 684, 686, 687, 778, 779, 780

Microbyte Corp. v. New Jersey State Golf Ass'n, 1986-2 Trade Cas. (CCH) ¶ 67,228 (D.N.J. 1986), 144, 153, 154, 158

Micros Sys. v. Portland Cash Register Sys., 1985-1 Trade Cas. (CCH) ¶ 66,353 (D. Or. 1984), 97, 98

Mid-America ICEE, Inc. v. John E. Mitchell Co., 1973-2 Trade Cas. (CCH) ¶ 74,681 (D. Or. 1973), 141, 155

Mid-Atlantic Toyota Antitrust Litig., 516 F. Supp. 1287 (D. Md. 1981), aff'd, 704 F.2d 125 (4th Cir. 1983), 699

Mid City Chevrolet, Inc. 95 F.T.C. 371 (1980), 499

Midcon Corp., 107 F.T.C. 48 (1986), 345, 346, 347, 348, 1067

Midcon Corp., Dkt. No. 9198, 5 TRADE REG. REP. (CCH) ¶ 22,510 (Feb. 2, 1988), 1067

Midcon Corp., Dkt. No. 9198, 5 TRADE REG. REP. (CCH) ¶ 22,708 (July 18, 1989), 1067

Midcon Corp. v. Freeport-McMoran, Inc., 625 F. Supp. 1475 (N.D. Ill. 1986), 317, 363, 367, 369

Midland Telecasting Co. v. Midessa Television Co., 617 F.2d 1141 (5th Cir. 1980), 1054

Midland-Ross Corp., 96 F.T.C. 172 (1980), 398

Mid-South Distrib. v. FTC, 287 F.2d 512 (5th Cir.), cert. denied, 368 U.S. 838 (1961), 404, 429, 448

Mid-South Grizzlies v. NFL, 550 F. Supp. 558 (E.D. Pa. 1982), aff'd, 720 F.2d 772 (3d Cir. 1983), cert. denied, 467 U.S. 1215 (1984), 247

Mid-South Grizzlies v. NFL, 720 F.2d 772 (3d Cir. 1983), cert. denied, 467 U.S. 1215 (1984), 91

Midtec Paper Corp. v. United States, 857 F.2d 1487 (D.C. Cir. 1988), 1146

Mid-Texas Communs. Sys. v. AT&T, 615 F.2d 1372, cert. denied, 449 U.S. 912 (1980), 218, 1049

Midwest Communs. v. Minnesota Twins, Inc., 779 F.2d 444 (8th Cir. 1985), cert. denied, 476 U.S. 1163 (1986), 138, 647

Midwest Constr. Co. v. Illinois Dep't of Labor, 684 F. Supp. 991 (N.D. Ill. 1988), 980, 994

Midwest Corp., 38 F.C.C.2d 897 (1973), recon. denied, 53 F.C.C.2d 294 (1975), 1042

Midwest Milk Monopolization Litig., 380 F. Supp. 880 (W.D. Mo. 1974), 1025

Mid-West Paper Prods. Co. v. Continental Group, 596 F.2d 573 (3d Cir. 1979), 655, 657, 661, 664, 665

Midwest Radio Co. v. Forum Publishing Co., 1989-2 Trade Cas. (CCH) ¶ 68,675 (D.N.D 1989), 212

Midwest Radio Co. v. Forum Publishing Co., 1990-1 Trade Cas. (CCH) ¶ 69,082 (D.N.D. 1989), 199, 200, 223, 252

Midwest Radio Co. v. Forum Publishing Co., 942 F.2d 1294 (8th Cir. 1991), 708

Midwestern Waffles, Inc. v. Waffle House, Inc., 734 F.2d 705 (11th Cir. 1984), 123, 128, 132, 136, 142, 144, 150, 161, 661

Mid-West Underground Storage, Inc. v. Porter, 717 F.2d 493 (10th Cir. 1983), 77, 96

Milchförderungsfonds, 28 O.J. EUR. COMM. (No. L 35) 35 (1985), [1982-1985 Transfer Binder] COMMON MKT. REP. (CCH) ¶ 10,649, 935

Military Servs. Realty v. Realty Consultants, 823 F.2d 829 (4th Cir. 1987), 97, 222

Millcarek v. Miami Herald Publishing Co., 388 F. Supp. 1002 (S.D. Fla. 1975), 192

Millen Indus. v. Coordination Council for N. Am. Affairs, 855 F.2d 879 (D.C. Cir. 1988), 901

Miller, Anderson, Nash, Yerke & Weiner v. United States Dep't of Energy, 499 F. Supp. 767 (D. Ore. 1980), 565

Miller & Son Paving v. Wrightstown Township Civic Ass'n, 443 F. Supp. 1268 (E.D. Pa. 1978), 94

Miller Insituform, Inc. v. Insituform of N. Am., Inc., 605 F. Supp. 1125 (M.D. Tenn. 1985), aff'd, 830 F.2d 606 (6th Cir. 1987), cert. denied, 484 U.S. 1064 (1988), 818, 823, 827, 830, 835

Miller Int'l Schallplatten GmbH v. Commission, Case 19/77, [1978] E.C.R. 131, [1977-1978 Transfer Binder] COMMON MKT. REP. (CCH) ¶ 8439, 924, 929, 939

Miller Motors, Inc. v. Ford Motor Co., 149 F. Supp. 790 (M.D.N.C. 1957), aff'd, 252 F.2d 441 (4th Cir. 1958), 184, 693

Miller Motors, Inc. v. Ford Motor Co., 252 F.2d 441 (4th Cir. 1958), 131, 165, 166

Miller v. Granados, 529 F.2d 393 (5th Cir. 1976), 138

Miller v. Hedlund, 1983-2 Trade Cas. (CCH) ¶ 65,754 (D. Or. 1983), 712, 715

Miller v. Hedlund, 813 F.2d 1344 (9th Cir. 1986), cert. denied, 484 U.S. 1061 (1988), 65, 973

Miller v. Honda Motor Co., 779 F.2d 769 (1st Cir. 1985), 873

Miller v. Indiana Hosp., 562 F. Supp. 1259 (W.D. Pa. 1983), 25

Miller v. Indiana Hosp., 843 F.2d 139 (3d Cir.), cert. denied, 488 U.S. 870 (1988), 26, 54, 92, 702, 707

Miller v. Indiana Hosp., 930 F.2d 334 (3d Cir. 1991), 974

Miller v. W.H. Bristow, Inc., 739 F. Supp. 1044 (D.S.C. 1990), 103

Mills v. Electric Auto-Lite, 396 U.S. 375 (1970), 781, 787

Milos v. Ford Motor Co., 317 F.2d 712 (3d Cir.), cert. denied, 375 U.S. 896 (1963), 184

Milsen Co. v. Southland Corp., 454 F.2d 363 (7th Cir. 1971), 141, 678

Milwaukee Elec. Tool Corp. v. McGrath & Durk, Inc., 519 N.Y.S.2d 905, 133 A.2d 535 (N.Y. App. Div. 1987), 792

Minersville Coal Co. v. Anthracite Export Ass'n, 55 F.R.D. 426 (M.D. Pa. 1971), 713

Ministère Public v. Asjes and others, Joined Cases 209-213/84, [1986] E.C.R. 1425, [1985-1986 Transfer Binder] COMMON MKT. REP. (CCH) ¶ 14,287, 961

Ministry of Supply, Cairo v. Universe Tankships, Inc., 708 F.2d 80 (2d Cir. 1983), 900

Minneapolis & St. L. Ry. v. United States, 361 U.S. 173 (1959), 1141

Minneapolis-Honeywell Regulator Co., 44 F.T.C. 351 (1948), rev'd, 191 F.2d 786 (7th Cir. 1951), cert. dismissed, 344 U.S. 206 (1952), 421

Minneapolis-Honeywell Regulator Co. v. FTC, 191 F.2d 786 (7th Cir. 1951), cert. dismissed, 344 U.S. 206 (1952), 521

Minnesota Mining & Mfg. Co. v. Research Medical, Inc., 691 F. Supp. 1305 (D. Utah 1988), 258

Minnesota Mining & Mfg. v. New Jersey Wood Finishing Co., 381 U.S. 311 (1965), 684, 685

Minnesota Power & Light Co., 11 F.E.R.C. (CCH) ¶ 61,313 (1980), 1072

Minnesota v. United States Steel Corp., 44 F.R.D. 559 (D. Minn. 1968), 695

Minpeco, SA v. Conticommodity Servs., 116 F.R.D. 517 (S.D.N.Y.), aff'd sub nom. Korwek v. Hunt, 827 F.2d 874 (2d Cir. 1987), 887

Minpeco, SA v. Conticommodity Servs., 673 F. Supp. 684 (S.D.N.Y. 1987), 1106

Minpeco, SA v. Conti Commodity Servs., 1988-1 Trade Cas. (CCH) ¶ 67,885 (S.D.N.Y. 1988), 794

Miranda v. Arizona, 384 U.S. 436 (1966), 566

Miriam Maschek, Inc., 85 F.T.C. 536 (1975), 491

Mir v. Little Co. of Mary Hosp., 884 F.2d (9th Cir. 1988), 668, 695

Misco, Inc. v. United States Steel Corp., 784 F.2d 198 (6th Cir. 1986), 402

Mission Hills Condominium Ass'n M-1 v. Corley, 570 F. Supp. 453 (N.D. Ill. 1983), 138, 644

Mississippi River Corp. v. FTC, 454 F.2d 1083 (8th Cir. 1972), 319, 330

Mississippi River Fuel Corp., 69 F.T.C. 1186 (1966), 518

Mississippi v. Borden, Inc., No. 590-0272 (S.D. Miss. filed June 11, 1990), 605

Missouri Basin Mun. Power Agency v. Midwest Energy Co., 53 F.E.R.C. (CCH) ¶ 61,368 (1990), 1077, 1078

Missouri-Kan.-Tex. R.R. v. United States, 632 F.2d 392 (5th Cir. 1980), *cert. denied*, 451 U.S. 1017 (1981), 1142

Missouri Portland Cement Co. v. Cargill, Inc., 498 F.2d 851 (2d Cir.), *cert. denied*, 419 U.S. 883 (1974), 323, 328, 329, 335, 365, 366, 368, 369

Missouri v. Hunter, 459 U.S. 359 (1983), 596

Missouri v. Jenkins, 491 U.S. 274 (1989), 786

Missouri v. National Org. for Women, 620 F.2d 1301 (8th Cir.), *cert. denied*, 449 U.S. 842 (1980), 94, 1013

Mistretta v. United States, 488 U.S. 361 (1989), 596

Mitchell Bros. Film Group v. Cinema Adult Theater, 604 F.2d 852 (5th Cir. 1979), *cert. denied*, 445 U.S. 917 (1980), 846

Mitchell Cotts/Sofiltra, 30 O.J. EUR. COMM. (No. L 41) 31 (1987), [1985-1988 Transfer Binder] COMMON MKT. REP. (CCH) ¶ 10,852, 937

Mitchell v. Frank R. Howard Memorial Hosp., 853 F.2d 762 (9th Cir. 1988), *cert. denied*, 489 U.S. 1013 (1989), 24, 28

Mitchell v. United States Surgical Corp., 1976-1 Trade Cas. (CCH) ¶ 60,879 (S.D. Ohio 1976), 121, 130

Mitsubishi Motors Corp. v. Soler Chrysler-Plymouth, Inc., 473 U.S. 614 (1985), 787, 788, 840, 895-96

Mizlou Television Network v. NBC, 603 F. Supp. 677 (D.D.C. 1984), 98, 873

M.L.C., Inc. v. North Am. Philips Corp., 109 F.R.D. 134 (S.D.N.Y. 1986), 771

MLC, Inc. v. North Am. Philips Corp., 671 F. Supp. 246 (S.D.N.Y. 1987), 51, 83, 118, 119, 183, 188

M. Leff Radio Parts, Inc. v. Mattel, Inc., 706 F. Supp. 387 (W.D. Pa. 1988), 151, 158, 159

Mobil Oil Corp. v. Blanton, 471 U.S. 1007 (1985), 262

Mobil Oil Corp. v. W.R. Grace & Co., 367 F. Supp. 207 (D. Conn. 1973), 824

Mobil Oil Exploration & Producing Southeast, Inc. v. United Distrib. Cos., 111 S. Ct. 615 (1991), 1057

Modern Mktg. Serv., 71 F.T.C. 1676 (1967), 432

Modern Mktg. Serv., [1983-1987 Transfer Binder] TRADE REG. REP. (CCH) ¶ 22,158 (May 21, 1984), *dismissed*, Dkt. 3783 (Aug. 28, 1984), 435

Modrey v. American Gage & Mach. Co., 478 F.2d 470 (2d Cir. 1973), 826

Moët-Hennessy, 24 O.J. EUR. COMM. (No. L 94) 7 (1981), [1978-1981 Transfer Binder] COMMON MKT. REP. (CCH) ¶ 10,352, 939

Moffat v. Lane Co., 595 F. Supp. 43 (D. Mass. 1984), 9, 184, 185

Molinas v. NBA, 190 F. Supp. 241 (S.D.N.Y. 1961), 90

Moll v. U.S. Life Title Ins. Co., 113 F.R.D. 625 (S.D.N.Y. 1987), 722

Monahan's Marine, Inc. v. Boston Whaler, Inc., 866 F.2d 525 (1st Cir. 1989), 48, 53, 114

Monarch Asphalt Sales Co. v. Wilshire Oil Co., 511 F.2d 1073 (10th Cir. 1975), 687

Monarch Entertainment Bureau v. New Jersey Highway Auth., 715 F. Supp. 1290 (D.N.J.), *aff'd*, 893 F.2d 1331 (3d Cir. 1989), 246, 984, 992, 1008

Monarch Life Ins. Co. v. Loyal Protective Life Ins. Co., 326 F.2d 841 (2d Cir. 1963), *cert. denied*, 376 U.S. 952 (1964), 1117

Monfort of Colo., Inc. v. Cargill, Inc., 591 F. Supp. 683 (D. Colo. 1983), *aff'd*, 761 F.2d 570 (10th Cir. 1985), *rev'd*, 479 U.S. 104 (1986), 285, 288, 289, 294, 295, 300

Monfort of Colo., Inc. v. Cargill, Inc., 761 F.2d 570 (10th Cir. 1985), *rev'd on other grounds*, 479 U.S. 104 (1986), 292, 304, 308, 334

Mono-Therm Indus. v. FTC, 653 F.2d 1373 (10th Cir. 1981), 527, 529

Monroe Auto Equip. Co., 66 F.T.C. 276 (1964), 430

Monsanto Co. v. Spray-Rite Serv. Corp., 465 U.S. 752 (1984), 3, 4, 5, 11, 12, 13, 14, 15, 16, 17, 100, 101, 105, 107, 117, 180, 181, 613, 614, 635, 704, 705

Montana v. Superamerica, 559 F. Supp. 298 (D. Mont. 1983), 781

Montana v. United States, 440 U.S. 147 (1979), 775

Montauk-Carribbean Airways, Inc. v. Hope, 1985-2 Trade Cas. (CCH) ¶ 66,660, (E.D.N.Y. 1985) aff'd, 784 F.2d 91 (2d Cir.), cert. denied, 479 U.S. 872 (1986), 987, 988

Montgomery Ward & Co., 97 F.T.C. 363 (1981), modified, 691 F.2d 1322 (9th Cir. 1982), 540

Montgomery Ward & Co. v. FTC, 379 F.2d 666 (7th Cir. 1967), 465, 476, 489

Montreal Trading Ltd. v. Amax, Inc., 661 F.2d 864 (10th Cir. 1981), cert. denied, 455 U.S. 1001 (1982), 859, 896

Montvale Mgmt. Group v. Snowshoe Co., 1984-1 Trade Cas. (CCH) ¶ 65,990 (N.D. W.Va. 1984), 144, 145, 155, 210, 216, 242

Monument Builders v. American Cemetery Ass'n, 629 F. Supp. 1002 (D. Kan. 1986), 152

Monument Builders v. American Cemetery Ass'n, 891 F.2d 1473 (10th Cir. 1989), cert. denied, 110 S. Ct. 2168 (1990), 152, 272, 789

Moog Indus., 51 F.T.C. 931 (1955), aff'd, 238 F.2d 43 (8th Cir. 1958), aff'd per curiam, 355 U.S. 411 (1958), 430, 412

Moog Indus. v. FTC, 355 U.S. 411 (1958), 489

Moore v. Backus, 78 F.2d 571 (7th Cir.), cert. denied, 296 U.S. 640 (1935), 793

Moore v. Boating Indus. Ass'n, 754 F.2d 698 (7th Cir.), vacated, 474 U.S. 895 (1985), on remand, 819 F.2d 693 (7th Cir.), cert. denied, 484 U.S. 854 (1987), 45

Moore v. Boating Indus. Ass'n, 819 F.2d 693 (7th Cir.), cert. denied, 484 U.S. 854 (1987), 54, 87, 89, 90

Moore v. Illinois, 55 U.S. (14 How.) 13 (1852), 629

Moore v. Jas. H. Matthews & Co., 473 F.2d 328 (9th Cir. 1973), 704

Moore v. Jas. H. Matthews & Co., 550 F.2d 1207 (9th Cir. 1977), 131, 132, 135, 138, 139, 144, 146, 147, 152, 153, 154, 160, 161, 202

Moore v. Jas. H. Matthews & Co., 682 F.2d 830 (9th Cir. 1982), 670, 672

Moore v. Mead Serv. Co., 190 F.2d 540 (10th Cir. 1951), cert. denied, 342 U.S. 902 (1952), 426

Moore v. Mead's Fine Bread Co., 348 U.S. 115 (1954), 402, 414

Moore v. New York Cotton Exch., 270 U.S. 593 (1926), 542

Moore v. Southeast Toyota Distribs., 1982-2 Trade Cas. (CCH) ¶ 64,743 (N.D. Ala. 1982), 730, 734

Moosehead/Whitbread, Decision 90/186, 23 O.J. EUR. COMM. (No. L 100) 32 (1990), [1990] 1 CEC (CCH) 2127, 941, 947

Moraine Prods. v. ICI Am., Inc., 538 F.2d 134 (7th Cir.) cert. denied, 429 U.S. 941 (1976), 835

Moretrench Corp. v. FTC, 127 F.2d 792 (2d Cir. 1942), 465

Morey v. Doud, 354 U.S. 457 (1957), 627

Morgan Guaranty Trust Co. v. Republic of Palau, 702 F. Supp. 60 (S.D.N.Y. 1988), 901

Morgan Smith Automotive Prods., Inc. v. General Motors Corp., 54 F.R.D. 19 (E.D. Pa. 1971), 746, 748, 750, 757

Morgan, Strand, Wheeler & Biggs v. Radiology, Ltd., 924 F.2d 1484 (9th Cir. 1991), 45, 173, 199, 200, 208, 210, 268

Morgan v. Ponder, 892 F.2d 1355 (8th Cir. 1989), 227, 228, 232, 233, 235

Morning Pioneer, Inc. v. Bismarck Tribune Co., 493 F.2d 383 (8th Cir.), cert. denied, 419 U.S. 836 (1974), 410

Morris Elecs. Inc. v. Mattel, Inc., 595 F. Supp. 56 (N.D.N.Y. 1984), 438, 441

Morrison v. Murray Biscuit Co., 797 F.2d 1430 (7th Cir. 1986), 103, 123, 124, 125, 126, 189

Mortensen v. First Fed. Sav. & Loan Ass'n, 549 F.2d 884 (3d Cir. 1977), 28, 29

Morton Bldgs. v. Morton Bldgs., Inc., 531 F.2d 910 (8th Cir. 1976), 22

Morton Salt Co. v. G.S. Suppiger Co., 314 U.S. 488 (1942), 800, 813, 814, 815, 816, 832, 846

Morton v. Charles County Bd. of Educ., 373 F. Supp. 394 (D. Md. 1974), aff'd, 520 F.2d 871 (4th Cir.), cert. denied, 423 U.S. 1034 (1975), 695

Morton v. National Dairy Prods. Corp., 287 F. Supp. 753 (E.D. Pa. 1968), aff'd, 414 F.2d 403 (3d Cir. 1969), cert. denied, 396 U.S. 1006 (1970), 423, 424

Mosby v. American Medical Int'l, 656 F. Supp. 601 (S.D. Tex. 1987), 647

Motion Picture Patents Co. v. Universal Film Mfg. Co., 243 U.S. 502 (1917), 813, 817

Motive Parts Warehouse v. Facet Enter., 774 F.2d 380 (10th Cir. 1985), 21, 406, 414, 417, 437, 439, 442

Motor Carriers Labor Advisory Council v. Trucking Mgmt., 711 F. Supp. 216 (E.D. Pa. 1989), 644

Motor Vehicle Mfrs. Ass'n v. Abrams, 899 F2d. 1315 (2d Cir. 1990), *cert. denied*, 111 S. Ct. 1122 (1991), 623

Mountain Grove Cemetery Ass'n v. Norwalk Vault Co., 428 F. Supp. 951 (D. Conn. 1977), 1000

Mountain States Tel. & Tel. Co. v. District Court, 1989-2 Trade Cas. (CCH) ¶ 68,679 (Colo. 1989), 738, 739

Mount Pleasant v. Associated Elec. Coop., 838 F.2d 268 (8th Cir. 1988), 205

Mourning v. Family Publications Serv., 411 U.S. 356 (1973), 534

Movie 1 & 2 v. United Artists Communs., 909 F.2d 1245 (9th Cir. 1990), *cert. denied*, 111 S. Ct. 2852 (1991), 40, 63, 85, 268

Moviecolor Ltd. v. Eastman Kodak Co., 288 F.2d 80 (2d Cir.), *cert. denied*, 368 U.S. 821 (1961), 688, 692

Mozart Co. v. Mercedes-Benz of N. Am., Inc., 593 F. Supp. 1506 (N.D. Cal. 1984), *aff'd*, 833 F.2d 1342 (9th Cir. 1987), *cert. denied*, 488 U.S. 870 (1988), 140, 144, 146, 147, 153

Mozart Co. v. Mercedes Benz of N. Am., Inc., 833 F.2d 1342 (9th Cir. 1987), *cert. denied*, 488 U.S. 870 (1988), 135, 148, 152, 155, 156, 160, 161, 162, 776

Mr. Frank, Inc. v. Waste Mgmt., Inc., 1981-1 Trade Cas. (CCH) ¶ 63,945 (N.D. Ill. 1981), 649

Mr. Frank, Inc. v. Waste Mgmt., Inc., 591 F. Supp. 859 (N.D. Ill. 1984), 280, 749

Mr. Furniture Warehouse, Inc. v. Barclays Am./Commercial, Inc., 919 F.2d 1517 (11th Cir. 1990), 242

Mt. Hood Stages, Inc. v. Greyhound Corp., 555 F.2d 687 (9th Cir. 1977), *vacated on other grounds*, 437 U.S. 322 (1978), 682, 690

Mt. Hood Stages, Inc. v. Greyhound Corp., 616 F.2d 394 (9th Cir.), *cert. denied*, 449 U.S. 831 (1980), 694, 1021, 1022

Mt. Mansfield Television, Inc. v. FCC, 442 F.2d 470 (2d Cir. 1971), 1029, 1039

Mt. Vernon Sundat, Inc. v. Nissan Motor Corp., 1976-1 Trade Cas. (CCH) ¶ 60,842 (E.D. Va. 1976), 112

Mueller Co., 60 F.T.C. 120 (1962), *aff'd*, 323 F.2d 44 (7th Cir. 1963), *cert. denied*, 377 U.S. 923 (1964), 428

Mueller Co. v. FTC, 323 F.2d 44 (7th Cir. 1963), *cert. denied*, 377 U.S. 1923 (1964), 407

Muenster Butane, Inc. v. Stewart Co., 651 F.2d 292 (5th Cir. 1981), 41, 45, 47, 48, 118, 123, 124, 125, 126, 187

Mugler v. Kansas, 123 U.S. 623 (1887), 627

Mul-T-Lock Corp. v. Mul-T-Lock, Ltd., 1984-1 Trade Cas. (CCH) ¶ 65,855 (E.D.N.Y. 1984), 863

Mularkey v. Holsum Bakery, 120 F.R.D. 118 (D. Ariz. 1988), 718

Mullane v. Central Hanover Bank & Trust Co., 339 U.S. 306 (1950), 744

Mullis v. Arco Petroleum Corp., 502 F.2d 290 (7th Cir. 1974), 188, 190, 407

Multiflex, Inc. v. Samuel Moore & Co., 709 F.2d 980 (5th Cir. 1983), *cert. denied*, 465 U.S. 1100 (1984), 196, 265, 670, 672

Multiple Ownership, 50 F.C.C. 2d 1046 (1975), 1038

Mulvey v. Samuel Goldwyn Prods., 433 F.2d 1073 (9th Cir. 1970), *cert. denied*, 402 U.S. 923 (1971), 661

Municipal Bond Reporting Antitrust Litig., 672 F.2d 436 (5th Cir. 1982), 203

Municipal Elec. Ass'n v. SEC, 413 F.2d 1052 (D.C. Cir. 1969), 1076

Municipal Elec. Ass'n v. SEC, 419 F.2d 757 (D.C. Cir. 1969), 1076

Municipality of Anchorage v. Hitachi Cable, Ltd., 547 F. Supp. 633 (D. Alaska 1982), 434, 583, 702, 776

Municipal Utils Bd. v. Alabama Power Co., 934 F.2d 1493 (11th Cir. 1991), 973, 994, 1009

Munters Corp. v. Burgess Indus., 450 F. Supp. 1195 (S.D.N.Y. 1977), 828, 829, 830

Murphy Tugboat Co. v. Crowley, 658 F.2d 1256 (9th Cir. 1981), *cert. denied*, 455 U.S. 1018 (1982), 672, 674

Murphy Tugboat Co. v. Shipowners & Merchants Towboat Co., 467 F. Supp. 841 (N.D. Cal. 1979), *aff'd sub nom.* Murphy Tugboat Co. v. Crowley, 658 F.2d 1256 (9th Cir. 1981), *cert. denied*, 455 U.S. 1018 (1982), 203

Murphy v. Alpha Realty, Inc., 1977-2 Trade Cas. (CCH) ¶ 61,566 (N.D. Ill. 1977), 722, 723

Murphy v. Business Cards Tomorrow, Inc., 854 F.2d 1202 (9th Cir. 1988), 45, 47, 48, 118, 123, 124, 126, 147, 182, 192

Murray Space Shoe Corp. v. FTC, 304 F.2d 270 (2d Cir. 1962), 465

Murrow Furniture Galleries v. Thomasville Furniture Indus., 889 F.2d 524 (4th Cir. 1989), 44, 50, 51, 123, 124, 125, 271

Musick v. Burke, 913 F.2d 1390 (9th Cir. 1990), 24

Musik-Bertrieb Membran GmbH v. GEMA, Joined Cases 55 and 57/80, [1981] E.C.R. 147, [1979-1981 Transfer Binder] COMMON MKT. REP. (CCH) ¶ 8670, 946

Musique Diffusion Française SA v. Commission, Joined Cases 100-03/80, [1983] E.C.R. 1825, [1981-1983 Transfer Binder] COMMON MKT. REP. (CCH) ¶ 8880, 919, 922

Mutual Fund Investors, Inc. v. Putnam Management Co., 553 F.2d 620 (9th Cir. 1977), 704

M. Witmark & Sons v. Pastime Amusement Co., 298 F. 470 (E.D.S.C.), *aff'd*, 2 F.2d 1020 (4th Cir. 1924), 846

Myers v. Shell Oil Co., 96 F. Supp. 670 (S.D. Cal. 1951), 402

Mytinger & Casselberry, Inc., 57 F.T.C. 717 (1960), *aff'd*, 301 F.2d 534 (D.C. Cir. 1962), 174

N

NAACP v. Claiborne Hardware Co., 458 U.S. 886 (1981), 94, 1012

Nader v. Allegheny Airlines, 512 F.2d 527 (D.C. Cir. 1975), *rev'd*, 426 U.S. 290 (1976), 1156

Naifeh v. Ronson Art Metal Works, Inc., 218 F.2d 202 (10th Cir. 1954), 407

Naify v. McClatchy Newspapers, 599 F.2d 335 (9th Cir. 1979), 191

Nanavati v. Burdette Tomlin Memorial Hosp., 857 F.2d 96 (3d Cir. 1988), *cert. denied*, 489 U.S. 1078 (1989), 21

Nankin Hosp. v. Michigan Hosp. Serv., 361 F. Supp. 1199 (E. D. Mich. 1973), 185, 1111

Nara v. American Dental Ass'n, 526 F. Supp. 452 (W.D. Mich. 1981), 645

Nash County Bd. of Educ. v. Biltmore Co., 640 F.2d 484 (4th Cir.), *cert. denied*, 454 U.S. 878 (1981), 604, 631

Nashua Corp. v. RCA Corp., 431 F.2d 220 (1st Cir. 1970), 836

Nashville Milk Co. v. Carnation Co., 355 U.S. 373 (1958), 451, 645

Nassau-Suffolk Ice Cream, Inc. v. Integrated Resources, Inc., 114 F.R.D. 684 (S.D.N.Y. 1987), 789

Natcontainer Corp. v. Continental Can Co., 362 F. Supp. 1094 (S.D.N.Y. 1973), 701, 746, 747, 748

National Account Sys., 89 F.T.C. 282 (1977), 533

National Ass'n of Broadcasters v. FCC, 740 F.2d 1190 (D.C. Cir. 1984), 1042

National Ass'n of Pharmaceutical Mfrs. v. Ayerst Labs., 850 F.2d 904 (2d Cir. 1988), 222, 663

National Ass'n of Recycling Indus. v. American Mail Line, 720 F.2d 618 (9th Cir. 1983), *cert. denied*, 465 U.S. 1109 (1984), 1165

National Ass'n of Regulatory Util. Commissioners v. FCC, 880 F.2d 422 (D.C. Cir. 1989), 1047

National Ass'n of Theatre Owners v. FCC, 420 F.2d 194 (D.C. Cir. 1969), *cert. denied*, 397 U.S. 922 (1970), 1042

National Auto Brokers Corp. v. General Motors Corp., 1974-2 Trade Cas. (CCH) ¶ 75,281 (S.D.N.Y. 1974), 410

National Auto Brokers Corp. v. General Motors Corp., 376 F. Supp. 620 (S.D.N.Y. 1974), aff'd, 572 F.2d 953 (2d Cir. 1978), cert. denied, 439 U.S. 1072 (1979), 408, 437

National Auto Brokers Corp. v. General Motors Corp., 572 F.2d 953 (2d Cir. 1978), cert. denied, 439 U.S. 1072 (1979), 41, 124, 187

National Bancard Corp. v. VISA U.S.A., Inc., 596 F. Supp. 1231 (S.D. Fla. 1984), aff'd, 779 F.2d 592 (11th Cir.), cert. denied, 479 U.S. 923 (1986), 37, 38, 39, 48, 49, 50, 51, 52, 56, 380, 1091

National Bancard Corp. v. VISA U.S.A., Inc., 779 F.2d 592 (11th Cir.), cert. denied, 479 U.S. 923 (1986), 41, 45, 53, 77, 375, 380

National Bank of Can. v. Interbank Card Ass'n, 507 F. Supp. 1113 (S.D.N.Y. 1980), aff'd, 666 F.2d 6 (2d Cir. 1981), 38, 380, 383

National Bank of Can. v. Interbank Card Ass'n, 666 F.2d 6 (2d Cir. 1981), 857, 860

National Biscuit Co. v. FTC, 299 F. 733 (2d Cir.), cert. denied, 266 U.S. 613 (1924), 401

National Broiler Marketing Ass'n v. United States, 436 U.S. 816 (1978), 1027

National Cable Television Ass'n v. Broadcast Music, Inc., 772 F. Supp. 614 (D.D.C. 1991), 39, 48, 374

National Cash Register Corp. v. Arnett, 554 F. Supp. 1176 (D. Colo. 1983), 1001

National Classification Comm. v. United States, 746 F.2d 886 (D.C. Cir. 1984), 1128

National Coal Ass'n v. Hodel, 825 F.2d 523 (D.C. Cir. 1987), 1085

National Comm'n on Egg Nutrition, 88 F.T.C. 89 (1976), enforced as modified, 570 F.2d 157 (7th Cir. 1977), cert. denied, 439 U.S. 821 (1978), 467, 468

National Comm'n on Egg Nutrition v. FTC, 570 F.2d 157 (7th Cir. 1977), cert. denied, 439 U.S. 821 (1978), 456, 466, 491, 492, 493, 494

National Constructors Ass'n v. National Elec. Contractors Ass'n, 498 F. Supp. 510 (D. Md. 1980), modified, 678 F.2d 492 (4th Cir. 1982), cert. dismissed, 403 U.S. 1234 (1983), 715

National Customs Brokers & Forwarders Ass'n v. United States, 883 F.2d 93 (D.C. Cir. 1989), 1159

National Dairy Prods. Corp., 70 F.T.C. 79 (1966), aff'd, 395 F.2d 517 (7th Cir.), cert. denied, 393 U.S. 977 (1968), 422, 425

National Dairy Prods. Corp. v. FTC, 395 F.2d 517 (7th Cir.), cert. denied, 393 U.S. 977 (1968), 407, 422, 428, 429, 488, 489

National Dairy Prods. Corp. v. FTC, 412 F.2d 605 (7th Cir. 1969), 414

National Distillers & Chem. Corp. v. Brad's Machine Prods., Inc., 666 F.2d 492 (11th Cir. 1982), 415

National Dynamics Corp., 82 F.T.C. 488 (1973), remanded in part, 492 F.2d 1333 (2d Cir.), cert. denied, 419 U.S. 993 (1974), 466, 467, 472

National Elec. Contractors Ass'n v. National Constructors Ass'n, 678 F.2d 492 (4th Cir. 1982), 40, 66, 70

National Farmers Org. v. Associated Milk Producers, Inc., 850 F.2d 1286 (8th Cir. 1988), 665, 668, 671, 672, 673, 675

National Foam Sys. v. Urquhart, 202 F.2d 659 (3d Cir. 1953), 825, 833

National Gerimedical Hosp. & Gerontology Center v. Blue Cross, 452 U.S. 378 (1981), 1019

National Hairdressers' & Cosmetologists' Ass'n v. Philad Co., 4 F.R.D. 106 (D. Del. 1944), 740

National Hockey League v. Metropolitan Hockey Club, 427 U.S. 639 (1976), 767, 768

National Indem. Co., 92 F.T.C. 426 (1978), 537

National Indep. Theatre Exhibitors, Inc. v. Charter Fin. Group, 747 F.2d 1396 (11th Cir. 1984), cert. denied, 471 U.S. 1056 (1985), 179

National Indep. Theatre Exhibitors v. Buena Vista Distrib. Co., 748 F.2d 602 (11th Cir. 1984), cert. denied, 471 U.S. 1056 (1985), 665, 666

National Lead Co. v. FTC, 227 F.2d 825 (7th Cir. 1955), 489

National Lockwasher Co. v. George K. Garrett Co., 137 F.2d 255 (3d Cir. 1943), 828

National Macaroni Mfrs. Ass'n v. FTC, 345 F.2d 421 (7th Cir. 1965), 70, 391

National Marine Elec. Distribs., v. Raytheon Co., 778 F.2d 190 (4th Cir. 1985), 13, 186, 189

National Panasonic (UK) Ltd. v. Commission, Case 136/79, [1980] E.C.R. 2033, [1979-1981 Transfer Binder] COMMON MKT. REP. (CCH) ¶ 8682, 919

National Parks & Conservation Ass'n v. Morton, 498 F.2d 765 (D.C. Cir. 1974), 519

National Parts Warehouse, 63 F.T.C. 1692 (1963), aff'd sub nom. General Auto Supplies v. F.T.C., 346 F.2d 311 (7th Cir.), cert. dismissed, 382 U.S. 923 (1965), 424, 430, 446, 447

National Petroleum Refiners Ass'n v. FTC, 482 F.2d 672 (D.C. Cir. 1973), cert. denied, 415 U.S. 951 (1974), 525

National Reporting Co. v. Alderson Reporting Co., 763 F.2d 1020 (8th Cir. 1985), 197, 263, 266

National Retailer-Owned Grocers, 60 F.T.C. 1208 (1962), rev'd sub nom. Central Retailer-Owned Grocers v. FTC, 319 F.2d 410 (7th Cir. 1963), 433

National Ry. Utilization Corp. v. Association of Am. R.Rs., 1983-2 Trade Cas. (CCH) ¶ 65,671 (E.D. Pa. 1983), 758

National Soc'y of Professional Eng'rs v. United States, 435 U.S. 679 (1978), 1, 2, 30, 32, 33, 34, 35, 42, 43, 44, 46, 52, 54, 68, 87, 98, 379, 493

National Souvenir Center, Inc. v. Historic Figures, Inc., 728 F.2d 503 (D.C. Cir.), cert. denied, 469 U.S. 825 (1984), 792

National Sulphuric Acid Ass'n, Decision 89/408, 23 O.J. EUR. COMM. (No. L 260) 24 (1980), [1978-1981 Transfer Binder] COMMON MKT. REP. (CCH) ¶ 10,246, exemption renewed, 32 O.J. EUR. COMM. (No. L 190) 22 (1989), [1989] 2 CEC (CCH) 2006, 933

National Super Spuds, Inc. v. New York Mercantile Exch., 77 F.R.D. 361 (S.D.N.Y. 1977), 733

National Supply Co. v. Hillman, 57 F. Supp. 4 (W.D. Pa. 1944), 280

National Sys. Corp., 93 F.T.C. 58 (1979), 499

National Tea Co., 96 F.T.C. 42 (1980), 345

National Tea Co., 97 F.T.C. 338 (1981), 247, 347

National Tire Wholesale, Inc. v. Washington Post, 441 F. Supp. 81 (D.D.C. 1977), aff'd without opinion, 595 F.2d 888 (D.C. Cir. 1979), 410

National Treasury Employees Union v. Nixon, 521 F.2d 317 (D.C. Cir. 1975), 782

National Union Elec. Corp. v. Emerson Elec. Co., 1981-2 Trade Cas. (CCH) ¶ 64,274 (N.D. Ill. 1981), 574, 646

Nationwide Mut. Ins. Co. v. Automotive Serv. Councils, 1981-1 Trade Cas. (CCH) ¶ 63,958 (D. Del. 1981), 776

Natrona Serv. v. Continental Oil Co., 598 F.2d 1294 (10th Cir. 1979), 193

Natta v. Hogan, 392 F.2d 686 (10th Cir. 1968), 760

Natural Design, Inc. v. Rouse Co., 1985-1 Trade Cas. (CCH) ¶ 66,339 (Md. 1984), 635

Naxon Telesign Corp. v. Bunker Ramo Corp., 517 F. Supp. 804 (N.D. Ill. 1981), aff'd, 686 F.2d 1258 (7th Cir. 1982), 689, 828

Naylor v. Case & McGrath, Inc., 585 F.2d 557 (2d Cir. 1978), 542, 645

NBC v. United States, 47 F. Supp. 940 (S.D.N.Y. 1942), 1031

NBC v. United States, 319 U.S. 190 (1943), 1030, 1031

NBO Indus. Treadway Cos. v. Brunswick Corp., 523 F.2d 262 (3d Cir. 1975), vacated and remanded sub nom. Brunswick Corp. v. Pueblo Bowl-O-Mat, Inc., 429 U.S. 477 (1977), 335, 359

NCAA v. Board of Regents, 468 U.S. 85 (1984), 2, 30, 32, 33, 35, 39, 41, 46, 47, 50, 52, 62, 67, 74, 84, 90, 135, 373, 374, 375, 380, 390

NCR Corp. v. AT&T, No. C-3-91-33 (S.D. Ohio filed Jan. 22, 1991), 636

Nebbia v. New York, 291 U.S. 502 (1934), 627

Nebraska Dep't of Aeronautics v. CAB, 298 F.2d 286 (8th Cir. 1962), 1156

Nebraska-Iowa Car Wash, Inc. v. Mobil Oil Corp., 1976-1 Trade Cas. (CCH) ¶ 60,849 (N.D. Ia. 1976), 190

Nebraska v. Land Paving Co., 1986-1 Trade Cas. (CCH) ¶ 67,196 (D. Neb. 1985), 688

Nebraska v. Nintendo of Am., Inc., No. 91-CV 2498 (RWS) (S.D.N.Y. filed Apr. 10, 1991), 611

Nederlandsche Baden-Indus., Michelin NV v. Commission, Case 322/81, [1983] ECR 3461, [1983-1985 Transfer Binder] COMMON MKT. REP. (CCH) ¶ 14,031, 950-52

Nederlandsche Banden-Indus. Michelin, 24 O.J. EUR. COMM. (No. L 353) 33 (1981), [1978-1981 Transfer Binder] COMMON MKT. REP. (CCH) ¶ 10,340, aff'd sub nom. Nederlandsche Banden-Indus., Michelin NV v. Commission, Case 322/81, [1983] E.C.R. 3461, [1983-1985 Transfer Binder] COMMON MKT. REP. (CCH) ¶ 14,031, 956

Nederlandse Cement-Handelmaatschappij NV, 15 J.O. COMM. EUR. (No. L 22) 16 (1972), [1970-1972 Transfer Binder] COMMON MKT. REP. (CCH) ¶ 9493, 933

Needles v. F.W. Woolworth Co., 13 F.R.D. 460 (E.D. Pa. 1952), 747

Neeld v. National Hockey League, 594 F.2d 1297 (9th Cir. 1979), 85, 91

Nelligan v. Ford Motor Co., 262 F.2d 556 (4th Cir. 1959), 132

Nelson Radio & Supply Co. v. Motorola, Inc., 200 F.2d 911 (5th Cir. 1952), cert. denied, 345 U.S. 925 (1953), 22, 147, 182

Nelson v. Monroe Regional Medical Center, 925 F.2d 1555 (7th Cir.), cert. dismissed, 112 S. Ct. 285 (1991), 25, 659

Nelson v. Pacific Southwest Airlines, 399 F. Supp. 1025 (S.D. Cal. 1975), 280

Nelson v. United Credit Plan, Inc., 77 F.R.D. 54 (E.D. La. 1978), 695

Net Realty Holding Trust v. Franconia Properties, Inc., 1983-1 Trade Cas. (CCH) ¶ 65,222 (E.D. Va. 1983), 700

Neugebauer v. A.S. Abell Co., 474 F. Supp. 1053 (D. Md. 1979), 130

Neumann v. Reinforced Earth Co., 594 F. Supp. 139 (D.D.C. 1984), aff'd, 786 F.2d 424 (D.C. Cir.), cert. denied, 479 U.S. 851 (1986), 649

Neumann v. Reinforced Earth Co., 786 F.2d 424 (D.C. Cir.), cert. denied, 479 U.S. 851 (1986), 197, 206, 222, 258, 261, 264, 811, 998

Neumann v. Vidal, 1982-2 Trade Cas. (CCH) ¶ 64,933 (D.D.C. 1981), 749, 750, 751, 752, 876

New Amsterdam Cheese Corp. v. Kraftco Corp., 363 F. Supp. 135 (S.D.N.Y. 1973), 186

Newberry v. Washington Post Co., 438 F. Supp. 470 (D.D.C. 1977), 104

New Dyckman Theatre Corp. v. Radio-Keith-Orpheum Corp., 20 F.R.D. 36 (S.D.N.Y. 1955), 408

New England Motor Rate Bureau, 5 TRADE REG. REP. (CCH) ¶ 22,722 (Aug. 18, 1989), modified sub nom. New England Motor Rate Bureau v. FTC, 908 F.2d 1064 (1st Cir. 1990), 57, 58, 455, 456

New England Motor Rate Bureau v. FTC, 908 F.2d 1064 (1st Cir. 1990), 974, 925

Newhouse Broadcasting Corp., 59 F.C.C. 2d 218 (1976), 1038

New Jersey v. Emhart Corp., No. 15664 (D. Conn. Oct. 30, 1974), 604

New Jersey v. General Motors Corp., 1974-2 Trade Cas. (CCH) ¶ 75,338 (N.D. Ill.), appeal dismissed mem., 500 F.2d 1404 (7th Cir.), cert. denied, 419 U.S. 1080 (1974), 604

New Jersey v. Morton Salt Co., 387 F.2d 94 (3d Cir. 1967), cert. denied, 391 U.S. 967 (1968), 686, 687

New Jersey v. National Broiler Mktg. Ass'n, No. C75-362A (N.D. Ga. Dec. 30, 1976), 604

New Jersey Wood Finishing Co. v. Minnesota Mining & Mfg., 332 F.2d 346 (3d Cir. 1964), aff'd, 381 U.S. 311 (1965), 645, 684

New Medical Techniques, Inc., 110 F.T.C. 125 (1987), 474

New Mexico Navajo Ranchers Ass'n v. ICC, 702 F.2d 227 (D.C. Cir. 1983), 1134

New Mexico v. Scott & Fetzer Co., 1981-2 Trade Cas. (CCH) ¶ 64,439 (D.N.M. 1981), 608

New Motor Vehicle Bd. v. Orrin W. Fox Co., 439 U.S. 96 (1978), 621, 968, 969, 995

New Rapids Carpet Center, Inc., 90 F.T.C. 64 (1977), 534

News Am. Publishing, Inc. v. FCC, 844 F.2d 800 (D.C. Cir. 1988), 1036

New York Airlines v. Dukes County, 623 F. Supp. 1435 (D. Mass. 1985), 921

New York Central & Hudson R.R. v. United States, 212 U.S. 481 (1909), 594

New York Citizens Comm. on Cable TV v. Manhattan Cable TV, Inc., 651 F. Supp. 802 (S.D.N.Y. 1986), 1054

New York Life Ins. Co. v. Deer Lodge County, 231 U.S. 495 (1913), 1109

New York Shipping Ass'n v. FMC, 854 F.2d 1338 (D.C. Cir. 1988), cert. denied, 488 U.S. 1041 (1989), 1163

New York State Elec. & Gas Corp. v. FERC, 638 F.2d 388 (2d Cir. 1980), *cert. denied*, 454 U.S. 821 (1981), 1067, 1069

New York v. Amfar Asphalt Corp., 1987-1 Trade Cas. (CCH) ¶ 67,417 (E.D.N.Y. 1986), *aff'd sub nom.* New York v. Hendrickson Bros., 840 F.2d 1065 (2d Cir.), *cert. denied*, 488 U.S. 848 (1988), 611, 631, 640

New York v. Anheuser-Busch, Inc., 117 F.R.D. 349 (E.D.N.Y. 1987), 715, 734

New York v. Anheuser-Busch, Inc., 673 F. Supp. 664 (E.D.N.Y. 1987), 125

New York v. Anheuser-Busch, Inc., 1990-2 Trade Cas. (CCH) ¶ 69,184 (E.D.N.Y. 1990), 125, 613

New York v. Brooks Drug, Inc., No. 90-CV 4330 (SWK) (S.D.N.Y. filed June 28, 1990), 605

New York v. Brown, 721 F. Supp. 629 (D.N.J. 1989), 636

New York v. Cedar Park Concrete Corp., 665 F. Supp. 238 (S.D.N.Y. 1987), 604, 647, 755

New York v. Cedar Park Concrete Corp., 684 F. Supp. 1229 (S.D.N.Y. 1988), 611

New York v. Dairylea Cooperative, Inc., 570 F. Supp. 1213 (S.D.N.Y. 1983), 658

New York v. Dairylea Cooperative, Inc., 547 F. Supp. 306 (S.D.N.Y. 1982), *appeal dismissed*, 698 F.2d 567 (2d Cir. 1983), 608

New York v. Hendrickson Bros., 840 F.2d 1065 (2d Cir.), *cert. denied*, 488 U.S. 848 (1988), 603, 653, 665, 669, 673, 688, 693

New York v. Rochester Automobile Dealers Ass'n., Index No. 5803-90, Indict. No. 445-A (N.Y. Sup. Ct. May 16, 1990), 633

New York v. Salem Sanitary Carting Corp. 1989-2 Trade Cas. (CCH) ¶ 68,691 (E.D.N.Y. 1989), 729, 731

New York v. Salem Sanitary Carting Corp., No. CV-85-0208 (ILG) (E.D.N.Y. Nov. 16, 1989), 605

New York v. Sullivan Highway Prods., Inc., No. 89-CV 4218 (JFK) (S.D.N.Y. Dec. 21, 1989), 605

New York v. VISA, U.S.A., Inc., 1990-1 Trade Cas. (CCH) ¶ 69,016 (S.D.N.Y. 1990), 612

New York v. Yonkers Contracting Co., 90-CV 3779 (CES) (S.D.N.Y. filed June 4, 1990), 605

Newark Gardens, Inc. v. Michigan Potato Indus. Comm'n, 847 F.2d 1201 (6th Cir. 1988), 1025

Newberry v. Washington Post Co., 71 F.R.D. 25 (D.D.C. 1976), 719

Newberry v. Washington Post Co., 438 F. Supp. 470 (D.D.C. 1977), 56, 104, 107, 108, 109, 118, 124, 126, 127, 191, 192

Newburger, Loeb & Co. v. Gross, 563 F.2d 1057 (2d Cir. 1977), *cert. denied*, 434 U.S. 1035 (1978), 99

Newburgh Moire Co. v. Superior Moire Co., 237 F.2d 283 (3d Cir. 1956), 821, 822

Newhouse Broadcasting Corp., 59 F.C.C.2d 218 (1976), 1039

Newport Components, Inc. v. NEC Home Elecs. (U.S.A.), Inc., 671 F. Supp. 1525 (C.D. Cal. 1987), 876

NFL v. North Am. Soccer League, 459 U.S. 1074 (1982), 374

Niagara Frontier Tariff Bureau v. United States, 1 I.C.C.2d 317 (1984), *aff'd per curiam*, 780 F.2d 109 (D.C. Cir. 1986), 1128

Niagara Frontier Tariff Bureau v. United States, 826 F.2d 1186 (2d Cir. 1987), 1128

Nichols v. Mobile Bd. of Realtors, 675 F.2d 671 (5th Cir. 1982), 725, 726, 734, 737

Nichols v. Spencer Int'l Press, Inc., 371 F.2d 332 (7th Cir. 1967), 648

Nichols v. Stroh Brewery, 1990-1 Trade Cas. (CCH) ¶ 68,944 (M.D. Pa. 1989), 790

Nifty Foods Corp. v. Great Atl. & Pac. Tea Co., 614 F.2d 832 (2d Cir. 1980), 179, 202, 215, 265

Nintendo of Am., Inc., FTC file No. 901-0028 (Apr. 10, 1991), 101, 107, 611

Nippon Sheet Glass Co., 5 TRADE REG. REP. (CCH) ¶ 22,810 (July 26, 1990), 377, 381

Niresk Indus. v. FTC, 278 F.2d 337 (7th Cir.), *cert. denied*, 364 U.S. 883 (1960), 475, 490

NL Indus. v. Gulf & Western Indus., 650 F. Supp. 1115 (D. Kan. 1986), 431, 435

Nobel Scientific Indus. v. Beckman Instruments, Inc., 670 F. Supp. 1313 (D. Md. 1986), *aff'd without published opinion*, 831 F.2d 537 (4th Cir. 1987), *cert. denied*, 487 U.S. 1226 (1988), 135, 148

Noble v. McClatchy Newspapers, 533 F.2d 1081 (9th Cir. 1975), *cert. denied*, 433 U.S. 908 (1977), 121, 130

Nolan's R.V. Center, Inc., 95 F.T.C. 294 (1980), 540

Nordic Bank PLC v. Trend Group, Ltd., 619 F. Supp. 542 (S.D.N.Y. 1985), 139

Norfolk Monmart Co. v. Woodlawn, 394 U.S. 700 (1969), 704

Norman v. McKee, 431 F.2d 769 (9th Cir. 1970), *cert. denied*, 401 U.S. 912 (1971), 740

Norstar Bancorp, 70 Fed. Res. Bull. 164 (1984), 1094

North Am. Philips Co. v. Stewart Eng'g Co., 319 F. Supp. 335 (N.D. Cal. 1970), 834

North Am. Philips Corp., 107 F.T.C. 62 (1986), 474

North Am. Philips Corp., 111 F.T.C. 139 (1988), 469, 473, 474

North Am. Produce Corp. v. Nick Penachio Co., 705 F. Supp. 746 (E.D.N.Y. 1988), 103

North Am. Soccer League v. NFL, 465 F. Supp. 665 (S.D.N.Y. 1979), 90, 249

North Am. Soccer League v. NFL, 505 F. Supp. 659 (S.D.N.Y. 1980), *aff'd in part and rev'd in part*, 670 F.2d 1249 (2d Cir.), *cert. denied*, 459 U.S. 1074 (1982), 781

North Am. Soccer League v. NFL, 670 F.2d 1249 (2d Cir.), *cert. denied*, 459 U.S. 1074 (1982), 37, 46, 56, 396

North Carolina Elec. Membership Corp. v. Carolina Power & Light Co., 666 F.2d 50 (4th Cir. 1981), 1014

North Carolina State Bd. of Registration for Professional Eng'rs & Land Surveyors v. FTC, 615 F. Supp. 1155 (E.D.N.C. 1985), 507, 523

North Carolina Utils. Comm'n v. FCC, 537 F.2d 787 (4th Cir.), *cert. denied*, 429 U.S. 1027 (1976), 1028

North Carolina v. Alford, 400 U.S. 25 (1970), 580

North Carolina v. P.I.A. Asheville, Inc., 740 F.2d 274 (1984), *cert. denied*, 471 U.S. 1003 (1985), 1018

North Carolina v. Pearce, 395 U.S. 711 (1969), 581

North Central Watt Count, Inc. v. Watt Count Eng'g Sys., 678 F. Supp. 1305 (M.D. Tenn. 1988), 60

Northeastern Educ. Television v. Educational Television Ass'n, 1991-1 Trade Cas. (CCH) ¶ 69,330, (N.D. Ohio 1990), 206, 209

Northeastern Tel. Co. v. AT&T, 497 F. Supp. 230 (D. Conn. 1980), *rev'd on other grounds*, 651 F.2d 76 (2d Cir. 1981), *cert. denied*, 455 U.S. 943 (1982), 673

Northeastern Tel. Co. v. AT&T, 651 F.2d 76 (2d Cir. 1981), *cert. denied*, 455 U.S. 943 (1982), 225, 228, 229, 234, 236, 253, 254, 255, 671

Northeast Jet Center, Ltd. v. Lehigh-Northampton Airport Auth., 767 F. Supp. 672 (E.D. Pa. 1991), 928

Northeast Utils. Serv. Co., 50 F.E.R.C. (CCH) ¶ 61,266 (1990), 1074, 1075, 1076

Northeast Women's Ctr. v. McMonagla, 670 F. Supp. 1300 (E.D. Pa. 1987), 50

Northern Cal. Power Agency v. FPC, 514 F.2d 184 (D.C. Cir.) *cert. denied*, 423 U.S. 863 (1975), 1067

Northern Cal. Supermarkets v. Central Cal. Lettuce Producers Coop., 580 F.2d 369 (9th Cir. 1978), *cert. denied*, 439 U.S. 1090 (1979), 1027

Northern Feather Works, Inc. v. FTC, 234 F.2d 335 (3d Cir. 1956), 524

Northern Ind. Pub. Serv. Co., 42 F.E.R.C. (CCH) ¶ 61,245 (1988), 1078

Northern Miss. Communs. v. Jones, 792 F.2d 1330 (5th Cir. 1986), 270, 271

Northern Natural Gas Co., 48 F.E.R.C. (CCH) ¶ 61,232 (1989), 1061, 1062

Northern Natural Gas Co. v. FPC, 399 F.2d 953 (D.C. Cir. 1968), 1030

Northern Pac. Ry. v. United States, 356 U.S. 1 (1958), 1, 31, 33, 34, 35, 62, 81, 131, 133, 134, 143, 148, 150, 157, 162, 830, 831

Northern Sec. Co. v. United States, 193 U.S. 197 (1904), 569, 624

Northern v. McGraw Edison Co., 542 F.2d 1336 (8th Cir. 1976), *cert. denied*, 429 U.S. 1097 (1977), 141, 156, 162, 669, 849

North Penn Oil & Tire Co. v. Phillips Petroleum Co., 358 F. Supp. 908 (E.D. Pa. 1973), 190

Northrop Corp. v. McDonnell Douglas Corp., 498 F. Supp. 1112 (C.D. Cal. 1980), *rev'd*, 700 F.2d 506 (9th Cir.), *cert. denied*, 464 U.S. 849 (1983), 1109

Northrop Corp. v. McDonnell Douglas Corp., 705 F.2d 1030 (9th Cir.), *cert. denied*, 464 U.S. 849 (1983), 36, 38, 77, 375, 383, 907

North Tex. Producers Ass'n v. Young, 308 F.2d 235 (5th Cir. 1962), *cert. denied*, 372 U.S. 929 (1963), 649

North Tex. Producers Ass'n v. Metzger Dairies, 348 F.2d 189 (5th Cir. 1965), *cert. denied*, 382 U.S. 977 (1966), 1026

Northwestern Fruit Co. v. A. Levy & J. Zentner Co., 665 F. Supp. 869 (E.D. Cal. 1986), 65

Northwestern Ind. Tel. Co. v. FCC, 824 F.2d 1205 (D.C. Cir. 1987), 1055

Northwest Pipeline Corp., 48 F.E.R.C. (CCH) ¶ 61,231 (1989), 1062

Northwest Pipeline Corp., 52 F.E.R.C. (CCH) ¶ 61,053 (1990), 1062

Northwest Power Prods. v. Omark Indus., 576 F.2d 83 (5th Cir. 1978), *cert. denied*, 439 U.S. 1116 (1979), 35, 41, 47, 50, 55, 97, 180, 181, 187, 188

Northwest Publications v. Crumb, 752 F.2d 473 (9th Cir. 1985), 40, 665, 666

Northwest Wholesale Stationers, Inc. v. Pacific Stationery & Printing Co., 472 U.S. 284 (1985), 30, 31, 32, 34, 35, 39, 78, 79, 81, 82, 83, 85, 86, 89, 384, 385, 390, 448, 1026

Norton-Children's Hosps. v. James E. Smith & Sons, 658 F.2d 440 (6th Cir. 1981), 689

Norton Tire Co. v. Tire Kingdom Co., 116 F.R.D. 236 (S.D. Fla. 1987), 790

Norton Tire Co. v. Tire Kingdom Co., 858 F.2d 1533 (11th Cir. 1988), 265

Norton v. Curtiss, 433 F.2d 779 (C.C.P.A. 1970), 808

Norval Co., 77 F.T.C. 1742 (1970), 434

Novak v. General Elec. Co., 1967 Trade Cas. (CCH) ¶ 71,984 (S.D.N.Y. 1967), 766, 790

Novatel Communs. v. Cellular Tel. Supply, 1986-2 Trade Cas. (CCH) ¶ 67,412 (N.D. Ga. 1986), 19, 20, 408, 432

Nuarc Co. v. FTC, 316 F.2d 576 (7th Cir. 1963), 440

Nu Dimensions Int'l, Ltd., 81 F.T.C. 793 (1972), 478

Nungesser v. Commission, Case 258/78, [1982] E.C.R. 2015, [1981-1983 Transfer Binder] COMMON MKT. REP. (CCH) ¶ 8805, 947

Nurse Midwifery Assocs. v. Hibbett, 549 F. Supp. 1185 (M.D. Tenn. 1982), 1118

Nurse Midwifery Assocs. v. Hibbett, 577 F. Supp. 1273 (M.D. Tenn. 1983), 25, 27

Nurse Midwifery Assocs. v. Hibbett, 689 F. Supp. 799 (M.D. Tenn. 1988), 154

Nurse Midwifery Assocs. v. Hibbett, 918 F.2d 605 (6th Cir.), *modified on other grounds*, 927 F.2d 904 (6th Cir. 1990), *cert. denied*, 112 S. Ct. 406 (1991), 21

Nutricia, 26 O.J. EUR. COMM. (No. L 376) 22 (1983), [1982-1985 Transfer Binder] COMMON MKT. REP. (CCH) ¶ 10,567, 937

NV Club and NV GB-Inno-BM v. NV Elsevier Sequoia, [1980] 3 COMMON MKT. L. R. 258, 920

NV GB-INNO-BM v. Vereniging van de Kleinhandelaars in Tabak, Case 13/77, [1977] E.C.R. 2115, [1977-1978 Transfer Binder] COMMON MKT. REP. (CCH) ¶ 8442, 957

N.W. Control, Inc. v. Outboard Marine Corp., 333 F. Supp. 493 (D. Del. 1971), 161

O

Oahu Gas Serv. v. Pacific Resources Inc., 838 F.2d 360 (9th Cir.), *cert. denied*, 488 U.S. 870 (1988), 206, 209, 215, 223, 230, 244, 245, 249

Obendorf v. City & County of Denver, 900 F.2d 1434 (10th Cir. 1990), 985, 1009

Oberweis Dairy v. Associated Milk Producers, 553 F. Supp. 962 (N.D. Ill. 1982), 662, 777

Obron v. Union Camp Corp., 355 F. Supp. 902 (E.D. Mich. 1972), *aff'd per curiam*, 477 F.2d 542 (6th Cir. 1973), 656

O'Byrne v. Cheker Oil Co., 727 F.2d 159 (7th Cir. 1984), 408, 431

Occidental, Inc. v. A Certain Cargo of Petroleum, 577 F.2d 1196 (5th Cir. 1978), *cert. denied*, 444 U.S. 928 (1979), 902

Occidental Petroleum Corp., 101 F.T.C. 373 (1983), 167

Occidental Petroleum Corp., 109 F.T.C. 167 (1986), 345, 347, 348, 1066

Occidental Petroleum Corp., 111 F.T.C. 27 (1988), 313

Occidental Petroleum Corp., 1986-1 Trade Cas. (CCH) ¶ 67,071, 356

Occidental Petroleum Corp. v. Buttes Gas & Oil Co., 331 F. Supp. 92 (C.D. Cal. 1971), *aff'd*, 461 F.2d 1261 (9th Cir.), *cert. denied*, 409 U.S. 950 (1972), 902, 904, 913, 950, 1015

Ocean Spray Cranberries, Inc., 80 F.T.C. 975 (1972), 473

Ocean State Physicians Health Plan, Inc. v. Blue Cross & Blue Shield, 692 F. Supp. 52 (D.R.I. 1988), *aff'd*, 883 F.2d 1101 (1st Cir. 1989), *cert. denied*, 494 U.S. 1027 (1990), 212

Ocean State Physicians Health Plan, Inc. v. Blue Cross & Blue Shield, 883 F.2d 1101 (1st Cir. 1989), *cert. denied*, 494 U.S. 1027 (1990), 223, 224, 226, 1113, 1114, 1115, 1118

O'Connell v. Citrus Bowl, Inc., 99 F.R.D. 117 (E.D.N.Y. 1983), 405, 712, 728

Odishelidze v. Aetna Life & Casualty Co., 853 F.2d 21 (1st Cir. 1988), 19

Oetiker v. Jurid Werke, GmbH, 556 F.2d 1 (D.C. Cir. 1977), 806

Oetiker v. Jurid Werke GmbH, 671 F.2d 596 (D.C. Cir. 1982), 808, 809

Oetjen v. Central Leathers Co., 246 U.S. 297 (1918), 902

Office of Communication of United Church of Christ v. FCC, 707 F.2d 1413 (D.C. Cir. 1983), *modified on remand*, 96 F.C.C.2d 930 (1984), *vacated and remanded*, 779 F.2d 702 (D.C. Cir. 1985), *modified on remand*, 104 F.C.C.2d 505 (1986), 1029, 1044

Office of Personnel Mgmt. v. Richmond, 110 S. Ct. 2465 (1990), 964

Official Airline Guides, Inc. v. FTC, 630 F.2d 920 (2d Cir. 1980), *cert. denied*, 450 U.S. 917 (1981), 191, 248, 454, 462, 523, 825

Ogden Food Serv. Corp. v. Mitchell, 614 F.2d 1001 (5th Cir. 1980), 144

Ogilvie v. Fotomat Corp., 641 F.2d 581 (8th Cir. 1981), 17

Ohio AFL-CIO v. Insurance Rating Bd., 451 F.2d 1178 (6th Cir. 1971), *cert. denied*, 409 U.S. 917 (1972), 1115, 1116

Ohio Christian College, 80 F.T.C. 815 (1972), 456

Ohio-Sealy Mattress Mfg. Co. v. Duncan, 486 F. Supp. 1047 (N.D. Ill. 1980), 679

Ohio-Sealy Mattress Mfg. Co. v. Kaplan, 429 F. Supp. 139 (N.D. Ill. 1977), 869, 874

Ohio-Sealy Mattress Mfg. Co. v. Sealy, Inc., 585 F.2d 821 (7th Cir. 1978), *cert. denied*, 440 U.S. 930 (1979), 75, 114, 130, 131, 132, 159, 676

Ohio Valley Elec. Corp. v. General Elec. Co., 244 F. Supp. 914 (S.D.N.Y. 1965), 34, 691

Ohio v. Arthur Andersen & Co., 570 F.2d 1370 (10th Cir.), *cert. denied*, 439 U.S. 833 (1978), 770

Ohio v. Johnson, 467 U.S. 493 (1984), 583

Ohio v. Ohio Medical Indem., Inc., 1976-2 Trade Cas. (CCH) ¶ 61,128, (S.D. Ohio 1976), 1114

Ohio v. Richter Concrete Co., 69 F.R.D. 604 (S.D. Ohio 1975), 713

O. Hommel Co. v. Ferro Corp., 472 F. Supp. 793 (W.D. Pa. 1979), *rev'd on other grounds*, 659 F.2d 340 (3d Cir. 1981), *cert. denied*, 455 U.S. 1017 (1982), 448, 865

O. Hommel Co. v. Ferro Corp., 659 F.2d 340 (3d Cir. 1981), *cert. denied*, 455 U.S. 1017 (1982), 414, 415

Ohralik v. Ohio State Bar Ass'n, 436 U.S. 447 (1978) *cert. denied*, 455 U.S. 908 (1982), 492

OKC Corp. v. FTC, 455 F.2d 1159 (10th Cir. 1972), 359

Oklahoma *ex rel.* Nesbitt v. Allied Materials Corp., 312 F. Supp. 130 (W.D. Okla. 1968), 778

Oklahoma Press Publishing Co. v. Walling, 327 U.S. 186 (1946), 506, 507

Oksanen v. Page Memorial Hosp., 945 F.2d 696 (4th Cir. 1991), *petition for cert. filed*, 60 U.S.L.W. 3481 (U.S. Dec. 3, 1991), 21, 26, 92

Oksanen v. United States, 362 F.2d 74 (8th Cir. 1966), 599

Olin Corp., 5 TRADE REG. REP. (CCH) ¶ 22,857 (July 12, 1990), 289, 298, 306, 311, 312, 318

Oliver Bros. v. FTC, 102 F.2d 763 (4th Cir. 1939), 431

Oliveri v. Thompson, 803 F.2d 1265 (2d Cir. 1986), 789

Olivetti-Canon, 31 O.J. EUR. COMM. (No. L 52) 51 (1988), [1985-1988 Transfer Binder] COMMON MKT. REP. (CCH) ¶ 10,961, 937

Olmstead v. Amoco Oil Co., 725 F.2d 627 (11th Cir. 1984), 132

Oltz v. St. Peter's Community Hosp., 656 F. Supp. 760 (D. Mont. 1987), aff'd, 861 F.2d 1440 (9th Cir. 1988), 49, 177, 271, 272

Oltz v. St. Peter's Community Hosp., 861 F.2d 1440 (9th Cir. 1988), 21, 36, 37, 42, 46, 47, 54, 55, 174

Olympia Co. v. Celotex Corp., 597 F. Supp. 285 (E.D. La. 1984), aff'd, 771 F.2d 888 (5th Cir. 1985), 415, 420

Olympia Equip. Leasing Co. v. Western Union Tel. Co., 797 F.2d 370 (7th Cir. 1986), cert. denied, 480 U.S. 934 (1987), 224, 243, 244, 261, 668, 674

Olympia Food Market, Inc. v. Sheffield Farms Co., 1955 Trade Cas. (CCH) ¶ 68,064 (S.D.N.Y. 1955), 403

O'Malley v. American Petrofina, Inc., 1974-1 Trade Cas. (CCH) ¶ 75,097 (D. Minn. 1974), 438

O.M. Droney Beverage Co. v. Miller Brewing Co., 365 F. Supp. 1067 (D. Minn. 1973), 111

Omega, 13 J.O. COMM. EUR. (No. L 242) 22 (1970), [1970-1972 Transfer Binder] COMMON MKT. REP. (CCH) ¶ 9396, 941

Omega Satellite Prods. Co. v. City of Indianapolis, 694 F.2d 119 (7th Cir. 1982), 667, 678

Omni Capital Int'l v. Rudolf Wolff & Co., 484 U.S. 97 (1987), 877

Omni Outdoor Advertising, Inc. v. Columbia Outdoor Advertising, Inc., 891 F. 2d 1127 (4th Cir. 1989), rev'd sub nom. City of Columbia v. Omni Outdoor Advertising, Inc., 111 S. Ct. 1344 (1991), 201, 202, 259 977, 997

Omni Resource Dev. Corp. v. Conoco, Inc., 739 F.2d 1412 (9th Cir. 1984), 999, 1001

Onan Corp. v. GLT Indus., 1988 WL 2804 (N.D. Ill. Jan. 12, 1988), 766, 767

O'Neill v. Coca-Cola Co., 669 F. Supp. 217 (N.D. Ill. 1987), 332

O.N.E. Shipping Ltd. v. Flota Mercante Grancolombiana, SA, 830 F.2d 449 (2d Cir. 1987), cert. denied, 488 U.S. 923 (1988), 904, 1166

Opdyke Inv. Co. v. City of Detroit, 883 F.2d 1265 (6th Cir. 1989), 988, 999

Oppenheimer Fund, Inc. v. Sanders, 437 U.S. 340 (1978), 739

Optical Fibers, 29 O.J. EUR. COMM. (No. L 236) 30 (1986), [1985-1988 Transfer Binder] COMMON MKT. REP. (CCH) ¶ 10,813, 937

Optivision, Inc. v. Syracuse Shopping Center Assoc., 472 F. Supp. 665 (N.D.N.Y. 1979), 38, 273

Orange Front Paint Supply Co. v. Pur-All Paint Prods. Co., 1980-1 Trade Cas. (CCH) ¶ 63,154 (E.D.N.Y. 1980), 192

Oreck Corp. v. Whirlpool Corp., 579 F.2d 126 (2d Cir.), cert. denied, 439 U.S. 946 (1978), 37, 45, 47, 48, 50, 53, 54, 118, 180, 187, 188, 241

Oregon Restaurant & Beverage Ass'n v. United States, 429 F.2d 516 (9th Cir. 1970), 81

Organization of Minority Vendors v. Illinois Central Gulf R.R., 579 F. Supp. 574 (N.D. Ill. 1983), 79, 95

Original Appalachian Artworks, Inc. v. Granada Elecs., Inc., 640 F. Supp. 928 (S.D.N.Y. 1986), aff'd, 816 F.2d 68 (2d Cir.), cert. denied, 484 U.S. 847 (1987), 846

Original Appalachian Artworks, Inc. v. Granada Elecs., Inc., 816 F.2d 68 (2d Cir.) cert. denied, 484 U.S. 847 (1987), 1003

Original Appalachian Artworks, Inc. v. McCall Pattern Co., 649 F. Supp. 832 (N.D. Ga. 1986), aff'd, 825 F.2d 355 (11th Cir. 1987), 848

Orkin Exterminating Co., 108 F.T.C. 263 (1986), aff'd, 849 F.2d 1354 (11th Cir. 1988), cert. denied, 488 U.S. 1041 (1989), 487, 519

Orkin Exterminating Co. v. FTC, 849 F.2d 1354 (11th Cir. 1988), cert. denied, 488 U.S. 1041 (1989), 487, 522

Orlando of Calabria, Inc., 86 F.T.C. 631 (1975), 491

Orth-O-Vision, Inc., 69 F.C.C.2d 657 (1978), 1042

Orth-O-Vision, Inc. v. Home Box Office, 474 F. Supp. 672 (S.D.N.Y. 1979), 846

Osawa & Co. v. B&H Photo, 589 F. Supp. 1163 (S.D.N.Y. 1984), 843

Osborn v. Sinclair Ref. Co., 286 F.2d 832 (4th Cir. 1060), *cert. denied*, 366 U.S. 963 (1961), 146, 147, 162, 182

Oscar Gruss & Son v. Geon Indus., 89 F.R.D. 32 (S.D.N.Y. 1980), 766

O.S.C. Corp. v. Apple Computer, Inc., 601 F. Supp. 1274 (C.D. Cal. 1985), *aff'd*, 792 F.2d 1464 (9th Cir. 1986), 126

O.S.C. Corp. v. Apple Computer, Inc., 792 F.2d 1464 (9th Cir. 1986), 13, 55, 123, 132, 183, 186, 705, 707

O.S.C. Corp. v. Toshiba Am., Inc., 491 F.2d 1064 (9th Cir. 1974), 868, 870, 875

Ostrofe v. H.S. Crocker Co., 670 F.2d 1378 (9th Cir. 1982), *vacated*, 460 U.S. 1007 (1983), *aff'd on remand*, 740 F.2d 739 (9th Cir. 1984), *cert. denied*, 469 U.S. 1200 (1985), 662

Otherson v. United States Dep't of Justice, 711 F.2d 267 (D.C. Cir. 1983), 583

Ottensmeyer v. Chesapeake & Potomac Tel. Co., 756 F.2d 986 (4th Cir. 1985), 992

Otter Tail Power Co. v. United States, 410 U.S. 366 (1973), 179, 210, 246, 964, 993, 1019, 1068, 1070

Otto Milk Co. v. United Dairy Farmers Coop., 388 F.2d 789 (3d Cir. 1967), 1026

Outboard Marine Corp. v. Pezetel, 461 F. Supp. 384 (D. Del. 1978), 898, 901

Outboard Marine Corp. v. Pezetel, 474 F. Supp. 168 (D. Del. 1979), 1007, 1008

Outlet Communs. v. King World Prods., 685 F. Supp. 1570 (M.D. Fla. 1988), 132, 140, 153

Overhead Door Corp. v. Nordpal Corp., 1979-1 Trade Cas. (CCH) ¶ 62,595 (D. Minn. 1978), 114

Owens-Corning Fiberglass Corp., 97 F.T.C. 249 (1981), 345

Owens v. Aetna Life & Casualty Co., 654 F.2d 218 (3d Cir.), cert. denied, 454 U.S. 1092 (1981), 1114

Owens v. Pepsi Cola Bottling Co., 1989-2 Trade Cas. (CCH) ¶ 68,834 (N.C. Ct. App. 1989), 625

Owosso Broadcasting Co., 60 RAD. REG. 2d (P&F) 99 (1986), 1036

P

Paceco, Inc. v. Ishikawajima-Harima Heavy Indus. Co., 468 F. Supp. 256 (N.D. Cal. 1979), 430, 865

Pace Indus. v. Three Phoenix Co., 813 F.2d 234 (9th Cir. 1987), 695

Pacific Broadcasting Corp., 66 F.C.C. 2d 256 (1977), 1039

Pacific Coast Agric. Export Ass'n v. Sunkist Growers, 526 F.2d 1196 (9th Cir.), *cert. denied*, 425 U.S. 959 (1976), 214, 215, 671, 672, 786

Pacific Eng'g & Prod. Co. v. Kerr-McGee Corp., 1974-1 Trade Cas. (CCH) ¶ 75,054 (D. Utah 1974), *rev'd*, 551 F.2d 790 (10th Cir.), *cert. denied*, 434 U.S. 879 (1977), 413, 449

Pacific Eng'g & Prod. Co. v. Kerr-McGee Corp., 1976-1 Trade Cas. (CCH) ¶ 60,724 (D. Utah 1976), *rev'd*, 551 F.2d 790 (10th Cir.), *cert. denied*, 434 U.S. 879 (1977), 786

Pacific Eng'g & Prod. Co. v. Kerr McGee Corp., 551 F.2d 790 (10th Cir.), *cert. denied*, 434 U.S. 879 (1977), 228, 232, 414

Pacific Far East Line v. R.J. Reynolds Indus., 1981-2 Trade Cas. (CCH) ¶ 64,412 (N.D. Cal. 1981), *aff'd sub nom.* Wyle v. R.J. Reynolds Indus., 709 F.2d 585 (9th Cir. 1983), 769

Pacific Gas & Elec. Co., 38 F.E.R.C. (CCH) ¶ 61,242 (1987), 1070

Pacific Gas & Elec. Co., 47 F.E.R.C. (CCH) ¶ 61,121 (1989), 1070

Pacific Gas & Elec. Co., 50 F.E.R.C. (CCH) ¶ 61,339 (1990), 1070

Pacific Mailing Equip. Corp. v. Pitney Bowes, Inc., 499 F. Supp. 108 (N.D. Cal. 1981), 210, 674

Pacific Power & Light Co., 26 F.E.R.C. (CCH) ¶ 63,048 (1984), 1069

Pacific Seafarers, Inc. v. Pacific Far East Line, 404 F.2d 804 (D.C. Cir. 1968), *cert. denied*, 393 U.S. 1093 (1969), 1164

Pacific Stationery & Printing Co. v. Northwest Wholesale Stationers, Inc., 715 F.2d 1393 (9th Cir. 1983), rev'd, 472 U.S. 284 (1985), 82, 89

Pacific Tobacco Corp. v. American Tobacco Co., 338 F. Supp. 842 (D. Or. 1972), 866

Pacific W. Cable Co. v. City of Sacramento, 798 F.2d 353 (9th Cir. 1986), 679

Package Shop, Inc. v. Anheuser-Busch, Inc., 675 F. Supp. 894 (D.N.J. 1987), 669, 673

Packard Motor Car Co. v. Webster Motor Car Co., 243 F.2d 418 (D.C. Cir.), *cert. denied*, 335 U.S. 822 (1957), 118, 119, 200

Page Dairy Co., 50 F.T.C. 395 (1953), 411

Page v. Work, 290 F.2d 323 (9th Cir. 1961), *cert. denied*, 368 U.S. 875 (1961), 29

Paine, Webber, Jackson & Curtis, Inc. v. Malon S. Andrus, Inc., 486 F. Supp. 1118 (S.D.N.Y. 1980), 600

Painton & Co. v. Bourns, Inc., 442 F.2d 216 (2d Cir. 1971), 826

Palmer v. BRG, of Ga. Inc., 874 F.2d 1417 (11th Cir. 1989), *rev'd*, 111 S. Ct. 401 (1990), 722, 737, 790

Palmer v. BRG of Ga., Inc., 111 S. Ct. 401 (1990), 30, 98, 382

Palmer v. Roosevelt Lake Log Owners Ass'n, 651 F.2d 1289 (9th Cir. 1981), 24, 28

Pan Am. World Airways v. United States, 371 U.S. 296 (1963), 1017, 1154, 1155, 1156

Panhandle E. Pipe Line Co., 48 F.E.R.C. (CCH) ¶ 61,233 (1989), 1062

Panhandle E. Pipe Line Co., 52 F.E.R.C. (CCH) ¶ 61,048 (1990), 1062

Panhandle E. Corp., 5 TRADE REG. REP. (CCH) ¶ 22,680 (July 17, 1989), 1066

Pan-Islamic Trade Corp. v. Exxon Corp., 632 F.2d 539 (5th Cir. 1980), *cert. denied*, 454 U.S. 927 (1981), 9, 659

Panther Pumps & Equip. Co. v. Hydrocraft, Inc., 468 F.2d 225 (7th Cir. 1972), *cert. denied*, 411 U.S. 965 (1973), 836

Papercraft Corp. v. FTC, 307 F. Supp. 1401 (W.D. Pa. 1970), 511

Papercraft Corp. v. FTC, 472 F.2d 927 (7th Cir. 1973), 351

Papst Motoren GmbH v. Kanematsu-Goshu (U.S.A.) Inc., 629 F. Supp. 864, (S.D.N.Y. 1986), 802, 808, 809

Paragould Cablevision, Inc. v. City of Paragould, 930 F.2d 1310 (8th Cir.), *cert. denied*, 112 S. Ct. 430 (1991), 979, 983

Paralegal Inst., Inc. v. American Bar Ass'n, 475 F. Supp. 1123 (E.D.N.Y. 1979), 88

Paramount Famous Lasky Corp. v. United States, 282 U.S. 30 (1930), 79

Paramount Pictures Corp. v. Baldwin-Montrose Chem. Co., 1966 Trade Cas. (CCH) ¶ 71,678 (S.D.N.Y. 1966), 394, 395, 396, 399

Pargas, Inc. v. Empire Gas Corp., 423 F. Supp. 199 (D. Md.), *aff'd per curiam*, 546 F.2d 25 (4th Cir. 1976), 366, 370, 678

Parion Theatre Corp. v. RKO Theatres, 319 F. Supp. 378 (S.D.N.Y. 1970), 748

Pariser v. Christian Health Care Sys., 627 F. Supp. 39 (E.D. Mo. 1986), *aff'd in part and rev'd in part*, 816 F.2d 1248 (8th Cir. 1987), 29

Pariser v. Christian Health Care Sys., 816 F.2d 1248 (8th Cir. 1987), 25

Parke, Austin & Lipscomb, Inc. v. FTC, 142 F.2d 437 (2d Cir.), *cert. denied*, 323 U.S. 753 (1944), 477

Parke, Davis & Co. v. Probel, Case 24/67, [1968] E.C.R. 55, [1967-1970 Transfer Binder] COMMON MKT. REP. (CCH) ¶ 8054, 946, 948

Parker v. Brown, 317 U.S. 341 (1943), 603, 965, 966, 976, 1050, 1054

Parker v. Crown Cork & Seal Co., 677 F.2d 391 (4th Cir. 1982), *aff'd*, 462 U.S. 345 (1983), 696

Parker v. Crown Cork & Seal Co., 462 U.S. 345 (1983), 696

Park-In Theatres v. Paramount-Richards Theatres, 90 F. Supp. 730 (D. Del.), *aff'd per curiam*, 185 F.2d 407 (3d Cir. 1950), *cert. denied*, 341 U.S. 950 (1951), 813

Parklane Hoisery Co. v. Shore, 439 U.S. 322 (1979), 775, 776

Parks v. Watson, 716 F.2d 646 (9th Cir. 1983), 24, 643, 648, 649, 664

Park v. El Paso Bd. of Realtors, 764 F.2d 1053 (5th Cir. 1985), *cert. denied*, 474 U.S. 1102 (1986), 8, 10, 25, 671

Parkview Markets, Inc. v. Kroger Co., 1978-2 Trade Cas. (CCH) ¶ 62,373 (S.D. Ohio 1978), 655, 664

Parkway Gallery Furniture v. Kittinger/Pennsylvania House Group, 116 F.R.D. 46 (M.D.N.C. 1987), 763, 764

Parkway Gallery Furniture, Inc. v. Kittinger/Pennsylvania House Group, 1988-1 Trade Cas. (CCH) ¶ 67,970 (M.D.N.C. 1988), aff'd, 878 F.2d 801 (4th Cir. 1989), 106, 124, 126

Parkway Gallery Furniture, Inc. v. Kittinger/Pennsylvania House Group, 878 F.2d 801 (4th Cir. 1989), 8, 706

Parliament T.V. Tube Sales, 59 F.T.C. 127 (1961), 477

Parmelee Transp. Co. v. Keeshin, 186 F. Supp. 533 (N.D. Ill. 1960), aff'd, 292 F.2d 794 (7th Cir.), cert. denied, 368 U.S. 944 (1961), 391

Parmelee Transp. Co. v. Keeshin, 292 F.2d 794 (7th Cir.), cert. denied, 368 U.S. 944 (1961), 96

Parrish's Cake Decorating Supplies, Inc. v. Wilton Enters., 1984-1 Trade Cas. (CCH) ¶ 65,917 (N.D. Ill. 1984), modified, 1985-1 Trade Cas. (CCH) ¶ 66,630 (N.D. Ill. 1985), 335, 362

Parrish v. Cox, 586 F.2d 9 (6th Cir. 1978), 407, 408, 415

Parsons Steel, Inc. v. First Ala. Bank, 679 F.2d 242 (11th Cir. 1982), 1098

Parsons v. Ford Motor Co., 669 F.2d 308 (5th Cir.), cert. denied, 459 U.S. 832 (1982), 15

Partee v. San Diego Chargers Football Co., 34 Cal. 3d 378, 194 Cal. Rptr. 367, 668 P.2d 674 (1983), cert. denied, 466 U.S. 904 (1984), 622

Partmar Corp. v. Paramount Pictures Theatres Corp., 347 U.S. 89 (1954), 778

Partridge v. St. Louis Joint Stock Land Bank, 130 F.2d 281 (8th Cir. 1942), 740

Parts & Elec. Motors, Inc. v. Sterling Elec., Inc., 826 F.2d 712 (7th Cir. 1987), 136, 140, 153, 159, 162

Paschall v. Kansas City Star Co., 130 F.2d 281 (8th Cir. 1942), 740

Paschall v. Kansas City Star Co., 605 F.2d 403 (8th Cir. 1979), 665

Paschall v. Kansas City Star Co., 695 F.2d 322 (8th Cir. 1982), rev'd, 727 F.2d 692 (8th Cir.), cert. denied, 469 U.S. 872 (1984), 675, 676, 784

Paschall v. Kansas City Star Co., 727 F.2d 692 (8th Cir.), cert. denied, 469 U.S. 872 (1984) 191, 197, 245

Pastonelli Food Prods., Inc. v. Pillsbury Co., 1989-1 Trade Cas. (CCH) ¶ 68,572 (N.D. Ill. 1989), 689, 693

Patrick v. Burget, 800 F.2d 1498 (9th Cir.), rev'd, 486 U.S. 94 (1988), 973, 974

Patrick v. Burget, 486 U.S. 94 (1988), 43, 93, 972, 973

Patterson Dental Co. v. McGaughey, 1986-1 Trade Cas. (CCH) ¶ 66,931 (D. Or. 1985), 153, 155

Paulson Inv. Co. v. Norbay Sec., Inc., 603 F. Supp. 615 (D. Or. 1984), 876

Paul v. Pulitzer Publishing Co., 1974 Trade Cas. (CCH) ¶ 75,116 (E.D. Mo. 1974), 108

Paul v. Virginia, 75 U.S. 168 (1868), 1110

Pavelic & Leflore v. Marvel Entertainment Group, 110 S. Ct. 456 (1989), 790

Pavlak v. Church, 681 F.2d 617 (9th Cir. 1982), vacated and remanded, 463 U.S. 1201 (1983), 696

Paxman v. Campbell, 612 F.2d 848 (4th Cir. 1980), 715

Pay Less Drug Stores Northwest, Inc., 87 F.T.C. 1271 (1976), 480

Pay Less Drug Stores Northwest, Inc., 96 F.T.C. 197 (1980), 345

P.D.Q., Inc. v. Nissan Motor Corp., 61 F.R.D. 372 (S.D. Fla. 1973), 716, 722

Peacock Buick, 86 F.T.C. 1532 (1975), on reconsideration, 87 F.T.C. 379 (1976), aff'd mem., 553 F.2d 97 (4th Cir. 1977), 468, 1112

Pearl Brewing Co. v. Anheuser-Busch, Inc., 339 F. Supp. 945 (S.D. Tex. 1972), 111

Pearl Brewing Co. v. Jos. Schlitz Brewing Co., 415 F. Supp. 1122 (S.D. Tex. 1976), 698, 701

Pearson v. Ecological Science Corp., 522 F.2d 171 (5th Cir. 1975), cert. denied, 425 U.S. 912 (1976), 740

Peck v. General Motors Corp., 894 F.2d 844 (6th Cir. 1990), 681, 682

Peelers Co. v. Wendt, 260 F. Supp. 193 (W.D. Wash. 1966), 825

Peeler v. United States, 163 F.2d 823 (10th Cir. 1947), 599

Pemco Prods., Inc. v. General Mills, Inc., 155 F. Supp. 433 (N.D. Ohio 1957), *aff'd*, 261 F.2d 302 (6th Cir. 1958), 824, 825

Pendleton Constr. Corp. v. Rockbridge County, 652 F. Supp. 312 (W.D. Va. 1987) *aff'd*, 837 F.2d 178 (4th Cir. 1988), 1004

Pendleton Woolen Mills, Inc., 94 F.T.C. 229 (1979), 107

Penn Cent. Secs. Litig., 367 F. Supp. 1158 (E.D. Pa. 1973), 397

Penne v. Greater Minneapolis Area Bd. of Realtors, 604 F. 2d 1143 (8th Cir. 1979), 8

Pennsylvania Dental Ass'n v. Medical Serv. Ass'n, 574 F. Supp. 457 (M.D. Pa.), *aff'd without published opinion sub nom.* Commissioner v. Pennsylvania Dental Ass'n, 722 F.2d 731 (3d Cir. 1983), *cert. denied*, 465 U.S. 1026 (1984), 71

Pennsylvania Dental Ass'n v. Medical Serv. Ass'n, 745 F.2d 248 (3d Cir. 1984), *cert. denied*, 471 U.S. 1016 (1985), 196, 200, 202, 208

Pennsylvania Dental Ass'n v. Medical Serv. Ass'n, 815 F.2d 270 (3d Cir.), *cert. denied*, 484 U.S. 851 (1987), 52, 56, 94, 682, 705, 707

Pennsylvania *ex rel.* Zimmerman v. Pepsico, Inc., 836 F.2d 173 (3d Cir. 1988), 84, 85, 86, 613

Pennsylvania Power Co., 21 F.E.R.C. (CCH) ¶ 61,313 (1982), 1072

Pennsylvania v. Budget Fuel Co., 1988-2 Trade Cas. (CCH) ¶ 68,229 (E.D. Pa. 1988), 608

Pennsylvania v. Delaware Valley Citizens' Council for Clean Air, 478 U.S. 546 (1986), 783

Pennsylvania v. Lake Asphalt & Petroleum Co., 610 F. Supp. 885 (M.D. Pa. 1985), 689, 690, 691

Pennsylvania Water & Power Co. v. Consolidated Gas, Elec. Light & Power Co., 184 F.2d 552 (4th Cir.), *cert. denied*, 340 U.S. 906 (1950), 1068

Pennwalt Corp. v. Plough, Inc., 85 F.R.D. 257 (D. Del. 1979), 752, 753

Pennzoil Co. v. FERC, 645 F.2d 360 (5th Cir. 1981), *cert. denied*, 454 U.S. 1142 (1982), 1057

Penthouse Int'l, Ltd. v. Playboy Enters., 663 F.2d 371 (2d Cir. 1981), 769

Peoples Sav. Bank v. Stoddard, 359 Mich. 297, 102 N.W.2d 777 (1960), 622

People *ex rel.* Kelley v. Perrin's Marine Sales, 1979-2 Trade Cas. (CCH) ¶ 62,811 (Mich. Cir. Ct. 1979), 640

People v. Association of Contracting Plumbers, 57 Misc. 2d 256, 291 N.Y.S.2d 624 (1968), 638

People v. Building Maintenance Contractors' Ass'n, 41 Cal. 2d 719, 264 P.2d 31 (1953), 628

People v. Henson Robinson Co., 1974-1 Trade Cas. (CCH) ¶ 75,107 (Ill. Cir. Ct. 1974), 624

People v. Mobile Magic Sales, Inc., 1979-2 Trade Cas. (CCH) ¶ 62,940 (Cal. Ct. App. 1979), 641

People v. North Ave. Furniture & Appliance, Inc., 1982-2 Trade Cas. (CCH) ¶ 64,795 (Colo. 1982), 638

Pep Boys - Manny, Moe & Jack, Inc. v. FTC, 122 F.2d 158 (3d Cir. 1941), 464, 477

PepsiCo, Inc. v. FTC, 472 F.2d 179 (2d Cir. 1972), *cert. denied*, 414 U.S. 876 (1973), 513, 524

Perez v. University of Puerto Rico, 600 F.2d 1 (1st Cir. 1979), 781

Perfect Film & Chem. Corp., 78 F.T.C. 990 (1971), 480

Performance Marketers, Inc. v. Edelbrock Corp., 516 F. Supp. 936 (N.D. Tex. 1981), 193

Perfumer's Workshop, Ltd. v. Roure Bertrand du Pont, Inc., 1990-2 Trade Cas. (CCH) ¶ 69,102 (S.D.N.Y. 1990), 144, 873

Perington Wholesale v. Burger King Corp., 631 F.2d 1369 (10th Cir. 1979), 172, 173, 273

Periodical Publishers' Serv. Bureau v. FTC, 1973-2 Trade Cas. (CCH) ¶ 74,743 (D.D.C. 1972), 531

Peritz v. Liberty Loan Corp., 523 F.2d 349 (7th Cir. 1975), 696

Perkins v. Benguet Consol. Mining Co., 342 U.S. 437 (1952), 873, 874

Perkins v. Standard Oil, 487 F.2d 672 (9th Cir. 1973), 785

Perkins v. Standard Oil, 395 U.S. 642 (1969), 413, 440

Perkins v. Standard Oil, 399 U.S. 222 (1970), 782, 785

Perma Life Mufflers, Inc. v. International Parts Corp., 376 F.2d 692 (7th Cir. 1967), *rev'd*, 392 U.S. 134 (1968), 411

Perma Life Mufflers, Inc. v. International Parts Corp., 392 U.S. 134 (1968), 16, 17, 18, 373, 697, 698, 699

Perma-Maid Co. v. FTC, 121 F.2d 282 (6th Cir. 1941), 477

Perpetual Fed. Sav. & Loan Ass'n, 90 F.T.C. 608 (1977), *order withdrawn and complaint dismissed*, 94 F.T.C. 401 (1979), 393, 460

Perpetual Fed. Sav. & Loan Ass'n, 94 F.T.C. 401 (1979), 460

Perryton Wholesale v. Pioneer Distrib. Co., 353 F.2d 618 (10th Cir. 1965), *cert. denied*, 383 U.S. 945 (1966), 96

Perry v. Fidelity Union Life Ins. Co., 606 F.2d 468 (5th Cir. 1979), cert. denied, 446 U.S. 987 (1980), 1112, 1113

Personal Drug Co., 50 F.T.C. 828 (1954), *aff'd*, 218 F.2d 817 (2d Cir. 1955), 469

Pete Thoesen Tractor & Equip. Repair Co. v. City of Chicago, 101 F.R.D. 734 (N.D. Ill. 1984), 431

Peter Satori, Inc. v. Studebaker-Packard Corp., 1964 Trade Cas. (CCH) ¶ 71,309 (S.D. Cal. 1964), 426

Pet, Inc. v. Kysor Indus. Corp., 404 F. Supp. 1252 (W.D. Mich. 1975), 702

Petition of Emprise Corp., 344 F. Supp. 319 (W.D.N.Y. 1972), 507

Peto v. Howell, 101 F.2d 353 (7th Cir. 1939), 1107

Peto v. Madison Square Garden Corp., 384 F.2d 682 (2d Cir. 1967), *cert. denied*, 390 U.S. 989 (1968), 686

Petroleum Exch. of London Ltd., 30 O.J. EUR. COMM. (No. L 3) 27 (1987), [1985-1988 Transfer Binder] COMMON MKT. REP. (CCH) ¶ 10,848, 936

Petroleum for Contractors, Inc. v. Mobil Oil Corp., 1978-2 Trade Cas. ¶ 62,151 (S.D.N.Y. 1978), 403, 404

Petroleum for Contractors, Inc. v. Mobil Oil Corp., 493 F. Supp. 320 (S.D.N.Y. 1980), 176, 416

Petroleum Products Antitrust Litig., 1991-2 Trade Cas. (CCH) ¶ 69,669 (C.D. Cal. 1991), 691, 692

Petrol Stops Northwest v. Continental Oil Co., 1978-2 Trade Cas. (CCH) ¶ 62,304 (D. Ariz. 1978), 654

Petrol Stops Northwest v. Continental Oil Co., 647 F.2d 1005 (9th Cir.), *cert. denied*, 454 U.S. 1098 (1981), 756

Petruzzi's IGA Supermarkets v. Darling-Delaware Co., 1988-1 Trade Cas. (CCH) ¶ 67,989 (M.D. Pa. 1987), 740

Pettibone Corp. v. Caterpillar Tractor Co., 1974-2 Trade Cas. (CCH) ¶ 75,419 (D. Neb. 1974), 565

Pettway v. American Cast Iron Pipe Co., 576 F.2d 1157 (5th Cir. 1978), *cert. denied*, 439 U.S. 1115 (1979), *cert. dismissed*, 467 U.S. 1247 (1984), 742

Peugeot-Ecosystem, Commission Press Release, IP (90) 233, (Mar. 27, 1990), *aff'd sub nom.* Automobiles Peugeot SA et Peugeot SA v. Commission, Case T-23/90R, [1990] E.C.R. II 195 and Automobiles Peugeot SA et Peugeot SA (Ct. First Instance 1991), 920

P.F. Collier & Son Corp. v. FTC, 427 F.2d 261 (6th Cir.), *cert. denied*, 400 U.S. 926 (1970), 491, 496

Pfiffner v. Roth, 1986-1 Trade Cas. (CCH) ¶ 66,903 (Iowa 1985), 637

Pfizer, Inc., 81 F.T.C. 23 (1972), 467, 470, 484

Pfizer, Inc. v. Eurim-Pharm GmbH, Case 1/81 [1981] E.C.R. 2913, [1979-1981 Transfer Binder] COMMON MKT. REP. (CCH) ¶ 8737, 945

Pfizer, Inc. v. Government of India, 434 U.S. 308 (1978), 742

Pfizer, Inc. v. Lord, 447 F.2d 122 (2d Cir. 1971), 711

Pfotzer v. Aqua Sys., 162 F.2d 779 (2d Cir. 1947), 778

Pharmeceutische Handelsconventie, SNPE-LEL, 21 O.J. EUR. COMM. (No. L 191) 41 (1978), [1978-1981 Transfer Binder] COMMON MKT. REP. (CCH) ¶ 10,064, 932

Pharmon v. Hoechst, Case 19/84, [1985] E.C.R. 2281, [1985-1986 Transfer Binder] COMMON MKT. REP. (CCH) ¶ 14,206, 946

Phi Delta Theta Fraternity v. J.A. Buchroeder & Co., 251 F. Supp. 968 (W.D. Mo. 1966), 847

Phil Tolkan Datsun v. Greater Milwaukee Datsun Dealers' Advertising Ass'n, 672 F.2d 1280 (7th Cir. 1982), 87

Philad Co. v. Lechler Labs., 107 F.2d 747 (2d Cir. 1939), 832

Philadelphia Carpet Co., 64 F.T.C. 762 (1964), aff'd, 342 F.2d 994 (3d Cir. 1965), 424, 425

Philadelphia Elec. Co. v. Anaconda Am. Brass Co., 42 F.R.D. 324 (E.D. Pa. 1967), 739, 740

Philadelphia Elec. Co. v. Anaconda Am. Brass Co., 275 F. Supp. 146 (E.D. Pa. 1967), 760

Philadelphia Elec. Co. v. Anaconda Am. Brass Co., 43 F.R.D. 452 (E.D. Pa. 1968), 695, 713

Philadelphia Fast Foods, Inc. v. Popeye's Famous Fried Chicken, Inc., 647 F. Supp. 216 (E.D. Pa. 1986), aff'd sub nom. without opinion Philadelphia Fast Food Partnership v. A. Copeland Enters., 806 F.2d (3d Cir. 1986), cert. denied, 481 U.S. 1016 (1987), 61, 84, 85, 118, 124, 126

Philadelphia Hous. Auth. v. American Radiator & Standard Sanitary Corp., 323 F. Supp. 364 (E.D. Pa. 1970), aff'd sub nom. Ace Heating & Plumbing Co. v. Crane Co., 453 F.2d 30 (3d Cir. 1970), 744

Philadelphia World Hockey Club v. Philadelphia Hockey Club, 351 F. Supp. 462 (E.D. Pa. 1972), 91, 209, 217, 225

Philco Corp. v. RCA, 186 F. Supp. 155 (E.D. Pa. 1960), 690, 693

Philip Morris, Inc., 82 F.T.C. 16 (1973), 485

Philip Morris/Rembrandt/Rothmans, aff'd sub nom. British American Tobacco Co. and R.J. Reynolds Indus. v. Commission, Joined Cases 142 and 156/84, [1987] E.C.R. 4487, [1987-1988 Transfer Binder] COMMON MKT. REP. (CCH) ¶ 14,405, 938

Philip Morris v. Commission, Case 730/79, [1980] E.C.R. 2671 [1979-1981 Transfer Binder] COMMON MKT. REP. (CCH) ¶ 8695, 923

Philip R. Consolo v. Grace Lines, 4 F.M.C. 293 (1953), 1157

Phillips Petroleum Co., 84 F.T.C. 1666 (1974), 166

Phillips Petroleum Co. v. Shutts, 472 U.S. 797 (1985), 733

Phillips Petroleum Co. v. Wisconsin, 347 U.S. 672 (1954), 1056, 1057

Phillips v. Crown Cent. Petroleum Corp., 395 F. Supp. 735 (D. Md. 1975), 109, 131, 132, 161

Phillips v. Crown Cent. Petroleum Corp., 602 F.2d 616 (4th Cir. 1979), cert. denied, 444 U.S. 1074 (1980), 109, 110, 152, 153, 154, 181, 655, 668, 674, 678

Phillips v. Vandygriff, 711 F.2d 1217 (5th Cir. 1983), cert. denied, 469 U.S. 821 (1984), 85, 86

Phoenix Coal Co. v. Commissioner, 14 T.C.M. (CCH) 96 (1955), aff'd, 231 F.2d 420 (2d Cir. 1956), 794

Phonetele, Inc. v. AT&T, 664 F.2d 716 (9th Cir. 1981), cert. denied, 459 U.S. 1145 (1983), 135, 160, 1018, 1049

Phosphate Export Ass'n, 42 F.T.C. 555 (1946), 914, 915

Phototron Corp. v. Eastman Kodak Co., 842 F.2d 95 (5th Cir.), cert. denied, 486 U.S. 1023 (1988), 363, 366, 651, 678

Photovest Corp. v. Fotomat Corp., 606 F.2d 704 (7th Cir. 1979), cert. denied, 445 U.S. 917 (1980), 141, 146, 147, 157, 204, 262, 264

Piambino v. Bailey, 610 F.2d 1306 (5th Cir.), cert. denied, 449 U.S. 1111 (1980), 744

Pick Mfg. Co. v. General Motors Corp., 80 F.2d 641 (7th Cir. 1935), aff'd per curiam, 299 U.S. 3 (1936), 161, 166

Piedmont Label Co. v. Sun Garden Packing Co., 598 F.2d 491 (9th Cir. 1979), 867

Pierce v. Commercial Warehouse, 876 F.2d 86 (11th Cir. 1989), cert. denied, 110 S. Ct. 841 (1990), 429

Pierce v. Ramsey Winch Co., 753 F.2d 416 (5th Cir. 1985), 181, 675

Pike v. Bruce Church, Inc., 397 U.S. 137 (1970), 621

Pilkington Bros. PLC, 103 F.T.C. 707 (1984), 890

Pillar Corp. v. Enercon Indus. Corp., 694 F. Supp. 1353 (E.D. Wis. 1988), 860

Pillar Corp. v. Enercon Indus. Corp., 1989-1 Trade Cas. (CCH) ¶ 68,597 (E.D. Wis. 1989), 873

Pillsbury Co., 93 F.T.C. 966 (1979), 314, 315, 316, 317

Pillsbury Co. v. Conboy, 459 U.S. 248 (1982), 771, 772

Pillsbury Mills, Inc., 50 F.T.C. 555 (1953), 307

Pinhas v. Summit Health, Ltd., 894 F.2d 1024 (9th Cir. 1989), aff'd, 111 S. Ct. 1842 (1991), 24, 974

Pink Supply Corp. v. Hiebert, Inc., 612 F. Supp. 1334 (D. Minn. 1985), aff'd, 788 F.2d 1313 (8th Cir. 1986), 16, 22

Pink Supply Corp. v. Hiebert, Inc., 788 F.2d 1313 (8th Cir. 1986), 22

Pinney Dock & Transp. Co. v. Penn Cent. Corp., 838 F.2d 1445 (6th Cir.), cert. denied, 488 U.S. 880 (1988), 623, 625, 663, 688, 689, 1017, 1021

Pinros & Gar Corp., 77 F.T.C. 1322 (1970), 473

Pipe Fittings & Valve Export Ass'n, 45 F.T.C. 917 (1948), 915

Piper Aircraft Co. v. Reyno, 454 U.S. 235 (1981), 866

Pireno v. New York State Chiropractic Ass'n, 1979-2 Trade Cas. (CCH) ¶ 62,758 (S.D.N.Y. 1979), rev'd and remanded, 650 F.2d 387 (2d Cir. 1981), aff'd sub nom. Union Labor Life Ins. Co. v. Pireno, 458 U.S. 119 (1982), 1118

Pitchford Scientific Instruments Corp. v. PEPI, Inc., 440 F. Supp. 1175 (W.D. Pa. 1977), aff'd, 582 F.2d 1275 (3d Cir. 1978), cert. denied, 440 U.S. 981 (1979), 783, 785, 786

Pitchford Scientific Instruments Corp. v. PEPI, Inc., 531 F.2d 92 (3d Cir. 1975), cert. denied, 426 U.S. 935 (1976), 62, 75, 109, 119, 121, 128, 164, 165, 170, 173, 665, 670, 671, 782, 786

Pitney Bowes, Inc. v. Mestre, 701 F.2d 1365 (11th Cir.), cert. denied, 464 U.S. 893 (1983), 825

Pittsburgh Corning Europe, 15 J.O. COMM. EUR. (No. L 272) 35 (1972), [1970-1972 Transfer Binder] COMMON MKT. REP. (CCH) ¶ 9539, 942, 943

Pittsburgh Plate Glass Co. v. United States, 260 F.2d 397 (4th Cir. 1958), aff'd, 360 U.S. 395 (1959), 8

Pittsburgh Plate Glass Co. v. United States, 360 U.S. 395 (1959), 590

P.J. Taggares Co. v. New York Mercantile Exch., 476 F. Supp. 72 (S.D.N.Y. 1979), 88, 89

Plastic Packaging Materials, Inc. v. Dow Chemical Co., 327 F. Supp. 213 (E.D. Pa. 1971), 130

Plaza Club, 80 F.T.C. 62 (1972), 478

P. Leiner Nutritional Prods. Corp., 105 F.T.C. 291 (1985), 473

Plekowski v. Ralston Purina Co., 68 F.R.D. 443 (M.D. Ga. 1975), appeal dismissed, 557 F.2d 1218 (5th Cir. 1977), 718, 733

Plekowski v. Ralston-Purina Co., 557 F.2d 1218 (5th Cir. 1977), 736

Plueckhahn v. Farmers Ins. Exch., 749 F.2d 241 (5th Cir.) cert. denied, 473 U.S. 905 (1985), 45, 47, 53, 78, 84, 85, 86

Plum Tree, Inc. v. N.K. Winston Corp., 351 F. Supp. 80 (S.D.N.Y. 1972), 408

Plum Tree, Inc. v. Rouse Co., 58 F.R.D. 373 (E.D. Pa. 1972), 717

Plymouth Dealers' Ass'n v. United States, 279 F.2d 128 (9th Cir. 1960), 64, 69

Pocahontas Supreme Coal Co. v. Bethlehem Steel Corp., 828 F.2d 211 (4th Cir. 1987), 397, 643, 661, 682, 690, 692, 706, 790

Pogue v. International Indus., 524 F.2d 342 (6th Cir. 1975), 103

Polansky v. TWA, 523 F.2d 332 (3d Cir. 1975), 1156

Polk Bros. v. Forest City Enters., 776 F.2d 185 (7th Cir. 1985), 39, 41, 51, 52, 77, 98, 126, 382

Poller v. CBS, 368 U.S. 464 (1962), 702, 703

Pollock v. Citrus Assocs. of the N.Y. Stock Exch., 512 F. Supp. 711 (S.D.N.Y. 1981), 662

Polydor Ltd. v. Harlequin Record Shops, Case 270/80, [1982] E.C.R. 329, [1981-1983 Transfer Binder] COMMON MKT. REP. (CCH) ¶ 8806, 946

Polygram Records, Inc., 108 F.T.C. 112 (1986), 349, 352

Polypropylene, 29 O.J. EUR. COMM. (No. L 230) 1 (1986), [1985-1988 Transfer Binder] COMMON MKT. REP. (CCH) ¶ 10,782, 932

Polytechnic Data Corp. v. Xerox Corp., 362 F. Supp. 1 (N.D. Ill. 1973), 15

Poncy v. Johnson & Johnson, 414 F. Supp. 551 (S.D. Fla. 1976), 751

Pontarelli Limousine, Inc. v. City of Chicago, 623 F. Supp. 281 (N.D. Ill. 1985), 988

Pontarelli Limousine, Inc. v. City of Chicago, 652 F. Supp. 1428 (N.D. Ill. 1987), 754, 757, 758

Pontius v. Children's Hosp., 552 F. Supp. 1352 (W.D. Pa. 1982), 92

Pope v. Mississippi Real Estate Comm'n, 695 F. Supp. 253 (N.D. Miss. 1988), aff'd, 872 F.2d 127 (5th Cir. 1989), 25, 42

Pope v. Mississippi Real Estate Comm'n, 872 F.2d 127 (5th Cir. 1989), 37, 38, 39, 88, 131

Porter & Dietsch, Inc. v. FTC, 605 F.2d 294 (7th Cir. 1979), cert. denied, 445 U.S. 950 (1980), 464, 466, 467, 468, 474, 489, 492

Porto Rican Am. Tobacco Co. v. American Tobacco Co., 30 F.2d 234 (2d Cir.), cert. denied, 279 U.S. 858 (1929), 401, 420

Port Terminal & Warehousing v. John S. James Co., 695 F.2d 1328 (11th Cir. 1983), 783

Portwood v. FTC, 418 F.2d 419 (10th Cir. 1969), 479, 491

Posadas de Puerto Rico Assocs. v. Tourism Co., 478 U.S. 328 (1986), 492

Poster Exch. v. National Screen Serv. Corp., 362 F.2d 571 (5th Cir.), cert. denied, 385 U.S. 948 (1966), 179

Potters Medical Center v. City Hosp. Ass'n, 800 F.2d 568 (6th Cir. 1986), 18, 21, 22, 196, 259, 264, 708, 1004

Potts v. Jos. Schlitz Brewing Co., 1977-2 Trade Cas. (CCH) ¶ 61,538 (N.D. Okla. 1977), 687

Powell v. NFL, 678 F. Supp. 777 (D. Minn. 1988), 1123, 1124

Powell v. NFL, 690 F. Supp. 812 (D. Minn. 1988), 1123, 1124

Powell v. NFL, 1989-1 Trade Cas. (CCH) ¶ 68,452 (D. Minn. 1989), 718

Powell v. NFL, 888 F.2d 559 (8th Cir. 1989), cert. denied, 111 S. Ct. 711 (1991), 91, 1123, 1124

Power Conversion, Inc. v. Saft Am., Inc., 672 F. Supp. 224 (D. Md. 1987), 63, 1108

Power East Ltd. v. Transamerica Delaval Inc., 558 F. Supp. 47 (S.D.N.Y.), aff'd without pub. op., 742 F.2d 1439 (2d Cir. 1983), 860

Power Replacements Corp. v. Air Preheater Co., 356 F. Supp. 872 (E.D. Pa. 1973), 209

Power Test Petroleum Distribs. v. Calcu Gas, Inc., 754 F.2d 91 (2d Cir. 1985), 142, 158, 849,

Practical Concepts, Inc. v. Republic of Bolivia, 811 F.2d 1543 (D.C. Cir. 1987), 901

Precision Instrument Mfg. Co. v. Automotive Maintenance Mach. Co., 324 U.S. 806 (1945), 800, 801, 810

Precision Shooting Equip. Co. v. Allen, 646 F.2d 313 (7th Cir.), cert. denied, 454 U.S. 964 (1981), 836

Preferred Communs. v. City of Los Angeles, 754 F.2d 1396 (9th Cir. 1985), 476, 966, 985, 1054

Preformed Line Prods. Co. v. Fanner Mfg. Co., 328 F.2d 265 (6th Cir.) cert. denied, 379 U.S. 846 (1964), 816

Preiffer v. New England Patriots Football Club, 1973-1 Trade Cas. (CCH) ¶ 74,267 (D. Mass. 1972), 139

Premier Elec. Constr. Co. v. National Elect. Contractors Ass'n, 814 F.2d 358 (7th Cir. 1987), 40, 53, 66, 70, 186, 373, 374, 381, 711, 994, 1000, 1002, 1003

Pretz v. Holstein Freisan Ass'n, 698 F. Supp. 1531 (D. Kan. 1988), 41, 42, 83, 87, 89, 90

Princeton Community Phone Book, Inc. v. Bate, 582 F.2d 706 (3d Cir.), cert. denied, 439 U.S. 966 (1978), 967

Principe v. McDonald's Corp., 631 F.2d 303 (4th Cir. 1980), cert. denied, 451 U.S. 970 (1981), 141, 142, 162, 849

Printing Plate Supply Co. v. Crescent Engraving Co., 246 F. Supp. 654 (W.D. Mich. 1965), 816

Pritchard-Keang Nam Corp. v. Jaworski, 751 F.2d 277 (8th Cir. 1984), 764

Pritt v. Blue Cross & Blue Shield, Inc., 699 F. Supp. 81 (S.D.W.Va. 1988), 1111

Procter & Gamble Co., 63 F.T.C. 1465 (1963), rev'd, 358 F.2d 74 (6th Cir. 1966), rev'd, 386 U.S. 568 (1967), 360

Proctor v. State Farm Mut. Auto. Ins. Co., 561 F.2d 262 (D.C. Cir. 1977), vacated, 440 U.S. 942 (1979), on remand, 1980-81 Trade Cas. (CCH) ¶ 63,591 (D.D.C. 1980), aff'd, 675 F.2d 308 (D.C. Cir.), cert. denied, 459 U.S. 839 (1982), 1118

Proctor v. State Farm Mut. Auto. Ins. Co., 675 F.2d 308 (D.C. Cir.), cert. denied, 459 U.S. 839 (1982), 1111, 1113

Procureur de la République and Others v. Bruno Giry and Guerlain SA, Joined Cases 253/78 and 1 to 3/79, [1980] E.C.R. 2357, [1979-1981 Transfer Binder] COMMON MKT. REP. (CCH) ¶ 8712, 922

Product Promotions, Inc. v. Cousteau, 495 F.2d 483 (5th Cir. 1974), 872

Products Liab. Ins. Agency v. Crum & Forster Ins. Co., 682 F.2d 660 (7th Cir. 1982), 55, 181

Professional Adjusting Sys. of Am. v. General Adjustment Bureau, 373 F. Supp. 1225 (S.D.N.Y. 1974), 746, 749

Professional Adjusting Sys. of Am. v. General Adjustment Bureau, 1975-2 Trade Cas. (CCH) ¶ 60,497 (S.D.N.Y. 1975), 766

Professional and Business Men's Life Ins. Co. v. Banker's Life Co., 163 F. Supp. 274 (D. Mont. 1958), 1115

Professional Beauty Supply v. National Beauty Supply, 594 F.2d 1179 (8th Cir. 1979), 639

Program Eng'g, Inc. v. Triangle Publications, 634 F.2d 1188 (9th Cir. 1980), 28

Pronuptia, Case 161/84, [1986] E.C.R. 353, [1985-1986 Transfer Binder] COMMON MKT. REP. (CCH) ¶ 14,245, 941

Pronuptia, 30 O.J. EUR. COMM. (No. L 12) 39 (1987), [1985-1988 Transfer Binder] COMMON MKT. REP. (CCH) ¶ 10,854, 941

Protect Our Mountain Environment, Inc. v. District Court, 677 P.2d 1361 (Colo. 1984), 638

Protectoseal Co. v. Barancik, 484 F.2d 585 (7th Cir. 1973), 395, 398

Prudential New York Theatres v. Radio City Music Hall Corp., 271 F. Supp. 762 (S.D.N.Y. 1967), 748

Prym-Beka, 16 O.J. EUR. COMM. (No. L 296) 24 (1973), [1973-1975 Transfer Binder] COMMON MKT. REP. (CCH) ¶ 9609, 923, 934

P. Stone, Inc. v. Koppers Co., 94 F.R.D. 662 (M.D. Pa. 1982), 769

Public Serv. Co. of Colo., 92 F.T.C. 343 (1978), 534

Public Serv. Co. of Ind., 42 F.E.R.C. (CCH) ¶ 61,243 (1988), 1078

Public Serv. Co. of Ind., Inc., Op. No. 349, 51 F.E.R.C. (CCH) ¶ 61,367 (1990), 1070

Public Serv. Co. v. General Elec. Co., 315 F.2d 306 (10th Cir.), cert. denied, 374 U.S. 809 (1963), 688, 689

Pueblo Aircraft Serv. v. City of Pueblo, 679 F.2d 805 (10th Cir. 1982), cert. denied, 459 U.S. 1126 (1983), 972, 983

Puerto Rico Maritime Shipping Auth. v. ICC, 645 F.2d 1102 (D.C. Cir. 1981), 1161

Puerto Rico Maritime Shipping Auth. v. Valley Freight Sys., 856 F.2d 546 (3d Cir. 1988), 1161

Pumps & Power Co. v. Southern States Indus., 787 F.2d 1252 (8th Cir. 1986), 10, 13, 14

Purex Corp. v. General Foods Corp., 318 F. Supp. 322 (C.D. Cal. 1970), 697, 701

Purex Corp. v. Procter & Gamble Co., 308 F. Supp. 584 (C.D. Cal. 1970), aff'd on other grounds, 453 F.2d 288 (9th Cir. 1971), cert. denied, 405 U.S. 1065 (1972), 570

Purex Corp. v. Procter & Gamble Co., 453 F.2d 288 (9th Cir. 1971), cert. denied, 405 U.S. 1065 (1972), 777

Purex Corp. v. Procter & Gamble Co., 664 F.2d 1105 (9th Cir. 1981), cert. denied, 456 U.S. 983 (1982), 270, 365, 371

Puritan-Bennett Aero Sys. Co., 110 F.T.C. 86 (1987), aff'd mem., 817 F.2d 102 (4th Cir. 1987), reprinted in 1987-1 Trade Cas. (CCH) ¶ 67,546, 468, 474

Purolator Prods., Inc., 65 F.T.C. 8 (1964), aff'd, 352 F.2d 874 (7th Cir. 1965), cert. denied, 389 U.S. 1045 (1968), 430

Purolator Prods., Inc. v. FTC, 352 F.2d 874 (7th Cir. 1965), cert. denied, 389 U.S. 1045 (1968), 429

Q

Q.T. Markets, Inc. v. Fleming Cos., 394 F. Supp. 1102 (D. Colo. 1975), 156

Q-Tips, Inc. v. Johnson & Johnson, 109 F. Supp. 657 (D.N.J. 1951), *modified*, 207 F. 2d 509 (3d Cir. 1953), *cert. denied*, 347 U.S. 935 (1954), 823

Quadrozzi v. City of New York, 1989-2 Trade Cas. ¶ 68,668 (S.D.N.Y. 1989), 789

Quaker Oats Co., 66 F.T.C. 1131 (1964), 412

Quaker State Foods Corp. v. F.M. Stamper Co., 1965 Trade Cas. (CCH) ¶ 71,345 (E.D.N.Y. 1965), 746, 751, 752

Quaker State Oil Ref. Corp., 419 F. Supp. 479, 494 (W.D. Pa. 1976), 186

Quality Auto Body, Inc. v. Allstate Ins. Co., 1980-2 Trade Cas. (CCH) ¶ 63,507 (N.D. Ill. 1980) *aff'd*, 660 F.2d 1195 (7th Cir. 1981), *cert. denied*, 455 U.S. 1020 (1982), 1117

Quality Auto Body, Inc. v. Allstate Ins. Co., 660 F.2d 1195 (7th Cir. 1981), *cert. denied*, 455 U.S. 1020 (1982), 45, 115

Quality Bakers of Am. v. FTC, 114 F.2d 393 (1st Cir. 1940), 431, 436

Quality Mercury, Inc. v. Ford Motor Co., 542 F.2d 466 (8th Cir. 1976), *cert. denied*, 433 U.S. 914 (1977), 119

Quality Prefab., Inc. v. Daniel J. Keating Co., 675 F.2d 77 (3d Cir. 1982), 769

Queen Ins. Co. v. State, 86 Tex. 250, 24 S.W. 397 (1893), 619

Quincy Cable TV, Inc. v. FCC, 768 F.2d 1434 (D.C. Cir. 1985), *cert. denied*, 476 U.S. 1169 (1986), 1052

Quinn v. Kent Gen. Hosp., 617 F. Supp. 1226 (D. Del. 1985), 32, 92, 971

Quinn v. Kent Gen. Hosp., 673 F. Supp. 1367 (D. Del. 1987), 25

Quinn v. Mobil Oil Co., 375 F.2d 273 (1st Cir.), *cert. dismissed*, 389 U.S. 801 (1967), 103

Quinonez v. National Ass'n of Sec. Dealers, 540 F.2d 824 (5th Cir. 1976), 1104

Quonset Real Estate v. Paramount Film Distrib., 50 F.R.D. 240 (S.D.N.Y. 1970), 746, 747

R

Rabiner & Jontow, Inc., 70 F.T.C. 638 (1966), *aff'd*, 386 F.2d 667 (2d Cir. 1967), *cert. denied*, 390 U.S. 1004 (1968), 437

Racetrac Petroleum, Inc. v. Prince George's County, 601 F. Supp. 892 (D. Md. 1985) *aff'd*, 786 F.2d 202 (4th Cir. 1986), 1005

Rader v. Balfour, 440 F.2d 469 (7th Cir.), *cert. denied*, 404 U.S. 983 (1971), 645, 684, 685, 686

Radial Lip Mach., Inc. v. International Carbide Corp., 76 F.R.D. 224 (N.D. Ill. 1977), 773

Radiant Burners, Inc. v. Peoples Gas Light & Coke Co., 364 U.S. 656 (1961), 78, 80, 88, 89

Radio Mfg. Co. v. Hazeltine Research, Inc., 339 U.S. 827 (1950), 836

Radovich v. NFL, 352 U.S. 445 (1957), 373, 648

Rafferty v. NYNEX Corp., 1990-2 Trade Cas. (CCH) ¶ 69,114 (D.D.C. 1990), 646, 662

Raiport Co. v. General Motors Corp., 366 F. Supp. 328 (E.D. Pa. 1973), *aff'd* 547 F.2d 1163 (3d Cir. 1977), 179

Ralph C. Wilson Indus. v. ABC, 598 F. Supp. 694 (N.D. Cal. 1984), *aff'd sub nom.* Ralph G. Wilson Indus. v. Chronicle Broadcasting Co., 794 F.2d 1359 (9th Cir. 1986), 48, 178

Ralph C. Wilson Indus. v. Chronicle Broadcasting Co., 794 F.2d 1359 (9th Cir. 1986), 9, 49, 118

Ralston v. Volkswagenwerk AG, 61 F.R.D. 427 (W.D. Mo. 1973), 735

Ramos v. Lamm, 713 F.2d 546 (10th Cir. 1983), *cert. denied*, 474 U.S. 823 (1985), 782

Ramsburg v. American Inv. Co., 231 F.2d 333 (7th Cir. 1956), 644

R & G Affiliates v. Knoll Int'l, 587 F. Supp. 1395 (S.D.N.Y. 1984), 108, 144, 155, 159

Rand v. Anaconda Ericsson, Inc., 794 F.2d 843 (2d Cir.), *cert. denied*, 479 U.S. 987 (1986), 661

Rangen, Inc. v. Sterling Nelson & Sons, 351 F.2d 851 (9th Cir. 1965), *cert. denied*, 383 U.S. 936 (1966), 404, 432, 434, 436, 993

Rank/SOPELEM, 18 O.J. EUR. COMM. (No. L 29) 20 (1975), [1973-1975 Transfer Binder] COMMON MKT. REP. (CCH) ¶ 9707, 934

Rankin County Cablevision v. Pearl River Valley Water Supply Dist., 692 F. Supp. 691 (S.D. Miss. 1988), 409, 1053

Rapperswill Corp., 89 F.T.C. 71 (1977), 491

Rasmussen v. American Dairy Ass'n, 472 F.2d 517 (9th Cir. 1972), *cert. denied*, 412 U.S. 950 (1973), 27, 28, 29

Rasoulzadeh v. Associated Press, 574 F. Supp. 854 (S.D.N.Y. 1983), *aff'd without published opinion*, 767 F.2d 908 (2d Cir. 1985), 903

Ratino v. Medical Serv., 718 F.2d 1260 (4th Cir. 1983), 40, 70, 704, 1111

Raul Int'l Corp. v. Sealed Power Corp., 586 F. Supp. 349 (D.N.J. 1984), *aff'd without published opinion*, 822 F.2d 54 (3d Cir. 1987), 449, 865

Rayex Corp. v. FTC, 317 F.2d 290 (2d Cir. 1963), 522

Raymond Lee Org., Inc., 92 F.T.C. 489 (1978), *aff'd sub nom.* Lee v. FTC, 679 F.2d 905 (D.C. Cir. 1980), 465. 466, 492

Raymond-Nagoya, 15 J.O. COMM. EUR. (No. L 143) 39 (1972), [1970-1972 Transfer Binder] COMMON MKT. REP. (CCH) ¶ 9513, 948

Raymond v. Avon Prods. Inc., 1978-1 Trade Cas. (CCH) ¶ 62,076 (N.Y. Sup. Ct. 1978), 449

Raytheon Prod. Corp. v. Commissioner, 144 F.2d 110 (1st Cir.), *cert. denied*, 323 U.S. 779 (1944), 794

Ray v. Indiana & Mich. Elec. Co., 606 F. Supp. 757 (N.D. Ill. 1984), *aff'd*, 758 F.2d 1148 (7th Cir. 1985), 239, 1073

Ray v. United Family Life Ins. Co., Inc., 430 F. Supp. 1353 (W.D.N.C. 1977), 1118

Razorback Ready Mix Concrete Co. v. Weaver, 761 F.2d 484 (8th Cir. 1985), 990, 999, 1001

RCA v. Andrea, 90 F.2d 612 (2d Cir. 1937), 820

R.C. Bigelow, Inc. v. Unilever N.V., 867 F.2d 102 (2d Cir.), *cert. denied*, 493 U.S. 815 (1989), 299, 362, 367, 370, 651, 676, 682

R.C. Dick Geothermal Corp. v. Thermogenics, Inc., 566 F. Supp. 1104 (N.D. Cal. 1983), 214

R.C. Dick Geothermal Corp. v. Thermogenics, Inc., 890 F.2d 139 (9th Cir. 1989), 37, 47, 661

RCM Supply v. Hunter Douglas, Inc., 686 F.2d 1074 (4th Cir. 1982), 282

R.D. Imports Ryno Indus. v. Mazda Distribs. (Gulf), 807 F.2d 1222 (5th Cir.) *cert. denied*, 484 U.S. 818 (1987), 159

Reaemco, Inc. v. Allegheny Airlines, 496 F. Supp. 546 (S.D.N.Y. 1980), 1011

REA Express, Inc. v. CAB, 507 F.2d 42 (2d Cir. 1974), 1156

Rea v. Ford Motor Co., 355 F. Supp. 842 (W.D. Pa. 1973), *rev'd*, 497 F.2d 577 (3d Cir.), *cert. denied*, 419 U.S. 868 (1974), 113, 408, 438

Reazin v. Blue Cross & Blue Shield, 635 F. Supp. 1287 (D. Kan. 1986), *aff'd* 899 F.2d 951 (10th Cir.), *cert. denied*, 110 S. Ct. 3241 (1990), 93

Reazin v. Blue Cross & Blue Shield, 663 F. Supp. 1360 (D. Kan. 1987), *aff'd* 899 F.2d 951 (10th Cir.), *cert. denied*, 110 S. Ct. 3241 (1990), 60, 214, 325, 326, 332, 335, 363, 971, 1113, 1116

Reazin v. Blue Cross & Blue Shield, 899 F.2d 951 (10th Cir.), *cert. denied*, 110 S. Ct. 3241 (1990), 4, 41, 46, 49, 50, 197, 215, 216, 217, 223, 663

Rebel Oil Co. v. Atlantic Richfield Co., 1990-2 Trade Cas. (CCH) ¶ 69,258 (D. Nev. 1990), 749

Reborn Enters. v. Fine Child, Inc., 590 F. Supp. 1423 (S.D.N.Y. 1984), *aff'd per curiam*, 754 F.2d 1072 (2d Cir. 1985), 107, 109, 110, 144, 185

Record Club of Am. v. CBS, 310 F. Supp. 1241 (E.D. Pa. 1970), 408

Red Apple Supermarkets v. Deltown Foods, Inc., 419 F. Supp. 1256 (S.D.N.Y. 1976), 403

Red Diamond Supply v. Liquid Carbonic Corp., 637 F.2d 1001 (5th Cir.), *cert. denied*, 454 U.S. 822 (1981), 45, 123, 125, 126, 128

Redd v. Shell Oil Co., 524 F.2d 1054 (10th Cir. 1975), *cert. denied*, 425 U.S. 912 (1976), 121, 141, 156, 160, 161, 190, 849

Redmond v. Missouri W. State College, 1988-2 Trade Cas. (CCH) ¶ 68,323 (W.D. Mo. 1988), 206, 265

Reed Bros. v. Monsanto Inc., 525 F.2d 486 (8th Cir. 1975), *cert. denied*, 423 U.S. 1055 (1976), 76, 130, 184

Refrigeration Eng'g Corp. v. Frick Co., 370 F. Supp. 702 (W.D. Tex. 1974), 141, 172, 175, 178, 424

Regency Oldsmobile, Inc. v. General Motors Corp., 723 F. Supp. 250 (D.N.J. 1989), 206, 265, 266, 272

Regents of Univ. of Cal. v. ABC, 747 F.2d 511 (9th Cir. 1984), 40, 81, 384

Regina Corp. v. FTC, 322 F.2d 765 (3d Cir. 1963), 108, 475, 494

Regional Refuse Sys. v. Inland Reclamation Co., 842 F.2d 150 (6th Cir. 1988), 769

Registered Physical Therapists, Inc. v. Intermountain Health Care, Inc., 1988-2 Trade Cas. ¶ 68,233 (D. Utah 1988), 42, 83

Regular Common Carrier Conference v. United States, 820 F.2d 1323 (D.C. Cir. 1987), 1131, 1144

Reichhold Chems., Inc., 91 F.T.C. 246 (1978), aff'd mem., 598 F.2d 616 (4th Cir. 1979), 309, 314, 315

Reich v. Reed Tool Co., 582 S.W.2d 549 (Tex. Ct. App. 1979), cert. denied, 446 U.S. 946 (1980), 826

Reines Distribs. v. Admiral Corp., 256 F. Supp. 581 (S.D.N.Y. 1966), 408

Re Inter-City Truck Lines (Canada), 133 D.L.R.3d 134 (Ont. H. Ct. J. 1982), 885

Reisman v. Caplin, 375 U.S. 440 (1964), 508

Reisner v. General Motors Corp., 511 F. Supp. 1167 (S.D.N.Y. 1981), aff'd, 671 F.2d 91 (2d Cir.), cert. denied, 459 U.S. 858 (1982), 135, 148, 154, 158

Reisner v. General Motors Corp., 671 F.2d 91 (2d Cir.), cert. denied, 459 U.S. 858 (1982), 757

Reiter v. Sonotone Corp., 486 F. Supp. 115 (D. Minn. 1980), 656, 657, 664, 678

Reiter v. Sonotone Corp., 442 U.S. 330 (1979), 649

Reliable Mortgage Corp., 85 F.T.C. 21 (1975), 534

Reliance Molded Plastics, Inc. v. Jiffy Prods., 215 F. Supp. 402 (D.N.J. 1963), aff'd per curiam, 337 F.2d 857 (3d Cir. 1964), 829

Remia BV, Case 42/84, [1985] E.C.R. 2545, [1985-1986 Transfer Binder] COMMON MKT. REP. (CCH) ¶ 14,217, 937

Remington Prods., Inc. v. North Am. Philips Corp., 717 F. Supp. 36 (D. Conn. 1989), 287, 363

Remington Prods., Inc. v. North Am. Philips Corp., 755 F. Supp. 52 (D. Conn. 1991), 363, 651

Remington Prods., Inc. v. North Am. Philips Corp., 763 F. Supp. 683 (D. Conn. 1991), 770

Remington Rand Corp.-Delaware v. Business Sys., 830 F.2d 1260 (3d Cir. 1987), 906

Removatron Int'l Corp., 111 F.T.C. 206 (1988), aff'd, 884 F.2d 1489 (1st Cir. 1989), 467, 468, 473

Removatron Int'l Corp. v. FTC, 884 F.2d 1489 (1st Cir. 1989), 468, 488, 489

Rentacolor, Inc., 103 F.T.C. 400 (1984), 535

Rental Car, Inc. v. Westinghouse Elec. Corp., 496 F. Supp. 373 (D. Mass. 1980), 716, 720, 727

Repp v. F.E.L. Publications, 688 F.2d 441 (7th Cir. 1982), 661

Republic Molding Corp. v. B. W. Photo Utils., 319 F.2d 347 (9th Cir. 1963), 814

Republic of Iraq v. First Nat'l City Bank, 353 F.2d 47 (2d Cir. 1965), aff'g, 241 F. Supp. 567 (S.D.N.Y.), cert. denied, 392 U.S. 1027 (1966), 907

Republic of Texas Corp. v. Board of Governors, 649 F.2d 1026 (5th Cir. 1981), 1095

Republic of the Philippines v. Marcos, 806 F.2d 344 (2d Cir. 1986), 906, 908

Republic of the Philippines v. Marcos, 862 F.2d 1355 (9th Cir.), cert. denied, 490 U.S. 1035 (1989), 903, 907

Republic of Vietnam v. Pfizer, Inc., 556 F.2d 892 (8th Cir. 1977), 645

Republic Packaging Corp. v. Harvey Indus., 406 F. Supp. 379 (N.D. Ill. 1976), 408

Reserve Supply Corp. v. Owens-Corning Fiberglas Corp., 639 F. Supp. 1457 (N.D. Ill. 1986), 420, 653

Resort Car Rental Sys. v. FTC, 518 F.2d 962 (9th Cir.), cert. denied, 423 U.S. 827 (1975), 491

Response of Carolina, Inc. v. Leasco Response, Inc., 537 F.2d 1307 (5th Cir. 1976), 121, 130, 143, 144, 146, 253

Retail Serv. Assocs. v. Conagra Pet Prods. Co., 759 F. Supp. 976 (D. Conn. 1991), 50, 118, 187, 188

Reuben H. Donnelley Corp., 95 F.T.C. 1 (1980), 507

Reuben H. Donnelley Corp. v. FTC, 580 F.2d 264 (7th Cir. 1978), 520

Reuter/BASF, 19 O.J. Eur. Comm. (No. L 254) 40 (1976), [1976-1978 Transfer Binder] Common Mkt. Rep. (CCH) ¶ 9862, 929, 937

Revco D.S., Inc., 67 F.T.C. 1158 (1965), 475

Rex Chainbelt, Inc. v. Harco Prods., Inc., 512 F.2d 993 (9th Cir.), *cert. denied*, 423 U.S. 831 (1975), 144, 833

Rex Sys. v. Holiday, 814 F.2d 994 (4th Cir. 1987), 965

Reynolds Metals Co. v. Columbia Gas Sys., No. 87-0446-R (E.D. Va. Aug. 17, 1988), 1065

Reynolds Metals Co. v. Commonwealth Gas Servs., 682 F. Supp. 291 (E.D. Va. 1988), 971

Reynolds Metals Co. v. FTC, 309 F.2d 223 (D.C. Cir. 1962), 285, 289, 294, 331, 360

Reynolds v. NFL, 584 F.2d 280 (8th Cir. 1978), 91, 724

RFD Publications v. Oregonian Publishing Co., 749 F.2d 1327 (9th Cir. 1984), 233

Rhinechem Corp., 93 F.T.C. 233 (1979), 276

R.H. Macy & Co. v. FTC, 326 F.2d 445 (2d Cir. 1964), 437, 438, 442, 445, 446, 459, 461, 494

Rhodes Pharmacal Co. v. FTC, 208 F.2d 382 (7th Cir. 1953), *rev'd in part to reinstate FTC order*, 348 U.S. 940 (1955), 466, 471, 513

Ricaud v. American Metal Co., 246 U.S. 304 (1918), 902, 909

Ricchetti v. Meister Brau, Inc., 431 F.2d 1211 (9th Cir. 1970), *cert. denied*, 401 U.S. 939 (1971), 185, 188, 193

Ricci v. Chicago Mercantile Exch., 409 U.S. 289 (1973), 1022, 1023, 1106

Rice v. Santa Fe Elevator Corp., 331 U.S. 218 (1947), 625

Richard Hoffman Corp. v. Integrated Bldg. Sys., 581 F. Supp. 367 (N.D. Ill. 1984), 30, 96

Richard Short Oil Co. v. Texaco, Inc., 799 F.2d 415 (8th Cir. 1986), 413, 417, 430, 450

Richardson v. Florida Bar, 1990-2 Trade Cas. (CCH) ¶ 69,111 (D.D.C. 1990), 967

Richardson v. United States, 577 F.2d 447 (8th Cir. 1978), *cert. denied*, 442 U.S. 910 (1979), 581

Richardson v. Volkswagenwerk, AG, 552 F. Supp. 73 (W.D. Mo. 1982), 877

Richards v. Neilsen Freight Lines, 810 F.2d 898 (9th Cir. 1987), 9, 705, 707, 1122, 1125, 1126, 1130

Richfield Oil Corp. v. Karseal Corp., 271 F.2d 709 (9th Cir. 1959), *cert. denied*, 361 U.S. 961 (1960), 671

Richmond Power & Light v. FERC, 574 F.2d 610 (D.C. Cir. 1978), 1069

Rich Prod./Jus-rol, 31 O.J. Eur. Comm. (No. L 69) 21 (1988), [1985-1988 Transfer Binder] Common Mkt. Rep. (CCH) ¶ 10,956, 950

Rich v. Kis Cal., Inc., 121 F.R.D. 254 (M.D.N.C. 1988), 885

Richter Concrete Corp. v. Hilltop Basic Resources, Inc., 547 F. Supp. 893 (S.D. Ohio 1981), *aff'd sub nom.*, Richter Concrete Corp. v. Hilltop Concrete Corp., 691 F.2d 818 (6th Cir. 1982), 2, 215

Richter Concrete Corp. v. Hilltop Concrete Corp., 691 F.2d 818 (6th Cir. 1982), 197, 236, 260, 265, 270

Rickards v. Canine Eye Registration Found., 704 F.2d 1449 (9th Cir.), *cert. denied*, 464 U.S. 994 (1983), 132

Rickards v. Canine Eye Registration Found., 783 F.2d 1329 (9th Cir.), *cert. denied*, 479 U.S. 851 (1986), 222, 258, 268, 998

Rickles, Inc. v. Frances Denney Corp., 508 F. Supp. 4 (D. Mass. 1980), 444

Riedel Int'l v. St. Helens Invs., 633 F. Supp. 117 (D. Or. 1985), 750, 751

Rigler v. FTC, 1980-81 Trade Cas. (CCH) ¶ 63,730 (D.D.C. 1981), 517

Ringtown Wilbert Vault Works v. Schuylkill Memorial Park Inc., 650 F. Supp. 823 (E.D. Pa. 1986), 139, 153, 154, 158

Rio Tinto Corp. v. Westinghouse Elec. Corp., [1978] 2 W.L.R. 81 (House of Lords 1977), 884

Rio Vista Oil, Ltd. v. Southland Corp., 667 F. Supp. 757 (D. Utah 1987), 19, 28

Riss & Co. v. Association of Am. R.R., 190 F. Supp. 10, (D.D.C. 1960), *aff'd in part, rev'd in part*, 299 F.2d 133 (D.C. Cir.), *cert. denied*, 370 U.S. 916 (1962), 668

Riss & Co. v. Association of Am. R.R., 299 F.2d 133 (D.C. Cir.), *cert. denied*, 370 U.S. 916 (1962), 668

Riverview Invs., Inc. v. Ottawa Community Improvement Corp., 899 F.2d 474 (6th Cir.), *cert. denied*, 111 S. Ct. 151 (1990), 7, 706, 986

RJM Sales & Marketing v. Banfi Products Corp., 546 F. Supp. 1368 (D. Minn. 1982), 662

R.J. Reynolds Tobacco Co., 111 F.T.C. 539 (1988), 466

RKO Gen., Inc. (WNAC-TV), 78 F.C.C.2d 1 (1980) *aff'd in part, rev'd in part*, RKO Gen., Inc. v. FCC, 670 F.2d 215 (D.C. Cir. 1981), *cert. denied*, 456 U.S. 927 (1982), 1031, 1032

RKO Gen., Inc., 82 F.C.C.2d 291 (1980), *vacated in part and remanded sub nom.* New S. Media Corp. v FCC, 685 F.2d 708 (D.C. Cir. 1982), 1032

RKO Gen., Inc. (KHJ-TV), 78 F.C.C.2d 355 (1980), 1032

RKO Gen., Inc. (WOR-TV), 92 F.C.C.2d 303 (1983), 1032

RKO Gen., Inc. (KHJ-TV), 2 F.C.C. Rcd 4807 (1987), 1031, 1032

RKO Gen., Inc. (WHBQ), 3 F.C.C. Rcd 5055 (1988), 1032

RKO Gen., Inc. (KHJ-TV), 3 F.C.C. Rcd 5057 (1988), *appeal dismissed sub nom.* Los Angeles Television v. FCC, No. 88-1673 (D.C. Cir. Aug. 4, 1989), 1032

RKO Gen., Inc. (WGMS), 3 F.C.C. Rcd 5262 (1988), 1032

RKO Gen., Inc. (WRKO), 3 F.C.C. Rcd 6603 (1988), 1032

RKO Gen., Inc. v. FCC, 670 F.2d 215 (D.C. Cir. 1981), *cert. denied*, 456 U.S. 927 (1982), 1032

Robbins Flooring, Inc. v. Federal Floors, Inc., 445 F. Supp. 4 (E.D. Pa. 1977), 405, 438

Robertson v. NBA, 67 F.R.D. 691 (S.D.N.Y. 1975), 735, 745

Robertson v. NBA, 389 F. Supp. 867 (S.D.N.Y. 1975), 622

Robertson v. NBA, 556 F.2d 682 (2d Cir. 1977), 724, 743

Roberts v. Elaine Powers Figure Salons, Inc., 708 F.2d 1476 (9th Cir. 1983), 50, 132, 141, 849

Roberts v. Exxon Corp., 427 F. Supp. 389 (W.D. La. 1977), 102, 103

Robert's Waikiki U-Drive, Inc. v. Budget Rent-A-Car Sys., 491 F. Supp. 1199 (D. Haw. 1980), *aff'd*, 732 F.2d 1403 (9th Cir. 1984), 54, 147

Robert's Waikiki U-Drive, Inc. v. Budget Rent-A-Car Sys., 732 F.2d 1403 (9th Cir. 1984), 45, 49, 132, 144, 151, 159

Robinson v. Intergraph Corp., 1988-2 Trade Cas. (CCH) ¶ 68,138, (E.D. Mich. 1988), 205, 206, 284, 305

Robinson v. Magovern, 456 F. Supp. 1000 (W.D. Pa. 1978), 55

Robinson v. Magovern, 521 F. Supp. 842 (W.D. Pa. 1981), *aff'd*, 688 F.2d 824 (3d Cir.), *cert. denied*, 459 U.S. 971 (1982), 272

Robinson v. Stanley Home Prods., Inc., 272 F.2d 601 (1st Cir. 1959), 434

Robintech, Inc. v. Chemidus Wavin, Ltd., 628 F.2d 142 (D.C. Cir. 1980), 814, 827, 830

Rocform Corp. v. Acitelli-Standard Concrete Wall, Inc., 367 F.2d 678 (6th Cir. 1966), 826

Roche Holding Ltd., 5 TRADE REG. REP. (CCH) ¶ 22,879 (Nov. 28, 1990), 324, 326, 345, 349

Rockland Physician Assocs. v. Gorden, 616 F. Supp. 945 (S.D.N.Y. 1985), 174

Rockwell Int'l Corp. v. H. Wolfe Iron and Metal Co., 576 F. Supp. 511 (W.D. Pa. 1983), 771

Rod Baxter Imports v. Saab-Scania of Am., Inc., 489 F. Supp. 245 (D. Minn. 1980), 406

Rodgers v. United States Steel Co., 70 F.R.D. 639 (W.D. Pa.), *appeal dismissed*, 541 F.2d 365 (3d Cir. 1976), 743

Rodrigue v. Chrysler Motors Corp., 421 F. Supp. 903 (E.D. La. 1976), 132

Roesch, Inc. v. Star Cooler Corp., 671 F.2d 1168 (8th Cir. 1982), *aff'd by an equally divided court en banc*, 712 F.2d 1235 (1983), *cert. denied*, 466 U.S. 926 (1984), 107

Rogers v. Douglas Tobacco Bd. of Trade, 244 F.2d 471 (5th Cir. 1957), 793

Rohm & Haas Co. v. Dawson Chem. Co., 557 F. Supp. 739 (S.D. Tex), *rev'd on other grounds*, 722 F.2d 1556 (Fed. Cir. 1983), *cert. denied*, 469 U.S. 851 (1984), 818

Rohm & Haas Co. v. Dawson Chem. Co., 635 F. Supp. 1211 (S.D. Tex. 1986), 809, 811, 812

Rohm & Haas Co. v. Owens-Corning Fiberglass Corp., 196 U.S.P.Q. (BNA) (N.D. Ala. 1977), 833

Rohrer v. Sears, Roebuck & Co., 1975-1 Trade Cas. (CCH) ¶ 60,352 (E.D. Mich. 1975), 404

Roland Mach. Co. v. Dresser Indus., 749 F.2d 380 (7th Cir. 1984), 49, 53, 109, 170, 172, 173, 176, 177, 178, 179, 367, 677, 678

Romaco, Inc. v. Crown Cent. Petroleum Corp., 1973-2 Trade Cas. (CCH) ¶ 74,694 (M.D. Ala. 1973), 190

Ron Tonkin Gran Turismo, Inc. v. Fiat Distrib., 637 F.2d 1376 (9th Cir.), *cert. denied*, 454 U.S. 831 (1981), 38, 79, 118, 147, 182, 187, 188, 192

Ronwin v. State Bar of Ariz., 686 F.2d 692, (9th Cir. 1981), *rev'd sub nom.*, Hoover v. Ronwin, 466 U.S. 558 (1984), 29, 982

Roofing Felt, 29 O.J. EUR. COMM. (No. L 232) 15 (1986), [1985-1988 Transfer Binder] COMMON MKT. REP. (CCH) ¶ 10,805, 932

Roofire Alarm Co. v. Royal Indem. Co., 313 F.2d 635 (6th Cir.), *cert. denied*, 373 U.S. 949 (1963), 88

Rooney v. Columbia Pictures Indus., 538 F. Supp. 211 (S.D.N.Y.), *aff'd*, 714 F.2d 117 (2d Cir. 1982), *cert. denied*, 460 U.S. 1084 (1983), 791

Rooney v. Columbia Pictures Indus., 714 F.2d 117 (2d Cir. 1982), *cert. denied*, 460 U.S. 1084 (1983), 791

Roorda v. American Oil Co., 446 F. Supp. 939 (W.D.N.Y. 1978), 403

Roorda v. American Oil Co., 1981-1 Trade Cas. (CCH) ¶ 64,153 (W.D.N.Y. 1981), 429

Roper v. Consurve, Inc., 578 F.2d 1106 (5th Cir. 1978), *aff'd sub nom.* Deposit Guaranty Nat'l Bank v. Roper, 445 U.S. 326 (1980), 717

Rosebrough Monument Co. v. Memorial Park Cemetery Ass'n, 666 F.2d 1130 (8th Cir. 1981), *cert. denied*, 457 U.S. 1111 (1982), 27, 45, 54, 70, 139, 152, 153, 154, 665, 669, 672, 679

Rose Confections, Inc. v. Ambrosia Chocolate Co., 816 F.2d 381 (8th Cir. 1987), 416, 419, 420, 450, 647, 666, 667, 671, 672, 673

Rosefielde v. Falcon Jet Corp., 701 F. Supp. 1053 (D.N.J. 1988), 73

Rosemont Cogeneration Joint Venture v. Northern States Power Co., 1991-1 Trade Cas. (CCH) ¶ 69,351 (D. Minn. 1991), 971

Rosenberg v. Healthcorp Affiliates, 663 F. Supp. 222 (N.D. Ill. 1987), 25

Rosenfeld v. Hartford Fire Ins. Co., 1988-1 Trade Cas. (CCH) ¶ 68,015 (S.D.N.Y. 1988), 710

Ross-Bart Post Theatre v. Eagle Lion Films, 140 F. Supp. 401 (E.D. Va. 1954), 867

Ross v. Bremer, 1982-2 Trade Cas. (CCH) ¶ 64,747 (W.D. Wash. 1982), 1004

Rothery Storage & Van Co. v. Atlas Van Lines, 597 F. Supp. 217 (D.D.C. 1984), *aff'd*, 792 F.2d 210 (D.C. Cir. 1986), *cert. denied*, 479 U.S. 1033 (1987), 53

Rothery Storage & Van Co. v. Atlas Van Lines, 792 F.2d 210 (D.C. Cir. 1986), *cert. denied*, 479 U.S. 1033 (1987), 1, 21, 37, 39, 41, 43, 45, 46, 48, 49, 51, 53, 56, 77, 78, 86, 205, 375, 379, 381, 385, 1130

Roth Office Equip. Co. v. G.F. Business Equip. Co., 1975-2 Trade Cas. (CCH) ¶ 60,563 (S.D. Ohio 1975), 184, 187

Rowe Furniture Corp. v. Serta, Inc., 1982-83 Trade Cas. (CCH) ¶ 64,993 (N.D. Ill. 1982), 81, 778

Rowe v. Hamrah, 1984-2 Trade Cas. (CCH) ¶ 66,119 (E.D. Cal. 1984), 409

Royal Crown Cola Co. v. Coca-Cola Co., 1967 Trade Cas. (CCH) ¶ 72,176 (N.D. Ga. 1967), 747

Royal Crown Cola Co. v. Coca-Cola Co., 53 ANTITRUST & TRADE REG. REP. (BNA) 1002 (M.D. Ga. Dec. 11, 1987), 780

Royal Crown Cola Co. v. Coca-Cola Co., 887 F.2d 1480 (11th Cir. 1989), *cert. denied*, 110 S. Ct. 3258 (1990), 361

Royal Drug Co. v. Group Life and Health Ins. Co., 737 F.2d 1433 (5th Cir. 1984), *cert. denied*, 469 U.S. 1160 (1985), 7, 37, 38, 85, 115, 1113

Royal Furniture Co., 93 F.T.C. 422 (1979), 532

Royal Indus. v. St. Regis Paper Co., 420 F.2d 449 (9th Cir. 1969), 821

Royal Printing Co. v. Kimberly-Clark Corp., 621 F.2d 323 (9th Cir. 1980), 657

Royal Serv. v. Goody Prod., 1986-1 Trade Cas. (CCH) ¶ 66,907 (E.D. Cal. 1985), *aff'd without published opinion*, 865 F.2d 1271 (9th Cir. 1989), 414, 430, 647

R.R. Donnelly & Sons Co. v. FTC, 931 F.2d 430 (7th Cir. 1991), 523

RSE, Inc. v. H&M, Inc., 90 F.R.D. 185 (M.D. Pa. 1981), 793

RSE, Inc. v. Penney Supply, 489 F. Supp. 1227 (M.D. Pa. 1980), 404

RSR Corp., 88 F.T.C. 8007 (1976), *aff'd*, 602 F.2d 1317 (9th Cir. 1979), *cert. denied*, 445 U.S. 927 (1980), 288

RSR Corp. v. FTC, 602 F.2d 1317 (9th Cir. 1979), *cert. denied*, 445 U.S. 927 (1980), 285, 287, 293, 294, 295, 296, 319, 359, 521

RTE Corp. v. Dow Corning Corp., 1986-2 Trade Cas. (CCH) ¶ 67,371 (E.D. Wis. 1986), 693

RTE v. Commission, Case T-69/89, (Ct. First Instance 1991), *appeal filed*, 944, 952, 953

Ruddy Brook Clothes, Inc. v. British & Foreign Marine Ins. Co., 195 F.2d 86 (7th Cir.), *cert. denied*, 344 U.S. 816 (1952), 86

Rudner v. Abbott Labs., 664 F. Supp. 1100 (N.D. Ohio 1987), 448

Ruiz v. Transportes Aeros Militares Ecuadorianos, 103 F.R.D. 458 (D.D.C. 1984), 871, 876

Runnels v. TMSI Contractors, Inc., 764 F.2d 417 (5th Cir. 1985), 869

Rural Tel. Serv. Co. v. Feist Publications, 737 F. Supp. 610 (D. Kan. 1990), 212, 242, 248, 251

Rush-Presbyterian-St. Luke's Medical Center v. Hellenic Republic, 877 F.2d 574 (7th Cir.), *cert. denied*, 110 S. Ct. 333 (1989), 900, 901

Russell v. United States, 369 U.S. 749 (1962), 584

Russ' Kwik Car Wash v. Marathon Petroleum Co., 772 F.2d 214 (6th Cir. 1985), 408

Russ Togs, Inc. v. Grinnell Corp., 426 F.2d 850 (2d Cir.), *cert. denied*, 400 U.S. 878 (1970), 686

Rutledge v. Boston Woven Hose & Rubber Co., 526 F.2d 248 (9th Cir. 1978), 689, 690, 691, 693

Rutledge v. Electric Hose & Rubber Co., 327 F. Supp. 1267 (C.D. Cal. 1971), *aff'd*, 511 F.2d 668 (9th Cir. 1975), 448

Rutledge v. Electric Hose & Rubber Co., 511 F.2d 668 (9th Cir. 1975), 437

Rutman Wine Co. v. E & J Gallo Winery, 829 F.2d 729 (9th Cir. 1987), 37, 54, 118, 180, 183, 188, 437, 449, 652

R.W. Int'l, Inc. v. Borden Interamerica, Inc., 673 F. Supp. 654 (D.P.R. 1987), 98

Ryals v. National Car Rental Sys., 404 F. Supp. 481 (D. Minn. 1975), 167, 168

Ryan v. Commissioner, 568 F.2d 531 (7th Cir. 1977), *cert. denied*, 439 U.S. 820 (1978), 592

Ryder Sys., 90 F.T.C. 921 (1977), 515

Ryko Mfg. Co. v. Eden Servs., 823 F.2d 1215 (8th Cir. 1987), *cert. denied*, 484 U.S. 1026 (1988), 50, 60, 78, 114, 124, 125, 126, 128, 170, 172, 173, 176, 177, 178, 182

S

SABA, 19 O.J. Eur. Comm. (No. L 28) 19 (1976), [1976-1978 Transfer Binder] Common Mkt. Rep. (CCH) ¶ 9802, 941-2

SABA, 26 O.J. Eur. Comm. (No. L 376) 41 (1983), [1982-1985 Transfer Binder] Common Mkt. Rep. (CCH) ¶ 10,568, 940

Sablosky v. Paramount Film Distrib. Corp., 137 F. Supp. 929 (E.D. Pa. 1955), 779

SA Brasserie de Haecht v. Wilkin-Janssen, Case 48/72, [1973] E.C.R. 77, [1971-1973 Transfer Binder] Common Mkt. Rep. (CCH) ¶ 8170, 926

Sabre Farms v. Bergendahl, 103 F.R.D. 8 (D. Or. 1984), 878

Sabre Shipping Corp. v. American President Lines, 285 F. Supp. 949 (S.D.N.Y. 1968), *cert. denied sub nom.* Japan Line v. Sabre Shipping Corp., 407 F.2d 173 (2d Cir.), *cert. denied*, 395 U.S. 922 (1969), 857, 911, 1165

Sabre Shipping v. American President Lines, 1969 Trade Cas. (CCH) ¶ 72,703 (S.D.N.Y. 1969), 746

SACEM v. Lucazeau, Joined Cases 110, 241-242/88, [1989] E.C.R. 2811, [1990] 2 CEC (CCH) 856, 956

SA Cimenteries CBR v. Commission, Joined Cases 8-11/66, [1967] E.C.R. 75, [1967-1970 Transfer Binder] COMMON MKT. REP. (CCH) ¶ 8052, 926

SA CNL-Sucal NV v. Hag GF AG, Case 10/89, (Eur. Comm. Ct. J. 1990), 945

SA Compagnie Générale pour la Diffusion de la Télévision Coditel v. SA Ciné Vog Films, Case 62/79, [1980] E.C.R. 881, [1979-1981 Transfer Binder] COMMON MKT. REP. (CCH) ¶ 8662, 947

Sacramento Coca-Cola Bottling Co. v. Chauffeurs, Teamsters & Helpers Local No. 150, 440 F.2d 1096 (9th Cir.), cert. denied, 404 U.S. 826 (1971), 1010

SA ETA Fabriques d'Ebauches, Case 31/85, [1985] E.C.R. 3933, [1985-1986 Transfer Binder] COMMON MKT. REP. (CCH) ¶ 14,276, 941

SAFCO, 15 J.O. COMM. EUR. (No. L 13) 44 (1971), [1970-1972 Transfer Binder] COMMON MKT. REP. (CCH) ¶ 9487, 923, 933

Safeway Stores, 91 F.T.C. 975 (1978), 480

Safeway Stores v. Oklahoma Retail Grocers Ass'n, 360 U.S. 334 (1959), 627

Safeway Stores v. Vance, 355 U.S. 389 (1958), 645

Sage Int'l, Ltd. v. Cadillac Gage Co., 507 F. Supp. 939 (E.D. Mich. 1981), 1001, 1006

Sage Int'l, Ltd. v. Cadillac Gage Co., 534 F. Supp. 896 (E.D. Mich. 1981), 903, 904, 907

Sager Glove Corp. v. Commissioner, 311 F.2d 210 (7th Cir. 1962), cert. denied, 373 U.S. 910 (1963), 794

Sahm v. V-1 Oil Co., 402 F.2d 69 (10th Cir. 1968), 110, 181

SA Lancôme v. Etos BV, Case 99/79, [1980] E.C.R. 2511, [1979-1981 Transfer Binder] COMMON MKT. REP. (CCH) ¶ 8714, 922, 926, 940

Salco Corp. v. General Motors Corp., 517 F.2d 567 (10th Cir. 1975), 129, 271-72

Salomon SA v. Alpina Sports Corp., 737 F. Supp. 720 (D.N.H. 1990), 1001

Salonia v. Poidomani, Case 126/80, [1981] E.C.R. 1563, [1979-1981 Transfer Binder] COMMON MKT. REP. (CCH) ¶ 8758, 940

Salt River Project Agric. Improvement & Power Dist. v. United States, 762 F.2d 1053 (D.C. Cir. 1985), 1135

Sample, Inc. v. Pendelton Woolen Mills, Inc., 704 F. Supp. 498 (S.D.N.Y. 1989), 109, 183

SA Musiques Diffusion Française v. Commission, Joined Cases 100-03/80, [1983] E.C.R. 1825, [1981-1983 Transfer Binder] COMMON MKT. REP. (CCH) ¶ 8880, 939

San Antonio Tel. Co. v. AT&T, 68 F.R.D. 435 (W.D. Tex. 1975), 722, 731

San Antonio Tel. Co. v. AT&T, 499 F.2d 349 (5th Cir. 1974), 868, 869

Sandcrest Outpatient Servs. v. Cumberland County Hosp. Sys., 853 F.2d 1139 (4th Cir. 1988), 978, 987

Sanderson v. Winner, 507 F.2d 477 (10th Cir. 1974), cert. denied, 421 U.S. 914 (1975), 722

Sandles v. Ruben, 89 F.R.D. 635 (S.D. Fla. 1981), 727

Sandoz, 30 O.J. EUR. COMM. (No. L 222) 28 (1987), [1985-1988 Transfer Binder] COMMON MKT. REP. (CCH) ¶ 10,907, aff'd sub nom. Sandoz Prodotti Farmaceutici SpA v. Commission, Case 277/87, [1990] E.C.R. I 45, 939

Sandsend Financial Consultants v. Wood, 743 S.W.2d 364 (Tex. Ct. App. 1988), 885

Sandura Co. v. FTC, 339 F.2d 847 (6th Cir. 1964), 120, 490, 491

San Juan Racing Ass'n v. Asociacion de Jinetes de Puerto Rico, 590 F.2d 31 (1st Cir. 1979), 1022

San-Mar Labs., 95 F.T.C. 236 (1980), 499

San Marino Elec. Corp. v. George J. Meyer Mfg. Co., 155 U.S.P.Q. (BNA) 617 (C.D. Cal. 1967), aff'd, 422 F.2d 1285 (9th Cir. 1970), 826

Sano Petroleum Corp. v. American Oil Co., 187 F. Supp. 345 (S.D.N.Y. 1960), 430, 431, 438

Sanofi, SA v. Med-Tech Veterinarian Prods., Inc., 222 U.S.P.Q. (BNA) 143 (D. Kan. 1983), 821

Santa Clara Valley Distrib. Co. v. Pabst Brewing Co., 556 F.2d 942 (9th Cir. 1977), 107, 108, 110, 130

Santa Fe-Pomeroy, Inc. v. P & Z Co., 569 F.2d 1084 (9th Cir. 1978), 805, 806

Santa Fe Southern Pac. Corp.-Control-Southern Pac. Trans. Co., 2 I.C.C. 2d 709 (1986), *petition to reopen denied*, 3 I.C.C. 926 (1987), 1142

Santobello v. New York, 404 U.S. 257 (1971), 581

Sapienza v. New York News, 481 F. Supp. 671 (S.D.N.Y. 1979), 172

Sapiro v. Hartford Fire Ins. Co., 452 F.2d 215 (7th Cir. 1972), 768

Sargent-Welch Scientific Co. v. Ventron Corp., 1973-2 Trade Cas. (CCH) ¶ 74,791 (N.D. Ill. 1973), 747

Sargent-Welch Scientific Co. v. Ventron Corp., 567 F.2d 701 (7th Cir. 1977), *cert. denied*, 439 U.S. 822 (1978), 109, 191, 221, 251

Sarin v. Samaritan Health Center, 813 F.2d 755 (6th Cir. 1987), 25

SA Télémarketing v. Télédiffusion, Case 311/84, [1985] E.C.R. 3261, [1985-1986 Transfer Binder] COMMON MKT. REP. (CCH) ¶ 14,246, 954

Satellite Fin. Planning Corp. v. First Nat'l Bank, 633 F. Supp. 386 (D. Del. 1986), 47, 131, 169, 173, 177

Satellite T Assoc. v. Continental Cablevision, Inc., 586 F. Supp. 973 (E.D. Va. 1982), *aff'd sub nom.*, Satellite Television & Associated Resources, Inc. v. Continental Cablevision, Inc., 714 F.2d 351 (4th Cir. 1983), *cert. denied*, 465 U.S. 1027 (1984), 1053

Satellite Television & Associated Resources, Inc. v. Continental Cablevision, 714 F.2d 351 (4th Cir. 1983), *cert. denied*, 465 U.S. 1027 (1987), 172, 173, 175, 177

Satellite Television Corp., 91 F.C.C.2d 953 (1982), 1042

Saturday Evening Post Co. v. Rumbleseat Press, Inc., 816 F.2d 1191 (7th Cir. 1987), 800, 836, 845

Sausalito Pharmacy, Inc. v. Blue Shield, 544 F. Supp. 230 (N.D. Cal. 1981), *aff'd per curiam*, 677 F.2d 47 (9th Cir.), *cert. denied*, 459 U.S. 1016 (1982), 115

Savage v. Waste Mgmt., Inc., 623 F. Supp. 1505 (D.S.C. 1985), 1011

Savannah Electric & Power Co., 42 F.E.R.C. (CCH) ¶ 61,240 (1988), 1078

Savannah Theatre Co. v. Lucas & Jenkins, 10 F.R.D. 461 (N.D. Ga. 1943), 752

Savin Corp. v. Heritage Copy Prods., Inc., 661 F. Supp. 463 (M.D. Pa. 1987), 873

Saylor v. Lindsley, 274 F. Supp. 253 (S.D.N.Y. 1967), *rev'd*, 391 F.2d 965 (2d Cir. 1968), 740

Saylor v. Lindsley, 391 F.2d 965 (2d Cir. 1968), 740

Scanlan v. Anheuser-Busch, Inc., 388 F.2d 918 (9th Cir.), *cert. denied*, 391 U.S. 916 (1968), 188

Scardino Milk Distribs. v. Wanzer & Sons, 1976-2 Trade Cas. (CCH) ¶ 61,173 (N.D. Ill. 1972), 403

Scarminach v. Goldwell GmbH, 531 N.Y.S.2d 188 (N.Y. Sup. Ct. 1988), 885

Schaben v. Samuel Moore & Co., 606 F.2d 831 (8th Cir. 1979), 184, 190

Schachar v. American Academy of Ophthalmology, 1988-1 Trade Cas. (CCH) ¶ 67,986 (N.D. Ill. 1988), *aff'd*, 870 F.2d 397 (7th Cir. 1989), 51

Schachar v. American Academy of Ophthalmology, 870 F.2d 397 (7th Cir. 1989), 1, 41, 43, 54, 86, 993

Schechtman v. Wolfson, 244 F.2d 537 (2d Cir. 1957), 398, 787

Schenker v. Pepperidge Farm, 1963 Trade Cas. (CCH) ¶ 70,974 (S.D.N.Y. 1963), 746, 749, 751

Schiessle v. Stephens, 525 F. Supp. 763 (N.D. Ill. 1982), 982

Schine Chain Theatres v. United States, 334 U.S. 110 (1948), 18, 358, 845

Schlegel/CPIO, 26 O.J. EUR. COMM. (No. L 351) 20 (1983), [1982-1985 Transfer Binder] COMMON MKT. REP. (CCH) ¶ 10,545, 942

Schlegel Mfg. Co. v. USM Corp., 525 F.2d 775 (6th Cir. 1975), *cert. denied*, 425 U.S. 912 (1976), 836

Schlumberger Ltd., 95 F.T.C. 913 (1980), 345

Schmidt v. Columbia Pictures Indus., 1986-2 Trade Cas. (CCH) ¶ 67,323 (D. Nev. 1986), 748, 749, 751

Schmidt v. Commission, Case 210/81, [1983] E.C.R. 3045, [1983-1985 Transfer Binder] COMMON MKT. REP. (CCH) ¶ 14,009, 921

Schmidt v. Polish People's Republic, 579 F. Supp. 23 (S.D.N.Y), aff'd, 742 F.2d 67 (2d Cir. 1984), 871

Schnabel v. Volkswagen of Am., Inc., 185 F. Supp. 122 (N.D. Iowa 1960), 646

Schnapps Shop, Inc. v. H. W. Wright & Co., 377 F. Supp. 570 (D. Md. 1973), 109

Schoenkopf v. Brown & Williamson Tobacco Corp., 637 F.2d 205 (3d Cir. 1980), 6

School Dist. of Philadelphia v. Harper & Row Publishers, Inc., 267 F. Supp. 1001 (E.D. Pa. 1967), 737

School Dist. v. Kurtz Bros., 240 F. Supp. 361 (E.D. Pa. 1965), 869

Schooner Exchange v. M'Faddon, 11 U.S. (7 Cranch) 116 (1812) (Marshall, C.J.), 899

Schuler v. Better Equip. Launder Center, Inc., 74 F.R.D. 85 (D. Mass. 1977), 727

Schwarzkopf Dev. Corp. v. Ti-Coating, Inc., 800 F.2d 240 (Fed. Cir. 1986), 851

Schwartz v. Commonwealth Land Title Ins. Co., 374 F. Supp. 564 (E.D. Pa.), opinion supplemented by 384 F. Supp. 302 (E.D. Pa. 1974), 1115

Schwartz v. Jamesway Corp., 660 F. Supp. 138 (E.D.N.Y. 1987), 789

Schwegmann Bros. v. Calvert Distillers Corp., 341 U.S. 384 (1951), 63, 101

Schweiker v. Hansen, 450 U.S. 785 (1981), 964

Schweizer v. Local Joint Executive Bd., 121 Cal. App. 2d 45, 262 P.2d 568 (1953), 638

Schwimmer v. Sony Corp., 471 F. Supp. 793 (E.D.N.Y. 1979), aff'd, 637 F.2d 41 (2d Cir. 1980), 898

Schwimmer v. Sony Corp., 637 F.2d 41 (2d Cir. 1980), 408, 655

Schwimmer v. Sony Corp., 677 F.2d 946 (2d Cir.), cert. denied, 459 U.S. 1007 (1982), 11

Schwing Motor Car Co. v. Hudson Sales Corp., 138 F. Supp. 899 (D. Md.), aff'd per curiam, 239 F.2d 176 (4th Cir. 1956), cert. denied, 355 U.S. 823 (1957), 118, 119

Sciambra v. Graham News, 892 F.2d 411 (5th Cir. 1990), 781

Sciambra v. Graham News Co., 841 F.2d 651 (5th Cir. 1988), 670, 769

Science Prods. Co. v. Chevron Chem. Co., 384 F. Supp. 793 (N.D. Ill. 1974), 203

Scientific Mfg. Co. v. FTC, 124 F.2d 640 (3d Cir. 1941), 477

SCM Corp. v. FTC, 565 F.2d 807 (2d Cir. 1977), 398, 399, 679

SCM Corp. v. Radio Corp. of Am., 318 F. Supp. 433 (S.D.N.Y. 1970), 828, 836

SCM Corp. v. Xerox Corp., 70 F.R.D. 508 (D. Conn.), appeal dismissed, 534 F.2d 1031 (2d Cir. 1976), 565

SCM Corp. v. Xerox Corp., 463 F. Supp. 983 (D. Conn. 1978), aff'd in part and remanded, 645 F.2d 1195 (2d Cir. 1981), cert. denied, 455 U.S. 1016 (1982), 685

SCM Corp. v. Xerox Corp., 463 F. Supp. 983 (D. Conn. 1978), remanded, 599 F.2d 32 (2d Cir.), on remand 474 F. Supp. 589 (D. Conn. 1979), aff'd, 645 F.2d 1195 (2d Cir. 1981), cert. denied, 455 U.S. 1016 (1982), 804, 821

SCM Corp. v. Xerox Corp., 645 F.2d 1195, (2d Cir. 1981), cert. denied, 455 U.S. 1016 (1982), 279, 685, 802, 803, 804

SCM v. Brothers Int'l Corp., 316 F. Supp. 1328 (S.D.N.Y. 1970), 870

Scooper Dooper, Inc. v. Kraftco Corp., 494 F.2d 840 (3d Cir. 1974), 121

Scott Medical Supply Co. v. Bedsole Surgical Supplies, 488 F.2d 934 (5th Cir. 1974), 186

Scott Paper Co., 63 F.T.C. 2240 (1963), 511

Scott v. City of Sioux City, 736 F.2d 1207 (8th Cir. 1984), cert. denied, 471 U.S. 1003 (1985), 985

Scott v. United States, 419 F.2d 264 (D.C. Cir. 1969), 581, 582

Scranton Constr. Co. v. Litton Indus. Leasing Corp., 494 F.2d 778 (5th Cir. 1974), cert. denied, 419 U.S. 1105 (1975), 27

Scriptomatic, Inc. v. Agfa-Gevaert, Inc., 1973-1 Trade Cas. (CCH) ¶ 74,594 (S.D.N.Y. 1973), 870, 876, 877

S.D. Collectibles, Inc. v. Plough, Inc., 952 F.2d 211 (8th Cir. 1991), 662

SDI Reading Concrete, Inc. v. Hilltop Basic Resources, Inc., 576 F. Supp. 525 (S.D. Ohio 1983), 406, 657

Seaboard A.L.R.R. v. United States, 382 U.S. 154 (1965), 1141

Seaboard Coast Line R.R. v. United States, 724 F.2d 1482 (11th Cir. 1984), 1137

Seaboard Supply Co. v. Congoleum Corp., 770 F.2d 367 (3d Cir. 1985), 84, 85, 114, 118, 183, 408, 434, 435

Seagood Trading Corp. v. Jerrico, Inc., 924 F.2d 1555 (11th Cir. 1991), 8, 31, 37, 41, 47, 52, 53, 62, 84, 178, 179, 182, 185, 186, 187, 190, 270

Sea-Land Serv. v. Alaska R.R., 1980-2 Trade Cas. (CCH) ¶ 63,481 (D.D.C. 1980), aff'd, 659 F.2d 243 (D.C. Cir. 1981), cert. denied, 455 U.S. 919 (1982), 1022

Sea-Land Serv. v. Alaska R.R., 659 F.2d 243 (D.C. Cir. 1981), cert. denied, 455 U.S. 919 (1982), 965

Sea-Land Serv. v. FMC, 653 F.2d 544 (D.C. Cir. 1991), 1163

Sealy Mattress Co. v. Sealy, Inc., 789 F.2d 582 (7th Cir. 1986), 847

Sears, Roebuck & Co., 95 F.T.C. 406 (1980), enforced, 676 F.2d 385 (9th Cir. 1982), 466, 498

Sears, Roebuck & Co. v. Stiffel Co., 376 U.S. 225 (1964), 799, 850

Sears, Roebuck & Co. v. FTC, 676 F.2d 385 (9th Cir. 1982), 489

Seasongood v. K&K Ins. Agency, 548 F.2d 729 (8th Cir. 1977), 1115

Seattle Totems Hockey Club v. National Hockey League, 783 F.2d 1347 (9th Cir.), cert. denied, 479 U.S. 932 (1986), 196

Seaward Yacht Sales v. Murray Chris-Craft Cruisers, Inc., 701 F. Supp. 766 (D. Or., 1988), 164, 165

Seawinds, Ltd. v. Ned Lloyd Lines, BV, 80 Bankr. 181 (N.D. Cal. 1987) aff'd, 846 F.2d 586 (9th Cir.), cert. denied, 488 U.S. 891 (1988), 1157, 1166

Seay Bros. v. City of Albuquerque, 601 F. Supp. 1518 (D.N.M. 1985), 982

Secatore's Inc. v. Esso Standard Oil Co., 171 F. Supp. 665 (D. Mass. 1959), 431

Secretary of Labor v. Fitzsimmons, 805 F.2d 682 (7th Cir. 1986), 717

Security Fire Door Co. v. County of Los Angeles, 484 F.2d 1028 (9th Cir. 1973), 96

Security Tire & Rubber Co. v. Gates Rubber Co., 598 F.2d 962 (5th Cir.), cert. denied, 444 U.S. 942 (1979), 408

SEC v. Arthur Young & Co., 584 F.2d 1018 (D.C. Cir. 1978), cert. denied, 439 U.S. 1071 (1979), 506

SEC v. Banca Della Svizzera Italiana, 92 F.R.D. 111 (S.D.N.Y. 1981), 888

SEC v. Everest Mgmt. Corp., 87 F.R.D. 100 (S.D.N.Y. 1980), 758

SEC v. First Fin. Group of Texas, 659 F.2d 660 (5th Cir. 1981), 767

SEC v. International Swiss Inv. Corp., 895 F.2d 1272 (9th Cir. 1990), 878

SEC v. National Sec., Inc., 393 U.S. 453 (1969), 1111, 1115

Seeburg Corp. v. FTC, 1966 Trade Cas. (CCH) ¶ 71,955 (E.D. Tenn. 1966), aff'd, 425 F.2d 124 (6th Cir.), cert. denied, 400 U.S. 866 (1970), 514

Segal v. AT&T, 606 F.2d 842 (9th Cir. 1979), 1021

Seglin v. Esau, 1984-1 Trade Cas. (CCH) ¶ 65,835 (N.D. Ill. 1984), aff'd on other grounds, 769 F.2d 1274 (7th Cir. 1985), 85

Seglin v. Esau, 769 F.2d 1274 (7th Cir. 1985), 25, 30

Seidenstein v. National Medical Enters., 769 F.2d 1100 (5th Cir. 1985), 206

SEIFA, 12 J.O. COMM. EUR. (No. L 173) 8 (1969), [1965-1969 Transfer Binder] COMMON MKT. REP. (CCH) ¶ 9315; C.F.A., 11 J.O. COMM. EUR. (No. L 276) 29 (1968), [1965-1969 Transfer Binder] COMMON MKT. REP. (CCH) ¶ 9268, 933

Seiffer v. Topsy's Int'l, 70 F.R.D. 622 (D. Kan. 1976), 783

Seligson v. Plum Tree, Inc., 55 F.R.D. 259 (E.D. Pa. 1972), 713

Seligson v. Plum Tree, Inc., 61 F.R.D. 343 (E.D. Pa. 1973), 718

Semke v. Enid Automobile Dealers Ass'n, 320 F. Supp. 445 (W.D. Okla. 1970), rev'd, 456 F.2d 1361 (10th Cir. 1972), 787

Semke v. Enid Automobile Dealers Ass'n, 456 F.2d 1361 (10th Cir. 1972), 699, 787

Semmes Motors, Inc. v. Ford Motor Co., 429 F.2d 1197 (2d Cir. 1970), 678

Senate Select Comm. on Secret Military Assistance to Iran v. Secord, 664 F. Supp. 562 (D.D.C. 1987), 889

Senza-Gel Corp. v. Seiffhart, 803 F.2d 661 (Fed. Cir. 1986), 815

Serlin Wine & Spirit Merchants, Inc. v. Healy, 512 F. Supp. 936 (D. Conn.), *aff'd sub nom.* Morgan v. Division of Liquor Control, 664 F.2d 353 (2d Cir. 1981), 969

Serpa v. Jolly King Restaurants, 62 F.R.D. 626 (S.D. Cal. 1974), 141

Service & Training, Inc. v. Data Gen. Corp., 737 F. Supp. 334 (D. Md. 1990), 140

Service Eng'g Co. v. Southwest Marine, Inc., 719 F. Supp. 1500 (N.D. Cal. 1989), 1007

ServiceMaster, Decision 88/604, 31 O.J. EUR. COMM. (No. L 332) 38 (1988), [1989] 1 CEC (CCH) 2287, 941

Service Merchandise Co. v. Boyd Corp., 722 F.2d 945 (1st Cir. 1983), 40, 77

Service One Int'l Corp., 106 F.T.C. 528 (1985), 532

Service Spring, Inc. v. Cambria Spring Co., 1984-1 Trade Cas. (CCH) ¶ 65,802 (N.D. Ill. 1984), 721

Sessions Tank Liners, Inc. v. Joor Mfg., 827 F.2d 458 (9th Cir. 1987), *vacated*, 487 U.S. 1213 (1988), *on remand*, 852 F.2d 484 (9th Cir. 1988), 259, 995, 1009

Seven Gables Corp. v. Sterling Recreation Org. Co., 1987-1 Trade Cas. (CCH) ¶ 67,637 (W.D. Wash. 1987), 270

Seven-Up Co. v. FTC, 478 F.2d 755 (8th Cir.), *cert. denied*, 414 U.S. 1013 (1973), 524

Seven-Up Co. v. No-Cal Corp., 183 U.S.P.Q. (BNA) 165 (E.D.N.Y. 1974), 847, 848

Sewell Plastics, Inc. v. Coca-Cola Co., 720 F. Supp. 1186 (W.D.N.C. 1988), *aff'd mem.*, 912 F.2d 463 (4th Cir. 1990), *cert. denied*, 111 S. Ct. 1019 (1991), 37, 38, 47, 48, 50, 176, 177, 179, 376, 391

Shafer v. Bulk Petroleum Corp., 569 F. Supp. 621 (E.D. Wis. 1983), 137

Shafer v. Farmers' Grain Co., 268 U.S. 189 (1925), 621

Shafi v. St. Francis Hosp., 1991-1 Trade Cas. (CCH) ¶ 69,500 (4th Cir. 1991), 151, 173

Shahawy v. Harrison, 778 F.2d 636 (11th Cir. 1985), 24

Shahawy v. Harrison, 875 F.2d 1529 (11th Cir. 1989), 974

Shah v. Memorial Hosp., 1988-2 Trade Cas. (CCH) ¶ 68,199, (W.D. Va. 1988), 974

Shaklee Corp., 84 F.T.C. 1593 (1974), 491-492

Shangri-La Mfg. Co. v. Anchor Hocking Glass Corp., 1967 Trade Cas. (CCH) ¶ 72,164 (S.D.N.Y. 1967), 703

Shared Network Technologies, Inc. v. Taylor, 669 F. Supp. 422 (N.D. Ga. 1987), 435

Sharkey v. Security Bank & Trust Co., 651 F. Supp. 1231 (D. Minn. 1987), 1098

Sharon Steel Corp. v. Chase Manhattan Bank, N.A., 691 F.2d 1039 (2d Cir. 1982), *cert. denied*, 460 U.S. 1012 (1983), 1089

Sharon Steel Corp. v. Chase Manhattan Bank, N.A., 88 F.R.D. 38 (S.D.N.Y. 1980), 649

Sharon v. Time, Inc., 599 F. Supp. 538 (S.D.N.Y. 1984), 888

Shawkee Mfg. Co. v. Hartford-Empire Co., 322 U.S. 271, (1944), 810

Shaw's, Inc. v. Wilson-Jones Co., 105 F.2d 331 (3d Cir. 1939), 407

Shaw v. Mobil Oil Corp., 60 F.R.D. 566 (D.N.H. 1973), 734

Shaw v. Orem City, 117 Utah 288, 214 P.2d 888 (1950), 627

Shaw v. Rolex Watch U.S.A., Inc., 673 F. Supp. 674 (S.D.N.Y. 1987), 20, 271

Shaw v. Russell Trucking Line, 542 F. Supp. 776 (W.D. Pa. 1982), 662

Shearson/American Express, Inc. v. McMahon, 482 U.S. 220 (1987), 788, 789

Shea v. Donohoe Constr., 795 F.2d 1071 (D.C. Cir. 1986), 770

Sheftelman v. Jones, 667 F. Supp. 859 (N.D. Ga. 1987), 716, 726

Sheldon Pontiac v. Pontiac Motor Division, 418 F. Supp. 1024 (D.N.J. 1976), *aff'd without published opinion*, 566 F.2d 1170 (3d Cir. 1977), 129

Shell Oil Co., 95 F.T.C. 357 (1980), 534

Shell Oil Co. v. Younger, 587 F.2d 34 (9th Cir. 1978), *cert. denied*, 440 U.S. 947 (1979), 622, 625

Shelton v. Pargo, Inc., 582 F.2d 1298 (4th Cir. 1978), 740, 743

Shepherd Intelligence Sys. v. Defense Technologies, Inc., 702 F. Supp. 365 (D. Mass. 1988), 1004

Shepherd Park Citizens Ass'n v. General Cinema Beverages of Washington, D.C., Inc., 1990-2 Trade Cas. (CCH) ¶ 69,287 (D.C. 1990), 608

Sherin v. Gould, 679 F. Supp. 473 (E.D. Pa. 1987), 741

Sherman College of Straight Chiropractic v. American Chiropractic Ass'n, 654 F. Supp. 716 (N.D. Ga. 1986), aff'd, 813 F.2d 349 (11th Cir.), cert. denied, 484 U.S. 854 (1987), 43, 92

Sherman v. British Leyland Motors, Ltd., 601 F.2d 429 (9th Cir. 1979), 47, 50, 76, 124, 128

Sherman v. Weber Dental Mfg. Co., 285 F. Supp. 114 (E.D. Pa. 1968), 121

Sherwin Williams Co., 86 F.T.C. 25 (1943), 428

Shields-Jetco, Inc. v. Torti, 314 F. Supp. 1292 (D.R.I. 1970), aff'd, 436 F.2d 1061 (1st Cir. 1971), 825

Shimazaki Communs. v. AT&T, 647 F. Supp. 10 (S.D.N.Y. 1986), 687

Shin Nippon Koki Co. v. Irvin Indus., 186 U.S.P.Q. (BNA) 296 (N.Y. Sup. Ct. 1975), 850

Shin Nippon Koki Co. v. Irvin Indus., 1975-1 Trade Cas. (CCH) ¶ 60,347 (N.Y. Sup. Ct. 1975), 842

Shires v. Magnavox Co., 432 F. Supp. 231 (E.D. Tenn. 1976), 793

Shoe Barn, Ltd. v. Acme Boot Co., 1979-2 Trade Cas. (CCH) ¶ 62,864 (E.D. Pa. 1979), 712

Shop & Save Food Markets v. Pneumo Corp., 683 F.2d 27 (2d Cir.), cert. denied, 459 U.S., 1038 (1982), 136, 143, 144, 147, 158

Shoppin' Bag of Pueblo, Inc. v. Dillon Cos., 783 F.2d 159 (10th Cir. 1986), 197, 215, 260, 262, 263, 266

Shrader v. Horton, 471 F. Supp. 1236 (W.D. Va. 1979) aff'd, 626 F.2d 1163 (4th Cir. 1980), 983

Shreve Equip., Inc. v. Clay Equip. Corp., 650 F.2d 101 (6th Cir.), cert. denied, 454 U.S. 897 (1981), 406, 665

Shreveport Macaroni Mfg. Co. v. FTC, 321 F.2d 404 (5th Cir. 1963), cert. denied, 375 U.S. 971 (1964), 404

Shulman v. Continental Bank, 513 F. Supp. 979 (E.D. Pa. 1981), 1098

Shulton, Inc. v. Optel Corp., 1987-1 Trade Cas. (CCH) ¶ 67,436 (D.N.J. 1986), 78, 115, 127, 129, 865

Shumate & Co. v. New York Stock Exch., 486 F. Supp. 1333 (N.D. Tex. 1980), 1102

Shumate v. National Ass'n of Sec. Dealers, 509 F.2d 147 (5th Cir. 1975), 595

SHV-Chevron, 18 O.J. EUR. COMM. (No. L 38) 14 (1975), [1973-1975 Transfer Binder] COMMON MKT. REP. (CCH) ¶ 9709, 938

Siebert v. FTC, 367 F.2d 364 (2d Cir. 1966), 476

Siegel v. Chicken Delight, Inc., 448 F.2d 43 (9th Cir. 1971), cert. denied, 405 U.S. 955 (1972), 119, 120, 134, 138, 141, 155, 160, 161, 670, 848, 849

Siemens/Fanuc, 28 O.J. EUR. COMM. (No. L 376) 29 (1985), [1985-1988 Transfer Binder] COMMON MKT. REP. (CCH) ¶ 10,765, 932

Sierra Wine & Liquor Co. v. Heublein, Inc., 626 F.2d 129 (9th Cir. 1980), 193

SI Handling Sys. v. Heisley, 658 F. Supp. 362 (E.D. Pa. 1986), 54

Silhouette Nat'l Health Spas, Inc., 84 F.T.C. 323 (1974), 478

Silver v. New York Stock Exch., 373 U.S. 341 (1963), 78, 80, 82, 88, 373, 1100, 1101, 1102

Simco Sales Serv. v. Air Reduction Co., 213 F. Supp. 505 (E.D. Pa. 1963), 778

Simeon Mgmt. Corp., 87 F.T.C. 1184 (1976), aff'd, 579 F.2d 1137 (9th Cir. 1978), 492

Simeon Mgmt. Corp. v. FTC, 579 F.2d 1137 (9th Cir. 1978), 467, 474

Simer v. Rios, 661 F.2d 655 (7th Cir. 1981), cert. denied, 456 U.S. 917 (1982), 740

Simmons v. ICC, 697 F.2d 326 (D.C. Cir. 1982), 1133

Simmons v. ICC, 760 F.2d 126, (7th Cir. 1985), 1132

Simmons v. ICC, 784 F.2d 242 (7th Cir. 1985), 1134

Simplified Renewal Application, 87 F.C.C.2d 1127 (1981), aff'd sub nom. Black Citizens For a Fair Media v. FCC, 719 F.2d 407 (D.C. Cir. 1983), cert. denied, 467 U.S. 1255 (1984), 1044

Simpson v. Union Oil Co., 411 F.2d 897 (9th Cir.), *rev'd*, 396 U.S. 13 (1969), 698
Simpson v. Union Oil Co., 377 U.S. 13 (1964), 101, 102, 103, 110, 181, 340
Singer Mfg. v. Brother Intern Corp., 191 F. Supp. 322 (S.D.N.Y. 1960), 747
Singer v. A. Hollander & Son, 202 F.2d 55 (3d Cir. 1953), 701
Sirdar-Phildar, 18 O.J. EUR. COMM. (No. L 125) 27 (1975), [1973-1975 Transfer Binder] COMMON MKT. REP. (CCH) ¶ 9741, 945, 946
Sirena Srl v. Eda GmbH, Case 40/70, [1971] E.C.R. 69, [1971-1973 Transfer Binder] COMMON MKT. REP. (CCH) ¶ 8101, 946, 952
Sitkin Smelting & Ref. Co. v. FMC Corp., 575 F.2d 440 (3d Cir.), *cert. denied*, 439 U.S., 41, 47, 48, 55, 96, 115
S. Kane & Son v. W.R. Grace & Co., 623 F. Supp. 162 (E.D. Pa. 1985), 988
Skepton v. County of Bucks, 613 F. Supp. 1013 (E.D. Pa. 1985), 988
SKF Indus., 94 F.T.C. 6 (1979), 128, 293, 393
Skil Corp. v. Black & Decker Mfg., 351 F. Supp. 65 (N.D. Ill. 1972), 701
Skinner v. United States Steel Corp., 233 F.2d 762 (5th Cir. 1956), 402, 404, 438
S. Klein, Inc., 95 F.T.C. 387 (1978), 533
Skokie Gold Standard Liquors, Inc. v. Joseph E. Seagram & Sons, 661 F. Supp. 1311 (N.D. Ill. 1986), 107
Skouras Theatre Corp. v. Radio-Keith-Orpheum Corp., 193 F. Supp. 401 (S.D.N.Y. 1961), 686
Skyview Distrib. v. Miller Brewing Co., 620 F.2d 750 (10th Cir. 1980), 16, 189
Slocumb Indus. v. Chelsea Indus., 1984-1 Trade Cas. (CCH) ¶ 65,932 (E.D. Pa. 1984), 203, 206
Slough v. FTC, 396 F.2d 870 (5th Cir.), *cert. denied*, 393 U.S. 980 (1968), 489
Smith Int'l, Inc. v. Kennametal, Inc., 621 F. Supp. 79 (N.D. Ohio 1985), 821, 827, 829
SmithKline Corp., 96 F.T.C. 612 (1980), 345, 348
SmithKline Corp. v. Eli Lilly & Co., 427 F. Supp. 1089 (E.D. Pa. 1976), *aff'd*, 575 F.2d 1056 (3d Cir.), *cert. denied*, 439 U.S. 838 (1978), 198
SmithKline Corp. v. Eli Lilly & Co., 575 F.2d 1056 (3d Cir.), *cert. denied*, 439 U.S. 838 (1978), 143, 146, 251
SmithKline Diagnostics, Inc. v. Helena Labs., 859 F.2d 878 (Fed. Cir. 1988), 810
Smith Mach. Co. v. Hesston Corp., 1985-1 Trade Cas. (CCH) ¶ 66,469 (N.M. 1985), 38, 164, 635
Smith Mach. Co. v. Hesston Corp., 1987-1 Trade Cas. (CCH) ¶ 67,563 (D.N.M. 1987), *aff'd*, 878 F.2d 1290 (10th Cir. 1989), *cert. denied*, 110 S. Ct. 1119 (1990), 133, 134, 152, 154, 159
Smith Mach. Co. v. Hesston Corp., 878 F.2d 1290 (10th Cir. 1989), *cert. denied*, 110 S. Ct. 1119 (1990), 635
Smith v. Combustion Eng'g, 856 F.2d 196 (6th Cir. 1988) *cert. denied*, 489 U.S. 1054 (1989), 992
Smith v. Mobil Oil Corp., 667 F. Supp. 1314 (W.D. Mo. 1987), 141, 142, 143, 727, 849
Smith v. Northern Mich. Hosps., 703 F.2d 942 (6th Cir. 1983), 55, 170, 173
Smith v. Pro Football, Inc., 593 F.2d 1173 (D.C. Cir. 1978), 39, 43, 45, 46, 47, 52, 53, 56, 85, 90, 91
Smith v. Scrivner-Boogaart, Inc., 447 F.2d 1014 (10th Cir. 1971), *cert. denied*, 404 U.S. 1059 (1972), 172
Smith v. Toyota Motor Sales, U.S.A., 1977-1 Trade Cas. (CCH) ¶ 61,252 (N.D. Cal. 1977), 728
Smokey's v. American Honda Motor Co., 453 F. Supp. 1265 (E.D. Okla. 1978), 866
Snap-On Tools Corp. v. FTC, 321 F.2d 825 (7th Cir. 1963), 98, 120, 129
Snyco, Inc. v. Penn Cent. Corp., 551 F. Supp. 949 (E.D. Pa. 1982), 365
Soap Opera Now, Inc. v. Network Publishing Co., 737 F. Supp. 1338 (S.D.N.Y. 1990), 199, 201, 247, 248, 252
Societe Internationale Pour Participations Industrielles et Commerciales, SA v. Rogers, 357 U.S. 197 (1958), 768, 886, 887
Societe Nationale Industrielle Aerospatiale v. United States District Court, 482 U.S. 522 (1987), 881, 884, 885, 887

Société de Vente de Ciments et Bétons de l'Est, SA and Kerpen & Kerpen GmbH & Co. KG, Case 319/82, [1983] E.C.R. 4173, [1983-1985 Transfer Binder] COMMON MKT. REP. (CCH) ¶ 14,043, 930

Soda-Ash-ICI, Decision 91/300, 34 O.J. EUR. COMM. (No. L 152) 40 (1991), [1991] 2 CEC (CCH) 2053, 956

Soda-Ash-Solvay, ICI, Decision 91/299, 34 O.J. EUR. COMM. (No. L 152) 21 (1991), [1991] 2 CEC (CCH) 2029, 956

Soda-Ash-Solvay, ICI, Decision 91/297, 34 O.J. EUR. COMM. (No. L 152) 1 (1991), [1991] 2 CEC (CCH) 2003, 932, 951, 953

Sofa Gallery, Inc. v. Mohasco Upholstered Furniture Corp., 639 F. Supp. 677 (D. Minn. 1986), 444

Sola Elec. Co. v. Jefferson Elec. Co., 317 U.S. 173 (1942), 837

Soletanche & Rodio, Inc. v. Brown & Lambrecht Earth Movers, Inc., 99 F.R.D. 269 (N.D. Ill. 1983), 887, 888

Solinger v. A&M Records, Inc., 586 F.2d 1304 (9th Cir. 1978), cert. denied, 441 U.S. 908 (1979), 649

Solomon v. Houston Corrugated Box Co., 526 F.2d 389 (5th Cir. 1976), 186

Sol S. Turnoff Drug Distribs. v. N.V. Nederlandsche C.V.C. Indus., 55 F.R.D. 347 (E.D. Pa. 1972), 752

Sonesta Int'l Hotels Corp. v. Wellington Assocs., 483 F.2d 247 (2d Cir. 1973), 369

Sonitrol of Fresno, Inc. v. AT&T, 1986-1 Trade Cas. (CCH) ¶ 67,080 (D.D.C. 1986), 20

Sopelem/Vickers, 21 O.J. EUR. COMM. (No. L 70) 47 (1978), [1976-1978 Transfer Binder] COMMON MKT. REP. (CCH) ¶ 10,014, 934, 935

Sorisio v. Lenox, Inc., 701 F. Supp. 950 (D. Conn.), aff'd, 863 F.2d 195 (2d. Cir. 1988), 109, 110

Sound Ship Bldg. Corp. v. Bethlehem Steel Corp., 387 F. Supp. 252 (D.N.J. 1975), aff'd, 533 F.2d 96 (3d Cir.), cert. denied, 429 U.S. 860 (1976), 98, 199

Soundtrack Chevelle, 88 F.T.C. 517 (1976), 490

South Carolina State Highway Dep't v. Barnwell Bros., 303 U.S. 177 (1938), 621

South Dakota v. Kansas City S. Indus., 880 F.2d 40 (8th Cir. 1989), cert. denied, 493 U.S. 1023 (1990), 614, 999

South End Oil Co. v. Texaco, Inc., 237 F. Supp. 650 (N.D. Ill. 1965), 184

South-East Coal Co. v. Consolidation Coal Co., 434 F.2d 767 (6th Cir. 1970), cert. denied, 402 U.S. 983 (1971), 666, 672, 699

Southeastern Power Admin. v. Kentucky Utils. Co., 25 F.E.R.C. (CCH) ¶ 61,204 (1983), 1069

Southern Blowpipe & Roofing Co. v. Chattanooga Gas Co., 360 F.2d 79 (6th Cir. 1966), cert. denied, 393 U.S. 844 (1968), 703

Southern Cal. Edison Co., 40 F.E.R.C. (CCH) ¶ 61,371 (1987), 1072

Southern Cal. Edison Co., 47 F.E.R.C. (CCH) ¶ 61,196 (1989), 1075

Southern Concrete Co. v. United States Steel Corp., 535 F.2d 313 (5th Cir. 1976), cert. denied, 429 U.S. 1096 (1977), 167

Southern Distrib. Co. v. Southdown, Inc., 574 F.2d 824 (5th Cir. 1978), 179

Southern Motor Carriers Rate Conference, Inc. v. United States, 471 U.S. 48 (1985), 970, 979, 1129

Southern Natural Gas Co., 51 F.E.R.C. (CCH) ¶ 61,186 (1990), reh'g denied, 54 F.E.R.C. (CCH) ¶ 61,098 (1991), 1062

Southern Pac. Communs. Co. v. AT&T, 556 F. Supp. 825 (D.D.C. 1983), aff'd, 740 F.2d 980 (D.C. Cir. 1984), cert. denied, 470 U.S. 1005 (1985), 216, 218, 219, 231, 233, 250, 669, 1018, 1049

Southern Pac. Communs. Co. v. AT&T, 567 F. Supp. 326 (D.D.C. 1983), aff'd, 740 F.2d 1011 (D.C. Cir. 1984), cert. denied, 470 U.S. 1005 (1985), 776

Southern Pac. Transp. Co. v. ICC, 736 F.2d 708 (D.C. Cir. 1984), cert. denied, 469 U.S. 1208 (1985), 1142

Southern Pac. Transp. Co. v. ICC, 871 F.2d 838 (9th Cir. 1989), 1134

Southern Pines Chrysler-Plymouth, Inc. v. Chrysler Corp., 826 F.2d 1360 (4th Cir. 1987), 139, 165, 166, 670, 671

Southern Snack Foods, Inc. v. J&J Snack Foods Corp., 79 F.R.D. 678 (D.N.J. 1978), 713, 718, 720

Southgate Brokerage Co. v. FTC, 150 F.2d 607 (4th Cir.), cert. denied, 326 U.S. 774 (1945), 433, 436

Southaven Land Co. v. Malone & Hyde, Inc., 715 F.2d 1079 (6th Cir. 1983), 660

Southland Corp., 102 F.T.C. 1337 (1983), 167

Southmark Corp. v. Life Investors, Inc. 851 F.2d 763 (5th Cir. 1988), 878

Southwestern Sheet Metal Workers, Inc. v. Semco Mfg., 788 F.2d 1144 (5th Cir. 1986), cert. denied, 480 U.S. 917 (1987), 647

Southwest Marine, Inc. v. Campbell Indus., 732 F.2d 744 (9th Cir.), cert. denied, 469 U.S. 1072 (1984), 700

Southwest Marine, Inc. v. Campbell Indus., 811 F.2d 501 (9th Cir. 1987), 781

Southwest Suburban Bd. of Realtors v. Beverly Area Planning Ass'n, 830 F.2d 1374 (7th Cir. 1987), 644, 661, 662

Southwest Sunsites, Inc. v. FTC, 785 F.2d 1431 (9th Cir.), cert. denied, 479 U.S. 828 (1986), 472, 492, 521

South-West Utils., Inc. v. South Cent. Bell Tel. Co., 1977-1 Trade Cas. (CCH) ¶ 61,303 (La. Ct. App. 1976), 638

Souza v. Estate of Bishop, 594 F. Supp. 1480 (D. Haw. 1984), aff'd, 799 F.2d 1327 (9th Cir. 1986), 159

Souza v. Estate of Bishop, 821 F.2d 1332 (9th Cir. 1987), 6, 8, 139

Spain Equip. Co. v. Nissan Motor Corp., 1980-1 Trade Cas. (CCH) ¶ 63,135 (N.D. Ala. 1980), 712, 717, 721, 728

Spanish Int'l Communs. Corp. v. Leibowitz, 608 F. Supp. 178 (S.D. Fla.), aff'd mem., 778 F.2d 791 (11th Cir. 1985), 1000

Spartan Grain & Mill Co. v. Ayers, 581 F.2d 419 (5th Cir. 1978), cert. denied, 444 U.S. 831 (1979), 135, 148, 154, 166, 167, 336

Spartan Grain & Mill Co. v. Ayers, 735 F.2d 1284 (11th Cir. 1984), cert. denied, 469 U.S. 1109 (1985), 150

Special Equip. Co. v. Coe, 324 U.S. 370 (1945), 800

Specialty Composites v. Cabot Corp., 845 F.2d 981 (Fed. Cir. 1988), 810

Spectrofuge Corp. v. Beckman Instruments, Inc., 575 F.2d 256 (5th Cir. 1978), cert. denied, 440 U.S. 939 (1979), 15, 201, 203, 262

Speed Shore Corp. v. Denda, 197 U.S.P.Q. (BNA) 526 (C.D. Cal. 1977), aff'd, 605 F.2d 469 (9th Cir. 1979), 854

Spencer v. Sun Oil Co., 94 F. Supp. 408 (D. Conn. 1950), 403, 404

Sperry Corp., 98 F.T.C. 4 (1981), 499

Sperry Prods., Inc. v. Aluminum Co. of Am., 171 F. Supp. 901 (N.D. Ohio 1959), aff'd in part and rev'd in part, 285 F.2d 911 (6th Cir. 1960), cert. denied, 368 U.S. 890 (1961), 806, 814-15

Spiegel, Inc., 86 F.T.C. 425 (1975), aff'd, 540 F.2d 287 (7th Cir.), modified, 88 F.T.C. 1001 (1976), 485

Spiegel, Inc. v. FTC, 411 F.2d 481 (7th Cir. 1969), 465, 475, 494

Sportmart, Inc. v. Frisch, 537 F. Supp. 1254 (N.D. Ill. 1982), 868, 869, 873, 875

Sportmart, Inc. v. Wolverine World Wide, Inc., 601 F.2d 313 (7th Cir. 1979), 575

Sports Center, Inc. v. Riddell, Inc., 673 F.2d 786 (5th Cir. 1982), 123, 126

Sports Form, Inc. v. UPI, 686 F.2d 750 (9th Cir. 1982), 677, 678

Spray-Rite Serv. Corp. v. Monsanto Co., 684 F.2d 1226 (7th Cir. 1982), aff'd on other grounds, 465 U.S. 752 (1984), 11, 783, 785

Springs Mills, Inc. v. Ultracashmere House, Ltd., 532 F. Supp. 1203 (S.D.N.Y.), rev'd, 689 F.2d 1127 (2d Cir. 1982), 541

SPRL Louis Eraw-Jacquery v. Société Coopérative la Hesbignonne, Case 27/87, [1988] E.C.R. 1919, [1989] 2 CEC (CCH) 637, 939

Square D Co. v. Niagara Frontier Tariff Bureau, 1984-1 Trade Cas. (CCH) ¶ 65,825 (D.D.C. 1984), 866, 870

Square D Co. v. Niagara Frontier Tariff Bureau, 760 F.2d 1347 (2d Cir. 1985), aff'd, 476 U.S. 409 (1986), 1020, 1160

Square D Co. v. Niagara Frontier Tariff Bureau, 476 U.S. 409 (1986), 1020, 1129, 1159

Square D Co. v. Schneider SA, 760 F. Supp. 362 (S.D.N.Y. 1991), 364, 393, 395, 396, 397, 398, 663

St. Bernard Gen. Hosp. v. Hospital Serv. Ass'n, 618 F.2d 1140 (5th Cir. 1980), 1111

St. Bernard Gen. Hosp. v. Hospital Serv. Ass'n, 712 F.2d 978 (5th Cir. 1983), cert. denied, 466 U.S. 970 (1984), 26, 40, 70, 85, 87

St. Joseph's Hosp. v. Hospital Auth. of Am., 620 F. Supp. 814 (S.D. Ga. 1985), vacated and remanded sub nom. St. Joseph's Hosp. v. Hospital Corp. of Am., 795 F.2d 948 (11th Cir. 1986), 15

St. Joseph's Hosp. v. Hospital Corp. of Am., 795 F.2d 948 (11th Cir. 1986), 21, 22, 1007

St. Jude Medical, Inc. v. Intermedics, Inc., 1985-1 Trade Cas. (CCH) ¶ 66,623 (D. Minn. 1985), 279, 335

St. Jude Medical, Inc. v. Intermedics, Inc., 623 F. Supp. 1294 (D. Minn. 1985), 252

St. Paul Fire & Marine Ins. Co. v. Barry, 438 U.S. 531 (1978), 1117

St. Regis Paper Co. v. United States, 368 U.S. 208 (1961), 505, 509

Standard Brands, Inc., 82 F.T.C. 1176 (1973), 473

Standard Distrib., Inc. v. FTC, 211 F.2d 7 (2d Cir. 1954), 525, 531

Standard Motor Prods., Inc., 54 F.T.C. 814 (1957), aff'd, 265 F.2d 674 (2d Cir.), cert. denied, 361 U.S. 816 (1959), 430

Standard Motor Prods., Inc., 68 F.T.C. 1248 (1965), enforcement denied, 371 F.2d 613 (2ds Cir. 1967), 423

Standard Oil Co., 41 F.T.C. 263 (1945), modified, 43 F.T.C. 56 (1946), modified and aff'd, 173 F.2d 210 (7th Cir. 1949), rev'd and remanded, 340 U.S. 231 (1951), modified, 49 F.T.C. 923 (1953), rev'd, 233 F.2d 649 (7th Cir. 1956), aff'd, 355 U.S. 396 (1958), 426

Standard Oil Co., 84 F.T.C. 1401 (1974) modified and enforced, 577 F.2d 653 (9th Cir. 1978), 470, 473-74

Standard Oil Co. v. California, 337 U.S. 293 (1949), 330

Standard Oil Co. v. FTC, 1980-2 Trade Cas. (CCH) ¶ 63,566 (N.D. Ind. 1980), vacated and dismissed as moot, Nos. 80-2479, 80-2701 (7th Cir. Oct. 13, 1981), 510

Standard Oil Co. v. FTC, 577 F.2d 653 (9th Cir. 1978), 469, 470, 482, 492, 494

Standard Oil Co. v. FTC, 596 F.2d 1381 (9th Cir. 1979), rev'd, 449 U.S. 232 (1980), 524

Standard Oil Co. v. FTC, 340 U.S. 231 (1951), 403, 417, 419, 426

Standard Oil Co. v. Moore, 251 F.2d 188 (9th Cir. 1957), cert. denied, 356 U.S. 975 (1958), 670

Standard Oil Co. v. Tennessee ex rel. Cates, 217 U.S. 413 (1910), 624

Standard Oil Co. v. United States, 221 U.S. 1 (1911), 1, 2, 30, 62, 227

Standard Oil Co. v. United States, 283 U.S. 163 (1931), 41, 818, 823, 824, 827, 837, 854

Standard Oil Co. v. United States, 337 U.S. 293 (1949), 134, 161, 170, 177, 178, 179, 198, 208, 831

Stan Kane Home Improvement Center v. Martin Paint Stores, 1975-1 Trade Cas. (CCH) ¶ 60,379 (S.D.N.Y. 1975), 156

Stanley Works v. FTC, 469 F.2d 498 (2d Cir. 1972), cert. denied, 412 U.S. 928 (1973), 304

Stan Togut Corp. v. Hobart Mfg. Co., 398 F. Supp. 1323 (S.D.N.Y. 1974), 103, 121

Stanzler v. Loew's Theatre & Realty Corp., 19 F.R.D. 286 (D.R.I. 1955), 747, 752

Star Lines v. Puerto Rico Maritime Shipping Auth., 442 F. Supp. 1201 (S.D.N.Y. 1978), 868

Starview Outdoor Theatre v. Paramount Film Distrib. Corp., 254 F. Supp. 855 (N.D. Ill. 1966), 693

State ex rel. Atty. Gen. v. Standard Oil Co., 49 Ohio St. 137, 30 N.E. 279 (1892), 619

State *ex rel.* Blumenthal v. BPS Petroleum Distrib., No. 3:91CV00173 (WWE) (Conn. Dist. Ct. filed Mar. 26, 1991), 633

State *ex rel.* Van de Kamp v. Texaco, Inc., 1985-2 Trade Cas. (CCH) ¶ 66,858 (Cal. Ct. App. 1985), *aff'd*, 1988-2 Trade Cas. (CCH) ¶ 68,288 (Cal. 1988), 636

State *ex rel.* Van de Kamp v. Texaco, Inc., 1988-2 Trade Cas. (CCH) ¶ 68,288 (Cal. 1988), 606, 636

State of New York v. Hendrickson Bros., 840 F.2d 1065 (2d Cir.), *cert. denied*, 488 U.S. 848 (1988), 688

Statesman Life Ins. Co., 74 F.T.C. 1322 (1968), 1116

State Theatre Co. v. Tri-States Theatre Corp., 11 F.R.D. 381 (D. Neb. 1951), 767

State v. Allied Chem. & Dye Corp., 9 Wis. 2d 290, 101 N.W.2d 133 (1960), 622

State v. Anesthesia Professional Ass'n, 1984-2 Trade Cas. (CCH) ¶ 66,081 (Me. 1984), 641

State v. Associated Milk Producers, 1974-2 Trade Cas. (CCH) ¶ 75,269 (Tex. Dist. Ct. 1974), 640

State v. Atex Gas, Inc., No. A25324 CV (Tex. Dist. Ct. filed July 13, 1990), 633

State v. BPS Petroleum Distrib., No. 3:91CV00173 (WWE) (Conn. Dist. Ct. filed Mar. 26, 1991), 633

State v. Bulova Watch Co., 1980-2 Trade Cas. (CCH) ¶ 63,397 (Alaska Super. Ct. 1978), 640

State v. Coca-Cola Bottling Co., No. 84 CI-15586 (Tex. Dist. Ct. Jan. 8, 1985), 637

State v. Coca-Cola Bottling Co., 1986-1 Trade Cas. (CCH) ¶ 67,169 (Tex. Dist. Ct. 1986), 612

State v. Coca-Cola Bottling Co., 697 S.W.2d 677 (Tex. App. 1985 writ ref'd n.r.e.), *appeal dismissed*, 478 U.S. 1029 (1986), 278, 622, 637

State v. Connors Bros., 1988-2 Trade Cas. (CCH) ¶ 68,237 (Me. Super. Ct. 1988), 612

State v. Dosch-King Co., 1988-1 Trade Cas. (CCH) ¶ 68,087 (Conn. Super. Ct. 1988), 611

State v. Exxon Corp., 1987-1 Trade Cas. (CCH) ¶ 67,579 (Conn. Super. Ct. 1987), 633, 636

State v. Flying J. Petroleum, Inc., No. 900906128 CV (Utah Dist. Ct. filed Oct. 24, 1990), 633

State v. Georgia Pacific Co., No. CV-90-8 (Me. Supr. Ct. filed Jan. 5, 1990), 633

State v. Hossan-Maxwell, 181 Conn. 655 (1980), 635

State v. Humboldt Petroleum, Inc., No. E73199M (Cal. Mun. Ct. filed Sept. 6, 1990), 633

State v. Insurance Servs. Office, Inc., 1989-2 Trade Cas. (CCH) ¶ 68,870 (Tex. Dist. Ct. 1989), 612

State v. Insurance Servs. Office, Inc., 1989-2 Trade Cas. (CCH) ¶ 68,871 (Tex. Dist. Ct. 1989), 612

State v. Insurance Servs. Office, Inc., 1991-1 Trade Cas. (CCH) ¶ 69,385 (Tex. Dist. Ct. 1991), 612

State v. Lancashire Fire Ins. Co., 66 Ark. 466, 51 S.W. 633 (1899), 628

State v. Levi Strauss & Co., 1986-1 Trade Cas. (CCH) ¶ 67,018 (Cal. 1986), 604

State v. Mystic Bituminous Prods. Co., 1988-1 Trade Cas. (CCH) ¶ 68,086 (Conn. Super. Ct. 1988), 611

State v. National Ass'n of Realtors, 1987-1 Trade Cas. (CCH) ¶ 67,484 (Conn. Super. Ct. 1986), 611

State v. New York Movers Tariff Bureau, 48 Misc. 2d 225, 264 N.Y.S.2d 931 (1965), 638

State v. Scioscia, 1985-1 Trade Cas. (CCH) ¶ 66,598 (N.J. Super. Ct. App. Div.), *cert. denied*, 101 N.J. 277, 501 A.2d 942 (1985), 637

State v. Southeast Tex. Ch. of Nat'l Elec. Contractor's Ass'n, 358 S.W.2d 711 (Tex. Civ. App. 1962, writ ref'd n.r.e.), *cert. denied*, 372 U.S. 965 (1963), 622

State Wholesale Grocers v. Great Atl. & Pac. Tea Co., 258 F.2d 831 (7th Cir. 1958), *cert. denied*, 358 U.S. 947 (1959), 440, 442, 443

Station WWSM, 31 F.C.C. 2d 584 (1971), 1037

Staub v. Harris, 626 F.2d 275 (3d Cir. 1980), 538

Stavrides v. Mellon Nat'l Bank & Trust Co., 353 F. Supp. 1072 (W.D. Pa.), *aff'd*, 487 F.2d 953 (3d Cir. 1973), 69, 168

St. Bernard General Hosp. v. Hospital Serv. Ass'n, 712 F.2d 978 (5th Cir. 1983), 70

Steadman v. SEC, 450 U.S. 91 (1981), 522

Stearns v. Genrad, Inc., 564 F. Supp. 1309 (M.D.N.C. 1983), *aff'd*, 752 F.2d 942 (4th Cir., 1984), 176, 178, 199

Stearns v. Genrad, Inc., 752 F.2d 942 (4th Cir. 1984), 182

Stegeman v. Aetna Ins. Co., 1980-1 Trade Cas. (CCH) ¶ 63,256 (E.D. Mich. 1980), 690, 692, 693

Steiner v. 20th Century-Fox Film Corp., 232 F.2d 190 (9th Cir. 1956), 661

Steinike & Weinlig v. Germany, Case 78/76, [1977] E.C.R. 595 [1977-1978 Transfer Binder] COMM. MKT. REP. (CCH) ¶ 8402, 923

Stenberg v. Cheker Oil Co., 573 F.2d 921 (6th Cir. 1978), 667, 678, 679

Stephen Jay Photography, Inc. v. Olan Mills, Inc., 903 F.2d 988 (4th Cir. 1990), 144, 435

Stephens Theatre Corp. v. Loew's, Inc., 17 F.R.D. 494 (E.D.N.Y. 1955), 746, 747

Stepp v. Ford Motor Credit Co., 623 F. Supp. 583 (E.D. Wis. 1985), 133, 199, 204, 662

Stergios Delimitis v. Henninger Bräu AG, Case 234/89 (Eur. Comm. Ct. J. 1991), 922, 930

Sterling Beef Co. v. City of Fort Morgan, 810 F.2d 961 (10th Cir. 1987), 983

Sterling Drug, Inc., 80 F.T.C. 477 (1972), 288, 335

Sterling Drug, Inc., 102 F.T.C. 395 (1983), *aff'd*, 741 F.2d 1146 (9th Cir. 1984), *cert. denied*, 470 U.S. 1084 (1985), 467, 474

Sterling Drug, Inc. v. FTC, 741 F.2d 1146 (9th Cir. 1984), *cert. denied*, 470 U.S. 1084 (1985), 488, 489, 522

Sterman v. Transamerica Title Ins. Co., 119 Ariz. 268, 580 P.2d 729 (1978), 639

Stevens v. Zenith Distrib. Corp., 568 F. Supp. 1200 (W.D. Mo. 1983), 407, 437

Stewart Aviation Co. v. Piper Aircraft Corp., 372 F. Supp. 876 (M.D. Pa. 1974), 683

Stewart-Warner Corp. v. Staley, 42 F. Supp. 140 (W.D. Pa. 1941), 803

Stichting Sigarettenindustrie, Joined Cases 240-242, 261-62, 268 & 269/82, [1985] E.C.R. 3831, [1985-1986 Transfer Binder] COMMON MKT. REP. (CCH) ¶ 14,265, 932

Stifel, Nicolaus & Co. v. Dain, Kalman & Quail, Inc., 578 F.2d 1256 (8th Cir. 1978), 48, 97

Stitt Spark Plug Co. v. Champion Spark Plug Co., 840 F.2d 1253 (5th Cir.), *cert. denied*, 488 U.S. 890 (1988), 176, 177, 178, 233, 414, 415, 706, 707

Stone v. William Beaumont Hosp., 782 F.2d 609 (6th Cir. 1986), 24, 25

Story Parchment Co. v. Paterson Parchment Paper Co., 282 U.S. 555 (1931), 647, 665, 668, 671, 672

Strategic Mktg. Servs. v. Cut & Curl, Inc., 1977-2 Trade Cas. (CCH) ¶ 61,788 (D. Conn. 1977), 1000

Stratmore v. Goodbody, 866 F.2d 189 (6th Cir.), *cert. denied*, 490 U.S. 1066 (1989), 39, 42, 45, 47, 380, 708

Straus & Straus v. American Publishers' Ass'n, 231 U.S. 222 (1913), 622, 845

Strax v. Commodity Exch., 524 F. Supp. 123 (N.D. Tex. 1983), 662

Strobl v. New York Mercantile Exch., 768 F.2d 22 (2d Cir.), *cert. denied*, 474 U.S. 1006 (1985), 1018

Structural Laminates, Inc. v. Douglas Fir Plywood Ass'n, 261 F. Supp 154 (D. Or. 1966), *aff'd per curiam*, 399 F.2d 155 (9th Cir. 1968), *cert. denied*, 393 U.S. 1024 (1969), 88

Structure Probe, Inc. v. Franklin Inst., 450 F. Supp 1272 (E.D. Pa. 1978), *aff'd mem.*, 595 F.2d 1214 (3d Cir. 1979), 211, 260

Struthers Scientific & Int'l Corp. v. General Foods Corp., 334 F. Supp. 1329 (D. Del. 1971), 808

Students Book Co. v. Washington Law Book Co., 232 F.2d 49 (D.C. Cir. 1955), *cert. denied*, 350 U.S. 988 (1956), 408

Stull v. Bayard, 561 F.2d 429 (2d Cir. 1977), *cert. denied*, 434 U.S. 1035 (1978), 696

Stupell Originals, Inc., 67 F.T.C. 173 (1965), 468, 469

Subrink Broadcasting, Inc., 42 F.C.C.2d 271 (1973), 1033

Suburban Beverages, Inc. v. Pabst Brewing Co., 462 F. Supp. 1301 (E.D. Wis. 1978), 182

Suburban Propane Gas Corp., 73 F.T.C. 1269 (1968), 446, 447

Suckow Borax Mines Consol., Inc. v. Borax Consol. Ltd., 185 F.2d 196 (9th Cir. 1950), *cert. denied*, 340 U.S. 943, *reh. denied*, 688, 692

Sugar Inst. v. United States, 297 U.S. 553 (1936), 65, 67, 71, 405

Sugar Land Tel. Co., 76 F.C.C.2d 19 (1980), 1054

Sulfur Export Corp., 43 F.T.C. 820 (1947), 915

Sulmeyer v. Coca-Cola Co., 515 F.2d 835 (5th Cir. 1975), *cert. denied*, 424 U.S. 934 (1976), 165

Sulmeyer v. Seven-Up Co., 411 F. Supp. 635 (S.D.N.Y. 1976), 121

Summey v. Ford Motor Credit Co., 449 F. Supp. 132 (D.S.C. 1976), *aff'd mem.*, 573 F.2d 1306 (4th Cir. 1978), 542, 646

Summey v. Ford Motor Credit Co., 573 F.2d 1306 (4th Cir. 1978), 646

Summit Health, Ltd. v. Pinhas, 111 S. Ct. 1842 (1991), 25, 54

Sum of Squares, Inc. v. Market Research Corp., 401 F. Supp. 53 (S.D.N.Y. 1975), 186

Sunbeam Corp., 67 F.T.C. 20 (1965), 443

Sunbury Wire Rope Mfg. v. U.S. Steel Corp., 129 F. Supp. 425 (E.D. Pa. 1955), 869

Sun Commun. v. Waters Publications, 466 F. Supp. 387 (W.D. Mo. 1979), 410

Sun Cosmetic Shoppe v. Elizabeth Arden Sales Corp., 178 F.2d 150 (2d Cir. 1949), 404

Sundance Land Corp. v. Community First Fed. Sav. & Loan Ass'n, 1988-Trade Cas. (CCH) ¶ 67,924 (9th Cir. 1988), 1098

Sun Down Inc. v. United States, 766 F. Supp. 463 (E.D. Va. 1991), 758

Sun Dun, Inc. v. Coca-Cola Co., 740 F. Supp. 381 (D. Md. 1990), 195

Sunergy Communities Corp. v. Aristek Properties, Ltd., 535 F. Supp. 1327 (D. Colo. 1982), 1004

Sunkist Growers v. FTC, 464 F. Supp. 302 (C.D. Cal. 1979), 523, 524, 525

Sunkist Growers v. Winckler & Smith Citrus Prods. Co., 370 U.S. 19 (1962), 1026

Sun Newspapers v. Minneapolis Star & Tribune Co., 1977-1 Trade Cas. (CCH) ¶ 61,254 (D. Minn. 1976), 689

Sun Newspapers v. Omaha World-Herald Co., 1983-2 Trade Cas. (CCH) ¶ 65,522 (D. Neb.), *modified and aff'd per curiam*, 713 F.2d 428 (8th Cir. 1983), 326, 365

Sun Newspapers v. Omaha World-Herald Co., 713 F.2d 428 (8th Cir. 1983), 251

Sun Oil Co., 55 F.T.C. 955 (1959), *set aside*, 294 F.2d 465 (5th Cir. 1961), *rev'd*, 371 U.S. 505 (1963), 420

Sun Oil Co., 84 F.T.C. 247 (1974), 466

Sun Oil v. Vickers Ref. Co., 414 F.2d 383 (8th Cir. 1969), 72

Sunrise Toyota Ltd. v. Toyota Motor Co., 55 F.R.D. 519 (S.D.N.Y. 1972), 713, 867

Sunshine Art Studios, Inc., 81 F.T.C. 836 (1972), 475

Sunshine Art Studios v. FTC, 481 F.2d 1171 (1st Cir. 1973), 469

Sun Theatre Corp. v. RKO Radio Pictures, 213 F.2d 284 (7th Cir. 1954), 686, 687

Sun Valley Disposal Co. v. Silver State Disposal Co., 420 F.2d 341 (9th Cir. 1969), 29

Sun-hand Nurseries, Inc., v. Southern Ca. Dis. Council of Laborers, 793 F.2d 1110 (9th Cir. 1986), *cert. denied*, 479 U.S. 1090 (1987), 1126

Superior Bedding Co. v. Serta Assocs., 353 F. Supp. 1143 (N.D. Ill. 1972), 130

Superior Beverage Co. v. Owens-Illinois, Inc., 1987-1 Trade Cas. (CCH) ¶ 67,461 (N.D. Ill. 1987), 726, 735

Superior Beverage Co. v. Owens-Illinois, Inc., No. 83-C-0512 (N.D. Ill. Feb. 18, 1988) (U.S. DIST. LEXIS 9094), 719, 726, 738

Superior Beverage/Glass Container, 133 F.R.D. 119 (N.D. Ill. 1991), 786

Superior Coal Co. v. Ruhrkohle, AG, 83 F.R.D. 414 (E.D. Pa. 1979), 875, 876

Supermarket Broadcasting Network, Inc., 78 F.T.C. 22 (1971), 441

Supermarket of Homes, Inc. v. San Fernando Valley Bd. of Realtors, 786 F.2d 1400 (9th Cir. 1986), 8, 49, 73, 86, 268

Supermarkets Gen. Corp. v. Grinnell Corp., 490 F.2d 1183 (2d Cir. 1974), 738

Super Premium Ice Cream, 691 F. Supp. at 1267, 183, 187

Supra USA, Inc. v. Samsung Elec. Co., 1987-2 Trade Cas. ¶ 67,760 (S.D.N.Y. 1987), 408

Surf Sales Co. v. FTC, 259 F.2d 744 (7th Cir. 1958), 483

Surgidev Corp. v. Eye Technology, Inc., 625 F. Supp. 800 (D. Minn. 1986), 1001

Surprise Brassiere Co., 71 F.T.C. 868 (1967), aff'd, 406 F.2d 711 (5th Cir. 1969), 437, 443

Susser v. Carvel Corp., 206 F. Supp. 636 (S.D.N.Y. 1962), aff'd, 332 F.2d 505 (2d Cir. 1964), cert. dismissed, 381 U.S. 125 (1965), 108

Susser v. Carvel Corp., 332 F.2d 505 (2d Cir. 1964), cert. dismissed, 381 U.S. 125 (1965), 107, 131, 141, 155, 156, 161, 179, 849

Sutliff, Inc. v. Donovan Cos., 727 F.2d 648 (7th Cir. 1984), 97

Swanee Paper Corp. v. FTC, 291 F.2d 833 (2d Cir. 1961), cert. denied, 368 U.S. 987 (1962), 494

Sweeney v. Athens Regional Medical Center, 709 F. Supp. 1563 (M.D. Ga. 1989), 24, 92, 93, 660, 971

Swerdloff v. Miami Nat'l Bank, 584 F.2d 54 (5th Cir. 1978), 1098

Swift & Co. v. United States, 196 U.S. 375 (1905), 262

Switzer Bros. v. Locklin, 297 F.2d 39 (7th Cir. 1961), cert. denied, 369 U.S. 851 (1962), 852

Swofford v. B & W, Inc., 251 F. Supp. 811, (S.D. Tex. 1966), aff'd, 395 F.2d 362 (5th Cir.), cert. denied, 393 U.S. 935 (1968), 806

Sylvania Elec. Prods., Inc., 51 F.T.C. 282 (1954), 411, 421, 424

Synthetic Fibres, 27 O.J. EUR. COMM. (No. L 207) 17 (1984), [1982-1985 Transfer Binder] COMMON MKT. REP. (CCH) ¶ 10,606, 923, 937

Syracuse Peace Council, 2 F.C.C. Rcd 5043 (1987), recon. denied, 3 F.C.C. Rcd 2035 (1988), 1028

Syufy Enters. v. American Multicinema, Inc., 793 F.2d 990 (9th Cir. 1986), cert. denied, 479 U.S. 1031 (1987), 199, 201, 202, 217, 268, 270, 271, 272, 672

T

Taggart v. Rutledge, 657 F. Supp 1420 (D. Mont. 1987), aff'd, 852 F.2d 1290 (9th Cir. 1988), 148, 169, 402, 404

Tamaron Distrib. Corp. v. Weiner, 418 F.2d 137 (7th Cir. 1969), 22, 103

Tambone v. Memorial Hosp. for McHenry County, 635 F. Supp. 508 (N.D. Ill. 1986, aff'd, 825 F.2d 1132 (7th Cir. 1987), 972

Tambone v. Simpson, 91 Ill. App. 3d 865, 46 Ill. Dec. 649, 414 N.E.2d 533 (1980), 631

TAM, Inc. v. Gulf Oil Corp., 553 F. Supp. 499 (E.D. Pa. 1983), 177

Tampa Elec. Co. v. Nashville Coal Co., 365 U.S. 320 (1961), 169, 170, 171, 172, 176, 178, 198, 208, 209, 210, 294

T&N PLC, 5 TRADE REG. REP. (CCH) ¶ 22,869 (Nov. 8, 1990), 348

Tarleton v. Meharry Medical College, 717 F.2d 1523 (6th Cir. 1983), 22, 28, 29

Tashof v. FTC, 437 F.2d 707 (D.C. Cir. 1970), 491, 533

Tasty Baking Co. v. Ralston Purina, Inc., 653 F. Supp. 1250 (E.D. Pa. 1987), 212, 263, 289, 294, 296, 305, 362, 368, 664

Taxi Weekly, Inc. v. Metropolitan Taxicab Bd. of Trade, 539 F.2d 907 (2d Cir. 1976), 668, 771

Taylor v. Anderson, 234 U.S. 74 (1914), 852

Taylor v. Meirick, 712 F.2d 1112 (7th Cir. 1983), 682

Tchacosh Co. Ltd. v. Rockwell International Corp., 766 F.2d 1333 (9th Cir. 1985), 907

TCI Cablevision, Inc. v. City of Jefferson, 604 F. Supp. 845 (W.D. Mo. 1984), 988

TEAC Corp., 104 F.T.C. 634 (1984), 122

Technical Chem. Co. v. IG-LO Prods., 812 F.2d 222 (5th Cir. 1987), 767, 768, 769

Technical Learning Collective, Inc. v. Dailmer-Benz AG, 1980-1 Trade Cas. (CCH) ¶ 63,006 (D. Md. 1980), 716

Technical Learning Collective, Inc. v. Daimler-Benz AG, 1980-81 Trade Cas. (CCH) ¶ 63,612 (D. Md. 1980), 657, 699

Technicon Instruments Corp. v. Alpkem Corp., 866 F.2d 417 (Fed. Cir. 1989), 258, 808

Technicon Medical Info. Sys. v. Green Bay Packaging, 480 F. Supp. 124 (E.D. Wis. 1979), 259

Technograph Printed Circuits, Ltd. v. Bendix Aviation Corp., 218 F. Supp. 1, 50 (D. Md. 1963), *aff'd per curiam*, 327 F.2d 497 (4th Cir.), *cert. denied*, 379 U.S. 826 (1964), 835, 850

TEKO (German Machinery Breakdown Insurance), Decision 90/22, 33 O.J. EUR. COMM. (No. L 13) 34 (1990), [1990] 1 CEC (CCH) 2045, 936

Tekton, Inc. v. Builders Bid Serv., 676 F.2d 1352 (10th Cir. 1982), 70

Telecom Plus v. Local No. 3, 719 F.2d 613 (2d Cir. 1983), 1023

Telectronics Proprietary, Ltd. v. Medtronic, Inc., 687 F. Supp. 832 (S.D.N.Y. 1988), 271, 279, 701

Teleflex Indus. Prods. v. Brunswick Corp., 293 F. Supp. 106 (E.D. Pa. 1968), *order vacated*, 410 F.2d 380 (3d Cir. 1969), 160, 161

Teleprompter Corp. 87 F.C.C.2d 531 (1981), *aff'd*, 89 F.C.C.2d 417 (1982), 1052

Teleprompter Corp., 89 F.C.C.2d 417 (1982), 1037

Telerate Sys. v. Caro, 689 F. Supp. 221 (S.D.N.Y. 1988), 135, 140, 144, 148, 157, 158, 159, 203, 212, 216

Telex Corp. v. IBM, 367 F. Supp. 258 (N.D. Ok. 1973), *rev'd*, 510 F.2d 894 (10th Cir.), *cert. dismissed*, 423 U.S. 802 (1975), 143, 203, 205, 223, 253, 254, 257, 849

Telex Corp. v. IBM, 510 F.2d 894 (10th Cir.), *cert. denied*, 423 U.S. 802 (1975), 200, 203, 205, 223, 253, 257, 849

Tempkin v. Lewis-Gale Hosp., 1989-2 Trade Cas. (CCH) ¶ 68,865 (W.D. Va. 1989), 93

Tempo Music, Inc. v. Myers, 407 F.2d 503 (4th Cir. 1969), 575, 845

Tennant Co. v. Hako Minuteman, Inc., 651 F. Supp. 945 (N.D. Ill. 1986), 811, 812

Tenneco, Inc., 98 F.T.C. 464 (1981), *rev'd*, 689 F.2d 346 (2d Cir. 1982), 288, 322, 323, 329

Tenneco, Inc. v. FTC, 689 F.2d 346 (2d Cir. 1982), 276, 285, 323, 325, 326, 329

Tennessee *ex rel.* Leech v. Highland Memorial Cemetery, Inc., 489 F. Supp. 65 (E.D. Tenn. 1980), 69, 608

Tepea BV v. Commission, Case 28/77, [1978] E.C.R. 1391, [1977-1978 Transfer Binder] COMMON MKT. REP. (CCH) ¶ 8467, 929, 946

Terra Comfort Corp., 52 F.E.R.C. (CCH) ¶ 61,241 (1990), 1070

Terrapin (Overseas) Ltd. v. Terranova Industrie C.A. Kapferer & Co., Case 119/75, [1976] E.C.R. 1039, [1976 Transfer Binder] COMMON MKT. REP. (CCH) ¶ 8362, 945

Terrell v. Household Goods Carriers' Bureau, 494 F.2d 16 (5th Cir.), *cert. dismissed*, 419 U.S. 987 (1974), 673

Terry's Floor Fashions, Inc. v. Burlington Indus., 763 F.2d 604 (4th Cir. 1985), 14, 407

Tetra Pak, 31 O.J. EUR. COMM. (No. L 272) 27 (1988), [1985-88 Transfer Binder] COMMON MKT. REP. (CCH) ¶ 11,015, *aff'd sub nom.* Tetra Pak Rausing v. Commission, Case T-51/89, [1990] E.C.R. II 309, [1990] 2 CEC (CCH) 409, 950, 958

Tetra Pak Rausing v. Commission, Case T-51/89, [1990] E.C.R. II 309, [1990] 2 CEC (CCH) 409, 954

Texaco, Inc., [1979-1987 Complaints & Orders Transfer Binder] TRADE REG. REP. (CCH) ¶ 22,146 (May 2, 1984), 343

Texaco, Inc. & Getty Oil, Inc., 104 F.T.C. 241 (1984), 345, 347, 348, 349

Texaco, Inc. v. FTC, 336 F.2d 754 (D.C. Cir. 1964), *vacated and remanded*, 381 U.S. 739 (1965), 510

Texaco Inc. v. Hasbrouck, 110 S. Ct. 2535 (1990), 405, 411, 421, 428

Texaco Puerto Rico, Inc. v. Medina, 834 F.2d 242 (1st Cir. 1987), 708

Texasgulf, Inc. v. Canada Dev. Corp., 366 F. Supp. 374 (S.D. Tex. 1973), 281

Texas Gulf-Sulphur Co. v. J.R. Simplot Co., 418 F.2d 793 (9th Cir. 1969), 406

Texas Indus., 67 F.T.C. 1378 (1965), 511

Texas Indus. v. Radcliff Materials, Inc., 451 U.S. 630 (1981), 793, 794

Texas Trading & Milling Co. v. Federal Republic of Nig., 647 F.2d 300 (2d Cir. 1981), *cert. denied*, 454 U.S. 1148 (1982), 871, 876, 900, 903, 907

Texas Utilities Co. v. Santa Fe Indus., 1986-1 Trade Cas. (CCH) ¶ 67,094 (D.N.M. 1986), 681

Texas v. Allan Constr. Co., 851 F.2d 1526 (5th Cir. 1988), 688, 690, 693

Texas v. United States, 730 F.2d 339 (5th Cir.), *cert. denied,* 469 U.S. 892 (1984), 1131

Texas v. United States Steel Corp., 546 F.2d 626 (5th Cir.), *cert. denied,* 434 U.S. 889 (1977), 756

TH. Goldschmidt AG v. Smith, 676 S.W.2d 443 (Tex. App. 1 Dist. 1984, no writ), 884

T. Harris Young & Assocs. v. Marquette Elecs., Inc., 931 F.2d 816 (11th Cir.), *cert. denied,* 112 S. Ct. 658 (1991), 143

Thatcher Enters. v. Cache County Corp., 902 F.2d 1472 (10th Cir. 1990), 987

Theatre Enters. v. Paramount Film Distrib. Corp., 346 U.S. 537 (1954), 6, 780

Theatre Party Assocs. v. Shubert Org., 695 F. Supp. 150 (S.D.N.Y. 1988), 201, 206

The 'In' Porters, SA v. Hanes Printables, Inc., 663 F. Supp. 494 (M.D.N.C. 1987), 858

THI-Hawaii, Inc. v. First Commerce Fin. Corp., 627 F.2d 991 (9th Cir. 1980), 700

Thillens, Inc. v. Community Currency Exch. Ass'n, 97 F.R.D. 668 (N.D. Ill. 1983), 715

Thillens, Inc. v. Fryzel, 712 F. Supp. 1319 (N.D. Ill. 1989), 978

Thill Sec. Corp. v. New York Stock Exch., 473 F. Supp. 1364 (E.D. Wis. 1979), *aff'd,* 633 F.2d 65 (7th Cir. 1980), 551, 1103

Thill Sec. Corp. v. New York Stock Exch., 433 F.2d 264 (7th Cir. 1970), *cert. denied,* 401 U.S. 994 (1971), 555, 1101

Thiret v. FTC, 512 F.2d 176 (10th Cir. 1975), 489, 490, 521

Thomas A. Dardas, 104 F.T.C. 562 (1984), 473

Thomas E. Hoar, Inc. v. Sara Lee Corp., 1988-2 Trade Cas. (CCH) ¶ 68,225 (E.D.N.Y. 1988), 770

Thomas J. Kline, Inc. v. Lorillard, Inc., 878 F.2d 791 (4th Cir. 1989), *cert. denied,* 110 S. Ct. 1120 (1990), 405

Thomason v. Mitsubishi Elec. Sales Am., 701 F. Supp. 1563 (N.D. Ga. 1989), 660, 662

Thomas v. Amerada Hess Corp., 393 F. Supp. 58 (M.D. Pa. 1975), 190, 441

Thomas v. Collins, 323 U.S. 516 (1945), 989

Thomasville Chair Co., 58 F.T.C. 441, *set aside,* 306 F.2d 541 (5th Cir. 1962), 425

Thomasville Chair Co., 63 F.T.C. 1048 (1963), 425, 433

Thomasville Chair Co. v. FTC, 306 F.2d 541 (5th Cir. 1962), 423, 425, 432

Thompson Medical Co., 104 F.T.C. 648 (1984), *aff'd,* 791 F.2d 189 (D.C. Cir. 1986), *cert. denied,* 479 U.S. 1086 (1987), 465, 467, 468, 470, 471

Thompson Medical Co. v. FTC, 791 F.2d 189 (D.C. Cir. 1986), *cert. denied,* 479 U.S. 1086 (1987), 473, 492

Thompson Prods., Inc., 55 F.T.C. 1252 (1959), 424

Thompson v. Board of Education, 709 F.2d 1200 (6th Cir. 1983), 715

Thompson v. Metropolitan Multi-List, Inc., 1990-2 Trade Cas. (CCH) ¶ 69,173 (N.D. Ga. 1990), *rev'd,* 934 F.2d 1566 (11th Cir. 1991), 138, 163

Thompson v. Metropolitan Multi-List, Inc., 934 F.2d 1566 (11th Cir. 1991), 78, 87, 88, 131, 136, 137, 140, 144, 147, 152, 154, 158

Thompson v. Midwest Found. Indep. Physicians Ass'n, 117 F.R.D. 108 (S.D. Ohio 1987), 714, 716, 718, 719, 722, 723, 727, 729, 734, 735, 737, 739

Thompson v. T.F.I. Cos., 64 F.R.D. 140 (N.D. Ill. 1974), 713, 718, 720

Thompson v. Wise Gen. Hosp., 707 F. Supp. 849 (W.D. Va. 1989), *aff'd mem.,* 896 F.2d 547 (5th Cir.), *cert. denied,* 111 S. Ct. 132 (1990), 25

Thomsen v. Cayser, 243 U.S. 66 (1917), 856

Thomsen v. Western Elec. Co., 680 F.2d 1263 (9th Cir.), *cert. denied,* 459 U.S. 991 (1982), 17

Thomson v. Commissioner, 406 F.2d 1006 (9th Cir. 1969), 794, 795

Thoms v. Sutherland, 52 F.2d 592 (3d Cir. 1931), 850

3 P.M., Inc. v. Basic Four Corp., 591 F. Supp. 1350 (E.D. Mich. 1984), 135, 148, 153, 155

305 East 24th Owners Corp. v. Parman Co., 714 F. Supp. 1296 (S.D.N.Y. 1989), 25, 138, 140, 153, 158

324 Liquor Corp. v. Duffy, 479 U.S. 335 (1987), 101, 972, 973

Three Movies of Tarzana v. Pacific Theaters, 828 F.2d 1395 (9th Cir. 1987), *cert. denied*, 484 U.S. 1066 (1988), 49, 52, 119, 183, 185, 186

Three-Way Corp. v. ICC, 792 F.2d 232 (D.C. Cir.), *cert. denied*, 479 U.S. 985 (1986), 1130

Thurman Indus. v. Pay 'N Pak Stores, 709 F. Supp. 985 (W.D. Wash.), *motion for reconsideration granted in part*, 1987-2 Trade Cas. (CCH) ¶ 67,676 (W.D. Wash. 1987), *aff'd*, 875 F.2d 1369 (9th Cir. 1989), 402, 404, 423, 433, 444, 447

Thurman Indus. v. Pay 'N Pak Stores, 1987-2 Trade Cas. (CCH) ¶ 67,676 (W.D. Wash. 1987), *aff'd*, 875 F.2d 1369 (9th Cir. 1989), 423

Thurman Indus. v. Pay 'N Pak Stores, 875 F.2d 1369 (9th Cir. 1989), 42, 45, 46, 47, 52, 201, 205, 207, 208, 259, 268, 269

Ticor Title Ins. Co., 5 TRADE REG. REP. (CCH) ¶ 22,744 (Oct. 19, 1989), *vacated*, 922 F.2d 1122 (3d Cir. 1991), *cert. granted*, 60 U.S.L.W. 3257 (U.S. Oct. 7, 1991) (No. 91-72), 1112, 1113

Ticor Title Ins. Co. v. FTC, 814 F.2d 731 (D.C. Cir. 1987), 509

Ticor Title Ins. Co. v. FTC, 922 F.2d 1122 (3d Cir. 1991), *cert. granted*, 60 U.S.L.W. 3257 (U.S. Oct. 7, 1991) (No. 91-72), 971, 975, 1112, 1113, 1114

Tic-X-Press, Inc. v. Omni Promotions Co., 815 F.2d 1407 (11th Cir. 1987), 136, 144, 146, 147, 153, 154, 157, 158, 782, 787

Tidewater Oil Co. v. United States, 409 U.S. 151 (1972), 352

Tidmore Oil Co. v. BP Oil Co., 932 F.2d 1384 (11th Cir.), *cert. denied*, 112 S. Ct. 339 (1991), 16, 180

Tiedemann v. The Signe, 37 F. Supp. 819 (E.D. La. 1941), 881

Tiftarea Shopper, Inc. v. Georgia Shopper, Inc., 786 F.2d 1115 (11th Cir. 1986), 18, 21

Tiger Trash v. Browning-Ferris Indus., 560 F.2d 818 (7th Cir. 1977), *cert. denied*, 434 U.S. 1034 (1978), 868

Tigner v. Texas, 310 U.S. 141 (1940), 1024

Tillamook Cheese and Dairy Ass'n v. Tillamook County Creamery Ass'n, 358 F.2d 115 (9th Cir. 1966), 1025

Tillie Lewis Foods, Inc., 65 F.T.C. 1099 (1964), 434

Timberlane Lumber Co. v. Bank of Am. Nat'l Trust & Savings Ass'n, 574 F. Supp. 1453 (N.D. Cal. 1983), *aff'd*, 749 F.2d 1378 (9th Cir. 1984), *cert. denied*, 472 U.S. 1032 (1985) 859

Timberlane Lumber Co. v. Bank of Am. Nat'l Trust & Savings Ass'n, 549 F.2d 597 (9th Cir. 1976), 843, 858-59, 863, 892, 905-06, 908, 909

Timberlane Lumber Co. v. Bank of Am. Nat'l Trust & Savings Ass'n, 749 F.2d 1378 (9th Cir. 1984), *cert. denied*, 472 U.S. 1032 (1985), 857, 859

Times Mirror Co., 100 F.T.C. 252 (1982), 515

Times Mirror Co. v. FTC, 1979-2 Trade Cas. (CCH) ¶ 62,756 (C.D. Cal. 1979), 410

Times-Picayune Publishing Co. v. United States, 345 U.S. 594 (1953), 44, 54, 136, 137, 145, 148, 163, 200, 260, 276, 830, 831

Timken Roller Bearing Co. v. FTC, 299 F.2d 839 (6th Cir.), *cert. denied*, 371 U.S. 861 (1962), 182

Timken Roller Bearing Co. v. United States, 341 U.S. 593 (1951), 18, 74, 275, 373, 382, 828, 843, 847

Tim W. Koerner & Assocs. v. Aspen Labs, 492 F. Supp. 294 (S.D. Tex. 1980), *aff'd*, 683 F.2d 416 (5th Cir. 1982), 364

Tingley Rubber Corp., 96 F.T.C. 340 (1980), 113

Tinnerman Prods., Inc. v. George K. Garrett Co., 185 F. Supp. 151 (E.D. Pa. 1960), *aff'd*, 292 F.2d 137 (3d Cir.), *cert. denied*, 368 U.S. 833 (1961), 821-22

Tipp-Ex, 30 O.J. EUR. COMM. (No. L 222) 1 (1987), [1985-1988 Transfer Binder] COMMON MKT. REP. (CCH) ¶ 10,899, *aff'd sub nom.* Tipp-Ex GmbH & Co. KG v. Commission, Case 279/87, [1990] E.C.R. 261, 939

Tire Sales Corp. v. Cities Serv. Oil Co., 637 F.2d 467 (7th Cir. 1980), *cert. denied*, 451 U.S. 920 (1981), 667

Todhunter-Mitchell & Co. v. Anheuser-Busch, Inc., 375 F. Supp. 610 (E.D. Pa. 1974), 121

Todhunter-Mitchell & Co. v. Anheuser-Busch, Inc., 383 F. Supp. 586 (E.D. Pa. 1974), 857

Todorov v. DCH Healthcare Auth., 921 F.2d 1438 (11th Cir. 1991), 4, 5, 6, 7, 9, 10, 33, 271

Toledo Edison Co., 10 N.R.C. 265 (1979), 751, 1081

Toltecs/Dorcet, 25 O.J. EUR. COMM. (No. L 379) 19 (1982), [1982-1985 Transfer Binder] COMMON MKT. REP. (CCH) ¶ 10,459, aff'd sub nom. BAT Cigaretten-Fabriken GmbH, Case 35/83, [1985] E.C.R. 363, [1983-1985 Transfer Binder] COMMON MKT. REP. (CCH) ¶ 14,151, 945

Tomac, Inc. v. Coca-Cola Co., 418 F. Supp. 359 (C.D. Cal. 1976), 121

Tominaga v. Shepherd, 682 F. Supp. 1489 (C.D. Cal. 1988), 135, 148, 152

Top-All Varieties v. Hallmark Cards, Inc., 301 F. Supp. 703 (S.D.N.Y. 1969), 187, 192

Topps Chewing Gum, Inc. v. Major League Baseball Players Ass'n, 641 F. Supp. 1179 (S.D.N.Y. 1986), 85, 678

Tose v. First Pa. Bank, N.A., 648 F.2d 879 (3d Cir.), cert. denied, 454 U.S. 893 (1981), 38, 54, 1089

Totaltape, Inc. v. National Ass'n of State Bds. of Accountancy, 1987-1 Trade Cas. (CCH) ¶ 67,471 (S.D.N.Y. 1987), 133, 774

Totes, Inc., 96 F.T.C. 335 (1980), 113

Touchett v. E Z Paintr Corp., 150 F. Supp. 384 (E.D. Wis. 1957), 814

Tower Loan of Miss., F.T.C. No. D 9241 (Jun. 27, 1990), 535

Town of Concord v. Boston Edison Co., 676 F. Supp. 396 (D. Mass 1988), 410

Town of Concord v. Boston Edison Co., 721 F. Supp. 1456 (D. Mass. 1989), rev'd, 915 F.2d 17 (1st Cir. 1990), cert. denied, 111 S. Ct. 1337 (1991), 199, 208, 210, 211, 212, 240

Town of Concord v. Boston Edison Co., 915 F.2d 17 (1st Cir. 1990), cert. denied, 111 S.Ct. 1337 (1991), 222, 238, 240, 241, 1073

Town of Hallie v. City of Chippewa Falls, 105 Wis. 2d 533, 314 N.W.2d 321 (1982), 637

Town of Hallie v. City of Eau Claire, 700 F.2d 376 (7th Cir. 1983), aff'd, 471 U.S. 34 (1985), 982, 986

Town of Hallie v. City of Eau Claire, 471 U.S. 34 (1985), 972, 982, 983, 986

Town of Massena v. Niagara Mohawk Power Corp., 1980-2 Trade Cas. (CCH) ¶ 63,526 (N.D.N.Y. 1980), 1071

Town of Susquehanna v. H&M, Inc., 98 F.R.D. 658 (M.D. Pa. 1983), 714

Town Sound & Custom Tops, Inc. v. Chrysler Motor Corp., 743 F. Supp 353 (E.D. Pa. 1990), 135, 151, 153, 154, 163

Toys "R" Us, Inc. v. R.H. Macy & Co., 728 F. Supp. 230 (S.D.N.Y. 1990), 189

Trabert & Hoeffer, Inc. v. Piaget Watch Corp., 633 F.2d 477 (7th Cir. 1980), 670, 676, 678

Trace X Chem. v. Canadian Indus., 738 F.2d 261 (8th Cir. 1984), cert. denied, 469 U.S. 1160 (1985), 222

Tractor Training Serv. v. FTC, 227 F.2d 420 (9th Cir. 1955), cert. denied, 350 U.S. 1005 (1956), 478

Trade Dev. Bank v. Continental Ins. Co., 469 F.2d 35 (2d Cir. 1972), 887

Trade-Mark Cases, 100 U.S. 82 (1879), 847

Trailer Marine Transport Corp. v. FMC, 602 F.2d 379 (D.C. Cir. 1979), 1161

Trailways v. CAB, 412 F.2d 926 (1st Cir. 1969), 1156

Trakas v. Quality Brands, Inc., 759 F.2d 185 (D.C. Cir. 1985), vacated, 812 F.2d 745 (D.C. Cir. 1987), 770

Transamerica Computer Co. v. IBM, 481 F. Supp. 965 (N.D. Cal. 1979), aff'd, 698 F.2d 1377 (9th Cir.), cert. denied, 464 U.S. 955 (1983), 143

Transamerica Computer Co. v. IBM, 698 F.2d 1377 (9th Cir.), cert. denied, 464 U.S. 955 (1983), 230, 254, 255, 261, 415

Transamerican S.S. Corp. v. Somali Democratic Republic, 590 F. Supp. 968 (D.D.C. 1984), aff'd in part and rev'd in part, 767 F.2d 998 (D.C. Cir. 1985), 876, 871

Transcontinental Bus Sys. v. CAB, 383 F.2d 466 (5th Cir. 1967), 1156

Transcontinental Gas Pipe Line Corp. v. State Oil & Gas Bd., 474 U.S. 409 (1986), 1057

Transitron Elec. Corp. v. Hughes Aircraft Co., 649 F.2d 871 (1st Cir. 1981), 836

TransKentucky Transp. R.R. v. Louisville & N. R.R., 581 F. Supp. 759 (E.D. Ky. 1983), 1008, 1023

Transnor (Bermuda) Ltd. v. BP N. Am. Petroleum, 738 F. Supp. 1472 (S.D.N.Y. 1990), 858, 861

Transocean Marine Paint Ass'n, 10 J.O. COMM. EUR. (No. L 163) (1967) [1965-1969 Transfer Binder] COMMON MKT. REP. (CCH) ¶ 9188, *renewed with conditions*, 17 O.J. EUR. COMM. (No. L 19) 18 (1974), [1973-1975 Transfer Binder] COMMON MKT. REP. (CCH) ¶ 9628, *rev'd in part*, Case 17/74, [1974] E.C.R. 1063, [1974 Transfer Binder] COMMON MKT. REP. (CCH) ¶ 8241, *revised*, 18 O.J. EUR. COMM. (No. L 286) 24 (1975), [1973-1975 Transfer Binder] COMMON MKT. REP. (CCH) ¶ 9783, *exemption renewed*, 23 O.J. EUR. COMM. (No. L 39) 73 (1979), [1978-1981 Transfer Binder] COMMON MKT. REP. (CCH) ¶ 10,186, *renewed*, Decision 88/635, 31 O.J. EUR. COMM. (No. L 351) 40 (1988), [1989] 1 CEC (CCH) 2003, 936

Transource Int'l, Inc. v. Trinity Indus., 725 F.2d 274 (5th Cir. 1984), 6, 98, 206

Transpacific Westbound Rate Agreement v. FMC, 938 F.2d 1025 (9th Cir. 1991), 1162

Transparent-Wrap Mach. Corp. v. Stokes & Smith Co., 329 U.S. 637, *on remand*, 161 F.2d 565 (2d Cir.), *cert. denied*, 331 U.S. 837 (1947), 800, 804, 805, 814

Trans Union Credit Information Co., 102 F.T.C. 1109 (1983), 536

Trans World Accounts, Inc., 90 F.T.C. 350 (1977), *rev'd in part*, 594 F.2d 212 (9th Cir. 1979), 532

Trans World Accounts, Inc. v. FTC, 594 F.2d 212 (9th Cir. 1979), 489

Trans World Airlines v. American Coupon Exch., 682 F. Supp. 1476 (C.D. Cal. 1988), *aff'd in part and vacated in part*, 913 F.2d 676 (9th Cir. 1990), 35, 38, 39, 183, 186, 245

Trans World Airlines v. Mattox, 897 F.2d 773 (5th Cir.), *cert. denied*, 111 S. Ct. 307 (1990), 623

Travelers Health Ass'n v. Virginia, 339 U.S. 643 (1950), 874

Travelers Ins. Co. v. Blue Cross, 481 F.2d 80 (3d Cir.), *cert. denied*, 414 U.S. 1093 (1973), 1118

Travel King, Inc., 86 F.T.C. 715 (1975), 469

Traweek v. City & County of San Francisco, 920 F.2d 589 (9th Cir. 1990), 966, 978, 985

Treasurer, Inc. v. Philadelphia Nat'l Bank, 682 F. Supp. 269 (D.N.J. 1988), *aff'd mem.*, 853 F.2d 921 (3d Cir. 1988), 829, 1090

Treasure Valley Potato Bargaining Ass'n v. Ore-Ida Foods, Inc., 497 F.2d 203 (9th Cir.), *cert. denied*, 419 U.S. 999 (1974), 64, 1028

Trecker v. Manning Implement, Inc., 73 F.R.D. 554 (N.D. Iowa 1976), 724

Triangle Conduit & Cable Co. v. FTC, 168 F.2d 175 (7th Cir. 1948), *aff'd sub nom.* Clayton Mark & Co. v. FTC, 336 U.S. 956 (1949), 65

Triangle Publications, 29 F.C.C. 315 (1960), *aff'd*, 291 F.2d 342 (D.C. Cir. 1961), 1043

Triangle Publications v. FCC, 291 F.2d 342 (D.C. Cir. 1961), 1043

Tri-Continental Fin. Corp. v. Tropical Marine Enters., 265 F.2d 619 (5th Cir. 1959), 98, 99

Trident Neuro-Imaging Lab. v. Blue Cross & Blue Shield, Inc., 568 F. Supp. 1474 (D.S.C. 1983), 1113

Triebwasser & Katz v. AT&T, 535 F.2d 1356 (2d Cir. 1976), 366, 677, 679

Triple M Roofing Corp. v. Termco, Inc., 753 F.2d 242 (2d Cir. 1985), 206

Tripoli Co. v. Wella Corp., 425 F.2d 932 (3d Cir.), *cert. denied*, 400 U.S. 831 (1970), 121

Tripper Corp. v. Chrysler Corp., 484 F. Supp. 507 (N.D. Cal. 1980), 192

Tri-State Executive Air, Inc. v. Tri-State Airport Auth., 1986-2 Trade Cas. (CCH) ¶ 67,257 (S.D. W.Va. 1985), 982

Tri-Valley Packing Ass'n v. FTC, 329 F.2d 694 (9th Cir. 1964), *on remand*, 70 F.T.C. 223 (1966), *modified and aff'd sub nom.* Tri-Valley Growers v. FTC, 411 F.2d 985 (9th Cir.), *cert. denied*, 396 U.S. 929 (1969), 406, 442

Trixler Brokerage Co. v. Ralston Purina Co., 505 F.2d 1045 (9th Cir. 1974), 191, 192

Troxel Mfg. Co. v. Schwinn Bicycle Co., 465 F.2d 1253 (6th Cir. 1972), *later appeal*, 489 F.2d 968 (6th Cir. 1973), *cert. denied*, 416 U.S. 939 (1974), 800, 836

Trucking Unlimited v. California Motor Transp. Co., 1967 Trade Cas. (CCH) ¶ 72,298 (N.D. Cal. 1967), 1005

Truck Treads, Inc. v. Armstrong Rubber Co., 818 F.2d 427 (5th Cir. 1987), 768, 769

TRW Inc. 93 F.T.C. 325 (1979), *aff'd in part and rev'd in part*, 647 F.2d 942 (9th Cir. 1981), 393, 395, 396

TRW Inc. v. FTC, 647 F.2d 942 (9th Cir. 1981), 394, 395, 396, 398, 399, 489, 494, 679, 680

Tucson Elec. Power Co., 44 F.E.R.C. (CCH) ¶ 61,441 (1988), 1074, 1075

Tugboat, Inc. v. Mobile Towing Co., 534 F.2d 1172 (5th Cir. 1976), 665

Tunis Bros. Co. v. Ford Motor Co., 696 F. Supp. 1056 (E.D. Pa. 1988), 118, 127, 128

Tunis Bros. Co. v. Ford Motor Co., 763 F.2d 1482 (3d Cir. 1985), *vacated*, 475 U.S. 1105 (1986), *remanded*, 823 F.2d 49 (3d Cir. 1987), *cert. denied*, 484 U.S. 1060 (1988), 21, 127

Tunis Bros. Co. v. Ford Motor Co., 823 F.2d 49 (3d Cir. 1987), *cert. denied*, 484 U.S. 1060 (1988), 13, 14, 127, 707

Turf Paradise, Inc. v. Arizona Downs, 670 F.2d 813 (9th Cir.), *cert. denied*, 456 U.S. 1011 (1982), 24, 77

Turmenne v. White Consol. Indus., 1967 Trade Cas. (CCH) ¶ 72,128 (D. Mass. 1967), 746

Turmenne v. White Consol. Indus., 266 F. Supp. 35 (D. Mass. 1967), 747

Turner Glass Corp. v. Hartford Empire Co., 173 F.2d 49 (7th Cir.), *cert. denied*, 338 U.S. 830 (1949), 829

Turner v. Johnson & Johnson, 809 F.2d 90 (1st Cir. 1986), 365

Turoff v. May Co., 531 F.2d 1357 (6th Cir. 1976), 723

TV Communs. Network v. ESPN, Inc., 1991-Trade Cas. (CCH) ¶ 69,476 (D. Col. 1991), 409

TV Signal Co. v. AT&T, 1981-1 Trade Cas. (CCH) ¶ 63,944 (D.S.D. 1981), 179, 210

TV Signal Co. v. AT&T, 462 F.2d 1256 (8th Cir. 1972), 409, 1053

TWA v. Hughes, 332 F.2d 602 (2d Cir. 1964), *cert. dismissed*, 380 U.S. 248 (1965), 1156

TWA v. Mattox, 712 F. Supp. 99 (W.D. Tex. 1989), *aff'd*, 897 F.2d 773 (5th Cir.), *cert. denied*, 111 S.Ct. 307 (1990), 1153, 1294

T.W. Elec. Serv. v. Pacific Elec. Contractors Ass'n, 809 F.2d 626 (9th Cir. 1987), 49, 708

Twentieth Century-Fox Film Corp. v. Brookside Theatre Corp., 194 F.2d 846 (8th Cir.), *cert. denied*, 343 U.S. 942 (1952), 686, 688

Twentieth Century-Fox Film Corp. v. Goldwyn, 328 F.2d 190 (9th Cir.), *cert. denied*, 379 U.S. 880 (1964), 782

Twentieth Holdings Corp., 1 F.C.C. Rcd 1201 (1986), 1036

Twin City Sportservice, Inc. v. Charles O. Finley & Co., 512 F.2d 1264 (9th Cir. 1975), *after remand*, 676 F.2d 1291 (9th Cir.), *cert. denied*, 459 U.S. 1009 (1982), 137, 202, 204, 214

Twin City Sportservice Inc. v. Charles O. Finley & Co., 676 F.2d 1291 (9th Cir.), *cert. denied*, 459 U.S. 1009 (1982), 172, 177, 783

Twin Labs. v. Weider Health & Fitness, 720 F. Supp. 31 (S.D.N.Y. 1989), *aff'd*, 900 F.2d 566 (2d Cir. 1990), 248

Twin Labs. v. Weider Health & Fitness, 900 F.2d 566 (2d Cir. 1990), 249, 252, 264

Twinsburg-Miller Corp. v. J.P. Stevens & Co., 1964 Trade Cas. (CCH) ¶ 70,986 (S.D.N.Y. 1963), 746

Typhoon Car Wash, Inc. v. Mobil Oil Corp., 770 F.2d 1085 (Temp. Emer. Ct. App.), *cert. denied*, 474 U.S. 981 (1985), 422, 424

U

U-Filler-Up Inc. v. Crown Cent. Petroleum Corp., 1973-2 Trade Cas. (CCH) ¶ 74,612 (M.D.N.C.), *rev'd*, 483 F.2d 1014 (4th Cir. 1973), 190

Ukiah Valley Medical Center v. FTC, 911 F.2d 261 (9th Cir. 1990), 456, 523

Umdenstock v. American Mortgage & Inv. Co., 495 F.2d 589 (10th Cir. 1974), 704

Umphres v. Shell Oil Co., 512 F.2d 420 (5th Cir.), *cert. denied*, 423 U.S. 929 (1975), 146

Uncle Ben's, Inc., 89 F.T.C. 131 (1977), 485

Underhill v. Hernandez, 168 U.S. 250 (1897), 902, 906

Ungar v. Dunkin' Donuts, 68 F.R.D. 65 (E.D. Pa. 1975), *rev'd*, 531 F.2d 1211 (3d Cir.), *cert. denied*, 429 U.S. 823 (1976), 718

Ungar v. Dunkin' Donuts, 531 F.2d 1211 (3d Cir.), *cert. denied*, 429 U.S. 823 (1976), 134, 136, 141, 144, 145, 146, 156, 728, 736

Unibrand Tire & Prod. Co. v. Armstrong Rubber Co., 429 F. Supp. 470 (W.D.N.Y. 1977), 134

Unijax, Inc. v. Champion Int'l, Inc., 683 F.2d 678 (2d Cir. 1982), 144, 146, 164, 185

Unioil, Inc. v. E.F. Hutton & Co., 809 F.2d 548 (9th Cir. 1986), *cert. denied*, 478 U.S. 823 (1987), 789

Union Bag-Camp Paper Corp. v. FTC, 233 F. Supp. 660 (S.D.N.Y. 1964), 511

Union Camp Corp. v. Lewis, 385 F.2d 143 (4th Cir. 1967), 763

Union Carbide & Carbon Corp. v. Nisely, 300 F.2d 561 (10th Cir. 1961), *cert. denied*, 371 U.S. 801 (1962), 673, 683, 685

Union Carbide Corp., 5 TRADE REG. REP. (CCH) ¶ 22,961 (Mar. 18, 1991), 515

Union Carbide Corp., 59 F.T.C. 614 (1961), 285, 359, 360

Union Carbide Corp., 79 F.T.C. 124 (1971), 482

Union Carbide Corp. v. Dow Chem. Co., 619 F. Supp. 1036 (D. Del. 1985), 764

Union City Barge Lines v. Union Carbide Corp., 823 F.2d 129 (5th Cir. 1987), 97

Uniondale Beer Co. v. Anheuser-Busch, Inc., 117 F.R.D. 340 (E.D.N.Y. 1987), 714, 715, 721, 725, 727, 730, 733, 737

Union Electric Co., 25 F.E.R.C. (CCH) ¶ 61,394 (1983), 1075

Union Labor Life Ins. Co. v. Pireno, 458 U.S. 119 (1982), 1111, 1112

Union Leader Corp. v. Newspapers of New England, Inc., 180 F. Supp. 125 (D. Mass. 1959), *rev'd in part and aff'd in part*, 284 F.2d 582 (1st Cir. 1960), *cert. denied*, 365 U.S. 833 (1961), 225

Union Leader Corp. v. Newspapers of New England, Inc., 284 F.2d 582 (1st Cir. 1960), *cert. denied*, 365 U.S. 833 (1961), 217, 313

Union Pa. R. v. ICC, 867 F.2d 646 (D.C. Cir. 1989), 1135, 1136, 1165, 1173

Union Planters Corp., 73 Fed. Res. Bull. 469 (1987), 1094

Uniroyal, Inc. v. Hoff & Thames, Inc., 511 F. Supp. 1060 (S.D. Miss. 1981), 407, 416, 423, 424

Uniroyal, Inc. v. Jetco Auto Serv., 461 F. Supp. 350 (S.D.N.Y. 1978), 634

United Airlines, Inc. v. McDonald, 432 U.S. 385 (1977), 737

United Air Lines v. Austin Travel Corp., 681 F. Supp. 176 (S.D.N.Y. 1988), *aff'd*, 867 F.2d 737 (2d Cir. 1989), 158, 172

United Air Lines v. Austin Travel Corp., 867 F.2d 737 (2d Cir. 1989), 159, 173, 176, 183, 214, 702

United Air Lines v. CAB, 766 F.2d 1107 (7th Cir. 1985), 1154

United Artists Associated v. NWL Corp., 198 F. Supp. 953 (S.D.N.Y. 1961), 846

United Artists Corp. v. Masterpiece Prods., 221 F.2d 213 (2d Cir. 1955), 854

United Banana Co. v. United Fruit Co., 245 F. Supp. 161 (D. Conn. 1965), *aff'd per curiam*, 362 F.2d 849 (2d Cir. 1966), 225

United Bank, Ltd. v. Cosmic Int'l, Inc., 542 F.2d 868 (2d Cir. 1976), 907

United Banks of Color., Inc., 73 Fed. Res. Bull. 383 (1987), 1094

United Biscuit Co. v. FTC, 350 F.2d 615 (7th Cir. 1965), *cert. denied*, 383 U.S. 926 (1966), 416

United Brands Co. v. Commission, Case 27/76, [1978] E.C.R. 207, [1977-1978 Transfer Binder] COMMON MKT. REP. (CCH) ¶ 8429, 951, 952, 954, 956

United Community Enters., 37 F.C.C.2d 953 (1972), 1037

United Drug Co. v. Theodore Rectanus Co., 248 U.S. 90 (1918), 847

United Egg Producers v. Bauer Int'l Corp., 312 F. Supp. 319 (S.D.N.Y. 1970), 718

United Fidelity & Guar. Co. v. DiMassa, 496 F. Supp. 71 (E.D. Pa. 1980), *aff'd*, 734 F.2d 3 (3d Cir. 1984), 695

United Indep. Flight Officers v. United Air Lines, 756 F.2d 1274 (7th Cir. 1985), 737

United Int'l Pictures (UIP), Decision, 89/467, 32 O.J. Eur. Comm. (No. L 226) 25 (1989), [1989] 2 CEC (CCH) 2019, 937

United Mine Workers v. Illinois State Bar Assn., 389 U.S. 217 (1967), 989

United Mine Workers v. Pennington, 325 U.S. 797 (1945), 1121

United Mine Workers v. Pennington, 381 U.S. 657 (1965), 257, 638, 899, 912, 990, 991, 1012, 1053, 1121

United Nat'l Records, Inc. v. MCA, Inc., 99 F.R.D. 178 (N.D. Ill. 1983), 727

United Nat'l Records, Inc. v. MCA, Inc., 101 F.R.D. 323 (N.D. Ill. 1984), 722, 725, 727, 730

United Nat'l Records, Inc. v. MCA, Inc., 609 F. Supp. 33 (N.D. Ill. 1984), 689, 690, 692

United Nuclear Corp. v. Combustion Eng'g, Inc., 302 F. Supp. 539 (E.D. Pa. 1969), 280, 281, 319, 323, 331, 1081

United Nuclear Corp. v. General Atomic Co., 96 N.M. 155, 629 P.2d 231 (1980), *appeal dismissed*, 451 U.S. 901 (1981), 888, 905, 908, 910

United Shoe Mach. Corp. v. United States, 258 U.S. 451 (1922), 131, 134

United States Cellular Operating Co., 3 F.C.C. Rcd 5345 (1988), 1030

United States Dep't of Justice v. Julian, 486 U.S. 1 (1988), 596

United States *ex rel.* Woodard v. Tynan, 757 F.2d 1085 (10th Cir. 1985), 758

United States Football League v. NFL, 1986-1 Trade Cas. (CCH) ¶ 67,153 (S.D.N.Y. 1986), 670

United States Football League v. NFL, 634 F. Supp. 1155 (S.D.N.Y. 1986), 1011, 1015

United States Football League v. NFL, 644 F. Supp. 1040 (S.D.N.Y. 1986), *aff'd*, 842 F.2d 1335 (2d Cir. 1988), *cert. denied*, 110 S. Ct. 116 (1990), 207, 222, 669

United States Football League v. NFL, 842 F.2d 1335 (2d Cir. 1988), *cert. denied*, 110 S. Ct. 116 (1990), 54, 91, 215, 220, 221, 223, 224, 247, 666, 667, 668, 674, 675, 1014

United States Football League v. NFL, 887 F.2d 408 (2d Cir. 1989), *cert. denied*, 493 U.S. 1071 (1990), 781, 782, 783, 784, 786

United States Gypsum Co. v. National Gypsum Co., 387 F.2d 799 (7th Cir. 1967), *cert. denied*, 390 U.S. 988 (1968), 833

United States Gypsum Co. v. National Gypsum Co., 352 U.S. 457 (1957), 813, 814, 816

United States Indus. v. United States Dist. Court, 345 F.2d 18 (9th Cir.), *cert. denied*, 382 U.S. 814 (1965), 597

United States Movidyn Corp. v. Hercules, Inc., 388 F. Supp. 1146 (D. Minn. 1975), 808

United States Navigation Co. v. Cunard S.S. Co., 284 U.S. 474 (1932), 1160, 1165

United States Retail Credit Ass'n v. FTC, 300 F.2d 212 (4th Cir. 1962), 464

United States Rubber Co., 28 F.T.C. 1489 (1939), 411

United States Rubber Co., 46 F.T.C. 998 (1950), 411, 423

United States Steel Corp., 8 F.T.C. 1 (1924), 401

United States Steel Corp., 74 F.T.C. 1270 (1968), 313

United States Steel Corp. v. Fortner Enters., 429 U.S. 610 (1977), 136, 149, 150, 153, 260

United States Steel Corp. v. FTC, 426 F.2d 592 (6th Cir. 1970), 315, 331, 334

United States Trotting Ass'n v. Chicago Downs Ass'n, 665 F.2d 781 (7th Cir. 1981), 35, 45, 56, 85, 87, 90

United States v. (Under Seal), 714 F.2d 347 (4th Cir.), *cert. dismissed*, 464 U.S. 978 (1983), 566, 567, 581

United States v. A. Schrader's Son, Inc., 252 U.S. 85 (1920), 11, 101

United States v. Abbott Labs, 505 F.2d 565 (4th Cir. 1974), *cert. denied*, 420 U.S. 990 (1975), 567

United States v. ABC, 1977-2 Trade Cas. (CCH) ¶ 61,580 (C.D. Cal. 1977), 1021, 1030, 1040

United States v. ABC, 1981-1 Trade Cas. (CCH) ¶ 64,150 (C.D. Cal. 1980), 571, 1040

United States v. ACB Sales & Serv., 590 F. Supp. 561 (D. Ariz. 1984), 538

United States v. ACB Sales & Serv., 683 F. Supp. 734 (D. Ariz. 1987), 496, 538, 539

United States v. Acorn Eng'g Co., 1981-2 Trade Cas. (CCH) ¶ 64,197 (N.D. Cal. 1981), 355, 357

United States v. Addyston Pipe & Steel Co., 85 F. 271 (6th Cir. 1898), *aff'd as modified*, 175 U.S. 211 (1899), 98, 379

United States v. Aero Ltd. Partnership, 1991-1 Trade Cas. (CCH) ¶ 69,451 (D.D.C. 1991), 344

United States v. Aero Mayflower Transit Co., 831 F.2d 1142 (D.C. Cir. 1987), 553

United States v. Aeroquip Corp., 1966 Trade Cas. (CCH) ¶ 71,692 (E.D. Mich. 1966), 587, 588

United States v. Agri-Mark, Inc., 1981-1 Trade Cas. (CCH) ¶ 63,967 (D. Vt. 1981), 178

United States v. Agri-Mark, Inc., 512 F. Supp. 737 (D. Vt. 1981), 350, 573

United States v. Agurs, 427 U.S. 97 (1976), 589, 599

United States v. Airco, Inc., 386 F. Supp. 915 (S.D.N.Y. 1974), 168

United States v. Alaska Bd. of Registration for Architects, Eng'rs & Land Surveyors, 1985-1 Trade Cas. (CCH) ¶ 66,423 (D. Alaska 1984), 68

United States v. Alcan Aluminum, Ltd., 605 F. Supp. 619 (W.D. Ky. 1985), 350, 377, 387, 570

United States v. Allegheny Bottling Co., 870 F.2d 655 (4th Cir. 1989), *reported in* 56 ANTITRUST & TRADE REG. REP. (BNA) 77 (Jan. 19, 1989), *rev'g in part* 695 F. Supp. 856 (E.D. Va. 1988), 597

United States v. Allied Publishers Serv., 1982-83 Trade Cas. (CCH) ¶ 64,983 (E.D. Cal. 1982), 497

United States v. Alton Box Board Co., 1977-1 Trade Cas. (CCH) ¶ 61,336 (N.D. Ill. 1977), 597

United States v. Aluminum Co. of Am., 91 F. Supp. 333 (S.D.N.Y. 1950), 806

United States v. Aluminum Co. of Am., 233 F. Supp. 718 (E.D. Mo. 1964), 331

United States v. Aluminum Co. of Am., 247 F. Supp. 308 (E.D. Mo. 1964), *aff'd*, 382 U.S. 12 (1965), 360

United States v. Aluminum Co. of Am., 148 F.2d 416 (2d Cir. 1945), 196, 198, 212, 219, 220, 221, 225, 237, 251, 260, 801, 803, 856, 896

United States v. Aluminum Co. of Am., 377 U.S. 271 (1964), 284, 286, 304

United States v. Aluminum Ltd., 268 F. Supp. 758 (D.N.J. 1966), 751

United States v. AMAX, Inc., 402 F. Supp. 956 (D. Conn. 1975), 299, 305, 329

United States v. AMAX, Inc., 1977-1 Trade Cas. (CCH) ¶ 61,467 (N.D. Ill. 1977), 912, 1015

United States v. American Airlines, 570 F. Supp. 654 (N.D. Tex. 1983), 555

United States v. American Airlines, 743 F.2d 1114 (5th Cir. 1984), *cert. dismissed*, 474 U.S. 1001 (1985), 195, 555

United States v. American Bell Tel. Co., 128 U.S. 315 (1888), 807

United States v. American Bldg. Maintenance Indus., 422 U.S. 271 (1975), 279

United States v. American Can Co., 87 F. Supp. 18 (N.D. Cal. 1949), 169, 177

United States v. American Can Co., 1950-51 Trade Cas. (CCH) ¶ 62, 679 (N.D. Cal. 1950), 853

United States v. American Collection Sys., Civ. No. 79-6691-Civ.-ALH (S.D. Fla. Jan. 16, 1980), 538

United States v. American Cyanamid Co., 1975-2 Trade Cas. (CCH) ¶ 60,608 (S.D.N.Y.), *modified*, 1975-2 Trade Cas. (CCH) ¶ 60,619 (S.D.N.Y. 1975), 589

United States v. American Cyanamid Co., 719 F.2d 558 (2d Cir. 1983), *cert. denied*, 465 U.S. 1101 (1984), *on remand*, 598 F. Supp. 1516 (S.D.N.Y. 1984), 306, 351, 574, 577, 579

United States v. American Greetings Corp., 168 F. Supp. 45 (N.D. Ohio 1958), *aff'd per curiam*, 272 F.2d 945 (6th Cir. 1959), 497

United States v. American Hosp. Supply Corp., 1987-1 Trade Cas. (CCH) ¶ 67,609 (N.D. Ill. 1987), 350, 497

United States v. American Inst. of Architects, 1972 Trade Cas. (CCH) ¶ 73,981 (D.D.C.), modified, 1972-2 Trade Cas. (CCH) ¶ 74,074 (D.D.C. 1972), 68

United States v. American Inst. of Architects, 1990-2 Trade Cas. (CCH) ¶ 69,256 (D.D.C. 1990), 68

United States v. American Inst. of Certified Pub. Accountants, 1972 Trade Cas. (CCH) ¶ 74,007 (D.D.C. 1972), 68

United States v. American Linen Supply Co., 141 F. Supp. 105 (N.D. Ill. 1956), 155

United States v. American Linseed Oil Co., 262 U.S. 371 (1923), 67, 69, 71, 405

United States v. American Oil Co., 259 F. Supp. 851 (D.N.J. 1966), 588

United States v. American Oil Co., 286 F. Supp. 742 (D.N.J. 1968), 589

United States v. American Oil Co., 291 F. Supp. 968 (D.N.J. 1968), 585

United States v. American Pharmaceutical Ass'n, 1981-2 Trade Cas. (CCH) ¶ 64,168 (W.D. Mich. 1981), 69

United States v. American Radiator & Standard Sanitary Corp., 433 F.2d 174 (3d Cir. 1970), *cert. denied*, 401 U.S. 948 (1971), 65, 67, 69, 589, 595

United States v. American Safety Razor Co., 1991-1 Trade Cas. (CCH) ¶ 69,355 (E.D. Pa. 1991), 349

United States v. American Smelting & Ref. Co., 182 F. Supp. 834 (S.D.N.Y. 1960), 66, 390

United States v. American Soc'y of Civil Eng'rs, 1972 Trade Cas. (CCH) ¶ 73,950 (S.D.N.Y. 1972), 68

United States v. American Soc'y of Composers, Authors, & Publishers, 586 F. Supp. 727 (S.D.N.Y. 1984), 40, 374

United States v. American Soc'y of Composers, Authors, & Publishers, 341 F.2d 1003 (2d Cir.), *cert. denied*, 382 U.S. 877 (1965), 574, 646

United States v. American Steel Foundries, 1955 Trade Cas. (CCH) ¶ 68,156 (N.D. Ohio 1955), 852

United States v. American Technical Indus., 1974-1 Trade Cas. (CCH) ¶ 74,873 (M.D. Pa. 1974), 283, 284, 286, 355

United States v. American Tobacco Co., 221 U.S. 106 (1911), 30, 227, 856

United States v. Ames Sintering Co., 927 F.2d 232 (6th Cir. 1990), 66, 556

United States v. Amoco Oil Co., No. 80-1071 (D.D.C. Apr. 29, 1980), 538

United States v. Amrep Corp., 1977-2 Trade Cas. (CCH) ¶ 61,785 (S.D.N.Y. 1977), 505

United States v. Andrew Carlson & Sons, 1980-2 Trade Cas. (CCH) ¶ 63,424 (E.D.N.Y. 1980), 571, 574

United States v. Anthracite Export Ass'n, 1970 Trade Cas. (CCH) ¶ 73,348 (M.D. Pa. 1970), 914

United States v. Anzelmo, 319 F. Supp. 1106 (E.D. La. 1970), 567

United States v. Aquafredda, 834 F.2d 915 (11th Cir. 1987), *cert. denied*, 485 U.S. 980 (1988), 26, 65, 74, 598

United States v. ARA Servs., 1979-2 Trade Cas. (CCH) ¶ 62,861 (E.D. Mo. 1979), 572, 573

United States v. Archer, 355 F. Supp. 981 (S.D.N.Y. 1972), *rev'd*, 486 F.2d 670 (2d Cir. 1973), 567

United States v. Archer-Daniels-Midland Co., 584 F. Supp. 1134 (S.D. Iowa 1984), *aff'd*, 785 F.2d 206 (8th Cir. 1986), *cert. denied*, 481 U.S. 1028 (1987), 280

United States v. Archer-Daniels-Midland Co., 695 F. Supp. 1000 (S.D. Iowa 1987), *rev'd*, 866 F.2d 242 (8th Cir. 1988), *cert. denied*, 493 U.S. 809 (1989), 302, 307

United States v. Archer-Daniels-Midland Co., 785 F.2d 206 (8th Cir. 1986), *cert. denied*, 481 U.S. 1028 (1987), 600

United States v. Archer-Daniels-Midland Co., 866 F.2d 242 (8th Cir. 1988), *cert. denied*, 493 U.S. 809 (1989), 284

United States v. Archer-Daniels-Midland Co., 1991-2 Trade Cas. (CCH) ¶ 69,647 (S.D. Iowa 1991), 311, 312

United States v. Arcole Midwest Corp., Nos. 77 CR 190, 77 CR 191, 77 C 3638 (N.D. Ill. Nov. 16, 1979), 590

United States v. Armored Transp., Inc., 629 F.2d 1313 (9th Cir. 1980), *cert. denied*, 450 U.S. 965 (1981), 585

United States v. Armour & Co., 402 U.S. 673 (1971), 575

United States v. Armour & Co., 420 U.S. 223 (1975), 575

United States v. Arnold, Schwinn & Co., 291 F. Supp. 564 (N.D. Ill. 1968), *vacated*, 442 F. Supp. 1366 (N.D. Ill. 1977), 129, 130

United States v. Arnold, Schwinn & Co., 388 U.S. 365 (1967), 41, 44, 46, 117, 120, 121, 127, 128, 187, 830

United States v. Ashland Oil, Inc., 457 F. Supp. 661 (W.D. Ky. 1978), 585

United States v. Associated Dry Goods Corp., ANTITRUST & TRADE REG. REP. (BNA) No. 994 (S.D.N.Y. Nov. 26, 1980), 534

United States v. Associated Milk Producers, 394 F. Supp. 29 (W.D. Mo. 1975), aff'd, 534 F.2d 113 (8th Cir.), cert. denied, 429 U.S. 940 (1976), 573, 578

United States v. Associated Patents, Inc., 134 F. Supp. 74 (E.D. Mich. 1955), aff'd mem. sub nom. Mac Inv. Co. v. United States, 350 U.S. 960 (1956), 805

United States v. Association of Eng'g Geologists, 1985-1 Trade Cas. (CCH) ¶ 66,349 (C.D. Cal. 1984), 68

United States v. AT&T, 524 F. Supp. 1336 (D.D.C. 1981), 203, 207, 216, 256, 1014, 1015

United States v. AT&T, 1982-1 Trade Cas. (CCH) ¶ 64,521 (D.D.C. 1982), 572

United States v. AT&T, 1982-1 Trade Cas. (CCH) ¶¶ 64,522, 64,623 (D.D.C. 1982), 574

United States v. AT&T, 1982-2 Trade Cas. (CCH) ¶ 64,727 (D.D.C. 1982), 573

United States v. AT&T, 1982-2 Trade Cas. (CCH) ¶¶ 64,726, 64,979 (D.D.C. 1982), 574

United States v. AT&T, 552 F. Supp. 131 (D.D.C. 1982), aff'd sub nom. Maryland v. United States, 460 U.S. 1001 (1983), 574, 577, 578, 1045, 1055

United States v. AT&T, 673 F. Supp. 525 (D.D.C. 1987), 1055

United States v. AT&T, 642 F.2d 1285 (D.C. Cir. 1980), 565, 762

United States v. Atlantic Richfield Co., 297 F. Supp. 1061, injunction vacated, 297 F. Supp. 1075 (S.D.N.Y. 1969), aff'd mem. sub nom. Bartlett v. United States, 401 U.S. 986 (1971), 308, 353, 356, 359

United States v. Atlantic Richfield Co., 1991-1 Trade Cas. (CCH) ¶ 69,318 (D.D.C. 1991), 344

United States v. Atomic Fire Equip. Co., 57 F.R.D. 531 (N.D. Ohio 1973), 585

United States v. Australian Land Title, Ltd., 92 F.T.C. 362 (1978), 499

United States v. Automatic Fire Alarm Co., 1969 Trade Cas. (CCH) ¶ 72,696 (D.R.I. 1968), 574

United States v. Automobile Mfrs. Ass'n, 1969 Trade Cas. (CCH) ¶ 72,907 (C.D. Cal. 1969), modified and replaced sub nom. Motor Vehicle Mfrs. Ass'n, 1982-83 Trade Cas. (CCH) ¶ 65,088 (C.D. Cal 1982), 388

United States v. Automobile Mfrs. Ass'n, 307 F. Supp. 617 (C.D. Cal. 1969), aff'd in part and appeal dismissed in part sub nom. Grossman v. Automobile Mfrs. Ass'n., 397 U.S. 248 (1970), 839

United States v. Azzarelli Constr. Co., 459 F. Supp. 146 (E.D. Ill. 1978), aff'd, 612 F.2d 292 (7th Cir. 1979), cert. denied, 447 U.S. 920 (1980), 590

United States v. Baggot, 463 U.S. 476 (1982), 754

United States v. Bagley, 473 U.S. 667 (1985), 589

United States v. Baker Hughes Inc., 1990-1 Trade Cas. (CCH) ¶ 68,976 (D.D.C. 1990), 344

United States v. Baker Hughes Inc., 731 F. Supp. 3 (D.D.C.), aff'd, 908 F.2d 981 (D.C. Cir. 1990), 311, 313, 353, 863

United States v. Baker Hughes Inc., 908 F.2d 981 (D.C. Cir. 1990), 305, 307, 309, 310

United States v. Bakersfield Assoc. Plumbing Contractors, Inc., 1958 Trade Cas. (CCH) ¶ 69,087 (S.D. Cal. 1958), modified, 1959 Trade Cas. (CCH) ¶ 69,266 (S.D. Cal. 1959), 64

United States v. Baldwin-United Corp., 1982-2 Trade Cas. (CCH) ¶ 64,788 (S.D. Ohio 1982), 345, 347

United States v. Baltimore & O.R.R., 538 F. Supp. 200 (D.D.C. 1982), aff'd sub nom. United States v. Bessemer & Lake Erie R.R., 717 F.2d 593 (D.C. Cir. 1983), 585, 1129

United States v. Baltimore & O.R.R., 543 F. Supp. 821 (D.D.C. 1982), 583

United States v. Bank of Va., 1966 Trade Cas. (CCH) ¶ 71,947 (E.D. Va., 1966), 1091

United States v. B&M Used Cars, 114 F.R.D. 55 (W.D.N.C. 1987), 758

United States v. Barclays Am. Corp., No. C-C-91-0014-MU (W.D.N.C. Jan. 17, 1991), 537

United States v. Basic Constr. Co., 711 F.2d 570 (4th Cir.), cert. denied, 464 U.S. 956 (1983), 595

United States v. Bausch & Lomb Optical Co., 45 F. Supp. 387 (S.D.N.Y. 1942), *aff'd by an equally divided Court*, 321 U.S. 707 (1944), 117

United States v. Bausch & Lomb Optical Co., 321 U.S. 707 (1944), 11, 101, 114, 119, 847

United States v. Beachner Constr. Co., 729 F.2d 1278 (10th Cir. 1984), 586

United States v. Beasley, 550 F.2d 261 (5th Cir.), *cert. denied*, 434 U.S. 863 (1977), 567

United States v. Beatrice Foods Co., 351 F. Supp. 969 (D. Minn. 1972), *aff'd*, 493 F.2d 1259 (8th Cir. 1974), *cert. denied*, 420 U.S. 961 (1975), 488

United States v. Bechtel Corp., 1979-1 Trade Cas. (CCH) ¶ 62,430 (N.D. Cal. 1979), *aff'd*, 648 F.2d 660 (9th Cir.), *cert. denied*, 454 U.S. 1083 (1981), 573

United States v. Bekaert Steel Wire Corp., 1985-2 Trade Cas. (CCH) ¶ 66,836 (D. Md. 1985), 593, 771

United States v. Beneficial Corp., 1980-1 Trade Cas. (CCH) ¶ 63,136 (N.D. Ill. 1979), 345

United States v. Ben M. Hogan Co., 686 F. Supp. 717 (E.D. Ark. 1988), 597, 598

United States v. Ben M. Hogan Co., 769 F.2d 1293 (8th Cir. 1985), *vacated*, 478 U.S. 1016 (1986), 583, 589, 590

United States v. Benson, 836 F.2d 1133 (8th Cir. 1988), 581

United States v. Berger Indus., 1985-1 Trade Cas. (CCH) ¶ 66,587 (E.D. Pa. 1983), 74

United States v. Bessemer & Lake Erie R.R., 717 F.2d 593 (D.C. Cir. 1983), 580, 585, 1017, 1129, 1139

United States v. Besser Mfg. Co., 96 F. Supp. 304 (E.D. Mich. 1951), *aff'd*, 343 U.S. 444 (1952), 803, 805, 812, 835, 838

United States v. Besser Mfg. Co., 125 F. Supp. 710 (D. Mich. 1954), 577

United States v. Bestway Disposal Corp., 681 F. Supp. 1027 (W.D.N.Y. 1988), 585, 587, 588, 589, 601

United States v. Bestway Disposal Corp., 724 F. Supp. 62 (W.D.N.Y. 1988), 598

United States v. Bethlehem Steel Corp., 168 F. Supp. 576 (S.D.N.Y. 1958), 211, 282, 287, 294, 320

United States v. Bi-Co Pavers, Inc., 741 F.2d 730 (5th Cir. 1984), 583, 589, 598

United States v. Binney & Smith, Inc., 1980-81 Trade Cas. (CCH) ¶ 63,747 (N.D. Ohio 1980), 778

United States v. Bird Corp., 1972 Trade Cas. (CCH) ¶ 74,055 (E.D.N.Y. 1972), 121

United States v. Birdman, 602 F.2d 547 (3rd Cir. 1979), *cert. denied*, 444 U.S. 1032 (1980), 568

United States v. Black & Decker Mfg. Co., 430 F. Supp. 729 (D. Md. 1976), 284, 285, 287, 298, 302, 314, 315, 316, 326, 323, 327, 328, 329, 335, 356

United States v. Blankenheim, Crim. No. 74-182-CBR (N.D. Cal. 1974), 597

United States v. Blitz, 179 F. Supp. 80 (S.D.N.Y. 1959), *rev'd in part*, 282 F.2d 465 (2d Cir. 1960), 119

United States v. Blue Bell, Inc., 395 F. Supp. 538 (M.D. Tenn. 1975), 285, 316

United States v. BNS Inc., 1988-2 Trade Cas. (CCH) ¶ 68,209 (C.D. Cal.), *aff'd*, 858 F.2d 456 (9th Cir. 1988), 344, 348

United States v. BNS Inc., 848 F.2d 945 (9th Cir.), *modified*, 858 F.2d 456 (9th Cir. 1988), 356

United States v. BNS Inc., 858 F.2d 456 (9th Cir. 1988), 350, 361, 573, 578, 677, 678

United States v. Board of Trade of the City of Chicago, Inc., 1974-1 Trade Cas. (CCH) ¶ 75,071 (N.D. Ill. 1974), 1105

United States v. Boch Oldsmobile, Inc., No. CA-86-1223-MA (D. Mass Apr. 29, 1986), 534

United States v. Boch Toyota, Inc., No. CA-86-1222-MA (D. Mass Apr. 29, 1986), 534

United States v. Book-of-the-Month Club, Inc., [1976-1979 Transfer Binder] TRADE REG. REP. (CCH) ¶ 21,474 (S.D.N.Y. Sept. 6, 1978), 498

United States v. Borden Co., 308 U.S. 188 (1939), 1025

United States v. Borden Co., 370 U.S. 460 (1962), 421, 422, 424

United States v. Borden, Inc., 1976-2 Trade Cas. (CCH) ¶ 61,177 (D. Ariz. 1976), 757

United States v. Borden, Inc., 6 TRADE REG. REP. (CCH) ¶ 45,090 (Case No. 3694) (M.D. Fla. 1990), 561, 597

United States v. Bostic, 336 F. Supp. 1312 (D.S.C.), *aff'd per curiam*, 473 F.2d 1388 (4th Cir. 1972), *cert. denied*, 411 U.S. 966 (1973), 488

United States v. Bowler, 585 F.2d 851 (7th Cir. 1978), 581

United States v. Bowman, 370 U.S. 460 (1962), 421, 425

United States v. Braasch, 505 F.2d 139 (7th Cir. 1974), *cert. denied*, 421 U.S. 910 (1975), 567

United States v. Braniff Airways, 428 F. Supp. 579 (W.D. Tex. 1977), 567, 585

United States v. Braniff Airways, 453 F. Supp. 724 (W.D. Tex. 1978), 1018

United States v. Braswell, 1981-2 Trade Cas. (CCH) ¶ 64,325 (N.D. Ga. 1981), 497

United States v. Brighton Bldg. & Maintenance Co., 431 F. Supp. 1118 (N.D. Ill. 1977), 582

United States v. Brighton Bldg. & Maintenance Co., 598 F.2d 1101 (7th Cir.), *cert. denied*, 444 U.S. 840 (1979), 57, 63, 555

United States v. Brink's, Inc., 1979-2 Trade Cas. (CCH) ¶ 62,902 (N.D. Ga. 1979), 73

United States v. Broce, 781 F.2d 792 (10th Cir. 1986), 586

United States v. Brookman Co., 229 F. Supp. 862 (N.D. Cal. 1964), 644

United States v. Brookman Co., 1965 Trade Cas. (CCH) ¶ 71,533 (N.D. Cal. 1965), 582

United States v. Brown, 936 F.2d 1042 (9th Cir. 1991), 40, 63, 76

United States v. Brown Shoe Co., 1956 Trade Cas. (CCH) ¶ 68,244 (E.D. Mo. 1956), *adjudicated on the merits*, 370 U.S. 294 (1962), 353, 355

United States v. Bruzgo, 373 F.2d 383 (3d Cir. 1967), 566

United States v. Burch, 873 F.2d 765 (5th Cir. 1989), 595

United States v. Burgstiner, No. CU491-044 (S.D. Ga. filed Feb. 7, 1991), 73

United States v. Burke, 781 F.2d 1234 (7th Cir. 1985), 566

United States v. Burns, 684 F.2d 1066 (2d Cir. 1982), *cert. denied*, 459 U.S. 1174 (1983), 592

United States v. Cadillac Overall Supply Co., 568 F.2d 1078 (5th Cir.), *cert. denied*, 437 U.S. 903 (1978), 76, 595

United States v. California Rice Exporters, Cr. 32879 (N.D. Cal. 1952), 914

United States v. Calmar Inc., 612 F. Supp. 1298 (D.N.J. 1985), 217, 288, 302, 305, 307, 309, 353

United States v. Campbell Hardware, Inc., 470 F. Supp. 430 (D. Mass. 1979), 584, 585

United States v. Capaldo, 402 F.2d 821 (2d Cir. 1968), *cert. denied*, 394 U.S. 989 (1969), 564

United States v. Capital Credit Corp., ANTITRUST & TRADE REG. REP. (BNA) No. 956, at A-14 (D.D.C. Mar. 13, 1980), 538

United States v. Capitol Serv., 1981-1 Trade Cas. (CCH) ¶ 63,972 (E.D. Wisc. 1981), 749

United States v. Capitol Serv., 756 F.2d 502 (7th Cir.), *cert. denied*, 474 U.S. 945 (1985), 40, 63, 76, 85

United States v. Capitol Thrift and Loan Ass'n, No. C-86-1148 (N.D. Cal. Mar. 12, 1986), 537

United States v. Cargo Serv. Stations, Inc., 657 F.2d 676 (5th Cir. 1981), *cert. denied*, 455 U.S. 1017 (1982), 22, 28, 57

United States v. Carilion Health Sys., 707 F. Supp. 840 (W.D. Va.), *aff'd mem.*, 892 F.2d 1042 (4th Cir. 1989), 279, 290, 320, 456

United States v. Carrols Dev. Corp., 454 F. Supp. 1215 (N.D.N.Y. 1978), 360, 578, 579

United States v. Carrols Dev. Corp., 1982-1 Trade Cas. (CCH) ¶ 64,510 (N.D.N.Y. 1981), 577

United States v. Carter, 15 F.R.D. 367 (D.D.C. 1954), 750

United States v. Carter Prods., Inc., 28 F.R.D. 373 (S.D.N.Y. 1961), 750

United States v. Cash Flow, Inc., Civ. No. D-80-485 (D. Conn. Oct. 31, 1980), 538

United States v. CBS, 1977-1 Trade Cas. (CCH) ¶ 61,327 (C.D. Cal. 1977), 1021, 1030, 1040

United States v. CBS, 459 F. Supp. 832 (C.D. Cal. 1978), 1040

United States v. CBS, No. 74-3599-RJK (C.D. Cal. March 10, 1978), 762

United States v. CBS, 1980-81 Trade Cas. (CCH) ¶ 63,594 (C.D. Cal. 1980), *modified*, 1988-2 Trade Cas. (CCH) ¶ 68,284 (C.D. Cal. 1986), 571, 1040

United States v. CBS, 1981-2 Trade Cas. (CCH) ¶ 64,227 (C.D. Cal. 1981), 575

United States v. CBS, 103 F.R.D. 365 (C.D. Cal. 1984), 766

United States v. CBS, 1988-2 Trade Cas. (CCH) ¶ 68,284 (C.D. Cal. 1986), 571

United States v. CBS, 666 F.2d 364 (9th Cir.), *cert. denied*, 457 U.S. 1118 (1982), 766

United States v. Central Adjustment Bureau, 667 F. Supp. 370 (N.D. Tex. 1986), *aff'd as modified*, 823 F.2d 880 (5th Cir. 1987), 538

United States v. Central Contracting Co., 527 F. Supp. 1101 (E.D. Va. 1981), 573

United States v. Central Contracting Co., 537 F. Supp. 571 (E.D. Va. 1982), 572

United States v. Central State Bank, 564 F. Supp. 1478 (W.D. Mich. 1983), 1092

United States v. Central State Bank, 621 F. Supp. 1276 (W.D. Mich. 1985), *aff'd per curiam*, 817 F.2d 22 (6th Cir. 1987), 275, 276, 289, 295, 296, 1089

United States v. Champion Int'l Corp., 557 F.2d 1270 (9th Cir.), *cert. denied*, 434 U.S. 938 (1977), 64, 1109

United States v. Charmer Indus., 711 F.2d 1164 (2d Cir. 1983), 596, 598

United States v. Chase Manhattan Bank, NA, 590 F. Supp. 1160 (S.D.N.Y. 1984), 888

United States v. Chase Manhattan Bank, NA, 584 F. Supp. 1080 (S.D.N.Y. 1984), 887

United States v. Chas. Pfizer & Co., 245 F. Supp. 737 (E.D.N.Y. 1965), 270

United States v. Chas. Pfizer & Co., 246 F. Supp. 464 (E.D.N.Y. 1965), 201

United States v. Chas. Pfizer & Co., 281 F. Supp. 837 (S.D.N.Y. 1969), *rev'd*, 426 F.2d 32 (2d Cir. 1970), 34

United States v. Chas. Pfizer & Co., 404 U.S. 548 (1972), 743

United States v. Chicago Title & Trust Co., 242 F. Supp. 56 (N.D. Ill. 1965), 1116

United States v. Chicago Tribune-N.Y. News Syndicate, 309 F. Supp. 1301 (S.D.N.Y. 1970), 119

United States v. Chrysler Corp., 232 F. Supp. 651 (D.N.J. 1964), 353

United States v. Chrysler Corp., 1983-2 Trade Cas. (CCH) ¶ 65,710 (N.D. Ind. 1983), 577

United States v. Ciba Corp., 1972 Trade Cas. (CCH) ¶ 74,026 (D.N.J. 1971), 753, 880

United States v. CIBA GEIGY Corp., 508 F. Supp. 1118 (D.N.J. 1976), *final judgment*, 1980-81 Trade Cas. (CCH) ¶ 63,813 (D.N.J. 1981), 128, 828, 829

United States v. Cincinnati Milling Mach. Co., 1954 Trade Cas. (CCH) ¶ 67,733 (E.D. Mich. 1954), 69

United States v. Cinemette Corp. of Am., 687 F. Supp. 976 (W.D. Pa. 1988), 554, 555, 584

United States v. Cities Serv. Co., 289 F. Supp. 133 (D. Mass. 1968), 356

United States v. Citizens & S. Nat'l Bank, 422 U.S. 86 (1975), 17, 73, 299, 318

United States v. City Fin. Corp., No. 1:90-CV-246 (N.D. Ga. Feb. 2, 1990), 537

United States v. City Linen, Coat & Apron Supply Serv., 1980-1 Trade Cas. (CCH) ¶ 63,133 (S.D. Fla. 1979), 571

United States v. Cleveland Trust Co., 392 F. Supp. 699 (N.D. Ohio 1974), *aff'd mem.*, 513 F.2d 633 (6th Cir. 1975), 397, 398, 399

United States v. Cleveland Trust Co., 1975-2 Trade Cas. (CCH) ¶ 60,611 (N.D. Ohio 1975), 398

United States v. Climatemp, Inc., 482 F. Supp. 376 (N.D. Ill. 1979), *aff'd mem.*, 705 F.2d 461 (7th Cir.), *cert. denied*, 462 U.S. 1134 (1983), 584, 587, 588, 590, 591

United States v. Coca-Cola Bottling Co., 1978-2 Trade Cas. (CCH) ¶ 62,277, (C.D. Cal. 1978), 345

United States v. Coca-Cola Bottling Co., 1980-81 Trade Cas. (CCH) ¶ 63,664 (C.D. Cal. 1980), 351

United States v. Coca-Cola Bottling Co., 575 F.2d 222 (9th Cir.), *cert. denied*, 439 U.S. 959 (1978), 355, 360

United States v. Coca-Cola Bottling Co. of Miami, No. 89-6097-CR (S.D. Fla. 1989), 561

United States v. Coffman, 567 F.2d 960 (10th Cir. 1977), 580

United States v. Coit Int'l Inc., 1982-1 Trade Cas. (CCH) ¶ 64,648 (N.D. Tex. 1981), 509

United States v. Colgate & Co., 250 U.S. 300 (1919), 3, 11, 12, 100, 241, 242

United States v. Columbia Artists Mgmt., Inc., 662 F. Supp. 865 (S.D.N.Y. 1987), 577

United States v. Columbia Pictures Corp., 189 F. Supp. 153 (S.D.N.Y. 1960), 56, 280, 376, 379, 804

United States v. Columbia Pictures Indus., 507 F. Supp. 412 (S.D.N.Y. 1980), *aff'd without opinion*, 659 F.2d 1063 (2d Cir., 1981), 40, 52, 81, 373, 381, 390, 1052

United States v. Columbia Steel Co., 334 U.S. 495 (1948), 44, 54, 209, 213, 275

United States v. Combustion Eng'g, Inc., 1971 Trade Cas. (CCH) ¶ 73,648 (D. Conn. 1971), 360

United States v. Concentrated Phosphate Export Ass'n, 393 U.S. 199 (1968), 680, 864, 914

United States v. Connecticut Nat'l Bank, 418 U.S. 656 (1974), 289, 293

United States v. Connecticut Package Stores Ass'n, 1975-1 Trade Cas. (CCH) ¶ 60,174 (D.D.C. 1975), 576, 577

United States v. Consolidated Car-Heating Co., 87 U.S.P.Q. (BNA) 20 (S.D.N.Y. 1950), 833

United States v. Consolidated Foods Corp., 1978-1 Trade Cas. (CCH) ¶ 62,063 (E.D. Pa. 1978), 335

United States v. Consolidated Foods Corp., 1978-1 Trade Cas. (CCH) ¶ 62,110 (E.D. Pa. 1978), 353

United States v. Consolidated Foods Corp., 455 F. Supp. 108 (E.D. Pa. 1978), 317

United States v. Consolidated Laundries Corp., 291 F.2d 563 (2d Cir. 1961), 76, 270, 271, 272, 599

United States v. Container Corp., 1970 Trade Cas. (CCH) ¶ 73,091 (M.D.N.C. 1970), 72

United States v. Container Corp., 393 U.S. 333 (1969), 67, 71, 72, 1109

United States v. Continental Can Co., 1964 Trade Cas. (CCH) ¶ 71,264 (S.D.N.Y. 1964), 351

United States v. Continental Can Co., 128 F. Supp. 932 (N.D. Cal. 1955), 577

United States v. Continental Can Co., 378 U.S. 441 (1964), 284, 287, 294, 300

United States v. Continental Group, 603 F.2d 444 (3d Cir. 1979), cert. denied, 444 U.S. 1032 (1980), 57, 555

United States v. Continental Oil Co., 1965 Trade Cas. (CCH) ¶ 71,557 (D.N.M. 1965), 280

United States v. Converse Rubber Corp., 1972 Trade Cas. (CCH) ¶ 74,101 (D. Mass. 1972), 349

United States v. Cooper, 1976-1 Trade Cas. (CCH) ¶ 60,952 (S.D. Tex. 1976), 398

United States v. Cooper Corp., 312 U.S. 600 (1941), 645

United States v. Cooperative Theatres, 845 F.2d 1367 (6th Cir. 1988), 31, 40, 63, 76, 85, 554, 598

United States v. Country Lake Foods, Inc., 754 F. Supp. 669 (D. Minn. 1990), 298, 307, 311, 313, 320

United States v. Countryside Farms, 428 F. Supp. 1150 (D. Utah 1977), 586, 587

United States v. Crescent Amusement Co., 323 U.S. 173 (1944), 18, 79, 845

United States v. Critical Indus., Crim. No. 90-00318 (D.N.J. filed July 24, 1990), 556

United States v. Critical Indus., Dkt. No. 90-CR-318 (D.N.J. Aug. 16, 1991), 67

United States v. Crocker Nat'l Corp., 422 F. Supp. 686 (N.D. Cal. 1976), 395

United States v. Crocker Nat'l Corp., 656 F.2d 428 (9th Cir. 1981), rev'd sub nom. Bank America Corp. v. United States, 462 U.S. 122 (1983), 395, 397, 1116

United States v. Crowell, Collier & MacMillan, Inc., 361 F. Supp. 983 (S.D.N.Y. 1973), 335

United States v. Crown Zellerbach Corp., 141 F. Supp. 118 (N.D. Ill. 1956), 828

United States v. Crystal Ford, Ltd., 1988-2 Trade Cas. (CCH) ¶ 68,148 (D. Md. 1988), 529

United States v. Cuisinarts, Inc., 1981-1 Trade Cas. (CCH) ¶ 63,979 (D. Conn. 1981), 107, 554

United States v. Culbro Corp., 1977-1 Trade Cas. (CCH) ¶ 61,514 (S.D.N.Y. 1977), 353

United States v. Culbro Corp., 436 F. Supp. 746 (S.D.N.Y. 1977), 353, 355, 356

United States v. Culbro Corp., 1978-2 Trade Cas. (CCH) ¶ 62,274 (S.D.N.Y. 1978), 349

United States v. Culbro Corp., 504 F. Supp. 661 (S.D.N.Y. 1981), 313, 315, 577

United States v. Dairymen, Inc., 1983-2 Trade Cas. (CCH) ¶ 65,651 (W.D. Ky. 1983), aff'd, 177

United States v. Dairymen, Inc., 1985-1 Trade Cas. (CCH) ¶ 66,638 (6th Cir.), cert. denied, 474 U.S. 822 (1985), 177

United States v. Dairymen, Inc., 660 F.2d 192 (6th Cir. 1981), 211, 261, 1026

United States v. Danenza, 528 F.2d 390 (2d Cir. 1975), 562

United States v. Data Card Corp., 1987-1 Trade Cas. (CCH) ¶ 67,437 (D.D.C. 1987), 345, 346, 348

United States v. David E. Thompson, Inc., 621 F.2d 1147 (1st Cir. 1980), 582, 583

United States v. Davis, 767 F.2d 1025 (2d Cir. 1985), 889

United States v. Deerfield Specialty Papers, Inc., 501 F. Supp. 796 (E.D. Pa. 1980), 585, 587, 588, 589

United States v. Del Monte Corp., [1983-1987 Transfer Binder] TRADE REG. REP. (CCH) ¶ 22,307 (N.D. Cal. Nov. 18, 1985), 497

United States v. DePalma, 461 F. Supp. 778 (S.D.N.Y. 1978), 566

United States v. Deutsches Kalisyndikat Gesellschaft, 31 F.2d 199 (S.D.N.Y. 1929), 899

United States v. Dewey's Rubbish Serv., 6 TRADE REG. REP. (CCH) ¶ 45,089 (Case No. 3678) (S.D. Cal. 1990), 597

United States v. Diebold, Inc., 1977-2 Trade Cas. (CCH) ¶ 61,736 (N.D. Ohio 1976), 890

United States v. Diebold, Inc., 369 U.S. 654 (1962), 314, 703

United States v. Disston, 612 F.2d 1035 (7th Cir. 1980), 599

United States v. Dixie Readers' Serv., [1983-1987 Transfer Binder] TRADE REG. REP. (CCH) ¶ 22,306 (S.D. Miss. Nov. 14, 1985), 497

United States v. Domtar Indus., 1987-1 Trade Cas. (CCH) ¶ 67,639 (N.D. Cal. 1987), 345, 347

United States v. Doss, 563 F.2d 265 (6th Cir. 1977), 567

United States v. Dow Chem. Co., 1987-2 Trade Cas. (CCH) ¶ 67,684 (N.D. Ill. 1987), 345, 347

United States v. Dubilier Condenser Corp., 289 U.S. 178 (1933), 801

United States v. Dynalectric Co., Crim. No. 86-350A (N.D. Ga. 1986), 561

United States v. Dynalectric Co., 859 F.2d 1559 (11th Cir. 1988), cert. denied, 490 U.S. 1006 (1989), 66, 373

United States v. Eagle Elec. Mfg. Co., 1980-1 Trade Cas. (CCH) ¶ 63,215 (D. Mass. 1980), 571

United States v. Eaton Yale & Towne, Inc., 1972 Trade Cas. (CCH) ¶ 74,012 (D. Conn. 1972), 121

United States v. Echeles, 352 F.2d 892 (7th Cir. 1965), 584

United States v. Echols, 542 F.2d 948 (5th Cir. 1976), cert. denied, 431 U.S. 904 (1977), 567

United States v. E.C. Knight Co., 156 U.S. 1 (1895), 23

United States v. E.I. du Pont de Nemours & Co., 118 F. Supp. 41 (D. Del. 1953), aff'd, 351 U.S. 377 (1956), 380, 803, 805, 821, 823, 842, 850

United States v. E.I. du Pont de Nemours & Co., 177 F. Supp. 1 (N.D. Ill. 1959), modified, 366 U.S. 316 (1961), 360

United States v. E.I. du Pont de Nemours & Co., 1980-81 Trade Cas. (CCH) ¶ 63,570 (N.D. Ohio 1980), 113

United States v. E.I. du Pont de Nemours & Co., 1982-1 Trade Cas. (CCH) ¶ 64,479 (D.D.C. 1981), 570

United States v. E.I. duPont de Nemours & Co., 351 U.S. 377 (1956), 192, 196, 197, 198, 199, 200, 201, 202, 207, 209, 213, 383

United States v. E.I. du Pont de Nemours & Co., 353 U.S. 586 (1957), 280, 281, 282, 330

United States v. E.I. du Pont de Nemours & Co., 366 U.S. 316 (1961), 350, 358, 359, 680

United States v. Eighty-Nine (89) Bottles of "Eau de Joy," 797 F.2d 767 (9th Cir. 1986), 843

United States v. El Paso Natural Gas Co., 376 U.S. 651 (1964), 314, 328, 329, 360, 1066

United States v. Electrical Apparatus Export Ass'n, 1946-47 Trade Cas. (CCH) ¶ 57,546 (S.D.N.Y. 1947), 914

United States v. Empire Gas Corp., 393 F. Supp. 903 (W.D. Mo. 1975), aff'd, 537 F.2d 296 (8th Cir. 1976), cert. denied, 429 U.S. 1122 (1977), 168

United States v. Empire Gas Corp., 537 F.2d 296 (8th Cir. 1976), cert. denied, 429 U.S. 1122 (1977), 99, 203, 204, 211, 260, 264, 265, 266, 267

United States v. Encore House Inc., [1983-1987 Transfer Binder] TRADE REG. REP. (CCH) ¶ 22,289 (S.D.N.Y. Sept. 25, 1985), 497

United States v. Endicott, 869 F.2d 452 (9th Cir. 1989), 598

United States v. Equity Group Holdings, 1991-1 Trade Cas. (CCH) ¶ 69,320 (D.D.C. 1991), 344

United States v. Essex Group, 1980-2 Trade Cas. (CCH) ¶ 63,296 (C.D. Cal. 1980), 571

United States v. E. Stewart Mitchel, Inc., 4 TRADE REG. REP. (CCH) ¶ 45,082 (Case No. 2979) (N.D. Va. 1982), 597

United States v. Evans & Assocs. Constr. Co., 1987-1 Trade Cas. (CCH) ¶ 67,464 (W.D. Okla. 1987), rev'd, 839 F.2d 656 (10th Cir. 1988), on rehearing, 857 F.2d 720 (10th Cir. 1988), 568
United States v. Evans & Assocs. Constr. Co., 839 F.2d 656 (10th Cir. 1988), 587, 590, 756
United States v. Everest & Jennings Int'l, 1979-1 Trade Cas. (CCH) ¶ 62,508 (C.D. Cal. 1979), 890
United States v. Exchange Fin. Co., No. 90-0174 (M.D. Tenn. Mar. 7, 1990), 537
United States v. Exxon Corp., [1979-1983 Transfer Binder] TRADE REG. REP. (CCH) ¶ 21,707 (D.D.C. Mar. 24, 1980), 498
United States v. Falstaff Brewing Corp., 383 F. Supp. 1020 (D.R.I. 1974), 323
United States v. Falstaff Brewing Corp., 410 U.S. 526 (1973), 322, 324, 327, 328
United States v. Farbenfabriken Bayer AG, 1969 Trade Cas. (CCH) ¶ 72,918 (D.D.C. 1969), 830
United States v. FCC, 652 F.2d 72 (D.C. Cir. 1980), 335, 376, 377, 1030
United States v. Finis P. Ernest, Inc., 509 F.2d 1256 (7th Cir.), cert. denied, 423 U.S. 893 (1975), 27, 63
United States v. Fireside Thrift Co., No. C-86-2379 (N.D. Cal. Sept. 2, 1986), 537, 539
United States v. First City Fin. Corp., Ltd., 1988-1 Trade Cas. (CCH) ¶ 67,697 (D.D.C. 1988), 344
United States v. First City Nat'l Bank, 386 U.S. 361 (1967), 1092, 1095
United States v. First Fed. Credit Control, Inc., ANTITRUST & TRADE REG. REP. (BNA) No. 1062 (N.D. Ohio Mar. 11, 1982), 538
United States v. First Hawaiian Inc., Civ. Doc. No. 90-00904 DAE (D. Haw. filed Dec. 28, 1990), 289
United States v. First Nat'l Bank, 310 F. Supp. 157 (D. Md. 1970), 1092
United States v. First Nat'l Bank & Trust Co., 376 U.S. 665 (1964), 275, 276, 569, 1089
United States v. First Nat'l Bankcorp., 329 F. Supp. 1003 (1971), 295
United States v. First Nat'l Bank of Chicago, 699 F.2d 341 (7th Cir. 1983), 888
United States v. First Nat'l City Bank, 396 F.2d 897 (2d Cir. 1968), 881, 887
United States v. First Nat'l State Bancorp., 499 F. Supp. 793 (D.N.J. 1980), 289, 294, 297, 323, 329, 356
United States v. Fischbach & Moore, Inc., 1984-1 Trade Cas. (CCH) ¶ 65,874 (W.D. Wash. 1983), 585
United States v. Fischbach & Moore, Inc., 576 F. Supp. 1384 (W.D. Pa. 1983), 587, 588, 589
United States v. Fischbach & Moore, Inc., 750 F.2d 1183 (3d Cir. 1984), cert. denied, 470 U.S. 1029 (1985), 23, 25, 27, 28, 597
United States v. Fischbach & Moore, Inc., 776 F.2d 839 (9th Cir. 1985), 756, 760
United States v. Fitapelli, 786 F.2d 1461 (11th Cir. 1986), 23, 584, 598
United States v. Flav-O-Rich, Inc., 6 TRADE REG. REP. (CCH) ¶ 45,091 (Case No. 3815) (M.D. Fla. 1990), 561, 597
United States v. Fleet/Norstar Fin. Group, Civ. Doc. No. 91-0221-P (D. Me. filed July 5, 1991), 290, 1096
United States v. Floersheim, 1980-2 Trade Cas. (CCH) ¶ 63,368 (C.D. Cal. 1980), aff'd, No. 80-5444 (9th Cir. July 23, 1981), 496
United States v. Flom, 558 F.2d 1179 (5th Cir. 1977), 63, 588
United States v. Florida Power Corp., 1971 Trade Cas. (CCH) ¶ 73,637 (M.D. Fla. 1971), 1068
United States v. FMC Corp., 306 F. Supp. 1106 (E.D. Pa. 1969), 72
United States v. F.M.C. Corp., 1979-2 Trade Cas. (CCH) ¶ 62,901 (D. Mass. 1979), 892
United States v. Foley, 598 F.2d 1323 (4th Cir. 1979), cert. denied, 444 U.S. 1043 (1980), 3, 555, 590
United States v. Ford Motor Co., 24 F.R.D. 65 (D.D.C. 1959), 588
United States v. Ford Motor Co., 315 F. Supp. 372 (E.D. Mich. 1970), aff'd, 405 U.S. 562 (1972), 360

United States v. Foremost-McKesson, Inc., 1976-2 Trade Cas. (CCH) ¶ 61,165 (D. Nev. 1976), 357

United States v. Forest City Enters., [1976-1979 Transfer Binder] TRADE REG. REP. (CCH) ¶ 21,306 (S.D. Ohio May 19, 1977), 498

United States v. Foster Bam, 1976-1 Trade Cas. (CCH) ¶ 60,734 (D. Conn. 1976), 398

United States v. Friedman, 532 F.2d 928 (3d Cir. 1976), 767

United States v. Frito-Lay, Inc., 1975 Trade Cas. (CCH) ¶ 60,265 (C.D. Cal. 1975), 576

United States v. Fuel Oil Dealers' Div., 1968 Trade Cas. (CCH) ¶ 72,619 (E.D. Pa. 1968), 587

United States v. GAF Corp., 596 F.2d 10 (2d Cir. 1979), 560

United States v. Gasoline Retailers Ass'n, 285 F.2d 688 (7th Cir. 1961), 69

United States v. G.B. Enters., 5 TRADE REG. REP. (CCH) ¶ 22,463 (D.D.C. July 27, 1987), 478

United States v. General Contractor's Ass'n, 1988-1 Trade Cas. (CCH) ¶ 68,019 (D. Haw. 1988), 570, 571

United States v. General Dyestuff Corp., 57 F. Supp. 642 (S.D.N.Y. 1944), 75, 384

United States v. General Dynamics Corp., 258 F. Supp. 36 (S.D.N.Y. 1966), 167, 168, 336

United States v. General Dynamics Corp., 341 F. Supp. 534 (N.D. Ill. 1972), aff'd, 415 U.S. 486 (1974), 289, 295

United States v. General Dynamics Corp., 828 F.2d 1356 (9th Cir. 1987), 1021

United States v. General Dynamics Corp., 415 U.S. 486 (1974), 295, 299, 300, 313, 315, 318, 896

United States v. General Elec. Co., 80 F. Supp. 989 (S.D.N.Y. 1948), 806, 896

United States v. General Elec. Co., 82 F. Supp. 753 (D.N.J. 1949), 102, 803, 805, 806, 823, 842, 857, 896

United States v. General Elec. Co., 115 F. Supp. 835 (D.N.J. 1953), 853

United States v. General Elec. Co., 1962 Trade Cas. (CCH) ¶¶ 70,342, 70,428, 70,546 (S.D.N.Y. 1962), 891

United States v. General Elec. Co., 209 F. Supp. 197 (E.D. Pa. 1962), 645

United States v. General Elec. Co., 358 F. Supp. 731 (S.D.N.Y. 1973), 102

United States v. General Elec. Co., 1974-1 Trade Cas. (CCH) ¶ 74,952 (S.D.N.Y. 1974), 102

United States v. General Elec. Co., 1977-2 Trade Cas. (CCH) ¶¶ 61,660-61 (E.D. Pa. 1977), 73

United States v. General Elec. Co., 272 U.S. 476 (1926), 102, 821

United States v. General Instrument Corp., 1953 Trade Cas. (CCH) ¶ 67,574 (D.N.J. 1953), 853

United States v. General Mills Fun Group, [1979-1983 Transfer Binder] TRADE REG. REP. (CCH) ¶ 21,641 (D. Minn. May 23, 1979), 498

United States v. General Motors, 1965 Trade Cas. (CCH) ¶ 71,624 (E.D. Mich. 1965), 852

United States v. General Motors Corp., Crim. No. 47,140 (E.D. Mich., Feb. 14, 1973), 589

United States v. General Motors Corp., 1974-2 Trade Cas. (CCH) ¶ 75,253 (E.D. Mich. 1974), 74, 600

United States v. General Motors Corp., 384 U.S. 127 (1966), 3, 11, 61, 62, 78, 80

United States v. General Shoe Corp., 1956 Trade Cas. (CCH) ¶ 68,271 (M.D. Tenn. 1956), 349

United States v. Georgia Telco Credit Union, No. C-80-117A (N.D. Ga. July 18, 1980), 537

United States v. Georgia Waste Sys., 731 F.2d 1580 (11th Cir. 1984), 592, 593

United States v. Germann, 370 F.2d 1019 (2d Cir. 1967), 562, 880

United States v. G. Heileman Brewing Co., 345 F. Supp. 117 (E.D. Mich. 1972), 314, 315, 355

United States v. Ghidoni, 732 F.2d 814 (11th Cir.), cert. denied, 469 U.S. 932 (1984), 889

United States v. Gibson, Dkt. No. 89-CR-747 (N.D. Ohio Apr. 9, 1990), 66

United States v. Gillen, 599 F.2d 541 (3d Cir.), cert. denied, 444 U.S. 866 (1979), 555

United States v. Gillette Co., 406 F. Supp. 713 (D. Mass. 1975), 573

United States v. Gimbel Bros., 202 F. Supp. 779 (E.D. Wis. 1962), 290

United States v. Glaxo Group, 302 F. Supp. 1 (D.D.C. 1969), rev'd, 410 U.S. 52 (1973), 121, 829

United States v. Glaxo Group, 410 U.S. 52 (1973), 837, 852

United States v. Gonzalez, 804 F.2d 691 (11th Cir. 1986), 584, 585

United States v. Goodman, 850 F.2d 1473 (11th Cir. 1988), 34, 40

United States v. Gravely, 840 F.2d 1156 (4th Cir. 1988), 22, 554, 592

United States v. Greater Buffalo Press, Inc., 402 U.S. 549 (1971), 314, 315, 359, 360

United States v. Greyhound Corp., 1957 Trade Cas. (CCH) ¶ 68, 756 (N.D. Ill. 1957), 853

United States v. Greyhound Corp., 508 F.2d 529 (7th Cir. 1974), 574

United States v. Griffith, 334 U.S. 100 (1948), 18, 195, 196, 217, 220, 251, 845

United States v. Grinnell Corp., 30 F.R.D. 358 (D.R.I. 1962), 550, 746, 747

United States v. Grinnell Corp., 305 F. Supp. 285 (S.D.N.Y. 1969), 683, 775

United States v. Grinnell Corp., 384 U.S. 563 (1966), 195, 196, 198, 204, 207, 209, 211, 213,
  219, 220, 275, 290, 749, 750

United States v. GTE Corp., 1985-1 Trade Cas. (CCH) ¶ 66,355 (D.D.C. 1984), 1046

United States v. GTE Corp., 603 F. Supp. 730 (D.D.C. 1984), 570

United States v. Haim, 218 F. Supp. 922 (S.D.N.Y. 1963), 562

United States v. Hammermill Paper Co., 429 F. Supp. 1271 (W.D. Pa. 1977)295, 296, 332

United States v. Hart, 457 F.2d 1087 (10th Cir.), cert. denied, 409 U.S. 861 (1972), 580

United States v. Healthco, Inc., 387 F. Supp. 258 (S.D.N.Y.), aff'd mem., 535 F.2d 1243 (2d Cir.
  1975), 308

United States v. Hemphill, 544 F.2d 341 (8th Cir. 1976), cert. denied, 430 U.S. 967 (1977), 598

United States v. Henderson, 693 F.2d 1028 (11th Cir. 1982), 4

United States v. Hertz Corp., 1981-1 Trade Cas. (CCH) ¶ 64,023 (S.D. Fla. 1981), 526, 529, 539

United States v. Hilton Hotels Corp., 467 F.2d 1000 (9th Cir. 1972), cert. denied, 409 U.S. 1125
  (1973), 81, 595

United States v. H. M. Prince Textiles, Inc., 262 F. Supp. 383 (S.D.N.Y. 1966), 496

United States v. Holloway, 778 F.2d 653 (11th Cir. 1985), cert. denied, 476 U.S. 1158 (1986),
  566

United States v. Holophane Co., 119 F. Supp. 114 (S.D. Ohio), 1954 Trade Cas. (CCH)
  ¶ 67,679 (S.D. Ohio 1954), aff'd per curiam, 352 U.S. 903 (1956), 839, 891, 896

United States v. Home Diathermy Co., 1960 Trade Cas. (CCH) ¶ 69,601 (S.D.N.Y. 1959), 497

United States v. Horvath, 731 F.2d 557 (8th Cir. 1984), 764

United States v. Hospital Affiliates Int'l, Inc., 1980-81 Trade Cas. (CCH) ¶ 63,721 (E.D. La.
  1980), 300, 357

United States v. Household Fin. Corp., 602 F.2d 1255 (7th Cir. 1979), cert. denied, 444 U.S.
  1044 (1980), 289

United States v. Household Goods Movers Investigation, 184 F. Supp. 689 (D.D.C. 1960), 563

United States v. Hsieh Hui Mei Chen, 754 F.2d 817 (9th Cir.), cert. denied, 471 U.S. 1139
  (1985), 585

United States v. Huck Manufacturing Co., 382 U.S. 197 (1965), 821

United States v. Hughes Tool Co., 1987-2 Trade Cas. (CCH) ¶ 67,698 (D.D.C. 1987), 344, 570

United States v. Hughes Tool Co., 415 F. Supp. 637 (C.D. Cal. 1976), 290, 323, 329

United States v. Hunterdon County Trust Co., 1962 Trade Cas. (CCH) ¶ 70,623 (D.N.J. 1962),
  1089

United States v. Hutcheson 312 U.S. 219 (1941), 1120

United States v. IBM, 1956 Trade Cas. (CCH) ¶ 68,245 (S.D.N.Y. 1956), 852

United States v. IBM, 62 F.R.D. 507 (S.D.N.Y. 1974), 766

United States v. IBM, 62 F.R.D. 526 (S.D.N.Y. 1974), 766

United States v. IBM, 66 F.R.D. 180 (S.D.N.Y. 1974), 747, 750, 751

United States v. IBM, 1975-1 Trade Cas. (CCH) ¶ 60,104 (S.D.N.Y. 1975), 256

United States v. IBM, 687 F.2d 591 (2d Cir. 1982), 574

United States v. ICC, 396 U.S. 491 (1970), 1141

United States v. Illinois Podiatry Soc'y, 1977-2 Trade Cas. (CCH) ¶ 61,767 (N.D. Ill. 1977), 573

United States v. Imperial Chem. Indus., 1956 Trade Cas. (CCH) ¶ 68,435 (S.D.N.Y. 1956), 852

United States v. Imperial Chem. Indus., 1957 Trade Cas. (CCH) ¶ 68,859 (S.D.N.Y. 1957), 577

United States v. Imperial Chem. Indus., 100 F. Supp. 504 (S.D.N.Y. 1951), *supplemental opinion on remedies*, 105 F. Supp. 215 (S.D.N.Y. 1952), 384, 839, 842, 850, 873, 889, 890, 891, 892

United States v. Imperial Chem. Indus., 105 F. Supp. 215 (S.D.N.Y. 1952), 852, 853

United States v. Imperial Chem. Indus., 254 F. Supp. 685 (S.D.N.Y. 1966), 853

United States v. Inco, Ltd., 1978-1 Trade Cas. (CCH) ¶ 61,869 (E.D. Pa. 1978), 891

United States v. Industrial Asphalt, 1987-2 Trade Cas. (CCH) ¶ 67,826 (C.D. Cal. 1987), 345, 346

United States v. Ingersoll-Rand Co., 218 F. Supp. 530 (W.D. Pa.), *aff'd*, 320 F.2d 509 (3d Cir. 1963), 167, 336

United States v. Ingersoll-Rand Co., 320 F.2d 509 (3d Cir. 1963), 336, 353

United States v. International Boxing Club, 178 F. Supp. 469 (S.D.N.Y. 1959), 576, 577

United States v. International Boxing Club, 220 F. Supp. 425 (S.D.N.Y. 1963), 577

United States v. International Harvester Co., 564 F.2d 769 (7th Cir. 1977), 317

United States v. International Harvester Co., 274 U.S. 693 (1927), 577

United States v. International Paper Co., Crim. No. H-78-11 (S.D. Tex. 1978), 594, 597

United States v. Interstate Dress Carriers, 280 F.2d 52 (2d Cir. 1960), 758

United States v. Iowa Beef Processors, Inc., 1974 Trade Cas. (CCH) ¶ 75,014 (N.D. Iowa), *aff'd*, 419 U.S. 806 (1974), 576, 577

United States v. ITT, 306 F. Supp. 766 (D. Conn. 1969), *appeal dismissed*, 404 U.S. 801 (1971), 167, 333

United States v. ITT, 1971 Trade Cas. (CCH) ¶ 73,619 (N.D. Ill. 1971), 332, 336

United States v. ITT Continental Baking Co., 485 F.2d 16, (10th Cir. 1975), *rev'd on other grounds*, 420 U.S. 223 (1975), 280

United States v. ITT Continental Baking Co., 420 U.S. 223 (1975), 575

United States v. Ivaco, Inc., 704 F. Supp. 1409 (W.D. Mich. 1989), 283, 285, 288, 290, 302, 305, 308, 313, 317, 318, 319, 320, 353, 376, 377, 387

United States v. James, 576 F.2d 1121 (5th Cir. 1978), *cert. denied*, 442 U.S. 917 (1979), 594

United States v. Jantzen, Inc., 1966 Trade Cas. (CCH) ¶ 71,887 (D. Or. 1966), 69

United States v. Jas. H. Matthews & Co., 1989-1 Trade Cas. (CCH) ¶ 68,441 (W.D. Pa. 1989), 217

United States v. J.B. Williams Co., 498 F.2d 414 (2d Cir. 1974), 496

United States v. J.I. Case Co., 101 F. Supp. 856 (D. Minn. 1951), 164, 165, 166

United States v. Jerrold Elecs. Corp., 187 F. Supp. 545 (E.D. Pa. 1960), *aff'd per curiam*, 365 U.S. 567 (1961), 133, 136, 137, 138, 160

United States v. J.L. Hammet Co., 1964 Trade Cas. (CCH) ¶ 71,178 (E.D. Pa. 1964), 64, 1109

United States v. J.M. Huber Corp., 179 F. Supp. 570 (S.D.N.Y. 1959), 588

United States v. John Doe, Inc. I, 481 U.S. 102 (1987), 600, 754, 755, 756, 758

United States v. John Scher Presents, Inc. 746 F.2d 959 (3d Cir. 1984), 597

United States v. Johns Manville Corp., 259 F. Supp. 440 (E.D. Pa. 1966), 1010

United States v. Joint-Traffic Ass'n, 171 U.S. 505 (1898), 63

United States v. Jones, 590 F. Supp. 233 (N.D. Ga. 1984), 591

United States v. Jones, 839 F.2d 1041 (5th Cir.), *cert. denied*, 486 U.S. 1024 (1988), 584, 585

United States v. Jordan, 870 F.2d 1310 (7th Cir.), *cert. denied*, 110 S. Ct. 101 (1989), 581

United States v. Jos. Schlitz Brewing Co., 253 F. Supp. 129 (N.D. Cal.), *aff'd*, 385 U.S. 37 (1966), 285, 308, 359, 865

United States v. JS&A Group, 716 F.2d 451 (7th Cir. 1983), 525, 526, 529

United States v. Kahan & Lessin Co., 695 F.2d 1122 (9th Cir. 1982), 566

United States v. Kahaner, 204 F. Supp. 921 (S.D.N.Y. 1962), 567

United States v. Karns, 1963 Trade Cas. (CCH) ¶ 70,950 (S.D.N.Y. 1963), 496

United States v. Kelly, 464 F.2d 709 (5th Cir. 1972), 591

United States v. Kempler Indus., Cr. No. 89-644 (N.D. Ill. July 24, 1989), 391

United States v. Kennecott Copper Corp., 231 F. Supp. 95 (S.D.N.Y. 1964), *aff'd*, 381 U.S. 414 (1965), 320

United States v. Kennecott Copper Corp., 249 F. Supp. 154 (S.D.N.Y. 1965), 351

United States v. Kerasotes Ill. Theatres, 650 F. Supp. 963 (C.D. Ill. 1987), 555

United States v. Kimberly-Clark Corp., 264 F. Supp. 439 (N.D. Cal. 1967), 294, 296, 330

United States v. Koppers Co., Crim. No. 79-85 (D. Conn. 1980), 594

United States v. Koppers Co., 652 F.2d 290 (2d Cir.), *cert. denied*, 454 U.S. 1083 (1981), 63, 76, 128, 1108, 1109

United States v. Korfant, 771 F.2d 660 (2d Cir. 1985), 586

United States v. Kouba, 632 F. Supp. 937 (D.N.D. 1986), 565

United States v. Krasnov, 143 F. Supp. 184 (E.D. Pa. 1956), *aff'd per curiam*, 355 U.S. 5 (1957), 835, 838

United States v. Kurzer, 422 F. Supp. 487 (S.D.N.Y. 1976), 591

United States v. Kurzer, 534 F.2d 511 (2d Cir. 1976), 591

United States v. Landmark Fin. Servs., No. N-84-3510 (D. Md. Dec. 10, 1986), 537

United States v. Lara-Hernandez, 588 F.2d 272 (9th Cir. 1978), 598

United States v. Leggett & Platt, Inc., 1979-1 Trade Cas. (CCH) ¶ 62,453 (C.D. Ohio 1978), 345

United States v. Leverage Funding Sys., 637 F.2d 645 (9th Cir. 1980), *cert. denied*, 452 U.S. 961 (1981), 585

United States v. Lever Bros., 216 F. Supp. 887 (S.D.N.Y. 1963), 279, 285, 316, 804

United States v. Libbey-Owens-Ford Glass Co., 1973-2 Trade Cas. (CCH) ¶ 74,794 (N.D. Ohio 1973), 576

United States v. Line Material Co., 333 U.S. 287 (1948), 821, 838

United States v. Loew's, Inc., 1952-53 Trade Cas. (CCH) ¶ 67,228 (S.D.N.Y. 1952), 571

United States v. Loew's Inc., 1972 Trade Cas. (CCH) ¶ 74,017 (S.D.N.Y. 1972), 138

United States v. Loew's, Inc., 1980-81 Trade Cas. (CCH) ¶ 63,662 (S.D.N.Y. 1980), 577

United States v. Loew's, Inc., 882 F.2d 29 (2d Cir. 1989), 332

United States v. Loew's Inc., 371 U.S. 38 (1962), 131, 133, 138, 143, 144, 146, 149, 157, 801, 831, 834, 838

United States v. London, 424 F. Supp. 556 (D. Md. 1976), *aff'd*, 556 F.2d 709 (4th Cir. 1977), *cert. denied*, 436 U.S. 930 (1978), 598

United States v. Long Island Fence Ass'n, 1959 Trade Cas. (CCH) ¶ 69,414 (E.D.N.Y. 1959), 588

United States v. Lonrho, PLC, 1988-2 Trade Cas. (CCH) ¶ 68,232 (D.D.C. 1988), 570

United States v. Lousiana-Pacific Corp., 1990-1 Trade Cas. (CCH) ¶ 69,077 (D. Or. 1990), 515

United States v. Louisiana-Pacific Corp., 554 F. Supp. 504 (D. Or. 1982), *rev'd in part and vacated in part*, 754 F.2d 1445 (9th Cir. 1985), *on remand*, 654 F. Supp. 962 (D. Or. 1987), *appeal dismissed*, 846 F.2d 43 (9th Cir. 1988) 348, 496

United States v. Louisiana-Pacific Corp., 754 F.2d 1445 (9th Cir. 1985) *remanded*, 654 F. Supp. 962 (D. Or. 1987), *appeal dismissed*, 846 F.2d 43 (9th Cir. 1988), 351, 515

United States v. Love, 6 TRADE REG. REP. (CCH) ¶ 45,090 (Case No. 3703) (N.D. Fla. 1990), 596

United States v. Lowenstein & Sons, 1970 Trade Cas. (CCH) ¶ 73,251 (S.D.N.Y. 1970), 107

United States v. LTV Corp., 1984-2 Trade Cas. (CCH) ¶ 66,133 (D.D.C.), *appeal dismissed*, 746 F.2d 51 (D.C. Cir. 1984), 296, 301, 317, 321, 345, 346, 348, 350

United States v. LTV Corp., 746 F.2d 51 (D.C. Cir. 1984), 578

United States v. Lucky Lager Brewing Co., 209 F. Supp. 665 (D. Utah 1962), 576, 577

United States v. Mahar, 550 F.2d 1005 (5th Cir. 1977), 602

United States v. Maine Lobstermen's Ass'n, 160 F. Supp. 115 (D. Me. 1957), 585

United States v. Mandel, 415 F. Supp. 1033 (D. Md. 1976), 565, 567

United States v. Mandujano, 425 U.S. 564 (1976), 564, 566

United States v. Manufacturers Hanover Trust Co., 240 F. Supp. 867 (S.D.N.Y. 1965), 285, 320

United States v. Mapco Gas Prod., 709 F. Supp. 895 (E.D. Ark. 1989), 582, 583

United States v. Marine Bancorporation, 418 U.S. 602 (1974), 293, 294, 295, 296, 297, 322, 323, 324, 325, 326, 327, 328, 329

United States v. Markham, 537 F.2d 187 (5th Cir. 1976), *cert. denied*, 429 U.S. 1041 (1977), 807, 837

United States v. Martin Linen Supply Co., 430 U.S. 564 (1977), 599, 600

United States v. Martin Marietta Corp., 1980-81 Trade Cas. (CCH) ¶ 63,109 (N.D. Ill. 1979), 345

United States v. Martin Marietta Corp., 1980-81 Trade Cas. (CCH) ¶ 63,673 (N.D. Ill. 1980), 344

United States v. Martino, 825 F.2d 754 (3d Cir. 1987), 567

United States v. Maryland & Va. Milk Producers Ass'n, 90 F. Supp. 681 (D.D.C. 1950), *rev'd*, 193 F.2d 907 (D.C. Cir. 1951), 1025

United States v. Maryland & Va. Milk Producers Ass'n, 167 F. Supp. 799 (D.D.C. 1958), *aff'd in part, rev'd and remanded in part*, 362 U.S. 458 (1960), 314

United States v. Masonite Corp., 316 U.S. 265 (1942), 822

United States v. Mazurie, 419 U.S. 544 (1975), 628

United States v. McCarraher, Cr. No. 87-4 (E.D. Pa. Jan. 7, 1987), 390

United States v. McDaniel, 482 F.2d 305 (8th Cir. 1973), 591

United States v. McDonough Co., 1959 Trade Cas. (CCH) ¶ 69,482 (D. Ohio 1959), 596

United States v. McKesson & Robbins, Inc., 351 U.S. 305 (1956), 128, 1017

United States v. McPartlin, 595 F.2d 1321 (7th Cir.), *cert. denied*, 444 U.S. 833 (1979), 565

United States v. Mechanik, 475 U.S. 66 (1986), 567

United States v. Melvin, 650 F.2d 641 (5th Cir. 1981), 565

United States v. Memphis Retail Appliance Dealers Ass'n, 1957 Trade Cas. (CCH) ¶ 68,704 (W.D. Tenn. 1957), 64

United States v. Mercedes-Benz of N. Am., Inc., 517 F. Supp. 1369 (N.D. Cal. 1981), 152, 153, 155, 156, 157, 160

United States v. Mercedes-Benz of N. Am., 547 F. Supp. 399 (N.D. Cal. 1982), 574

United States v. Merck & Co., 1980-81 Trade Cas. (CCH) ¶ 63,682 (S. D. Cal. 1980), 344

United States v. Michaelson, 552 F.2d 472 (2d Cir. 1977), 582

United States v. Mid-America Dairymen, Inc., 1977-1 Trade Cas. (CCH) ¶ 61,508 (W.D. Mo. 1977), 573

United States v. Middlebrooks, 618 F.2d 273 (5th Cir. 1980), 4

United States v. Miller, 771 F.2d 1219 (9th Cir. 1985), 554, 583, 585, 590

United States v. Miller, 871 F.2d 488 (4th Cir. 1989), 595

United States v. Minnesota Mining & Mfg. Co., 1950-51 Trade Cas. (CCH) ¶ 62,724 (D. Mass. 1950), 853

United States v. Minnesota Mining & Mfg. Co., 92 F. Supp. 947 (D. Mass. 1950), 384, 914, 915

United States v. Missouri Valley Constr. Co., 741 F.2d 1542 (8th Cir. 1984), 597

United States v. MMR Corp. (LA), 907 F.2d 489 (5th Cir. 1990), *cert. denied*, 111 S. Ct. 1388 (1991), 63, 66

United States v. Mobile Materials, Inc., 871 F.2d 902 (10th Cir.), *cert. denied*, 493 U.S. 1043 (1989), 583, 586, 588, 596

United States v. Mobile Materials, Inc., 881 F.2d 866 (10th Cir. 1989), 593, 594, 598

United States v. Molbe Shoes, Inc., [1983-1987 Transfer Binder] TRADE REG. REP. (CCH) ¶ 22,439 (S.D.N.Y. 1987), 479

United States v. Moore, 822 F.2d 35 (8th Cir. 1987), 582

United States v. Morgan Drive Away, Inc., 1974-1 Trade Cas. (CCH) ¶ 74,888 (D.D.C. 1974), 1129

United States v. Morton Salt Co., 235 F.2d 573 (10th Cir. 1956), 7

United States v. Morton Salt Co., 338 U.S. 632 (1950), 505, 506

United States v. Motor Vehicle Mfrs. Ass'n, 1981-2 Trade Cas. (CCH) ¶ 64,370 (C.D. Cal. 1981), 574, 578, 579

United States v. Motor Vehicle Mfrs. Ass'n, 643 F.2d 644 (9th Cir. 1981), 575, 576

United States v. M.P.M., Inc., 397 F. Supp. 78 (D. Colo. 1975), 295, 296, 307, 308, 313, 315, 317

United States v. Mrs. Smith's Pie Co., 440 F. Supp. 220 (E.D. Pa. 1976), 209, 211, 283, 285, 286

United States v. National Ass'n of Broadcasters, 1982-83 Trade Cas. (CCH) ¶¶ 65,049-50 (D.D.C. 1982), 1034

United States v. National Ass'n of Broadcasters, 536 F. Supp. 149 (D.D.C. 1982), 40, 47, 48, 69, 1034

United States v. National Ass'n of Sec. Dealers, 422 U.S. 694 (1975), 1102, 1103, 1104

United States v. National Bank & Trust Co., 1984-2 Trade Cas. (CCH) ¶ 66,074 (N.D.N.Y. 1984), 344, 1093, 1096

United States v. National Dairy Prods. Corp., 372 U.S. 29 (1963), 451, 628

United States v. National Fin. Adjusters, Inc., 1985-2 Trade Cas. (CCH) ¶ 66,856 (E.D. Mich. 1985), 577

United States v. National Lead Co., 63 F. Supp. 513 (S.D.N.Y. 1945), aff'd, 332 U.S. 319 (1947), 384, 805, 828, 838, 842, 896

United States v. National Lead Co., 332 U.S. 319 (1947), 75, 805, 844, 853, 890, 891

United States v. National Malleable Steel Casting Co., 1957 Trade Cas. (CCH) ¶ 68,890 (N.D. Ohio 1957), aff'd per curiam, 358 U.S. 38 (1958), 88

United States v. National Medical Enters., 1987-1 Trade Cas. (CCH) ¶ 67,640 (E.D. Cal. 1987), 349

United States v. National Peanut Cleaners & Shellers Ass'n, 1932-39 Trade Cas. (CCH) ¶ 55,220 (E.D. Va. 1939), 577

United States v. National Trailer Rental Sys., 156 F. Supp. 800 (D. Kan.), aff'd per curiam, 355 U.S. 10 (1957), 69

United States v. National Siding Corp., [1979-1983 Transfer Binder] TRADE REG. REP. (CCH) ¶ 21,704 (N.D. Ala. Dec. 4, 1979), 498

United States v. Navajo Freight Lines, 339 F. Supp. 554 (D. Colo. 1971), 1131

United States v. NBC, 1974 Trade Cas. (CCH) ¶ 74,885 (C.D. Cal. 1974), 1021, 1023, 1030, 1040

United States v. NBC, Civ. No. 74-3601-RJK (C.D. Cal. June 20, 1977), aff'd without published opinion, 603 F.2d 227 (9th Cir.), cert. denied, 444 U.S. 991 (1979), 574

United States v. NBC, 449 F. Supp. 1127 (C.D. Cal. 1978), 571, 573, 574, 578, 1040

United States v. NBC, 1986-1 Trade Cas. (CCH) ¶ 66,956 (C.D. Cal. 1984), 1040

United States v. NBC, 603 F.2d 227 (9th Cir.), cert. denied, 444 U.S. 991 (1979), 578

United States v. New Wrinkle, Inc., 342 U.S. 371 (1952), 822

United States v. Newmont Mining Corp., 34 F.R.D. 504 (S.D.N.Y. 1964), 680

United States v. New York Coffee & Sugar Exchange, 1979-1 Trade Cas. (CCH) ¶ 62,665 (S.D.N.Y. 1979), 1106

United States v. New York Great Atl. & Pac. Tea Co., 1985-1 Trade Cas. ¶ 66,546 (S.D.N.Y. 1985), 577

United States v. Nissan Motor Corp., 1973-1 Trade Cas. (CCH) ¶ 74,333 (N.D. Cal. 1973), 113

United States v. Nixon, 418 U.S. 683 (1974), 589

United States v. Nobles, 422 U.S. 225 (1975), 763

United States v. Noriega, 746 F. Supp. 1506 (S.D. Fla. 1990), 906

United States v. Norman M. Morris Corp., 1976-1 Trade Cas. ¶ 60,894, (S.D.N.Y. 1976), decree terminated by consent, 1983-1 Trade Cas. ¶ 65,442 (S.D.N.Y. 1981), 890

United States v. Norris, 281 U.S. 619 (1930), 580

United States v. North Am. Salt Co., 1990-2 Trade Cas. (CCH) ¶ 69,143 (N.D. Ill. 1990), 345

United States v. North Dakota Hosp. Ass'n, 640 F. Supp. 1028 (D.N.D. 1986), 23, 24, 25, 43, 65, 66, 94, 1010

United States v. Northern Cal. Pharmaceutical Ass'n, 235 F. Supp. 378 (N.D. Cal. 1964), 577

United States v. Northwest Indus., 301 F. Supp. 1066 (N.D. Ill. 1969), 333, 355

United States v. Northwestern Nat'l Bank, 1964 Trade Cas. (CCH) ¶ 71,022 (D. Minn. 1964), 1089

United States v. Nu-Phonics, Inc., 433 F. Supp. 1006 (E.D. Mich. 1977), 34

United States v. NV Nederlandsche Combinatie Voor Chemische Industrie, 1970 Trade Cas. (CCH) ¶ 73,181 (S.D.N.Y. 1970), 574

United States v. Olympia Provision & Baking Co., 282 F. Supp. 819 (S.D.N.Y. 1968), *aff'd per curiam*, 393 U.S. 480 (1969), 70

United States v. Omni Int'l Corp., 634 F. Supp. 1414 (D. Md. 1986), 568

United States v. O.M. Scott & Sons, 303 F. Supp. 141 (D.D.C. 1969), 107, 108

United States v. Oregon State Bar, 385 F. Supp. 507 (D. Or. 1974), 556

United States v. Oregon State Medical Soc'y, 343 U.S. 326 (1952), 679, 680

United States v. Otter Tail Power Co., 360 F. Supp. 451 (D. Minn. 1973), *aff'd*, 417 U.S. 901 (1974), 1003

United States v. Otter Tail Power Co., 410 U.S. 366 (1973), 246

United States v. Owens-Corning Fiberglass Corp., 178 F. Supp. 325 (N.D. Ohio 1959), 577

United States v. Owens-Corning Fiberglass Corp., 1978-2 Trade Cas. (CCH) ¶ 62,534 (N.D. Ohio 1978), 577

United States v. Owens-Illinois Glass Co., 1963 Trade Cas. (CCH) ¶ 70,808 (N.D. Ohio 1963), 348

United States v. Pabst Brewing Co., 183 F. Supp. 220 (E.D. Wis. 1960), 360

United States v. Pabst Brewing Co., 296 F. Supp. 994 (E.D. Wis. 1969), 315, 316

United States v. Pabst Brewing Co., 384 U.S. 546 (1966), 209, 293, 294, 295, 296, 297, 300, 303

United States v. Pacific & Arctic Ry. & Navigation Co., 228 U.S. 87 (1913), 856

United States v. Pacific Dunlop Holdings, Inc., 1990-1 Trade Cas. (CCH) ¶ 69,087 (E.D. Pa. 1989), 570

United States v. Pacific Telesis Group, 7 TRADE REG. REP. (CCH) ¶ 50,701 (C.D. Cal. Feb. 28, 1986), 570

United States v. Pan Am. World Airways, 193 F. Supp. 18, 36 (S.D.N.Y. 1961), *rev'd*, 371 U.S. 296 (1963), 372

United States v. Papercraft Corp., 540 F.2d 131 (3d Cir. 1976), 496, 497

United States v. Pappadio, 346 F.2d 5 (2d Cir. 1965), *vacated*, 384 U.S. 364 (1966), 566

United States v. Paramount Pictures, 1948-49 Trade Cas. (CCH) ¶ 62,377 (S.D.N.Y. 1949), 571

United States v. Paramount Pictures, 333 F. Supp. 1100 (S.D.N.Y. 1971), 578, 579

United States v. Paramount Pictures, 334 U.S. 131 (1948), 196, 205, 213, 217, 220, 251, 271, 569, 834, 845, 852

United States v. Parelius, 83 F. Supp. 617 (D. Haw. 1949), 598

United States v. Parke, Davis & Co., 362 U.S. 29 (1960), 11, 101, 107, 108

United States v. Parker-Rust-Proof Co., 61 F. Supp. 805 (E.D. Mich. 1945), 823

United States v. Patten, 226 U.S. 525 (1913), 1107

United States v. Paul B. Elder Co., 1974-2 Trade Cas. (CCH) ¶ 75,238 (D. Del. 1974), 509

United States v. Paxson, 861 F.2d 730 (D.C. Cir. 1988), 760

United States v. P.C. Network, Inc., [1983-1987 Transfer Binder] TRADE REG. REP. (CCH) ¶ 22,438 (N.D. Ill. Mar. 20, 1987), 479

United States v. Penick & Ford, Ltd., 242 F. Supp. 518 (D.N.J. 1965), 336

United States v. Penn-Olin Chem. Co., 217 F. Supp. 110 (D. Del. 1963), 377

United States v. Penn-Olin Chem. Co., 246 F. Supp. 917 (D. Del. 1965), *aff'd per curiam*, 389 U.S. 308 (1967), 327, 378

United States v. Penn-Olin Chem. Co., 378 U.S. 158 (1964), 275, 276, 280, 297, 324, 328, 372, 373, 376, 377, 378

United States v. Pennsalt Chems. Corp., 1967 Trade Cas. (CCH) ¶ 71,982 (E.D. Pa. 1967), 571

United States v. Pennsylvania Refuse Removal Ass'n, 242 F. Supp. 794 (E.D. Pa. 1965), *aff'd*, 357 F.2d 806 (3d Cir.), *cert. denied*, 384 U.S. 961 (1966), 68

United States v. Pennsylvania Refuse Removal Ass'n, 357 F.2d 806 (3d Cir.), *cert. denied*, 384 U.S. 961 (1966), 76

United States v. Pennzoil Co., 252 F. Supp. 962 (W.D. Pa. 1965), 285, 286

United States v. Pepe, 367 F. Supp. 1365 (D. Conn. 1973), 564

United States v. Pepsi-Cola Bottling Co. of Walla Walla, 1991-1 Trade Cas. (CCH) ¶ 69,394 (9th Cir. 1991), 596

United States v. Perez, 823 F.2d 854 (5th Cir. 1987), 594

United States v. Pfizer, 246 F. Supp. 464 (E.D.N.Y. 1965), 177

United States v. Phelps Dodge Indus., 589 F. Supp. 1340 (S.D.N.Y. 1984), 64

United States v. Philadelphia Nat'l Bank, 374 U.S. 321 (1963), 276, 289, 290, 294, 296, 300, 304, 314, 319, 748, 1018, 1089, 1091

United States v. Philco Corp., 1956 Trade Cas. (CCH) ¶ 68,409 (E.D. Pa. 1956), 130

United States v. Phillipsburg Nat'l Bank & Trust Co., 399 U.S. 350 (1970), 289, 394, 296, 300, 1092

United States v. Phillips Petroleum Co., 367 F. Supp. 1226 (C.D. Cal. 1973), *aff'd mem.*, 418 U.S. 906 (1974), 315, 316, 322, 326, 327, 328, 329, 351, 360

United States v. Pitney-Bowes, Inc., 1959 Trade Cas. (CCH) ¶ 69,235 (D. Conn. 1959), 852

United States v. Pittsburgh Area Pontiac Dealers, Inc., 1978-2 Trade Cas. (CCH) ¶ 62,233 (W.D. Pa. 1978), 64

United States v. Plitt S. Theatres, 1987-2 Trade Cas. (CCH) ¶ 67,681 (W.D.N.C. 1987), 555

United States v. Plitt S. Theatres, 671 F. Supp. 1095 (W.D.N.C. 1987), 555

United States v. Pogue, 865 F.2d 226 (10th Cir. 1989), 581

United States v. Portac, Inc., 869 F.2d 1288 (9th Cir. 1989), 584, 595

United States v. Porter, 764 F.2d 1 (1st Cir. 1985), *cert. denied*, 481 U.S. 1048 (1987), 584

United States v. Portsmouth Paving Corp., 694 F.2d 312 (4th Cir. 1982), 34, 63

United States v. Potamkin Cadillac Corp., 689 F.2d 379 (2d Cir. 1982), 509

United States v. Powell, 379 U.S. 48 (1964), 506

United States v. Prescon Corp., 695 F.2d 1236 (10th Cir. 1982), 597

United States v. Price Bros. Co., 721 F. Supp. 869 (E.D. Mich. 1989), 547

United States v. Prince, 1976-2 Trade Cas. (CCH) ¶ 61,038 (5th Cir. 1976), 582

United States v. Procter & Gamble Co., 187 F. Supp. 55 (D.N.J. 1960), 567

United States v. Procter & Gamble Co., 356 U.S. 677 (1958), 565, 755, 757

United States v. Provident Nat'l Bank, 280 F. Supp. 1 (E.D. Pa. 1968), 1092

United States v. Pruim, 6 TRADE REG. REP. (CCH) ¶ 45,089 (Case No. 3669) (D. Ill. 1990), 596

United States v. Purolator Sec., Inc., Crim. No. 78-80367 (E.D. Mich. 1978), 582

United States v. Quality Cars Inc., 5 TRADE REG. REP. (CCH) ¶ 22,460 (N.D. Tex. July 22, 1987), 478

United States v. Ramsey, 785 F.2d 184 (7th Cir.), *cert. denied*, 476 U.S. 1186 (1986), 564

United States v. Rath, 406 F.2d 757 (6th Cir.), *cert. denied*, 394 U.S. 920 (1969), 567

United States v. RCA, 46 F. Supp. 654 (D. Del. 1942), 577

United States v. RCA, 1958 Trade Cas. (CCH) ¶ 69,164 (S.D.N.Y. 1958), 852

United States v. RCA, 358 U.S. 334 (1959), 964, 1029, 1030, 1050

United States v. R. Hoe & Co., 1955 Trade Cas. ¶ 68,215, (S.D.N.Y. 1955), 890

United States v. R.J. Reynolds Tobacco Co., 268 F. Supp. 769 (D.N.J. 1966), 750, 751

United States v. Reader's Digest Ass'n, 464 F. Supp. 1037 (D. Del. 1979), *aff'd*, 662 F.2d 955 (3d Cir. 1981), *cert. denied*, 455 U.S. 908 (1982), 496

United States v. Reader's Digest Ass'n, 662 F.2d 955 (3d Cir. 1981), *cert. denied*, 455 U.S. 908 (1982), 493, 494

United States v. Realty Multi-List, Inc., 629 F.2d 1351 (5th Cir. 1980), 33, 38, 39, 45, 46, 52, 79, 87, 88, 375, 385

United States v. Reed Roller Bit Co., 274 F. Supp. 573 (W.D. Okla. 1967), 315, 316, 358, 359, 360

United States v. Reliance Group Holdings, Inc., 1990-2 Trade Cas. (CCH) ¶ 69,248 (D.D.C. 1990), 344

United States v. Revlon, Inc., 1975-1 Trade Cas. (CCH) ¶ 60,202, 1975-2 Trade Cas. (CCH) ¶ 60,583 (S.D.N.Y. 1975), 129

United States v. Riccobene, 451 F.2d 586 (3d Cir. 1971), 567

United States v. Rice, 550 F.2d 1364 (5th Cir.), *cert. denied*, 434 U.S. 954 (1977), 584

United States v. Rice Growers Ass'n, 1986-2 Trade Cas. (CCH) ¶ 67,288 (E.D. Cal. 1986), 292, 294, 295, 296, 317, 319

United States v. RMI Co., 467 F. Supp. 915 (W.D. Pa. 1979), 568, 602

United States v. Robertshaw-Fulton Controls Co., 1957 Trade Cas. (CCH) ¶ 68,592 (W.D. Pa. 1957), 349

United States v. Rocco, 587 F.2d 144 (3rd Cir. 1978), *cert. denied*, 440 U.S. 972 (1979), 592

United States v. Rockford Memorial Corp., 717 F. Supp. 1251 (N.D. Ill. 1989), *aff'd*, 898 F.2d 1278 (7th Cir.), *cert. denied*, 111 S. Ct. 295 (1990), 285, 290, 300, 320

United States v. Rockford Memorial Corp., 898 F.2d 1278 (7th Cir.), *cert denied*, 111 S. Ct. 295 (1990), 276, 279, 456, 1018

United States v. Rock Island Motor Transit Co., 340 U.S. 419 (1951), 1144

United States v. Rock Royal Coop., 307 U.S. 533 (1939), 1025

United States v. Rockwell Int'l Corp., 1978 Trade Cas. (CCH) ¶ 62,402 (E.D. Pa. 1978), 568, 582

United States v. Rockwell Int'l Corp., 1981-1 Trade Cas. (CCH) ¶ 63,875, (W.D. Pa. 1980), 281, 345, 347

United States v. Rohm & Haas Co., 1987-1 Trade Cas. (CCH) ¶ 67,444 (D.D.C. 1987), 344

United States v. Roll Mfrs. Inst., 1955 Trade Cas. (CCH) ¶ 68,110 (W.D. Pa. 1955), 69

United States v. Roscoe Moss Corp., 1988-1 Trade Cas. (CCH) ¶ 68,040 (D.D.C. 1988), 344

United States v. Rosendin Elec., Inc., 122 F.R.D. 219 (N.D. Cal. 1987), 759

United States v. Rosendin Elec., Inc., 1989-2 Trade Cas. (CCH) ¶ 68,809 (N.D. Cal. 1987), *aff'd*, 852 F.2d 1290 (9th Cir. 1988), 619

United States v. Rubbish Removal, Inc., 1985-1 Trade Cas. (CCH) ¶ 66,617 (N.D.N.Y. 1985), 567, 583

United States v. Safety First Prods. Corp., 1972 Trade Cas. (CCH) ¶ 74,223 (S.D.N.Y. 1972), 121

United States v. Saf-T-Boom Corp., 164 U.S.P.Q. (BNA) 283 (E.D. Ark.), *aff'd per curiam*, 431 F.2d 737 (8th Cir. 1970), 807

United States v. Saks & Co., 426 F. Supp. 812 (S.D.N.Y. 1976), 505, 758

United States v. Sargent Elec. Co., 785 F.2d 1123 (3d Cir.), *cert. denied*, 479 U.S. 819 (1986), 63, 586

United States v. Savannah Cotton & Naval Stores Exch., 192 F. Supp. 256 (S.D. Ga. 1960), *aff'd*, 365 U.S. 298 (1961), 577

United States v. Sav-Cote Chem. Labs., 1971 Trade Cas. (CCH) ¶ 73,439 (D.N.J. 1969), 496

United States v. Schine, 260 F.2d 552 (2d Cir. 1958), *cert. denied*, 358 U.S. 934 (1959), 574

United States v. Scophony Corp., 69 F. Supp. 666 (S.D.N.Y. 1946), *rev'd,* 333 U.S. 795 (1949), 867

United States v. Scophony Corp., 333 U.S. 795 (1948), 867, 868, 869, 878

United States v. Scott, 437 U.S. 82, *reh'g denied*, 439 U.S. 883 (1978), 599

United States v. Sealy, Inc., 388 U.S. 350 (1967), 62, 70, 75, 80, 382, 828, 847

United States v. Sears, Roebuck & Co., 111 F. Supp. 614 (S.D.N.Y. 1953), 395

United States v. Security Pac. Fin. Sys. and Sec. Pac. Fin. Corp., No. 83-2647N (S.D. Cal. Dec. 21, 1983), 537

United States v. Sells Eng'g, Inc., 463 U.S. 418 (1983), 567, 754, 755, 757

United States v. Serta Assocs., 296 F. Supp. 1121 (N.D. Ill. 1968), *aff'd mem.*, 393 U.S. 534 (1969), 64, 112

United States v. Serubo, 604 F.2d 807 (3d Cir. 1979), 568

United States v. Service Corp. Int'l, 1991-1 Trade Cas. (CCH) ¶ 69,289 (D.D.C. 1991), 344

United States v. Seville Indus. Mach. Corp., 696 F. Supp. 986 (D.N.J. 1988), 63, 390, 584

United States v. Shandell, 800 F.2d 322 (2d Cir. 1986), 592

United States v. Shapiro, 103 F.2d 775 (2d Cir. 1939), 596

United States v. Shaw-Walker Co., 1962 Trade Cas. (CCH) ¶ 70,491 (W.D.N.Y. 1962), 69

United States v. Siemens Corp., 621 F.2d 499 (2d Cir. 1980), 322, 346, 347, 359

United States v. Simmonds Precision Prods., 319 F. Supp. 620 (S.D.N.Y. 1970), 578

United States v. Simmons Co., 1970 Trade Cas. (CCH) ¶ 73,164 (S.D. Ohio 1970), 107

United States v. Singer Mfg. Co., 374 U.S. 174 (1963), 803, 838, 842, 854

United States v. Sisal Sales Corp., 274 U.S. 268 (1927), 856, 903, 905

United States v. Smith, 532 F.2d 158 (10th Cir. 1976), 592

United States v. Smith Grading & Paving, Inc., 760 F.2d 527 (4th Cir.), *cert. denied*, 474 U.S. 1005 (1985), 57, 555, 590

United States v. Society of Indep. Gasoline Marketers of Am., 1977-2 Trade Cas. (CCH) ¶ 61,753 (D. Md. 1977), 582

United States v. Society of Indep. Gasoline Marketers of Am., 624 F.2d 461 (4th Cir. 1979), *cert. denied*, 449 U.S. 1078 (1981), 555, 589, 593

United States v. Socony-Vacuum Oil Co., 310 U.S. 150 (1940), 4, 31, 34, 62, 67, 85, 963, 964

United States v. South-Eastern Underwriters Ass'n, 322 U.S. 533 (1944), 22, 622, 1110

United States v. Southern Motor Carriers Rate Conference, Inc. 439 F. Supp. 29 (N.D. Ga. 1977), *aff'd en banc*, 702 F.2d 532 (5th Cir. 1983), *rev'd*, 471 U.S. 48 (1985), 1022

United States v. Southern Motor Carriers Rate Conference, Inc., 467 F. Supp. 471, (N.D. Ga. 1979), *aff'd*, 672 F.2d 469 (5th Cir. Unit B 1982), *rev'd*, 471 U.S. 48(1985), 1139

United States v. Southern Motor Carriers Rate Conference, Inc., 672 F.2d 469 (5th Cir. 1982), *rev'd*, 471 U.S. 48 (1985), 1012

United States v. Southern Motor Carriers Rate Conference, Inc., 702 F.2d 532 (5th Cir. 1983), *rev'd*, 471 U.S. 48 (1985), 970

United States v. Southland Corp., 6 TRADE REG. REP. (CCH) ¶ 45,090 (Case No. 3695) (M.D. Fla. 1990), 561, 597

United States v. Spectra-Physics, Inc., 46 FED. REG. 31,095 (1981), 358

United States v. Standard Oil Co. (New Jersey), 23 F.R.D. 1 (S.D.N.Y. 1958), 888

United States v. Standard Oil, Co., 1964 Trade Cas. (CCH) ¶ 70,984 (S.D.N.Y. 1963), 577

United States v. Standard Oil Co., 1963 Trade Cas. (CCH) ¶ 70,819 (S.D.N.Y. 1963), 571

United States v. Standard Oil Co., 253 F. Supp. 196 (D.N.J. 1966), 331

United States v. Standard Oil Co., 1969 Trade Cas. ¶ 72,742 (S.D.N.Y. 1968), 892

United States v. Standard Oil Co., 362 F. Supp. 1331 (N.D. Cal. 1972), *aff'd*, 412 U.S. 924 (1983), 176

United States v. Standard Tallow Corp., 1988-1 Trade Cas. (CCH) ¶ 67,913 (S.D.N.Y. 1988), 571

United States v. Standard Ultramarine & Color Co., 137 F. Supp. 167 (S.D.N.Y. 1955), 582

United States v. Stanford, 589 F.2d 285 (7th Cir. 1978), *cert. denied*, 440 U.S. 983 (1979), 758, 759

United States v. Stewart Mechanical Enters., 1979-2 Trade Cas. (CCH) ¶ 61,904 (W.D. Ky. 1979), 574

United States v. Stoeco Homes, Inc., 359 F. Supp. 672 (D.N.J. 1973), *vacated and remanded*, 498 F.2d 597 (3d Cir. 1974), *cert. denied*, 420 U.S. 927 (1975), 502

United States v. Stop & Shop Co., 1985-2 Trade Cas. (CCH) ¶ 66,689 (D. Conn. 1984), 40, 65

United States v. Storer Broadcasting Co., 351 U.S. 192 (1956), 1034, 1035

United States v. STP Corp., [1976-1979 Transfer Binder] TRADE REG. REP. (CCH) ¶ 21,390 (S.D.N.Y. Feb. 9, 1978), 496

United States v. Stroh Brewery Co., 1982-2 Trade Cas. (CCH) ¶ 64,804 (D.D.C. 1982), 573, 578

United States v. Stroh Brewery Co., 1982-83 Trade Cas. (CCH) ¶ 65,037, (D.D.C. 1982), *modified*, 1983-2 Trade Cas. (CCH) ¶ 65,627 (D.D.C. 1983), 344, 345, 347, 359

United States v. Studiengesellschaft Kohle, mbH, 670 F.2d 1122 (D.C. Cir. 1981), 39, 814, 820, 827, 830

United States v. Suntar Roofing, Inc., 709 F. Supp. 1526 (D. Kan. 1989), *aff'd*, 897 F.2d 469 (10th Cir. 1990), 555, 598, 599, 602

United States v. Suntar Roofing, Inc., 897 F.2d 469 (10th Cir. 1990), 31, 40, 76

United States v. Sweig, 316 F. Supp. 1148 (S.D.N.Y. 1970), 567

United States v. Swift & Co., 189 F. Supp. 885 (N.D. Ill. 1960), *aff'd*, 367 U.S. 909 (1961), 577

United States v. Swift & Co., 1975-1 Trade Cas. (CCH) ¶ 60,201 (N.D. Ill. 1975), 575, 577

United States v. Swift & Co., 286 U.S. 106 (1932), 576

United States v. Sysco Food Servs., No. H-91-00112 (S.D. Tex. 1991), 561

United States v. Sysco Food Servs., 6 TRADE REG. REP. (CCH) ¶ 45,091 (Case No. 3813) (S.D. Tex. 1991), 597

United States v. Syufy Enters., 712 F. Supp. 1386 (N.D. Cal. 1989), *aff'd*, 903 F.2d 659 (9th Cir. 1990), 203, 282, 285

United States v. Syufy Enters., 903 F.2d 659 (9th Cir. 1990), 196, 201, 217, 218, 221, 223, 226, 268, 307, 309, 312

United States v. Tallant, 407 F. Supp. 878 (N.D. Ga. 1975), 567

United States v. Taylor, 487 U.S. 326 (1988), 586

United States v. Taylor Forge & Pipe Works, 1964 Trade Cas. (CCH) ¶ 71,277 (S.D.N.Y. 1964), 588

United States v. Tedesco, 441 F. Supp. 1336 (M.D. Pa. 1977), 584, 585, 587

United States v. Tengelmann Warenhandelsgesellschaft, 1989-1 Trade Cas. (CCH) ¶ 68,623 (D.D.C. 1989), 344, 570, 897

United States v. Terminal Railroad Ass'n, 224 U.S. 383 (1912), 246, 384, 385

United States v. Texas State Bd. of Public Accountancy, 464 F. Supp. 400 (W.D. Tex. 1978), *modified*, 592 F.2d 919 (5th Cir.), *cert. denied*, 444 U.S. 925 (1979), 68, 970, 982

United States v. Theodore Weiswasser, [1983-1987 Transfer Binder] TRADE REG. REP. (CCH) ¶ 22,287 (W.D. Wash. Sept. 6, 1985), 502

United States v. Third Nat'l Bank, 390 U.S. 171 (1968), 314, 1092

United States v. Tidewater Marine Serv., 284 F. Supp. 324 (E.D. La. 1968), 286, 308

United States v. Times Mirror Co., 274 F. Supp. 606 (C.D. Cal. 1967), 285, 290

United States v. Timken Roller Bearing Co., 83 F. Supp. 284 (N.D. Ohio 1949), *modified and aff'd*, 341 U.S. 593 (1951), 842, 850, 897

United States v. Title Ins. Rating Bureau, 700 F.2d 1247 (9th Cir. 1983), *cert. denied*, 467 U.S. 1240 (1984), 970, 1113

United States v. Topco Assocs., 1973-1 Trade Cas. (CCH) ¶ 74,391 (N.D. Ill.), *aff'd*, 414 U.S. 801 (1973), 130, 382

United States v. Topco Assocs., 405 U.S. 596 (1972), 1, 30, 35, 47, 62, 75, 76, 382, 390, 843, 847

United States v. Topco Assocs., 414 U.S. 801 (1973), *aff'g*, 1973-1 Trade Cas. (CCH) ¶ 74,391 (N.D. Ill. 1972), 76

United States v. Tracinda Inv. Corp., 477 F. Supp. 1093 (C.D. Cal. 1979), 279, 281, 285, 307, 308

United States v. Tramunti, 500 F.2d 1334 (2d Cir.), *cert. denied*, 419 U.S. 1079 (1974), 592

United States v. Trenton Potteries Co., 273 U.S. 392 (1927), 31, 62, 63

United States v. Tri-Texas, Inc., [1979-1983 Transfer Binder] TRADE REG. REP. (CCH) ¶ 21,390 (S.D.N.Y. Feb. 9, 1978), 498

United States v. Trump, No. 88-0929 (D.D.C. April 5, 1989), 344

United States v. Tuff-Tire Am., Inc., [1983-1987 Transfer Binder] TRADE REG. REP. (CCH) ¶ 22,440 (M.D. Fla. Mar. 13, 1987), 497

United States v. Twentieth Century Fox Film Corp., 882 F.2d 656 (2d Cir. 1989), *cert. denied*, 110 S. Ct. 772 (1990), 574

United States v. Union Camp Corp., 1969 Trade Cas. (CCH) ¶ 72,689 (E.D. Va. 1969), 807

United States v. Union Circulation Co., 1983-1 Trade Cas. (CCH) ¶ 65,372 (N.D. Ga. 1983), 497

United States v. Union Oil Co., 343 F.2d 29 (9th Cir. 1965), 556

United States v. Uniroyal, Inc., 300 F. Supp. 84 (S.D.N.Y. 1969), 108

United States v. United Artists Theatre Circuit, 1980-2 Trade Cas. (CCH) ¶ 63,549 (E.D.N.Y. 1980), 576, 577

United States v. United Engr. & Foundry Co., 1952-1953 Trade Cas. ¶ 67,368, (W.D. Pa. 1952) (same), 890

United States v. United Fruit Co., 1958 Trade Cas. (CCH) ¶ 68,941 (E.D. La. 1958), 69

United States v. United Fruit Co., 1978-1 Trade Cas. (CCH) ¶ 62,001, (E.D. La. 1978), 892

United States v. United Liquors Corp., 149 F. Supp. 609 (W.D. Tenn. 1956), aff'd per curiam, 352 U.S. 991 (1957), 65, 66

United States v. United Shoe Mach. Corp., 110 F. Supp. 295 (D. Mass. 1953), aff'd per curiam, 347 U.S. 521 (1954), 196, 198, 217, 750, 853

United States v. United Shoe Mach. Corp., 247 U.S. 32 (1918), 802, 818

United States v. United Shoe Mach. Corp., 391 U.S. 244 (1968), 577

United States v. United States Alkali Export Ass'n, 58 F. Supp. 785 (S.D.N.Y. 1944), aff'd, 325 U.S. 196 (1945), later proceeding, 86 F. Supp. 59 (S.D.N.Y. 1949), 914, 916

United States v. United States Alkali Export Ass'n, 86 F. Supp. 59 (S.D.N.Y. 1949), 75, 897

United States v. United States Alkali Export Ass'n, 325 U.S. 196 (1945), 915

United States v. United States Gypsum Co., 333 U.S. 364 (1948), 803, 822, 823, 835, 837, 838

United States v. United States Gypsum Co., 340 U.S. 76 (1950), 852

United States v. United States Gypsum Co., 438 U.S. 422 (1978), 36, 54, 57, 67, 72, 417, 554, 594

United States v. United States Steel Corp., 1964 Trade Cas. (CCH) ¶ 71,212 (S.D.N.Y. 1964), 588

United States v. United States Steel Corp., 1964 Trade Cas. (CCH) ¶ 71,276 (S.D.N.Y. 1964), 588

United States v. United Technologies Corp., 1977-2 Trade Cas. (CCH) ¶ 61,647 (N.D. Ohio 1977), 283

United States v. United Technologies Corp., 466 F. Supp. 196 (N.D.N.Y. 1979), 335, 356, 357

United States v. United Technologies Corp., 1980-81 Trade Cas. (CCH) ¶ 63,792 (N.D.N.Y. 1981), 349, 574

United States v. United Tote, Inc., 1991-1 Trade Cas. (CCH) ¶ 69,300 (D. Del. 1991), 355

United States v. United Tote, Inc., 768 F. Supp. 1064 (D. Del. 1991), 302, 305, 308, 309, 311

United States v. Universal Wool Batting Corp., 1961 Trade Cas. (CCH) ¶ 70,168 (S.D.N.Y. 1961), 496

United States v. Univis Lens Co., 316 U.S. 241 (1942), 822, 828

United States v. Upjohn Co., 600 F.2d 1223 (6th Cir. 1979), rev'd, 449 U.S. 383 (1981), 760

United States v. Vehicular Parking, Ltd., 54 F. Supp. 828 (D. Del.), modified, 56 F. Supp. 297 (D. Del. 1944), modified, 61 F. Supp. 656 (D. Del. 1945), 803, 822, 837

United States v. Vehicular Parking, Ltd., 61 F. Supp. 656 (D. Del. 1945), 852

United States v. Vetco Inc., 644 F.2d 1324 (9th Cir.), cert. denied, 454 U.S. 1098 (1981), 888

United States v. Vetco Inc., 691 F.2d 1281 (9th Cir.), cert. denied, 454 U.S. 1098 (1981), 863

United States v. Vinson, 606 F.2d 149 (6th Cir. 1979), cert. denied, 444 U.S. 1074 (1980), 594

United States v. Virginia National Bankshares, Inc., 1982-2 TRADE CAS. (CCH) ¶ 64,871 (W.D. Va. 1982), 1092

United States v. Von's Grocery Co., 384 U.S. 270 (1966), 300, 303, 304, 314

United States v. Wachovia Corp., 313 F. Supp. 632 (W.D.N.C. 1970), 356

United States v. Walser Motor, Inc., No. 3-85-1898 (D. Minn., Apr. 29, 1987), 534

United States v. Ward, Crim. No. 78-437 (E.D. La. 1978), 582

United States v. Warren Five Cents Sav. Bank, 1980-81 Trade Cas. (CCH) 1090 ¶ 63,772 (D. Mass. 1981), 1089

United States v. Washington, 586 F.2d 1147 (7th Cir. 1978), 4

United States v. Washington, 431 U.S. 181 (1977), 566

United States v. Waste Mgmt., Inc., 588 F. Supp. 498 (S.D.N.Y. 1983), *rev'd*, 743 F.2d 976 (2d Cir. 1984), 359

United States v. Waste Mgmt., Inc., 1989-1 Trade Cas. (CCH) ¶ 68,481 (W.D. Tex. 1988), 344, 348, 571

United States v. Waste Mgmt., Inc., 743 F.2d 976 (2d Cir. 1984), 285, 295, 296, 300, 305, 307, 309

United States v. Watchmakers of Switz. Information Center, Inc., 133 F. Supp. 40 (S.D.N.Y. 1955), 867, 873

United States v. Watchmakers of Switz. Information Center, Inc., 1963 Trade Cas. (CCH) ¶ 70,600 (S.D.N.Y. 1962), *order modified*, 1965 Trade Cas. (CCH) ¶ 71,352 (S.D.N.Y. 1965), 857, 890, 891, 892, 909, 910

United States v. Wells, 163 F. 313 (D. Idaho 1908), 566, 568

United States v. Western Elec. Co., 1956 Trade Cas. (CCH) ¶ 68,246 (D.N.J. 1956), 852

United States v. Western Elec. Co., 592 F. Supp. 846 (D.D.C. 1984), *appeal dismissed*, 777 F.2d 23 (D.C. Cir. 1985), 573

United States v. Western Elec. Co., 604 F. Supp. 256 (D.D.C. 1984), 1045

United States v. Western Elec. Co., 673 F. Supp. 525 (D.D.C. 1987), *aff'd in part, rev'd in part*, 900 F.2d 283 (D.C. Cir.), *cert. denied*, 111 S. Ct. 283 (1990), 1047

United States v. Western Elec. Co., 1989-2 Trade Cas. (CCH) ¶ 68,737 (D.D.C. 1989), 575

United States v. Western Elec. Co., 1990-1 Trade Cas. (CCH) ¶ 68,973 (D.C. Cir. 1990), 577

United States v. Western Elec. Co., 767 F. Supp. 308, (D.D.C. 1991), *stay vacated*, 1991-2 Trade Cas. (CCH) ¶ 69,610 (D.C. Cir. 1991), 1045

United States v. Western Elec. Co., 894 F.2d 430 (D.C. Cir. 1990), 575

United States v. Western Elec. Co., 900 F.2d 283 (D.C. Cir.), *cert. denied*, 111 S. Ct. 283 (1990), 1045

United States v. Westinghouse Elec. Corp., 1977-2 Trade Cas. (CCH) ¶ 61,661 (E.D. Pa. 1977), 555, 571

United States v. Westinghouse Elec. Corp., 471 F. Supp. 532 (N.D. Cal. 1978), *aff'd*, 648 F.2d 642 (9th Cir. 1981), 145, 147, 843

United States v. Westinghouse Elec. Corp., 1988-1 Trade Cas. (CCH) ¶ 68,012 (D.D.C. 1988), 573, 574

United States v. Westinghouse Elec. Corp., 1988-2 Trade Cas. (CCH) ¶ 68,328 (D.D.C. 1988), 579

United States v. Westinghouse Elec. Corp., 1988-2 Trade Cas. (CCH) ¶ 68,327 (D.D.C), *modified*, 1988-2 Trade Cas. (CCH) ¶ 68,328 (D.D.C. 1988), 344

United States v. Westinghouse Elec. Corp., 1989-1 Trade Cas. (CCH) ¶ 68,607 (S.D.N.Y. 1989), 344, 346, 349, 571

United States v. Westinghouse Elec. Corp., 648 F.2d 642 (9th Cir. 1981), 770, 819, 841

United States v. W.F. Brinkley & Son Constr. Co., 783 F.2d 1157 (4th Cir. 1986), 63, 64, 554, 555, 1108

United States v. Wheelabrator-Frye, Inc., 1981-1 Trade Cas. (CCH) ¶ 64,018 (D.D.C. 1981), 345

United States v. White Consol. Indus., 323 F. Supp. 1397 (N.D. Ohio 1971), 336

United States v. White Motor Co., 194 F. Supp. 562 (N.D. Ohio 1961), *rev'd*, 372 U.S. 253 (1963), 120

United States v. White Motor Co., 1964 Trade Cas. (CCH) ¶ 71,195 (N.D. Ohio 1964), 120

United States v. White Ready-Mix Concrete Co., 449 F. Supp. 808 (N.D. Ohio 1978), 587

United States v. White Ready-Mix Concrete Co., 1981-2 Trade Cas. (CCH) ¶ 64,237 (N.D. Ohio 1981), 758

United States v. Wholesale Tobacco Distribs., 1977-1 Trade Cas. (CCH) ¶ 61,535 (S.D.N.Y. 1977), 588

United States v. Wickes Cos., No. 88-0782 (D.D.C. Apr. 12, 1988), 344

United States v. William Anderson Co., 698 F.2d 911 (8th Cir. 1982), 597

United States v. Wilson Chem. Co., 1962 Trade Cas. (CCH) ¶ 70,478 (W.D. Pa. 1962), *aff'd per curiam*, 319 F.2d 133 (3d Cir. 1963), 496

United States v. Wilson Sporting Goods Co., 288 F. Supp. 543 (N.D. Ill. 1968), 290, 334, 357

United States v. Women's Sportswear Mfg. Ass'n, 336 U.S. 460 (1949), 23, 26

United States v. Work Wear Corp., 1975-2 Trade Cas. (CCH) ¶ 60,431 (N.D. Ohio 1975), 577

United States v. Wright, 873 F.2d 437 (1st Cir. 1989), 595

United States v. Wright Contracting Co., 728 F.2d 648 (4th Cir. 1984), 597

United States v. W.T. Grant Co., 345 U.S. 629 (1953), 398, 399, 679, 680

United States v. Yellow Cab Co., 332 U.S. 218 (1947), 18, 270

United States v. Yoder Bros., 1989-2 Trade Cas. (CCH) ¶ 68,723 (N.D. Ohio 1986), 103, 111, 576, 577

United States v. Yonkers Contracting Co., 706 F. Supp. 296 (S.D.N.Y. 1989), 586, 598

United States v. Young Bros., 728 F.2d 682 (5th Cir.), *cert. denied*, 469 U.S. 881 (1984), 22, 25, 27, 593, 598

United States v. Zolin, 491 U.S. 554 (1989), 762, 763, 765

United Telephone Co. v. Johnson Publishing Co., 855 F.2d 604 (8th Cir. 1988), 846

United Transp. Union v. ICC, 891 F.2d 908 (D.C. Cir. 1989), *cert. denied*, 110 S. Ct. 3271 (1990), 1133

Unity Ventures v. County of Lake, 1984-1 Trade Cas. (CCH) ¶ 65,883 (N.D. Ill. 1983), *judgment n.o.v. granted*, 631 F. Supp. 181 (N.D. Ill. 1986), *aff'd*, 841 F.2d 770 (7th Cir.), *cert. denied*, 488 U.S. 891 (1988), 987

Unity Ventures v. County of Lake, 631 F. Supp. 181 (N.D. Ill. 1986), *aff'd*, 841 F.2d 770 (7th Cir.), *cert. denied*, 488 U.S. 891 (1988), 989

Universal Amusements Co. v. General Cinema Corp., 635 F. Supp. 1505 (S.D. Tex. 1985), 87, 647

Universal Analytics, Inc. v. MacNeal-Schwendler Corp., 707 F. Supp. 1170 (C.D. Cal. 1989), *aff'd*, 914 F.2d 1256 (9th Cir. 1990), 97, 222, 261

Universal Analytics, Inc. v. MacNeal-Schwendler Corp., 914 F.2d 1256 (9th Cir. 1990), 226

Universal Brands, Inc. v. Philip Morris, Inc., 546 F.2d 30 (5th Cir. 1977), 179, 181, 191

Universal Camera Corp. v. NLRB, 340 U.S. 474 (1951), 521

Universal Credit Acceptance Corp., 82 F.T.C. 570 (1973), *modified sub nom.* Heater v. FTC, 503 F.2d 321 (9th Cir. 1971),478

Universal Lite Distribs. v. Northwest Indus., 452 F. Supp. 1206 (D. Md. 1978), *modified*, 602 F.2d 1173 (4th Cir. 1979), 414

Universal-Rundle Corp., 65 F.T.C. 924 (1964), *order set aside*, 352 F.2d 831 (7th Cir. 1965), *rev'd and remanded*, 387 U.S. 244 (1967), 412

Universal-Rundle Corp. v. FTC, 382 F.2d 285 (7th Cir. 1967), 415, 430

Universal Training Servs., 94 F.T.C. 167 (1979), 499

Unocal Corp. v. Mesa Petroleum Co., 616 F. Supp. 149 (W.D. La. 1985), 317

UNR Indus. v. Continental Ins. Co., 607 F. Supp. 855 (N.D. Ill. 1984), 69, 1114, 1118

Upjohn Co. v. United States, 449 U.S. 383 (1981), 760, 761

Urban Elec. Supply & Equip. Corp. v. New York Convention Center Dev., 105 F.R.D. 92 (E.D.N.Y. 1985), 768, 769

Urquhart v. United States, 109 F. Supp. 409 (Ct. Cl. 1953), 833

U.S. Anchor Mfg. v. Rule Indus., 717 F. Supp. 1565 (N.D. Ga. 1989), 228, 236

USA Petroleum Co. v. Atlantic Richfield Co., 859 F.2d 687 (9th Cir. 1988), *rev'd*, 110 S. Ct. 1884 (1990), 104, 614

U.S. Gen. Supply Corp., 80 F.T.C. 857 (1972), 479

USM Corp. v. SPS Technologies, Inc., 694 F.2d 505, (7th Cir. 1982), *cert. denied*, 462 U.S. 1107 (1983), 800, 802, 813, 815, 816, 824, 825, 831

USM Corp. v. Standard Pressed Steel Co., 453 F. Supp. 743 (N.D. Ill. 1978), *aff'd in part and vacated in part*, 694 F.2d 505 (7th Cir. 1982), *cert. denied*, 462 U.S. 1107 (1983), 836

U.S. Philips Corp. v. Windmere Corp., 680 F. Supp. 361 (S.D. Fla. 1987), 236

USS-Posco Indus. v. Contra Costa County Bldg. & Constr. Trades Council, 721 F. Supp. 239 (N.D. Cal. 1989), 999

Utah Gas Pipelines Corp. v. El Paso Natural Gas Co., 233 F. Supp. 955 (D. Utah 1964), 649

Utah Pie Co. v. Continental Baking Co., 386 U.S. 685 (1967), 227, 414

Utah Power & Light Co., 41 F.E.R.C. (CCH) ¶ 61,283 (1987), 1075

Utah Power & Light Co., 45 F.E.R.C. (CCH) ¶ 61,095 (1989), 1074

Utah v. American Pipe & Constr. Co., 49 F.R.D. 17 (C.D. Cal. 1969), 713

Utilities Servs. Eng'g, Inc. v. Colorado Bldg. & Constr. Trades Council, 549 F.2d 173 (10th Cir. 1977), 1120

V

Vacuum Interrupters Ltd., 20 O.J. EUR. COMM. (No. L 48) 32 (1977), [1976-1978 Transfer Binder] COMMON MKT. REP. (CCH) ¶ 9926, 929

Vaessen-Moris, 22 O.J. EUR. COMM. (No. L 19) 32 (1979), [1978-1981 Transfer Binder] COMMON MKT. REP. (CCH) ¶ 10,107, 925, 943

VAG v. Magne, Case 10/86, [1986] E.C.R. 4071, [1985-1986 Transfer Binder] COMMON MKT. REP. (CCH) ¶ 14,390, 941

Valasco Prods. Co. v. Lloyd A. Fry Roofing Co., 346 F.2d 661 (6th Cir.), cert. denied, 382 U.S. 904 (1965), 414

Valdan Sportswear v. Montgomery Ward & Co., 591 F. Supp. 1188 (S.D.N.Y. 1984), 770

Valin Corp. v. Ametek, Inc., 1986-1 Trade Cas. (CCH) ¶ 67,125 (N.D. Cal. 1986), 186

Valley Bank of Nevada v. Plus Sys., 914 F.2d 1186 (9th Cir. 1990), 627

Valley Liquors, Inc. v. Renfield Importers, 678 F.2d 742 (7th Cir. 1982), 51, 124

Valley Liquors, Inc. v. Renfield Importers, 822 F.2d 656 (7th Cir.), cert. denied, 484 U.S. 977 (1987), 8, 16, 51, 191, 214, 707, 708

Valley Plymouth v. Studebaker-Packard Corp., 219 F. Supp. 608 (S.D. Cal. 1963), 406, 426

Vanadium Corp. of Am. v. Susquehanna Corp., 203 F. Supp. 686 (D. Del. 1962), 281

Van Allen v. Circle K Corp., 58 F.R.D. 562 (C.D. Cal. 1972), 713

Van Bokkelen v. Grumman Aerospace Corp., 432 F. Supp. 329 (E.D.N.Y. 1977), 904, 907

Vanco Beverages, Inc. v. Falls City Indus., 654 F.2d 1224 (7th Cir. 1981), rev'd, 460 U.S. 428 (1983), 670

Vandervelde v. Put & Call Brokers & Dealers Ass'n, 344 F. Supp. 118 (S.D.N.Y. 1972), 66, 783, 785, 793, 1104

V. & L. Cicione, Inc. v. C. Schmidt & Sons, 403 F. Supp. 643 (E.D. Pa. 1975), aff'd without published opinion, 565 F.2d 154 (3d Cir. 1977), 130, 272

Van Dyk Research Corp. v. Xerox Corp., 478 F. Supp. 1268 (D.N.J. 1979), aff'd, 631 F.2d 251 (3d Cir. 1980), cert. denied, 452 U.S. 905 (1981), 380, 383

Van Dyk Research Corp. v. Xerox Corp., 631 F.2d 251 (3d Cir. 1980), cert. denied, 452 U.S. 905 (1981), 667

Van Horn v. Trickey, 840 F.2d 604 (8th Cir. 1988), 741

Vanity Fair Paper Mills, Inc. v. FTC, 311 F.2d 480 (2d Cir. 1962), 442, 443, 490

Van-S-Aviation v. Piper Aircraft Corp., 101 F.R.D. 759 (W.D. Mo. 1984), 722

Van Zuylen Frères v. Hag AG, Case 192/73, [1974] E.C.R. 731, [1974 Transfer Binder] COMMON MKT. REP. (CCH) ¶ 8230, 945

Vapor Corp. v. Westcode, Inc., 12 U.S.P.Q.2d (BNA) 1218 (E.D. Pa. 1989), 258

Varney v. Coleman Co., 385 F. Supp. 1337 (D.N.H. 1974), 186, 192, 329

Vasiliow Co. v. Anheuser-Busch, Inc., 117 F.R.D. 345 (E.D.N.Y. 1987), 647, 714, 715, 720, 724, 727, 729, 734

VBBB/VBVB (Dutch Language Books), 25 O.J. EUR. COMM. (No. L 54) 36 (1982), [1978-1981 Transfer Binder] COMMON MKT. REP. (CCH) ¶ 10,351, 942

VBBB v. Eldi Records BV, Case 106/79, [1980] E.C.R. 1137, [1979-1981 Transfer Binder] COMMON MKT. REP. (CCH) ¶ 8646, 932

Vegetable Parchment Producers, 20 O.J. EUR. COMM. (No. L 70) 54 (1977), [1976-1978 Transfer Binder] COMMON MKT. REP. (CCH) ¶ 10,016, 933

Velcro/Aplix, 28 O.J. EUR. COMM. (No. L 233) 22 (1985), [1985-1988 Transfer Binder] COMMON MKT. REP. (CCH) ¶ 10,719, 949

Veltman v. Norman Simon, Inc., 1977-1 Trade Cas. (CCH) ¶ 61,273 (S.D.N.Y. 1977), 826

Vendo Co. v. Lektro-Vend Corp., 433 U.S. 623 (1977), 258, 1000

Venus Foods, Inc., 57 F.T.C. 1025 (1960), 434

Venzie Corp. v. United States Mineral Prods. Co., 521 F.2d 1309 (3d Cir. 1975), 121, 131, 132, 191

Verband der Sachversicherer v. Commission, Case 45/85, [1987] E.C.R. 405, [1987-1988 Transfer Binder] COMMON MKT. REP. (CCH) ¶ 14,413, 925, 929, 936

Vereniging van Cementhandelaren v. Commission, Case 8/72, [1972] E.C.R. 977, [1971-1973 Transfer Binder] COMMON MKT. REP. (CCH) ¶ 8179, 929

Verlinden BV v. Central Bank of Nig., 461 U.S. 480 (1983), 900

Vermont v. Cayuga Rock Salt Co., 276 F. Supp. 970 (D. Me. 1967), 686

Vermont v. Densmore Brick Co., 1980-2 Trade Cas. (CCH) ¶ 63,347 (D. Vt. 1980), 657

Verson Wilkins Ltd. v. Allied Prods. Corp., 723 F. Supp. 1 (N.D. Ill. 1989), 39, 99

Vetter Corp. v. American Honda Motor Co., 1984-2 Trade Cas. (CCH) ¶ 66,158 (N.D. Ill. 1984), 163

VHF TV Top 100 Market, 81 F.C.C.2d 233 (1980), recon. denied, 90 F.C.C.2d 160 (1982), 1042

Viacom Int'l, Inc. v. Time, Inc., 89 Civ. 3139 JMW (S.D.N.Y., complaint filed May 9, 1989), 1054

Vial v. First Commerce Corp., 564 F. Supp. 650 (E.D. La. 1983), 1092

Vichy, Decision 91/153, 35 O.J. EUR. COMM. (No. L 75) 57 (1991), [1991] 1 CEC (CCH) 2062, 926

Victoria Oil Co. v. Lancaster Corp., 587 F. Supp. 429 (D. Colo. 1984), 681

Victorian House, Inc. v. Fisher Camuto Corp., 769 F.2d 466 (8th Cir. 1985), 13, 14, 22, 181

Video Int'l Prod., Inc. v. Warner-Amex Cable Communs., 858 F.2d 1075 (5th Cir. 1988), 1004, 1053

Viking Theatre Corp. v. Warner Bros. Pictures Distrib. Corp., 264 F. Supp. 665 (E.D. Pa. 1967), 778

Viking Travel, Inc. v. Air France, 462 F. Supp. 28 (E.D.N.Y. 1978), 662

Viking Travel, Inc. v. Air France, 1982-2 Trade Cas. (CCH) ¶ 64,915 (E.D.N.Y. 1982), 713, 714, 719, 721

Vilastor Kent Theatre Corp. v. Brandt, 18 F.R.D. 199 (S.D.N.Y. 1955), 751

Village of Bolingbrook v. Citizens Utils. Co., 864 F.2d 481 (7th Cir. 1988), 1001

Village of Hoffman Estates v. Flipside, Hoffman Estates, Inc., 455 U.S. 489 (1982), 628

Villeroy & Boch, 28 O.J. EUR. COMM. (No. L 376) 15 (1985), [1985-1988 Transfer Binder] COMMON MKT. REP. (CCH) ¶ 10,758, 940

Virginia Academy of Clinical Psychologists v. Blue Shield, 501 F. Supp. 1232 (E.D. Va. 1980), 676

Virginia Academy of Clinical Psychologists v. Blue Shield, 543 F. Supp. 126 (E.D. Va. 1982), 783, 787

Virginia Academy of Clinical Psychologists v. Blue Shield, 624 F.2d 476 (4th Cir. 1980), 71, 1111

Virginia Excelsior Mills, Inc. v. FTC, 256 F.2d 538 (4th Cir. 1958), 384, 390

Virginia State Bd. of Pharmacy v. Virginia Citizens Consumers Council, Inc., 425 U.S. 748 (1976), 493

Virtue v. Creamery Package Mfg. Co., 227 U.S. 8 (1913), 821

Vista Chem. Co. v. Atchison, T. & S.F. Ry., 5 I.C.C.3d 331 (1989), 1140

Vitagraph, Inc. v. Grobaski, 46 F.2d 813 (W.D. Mich. 1931), 846

Viviano Macaroni Co. v. FTC, 411 F.2d 255 (3d Cir. 1969), 420, 437

Vogel v. American Soc'y of Appraisers, 744 F.2d 598 (7th Cir. 1984), 36, 39, 65, 85, 375, 390

Völk v. Vervaecke, Case 5/69, [1969] E.C.R. 295, [1967-1970 Transfer Binder] COMMON MKT.
REP. (CCH) ¶ 8074, 928, 930

Volkart Bros. v. Freeman, 311 F.2d 52 (5th Cir. 1962), 1106

Volkswagen of Am., 103 F.T.C. 536 (1984), 517, 889

Volkswagenwerk AG v. FMC, 390 U.S. 261 (1968), 1163, 1164

Volkswagenwerk Aktiengesellschaft v. Schlunk, 486 U.S. 694 (1988), 878

Vollrath Co. v. Sammi Corp., 1990-1 Trade Cas. (CCH) ¶ 68,955 (C.D. Cal. 1989), 227, 228,
234, 236, 237, 271

Volvo N. Am. Corp. v. Men's Int'l Professional Tennis Council, 857 F.2d 55 (2d Cir. 1988), 260,
270, 271, 368

Vorhees v. Fischer & Krecke, 697 F.2d 574 (4th Cir. 1983), 877

VTR, Inc. v. Goodyear Tire & Rubber Co., 303 F. Supp. 773 (S.D.N.Y. 1969), 364, 649

VZW Vereniging van Vlaamse Reisbureaus v. VZW Sociale Dienst, Case 311/85, [1987] E.C.R.
3801, [1987-1988 Transfer Binder] COMMON MKT. REP. (CCH) ¶ 14,499, 943

W

Wachovia Bank & Trust Co. v. National Student Mktg. Corp., 650 F.2d 342 (D.C. Cir. 1980),
cert. denied, 452 U.S. 954 (1981), 697

Wagner v. Central La. Elec. Co., 99 F.R.D. 279 (E.D. La. 1983), 712, 714, 719, 727

Wagner v. Central La. Elec. Co., 102 F.R.D. 196 (E.D. La. 1984), 712

Wainwright v. Kraftco Corp., 54 F.R.D. 532 (N.D. Ga. 1972), 735

Waldbaum v. Worldvision Enters., 84 F.R.D. 95 (S.D.N.Y. 1979), 600

Waldo v. North Am. Van Lines, 102 F.R.D. 807 (W.D. Pa. 1984), 146, 170, 173, 712, 728

Waldo v. North Am. Van Lines, 669 F. Supp. 722 (W.D. Pa. 1987), 645, 1018

Waldorf Shopping Mall, Inc. v. Great Atl. & Pac. Tea Co., 1984-1 Trade Cas. (CCH) ¶ 65,976
(Md. Cir. Ct. 1984), 639

Waldron v. British Petroleum Co., 231 F. Supp. 72 (S.D.N.Y. 1964), 649

Walker Oil Co. v Hudson Oil Co., 414 F.2d 588 (8th Cir. 1969), cert. denied, 396 U.S. 1042
(1970), 403, 404

Walker Process Equip., Inc. v. Food Mach. & Chem. Corp., 382 U.S. 172 (1965), 36, 197, 258,
266, 750, 802, 807, 808, 809, 993, 1006

Walker v. U-Haul Co., 734 F.2d 1068 (5th Cir. 1984), 704

Wall Prods. Co. v. National Gypsum Co., 326 F. Supp. 295 (N.D. Cal. 1971), 72

Wall Prods. Co. v. National Gypsum Co., 357 F. Supp. 832 (N.D. Cal. 1973), 671

Wallace Clark & Co. v. Acheson Indus., 532 F.2d 846 (2d Cir.), cert. denied, 524 U.S. 976
(1976), 836

Wall v. City of Athens, 663 F. Supp. 747 (M.D. Ga. 1987), 979, 981, 984

Walpa Const. Corp. v. Mobile Paint Mfg. Co., 701 F. Supp. 23 (D.P.R. 1988), 50

Walsh v. Ford Motor Co., 807 F.2d 1000 (D.C. Cir. 1986), cert. denied, 482 U.S. 915 (1987), on
remand, 130 F.R.D. 260 (D.D.C. 1990), 540

Walter Kidde & Co., [1973-1976 Complaints & Orders Transfer Binder] TRADE REG. REP.
(CCH) ¶ 21,126 (June 29, 1976), 349

Walter Switzer, Inc., 89 F.T.C. 163 (1977), 541

Waltham Watch Co. v. FTC, 318 F.2d 28 (7th Cir.), cert. denied, 375 U.S. 944 (1963), 477

WANO-Schwarzpulver, 21 O.J. EUR. COMM. (No. L 322) 26 (1978), [1978-1981 Transfer
Binder] COMMON MKT. REP. (CCH) ¶ 10,089, 938

Ward Labs. v. FTC, 276 F.2d 952 (2d Cir.), cert. denied, 364 U.S. 827 (1960), 469

Wardell v. Certified Oil Co., 1982-1 Trade Cas. (CCH) ¶ 64,477 (S.D. Ohio 1981), 728

Ware v. Trailer Mart, Inc., 623 F.2d 1150 (6th Cir. 1980), 138, 147, 154

Warner Amex Cable Communs. v. ABC, 499 F. Supp. 537 (S.D. Ohio 1980), 38

Warner Communs., 51 F.C.C.2d 1079 (1975), 1030

Warner Communs., 108 F.T.C. 105 (1986), 349, 352

Warner-Jenkinson Co. v. Allied Chem. Corp., 477 F. Supp. 371 (S.D.N.Y. 1979), aff'd mem., 633 F.2d 208 (2d Cir. 1980), 823

Warner-Jenkinson Co. v. Allied Chem. Corp., 567 F.2d 184, 188 (2d Cir. 1977), 836

Warner-Lambert Co., 86 F.T.C. 1398 (1975), aff'd as modified, 562 F.2d 749 (D.C. Cir. 1977), cert. denied, 435 U.S. 950 (1978), 470-471, 473

Warner-Lambert Co. v. FTC, 562 F.2d 749 (D.C. Cir. 1977), cert. denied, 435 U.S. 950 (1978), 490, 491, 492, 493, 494

Warren Corp. v. Goldwert Textile Sales, Inc., 581 F. Supp. 897 (S.D.N.Y. 1984), 541

Warriner Hermetics, Inc. v. Copeland Refrigeration Corp., 463 F.2d 1002 (5th Cir.), cert. denied, 409 U.S. 1086 (1972), 141, 155, 160, 849

Washington Crab Ass'n, 66 F.T.C. 45 (1964), 1028

Washington Gas Light Co. v. Virginia Elec. & Power Co., 438 F.2d 248 (4th Cir. 1971), 139

Washington Metro. Area Transit Comm'n v. Holiday Tours, Inc., 559 F.2d 841 (D.C. Cir. 1977), 366

Washington Mut. Sav. Bank v. FDIC, 482 F.2d 459 (9th Cir. 1973), 1095

Washington Natural Gas Co. v. Public Util. Dist. No. 1, 1970 Trade Cas. (CCH) ¶ 73,083 (Wash. 1969), 637

Washington Osteopathic Medical Ass'n v. King County Medical Serv. Corp., 1971 Trade Cas. (CCH) ¶ 73,442 (Wash. 1970), 638

Washington Star Communs., 57 F.C.C.2d 475 (1976), 1039

Washington State Bowling Proprietors Ass'n v. Pacific Lanes, Inc., 356 F.2d 371 (9th Cir.), cert. denied, 384 U.S. 963 (1966), 81

Washington State Elec. Contractors Ass'n v. Forrest, 930 F.2d 736 (9th Cir.), cert. denied, 112 S. Ct. 439 (1991), 980

Washington Trotting Ass'n v. Pennsylvania Harness Horsemen's Ass'n, 428 F. Supp. 122 (W.D. Pa. 1977), 81

Washington v. American Pipe & Constr. Co., 41 F.R.D. 59 (D. Wash. 1966), 597

Washington v. American Pipe & Constr. Co., 280 F. Supp. 802 (W.D. Wash. 1968), 662

Washington v. Sterling Theatres Co., 64 Wash. 2d 761, 394 P.2d 226 (1964), 622

Washington v. Texaco Ref. & Marketing, Inc., 1991-1 Trade Cas. (CCH) ¶ 69,345 (W.D. Wash. 1991), 278, 345, 612

Washington v. Wyman, 54 F.R.D. 266 (S.D.N.Y. 1971), 739

Washington Whey Co. v. Fairmont Foods Co., 72 F.R.D. 180 (D. Neb. 1976), 774

Water Transp. Ass'n v. ICC, 715 F.2d 581 (D.C. Cir. 1983), cert. denied, 465 U.S. 1006 (1984), 1143

Waters-Pierce Oil Co. v. Texas, 212 U.S. 86 (1909), 622

Waters v. National Farmers Org., 328 F. Supp. 1229 (S.D. Ind. 1971), 433

Watson Packer, Inc. v. Dresser Indus., 193 U.S.P.Q. (BNA) (N.D. Tex. 1977), 833

Watson v. Buck, 313 U.S. 387 (1941), 622

Ways & Means, Inc. v. IVAC Corp., 506 F. Supp. 697 (N.D. Cal. 1979), aff'd, 638 F.2d 143 (9th Cir. 1981), cert. denied, 454 U.S. 895 (1982), 144

WCVL, Inc., 55 F.C.C.2d 879 (1975), 1037

Wearly v. FTC, 616 F.2d 662 (3d Cir.), cert. denied, 449 U.S. 822 (1980), 508

Weatherby v. RCA Corp., 1988-1 Trade Cas. (CCH) ¶ 68,077 (N.D.N.Y. 1986), 1114

Weatherby v. RCA Corp., 1988-1 Trade Cas. (CCH) ¶ 68,078 (N.D.N.Y. 1986), 661, 662, 1118

Weather-Wise Co. v. Aeroquip Corp., 468 F.2d 716 (5th Cir.), cert. denied, 410 U.S. 990 (1972), 186, 191, 192

Webb-Crawford Co. v. FTC,109 F.2d 268 (5th Cir.), cert. denied, 310 U.S. 638 (1940), 436

Webb v. Fury, 167 W. Va. 434, 282 S.E.2d 28 (1981), 638

Webb v. Primo's Inc., 706 F. Supp. 863 (N.D. Ga. 1988), 144

Webb v. Utah Tour Brokers Ass'n, 568 F.2d 670 (10th Cir. 1977), 81, 673, 1015

Webster County Memorial Hosp., Inc. v. UMW Welfare & Retirement Fund of 1950, 536 F.2d 419 (D.C. Cir. 1976), 390, 391

Webster Rosewood Corp. v. Schine Chain Theatres, 263 F.2d 533 (2d Cir.), *cert. denied*, 360 U.S. 912 (1959), 780

Webster v. Sinclair Ref. Co., 338 F. Supp. 248 (S.D. Ala. 1971), 72

Weeks Dredging & Contracting, Inc. v. American Dredging Co., 451 F. Supp. 468 (E.D. Pa. 1978), 285, 286, 287, 295

Weider Health & Fitness, Inc., 106 F.T.C. 584 (1985), 499

Weight-Rite Golf Corp. v. United States Golf Ass'n, 766 F. Supp. 1104 (M.D. Fla. 1991), 50, 89

Weight Watchers of Phila., Inc. v. Weight Watchers, Int'l, Inc., 455 F.2d 770 (2d Cir. 1972), 743, 744

Weight Watchers of Rocky Mountain Region, Inc. v. Weight Watchers, Inc., 1976-2 Trade Cas. (CCH) ¶ 61,157 (E.D.N.Y. 1976), 107, 108

Weinberger v. Retail Credit Co., 498 F.2d 552 (4th Cir. 1974), 681, 688, 689, 691, 712

Weiss v. Chalker, 55 F.R.D. 168 (S.D.N.Y. 1972), 742

Weiss v. York Hosp., 628 F.Supp. 1392 (M.D. Pa. 1986), 784

Weiss v. York Hosp., 745 F.2d 786 (3d Cir. 1984), *cert. denied*, 470 U.S. 1060 (1985), 21, 25, 27, 28, 43, 79, 85, 86, 199, 207, 213, 715, 724, 784

Weit v. Continental Ill. Nat'l Bank & Trust Co., 641 F.2d 457 (7th Cir. 1981), *cert. denied*, 455 U.S. 988 (1982), 1015, 1089

Welch v. American Psychoanalytic Ass'n, 1986-1 Trade Cas. (CCH) ¶ 67,037 (S.D.N.Y. 1986), 87, 92, 93

Well Surveys, Inc. v. McCullough Tool Co., 199 F. Supp. 374, (N.D. Okla. 1961), *aff'd*, 343 F.2d 381 (10th Cir. 1965), *cert. denied*, 383 U.S. 933 (1966), 805

Wells Fargo & Co., 72 Fed. Res. Bull. 424 (1986), 1096

Wells Real Estate, Inc. v. Greater Lowell Bd. of Realtors, 850 F.2d 803 (1st Cir.), *cert. denied*, 488 U.S. 955 (1988), 25, 147, 158

Wendkos v. ABC Consol. Corp., 379 F. Supp. 15 (E.D. Pa. 1974), 133, 170, 684

Weser v. Professional Golfers' Ass'n, 1979-2 Trade Cas. (CCH) ¶ 62,740 (N.D. Ill. 1979), *aff'd*, 1980-2 Trade Cas. (CCH) ¶ 63,530 (10th Cir. 1980), 2

West Coast Hotel Co. v. Parrish, 300 U.S. 379 (1937), 627

West Tex. Transmission, L.P. v. Enron Corp., 1989-1 Trade Cas. (CCH) ¶ 68,424 (W.D. Tex. 1988), 346

West v. Multibanco Comermex, SA, 807 F.2d 820 (9th Cir.), *cert. denied*, 482 U.S. 906 (1987), 901

West Virginia v. Chas. Pfizer & Co., 440 F.2d 1079 (2d Cir.), *cert. denied*, 404 U.S. 871 (1971), 744

Westborough Mall, Inc. v. City of Cape Girardeau, 693 F.2d 733 (8th Cir. 1982) *cert. denied*, 461 U.S. 945 (1983), 977, 982, 983

Westchester Radiological Assocs. v. Empire Blue Cross & Blue Shield, 707 F. Supp. 708 (S.D.N.Y.), *aff'd*, 884 F.2d 707 (2d Cir. 1989), *cert. denied*, 110 S. Ct. 1169 (1990), 93, 196, 220

Western Coal Traffic League v. United States, 719 F.2d 772 (5th Cir. 1983), *cert. denied*, 466 U.S. 953 (1984), 1135

Western Concrete Structures Co. v. Mitsui & Co. (U.S.A.), 760 F.2d 1013 (9th Cir.), *cert. denied*, 474 U.S. 903 (1985), 115, 116, 222, 898, 899

Western Electric Co. v. Stewart-Warner Corp., 631 F.2d 333 (4th Cir. 1980), *cert. denied*, 450 U.S. 971 (1981), 824

Western Fruit Growers Sales Co. v. FTC, 322 F.2d 67 (9th Cir. 1963), *cert. denied*, 376 U.S. 907 (1964), 434

Western Fuels Ass'n v. Burlington N. R., 102 F.R.D. 201 (D. Wyo. 1984), 565

Western Geophysical Co. of Am. v. Bolt Assocs., 50 F.R.D. 193 (D. Conn. 1970), *appeal dismissed*, 440 F.2d 765 (2d Cir. 1971), 854

Western Mountain Oil, Inc. v. Gulf Oil Corp., 575 F. Supp. 813 (D. Nev.), *aff'd*, 726 F.2d 765 (Temp. Emer. Ct. App. 1983), 692

Western Power Sports, Inc. v. Polaris Indus. Partners, 1990-1 Trade Cas. (CCH) ¶ 68,990 (D. Idaho 1990), 151, 164

Western Radio Corp. v. FTC, 339 F.2d 937 (7th Cir. 1964), *cert. denied*, 381 U.S. 938 (1965), 473

Western Shoe Gallery, Inc. v. Duty Free Shoppers, Ltd., 593 F. Supp. 348 (N.D. Cal. 1984), 691

Western Waste Serv. Sys. v. Universal Waste Control, 616 F.2d 1094 (9th Cir.), *cert. denied*, 449 U.S. 869 (1980), 24, 27, 28, 29

Western Wholesale Liquor Co. v. Gibson Wine Co., 372 F. Supp. 802 (D.S.D. 1974), 186

Westinghouse Broadcasting Co., 44 F.C.C. 2778 (1962), 1031

Westinghouse Credit Corp., 94 F.T.C. 1280 (1979), 536, 537

Westinghouse Credit Corp. v. Mountain States Mining & Milling Co., 37 F.R.D. 348 (D. Colo. 1965), 752, 753

Westinghouse Elec. & Mfg. Co. v. Cutting & Washington Radio Corp., 294 F. 671 (2d Cir. 1923), 828

Westinghouse Elec. Corp. v. Bulldog Elec. Prods. Co., 179 F.2d 139 (4th Cir. 1950), 816

Westinghouse Elec. Corp. v. City of Burlington, 326 F.2d 691 (D.C. Cir. 1964), 688

Westinghouse Elec. Corp. v. Pacific Gas & Elec. Co., 326 F.2d 575 (9th Cir. 1964), 693

Westmac, Inc. v. Smith, 797 F.2d 313 (6th Cir. 1986), *cert. denied*, 479 U.S. 1035 (1987), 1002

Westman Comm'n Co. v. Hobart Int'l Inc., 796 F.2d 1216 (10th Cir. 1986), *cert. denied*, 486 U.S. 1005 (1988), 45, 49, 50, 53, 84, 86, 180, 181, 183, 186, 187, 189, 192, 208, 217

Westpoint Pepperell, Inc. v. Rea, 1980-2 Trade Cas. (CCH) ¶ 63,341 (N.D. Cal. 1980), 186

Weyerhaueser Co., 106 F.T.C. 172 (1985), 293, 306, 310

WFLI, Inc., 13 F.C.C.2d 846 (1968), 1033, 1034

W. Goebel Porzellanfabrik v. Action Indus., 589 F. Supp. 763 (S.D.N.Y. 1984), 846, 1003

W.H. Brady Co. v. Lem Prods., 659 F. Supp. 1355 (N.D. Ill. 1987), 143, 1003

Wheeling-Pittsburgh Steel Corp. v. ICC, 723 F.2d 346 (3d Cir. 1983), 1133

Whims Appliance Serv. v. General Motors Corp., 1978-1 Trade Cas. (CCH) ¶ 62,093 (N.D. Ohio 1978), 542, 645

Whitaker Cable Corp., 51 F.T.C. 958 (1955), *aff'd*, 239 F.2d 253 (7th Cir. 1956), *cert. denied*, 353 U.S. 938 (1957), 430

Whitaker Cable Corp. v. FTC, 239 F.2d 253 (7th Cir. 1956), *cert. denied*, 353 U.S. 938 (1957), 412

Whitcom Investment Co., 92 F.C.C.2d 1067 (1983), 1037

White & White, Inc. v. American Hosp. Supply Corp., 540 F. Supp. 951 (W.D. Mich. 1982), *rev'd*, 723 F.2d 495 (6th Cir. 1983), 176

White & White, Inc. v. American Hosp. Supply Corp., 723 F.2d 495 (6th Cir. 1983), 50, 197, 265, 390

White & White, Inc. v. American Hosp. Supply Corp., 786 F.2d 728 (6th Cir. 1986), 780

White Bag Co. v. International Paper Co., 579 F.2d 1384 (4th Cir. 1974), 190, 214, 265

White Cap Co. v. Owens-Illinois Glass Co., 203 F.2d 694 (6th Cir.), *cert. denied*, 346 U.S. 876 (1953), 816

White Consol. Indus. v. Whirlpool Corp., 612 F. Supp. 1009 (N.D. Ohio), *vacated*, 619 F. Supp. 1022 (N.D. Ohio 1985), *aff'd*, 781 F.2d 1224 (6th Cir. 1986), 294, 302, 303, 359, 365, 367

White Consol. Indus. v. Whirlpool Corp., 619 F. Supp. 1022 (N.D. Ohio 1985), *aff'd*, 781 F.2d 1224 (6th Cir. 1986), 294, 370

White Directory v. Rochester Tel. Corp., 714 F. Supp. 65 (W.D.N.Y. 1989), 252

White Indus. v. Cessna Aircraft Co., 845 F.2d 1497 (8th Cir.), *cert. denied*, 488 U.S. 856 (1988), 430, 450, 666

White Lead, 21 O.J. EUR. COMM. (No. L 21) 16 (1978), [1978-1981 Transfer Binder] COMMON MKT. REP. (CCH) ¶ 10,111, 932, 933

White Motor v. United States, 372 U.S. 253 (1963), 34, 35, 60, 120, 128

White v. Hearst Corp., 669 F.2d 14 (1st Cir. 1982), 50, 180, 188, 191

White v. Mapco Gas Prods., 116 F.R.D. 498 (E.D. Ark. 1987), 754, 755

White v. Rockingham Radiologists, Ltd., 820 F.2d 98 (4th Cir. 1987), 131, 133, 143, 198

Whitlock v. Under Sea Indus., 1984-1 Trade Cas. (CCH) ¶ 65,847 (C.D. Cal. 1984), 657

Whittaker Corp. v. Edgar, 535 F. Supp. 933 (N.D. Ill. 1982), 363

Wickard v. Filburn, 317 U.S. 111 (1942), 23

Wicker v. Union County Gen. Hosp., 673 F. Supp. 177 (N.D. Miss. 1987), 971, 988

Widger Chem. Corp. v. Chemfil Corp., 601 F. Supp. 845 (E.D. Mich. 1985), 873

Wilcox Dev. Co. v. First Interstate Bank, NA, 97 F.R.D. 440 (D. Or. 1983), 712, 713, 716, 724, 730

Wilcox Dev. Co. v. First Interstate Bank, NA, 605 F. Supp. 592 (D. Or. 1985), *aff'd and remanded*, 815 F.2d 522 (9th Cir. 1987), 1089

Wilcox v. First Interstate Bank, NA, 815 F.2d 522 (9th Cir. 1987), 7, 8, 9, 73

Wilder Enters. v. Allied Artists Pictures, 632 F.2d 1135 (4th Cir. 1980), 745, 746, 747

Wileman Bros. & Elliott, Inc. v. Giannini, 909 F.2d 332 (9th Cir. 1990), 1020

Wilhelm v. Bundeskartellamt, Case 14/68, [1969] E.C.R. 1, [1967-1970 Transfer Binder] COMMON MKT. REP. (CCH) ¶ 8056, 922

Wilk v. American Medical Ass'n, 671 F. Supp. 1465 (N.D. Ill. 1987), *aff'd*, 895 F.2d 352 (7th Cir.), *cert. denied*, 110 S. Ct. 2621 (1990), 48, 93

Wilk v. American Medical Ass'n, 719 F.2d 207 (7th Cir. 1983), *cert. denied*, 467 U.S. 1210 (1984), *on remand*, 671 F. Supp. 1465 (N.D. Ill. 1987), *aff'd*, 895 F.2d 352 (7th Cir.), *cert. denied*, 110 S. Ct. 2621 (1990), 40, 85, 92

Wilk v. American Medical Ass'n, 895 F.2d 352 (7th Cir.), *cert. denied*, 110 S. Ct. 2621 (1990), 31, 33, 36, 37, 46, 48, 51, 52, 56, 92, 93, 675, 676, 679, 680

Wilkerson v. Bowen, 828 F.2d 117 (3d Cir. 1987), 717

Willard Dairy Corp. v. National Dairy Prods. Corp., 309 F.2d 943 (6th Cir. 1962), *cert. denied*, 373 U.S. 934 (1963), 403

William Cohen & Son v. All American Hero, Inc., 693 F. Supp. 201 (D.N.J. 1988), 56, 141

William Goldman Theatres v. Loew's, Inc., 69 F. Supp. 103 (E.D. Pa. 1946), *aff'd per curiam*, 164 F.2d 1021 (3d Cir.), *cert. denied*, 334 U.S. 811 (1948), 669

William Goldman Theatres v. Loew's, Inc., 150 F.2d 738 (3d Cir. 1945), 210

William Goldman Theatres v. Metro-Goldwyn-Mayer, Inc., 54 F.R.D. 201 (E.D. Pa. 1971), 749

William H. Rorer, Inc. v. FTC, 374 F.2d 622 (2d Cir. 1967), 489, 490

William Inglis & Sons Baking Co. v. ITT Continental Baking Co., 461 F. Supp. 410 (N.D. Cal. 1978), *aff'd in part and rev'd in part*, 668 F.2d 1014 (9th Cir. 1981), *cert. denied*, 459 U.S. 825 (1982), 412

William Inglis & Sons Baking Co. v. Continental Baking Co., 942 F.2d 1332 (9th Cir. 1991), 414

William Inglis & Sons Baking Co. v. ITT Continental Baking Co., 526 F.2d 86 (9th Cir. 1975), 367

William Inglis & Sons Baking Co. v. ITT Continental Baking Co., 668 F.2d 1014 (9th Cir. 1981), *cert. denied*, 459 U.S. 825 (1982), 16, 229, 230, 235, 236, 261, 268, 269, 402, 403, 414, 415, 419, 666, 667

Williams & Co. v. Williams & Co.-East, Inc., 377 F. Supp. 418 (C.D. Cal. 1974), 129

Williams & Co. v. Williams & Co.-East, Inc., 542 F.2d 1053 (9th Cir. 1976), *cert. denied*, 433 U.S. 908 (1977), 121

Williams Elec. Co. v. Honeywell, Inc., 1991-1 Trade Cas. (CCH) ¶ 69,473 (N.D. Fla. 1991), 965

Williamson v. Lee Optical of Oklahoma, Inc., 348 U.S. 483 (1955), 627

Williams Pipe Line Co., 21 F.E.R.C. (CCH) ¶ 61,260 (1982), *cert. denied* 469 U.S. 1034 (1984), 1079

Williams v. Canon, Inc., 432 F. Supp. 376 (C.D. Cal. 1977), 868, 870, 878

Williams v. Curtiss-Wright Corp., 694 F.2d 300 (3d Cir. 1982), 903, 904, 906

Williams v. St. Joseph Hosp., 629 F.2d 448 (7th Cir. 1980), 27, 81

Willow Run Garden Shop v. Mr. Christmas, Inc., 1973-2 Trade Cas. (CCH) ¶ 74,816 (D.N.J. 1973), *rev'd without published opinion*, 500 F.2d 1401 (3d Cir. 1974), 426

Will v. Comprehensive Accounting Corp., 776 F.2d 665 (7th Cir. 1985), *cert. denied*, 475 U.S. 1129 (1986), 150, 151, 154, 156, 158, 159

Wilmar Poultry Co. v. Morton-Norwich Prods., Inc., 1974-2 Trade Cas. (CCH) ¶ 75,292 (D. Minn. 1974), *aff'd*, 520 F.2d 289 (8th Cir. 1975), *cert. denied*, 424 U.S. 915 (1976), 693

Wilmar Poultry Co. v. Morton-Norwich Prods., Inc., 520 F.2d 289 (8th Cir. 1975), *cert. denied*, 424 U.S. 915 (1976), 692

Wilmorite v. Eagan Real Estate, Inc., 454 F. Supp. 1124 (N.D.N.Y. 1977) *aff'd mem.*, 578 F.2d 1372 (2d Cir.), *cert. denied*, 439 U.S. 983 (1978), 1005

Wilson P. Abraham Constr. Corp. v. Armco Steel Corp., 559 F.2d 250 (5th Cir. 1977), 565

Wilson v. I.B.E. Indus., 510 F.2d 986 (5th Cir. 1975), 130, 180, 184, 186, 187

Wilson v. Morris, 699 F.2d 926 (7th Cir. 1983), 602

Windham v. American Brands, Inc., 539 F.2d 1016 (4th Cir. 1976), 712

Windham v. American Brands, Inc., 565 F.2d 59 (4th Cir. 1977), *cert. denied*, 435 U.S. 968 (1978), 712, 728, 729, 730, 733

Windsurfing Int'l, 26 O.J. EUR. COMM. (No. L 229) 1 (1983), [1982-1985 Transfer Binder] COMMON MKT. REP. (CCH) ¶ 10,515, *aff'd sub nom.* Windsurfing Int'l Inc. v. Commission, Case 193/83, [1986] E.C.R. 611, [1985-1986 Transfer Binder] COMMON MKT. REP. (CCH) ¶ 14,271, 949

Windsurfing Int'l, Inc. v. AMF, Inc., 782 F.2d 995 (Fed. Cir.) *cert. denied*, 477 U.S. 905 (1986), 814, 815, 831, 836

Windy City Circulating Co. v. Charles Levy Circulating Co., 550 F. Supp. 960 (N.D. Ill. 1982), 429, 439

Windy City Circulating Co. v. Chas. Levy Circulating Co., 1985-2 Trade Cas. (CCH) ¶ 66,865 (N.D. Ill. 1985), 364

Winklemann v. New York Stock Exch., 445 F.2d 786 (3d Cir. 1971), 676

Winn v. Edna Hibel Corp., 858 F.2d 1517 (11th Cir., 1988), 183, 184

Winter Hill Frozen Foods & Servs. v. Haagan-Dazs Co., 691 F. Supp. 539 (D. Mass. 1988), 51, 125, 180, 181

Winterland Concessions Co. v. Trela, 735 F.2d 257 (7th Cir. 1984), 998, 1000, 1004

Winters v. Indiana & Mich. Elec. Co., 1979-2 Trade Cas. (CCH) ¶ 62,797 (N.D. Ind. 1979), 968

Winther v. DEC Int'l, Inc., 625 F. Supp. 100 (D. Colo. 1985), 662

Wire Mesh Prods., Inc. v. Wire Belting Ass'n, 520 F. Supp. 1004 (E.D. Pa. 1981), 413

Wisconsin Elec. Power Co., 59 F.P.C. 1196 (1977), 1075

Wisconsin Liquor Co. v. Park & Tilford Distillers Corp., 267 F.2d 928 (7th Cir. 1959), 270-71

Wisconsin v. Milwaukee Braves, Inc., 31 Wis. 2d 699, 144 N.W.2d 1, *cert. denied*, 385 U.S. 990 (1966), 622

Wisdom Rubber Indus. v. Johns-Manville Sales Corp., 415 F. Supp. 363 (D. Haw. 1976), 188

WIXT Television, Inc. v. Meredith Corp., 506 F. Supp. 1003 (N.D.N.Y. 1980), 168, 1004

W. J. Seufert Land Co. v. National Restaurant Supply Co., 266 Ore. 92, 511 P.2d 363 (1973), 625

W.L. Gore & Assocs. v. Carlisle Corp., 381 F. Supp. 680 (D. Del. 1975), *aff'd in relevant part*, 529 F.2d 614 (3d. Cir. 1976), 167, 168

W.L. Gore & Assocs. v. Carlisle Corp., 529 F.2d 614 (3d Cir. 1976), 823

Wm. A. Meier Glass Co. v. Anchor Hocking Glass Corp., 11 F.R.D. 487 (W.D. Pa. 1951), 747

Wm. T. Thompson Co. v. General Nutrition Corp., 104 F.R.D. 119 (C.D. Cal. 1985), 767, 770

Wolfe v. National Lead Co., 225 F.2d 427 (9th Cir.), *cert. denied*, 350 U.S. 915 (1955), 670

Wolfson v. Artisans Sav. Bank, 83 F.R.D. 547 (D. Del. 1979), 689

Wolf v. Ford Motor Co., 829 F.2d 1277 (4th Cir. 1987), 623

Wolf v. TWA, 544 F.2d 134 (3d Cir.), *cert. dismissed*, 380 U.S. 248 (1976), 1156

Wolf v. Wagner Spray Tech Corp., ¶ 715 F. Supp. 504 (S.D.N.Y. 1989), 688, 691, 692

Wood v. Combustion Eng'g, Inc., 643 F.2d 339 (5th Cir. 1981), 697

Wood v. NBA, 809 F.2d 954 (2d Cir. 1987), 91, 1124

Woods Exploration & Prod. Co. v. Aluminum Co. of Am., 438 F.2d 1286 (5th Cir. 1971) *cert. denied*, 404 U.S. 1047 (1972), 207, 213, 259, 622, 631, 1006, 1063

Woolen v. Surtran Taxicabs, Inc., 461 F. Supp. 1025 (N.D. Tex. 1978), 968

Woolen v. Surtran Taxicabs, Inc., 615 F. Supp. 344 (N.D. Tex. 1985) *aff'd per curiam*, 801 F.2d 159 (5th Cir. 1986), *cert. denied*, 480 U.S. 931 (1987), 994

Woolen v. Surtran Taxicabs, Inc., 801 F.2d 159 (5th Cir. 1986), *cert. denied*, 480 U.S. 931 (1987), 971, 988

Workman v. State Farm Mut. Auto Ins. Co., 520 F. Supp. 610 (N.D. Cal. 1981), 1118

World Airlines v. American Coupon Exch., 682 F. Supp. 1476, (C.D. Cal. 1988), *aff'd*, 913 F.2d 676 (1990), 183, 186

World Arrow Tourism Enters. v. Trans World Airlines, 582 F. Supp. 808 (S.D.N.Y. 1984), 215

World of Sleep, Inc. v. La-Z-Boy Chair, Co., 1982-2 Trade Cas. (CCH) ¶ 64,854 (D. Colo. 1982), 784, 786

World of Sleep, Inc. v. La-Z-Boy Chair Co., 756 F.2d 1467 (10th Cir.), *cert. denied*, 474 U.S. 823 (1985), 40, 437, 449, 450, 782

World of Sleep, Inc. v. Stearns & Foster Co., 525 F.2d 40 (10th Cir. 1975), 121

Worldwide Television Corp. v. FTC, 352 F.2d 303 (3d Cir. 1965), *cert. denied*, 384 U.S. 928 (1966), 480

World-Wide Volkswagen Corp. v. Autobahn Motors Co., 1980-81 Trade Cas. (CCH) ¶ 63,601 (S.D.N.Y. 1980), 405

World-Wide Volkswagen Corp. v. Woodson, 444 U.S. 286 (1980), 872, 875

Worthen Bank & Trust Co. v. National BankAmericard, Inc., 345 F. Supp. 1323 (E.D. Ark. 1972), 713

Worthen Bank & Trust Co. v. National BankAmericard, Inc., 485 F.2d 119 (8th Cir. 1973), *cert. denied*, 415 U.S. 918 (1974), 38, 380, 383, 1089, 1091

Wrede v. AT&T, 1985-1 Trade Cas. (CCH) ¶ 66,563 (M.D. Ga. 1984), 776

Wright-Patt Credit Union, Inc., 106 F.T.C. 354 (1985), 536

Wright v. Southern Mono Hosp. Dist., 631 F. Supp. 1294 (E.D. Cal. 1986), 29, 173

Writers' Guild of Am. v. ABC, 609 F.2d 355 (9th Cir. 1979), *cert. denied*, 449 U.S. 824 (1980), 1030

W.S. Kirkpatrick & Co. v. Environmental Tectonics Corp., 493 U.S. 400 (1990), 861, 901-05, 908

Wyle v. Bank Melli, 577 F. Supp. 1148 (N.D. Cal. 1983), 900

Wyle v. R.J. Reynolds Indus., 709 F.2d 585 (9th Cir. 1983), 698, 768, 770

Wyndham Assocs. v. Bintliff, 398 F.2d 614 (2d Cir.), *cert. denied*, 393 U.S. 977 (1968), 711

X

Xerox Corp., 86 F.T.C 364 (1975), 256

Xerox Corp. v. SCM Corp., 576 F.2d 1057 (3d Cir. 1978), 853

Xerox v. IBM, 64 F.R.D. 367 (S.D.N.Y. 1974), 762

Xeta, Inc. v. Atex, Inc., 825 F.2d 604 (1st Cir. 1987), 851

Xeta, Inc. v. Atex, Inc., 852 F.2d 1280 (Fed. Cir. 1988), 402, 404, 406

X/Open Group, 30 O.J. Eur. Comm. (No. L 35) 36 (1987), [1985-1988 Transfer Binder] Common Mkt. Rep. (CCH) ¶ 10,865, 936

Y

Yaffe v. Detroit Steel Corp., 50 F.R.D. 481 (N.D. Ill. 1970), 740

Yaffe v. Powers, 454 F.2d 1362 (1st Cir. 1972), 732

Yamaha Int'l Corp., 86 F.T.C. 973 (1975), 492

Yamaha Motor Co. v. FTC, 657 F.2d 971 (8th Cir. 1981), *cert. denied*, 456 U.S. 915 (1982), 276, 285, 294, 325, 326, 373, 378, 382, 383, 459

Yanai v. Frito Lay, Inc., 61 F.R.D. 349 (N.D. Ohio 1973), 729, 732

Y&Y Popcorn Supply Co. v. ABC Vending Corp., 263 F. Supp. 709 (E.D. Pa. 1967), 777, 779

Yellow Cab Co. v. Production Workers Union, 1980-81 Trade Cas. (CCH) ¶ 63,839 (Ill. App. Ct. 1980), 641

Yellow Pages Cost Consultants v. GTE Directors, 951 F.2d 1158 (9th Cir. 1991), 662, 675

Yentsch v. Texaco, Inc., 630 F.2d 46 (2d Cir. 1980) 104, 108, 109, 110, 132, 136, 144, 153, 154, 158, 181

Yoder Bros. v. California-Florida Plant Corp., 537 F.2d 1347 (5th Cir. 1976), *cert. denied*, 429 U.S. 1094 (1977), 81, 202, 205, 214, 644, 684, 687

Young & Rubicam/Zemp, Inc., 105 F.T.C. 317 (1985), 473

Young v. Katz, 447 F.2d 431 (5th Cir. 1971), 743

Younger v. Jensen, 26 Cal. 3d 397, 161 Cal. Rptr. 905, 605 P.2d 813 (1980), 624

Yves Rocher, 30 O.J. EUR. COMM. (No. L 8) 49 (1987), [1985-1988 Transfer Binder] COMMON MKT. REP. (CCH) ¶ 10,855, 941

Yves Saint-Laurent Parfums, 33 O.J. EUR. COMM. (No. C 320) 11 (1990), 940

Z

Zajicek v. Koolvent Metal Awning Corp. of Am., 283 F.2d 127 (9th Cir. 1960), *cert. denied*, 365 U.S. 859 (1961), 806

Zanussi, 21 O.J. EUR. COMM. (No. L 322) 36 (1978), [1978-1981 Transfer Binder] COMMON MKT. REP. (CCH) ¶ 10,090, 941

Zapata Gulf Marine Corp. v. Puerto Rico Maritime Shipping Auth., 682 F. Supp. 1345 (E.D. La. 1988), 980

Zapata Gulf Marine Corp. v. Puerto Rico Maritime Shipping Auth., 1989 U.S. DIST. LEXIS 13650 (E.D. La. 1989), 218, 227

Zapata Gulf Marine Corp. v. Puerto Rico Maritime Shipping Auth., 133 F.R.D. 481 (E.D. La. 1990), 646

Zavaletta v. American Bar Ass'n, 721 F. Supp. 96 (E.D. Va. 1989), 991

Zedan v. Kingdom of Saudi Arabia, 849 F.2d 1511 (D.C. Cir. 1988), 900

Zeltser v. Hunt, 90 F.R.D. 65 (S.D.N.Y. 1981), 712

Zenith Labs., Inc. v. Carter-Wallace, Inc., 64 F.R.D. 159 (D.N.J. 1974), *aff'd*, 530 F.2d 508 (3d Cir.), *cert. denied*, 429 U.S. 828 (1976), 736

Zenith Labs., Inc. v. Carter-Wallace, Inc., 530 F.2d 508 (3d Cir.), *cert. denied*, 429 U.S. 828 (1976), 676

Zenith Radio Corp. v. Hazeltine Research, Inc., 395 U.S. 100 (1969), 365, 647, 665, 667, 668, 671, 672, 676, 679, 800, 801, 814, 820, 823, 824, 838

Zenith Radio Corp. v. Hazeltine Research, Inc., 401 U.S. 321 (1971), 681, 682, 686, 746, 842

Zenith Radio Corp. v. Matsushita Elec. Indus. Co., 402 F. Supp. 244 (E.D. Pa. 1975), *petition denied*, 521 F.2d 1399 (3d Cir. 1975), 878

Zenith Radio Corp. v. Matsushita Elec. Indus. Co., 402 F. Supp. 262 (E.D. Pa. 1975), 866, 868, 870

Zenith Radio Corp. v. Matsushita Elec. Indus. Co., 494 F. Supp. 1161 (E.D. Pa. 1980), 857, 860

Zenith Radio Corp. v. Matsushita Elec. Indus., 494 F. Supp. 1246 (E.D. Pa. 1980), 655

Zenith Radio Corp. v. Matsushita Elec. Indus. Co., 723 F.2d 238 (3d Cir. 1983), *rev'd sub nom.* Matsushita Elec. Indus. Co. v. Zenith Radio Corp., 475 U.S. 574 (1986), 865

Zenith Radio Corp. v. Radio Corp. of Am., 106 F. Supp. 561 (D. Del. 1952), 854

Zernicek v. Brown & Root, Inc., 826 F.2d 415 (5th Cir. 1987), *cert. denied*, 484 U.S. 1043 (1988), 900

Zestee Foods, Inc. v. Fruehauf Corp., 390 F. Supp. 595 (N.D. Okla. 1974), 434

Zidell Explorations, Inc. v. Conval Int'l, Ltd., 719 F.2d 1465 (9th Cir. 1983), 40, 189

Zilmmer Paper Prods., Inc. v. Berger & Montague, P.C., 758 F.2d 86 (3d Cir.), *cert. denied*, 474 U.S. 902 (1985), 738, 744

Zimmerman v. NFL, 632 F. Supp. 398 (D.D.C. 1986), 1124

Zinc Producer Group, 27 O.J. EUR. COMM. (No. L 220) 27 (1984), [1982-1984 Transfer Binder] COMMON MKT. REP. (CCH) ¶ 10,617, 927

Zinc Producers, 25 O.J. EUR. COMM. (No. L 362) 40 (1982), [1982-1985 Transfer Binder] COMMON MKT. REP. (CCH) ¶ 10,447, 932

Zinser v. Continental Grain Co., 660 F.2d 754 (10th Cir. 1981), *cert. denied*, 455 U.S. 941 (1982), 654

Zisman v. Sieger, 106 F.R.D. 194 (N.D. Ill. 1985), 877, 878

Zlotnick the Furrier, Inc., 48 F.T.C. 1068 (1952), 483

Zoslaw v. CBS, 1977-2 Trade Cas. (CCH) ¶ 61,757 (N.D. Cal. 1977), 403

Zoslaw v. MCA Distrib. Corp., 594 F. Supp. 1022 (N.D. Cal. 1984), 420

Zoslaw v. MCA Distrib. Corp., 693 F.2d 870 (9th Cir. 1982), *cert. denied*, 460 U.S. 1085 (1983), 64, 73, 114, 185, 188, 403, 404, 408, 444

Züchner v. Bayerische Vereinsbank, Case 172/80, [1981] E.C.R. 2021, [1979-1981 Transfer Binder] COMMON MKT. REP. (CCH) ¶ 8706, 931

Zuckerman v. Yount, 362 F. Supp. 858 (N.D. Ill. 1973), 88, 89

Zwicker v. J. I. Case Co., 596 F.2d 305 (8th Cir. 1979), 406, 443

Zylstra v. Safeway Stores, Inc., 578 F.2d 102 (5th Cir. 1978), 723, 736

INDEX

ADMINISTRATIVE AGENCIES (*see* Exemptions; Regulated Industries)
ADVISORY OPINIONS (*see* Antitrust Division; Federal Trade Commission)
AGREEMENT (*see* Concerted Action)
AGRICULTURAL COOPERATIVES (*see* Regulated Industries)
ANCILLARY RESTRAINTS, 74, 76-77 (*see also* Covenants Not to Compete; Joint Ventures)
ANTITRUST DIVISION (*see also* Mergers and Acquisitions)
   Antitrust Cooperation Agreements, 894-95
   Bilateral Agreements, 894-95
      European Economic Community, 895
   Business Review Letters, 548-50
   Civil Investigative Demands, 556-60
   Clearance Procedures, 547
   Consent Decrees, 569-79
      Antitrust Division procedure, 570
      Antitrust Procedures and Penalties Act, 572
      approval, procedures for, 573-74
      approval, standard for, 573
      competitive impact statement, 572-73
      contempt, 574
      intervention, 578-79
      legal effect, 569-70
      modification, 575-77
      public comment, 572-73
      Tunney Act, 572
   Damages Actions, 579
   Freedom of Information Act, 560
   Guidelines, 548
   Indictment, Effect of Cooperation on, 568
   Indictment, Opportunity for Meeting Prior to, 568-69
   Investigations, Commencement of, 552-53
   Investigations, Criminal, 553-56
   Investigations, Merger, 560
   Nolo Contendere Pleas, Policy on, 582
   Organization, 545-47, 552
      clearance procedures, 547
      economists, 547

   field offices, 545-46
   legislative matters, 552
   office of operations, 546-47
   Washington sections, 545-46
   Plea Bargains, 581
   Sentencing Guidelines, 597
   Speeches, 548
   Use Immunity, 593
ANTITRUST INJURY (*see also* Private Antitrust Suits – Injury)
   Monopolization Cases, 196
   Merger Cases, 362-63
   Private Suits, 650-52
   Robinson-Patman Cases, 449
   Vertical Price Restrictions, 104-05
ANTITRUST PROCEDURES AND PENALTIES ACT, 572
APPEARANCE AND IMAGE STANDARDS (*see* Vertical Refusals to Deal)
ARBITRATION, 787-88
   Domestic Transactions, 788
   International Transactions, 788
AREA OF PRIMARY RESPONSIBILITY (*see* Vertical Nonprice Restrictions)
ATTEMPTS TO MONOPOLIZE (*see* Monopolization)
ATTORNEY-CLIENT PRIVILEGE, 760-66 (*see also* Criminal Enforcement)
   Control Group Test, 760-61
   Crime/Fraud Exception, 762-66
   In Camera Review, 764-66
   Subject Matter Test, 760
   Upjohn Test, 760-62
   Waiver, 762
ATTORNEYS' FEES, 780-87
   Appellate Work, 785
   Defendant, 781-82
   Lodestar Method, 782-85
   Paralegal Fees, 786
   Successful Plaintiff, 780-87
   Unsuccessful Plaintiff, 787

BID RIGGING, 44, 1108-09 (*see also* Per Se Rule; Price Fixing)
   Government Contracts, 1108-09
BOYCOTT (*see* Concerted Refusal to Deal)
BUSINESS JUSTIFICATION, PURPOSE OR REASONS (*see* Rule of Reason; Tying; Vertical Refusals to Deal)

BUYING COOPERATIVE (*see* Concerted
    Refusal to Deal – Purchasing
    Cooperative; Joint Venture – Joint
    Buying Arrangements)
CAPPER-VOLSTEAD ACT (*see* Regulated
    Industries)
CIVIL INVESTIGATIVE DEMANDS, 556-60
    Document Production, 559
    Documents, Return of, 560
    Information Obtained, Disclosure of,
        560
    Information Obtained, Uses of, 559-60
    Petition to Modify or Set Aside, 557-59
    Procedures for Issuance, 556
    Scope, 556-57
    Scope, Negotiations, 557
    Testimony, 559
CLASS ACTIONS (*see* Private Antitrust
    Suits)
CLAYTON ACT, § 3 (*see* Tying)
CLAYTON ACT, § 7 (*see* International
    Antitrust; Mergers and Acquisitions;
    Private Antitrust Suits)
CLAYTON ACT, § 10, 1145
COLGATE DOCTRINE (*see* Resale Price
    Maintenance)
COLLATERAL ESTOPPEL (*see* Private
    Antitrust Suits)
COMMERCE (*see* Foreign Commerce;
    Interstate Commerce)
CONCENTRATION (*see* Market Power;
    Market Share; Mergers and
    Acquisitions – Concentration
    Measures)
CONCERTED ACTION, 2-13, 15-17, 67, 69,
    100, 105-06 (*see also* Conspiracy,
    Proof of; Horizontal Restraint or
    Agreement; Intraenterprise
    Conspiracy)
    Acquiescence in Conduct, 16-17
    Circumstantial Evidence of, 4-10, 12
    Dealer Termination, 105-06
    Distribution Network, 15
    Express Agreement, 3-4
    Independent Action, 12-13, 100
    Indirectly Controlling Prices, 69 (*see
        also* Price Fixing – Actions Indirectly
        Affecting Price)
    Price Fixing, 67 (*see also* Price Fixing)
    Unilateral Conduct, 11 (*see also*
        Independent Action)

CONCERTED REFUSAL TO DEAL, 77-95,
    Association Procedural Safeguards, 89-
        90
    "Classic Boycott," 84-86
    First Amendment, 84, 94 (*see also
        Noerr-Pennington* Doctrine)
    Health Care Associations and
        Hospitals, 91-94
    Horizontal Price Fixing, 84
    Horizontal Refusal to Deal, 77, 80-82
    Industry Self-Regulation, 86-87
    Market Power, 82-84
    Noneconomic Boycotts, 94-95 (*see also
        Noerr-Pennington* Doctrine)
    Per Se Rule, 78-82, 84-85
    Purchasing Cooperative, 82-83
    Rule of Reason, 78, 83, 89-80
    Sports League, 90-91
    Standard and Certification Programs,
        88
CONSCIOUS PARALLELISM, 5-7 (*see also*
    Concerted Action – Circumstantial
    Evidence of)
CONSENT DECREES (*see* Antitrust
    Division)
CONSIGNMENT (*see* Vertical Price
    Restrictions)
CONSPIRACIES TO ELIMINATE A
    COMPETITOR BY UNFAIR MEANS
    (*see Pick-Barth* Doctrine)
CONSPIRACY (*see* Concerted Action;
    Horizontal Restraint or Agreement;
    Monopolization – Conspiracy to
    Monopolize; *Pick-Barth* Doctrine)
CONSPIRACY, PROOF OF, 2-17
COOPERATIVE ADVERTISING (*see* Price
    Fixing)
COPPERWELD DOCTRINE (*see*
    Intraenterprise Conspiracy)
COVENANTS NOT TO COMPETE, 98-99
    Ancillary Restraint, 98-99
    Reasonableness of, 98-99
CRIMINAL ENFORCEMENT (*see also*
    Robinson-Patman Act; State
    Antitrust Enforcement)
    Acquittal, 598
    Appeals, 599-600
    Arraignment, 580
    Arrest Warrant, 579
    Attorney-Client Privilege, 565
        joint defense privilege, 565

CRIMINAL ENFORCEMENT (*continued*)
  Conflicts of Interest, 600-02
    disqualification for potential conflict, 601-02
    multiple representation, 600-01
    waiver by client, 602
  Criminal Remedies, 561 (*see also* Sentencing)
  Discovery, 587-91
    bill of particulars, 587-88
    Brady material, 589-90
    defendant's grand jury testimony, 587
    exculpatory material, 587-89
    government witnesses, statements of, 590
    grand jury testimony, 590-91
    impeachment material, 589-90
    Jencks Act, 590
    subpoenas, 588-89
  Double Jeopardy, 585-86
  Evidence, 593-94
    coconspirator statements, 593-94
  Grand Jury, 562-69, 585, 590-91, 600, 754-60
    abuse, conduct alleged to be, 566-67
    abuse, prejudice required to obtain dismissal for, 567-68
    cooperation, 568
    indictment, Antitrust Division policy on, 568
    indictment, opportunity for meeting prior to, 568-69
    irregularities, basis to quash indictment, 585
    leniency, 568-69
    materials, use in civil proceeding, 600, 754-60
    subpoenas, 562-64
    targets, notification of, 566
    testimony, consultation with counsel, 564-65
    testimony, discovery in criminal cases of, 590-91
    testimony, joint defense privilege, 565
    witness interviews, 565-66
  Grand Jury Materials, 754-60
    debriefing materials, 760
    disclosure, 754
    documents, 758
    particularized need, 756
    proper court, 759
    testimony, 755
    work product privilege, 760
  Immunity, 591-93
    transactional, 591
    use, 591-93 (*see also* Use Immunity)
  Intent, 554, 594-95
    antitrust compliance programs, 594-95
    criminal, 554
  Investigations, 561
    remedies, 561
  Joinder, 584-85
  New Trial, 598-99
  Pleas, 580-83
    court, role of, 581
    guilty plea, 580
    guilty plea, consequences of, 582
    nolo contendere, 580, 582, 583
    nolo contendere, Antitrust Division policy, 582
    plea bargains, 581
    use in other proceedings, 583
    withdrawal, 582
  Pretrial Release, 580
    bail, 580
  Sentencing, 595-97
    Antitrust Division Guidelines, 597
    presentencing reports, 595-97
    Sentencing Commission Guidelines, 596-97
    Sentencing Reform Act of 1984, 596
    Sherman Act penalties, 596
  Severance, 584-85
  Speedy Trial Act, 586
  Use Immunity, 591-93
    Antitrust Division procedures, 593
    procedures for obtaining, 592
    scope, 591-92
  Venue, Criminal Cases, 585
  Wire and/or Mail Fraud, 66-67
CUSTOMER ALLOCATIONS (*see* Horizontal Restraint or Agreement; Per Se Rule; Territorial Allocation and Customer Restrictions)

DAMAGES (*see* Antitrust Division; Mergers and Acquisitions; Private Antitrust Suits)
DEALER ASSISTANCE PROGRAMS (*see* Vertical Price Restrictions)
DEALER TERMINATION (*see* Horizontal Restraint or Agreement; Vertical Refusals to Deal)

DISCOVERY (*see* International Antitrust, Procedural Issues; Private Antitrust Suits)

DISCRIMINATION (*see* European Economic Community – Competition Law; Robinson Patman Act)

DISTRIBUTION RESTRAINTS (*see* Resale Price Maintenance; Territorial Allocation and Customer Restrictions; Vertical Nonprice Restrictions; Vertical Price Restrictions)

DUAL DISTRIBUTION (*see* Horizontal Restraint or Agreement; Vertical Nonprice Restrictions)

EFFICIENCIES (*see* Joint Ventures; Mergers and Acquisitions – Efficiencies; Rule of Reason)

ENTRY (*see* Mergers and Acquisitions; Monopolization)

EUROPEAN ECONOMIC COMMUNITY
 Composition, 918-19
 Court of Justice, 920
 Court of First Instance, 920
 Enforcement Responsibilities, 918

EUROPEAN ECONOMIC COMMUNITY –
 ANTITRUST POLICY, 922-24
 Differences from United States, 923
 Goals, 922
 Market Structure, Role of, 923
 Regulated Monopolies, 923-24
 State Aid, Limitations on, 923-24

EUROPEAN ECONOMIC COMMUNITY –
 COMPETITION LAW
 Abuse of Dominant Position, 950-58
  abuse generally, 953-54
  collective dominance, 952
  discrimination, 957
  dominance, indicia of, 952-53
  dominant position, 951
  market definition, 951-52
  market share, 953
  practices prohibited, 950
  pricing conduct, 956-57
  refusal to deal, 954-56
  relationship to Article 85, 954
  tying, 959
 Article 85, 931-50 (*see also* Restrictive Agreements)
 Article 86 (*see* Abuse of Dominant Position)

Block Exemptions, 922, 926-27, 936, 939-42, 942-45, 948-50, 950-51
  concerted practice, 922
  exclusive distribution, 940
  exclusive purchasing, 942
  franchises, 941-42
  know-how licensing, 949-50
  patent licensing, 948
  research and development, 936
 Horizontal Restrictions, 932-39
  concentrative joint venture, 937-38
  cooperative joint venture, 937-38
  customer allocation, 932
  information exchange, 933
  investment in competitor, 939
  joint advertising, 936-37
  joint purchasing agreements, 933
  joint sales agencies, 933
  market division, 932
  output restrictions, 932
  price fixing, 933
  reciprocal dealing, 932
  research and development, 935-36
  sale of business, noncompetition agreement, 937
  software standards, 936-37
  specialization agreements, 935
  trademarks, 936-37
 Industrial Property, 944-50
  copyrights, 946
  exclusive territories, 946-47
  exhaustion of rights, 946
  licensing, 947, 948-49
  patent licensing, block exemption, 948
  patents, 946
  rights under national law, limits on trademarks, 944-46
  subcontracting, 945
 Intellectual Property Rights, 945
 Mergers and Acquisitions, 958-61
  abuse of dominant position, 958-59
  ancillary restrictions, 960
  community dimension, concentrations with, 961
  concentrations, 960
  national law, applicability of, 960
  prenotification, 960
  private enforcement, 961
  regulation, 959
  thresholds, 960
 National Antitrust Enforcement, 921-22

EUROPEAN ECONOMIC COMMUNITY –
    COMPETITION LAW (*continued*)
Negative Clearance and Exemptions,
    922, 924-26
    application, 925-26
    effect, 926
    exemption, individual, 926
    exemption, standard for obtaining,
        925-26
    notices, 925
    notification, 926
    provisional validity, 926
    time period, 925
Regulations, 918-20
Remedies
    fines, 918
    injunctions, 918
Reports, 918-20
Restrictive Agreements, 931-32 (*see
    also* Horizontal Restrictions;
    Industrial Property; Vertical
    Restraints)
    concerted action, 931
    effect on trade, 932
    intraenterprise conspiracy, 931
    prohibited practices, 931
Vertical Restraints, 939-44
    exclusive distributorships, 939-40
    franchises, 941-42
    miscellaneous practices, 943-44
    parallel trade, 940
    requirements contracts, 942-43
    resale price maintenance, 942-43
    selective distribution, 940-41
    territorial restrictions, 939
    tying, 943
EUROPEAN ECONOMIC COMMUNITY –
    JURISDICTION, 927-30, 933
Appreciable Effect on Trade
    Between the Member States, 933
Appreciable Impact on Competition,
    933
Export Trade, 928, 929-30
Extraterritorial Acts, 927-28
Trade Between Member States, 927,
    928-30
EXCHANGING PRICE INFORMATION (*see
    Price Fixing)
EXCLUSIVE DEALING, 169-79
Anticompetitive Effect, 173-74
Clayton Act, § 3, 169-70, 172, 174
Competitive Effect of, 170

Exclusive Distributorship, Distinguished
    from, 169
FTC Act, § 5, 169, 174-76
Interbrand Competition, 175
Market Foreclosure, 171-72, 174
Qualitative Substantiality Test, 171
Quantitative Substantiality Test, 170
Requirements Contracts, 169-70
Rule of Reason, 175, 178
Tying Arrangements, Compared with,
    169
EXCLUSIVE DISTRIBUTORSHIPS, 117-19,
    169, 183 (*see also* Exclusive Dealing;
    Territorial Allocation and Customer
    Restrictions; Vertical Nonprice
    Restrictions)
Exclusive Dealing, Distinguished from,
    169
Interbrand Competition, 119
EXEMPTIONS
Export Trade (*see* International
    Antitrust – Export Trading Company
    Act)
Express Exemptions, 1016-17
Implied Exemptions, 1018-19
Implied Repeal of Antitrust Laws,
    1016-19

FEDERAL TRADE COMMISSION
    (CHAPTER V)
Consumer Credit, 532-40
    Consumer Leasing Act, 535
    Electronic Fund Transfer Act, 539
    Equal Credit Opportunity Act,
        537-38
    Fair Credit Billing Act, 535
    Fair Credit Reporting Act, 535-37
    Fair Debt Collection Practices Act,
        538-39
    Federal Trade Commission Act, 532-
        33
    Holder in Due Course Rule, 539
    Truth-in-Lending Act, 533-35
Deceptive Acts and Practices, 464-82,
    492-94
    actual deception, 464-66
    business, employment, and sales
        practices, 478-81
    business or trade status, 477
    business torts, 477-78
    commercial speech, 466-67, 492-93
    endorsements and testimonials,
        474-75

FEDERAL TRADE COMMISSION –
  Deceptive Acts and Practices
  (*continued*)
  guarantees, 475
  material facts, failure to disclose,
    468-69
  meaning of representations, 469-71
  1983 Policy Statement, 471-72
  origin of products, 476-77
  pricing claims, 475-76
  product characteristics, 472-74
  scienter, 464
  substantiation, 467-68
  television advertising, 480-82
  Labeling, 541-42
    Fair Packaging and Labeling Act,
      541
    FTC Act regulation, 541-52
    wool, textiles, and fur labeling,
      541
  Merger Enforcement (*see* Mergers and
    Acquisitions – Federal Trade
    Commission)
  Procedure, 504-24, 530-32
    advisory opinions, 530-31
    advocacy, 532
    confidential information, 516-20
    discovery, 510-13
    enforcement policy statements, 531
    evidence, 513
    industry guides, 531
    intervention, 512-13
    investigative procedure, 504-09
    judicial review, final orders, 521-23
    judicial review, interlocutory, 523-24
    modification of orders, 515-16
    privileges and immunity, 513-14
    separation of functions, 509-10
    settlement, 514-15
  Remedies, 487-504 (*see also*
    Mergers and Acquisitions)
    cease and desist orders, 488-92,
      493-95
    civil penalties, 495-98
    consumer redress, 498-501
    corrective advertising, 492
    injunctions, 501-04
    trade regulation rules, 495
  Rulemaking, 524-30
    authority, 524-25
    judicial review, 529-30
    Magnuson-Moss, 525-26
    procedures, 526-28

  State "Little FTC Acts," 543-44
  Unfair Acts and Practices, 482-87
    cigarette labeling rule,
      483-84
    examples, 484-87
    general standards, 482-83
    1980 Policy Statement, 483-84
  Warranties, 539-40
FEDERAL TRADE COMMISSION ACT
  Commerce Requirement, 454-55
  Construction with other Statutes, 457
  Exclusive Dealing, 169, 174-76
  Foreign Commerce, 864
  Generally, 453-63, 542-43
  Merger Cases, 276, 353-55, 372, 392
  Policies of other Statutes, 457-63
  Private Right of Action, 542-43
  Private Suits, 645, 684
  Profit Requirement, 455-56
  Public Interest Requirement, 455
  Restraints of Trade, 68, 133-34, 169,
    174-76
  Structure, 453-54
  Wheeler-Lea Amendments, 453, 464
FEDERAL TRADE COMMISSION ACT, § 5,
  68, 133-34, 169, 174-76
FILED RATE DOCTRINE, 1019-21, 1073
  Suits by Competitors, 1020-21
FIRST AMENDMENT, 990-92, 996 (*see also*
  Noerr-Pennington Doctrine)
FOREIGN COMMERCE (*see* International
  Antitrust)
FRANCHISES (*see* Territorial Allocation
  and Customer Restrictions; Tying;
  Vertical Nonprice Restrictions)
FREEDOM OF INFORMATION ACT, 560
  Civil Investigative Demands, 560
FREE RIDING (*see* Rule of Reason;
  Vertical Nonprice Restrictions;
  Vertical Refusals to Deal)
FULL LINE FORCING (*see* Tying)

GEOGRAPHIC MARKET DEFINITION, 44
  208-11, 282, 291, 293-98 (*see also*
  Market Definition)
  Department of Justice Approach,
    297-98
  Foreign Competitors, 298
  FTC Approach, 298
  Monopolization Cases, 208-11
  NAAG Approach, 298
  Sales Patterns, 295
  "Section of the Country," 282, 293

GEOGRAPHIC MARKET DEFINITION
  (*continued*)
  Submarkets, 297-98
  Transportation Costs, 295-96
GOVERNMENT CONTRACTS, 1107-09
  Bid Rigging, 1108-09
  Customer Allocation, 1109
  Federal Acquisition Regulation,
    1107-08
  Procurement Policy, 1107
  Teaming Agreements, 1109
  Territorial Allocation, 1109
GRAND JURY (*see* Criminal Enforcement;
  Private Antitrust Suits)
GROUP BOYCOTTS (*see* Concerted
  Refusal to Deal)

HEALTH CARE ASSOCIATIONS AND
  HOSPITALS (*see* Concerted Refusals
  to Deal)
HORIZONTAL RESTRAINT OR
  AGREEMENT, 2, 60-62, 74-77, 1109
  (*see also* Territorial Allocation and
  Customer Restrictions)
  Customer Allocations, 2, 74-77
  Dealer Termination, 61
  Dual Distribution, 62
  Government Contracts, 1109
  Output Restrictions, 74
  Rule of Reason, 76-77
  Territorial Allocations, 2, 74-77
  Vertical Restraint, Distinguished
    from, 60-61

IMMUNITY
  Damages Immunity
    local government officials, 987
    local governments, 987
  Federal Agencies
    immunity of, 965
  Federal Officials
    approval of conduct by, 963-64
    immunity of, 965
INDUSTRY SELF-REGULATION (*see*
  Concerted Refusal to Deal)
INJUNCTIVE RELIEF (*see* Mergers and
  Acquisitions; Private Antitrust Suits)
INJURY (*see* Antitrust Injury; Private
  Antitrust Suits)
INTELLECTUAL PROPERTY (CHAPTER IX)
  Arbitration, 840
  Copyright
    defined, 844

  misuse, 845
  Noerr-Pennington doctrine, 846-47
  restrictions on import, 843
Copyright Licenses
  package licenses, 834
Crosslicensing, 837-39
Customer Restrictions, 827
Exhaustion, 828
Export Trading Company Act, 840
Federal Circuit Patent Claims,
  jurisdiction over, 851
Field of Use Restrictions, 828-30
First Sale Doctrine, 828
Foreign Trade Antitrust Improvements
  Act, 840, 843
Grantbacks
  defined, 804
  Department of Justice enforcement,
    806
  exclusive, 805-06
  rule of reason, 805
International Guidelines
  patents, foreign licensing, 839-44
  patents, market power, 802-03
Know-how, Licensing
  Department of Justice position, 839-
    40, 842
  international agreements, 840
  statutes, 840
  territorial restrictions, 842
Lanham Act
  incontestability, 848
Location Clauses, 827
National Cooperative Research Act,
  840
No-Contest Clause, 835-37
Noerr-Pennington Doctrine, 846-47
Package Licensing, 834 (*see also*
  Copyright Licenses; Patent
  Licenses)
Patent Licenses (*see also* Grantbacks)
  agreement not to contest validity,
    835-37
  boycott, 839
  crosslicensing, 837-39
  customer restrictions, 827
  Department of Justice position,
    819-20
  exclusivity, 820
  field of use restrictions, 828-30
  first sale doctrine, 828
  geographic restrictions, 827-28
  location clauses, 827

INTELLECTUAL PROPERTY – Patent
      Licenses (*continued*)
   nine no-no's, 819
   package licensing, 834-35
   patent pools, 837-39
   price limitations, 821
   quantity limitations, 822
   refusal to license, 818
   royalties, based on use, 826
   royalties, discriminatory, 824-25
   royalties, fixing, 827
   royalties, postexpiration, 825-26
   royalties, preissuance, 826
   royalties, unrelated to use, 823-24
   territorial restrictions, 827-28
Patent Misuse
   applicability of antitrust rules, 815-16
   collection of royalties, 816
   consequences, 816
   contributory infringement, 816-18
   defined, 813
   historical development, 813-14
   purge of, 816
   statutory limitations on, 816-17
   statutory limits on, 815
   tying, 831
Patent Pools, 837-39 (*see also* Patent
   Licenses)
Patents
   antitrust violations, remedies for,
      852-53
   appellate jurisdiction, 81
   as monopoly, 801
   contributory infringement, 817
   direct infringement, 816
   Federal Circuit, 851
   market power, 801-03, 815
   misuse and antitrust rules, 815-16
   nonuse, 818
   nonuse, agreement for, 819
   settlement of infringements and
      interferences, 854
   special antitrust rules for, 800
Patents, Acquisition
   assignment, 803
   Clayton Act, § 7, applicability of, 804
   grantbacks, 804-06 (*see also*
      Grantbacks)
   internal development, 803
   National Cooperative Research Act,
      804
   transferability, 804

Patents, Fraudulent Procurement
   as antitrust violation, 807
   fraud, definition of, 808-09
   inequitable conduct, 809-10
   monopolization, 807-08
   unenforceability, 806-07
Patents, Invalid
   damages, 813
   enforcement of as antitrust violation,
      811-12
   Noerr-Pennington doctrine, 812
   subjective belief in validity, 812
Patents, Licensing Foreign Patents
   Department of Justice position, 839-
      40
   international agreements, 840
   statutes, 840
   territorial restrictions, 841-42
Robinson-Patman Act
   royalties, discriminatory, 824
Royalties, 823-24 (*see also* Patent
   Licenses)
Territorial Restrictions, 827-28
   (*see also* Know-how, Licensing;
      Patent Licenses)
Trade Secrets (*see also* Know-
   how, Licensing)
   bad faith assertion of, 850
   licenses, 850
   state law, 849
Trademark
   defined, 847
   incontestability, 848
   licensing, 847
   misuse, 847
   restrictions on import, 842
   tying arrangements, 848-49 (*see also*
      Tying)
Tying Arrangements
   antitrust violation, 833
   copyright, market power, 831
   defined, 830
   market power, 831
   misuse, 831-32 (*see also* Patent
      Misuse)
   patent, market power, 831
   statutory limitations, 832
INTERBRAND COMPETITION (*see* Exclusive
      Dealing; Exclusive
      Distributorships; Rule of Reason;
      Territorial Allocation and
      Customer Restrictions; Vertical
      Nonprice Restrictions)

INTERLOCKING DIRECTORATES, 392-99
  Antitrust Amendments Act of 1990,
    392, 394, 396
  Clayton Act, § 8, 392-99
  Depository Institution Management
    Interlocks Act, 392
  Enforcement and Policy, 398-99
  Indirect Interlocks, 396-97
INTERNATIONAL ANTITRUST
  Act of State Doctrine, 901-09
    effect, 901-02
    exceptions, 907-09
    intellectual property rights, 906, 907
    judicial decrees, 906
  Antitrust Cooperation Agreements,
    894-95
  Arbitration, 895-96
  Clayton Act, § 7, 864-65
  Comity
    discovery, 866 (see also International
      Antitrust – Procedural Issues)
    Foreign Trade Antitrust
      Improvements Act, 861
    intended effects test, 859-60
    jurisdiction, 858-63
    Restatement of Foreign Relations
      Law, 862
    Timberlane doctrine, 858-59
    United States as party, 862
  Defense Production Act, 918 (see also
    National Defense)
  Dumping, 898
  Export Trading Company Act, 916-17
  Extraterritoriality, 892-94
    blocking statutes, 893-94
  Federal Trade Commission Act, 864
  Foreign Sovereign Compulsion, 909-11
    compelled conduct, 910
  Foreign Sovereign Immunity Act,
    899-901
    commercial activity, 899-901
  Foreign Trade Antitrust Improvements
    Act, 857-58, 861-64
    comity, 861-62
    Department of Justice
      interpretation, 863-64
    injuries compensable, 858
    jurisdictional test, 857-58
    standing, 858
  Injunctions, 889-90
  Intellectual Property, 897-98
    international licensing, 897-98

International Guidelines, 863
National Defense, 918
Petitioning Foreign Governments,
    898-99, 912-13
  Antitrust Division position, 913
  discovery privilege, 913
  Noerr-Pennington, 912-13
  sham litigation, 898-99
Premerger Notification, 897
  acquisition by firm controlled by
    foreign government, 897
  acquisition of foreign assets, 897
  acquisition by foreign government,
    897
Relief, 889-92, 895-96
  arbitration, 895-96
  comity, 891-92
  injunctions, 889
Restraints Approved by U.S. Executive
    Branch, 911-12
  authority to confer immunity, 911-12
  import restraints, 912
  private parties, 912
Robinson-Patman Act, 865
  foreign commerce, 865
  subject matter jurisdiction, 865
Statutory Exemptions, 914 (see also
    Export Trading Company Act;
    National Defense;
    Webb-Pomerene Act)
Trade Laws, 899
Webb-Pomerene Act, 914-16
  activities protected, 915
  registration, 916
INTERNATIONAL ANTITRUST,
  PROCEDURAL ISSUES
Blocking Statutes, 886, 893-94
  discovery, 886
  relief, 893-94
Discovery Abroad, 879-89
  blocking statutes, 886
  foreign law limitations, effect of,
    885-87
  Hague Convention on the Taking of
    Evidence Abroad, 882, 884-85
  letters rogatory, 881-84
  limitations on pretrial discovery,
    882-84
  nonparties, 881
  parties to the action, 879-81
  privileges, 884
  procedure, 882

INTERNATIONAL ANTITRUST,
   PROCEDURAL ISSUES – Discovery
   Abroad (*continued*)
  relation to Federal Rules of Civil
    Procedure, 884-85
  reservations, 882-84
  sanctions, 886-87
  subpoenas to U.S. citizens or
    residents, 881
  Nonresident Defendants, 874-77
  Personal Jurisdiction, 871-77
   aggregate contacts, 875-77
   challenges to jurisdiction, 874
   effect in forum, 875
   fairness, 872
   minimum contacts test, 871-74
   national contacts, 875-77
   nonresident defendants, 874-77
   service of process, 875-77
   transacting business, 874-75
   venue, relationship to, 873-74
  Service of Process, 877-79
   Clayton Act, 877
   extraterritorial, 877-78
   Hague Service Convention, 878
   method, 878
   subsidiary of foreign parent, 878-79
  Standing, 858
   Foreign Trade Antitrust
    Improvements Act, 858
  Subject Matter Jurisdiction, 856-67
   Alcoa doctrine, 856-67
   Clayton Act, § 3, 865
   Clayton Act, § 7, 864-65
   comity, 858-63
   International Guidelines, 863-64
   Federal Trade Commission Act, 864
   Foreign Trade Antitrust
    Improvements Act, 856-58, 861,
    863-64
   Restatement of Foreign Relations
    Law, 862
   Robinson-Patman Act, 865
   Sherman Act, 856-57, 859-64
   simultaneous proceedings in two
    countries, 863
   United States as party, 862
   United States as purchaser, 864
  Venue, 866-71
   antitrust venue provisions, 866-67
   corporations, 866-67
   foreign state as defendant, 871
   forum non conveniens, 866

   general venue statute, 869-71
   individuals, 866-67
   transacts business, 867-69
INTERNATIONAL GUIDELINES, 278, 298,
   386, 389, 802-03, 839-44 (*see also*
   Intellectual Property)
  Licensing Foreign Patents, 839-44
  Patents, Market Power, 802-03
INTERSTATE COMMERCE, 22-27, 28, 196,
   402-04
  "Affecting" Commerce, 23-25, 28
  "In" Commerce, 23
  Monopolization Cases, 196
  Robinson-Patman Cases, 402-04
INTRABRAND COMPETITION (*see* Rule of
   Reason; Territorial Allocation and
   Customer Restrictions)
INTRAENTERPRISE CONSPIRACY, 17-22,
   270-71
  Copperweld Doctrine, 18-21
  Monopolization Cases, 270-71
  Officers, Agents and Employees, 18,
   21-22

JOINT VENTURES, 74, 339, 372-92 (*see
   also* Regulated Industries – Joint
   Ventures in Regulated Markets)
  Collateral Restraints, 378-87
   ancillary restraints, 379
   customer restraints, 381-84
   Department of Justice and FTC
    approaches, 386-87
   restraints on access, 384-86
   restraints on price and output,
    379-81
   territorial and customer restraints,
    381-84
  Formation of a Joint Venture, 372-76
   creation of new product, 374-76
   integrative efficiencies, 372-73
   market power, 376-78, 385
  Joint Buying Arrangements, 389-92
   (*see also* Concerted Refusal to
   Deal – Purchasing Cooperative)
   Department of Justice approach, 74,
    391-92
  Joint Selling Arrangements, 389-92
  National Cooperative Research Act,
   388-89
  Per Se Rule, 373-74, 385, 390
  Production Joint Ventures, 377-78, 387
  Research Joint Ventures, 388-89
  Spillover Market, 386

JUSTICE DEPARTMENT (*see* Antitrust
    Division)

KEOGH Doctrine, 1019-21, 1130-39
    Suits by Competitors, 1020-21

LABOR UNIONS, 1119-26
    Labor Group, 1120-21
    Nonstatutory Exemption, 1121-26
    National Labor Relations Act, 1124-26
    Norris-La Guardia Act, 1120
    Statutory Exemption, 1119-21
LOCAL GOVERNMENT ANTITRUST ACT
        OF 1984, 984, 987-88
    Attorneys' Fees, 988
    Damages Immunity, 984
    Injunctive Relief, 987-88
    Retroactive Application, 988
    Scope of, 987
LOCATION CLAUSES (*see* Territorial
        Allocation and Customer
        Restrictions; Vertical Nonprice
        Restrictions)

MARKET DEFINITION, 44, 46, 199-211,
        266, 282-89 (*see also* Geographic
        Market Definition; Product Market
        Definition)
    Attempt to Monopolize, 266
    Cluster Markets, 207-08
    Cross-Elasticity of Demand, 201-02,
        282-87
    Cross-Elasticity of Supply, 202-04, 287
    Merger Cases, 282
    Production Substitutability, 202-04,
        287-88
    Reasonable Interchangeability of Use,
        200-02
    Single Product Markets, 206-07
    Submarkets, 204-05, 208, 288-89
    Summary Judgment, 199
    Type, Grade, or Quality Differences,
        205
MARKET DIVISION (*see* Horizontal
        Restraint or Agreement; Territorial
        Allocations and Customer
        Restrictions)
MARKET FORECLOSURE (*see* Exclusive
        Dealing)
MARKET POWER (*see also*
        Monopolization – Monopoly Power)
    Compare to Monopoly Power, 212

Joint Ventures, 376-78, 385
    Merger Cases, 276, 299-300
    Monopolization Cases, 50, 82-83, 212
    Restraints of Trade, 50-51, 58-59
    Tying Cases, 163
MARKET SHARE, 212-14, 263-64, 299-307
    Attempt to Monopolize Cases, 263-64
    Merger Cases, 299-307
    Monopoly Power, 212-14
MAXIMUM RESALE PRICES, 104-05 (*see
        also* Per Se Rule; Price Fixing)
MCCARRAN-FERGUSON ACT, 1110-18
    Availability of Exemption, 1110
    Boycott Exception, 1117-18
    Business of Insurance, 1110-14
    Coercion, 1118
    Effectiveness of State Regulation, 1115
    Interstate Commerce, 1110
    Intimidation, 1118
    State Regulation Requirement,
        1114-16
MERGERS AND ACQUISITIONS
        (CHAPTER III)
    Antitrust Injury, 362-63
    Burden of Proof, 325-26
    Clayton Act
        acquisition of not-for-profit entities,
            279
        partial acquisitions, 280-81
        Section 7, 275-82, 293, 298-99, 303,
            305, 313, 317, 322, 324, 351, 357,
            364, 371, 377
        "solely for investment" exception,
            281
    Collusion, 311-12
    Concentration Measures (*see also*
        Market Share)
        capacity, 300-01
        concentration ratios, 301-02
        Department of Justice approach,
            300-03, 305-07, 310-11
        foreign firms, 301
        four-firm ratio, 301-02
        FTC approach, 305-06, 310-12
        General Dynamics, 300
        Herfindahl-Hirschman Index, 301-02
        judicial approaches, 303-05
        market share, 299-300, 303-05
        NAAG approach, 306
        Philadelphia National Bank, 304
        presumption of illegality, 304-05
        sales, 299-300

MERGERS AND ACQUISITIONS
  (continued)
  Conglomerate Acquisitions, 333-34,
    335-37
    entrenchment doctrine, 334
    federal agency enforcement, 337
    reciprocity theory, 335-36
  Consent Decrees, 321, 338, 344,
    349-51
  Cross-Elasticity, 202-04, 282, 287
    of demand, 282
    of production, 287
    of supply, 202-04, 287
  Damages, 361, 371
    treble damages, 361
  Defenses to Merger Enforcement
    ease of entry, 299, 307-11, 322-24
    efficiencies, 319-22, 331-33, 372-76
    failing or impaired company
      doctrine, 313-18
    national security, 337
    Newspaper Preservation Act, 318
    power buyers, 311-12
  Department of Justice (see also
    Concentration Measures;
    Divestiture; Efficiencies; Entry;
    Failing or Impaired Company;
    Permanent Injunctive Relief;
    Potential Competition;
    Preliminary Injunctive Relief;
    Vertical Acquisition)
    enforcement, 337
    International Guidelines, 277-78,
      386, 389
    1984 Merger Guidelines, 277-78,
      290-92, 297-98, 300-02, 305-07,
      311-12, 320-21, 324, 328, 332-33,
      337
    1992 Merger Guidelines (see
      Appendix F)
  Divestiture, 337, 338, 344-51, 358-60,
    368, 371
  Economies of Scale, 372
  Efficiencies, 319-22, 331-33, 372-76
    Department of Justice approach,
      320-21
    FTC approach, 321-22
    NAAG approach, 322
    standards, 319-20
  Entry, 299, 307-11, 322-24, 327-28
    barriers to entry, 308-09
    de novo entry, 327-28
    Department of Justice approach, 310

  FTC approach, 309-11
  NAAG approach, 311
  toehold acquisitions, 328
  Exon-Florio Amendment, 337
  Failing or Impaired Company, 313-18
    Department of Justice approach, 316
    FTC approach, 316
    General Dynamics, 318
    impaired company, 317-18
    Newspaper Preservation Act, 318
    requirements, 313-16
  Federal Trade Commission Act, 276,
    353-55, 372, 392
  Federal Trade Commission (see also
    Concentration Measures;
    Divestiture; Efficiencies; Entry;
    Failing or Impaired Company;
    Permanent Injunctive Relief;
    Potential Competition;
    Preliminary Injunctive Relief)
    consent orders, 346
    enforcement, 337-38
    premerger notification, 338-44
    statement concerning horizontal
      mergers, 278, 305-06, 312
  Herfindahl-Hirschman Index, 301-03,
    305-06 (see also Concentration
    Measures)
  Hold Separate Orders, 355-57
  Horizontal Mergers, 298-322 (see also
    Concentration Measures; Market
    Share)
    enforcement concerns, 298-99
    role of "other factors," 299
  Injunctive Relief, 337-38, 351-58,
    365-67, 370-71 (see also
    Permanent Injunctive Relief;
    Preliminary Injunctive Relief)
  Market Concentration (see
    Concentration Measures)
  Market Definition, 282 (see also
    Geographic Market Definition,
    Product Market Definition)
  Merger Guidelines (see also
    Department of Justice)
  Newspaper Preservation Act, 318
  Noncompetitive Performance, 312-13
  Permanent Injunctive Relief, 337,
    358-61, 370-71
    private parties, 370-71
  Potential Competition, 322-29, 377
    actual potential competition, 324-28
    actual potential entrant theory, 322

MERGERS AND ACQUISITIONS – Potential
        Competition (*continued*)
    Department of Justice approach,
        324, 328
    FTC approach, 324, 328
    perceived potential competition,
        328-29
    perceived potential entrant theory,
        322, 329
    Preliminary Injunctive Relief, 337-38,
        351-58, 365-71
    balance of equities, 354
    Department of Justice actions,
        352-53
    FTC actions, 353-55
    hold separate orders, 355-57
    likelihood of success on the merits,
        354, 367
    private parties, actions by, 365-71
    public interest, 353
    relative hardship, 369
    rescission, 357-58
    standard for issuance, 353
    Premerger Notification, 277, 338-44,
        358, 897
    confidential treatment, 343
    enforcement actions, 343-44
    filing requirements, 338-40
    foreign acquisitions, 897
    in-commerce test, 339
    injunctive relief, 358
    NAAG Voluntary Premerger
        Disclosure Compact, 343
    scope of, 340
    second requests, 342-43
    size-of-the-parties test, 339
    size-of-the-transaction test, 339
    substantial compliance, 342-43
    waiting period, 341-43
    Private Enforcement of § 7, 278-79,
        361-71
    attorneys' fees, 361
    divestiture, 371
    injunctive relief, 370
    preliminary relief, 365-69
    standing, 362-65
    Rescission, 357-58 (*see also* Preliminary
        Injunctive Relief)
    Remedies (*see* Damages; Divestiture;
        Hold Separate Order; Preliminary
        Injunction; Permanent Injunction;
        Recission)
    Rule of Reason, 373-75, 385-87, 390

    Sherman Act, 275-76, 372, 378, 384,
        393, 395
    State Merger Enforcement, 311, 322,
        371-72 (*see also* State Antitrust
        Enforcement)
    NAAG Merger Guidelines, 278-79,
        292, 298, 301, 306, 322, 371-72
    NAAG Voluntary Premerger
        Disclosure Compact, 279, 343,
        371-72
    Stock Acquisitions, 279-81
    investment exception, 281
    Vertical Acquisitions, 330-33
    Department of Justice approach,
        331-33
    foreclosure theory, 330-32
MINIMUM RESALE PRICES, 100-02 (*see
        also* Price Fixing; Resale Price
        Maintenance)
MONOPOLIZATION (CHAPTER II)
    Abuse of Process, 257-59
    Anticompetitive Conduct, 219-59,
        261-62
    abuse of process, 257-59
    attempt to monopolize, 261-62
    business torts, 222
    duty to predisclose, 255
    economic irrationality, 222-24
    essential facility, 246-50
    intent, 224-26
    legitimate business purpose, 222-24
    leveraging, 250
    miscellaneous anticompetitive
        conduct, 226
    patent infringement actions, 258
    predatory pricing, 226
    price squeeze, 237-41
    product introduction, 253-57
    product preannouncement, 256
    product promotion, 256
    refusal to deal, 241-46
    "thrust upon" defense, 220-21
    Antitrust Injury, 196
    Areeda-Turner Test, 227-29 (*see also*
        Predatory Pricing)
    Attempt to Monopolize, 259-69
    anticompetitive conduct, 261-62
    dangerous probability of success,
        262-69
    elements, 259
    market share, 263-64
    relevant market, 266
    specific intent, 260-61

MONOPOLIZATION (*continued*)
  Business Torts, 222
  Conspiracy to Monopolize, 270-73
    Copperweld doctrine, 271
    dangerous probability of success,
      272-73
    elements, 270
    specific intent, 271-72
  Elements of Offense, 220-21
  Entry, Ease of, 216-18 (*see also*
      Monopoly Power)
    barrier to entry, 216
    monopoly power, 216-18
  Essential Facilities Doctrine, 246-50
      (*see also* Anticompetitive
      Conduct)
  Filed-Rate Doctrine, 239-40 (*see also*
      Price Squeeze)
  Intent, 220-21, 224-26, 234-36, 260-61,
      271-72
    attempt to monopolize, 260-61
    conspiracy to monopolize, 271-72
    monopolization, 220-21, 224-26
    predatory pricing, 234-36
    specific intent, 220-21, 260-61,
      271-72
  Interstate Commerce, 196
  Intraenterprise Conspiracy, 270-71 (*see
      also* Conspiracy to Monopolize)
  Leveraging, 250-52 (*see also*
      Anticompetitive Conduct)
  Monopoly Power, 196-97, 211-14,
      216-18, 263-64
    barrier to entry, 216-18
    compared to market power, 212
    defined, 196-97
    direct proof of, 211-12
    duration, 197
    entry, 216-18
    market share, 212-14, 263-64
    regulation, 240-41
    supranormal profits, 216
  Monopsony, 196, 227
    in general, 196
    predatory pricing, 227
  Noerr-Pennington, 240, 257-59
    abuse of process, 257-59
    price squeeze, 240
  Patent Infringement Actions, 258 (*see
      also* Intellectual Property –
      Patents)

  Predatory Pricing, 227-37
    Areeda-Turner test, 227-29
    defined, 227
    entry, 236-37
    fully distributed cost, 232-33
    intent, 234-36
    limit pricing, 227, 230
    long run incremental cost, 232-33
    market structure, 236-37
    monopsony, 227
    price cuts, 227, 230
    price-cost analysis, 227-34
    recoupment, 236-37
    variable versus fixed costs, 228-29
  Price Squeeze, 237-41
    filed rate doctrine, 239-40
  Refusal to Deal, 242-46 (*see also*
      Anticompetitive Conduct; Vertical
      Refusals to Deal)
    essential facilities doctrine, 246
    intent test, 242-46
    legitimate business purpose, 244-45
  Sham Litigation, 257-58 (*see also*
      Noerr-Pennington Abuse of Process)
  Shared Monopoly, 195
  Specific Intent, 220-21, 260-61, 271-72
      (*see also* Intent)
  State Action, 240
    price squeeze, 240
  Submarkets, 204-05 (*see also* Market
      Definition)
  Summary Judgment, 199
    market definition, 199
  "Thrust Upon" Defense, 220-21

NATIONAL ACCOUNTS PROGRAMS (*see*
      Price Fixing – Vertical Price
      Restrictions)
NATIONAL COOPERATIVE RESEARCH
      ACT, 388-89, 840 (*see also* Joint
      Ventures)
NOERR-PENNINGTON DOCTRINE, 4, 989-
      1016 (*see also* Concerted Refusal to
      Deal – Noneconomic Boycotts;
      International Antitrust;
      Monopolization)
  Access-Barring Activities, 1005-06
  Admissibility of Evidence, 1014-15
  Baseless Petitioning, 999-1000
  Basis of Doctrine, 990-91
  Boycotts, 996, 1012-14

NOERR-PENNINGTON DOCTRINE
  (*continued*)
  Bribery of Public Officials, 1009
  Commercial Exception, 1009-11
  Conspiracy Exception, 997-98, 1008-09
  Defendant's Intent, 1002-03
  Discovery, 1014
  First Amendment, 990-92
  Foreign Governments, Petitioning of,
    1015-16
  Lobbying, 990
  Misrepresentations, 1006-08
  Petitioning Adjudicative Bodies, 992
  Petitioning Foreign Governments,
    1015-16
  Political Boycotts, 1012-14
  Political Corruption, 1009
  Sham Exception, 991-93, 995, 997-1006
  Single Baseless Case, 1000-01
  Soliciting Administrative Action, 991-92
  Standard Setting Activities, 993-95
  Successful Petitioning, 1003-05
  Tariff Filings, 1011-12
  Threats of Litigation, 1001
  Trade Associations, 993-94
  Unethical Petitioning, 955

OLIGOPOLY (*see* Market Power; Mergers
    and Acquisitions; Monopolization)
OUTPUT RESTRICTIONS (*see* Horizontal
    Restraint or Agreement; Per Se
    Rule)

PATENT LICENSES (*see* Intellectual
    Property)
PATENTS (*see* Intellectual Property)
PARALLEL CONDUCT (*see* Concerted
    Action – Circumstantial Evidence of)
PER SE RULE, 31, 33-41, 58-59, 63-67,
    74-77, 79-80, 82-86, 95-97, 100-01,
    103-06, 116, 131-36, 373-74, 385,
    390 (*see also* Rule of Reason –
    Particular Substantive Titles)
  Ancillary Restraint, 38-39
  Bid Rigging, 33
  "Classic Boycott," 84-86
  Conspiracies to Eliminate Competitor
    by Unfair Means, 97
  Customer Allocation, 74
  Customer Restrictions, 76
  Group Boycotts, 33-34, 79-80, 82-83
  Horizontal Customer Allocation, 76-77
  Horizontal Territorial Allocation, 76-77

Hybrid Standard, 31
Joint Ventures, 373-74, 385, 390
Maximum Resale Prices, 66, 103-105
"Naked" Restraint, 35, 58-59, 76-77
Output Restrictions, 40-41, 74
Price Fixing, 33, 40-41, 63-65, 67
Resale Price Maintenance, 100-01, 116
Tying, 33, 131-36
Underlying Economic Rationale, 38-39
Vertical Price Agreements, 100, 105-06
PICK-BARTH DOCTRINE, 95-97
PRICE DISCRIMINATION (*see* Robinson-
    Patman – Discrimination)
PRICE FIXING (*see also* Bid Rigging;
    Concerted Action; Per Se Rule;
    Resale Price Maintenance)
  Actions Indirectly Affecting Price,
    67-71 (*see also* Concerted Action)
  Ancillary to Procompetitive Purpose,
    62
  Antitrust Injury, 104-05
  Bid Rigging, 63-64, 67
  Coercive Tactics, 108-10
  Commodities Futures, 1106
  Consignment, 102-03
  Cooperative Advertising, 64, 110,
    112-13
  Dealer Assistance Programs, 105,
    110-11
  Dealer Termination, 105
  Exchanging Price Information, 71
  Government Contracts, 1109
  Horizontal Price Fixing, 62-67
  Maximum Prices, 66
  Maximum Resale Prices, 103-04
  Minimum Quantities, 69-70
  National Accounts Programs, 113-14
  Per Se Rule, 62-64, 66, 72
  Price Pass-Through, 112
  Price Promotion, 110-12
  Quotas, 69
  Resale Price Maintenance, 100-01 (*see
    also* Resale Price Maintenance;
    Territorial Allocation and
    Customer Restrictions; Vertical
    Refusals to Deal)
  Rule of Reason, 68
  Structural Conspiracies, 71
  Suggested Resale Prices, 107-08,
    111-12
  Territorial and Customer Restrictions,
    114
  Uniform Price Lists, 64

PRICE FIXING (*continued*)
  Uniform Standards, 69
  Vertical Price Restrictions, 100-08,
    110-14
  Vertical Refusal to Deal, 105
PRICE PROMOTION (*see* Price Fixing;
  Rule of Reason; Vertical Price
  Restrictions)
PRIMARY JURISDICTION, 1021-23 (*see*
  also Regulated Industries –
  Jurisdiction)
PRIVATE ANTITRUST SUITS (CHAPTER
  VIII)
  Antitrust Injury, 650-52
  Antitrust Laws Defined, 645-46
  Automobile Dealers Day-in-Court Act,
    645-46
  Bifurcation of Trials, 773-74
  Class Actions, 644, 695-97, 712-45
    adequacy of representation, 717-23
    certification procedure, 734-37
    common questions, 714-15
    conflicts, 717-20
    costs of notice, 737-39
    dismissal and compromise, 739-45
    effect of judgment, 733
    notice of dismissal or compromise,
      739-44
    notice of suit, 737-39
    numerosity, 713-14
    person entitled to sue, 643-45
    persons bound, 733
    predominance of common questions,
      725-28
    prerequisites to suit, 712
    procedures, 733-34
    representatives, 715
    Rule 23(b)(1) classes, 723-24
    Rule 23(b)(3) classes, 724
    rulings, appeal from, 736-37
    settlements, 739-45
    statute of limitations, 695
    subclasses, 719
    superiority, 729-33
    tolling, 695
    typicality, 715
  Clayton Act
    generally, 643, 645-46
    Section 4, 646-63
    Section 4A, 645
    Section 4B, 680-82
    Section 5(i), 682-87

    Section 7, 650, 684
    Section 16, 643, 645, 663-65
  Collateral Estoppel, 775-76
  Complex Cases, 772-73
  Contract, Antitrust Violation as
    Defense, 791
  Contribution, 793-94
  Cost-Plus Contract, 653 (*see also*
    Indirect Purchaser)
  Costs, 780
  Damages
    "before and after" theory, 671
    burden of proof, 667-69
    business or property, 647-49
    calculation of, 669-71
    disaggregation, 674-75
    duplicative recovery, 658-59
    evidence, sufficiency, 673
    expert testimony, 674
    foreseeability, 658
    "going concern" value, 670
    lost profits, 672
    market share, 671
    mitigation, 675
    monopolistic overcharge cases, 669
    nominal, 781
    price-fixing cases, 669
    proving by various methodologies,
      669-74
    recovery by foreign governments,
      645
    segregation, 674-75
    tax treatment of, 794-97
    treble, 645
    tying cases, 669
    yardstick approach, 671
  Death of a Party, 793
  Defenses
    antitrust violation, breach of contract
      suit, 791-92
    in pari delicto, 697-700
    pass-on, 653-58
    statute of limitations, 681-97 (*see*
     also Statute of Limitations)
    unclean hands, 701-02
  Disaggregation (*see* Damages)
  Discovery, 745-72
    attorney-client privilege, 760-66
    conditioned discovery, 766
    corporate affiliates, 752-54
    costs, 766
    fifth amendment problems, 771-72

PRIVATE ANTITRUST SUITS –
    Discovery (*continued*)
      foreign discovery, 753 (*see also*
        International Antitrust,
        Procedural Issues)
      grand jury materials, 754-60
      reasonable period, 747
      relevant market, 747-52
      relevant time period, 745-48
      sanctions for failure to make, 767-71
      Upjohn test, 760-62
      work product privilege, 760
    Federal Trade Commission Act, 645,
      684
    Fifth Amendment, 771-72
    Fraudulent Concealment, 688-93
      affirmative acts, 689
      discovery, 689
      due diligence, 693
      knowledge of, 692
      public records, 691-93
      self-concealing, 689
    Government Judgments, Use in Private
      Litigation, 775-80
      collateral estoppel, 775-76
      consent judgments, 779
      governments, actions by, 645
      prima facie effect, 777
    Grand Jury Materials, 754-60
      debriefing materials, 760
      disclosure, 754
      documents, 758
      particularized need, 756
      proper court, 759
      testimony, 755
      work product privilege, 760
    In Pari Delicto, 697
    Indirect Purchaser, 653-58
      cost-plus contract, 653-56
      pass-on defense, 653-55
      preemption by state law, 658
      regulated utilities, 656
      remoteness, 652-63
    Injunctive Relief, 675-80
      abandonment of challenged conduct,
        679
      destruction of goodwill, 678
      discriminatory treatment, 678
      divestiture, 680
      irreparable harm, 676, 677
      likelihood of success, 676
      mergers and acquisitions, 678
      permanent, 679
      preliminary, 676 (*see also*
        preliminary injunctions)
      public interest standard, 676
      standing, 663-65
      state statutes and regulations, 678
      status quo, preservation of, 677
      terminations, 678
      utility rates, 678
    Injury (*see also* Antitrust Injury;
      Standing to Sue)
      antitrust injury, 650-52
      fact of damage, 647
      impact, 647
      indirect injury, 653
      material cause, 647
      proof of injury, 665-67
    Judicial Panel on Multidistrict
      Litigation, 708
    Jury Trials, 772-73
    Mitigation (*see* Damages)
    Multidistrict Litigation, 708-11
      choice of transferee court, 710
      factors for transfer, 709
      jurisdiction of transferee court, 710
      power of transferee court, 711
      venue in transferee court, 710
    Pass-On Defense (*see also* Indirect
      Purchaser)
      assignment of claims, 654
      coconspirator exception, 657
      defensive use, 653
      offensive use, 653, 654
      state laws, 658
    Person, Definition, 643-45
      association, 643
      class action, 644
      corporation, 643
      foreign government, 645
      individual, 643
      partnership, 643
      private person, 643
      United States, 645
    Predatory Pricing, 651
    Preemption, 658
    Preliminary Injunctions, 676-79
      cases denying, 678
      cases granting, 678
      standard for obtaining, alternative,
        677
      standard for obtaining, traditional,
        676
    Remoteness, 652, 658 (*see also*
      Indirect Purchaser)

PRIVATE ANTITRUST SUITS (*continued*)
    Robinson-Patman Act, 645, 667
    Rule 11, 789-91
    Sanctions, 789-91
    Standing to Sue, 648, 652-65 (*see also*
        Antitrust Injury; Injury)
        broker, 662
        Clayton Act, § 16, 663
        employee, 661-62
        lack of, 660-61
        licensor, 661
        miscellaneous plaintiffs, 661-63
        preparedness to enter, 648
        remoteness, 652-63
        sales agent, 662
        target of takeover, 662-63
        umbrella theory, 661
        unions, 659-60
        zone of interests test, 659
    Statute of Limitations, 681-97 (*see also*
        Fraudulent Concealment; Tolling
        of Statute of Limitations)
        accrual of action, 681
        discovery of cause of action, 689
        due diligence, 693
        lack of knowledge, 691
        tolling, 682
        Uniform Statute of Limitations, 680-
        82
    Summary Judgment, 702-08
        economic plausibility, 705
        Matsushita test, 705-08
        Monsanto test, 704-08
        permissible inferences, 704-05
        Poller test, 702-03
    Tax Treatment of Damages, 794-97
        defendant's payments, 795
        plaintiff's recovery, 794
    Tolling of Statute of Limitations,
        688-95 (*see also* Statute of
        Limitations)
        class actions, 695
        equitable tolling, 693
        fraudulent concealment, 688-89
        government actions, 682-83
    Treble Damage Action, 643
    Unclean Hands, 701-02 (*see also*
        Defenses)
PRODUCT MARKET DEFINITION, 44,
    199-208 282-93 (*see also* Market
    Definition)
    Cluster Markets, 289-90

Cross-Elasticity of Demand, 201-02,
    282-87
Cross-Elasticity of Supply, 202-04, 287
Department of Justice Approach,
    290-92
FTC Approach, 292
Imperfect Substitutes, 293
Interchangeability of Use, 282-87
"Line of Commerce" Element, 282
Monopolization Cases, 199-208
NAAG Approach, 292
Production Substitutability, 202-04,
    287-88
Single Product Markets, 206-07
Submarkets, 204-05, 208, 288-89
PROFIT PASSOVER ARRANGEMENTS (*see*
    Vertical Nonprice Restrictions)
PURCHASING COOPERATIVE (*see*
    Concerted Refusal to Deal)

QUALITY STANDARDS (*see* Vertical
    Refusals to Deal)

RECIPROCAL DEALING, 166-68
REFUSAL TO DEAL (*see* Concerted
    Refusal to Deal)
REGULATED INDUSTRIES (CHAPTER XI)
    Agricultural Cooperatives, 1024-28
    Air Transportation, 1145-57
        airline mergers, 1147-49
        contestability theory, 1149
        CRS joint venture, 1150-51
        preemption of state regulation,
            1152-54
        unfair competition, 1154-57
    Atomic Energy Act, 1081
    AT&T Consent Decree, 1045-46, 1055
    Bank Merger Act of 1966, 1092-95
    Broadcasting, 1028-44
        anticompetitive use of broadcast
            facilities, 1034
        application of antitrust laws to,
            1029-30
        consideration of competitive factors,
            1030-31
        cross-ownership rules, 1036-37
        deregulation of, 1042-44
        joint sales practices, 1033-34
        multiple ownership rules, 1035-37,
            1039
        regulation of licensing, 1031-32
        television networks, 1039-42

REGULATED INDUSTRIES (*continued*)
  Cable Television, 1050-55
    AT&T consent decree, 1055
    consideration of competitive factors,
      1051-52, 1055
    essential facilities doctrine, 1054
    licensing, 1052
    Noerr-Pennington, 1053-54
    nonprice predation, 1053-54
    predatory pricing, 1053
    preemption by FCC, 1051
    price discrimination, 1053
    state action, 1054
    telephone company ownership of,
      1055
    tying, 1054-55
    vertical integration, 1052-53
  Capper-Volstead Act, 1024-25, 1028
  Commodity Exchange Act, 1107
    cornering, 1107
    manipulation of prices, 1107
  Commodities Futures, 1104-07
    antitrust immunity, 1106-07
  Commodity Futures Trading
      Commission, 1104-06
    cornering, 1107
    manipulation of prices, 1107
    price fixing, 1106
  Communications Act of 1934, 1028
  Electric Power, 1067-79
    antitrust immunity, 1068
    antitrust policy, regulatory
      consideration, 1067-68, 1072-73
    essential facilities doctrine, 1071
    implied immunity, 1070-71
    mergers and acquisitions, 1075-79
    monopoly leveraging, 1074
    price squeeze, 1071-74
    refusal to wheel, 1071
    regulation of, 1067
    wheeling, FERC authority to
      compel, 1069-70
  Essential Facilities Doctrine, 1054,
      1065-66, 1071, 1140-41
    cable television, 1054
    electric power transmission lines,
      1071
    natural gas pipelines, 1065-66
    railroad lines, 1040-41
  Federal Coal Leases, 1083-85
    Department of Justice review,
      1084-85

  Federal Energy Leases, 1087-89
    antitrust review of, 1087-89
  Federal Offshore Oil and Gas Leases,
      1085-87
    antitrust review of, 1085-86
    Department of Justice review,
      1086-87
  Federal Power Act, 1067-68
  Federal Regulation, Effect of, 1016
  Financial Institutions, 1090-99
    bank holding company mergers,
      1095-96
    bank mergers, 1092-95
    bank mergers, standard of review,
      1093-95
    Clayton Act, § 8, 1099
    Garn-St Germain Depository
      Institution Act, 1099
    interlocking directorates, 1099
    Investment Company Act of 1940,
      1099
    joint ventures, 1090-92
    Management Interlocks Act, 1099
    savings and loan company mergers,
      1096
    tying, 1097-99
  Insurance (*see* McCarran-Ferguson
      Act)
  Interstate Commerce Commission,
      1128-45
    motor carriers, regulation of,
      1128-31
    rail transportation, regulation of,
      1131-45
  Joint Ventures in Regulated Markets,
      1050-51, 1090-92
    computer reservation systems, 1151
    financial institutions, 1090-92
  Jurisdiction, 1017, 1021-23
    exclusive jurisdiction of agency, 1017
    primary jurisdiction of agency,
      1021-23
  Mergers and Acquisitions
    airlines, 1148-50
    bank holding companies, 1095-96
    banks, 1092-95
    bridge banks, 1096-97
    credit unions, 1097
    electric utilities, 1075-79
    motor carriers, 1130-31
    rail carriers, 1141-45
    savings and loan companies, 1096

REGULATED INDUSTRIES (*continued*)
  Motor Carriers, 1127-31
    Clayton Act, § 16, 1130
    collective ratemaking, state action
      immunity for, 1129
    entry, regulation of, 1127
    Interstate Commerce Commission,
      regulation by, 1127
    Keogh doctrine, 1130
    mergers, 1130-31
    pooling agreements, 1130-31
    rate bureaus, 1128-29
    rate bureaus, statutory immunity,
      1129-30
    rates, regulation of, 1127-28
  National and Naval Petroleum
    Reserves, 1087
    antitrust review of leases, 1087
  Natural Gas, 1056-67
    antitrust policy, regulatory
      consideration of, 1056-57
    bypass of traditional suppliers,
      1061-62
    essential facilities doctrine, 1065-66
    FERC, regulation by, 1056
    mergers and acquisitions, 1066-67
    monopsony power of pipelines, 1060
    open access transportation of,
      1058-61
    refusal to transport, 1063-66
    standing of indirect purchasers,
      1062-63
    take-or-pay contracts, 1060-61
    wellhead prices, deregulation of,
      1057-58
  Nuclear Power, 1083
    antitrust laws, applicability of, 1081
    antitrust prelicensing review of
      facilities, 1081-83
    NRC regulation, 1081
  Ocean Common Carriers, 1157-66
    agreements, regulation of, 1162-64
    antitrust immunity, 1164-66
    entry, regulation of, 1158-59
    Federal Maritime Commission
      regulation of, 1157-58
    mergers and acquisitions, 1158
    rates, regulation of, 1159-61
    Shipping Act of 1984, 1157-58
  Oil Pipelines, 1079-81
    deepwater port licensing, 1080-81
    FERC regulation, 1079-81

    market power measurement, 1080
  Price Squeeze, 1071-74
    regulated industries, 1071-74
  Public Utility Regulatory Policies Act
    of 1978, 1069, 1076
  Rail Transportation, 1131-45
    competitive access to, 1140
    entry, regulation of, 1134-35
    essential facilities doctrine,
      1140-41
    ICC, 1131-32
    Keogh doctrine, 1139
    negotiated rates, 1137-38
    railroad mergers, 1141-45
    rate agreements, 1138-40
    rate bureaus, 1138
    rate discrimination, 1137
    rates, regulation of, 1134-37
    regulation, exemption from,
      1132-34
    Staggers Rail Act, 1134
  Refusals to Deal, 1063-66, 1070-71
    denial of access to electric
      transmission lines, 1070-71
    denial of access to pipeline
      transportation, 1063-66
    legitimate business justification,
      1064-65, 1071
  Securities Exchange Commission,
    Regulated Activities, 1101-04
    applicability of antitrust laws, 1101
    implied antitrust immunity,
      1101-04
  Telecommunications Common
    Carriers, 1045-50
    antitrust immunity, 1049-50
    FCC regulation of, 1047-49
    state regulation of, 1049-50
REQUIREMENTS CONTRACTS (*see*
  Exclusive Dealing)
RELEVANT MARKET (*see* Geographic
  Market Definitions; Market
  Definition; Product Market
  Definition; Rule of Reason)
RESALE PRICE MAINTENANCE, 11-12, 16,
  100-02, 107-08, 114-15
  Colgate Doctrine, 11-12
  Minimum Resale Price, 100-02
  Per Se Rule, 102, 114-15
  Suggested Resale Prices, 107-08,
    111-12
  Vertical Termination, 11-12, 16

ROBINSON-PATMAN ACT (CHAPTER IV)
  Advertising and Promotional
      Allowances and Services, 436-44
    availability defense, 442
    contemporaneous sales, 442
    discrimination between customers,
      439
    Fred Meyer guides, 440-41
    proportional equality, 442, 444
    resale, requirement of, 437-39
  Antitrust Injury, 449
  Availability Defense, 406-07, 442-44
  Brokerage, 431-36
    "discounts in lieu" of brokerage,
      432-34
    "for services rendered," 435-36
    payments to agents, 434-35
  Buyer Liability for Price
      Discrimination, 444-48
    burden of proof, 446-47
    derivative liability, 444
    meeting competition defense, 447-48
    "trade experience" evidence, 445-46
  Changing Conditions Defense, 426-27
  Commerce Requirement, 402-04
  Commodities, as Element of § 2(a)
      Violation, 409-10
  Competitive Injury, 413-17, 428 (*see
      also* Primary Line Injury;
      Secondary Line Injury)
    Morton Salt Inference, 416, 428
    primary line, 414-15
    secondary line, 415-17
  Cost Justification Defense, 420-26
    brokerage allowance, 425
    chain stores, 422
    classification of customers, 420-22
    proof of cost savings, 423-24, 425
    types of cost savings, 424-25
  Criminal Enforcement, 450-51
  Discrimination as Element of a § 2(a)
      Violation, 405-08
    availability defense, 406-07
    contemporaneous sales, 406
    delivered pricing, 405
    indirect purchasers, 408
    nonsale transactions, 408
    offer, 407
    price discrimination, 404-05
    refusal to deal, 407
    terms of sale, 405
  Elements of § 2(a) Violation, 404
  Enforcement, 401-02

Exemptions, 448-49
    cooperatives, 448
    exports, 448
    government sales, 449
    nonprofit institutions, 448
  Export Exemption, 448-49
  Fred Meyer Guides, 440-41 (*see also*
      Advertising and Promotional
      Allowances and Services)
  Functional Discounts, 427-31
    indirect purchasers doctrine, 429
    Morton Salt inference, 428
    reasonableness of functional
      discounts, 427-29
    retailer-owned wholesaler, 429-30
  Government Sales Exemption from
      Robinson-Patman, 449
  Injury, 449-50 (*see also* Primary Line
      Injury; Secondary Line Injury)
    antitrust injury, 449-50
    causation, 450
  Interstate Commerce, 402-04
  Like Grade and Quality, as Element
      of § 2(a) Violation, 410-13
    brand names, 410-11
    manufacturing costs, 412
    packaging, 412
    product lines, 412
    warranties, 412
  Meeting Competition Defense, 417-21,
      447
    area-wide pricing, 418-19
    attracting new customers, 419-20
    good faith, 417-18
    prices of customer's competitors,
      420
  Nonprofit Institutions Exemption, 448
  Price Discrimination, 404-05 (*see also*
      Discrimination)
    credit terms, 405
  Primary Line Injury, 414-15
    predatory intent, 414-15
  Private Rights of Action, 449
  Promotional and Advertising
      Allowances (*see* Advertising and
      Promotional Allowances and
      Services)
  Sales to Two Purchasers, as Element
      of § 2(a) Violation, 407-08
    indirect purchases, 408
    nonsale transactions, 408
    offers, 407
    refusals to deal, 407

ROBINSON-PATMAN ACT (*continued*)
  Secondary Line Injury, 415-17, 427-30
    functional discounts, 427
    indirect purchaser doctrine, 429
    Morton Salt inference, 416, 428
    retailer-owned wholesaler, 429-30
RULE OF REASON, 41-48, 50-54, 56-59,
    100, 105-06, 110-11, 114-17, 120-23,
    175, 178, 373-75, 385-87, 390 (*see*
    also Per Se Rule)
  Anticompetitive Effect, 53-54, 105
  Anticompetitive Purpose or Intent, 54,
    106
  Balancing Analysis, 53, 58
  Business Purpose, 47, 56
  Effect on Competition, 42-43, 46-47,
    49, 51-52
  Efficiencies, 42-43
  Exclusive Dealing, 175, 178
  Free Riding, 53 (*see also* Vertical
    Nonprice Restrictions; Vertical
    Refusals to Deal)
  Horizontal Restraints, 57-58
  Hybrid Standard, 30-32
  Interbrand and Intrabrand
    Competition, Balance of, 122-23
  Interbrand Competition, 52
  Intrabrand Competition, 52
  Joint Ventures, Analysis of, 373-75,
    385-87, 390
  Market Failure, 53
  Market Power, 50-51, 58-59
  Market Structure, 48-50
  Price Promotion, 110-11
  Relevant Market, 44, 46
  Territorial and Customer Restrictions,
    114-15, 120, 123, 127-28 (*see also*
    Territorial Allocation and
    Customer Restrictions)
  Truncated Rule of Reason, 51
  Tying, 163
  Vertical Nonprice Restraints, 100, 106,
    116-17, 121 (*see also* Vertical
    Nonprice Restrictions)

SHERMAN ACT, § 1
  Anticompetitive Effect, 55-56
  Anticompetitive Purpose or Intent,
    55-56
  Concerted Action, 2-3
  Elements of Violation of, 2
  Independent Action or Conduct, 3
  Joint Ventures, 276

Mergers and Acquisitions (*see* Mergers
  and Acquisitions – Sherman Act)
Purposes of, 1, 44
Unilateral Conduct, 2
Vertical Refusals to Deal, 179-80
SPORTS LEAGUES, 90-91 (*see also*
  Concerted Refusal to Deal)
STANDARDS AND CERTIFICATION
  PROGRAMS (*see* Concerted Refusal
  to Deal)
STATE ACTION
  Active Supervision Requirement,
    972-76, 985-86
  Acts of State Supreme Court, 968
  Acts of State Bar, 967
  Bribery of Public Officials, 978
  Clear Articulation Requirement,
    970-72, 982-85
  Commercial Exception, 978-79
  Compulsion Requirement, 967, 970-71
  Conspiracy Exception, 976-77
  Corruption of Public Officials, 978
  Defined, 965
  Federalism, Principles of, 966
  Foreseeability Standard, 983-84
  Home Rule Statutes, 981-82
  Immunity, Limitations on, 976-79
  Insurance, 971, 975-76
  Judicial Review of Conduct, 974
  Midcal Test, 969-70
  Motor Carrier Rate Bureaus, 1129
  Parker Doctrine, 965-66
  Peer Review Decisions, 973-74
  Rate Bureaus, 970-71, 974-75
  State Agencies, 979-80
  State Departments, 979-80
  State Political Subdivisions, 981-86
  State Sovereignty, 966
STATE ANTITRUST ENFORCEMENT
  (CHAPTER VII) (*see also* Federal
  Trade Commission – State "Little
  FTC Acts"; Mergers and
  Acquisitions – State Antitrust
  Enforcement)
  Constitutional Issues, 621-33
    commerce clause, 621-22
    double jeopardy clause, 629
    double recovery, 629-32
    due process clause, 627-29
    equal protection clause, 626-27
    state premerger notification statutes,
      632-33
    supremacy clause, 622-26

STATE ANTITRUST ENFORCEMENT
(*continued*)
Coordination among States, 608-19,
279, 371-72, 641-15
amicus briefs, 613-14
coordinated investigations and
litigation, 609-10
Executive Working Group for
Antitrust (EWG), 618-19
horizontal price fixing and bid
rigging, 611
joint ventures, 612-13
legislative positions, 614
mergers, 611-12
Multistate Task Force, 608-09
NAAG Merger Guidelines, 617-18
NAAG Vertical Restraints
Guidelines, 615-16
NAAG Voluntary Pre-Merger
Disclosure Compact, 279, 371-72,
614-15 (*see* Premerger
Notification)
resale price maintenance, 610-11
tying, 611
Unlawful Boycotts, 612
vertical territorial restrictions, 613
Criminal Sanctions (*see* Remedies)
Damages (*see* Parens Patriae Actions;
Remedies; State Actions as a
"Private Person")
Exemptions and Defenses, 637-39
contribution, 639
government immunity, 637
insurance, 638-39
labor, 638
Noerr-Pennington, 638
primary jurisdiction, 638
state action, 612, 637
unclean hands and in pari delicto,
639
Parens Patriae Actions, 606-08 (*see
also* Remedies)
damages, 607-08
limitations, 607
Preemption of State Law (*see*
Constitutional Issues – Supremacy
Clause)
Premerger Notification, 632
Remedies, 639-41
civil penalties, 640
criminal, 639
damages, 640-41

forfeiture of right to do business,
641
injunctions, 641
parens patriae actions, 641
State Attorneys General, Disclosure to,
614-15, 632-33 (*see also*
Coordination among States)
State Actions as a "Private Person"
under Federal Law, 603-06
class actions, 604
injunctive relief, 605-06
treble damage suits, 603-05
State and Federal Antitrust Laws,
Differences between, 633-36
horizontal restraints, 634
indirect purchaser standing, 625-26,
640-41
mergers, 617, 636
monopolies, 635
price discrimination, 635-36
vertical restraints, 616, 634-35
State Antitrust Laws, Historical
Development of, 619-21
STANDING TO SUE (*see* Private Antitrust
Suits)
STATUTE OF LIMITATIONS (*see* Private
Antitrust Suits)
STRUCTURAL CONSPIRACY (*see* Price
Fixing – Actions Indirectly Affecting
Price)
SUGGESTED RESALE PRICES (*see* Price
Fixing; Resale Price Maintenance)
SUMMARY JUDGMENT (*see* Private
Antitrust Suits)

TERRITORIAL ALLOCATION AND
CUSTOMER RESTRICTIONS, 76, 119-
26 (*see also* Horizontal Restraint or
Agreement; Vertical Nonprice
Restraints)
Among Potential Competitors, 76
Effect on Interbrand and Intrabrand
Competition, 119-24
Franchises, 120
Location Clauses, 121-22
Resale Price Maintenance, as Part of,
119
Rule of Reason, 120
TRUNCATED RULE OF REASON (*see* Rule
of Reason)
TYING, 131-69, 1097-99
Bank Holding Company Act, 1097-99

TYING (*continued*)
Business Justification, 135, 160, 162
Clayton Act, § 3, 133
Coercion, 144-148
Competition, Effects on, 158-59
Conditioning, 143-46
Defenses, 160-62
Economic Interest, 131
Economic Power, 148-50, 152-53, 155-56
Elements of Violation, 136-59
Exclusive Dealing, Compared with, 169
Federal Trade Commission Act, § 5, 133-34
Forcing (*see* Coercion)
Foreclosure, 158-59
Franchising, 141-42, 156-57
Full Line Forcing, 164-66
Intellectual Property (*see* Intellectual Property)
Lock-In, 152
Market Power, 163
Market Share, 151
Per Se Rule, 33, 134-35
Rule of Reason, 163
Savings and Loan Institutions, 1099
Separate Products, 136-41
Sherman Act, § 1 and § 2, 133
Substantial Amount of Commerce, 157
Tied Product, 157-59
Trademarks, 140-42, 155-57
Two Products (*see* Separate Products)
Uniqueness, 153-54

UNFAIR METHODS OF COMPETITION, 65
Basing Point Pricing, 65

VERTICAL NONPRICE RESTRICTIONS, 52, 100, 104-05, 116-31, 331
Area of Primary Responsibility, 117, 129
Dual Distribution, 127
Efficiencies, 52
Exclusive Distributorship, 117-18
Franchises, 120
Free Riders, 117
Interbrand Competition, Promotion of, 122-23
Location Clauses, 117, 122, 129
Profit Pass-Over Arrangements, 117, 130
Rule of Reason, 100, 116-17, 121, 123
Territorial and Customer Restrictions, 117, 119-20, 123-24, 127
VERTICAL REFUSALS TO DEAL, 180-93
(*see also* Exclusive Distributorships; Monopolization; Refusal to Deal; Rule of Reason; Vertical Nonprice Restraints)
Allocation of Scarce Supplies, 185
Appearance and Image Standards, 183-84
Business Reasons, 190, 192
Distribution Network, 185-86
Exclusive Distributorship, 183-84
Free Riders, 185-86,
Noncommercial Reasons, 185
Purpose and Effect of, 180, 185, 188-89, 193
Quality Standards, 184-85
Rule of Reason, 185
Sufficient Distribution, 183-84
Unsatisfactory Dealer Performance, 183-84
Vertical Integration, 191
Vertical Terminations, 188, 189
VERTICAL TERMINATIONS (*see* Resale Price Maintenance; Vertical Refusals to Deal)

WIRE AND/OR MAIL FRAUD, 66-67